CRIMINAL LAW
CASES, CONTROVERSIES AND PROBLEMS

■ ■ ■

Joseph E. Kennedy
Martha Brandis Professor of Law
University of North Carolina School of Law

AMERICAN CASEBOOK SERIES®

American Casebook Series is a trademark registered in the U.S. Patent and Trademark Office.

© 2019 LEG, Inc. d/b/a West Academic
    444 Cedar Street, Suite 700
    St. Paul, MN 55101
    1-877-888-1330

West, West Academic Publishing, and West Academic are trademarks of West Publishing Corporation, used under license.

Printed in the United States of America

ISBN: 978-1-64020-071-5

*For Tom, Sam, and Christina, who have taught
me more than they will ever realize.*

PREFACE

———

I am jealous. You are about to begin a journey that I began over thirty years ago as a first year law student waiting anxiously in his criminal law class wondering if he would earn the unwanted distinction of being the first one in his section to be called on by the professor. Since then I have studied criminal law, practiced criminal law and taught criminal law almost continuously. It has been a marvelous journey because you cannot do any of those three things without learning to think more clearly about the law, our society and ultimately the meaning of good and evil.

I tell my students that I don't care what they think but that I do care very much how they think. If you take this journey for all that it is worth, it will change how you think about questions of fundamental importance to law and justice. In the process you will also develop those habits of mind that we refer to as "thinking like a lawyer." And yes, you will also learn the doctrines of the criminal law.

And it will be an interesting trip! Vexing issues of race, class and gender; philosophical debates about the nature of right and wrong; difficult divisions of power between legislators, judges, prosecutors and juries; and countless stories of tragic choices made by real people and the consequences that ensued. You will soon see that the most difficult issues the criminal law confronts involve dilemmas—choices between rival goods—and you will come to appreciate the importance and the meaning of those choices.

Despite the seriousness of the subject matter, you will discover the tone of my own writing in this book to be somewhat lighthearted, especially in my choice of funny or quirky examples to illustrate key concepts. I learned while practicing criminal law that a sense of humor was an essential survival tool. I have also learned during my years of teaching that even bad jokes can help students remember concepts that are abstract and esoteric. And boy, do I know a lot of bad jokes.

Think of this book as a map, me as the slightly irreverent mapmaker, and your professor as your essential guide for this journey. Buckle up—this is going to be quite a ride!

JOSEPH KENNEDY

February 9, 2019

ACKNOWLEDGMENTS

Countless faculty and staff colleagues, research assistants and students helped me write this textbook. At various points in time, Debra Edge, Tyla Olson, Samantha Owen, Andrew Swanson and Rebecca Wilson provided invaluable manuscript support. A number of talented research assistants contributed research memoranda and important comments on drafts: James Jordan, Caitlin Haff, Saverio Longobardo and Evelyn Yarborough. Bonnie Karlen of West Academic Publishing nudged, encouraged and guided me through the publication process, and Laura Holle and Daniel Buteyn thoroughly edited the entire manuscript.

I have been blessed with wonderful colleagues at UNC over the years who helped me develop and refine my thinking about criminal law and who continue to encourage and inspire me: Carissa Hessick, Eisha Jain, Joan Krause, Arnold Loewy, Robert Mosteller, Eric Muller and Richard Myers. Sarah Beale of Duke Law and the late—and sorely missed—Andrew Taslitz of Howard Law deserve special credit for convincing me that writing a textbook was something that I could and should do.

I must also acknowledge an intellectual debt to three giant figures in criminal law scholarship whose comprehensive treatments of criminal law doctrine gave me a foundation upon which to build: Joshua Dressler, Wayne LaFave, and Paul Robinson.

Finally, this book never would have seen completion without the love and encouragement of my colleague and partner in life, Maria Savasta-Kennedy.

Disclaimer

Some of the practice problems in this text were inspired by real events, but the names and facts of those problems have been changed.

FOREWORD: FOR FIRST YEAR LAW STUDENTS

"If the world were perfect it wouldn't be."

—Yogi Berra

Don't be fooled by all those lawyer jokes. People make jokes about lawyers because they know they can't do without us and because we remind them of the conflicts and disputes that need resolving, conflicts that sometimes reflect the darker side of people and society. Tell me, do you think that our society needs more or less people who are fair enough to see both sides of an argument, patient enough to think through all the angles of a difficult problem, and trained to look for a balance between competing perspectives?

We do important work. We make agreements, resolve disputes, and help keep society running in an orderly, humane, and fair way. None of this works perfectly, but it wouldn't work at all without us. Doing what we do requires not only knowledge of the law but also the special set of mental habits that we collectively refer to as "thinking like a lawyer" that you begin learning in your first year of law school.

There are times in many people's lives when they work hard at something pointless just to get by. Law school is not that. It matters. You will learn something special and valuable. You will change how you think in a way that makes the world a more interesting place and you a more valuable part of it.

And, once you get through the first year of law school, the odds are huge that you will graduate from law school and eventually become a lawyer. Being a lawyer can be a great thing. It is a job where you get to help people while doing interesting work and earning a good living.

Grammar experts like to say that only Superman does good and the rest of us do well. As a lawyer you can do both. Welcome to the real Justice League.

SUMMARY OF CONTENTS

―――――――――

PREFACE V

ACKNOWLEDGMENTS VII

FOREWORD: FOR FIRST YEAR LAW STUDENTS IX

TABLE OF CASES XXIX

Chapter 1. An Overview of Criminal Law 1
A.   The Structure of the Criminal Law 1

Chapter 2. The Criminal Process 7
A.   From Investigation Through Trial 7
B.   The Appellate Process 8
C.   Common Procedural Postures 9
D.   Prosecutorial Discretion and Plea Bargaining 12
E.   Sentencing 12
F.   Professional Ethics 13
G.   Case in Context 14
H.   Special Focus: Prostitution and Sex Trafficking 17

Chapter 3. Philosophies of Punishment 29
A.   Retribution 30
B.   Major Utilitarian Theories of Punishment: Deterrence and
     Incapacitation 32
C.   Minor Utilitarian Theories 34
D.   The Bottom Line: Mixed Theories 35
E.   Case in Context 37
F.   Special Focus: Punishment and Addiction 43

Chapter 4. Statutory Interpretation and Sources of Law 55
A.   Common Law 56
B.   The Model Penal Code 56
C.   U.S. Constitutional Law and Federal Criminal Law....................... 57
D.   Statutory Interpretation 58
E.   Special Focus: Statutory Interpretation and White Collar Crime 75
F.   Constitutional Constraints: Legality, Vagueness and Overbreadth 95
G.   Special Focus: Sexual Autonomy.. 118

Chapter 5. The Guilty Hand 125
A.   The Requirement of a Voluntary Act 125
B.   Status Offenses 127
C.   How the Voluntary Act Doctrine Often Operates in Practice 128
D.   The Philosophy Behind the Voluntary Act Requirement 138

E.   Omission Liability 139
F.   An Important Limitation on Criminal Omission Liability 141
G.   The Philosophy Behind Limited Omission Liability 141
H.   Possessory Offenses 145
I.   Special Focus: Drug Possession 145
J.   Special Focus: Digital Possession 154
K.   Model Penal Code 165

Chapter 6. The Guilty Mind **167**
A.   Model Penal Code Mental State Definitions 168
B.   Common Law Mental States 171
C.   Specific vs. General Intent 173
D.   Special Focus: Mental States and Online Threats 180
E.   Conditional Intent 195
F.   Wilful Blindness 201
G.   Special Focus: Hate Crimes 204
H.   Analyzing Mental State Requirements 212
I.   Strict Liability in Common Law Jurisdictions 216
J.   Public Welfare Offenses 226
K.   Special Focus: Environmental Crime 236
L.   Special Focus: Drug Crime and Mental States 249

Chapter 7. Mistakes and the Guilty Mind **267**
A.   Mistake of Fact Doctrine Reflects but Does Not Change an Offense's
      Mental State Requirements 267
B.   Mistakes of Fact Do Not Have to Be Reasonable 268
C.   The Common Law Distinction Between Specific and General Intent
      with Respect to Mistakes 272
D.   Mistakes of Law Generally Are Not a Defense 272
E.   Malum Prohibitum Crimes and Mistakes of Law 273
F.   Mistakes of Law Defenses 281
G.   Model Penal Code 294

Chapter 8. Intoxication **297**
A.   Overview 297
B.   Intoxication as a General Mental State Defense 298
C.   Minority Rules 304
D.   Intoxication as a Conduct Defense 311
E.   Intoxication and Murder 311
F.   Intoxication and Timing 312
G.   Intoxication and Defensive Force 312
H.   Intoxication and Insanity 312
I.   Involuntary Intoxication 313
J.   Involuntary Intoxication and Temporary Insanity 318

Chapter 9. Homicide: An Overview **321**
A.   Intentional Killings 321

B.   Unintentional Killings 322
C.   Murder 322
D.   Manslaughter 322
E.   Degrees of Murder... 322
F.   Common Law Murder 323
G.   Model Penal Code 324

Chapter 10. Intent to Kill Murder **327**
A.   Intent to Kill 327
B.   Intent to Grievously Injure Murder 331

Chapter 11. Premeditated and Deliberate Murder **335**
A.   Premeditation and Deliberation Defined.................................. 335
B.   Model Penal Code 337
C.   Cases in Context.. 337

Chapter 12. Voluntary Manslaughter **355**
A.   Statutory Examples 356
B.   Elements of Provocation 356
C.   Adequacy of Provocation 358
D.   Reasonableness of Cooling Off Period 369
E.   Model Penal Code and EMED 381

Chapter 13. Unintentional Killings **391**
A.   Involuntary Manslaughter 391
B.   Depraved Heart Murder 411

Chapter 14. Felony Murder **431**
A.   Policies Behind the Felony Murder Doctrine 432
B.   Statutory Variations 432
C.   The Basic Rule... 433
D.   Overview of Felony Murder Limits 438
E.   Limits on Types of Felonies 439
F.   Limiting Felony Murder to Independent Felonies.................... 447
G.   Limits on the Causal Relationship Between the Felony and the
     Resulting Death.. 451
H.   Killings Committed by Non-Felons 469
I.   Other Types of Felony Murder Liability 473
J.   Misdemeanor or Unlawful Act Manslaughter 476

Chapter 15. Causation **483**
A.   Overview of the Elements... 483
B.   Actual Causation 484
C.   Proximate Cause 488
D.   Model Penal Code 499
E.   Special Focus: Assisted Suicide.. 501

Chapter 16. Inchoate Crimes Overview and Solicitation..................509
A. Overview 509
B. Solicitation 510
C. Solicitation as an Attempt? 516
D. Merger... 517

Chapter 17. Conspiracy...519
A. The Crime Is the Agreement 519
B. Policies Behind Conspiracy Doctrine 519
C. The Elements of Conspiracy: An Overview 520
D. The Guilty Hand: The Agreement... 521
E. The Guilty Mind: Intent to Agree and Intent to Achieve 526
F. Liability for Other Crimes 545
G. Abandoning or Withdrawing from a Conspiracy..................... 549
H. Duration of the Conspiracy... 554
I. Merger.. 558
J. Wharton's Rule 558
K. Unilateral vs. Bilateral Conspiracies..................................... 558
L. Scope of the Conspiracy 559
M. Model Penal Code 560

Chapter 18. Attempt...563
A. An Overview of the Elements 563
B. Sentencing 564
C. Complete Attempts and "Moral Luck" 564
D. Conduct Required for Attempt 565
E. Mental State Required for Attempt 576
F. Renunciation or Withdrawal 582
G. Impossibility 586
H. Model Penal Code 600

Chapter 19. Complicity and Liability for Crimes of Others...............603
A. Overview of the Elements.. 603
B. Philosophical and Policy Considerations 604
C. Common Law Terminology... 604
D. The Guilty Hand: Assistance... 606
E. The Guilty Hand: Acts of Encouragement.............................. 625
F. The Guilty Mind 631
G. Natural and Probable Consequences 644
H. Abandonment/Withdrawal... 649
I. Model Penal Code 653
J. Vicarious and Enterprise Liability Distinguished 655

Chapter 20. Defensive Force...659
A. Justification vs. Excuse... 659
B. Overview of the Elements.. 660
C. Model Penal Code 674

D. Imminence of Harm 676
E. Domestic Violence and Syndrome Evidence............................ 677
F. Necessity of Force... 688
G. Stand Your Ground and the Duty to Retreat 689
H. Protection of Property and Home.. 691
I. Proportionate Force.. 697
J. Initial Aggressor Rules 697
K. Protection of Others 709
L. Imperfect Self Defense.. 710
M. Model Penal Code Sections.. 711

Chapter 21. Duress and Necessity.. 715
A. Elements of Duress 716
B. Elements of the Necessity Defense 718
C. Cases in Context... 720

Chapter 22. Insanity and Related Defenses 733
A. Diminished Capacity and Partial Responsibility 733
B. Overview of the Elements of Insanity...................................... 735
C. Procedural Background... 736
D. Mental Disease or Defect 737
E. M'Naghten Test 738
F. Arguing About Delusional Beliefs... 753
G. M'Naghten Criticisms and Responses 764
H. The Model Penal Code 766

Chapter 23. Rape 777
A. The Challenges and Rewards of Rape Law 777
B. Overview of Elements 779
C. The Predicate Sexual Act.. 781
D. Force.. 781
E. Lack of Capacity 782
F. Non-Consent 782
G. Acquaintance Rape and Marital Rape 784
H. Mental State as to Consent 784
I. Degrees of Rape 784
J. The MPC 784
K. Cases in Context... 785

Chapter 24. Miscellaneous Crimes Against the Person 819
A. Assault and Battery Distinguished... 819
B. Battery 819
C. Assault 820
D. Stalking.. 829
E. False Imprisonment 835
F. Kidnapping 835

Chapter 25. Property Crimes **839**
A.   Larceny 840
B.   Embezzlement 843
C.   Obtaining Property by False Pretenses 843
D.   Forgery and Writing Bad Checks 844
E.   Consolidated Theft Statutes 845
F.   Robbery 854
G.   Burglary 859

Appendix. The Ultimate Practice Problem **875**

INDEX 881

TABLE OF CONTENTS

PREFACE V

ACKNOWLEDGMENTS VII

FOREWORD: FOR FIRST YEAR LAW STUDENTS IX

TABLE OF CASES XXIX

Chapter 1. An Overview of Criminal Law 1
A.   The Structure of the Criminal Law.. 1
     1.   The Guilty Hand... 2
     2.   The Guilty Mind 2
     3.   Moved by 2
     4.   The Required Circumstances.. 2
     5.   Example: The Case of the Burgling Butt............................. 3
     6.   Sometimes Causing a Bad Result 4
     7.   In the Absence of a Justification or an Excuse................... 5

Chapter 2. The Criminal Process... 7
A.   From Investigation Through Trial 7
B.   The Appellate Process 8
C.   Common Procedural Postures 9
     1.   Errors in Jury Instructions.. 9
     2.   Motions to Dismiss Before Trial 9
     3.   Motions to Dismiss During Trial and Challenges to Sufficiency of
          the Evidence.. 9
     4.   Evidentiary Rulings 10
     5.   Appeals by the Prosecution.. 10
     6.   Jury Nullification 11
D.   Prosecutorial Discretion and Plea Bargaining 12
E.   Sentencing 12
F.   Professional Ethics.. 13
G.   Case in Context 14
     Christopher C. Owens, Jr. v. State of Maryland 14
H.   Special Focus: Prostitution and Sex Trafficking 17
     The People of the State of New York v. Carol Link and Debra
          Meltsner 17
     U.S. v. Carson 21

Chapter 3. Philosophies of Punishment 29
A.   Retribution... 30
B.   Major Utilitarian Theories of Punishment: Deterrence and
     Incapacitation 32
C.   Minor Utilitarian Theories 34

D. The Bottom Line: Mixed Theories..35
   Practice Problem 3.1: The Sentencing Game 36
E. Case in Context 37
   The Queen v. Dudley & Stephens 37
   Practice Problem 3.2: Flight 93 42
F. Special Focus: Punishment and Addiction 43
   Robison v. California...43
   Powell v. Texas...50

Chapter 4. Statutory Interpretation and Sources of Law 55
A. Common Law...56
B. The Model Penal Code 56
C. U.S. Constitutional Law and Federal Criminal Law...............57
D. Statutory Interpretation..58
   United States of America v. Hilton A. Lake 59
   United States of America v. David Nosal 63
E. Special Focus: Statutory Interpretation and White Collar Crime 75
   John L. Yates v. United States..76
   James Brogan v. United States 89
F. Constitutional Constraints: Legality, Vagueness and Overbreadth.......95
   State of Vermont v. Rebekah S. VanBuren 96
   City of Chicago v. Jesus Morales et al. 111
G. Special Focus: Sexual Autonomy...118
   Lawrence v. Texas...118
   Practice Problem 4.0: Criminal Keystrokes.........................124

Chapter 5. The Guilty Hand..125
A. The Requirement of a Voluntary Act 125
   1. Reflexes Are Not Voluntary..126
   2. Acts Done While Sleepwalking and Under Hypnosis Might Not Be Voluntary 126
   3. Acts Done Under Duress Are "Voluntary" 126
   4. Acts Done Habitually Are Considered "Voluntary".......127
B. Status Offenses...127
C. How the Voluntary Act Doctrine Often Operates in Practice 128
   Martin v. State 128
   People v. Decina 129
   People v. Grant 134
   Practice Problem 5.1: Traumatic Touching 138
D. The Philosophy Behind the Voluntary Act Requirement 138
E. Omission Liability...139
   1. Statutory Duties 139
   2. Contractual Duties 140
   3. Status Relationships 140
   4. Duties Voluntarily Assumed..140
   5. Creation of a Risk of Peril...141
F. An Important Limitation on Criminal Omission Liability 141

G. The Philosophy Behind Limited Omission Liability 141
     Jones v. United States 142
H. Possessory Offenses... 145
I. Special Focus: Drug Possession... 145
     The State v. Joe Frank Matarazzo.. 145
     United States of America v. Rafael Angel Zavala Maldonado 147
J. Special Focus: Digital Possession.. 154
     State of South Dakota v. Todd David Linson 155
     State of Oregon v. Barry Lowell Barger 159
K. Model Penal Code... 165
     Practice Problem 5.2: Left Holding the Bag 166

Chapter 6. The Guilty Mind **167**
A. Model Penal Code Mental State Definitions 168
     M.P.C. § 2.02. General Requirements of Culpability.......................... 168
B. Common Law Mental States 171
     Regina v. Faulkener... 171
C. Specific vs. General Intent.. 173
     State of Vermont v. James Riley 175
     State v. Richardson 177
D. Special Focus: Mental States and Online Threats............................. 180
     Anthony Douglas Elonis v. United States 180
E. Conditional Intent... 195
     Francois Holloway, aka Abdu Ali v. United States............................. 195
F. Wilful Blindness 201
     United States v. Jewell 201
G. Special Focus: Hate Crimes.. 204
     United States of America v. Miller... 204
H. Analyzing Mental State Requirements... 212
     1. Model Penal Code Default Rules 213
         M.P.C. § 2.02. General Requirements of Culpability 213
     Practice Problem 6.1: Home Alone... 215
     2. Common Law Default Rules 215
     Practice Problem 6.2: Cold-Calling Crime 216
I. Strict Liability in Common Law Jurisdictions 216
     Regina v. Prince... 217
     Dean v. United States 222
J. Public Welfare Offenses... 226
     Morissette v. United States 228
     Practice Problem 6.3: Statutory Smorgasbord 236
K. Special Focus: Environmental Crime.. 236
     United States of America v. Michael H. Weitzenhoff; Thomas W.
         Mariani.. 236
L. Special Focus: Drug Crime and Mental States 249
     State of Florida v. Luke Jarrod Adkins, et al. 249
     People v. Ryan 262
     Practice Problem 6.4: Dubious Downloading 266

Chapter 7. Mistakes and the Guilty Mind 267
A. Mistake of Fact Doctrine Reflects but Does Not Change an Offense's
  Mental State Requirements.. 267
B. Mistakes of Fact Do Not Have to Be Reasonable 268
  People v. Navarro 269
C. The Common Law Distinction Between Specific and General Intent
  with Respect to Mistakes 272
D. Mistakes of Law Generally Are Not a Defense 272
  Practice Problem 7.1: A Sharp Distinction 273
E. Malum Prohibitum Crimes and Mistakes of Law 273
  People v. Marrero 274
F. Mistakes of Law Defenses 281
  United States of America v. Dennis Moran 281
  People v. Bray.. 289
G. Model Penal Code.. 294
  § 2.04. Ignorance or Mistake 294
  Practice Problem 7.2: Monumental Mistakes.. 295

Chapter 8. Intoxication 297
A. Overview 297
B. Intoxication as a General Mental State Defense 298
M.P.C. § 2.08. Intoxication 299
  State v. Cameron... 300
C. Minority Rules... 304
  Montana v. Egelhoff 305
D. Intoxication as a Conduct Defense 311
E. Intoxication and Murder... 311
F. Intoxication and Timing 312
G. Intoxication and Defensive Force... 312
H. Intoxication and Insanity 312
  1. Temporary Insanity... 312
  2. Settled Insanity Resulting from Intoxicating Substances............. 312
  3. Intoxicated While Insane 313
I. Involuntary Intoxication 313
  1. Coerced Intoxication.. 313
  2. Pathological Intoxication 313
  Commonwealth of Pennsylvania v. Karen Smith 314
J. Involuntary Intoxication and Temporary Insanity 318
  Practice Problem 8.0: "Just Take Two Pills and Call Your Lawyer in
  the Morning" 318

Chapter 9. Homicide: An Overview 321
A. Intentional Killings 321
B. Unintentional Killings 322
C. Murder 322
D. Manslaughter 322
E. Degrees of Murder... 322

F. Common Law Murder 323
G. Model Penal Code 324
   § 210.2. Murder 324
   § 210.3. Manslaughter 324
   § 210.4. Negligent Homicide 325
   Practice Problem 9.0: Interpreting Murder 325

Chapter 10. Intent to Kill Murder **327**
A. Intent to Kill 327
   Robert Francis, Warden v. Raymond Lee Franklin 328
B. Intent to Grievously Injure Murder 331
   Practice Problem 10.0: Mezcal Murder? 332

Chapter 11. Premeditated and Deliberate Murder **335**
A. Premeditation and Deliberation Defined 335
   1. Failed Excuses 336
   2. Earmarks of Premeditation and Deliberation 336
B. Model Penal Code 337
   Article 210. Criminal Homicide 337
      § 210.2. Murder 337
C. Cases in Context 337
   State v. Bingham 337
   Watson v. U.S. 340
   Commonwealth v. Carroll 345
   Practice Problem 11.0: O Pioneers 349

Chapter 12. Voluntary Manslaughter **355**
A. Statutory Examples 356
B. Elements of Provocation 356
C. Adequacy of Provocation 358
   Illinois v. Walker 359
   Girouard v. Maryland 362
   Brooks v. State 366
D. Reasonableness of Cooling Off Period 369
   State v. Gounagias 369
   People v. Ellena Starr Nesler 373
   People v. Albert Joseph Berry 375
E. Model Penal Code and EMED 381
   Model Penal Code Section 210.3 381
   American Law Institute, Model Penal Code and Commentaries 381
   People v. Casassa 383
   Practice Problem 12.0: A Fatal Reunion 387

Chapter 13. Unintentional Killings **391**
A. Involuntary Manslaughter 391
   The People of the State of Colorado v. Nathan Hall 392
   Practice Problem 13.1: Texting and Dying 404

The State of Washington v. Williams 405
Practice Problem 13.2: Ember Alert 410
B. Depraved Heart Murder 411
Mayes v. Illinois.. 412
People v. Marjorie Knoller 415
   1. Model Penal Code and Reckless Murder 424
      Section 210.2. Murder 424
      Kansas v. John P. Doub, III.. 424
Practice Problem 13.3: A Murderous Beef? 429

Chapter 14. Felony Murder.. 431
A. Policies Behind the Felony Murder Doctrine 432
B. Statutory Variations 432
C. The Basic Rule.. 433
West Virginia v. Paul Emerson Sims 433
People v. Archie Fuller.. 436
D. Overview of Felony Murder Limits 438
E. Limits on Types of Felonies 439
   1. Enumeration.. 439
   2. The Inherently Dangerous Felony Rule..................................... 439
      Hines v. The State of Georgia... 440
      The People v. Evert Keith Howard.. 443
F. Limiting Felony Murder to Independent Felonies............................. 447
The People v. Linda Lee Smith 448
G. Limits on the Causal Relationship Between the Felony and the
   Resulting Death... 451
   1. Time and Place Rules.. 452
      The People of the State of New York v. Gladman 452
   2. Logical Relationship Rules 456
      People v. Cavitt... 457
   3. Causation Rules 461
      State v. Martin.. 462
H. Killings Committed by Non-Felons 469
Kansas v. Sanexay Sophophone 470
I. Other Types of Felony Murder Liability.. 473
Model Penal Code Section 210.2. Murder.. 474
Model Penal Code, Comment to 210.2 474
Practice Problem 14.1: A Very Tarantino Felony............................... 475
J. Misdemeanor or Unlawful Act Manslaughter................................... 476
U.S. v. Earl E. Walker.. 476
Practice Problem 14.2: Deadly Dealings.. 479
Practice Problem 14.3: 911 Murder.. 480
Practice Problem 14.4: Murderous Beef Redux................................. 481

Chapter 15. Causation 483
A. Overview of the Elements... 483

B. Actual Causation 484
    1. Multiple Actual Causes and Substantial Factors 484
    2. The Year and a Day Rule 485
        Regina v. Martin Dyos 485
C. Proximate Cause 488
    1. Unexpected Victims and Transferred Intent................... 489
    2. Intervening Causes 489
    3. Dependent Intervening Causes 490
    4. Pre-existing Weakness of the Victim 490
    5. Independent (or Coincidental) Intervening Causes 491
    6. Pulling the Plug on Life Support.................................... 491
        Commonwealth v. Root 492
        State v. Echols 498
D. Model Penal Code.. 499
E. Special Focus: Assisted Suicide... 501
    People v. Kevorkian... 501
    Practice Problem 15.0: Death by Text Message 505

Chapter 16. Inchoate Crimes Overview and Solicitation **509**
A. Overview 509
B. Solicitation 510
    1. An Historical Example 510
    2. First Amendment Limits 511
        New York v. Robert Quentin & John Garcia 511
        United States of America v. William White.................... 513
C. Solicitation as an Attempt? 516
    Model Penal Code.. 516
        § 5.02. Criminal Solicitation 516
D. Merger 517
    Practice Problem 16.0: "Do You Want to Go?"................... 517

Chapter 17. Conspiracy... **519**
A. The Crime Is the Agreement 519
B. Policies Behind Conspiracy Doctrine 519
C. The Elements of Conspiracy: An Overview 520
D. The Guilty Hand: The Agreement.. 521
    1. The Guilty Hand: Overt Act... 522
    Commonwealth of Pennsylvania v. Charles Azim 523
    United States v. Fitz 524
E. The Guilty Mind: Intent to Agree and Intent to Achieve 526
    People v. Swain 528
    1. Purposeful vs. Knowing Assistance................................ 532
        People v. Lauria 533
    2. Attendant Circumstances 541
        United States v. Feola 541
    3. The Corrupt Motive Doctrine 545

F.   Liability for Other Crimes 545
       United States of America v. Diaz 546
G.   Abandoning or Withdrawing from a Conspiracy 549
       The People v. David Wayne Sconce 550
H.   Duration of the Conspiracy 554
       United States v. Recio 554
I.   Merger 558
J.   Wharton's Rule 558
K.   Unilateral vs. Bilateral Conspiracies 558
L.   Scope of the Conspiracy 559
M.   Model Penal Code 560
       Section 5.03. Criminal Conspiracy 560
       Practice Problem 17.0: The Long Game 561

Chapter 18. Attempt 563
A.   An Overview of the Elements 563
B.   Sentencing 564
C.   Complete Attempts and "Moral Luck" 564
D.   Conduct Required for Attempt 565
       People v. Murray 568
       U.S. v. Jackson, Scott, & Allen 569
       Practice Problem 18.1: Fatal Feedback 575
E.   Mental State Required for Attempt 576
     1.   Attempted Result Crimes 576
          South Dakota v. Lyerla 577
     Practice Problem 18.2: Hunter's Squabble 580
     2.   Attempted Felony Murder 580
     3.   Attempted Manslaughter 580
     4.   Attempted Reckless or Negligent Conduct Crimes 581
     5.   Purpose vs. Knowledge 581
     6.   Attendant Circumstances 581
     7.   Model Penal Code Mental State Requirements for Attempt 582
F.   Renunciation or Withdrawal 582
       People v. Staples 583
G.   Impossibility 586
     1.   Factual vs. Legal Impossibility 586
          People v. Dlugash 587
     2.   The Breakdown of the Distinction Between Factual and Legal
          Impossibility 591
     3.   The Model Penal Code and Pure Legal Impossibility 591
          People v. Thousand 592
     4.   The Modern Approach 599
     5.   Inherent Impossibility 600
H.   Model Penal Code 600
       § 5.01. Criminal Attempt 601
       Practice Problem 18.3: Criminal Collaboration 602

Chapter 19. Complicity and Liability for Crimes of Others............. 603
A. Overview of the Elements.. 603
B. Philosophical and Policy Considerations 604
C. Common Law Terminology... 604
    1. Acquittal of the Principal... 606
D. The Guilty Hand: Assistance... 606
    State v. Ochoa.. 607
    State v. Tally.. 613
    State of West Virginia v. Kevin Dwayne Hoselton 621
E. The Guilty Hand: Acts of Encouragement................................... 625
    1. Solicitation and Conspiracy 625
    2. Mere Presence Not Enough 626
    3. Assistance by Omission... 627
       State ex rel. V.T. 627
    4. Aiding and Abetting 629
       Wilcox v. Jeffery 629
    Practice Problem 19.1: Facebook Dead 631
F. The Guilty Mind 631
    1. Purpose vs. Knowledge... 632
       The People v. Timothy Mark Beeman............................. 633
    Practice Problem 19.2: A Felonious Ride? 638
    2. Complicity for Recklessness or Negligence...................... 639
       The State of Washington v. Christine Hopkins............... 639
    3. The Alternate Rule for Complicity Mental States........... 644
G. Natural and Probable Consequences 644
    State of Maine v. William Linscott 645
H. Abandonment/Withdrawal 649
    The State of New Hampshire v. Paul Formella 650
I. Model Penal Code.. 653
    MPC § 2.06. Liability for Conduct of Another; Complicity 653
J. Vicarious and Enterprise Liability Distinguished 655
    Practice Problem 19.3: The Spice Boys 655
    Practice Problem 19.4: 911 Murder Redux.............................. 657

Chapter 20. Defensive Force.. 659
A. Justification vs. Excuse.. 659
B. Overview of the Elements... 660
    1. Used Against an Unlawful Force.. 660
    2. Actual Fear 661
    3. Reasonable Fear 661
       a. A Reasonable Fear Does Not Have to Be Correct.......... 661
       b. A Fear Cannot Be Unreasonable Even if Correct.......... 662
       c. Who Is the Reasonable Person, and What Is Reasonable
          Fear?.. 662
          People v. Goetz.. 663
    Practice Problem 20.1: Hating History 668

    4.   Subjective Reasonableness as a Standard for an Excuse 669

        State v. Wanrow 671

C. Model Penal Code 674

    1.   Actual but Unreasonable Fears 675

D. Imminence of Harm 676

    1.   Immediacy vs. Necessity 676

E. Domestic Violence and Syndrome Evidence 677

    State of North Carolina v. Judy Ann Laws Norman 678

    State of North Dakota v. Janice Leidholm 682

F. Necessity of Force 688

G. Stand Your Ground and the Duty to Retreat 689

    1.   The Castle Exception 690

H. Protection of Property and Home 691

    State of New Mexico v. Cecil Boyett 692

I. Proportionate Force 697

J. Initial Aggressor Rules 697

    The People v. Kelsey Dru Gleghorn 699

    United States of America v. Bennie L. Peterson 702

    Practice Problem 20.2: Concealed Culpability 709

K. Protection of Others 709

L. Imperfect Self Defense 710

M. Model Penal Code Sections 711

    § 3.04. Use of Force in Self-Protection 711

    § 3.05. Use of Force for the Protection of Other Persons 712

    Practice Problem 20.3: Fatal Flashback 713

Chapter 21. Duress and Necessity **715**

A. Elements of Duress 716

    1.   Duress Under the Model Penal Code 717

        § 2.09. Duress 717

    2.   Prison Escapes 718

B. Elements of the Necessity Defense 718

    Practice Problem 21.1: A Turn for the Worse? 720

C. Cases in Context 720

    United States of America v. Juan Manuel Contento-Pachon 720

    Practice Problem 21.2: Desert in the Desert 724

    Illinois v. Unger 724

    1.   Necessity Under the Model Penal Code 728

        § 3.02. Justification Generally: Choice of Evils 729

    Practice Problem 21.3: Going Viral 730

Chapter 22. Insanity and Related Defenses **733**

A. Diminished Capacity and Partial Responsibility 733

    1.   Diminished Capacity 734

    Model Penal Code 734

        § 4.02. Evidence of Mental Disease or Defect Admissible

        When Relevant to Element of the Offense 734

2. Partial Responsibility 735
B. Overview of the Elements of Insanity 735
C. Procedural Background 736
　1. Competency Distinguished 737
D. Mental Disease or Defect 737
E. M'Naghten Test 738
　Eric Michael Clark v. Arizona 740
F. Arguing About Delusional Beliefs 753
　1. Deific Commands 754
　　Colorado v. Robert Pasqual Serravo 754
G. M'Naghten Criticisms and Responses 764
　1. The Irresistible Impulse Test and the Role of Volition 765
　2. The Durham "Product" Test and the Scope of Psychiatric
　　Expertise 765
H. The Model Penal Code 766
　§ 4.01. Mental Disease or Defect Excluding Responsibility 766
　1. The Hinckley Verdict and the Return of M'Naghten 768
　United States of America v. Robert Lyons 768
　Practice Problem 22.0: Friends, Lovers, and Zombies 775

Chapter 23. Rape 777
A. The Challenges and Rewards of Rape Law 777
B. Overview of Elements 779
C. The Predicate Sexual Act 781
D. Force 781
E. Lack of Capacity 782
F. Non-Consent 782
G. Acquaintance Rape and Marital Rape 784
H. Mental State as to Consent 784
I. Degrees of Rape 784
J. The MPC 784
K. Cases in Context 785
　Rusk v. State 785
　State v. Rusk 791
　The People of the State of New York v. Eric Dorsey 792
　Commonwealth of Pennsylvania v. Robert A. Berkowitz 800
　In the Interest of M.T.S. 811
　Practice Problem 23.0: Defining Rape 818

Chapter 24. Miscellaneous Crimes Against the Person 819
A. Assault and Battery Distinguished 819
B. Battery 819
C. Assault 820
　1. Attempted Battery Assault 820
　2. Intent to Frighten Assault 821
　　Commonwealth v. Albert J. Henson 822

      3. Aggravated Assaults 825
        The People of the State of Illinois v. William J. Conley 826
  D. Stalking 829
      The State of New Hampshire v. Frank Simone 830
  E. False Imprisonment 835
  F. Kidnapping 835
      Practice Problem 24.0: Just for Kicks 835

Chapter 25. Property Crimes **839**
  A. Larceny 840
      1. Taking 840
      2. Larceny by Trick 840
      3. Asportation 840
      4. Personal Property 841
      5. Another's Property 841
      6. Intent to Permanently Deprive 841
      7. Good Faith Mistakes 842
      8. Doctrine of Continuing Trespass 842
  B. Embezzlement 843
  C. Obtaining Property by False Pretenses 843
      1. Larceny by Trick Distinguished 844
  D. Forgery and Writing Bad Checks 844
  E. Consolidated Theft Statutes 845
      Commonwealth v. James O. Mills 845
      Practice Problem 25.1: Drunken Dealings at Downton Abbey 854
  F. Robbery 854
      1. From Person or Presence 855
      2. Through Force or Intimidation 855
      3. Mental State 856
      4. Attempted Robbery 856
      5. Aggravated Robbery 856
        Lear v. State 856
  G. Burglary 859
      1. Breaking 859
      2. Entering 860
      3. Felonious or Larcenous Intent 860
      4. Burglary as an Anticipatory Offense 860
        State of Maine v. Dale Thibeault 861
        State of Minnesota v. Peter Allen Colvin 866
      Practice Problem 25.2: Murderous Munchies? 873

Appendix. The Ultimate Practice Problem **875**
Psycho-Survivor 875

INDEX 881

TABLE OF CASES

The principal cases are in bold type.

Abeyta, State v., 694
Ables, Commonwealth v., 806
Acevedo, United States v., 152
Acosta, People v., 265
Adkins, State v., 249, 258
Allweiss, People v., 794
Anderson, State v., 648
Andrews, Commonwealth v., 848
Arata, State v., 339
Armstrong, State v., 648
Arzate-Nunez, United States v., 71
Ashcroft v. Free Speech Coalition, 514
Atencio, United States v., 721
Austin v. United States, 341
Autterson, People v., 291
Avery, State v., 694
Azim, Commonwealth v., 523
Bailey, State v., 693
Baker, United States v., 573
Balint, United States v., 186, 230, 233, 252
Ballem, Commonwealth v., 347
Barger, State v., 157, **159**, 161
Barker, United States v., 277, 278
Barnes v. State, 232
Barnes, State v., 163, 164
Barry, Commonwealth v., 850
Barry, State v., 156
Bass, United States v., 71, 774
Bates v. United States, 223
Bausch, State v., 156
Beardsley, People v., 144
Beeman, People v., 633
Behrman, United States v., 229, 233
Beltran, People v., 635
Berklowitz, Commonwealth v., 807
Berkowitz, Commonwealth v., 800
Berry, People v., 375
Billa, People v., 458
Bily, United States v., 285
Bingham, State v., 337
Bissett, People v., 360
Blake v. United States, 769, 771
Blakeney, State v., 176
Blue, State v., 694
Bolanger, People v., 636
Booker, United States v., 751
Borchers, People v., 378
Boren, United States v., 64
Boss, People v., 459
Bostic v. United States, 341

Boutin, State v., 175
Boyett, State v., 692
Brandenburg v. Ohio, 514
Brawner, United States v., 761
Bray, People v., 289
Brinkley v. United States, 770, 771
Broadcast Music, Inc. v. Xanthas, Inc., 285
Brogan v. United States, 89
Brooks v. State, 366
Brown v. State, 858
Brown, People v., 652
Brown, State v., 257
Brown, United States v., 222
Bufarale, People v., 378
Burch, People v., 291
Burns, United States v., 62
Burton, People v., 450
Cabaccang, United States v., 71
Cable/Home Communication v. Network Productions, 285
Cabral, People v., 635
Callanan v. United States, 548
Calzada, People v., 450
Cameron, State v., 300
Campos, State v., 694
Canola, State v., 466
Carroll, Commonwealth v., 345
Carson, United States v., 21
Carter v. State, 365
Carter v. United States, 189
Carter, People v., 454
Casassa, People v., 383
Castillo, People v., 379
Castro, United States v., 555
Cavitt, People v., 457
Chalmers, State v., 426
Chapdelaine, United States v., 153
Chavez, State v., 743
Cheek v. United States, 283
Chicago, City of v. Morales, 111
Chicone v. State, 250, 251
Clark v. Arizona, 740
Clark, People v., 701
Claudio, Commonwealth v., 853
Cleaves, People v., 502
Coates v. Cincinnati, 115
Coffin v. United States, 259
Cohen v. California, 515
Coleman, People v., 798
Collins, Commonwealth v., 316

xxix

Colon, Commonwealth v., 853
Colvin, State v., 866
Conley, People v., 375, 378, 379, **826**
Connally, State v., 162
Connick v. Myers, 109
Connors, People v., 198
Contento-Pachon, United States v., 720
Contes, People v., 262
Cookson, State v., 863
Corcoran, Commonwealth v., 848, 849
Corley, People v., 274
Cornell, United States v., 307
Couch, State v., 693
Cox v. State, 192, 364
Crawford v. United States, 342
Crenshaw, State v., 762, 764
Crimmins, United States v., 542, 543, 545
Cruz, United States v., 555
Curtis, People v., 694
Dahlberg v. People, 827
Daniels, People v., 291
Darby, United States v., 192
Davis v. State, 364
Davis v. United States, 261, 772
Davis, People v., 726
Dean v. United States, 222
Decina, People v., 129
Deso, State v., 176
Devine, People v., 270
Diamond Power Int'l, Inc. v. Davidson, 70
Diaz, United States v., 546
DiNovo, United States v., 153
Diodoro, Commonwealth v., 158
Dlugash, People v., 587
Doepel v. United States, 341
Dolan v. People, 454
Domanski, Commonwealth v., 849
Donough, Commonwealth v., 347
Donovan, Commonwealth v., 849
Dorman, Commonwealth v., 810
Dorsey, People v., 792
Dotterweich, United States v., 52, 186, 234
Doub, State v., 424
Drew, United States v., 69
Drum, Commonwealth v., 347
Dun & Bradstreet, Inc. v. Greenmoss Builders, Inc., 101
Earl, People v., 438
Earnest, Commonwealth v., 348
Echeverri, United States v., 153
Echols, State v., 498
Edwards v. California, 44
EF Cultural Travel BV v. Explorica, Inc., 73
Elonis v. United States, 180

Farmer v. Brennan, 189
Farren, Commonwealth v., 232
Faulkener, Regina v., 171
Faulkner, State v., 364
Feola, United States v., 541
Fiorentino, People v., 385
Fitz, United States v., 524
Fitzgerald Publishing Co., Inc. v. Baylor Publishing Co., Inc., 285
Flores, People v., 798
Formella, State v., 650
Francis v. Franklin, 328
Frank, Commonwealth v., 806
Frazier, State v., 624
Freed, United States v., 246, 253
Fries, State v., 162
Frontiero v. Richardson, 674
Fuller, People v., 436
Gaines, State v., 162
Gappins, State v., 678
Gardner v. People, 274
Gemma, United States v., 26
Giaccio v. Pennsylvania, 114
Ginzburg v. United States, 110
Giro, People v., 454
Girouard v. Maryland, 362
Gladman, People v., 452
Gleghorn, People v., 699
Goetz, People v., 663
Goldberg v. State, 789
Gonzales, United States v., 90
Goodall, State v., 647
Gordon, United States v., 722, 723
Gorshen, People v., 379
Gounagias, State v., 369
Graham, People v., 379
Grant, People v., 134
Green v. United States, 770
Guido, State v., 368
Guiteau's Case, 763
Hall v. United States, 341
Hall, People v., 392
Hansen, People v., 446
Harmon, People v., 726
Harper, State v., 623
Harris v. United States, 223, 341
Hays, Commonwealth v., 850
Hazel v. State, 787, 789
Head v. United States, 341
Hecker, People v., 701
Heller, Commonwealth v., 347
Hemphill v. United States, 341
Heng Awkak Roman, United States v., 573
Henson, Commonwealth v., 822
Hernandez, People v., 291, 579
Hicks v. United States, 636
Hicks, Commonwealth v., 317
High, State v., 862

Hines v. State, 440
Holloway v. United States, 195
Holman v. Johnson, 540
Holmes, United States v., 40
Homeyer, Commonwealth v., 347
Hood, People v., 636
Hopkins, State v., 639
Hopt v. People, 307
Hoselton, State v., 621
Houston v. Hill, 117
Howard v. United States, 771
Howard, People v., 443
Hsu, United States v., 596
Huter, People v., 453
Illinois v. Walker, 359
Iniguez, People v., 105
International Airport Ctrs., LLC v. Citrin, 70
International Ass'n of Machinists & Aerospace Workers v. Werner-Masuda, 70
International Minerals & Chem. Corp., United States v., 240, 247, 253
Irvin, Commonwealth v., 809
Jackson v. United States, 344
Jackson v. Virginia, 17, 849
Jackson, People v., 454
Jackson, United States v., 569
Jacobson v. Massachusetts, 45
Jaurequi, People v., 48
Jeffries, Commonwealth v., 179
Jewell, United States v., 201
John Hancock Mut. Life Ins. Co. v. Harris Trust and Sav. Bank, 197
John, United States v., 70, 73
Johnson, Commonwealth v., 850
Johnson, People v., 445
Johnson, State v., 648
Jones v. United States, 65, 142, 341
Jones, Commonwealth v., 347
Joseph G., In re, 503
Judge, State v., 578
Kain, United States v., 157
Kalinowski, Commonwealth v., 849
Kelley, Commonwealth v., 848
Kelly, Commonwealth v., 848
Kelso, People v., 450
Kenneally, Commonwealth v., 848, 849, 850
Kent v. Dulles, 113
Kevorkian, People v., 501
Key, Commonwealth v., 853
Kimball, State v., 648
Kimble, People v., 459
King, Commonwealth v., 848, 849, 850, 851
King, People v., 635
Knoller, People v., 415

Kolender v. Lawson, 114, 115, 116
Kozminski, United States v., 69
Labrum, State v., 628
Lacey, People v., 652
Lake, United States v., 59
Lamare, United States v., 152
Lambert v. California, 254
Laney v. United States, 708
Lanzetta v. New Jersey, 114
Larson, State v., 871
Latimore, Commonwealth v., 849
Lauria, People v., 533
Lawrence v. Texas, 118
Lear v. State, 856
Ledford, State v., 180
Leidholm, State v., 682
Leonard, Commonwealth v., 852
Lewis v. United States, 557
Lewis, People v., 459
Liberty, Commonwealth v., 849
Link, People v., 17
Linscott, State v., 645
Linson, State v., 155
Liparota v. United States, 240
Littlefield, State v., 833
Logan, People v., 377, 380
Long, People v., 379
Lopes, State v., 628
Loustaunau, People v., 701
Lovercamp, People v., 726
LVRC Holdings LLC v. Brekka, 63, 72
Lyerla, State v., 577
Lyons, United States v., 768, 769, 775
M.T.S., In the Interest of, 811
Maldonado v. Morales, 74
Marbury v. Madison, 187
Marrero, People v., 274
Marsh v. People, 156
Martin Dyos, Regina v., 485
Martin v. State, 128
Martin, State v., 462
Martinez, State v., 578
Marwig, People v., 454
Matarazzo, State v., 145
Matlock, People v., 503
Mattison, People v., 450
Mayes v. Illinois, 412
McFadden, State v., 642
McKinney, State v., 159
McMillian, United States v., 26
Meadows, Commonwealth v., 808, 810
Medlin, State v., 251
Melton, Commonwealth v., 347
Mendoza, People v., 291
Mercer, State v., 159
Mesa, People v., 700
Mickelson v. Barnet, 850
Micklus, United States v., 723

Miller, United States v., 204
Mills, Commonwealth v., 845, 850
Mitchell v. United States, 477
Mizell, People v., 265
Monahan, Commonwealth v., 849, 852
Montana v. Egelhoff, 305, 742
Montgomery, State v., 459
Montsdoca v. State, 858
Moore, Commonwealth v., 347
Morales, State v., 122
Moran, Commonwealth v., 807
Moran, United States v., 281
Moretti, State v., 596
Morissette v. United States, 185, **228**, 249, 280, 636
Morse, People v., 379
Mosher, People v., 375, 379
Mott, State v., 741, 744
Murdock, United States v., 284
Murphy v. Waterfront Comm'n of N.Y. Harbor, 91
Murray, People v., 568
Nadal-Ginard, Commonwealth v., 848, 850
Natal, United States v., 88
National Carbide Corp., Commissioner v., 80
Navarro, People v., 269
Neese, People v., 291
Nelson, Commonwealth v., 347
Nesler, People v., 373
New v. State, 158
New York Times Co. v. Sullivan, 101
Newbegin, State v., 862
Nichols, Commonwealth v., 232
Norman, State v., 678
Northrop, People v., 450
Nosal, United States v., 63
Oare, State v., 163
Ochoa, State v., 607
Orbit One Commc'ns, Inc. v. Numerex Corp., 70
Overbey, State v., 156
Owens v. State, 14
Palmer, Commonwealth v., 315
Parsons, State v., 857
Paternostro v. United States, 90
Patrick, People v., 637
Patrick, United States v., 721
Patterson v. New York, 307, 330, 742
Peacher, State ex rel. v. Sencindiver, W.Va., 435
Pearsall, Commonwealth v., 810
Pellegrino, State v., 695
Pembliton, Regina v., 172
Peoni, United States v., 623
Perez, People v., 578, 579, 702
Perna v. Pirozzi, 816
Peterson, United States v., 702

Pfeiffer v. Salas, 853
Phillips, Commonwealth v., 347
Phillips, People v., 446
Pinkerton v. United States, 548
Planned Parenthood of Columbia/Willamette, Inc. v. American Coalition of Life Activists, 514, 515
Planned Parenthood of Southeastern Pa. v. Casey, 122
Playboy Entm't Grp., Inc., United States v., 100
Poindexter, Commonwealth v., 806
Porter, State v., 178, 611
Poss, State v., 578
Powell v. Texas, 50, 308
Powell, State v., 612
Powerex Corp. v. Reliant Energy Servs., Inc., 67
Price, People ex rel. v. Sheffield Farms-Slawson-Decker Co., 233
Primeaux, State v., 578
Prince, Regina v., 217
Pulido, People v., 457
Queen, The v. Dudley & Stephens, 37
Quentin, People v., 511
R.A.V. v. St. Paul, 190
Ragansky v. United States, 192
Ramirez v. Territory, 858
Rash, State v., 578
Ratzlaf v. United States, 240, 246
RCA/Ariola Int'l, Inc. v. Thomas & Grayston Co., 285
Recio, United States v., 554
Redline, Commonwealth v., 472
Reese, United States v., 115
Reisman, People v., 263
Rex v. Gnosil, 857
Reynolds v. State, 858
Rhode Island Recreation Center v. Aetna Casualty and Surety Co., 721
Rhodes, Commonwealth v., 805, 806, 807, 808, 809
Richardson, State v., 177
Richardson, United States v., 722
Richland, State v., 106
Riley, State v., 157, **175**
Riverside Bayview Homes, Inc., United States v., 242
Roberts, People v., 502
Robertson, People v., 446
Robinson, State v., 425, 642, 643
Robison v. California, 43
Roby, People v., 232
Rodriguez, United States v., 69, 73
Rodriguez-Rios, United States v., 90, 94
Rogers v. United States, 186

Romm, United States v., 157
Root, Commonwealth v., 492
Rose, United States v., 284
Rosen v. United States, 192
Rough, Commonwealth v., 808
Ruppert, Commonwealth v., 806
Rusk v. State, 785
Rusk, State v., 791
Russell, United States v., 64
Russello v. United States, 224
Ryan, Commonwealth v., 850
Ryan, People v., 262
Rye, State v., 695
Sandstrom v. Montana, 331, 636
Santos, United States v., 70
Satchell, People v., 448
Schindler Elevator Corp. v. United
    States ex rel. Kirk, 84
Schmidt, People v., 759, 764
Sconce, People v., 550
Scott v. State, 250, 251
Scott v. United States, 477
Sears, People v., 449
Sedeno, People v., 380
Serravo, People v., 754
Shamrock Foods Co. v. Gast, 70
Shelton v. Sec'y, Dep't of Corr., 252,
    257
Sherman v. United States, 93
Shevlin-Carpenter Co. v. Minnesota,
    253
Shockley, People v., 450
Shults, Commonwealth v., 347
Shuttlesworth v. Birmingham, 115
Simon, State v., 686
Simone, State v., 830
Sims, State v., 433
Slaney, Commonwealth v., 823
Small, People v., 379, 623
Small, State v., 833
Smiley v. Kansas, 116
Smith v. California, 44, 254
Smith v. Goguen, 117
Smith v. United States, 224
Smith, Commonwealth v., 314
Smith, People v., 263, **448**, 701, 702
Snow, Commonwealth v., 850, 851
Snyder v. Phelps, 102, 109
Sophophone, State v., 470
Spriggs, Commonwealth v., 652
Staples, People v., 583
Staples, United States v., 225, 240,
    245, 246
Stevens, United States v., 69, 109
Stevick v. Commonwealth, 807
Stobo, United States v., 192
Stuart, People v., 291
Swain, People v., 528
Tally, State v., 613

Taylor v. Illinois, 306
Taylor, People v., 450
Teague, United States v., 73
Tenement House Department of City
    of New York v. McDevitt, 232
Terminiello v. Chicago, 45
Terry, People v., 726
Terry, State v., 815
Thibeault, State v., 861
Thomas, United States v., 596
Thousand, People v., 592
Todaro, Commonwealth v., 317
Turner v. United States, 256
Ulster County Court v. Allen, 330
Unger, People v., 724
United States Gypsum Co., United
    States v., 225
University of Tex. Sw. Med. Ctr. v.
    Nassar, 210
V.T., State ex rel., 627
Valentine, People v., 377
Valles, People v., 666
VanBuren, State v., 96
Vasquez, People v., 458, 636
Vigilante, State v., 368
Virginia v. Black, 190
Vogel, People v., 291
Volk, Commonwealth v., 523
Waite, Commonwealth v., 232
Walker, People v., 701
Walker, United States v., 476
Walsh, People v., 454
Wanrow, State v., 671, 686
Ward, State v., 364
Washington, People v., 451
Washington, State v., 257
Watson v. United States, 223, **340**
Watson, Commonwealth v., 853
Watson, People v., 380, 446, 638
Watts v. United States, 188, 192
Weiss, People v., 274
Weitzenhoff, United States v., 236,
    244
Weller, State v., 164
West v. State, 14
Wetmore, People v., 270
Whipple v. Martinson, 44
White, Commonwealth v., 823, 824,
    825
White, United States v., 513
Whitehead v. State, 364
Wiener, United States v., 94
Wiggins v. State, 14
Wight, United States v., 153
Wilcox v. Jeffery, 629
Will, People v., 612
Williams v. Fears, 113
Williams v. Taylor, 223
Williams, Commonwealth v., 806

Williams, People v., 446
Williams, State v., 405
Williams-Yulee v. Fla. Bar, 100
Wilson v. State, 14
Wilson, People v., 449
Wiltberger, United States v., 70
Winegan v. State, 789
Wingler, State v., 681
Winkler, United States v., 156
Winship, In re, 647
Winston, People v., 291, 292
Wion v. United States, 771
Worden v. State, 157
X-Citement Video, United States v.,
   186, 255
Yanik, People v., 794, 799
Yates v. United States, 76
Young, State v., 459
**Zavala Maldonado, United States
   v., 147**

CRIMINAL LAW
CASES, CONTROVERSIES AND PROBLEMS

CHAPTER 1

AN OVERVIEW OF CRIMINAL LAW

■ ■ ■

Criminal Law should be your favorite subject in your first year of law school. I will admit that I am biased on this question. I love criminal law. I practiced criminal law; I teach criminal law; I write about criminal law. Let me offer you three objective reasons though why criminal law should be your favorite 1L subject.

1. *Criminal Law involves something Familiar and Interesting.* We are not talking about something unfamiliar, such as transactions involving widgets or "springing future interests." Our society is fascinated with crime and punishment, and our media saturates us with depictions of true and fictional crime. We all intuitively understand what crime is about—hurting people or messing with their stuff.

2. *Criminal Law involves Good and Evil.* Criminal law forces us to wrestle with how we define and differentiate between different degrees of evil. This provides criminal law with an organizing theme that is both familiar and interesting.

3. *Criminal Law enjoys a Coherent Structure.* You can sum up the basic structure of the criminal law in one sentence (which I will give you in the very next section). You can then use this sentence to organize your study of any criminal law doctrine and to analyze any criminal law problem. Not to say that the criminal law is simple. It will take you an entire semester to learn all the doctrines necessary to fully understand what this sentence means. But the structure of the criminal law brings a welcome order to its complexity. This order is particularly valuable to students in their first year of legal study.

A. THE STRUCTURE OF THE CRIMINAL LAW

Here is the sentence that sums up the basic structure of the criminal law. This sentence tells you what criminal liability requires.

The Guilty Hand moved by the Guilty Mind, under the required Circumstances, that sometimes causes a Result in the absence of a Justification or Excuse.

1

Quite a mouthful I admit, but it reflects a structure that is beautiful in its simplicity. Every word in this sentence does a lot of work, but the sentence will work for you on any criminal law case or question if you really learn what it means. Let's break it down into fundamental parts. In doing so, we will preview some important concepts that we will develop later.

1.   THE GUILTY HAND

This phrase refers to the "doing" part of a crime. All crimes require some sort of action. There is no such thing as a "thought crime," a crime that you can commit by thinking bad thoughts. You might have the guiltiest mental state imaginable ("I so want to kill him!"), but if you do not do what the crime requires you cannot be guilty. No conduct, no criminal liability.

2.   THE GUILTY MIND

This phrase refers to the mental state requirement of a crime. Oliver Wendell Holmes famously referred to the importance of mental states when he observed that "even a dog knows the difference between being tripped over and kicked." The criminal law relies heavily on the definitions of different mental states to determine whether a crime has occurred and to distinguish more serious from less serious crime. Even if the defendant performs the conduct required for the crime, she will not be guilty if she does not perform that conduct with the required mental state.

3.   MOVED BY

This phrase refers to the concurrence requirement. With very few exceptions, the guilty mind must exist at the same moment that the conduct is performed. Moreover, the guilty mind must move the guilty hand in the sense that the conduct must be caused or generated by the required mental state. Wishing someone dead at the moment you bump into him and knock him off a cliff would not be murder if the bump was neither intentional nor extremely reckless.

4.   THE REQUIRED CIRCUMSTANCES

This phrase refers to what is more formally described as the "attendant circumstances" of a crime. Some crimes—certainly not all—require certain circumstances to exist in order for the crime to take place. For example, some criminal statutes make it a special crime to do certain things on or near a school where children attend. These laws are typically passed to give special protection to children by making what is already a crime—selling illegal drugs, for example—a more serious crime within some specified distance of a school. The language of the statute requiring that the sale of drugs take place within a certain number of yards of a school is an attendant circumstance.

5.   EXAMPLE: THE CASE OF THE BURGLING BUTT

Before we go any further, let's work through an example involving the first four elements of our sentence. We will discuss burglary at greater length later, but a simplified statement of the elements of burglary follows.

Breaking and

Entering

A Dwelling

Of Another

At Night

With the Intent to commit a Felony or Larceny therein

Assume that one Friday night when you are leaving your apartment to go out, you notice that your next-door neighbor appears to have left the door to his apartment slightly ajar. He is a bit absentminded and has done this before. Usually, you just pull the door closed for him. But not this night. This night you are feeling curious, dare I say snoopy. You decide that you are going to sneak into his apartment and look around. You try to slip through the opening of the door without touching it, but your butt hits the door as you go through, and it swings open a bit more. You are sitting on his couch, browsing through his magazines when you see a beautiful diamond ring on his coffee table. Deciding to steal it, you grab the ring and leave his apartment.

Have you committed the crime of burglary? To answer that question you need to know a little more about how the criminal law defines some of the elements. The conduct required is breaking and entering. The attendant circumstances are that the structure entered must be a dwelling of another, and the entry must be accomplished at night. Well, we have the entry of a dwelling of another at night. Is the element of breaking present though? As we will learn, many jurisdictions define a breaking to include enlargement of any opening. So when your butt hit the door, you performed a breaking. Therefore, we have the guilty hand (or in this case the guilty butt), and we have the required circumstances. What about the mental state?

Here is where things get even more interesting. Burglary requires that you break and enter with the intent to commit a felony or larceny therein. Larceny is essentially stealing, so you supplied the required guilty mind when you decided to steal the ring. Nonetheless, the crime of burglary did not occur on these facts. What is missing? The concurrence requirement. At the moment you broke and entered, you did not intend to steal anything. Your guilty butt was not moved by the required guilty mind of a felon or a thief. You only decided to steal after the conduct that constitutes burglary was complete.

Does this mean you committed no crime? Of course not. You committed criminal trespass and larceny, so you are a trespasser and a thief but not a burglar because of the absence of concurrence between the guilty hand and the guilty mind.

Concurrence also works in the opposite direction. Assume this time that you saw the ring through a window while walking by and decided that you would enter the apartment in order to steal it. In this case, your guilty butt is moved by the required guilty mind of a thief. But this time you change your mind after you have entered the apartment. You say to yourself, "hey, I am a law student; I can't go around stealing from my neighbor's apartment." Have you committed the crime of burglary? Yes! You committed the crime of burglary when your guilty butt hit the door with the concurrent larcenous intent required. The fact that you did not go through with the larceny does not "undo" the burglary you already committed.

Now, let's return to the other elements of our simple sentence.

6.   SOMETIMES CAUSING A BAD RESULT

"Sometimes" does not sound very legal. However, the vast majority of crimes do not require results. For example, the crime of larceny requires the conduct of taking the property of another. Taking, in turn, requires you to move the property at least some slight distance. That movement is not thought to be a result, but part of the "doing" part of the offense. What, then, does the criminal law consider to be a result? Homicide crimes provide easy examples.

Homicide, by definition, involves the killing of a human being. Killing is conduct causing death. If death does not result from the conduct, then no homicide takes place. If you took a shot at me with a high-powered rifle intending to kill me but missed, you could not be guilty of murder. While you had the guilty hand (trigger finger, in this case) and the guilty mind (an intent to kill) required for murder, you did not have the bad result (death of a human being) that murder and all other homicide crimes require. Attempted murder? Yes, but attempted murder is not considered a result crime for the very reason that the result of death is not required.

If the crime does require a result, two things must exist. First, the result must occur. In the example given, I must die. Second, the bad result must have been caused by the guilty hand. Imagine now that you shot me with a high-powered rifle from a great distance with the intent to kill, but during the time it took the bullet to travel towards my head I was struck by lightning and died instantaneously. You would not be guilty of murder because the bullet you launched entered the brain of a corpse. The intended result of my death occurred, but it was not caused by your conduct. Again, you would be guilty only of attempted murder. The bottom line is that causation is an issue in criminal law only in those cases where the crimes require results.

All first-year criminal law courses spend a lot of time studying homicide, so you would be forgiven for thinking that result crimes are common. It bears emphasis that the majority of crimes do not require results, although the distinction between results and conduct is not always obvious. Assault with intent to inflict serious injury is not a result crime, for example. It requires you to assault someone with the intent to seriously injure them. The crime of assault inflicting serious bodily injury, on the other hand, does require the result of serious bodily injury to have been caused by the assault.

7. IN THE ABSENCE OF A JUSTIFICATION OR AN EXCUSE

If, up to this point, any one thing in our sentence is missing, that omission constitutes a defense. If you lack the guilty hand or the guilty mind or the attendant circumstances or causation of the required result, then you are not guilty of the crime. Certain general defenses may preclude criminal liability even if all elements of the crime are otherwise present. These general defenses are divided into two different categories: justifications and excuses.

The clearest example of a justification is self-defense. Assume you shot someone in the head with the intent to kill him and that he died as a result. Ordinarily that would be murder, but in this case the reason you shot the person was because he was charging at you with a whirring chainsaw, screaming that he was going to cut you in half. You did not need to read this book to realize that intentionally killing the chainsaw attacker would be justified on the grounds of self-defense. No crime occurs because you were justified in what you did.

Justifications are limited to those defenses where society either tolerates or approves of certain behavior that would otherwise be a crime. Society cheers when you kill the chainsaw attacker because society is glad that you defended yourself. When you can imagine society clapping in the background, the defense involved is always a justification.

Excuses, on the other hand, involve very different types of defenses. The clearest example of an excuse defense is insanity. Let's say that you shoot someone in the head intending to kill him because you believe him to be the vanguard of an alien invasion bent on exterminating the human race. You believe this because you suffer from paranoid schizophrenia. The person you shoot is not, of course, an alien invader. You would be excused from criminal responsibility for what would otherwise be murder on the grounds that you were legally insane at the time of the killing. Excuses, unlike justifications, do not involve conduct that society approves of or tolerates. No one claps when you kill an innocent person as a result of your mental illness. Excuse defenses are essentially concessions to human frailties. Excuses relieve you from criminal responsibility even though your conduct was not justified.

Note the repeated emphasis on criminal responsibility. An insane killer could still be civilly responsible for his actions. In fact, people who commit serious violent acts as the result of insanity are often involuntarily committed to mental institutions under civil statutes. The difference between civil and criminal responsibility will be something that we will talk more about when we discuss the purposes of criminal punishment.

So, once you have checked to see whether any justifications or excuses apply, you are done with your criminal law analysis. As promised, the whole of criminal law fits in one, easy-to-remember sentence, but it will take the rest of this book and an entire semester to learn how to use that sentence.

CHAPTER 2

THE CRIMINAL PROCESS

■ ■ ■

This chapter provides necessary background, but only background. This course covers the substantive criminal law, which concerns the definition of crimes and defenses. Still, understanding a little criminal procedure will be necessary to understanding the substantive criminal law you will be reading about in the cases that you study. This short chapter will give you the minimum you need to know to understand what you read in this textbook and what you discuss in this class.

A. FROM INVESTIGATION THROUGH TRIAL

The criminal process begins with the investigation of a crime by the police, usually culminating in an arrest. After a person is arrested (but occasionally before), a formal document specifying the accused crimes is filed in court. This document can be called different things: criminal charges, a criminal complaint, an information, or an indictment.

The filing of that document initiates formal courtroom proceedings against the person charged, the defendant. These proceedings adjudicate the defendant's guilt or innocence of the charges filed. The central phase of these proceedings is the trial. At the trial, the prosecution must present the evidence supporting the charges against the defendant. The defendant has a right to confront the evidence against him. He can do this by making legal objections to the introduction of the evidence based on the rules of evidence (which you usually will not study until your second year of law school). He can also cross-examine the witnesses who testify against him. The defendant also has the right to present evidence in his defense. He can call witnesses to testify on his behalf, seek to introduce documents or tangible things to support his defense, or even testify. His evidence and witnesses, of course, are also subject to objections and cross-examination by the prosecution.

The defendant is presumed innocent until proven guilty. This means that the prosecution has the burden of proof on all elements of each charge. The defendant does not have to produce any evidence to be entitled to be found not guilty (which is called an acquittal.) The prosecutor must prove each element of a crime beyond a reasonable doubt. The beyond a reasonable doubt standard is the highest legal standard of proof. A preponderance of the evidence standard is the standard of proof required in a civil lawsuit. That requires the party with the burden of proof to prove that their case is "more probable than not," a probability of slightly over 50%. Clear and convincing evidence is higher than preponderance of the evidence and is the standard commonly used when family members wish to withdraw life support from a comatose relative. The beyond a reasonable doubt standard, although never expressed in percentage terms, is understood to be even higher than clear and convincing evidence.

The defendant also has a right against self-incrimination. This means that the prosecutor cannot call him to the stand and force him to answer questions. The prosecutor cannot even comment on a defendant's decision not to testify. (Such as "don't you think he would have testified if he had a good explanation for the blood on his hands?") If the defendant does not testify, the judge will instruct the jury not to consider it as evidence of either guilt or innocence.

The jury is the finder of fact in most criminal trials. The judge instructs the jury on the law, and the jury applies the law to the facts. In a criminal case, the judge defines the elements of the crime and the elements of any applicable defenses for the jury. The jury then decides whether the defendant has been proven guilty of the crimes charged beyond a reasonable doubt. When a jury returns a verdict of not guilty, they are not declaring that they have found the defendant to be innocent. Instead, they have decided that the prosecution has not proven the defendant guilty beyond a reasonable doubt.

B. THE APPELLATE PROCESS

After a trial is concluded, either side may appeal the case to a court of appeals (known as an appellate court), but the grounds for appeal are very limited. Courts of appeals do not hear evidence or conduct trials. No witnesses are called. Rather the appellate court reviews the transcript of the trial, documents admitted into evidence, and other relevant court documents. The appellate court may allow the attorneys a brief opportunity to argue orally before them, but their decision is based largely on the written record of the trial and the written arguments (called "briefs") of the lawyers arguing the appeal.

Generally speaking, appellate courts do not review questions of fact; they review questions of law. For example, they generally will not second-guess a jury's decision to believe or not believe a certain witness because the system places more trust in the jury's ability to evaluate the witness's live testimony than in an appellate judge's ability to assess credibility based on reading a transcript.

When an appellate court considers an appeal, it does not review the entire record of the proceedings looking for any possible legal error. Instead, it requires the appealing party to identify specific legal issues that the appellate court should consider. The appealing party will allege that the judge below made an error of law, and this will be the issue that the appellate court will consider.

Virtually all of the cases that you read in your textbook will be appellate decisions written by these appellate judges who read transcripts and briefs but who hear no live testimony. This is key to understanding the nature of the appellate decisions they write. They are not retrying the case based on their review of the documents. Rather, they are trying to determine whether the law was followed.

C. COMMON PROCEDURAL POSTURES

The specific type of legal error raised in the appeal is often referred to as the "procedural posture" of the case. Understanding the most common procedural postures of criminal cases on appeal will help you better learn the substantive criminal law from these appellate cases.

1. ERRORS IN JURY INSTRUCTIONS

This type of issue is a favorite for the textbook authors who select cases for inclusion in a textbook because jury instructions frame the issue of substantive law so clearly for the reader. Since the jury relies on the judge to correctly define the crime and the applicable defenses, a jury instruction error poisons the entire process. Often, it is only when judges wrestle with how to express a legal concept to a jury that we learn what that legal concept means. Jury instructions are where the rubber hits the road.

2. MOTIONS TO DISMISS BEFORE TRIAL

A motion to dismiss before the trial begins is usually directed at the complaint or other charging document filed by the prosecutor. One reason to require the filing of such a document is to force the prosecutor to give the defendant fair notice of what he is being accused of. Prosecutors are required to give the defendant not only a list of the accused crimes but also a series of specific allegations spelling out the things he did and the specific laws that were broken. A failure to be sufficiently specific or a failure to correctly state the law results in dismissal of the complaint. These motions to dismiss do not challenge the truth of the charge. Such a motion usually argues that, even if every fact alleged in the complaint is true, the defendant is not guilty as a matter of law.

3. MOTIONS TO DISMISS DURING TRIAL AND CHALLENGES TO SUFFICIENCY OF THE EVIDENCE

Motions to dismiss during trial are very different matters. Evidence has been produced, and usually the defendant is moving to dismiss a charge on the grounds that no reasonable juror could find this charge to have been proved beyond a reasonable doubt as a matter of law. Sometimes these motions are made before the jury begins to deliberate on the rationale that the jury should not get a chance to make the mistake of returning a verdict that is not supported by the evidence. Sometimes these motions are made after a jury returns a verdict of guilty, arguing that the jury failed to see that the evidence of guilt was insufficient as a matter of law. Such motions are a modest form of second-guessing of the jury by the trial judge. These motions must argue that no reasonable juror could have found the defendant guilty even if one gave the prosecution the benefit of every reasonable inference that could be drawn in its favor.

4. EVIDENTIARY RULINGS

These tend to be the least common procedural postures in criminal law textbook cases because the law of evidence is quite complicated and the subject of a different course. Sometimes, though, the evidentiary issue is straightforward because it flows directly from a mistaken interpretation of the substantive criminal law. Relevance, for example, is a fundamental requirement for admissible evidence. If evidence is not relevant to an element of the criminal charge, then it should not be admitted. If the judge gets the definition of the legal element of the charge wrong, this error will sometimes manifest itself in a decision to admit or not to admit a particular piece of evidence on relevance grounds.

5. APPEALS BY THE PROSECUTION

The prosecution and the defense can appeal legal errors. Sometimes a jury instruction error will hurt the prosecution. Sometimes a trial judge will grant a motion to dismiss that she should not have granted. Sometimes a trial judge will refuse to admit a piece of evidence that should have been admitted. Prosecutors can appeal these types of error.

There is one type of error that a prosecutor cannot appeal, however. As mentioned above, a defendant can challenge the sufficiency of the evidence supporting a jury's finding of guilty by arguing that no reasonable juror could have so found even if you give the prosecution the benefit of all inferences that could be reasonably drawn in their favor. A prosecutor, however, cannot challenge an acquittal on the grounds that no reasonable juror could have found the defendant not guilty. If allowed, such an appeal would give the prosecution a second chance to prove the defendant guilty, violating the Double Jeopardy Clause of the Fifth Amendment to the U.S. Constitution. The Double Jeopardy Clause prohibits a sovereign (government) from putting a person on trial twice for the same offense. It does not apply to juries that fail to reach a verdict ("hung juries") but does apply whenever a verdict is returned. This clause was written into the Constitution's Bill of Rights to limit government power. Without it the government could try people again and again until they found a jury willing to find the defendant guilty. Being subject to successive trials for the same offense was thought to be an abuse of government power.

So, prosecutors cannot appeal an acquittal on the grounds that the evidence of guilt was overwhelming. The jury gets the last word against the prosecutor (but not against the defendant).

6. JURY NULLIFICATION

An incident of the Double Jeopardy Clause is that a jury has the power—although not the right—to ignore the law in returning a verdict of not guilty. If the jury votes not guilty, there is nothing the prosecutor or the judge can do to challenge the jury's decision that the crime was not proved beyond a reasonable doubt even if the prosecution has presented overwhelming and indisputable evidence.

Does this ever happen? Yes. Why would a jury do such a thing? Usually because they disagree with the law that the defendant has been accused of breaking. For this reason, this practice is called "jury nullification" because the jury is, in effect, nullifying the law that the prosecution seeks to enforce.

Is jury nullification a good or a bad thing? That may depend on what you think of the law being broken. Before the civil war, juries in northern states would sometimes refuse to convict people who helped escaped slaves despite overwhelming evidence of guilt. On the other hand, southern juries during the civil rights movement in the fifties sometimes refused to convict white supremacists of violent crimes against civil rights workers despite equally overwhelming evidence of guilt.

The position of the law is that jury nullification is an inevitable power of juries given the existence of the double jeopardy clause but that it is not a right of juries. For this reason, judges will not allow defense counsel to inform juries of their power to ignore the law if they wish to return a verdict of not guilty.

Note that jury nullification is a "one-way-ratchet" in that it benefits only the defense. A jury verdict that convicts despite overwhelming evidence of innocence could be challenged on sufficiency of the evidence grounds by the defense, as described above.

The power of the jury to nullify the law provides an important check on the power of the legislature to declare conduct criminal. If the legislature gets too far out of touch with "the conscience of the community," then prosecutors will be unable to obtain convictions and the overall legitimacy of the criminal law will suffer.

D. PROSECUTORIAL DISCRETION AND PLEA BARGAINING

One of the most notable aspects of our system of criminal justice is the enormous discretion exercised by prosecutors. The principal source of that power is the prosecutor's control over the criminal complaint or other charging document. No judge or private party can tell a prosecutor which defendants to charge and which crimes to charge the defendants with. As mentioned above, the complaint must allege acts that the legislature has declared to be criminal. Criminal statutes are very broad, though, and prosecutors could theoretically charge a lot more people with a lot more crimes than they do or can, given the limited resources that exist for the prosecution of crime.

This control over the complaint continues throughout the criminal process. You are probably aware of the practice of plea bargaining. One common form of plea bargaining is when a defendant pleads guilty to a reduced charge. It is solely in the power of the prosecutor to reduce the charge stated in the complaint before trial. If the prosecutor does not wish to offer a reduced charge, then the defendant must take his chances by going to trial. There, the judge or jury could find him not guilty of some or all of the charges stated in the complaint, or guilty of a lesser charge.

The vast majority of criminal cases are plea-bargained and relatively few go to trial. The nature of the plea bargains offered and accepted, however, turn to some degree on the parties' predictions of what would happen at trial. So, an understanding of how the criminal law applies to a set of facts remains essential.

E. SENTENCING

Sentencing, in contrast, has traditionally been the province of the judge, not the prosecutor. If a defendant is found guilty, the judge will listen to argument and evidence from both the prosecutor and the defense as to what the appropriate sentence should be. The sentencing range for a criminal offense is defined by the legislature, and the judge has discretion to sentence the defendant anywhere within that range.

Legislatures in many jurisdictions have made sentencing much more determinate in the last few decades. A determinate sentencing system is one in which the charge for which you are convicted—usually in combination with any prior criminal record—narrowly defines the range of sentences that the judge may impose. For example, under indeterminate sentencing systems, it might be up to the judge to sentence a first offender to anywhere from two to ten years for a given offense. A more determinate sentencing system might allow a range of only five to seven years for the same crime.

Determinate sentencing systems transfer some of the judge's sentencing power to the prosecutor. Since the charge greatly determines the sentence and since most cases are plea-bargained, the judge's discretion at sentencing is much more limited, and the prosecutor's power to shape the sentence during plea bargaining is much greater.

Exam Tip: Distinguishing One Crime from Another

Since the crime you are charged with plays a greater role in determining your sentence, it is more important than ever to be able to distinguish one crime from another. For this reason, many criminal law exams contain fact patterns which raise issues about several possible crimes. This allows the professor to assess the ability of the student to understand the differences between crimes and how a single course of action might violate different criminal laws.

F. PROFESSIONAL ETHICS

One final bit of background needs to be discussed. All lawyers, including prosecutors and criminal defense lawyers, operate under rules of professional ethics. These rules guide and constrain how lawyers do their jobs. Like criminal procedure, professional ethics is the subject of an entire course of its own. Sometimes professors like to introduce the subject by integrating an ethical discussion into a discussion of a particular case or doctrine. Two recurring issues of professional ethics particular to criminal law are worth brief mention. One concerns prosecutors and the other criminal defense lawyers.

The criminal defense issue is a simple one that most people intuitively see. How can a lawyer defend someone of a crime whom they know to be guilty? Here an important difference emerges between criminal and civil cases. If the government truly has the burden of proving the defendant guilty of all elements of the charge beyond a reasonable doubt, then a guilty defendant need never take the witness stand in order to challenge that burden. In a civil case, in contrast, one side can force the other side to testify at or before trial, so a clearly guilty (or "liable" in civil terminology) defendant has nowhere to hide.

If you accept that the prosecution should bear this burden in criminal cases, then you must permit lawyers to defend people they know to be guilty. Criminal lawyers cannot put such people on the witness stand because guilty defendants will either perjure themselves or admit guilt. But the criminal lawyer can and must challenge the prosecution's evidence at trial in order to guarantee that the only people convicted have been proved guilty beyond a reasonable doubt.

The prosecution issue is less obvious but no less important. Are prosecutors partisans in an adversary system, or are they also public officials who have an obligation to seek justice? If a prosecutor thinks someone probably committed a crime but still has a reasonable doubt as to a defendant's guilt, should she dismiss the charge, or should she submit the evidence to a jury of twelve people and let them decide? In exercising her broad discretion, should a prosecutor seek to get the greatest number of convictions for the most serious crimes possible, or should she exercise personal judgment about who really deserves what type of punishment? These questions have no simple answers.

G. CASE IN CONTEXT

Burden of proof is one of the less intuitive concepts that students sometimes struggle with. Most readily understand the idea that prosecutors must prove defendants guilty, but they don't always appreciate what it means to prove each and every element of a crime.

CHRISTOPHER C. OWENS, JR. V. STATE OF MARYLAND

Court of Special Appeals of Maryland
93 Md.App. 162 (1992)

OPINION: This appeal presents us with a small gem of a problem from the borderland of legal sufficiency. It is one of those few occasions when some frequently invoked but rarely appropriate language is actually pertinent. Ironically, in this case it was not invoked. The language is, "[A] conviction upon circumstantial evidence alone is not to be sustained unless the circumstances are inconsistent with any reasonable hypothesis of innocence." West v. State, 312 Md. 197, 211–212, 539 A.2d 231 (1988); Wilson v. State, 319 Md. 530, 537, 573 A.2d 831 (1990); Wiggins v. State, 324 Md. 551, 565–566, 597 A.2d 1359 (1991).

We have here a conviction based upon circumstantial evidence alone. The circumstance is that a suspect was found behind the wheel of an automobile parked on a private driveway at night with the lights on and with the motor running. Although there are many far-fetched and speculative hypotheses that might be conjured up (but which require no affirmative elimination), there are only two unstrained and likely inferences that could reasonably arise. One is that the vehicle and its driver had arrived at the driveway from somewhere else. The other is that the driver had gotten into and started up the vehicle and was about to depart for somewhere else.

The first hypothesis, combined with the added factor that the likely driver was intoxicated, is consistent with guilt. The second hypothesis, because the law intervened before the forbidden deed could be done, is consistent with innocence. With either inference equally likely, a fact finder could not fairly draw the guilty inference and reject the innocent with the requisite certainty beyond a reasonable doubt. We are called upon, therefore, to examine the circumstantial predicate more closely and to ascertain whether there were any attendant and ancillary circumstances to render less likely, and therefore less reasonable, the hypothesis of innocence. Thereon hangs the decision.

The appellant, Christopher Columbus Owens, Jr., was convicted in the Circuit Court for Somerset County by Judge D. William Simpson, sitting without a jury, of driving while intoxicated. Upon this appeal, he raises the single contention that Judge Simpson was clearly erroneous in finding him guilty because the evidence was not legally sufficient to support such finding.

The evidence, to be sure, was meager. The State's only witness was Trooper Samuel Cottman, who testified that at approximately 11 P.M. on March 17, 1991, he drove to the area of Sackertown Road in Crisfield in response to a complaint that had been called in about a suspicious vehicle. He spotted a truck matching the description of the "suspicious vehicle." It was parked in the driveway of a private residence.

The truck's engine was running and its lights were on. The appellant was asleep in the driver's seat, with an open can of Budweiser clasped between his legs. Two more empty beer cans were inside the vehicle. As Trooper Cottman awakened him, the appellant appeared confused and did not know where he was. He stumbled out of the vehicle. There was a strong odor of alcohol on his breath. His face was flushed and his eyes were red. When asked to recite the alphabet, the appellant "mumbled through the letters, didn't state any of the letters clearly and failed to say them in the correct order." His speech generally was "slurred and very unclear." When taken into custody, the appellant was "very argumentative . . . and uncooperative." A check with the Motor Vehicles Administration revealed, moreover, that the appellant had an alcohol restriction on his license. The appellant declined to submit to a blood test for alcohol.

After the brief direct examination of Trooper Cottman (consuming but 3 1/2 pages of transcript), defense counsel asked only two questions, establishing that the driveway was private property and that the vehicle was sitting on that private driveway. The appellant did not take the stand and no defense witnesses were called. The appellant's argument as to legal insufficiency is clever. He chooses to fight not over the fact of drunkenness but over the place of drunkenness. He points out that his conviction was under the Transportation Article, which is limited in its coverage to the driving of vehicles on "highways" and does not extend to driving on a "private road or driveway."

We agree with the appellant that he could not properly have been convicted for driving, no matter how intoxicated, back and forth along the short span of a private driveway. The theory of the State's case, however, rests upon the almost Newtonian principle that present stasis on the driveway implies earlier motion on the highway. The appellant was not convicted of drunken driving on the private driveway, but of drunken driving on the public highway before coming to rest on the private driveway.

It is a classic case of circumstantial evidence. From his presence behind the wheel of a vehicle on a private driveway with the lights on and the motor running, it can reasonably be inferred that such individual either 1) had just arrived by way of the public highway or 2) was just about to set forth upon the public highway. The binary nature of the probabilities that a vehicular odyssey had just concluded or was just about to begin is strengthened by the lack of evidence of any third reasonable explanation, such as the presence beside him of an inamorata or of a baseball game blaring forth on the car radio. Either he was coming or he was going.

The first inference would render the appellant guilty; the second would not. Mere presence behind the wheel with the lights on and the motor running could give rise to either inference, the guilty one and the innocent one. For the State to prevail, there has to be some other factor to enhance the likelihood of the first inference and to diminish the likelihood of the second. We must look for a tiebreaker.

The State had several opportunities to break the game wide open but failed to capitalize on either of them. As Trooper Cottman woke the appellant, he asked him what he was doing there. The appellant responded that he had just driven the occupant of the residence home. Without explanation, the appellant's objection to the answer was sustained. For purposes of the present analysis, therefore, it is not in the case. We must look for a tiebreaker elsewhere.

Three beer cans were in evidence. The presence of a partially consumed can of beer between the appellant's legs and two other empty cans in the back seat would give rise to a reasonable inference that the appellant's drinking spree was on the downslope rather than at an early stage. At least a partial venue of the spree, moreover, would reasonably appear to have been the automobile. One does not typically drink in the house and then carry the empties out to the car. Some significant drinking, it may be inferred, had taken place while the appellant was in the car. The appellant's state of unconsciousness, moreover, enforces that inference. One passes out on the steering wheel after one has been drinking for some time, not as one only begins to drink. It is not a reasonable hypothesis that one would leave the house, get in the car, turn on the lights, turn on the motor, and then, before putting the car in gear and driving off, consume enough alcohol to pass out on the steering wheel. Whatever had been going on (driving and drinking) would seem more likely to have been at a terminal stage than at an incipient one.

Yet another factor would have sufficed, we conclude, to break the tie between whether the appellant had not yet left home or was already abroad upon the town. Without anything further as to its contents being revealed, it was nonetheless in evidence that the thing that had brought Trooper

Cottman to the scene was a complaint about a suspicious vehicle. The inference is reasonable that the vehicle had been observed driving in some sort of erratic fashion. Had the appellant simply been sitting, with his motor idling, on the driveway of his own residence, it is not likely that someone from the immediate vicinity would have found suspicious the presence of a familiar neighbor in a familiar car sitting in his own driveway. The call to the police, even without more being shown, inferentially augurs more than that. It does not prove guilt in and of itself. It simply makes one of two alternative inferences less reasonable and its alternative inference thereby more reasonable.

The totality of the circumstances are, in the last analysis, inconsistent with a reasonable hypothesis of innocence. They do not, of course, foreclose the hypothesis but such has never been required. They do make the hypothesis more strained and less likely. By an inverse proportion, the diminishing force of one inference enhances the force of its alternative. It makes the drawing of the inference of guilt more than a mere flip of a coin between guilt and innocence. It makes it rational and therefore within the proper purview of the factfinder. Jackson v. Virginia, 443 U.S. 307, 319, 99 S. Ct. 2781, 2789, 61 L. Ed. 2d 560, 573 (1979). We affirm.

DISCUSSION QUESTIONS

1.   Why does it matter whether this intoxicated driver was beginning or finishing his drive? Isn't he equally dangerous or blameworthy either way?

2.   The judge decides the case based on his assessment of which inference is more reasonable. Do you agree with the court's assumptions of what sorts of drinking behaviors are more or less likely? Could the court have made its decision without making some assumptions about drinking behavior?

3.   Why wasn't the defendant's home address part of the evidence in the case? Why couldn't the trial judge, or even the appellate court, simply look up the defendant's address from court records?

H. SPECIAL FOCUS: PROSTITUTION AND SEX TRAFFICKING

Prostitution is typically a misdemeanor offense. The following procedural case required a court to decide just how serious a misdemeanor it is.

THE PEOPLE OF THE STATE OF NEW YORK V. CAROL LINK AND DEBRA MELTSNER

Criminal Court of the City of New York, New York County
107 Misc.2d 973 (1981)

Defendants, Carol Link and Debra Meltsner, are charged with the crime of prostitution. They have moved for trial by jury, claiming that CPL

340.40 (subd 2) (which directs that the trial shall be before a single Judge) is unconstitutional, first, because prostitution is not a "petty" but a "serious" offense requiring trial by jury under the Federal Constitution, second, because that section denies them "equal protection" by withholding the right to trial by jury in class B misdemeanor trials in New York City while permitting jury trials of such cases in the remainder of the State.

I

Whether a crime is serious or petty can be determined by several criteria. In *Duncan v Louisiana*, the Supreme Court held that the length of any sentence of imprisonment that may be imposed is a major but not exclusive criterion. In *Baldwin v New York*, the court held that exposure to incarceration for more than six months conclusively establishes the crime charged as serious.

Both *Duncan* and *Baldwin* certified the continuing validity of earlier holdings that the nature of an offense and a defendant's exposure to disabilities other than incarceration may also qualify that offense as serious.

Thereafter, the Supreme Court decided *Codispoti v Pennsylvania*, involving a criminal contempt conviction. The opinion contained language which the District Attorney herein relies upon in opposing defendant's motion: "our decisions have established a fixed dividing line between petty and serious offenses: those crimes carrying a sentence of more than six months are serious crimes and those carrying a sentence of six months or less are petty crimes." The District Attorney then argues that inasmuch as convicted prostitutes may be jailed for up to only three months, prostitution is *ipso facto* a petty offense.

To the contrary, I hold that in *Codispoti*, the fixed dividing line of six months was only intended to be the criterion of whether or not an offense is serious where it is not otherwise inherently serious apart from the sentence to which the defendant is exposed.

Taylor v Hayes announced the same day as *Codispoti*, explicitly recognized that some crimes are serious " 'regardless of the penalty involved.' " In *Ludwig v Massachusetts*, the court again observed that the length of the defendant's exposure to jail is "usually" but not exclusively the measure of the seriousness of the charge. In *Scott v Illinois*, the court again noted that even as to offenses carrying incarceration of six months or less, trial by jury is only unnecessary " 'if they otherwise qualify as petty offenses' ".

II

Like the institution of marriage itself, prostitution is older than the common law. The District Attorney does not dispute that even if there were no incarceration involved, a prostitution conviction results in profound consequences for the person convicted. From biblical times and throughout the world today, to mark a woman a prostitute is to designate her a pariah. Whether she is described as a "hustler," a "hooker," a "bawd" or a "harlot," a "biffer," a "trull," "pigmeat" or a "whore," the prostitute bears the opprobrium of "the fallen woman". Conviction exposes her to banishment by deportation to a foreign land; to denial of entry into America; to summary divorce at the inception of her husband; to being declared an unfit mother and deprived of the custody and visitation of her children; to expulsion from her residence; to exclusion from many forms of endeavor; and, with every expectation that her word of accusation will carry little weight in court (for, who would believe her?), to being freely raped.

Judges have described prostitutes as "malodorous and evil characters," perpetrators of "evil and wrongdoing," underminers of "public morals and decency

At bottom, however, the quintessential thrust of the label "prostitute" is to denominate the creature to whom it is affixed as, through and through, unprincipled, a low life, one who would sell out any loyalty, desecrate any covenant, and, literally as well as characterologically as one willing to do just about anything for the right price. It is well-nigh inevitable that a woman so branded will be banned from the office, the factory, the home and the church. Ultimately, as defendants claim without dispute, the convicted prostitute is likely to despise herself.

If there is a class of cases more eligible than prostitution for designation as "serious", notwithstanding that incarceration for more than six months is not in the picture, I have yet to find it.

III

Ironically, the governmental authorities of New York County treat the crime of prostitution as serious. Desk appearance tickets in lieu of arrest, used in a wide variety of misdemeanor cases including many involving moral turpitude and violence, are never used in prostitution cases. Accused prostitutes are always subjected to formal arrest.

The Criminal Justice Agency routinely interviews defendants and submits reports to the arraigning Magistrate in every felony category and in every type of misdemeanor case except one, concerning defendants' eligibility to be released upon their own recognizance. The one exception is the case of prostitution, where those steps are never taken.

Adjournments in contemplation of dismissal are granted upon the application of the District Attorney to first offenders in a wide variety of misdemeanor cases. The District Attorney never makes this application in prostitution cases.

Likewise, the District Attorney freely consents to the acceptance of guilty pleas to reduced charges in countless categories of crime but never in prostitution cases.

Only in prostitution cases does the District Attorney have a uniform and unremitting policy of opposing all defense motions to dismiss first offender cases in the interests of justice. No matter how desperate were the circumstances which brought the offense into being, no matter how catastrophic are the predictable consequences of conviction to the first offender, the District Attorney's unvarying position is that dismissal should be denied on account of prostitution's adverse impact upon the quality of life in New York County.

The District Attorney thus shares with the community the disapprobation for those who mock and degrade sex by selling it commercially. Having shown the seriousness with which prostitution is regarded by the community and its designated officials, the District Attorney should not now say that such conduct is minor and that the attendant safeguard of trial by jury, before those accused can be convicted and branded, may be brushed aside.

IV

The court finds that prostitution, no matter how lightly punished, is a serious crime and may not be prosecuted without the right to trial by jury. To the extent that CPL 340.40 (subd 2) makes such trial unavailable in New York County, to wit, to these two defendants, that section contravenes the Sixth and Fourteenth Amendments to the Federal Constitution and is null. In light of this resolution of the motion, it is unnecessary to reach and pass upon defendants' "equal protection" claim.

DISCUSSION QUESTIONS

1.   What are the practical differences between being entitled to a jury trial as opposed to a "bench" trial where the judge also sits as jury?

2.   Do you agree that those accused of prostitution are entitled to jury trials?

3.   What criteria should courts use generally to decide when a jury trial is required?

Case in Context

Sex trafficking is a much more serious offense than mere prostitution itself. In the following case the court had to make evidentiary decisions that ultimately would shape how a jury might think about what sex trafficking really means.

U.S. V. CARSON

United States Court of Appeals, Seventh Circuit
870 F.3d 584 (2017)

A jury convicted McKenzie Carson of four counts of violating the federal sex trafficking statute. Three of those counts alleged that Carson engaged in sex trafficking with knowledge that the victims were forced, threatened or coerced. The other count alleged that Carson was involved in the sex trafficking of a person under the age of eighteen. He asks this court to reverse his conviction and remand for a new trial, claiming that he was prevented from eliciting relevant testimony from his victims [and] that he was precluded from effectively cross examining a key witness. We find no reversible error and thus affirm the decision of the district court.

I.

Toward the end of 2009, Kaitlin Fratto's neighbor, Christopher Richardson asked her if she would be interested in working in an escort business run by his acquaintance, McKenzie Carson. Fratto, although only seventeen years old, was in need of money and expressed interest in the job. Richardson brokered a meeting, but not before telling Carson that Fratto was seventeen, as he worried that both of them could get "into potentially a lot of trouble" if Fratto worked as an escort while a minor. Tr. 12/2/13 at 165 (R. 161, pageID 1495). Richardson drove Fratto to a Motel 6 in Joliet to meet Carson, reminding him again that Fratto was seventeen. Despite the warning, Carson asked Fratto to remove her clothing, took her to the bathroom and raped her, threatening to kill her if she told anyone. After the rape, another woman, Katie Smego arrived, and the four left for another hotel where Carson took provocative photographs of Fratto and Smego, including some in which the two were naked. Carson used the photographs to post advertisements for prostitution services on the website Backpage.com.

In the two day period after Carson posted the advertisements, Carson arranged one commercial sex transaction for Fratto and two for Smego. He also arranged to have another man take more photographs of Fratto for additional advertisements on Backpage.com. As the photographs were being taken, Richardson reminded Carson that Fratto was only seventeen. After the photo session, Richardson drove Fratto to and from three or four more commercial sex transactions that night. Carson directed Richardson where to deliver the money Fratto earned, but when Richardson insisted that some of the money was his, a heated argument ensued in which Carson told Richardson that if Richardson did not bring both Fratto and the money back to him, "I'll kill you, I'll kill your kids, I'll kill your family." Tr. 12/2/13 at 183 (R. 161, pageID 1513). Richardson relayed the threats to Fratto who stayed with Richardson instead of returning to Carson. Carson continued to call throughout the night, issuing more threats and threatening to kill Fratto if he did not get his money, and at one point telling Fratto that he had killed Smego.

Eventually Fratto agreed to continue working for Carson, during which time she traded sex for money three or four times a day. During the time Carson was trafficking Fratto, he flattered her by telling her she was "his top notch bitch," that she was pretty, and would get rich modeling. Tr. 12/3/13 at 410–11 (R. 162, pageID 1740–41). He also tried to isolate Fratto from her mother, took her battery out of her phone and told her "he didn't want [her] talking to nobody, and he didn't want nobody to know where [she] was." *Id.* at 403 (R. 162, pageID 1733).

Fratto testified that she told Carson that she was seventeen and even showed him her identification card. In response, she testified that he said, "it was alright, that [they] would just have to keep it under the radar until [she] turned 18." *Id.*

Unlike Fratto, the remaining . . . victims were not minors, but they were easily manipulable for other reasons. All of them were long-time drug addicts, homeless, desperate for drugs and had nowhere to go.

Veronica Del Valle was in just such a desperate state when she met Carson. She testified that she had been using crack cocaine since the age of twelve, and at the height of her addiction any interruption left her throwing up, sweating, unable to sleep and eat. In late 2009 and early 2010 she was living in a crack house when another woman suggested she could work as a prostitute for Carson. On two occasions in 2010 Del Valle left the crack house with Carson who took her to a hotel, took seductive pictures of her for advertisements he posted on Backpage.com and supplied her with drugs. In the summer of 2010, he located her at the crack house again, bought her drugs and convinced her to work as a prostitute, promising that she would keep the money she earned and that she could decide for herself when she wanted to work. Del Valle ended up working for Carson for five to six months, engaging in commercial sex transactions up to as many as five times a day, staying with Carson at hotels, and using drugs that he provided for her.

Del Valle testified that Carson took most of her money, took away her personal cell phone and gave her a phone she could use for "business" only. He checked her phone regularly to see if anybody out of the ordinary was calling her and told her he would use the phone's GPS to find her, which, in fact, he did one night when Del Valle tried to leave. Using the GPS to track her, he ran up and down a street at 3 a.m. screaming her name. He also took away her shoes and clothes to keep her from leaving the hotel where she stayed. But that was not enough control for Carson. He beat her with belts, slapped her face, anally raped her, gave her black eyes and cut lips and told her that if she "were to leave, he would kill [her] grandmother and [her] children." Tr. 12/4/13 at 548 (R. 163, pageID 1879).

Like Del Valle, Jessica Sikora was a heroin addict who experienced severe withdrawal—vomiting, sweating, and pain—when she stopped using heroin. Sikora testified that she too met Carson in 2010 when she was homeless. When another woman told Sikora that Carson could get her a job and a place to live, Sikora got into a car with Carson who took her straight to Chicago's west side to buy her heroin and then to a hotel where she met Del Valle. Carson promised he could "hook [her] up with dates," that she would make money, he would buy her drugs, cosmetics, anything she needed, and give her a place to stay. Sikora knew she had nowhere to go and decided to stay. What she did not count on was the fact that Carson would require her to give him all of the money she earned, ordering her to strip naked so she could not hide money; that he would beat her with his hands, with a belt, with an extension cord; that he would hold a knife to her throat; and rape her orally, vaginally and anally, including one time while a woman and her newborn child watched. At one point, when she said she was too tired to work, Carson punched her in the eye leaving her with a permanently broken blood vessel.

In addition to the testimony described above, the jury also heard from Margaret Hurley, who testified that from January through March 2010, Carson paid her to drive the women to their commercial sex transactions and retrieve drugs for them. She also testified that she saw Carson beat his victims, including Del Valle. Hurley testified that, as with the other women, Carson took pictures of her that he posted in advertisements on Backpage.com, but she never testified that she worked as a prostitute for Carson.

The government also called Dr. Sharon Cooper, a sex trafficking expert who helped explain how the desperate situations in which victims find themselves make them easy targets for sex trafficking. Cooper testified that sex traffickers select victims who demonstrate vulnerabilities including homelessness, substance abuse, mental health issues, and histories of physical, emotional or sexual abuse. A typical trafficker recruits victims by telling them that he loves them, promising them a better life, providing them with shelter and drugs, and lying to them about the nature of the job. Traffickers often use one victim to recruit other victims as victims are more likely to trust someone of a similar age and gender than a stranger of the opposite gender.

Cooper testified that traffickers control their victims through physical violence, sexual violence, psychological violence and grooming. Traffickers, she testified, groom victims with promises and compliments, but escalate to physical abuse, sexual assault and death threats. Often the trafficker will abuse a more experienced prostitute while younger victims watch. They also use psychological violence such as tearing a victim down, telling them they are worthless, socially isolating them, and controlling them financially and by taking advantage of a victim's drug dependency. Cooper noted that traffickers tend to be more violent with adult women because children and minors are far easier to intimidate.

Importantly for this case, and for a general understanding of the complexity of trafficking in general, Cooper explained that victims often stay with their traffickers—or leave and then return—because they believe they have nowhere to go; that there is no one else out there for them, and no other options for them; they feel ashamed and guilty and stigmatized, thinking that they will not be accepted elsewhere. They are also afraid that if they leave, the trafficker will find them and harm them even more egregiously.

Given the testimony of Dr. Cooper, it was not surprising that the jury heard testimony that could be construed as evidence that the victims had chosen their lot. For example, the jury heard evidence that Fratto and Del Valle both left Carson and then returned, and that at times both could have left but did not do so. The jury heard evidence intended to convince them that these women willingly agreed to work as prostitutes. But whether they willingly agreed to essentially become enslaved—that is, to turn over all of their money and freedom and suffer abuse—is another question, and the one at the heart of the sex trafficking statute, of course. . . .

The jury convicted Carson on all four counts of violating the federal sex-trafficking statute, and Carson had the opportunity at sentencing to submit expert testimony about his Bipolar I Disorder, his problems with drug abuse, and his abusive family background. Despite Carson's submissions, the district court sentenced Carson to forty-seven years' imprisonment and five years of supervised release on each count, with the sentences to run concurrently. The court sentenced Carson below the Sentencing Guideline recommendation of life and below the government's recommended 55-year sentence.

II.

The federal sex trafficking statute under which Carson was indicted reads as follows:

> **(a)** Whoever knowingly—in reckless disregard of the fact, that means of force, threats of force, fraud, coercion described in subsection (e)(2), or any combination of such means will be used to cause the person to engage in a commercial sex act, or that the person has not attained the age of 18 years and will be caused to engage in a commercial sex act, shall be punished as provided in subsection (b). 18 U.S.C. § 1591(a).

The government charged Carson with trafficking Fratto under both the coercion and age provisions. Counts 2–4 charged Carson with trafficking Lazzar, Sikora and Del Valle under the coercion provision.

A.   Evidence of victims' prior acts of prostitution.

Before the district court, Carson argued that evidence of his awareness of the victim's past prostitution had a direct bearing on his defense, that he subjectively believed that the women were not coerced into engaging in commercial sex acts, but rather did so willingly. . . . that the fact of their prior prostitution was relevant to his state of mind, that is, whether he acted "knowingly, or in reckless disregard of the fact, that means of force, threats of force, . . . coercion . . ., or any combination of such means will be used to cause the person to engage in a commercial sex act" as forbidden by the statute under which he was charged, 18 U.S.C. § 1591(a). . . . In this case, whether the victims had previously worked as prostitutes was irrelevant to the required *mens rea* for the crime.

Recall that § 1591 requires that Carson knowingly or recklessly disregarded the fact that force, threats of force, and coercion, and any combination of such means, would be used to cause any of his victims—Fratto, Del Valle, Sikora and Lazzar—to engage in a commercial sex act. See 18 U.S.C. § 1591(a). Whether they had previously worked as prostitutes was irrelevant to the required *mens rea* above. First, as the government points out, Carson proffered no evidence to the district court that his victims had voluntarily engaged in commercial sex transactions on other occasions. Unless he knew that the victims had voluntarily done so in the past, he could not have reason to believe they would do so in the future. In other words, voluntary prostitution is a completely separate act from commercial sex transactions that occur as the result of force or coercion in the context of sex trafficking, and Carson offered no evidence that the women he victimized had engaged in the voluntary act as opposed to having been victims before, or more importantly, that he knew that the prior acts were voluntary. If anything, Carson must have known that whatever traits made these women easy targets for his coercion, would have made them easy targets for others as well.

Second, even if Carson could demonstrate that his victims had willingly and voluntarily worked as prostitutes in the past, based on the overwhelming evidence at trial, Carson could not plausibly argue that his victims willingly worked for him or that he thought his victims were willingly working for him. The government presented example after example of compelling evidence of coercion—evidence that Carson beat and raped the victims, that he threatened to stalk and kill them and their families, the manner in which he isolated them from the outside world, confiscating their telephones, money, identification, clothes, shoes, and manipulating them with false promises and controlling their access to the drugs for which they were physically and mentally dependent. Whether they had worked as prostitutes previously would have no effect on whether Carson knew (or recklessly disregarded the fact) that force, threats of force or coercion would have caused his victims to engage in commercial sex acts under his "employ." This is particularly true because Carson was the one using force, threatening, and coercing them. Had Carson truly subjectively believed (whether correctly or not) that the victims were voluntarily working for him as prostitutes, he would have had no reason to rape, beat and threaten them, to take their telephones, clothing, shoes and control their access to drugs.

Force and coercion can be complicated topics. Sometimes, for example, a minor can be forced into sex trafficking by fraud alone. See, e.g., *United States v. McMillian*, 777 F.3d 444, 447 (7th Cir.), *cert. denied*, ___ U.S. ___, 135 S.Ct. 2392, 192 L. Ed. 2d 176 (2015). Women in desperate circumstances find themselves in situations where they are without homes, in need of drugs or food or protection and must make difficult decisions. The victims in this case certainly were in this category. Each one was inextricably hooked on illegal drugs and without resources or anywhere to go. Sometimes women in such dire circumstances voluntarily exchange sex to obtain the things they desperately need. But there is nothing voluntary when they are forced to do so by another person. And there is nothing blurry or in the grey area when the coercion involves, rape, brutal physical violence, abrupt withholding of drugs to cause severe withdrawal symptoms, death threats, taking women's phones and clothing and following them with GPS technology. No rational person could witness such force and coercion, let alone inflict it himself, without knowing or recklessly disregarding the fact that the threats and force of threats and coercion, or any combination of them, caused these women to engage in commercial sex acts.

For the same reasons, a number of other circuit courts have similarly held that acts of prior prostitution are irrelevant to a charge under § 1591(a) and thus barred. Most recently, the First Circuit, in a case where the defendant was making the same *mens rea* argument in a sex trafficking case, noted that similar evidence of prior prostitution was "either entirely irrelevant or of such slight probative value in comparison to its prejudicial effect that a decision to exclude it would not violate [the defendant's] constitutional rights." *United States v. Gemma*, 818 F.3d 23, 34 (1st Cir.), *cert. denied*, ___ U.S. ___, 137 S.Ct. 410, 196 L.Ed.2d 319 (2016). The court went on to note that the victim's participation in prostitution before or after doing so with the defendant had no relevance as to whether this particular defendant used force and the threat of force to cause her to engage in commercial sex. *Id.*

The district court did not err in barring evidence of prior commercial sex acts by the victims in this case.

DISCUSSION QUESTIONS

1. Carson is a terribly unsympathetic defendant who committed monstrous acts of violence, but should the jury have been allowed to at least

consider evidence about the victims' prior acts of prostitution in deciding whether he coerced them?

2.   Can a judge effectively shape the definition of a crime or a defense by deciding what evidence to admit and exclude? Should they? What is the alternative?

3.   Should judges in general err on the side of letting juries hear more or less evidence? Is it better for jurors to hear anything that might possibly be relevant to their decision, or should we limit what they learn to only things that bear directly on that decision?

CHAPTER 3

PHILOSOPHIES OF PUNISHMENT

■ ■ ■

Law is not philosophy, yet you must understand a few things about philosophies of criminal punishment to understand criminal law. Philosophies of punishment all begin with the same question: why punish? Most people see this as a rather academic question because they cannot imagine a society in which people who did bad things were not punished. Philosophers, of course, build their castles of thought from the ground up, so they require punishment to have some purpose that justifies it. This is a useful exercise for lawyers because interpreting the law often requires interpreting it in light of some imagined purpose.

Judges and lawyers have, for many generations, found it useful and often indispensable to think philosophically about the criminal law because it has many purposes that often conflict with one another. So, making arguments about how the criminal law should be interpreted is easier if you can think about how different interpretations serve or frustrate different purposes of punishment.

That being said, lawyers (and law students) should be careful to use philosophy and not be used by it. Law is not philosophy. Oliver Wendell Holmes once famously said that "the life of the law is experience." Purely philosophical arguments rarely triumph over arguments grounded in a society's experience. Moreover, criminal law, more than any other subject, is driven by moral intuitions about right and wrong. These moral intuitions are deeply rooted, often conflict with one another, and are sometimes not rational. So, the philosopher's quest to rationalize criminal punishment is doomed from the start. Our moral intuitions are too strong to be tamed and too messy to be neatly organized.

How then do lawyers use philosophy in the criminal law? Different philosophies of punishment help us to think systematically about our moral intuitions. They organize our thinking in a way that helps us identify the most important arguments for and against interpreting the criminal law in various ways. More specifically, they provide a vocabulary for certain types of arguments that has become almost indispensable. It is impossible to read very far in a criminal law textbook without coming across the terms deterrence and retribution because these terms provide useful shorthand for referring to big ideas that are complex yet familiar.

So learn the basics of the philosophies of punishment at the beginning of this course! It will better equip you to understand and argue about the criminal law doctrines that this course covers.

A. RETRIBUTION

Let's start with what is perhaps the most intuitive purpose of punishment. We punish people who commit crime because they deserve it. Punishment is simply one's "just desert." This intuition is the heart of the theory of retribution. Society punishes offenders in retribution for the crimes they commit because they are morally worthy of blame.

Before going any further, we should make sure that we really understand what a purely retributive system of punishment requires. Let's borrow an example from Immanuel Kant, a nineteenth century philosopher who heavily influenced retributive theories. Imagine that a jailer and a murderer were the last two people left on earth. The jailer was dying, and the murderer had not yet been punished. Should the jailer punish the murderer before the jailer dies even though there will be no one left for the murderer to harm? Pure retributivists would have the jailer punish the murderer before the jailer dies because retributivists believe that desert alone—and not preventing any future consequence—justifies punishment.

A pure retributivist approach also rules out punishing people on grounds other than moral desert. Following the second version of Kant's categorical imperative, retributivists refuse to treat people as means to greater ends. Strictly speaking, this means that we should not punish people to deter others from committing the same crime or even to keep society safe. We should only punish them when—and to the extent—they morally deserve it.

But this simple intuition quickly grows complex when given further thought. There are different ways of thinking about why one "deserves" punishment that often conflict with one another. One way of thinking about desert emphasizes choice. You deserve to be punished when you steal from someone or deliberately injure them because you chose to hurt them. A different way of thinking about desert emphasizes harm. Society should punish you in response to the harm that you caused.

The tension between choice-based and harm-based versions of retributivism is easily illustrated. Return to the example of the mentally ill person who kills another because his schizophrenia leads him to believe that the victim is an alien invader bent on the destruction of all humanity. He did not "choose" to kill another human being. He did not even believe that he was killing a human being, and he believed that the killing was necessary to protect himself and everyone else from destruction. Choice-based retributivism would excuse his behavior from criminal responsibility, but a purely harm-based retributivism would not. Since the person he killed was entirely innocent, he would deserve to be punished for taking innocent life.

Choice-based retributivism is not necessarily more or less lenient than harm-based retributivism. Someone deliberately tries to shoot you in the head, but he misses his shot. A purely-choice based retributivism would punish the shooter as severely as if he had killed you because the blameworthiness of his choice in both instances is the same. A harm-based retributivism would justify lesser punishment on the grounds that an attempted murder inflicts less harm than a successful one. Our moral intuitions about choice and harm are both very strong, and neither consistently trumps the other when they come into conflict in the interpretation of the criminal law.

Choice-based retributivism often generates arguments for and against punishment in the very same case because our moral intuitions about choice are also very complex. Choice-based retributivism concerns itself with the blameworthiness or culpability of the choice made, yet choices have more than one dimension. Imagine that a child grows up in a home where he suffers violent abuse at the hands of his parents on a regular basis. As an adult, he abuses his own children when they disobey him. He is particularly morally blameworthy because he chooses to harm children who are vulnerable and entrusted to his care. Yet his choice is heavily influenced by factors that he did not choose. His beatings as a child may have conditioned him to act violently, possibly on a deep, neurological level. Retributivists could make arguments for and against offering such an offender an excuse to mitigate his liability. To put it slightly differently, choice-based retributivism concerns itself both with the blameworthiness of the act—beating an innocent child—as well as the blameworthiness of the actor—a past victim of child abuse himself.

This sort of choice-retributivism—often described in terms of "culpability" or "moral blameworthiness" has greatly influenced the development of American criminal law. Culpability concerns mark the most consistent line between the civil and the criminal law. Historically, we criminalize those things that we deem worthy of moral condemnation, leaving the civil law to make life more orderly, efficient, and fair. The decision to punish intentional criminal acts more seriously than acts committed accidentally reflects the basic moral intuition that the person who kicks the dog is more culpable than the person who trips over the dog. As you will learn in coming chapters, we excuse or mitigate criminal liability in a number of different ways when the offender labored under a condition that limited his ability to make the right choice. For example, we excuse criminal liability completely in cases of insanity; we often preclude criminal liability for many serious offenses if intoxication negated the person's ability to think; we reduce murder to manslaughter under circumstances where the offender reasonably lost control of his emotions.

Often, what ultimately lies at the heart of choice-based retributivism is a concern not only with the moral blameworthiness of the act but also with the character of the actor. Imagine an offender who commits a terrible crime in her youth but who escapes justice for many decades. During the intervening years she commits no further crimes, and dedicates herself to numerous good works in the community. When she is finally caught, should the prosecutor and judge consider her blameless life and many good works during those intervening years? Some would argue that the offender's subsequent good conduct informs our understanding of her blameworthiness at the time of the earlier crime. Her well-lead life reveals that her earlier crime did not reflect her essential moral quality as a person. Others would argue that she had obviously changed during the intervening years. As a result, she no longer deserves the same punishment because she is not the same blameworthy person that she was. Most, however, would argue against completely excusing her from any criminal liability for her earlier crime because the harm she inflicted on society needs to be punished, which is an argument that appeals to our harm-based retributivist intuitions.

So, retributive intuitions are influential but complex. They spring from different intuitions about desert and generate arguments both for and against criminal liability in the very same cases.

B. MAJOR UTILITARIAN THEORIES OF PUNISHMENT: DETERRENCE AND INCAPACITATION

Utilitarianism holds that we punish crime in order to promote the greatest good for the greatest number of people. Note at the outset that this makes punishment a means to some greater end, not something that is an end unto itself because people "deserve" punishment for crimes. Such means/ends theories are called "consequentialist" theories because they justify things in terms of the consequences they promote. Utilitarianism is the most commonly invoked consequentialist theory in punishment because the idea of promoting the greatest good for the greatest number of people has wide appeal.

The two most common utilitarian punishment theories are deterrence and incapacitation. Deterrence justifies punishment on the grounds—and to the extent that—it deters people from committing crime in the future. There are, in turn, two different types of deterrence recognized. Specific deterrence refers to the idea that punishing an offender deters that specific offender from committing crime in the future. General deterrence refers to the idea that punishment deters people in general from offending in the future. Incapacitation, on the other hand, justifies punishment on the grounds that it stops, or incapacitates people from committing crimes—usually by imprisoning them.

What both incapacitation and deterrence have in common is that they hold that punishment is justified by the need to reduce crime. We punish people to deter others from committing crime, or we incapacitate them to reduce crime. Reducing crime, of course, serves the greatest good of society because crime, by definition, is something that society has decided is bad. Punishment is the means to the ends of reducing or preventing crime.

A pure theory of deterrence would justify the punishment of a completely innocent person just to deter others from crime. Imagine, for example, that we decided to deter the assassination of political leaders by executing not only the assassin but also the members of the assassin's immediate family. This certainly might deter some would-be assassins, but it would accomplish this at the cost of punishing innocent people (assuming that the family members played no part in the assassination).

General deterrence also justifies punishing someone whom you believed would never offend again. Imagine that an elderly person commits a mercy killing of a beloved spouse who suffered in terrible agony from a terminal disease. Even though he is unlikely to kill or offend again, general deterrence requires punishing him for murder in order to deter others from committing similar killings in the future.

Deterrence, like retribution, generates arguments for differing degrees of punishment. Offenders who have completely lost control of themselves as the result of mental illness or extreme emotional states, for example, arguably cannot be deterred at the moment they commit their offenses. If the only purpose of punishment is deterrence, then their punishment should at least be reduced, if not foregone altogether.

Deterrence influences punishment in multiple ways. Generally speaking, it justifies punishment for less blameworthy mental states than retribution. Deterrence justifies criminal liability for accidental harms on the grounds that punishment will teach people to be more careful. It also justifies so-called "strict liability" offenses where the offender does not have a blameworthy mental state. For example, strict liability for criminal violations of food and drug laws is often justified on the grounds that strict liability deters people from endangering the public safety. Such arguments, however, only go so far. Many argue that since you cannot deter people from doing things that they do not intend or are at least aware of, punishment for accidental harms should be strictly limited. Criminal violations of food and safety regulations, for example, usually carry light penalties.

Deterrence, however, can also generate a different type of argument in favor of narrowing criminal liability. The term over-deterrence refers to the prospect of discouraging people from doing things that are not wrongful or harmful and that are often important and useful. For example, if we make food safety regulations too strict and the penalties too severe, then we will deter prudent people from going into food industries. They will fear being criminally punished some day for something that was not their fault.

Incapacitation and deterrence often operate side by side. Both justify imprisonment of people who are dangerous but not altogether blameworthy on the grounds of reducing the danger of future offenses against the public. Incapacitation, however, can justify the incarceration of people who cannot be deterred. Return to the example of our offender who was violently abused as a child. Imagine now that, as a result of his past abuse, he suffers from an explosive temper and commits a serious of random assaults against strangers with whom he gets into arguments. Even though this particular offender and all other offenders who suffer from his condition might not be deterrable, many would support punishment on the grounds that he is a threat to public safety. Imprisoning him deters no one, but the act does make the public safer by keeping him away from others.

Deterrence is premised on certain assumptions about human behavior. Deterrence imagines that offenders engage in some of cost-benefit analysis, weighing the prospects of punishment against their motivations for committing a crime. Whether offenders actually think this way in general or in certain types of cases continues to be the subject of robust debate.

C. MINOR UTILITARIAN THEORIES

Deterrence and retribution are the two theories that influence the criminal law the most, but a few other utilitarian theories compete for a very distant third place.

Rehabilitation proponents believe that the purpose of punishment should be to rehabilitate offenders. Rehabilitation means some program of treatment or education that makes the offender less likely to offend again. Rehabilitation is not offered as an end unto itself, but as a means of making society happier and healthier by curing its most troubled members of the ills that lead them to commit crime. Ironically, rehabilitation could support broader criminal liability than deterrence or retribution since even people who don't deserve criminal liability or who aren't susceptible to deterrence would still be found guilty in order to facilitate their treatment. The one place where rehabilitation still exerts meaningful influence is juvenile court, the rationale for which lies in the idea that juvenile delinquents should be helped to change their ways before they mature into adults.

Rehabilitation was briefly influential during the nineteen fifties and sixties but has been almost completely eclipsed by retribution and deterrence since then. Rehabilitation requires that offenders receive some form of meaningful treatment, an expensive proposition that rarely commands strong political support. Rehabilitation lost popularity because it was seen as minimizing the offender's responsibility for his offense (even though many treatment programs emphasize personal responsibility). It remains an important consideration at sentencing for certain types of offenses that involve treatable conditions, such as mental illness or substance abuse.

Rehabilitation may be making a bit of a comeback, particularly with respect to drug crimes. In such instances rehabilitation serves as an argument against punishment altogether. If a certain type of behavior is seen as an outgrowth of a mental health or substance abuse problem, for example, defense lawyers will argue that the person should not be prosecuted if she can avail herself of treatment. Many proponents of drug legalization or decriminalization argue that those who abuse drugs or alcohol should be treated, not convicted of drug possession or use.

Restorative justice is a philosophy that sees the purpose of punishment as repairing the harm done by the offense and, in so doing, restoring the state of affairs that existed before the crime had been committed. Restorative justice emphasizes restitution to the victim, apologies and expressions of remorse by the offender, and reconciliation where possible between victim and offender. The animating premise of restorative justice is that crime constitutes a breach in the harmony of the community, and that restoration of that harmony should be punishment's paramount purpose. Restorative justice heavily favors various alternate dispute resolution mechanisms over adversarial courtroom proceedings.

Expressive punishment sees punishment's primary purpose as expressing society's denunciation of the crime. By denouncing criminal behavior, punishment acts as a safety valve for society's anger, thereby reducing the likelihood of private vengeance or vigilante justice. Stigmatizing the victim also affirms the values of the society and thereby promotes social cohesion. Finally, denunciation also vindicates the victim by expressing society's collective recognition of the wrong suffered.

D. THE BOTTOM LINE: MIXED THEORIES

In the development of the American criminal law, no one theory of punishment has ever conclusively prevailed over the others because the conflicting intuitions they appeal to remain strong. We care deeply about right and wrong, but we also care about being safe and deterring crime. We like the idea of rehabilitation, but we also feel the need to condemn certain behaviors. In practice, we mix and match the theories described, an approach that is described as a "mixed theory of punishment."

Remember that you are studying to be lawyers, not philosophers, so the lack of a single, unified theory need not trouble you. Lawyers need to be able to make and anticipate arguments. Philosophies of punishment are useful tools in that enterprise because they express and organize powerful ideas and intuitions. Using these theories to generate arguments for and against various interpretations is part of what makes the study of criminal law so interesting and enjoyable.

Practice Problem 3.1: The Sentencing Game

Sentencing decisions directly raise questions about the purpose of punishment. Defense lawyers often ask "what would be the point" of imprisoning someone for a crime whose harm cannot be undone. Prosecutors, on the other hand, routinely ask judges "to send a message" by giving harsh sentences. What sentence would be appropriate for the following three offenders? Why? What if you could only "spend" thirty years of prison in total on all three offenders? How would you allocate those prison years?

1. A political activist with a college degree and no prior criminal record plants a bomb in a campaign headquarters that detonates in the middle of the night, accidentally killing an employee who decided to spend the night sleeping on a couch in a reception area. The activist assumes a false identity and eludes capture for twenty-five years. During that time, she commits no further crimes and devotes herself to community service.

2. A decorated military veteran suffering from traumatic war injuries, debilitating post-traumatic stress syndrome and related substance abuse issues commits a series of violent assaults against strangers over trivial arguments. These violent assaults grow in seriousness over the years, and he graduates from probationary sentences to longer and longer stints in the county jail. While intoxicated, he shoots another intoxicated man in a restaurant who had mocked his disability and demeaned his patriotism.

3. A child suffers serious abuse and neglect at the hands of violent, alcoholic parents while growing up in a desperately poor urban neighborhood. During one beating, he suffers a traumatic head injury that impairs his cognitive functioning. He begins drinking hard alcohol that he finds around the house as a young teen, and eventually drops out of high school. He then begins using drugs and selling them for a street gang. While selling on a street corner late one night, he mistakes another young man approaching him for a member of a rival gang intending to rob him. He smashes the young man over the head with a heavy wine bottle, killing him. The victim grew up in the same general neighborhood, but was a college student visiting his mother during spring break. He wore a baseball cap from his college that displayed lettering that resembled the insignia of the rival gang. Evidence suggests

> that he was approaching the defendant to buy marijuana from
> him.

E. CASE IN CONTEXT

Cases that involve the most desperate circumstances often force judges and juries to confront fundamental questions about why we punish. The following famous case about cannibalism on the high seas was just such a case. Doctrinally, the case involved the defense of necessity. This defense is covered later in this text, but essentially it is a "lesser of two evils defense." For example, a hiker lost in a blizzard who broke into an unoccupied cabin in order to survive would have a necessity defense to the crime of criminal trespass. But should such a defense apply to murder?

THE QUEEN V. DUDLEY & STEPHENS
Queen's Bench Division
14 Q.B.D. 273 (1884)

Indictment for the murder of Richard Parker on the high seas within the jurisdiction of the Admirality.

At the trial before Huddleston, B., at the Devon and Cornwall Winter Assizes, November 7, 1884, the jury, at the suggestion of the learned judge, found the facts of the case in a special verdict which stated "that on July 5, 1884, the prisoners, Thomas Dudley and Edward Stephens, with one Brooks, all able-bodied English seamen, and the deceased also an English boy, between seventeen and eighteen years of age, the crew of an English yacht, a registered English vessel, were cast away in a storm on the high seas 1600 miles from the Cape of Good Hope, and were compelled to put into an open boat belonging to the said yacht. That in this boat they had no supply of water and no supply of food, except two 1 lb. tins of turnips, and for three days they had nothing else to subsist upon. That on the fourth day they caught a small turtle, upon which they subsisted for a few days, and this was the only food they had up to the twentieth day when the act now in question was committed. That on the twelfth day the turtle were entirely consumed, and for the next eight days they had nothing to eat. That they had no fresh water, except such rain as they from time to time caught in their oilskin capes. That the boat was drifting on the ocean, and was probably more than 1000 miles away from land. That on the eighteenth day, when they had been seven days without food and five without water, the prisoners spoke to Brooks as to what should be done if no succor came, and suggested that someone should be sacrificed to save the rest, but Brooks dissented, and the boy, to whom they were understood to refer, was not consulted. That on the 24th of July, the day before the act now in question, the prisoner Dudley proposed to Stephens and Brooks that lots should be cast who should be put to death to save the rest, but Brooks refused consent, and it was not put to the boy, and in point of fact there was no drawing of lots. That on that day the prisoners spoke of their having families, and suggested it would be better to kill the boy that their lives should be saved, and Dudley proposed that if there was no vessel in sight by the morrow morning the boy should be killed. That next day, the 25th of July, no vessel appearing, Dudley told Brooks that he had better go and have a sleep, and made signs to Stephens and Brooks that the boy had better be killed. The prisoner Stephens agreed to the act, but Brooks dissented from it. That the boy was then lying at the bottom of the boat quite helpless, and extremely weakened by famine and by drinking sea water, and unable to make any resistance, nor did he ever assent to his being killed. The prisoner Dudley offered a prayer asking forgiveness for them all if either of them should be tempted to commit a rash act, and that their souls might be saved. That Dudley, with the assent of Stephens, went to the boy, and telling him that his time was come, put a knife into his throat and killed him then and there; that the three men fed upon the body and blood of the boy for four days; that on the fourth day after the act had been committed the boat was picked up by a passing vessel, and the prisoners were rescued, still alive, but in the lowest state of prostration. That they were carried to the port of Falmouth, and committed for trial at Exeter. That if the men had not fed upon the body of the boy they would probably not have survived to be so picked up and rescued, but would within the four days have died of famine. That the boy, being in a much weaker condition, was likely to have died before them. That at the time of the act in question there was no sail in sight, nor any reasonable prospect of relief. That under these circumstances there appeared to the prisoners every probability that unless they then fed or very soon fed upon the boy or one of themselves they would die of starvation. That there was no appreciable chance of saving life except by killing someone for the others to eat. That assuming any necessity to kill anybody, there was no greater necessity for killing the boy than any of the other three men. But whether upon the whole matter by the jurors found the killing of Richard Parker by Dudley and Stephens be felony and murder the jurors are ignorant, and pray the advice of the Court thereupon, and if upon the whole matter the Court shall be of opinion that the killing of Richard Parker be felony and murder, then the jurors say that Dudley and Stephens were each guilty of felony and murder as alleged in the indictment."

From these facts, stated with the cold precision of a special verdict, it appears sufficiently that the prisoners were subject to terrible temptation, to sufferings which might break down the bodily power of the strongest man and try the conscience of the best. Other details yet more harrowing, facts still more loathsome and appalling, were presented to the jury, and are to be found recorded in my learned Brother's notes. But nevertheless this is clear, that the prisoners put to death a weak and unoffending boy upon the chance of preserving their own lives by feeding upon his flesh and blood after he was killed, and with the certainty of depriving him of any possible chance of survival. The verdict finds in terms that "if the men had not fed upon the body of the boy they would probably not have survived," and that, "the boy being in a much weaker condition was likely to have died before them." They might possibly have been picked up next day by a passing ship; they might possibly not have been picked up at all; in either case it is obvious that the killing of the boy would have been an unnecessary and profitless act. It is found by the verdict that the boy was incapable of resistance, and, in fact, made none; and it is not even suggested that his death was due to any violence on his part attempted against, or even so much as feared by, those who killed him. Under these circumstances the jury say that they are ignorant whether those who killed him were guilty of murder, and have referred it to this Court to determine what is the legal consequence which follows from the facts which they have found.

The learned judge then adjourned the assizes until the 25th of November at the Royal Courts of Justice. On the application of the Crown they were again adjourned to the 4th of December, and the case ordered to be argued before a Court consisting of five judges.

There remains to be considered the real question in the case—whether killing under the circumstances set forth in the verdict be or be not murder. The contention that it could be anything else was, to the minds of us all, both new and strange, and we stopped the Attorney General in his negative argument in order that we might hear what could be said in support of a proposition which appeared to us to be at once dangerous, immoral, and opposed to all legal principle and analogy. All, no doubt, that can be said has been urged before us, and we are now to consider and determine what it amounts to. First it is said that it follows from various definitions of murder in books of authority, which definitions imply, if they do not state, the doctrine, that in order to save your own life you may lawfully take away the life of another, when that other is neither attempting nor threatening yours, nor is guilty of any illegal act whatever towards you or anyone else. But if these definitions be looked at they will not be found to sustain this contention.

It is . . . clear . . . that the doctrine contended for receives no support from the great authority of Lord Hale. It is plain that in his view the necessity which justified homicide is that only which has always been and is now considered a justification. . . . Lord Hale regarded the private necessity which justified, and alone justified, the taking the life of another for the safeguard of one's own to be what is commonly called "self defence." (Hale's Pleas of the Crown, i. 478.)

But if this could be even doubtful upon Lord Hale's words, Lord Hale himself has made it clear. For in the chapter in which he deals with the exemption created by compulsion or necessity he thus expresses himself— "If a man be desperately assaulted and in peril of death, and cannot otherwise escape unless, to satisfy his assailant's fury, he will kill an innocent person then present, the fear and actual force will not acquit him of the crime and punishment of murder, if he commit the fact [sic], for he ought rather to die himself than kill an innocent; but if he cannot otherwise save his own life the law permits him in his own defence to kill the assailant, for by the violence of the assault, and the offence committed upon him by the assailant himself, the law of nature, and necessity, hath made him his own protector. . . ." (Hale's Pleas of the Crown, vol. i. 51.)

But, further still, Lord Hale in the following chapter deals with the position asserted by the casuists, and sanctioned, as he says, by Grotius and Puffendorf, that in a case of extreme necessity, either of hunger or clothing; "theft is no theft, or at least not punishable as theft, as some even of our own lawyers have asserted the same." "But," says Lord Hale, "I take it that here in England, that rule, at least by the laws of England, is false; and therefore, if a person, being under necessity for want of victuals or clothes, shall upon that account clandestinely and animo furandi steal another man's goods, it is felony, and a crime by the laws of England punishable with death." (Hale, Pleas of the Crown, i. 54.) If, therefore, Lord Hale is clear—as he is—that extreme necessity of hunger does not justify larceny, what would he have said to the doctrine that it justified murder?

Is there, then, any authority for the proposition which has been presented to us? Decided cases there are none. . . . The American case cited by my Brother Stephen in his Digest [United States v. Holmes, 26 F. Cas. 360, 1 Wall. Jr. 1 (C.C.E.D. Pa. 1842)], from Wharton on Homicide, in which it was decided, correctly indeed, that sailors had no right to throw passengers overboard to save themselves, but on the somewhat strange ground that the proper mode of determining who was to be sacrificed was to vote upon the subject by ballot, can hardly, as my Brother Stephen says, be an authority satisfactory to a court in this country. . . .

The one real authority of former time is Lord Bacon, who . . . lays down the law as follows: "Necessity carrieth a privilege in itself. Necessity is of three sorts—necessity of conservation of life, necessity of obedience, and necessity of the act of God or of a stranger. First of conservation of life; if a man steals viands to satisfy his present hunger, this is no felony nor larceny. So if divers be in danger of drowning by the casting away of some boat or barge, and one of them get to some plank, or on the boat's side to keep himself above water, and another to save his life thrust him from it, whereby he is drowned, this is neither se defendendo nor by misadventure, but justifiable." . . . Lord Bacon was great even as a lawyer; but it is permissible to much smaller men, relying upon principle and on the authority of others, the equals and even the superiors of Lord Bacon as lawyers, to question the soundness of his dictum. There are many conceivable states of things in which it might possibly be true, but if Lord Bacon meant to lay down the broad proposition that man may save his life by killing, if necessary, an innocent and unoffending neighbour, it certainly is not law at the present day. . . .

Now it is admitted that the deliberate killing of this unoffending and unresisting boy was clearly murder, unless the killing can be justified by some well recognised excuse admitted by the law. It is further admitted that there was in this case no such excuse, unless the killing was justified by what has been called "necessity." But the temptation to the act which existed here was not what the law has ever called necessity. Nor is this to be regretted. Though law and morality are not the same, and many things may be immoral which are not necessarily illegal, yet the absolute divorce of law from morality would be of fatal consequence; and such divorce would follow if the temptation to murder in this case were to be held by law an absolute defence of it. It is not so. To preserve one's life is generally speaking a duty, but it may be the plainest and the highest duty to sacrifice it. War is full of instances in which it is a man's duty not to live, but to die. The duty, in case of shipwreck, of a captain to his crew, of the crew to the passengers, of soldiers to women and children, as in the noble case of the Birkenhead; these duties impose on men the moral necessity, not of the preservation, but of the sacrifice of their lives for others, from which in no country, least of all, it is to be hoped, in England, will men ever shrink, as indeed, they have not shrunk. It is not correct, therefore, to say that there is any absolute or unqualified necessity to preserve one's life. Necesse est ut eam, non ut vivam, is a saying of a Roman officer quoted by Lord Bacon himself with high eulogy in the very chapter on necessity to which so much reference has been made. It would be a very easy and cheap display of commonplace learning to quote from Greek and Latin authors, from Horace, from Juvenal, from Cicero, from Euripides, passage after passage, in which the duty of dying for others has been laid down in glowing and emphatic language as resulting from the principles of heathen ethics; it is enough in a Christian country to remind ourselves of the Great Example whom we profess to follow. It is not needful to point out the awful danger of admitting the principle which has been contended for. Who is to be the judge of this sort of necessity? By what measure is the comparative value of lives to be measured? Is it to be strength, or intellect, or what? It is plain that the principle leaves to him who is to profit by it to determine the necessity which will justify him in deliberately taking another's life to save his own. In this case the weakest, the youngest, the most unresisting, was chosen. Was it more necessary to kill him than one of the grown men? The answer must be "No"—

So spake the Fiend, and with necessity,

The tyrant's plea, excused his devilish deeds.

It is not suggested that in this particular case the deeds were "devilish," but it is quite plain that such a principle once admitted might be made the legal cloak for unbridled passion and atrocious crime. There is no safe path for judges to tread but to ascertain the law to the best of their ability and to declare it according to their judgment; and if in any case the law appears to be too severe on individuals, to leave it to the Sovereign to exercise that prerogative of mercy which the Constitution has entrusted to the hands fittest to dispense it.

It must not be supposed that in refusing to admit temptation to be an excuse for crime it is forgotten how terrible the temptation was; how awful the suffering; how hard in such trials to keep the judgment straight and the conduct pure. We are often compelled to set up standards we cannot reach ourselves, and to lay down rules which we could not ourselves satisfy. But a man has no right to declare temptation to be an excuse, though he might himself have yielded to it, nor allow compassion for the criminal to change or weaken in any manner the legal definition of the crime. It is therefore our duty to declare that the prisoners' act in this case was willful murder, that the facts as stated in the verdict are no legal justification of the homicide; and to say that in our unanimous opinion the prisoners are upon this special verdict guilty of murder.

NOTE:

The Court then proceeded to pass sentence of death upon the prisoners

DISCUSSION QUESTIONS

1.   Should the criminal law promote the greatest good for the greatest number of people or protect innocent life at all costs?

2.   Would it have mattered it if they had drawn lots, and Parker had lost? What if Parker had begged to be killed, both to end his suffering and to save his shipmates?

3.   Why does the court punish Dudley and Stephens for doing what the court admits they might do themselves? The court expresses concern that creating an exception for Dudley and Stephens might create a "cloak" for "atrocious" crime. Shouldn't the court simply try and do justice in this case without worrying about the next case? Can it?

Practice Problem 3.2: Flight 93

On September 11th, 2001, terrorists hijacked Flight 93 with the intention of flying the plane into government buildings in Washington, D.C. After he learned of the hijacking of the plane, Vice President Cheney ordered that the plane be shot down by fighter jets before it could reach its target. By the time he gave the order, however, the passengers had already rushed the cockpit and the plane had crashed killing all on board. There were forty-four people on board, including the three hijackers. Many more might have died if the plane had crashed into a government building. Imagine that the passengers had not rushed the cockpit and that the plane had been shot down as the Vice President ordered. Would the Vice President have been guilty of murder? If not, what rule can you articulate that reconciles your decision with the decision in the Dudley and Stephens case?

F.   SPECIAL FOCUS: PUNISHMENT AND ADDICTION

In two cases in the nineteen sixties the Supreme Court wrestled with how the criminal law can regulate the consumption of intoxicating and addicting substances. In doing so, the Court had to wrestle with fundamental questions about what purposes punishing such behavior serves. The first case involved addiction to illegal narcotics, and the second case involved alcohol intoxication. Both involved a doctrinal distinction between a "status" and an "act." We will further discuss this doctrinal distinction in later chapters, but our present focus is on how the justices think about why we punish such crimes.

ROBISON V. CALIFORNIA
Supreme Court of the United States
370 U.S. 660 (1962)

MR. JUSTICE STEWART delivered the opinion of the Court.

A California statute makes it a criminal offense for a person to "be addicted to the use of narcotics." This appeal draws into question the constitutionality of that provision of the state law, as construed by the California courts in the present case.

The appellant was convicted after a jury trial in the Municipal Court of Los Angeles. The evidence against him was given by two Los Angeles police officers. Officer Brown testified that he had had occasion to examine the appellant's arms one evening on a street in Los Angeles some four months before the trial. The officer testified that at that time he had observed "scar tissue and discoloration on the inside" of the appellant's right arm, and "what appeared to be numerous needle marks and a scab which was approximately three inches below the crook of the elbow" on the appellant's left arm. The officer also testified that the appellant under questioning had admitted to the occasional use of narcotics.

Officer Lindquist testified that he had examined the appellant the following morning in the Central Jail in Los Angeles. The officer stated that at that time he had observed discolorations and scabs on the appellant's arms, and he identified photographs which had been taken of the appellant's arms shortly after his arrest the night before. Based upon more than ten years of experience as a member of the Narcotic Division of the Los Angeles Police Department, the witness gave his opinion that "these marks and the discoloration were the result of the injection of hypodermic needles into the tissue into the vein that was not sterile." He stated that the scabs were several days old at the time of his examination, and that the appellant was neither under the influence of narcotics nor suffering withdrawal symptoms at the time he saw him. This witness also testified that the appellant had admitted using narcotics in the past.

The appellant testified in his own behalf, denying the alleged conversations with the police officers and denying that he had ever used narcotics or been addicted to their use. He explained the marks on his arms as resulting from an allergic condition contracted during his military service. His testimony was corroborated by two witnesses.

The trial judge instructed the jury that the statute made it a misdemeanor for a person "either to use narcotics, or to be addicted to the use of narcotics . . . . That portion of the statute referring to the 'use' of narcotics is based upon the 'act' of using. That portion of the statute referring to 'addicted to the use' of narcotics is based upon a condition or status. They are not identical. . . . To be addicted to the use of narcotics is said to be a status or condition and not an act. It is a continuing offense and differs from most other offenses in the fact that [it] is chronic rather than acute; that it continues after it is complete and subjects the offender to arrest at any time before he reforms. The existence of such a chronic condition may be ascertained from a single examination, if the characteristic reactions of that condition be found present."

The judge further instructed the jury that the appellant could be convicted under a general verdict if the jury agreed either that he was of the "status" or had committed the "act" denounced by the statute. "All that the People must show is either that the defendant did use a narcotic in Los Angeles County, or that while in the City of Los Angeles he was addicted to the use of narcotics . . . ."

Under these instructions the jury returned a verdict finding the appellant "guilty of the offense charged." An appeal was taken to the Appellate Department of the Los Angeles County Superior Court, "the highest court of a State in which a decision could be had" in this case. 28 U.S.C. § 1257. See Smith v. California, 361 U.S. 147, 149; Edwards v. California, 314 U.S. 160, 171. Although expressing some doubt as to the constitutionality of "the crime of being a narcotic addict," the reviewing court in an unreported opinion affirmed the judgment of conviction, citing two of its own previous unreported decisions which had upheld the constitutionality of the statute. We noted probable jurisdiction of this appeal, 368 U.S. 918, because it squarely presents the issue whether the statute as construed by the California courts in this case is repugnant to the Fourteenth Amendment of the Constitution.

The broad power of a State to regulate the narcotic drugs traffic within its borders is not here in issue. More than forty years ago, in Whipple v. Martinson, 256 U.S. 41, this Court explicitly recognized the validity of that power: "There can be no question of the authority of the State in the exercise of its police power to regulate the administration, sale, prescription and use of dangerous and habit-forming drugs . . . . The right to exercise this power is so manifest in the interest of the public health and welfare, that it is unnecessary to enter upon a discussion of it beyond saying that it is too firmly established to be successfully called in question." 256 U.S., at 45.

Such regulation, it can be assumed, could take a variety of valid forms. A State might impose criminal sanctions, for example, against the unauthorized manufacture, prescription, sale, purchase, or possession of narcotics within its borders. In the interest of discouraging the violation of such laws, or in the interest of the general health or welfare of its inhabitants, a State might establish a program of compulsory treatment for those addicted to narcotics. Such a program of treatment might require periods of involuntary confinement. And penal sanctions might be imposed for failure to comply with established compulsory treatment procedures. Cf. Jacobson v. Massachusetts, 197 U.S. 11. Or a State might choose to attack the evils of narcotics traffic on broader fronts also—through public health education, for example, or by efforts to ameliorate the economic and social conditions under which those evils might be thought to flourish. In short, the range of valid choice which a State might make in this area is undoubtedly a wide one, and the wisdom of any particular choice within the allowable spectrum is not for us to decide. Upon that premise we turn to the California law in issue here.

It would be possible to construe the statute under which the appellant was convicted as one which is operative only upon proof of the actual use of narcotics within the State's jurisdiction. But the California courts have not so construed this law. Although there was evidence in the present case that the appellant had used narcotics in Los Angeles, the jury was instructed that they could convict him even if they disbelieved that evidence. The appellant could be convicted, they were told, if they found simply that the appellant's "status" or "chronic condition" was that of being "addicted to the use of narcotics." And it is impossible to know from the jury's verdict that the defendant was not convicted upon precisely such a finding.

The instructions of the trial court, implicitly approved on appeal, amounted to "a ruling on a question of state law that is as binding on us as though the precise words had been written" into the statute. Terminiello v. Chicago, 337 U.S. 1, 4. "We can only take the statute as the state courts read it." Id., at 6. Indeed, in their brief in this Court counsel for the State have emphasized that it is "the proof of addiction by circumstantial evidence . . . by the tell-tale track of needle marks and scabs over the veins of his arms, that remains the gist of the section."

This statute, therefore, is not one which punishes a person for the use of narcotics, for their purchase, sale or possession, or for antisocial or disorderly behavior resulting from their administration. It is not a law which even purports to provide or require medical treatment. Rather, we deal with a statute which makes the "status" of narcotic addiction a criminal offense, for which the offender may be prosecuted "at any time before he reforms." California has said that a person can be continuously guilty of this offense, whether or not he has ever used or possessed any narcotics within the State, and whether or not he has been guilty of any antisocial behavior there.

It is unlikely that any State at this moment in history would attempt to make it a criminal offense for a person to be mentally ill, or a leper, or to be afflicted with a venereal disease. A State might determine that the general health and welfare require that the victims of these and other human afflictions be dealt with by compulsory treatment, involving quarantine, confinement, or sequestration. But, in the light of contemporary human knowledge, a law which made a criminal offense of such a disease would doubtless be universally thought to be an infliction of cruel and unusual punishment in violation of the Eighth and Fourteenth Amendments.

We cannot but consider the statute before us as of the same category. In this Court counsel for the State recognized that narcotic addiction is an illness. Indeed, it is apparently an illness which may be contracted innocently or involuntarily. We hold that a state law which imprisons a person thus afflicted as a criminal, even though he has never touched any narcotic drug within the State or been guilty of any irregular behavior there, inflicts a cruel and unusual punishment in violation of the Fourteenth Amendment. To be sure, imprisonment for ninety days is not, in the abstract, a punishment which is either cruel or unusual. But the question cannot be considered in the abstract. Even one day in prison would be a cruel and unusual punishment for the "crime" of having a common cold.

We are not unmindful that the vicious evils of the narcotics traffic have occasioned the grave concern of government. There are, as we have said, countless fronts on which those evils may be legitimately attacked. We deal in this case only with an individual provision of a particularized local law as it has so far been interpreted by the California courts.

Reversed.

MR. JUSTICE CLARK, dissenting.

The Court finds § 11721 of California's Health and Safety Code, making it an offense to "be addicted to the use of narcotics," violative of due process as "a cruel and unusual punishment." I cannot agree.

The statute must first be placed in perspective. California has a comprehensive and enlightened program for the control of narcotism based on the overriding policy of prevention and cure. It is the product of an extensive investigation made in the mid-Fifties by a committee of distinguished scientists, doctors, law enforcement officers and laymen appointed by the then Attorney General, now Governor, of California . . .

Apart from prohibiting specific acts such as the purchase, possession and sale of narcotics, California has taken certain legislative steps in regard to the status of being a narcotic addict—a condition commonly recognized as a threat to the State and to the individual. The Code deals with this problem in realistic stages. At its incipiency narcotic addiction is handled under § 11721 of the Health and Safety Code which is at issue here. It provides that a person found to be addicted to the use of narcotics shall serve a term in the county jail of not less than 90 days nor more than one year, with the minimum 90-day confinement applying in all cases without exception. Provision is made for parole with periodic tests to detect readdiction.

The trial court defined "addicted to narcotics" as used in § 11721 in the following charge to the jury:

"The word 'addicted' means, strongly disposed to some taste or practice or habituated, especially to drugs. In order to inquire as to whether a person is addicted to the use of narcotics is in effect an inquiry as to his habit in that regard. Does he use them habitually. To use them often or daily is, according to the ordinary acceptance of those words, to use them habitually."

There was no suggestion that the term "narcotic addict" as here used included a person who acted without volition or who had lost the power of self-control. Although the section is penal in appearance—perhaps a carry-over from a less sophisticated approach—its present provisions are quite similar to those for civil commitment and treatment of addicts who have lost the power of self-control, and its present purpose is reflected in a statement which closely follows § 11721: "The rehabilitation of narcotic addicts and the prevention of continued addiction to narcotics is a matter of statewide concern." California Health and Safety Code § 11728.

Where narcotic addiction has progressed beyond the incipient, volitional stage, California provides for commitment of three months to two years in a state hospital. California Welfare and Institutions Code § 5355. For the purposes of this provision, a narcotic addict is defined as:

"any person who habitually takes or otherwise uses to the extent of having lost the power of self-control any opium, morphine, cocaine, or other narcotic drug as defined in Article 1 of Chapter 1 of Division 10 of the Health and Safety Code." California Welfare and Institutions Code § 5350.

This proceeding is clearly civil in nature with a purpose of rehabilitation and cure. Significantly, if it is found that a person committed under § 5355 will not receive substantial benefit from further hospital treatment and is not dangerous to society, he may be discharged—but only after a minimum confinement of three months. § 5355.1.

Thus, the "criminal" provision applies to the incipient narcotic addict who retains self-control, requiring confinement of three months to one year and parole with frequent tests to detect renewed use of drugs. Its overriding purpose is to cure the less seriously addicted person by preventing further use. On the other hand, the "civil" commitment provision deals with addicts who have lost the power of self-control, requiring hospitalization up to two years. Each deals with a different type of addict but with a common purpose. This is most apparent when the sections overlap: if after civil commitment of an addict it is found that hospital treatment will not be helpful, the addict is confined for a minimum period of three months in the same manner as is the volitional addict under the "criminal" provision. . .

The majority strikes down the conviction primarily on the grounds that petitioner was denied due process by the imposition of criminal penalties for nothing more than being in a status. This viewpoint is premised upon the theme that § 11721 is a "criminal" provision authorizing a punishment, for the majority admits that "a State might establish a program of compulsory treatment for those addicted to narcotics" which "might require periods of involuntary confinement." I submit that California has done exactly that. The majority's error is in instructing the California Legislature that hospitalization is the only treatment for narcotics addiction—that anything less is a punishment denying due process. California has found otherwise after a study which I suggest was more extensive than that conducted by the Court. . .

However, the case in support of the judgment below need not rest solely on this reading of California law. For even if the overall statutory scheme is ignored and a purpose and effect of punishment is attached to § 11721, that provision still does not violate the Fourteenth Amendment. The majority acknowledges, as it must, that a State can punish persons who purchase, possess or use narcotics. Although none of these acts are harmful to society in themselves, the State constitutionally may attempt to deter and prevent them through punishment because of the grave threat of future harmful conduct which they pose. Narcotics addiction—including the incipient, volitional addiction to which this provision speaks—is no different. California courts have taken judicial notice that "the inordinate use of a narcotic drug tends to create an irresistible craving and forms a habit for its continued use until one becomes an addict, and he respects no convention or obligation and will lie, steal, or use any other base means to gratify his passion for the drug, being lost to all considerations of duty or social position." People v. Jaurequi, 142 Cal. App. 2d 555, 561, 298 P. 2d 896, 900 (1956). Can this Court deny the legislative and judicial judgment of California that incipient, volitional narcotic addiction poses a threat of serious crime similar to the threat inherent in the purchase or possession of narcotics? And if such a threat is inherent in addiction, can this Court say that California is powerless to deter it by punishment? . . .

I would affirm the judgment.

MR. JUSTICE WHITE, dissenting.

If appellant's conviction rested upon sheer status, condition or illness or if he was convicted for being an addict who had lost his power of self-control, I would have other thoughts about this case. But this record presents neither situation. And I believe the Court has departed from its wise rule of not deciding constitutional questions except where necessary and from its equally sound practice of construing state statutes, where possible, in a manner saving their constitutionality.

I am not at all ready to place the use of narcotics beyond the reach of the States' criminal laws. I do not consider appellant's conviction to be a punishment for having an illness or for simply being in some status or condition, but rather a conviction for the regular, repeated or habitual use of narcotics immediately prior to his arrest and in violation of the California law. As defined by the trial court, addiction is the regular use of narcotics and can be proved only by evidence of such use. To find addiction in this case the jury had to believe that appellant had frequently used narcotics in the recent past. California is entitled to have its statute and the record so read, particularly where the State's only purpose in allowing prosecutions for addiction was to supersede its own venue requirements applicable to prosecutions for the use of narcotics and in effect to allow convictions for use where there is no precise evidence of the county where the use took place.

I respectfully dissent.

DISCUSSION QUESTIONS

1.   The majority rests its holding on a fine distinction between a status and an act. What if someone were intoxicated or under the influence of a controlled substance? Is that a status, or an act?

2.   Assuming that one can only become addicted to illegal drugs by using illegal drugs, why not allow states to punish such addiction?

3.   Do you think those addicted to illegal drugs would be better off being civilly confined against their will or arrested for a crime? Does it matter either way?

POWELL V. TEXAS

Supreme Court of the United States
392 U.S. 514 (1968)

MR. JUSTICE MARSHALL announced the judgment of the Court and delivered an opinion in which THE CHIEF JUSTICE, MR. JUSTICE BLACK, and MR. JUSTICE HARLAN join.

In late December 1966, appellant was arrested and charged with being found in a state of intoxication in a public place, in violation of Vernon's Ann. Texas Penal Code, Art. 477 (1952), which reads as follows:

'Whoever shall get drunk or be found in a state of intoxication in any public place, or at any private house except his own, shall be fined not exceeding one hundred dollars.'

The trial judge in the county court, sitting without a jury, made certain findings of fact, infra, at 2148, but ruled as a matter of law that chronic alcoholism was not a defense to the charge. He found appellant guilty, and fined him $50. There being no further right to appeal within the Texas judicial system, appellant appealed to this Court; we noted probable jurisdiction.

I

The principal testimony was that of Dr. David Wade, a Fellow of the American Medical Association, duly certificated in psychiatry. Dr. Wade sketched the outlines of the 'disease' concept of alcoholism; noted that there is no generally accepted definition of 'alcoholism'; alluded to the ongoing debate within the medical profession over whether alcohol is actually physically 'addicting' or merely psychologically 'habituating'; and concluded that in either case a 'chronic alcoholic' is an 'involuntary drinker,' who is 'powerless not to drink,' and who 'loses his self-control over his drinking.' He testified that he had examined appellant, and that appellant is a 'chronic alcoholic,' who 'by the time he has reached (the state of intoxication) * * * is not able to control his behavior, and (who) * * * has reached this point because he has an uncontrollable compulsion to drink.' Dr. Wade also responded in the negative to the question whether appellant has 'the willpower to resist the constant excessive consumption of alcohol.' He added that in his opinion jailing appellant without medical attention would operate neither to rehabilitate him nor to lessen his desire for alcohol.

On cross-examination, Dr. Wade admitted that when appellant was sober he knew the difference between right and wrong, and he responded affirmatively to the question whether appellant's act in taking the first drink in any given instance when he was sober was a 'voluntary exercise of his will.' Qualifying his answer, Dr. Wade stated that 'these individuals have a compulsion, and this compulsion, while not completely overpowering, is a very strong influence, an exceedingly strong influence, and this compulsion coupled with the firm belief in their mind that they are going to be able to handle it from now on causes their judgment to be somewhat clouded.'

Appellant testified concerning the history of his drinking problem. He reviewed his many arrests for drunkenness; testified that he was unable to stop drinking; stated that when he was intoxicated he had no control over his actions and could not remember them later, but that he did not become violent; and admitted that he did not remember his arrest on the occasion for which he was being tried. On cross-examination, appellant admitted that he had had one drink on the morning of the trial and had been able to discontinue drinking.

II

Despite the comparatively primitive state of our knowledge on the subject, it cannot be denied that the destructive use of alcoholic beverages is one of our principal social and public health problems.16 The lowest current informed estimate places the number of 'alcoholics' in America (definitional problems aside) at 4,000,000, and most authorities are inclined to put the figure considerably higher.

There is as yet no known generally effective method for treating the vast number of alcoholics in our society. Thus it is entirely possible that, even were the manpower and facilities available for a full-scale attack upon chronic alcoholism, we would find ourselves unable to help the vast bulk of our 'visible'-let alone our 'invisible'-alcoholic population.

However, facilities for the attempted treatment of indigent alcoholics are woefully lacking throughout the country. It would be tragic to return large numbers of helpless, sometimes dangerous and frequently unsanitary inebriates to the streets of our cities without even the opportunity to sober up adequately which a brief jail term provides. Presumably no State or city will tolerate such a state of affairs. Yet the medical profession cannot, and does not, tell us with any assurance that, even if the buildings, equipment and trained personnel were made available, it could provide anything more than slightly higher-class jails for our indigent habitual inebriates. Thus we run the grave risk that nothing will be accomplished beyond the hanging of a new sign-reading 'hospital'—over one wing of the jailhouse.

One virtue of the criminal process is, at least, that the duration of penal incarceration typically has some outside statutory limit; this is universally true in the case of petty offenses, such as public drunkenness, where jail terms are quite short on the whole. 'Therapeutic civil commitment' lacks this feature; one is typically committed until one is 'cured.' Thus, to do otherwise than affirm might subject indigent alcoholics to the risk that they may be locked up for an indefinite period of time under the same conditions as before, with no more hope than before of receiving effective treatment and no prospect of periodic 'freedom.'

Faced with this unpleasant reality, we are unable to assert that the use of the criminal process as a means of dealing with the public aspects of problem drinking can never be defended as rational. The picture of the penniless drunk propelled aimlessly and endlessly through the law's 'revolving door' of arrest, incarceration, release and re-arrest is not a pretty one. But before we condemn the present practice across-the-board, perhaps we ought to be able to point to some clear promise of a better world for these unfortunate people. Unfortunately, no such promise has yet been forthcoming. If, in addition to the absence of a coherent approach to the problem of treatment, we consider the almost complete absence of facilities and manpower for the implementation of a rehabilitation program, it is difficult to say in the present context that the criminal process is utterly lacking in social value. This Court has never held that anything in the Constitution requires that penal sanctions be designed solely to achieve therapeutic or rehabilitative effects, and it can hardly be said with assurance that incarceration serves such purposes any better for the general run of criminals than it does for public drunks.

Affirmed.

IV

The rule of constitutional law urged upon us by appellant would have a revolutionary impact on the criminal law, and any possible limits proposed for the rule would be wholly illusory. If the original boundaries of Robinson are to be discarded, any new limits too would soon fall by the wayside and the Court would be forced to hold the States powerless to punish any conduct that could be shown to result from a 'compulsion,' in the complex, psychological meaning of that term. The result, to choose just one illustration, would be to require recognition of 'irresistible impulse' as a complete defense to any crime; this is probably contrary to present law in most American jurisdictions.

The real reach of any such decision, however, would be broader still, for the basic premise underlying the argument is that it is cruel and unusual to punish a person who is not morally blameworthy. I state the proposition in this sympathetic way because I feel there is much to be said for avoiding the use of criminal sanctions in many such situations. See Morissette v. United States, supra. But the question here is one of constitutional law. The legislatures have always been allowed wide freedom to determine the extent to which moral culpability should be a prerequisite to conviction of a crime. E.g., United States v. Dotterweich, 320 U.S. 277, 64 S.Ct. 134, 88 L.Ed. 48 (1943). The criminal law is a social tool that is employed in seeking a wide variety of goals, and I cannot say the Eighth Amendment's limits on the use of criminal sanctions extend as far as this viewpoint would inevitably carry them.

But even if we were to limit any holding in this field to 'compulsions' that are 'symptomatic' of a 'disease,' in the words of the findings of the trial court, the sweep of that holding would still be startling. Such a ruling would make it clear beyond any doubt that a narcotics addict could not be punished for 'being' in possession of drugs or, for that matter, for 'being' guilty of using them. A wide variety of sex offenders would be immune from punishment if they could show that their conduct was not voluntary but part of the pattern of a disease. More generally speaking, a form of the insanity defense would be made a constitutional requirement throughout the Nation, should the Court now hold it cruel and unusual to punish a person afflicted with any mental disease whenever his conduct was part of the pattern of his disease and occasioned by a compulsion symptomatic of the disease.

DISCUSSION QUESTIONS

1.   Why is it justified to criminally punish someone for being intoxicated but not for being addicted?

2.   Do you think alcoholics would be better off if they could not be arrested for being intoxicated? Should we deal with public intoxication by alcoholics as a civil matter? Should that matter as to whether such punishment is constitutional?

3.   In Section IV the Court makes a classic "slippery slope" argument by saying in essence "if we prohibit this type of crime, we will have to prohibit many others. Is this true, or can principled distinctions be drawn between intoxication and committing other crimes such as buying illegal drugs under a compulsion born of addiction? If not, should such compulsion be a defense?

CHAPTER 4

STATUTORY INTERPRETATION
AND SOURCES OF LAW

■ ■ ■

Before you jump into the doctrines that define crimes and defenses, you must understand the sources of American criminal law. Today, most crimes and many defenses are defined by statute. Yet, at the beginning, American criminal law was heavily influenced by the common law of crimes that developed in England. The foundation of common law crimes in England helped create an American common law of crimes. Over time, more jurisdictions defined the criminal law through statutes that followed the common law and were passed by legislatures. In the middle of the last century, however, the American Law Institute developed a rival approach called the Model Penal Code. Explaining the role that the common law, the Model Penal Code, and modern criminal statutes play in American criminal law is one purpose of this chapter.

Moreover, this chapter will describe the principles that govern the creation and interpretation of statutes. First, judges read statutes more literally than they read common law cases because they are bound to give effect to the plain meaning of the legislature's chosen language. If the meaning of the statutory language is not plain, judges will then consider legislative intent and purpose. Second, the U.S. Constitution provides some modest limits on what legislatures can do when they create crimes: criminal statutes cannot be overly vague or overbroad and must provide clear notice of prohibited conduct. Although constitutional principles seldom arise in substantive criminal law, understanding the limits of statutory creation and interpretation is key to understanding how judges approach criminal statutes.

A basic idea to hold firmly in mind is that statues should be read word for word. This is where you start, but not necessarily where you end, in interpreting a statute. Even punctuation matters. In a possibly apocraphyl story the Czarina of Russia saved a man from exile by changing a comma. The warrant her husband the Czar wrote read "Pardon impossible, to be sent to Siberia." She changed the warrant to read "Pardon, impossible to be sent to Siberia." Remember the Czarina when you interpret statutes.

A. COMMON LAW

The English common law heavily influenced American criminal law. In England, judges, rather than the legislature, developed and defined crimes and defenses. These common law judges decided cases based on judge-made rules from earlier cases. Over time, the English Parliament began passing criminal statutes, and English colonists brought both types of law with them to the American colonies.

Although the English common law provided the foundation for American criminal law, it was a foundation that American judges and legislatures quickly began modifying. American judges issued their own common law decisions in criminal cases. More often, state legislatures passed statutes defining crimes and defenses, and by the end of the nineteenth century most states had passed comprehensive criminal codes.

Why then, if almost all crimes today are defined by statute, do we continue studying the common law? The answer is because the common law remains hugely influential in *interpreting* those criminal statutes. While many states essentially reduced the common law's definitions of crimes and defenses to statutory form, the terms and concepts they used in the statutes were left undefined. Not surprisingly then, judges interpreting these statutes look to the common law meaning of terms and concepts. For example, a modern homicide statute might define voluntary manslaughter as a killing committed upon "adequate provocation." Since provocation was a common law term, judges assume that the legislature intended for common law principles and precedents to guide its interpretation.

So, the common law guides the interpretation of many criminal statutes. Common law principles, however, do not *bind* a judge in the way that constitutional principles do. As we will discuss, a constitutional principle is one that a legislature may not violate. Since common law principles are not constitutional principles, a legislature may decide to deviate from the common law through statute. As long as the legislature makes this intent clear in plain language, a judge will follow that command. For example, a conspiracy at common law only required a conspiratorial agreement and no further action by the conspirators. A majority of American states, however, rejected that rule. Their legislatures defined criminal conspiracy as requiring an overt act in furtherance of the conspiratorial agreement.

B. THE MODEL PENAL CODE

Not surprisingly, people eventually asked whether it would make more sense to start over from scratch, rather than modify the common law approach on a piecemeal basis. Why use an approach to punishment that was developed hundreds of years ago? So, in the middle of the last century, the American Law Institute developed the Model Penal Code. The Model

Penal Code ("MPC") proved hugely influential. Slightly over thirty states adopted substantial parts of it. These jurisdictions are known as Model Penal Code jurisdictions, and they resort to the commentaries or cases from MPC jurisdictions, not common law jurisdictions, when deciding difficult issues. Even in non-MPC jurisdictions, many courts and legislatures will follow the Code's approach on some issues.

C. U.S. CONSTITUTIONAL LAW AND FEDERAL CRIMINAL LAW

The Constitution of the United States and the decisions of the Supreme Court interpreting it play a relatively minor role in a first-year criminal law course. The Constitution is the supreme law of the land, a "super law" that binds all other branches of government at both the state and local level. No legislative or executive branch of federal or state government may violate the Constitution, and the U.S. Supreme Court is the final authority on what the U.S. Constitution means. Constitutional law plays a small role in criminal law because the Constitution grants broad powers to legislatures at both the state and national level to define crimes. The Constitution provides many more limits on the procedures under which crime is investigated and adjudicated, but those are topics for second and third year courses.

Furthermore, federal criminal law plays a relatively minor role in criminal law. The vast majority of criminal law is state law, and the vast majority of criminal cases are brought in state courts. Federal criminal law is entirely statutory, and federal courts interpret these federal criminal statutes. U.S. Supreme Court cases interpreting federal statutes sometimes influence state courts confronting similar issues in interpreting state statutes. State courts, however, are not bound to follow the Supreme Court's lead on criminal law matters unless they concern constitutional issues.

Study Tip: Majority vs. Minority Rules

There is yet another way in which scholars, judges, and professors categorize legal rules. Major variations on fundamental issues have given rise to the concept of majority and minority rules. On important issues, judges and—more often—the authors of scholarly writings will identify the leading rule as the majority rule and the alternate approach as the minority rule. These categories often reflect the split between the common law approach and the MPC approach, but not always. Since common law jurisdictions often vary in their approaches, fundamental differences among common law jurisdictions will also sometimes be referred to as a majority and minority approaches. Also, sometimes rules will be described as part of "an emerging trend" or a "modern approach." Usually, this means that the rule has recently been adopted by a number of state legislatures or courts.

In the absence of majority and minority rules, judges and scholars acknowledge the lack of consensus among jurisdictions using language that students sometimes find maddening. In such cases, a judicial opinion or treatise (and even this textbook) will say, "many cases hold," "a few cases suggest," "some support exists for a rule that," or some other such qualifying language. There are many questions that appellate courts in various states have not resolved or even addressed in reported opinions.

D. STATUTORY INTERPRETATION

A statute is a law passed by a legislature and signed into law by the executive. Unless a criminal statute violates the U.S. Constitution (or the state's constitution), a court is bound to apply the law as the legislature wrote it. Statutes, however, inevitably contain gaps and ambiguities that require judges to interpret those statutes to resolve disputes about what they mean. In doing so, judges must honor the purpose and intent the legislature had when it passed the law. So a judge can't substitute her own judgment about whether the law is a good or bad idea. First, judges refer to the exact wording of the statute, reading the statute in a literal way. If the plain meaning of the statute is unclear, they will then, and only then, look beyond the text. This allegiance to the text is referred to as the plain meaning rule.

If the plain meaning is unclear, judges look at legislative history to determine what the legislature intended. Legislative history refers to the documents that were created or used by legislators as the bill was introduced, considered, and passed into law. Absent evidence of a specific legislative intent, courts look to the legislature's purpose in passing the statute, and often hear arguments from lawyers based on policy and philosophical considerations. Such resulting opinions are often included in criminal law textbooks. Cases that turn on the interpretation of legislative history, however, are not often included in criminal law textbooks (and not at all in this one) because resolution of such a narrow historical question does not illustrate much about the criminal law. Additionally, evidence of legislative history is often rare at the state level, especially with respect to statutory definitions of crimes that have been around for decades or more.

The plain meaning rule, along with the rule of lenity, is known as a "canon of statutory construction." The rule of lenity, which applies specially to criminal law cases, provides that ambiguities in statutes are to be resolved in favor of the criminal defendant. First-year law students, however, need to take both rules with a grain of salt. Instead of resolving interpretive disputes, these rules shape the language that lawyers use to make arguments and that judges use to justify decisions. A judge who does not wish to refer to legislative intent might say, "there is no need to cloud the meaning of a text that is clear." On the other hand, those wishing to consider legislative history will say that the meaning of the statutory text is cloudy. Likewise, those arguing for the prosecution will say that the rule of lenity does not apply because the meaning of the statute is plainly in their favor. Unlike baseball, a tie does not really go to the defender.

Study/Exam Tip

Anytime you see the language of a statute defining a crime in a case or exam question, highlight it. The language defining the crime at issue is often key to understanding the issues resolved by the case or raised by the fact pattern.

Case in Context

A five year sentence in the following case turns on the statutory interpretation of four words.

UNITED STATES OF AMERICA V. HILTON A. LAKE

United States Court of Appeals, Third Circuit
150 F.3d 269 (1998)

OPINION OF THE COURT

ALITO, CIRCUIT JUDGE.

This is an appeal from a judgment in a criminal case. After a jury trial, the defendant, Hilton A. Lake, was convicted under 18 U.S.C. § 924(c)(1) of using or carrying a firearm during and in relation to a crime of violence, namely, a carjacking (see 18 U.S.C. § 2119). Lake challenges his conviction on numerous grounds, the most substantial of which is that he did not violate the carjacking statute because, he argues, he did not take the motor vehicle in question "from the person or presence" of the victim. We reject this and Lake's other arguments, and we therefore affirm.

I.

The events that led to Lake's prosecution occurred at Little Magen's Bay in St. Thomas, United States Virgin Islands. The road to the beach at Little Magen's Bay ends at the top of a hill. There is a steep path bordered by vegetation and rocks that leads from the road down to the beach, and the road cannot be seen from the beach.

On the day in question, Lake hitchhiked to Little Magen's Bay and encountered Milton Clarke, who was sitting on the beach reading a newspaper. Lake asked whether Clarke owned a white car parked up on the road. Clarke said that he did, and Lake initially walked away. However, Lake returned a few moments later and asked to borrow the car. When Clarke refused, Lake stated that it was an emergency. Clarke again refused, and Lake walked off. When Lake returned yet again, Clarke said:

[L]isten, think about it. If I walked up to you and asked you, can I borrow your car[,] [a]re you going to lend it to me? Of course not.

So why don't you leave me the hell alone. I'm here to have a nice time. Just chill. Go someplace else.

App. 140A.

Lake walked off and sat on a rock, while Clarke anxiously watched him out of the corner of his eye, but Lake soon returned with the same request. When Clarke swore again, Lake asked if he could have a drink from Clarke's cooler. Clarke said: "[D]on't you get it? Leave me alone." Lake then lifted up his shirt, showed Clarke the handle of a gun, and said: "[Y]ou know what that is?" Clarke stood up and started backing away, but Lake pulled the gun from his waist band, put it against Clarke's face, and demanded the car keys. Clarke said that he did not have the keys and started walking toward the water with Lake following. Clarke waded into waist-deep water, and Lake walked out onto a promontory overlooking the water.

While Clarke was in the water, his friend, Pamela Croaker, appeared on the beach. Clarke shouted a warning, prompting Lake to approach Croaker. Lake demanded that Croaker surrender her car keys, and Croaker said: "I don't even know you. Why would I give you the keys to the car?" Lake then grabbed the keys, and the two wrestled for possession of the keys. When Croaker saw the gun, she surrendered the keys but asked to keep her house keys. Lake went up the steep path to the parking area where Croaker had parked her car out of sight of the beach. Lake then drove away in Croaker's car after leaving her house keys on the hood of Clarke's car. As we will discuss later in more detail, both Croaker and Clarke followed him up the path, but when they arrived, he was driving away.

Later that day, the police apprehended Lake in the stolen car at a McDonald's restaurant. When questioned by the police and an FBI agent, Lake stated that he had used a toy gun and that he had thrown it in a swamp. He refused to take the officers to the site where he had allegedly disposed of the gun, and when asked to tell the truth about whether the gun was really a toy, he responded that he "would think about it." The gun was never recovered.

Lake was indicted for carjacking, in violation of 18 U.S.C. § 2119, and for using and carrying a firearm during and in relation to a crime of violence (the carjacking), in violation of 18 U.S.C. § 924(c)(1). At the close of the evidence in his jury trial, Lake moved unsuccessfully for a judgment of acquittal. The jury subsequently returned a verdict of not guilty of the carjacking charge but guilty of the firearms offense. Lake was sentenced to imprisonment for 60 months plus a three-year term of supervised release. He then took this appeal.

B. *From the person or presence of another.* Lake maintains that the evidence did not show that he took Croaker's car "from [her] person or presence," as 18 U.S.C. § 2119 demands. Lake argues that he took her keys, not her car, from her person or presence and that the car was not in Croaker's presence when he took it because she could not see or touch the car at that moment.

The carjacking statute's requirement that the vehicle be taken "from the person or presence of the victim" "tracks the language used in other federal robbery statutes," Under these statutes, "property is in the presence of a person if it is 'so within his reach, observation or control, that he could if not overcome by violence or prevented by fear, retain his possession of it.' LaFave and Scott, *Substantive Criminal Law* § 8.11 at 443 (1986) (" 'Presence' in this connection is not so much a matter of eyesight as it is one of proximity and control: the property taken in the robbery must be close enough to the victim and sufficiently under his control that, had the latter not been subjected to violence or intimidation by the robber, he could have prevented the taking").

Here, as previously described, Lake took Croaker's car keys at gunpoint on the beach and then ran up the path and drove away in her car. Croaker pursued Lake but did not reach the parking area in time to stop him. Applying the definition of "presence" noted above, we conclude that a rational jury could have found that Croaker could have prevented the taking of her car if she had not been fearful that Lake would shoot or otherwise harm her. Croaker testified that the sight of Lake's gun caused her great fear. She stated that when she first saw the gun she "felt like [she] was going to let go of [her] bowels [and] faint." Although Croaker did not say in so many words that she hesitated for some time before pursuing Lake up the path, the sequence of events laid out in her testimony supports the inference that this is what occurred. Croaker stated that at the point when she surrendered the keys, Clarke "was struggling back through the water to come back," that she did not start to run up the path until Clarke emerged from the water. Clarke testified that, when Lake ran up the path, Croaker was "pulling herself together kind of." Clarke related that he "caught up to [Croaker] at the bottom of the paved driveway" and that the two of them proceeded up the path together. They reached the parking area in time for Croaker to see Lake driving away in her car but not in time to stop him. Both Croaker and Clarke stated that at this point they were very scared. Based on this testimony, a rational jury could infer that Croaker hesitated before pursuing Lake due to fear and that if she had not hesitated she could have reached the parking area in time to prevent Lake from taking her car without employing further force, violence, or intimidation. We do not suggest this inference was compelled, but because such an inference was rational, we hold that the evidence was sufficient.

BECKER, CHIEF JUDGE, dissenting.

When the defendant took the car keys from his victim, Pamela Croaker, Ms. Croaker's car was, in city terms, a block away, up the hill, out of sight. Under these circumstances, I would join an opinion upholding Lake's conviction for "keyjacking," or for both key robbery and grand larceny. I cannot, however, agree that he is guilty of carjacking. The majority draws upon federal robbery statutes to explicate how the vehicle (as opposed to its keys) may be considered to have been taken from the "person or presence of the victim." Disciples of the jurisprudence of pure reason may, in analytic terms, find this approach convincing. As I will explain below, I do not. At all events, my polestar is the plain meaning of words, and in my lexicon, Ms. Croaker's car cannot fairly be said to have been taken from her person or presence, hence I respectfully dissent.

The robbery statutes upon which the carjacking statute is based do not themselves define the phrase "from the person or presence of the victim." Webster's New International Dictionary defines presence as "the vicinity of, or area immediately near one." However, rather than relying on the plain meaning, the majority turns to a construction of the phrase "person or presence" adopted by the Ninth Circuit in *United States v. Burns,* 701 F.2d 840 (9th Cir.1983), where, in construing a federal robbery statute, that court reasoned that "property is in the presence of a person if it is 'so within his reach, inspection, observation or control, that he could if not overcome by violence or prevented by fear, retain his possession of it.' " *Id.* at 843. Based on this definition, the majority concludes that a rational jury "could infer that Croaker hesitated before pursuing Lake due to fear and that if she had not hesitated she could have reached the parking area in time to prevent Lake from taking her car without employing further force, violence, or intimidation." Maj. Op. at 273. This proves too much. If it is true that had Croaker not hesitated out of fear she could have followed Lake up the steep path leading from the secluded beach to the road, then it is equally true (barring physical limitations) that she could have followed him up that path and then halfway across St. Thomas. The fact that Croaker's car was nearby is thus not relevant; if she could have followed Lake up the hill, she could have followed him anywhere. I am aware, of course, that the craft of judging requires line-drawing, but I simply do not see how that endeavor can be principled when it is predicated on open-ended definitions of key statutory terms, especially where those terms admit of plain meaning.

DISCUSSION QUESTIONS

1.   Should the court be limited to the plain meaning of "in the presence of" as the dissent argues? What does "plain meaning" mean?

2.   Do you think that members of Congress contemplated the majority's interpretation of the phrase "in the presence of" when they voted on this statute? Should that matter?

3.   Do you think that the court's interpretation of the phrase "in the presence of" serves Congress' general purpose in passing the statute? What are

the advantages and disadvantages of interpreting statues with reference to a legislature's general purpose?

Case in Context

Most people would readily assume that computer hacking is a crime, but how should we define "hacking"? Under one possible definition discussed in the following case, we might all be hackers.

UNITED STATES OF AMERICA V. DAVID NOSAL

United States Court of Appeals, Ninth Circuit
676 F.3d 854 (2012)

KOZINSKI, CHIEF JUDGE:

Computers have become an indispensable part of our daily lives. We use them for work; we use them for play. Sometimes we use them for play at work. Many employers have adopted policies prohibiting the use of work computers for nonbusiness purposes. Does an employee who violates such a policy commit a federal crime? How about someone who violates the terms of service of a social networking website? This depends on how broadly we read the Computer Fraud and Abuse Act (CFAA), 18 U.S.C. § 1030.

FACTS

David Nosal used to work for Korn/Ferry, an executive search firm. Shortly after he left the company, he convinced some of his former colleagues who were still working for Korn/Ferry to help him start a competing business. The employees used their log-in credentials to download source lists, names and contact information from a confidential database on the company's computer, and then transferred that information to Nosal. The employees were authorized to access the database, but Korn/Ferry had a policy that forbade disclosing confidential information. The government indicted Nosal on twenty counts, including trade secret theft, mail fraud, conspiracy and violations of the CFAA. The CFAA counts charged Nosal with violations of 18 U.S.C. § 1030(a)(4), for aiding and abetting the Korn/Ferry employees in "exceed[ing their] authorized access" with intent to defraud.

Nosal filed a motion to dismiss the CFAA counts, arguing that the statute targets only hackers, not individuals who access a computer with authorization but then misuse information they obtain by means of such access. The district court initially rejected Nosal's argument, holding that when a person accesses a computer "knowingly and with the intent to defraud . . . [it] renders the access unauthorized or in excess of authorization." Shortly afterwards, however, we decided *LVRC Holdings LLC v. Brekka,* 581 F.3d 1127 (9th Cir.2009), which construed narrowly the phrases "without authorization" and "exceeds authorized access" in the

CFAA. Nosal filed a motion for reconsideration and a second motion to dismiss.

The district court reversed field and followed *Brekka's* guidance that "[t]here is simply no way to read [the definition of 'exceeds authorized access'] to incorporate corporate policies governing use of information unless the word alter is interpreted to mean misappropriate," as "[s]uch an interpretation would defy the plain meaning of the word alter, as well as common sense." Accordingly, the district court dismissed counts 2 and 4–7 for failure to state an offense. The government appeals. We have jurisdiction over this interlocutory appeal. 18 U.S.C. § 3731; *United States v. Russell,* 804 F.2d 571, 573 (9th Cir.1986). We review de novo. *United States v. Boren,* 278 F.3d 911, 913 (9th Cir.2002).

DISCUSSION

The CFAA defines "exceeds authorized access" as "to access a computer with authorization and to use such access to obtain or alter information in the computer that the accesser is not entitled so to obtain or alter." 18 U.S.C. § 1030(e)(6). This language can be read either of two ways: First, as Nosal suggests and the district court held, it could refer to someone who's authorized to access only certain data or files but accesses unauthorized data or files—what is colloquially known as "hacking." For example, assume an employee is permitted to access only product information on the company's computer but accesses customer data: He would "exceed [ ] authorized access" if he looks at the customer lists. Second, as the government proposes, the language could refer to someone who has unrestricted physical access to a computer, but is limited in the use to which he can put the information. For example, an employee may be authorized to access customer lists in order to do his job but not to send them to a competitor.

The government argues that the statutory text can support only the latter interpretation of "exceeds authorized access." In its opening brief, it focuses on the word "entitled" in the phrase an "accesser is not *entitled* so to obtain or alter." *Id.* § 1030(e)(6) (emphasis added). Pointing to one dictionary definition of "entitle" as "to furnish with a right," *Webster's New Riverside University Dictionary* 435, the government argues that Korn/Ferry's computer use policy gives employees certain rights, and when the employees violated that policy, they "exceed[ed] authorized access." But "entitled" in the statutory text refers to how an accesser "obtain[s] or alter[s]" the information, whereas the computer use policy uses "entitled" to limit how the information is used after it is obtained. This is a poor fit with the statutory language. An equally or more sensible reading of "entitled" is as a synonym for "authorized." So read, "exceeds authorized access" would refer to data or files on a computer that one is not authorized to access.

In its reply brief and at oral argument, the government focuses on the word "so" in the same phrase. *See* 18 U.S.C. § 1030(e)(6) ("accesser is not entitled *so* to obtain or alter" (emphasis added)). The government reads "so" to mean "in that manner," which it claims must refer to use restrictions. In the government's view, reading the definition narrowly would render "so" superfluous.

The government's interpretation would transform the CFAA from an anti-hacking statute into an expansive misappropriation statute. This places a great deal of weight on a two-letter word that is essentially a conjunction. If Congress meant to expand the scope of criminal liability to everyone who uses a computer in violation of computer use restrictions—which may well include everyone who uses a computer—we would expect it to use language better suited to that purpose. Under the presumption that Congress acts interstitially, we construe a statute as displacing a substantial portion of the common law only where Congress has clearly indicated its intent to do so. *See Jones v. United States,* 529 U.S. 848, 858, 120 S.Ct. 1904, 146 L.Ed.2d 902 (2000) ("[U]nless Congress conveys its purpose clearly, it will not be deemed to have significantly changed the federal-state balance in the prosecution of crimes." (internal quotation marks omitted)).

In any event, the government's "so" argument doesn't work because the word has meaning even if it doesn't refer to use restrictions. Suppose an employer keeps certain information in a separate database that can be viewed on a computer screen, but not copied or downloaded. If an employee circumvents the security measures, copies the information to a thumb drive and walks out of the building with it in his pocket, he would then have obtained access to information in the computer that he is not "entitled *so* to obtain." Or, let's say an employee is given full access to the information, provided he logs in with his username and password. In an effort to cover his tracks, he uses another employee's login to copy information from the database. Once again, this would be an employee who is authorized to access the information but does so in a manner he was not authorized "so to obtain." Of course, this all assumes that "so" must have a substantive meaning to make sense of the statute. But Congress could just as well have included "so" as a connector or for emphasis.

While the CFAA is susceptible to the government's broad interpretation, we find Nosal's narrower one more plausible. Congress enacted the CFAA in 1984 primarily to address the growing problem of computer hacking, recognizing that, "[i]n intentionally trespassing into someone else's computer files, the offender obtains at the very least information as to how to break into that computer system." S.Rep. No. 99–432, at 9 (1986), 1986 U.S.C.C.A.N. 2479, 2487 (Conf. Rep.). The government agrees that the CFAA was concerned with hacking, which is why it also prohibits accessing a computer "without authorization."

According to the government, *that* prohibition applies to hackers, so the "exceeds authorized access" prohibition must apply to people who are authorized to use the computer, but do so for an unauthorized purpose. But it is possible to read both prohibitions as applying to hackers: "[W]ithout authorization" would apply to *outside* hackers (individuals who have no authorized access to the computer at all) and "exceeds authorized access" would apply to *inside* hackers (individuals whose initial access to a computer is authorized but who access unauthorized information or files). This is a perfectly plausible construction of the statutory language that maintains the CFAA's focus on hacking rather than turning it into a sweeping Internet-policing mandate.

The government's construction of the statute would expand its scope far beyond computer hacking to criminalize any unauthorized use of information obtained from a computer. This would make criminals of large groups of people who would have little reason to suspect they are committing a federal crime. While ignorance of the law is no excuse, we can properly be skeptical as to whether Congress, in 1984, meant to criminalize conduct beyond that which is inherently wrongful, such as breaking into a computer.

The government argues that defendants here did have notice that their conduct was wrongful by the fraud and materiality requirements in subsection 1030(a)(4), which punishes whoever:

> knowingly and with intent to defraud, accesses a protected computer without authorization, or exceeds authorized access, and by means of such conduct furthers the intended fraud and obtains anything of value, unless the object of the fraud and the thing obtained consists only of the use of the computer and the value of such use is not more than $5,000 in any 1-year period.

18 U.S.C. § 1030(a)(4). But "exceeds authorized access" is used elsewhere in the CFAA as a basis for criminal culpability without intent to defraud. Subsection 1030(a)(2)(C) requires only that the person who "exceeds authorized access" have "obtain[ed] . . . information from any protected computer." Because "protected computer" is defined as a computer affected by or involved in interstate commerce—effectively all computers with Internet access—the government's interpretation of "exceeds authorized access" makes every violation of a private computer use policy a federal crime. *See id.* § 1030(e)(2)(B).

The government argues that our ruling today would construe "exceeds authorized access" only in subsection 1030(a)(4), and we could give the phrase a narrower meaning when we construe other subsections. This is just not so: Once we define the phrase for the purpose of subsection 1030(a)(4), that definition must apply equally to the rest of the statute pursuant to the "standard principle of statutory construction . . . that identical words and phrases within the same statute should normally be given the same meaning." *Powerex Corp. v. Reliant Energy Servs., Inc.,* 551 U.S. 224, 232, 127 S.Ct. 2411, 168 L.Ed.2d 112 (2007). The phrase appears five times in the first seven subsections of the statute, including subsection 1030(a)(2)(C). *See* 18 U.S.C. § 1030(a)(1), (2), (4) and (7). Giving a different interpretation to each is impossible because Congress provided a *single* definition of "exceeds authorized access" for all iterations of the statutory phrase. *See id.* § 1030(e)(6). Congress obviously meant "exceeds authorized access" to have the same meaning throughout section 1030. We must therefore consider how the interpretation we adopt will operate wherever in that section the phrase appears.

In the case of the CFAA, the broadest provision is subsection 1030(a)(2)(C), which makes it a crime to exceed authorized access of a computer connected to the Internet *without* any culpable intent. Were we to adopt the government's proposed interpretation, millions of unsuspecting individuals would find that they are engaging in criminal conduct.

Minds have wandered since the beginning of time and the computer gives employees new ways to procrastinate, by g-chatting with friends, playing games, shopping or watching sports highlights. Such activities are routinely prohibited by many computer-use policies, although employees are seldom disciplined for occasional use of work computers for personal purposes. Nevertheless, under the broad interpretation of the CFAA, such minor dalliances would become federal crimes. While it's unlikely that you'll be prosecuted for watching Reason.TV on your work computer, you *could* be. Employers wanting to rid themselves of troublesome employees without following proper procedures could threaten to report them to the FBI unless they quit. Ubiquitous, seldom-prosecuted crimes invite arbitrary and discriminatory enforcement.

Employer-employee and company-consumer relationships are traditionally governed by tort and contract law; the government's proposed interpretation of the CFAA allows private parties to manipulate their computer-use and personnel policies so as to turn these relationships into ones policed by the criminal law. Significant notice problems arise if we allow criminal liability to turn on the vagaries of private polices that are lengthy, opaque, subject to change and seldom read. Consider the typical corporate policy that computers can be used only for business purposes. What exactly is a "nonbusiness purpose"? If you use the computer to check the weather report for a business trip? For the company softball game? For your vacation to Hawaii? And if minor personal uses are tolerated, how can an employee be on notice of what constitutes a violation sufficient to trigger criminal liability?

Basing criminal liability on violations of private computer use polices can transform whole categories of otherwise innocuous behavior into federal crimes simply because a computer is involved. Employees who call family members from their work phones will become criminals if they send an email instead. Employees can sneak in the sports section of the *New York Times* to read at work, but they'd better not visit ESPN.com. And sudoku enthusiasts should stick to the printed puzzles, because visiting www.dailysudoku.com from their work computers might give them more than enough time to hone their sudoku skills behind bars.

The effect this broad construction of the CFAA has on workplace conduct pales by comparison with its effect on everyone else who uses a computer, smart-phone, iPad, Kindle, Nook, X-box, Blu-Ray player or any other Internet-enabled device. The Internet is a means for communicating via computers: Whenever we access a web page, commence a download, post a message on somebody's Facebook wall, shop on Amazon, bid on eBay, publish a blog, rate a movie on IMDb, read www.NYT.com, watch YouTube and do the thousands of other things we routinely do online, we are using one computer to send commands to other computers at remote locations. Our access to those remote computers is governed by a series of private agreements and policies that most people are only dimly aware of and virtually no one reads or understands.

For example, it's not widely known that, up until very recently, Google forbade minors from using its services. *See* Google Terms of Service, effective April 16, 2007–March 1, 2012, § 2.3, http://www.google.com/intl/en/policies/terms/archive/20070416 ("You may not use the Services and may not accept the Terms if . . . you are not of legal age to form a binding contract with Google. . . .") (last visited Mar. 4, 2012). Adopting the government's interpretation would turn vast numbers of teens and pre-teens into juvenile delinquents—and their parents and teachers into delinquency contributors. Similarly, Facebook makes it a violation of the terms of service to let anyone log into your account. *See* Facebook Statement of Rights and Responsibilities § 4.8 http://www.facebook.com/legal/terms ("You will not share your password, . . . let anyone else access your account, or do anything else that might jeopardize the security of your account.") (last visited Mar. 4, 2012). Yet it's very common for people to let close friends and relatives check their email or access their online accounts. Some may be aware that, if discovered, they may suffer a rebuke from the ISP or a loss of access, but few imagine they might be marched off to federal prison for doing so.

Or consider the numerous dating websites whose terms of use prohibit inaccurate or misleading information. *See, e.g.,* eHarmony Terms of Service § 2(I), http://www.eharmony.com/about/terms ("You will not provide inaccurate, misleading or false information to eHarmony or to any other user.") (last visited Mar. 4, 2012). Or eBay and Craigslist, where it's a violation of the terms of use to post items in an inappropriate category. *See, e.g.,* eBay User Agreement, http://pages.ebay.com/help/policies/user-agreement.html ("While using eBay sites, services and tools, you will not:

post content or items in an inappropriate category or areas on our sites and services . . . .") (last visited Mar. 4, 2012). Under the government's proposed interpretation of the CFAA, posting for sale an item prohibited by Craigslist's policy, or describing yourself as "tall, dark and handsome," when you're actually short and homely, will earn you a handsome orange jumpsuit.

Not only are the terms of service vague and generally unknown—unless you look real hard at the small print at the bottom of a webpage—but website owners retain the right to change the terms at any time and without notice. *See, e.g.,* YouTube Terms of Service § 1.B, http://www. youtube.com/t/terms ("YouTube may, in its sole discretion, modify or revise these Terms of Service and policies at any time, and you agree to be bound by such modifications or revisions.") (last visited Mar. 4, 2012). Accordingly, behavior that wasn't criminal yesterday can become criminal today without an act of Congress, and without any notice whatsoever.

The government assures us that, whatever the scope of the CFAA, it won't prosecute minor violations. But we shouldn't have to live at the mercy of our local prosecutor. *Cf. United States v. Stevens,* 559 U.S. 460, 130 S.Ct. 1577, 1591, 176 L.Ed.2d 435 (2010) ("We would not uphold an unconstitutional statute merely because the Government promised to use it responsibly."). And it's not clear we *can* trust the government when a tempting target comes along. Take the case of the mom who posed as a 17-year-old boy and cyber-bullied her daughter's classmate. The Justice Department prosecuted her under 18 U.S.C. § 1030(a)(2)(C) for violating MySpace's terms of service, which prohibited lying about identifying information, including age. *See United States v. Drew,* 259 F.R.D. 449 (C.D.Cal.2009). Lying on social media websites is common: People shave years off their age, add inches to their height and drop pounds from their weight. The difference between puffery and prosecution may depend on whether you happen to be someone an AUSA has reason to go after.

In *United States v. Kozminski,* 487 U.S. 931, 108 S.Ct. 2751, 101 L.Ed.2d 788 (1988), the Supreme Court refused to adopt the government's broad interpretation of a statute because it would "criminalize a broad range of day-to-day activity." *Id.* at 949, 108 S.Ct. at 2763. Applying the rule of lenity, the Court warned that the broader statutory interpretation would "delegate to prosecutors and juries the inherently legislative task of determining what type of . . . activities are so morally reprehensible that they should be punished as crimes" and would "subject individuals to the risk of arbitrary or discriminatory prosecution and conviction." *Id.* By giving that much power to prosecutors, we're inviting discriminatory and arbitrary enforcement.

We remain unpersuaded by the decisions of our sister circuits that interpret the CFAA broadly to cover violations of corporate computer use restrictions or violations of a duty of loyalty. *See United States v.*

Rodriguez, 628 F.3d 1258 (11th Cir.2010); *United States v. John,* 597 F.3d 263 (5th Cir.2010); *Int'l Airport Ctrs., LLC v. Citrin,* 440 F.3d 418 (7th Cir.2006). These courts looked only at the culpable behavior of the defendants before them, and failed to consider the effect on millions of ordinary citizens caused by the statute's unitary definition of "exceeds authorized access." They therefore failed to apply the long-standing principle that we must construe ambiguous criminal statutes narrowly so as to avoid "making criminal law in Congress's stead." *United States v. Santos,* 553 U.S. 507, 514, 128 S.Ct. 2020, 170 L.Ed.2d 912 (2008).

We therefore respectfully decline to follow our sister circuits and urge them to reconsider instead. For our part, we continue to follow in the path blazed by *Brekka,* 581 F.3d 1127, and the growing number of courts that have reached the same conclusion. These courts recognize that the plain language of the CFAA "target[s] the unauthorized procurement or alteration of information, not its misuse or misappropriation." *Shamrock Foods Co. v. Gast,* 535 F.Supp.2d 962, 965 (D.Ariz.2008) (internal quotation marks omitted); *see also Orbit One Commc'ns, Inc. v. Numerex Corp.,* 692 F.Supp.2d 373, 385 (S.D.N.Y.2010) ("The plain language of the CFAA supports a narrow reading. The CFAA expressly prohibits improper 'access' of computer information. It does not prohibit misuse or misappropriation."); *Diamond Power Int'l, Inc. v. Davidson,* 540 F.Supp.2d 1322, 1343 (N.D.Ga.2007) ("[A] violation for 'exceeding authorized access' occurs where initial access is permitted but the access of certain information is not permitted."); *Int'l Ass'n of Machinists & Aerospace Workers v. Werner-Masuda,* 390 F.Supp.2d 479, 499 (D.Md.2005) ("[T]he CFAA, however, do[es] not prohibit the unauthorized disclosure or use of information, but rather unauthorized access.").

CONCLUSION

We need not decide today whether Congress *could* base criminal liability on violations of a company or website's computer use restrictions. Instead, we hold that the phrase "exceeds authorized access" in the CFAA does not extend to violations of use restrictions. If Congress wants to incorporate misappropriation liability into the CFAA, it must speak more clearly. The rule of lenity requires "penal laws . . . to be construed strictly." *United States v. Wiltberger,* 18 U.S. (5 Wheat.) 76, 95, 5 L.Ed. 37 (1820). "[W]hen choice has to be made between two readings of what conduct Congress has made a crime, it is appropriate, before we choose the harsher alternative, to require that Congress should have spoken in language that is clear and definite." *Jones,* 529 U.S. at 858, 120 S.Ct. at 1912 (internal quotation marks and citation omitted).

The rule of lenity not only ensures that citizens will have fair notice of the criminal laws, but also that Congress will have fair notice of what conduct its laws criminalize. We construe criminal statutes narrowly so that Congress will not unintentionally turn ordinary citizens into criminals. "[B]ecause of the seriousness of criminal penalties, and because criminal punishment usually represents the moral condemnation of the community, legislatures and not courts should define criminal activity." *United States v. Bass,* 404 U.S. 336, 348, 92 S.Ct. 515, 30 L.Ed.2d 488 (1971). "If there is any doubt about whether Congress intended [the CFAA] to prohibit the conduct in which [Nosal] engaged, then 'we must choose the interpretation least likely to impose penalties unintended by Congress.'" *United States v. Cabaccang,* 332 F.3d 622, 635 n. 22 (9th Cir.2003) (quoting *United States v. Arzate-Nunez,* 18 F.3d 730, 736 (9th Cir.1994)).

This narrower interpretation is also a more sensible reading of the text and legislative history of a statute whose general purpose is to punish hacking—the circumvention of technological access barriers—not misappropriation of trade secrets—a subject Congress has dealt with elsewhere. *See supra* note 3. Therefore, we hold that "exceeds authorized access" in the CFAA is limited to violations of restrictions on *access* to information, and not restrictions on its *use.*

Because Nosal's accomplices had permission to access the company database and obtain the information contained within, the government's charges fail to meet the element of "without authorization, or exceeds authorized access" under 18 U.S.C. § 1030(a)(4). Accordingly, we affirm the judgment of the district court dismissing counts 2 and 4–7 for failure to state an offense. The government may, of course, prosecute Nosal on the remaining counts of the indictment.

AFFIRMED.

SILVERMAN, CIRCUIT JUDGE, with whom TALLMAN, CIRCUIT JUDGE concurs, dissenting:

This case has nothing to do with playing sudoku, checking email, fibbing on dating sites, or any of the other activities that the majority rightly values. It has everything to do with stealing an employer's valuable information to set up a competing business with the purloined data, siphoned away from the victim, knowing such access and use were prohibited in the defendants' employment contracts. The indictment here charged that Nosal and his co-conspirators knowingly exceeded the access to a protected company computer they were given by an executive search firm that employed them; that they did so with the intent to defraud; and further, that they stole the victim's valuable proprietary information by means of that fraudulent conduct in order to profit from using it. In ridiculing scenarios not remotely presented by *this* case, the majority does a good job of knocking down straw men—far-fetched hypotheticals involving neither theft nor intentional fraudulent conduct, but innocuous violations of office policy.

The majority also takes a plainly written statute and parses it in a hyper-complicated way that distorts the obvious intent of Congress. No other circuit that has considered this statute finds the problems that the majority does.

18 U.S.C. § 1030(a)(4) is quite clear. It states, in relevant part:

(a) Whoever—

(4) knowingly and with intent to defraud, accesses a protected computer without authorization, or exceeds authorized access, and by means of such conduct furthers the intended fraud and obtains anything of value . . .

shall be punished. . . .

Thus, it is perfectly clear that a person with *both* the requisite mens rea *and* the specific intent to defraud—but *only* such persons—can violate this subsection in one of two ways: first, by accessing a computer without authorization, or second, by exceeding authorized access. 18 U.S.C. § 1030(e)(6) defines "exceeds authorized access" as "to access a computer with authorization and to use such access to obtain or alter information in the computer that the accesser is not entitled so to obtain or alter."

"As this definition makes clear, an individual who is authorized to use a computer for certain purposes but goes beyond those limitations is considered by the CFAA as someone who has 'exceed[ed] authorized access.'" *LVRC Holdings LLC v. Brekka,* 581 F.3d 1127, 1133 (9th Cir.2009).

"[T]he definition of the term 'exceeds authorized access' from § 1030(e)(6) implies that an employee can violate employer-placed limits on accessing information stored on the computer and still have authorization to access that computer. The plain language of the statute therefore indicates that 'authorization' depends on actions taken by the employer." *Id.* at 1135. In *Brekka,* we explained that a person "exceeds authorized access" when that person has permission to access a computer but accesses information on the computer that the person is not entitled to access. *Id.* at 1133. In that case, an employee allegedly emailed an employer's proprietary documents to his personal computer to use in a competing business. *Id.* at 1134. We held that one does not exceed authorized access simply by "breach[ing] a state law duty of loyalty to an employer" and that, because the employee did not breach a contract with his employer, he could not be liable under the Computer Fraud and Abuse Act. *Id.* at 1135, 1135 n. 7.

This is not an esoteric concept. A bank teller is entitled to access a bank's money for legitimate banking purposes, but not to take the bank's money for himself. A new car buyer may be entitled to take a vehicle around the block on a test drive. But the buyer would not be entitled—he would "exceed his authority"—to take the vehicle to Mexico on a drug run. A person of ordinary intelligence understands that he may be totally prohibited from doing something *altogether,* or authorized to do something but prohibited from going *beyond* what is authorized. This is no doubt why the statute covers not only "unauthorized access," but also "exceed[ing] authorized access." The statute contemplates both means of committing the theft.

The majority holds that a person "exceeds authorized access" only when that person has permission to access a computer generally, but is *completely* prohibited from accessing a different portion of the computer (or different information on the computer). The majority's interpretation conflicts with the plain language of the statute. Furthermore, none of the circuits that have analyzed the meaning of "exceeds authorized access" as used in the Computer Fraud and Abuse Act read the statute the way the majority does. Both the Fifth and Eleventh Circuits have explicitly held that employees who knowingly violate clear company computer restrictions agreements "exceed authorized access" under the CFAA.

In *United States v. John,* 597 F.3d 263, 271–73 (5th Cir.2010), the Fifth Circuit held that an employee of Citigroup exceeded her authorized access in violation of § 1030(a)(2) when she accessed confidential customer information in violation of her employer's computer use restrictions and used that information to commit fraud. As the Fifth Circuit noted in *John,* "an employer may 'authorize' employees to utilize computers for any lawful purpose but not for unlawful purposes and only in furtherance of the employer's business. An employee would 'exceed[ ] authorized access' if he or she used that access to obtain or steal information as part of a criminal scheme." *Id.* at 271 (alteration in original). At the very least, when an employee "knows that the purpose for which she is accessing information in a computer is both in violation of an employer's policies and is part of[a criminally fraudulent] scheme, it would be 'proper' to conclude that such conduct 'exceeds authorized access.' " *Id.* at 273.

Similarly, the Eleventh Circuit held in *United States v. Rodriguez,* 628 F.3d 1258, 1263 (11th Cir.2010), that an employee of the Social Security Administration exceeded his authorized access under § 1030(a)(2) when he obtained personal information about former girlfriends and potential paramours and used that information to send the women flowers or to show up at their homes. The court rejected Rodriguez's argument that unlike the defendant in *John,* his use was "not criminal." The court held: "The problem with Rodriguez's argument is that his use of information is irrelevant if he obtained the information without authorization or as a result of exceeding authorized access." *Id.; see also EF Cultural Travel BV v. Explorica, Inc.,* 274 F.3d 577, 583–84 (1st Cir.2001) (holding that an employee likely exceeded his authorized access when he used that access to disclose information in violation of a confidentiality agreement).

The Third Circuit has also implicitly adopted the Fifth and Eleventh circuit's reasoning. In *United States v. Teague,* 646 F.3d 1119, 1121–22 (8th

Cir.2011), the court upheld a conviction under § 1030(a)(2) and (c)(2)(A) where an employee of a government contractor used his privileged access to a government database to obtain President Obama's private student loan records.

The indictment here alleges that Nosal and his coconspirators knowingly exceeded the authority that they had to access their employer's computer, and that they did so with the intent to defraud and to steal trade secrets and proprietary information from the company's database for Nosal's competing business. It is alleged that at the time the employee coconspirators accessed the database they *knew* they only were allowed to use the database for a legitimate business purpose because the co-conspirators allegedly signed an agreement which restricted the use and disclosure of information on the database except for legitimate Korn/Ferry business. Moreover, it is alleged that before using a unique username and password to log on to the Korn/Ferry computer and database, the employees were notified that the information stored on those computers were the property of Korn/Ferry and that to access the information without relevant authority could lead to disciplinary action and criminal prosecution. Therefore, it is alleged, that when Nosal's co-conspirators accessed the database to obtain Korn/Ferry's secret source lists, names, and contact information with the intent to defraud Korn/Ferry by setting up a competing company to take business away using the stolen data, they "exceed[ed their] authorized access" to a computer with an intent to defraud Korn/Ferry and therefore violated 18 U.S.C. § 1030(a)(4). If true, these allegations adequately state a crime under a commonsense reading of this particular subsection.

Furthermore, it does not advance the ball to consider, as the majority does, the parade of horribles that might occur under *different* subsections of the CFAA, such as subsection (a)(2)(C), which does not have the scienter or specific intent to defraud requirements that subsection (a)(4) has. *Maldonado v. Morales,* 556 F.3d 1037, 1044 (9th Cir.2009) ("The role of the courts is neither to issue advisory opinions nor to declare rights in hypothetical cases, but to adjudicate live cases or controversies.") (citation and internal quotation marks omitted). Other sections of the CFAA may or may not be unconstitutionally vague or pose other problems. We need to wait for an actual case or controversy to frame these issues, rather than posit a laundry list of wacky hypotheticals. I express no opinion on the validity or application of other subsections of 18 U.S.C. § 1030, other than § 1030(a)(4), and with all due respect, neither should the majority.

The majority's opinion is driven out of a well meaning but ultimately misguided concern that if employment agreements or internet terms of service violations could subject someone to criminal liability, all internet users will suddenly become criminals overnight. I fail to see how anyone can seriously conclude that reading ESPN.com in contravention of office policy could come within the ambit of 18 U.S.C. § 1030(a)(4), a statute explicitly requiring an intent to defraud, the obtaining of something of value by means of that fraud, while doing so "knowingly." And even if an imaginative judge can conjure up far-fetched hypotheticals producing federal prison terms for accessing word puzzles, jokes, and sports scores while at work, well, . . . that is what an as-applied challenge is for. Meantime, back to this case, 18 U.S.C. § 1030(a)(4) clearly is aimed at, and limited to, knowing and intentional fraud. Because the indictment adequately states the elements of a valid crime, the district court erred in dismissing the charges.

I respectfully dissent.

DISCUSSION QUESTIONS

1. Why didn't Congress just use the word "hacking" in the statute and allow judges or juries to interpret the term in a way that makes sense given the facts of the case before them?

2. Do you agree with the majority or the dissent's interpretation of "exceeds authorized access"?

3. The Computer Fraud and Abuse Act was passed in the 1990's. Since then the role of computers in our lives has changed more than most people could have imagined. Should the court base its interpretation on what Congress had in mind when the statute passed? On what Congress might intend today?

E. SPECIAL FOCUS: STATUTORY INTERPRETATION AND WHITE COLLAR CRIME

While crimes of violence and run of the mill property crimes such as theft, robbery and burglary have always captured the public's imagination, white collar crime arguably inflicts greater dollar costs on society. Defining these offenses is difficult, however, and raises many difficult questions of statutory interpretation.

Case in Context

One offense often charged in white collar cases is obstruction of justice. Do you think there is something "fishy" about the government's definition of that offense in the following case?

JOHN L. YATES V. UNITED STATES

Supreme Court of the United States
135 S.Ct. 1074 (2015)

Opinion

JUSTICE GINSBURG announced the judgment of the Court and delivered an opinion, in which THE CHIEF JUSTICE, JUSTICE BREYER, and JUSTICE SOTOMAYOR join.

John Yates, a commercial fisherman, caught undersized red grouper in federal waters in the Gulf of Mexico. To prevent federal authorities from confirming that he had harvested undersized fish, Yates ordered a crew member to toss the suspect catch into the sea. For this offense, he was charged with, and convicted of, violating 18 U.S.C. § 1519, which provides:

> "Whoever knowingly alters, destroys, mutilates, conceals, covers up, falsifies, or makes a false entry in any record, document, or tangible object with the intent to impede, obstruct, or influence the investigation or proper administration of any matter within the jurisdiction of any department or agency of the United States or any case filed under title 11, or in relation to or contemplation of any such matter or case, shall be fined under this title, imprisoned not more than 20 years, or both."

Section 1519 was enacted as part of the Sarbanes-Oxley Act of 2002, 116 Stat. 745, legislation designed to protect investors and restore trust in financial markets following the collapse of Enron Corporation. A fish is no doubt an object that is tangible; fish can be seen, caught, and handled, and a catch, as this case illustrates, is vulnerable to destruction. But it would cut § 1519 loose from its financial-fraud mooring to hold that it encompasses any and all objects, whatever their size or significance, destroyed with obstructive intent. Mindful that in Sarbanes-Oxley, Congress trained its attention on corporate and accounting deception and cover-ups, we conclude that a matching construction of § 1519 is in order: A tangible object captured by § 1519, we hold, must be one used to record or preserve information.

I

On August 23, 2007, the *Miss Katie,* a commercial fishing boat, was six days into an expedition in the Gulf of Mexico. Her crew numbered three, including Yates, the captain. Engaged in a routine offshore patrol to inspect both recreational and commercial vessels, Officer John Jones of the Florida Fish and Wildlife Conservation Commission decided to board the *Miss Katie* to check on the vessel's compliance with fishing rules. Although the *Miss Katie* was far enough from the Florida coast to be in exclusively federal waters, she was nevertheless within Officer Jones's jurisdiction. Because he had been deputized as a federal agent by the National Marine

Fisheries Service, Officer Jones had authority to enforce federal, as well as state, fishing laws.

Upon boarding the *Miss Katie,* Officer Jones noticed three red grouper that appeared to be undersized hanging from a hook on the deck. At the time, federal conservation regulations required immediate release of red grouper less than 20 inches long. 50 C.F.R. § 622.37(d)(2)(ii) (effective April 2, 2007). Violation of those regulations is a civil offense punishable by a fine or fishing license suspension. See 16 U.S.C. §§ 1857(1)(A), (G), 1858(a), (g).

Suspecting that other undersized fish might be on board, Officer Jones proceeded to inspect the ship's catch, setting aside and measuring only fish that appeared to him to be shorter than 20 inches. Officer Jones ultimately determined that 72 fish fell short of the 20-inch mark. A fellow officer recorded the length of each of the undersized fish on a catch measurement verification form. With few exceptions, the measured fish were between 19 and 20 inches; three were less than 19 inches; none were less than 18.75 inches. After separating the fish measuring below 20 inches from the rest of the catch by placing them in wooden crates, Officer Jones directed Yates to leave the fish, thus segregated, in the crates until the *Miss Katie* returned to port. Before departing, Officer Jones issued Yates a citation for possession of undersized fish.

Four days later, after the *Miss Katie* had docked in Cortez, Florida, Officer Jones measured the fish contained in the wooden crates. This time, however, the measured fish, although still less than 20 inches, slightly exceeded the lengths recorded on board. Jones surmised that the fish brought to port were not the same as those he had detected during his initial inspection. Under questioning, one of the crew members admitted that, at Yates's direction, he had thrown overboard the fish Officer Jones had measured at sea, and that he and Yates had replaced the tossed grouper with fish from the rest of the catch.

For reasons not disclosed in the record before us, more than 32 months passed before criminal charges were lodged against Yates. On May 5, 2010, he was indicted for destroying, concealing, and covering up undersized fish to impede a federal investigation, in violation of § 1519. By the time of the indictment, the minimum legal length for Gulf red grouper had been lowered from 20 inches to 18 inches. No measured fish in Yates's catch fell below that limit. The record does not reveal what civil penalty, if any, Yates received for his possession of fish undersized under the 2007 regulation.

Yates was tried on the criminal charges in August 2011. At the end of the Government's case in chief, he moved for a judgment of acquittal on the § 1519 charge. Pointing to § 1519's title and its origin as a provision of the Sarbanes-Oxley Act, Yates argued that the section sets forth "a documents offense" and that its reference to "tangible object[s]" subsumes "computer hard drives, logbooks, [and] things of that nature," not fish. App. 91–92.

Yates acknowledged that the Criminal Code contains "sections that would have been appropriate for the [G]overnment to pursue" if it wished to prosecute him for tampering with evidence. Yates insisted, did not.

The Government countered that a "tangible object" within § 1519's compass is "simply something other than a document or record." The trial judge expressed misgivings about reading "tangible object" as broadly as the Government urged: "Isn't there a Latin phrase [about] construction of a statute. . . . The gist of it is . . . you take a look at [a] line of words, and you interpret the words consistently. So if you're talking about documents, and records, tangible objects are tangible objects in the nature of a document or a record, as opposed to a fish." *Ibid.* The first-instance judge nonetheless followed controlling Eleventh Circuit precedent. While recognizing that § 1519 was passed as part of legislation targeting corporate fraud, the Court of Appeals had instructed that "the broad language of § 1519 is not limited to corporate fraud cases, and 'Congress is free to pass laws with language covering areas well beyond the particular crisis *du jour* that initially prompted legislative action.' Accordingly, the trial court read "tangible object" as a term "independent" of "record" or "document." For violating § 1519, the court sentenced Yates to imprisonment for 30 days, followed by supervised release for three years. App. 118–120. For life, he will bear the stigma of having a federal felony conviction.

On appeal, the Eleventh Circuit found the text of § 1519 "plain." 733 F.3d 1059, 1064 (2013). Because "tangible object" was "undefined" in the statute, the Court of Appeals gave the term its "ordinary or natural meaning," *i.e.,* its dictionary definition, "[h]aving or possessing physical form." *Ibid.* (quoting Black's Law Dictionary 1592 (9th ed. 2009)).

II

The Sarbanes-Oxley Act, all agree, was prompted by the exposure of Enron's massive accounting fraud and revelations that the company's outside auditor, Arthur Andersen LLP, had systematically destroyed potentially incriminating documents. The Government acknowledges that § 1519 was intended to prohibit, in particular, corporate document-shredding to hide evidence of financial wrongdoing. Brief for United States 46. Prior law made it an offense to "intimidat[e], threate[n], or corruptly persuad[e] *another person*" to shred documents. § 1512(b) (emphasis added). Section 1519 cured a conspicuous omission by imposing liability on a person who destroys records himself. See S.Rep. No. 107–146, p. 14 (2002) (describing § 1519 as "a new general anti shredding provision" and explaining that "certain current provisions make it a crime to persuade another person to destroy documents, but not a crime to actually destroy the same documents yourself"). The new section also expanded prior law by including within the provision's reach "any matter within the jurisdiction of any department or agency of the United States." *Id.,* at 14–15.

In the Government's view, § 1519 extends beyond the principal evil motivating its passage. The words of § 1519, the Government argues, support reading the provision as a general ban on the spoliation of evidence, covering all physical items that might be relevant to any matter under federal investigation.

Yates urges a contextual reading of § 1519, tying "tangible object" to the surrounding words, the placement of the provision within the Sarbanes-Oxley Act, and related provisions enacted at the same time, in particular § 1520 and § 1512(c)(1), see *infra,* at 1083, 1084–1085. Section 1519, he maintains, targets not all manner of evidence, but records, documents, and tangible objects used to preserve them, *e.g.,* computers, servers, and other media on which information is stored.

We agree with Yates and reject the Government's unrestrained reading. "Tangible object" in § 1519, we conclude, is better read to cover only objects one can use to record or preserve information, not all objects in the physical world.

A

The ordinary meaning of an "object" that is "tangible," as stated in dictionary definitions, is "a discrete . . . thing," Webster's Third New International Dictionary 1555 (2002), that "possess[es] physical form," Black's Law Dictionary 1683 (10th ed. 2014). From this premise, the Government concludes that "tangible object," as that term appears in § 1519, covers the waterfront, including fish from the sea.

Whether a statutory term is unambiguous, however, does not turn solely on dictionary definitions of its component words. Rather, "[t]he plainness or ambiguity of statutory language is determined [not only] by reference to the language itself, [but as well by] the specific context in which that language is used, and the broader context of the statute as a whole." Ordinarily, a word's usage accords with its dictionary definition. In law as in life, however, the same words, placed in different contexts, sometimes mean different things.

We have several times affirmed that identical language may convey varying content when used in different statutes, sometimes even in different provisions of the same statute. As the Court observed in *Atlantic Cleaners & Dyers,* 286 U.S., at 433, 52 S.Ct. 607:

> "Most words have different shades of meaning and consequently may be variously construed. . . . Where the subject matter to which the words refer is not the same in the several places where [the words] are used, or the conditions are different, or the scope of the legislative power exercised in one case is broader than that

exercised in another, the meaning well may vary to meet the purposes of the law, to be arrived at by a consideration of the language in which those purposes are expressed, and of the circumstances under which the language was employed."

In short, although dictionary definitions of the words "tangible" and "object" bear consideration, they are not dispositive of the meaning of "tangible object" in § 1519.

Supporting a reading of "tangible object," as used in § 1519, in accord with dictionary definitions, the Government points to the appearance of that term in Federal Rule of Criminal Procedure 16. That Rule requires the prosecution to grant a defendant's request to inspect "tangible objects" within the Government's control that have utility for the defense. See Fed. Rule Crim. Proc. 16(a)(1)(E).

Rule 16's reference to "tangible objects" has been interpreted to include any physical evidence. See 5 W. LaFave, J. Israel, N. King, & O. Kerr, Criminal Procedure § 20.3(g), pp. 405–406, and n. 120 (3d ed. 2007). Rule 16 is a discovery rule designed to protect defendants by compelling the prosecution to turn over to the defense evidence material to the charges at issue. In that context, a comprehensive construction of "tangible objects" is fitting. In contrast, § 1519 is a penal provision that refers to "tangible object" not in relation to a request for information relevant to a specific court proceeding, but rather in relation to federal investigations or proceedings of every kind, including those not yet begun. See *Commissioner v. National Carbide Corp.,* 167 F.2d 304, 306 (C.A.2 1948) (Hand, J.) ("words are chameleons, which reflect the color of their environment"). Just as the context of Rule 16 supports giving "tangible object" a meaning as broad as its dictionary definition, the context of § 1519 tugs strongly in favor of a narrower reading.

B

Familiar interpretive guides aid our construction of the words "tangible object" as they appear in § 1519.

We note first § 1519's caption: "Destruction, alteration, or falsification of records in Federal investigations and bankruptcy." That heading conveys no suggestion that the section prohibits spoliation of any and all physical evidence, however remote from records. Neither does the title of the section of the Sarbanes-Oxley Act in which § 1519 was placed, § 802: "Criminal penalties for altering documents." 116 Stat. 800. Furthermore, § 1520, the only other provision passed as part of § 802, is titled "Destruction of corporate audit records" and addresses only that specific subset of records and documents. While these headings are not commanding, they supply cues that Congress did not intend "tangible object" in § 1519 to sweep within its reach physical objects of every kind, including things no one would describe as records, documents, or devices closely associated with them. ("[T]he title of a statute and the heading of a section are tools available for the resolution of a doubt about the meaning of a statute." (internal quotation marks omitted)). If Congress indeed meant to make § 1519 an all-encompassing ban on the spoliation of evidence, as the dissent believes Congress did, one would have expected a clearer indication of that intent.

Section 1519's position within Chapter 73 of Title 18 further signals that § 1519 was not intended to serve as a cross-the-board ban on the destruction of physical evidence of every kind. Congress placed § 1519 (and its companion provision § 1520) at the end of the chapter, following immediately after the pre-existing § 1516, § 1517, and § 1518, each of them prohibiting obstructive acts in specific contexts. See § 1516 (audits of recipients of federal funds); § 1517 (federal examinations of financial institutions); § 1518 (criminal investigations of federal health care offenses). See also S.Rep. No. 107–146, at 7 (observing that § 1517 and § 1518 "apply to obstruction in certain limited types of cases, such as bankruptcy fraud, examinations of financial institutions, and healthcare fraud").

But Congress did not direct codification of the Sarbanes-Oxley Act's other additions to Chapter 73 adjacent to these specialized provisions. Instead, Congress directed placement of those additions within or alongside retained provisions that address obstructive acts relating broadly to official proceedings and criminal trials: Section 806, "Civil Action to protect against retaliation in fraud cases," was codified as § 1514A and inserted between the pre-existing § 1514, which addresses civil actions to restrain harassment of victims and witnesses in criminal cases, and § 1515, which defines terms used in § 1512 and § 1513. Section 1102, "Tampering with a record or otherwise impeding an official proceeding," was codified as § 1512(c) and inserted within the pre-existing § 1512, which addresses tampering with a victim, witness, or informant to impede any official proceeding. Section 1107, "Retaliation against informants," was codified as § 1513(e) and inserted within the pre-existing § 1513, which addresses retaliation against a victim, witness, or informant in any official proceeding. Congress thus ranked § 1519, not among the broad proscriptions, but together with specialized provisions expressly aimed at corporate fraud and financial audits. This placement accords with the view that Congress' conception of § 1519's coverage was considerably more limited than the Government's.

The words immediately surrounding "tangible object" in § 1519— "falsifies, or makes a false entry in any record [or] document"—also cabin the contextual meaning of that term. [W]e rely on the principle of *noscitur a sociis*—a word is known by the company it keeps—to "avoid ascribing to one word a meaning so broad that it is inconsistent with its accompanying words, thus giving unintended breadth to the Acts of Congress." (internal quotation marks omitted). ("a word is given more precise content by the neighboring words with which it is associated"). . . .

The *noscitur a sociis* canon operates here. "Tangible object" is the last in a list of terms that begins "any record [or] document." The term is therefore appropriately read to refer, not to any tangible object, but specifically to the subset of tangible objects involving records and documents, *i.e.,* objects used to record or preserve information.

This moderate interpretation of "tangible object" accords with the list of actions § 1519 proscribes. The section applies to anyone who "alters, destroys, mutilates, conceals, covers up, *falsifies,* or *makes a false entry in* any record, document, or tangible object" with the requisite obstructive intent. (Emphasis added.) The last two verbs, "falsif[y]" and "mak[e] a false entry in," typically take as grammatical objects records, documents, or things used to record or preserve information, such as logbooks or hard drives. See, *e.g.,* Black's Law Dictionary 720 (10th ed. 2014) (defining "falsify" as "[t]o make deceptive; to counterfeit, forge, or misrepresent; esp., to tamper with (a document, record, etc.)"). It would be unnatural, for example, to describe a killer's act of wiping his fingerprints from a gun as "falsifying" the murder weapon. But it would not be strange to refer to "falsifying" data stored on a hard drive as simply "falsifying" a hard drive. Furthermore, Congress did not include on § 1512(c)(1)'s list of prohibited actions "falsifies" or "makes a false entry in." See § 1512(c)(1) (making it unlawful to "alte[r], destro[y], mutilat[e], or concea[l] a record, document, or other object" with the requisite obstructive intent). That contemporaneous omission also suggests that Congress intended "tangible object" in § 1519 to have a narrower scope than "other object" in § 1512(c)(1).

A canon related to *noscitur a sociis, ejusdem generis,* counsels: "Where general words follow specific words in a statutory enumeration, the general words are [usually] construed to embrace only objects similar in nature to those objects enumerated by the preceding specific words." . . . Had Congress intended "tangible object" in § 1519 to be interpreted so generically as to capture physical objects as dissimilar as documents and fish, Congress would have had no reason to refer specifically to "record" or "document." The Government's unbounded reading of "tangible object" would render those words misleading surplusage.

Having used traditional tools of statutory interpretation to examine markers of congressional intent within the Sarbanes-Oxley Act and § 1519 itself, we are persuaded that an aggressive interpretation of "tangible object" must be rejected. It is highly improbable that Congress would have buried a general spoliation statute covering objects of any and every kind in a provision targeting fraud in financial record-keeping.

. . .

C

Finally, if our recourse to traditional tools of statutory construction leaves any doubt about the meaning of "tangible object," as that term is used in § 1519, we would invoke the rule that "ambiguity concerning the ambit of criminal statutes should be resolved in favor of lenity." That interpretative principle is relevant here, where the Government urges a reading of § 1519 that exposes individuals to 20-year prison sentences for tampering with *any* physical object that *might* have evidentiary value in *any* federal investigation into *any* offense, no matter whether the investigation is pending or merely contemplated, or whether the offense subject to investigation is criminal or civil. . . . In determining the meaning of "tangible object" in § 1519, "it is appropriate, before we choose the harsher alternative, to require that Congress should have spoken in language that is clear and definite."

For the reasons stated, we resist reading § 1519 expansively to create a coverall spoliation of evidence statute, advisable as such a measure might be. Leaving that important decision to Congress, we hold that a "tangible object" within § 1519's compass is one used to record or preserve information. The judgment of the U.S. Court of Appeals for the Eleventh Circuit is therefore reversed, and the case is remanded for further proceedings.

It is so ordered.

JUSTICE KAGAN, with whom JUSTICE SCALIA, JUSTICE KENNEDY, and JUSTICE THOMAS join, dissenting.

A criminal law, 18 U.S.C. § 1519, prohibits tampering with "any record, document, or tangible object" in an attempt to obstruct a federal investigation. This case raises the question whether the term "tangible object" means the same thing in § 1519 as it means in everyday language— any object capable of being touched. The answer should be easy: Yes. The term "tangible object" is broad, but clear. Throughout the U.S. Code and many States' laws, it invariably covers physical objects of all kinds. And in § 1519, context confirms what bare text says: All the words surrounding "tangible object" show that Congress meant the term to have a wide range. That fits with Congress's evident purpose in enacting § 1519: to punish those who alter or destroy physical evidence—*any* physical evidence—with the intent of thwarting federal law enforcement.

The plurality instead interprets "tangible object" to cover "only objects one can use to record or preserve information." *Ante,* at 1081. In my view, conventional tools of statutory construction all lead to a more conventional result: A "tangible object" is an object that's tangible. I would apply the statute that Congress enacted and affirm the judgment below.

I

While the plurality starts its analysis with § 1519's heading, see *ante,* at 1083 ("We note first § 1519's caption"), I would begin with § 1519's text. When Congress has not supplied a definition, we generally give a statutory term its ordinary meaning. See, *e.g., Schindler Elevator Corp. v. United States ex rel. Kirk,* 563 U.S. ___, ___, 131 S.Ct. 1885, 1891, 179 L.Ed.2d 825 (2011). As the plurality must acknowledge, the ordinary meaning of "tangible object" is "a discrete thing that possesses physical form." *Ante,* at 1081 (punctuation and citation omitted). A fish is, of course, a discrete thing that possesses physical form. See generally Dr. Seuss, One Fish Two Fish Red Fish Blue Fish (1960). So the ordinary meaning of the term "tangible object" in § 1519, as no one here disputes, covers fish (including too-small red grouper).

That interpretation accords with endless uses of the term in statute and rule books as construed by courts. Dozens of federal laws and rules of procedure (and hundreds of state enactments) include the term "tangible object" or its first cousin "tangible thing"—some in association with documents, others not. To my knowledge, no court has ever read any such provision to exclude things that don't record or preserve data; rather, all courts have adhered to the statutory language's ordinary (*i.e.,* expansive) meaning. For example, courts have understood the phrases "tangible objects" and "tangible things" in the Federal Rules of Criminal and Civil Procedure to cover everything from guns to drugs to machinery to . . . animals.

That is not necessarily the end of the matter; I agree with the plurality (really, who does not?) that context matters in interpreting statutes. We do not "construe the meaning of statutory terms in a vacuum." Rather, we interpret particular words "in their context and with a view to their place in the overall statutory scheme." And sometimes that means, as the plurality says, that the dictionary definition of a disputed term cannot control. But this is not such an occasion, for here the text and its context point the same way. Stepping back from the words "tangible object" provides only further evidence that Congress said what it meant and meant what it said.

Begin with the way the surrounding words in § 1519 reinforce the breadth of the term at issue. Section 1519 refers to "any" tangible object, thus indicating (in line with *that* word's plain meaning) a tangible object "of whatever kind." Webster's Third New International Dictionary 97 (2002). This Court has time and again recognized that "any" has "an expansive meaning," bringing within a statute's reach *all* types of the item (here, "tangible object") to which the law refers. And the adjacent laundry list of verbs in § 1519 ("alters, destroys, mutilates, conceals, covers up, falsifies, or makes a false entry") further shows that Congress wrote a statute with a wide scope. Those words are supposed to ensure—just as "tangible object" is meant to—that § 1519 covers the whole world of evidence-tampering, in all its prodigious variety.

Still more, "tangible object" appears as part of a three-noun phrase (including also "records" and "documents") common to evidence-tampering laws and always understood to embrace things of all kinds. The Model Penal Code's evidence-tampering section, drafted more than 50 years ago, similarly prohibits a person from "alter[ing], destroy[ing], conceal[ing] or remov[ing] any *record, document or thing*" in an effort to thwart an official investigation or proceeding. The Code's commentary emphasizes that the offense described in that provision is "not limited to conduct that [alters] a written instrument." Rather, the language extends to "any physical object." Consistent with that statement—and, of course, with ordinary meaning—courts in the more than 15 States that have laws based on the Model Code's tampering provision apply them to all tangible objects, including drugs, guns, vehicles and . . . yes, animals. Not a one has limited the phrase's scope to objects that record or preserve information.

The words "record, document, or tangible object" in § 1519 also track language in 18 U.S.C. § 1512, the federal witness-tampering law covering (as even the plurality accepts, see *ante,* at 1084) physical evidence in all its forms. Section 1512, both in its original version (preceding § 1519) and today, repeatedly uses the phrase "record, document, or other object"—most notably, in a provision prohibiting the use of force or threat to induce another person to withhold any of those materials from an official proceeding. § 18 U.S.C. § 1512(b)(2). That language, which itself likely derived from the Model Penal Code, encompasses no less the bloody knife than the incriminating letter, as all courts have for decades agreed. And typically "only the most compelling evidence" will persuade this Court that Congress intended "nearly identical language" in provisions dealing with related subjects to bear different meanings. Context thus again confirms what text indicates.

And legislative history, for those who care about it, puts extra icing on a cake already frosted. Section 1519, as the plurality notes, see *ante,* at 1079, 1081, was enacted after the Enron Corporation's collapse, as part of the Sarbanes-Oxley Act of 2002. But the provision began its life in a separate bill, and the drafters emphasized that Enron was "only a case study exposing the shortcomings in our current laws" relating to both "corporate and criminal" fraud. The primary "loophole[ ]" Congress identified, arose from limits in the part of § 1512 just described: That provision, as uniformly construed, prohibited a person from inducing another to destroy "record[s], document[s], or other object[s]"—of every type—but not from doing so himself. Congress (as even the plurality agrees.) enacted § 1519 to close that yawning gap. But § 1519 could fully achieve that goal only if it covered all the records, documents, and objects § 1512 did, as well as all the means of tampering with them. And so § 1519 was written to do exactly that—"to apply broadly to any acts to destroy or fabricate physical evidence," as long as performed with the requisite intent. S.Rep. No. 107–146, at 14. "When a person destroys evidence," the drafters explained, "overly technical legal distinctions should neither hinder nor prevent prosecution." *Id.*, at 7. Ah well: Congress, meet today's Court, which here invents just such a distinction with just such an effect.

As Congress recognized in using a broad term, giving immunity to those who destroy non-documentary evidence has no sensible basis in penal policy. A person who hides a murder victim's body is no less culpable than one who burns the victim's diary. A fisherman, like John Yates, who dumps undersized fish to avoid a fine is no less blameworthy than one who shreds his vessel's catch log for the same reason. Congress thus treated both offenders in the same way. It understood, in enacting § 1519, that destroying evidence is destroying evidence, whether or not that evidence takes documentary form.

II

A

The plurality searches far and wide for anything—*anything*—to support its interpretation of § 1519. But its fishing expedition comes up empty.

As an initial matter, this Court uses *noscitur a sociis* and *ejusdem generis* to resolve ambiguity, not create it. Those principles are "useful rule[s] of construction where words are of obscure or doubtful meaning." But when words have a clear definition, and all other contextual clues support that meaning, the canons cannot properly defeat Congress's decision to draft broad legislation.

Anyway, assigning "tangible object" its ordinary meaning comports with *noscitur a sociis* and *ejusdem generis* when applied, as they should be, with attention to § 1519's subject and purpose. Those canons require identifying a common trait that links all the words in a statutory phrase. In responding to that demand, the plurality characterizes records and documents as things that preserve information—and so they are. But just as much, they are things that provide information, and thus potentially serve as evidence relevant to matters under review. And in a statute pertaining to obstruction of federal investigations, that evidentiary function comes to the fore. The destruction of records and documents prevents law enforcement agents from gathering facts relevant to official inquiries. And so too does the destruction of tangible objects—of whatever kind. Whether the item is a fisherman's ledger or an undersized fish, throwing it overboard has the identical effect on the administration of justice. See *supra,* at 1094. For purposes of § 1519, records, documents, and (all) tangible objects are therefore alike.

And the plurality's invocation of § 1519's verbs does nothing to buttress its canon-based argument. See *ante,* at 1085–1086; *ante,* at 1089–1090 (opinion of ALITO, J.). The plurality observes that § 1519 prohibits "falsif[ying]" or "mak[ing] a false entry in" a tangible object, and no one can do those things to, say, a murder weapon (or a fish). *Ante,* at 1085. But of course someone can alter, destroy, mutilate, conceal, or cover up such a tangible object, and § 1519 prohibits those actions too. The Court has never before suggested that all the verbs in a statute need to match up with all the nouns. ("[T]he law does not require legislators to write extra language specifically exempting, phrase by phrase, applications in respect to which a portion of a phrase is not needed"). And for good reason. It is exactly when Congress sets out to draft a statute broadly—to include every imaginable variation on a theme—that such mismatches will arise. To respond by narrowing the law, as the plurality does, is thus to flout both what Congress wrote and what Congress wanted.

Finally, when all else fails, the plurality invokes the rule of lenity. See *ante,* at 1087. But even in its most robust form, that rule only kicks in when, "after all legitimate tools of interpretation have been exhausted, 'a reasonable doubt persists' regarding whether Congress has made the defendant's conduct a federal crime." No such doubt lingers here. The plurality points to the breadth of § 1519, see *ante,* at 1087, as though breadth were equivalent to ambiguity. It is not. Section 1519 *is* very broad. It is also very clear. Every traditional tool of statutory interpretation points in the same direction, toward "object" meaning object. Lenity offers no proper refuge from that straightforward (even though capacious) construction.

B

III

If none of the traditional tools of statutory interpretation can produce today's result, then what accounts for it? The plurality offers a clue when it emphasizes the disproportionate penalties § 1519 imposes if the law is read broadly. See *ante,* at 1087–1088. Section 1519, the plurality objects, would then "expose[ ] individuals to 20-year prison sentences for tampering with *any* physical object that *might* have evidentiary value in *any* federal investigation into *any* offense." *Ante,* at 1088. That brings to the surface the real issue: overcriminalization and excessive punishment in the U.S. Code.

Now as to this statute, I think the plurality somewhat—though only somewhat—exaggerates the matter. The plurality omits from its description of § 1519 the requirement that a person act "knowingly" and with "the intent to impede, obstruct, or influence" federal law enforcement. And in highlighting § 1519's maximum penalty, the plurality glosses over the absence of any prescribed minimum. (Let's not forget that Yates's sentence was not 20 years, but 30 days.) Congress presumably enacts laws with high maximums and no minimums when it thinks the prohibited conduct may run the gamut from major to minor. That is assuredly true of acts obstructing justice. Compare this case with the following, all of which properly come within, but now fall outside, § 1519: *McRae,* 702 F.3d, at 834–838 (burning human body to thwart murder investigation); *Maury,* 695 F.3d, at 243–244 (altering cement mixer to impede inquiry into amputation of employee's fingers); *United States v. Natal,* 2014 U.S. Dist. LEXIS 108852 (D.Conn., Aug. 7, 2014) (repainting van to cover up evidence of fatal arson). Most district judges, as Congress knows, will recognize differences between such cases and prosecutions like this one, and will try to make the punishment fit the crime. Still and all, I tend to think, for the reasons the plurality gives, that § 1519 is a bad law—too broad and undifferentiated, with too-high maximum penalties, which give prosecutors too much leverage and sentencers too much discretion. And I'd go further: In those ways, § 1519 is unfortunately not an outlier, but an emblem of a deeper pathology in the federal criminal code.

But whatever the wisdom or folly of § 1519, this Court does not get to rewrite the law. "Resolution of the pros and cons of whether a statute should sweep broadly or narrowly is for Congress." *Rodgers,* 466 U.S., at 484, 104 S.Ct. 1942. If judges disagree with Congress's choice, we are perfectly entitled to say so—in lectures, in law review articles, and even in dicta. But we are not entitled to replace the statute Congress enacted with an alternative of our own design.

I respectfully dissent.

DISCUSSION QUESTIONS

1.   How many different tools did the majority and dissent use to decide whether a fish could be a "tangible object" within the meaning of the statute? If you were a judge, which tools would you rely on most heavily?

2.   Should court's limit themselves to the "ordinary meaning" of a phrase such as "tangible object?"

3.   Does it make sense to interpret the phrase "tangible object" in light of the general goals of the *Sarbanes-Oxley Act*?

Case in Context

People often lie to investigators to cover things up. Sometimes those lies are crimes themselves. But should simply denying wrongdoing be a crime?

JAMES BROGAN V. UNITED STATES

Supreme Court of the United States
522 U.S. 398 (1998)

JUSTICE SCALIA delivered the opinion of the Court.

This case presents the question whether there is an exception to criminal liability under 18 U.S.C. § 1001 for a false statement that consists of the mere denial of wrongdoing, the so-called "exculpatory no."

I

While acting as a union officer during 1987 and 1988, petitioner James Brogan accepted cash payments from JRD Management Corporation, a real estate company whose employees were represented by the union. On October 4, 1993, federal agents from the Department of Labor and the Internal Revenue Service visited petitioner at his home. The agents identified themselves and explained that they were seeking petitioner's cooperation in an investigation of JRD and various individuals. They told petitioner that if he wished to cooperate, he should have an attorney contact the United States Attorney's Office, and that if he could not afford an attorney, one could be appointed for him.

The agents then asked petitioner if he would answer some questions, and he agreed. One question was whether he had received any cash or gifts from JRD when he was a union officer. Petitioner's response was at that point, the agents disclosed that a search of JRD headquarters had produced company records showing the contrary. They also told petitioner that lying to federal agents in the course of an investigation was a crime. Petitioner did not modify his answers, and the interview ended shortly thereafter.

Petitioner was indicted for accepting unlawful cash payments from an employer in violation of 29 U.S.C. §§ 186(b)(1), (a)(2) and (d)(2), and making a false statement within the jurisdiction of a federal agency in violation of 18 U.S.C. § 1001. He was tried, along with several co-defendants, before a jury in the United States District Court for the Southern District of New York, and was found guilty. The United States Court of Appeals for the Second Circuit affirmed the convictions. We granted certiorari on the issue of the "exculpatory no."

II

At the time petitioner falsely replied "no" to the Government investigators' question, 18 U.S.C. § 1001 (1988 ed.) provided:

"Whoever, in any matter within the jurisdiction of any department or agency of the United States knowingly and willfully falsifies, conceals or covers up by any trick, scheme, or device a material fact, or makes any false, fictitious or fraudulent statements or representations, or makes or uses any false writing or document knowing the same to contain any false, fictitious or fraudulent statement or entry, shall be fined not more than $10,000 or imprisoned not more than five years, or both."

By its terms, 18 U.S.C. § 1001 covers "any" false statement—that is, a false statement "of whatever kind," *United States v. Gonzales,* 520 U.S. 1, 5, 117 S.Ct. 1032, 1035 (1997) (internal quotation marks and citation omitted). The word "no" in response to a question assuredly makes a "statement," see, *e.g.,* Webster's New International Dictionary 2461 (2d ed.1950) (def. 2: "That which is stated; an embodiment in words of facts or opinions"), and petitioner does not contest that his utterance was false or that it was made "knowingly and willfully." In fact, petitioner concedes that under a "literal reading" of the statute he loses. Brief for Petitioner 5.

Petitioner asks us, however, to depart from the literal text that Congress has enacted, and to approve the doctrine adopted by many Circuits which excludes from the scope of § 1001 the "exculpatory no." The central feature of this doctrine is that a simple denial of guilt does not come within the statute. There is considerable variation among the Circuits concerning, among other things, what degree of elaborated tale-telling carries a statement beyond simple denial. In the present case, however, the Second Circuit agreed with petitioner that his statement would constitute a "true 'exculpatory n[o]' as recognized in other circuits," 96 F.3d, at 37, but aligned itself with the Fifth Circuit (one of whose panels had been the very first to embrace the "exculpatory no," see *Paternostro v. United States,* 311 F.2d 298 (C.A.5 1962)) in categorically rejecting the doctrine, see *United States v. Rodriguez-Rios,* 14 F.3d 1040 (C.A.5 1994) (en banc).

Petitioner's argument in support of the "exculpatory no" doctrine proceeds from the major premise that § 1001 criminalizes only those statements to Government investigators that "pervert governmental functions"; to the minor premise that simple denials of guilt to Government investigators do not pervert governmental functions; to the conclusion that § 1001 does not criminalize simple denials of guilt to Government investigators. Both premises seem to us mistaken. As to the minor: We cannot imagine how it could be true that falsely denying guilt in a Government investigation does not pervert a governmental function. Certainly the investigation of wrongdoing is a proper governmental function; and since it is the very *purpose* of an investigation to uncover the truth, any falsehood relating to the subject of the investigation perverts that function. It could be argued, perhaps, that a *disbelieved* falsehood does not pervert an investigation. But making the existence of this crime turn upon the credulousness of the federal investigator (or the persuasiveness of the liar) would be exceedingly strange; such a defense to the analogous crime of perjury is certainly unheard of. Moreover, as we shall see, the only support for the "perversion of governmental functions" limitation is a statement of this Court referring to the *possibility* (as opposed to the certainty) of perversion of function—a possibility that exists whenever investigators are told a falsehood relevant to their task.

The second line of defense that petitioner invokes for the "exculpatory no" doctrine is inspired by the Fifth Amendment. He argues that a literal reading of § 1001 violates the "spirit" of the Fifth Amendment because it places a "cornered suspect" in the "cruel trilemma" of admitting guilt, remaining silent, or falsely denying guilt. This "trilemma" is wholly of the guilty suspect's own making, of course. An innocent person will not find himself in a similar quandary (as one commentator has put it, the innocent person lacks even a "lemma," and even the honest and contrite guilty person will not regard the third prong of the "trilemma" (the blatant lie) as an available option. The *bon mot* "cruel trilemma" first appeared in Justice Goldberg's opinion for the Court in *Murphy v. Waterfront Comm'n of N.Y. Harbor,* 378 U.S. 52, 84 S.Ct. 1594, 12 L.Ed.2d 678 (1964), where it was used to explain the importance of a suspect's Fifth Amendment right to remain silent when subpoenaed to testify in an official inquiry. Without that right, the opinion said, he would be exposed "to the cruel trilemma of self-accusation, perjury or contempt." *Id.,* at 55. In order to validate the "exculpatory no," the elements of this "cruel trilemma" have now been altered—ratcheted up, as it were, so that the right to remain silent, which was the *liberation* from the original trilemma, is now *itself* a cruelty. We are not disposed to write into our law this species of compassion inflation.

Whether or not the predicament of the wrongdoer run to ground tugs at the heartstrings, neither the text nor the spirit of the Fifth Amendment confers a privilege to lie. "[P]roper invocation of the Fifth Amendment privilege against compulsory self-incrimination allows a witness to remain silent, but not to swear falsely." Petitioner contends that silence is an "illusory" option because a suspect may fear that his silence will be used against him later, or may not even know that silence is an available option. As to the former: It is well established that the fact that a person's silence can be used against him—either as substantive evidence of guilt or to impeach him if he takes the stand—does not exert a form of pressure that exonerates an otherwise unlawful lie. And as for the possibility that the person under investigation may be unaware of his right to remain silent: In the modern age of frequently dramatized "Miranda" warnings, that is implausible. Indeed, we found it implausible (or irrelevant) 30 years ago, unless the suspect was "in custody or otherwise deprived of his freedom of action in any significant way."

Petitioner repeats the argument made by many supporters of the "exculpatory no," that the doctrine is necessary to eliminate the grave risk that § 1001 will become an instrument of prosecutorial abuse. The supposed danger is that overzealous prosecutors will use this provision as a means of "piling on" offenses—sometimes punishing the denial of wrongdoing more severely than the wrongdoing itself. The objectors' principal grievance on this score, however, lies not with the hypothetical prosecutors but with Congress itself, which has decreed the obstruction of a legitimate investigation to be a separate offense, and a serious one. It is not for us to revise that judgment. Petitioner has been unable to demonstrate, moreover, any history of prosecutorial excess, either before or after widespread judicial acceptance of the "exculpatory no." And finally, if there is a problem of supposed "overreaching" it is hard to see how the doctrine of the "exculpatory no" could solve it. It is easy enough for an interrogator to press the liar from the initial simple denial to a more detailed fabrication that would not qualify for the exemption.Courts may not create their own limitations on legislation, no matter how alluring the policy arguments for doing so, and no matter how widely the blame may be spread. Because the plain language of § 1001 admits of no exception for an "exculpatory no," we affirm the judgment of the Court of Appeals.

It is so ordered.

JUSTICE GINSBURG, with whom JUSTICE SOUTER joins, concurring in the judgment.

Because a false denial fits the unqualified language of 18 U.S.C. § 1001, I concur in the affirmance of Brogan's conviction. I write separately, however, to call attention to the extraordinary authority Congress, perhaps unwittingly, has conferred on prosecutors to manufacture crimes. I note, at the same time, how far removed the "exculpatory no" is from the problems Congress initially sought to address when it proscribed falsehoods designed to elicit a benefit from the Government or to hinder Government operations.

I

At the time of Brogan's offense, § 1001 made it a felony "knowingly and willfully" to make "any false, fictitious or fraudulent statements or representations" in "any matter within the jurisdiction of any department or agency of the United States." 18 U.S.C. § 1001 (1988 ed.). That encompassing formulation arms Government agents with authority not simply to apprehend lawbreakers, but to generate felonies, crimes of a kind that only a Government officer could prompt.

This case is illustrative. Two federal investigators paid an unannounced visit one evening to James Brogan's home. The investigators already possessed records indicating that Brogan, a union officer, had received cash from a company that employed members of the union Brogan served. (The agents gave no advance warning, one later testified, because they wanted to retain the element of surprise. App. 5.) When the agents asked Brogan whether he had received any money or gifts from the company, Brogan responded "No." The agents asked no further questions. *After* Brogan just said "No," however, the agents told him: (1) the Government had in hand the records indicating that his answer was false;

and (2) lying to federal agents in the course of an investigation is a crime. Had counsel appeared on the spot, Brogan likely would have received and followed advice to amend his answer, to say immediately: "Strike that; I plead not guilty." But no counsel attended the unannounced interview, and Brogan divulged nothing more. Thus, when the interview ended, a federal offense had been completed—even though, for all we can tell, Brogan's unadorned denial misled no one. . . .

[This section] may apply to encounters between agents and their targets "under extremely informal circumstances which do not sufficiently alert the person interviewed to the danger that false statements may lead to a felony conviction." Because the questioning occurs in a noncustodial setting, the suspect is not informed of the right to remain silent. Unlike proceedings in which a false statement can be prosecuted as perjury, there may be no oath, no pause to concentrate the speaker's mind on the importance of his or her answers. As in Brogan's case, the target may not be informed that a false "No" is a criminal offense until *after* he speaks.

At oral argument, the Solicitor General forthrightly observed that § 1001 could even be used to "escalate completely innocent conduct into a felony." Tr. of Oral Arg. 36. More likely to occur, "if an investigator finds it difficult to prove some elements of a crime, she can ask questions about other elements to which she already knows the answers. If the suspect lies, she can then use the crime she has prompted as leverage or can seek prosecution for the lie as a substitute for the crime she cannot prove." Comment, False Statements to Federal Agents: Induced Lies and the Exculpatory No, 57 U. Chi. L.Rev. 1273, 1278 (1990) (footnote omitted). If the statute of limitations has run on an offense—as it had on four of the five payments Brogan was accused of accepting—the prosecutor can endeavor to revive the case by instructing an investigator to elicit a fresh denial of guilt. Prosecution in these circumstances is not an instance of Government "punishing the denial of wrongdoing more severely than the wrongdoing itself," *ante,* at 810; it is, instead, Government generation of a crime when the underlying suspected wrongdoing is or has become nonpunishable.

II

Even if the encompassing language of § 1001 precludes judicial declaration of an "exculpatory no" defense, the core concern persists: "The function of law enforcement is the prevention of crime and the apprehension of criminals. Manifestly, that function does not include the manufacturing of crime." *Sherman v. United States,* 356 U.S. 369, 372, 78 S.Ct. 819, 820, 2 L.Ed.2d 848 (1958). The Government has not been blind to this concern. Notwithstanding the prosecution in this case and the others cited Department of Justice has long noted its reluctance to approve § 1001 indictments for simple false denials made to investigators. Indeed, the Government once asserted before this Court that the arguments supporting the "exculpatory no" doctrine "are forceful even if not necessarily dispositive."

The Department of Justice has maintained a policy against bringing § 1001 prosecutions for statements amounting to an "exculpatory no." At the time the charges against Brogan were filed, the United States Attorneys' Manual firmly declared: "Where the statement takes the form of an 'exculpatory no,' 18 U.S.C. § 1001 does not apply regardless who asks the question." United States Attorneys' Manual & para;9–42.160 (Oct. 1, 1988). After the Fifth Circuit abandoned the "exculpatory no" doctrine in *United States v. Rodriguez-Rios,* 14 F.3d 1040 (1994) (en banc), the manual was amended to read: "It is the Department's policy that it is not appropriate to charge a Section 1001 violation where a suspect, during an investigation, merely denies his guilt in response to questioning by the government." United States Attorneys' Manual & para;9–42.160 (Feb. 12, 1996).

These pronouncements indicate, at the least, the dubious propriety of bringing felony prosecutions for bare exculpatory denials informally made to Government agents. Although today's decision holds that such prosecutions can be sustained under the broad language of § 1001, the Department of Justice's prosecutorial guide continues to caution restraint in each exercise of this large authority.

IV

The Court's opinion does not instruct lower courts automatically to sanction prosecution or conviction under § 1001 in all instances of false denials made to criminal investigators. The Second Circuit, whose judgment the Court affirms, noted some reservations. That court left open the question whether "to violate Section 1001, a person must know that it is unlawful to make such a false statement." *United States v. Wiener,* 96 F.3d 35, 40 (1996). And nothing that court or this Court said suggests that "the mere denial of criminal responsibility would be sufficient to prove such [knowledge]." *Ibid.* Moreover, "a trier of fact might acquit on the ground that a denial of guilt in circumstances indicating surprise or other lack of reflection was not the product of the requisite criminal intent," *ibid.,* and a jury could be instructed that it would be permissible to draw such an inference. Finally, under the statute currently in force, a false statement must be "materia[l]" to violate § 1001. See False Statements Accountability Act of 1996, Pub.L. 104–292, § 2, 110 Stat. 3459.

The controls now in place, however, do not meet the basic issue, *i.e.,* the sweeping generality of § 1001's language. Thus, the prospect remains that an overzealous prosecutor or investigator—aware that a person has committed some suspicious acts, but unable to make a criminal case—will create a crime by surprising the suspect, asking about those acts, and receiving a false denial. Congress alone can provide the appropriate instruction.

DISCUSSION QUESTIONS

1.   The average person might be surprised to learn that simply denying guilt in an interview when they are not under oath can be a crime. If so, should such common understandings shape how judges interpret statutes?

2.   The government essentially conceded that their interpretation would allow them to "manufacture crime" out of lies. Should judges try to limit government power when they interpret statutes, or should they defer to the decisions of duly elected legislators?

3.   Does a government investigator have to warn someone that lying to them is a crime?

F. CONSTITUTIONAL CONSTRAINTS: LEGALITY, VAGUENESS AND OVERBREADTH

Judges interpret statutes with an eye to certain constitutional limits. Basic to the constitutional notion of due process of law is the idea of legality, which means that crimes must be clearly defined in order to give people fair notice of what will be punished and to prevent arbitrary exercises of government power. Clauses of the Constitution specifically prohibit legislation that declares past conduct to be crimes (known as ex post facto laws) and legislation that declares particular people to be guilty of a crime (known as bills of attainder).

While bills of attainder are unheard of and ex post facto laws are rare, vagueness challenges are more common. Courts have held that the Due Process Clauses of the Fifth and Fourteenth Amendments to the Constitution forbid vague criminal laws. A criminal statute is constitutionally vague if it does not provide a person of ordinary intelligence with fair notice of prohibited conduct. Yet, criminal statutes are often general and are not required to precisely draw the line between criminal and non-criminal conduct. Rather, they must give you a fair idea of when you are "getting warmer," in the words of the old children's game. One English jurist put it best when he said, "Those who skate on thin ice can hardly expect to find a sign which will denote the precise spot where they may fall in."

The best way of understanding the vagueness standard is by understanding the constitutional values that clear statutes protect. Statutes that are unconstitutionally vague often threaten all of these values.

1.   Clear statutes prevent the legislative branch from unconstitutionally delegating its law-making function to the courts (Constitutionally, courts are intended to interpret rather than make the law, although it becomes a fine distinction).

2. Clear statutes give people fair notice of punishable conduct, giving them an opportunity to behave accordingly.

3. Clear statutes avoid giving arbitrary and potentially discriminatory powers of arrest and prosecution to the executive branch and law enforcement.

Overbreadth challenges are distinct from but related to vagueness challenges. Sometimes prosecutors will seek to save a law from a vagueness challenge by giving the law a clear yet sweeping meaning. For example, a prosecutor might argue that the loitering law described in the following case prohibits anyone from standing in one place on a public street for more than a moment. Yet, such a law would be so broad that it would effectively prohibit people from gathering together in public. Such a sweeping law would violate the First Amendment's Right of Assembly, and it would therefore be constitutionally overbroad.

Case in Context

The statute in the following case criminalized "revenge porn," and the court had to decide whether it violated the First Amendment.

STATE OF VERMONT V. REBEKAH S. VANBUREN

Supreme Court of Vermont
2018 WL 4177776 (2018)

ROBINSON, J.

This case raises a facial challenge to Vermont's statute banning disclosure of nonconsensual pornography. 13 V.S.A. § 2606. We conclude that the statute is constitutional on its face and grant the State's petition for extraordinary relief.

I. "Revenge-Porn," or Nonconsensual Pornography Generally

"Revenge porn" is a popular label describing a subset of nonconsensual pornography published for vengeful purposes. "Nonconsensual pornography" may be defined generally as "distribution of sexually graphic images of individuals without their consent." D. Citron & M. Franks, Criminalizing Revenge Porn, 49 Wake Forest L. Rev. 345, 346 (2014). The term "nonconsensual pornography" encompasses "images originally obtained without consent (e.g., hidden recordings or recordings of sexual assaults) as well as images originally obtained with consent, usually within the context of a private or confidential relationship." Id. The nonconsensual dissemination of such intimate images—to a victim's employer, coworkers, family members, friends, or even strangers—can cause "public degradation, social isolation, and professional humiliation for the victims." C. Alter, " 'It's Like Having an Incurable Disease': Inside the Fight Against Revenge Porn," Time.com, http://time.com/4811561/revenge-porn/ [https://perma.cc/G9UP-L984]. The images may haunt victims throughout their lives. Id. (describing lasting effects of having one's nude photos posted online and stating that "this type of cyber crime can leave a lasting digital stain, one that is nearly impossible to fully erase").

This problem is widespread, with one recent study finding that "4% of U.S. internet users—roughly 10.4 million Americans—have been threatened with or experienced the posting of explicit images without their consent." See Data & Society, "New Report Shows That 4% of U.S. Internet Users Have Been a Victim of 'Revenge Porn,'" (Dec. 13, 2016), https://datasociety.net/blog/2016/12/13/nonconsensual-image-sharing/ [https://perma.cc/26FC-937V]; see also C. Alter, supra (stating that "Facebook received more than 51,000 reports of revenge porn in January 2017 alone"). Revenge porn is overwhelmingly targeted at women. D. Citron & M. Franks, supra, at 353–54 (citing data that victims of revenge porn are overwhelmingly female).

Forty states, including Vermont, have enacted legislation to address this issue. See Cyber Civil Rights Initiative, 40 States + DC Have Revenge Porn Laws, https://www.cybercivilrights.org/revenge-porn-laws/ [https://perma.cc/83UK-KKUS] (collecting state statutes). Federal legislation has also been proposed. See Intimate Privacy Protection Act of 2016, H.R. 5896, 114th Cong. (2016), https://www.congress.gov/bill/114th-congress/house bill/5896 [https://perma.cc/RM6V-865X] (proposing to "amend the federal criminal code to make it unlawful to knowingly distribute a photograph, film, or video of a person engaging in sexually explicit conduct or of a person's naked genitals or post-pubescent female nipple with reckless disregard for the person's lack of consent if the person is identifiable from the image itself or from information displayed in connection with the image," with certain exceptions); Servicemember Intimate Privacy Protection Act, H.R. 1588, 115th Cong. (2017), https://www.congress.gov/bill/115th-congress/house-bill/1588 [https://perma.cc/7ZBK-KT49] (proposing to "amend the Uniform Code of Military Justice to prohibit the nonconsensual distribution of private sexual images").

II. Vermont's Statute

Vermont's law, enacted in 2015, makes it a crime punishable by not more than two years' imprisonment and a fine of $2,000 or both to "knowingly disclose a visual image of an identifiable person who is nude or who is engaged in sexual conduct, without his or her consent, with the intent to harm, harass, intimidate, threaten, or coerce the person depicted, and the disclosure would cause a reasonable person to suffer harm." 13 V.S.A. § 2606(b)(1). "Nude" and "sexual conduct" are both expressly defined. The law makes clear that "[c]onsent to recording of the visual image does not, by itself, constitute consent for disclosure of the image." Id. Violation of § 2606(b)(1) is a misdemeanor, unless a person acts "with the intent of disclosing the image for financial profit," in which case it is a felony.

Section 2606 does not apply to:

(1)   Images involving voluntary nudity or sexual conduct in public or commercial settings or in a place where a person does not have a reasonable expectation of privacy.

(2)   Disclosures made in the public interest, including the reporting of unlawful conduct, or lawful and common practices of law enforcement, criminal reporting, corrections, legal proceedings, or medical treatment.

(3)   Disclosures of materials that constitute a matter of public concern.

(4)   Interactive computer services, as defined in 47 U.S.C. § 230(f)(2), or information services or telecommunications services, as defined in 47 U.S.C. § 153, for content solely provided by another person. This subdivision shall not preclude other remedies available at law.

Id. § 2606(d)(1)–(4).

III. Facts and Proceedings Before the Trial Court

In late 2015, defendant was charged by information with violating 13 V.S.A. § 2606(b)(1). In support of the charge, the State submitted an affidavit from a police officer and a sworn statement from complainant, which was incorporated into the officer's affidavit by reference. The parties agreed that the trial court could rely on these affidavits in ruling on the motion to dismiss; the parties later stipulated to certain additional facts as well.

The police officer averred as follows. Complainant contacted police after she discovered that someone had posted naked pictures of her on a Facebook account belonging to Anthony Coon and "tagged" her in the picture. Complainant called Mr. Coon and left a message asking that the pictures be deleted. Shortly thereafter, defendant called complainant back on Mr. Coon's phone; she called complainant a "moraless pig" and told her that she was going to contact complainant's employer, a child-care facility. When complainant asked defendant to remove the pictures, defendant responded that she was going to ruin complainant and get revenge.

Complainant told police that she had taken naked pictures of herself and sent them to Mr. Coon through Facebook Messenger. She advised that the pictures had been sent privately so that no one else could view them. Defendant admitted to the officer that she saw complainant's pictures on Mr. Coon's Facebook account and that she posted them on Facebook using Mr. Coon's account. Defendant asked the officer if he thought complainant had "learned her lesson."

In her sworn statement, complainant provided additional details concerning the allegations above. She described her efforts to delete the pictures from Facebook and to delete her own Facebook account. Complainant stated that the night before the pictures were publicly posted, she learned through a friend that defendant was asking about her. Defendant described herself as Mr. Coon's girlfriend. Complainant asked Mr. Coon about defendant, and Mr. Coon said that defendant was obsessed with him and that he had never slept with her. Complainant "took it as him being honest so we moved on." The next day, complainant discovered that defendant posted her nude images on Mr. Coon's Facebook page. A judge found probable cause for the charge against defendant in December 2015.

In February 2016, defendant filed a motion to dismiss. She argued that 13 V.S.A. § 2606 violated the First Amendment to the U.S. Constitution because it restricted protected speech and it could not survive strict scrutiny. Defendant also asserted that complainant had no reasonable expectation of privacy because she took the pictures herself and messaged them to Mr. Coon without any promise on his part to keep the pictures private. Defendant cited 13 V.S.A. § 2606(d)(1), which provides an exception from liability for individuals who disclose "[i]mages involving voluntary nudity or sexual conduct in public or commercial settings or in a place where a person does not have a reasonable expectation of privacy."

The State opposed the motion. With respect to the First Amendment, the State argued that the expression covered by the statute was not protected speech, and alternatively, that the statute was narrowly tailored to achieve compelling State interests. As to defendant's second argument, the State asserted that complainant had a reasonable expectation of privacy in the pictures. It explained that complainant used an application that allows one Facebook user to privately send text messages to another Facebook user, and it argued that complainant reasonably expected that only Mr. Coon would access the pictures. The pictures only became public, the State contended, because defendant logged into Mr. Coon's Facebook account without permission, accessed his private messages, and then posted the pictures on Mr. Coon's public feed where other Facebook users could view them. The State further argued that the reasonable expectation of privacy contemplated by the statute concerned the "place" where the pictures were taken, not the method by which the pictures were initially shared. It argued that the method of initial publication was relevant to whether complainant consented to defendant's disclosure under § 2606(b)(1), but complainant unquestionably did not consent to the disclosures here. Finally, the State asserted that the question of whether complainant had a reasonable expectation of privacy—either when the pictures were first taken or when they were later sent to Mr. Coon—was a question of fact that was not appropriate for resolution on a motion to dismiss.

At the court's request, defendant and the State later stipulated to the following additional facts for purposes of the motion to dismiss: complainant sent the photographs to Mr. Coon on October 7, 2015. The photographs were posted on a public Facebook page on October 8, 2015. Complainant was not in a relationship with Mr. Coon at the time the photographs were sent to him. Defendant did not have permission to access Mr. Coon's Facebook account. Mr. Coon believed that defendant accessed his Facebook account through her telephone, which had Mr. Coon's password saved.

Within this factual context, the trial court considered defendant's facial challenge to 13 V.S.A. § 2606 under the First Amendment. The court concluded that § 2606 imposed a content-based restriction on protected speech, which required the State to show that the law is "narrowly tailored to promote a compelling Government interest," and there is no "less restrictive alternative" available that would serve the Government's purpose. United States v. Playboy Entm't Grp., Inc., 529 U.S. 803, 813, 120 S.Ct. 1878, 146 L.Ed.2d 865 (2000); see also Williams-Yulee v. Fla. Bar, ___ U.S. ___, 135 S.Ct. 1656, 1665–66, 191 L.Ed.2d 570 (2015) (explaining State bears burden of showing statute survives strict scrutiny). Assuming that a compelling governmental interest existed, the court concluded that the State failed to show that there were no less restrictive alternatives available, or to address why civil penalties, such as those set out in 13 V.S.A. § 2606(e), were not reasonable and effective alternatives. It thus concluded the statute did not survive strict scrutiny and dismissed the State's charges.

The court did not address defendant's assertion that complainant had no reasonable expectation of privacy in her nude photographs under 13 V.S.A. § 2606(d)(1). It did note, however, that the facts of this case were not a clear example of the "typical revenge porn case" because complainant sent the photographs to a person with whom she had a past but not present relationship. The court noted that complainant would not have known Mr. Coon's relationship status, the effect that such photographs might have on that relationship, or who might have access to his Facebook account.

The State challenges the court's dismissal of its charges through a petition for extraordinary relief requesting that we review the trial court's ruling that § 2606 is unconstitutional.

    . . . .

B.   Strict Scrutiny

Our conclusion that nonconsensual pornography does not fall into an existing or new category of unprotected speech does not end the inquiry. The critical question is whether the First Amendment permits the regulation at issue. See, e.g., Williams-Yulee, ___ U.S. ___, 135 S.Ct. at 1667–73 (acknowledging solicitation of campaign funds by judicial candidates is not category of unprotected speech under the First Amendment, but concluding restriction on such solicitations was constitutionally permitted because it was narrowly tailored to serve compelling State interest). The remaining question is whether § 2606 is narrowly tailored to serve a compelling State interest.

1. Compelling Interest

We conclude that the State interest underlying § 2606 is compelling. We base this conclusion on the U.S. Supreme Court's recognition of the relatively low constitutional significance of speech relating to purely private matters, evidence of potentially severe harm to individuals arising from nonconsensual publication of intimate depictions of them, and a litany of analogous restrictions on speech that are generally viewed as uncontroversial and fully consistent with the First Amendment.

Although we decline to identify a new category of unprotected speech on the basis of the above cases, the decisions cited above are relevant to the compelling interest analysis in that they reinforce that the First Amendment limitations on the regulation of speech concerning matters of public interest do not necessarily apply to regulation of speech concerning purely private matters. Time and again, the Supreme Court has recognized that speech concerning purely private matters does not carry as much weight in the strict scrutiny analysis as speech concerning matters of public concern, and may accordingly be subject to more expansive regulation.

In Dun & Bradstreet, Inc. v. Greenmoss Builders, Inc., a majority of Supreme Court justices concluded that the "recovery of presumed and punitive damages in defamation cases absent a showing of 'actual malice' does not violate the First Amendment when the defamatory statements do not involve matters of public concern." 472 U.S. 749, 762, 105 S.Ct. 2939, 86 L.Ed.2d 593 (1985); id. at 763–64, 105 S.Ct. 2939 (Burger, C.J., concurring); id. at 765–774, 105 S.Ct. 2939 (White, J., concurring). The plurality explained that the Court's conclusion in New York Times Co. v. Sullivan, 376 U.S. 254, 84 S.Ct. 710, 11 L.Ed.2d 686 (1964), that the First Amendment limits the reach of state defamation laws was based on the Constitution's solicitude for "freedom of expression upon public questions" and the view that "debate on public issues should be uninhibited, robust, and wide open." Dun & Bradstreet, Inc., 472 U.S. at 755, 105 S.Ct. 2939 (quotation omitted). The Court elaborated:

> The First Amendment was fashioned to assure unfettered interchange of ideas for the bringing about of political and social changes desired by the people. Speech concerning public affairs is more than self-expression; it is the essence of self-government. Accordingly, the Court has frequently affirmed that speech on public issues occupies the highest rung of the hierarchy of First Amendment values, and is entitled to special protection. In

contrast, speech on matters of purely private concern is of less First Amendment concern. As a number of state courts, including the court below, have recognized, the role of the Constitution in regulating state libel law is far more limited when the concerns that activated New York Times and Gertz are absent.

Id. at 759, 105 S.Ct. 2939 (alternations, citations, and quotations omitted).

The Court echoed these sentiments more recently and built on this analysis in Snyder v. Phelps, 562 U.S. 443, 131 S.Ct. 1207, 179 L.Ed.2d 172 (2011). In Snyder, the Westboro Baptist Church picketed on public land approximately 1,000 feet from a funeral service for a soldier killed in Iraq. The picketers displayed signs stating, among other things, "Thank God for Dead Soldiers," "God Hates You," and "Fags Doom Nations." Id. at 454, 131 S.Ct. 1207. The soldier's father could see the tops of the picket signs as he drove to the funeral, although he did not see what was written on them until watching a news broadcast later that night. He sued the church and its leaders (collectively "Westboro") for various torts, and a jury awarded him five million dollars in compensatory and punitive damages for intentional infliction of emotional distress, intrusion upon seclusion, and civil conspiracy.

The Court affirmed the appeals court's reversal and judgment for defendants on the basis that the speech was protected by the First Amendment. In reaching its conclusion, the Court explained, "Whether the First Amendment prohibits holding Westboro liable for its speech in this case turns largely on whether that speech is of public or private concern, as determined by all the circumstances of the case." Id. at 451, 131 S.Ct. 1207. After recounting the myriad reasons why speech concerning matters of public concern is "at the heart of the First Amendment's protection," id. at 451–52, 131 S.Ct. 1207, the Court considered the status of speech concerning purely private matters:

> Not all speech is of equal First Amendment importance, however, and where matters of purely private significance are at issue, First Amendment protections are often less rigorous. That is because restricting speech on purely private matters does not implicate the same constitutional concerns as limiting speech on matters of public interest. There is no threat to the free and robust debate of public issues; there is no potential interference with a meaningful dialogue of ideas; and the threat of liability does not pose the risk of a reaction of self-censorship on matters of public import.

Id. at 452, 131 S.Ct. 1207 (alternations, citations, and quotations omitted).

The Court acknowledged that "the boundaries of the public concern test are not well defined," and offered the following guiding principles:

> Speech deals with matters of public concern when it can be fairly considered as relating to any matter of political, social, or other concern to the community, or when it is a subject of legitimate news interest; that is, a subject of general interest and of value and concern to the public. The arguably inappropriate or controversial character of a statement is irrelevant to the question whether it deals with a matter of public concern.

Id. at 453, 131 S.Ct. 1207 (citations and quotations omitted).

Considering the content (though not the viewpoint) of the picketers' signs in context, the Court concluded that the messages plainly related to "broad issues of interest to society at large," rather than matters of "purely private concern." Id. at 454, 131 S.Ct. 1207 (quotation omitted). The signs conveyed Westboro's views concerning "the political and moral conduct of the United States and its citizens, the fate of our Nation, homosexuality in the military, and scandals involving the Catholic clergy"—all "matters of public import." Id. The signs conveyed the church's position on these issues in a manner designed "to reach as broad a public audience as possible." Id. Because "Westboro's speech was at a public place on a matter of public concern," it was "entitled to 'special protection' under the First Amendment," which could not "be overcome by a jury finding that the picketing was outrageous." Id. at 458, 131 S.Ct. 1207. The Court therefore set aside the jury verdict that imposed tort liability on Westboro for intentional infliction of emotional distress.

The proscribed speech in this case has no connection to matters of public concern. By definition, the proscribed images must depict nudity or sexual conduct, § 2606(b)(1); must be disseminated without the consent of the victim, id.; cannot include images in settings in which a person does not have a reasonable expectation of privacy, id. § 2606(d)(1); cannot include disclosures made in the public interest, including reporting concerning various specified matters, id. § 2606(d)(2); and may not constitute a matter of public concern, id. § 2606(d)(3). By definition, the speech subject to regulation under § 2606 involves the most private of matters, with the least possible relationship to matters of public concern.

Moreover, nonconsensual pornography is remarkably common, and the injuries it inflicts are substantial. A 2014 estimate set the number of websites featuring nonconsensual pornography at 3,000. Revenge Porn: Misery Merchants, The Economist (July 5, 2014), http://www.economist. com/news/international/21606307-how-should-online-publication-explicit-images-without-their-subjects-consent-be [https://perma.cc/93MV-KNWL]. That number has no doubt grown. One recent survey found that that two percent of U.S. internet users have been the victim of nonconsensual pornography—that is, someone actually posted an explicit video or image of them online without their consent. A. Lenhart, M. Ybarra, M. Price-Feeney, Data & Society Research Institute and Center for Innovative

Public Health Research, <u>Nonconsensual Image Sharing: One in 25 Americans Has Been a Victim of "Revenge Porn,"</u> 4 (Dec. 13, 2016), https://datasociety.net/pubs/oh/Nonconsensual_Image_Sharing_2016.pdf [https://perma.cc/3995-QXAH]. A survey of victims of nonconsensual pornography found that in over fifty percent of the cases the nude images were published alongside the victim's full name and social network profile, and over twenty percent of victims reported that their email addresses and telephone numbers appeared alongside the images. D. Citron & M. Franks, <u>supra</u>, at 350–51.

The harm to the victims of nonconsensual pornography can be substantial. Images and videos can be directly disseminated to the victim's friends, family, and employers; posted and "tagged" (as in this case) so they are particularly visible to members of a victim's own community; and posted with identifying information such that they catapult to the top of the results of an online search of an individual's name. In the constellation of privacy interests, it is difficult to imagine something more private than images depicting an individual engaging in sexual conduct, or of a person's genitals, anus, or pubic area, that the person has not consented to sharing publicly. The personal consequences of such profound personal violation and humiliation generally include, at a minimum, extreme emotional distress. See <u>id.</u> at 351 (citing data that over eighty percent of victims report severe emotional distress and anxiety). Amici cited numerous instances in which the violation led the victim to suicide. Moreover, the posted images can lead employers to fire victims. See, e.g., <u>Warren City Bd. of Educ.</u>, 124 Lab. Arb. Rep. (BNA) 532, 536–37 (2007) (arbitration decision upholding termination of teacher fired after ex-spouse distributed nude images online and in community). A Microsoft-commissioned survey found that an internet search is a standard part of most employers' hiring processes. Cross-tab, <u>Online Reputation in a Connected World</u>, 6 (2010) https://www.job-hunt.org/guides/DPD_Online-Reputation-Research_overview.pdf [https://perma.cc/QGV2-A9JX]. For that reason, nonconsensual pornography posted online can be a significant obstacle to getting a job. Moreover, the widespread dissemination of these images can lead to harassment, extortion, unwelcome sexual attention, and threats of violence. See D. Citron & M. Franks, <u>supra</u>, at 350–54. The government's interest in preventing any intrusions on individual privacy is substantial; it's at its highest when the invasion of privacy takes the form of nonconsensual pornography.

Finally, the government's interest in preventing the nonconsensual disclosure of nude or sexual images of a person obtained in the context of a confidential relationship is at least as strong as its interest in preventing the disclosure of information concerning that person's health or finances obtained in the context of a confidential relationship; content-based restrictions on speech to prevent these other disclosures are uncontroversial and widely accepted as consistent with the First

Amendment. Doctors who disclose individually identifiable health information without permission may be subject to a $50,000 fine and a term of imprisonment for up to a year. 42 U.S.C. § 1320d–6. Banks are prohibited from disclosing to third-parties nonpublic, personal information about their customers without first giving the customers a chance to "opt out." 15 U.S.C. § 6802(b). In fact, in <u>Vermont</u> financial institutions can only make such disclosures if customers "opt in." Reg. B–2018–01: Privacy of Consumer Financial and Health Information § 11, Code of Vt. Rules 21 010 016, http://www.lexisnexis.com/hottopics/codeofvtrules. A violation of this requirement is subject to a fine of up to $15,000. <u>Id.</u> § 24; 8 V.S.A. § 10205; 8 V.S.A. § 11601(a)(4). And nonconsensual disclosure of individuals' social security numbers in violation of U.S. law can subject the discloser to fines and imprisonment for up to five years. 42 U.S.C. § 408(a)(8). In these cases, it is obvious that the harm to be addressed flows from the disclosure of personal information. The fact that the disclosure requires speech, and that restriction of that speech is based squarely on its content, does not undermine the government's compelling interest in preventing such disclosures. From a constitutional perspective, it is hard to see a distinction between laws prohibiting nonconsensual disclosure of personal information comprising images of nudity and sexual conduct and those prohibiting disclosure of other categories of nonpublic personal information. The government's interest in protecting all from disclosure is strong.

For the above reasons, we conclude that the State interest underlying § 2606 is compelling. Accord <u>People v. Iniguez</u>, 247 Cal.App.4th Supp. 1, 202 Cal.Rptr.3d 237, 243 (App. Dep't Super. Ct. 2016) ("It is evident that barring persons from intentionally causing others serious emotional distress through the distribution of photos of their intimate body parts is a compelling need of society.").

2.   Narrowly Tailored

Section 2606 defines unlawful nonconsensual pornography narrowly, including limiting it to a confined class of content, a rigorous intent element that encompasses the nonconsent requirement, an objective requirement that the disclosure would cause a reasonable person harm, an express exclusion of images warranting greater constitutional protection, and a limitation to only those images that support the State's compelling interest because their disclosure would violate a reasonable expectation of privacy. Our conclusion on this point is bolstered by a narrowing interpretation of one provision that we offer to ensure that the statute is duly narrowly tailored. The fact that the statute provides for criminal as well as civil liability does not render it inadequately tailored.

The images subject to § 2606 are precisely defined, with little gray area or risk of sweeping in constitutionally protected speech. Nude images are defined as those showing genitalia, the pubic area, anus, or post-pubescent female nipple. 13 V.S.A. § 2606(a)(3). Sexual conduct involves contact between the mouth and penis, anus or vulva, or between two of the latter three; intrusion by any part of a person's body or object into the genital or anal opening of another with the intent to appeal to sexual desire; intentional touching (not through the clothing) of the genitals, anus or breasts of another with the intent of appealing to sexual desire, masturbation, bestiality, or sadomasochistic abuse for sexual purposes. See id. § 2606(a)(4); id. § 2821. The individual depicted in the image must be identifiable. Id. § 2606(b)(1).

Moreover, disclosure is only criminal if the discloser <u>knowingly</u> discloses the images without the victim's consent. Id. We construe this intent requirement to require knowledge of both the fact of disclosing, and the fact of nonconsent. See <u>State v. Richland</u>, 2015 VT 126, ¶¶ 9–11, 200 Vt. 401, 132 A.3d 702 (discussing presumption that statutory state-of-mind requirement applies to all elements of offense). Individuals are highly unlikely to accidentally violate this statute while engaging in otherwise permitted speech. In fact, § 2606 goes further, requiring not only knowledge of the above elements, but a specific intent to harm, harass, intimidate, threaten, or coerce the person depicted or to profit financially. 13 V.S.A. § 2606(b)(1), (2).

In addition, the disclosure must be one that would cause a <u>reasonable</u> person "physical injury, financial injury, or serious emotional distress." Id. § 2606(a)(2), (b)(1). The statute is not designed to protect overly fragile sensibilities, and does not reach even knowing, nonconsensual disclosures of images falling within the narrow statutory parameters unless disclosure would cause a reasonable person to suffer harm.

Two additional limitations assuage any concern that some content meeting all of these requirements may nonetheless implicate a matter of public concern. First, the statute does not purport to reach "[d]isclosures made in the public interest, including the reporting of unlawful conduct, or lawful and common practices of law enforcement, criminal reporting, corrections, legal proceedings, or medical treatment." Id. § 2606(d)(2). This broad and nonexclusive list of permitted disclosures is designed to exclude from the statute's reach disclosures that do implicate First Amendment concerns—those made in the public interest. Second, even if a disclosure is not made "in the public interest," if the materials disclosed "constitute a matter of public concern," they are excluded from the statute's reach. Id. § 2606(d)(3). The Legislature has made every effort to ensure that its prohibition is limited to communication of purely private matters with respect to which the State's interest is the strongest and the First Amendment concerns the weakest.

Finally, to ensure that the statute reaches only those disclosures implicating the right to privacy the statute seeks to protect, it expressly excludes "[i]mages involving voluntary nudity or sexual conduct in public or commercial settings or in a place where a person does not have a reasonable expectation of privacy." Id. § 2606(d)(1). Where an individual does not have a reasonable expectation of privacy in an image, the State's interest in protecting the individual's privacy interest in that image is minimal. The statute recognizes this fact.

In connection with this factor, we offer a narrowing construction, or clarification of the statute to ensure its constitutional application while promoting the Legislature's goals. See Tracy, 2015 VT 111, ¶ 28, 200 Vt. 216, 130 A.3d 196 (noting our obligation to construe statutes to avoid constitutional infirmities where possible, and to avoid facial challenges if there is readily apparent construction of statute that can rehabilitate constitutional infirmity). The statute's exclusion of otherwise qualifying images involving voluntary nudity or sexual conduct in settings in which a person does not have a reasonable expectation of privacy, 13 V.S.A. § 2606(d)(1), does not clearly reach images recorded in a private setting but distributed by the person depicted to public or commercial settings or in a manner that undermines any reasonable expectation of privacy. From the perspective of the statute's goals, there is no practical difference between a nude photo someone voluntarily poses for in the public park and one taken in private that the person then voluntarily posts in that same public park. Given the Legislature's clear intent to protect peoples' reasonable expectations of privacy in intimate images of them, and to exclude from the statute's reach those images in which a person has no such reasonable expectation, it seems clear that the Legislature intends its exclusion to apply to images the person has distributed to the public, as well as those recorded in public. This construction also ensures that the scope of the statute is no broader than necessary to advance the State's interest in protecting reasonable expectations of privacy with respect to intimate images.

Given this narrowing construction, as well as all the express limitations on the statute's reach built into § 2606, we conclude that it is narrowly tailored to advance the State's compelling interest.

We reject defendant's suggestion that civil penalties are necessarily less restrictive than criminal penalties, and that because the statute includes criminal penalties as well as the potential for civil liability it is broader than necessary to advance the State's interest. The Supreme Court has acknowledged that civil and criminal penalties do not stand in a clear hierarchy from the perspective of chilling speech. In Sullivan, the Court explained, "What a State may not constitutionally bring about by means of a criminal statute is likewise beyond the reach of its civil law of libel. The fear of [civil] damage awards . . . may be markedly more inhibiting than the fear of prosecution under a criminal statute." 376 U.S. at 277, 84 S.Ct. 710. In fact, the Court noted that people charged criminally enjoy greater procedural safeguards than those facing civil suit, and the prospect of steep civil damages can chill speech even more than that of criminal prosecution.

Id. See also Garrison, 379 U.S. at 67 n.3, 85 S.Ct. 209 ("Whether the libel law be civil or criminal, it must satisfy relevant constitutional standards.").

For the above reasons, the statute is narrowly tailored to advance the State's interests, does not penalize more speech than necessary to accomplish its aim, and does not risk chilling protected speech on matters of public concern. We accordingly conclude that 13 V.S.A. § 2606 is constitutional on its face.

SKOGLUND, J., dissenting.

Defendant raises a constitutional challenge to Vermont's version of a so-called "revenge porn" statute, 13 V.S.A. § 2606. The trial court found the statute abridges freedom of speech protected by the First Amendment and, thus, was unconstitutional. I agree and would affirm on that basis.

Section 2606, entitled "Disclosure of sexually explicit images without consent," was enacted in 2015 as part of a national attempt to criminalize revenge-porn dissemination, or what is sometimes described as "nonconsensual pornography," and thus safeguard sexual autonomy in the digital age. See generally R. Patton, Taking the Sting Out of Revenge Porn: Using Criminal Statutes to Safeguard Sexual Autonomy in the Digital Age, 16 Geo. J. of Gender & L. 407 (2015). It was an attempt to protect against the mortifying consequences of sexting—the making and sending of explicit pictures of oneself using digital devices. Forty states have acknowledged these issues and enacted legislation to address them. Cyber Civil Rights Initiative, 40 States + DC Have Revenge Porn Laws, https://www.cybercivil rights.org/revenge-porn-laws/ [https://perma.cc/83UK-KKUS] (collecting state statutes). Under Section 2606, Vermont prohibits "knowingly disclos[ing] a visual image of an identifiable person who is nude or who is engaged in sexual conduct, without his or her consent, with the intent to harm, harass, intimidate, threaten, or coerce the person depicted and the disclosure would cause a reasonable person to suffer harm." 13 V.S.A. § 2606(b)(1).

The affidavits and stipulated facts described the following. Complainant took photographs of herself while nude or partially nude and sent them to Anthony Coon's Facebook Messenger account. Coons and complainant were not in a relationship, nor did he request she send the photographs. The photographs themselves were not introduced into evidence—the parties agreed they met the definition of "nude" in § 2606(a)(3), but that they were not necessarily obscene. Though defendant did not have permission from Mr. Coon to access his Facebook account, she did so and discovered the photographs complainant sent. Defendant posted the photographs onto a public Facebook page and "tagged" complainant in them. For purposes of the motion to dismiss, defendant admitted that she did this for revenge and to get back at complainant for her prior relationship with Mr. Coon and for sending him the nude photographs.

The trial court found that the "merely 'nude' photographs" could not be considered obscene and therefore were a protected form of speech and not subject to the "narrow and well-defined classes of expression" that are seen to carry "so little social value . . . that the State can prohibit and punish such expression." Connick v. Myers, 461 U.S. 138, 147, 103 S.Ct. 1684, 75 L.Ed.2d 708 (1983). The court then reasoned that, in this content-discrimination case, because the images were not obscene, it had to review the statute and its prohibitions under a strict scrutiny basis. It further opined that the element of "revenge" in the statute did not allow for enlargement of unprotected speech under the First Amendment.

Section 2606 is not "narrowly tailored to promote a compelling Government interest." Id.; see also United States v. Stevens, 559 U.S. 460, 468–69, 130 S.Ct. 1577, 176 L.Ed.2d 435 (2010). Moreover, a less restrictive alternative exists. Playboy Entm't Grp., Inc., 529 U.S. at 813, 120 S.Ct. 1878. Therefore, I would affirm the trial court's order holding that the statute cannot survive strict scrutiny.

First, I do not agree that the government has a compelling interest. Does the statute relate to matters of public concern? Speech deals with matters of public concern when it can be "fairly considered as relating to any matter of political, social, or other concern to the community." Connick, 461 U.S. at 146, 103 S.Ct. 1684. I agree the speech protected by the statute cannot be considered as relating to matters of public concern and, thus, does not carry as much weight in the strict scrutiny analysis as speech concerning matters of public concern. "First Amendment protections are often less rigorous . . . because restricting speech on purely private matters does not implicate the same constitutional concerns as limiting speech on matters of public interest." Snyder v. Phelps, 562 U.S. 443, 452, 131 S.Ct. 1207, 179 L.Ed.2d 172 (2011). Can revenge porn cause extreme emotional distress? Oh, yes. However, while the majority finds a compelling State interest in preventing the nonconsensual disclosure of nude or sexual images of a person obtained in the context of a confidential relationship, I cannot agree that, in this day and age of the internet, the State can reasonably assume a role in protecting people from their own folly and trump First Amendment protections for speech.

Next, the statute fails to survive strict scrutiny because it is not narrowly tailored, nor does it provide the least restrictive means of dealing with the perceived problem. As explained above, the statute criminalizes dissemination of nude imagery or any sexual conduct of a person without that person's consent and with a bad motive. Reduced to its essential purpose, it criminalizes an invasion of personal privacy.

My primary war with the statute is simply this. The State has at its disposal less restrictive means to protect Vermonters against invasion of their privacy than subjecting a violator to a criminal penalty. Section 2606 does provide for a civil remedy. Subsection (e) provides plaintiff a private cause of action against a defendant who knowingly discloses, without the plaintiff's consent, an identifiable visual image of the plaintiff while he or she is nude or engaged in sexual conduct and the disclosure causes the plaintiff harm. It also provides for relief in the form of equitable relief, a temporary restraining order, a preliminary injunction or permanent injunction. While the State argued that the private right of action may fail to deter and punish publishers of nonconsensual pornography because "[m]ost victims lack resources to bring lawsuits, [and] many individual defendants are judgment-proof," the potential success of a private right of action is irrelevant in determining whether less restrictive alternative exists. One could always bring an action alleging intentional infliction of emotional distress. The Legislature could provide for triple damages and require that attorney's fees be awarded the prevailing party. There is a myriad of ways to provide protection to people short of criminal charges.

The statute's ambiguities concerning the scope of its coverage, even with the limiting interpretation crafted by the majority, coupled with its increased deterrent effect as a criminal statute, raise special First Amendment concerns because of its obvious chilling effect on free speech. "Criminal punishment by government, although universally recognized as a necessity in limited areas of conduct, is an exercise of one of government's most awesome and dangerous powers." Ginzburg v. United States, 383 U.S. 463, 477, 86 S.Ct. 969, 16 L.Ed.2d 31 (1966) (Black, J., dissenting). While disseminating "revenge porn" may be a repulsive and harmful action, the statute's attempt to criminalize this behavior runs afoul of the rights and privileges of the First Amendment. When content-based speech regulation is in question, exacting scrutiny is required. And, the burden placed on free speech due to its content is unacceptable if less restrictive alternatives would be at least as effective in achieving the statute's purposes. Civil avenues exist that can avenge an invasion of privacy or a deliberate infliction of emotional distress without criminalizing speech based on the content of the message. As the Supreme Court has said, "[s]tatutes suppressing or restricting speech must be judged by the sometimes inconvenient principles of the First Amendment." Alvarez, 567 U.S. at 715, 132 S.Ct. 2537. And, the First Amendment protects us all with an even hand.

I would affirm on this basis.

DISCUSSION QUESTIONS

1. Does this statute serve a compelling interest?

2. Is it narrowly tailored?

3. As a matter of policy, should this behavior be a crime, or is civil liability sufficient?

Case in Context

A number of jurisdictions created sweeping offenses to deal with the existence of criminal gangs. The Supreme Court heard a challenge to one such ordnance.

CITY OF CHICAGO V. JESUS MORALES ET AL.

Supreme Court of the United States
527 U.S. 41 (1999)

JUSTICE STEVENS announced the judgment of the Court and delivered the opinion of the Court with respect to Parts I, II, and V, and an opinion with respect to Parts III, IV, and VI, in which JUSTICE SOUTER and JUSTICE GINSBURG join.

In 1992, the Chicago City Council enacted the Gang Congregation Ordinance, which prohibits "criminal street gang members" from "loitering" with one another or with other persons in any public place. The question presented is whether the Supreme Court of Illinois correctly held that the ordinance violates the Due Process Clause of the Fourteenth Amendment to the Federal Constitution.

I

Before the ordinance was adopted, the city council's Committee on Police and Fire conducted hearings to explore the problems created by the city's street gangs, and more particularly, the consequences of public loitering by gang members. Witnesses included residents of the neighborhoods where gang members are most active, as well as some of the aldermen who represent those areas. Based on that evidence, the council made a series of findings that are included in the text of the ordinance and explain the reasons for its enactment.

The council found that a continuing increase in criminal street gang activity was largely responsible for the city's rising murder rate, as well as an escalation of violent and drug related crimes. It noted that in many neighborhoods throughout the city, " 'the burgeoning presence of street gang members in public places has intimidated many law abiding citizens.' " 177 Ill.2d 440, 445, 227 Ill.Dec. 130, 687 N.E.2d 53, 58 (1997). Furthermore, the council stated that gang members " 'establish control over identifiable areas . . . by loitering in those areas and intimidating others from entering those areas; and . . . [m]embers of criminal street gangs avoid arrest by committing no offense punishable under existing laws when they know the police are present. . . .' " *Ibid.* It further found that " 'loitering in public places by criminal street gang members creates a justifiable fear for the safety of persons and property in the area' " and that " '[a]ggressive action is necessary to preserve the city's streets and other public places so that the public may use such places without fear.' " Moreover, the council concluded that the city " 'has an interest in discouraging all persons from loitering in public places with criminal gang members.' " *Ibid.*

The ordinance creates a criminal offense punishable by a fine of up to $500, imprisonment for not more than six months, and a requirement to perform up to 120 hours of community service. Commission of the offense involves four predicates. First, the police officer must reasonably believe that at least one of the two or more persons present in a " 'public place' " is a " 'criminal street gang membe[r].' " Second, the persons must be " 'loitering,' " which the ordinance defines as "remain[ing] in any one place with no apparent purpose." Third, the officer must then order " 'all' " of the persons to disperse and remove themselves " 'from the area.' " Fourth, a person must disobey the officer's order. If any person, whether a gang member or not, disobeys the officer's order, that person is guilty of violating the ordinance. *Ibid.*

Two months after the ordinance was adopted, the Chicago Police Department promulgated General Order 92–4 to provide guidelines to govern its enforcement. That order purported to establish limitations on the enforcement discretion of police officers "to ensure that the anti-gang loitering ordinance is not enforced in an arbitrary or discriminatory way." Chicago Police Department, General Order 92–4, reprinted in App. to Pet. for Cert. 65a. The limitations confine the authority to arrest gang members who violate the ordinance to sworn "members of the Gang Crime Section" and certain other designated officers, and establish detailed criteria for defining street gangs and membership in such gangs. *Id.,* at 66a–67a. In addition, the order directs district commanders to "designate areas in which the presence of gang members has a demonstrable effect on the activities of law abiding persons in the surrounding community," and provides that the ordinance "will be enforced only within the designated areas." *Id.,* at 68a–69 a. The city, however, does not release the locations of these "designated areas" to the public.

II

During the three years of its enforcement, the police issued over 89,000 dispersal orders and arrested over 42,000 people for violating the ordinance. In the ensuing enforcement proceedings, 2 trial judges upheld the constitutionality of the ordinance, but 11 others ruled that it was invalid. In respondent Youkhana's case, the trial judge held that the "ordinance fails to notify individuals what conduct is prohibited, and it encourages arbitrary and capricious enforcement by police."

The Illinois Appellate Court affirmed the trial court's ruling in the *Youkhana* case, consolidated and affirmed other pending appeals in accordance with *Youkhana,* and reversed the convictions of respondents Gutierrez, Morales, and others. The Appellate Court was persuaded that the ordinance impaired the freedom of assembly of nongang members in violation of the First Amendment to the Federal Constitution and Article I of the Illinois Constitution, that it was unconstitutionally vague. . .

The Illinois Supreme Court affirmed. It held "that the gang loitering ordinance violates due process of law in that it is impermissibly vague on its face and an arbitrary restriction on personal liberties." 177 Ill.2d, at 447, 227 Ill.Dec. 130, 687 N.E.2d, at 59. . . .

. . .

We granted certiorari, 523 U.S. 1071, 118 S.Ct. 1510, 140 L.Ed.2d 664 (1998), and now affirm. Like the Illinois Supreme Court, we conclude that the ordinance enacted by the city of Chicago is unconstitutionally vague.

III

The basic factual predicate for the city's ordinance is not in dispute. As the city argues in its brief, "the very presence of a large collection of obviously brazen, insistent, and lawless gang members and hangers-on on the public ways intimidates residents, who become afraid even to leave their homes and go about their business. That, in turn, imperils community residents' sense of safety and security, detracts from property values, and can ultimately destabilize entire neighborhoods." The findings in the ordinance explain that it was motivated by these concerns. We have no doubt that a law that directly prohibited such intimidating conduct would be constitutional, but this ordinance broadly covers a significant amount of additional activity. Uncertainty about the scope of that additional coverage provides the basis for respondents' claim that the ordinance is too vague.

. . .

. . .The freedom to loiter for innocent purposes is part of the "liberty" protected by the Due Process Clause of the Fourteenth Amendment. We have expressly identified this "right to remove from one place to another according to inclination" as "an attribute of personal liberty" protected by the Constitution. *Williams v. Fears,* 179 U.S. 270, 274 (1900). Indeed, it is apparent that an individual's decision to remain in a public place of his choice is as much a part of his liberty as the freedom of movement inside frontiers that is "a part of our heritage" *Kent v. Dulles,* 357 U.S. 116, 126 (1958), or the right to move "to whatsoever place one's own inclination may direct" identified in Blackstone's Commentaries. 1 W. Blackstone, Commentaries on the Laws of England 130 (1765).

There is no need, however, to decide whether the impact of the Chicago ordinance on constitutionally protected liberty alone would suffice to support a facial challenge under the overbreadth doctrine. . . .For it is clear that the vagueness of this enactment makes a facial challenge appropriate.

Vagueness may invalidate a criminal law for either of two independent reasons. First, it may fail to provide the kind of notice that will enable ordinary people to understand what conduct it prohibits; second, it may

Recognizing that the ordinance does reach a substantial amount of innocent conduct, we turn, then, to its language to determine if it "necessarily entrusts lawmaking to the moment-to-moment judgment of the policeman on his beat." *Kolender v. Lawson,* 461 U.S., at 360, 103 S.Ct. 1855 (internal quotation marks omitted). As we discussed in the context of fair notice, see *supra,* at 1859–1860, this page, the principal source of the vast discretion conferred on the police in this case is the definition of loitering as "to remain in any one place with no apparent purpose."

As the Illinois Supreme Court interprets that definition, it "provides absolute discretion to police officers to decide what activities constitute loitering." 177 Ill.2d, at 457, 227 Ill.Dec. We have no authority to construe the language of a state statute more narrowly than the construction given by that State's highest court. "The power to determine the meaning of a statute carries with it the power to prescribe its extent and limitations as well as the method by which they shall be determined." *Smiley v. Kansas,* 196 U.S. 447, 455 (1905).

Presumably an officer would have discretion to treat some purposes— perhaps a purpose to engage in idle conversation or simply to enjoy a cool breeze on a warm evening—as too frivolous to be apparent if he suspected a different ulterior motive. Moreover, an officer conscious of the city council's reasons for enacting the ordinance might well ignore its text and issue a dispersal order, even though an illicit purpose is actually apparent.

It is true, as the city argues, that the requirement that the officer reasonably believe that a group of loiterers contains a gang member does place a limit on the authority to order dispersal. That limitation would no doubt be sufficient if the ordinance only applied to loitering that had an apparently harmful purpose or effect, or possibly if it only applied to loitering by persons reasonably believed to be criminal gang members. But this ordinance, for reasons that are not explained in the findings of the city council, requires no harmful purpose and applies to nongang members as well as suspected gang members. It applies to everyone in the city who may remain in one place with one suspected gang member as long as their purpose is not apparent to an officer observing them. Friends, relatives, teachers, counselors, or even total strangers might unwittingly engage in forbidden loitering if they happen to engage in idle conversation with a gang member.

Ironically, the definition of loitering in the Chicago ordinance not only extends its scope to encompass harmless conduct, but also has the perverse consequence of excluding from its coverage much of the intimidating conduct that motivated its enactment. As the city council's findings demonstrate, the most harmful gang loitering is motivated either by an apparent purpose to publicize the gang's dominance of certain territory, thereby intimidating nonmembers, or by an equally apparent purpose to conceal ongoing commerce in illegal drugs. As the Illinois Supreme Court has not placed any limiting construction on the language in the ordinance, we must assume that the ordinance means what it says and that it has no application to loiterers whose purpose is apparent. The relative importance of its application to harmless loitering is magnified by its inapplicability to loitering that has an obviously threatening or illicit purpose.

Finally, in its opinion striking down the ordinance, the Illinois Supreme Court refused to accept the general order issued by the police department as a sufficient limitation on the "vast amount of discretion" granted to the police in its enforcement. We agree. See *Smith v. Goguen,* 415 U.S. 566, 575, 94 S.Ct. 1242, 39 L.Ed.2d 605 (1974). That the police have adopted internal rules limiting their enforcement to certain designated areas in the city would not provide a defense to a loiterer who might be arrested elsewhere. Nor could a person who knowingly loitered with a well-known gang member anywhere in the city safely assume that they would not be ordered to disperse no matter how innocent and harmless their loitering might be.

VI

In our judgment, the Illinois Supreme Court correctly concluded that the ordinance does not provide sufficiently specific limits on the enforcement discretion of the police "to meet constitutional standards for definiteness and clarity." 177 Ill.2d, at 459, 227 Ill.Dec. 130, 687 N.E.2d, at 64. We recognize the serious and difficult problems testified to by the citizens of Chicago that led to the enactment of this ordinance. "We are mindful that the preservation of liberty depends in part on the maintenance of social order." *Houston v. Hill,* 482 U.S. 451, 471–472, 107 S.Ct. 2502, 96 L.Ed.2d 398 (1987). However, in this instance the city has enacted an ordinance that affords too much discretion to the police and too little notice to citizens who wish to use the public streets.

Accordingly, the judgment of the Supreme Court of Illinois is

Affirmed.

DISCUSSION QUESTIONS

1.   Is the court saying that the word "loiter" is itself unconstitutionally vague? Could a state constitutionally prohibit "loitering with an intent to intimidate"?

2.   Why didn't the city simply make it a crime to be a member of a criminal gang?

3.   Communities of color in Chicago were most affected by gang-related homicides, and many leaders in those communities supported this ordinance. Should that matter constitutionally?

G. SPECIAL FOCUS: SEXUAL AUTONOMY

The Supreme Court has over the years entertained constitutional challenges to laws criminalizing consensual sexual activity between members of the same sex. The following landmark case struck down such a statute on constitutional grounds.

LAWRENCE V. TEXAS
Supreme Court of the United States
539 U.S. 558 (2003)

JUSTICE KENNEDY delivered the opinion of the Court.

Liberty protects the person from unwarranted government intrusions into a dwelling or other private places. In our tradition the State is not omnipresent in the home. And there are other spheres of our lives and existence, outside the home, where the State should not be a dominant presence. Freedom extends beyond spatial bounds. Liberty presumes an autonomy of self that includes freedom of thought, belief, expression, and certain intimate conduct. The instant case involves liberty of the person both in its spatial and more transcendent dimensions.

I

The question before the Court is the validity of a Texas statute making it a crime for two persons of the same sex to engage in certain intimate sexual conduct.

In Houston, Texas, officers of the Harris County Police Department were dispatched to a private residence in response to a reported weapons disturbance. They entered an apartment where one of the petitioners, John Geddes Lawrence, resided. The right of the police to enter does not seem to have been questioned. The officers observed Lawrence and another man, Tyron Garner, engaging in a sexual act. The two petitioners were arrested, held in custody over night, and charged and convicted before a Justice of the Peace.

The complaints described their crime as "deviate sexual intercourse, namely anal sex, with a member of the same sex (man)." App. to Pet. for Cert. 127a, 139a. The applicable state law is Tex. Penal Code Ann. § 21.06(a) (2003). It provides: "A person commits an offense if he engages in deviate sexual intercourse with another individual of the same sex." The statute defines "[d]eviate sexual intercourse" as follows:

"(A) any contact between any part of the genitals of one person and the mouth or anus of another person; or

"(B) the penetration of the genitals or the anus of another person with an object." § 21.01(1).

The petitioners exercised their right to a trial de novo in Harris County Criminal Court. They challenged the statute as a violation of the Equal Protection Clause of the Fourteenth Amendment and of a like provision of the Texas Constitution. Tex. Const., Art. 1, § 3a. Those contentions were rejected. The petitioners, having entered a plea of nolo contendere, were each fined $200 and assessed court costs of $141.25. App. to Pet. for Cert. 107a–110a.

The petitioners were adults at the time of the alleged offense. Their conduct was in private and consensual.

II

We conclude the case should be resolved by determining whether the petitioners were free as adults to engage in the private conduct in the exercise of their liberty under the Due Process Clause of the Fourteenth Amendment to the Constitution. For this inquiry we deem it necessary to reconsider the Court's holding in Bowers.

The facts in Bowers had some similarities to the instant case. A police officer, whose right to enter seems not to have been in question, observed Hardwick, in his own bedroom, engaging in intimate sexual conduct with another adult male. The conduct was in violation of a Georgia statute making it a criminal offense to engage in sodomy. One difference between the two cases is that the Georgia statute prohibited the conduct whether or not the participants were of the same sex, while the Texas statute, as we have seen, applies only to participants of the same sex. Hardwick was not prosecuted, but he brought an action in federal court to declare the state statute invalid. He alleged he was a practicing homosexual and that the criminal prohibition violated rights guaranteed to him by the Constitution. The Court, in an opinion by Justice White, sustained the Georgia law. Chief Justice Burger and Justice Powell joined the opinion of the Court and filed separate, concurring opinions. Four Justices dissented. 478 U.S., at 199 (opinion of Blackmun, J., joined by Brennan, Marshall, and Stevens, JJ.); id., at 214 (opinion of Stevens, J., joined by Brennan and Marshall, JJ.).

The Court began its substantive discussion in Bowers as follows: "The issue presented is whether the Federal Constitution confers a fundamental right upon homosexuals to engage in sodomy and hence invalidates the laws of the many States that still make such conduct illegal and have done so for a very long time." Id., at 190. That statement, we now conclude, discloses the Court's own failure to appreciate the extent of the liberty at stake. To say that the issue in Bowers was simply the right to engage in certain sexual conduct demeans the claim the individual put forward, just as it would demean a married couple were it to be said marriage is simply about the right to have sexual intercourse. The laws involved in Bowers and here are, to be sure, statutes that purport to do no more than prohibit a particular sexual act. Their penalties and purposes, though, have more far-reaching consequences, touching upon the most private human conduct, sexual behavior, and in the most private of places, the home. The statutes do seek to control a personal relationship that, whether or not entitled to formal recognition in the law, is within the liberty of persons to choose without being punished as criminals.

This, as a general rule, should counsel against attempts by the State, or a court, to define the meaning of the relationship or to set its boundaries absent injury to a person or abuse of an institution the law protects. It suffices for us to acknowledge that adults may choose to enter upon this relationship in the confines of their homes and their own private lives and still retain their dignity as free persons. When sexuality finds overt expression in intimate conduct with another person, the conduct can be but one element in a personal bond that is more enduring. The liberty protected by the Constitution allows homosexual persons the right to make this choice.

Having misapprehended the claim of liberty there presented to it, and thus stating the claim to be whether there is a fundamental right to engage in consensual sodomy, the Bowers Court said: "Proscriptions against that conduct have ancient roots." Id., at 192. In academic writings, and in many of the scholarly amicus briefs filed to assist the Court in this case, there are fundamental criticisms of the historical premises relied upon by the majority and concurring opinions in Bowers. Brief for Cato Institute as Amicus Curiae 16–17; Brief for American Civil Liberties Union et al. as Amici Curiae 15–21; Brief for Professors of History et al. as Amici Curiae 3–10. We need not enter this debate in the attempt to reach a definitive historical judgment, but the following considerations counsel against adopting the definitive conclusions upon which Bowers placed such reliance.

At the outset it should be noted that there is no longstanding history in this country of laws directed at homosexual conduct as a distinct matter. Beginning in colonial times there were prohibitions of sodomy derived from the English criminal laws passed in the first instance by the Reformation Parliament of 1533. The English prohibition was understood to include relations between men and women as well as relations between men and men. See, e.g., King v. Wiseman, 92 Eng. Rep. 774, 775 (K. B. 1718) (interpreting "mankind" in Act of 1533 as including women and girls). Nineteenth-century commentators similarly read American sodomy, buggery, and crime-against-nature statutes as criminalizing certain relations between men and women and between men and men. See, e.g., 2 J. Bishop, Criminal Law § 1028 (1858); 2 J. Chitty, Criminal Law 47–50 (5th Am. ed. 1847); R. Desty, A Compendium of American Criminal Law 143 (1882); J. May, The Law of Crimes § 203 (2d ed. 1893). The absence of legal prohibitions focusing on homosexual conduct may be explained in part by noting that according to some scholars the concept of the homosexual as a distinct category of person did not emerge until the late

19th century. See, e.g., J. Katz, The Invention of Heterosexuality 10 (1995); J. D'Emilio & E. Freedman, Intimate Matters: A History of Sexuality in America 121 (2d ed. 1997) ("The modern terms homosexuality and heterosexuality do not apply to an era that had not yet articulated these distinctions"). Thus early American sodomy laws were not directed at homosexuals as such but instead sought to prohibit nonprocreative sexual activity more generally. This does not suggest approval of homosexual conduct. It does tend to show that this particular form of conduct was not thought of as a separate category from like conduct between heterosexual persons.

Laws prohibiting sodomy do not seem to have been enforced against consenting adults acting in private. A substantial number of sodomy prosecutions and convictions for which there are surviving records were for predatory acts against those who could not or did not consent, as in the case of a minor or the victim of an assault. As to these, one purpose for the prohibitions was to ensure there would be no lack of coverage if a predator committed a sexual assault that did not constitute rape as defined by the criminal law. Thus the model sodomy indictments presented in a 19th-century treatise, see 2 Chitty, supra, at 49, addressed the predatory acts of an adult man against a minor girl or minor boy. Instead of targeting relations between consenting adults in private, 19th-century sodomy prosecutions typically involved relations between men and minor girls or minor boys, relations between adults involving force, relations between adults implicating disparity in status, or relations between men and animals.

It was not until the 1970's that any State singled out same-sex relations for criminal prosecution, and only nine States have done so. Post-Bowers even some of these States did not adhere to the policy of suppressing homosexual conduct. Over the course of the last decades, States with same-sex prohibitions have moved toward abolishing them.

In summary, the historical grounds relied upon in Bowers are more complex than the majority opinion and the concurring opinion by Chief Justice Burger indicate. Their historical premises are not without doubt and, at the very least, are overstated.

It must be acknowledged, of course, that the Court in Bowers was making the broader point that for centuries there have been powerful voices to condemn homosexual conduct as immoral. The condemnation has been shaped by religious beliefs, conceptions of right and acceptable behavior, and respect for the traditional family. For many persons these are not trivial concerns but profound and deep convictions accepted as ethical and moral principles to which they aspire and which thus determine the course of their lives. These considerations do not answer the question before us, however. The issue is whether the majority may use the power of the State to enforce these views on the whole society through operation of the criminal law. "Our obligation is to define the liberty of all, not to mandate our own moral code." Planned Parenthood of Southeastern Pa. v. Casey, 505 U.S. 833, 850 (1992).

In our own constitutional system the deficiencies in Bowers became even more apparent in the years following its announcement. The 25 States with laws prohibiting the relevant conduct referenced in the Bowers decision are reduced now to 13, of which 4 enforce their laws only against homosexual conduct. In those States where sodomy is still proscribed, whether for same-sex or heterosexual conduct, there is a pattern of nonenforcement with respect to consenting adults acting in private. The State of Texas admitted in 1994 that as of that date it had not prosecuted anyone under those circumstances. State v. Morales, 869 S. W. 2d 941, 943.

Two principal cases decided after Bowers cast its holding into even more doubt. In Planned Parenthood of Southeastern Pa. v. Casey, 505 U.S. 833 (1992), the Court reaffirmed the substantive force of the liberty protected by the Due Process Clause. The Casey decision again confirmed that our laws and tradition afford constitutional protection to personal decisions relating to marriage, procreation, contraception, family relationships, child rearing, and education. Id., at 851. In explaining the respect the Constitution demands for the autonomy of the person in making these choices, we stated as follows:

"These matters, involving the most intimate and personal choices a person may make in a lifetime, choices central to personal dignity and autonomy, are central to the liberty protected by the Fourteenth Amendment. At the heart of liberty is the right to define one's own concept of existence, of meaning, of the universe, and of the mystery of human life. Beliefs about these matters could not define the attributes of personhood were they formed under compulsion of the State." Ibid.

Persons in a homosexual relationship may seek autonomy for these purposes, just as heterosexual persons do. The decision in Bowers would deny them this right.

. . .

The rationale of Bowers does not withstand careful analysis. In his dissenting opinion in Bowers Justice Stevens came to these conclusions:

"Our prior cases make two propositions abundantly clear. First, the fact that the governing majority in a State has traditionally viewed a particular practice as immoral is not a sufficient reason for upholding a law prohibiting the practice; neither history nor tradition could save a law prohibiting miscegenation from constitutional attack. Second, individual decisions by married persons, concerning the intimacies of their physical relationship, even when not intended to produce offspring, are a form of "liberty" protected by the Due Process Clause of the Fourteenth

Amendment. Moreover, this protection extends to intimate choices by unmarried as well as married persons." 478 U.S., at 216 (footnotes and citations omitted).

Justice Stevens' analysis, in our view, should have been controlling in Bowers and should control here.

Bowers was not correct when it was decided, and it is not correct today. It ought not to remain binding precedent. Bowers v. Hardwick should be and now is overruled.

The present case does not involve minors. It does not involve persons who might be injured or coerced or who are situated in relationships where consent might not easily be refused. It does not involve public conduct or prostitution. It does not involve whether the government must give formal recognition to any relationship that homosexual persons seek to enter. The case does involve two adults who, with full and mutual consent from each other, engaged in sexual practices common to a homosexual lifestyle. The petitioners are entitled to respect for their private lives. The State cannot demean their existence or control their destiny by making their private sexual conduct a crime. Their right to liberty under the Due Process Clause gives them the full right to engage in their conduct without intervention of the government. "It is a promise of the Constitution that there is a realm of personal liberty which the government may not enter." Casey, supra, at 847. The Texas statute furthers no legitimate state interest which can justify its intrusion into the personal and private life of the individual.

Had those who drew and ratified the Due Process Clauses of the Fifth Amendment or the Fourteenth Amendment known the components of liberty in its manifold possibilities, they might have been more specific. They did not presume to have this insight. They knew times can blind us to certain truths and later generations can see that laws once thought necessary and proper in fact serve only to oppress. As the Constitution endures, persons in every generation can invoke its principles in their own search for greater freedom.

The judgment of the Court of Appeals for the Texas Fourteenth District is reversed, and the case is remanded for further proceedings not inconsistent with this opinion.

It is so ordered.

DISCUSSION QUESTIONS

1.   What exactly is the holding of this case? Where is it stated?

2.   Justice Kennedy observes that attitudes towards same-sex acts have changed over time. Should constitutional law play a role in such change? What role?

3.   How far do the principles articulated in this case extend? What other sorts of crimes might this decision apply to?

Practice Problem 4.0: Criminal Keystrokes

You work as legislative counsel for your state's legislature. Recently a young high school boy committed suicide after suffering a sustained campaign of harassing posts on his social media page from his fellow students. The harassing posts began when another student posted a comment on the boy's page stating that he had sexually molested an elementary school boy while serving as a summer camp counselor. The statement was false and had begun as a joke by some of the dead boy's friends although the student who posted the initial accusation believed it to be true.

All social media sites prohibit the posting of harassing or false material in their terms of service,[1] but a member of your state legislature has introduced the following bills creating the crimes of cyberbullying and computer trespass. Analyze the two proposed bills. Your analysis should include a discussion of how the language of the statutes would be interpreted by courts, as well as a broader discussion of whether the resulting criminal liability would be too broad or too narrow. Illustrate your analysis by reference to the tragic case described above, and where appropriate, provide specific recommendations for amending the statutory language. Your state is a common law jurisdiction.

Cyberbullying

(a)   It shall be unlawful for any person to use a computer or computer network to plant any false statement tending to provoke—or that actually provokes—any third party to harass a minor.

(b)   Any person who violates this section shall be guilty of cyberbullying, which offense shall be punishable as a misdemeanor.

Computer Trespass

A person is guilty of computer trespass in the second degree, a misdemeanor, when he or she uses a computer service in violation of terms of service.

A person is guilty of computer trespass in the second degree, a felony, when he or she uses a computer service in violation of terms of service with the intent to commit a crime.

---

[1]   Terms of Service are the contractual provisions that a user of a social media site or an internet service provider must agree to in order to use the site or service.

CHAPTER 5

THE GUILTY HAND

■ ■ ■

The guilty hand component of a crime is often the most straightforward aspect of the analysis. In the simplest terms, one must identify the actions the defendant must perform in order to be guilty of the crime. . . . Different terminology exists for describing this "doing" part of criminal offenses. Some use the terms conduct or actus reus to refer to the actions the defendant must perform. Others include not only the actions performed but also the results caused (if any are required by the definition of the crime). Still others include attendant circumstances (such as the fact that burglaries at common law had to be performed at night). Therefore, remember that different judges and writers may use these terms differently . . . . For our purposes, we will use the term "guilty hand" to refer only to the defendant's actions.

A. THE REQUIREMENT OF A VOLUNTARY ACT

All crimes, with the exception of omission liability, require some voluntary act. So you can't think your way into criminal liability. A passage in the Catholic Liturgy asks forgiveness for thoughts, but in the criminal law thoughts without deeds do not create criminal liability. For example, in the movie *This is the End*, Jonah Hill prays to God for the death of one of his housemates. "Dear God," he prays, "I think Jay is one of your worst creations—please kill him!" As malicious as this prayer may be, it is not a crime. Even if Jonah confessed this heartfelt prayer to the police, he could not be found guilty of attempted murder. So, you must act—not just think—to be guilty of a crime.

Moreover, "voluntary" does not have the same meaning in the voluntary act doctrine as it does in ordinary, everyday conversation. This is the single most important—and counterintuitive—point to remember in this area. It is a term of art with a specialized meaning. Here, an act is voluntary if it is a willed muscular motion. This definition includes words and speech since your vocal cords do not move on their own.

Additionally, a related way of describing a voluntary act uses the idea of consciousness. In these terms, a voluntary act is the product of a conscious choice. Conversely, unconscious acts are not voluntary. Because volition and consciousness are so fundamental to human experience, most statutes define voluntary in negative terms. The Model Penal Code's catch-all definition of *involuntary*, for example, is "a bodily movement that otherwise is not a product of the effort or determination of the actor, either conscious or habitual." (MPC 2.01, 3(d)).

1. REFLEXES ARE NOT VOLUNTARY

The easiest example of an involuntary act is a reflex—an autonomous neurological response to external stimuli. Imagine that, at your doctor's office, instead of tapping your knee with that little hammer to test your reflexes, your doctor smashes your knee with a large rubber mallet. Reflexively, your leg shoots forward as you cry out in pain. There is some justice, however, because your foot catches your sadistic physician square in the groin, and he collapses to the ground. Since the required conduct—a harmful or offensive touching—was not performed voluntarily or consciously, you could not be prosecuted for the battery of your physician.

2. ACTS DONE WHILE SLEEPWALKING AND UNDER HYPNOSIS MIGHT NOT BE VOLUNTARY

A more controversial example is an act performed while sleepwalking or under hypnosis. If juries conclude that the defendant performed acts while asleep, some jurisdictions allow those acts to be considered involuntary. Further, a few jurisdictions (including the MPC) recognize a similar defense for acts resulting from hypnotic suggestion. Most jurisdictions, however, hold one responsible for what one does while asleep or under hypnosis on the theory that one would never do something while asleep or under hypnosis that one would not otherwise do.

Reflexive actions, sleepwalking, and hypnosis are relatively intuitive examples of conduct that might not be voluntary. Now, let's consider two types of conduct that an average person would consider involuntary or unconscious but which the law considers to be voluntary and the product of a conscious choice.

3. ACTS DONE UNDER DURESS ARE "VOLUNTARY"

Imagine that your professor lost his mind and ordered you at gun point to strike the student sitting next to you in class. If charged with battery or assault, could you successfully argue that there was no voluntary act? No! Actions performed under duress are considered voluntary for the purposes of the voluntary act doctrine. Your criminal liability will turn on whether you have satisfied the defense of duress, an excuse for criminal liability that we will cover later in the course (and which you should address separately if writing for the exam).

4. ACTS DONE HABITUALLY ARE CONSIDERED "VOLUNTARY"

Now imagine a chain-smoker goes to the hospital to visit his best friend, who—not coincidentally—is also a chain-smoker and dying of emphysema. The dying friend is in an oxygen tent, and there are signs everywhere warning, "highly flammable oxygen in use," and "smoking absolutely prohibited," as well as—for the truly dense—"smoking may result in fire and explosion." Distraught at seeing his friend laboring to breathe, our visiting chain-smoker does what chain smokers often do—he unconsciously takes out a cigarette and lights it. Only after the explosion that incinerated his dear friend did our chain-smoking defendant realize what he had done, as he noticed the remains of his cigarette clutched between his own charred fingers. Can he avoid criminal liability on the grounds that he did not voluntarily or consciously light his cigarette? No! Remember that "voluntary" and "conscious" are used as legal terms of art here. When we say in everyday conversation that we did something "unconsciously," we are referring to what the criminal law considers habitual behavior. Habitual behavior is considered conscious behavior for the purposes of the voluntary act doctrine. Our chain smoker's defense will turn on whether he had the mental state required for the crime, a subject for the next chapter.

B. STATUS OFFENSES

The voluntary act doctrine is one of the few areas where a common law principle enjoys constitutional status. As discussed in Chapter 4, in *Robison v. California*, the U.S. Supreme Court held that criminalizing a mere status violated the Eighth Amendment to the U.S. Constitution's prohibition of cruel and unusual punishments. In *Robinson*, the Court struck down a statute that made it a crime to be addicted to the use of narcotics. While the government is free to criminalize using, possessing, or being under the influence of an illegal drug, it cannot criminalize the state—or status—of being addicted. To do so, the Court reasoned, would be akin to prosecuting someone for being sick. In a later case, *Powell v. Texas*, the Court made clear, however, that it was not unconstitutional to criminalize behavior that resulted from an addiction. The defendant in *Powell* argued that his violation of a public intoxication statute was the involuntary result of his chronic alcoholism, but the Court distinguished the case from *Robinson* on the grounds that becoming intoxicated was conduct, not status. The Court squarely rejected the notion that acts committed as the result of an addiction are involuntary for the purposes of constitutional analysis.

C. HOW THE VOLUNTARY ACT DOCTRINE OFTEN OPERATES IN PRACTICE

As with many common law principles, the voluntary act requirement operates most often as a presumption of statutory interpretation. Judges presume that the legislature intended to require the defendant to perform at least one voluntary act for the crime, and they will interpret criminal statutes accordingly. The difficult cases involve questions about which acts, how many, and when those acts must be committed.

Case in Context

The court in the following case makes a choice about which acts must be voluntary.

MARTIN V. STATE
Court of Appeals of Alabama
31 Ala.App. 334 (1944)

SIMPSON, JUDGE.

Appellant was convicted of being drunk on a public highway, and appeals. Officers of the law arrested him at his home and took him onto the highway, where he allegedly committed the proscribed acts, viz., manifested a drunken condition by using loud and profane language.

The pertinent provisions of our statute are: "Any person who, while intoxicated or drunk, appears in any public place where one or more persons are present, * * * and manifests a drunken condition by boisterous or indecent conduct, or loud and profane discourse, shall, on conviction, be fined", etc. Code 1940, Title 14, Section 120.

Under the plain terms of this statute, a voluntary appearance is presupposed. The rule has been declared, and we think it sound, that an accusation of drunkenness in a designated public place cannot be established by proof that the accused, while in an intoxicated condition, was involuntarily and forcibly carried to that place by the arresting officer.

Conviction of appellant was contrary to this announced principle and, in our view, erroneous. It appears that no legal conviction can be sustained under the evidence, so, consonant with the prevailing rule, the judgment of the trial court is reversed and one here rendered discharging appellant.

Of consequence, our original opinion of affirmance was likewise laid in error. It is therefore withdrawn.

Reversed and rendered.

DISCUSSION QUESTIONS

1.   Does every act required for a crime have to be voluntary, or just one? Is "manifesting" a voluntary act? How do courts choose which acts have to be voluntary ones?

2.   What if Martin ended up on the street because he had been thrown out of a party because of his belligerent behavior?

3.   Imagine an epidemic of a highly contagious and highly lethal flu. Could a state criminalize sneezing or coughing in a public place?

Case in Context

The court in the following case finds a voluntary act by reaching into the past.

PEOPLE V. DECINA

Court of Appeals of New York
2 N.Y.2d 133 (1956)

FROESSEL, JUDGE.

At about 3:30 p. m. on March 14, 1955, a bright, sunny day, defendant was driving, alone in his car, in a northerly direction on Delaware Avenue in the city of Buffalo. The portion of Delaware Avenue here involved is 60 feet wide. At a point south of an overhead viaduct of the Erie Railroad, defendant's car swerved to the left, across the center line in the street, so that it was completely in the south lane, traveling 35 to 40 miles per hour.

It then veered sharply to the right, crossing Delaware Avenue and mounting the easterly curb at a point beneath the viaduct and continued thereafter at a speed estimated to have been about 50 or 60 miles per hour or more. During this latter swerve, a pedestrian testified that he saw defendant's hand above his head; another witness said he saw defendant's left arm bent over the wheel, and his right hand extended towards the right door.

A group of six schoolgirls were walking north on the easterly sidewalk of Delaware Avenue, two in front and four slightly in the rear, when defendant's car struck them from behind. One of the girls escaped injury by jumping against the wall of the viaduct. The bodies of the children struck were propelled northward onto the street and the lawn in front of a coal company, located to the north of the Erie viaduct on Delaware Avenue. Three of the children, 6 to 12 years old, were found dead on arrival by the medical examiner, and a fourth child, 7 years old, died in a hospital two days later as a result of injuries sustained in the accident.

After striking the children, defendant's car continued on the easterly sidewalk, and then swerved back onto Delaware Avenue once more. It continued in a northerly direction, passing under a second viaduct before it again veered to the right and remounted the easterly curb, striking and breaking a metal lamppost. With its horn blowing steadily, apparently because defendant was 'stopped over' the steering wheel, the car proceeded on the sidewalk until it finally crashed through a 7 1/4-inch brick wall of a grocery store, injuring at least one customer and causing considerable property damage.

When the car came to a halt in the store, with its horn still blowing, several fires had been ignited. Defendant was stooped over in the car and was 'bobbing a little'. To one witness he appeared dazed, to another unconscious, lying back with his hands off the wheel. Various people present shouted to defendant to turn off the ignition of his car, and 'within a matter of seconds the horn stopped blowing and the car did shut off'.

Defendant was pulled out of the car by a number of bystanders and laid down on the sidewalk. To a policeman who came on the scene shortly he appeared 'injured, dazed'; another witness said that 'he looked as though he was knocked out, and his arm seemed to be bleeding'. An injured customer in the store, after receiving first aid, pressed defendant for an explanation of the accident and he told her: 'I blacked out from the bridge'.

When the police arrived, defendant attempted to rise, staggered and appeared dazed and unsteady. When informed that he was under arrest, and would have to accompany the police to the station house, he resisted and, when he tried to get away, was handcuffed. The foregoing evidence was adduced by the People, and is virtually undisputed. Defendant did not take the stand nor did he produce any witnesses.

From the police station defendant was taken to the E. J. Meyer Memorial Hospital, a county institution, arriving at 5:30 P.M.

On the evening of that day, after an interne had visited and treated defendant and given orders for therapy, Dr. Wechter, a resident physician in the hospital and a member of its staff, came to his room.

He asked defendant how he felt and what had happened. Defendant, who still felt a little dizzy or blurry, said that as he was driving he noticed a jerking of his right hand, which warned him that he might develop a convulsion, and that as he tried to steer the car over to the curb he felt himself becoming unconscious, and he thought he had a convulsion. He was aware that children were in front of his car, but did not know whether he had struck them.

Defendant then proceeded to relate to Dr. Wechter his past medical history, namely, that at the age of 7 he was struck by an auto and suffered a marked loss of hearing. In 1946 he was treated in this same hospital for an illness during which he had some convulsions. Several burr holes were made in his skull and a brain abscess was drained. Following this operation defendant had no convulsions from 1946 through 1950. In 1950 he had four convulsions, caused by scar tissue on the brain. From 1950 to 1954 he experienced about 10 or 20 seizures a year, in which his right hand would jump although he remained fully conscious. In 1954, he had 4 or 5 generalized seizures with loss of consciousness, the last being in September, 1954, a few months before the accident. Thereafter he had more hospitalization, a spinal tap, consultation with a neurologist, and took medication daily to help prevent seizures.

On the basis of this medical history, Dr. Wechter made a diagnosis of Jacksonian epilepsy, and was of the opinion that defendant had a seizure at the time of the accident. Other members of the hospital staff performed blood tests and took an electroencephalogram during defendant's three-day stay there. The testimony of Dr. Wechter is the only testimony before the trial court showing that defendant had epilepsy, suffered an attack at the time of the accident, and had knowledge of his susceptibility to such attacks.

Defendant was indicted and charged with violating section 1053–a of the Penal Law. Following his conviction, after a demurrer to the indictment was overruled, the Appellate Division, while holding that the demurrer was properly overruled, reversed on the law, the facts having been 'examined' and found 'sufficient'.

We turn first to the subject of defendant's cross appeal, namely, that his demurrer should have been sustained, since the indictment here does not charge a crime. The indictment states essentially that defendant, knowing 'that he was subject to epileptic attacks or other disorder rendering him likely to lose consciousness for a considerable period of time', was culpably negligent 'in that he consciously undertook to and did operate his Buick sedan on a public highway' and 'while so doing' suffered such an attack which caused said automobile 'to travel at a fast and reckless rate of speed, jumping the curb and driving over the sidewalk' causing the death of 4 persons. In our opinion, this clearly states a violation of section 1053– a of the Penal Law. The statute does not require that a defendant must deliberately intend to kill a human being, for that would be murder. Nor does the statute require that he knowingly and consciously follow the precise path that leads to death and destruction. It is sufficient, we have said, when his conduct manifests a 'disregard of the consequences which may ensue from the act, and indifference to the rights of others. No clearer definition, applicable to the hundreds of varying circumstances that may arise, can be given. Under a given state of facts, whether negligence is culpable is a question of judgment.'

Assuming the truth of the indictment, as we must on a demurrer, this defendant knew he was subject to epileptic attacks and seizures that might strike at any time. He also knew that a moving motor vehicle uncontrolled on public highway is a highly dangerous instrumentality capable of unrestrained destruction. With this knowledge, and without anyone accompanying him, he deliberately took a chance by making a conscious choice of a course of action, in disregard of the consequences which he knew might follow from his conscious act, and which in this case did ensue. How can we say as a matter of law that this did not amount to culpable negligence within the meaning of section 1053–a?

To hold otherwise would be to say that a man may freely indulge himself in liquor in the same hope that it will not affect his driving, and if it later develops that ensuing intoxication causes dangerous and reckless driving resulting in death, his unconsciousness or involuntariness at that time would relieve him from prosecution under the statute. His awareness of a condition which he knows may produce such consequences as here, and his disregard of the consequences, renders him liable for culpable negligence, as the courts below have properly held. To have a sudden sleeping spell, an unexpected heart or other disabling attack, without any prior knowledge or warning thereof, is an altogether different situation, and there is simply no basis for comparing such cases with the flagrant disregard manifested here.

Accordingly, the Appellate Division properly sustained the lower court's order overruling the demurrer.

DESMOND, JUDGE (concurring in part and dissenting in part).

I agree that the judgment of conviction cannot stand but I think the indictment should be dismissed because it alleges no crime. Defendant's demurrer should have been sustained.

The indictment charges that defendant knowing that 'he was subject to epileptic attacks or other disorder rendering him likely to lose consciousness' suffered 'an attack and loss of consciousness which caused the said automobile operated by the said defendant to travel at a fast and reckless rate of speed' and to jump a curb and run onto the sidewalk 'thereby striking and causing the death' of 4 children. Horrible as this occurrence was and whatever necessity it may show for new licensing and driving laws, nevertheless this indictment charges no crime known to the New York statutes. Our duty is to dismiss it.

Section 1053–a of the Penal Law describes the crime of 'criminal negligence in the operation of a vehicle resulting in death'. Declared to be guilty of that crime is 'A person who operates or drives any vehicle of any kind in a reckless or culpably negligent manner, whereby a human being is killed'. The essentials of the crime are, therefore, first, vehicle operation in a culpably negligent manner, and, second, the resulting death of a person. This indictment asserts that defendant violated section 1053–a, but it then proceeds in the language quoted in the next-above paragraph of this opinion to describe the way in which defendant is supposed to have offended against that statute. That descriptive matter shows that defendant did not violate section 1053–a. No operation of an automobile in a reckless manner is charged against defendant. The excessive speed of the car and its jumping the curb were 'caused', says the indictment itself, by defendant's prior 'attack and loss of consciousness'. Therefore, what defendant is accused of is not reckless or culpably negligent driving, which necessarily connotes and involves consciousness and volition. The fatal assault by this car was after and because of defendant's failure of consciousness. To say that one drove a car in a reckless manner in that his unconscious condition caused the car to travel recklessly is to make two mutually contradictory assertions. One cannot be 'reckless' while unconscious. One cannot while unconscious 'operate' a car in a culpably negligent manner or in any other 'manner'. The statute makes criminal a particular kind of knowing, voluntary, immediate operation. It does not touch at all the involuntary presence of an unconscious person at the wheel of an uncontrolled vehicle. To negative the possibility of applying section 1053–a to these alleged facts we do not even have to resort to the rule that all criminal statutes are closely and strictly construed in favor of the citizen and that no act or omission is criminal unless specifically and in terms so labeled by a clearly worded statute.

Numerous are the diseases and other conditions of a human being which make it possible or even likely that the afflicted person will lose control of his automobile. Epilepsy, coronary involvements, circulatory diseases, nephritis, uremic poisoning, diabetes, Meniere's syndrome, a tendency to fits of sneezing, locking of the knee, muscular contractions any of these common conditions may cause loss of control of a vehicle for a period long enough to cause a fatal accident. An automobile traveling at only 30 miles an hour goes 44 feet in a second. Just what is the court holding here? No less than this: that a driver whose brief blackout lets his car run amuck and kill another has killed that other by reckless driving. But any such 'recklessness' consists necessarily not of the erratic behavior of the automobile while its driver is unconscious, but of his driving at all when he knew he was subject to such attacks. Thus, it must be that such a blackout-prone driver is guilty of reckless driving whenever and as soon as he steps into the driver's seat of a vehicle. Every time he drives, accident or no accident, he is subject to criminal prosecution for reckless driving or to revocation of his operator's license.

When section 1053–a was new it was assailed as unconstitutional on the ground that the language 'operates or drives any vehicle of any kind in a reckless or culpably negligent manner' was too indefinite since a driver could only guess as to what acts or omissions were meant. [G]iving section 1053–a the new meaning assigned to it permits punishment of one who did not drive in any forbidden manner but should not have driven at all, according to the present theory. No motorist suffering from any serious malady or infirmity can with impunity drive any automobile at any time or place, since no one can know what physical conditions make it 'reckless' or 'culpably negligent' to drive an automobile. Such a construction of a

Here, Dr. Ludin stated that his opinion would be different if the defendant was not telling the truth. Analysis of the record on appeal discloses facts on which the jury could base their opinion that the defendant was being untruthful.

First, defendant alleges that he cannot remember anything that occurred during the three-day period following his arrest. The doctor, however, testified that on December 14, 1974, defendant was alert, awake and in contact with reality. Officer Yarcho also stated that the defendant was alert and not confused when he was arrested. The defendant also responded in an appropriate manner when questioned about his personal history. Next, is Officer Yarcho's troubling testimony that defendant's arrest required a great deal of force. Such testimony coincides with Dr. Ludin's statement that a person having a psychomotor seizure exhibits a great deal of strength. This testimony, however, as the State points out, must be contrasted with Officer Yarcho's later testimony that it took four men to place the defendant in an ambulance at the jail, while he initially took the defendant into custody by himself. Furthermore, Officer Yarcho testified that defendant was much stronger during the jail incident than he was during the arrest. Finally, Officer Yarcho stated that in his opinion the defendant was in possession of his 'complete faculties' and 'normal' at the time of his arrest. The evidence showing that the defendant had a grand mal seizure at the jail does not necessarily reflect that the defendant also had a psychomotor seizure a short time before. While Dr. Ludin did say that sometimes a grand mal seizure is preceded by a psychomotor seizure, he did not say that this always occurs. . .

The term automatism is defined as the state of a person who, though capable of action, is not conscious of what he is doing. Automatism is not insanity. . . .[I]t is manifested by the performance of involuntary acts that can be of a simple or complex nature. Clinically, automatism has been identified in a wide variety of physical conditions including: epilepsy, organic brain disease, concussional states following head injuries, drug abuse, hypoglycemia and, less commonly, in some types of schizophrenia and acute emotional disturbance. Psychomotor epileptics not only engage in automatic or fugue-like activity, but they may also suffer convulsive seizures.

Section 4–1 of our Criminal Code provides:

A material element of every offense is a voluntary act, which includes an omission to perform a duty which the law imposes on the offender and which he is physically capable of performing.

While the Illinois Pattern Jury Instructions contain an instruction relating to this statute . . .that instruction was [not] read to the jury in this case. . . [W]e hold that the interests of justice require reversal of the defendant's convictions because the jury instructions are substantially defective in that they do not contain an instruction on the defense of involuntary conduct. We note that courts in other jurisdictions have held that the defendant, who introduces evidence of abnormal mental condition, bearing upon the state of mind required for the crime with which he is charged, is entitled to an instruction drawing the jury's attention to that evidence.

The entire record on appeal here, especially the testimony of Dr. Ludin, reflects that the defendant suffers from psychomotor epilepsy which is not insanity. The record reflects that the defendant may have been acting in a state of automatism when he attacked Officer Vonderahe on December 13, 1974. We therefore leave the factual resolution of this question to a jury that is properly instructed as to sections 4–1 and 4–3 through 4–7 of the Code.

This part of the case was especially helpful to understanding the voluntary act requirement. Although a voluntary act is an absolute requirement for criminal liability under section 4–1 of our Code. . .there is no requirement that every act preceding the actual commission of the offense be voluntary. Thus, the jury may, on remand, determine that the defendant attacked Officer Vonderahe while in a state of automatism, but that he nevertheless committed an offense for which he is criminally responsible if he had prior notice of his susceptibility to engage in violent involuntary conduct brought on by drinking alcoholic beverages or by some other conscious causal behavior. . . .

[The Illinois] Code provides for the affirmative defense of insanity and requires that every offense be the result of a voluntary act. Our legislature has provided that a person found not guilty of an offense by reason of insanity can be committed to a mental health facility for treatment, although no such provision applies to an alleged offender who commits an involuntary act. . .On remand, the defendant will again run the risk of being convicted for the offenses of aggravated battery or obstructing a police officer if the jury finds that he was not insane when he attacked Officer Vonderahe and that he either consciously committed the offense or recklessly brought about his alleged psychomotor epileptic seizure and its accompanying state of automatism. As some commentators have suggested, the jury plays an important role when the defense is raised:

[A]utomatism as a result of psychomotor seizures should be (a) valid criminal defense. The dearth of cases employing this defense suggests that the problem is one of proof. If one is sane immediately prior to and after the unlawful act is committed it is difficult to establish that a particular violent act occurred as a result of a psychomotor seizure.' (Barrow & Fabing, Epilepsy and the Law (1956), 92–93.)

If the jury finds that the defendant was sane but not responsible for the attack on Officer Vonderahe, then he cannot be committed for the offenses. We find this course to be mandated by our legislature which only provided for the commitment of persons who are criminally insane. . .

REVERSED AND REMANDED WITH DIRECTIONS.

DISCUSSION QUESTIONS

1.   Do you think that the court believed that Grant was suffering from psycho-motor epilepsy at the time he assaulted the police officer? If not, why does the court reverse the conviction?

2.   What is the voluntary act that the court suggests could support a conviction even if Grant was suffering an epileptic attack at the time of the assault?

3.   In both *Decina* and *Grant* the court reaches back in time to find a voluntary act. Do you agree with one but not the other? If so, can you articulate a principle that distinguishes the two cases?

The bottom line is that you should always look for at least one voluntary act in applying a criminal statute, but you can sometimes be creative in where and when you find that act.

Practice Problem 5.1: Traumatic Touching

Adrian is thirteen years old and has been placed by the state in a group home as the result of having been repeatedly sexually molested by a household member. Adrian has also been diagnosed with narcolepsy, a sleep disorder that sometimes makes a person sleep very, very deeply. Adrian falls asleep on the living room couch in the group home, which is a violation of the home rules. Adrian has been repeatedly told not to sleep on the couch by group home staff. On this occasion a staff member yells loudly for Adrian to wake up. When Adrian fails to wake up the staff member starts shaking Adrian's shoulders. After three or four shakes Adrian wakes up. As Adrian's eyes are opening Adrian hits the staff member very hard on the side of the head with a closed fist. Analyze Adrian's criminal liability for striking the staff member.

D. THE PHILOSOPHY BEHIND THE VOLUNTARY ACT REQUIREMENT

The voluntary act requirement serves a number of different purposes. First, people are usually not considered morally blameworthy for acts that they did not voluntarily perform. Choice lies at the heart of many of our intuitions about blameworthiness, and if someone did not will their muscles to move, they did not choose to do anything. Second, people cannot be deterred from involuntary actions because they have never weighed the costs and benefits of acting. Finally, the requirement of a voluntary act serves as a guarantee that we will never rely too much on mental state evidence for criminal liability. The "proof is in the pudding" as the saying goes, and requiring voluntary action reduces the chance that we will erroneously punish someone who is not dangerous or blameworthy.

E. OMISSION LIABILITY

The philosopher John Austin once said that there are two parts to an argument: the part where you say something and the part where you take it back. The same could be said of the law. The law is filled with general rules and specific exceptions, and one important exception exists to the voluntary act requirement: one may be criminally liable for failing to act in the face of a legal duty.

At the outset, note that criminal liability for omissions requires not a moral duty but a legal one. If you are sitting at Starbucks and see one patron strangle another to death over who gets to plug their laptop into the last remaining power outlet, you don't have to lift a finger to stop it. You don't even have to call 911. You can simply finish your coffee and go on about your day because no general legal duty exists to aid other people or to report crime. You obviously have a moral duty to do something, but moral duties do not give rise to criminal liability for omissions.

What sorts of legal duties create omission liability under the criminal law? To answer this question, imagine that you are drowning at a public beach. A crowd of people are watching you die. People are even filming your death on their phones and uploading it to YouTube, where it is instantaneously going viral (your fifteen seconds of fame!). But nobody lifts a finger to help you, despite the abundance of lifesaving equipment lying around. Who can be prosecuted for failing to come to your aid?

1. STATUTORY DUTIES

There is a police officer on the beach. She can be criminally prosecuted for failing to come to your aid because in most jurisdictions police officers have a statutory obligation to come to a person's aid in the event of an emergency. Just as she could not just walk by a person having a cardiac arrest on a public street, she can't ignore your plight.

The legislature can create legal duties for one person to aid another by statute. For example, certain categories of people have a statutory obligation to report child abuse in many states. Child abuse (and domestic violence) aside, such reporting statutes are rare. They usually limit the duty to certain types of people and certain types of situations.

More generally, the legislature can create a legal duty for you to do certain things. One easy example is paying taxes. Failing to file a tax return on income you earn is an omission to act in the face of a legal duty that is created by statute. Again, this sort of legal liability is the exception.

The vast majority of criminal statutes criminalize things that you do, not things that you don't.

2. CONTRACTUAL DUTIES

Can you believe it? The lifeguard is watching you drown, too. He has a really good view from that tall chair he sits in and is using it to good advantage as he films your death on his cell phone. He can be criminally prosecuted because his employment contract obliges him to come to the aid of people drowning. Remember that contracts may be oral or written, but all the requirements of a contract must be satisfied for a duty to arise under it.

3. STATUS RELATIONSHIPS

Here is the really bad news. Your mother is watching you drown, too. She is actually yelling, "I told you to stay with the swim lessons, but you had to try to become the big soccer star!" She can be prosecuted because the status relationship of parent to child creates a legal duty for her to come to your aid, and her omission to act in the face of that duty can be a crime.

The paradigm status relationships for the purposes of criminal liability are:

- Parent to child
- Spouse to spouse
- Employer to employee
- Ship captain to crew and passengers

A failure to come to someone's aid in the face of a legal duty arising from such a status relationship can give rise to criminal liability.

4. DUTIES VOLUNTARILY ASSUMED

While you are drowning, a swimmer who is an Olympic gold medalist decides to come to your rescue. He jumps out of his beach chair and announces loudly to the assembled crowd, "Hey, I have this," then gestures for everyone to get out of his way. He jogs towards the shore, but as his toes touch the water he jumps back out exclaiming, "Man, that is so much colder than all of those swimming pools I have spent my life in." He goes back to his beach chair.

The Olympic swimmer can be criminally prosecuted in many jurisdictions because he would be deemed to have voluntarily undertaken a rescue that he subsequently abandoned. Voluntary assumption of a legal duty creates a legal duty because such undertakings may have caused the victim to rely upon the aid or may have dissuaded others from helping.

5. CREATION OF A RISK OF PERIL

Actually, the reason you are drowning in the first place is that your bone-head college roommate pushed you off the edge of a pier as a joke, not knowing that you could not swim. Once in the water, you immediately scream, "I can't swim," and begin to drown. She stands there, exclaiming "wow, she can't swim; imagine that." She then turns and walks away, stepping over the lifesaving equipment lying on the pier. Your college roommate can be criminally prosecuted for failing to come to your aid because she created the risk of peril in the first place. One who puts another in danger does have a legal duty to come to their aide, and failing to do so creates criminal liability.

F. AN IMPORTANT LIMITATION ON CRIMINAL OMISSION LIABILITY

With respect to these legal duties, you must only aid another to the extent of your ability to safely do so. If you are not a strong swimmer, you do not have to risk your life to save another. That is why, in the hypothetical, I was careful to leave lifesaving equipment lying around. On the other hand, help is often just a phone call away in our cell-phone-carrying society, so failing to at least phone for help can easily give rise to criminal liability if a legal duty to aid exists.

G. THE PHILOSOPHY BEHIND LIMITED OMISSION LIABILITY

There are several different reasons the criminal law avoids prosecuting people for things they did not do, even where moral duties exist. You can watch the Starbucks strangulation take place in legal safety because judges and legislatures have historically feared the blurriness of the lines that would define a general duty to aid people or to report or prevent crime. What if you see someone pulled over on the side of the road staring blankly into space? Are they having a heart attack, did they just finish burying a murder victim by the side of the road, or are they trying to remember where they put the grocery list? You hear the neighbors next door engaged in a screaming argument. If they are actually hitting one another as they scream, would you be criminally liable for failing to call the police? The blurriness of these lines also raises questions about the role of government in society. If you think your roommate is selling illegal drugs, a duty to act or report could easily turn us into a nation of informers, something that might reduce crime but would also expand the power of the state at the expense of personal privacy and autonomy.

This next case features one of many horrific fact patterns you will encounter in your studies of criminal law and it illustrates the concept of a legal duty very well as a result.

Case in Context

The following case involves a terrible story of neglect, one that would seem to cry out for omission liability.

JONES V. UNITED STATES

United States Court of Appeals District of Columbia Circuit
308 F.2d 307 (1962)

WRIGHT, CIRCUIT JUDGE.

Appellant, together with one Shirley Green, was tried on a three-count indictment charging them jointly with (1) abusing and maltreating Robert Lee Green (2) abusing and maltreating Anthony Lee Green, and (3) involuntary manslaughter through failure to perform their legal duty of care for Anthony Lee Green, which failure resulted in his death. At the close of evidence, after trial to a jury, the first two counts were dismissed as to both defendants. On the third count, appellant was convicted of involuntary manslaughter. Shirley green was found not guilty.

Appellant urges several grounds for reversal. We need consider but two. First, appellant argues that there was insufficient evidence as a matter of law to warrant a jury finding of breach of duty in the care she rendered Anthony Lee. Alternatively, appellant argues that the trial court committed plain error in failing to instruct the jury that it must first find that appellant was under a legal obligation to provide food and necessities to Anthony Lee before finding her guilty of manslaughter in failing to provide them. The first argument is without merit. Upon the latter we reverse.

A summary of the evidence, which is in conflict upon almost every significant issue, is necessary for the disposition of both arguments. In late 1957, Shirley Green became pregnant, out of wedlock, with a child, Robert Lee, subsequently born August 17, 1958. Apparently to avoid the embarrassment of the presence of the child in the Green home, it was arranged that appellant, a family friend, would take the child to her home after birth. Appellant did so, and the child remained there continuously until removed by the police on August 5, 1960. Initially appellant made some motions toward the adoption of Robert Lee, but these came to naught, and shortly thereafter it was agreed that Shirley Green was to pay appellant $72 a month for his care. According to appellant, these payments were made for only five months. According to Shirley Green, they were made up to July, 1960.

Early in 1959 Shirley Green again became pregnant, this time with the child Anthony Lee, whose death is the basis of appellant's conviction. This child was born October 21, 1959. Soon after birth, Anthony Lee developed a mild jaundice condition, attributed to a blood income with his mother. The jaundice resulted in his retention in the hospital for three days beyond the usual time, or until October 26, 1959, when, on authorization signed by Shirley Green, Anthony Lee was released by the hospital to appellant's custody. Shirley Green, after a two or three day stay in the hospital, also lived with appellant for three weeks, after which she returned to her parents' home, leaving the children with appellant. She testified she did not see them again, except for one visit in March, until August 5, 1960. Consequently, though there does not seem to have been any specific monetary agreement with Shirley Green covering Anthony Lee's support, appellant had complete custody of both children until they were rescued by the police.

With regard to medical care, the evidence is undisputed. In March, 1960, appellant called a Dr. Turner to her home to treat Anthony Lee for a bronchial condition. Appellant also telephoned the doctor at various times to consult with him concerning Anthony Lee's diet and health. In early July, 1960, appellant took Anthony Lee to Dr. Turner's office where he was treated for 'simple diarhea.' At this time the doctor noted the 'wizened' appearance of the child and told appellant to tell the mother of the child that he should be taken to a hospital. This was not done.

On August 2, 1960, two collectors for the local gas company had occasion to go to the basement of appellant's home, and there saw the two children. Robert Lee and Anthony Lee at this time were age two years and ten months respectively. Robert Lee was in a 'crib' consisting of a framework of wood, covered with a fine wire screening, including the top which was hinged. The 'crib' was lined with newspaper, which was stained, apparently with feces, and crawling with roaches. Anthony Lee was lying in a bassinet and was described as having the appearance of a 'small baby monkey.' One collector testified to seeing roaches on Anthony Lee.

On August 5, 1960, the collectors returned to appellant's home in the company of several police officers and personnel of the Women's Bureau. At this time, Anthony Lee was upstairs in the dining room in the bassinet, but Robert Lee was still downstairs in his 'crib.' The officers removed the children to the D. C. General Hospital where Anthony Lee was diagnosed as suffering from severe malnutrition and lesions over large portions of his body, apparently caused by severe diaper rash. Following admission, he was fed repeatedly, apparently with no difficulty, and was described as being very hungry. His death, 34 hours after admission, was attributed without dispute to malnutrition. At birth, Anthony Lee weighed six pounds, fifteen ounces—at death at age ten months, he weighed seven pounds, thirteen ounces. Normal weight at this age would have been approximately 14 pounds.

Moreover, there is substantial evidence from which the jury could have found that appellant failed to obtain proper medical care for the child. Appellant relies upon the evidence showing that on one occasion she summoned a doctor for the child, on another took the child to the doctor's office, and that she telephoned the doctor on several occasions about the baby's formula. However, the last time a doctor saw the child was a month before fore his death, and appellant admitted that on that occasion the doctor recommended hospitalization. Appellant did not hospitalize the child, nor did she take any other steps to obtain medical care in the last crucial month. Thus there was sufficient evidence to go to the jury on the issue of medical care, as well as failure to feed.

Appellant also takes exception to the failure of the trial court to charge that the jury must find beyond a reasonable doubt, as an element of the crime, that appellant was under a legal duty to supply food and necessities to Anthony Lee.

The problem of establishing the duty to take action which would preserve the life of another has not often arisen in the case law of this country. The most commonly cited statement of the rule is found in People v. Beardsley, 150 Mich. 206, 113 N.W. 1128, 1129, 13 L.R.A., N.S., 1020:

'The law recognizes that under some circumstances the omission of a duty owed by one individual to another, where such omission results in the death of the one to whom the duty is owing, will make the other chargeable with manslaughter. * * * This rule of law is always based upon the proposition that the duty neglected must be a legal duty, and not a mere moral obligation. It must be a duty imposed by law or by contract, and the omission to perform the duty must be the immediate and direct cause of death. * * *'

There are critical issues of fact which must be passed on by the jury—specifically in this case, whether appellant had entered into a contract with the mother for the care of Anthony Lee or, alternatively, whether she assumed the care of the child and secluded him from the care of his mother, his natural protector. On both of these issues, the evidence is in direct conflict, appellant insisting that the mother was actually living with appellant and Anthony Lee, and hence should have been taking care of the child herself, while Shirley Green testified she was living with her parents and was paying appellant to care for both children.

In spite of this conflict, the instructions given in the case failed even to suggest the necessity for finding a legal duty of care. The only reference to duty in the instructions was the reading of the indictment which charged, inter alia, that the defendants 'failed to perform their legal duty.' A finding of legal duty is the critical element of the crime charged and failure to instruct the jury concerning it was plain error.

Reversed and remanded.

DISCUSSION QUESTIONS

1.   What was wrong with the jury instructions in this case?

2.   Why might that error be particularly important in cases of omissions with terrible facts?

3.   Why don't we create a general legal duty for adults to provide basic care for infants and small children in cases such as these?

H. POSSESSORY OFFENSES

Legislatures have created a wide range of possessory offenses, most notably in the long-waged war on drugs. In such offenses the simple act of possessing something constitutes either an entire crime or a key element of the crime. Yet courts have wrestled with what it means to legally possess something. Possessing something is a strange form of conduct because it involves not doing but having something. The criminal law recognizes two types of possession: actual and constructive. While actual possession requires physical custody, constructive possession is satisfied by having sufficient dominion and control.

I. SPECIAL FOCUS: DRUG POSSESSION

Drug offenses are often possessory in nature, and the War on Drugs has resulted in a number of decisions exploring the finer points of possession.

THE STATE V. JOE FRANK MATARAZZO

Supreme Court of South Carolina
262 S.C. 662 (1974)

Opinion

BUSSEY, JUSTICE:

At the June, 1973, term of the Court of General Sessions for Hampton County, the appellant Matarazzo was convicted of the offense of possession of a controlled substance (marijuana) with intent to distribute the same. He appeals from his conviction and resulting sentence to a two year term of imprisonment. He states and argues four questions on appeal and we shall first consider his contention that the evidence in the case was insufficient to support his conviction.

It is elementary that in deciding whether the court erred in failing to direct a verdict in favor of a defendant in a criminal case the appellate court is required to view the testimony in the light most favorable to the State. When a motion for a directed verdict is made the trial judge is concerned with the existence or non-existence of evidence, not with its weight, and although he should not refuse to grant such motion where the evidence merely raises a suspicion that the accused is guilty, it is his duty to submit the case to the jury, if there is any evidence, either direct or circumstantial, which reasonably tends to prove the guilt of the accused or from which guilt may be fairly and logically deduced.

We accordingly review and state the evidence in the light most favorable to the State. Appellant, then 20 years of age, in February, 1973, rented a trailer which became his abode in Hampton, South Carolina. Before coming to Hampton he had been a resident of Savannah, Georgia for the previous 16 years. He was employed by the Georgia-Pacific Company working on a job from late afternoon until about 2:30 a.m., five days a week. Living in appellant's trailer with him was one Russell Curl, age 19, a former employee of appellant in forestry work, and a 14 year old Negro boy, one Willie Mays. Neither Mays nor Curl were employed at the time of the alleged offense, both being non-paying guests in appellant's trailer home.

On Friday night, April 27, 1973, five law officers, including the Chief of the Hampton Police Department, acting on information from an informant, went to the appellant's trailer, knocked upon the door and were invited in. As the officers entered there were eleven persons in the living room of the trailer, Curl, Mays, and nine others who ranged in age from 13 to 18 years. A warm pipe was lying on the living room floor and the officers, one or more of them being familiar therewith, smelled burning marijuana. The appellant was at work and not present at the pot party. Curl who was known to the officers as an occupant of the trailer was promptly arrested. Mays, not known to the officers to be an occupant of the trailer, was later arrested as was the appellant.

The officers were armed with a search warrant, later ruled to be invalid, and in the course of a search of the trailer they found three bags of marijuana in the bathroom under the bathtub and a fourth bag underneath the couch in the living room near the spot where the pipe was found. Upon a motion to suppress, the three bags of marijuana found in the bathroom were excluded from the evidence, with only the bag found under the couch being admitted into evidence. There was other evidence, however, as will hereinafter appear, that four bags of marijuana were in the trailer at the time of Curl's arrest. These four bags had been in the trailer for several nights and their presence therein was known to the appellant. Both Mays and Curl testified that appellant knew of the presence of the marijuana, but denied that such was the property of the appellant. At one point, however, Mays in response to a leading question by the solicitor testified to the effect that the marijuana was the property of all three occupants of the trailer. At least one sale of $5.00 worth of marijuana was made by Willie.

The nine teen-agers who were attending the pot party as guests when the raid occurred were known to, and friends of, all three occupants of the trailer. The circumstances reflected by the evidence give rise to the inference that this was not the first party to be held at the trailer. At some time prior to the night of the raid, the chief of police went to the trailer and removed therefrom two 13 year old girls. Appellant was admittedly present at that time but contended that he was asleep and didn't know what the girls were doing there. Appellant admitted that he knew parties had taken place at his trailer but denied any knowledge that they were pot parties or that any children were participating therein.

Ordinarily articles in a dwelling are deemed to be in the constructive possession of the person controlling the dwelling. See 22A C.J.S. Criminal Law s 597, p. 379. See also the annotation im 91 A.L.R.2d 810, dealing particularly with possession and/or constructive possession in drug cases. There is abundant evidence, we think, to prove at least constructive possession of marijuana by the appellant and indeed his brief tacitly so concedes. Viewing the evidence in the light most favorable to the State we conclude that under all of the circumstances a fair and logical deduction therefrom is that such possession on the part of the appellant was with the intent to participate directly or indirectly in the distribution thereof. It follows that the trial court correctly denied appellant's motion for a directed verdict of not guilty.

Affirmed.

DISCUSSION QUESTIONS

1.   What evidence existed that the defendant exercised control over the drugs found?

2.   Should knowing something is in your car or in a common area of your residence be legally sufficient to support a finding of constructive possession? What are the advantages and disadvantages of such a broad definition of constructive possession?

3.   Could everyone at the party be found to have been in constructive possession of the drugs?

UNITED STATES OF AMERICA V. RAFAEL ANGEL ZAVALA MALDONADO

United States Court of Appeals, First Circuit
23 F.3d 4 (1994)

BOUDIN, CIRCUIT JUDGE.

On July 2, 1992, a jury convicted Rafael Angel Zavala Maldonado ("Zavala") of possession of cocaine with intent to distribute, in violation of 21 U.S.C. § 841(a)(1). On appeal, Zavala argues that the evidence was insufficient to support the conviction.... For the reasons set forth, we affirm.

I.

. . . . In January 1992, Ruben de los Santos ("Santos"), a seaman serving on board the M/V Euro Colombia, was in the port of Cartagena, Colombia. There, a drug dealer gave Santos sixteen packages of cocaine, amounting to a total of eight kilograms, and asked Santos to deliver them as instructed when the ship docked at the port of Ponce, Puerto Rico.

Santos had earlier been approached by American law enforcement agents attached to the Customs Service, and he accepted the cocaine in Cartagena with the approval of the agents, who intended to track the drugs to their destination. . . . Shortly thereafter, Santos under surveillance by federal agents and cooperating local police, went to the Hotel Melia in Ponce and asked at the front desk for Mr. Palestino. These last two steps complied with the instructions given to Santos in Catagena, by the dealer who had given him the cocaine, to deliver it to Palestino, at the Hotel Melia in Ponce.

When the clerk called from the desk to the room registered to Palestino, the defendant Zavala appeared and gestured to Santos to follow him to room 302. There Santos, who was carrying the cocaine in a bag, told Zavala that he had the drugs to be delivered to Palestino. Zavala said that he was a friend of Palestino and that Palestino would come to the hotel. Using a cellular telephone, Zavala then placed a call, purportedly to Palestino. Then at Santos' urging Zavala called a second time to ask Palestino to come quickly. Zavala asked Santos if they could put the cocaine in another hotel room, saying that he (Zavala) had other friends in the hotel, but Santos refused.

As time passed and Palestino still did not arrive, Santos became increasingly anxious and he proposed to Zavala that they go out of the room for a soda. Zavala agreed, Santos placed the bag with the cocaine in a closet or dressing room in room 302, and the two men left room 302 and entered the corridor. As they went down the stairs, the supervising customs agent detained them. When Santos explained that Palestino had still not arrived, Zavala was taken back to room 302 in custody, accompanied by Santos and one or more agents. There were several more calls to the room purportedly from Palestino, two or three on the cellular telephone and one on the hotel telephone; in each case Santos told the caller that Zavala was out or otherwise occupied.

Shortly after the final call, the operation came to an end. Law enforcement agents, it appears, had seen a car, with the driver using a cellular telephone, circling around the hotel. The driver then parked and went into the hotel. He proceeded with another individual to one of the hotel rooms and entered. When agents then knocked on the door of this room, the individuals inside exited through a window. After a chase they were caught, and a search of their car yielded a loaded nine millimeter pistol and $6,305 in cash.

This final episode was described in testimony at the trial. So far as we know, neither the driver nor the other man with him was charged. Possibly the police thought that the evidence was not quite strong enough to prove their participation in the drug deal. Zavala, however, was charged as previously described, and convicted on one count: possession with intent to distribute.

II.

Zavala's primary claim is that an acquittal should have been ordered on grounds of insufficient evidence to prove possession.

* * *

[T]he conviction for possession can stand only if a reasonable jury could find that Zavala did possess the cocaine within the meaning of 21 U.S.C. § 841. If the statute used the term "possess" as a lay juror might understand it prior to instructions from the judge, it might be a stretch to say that Zavala "possessed" the cocaine in the bag. There is no evidence that he even touched the bag or saw the cocaine or that he was ever alone in the room with it or that he had a practical opportunity to remove it from the hotel. These facts explain why Zavala's main argument on appeal is that his relationship to the cocaine cannot be deemed "possession."

The difficulty with the argument is that the concept of possession in the drug statute comes freighted with a history of interpretation. Congress was here concerned not with "possession" in a narrowly focused situation (*e.g.,* actual possession of a weapon on an aircraft) but with possession of drugs incident to their distribution. There is every reason to think that Congress wished to cast its net widely so that, assuming *mens rea,* a defendant proximately associated with the drugs would be reached by the statute. The prevailing interpretation of "possession," in the framework of the drug statutes, reflects that broad reach.

Under settled law, "possession" includes not merely the state of immediate, hands-on physical possession but also "constructive" possession, including possession through another, and joint as well as exclusive possession. Further these concepts can be combined so that, for example, "joint constructive possession" is quite as bad as having the drugs exclusively in one's own pocket. These concepts of constructive and joint possession are almost uniformly reflected in both decisions and in standard instructions.

"Constructive" possession is commonly defined as the power and intention to exercise control, or dominion and control, over an object not in one's "actual" possession. The "constructive possession" label may confuse jurors at first—drug trial juries routinely ask to be reinstructed on the definition of possession—but the underlying idea is important and not so difficult to grasp. Courts are saying that one can possess an object while it is hidden at home in a bureau drawer, or while held by an agent, or even while it is secured in a safe deposit box at the bank and can be retrieved only when a bank official opens the vault. The problem is not so much with the idea as with deciding how far it should be carried.

Here, we think is at least arguable that Zavala was *not* shown to possess the drugs while he and Santos were in the room together. Santos apparently had exclusive control of the bag during this period. It contained drugs for which he had not been paid; Zavala was not the named person to whom it was to be delivered; and Santos refused Zavala's suggestion that the bag be entrusted to Zavala's friends in another room. If the agents had broken into the room and arrested Zavala at this point, a directed verdict of acquittal might have been required.

But once both parties departed from the room leaving the drugs inside, the situation altered. It is not that Zavala got closer to the drugs—indeed, he moved further away from them—but rather that two other circumstances changed: first, Santos surrendered his actual possession of them; and second, with the acquiescence of both parties, the drugs were secured in Zavala's room. In the context of this case, we think that a jury could then find both requisites of constructive possession: that Zavala had sufficient power to control the drugs and an intention to exercise that power.

Turning first to the *power* to exercise control, we begin with the fact that the drugs were left in Zavala's room with his knowledge and consent while Zavala was awaiting the arrival of an accomplice to pay for them. It is fair to describe the location as Zavala's hotel room because he was effectively in occupation and the jury could reasonably infer that he could return there at will. The evidence showed that the room, although registered in Palestino's name, had been lent to two occupants. It was Zavala who emerged when Santos arrived at the hotel and the room was called; and it was Zavala who took Santos to the room to await "his friend" Palestino.

The location of drugs or firearms in a defendant's home or car is a common basis for attributing possession to the defendant. This is so even if the residence or room is shared by others. The cases do not say that possession is automatic but rather that the location of the object in a domain specially accessible to the defendant can (at least where knowledge is admitted or inferred) be enough to permit the jury to find possession.

Admittedly, Zavala's power to control in this case was diluted because Santos had not yet been paid and might well have resisted any attempt by Zavala to return to the room and carry away the drugs. But by the same token a jury could infer that drugs now stored in Zavala's hotel room, awaiting transfer to Zavala's accomplice, were at least as much within Zavala's power to control as within Santos' power. If each had an effective veto over the other, it would still be joint possession. Two drug dealers with cocaine in the back seat of their car might both possess it even though neither would let the other out of sight.

The issue of *intention* is quite as important as the issue of power. Someone might have effective power over drugs simply because they were located within reach while their true owner was temporarily absent; but if such a person had power over the drugs (say, as a temporary visitor to the room in which they were located) but had no intention to exercise that power, there might still be no crime. Here, Zavala's connection with the drugs stored in his hotel room was not at all innocent: the drugs were stored there for the purpose (so far as Zavala knew and intended) of facilitating their transfer to his accomplice, Palestino.

In many cases, intention and knowledge are inferred solely from the location of the drugs in an area to which the defendant has a priority of access. Here, Zavala's state of mind is established by independent evidence: his statements that Palestino would be there soon, his suggestion that the drugs be stored temporarily in another room, apparently with his confederates; and by the cellular telephone calls by Zavala and to him seemingly from Palestino. No reasonable jury could have had any doubt that Zavala was there to assist in the transmission of the drugs lodged in his room.

Assuming Zavala's guilty mind, it might still be argued that his precise intention was to aid in the storage and transfer of the drugs but not to "control" the drugs. We think this is too fine a distinction. Defendant's intention to have the drugs stored in his room, incident to their intended transfer to a confederate, seems to us an intention intimately related to his power to control the drugs. If a jury finds this to be constructive possession, we do not think that it has stretched the concept too far or betrayed the intention of Congress.

Finally, it is beside the point that Zavala's "possession" in the hallway was extremely brief and that Zavala probably could not have escaped with the drugs because of the police surveillance. That the police are present and ready to frustrate distribution does not make possession of drugs any less a crime, and a minute of possession is as much an offense as a year of possession. If Palestino himself had arrived and Santos had handed him the bag, he would be guilty of possession even if the police had burst into the room sixty seconds later. The completion of the crime does not require that the defendant have a sporting chance.

Affirmed.

COFFIN, SENIOR CIRCUIT JUDGE (dissenting).

I believe the court errs by expanding the definition of "constructive possession" beyond what is supported by the relevant caselaw, stretching the statutory reach of "possession" under 21 U.S.C. § 841(a)(1) dangerously and unnecessarily far.

My colleagues concede that it is at least arguable that Zavala was *not* shown to possess the drugs while he and Santos were in the room together; and that had the agents broken into the room and arrested Zavala at this point, a directed verdict of acquittal might have been required. They contend, however, that once Zavala, on Santos' suggestion, locked the drugs in his hotel room while the two men went to get a drink, Zavala "possessed" the drugs, by virtue of the facts that he had yielded actual possession of the drugs, and that he had priority of access to the room in which they were stored.

The court reaches this conclusion by relying on an interpretation of "constructive possession" which I cannot help thinking is both incorrect and overbroad. "Constructive possession," as the majority properly states, is established by showing that a person knowingly had the *power* and *intention* at a given time to exercise dominion and control over an object, either directly or through others. *See United States v. Acevedo,* 842 F.2d 502, 507 (1st Cir.1988) (emphasis added). The court, in turn, defines "power" in physical terms: in its view, the requisite "power" exists if the contraband is in a location specially accessible to a defendant, such as in one's home, hotel room, or car, or located within his or her reach.

I am persuaded that this reliance on physical power of access understates the law's requirements. Although, as the court points out, a lay person's understanding of "possession" is not helpful, I cannot so easily sidestep our and other courts' use of the word "dominion," which connotes ownership or a right to property. *Black's Law Dictionary* 486 (6th ed. 1990).

More importantly, in this and other circuits, the caselaw supports a reading of "power" as the *right* or *authority* to exercise control, or dominion and control, over something not in one's actual possession. . . . For example, in *Ocampo-Guarin,* we found sufficient evidence of "power" to establish constructive possession of a suitcase and the cocaine inside it, where the defendant carried baggage claim tickets "which represented her legal right to reclaim the luggage." 968 F.2d at 1410. Similarly, in *United States v. Lamare,* we upheld a finding of constructive possession of a firearm that had been left as collateral for a towing charge owed by the defendant, because the defendant "could have taken actual possession of the pistol at any time by paying the towing charge . . . and intended to do so." 711 F.2d at 5–6.

The fact that contraband is located in a place specially accessible to a defendant may be sufficient to establish a defendant's power to exercise dominion or control over it, and thus support a finding of constructive possession, if there is a showing that the defendant has the right or authority to exercise control over the object at issue, or if the record is silent as to his right or authority over the contraband. But here the very facts militating against a finding of constructive possession while Santos and Zavala were in the room together—the fact that the drugs had not been paid for, the fact that Zavala was not the intended recipient, and Santos' refusal to follow Zavala's suggestion to transfer them to another room—effectively refute any presumption that Zavala had any claim on the drugs.

None of the cases cited by the majority support the conclusion that, where knowledge is admitted or inferred, the location of contraband in a place specially accessible to a defendant, without more, is sufficient to establish constructive possession. For example, in *United States v. Echeverri,* 982 F.2d 675, 678 (1st Cir.1993), it was the "totality of the circumstances"—the fact that drugs and drug paraphernalia were found in plain view, only four feet from the defendant himself, together with the fact that the contraband was found in his apartment—that persuaded the court that the evidence was sufficient to support a finding of constructive possession. And in *United States v. Chapdelaine,* 989 F.2d 28, 33–34 (1st Cir.1993), the court found defendant in constructive possession of bullets found in his bedroom closet based, in part, on the fact that they matched those in a firearm found in defendant's actual possession.

In *United States v. Wight,* 968 F.2d 1393, 1397 (1st Cir.1992), the single case cited by the majority that approaches the situation before us, a jury convicted Wight, the passenger in a van in which a pistol was found between the driver's and the passenger's seat, of possessing the pistol during the drug trafficking crime, but acquitted the driver of the firearm possession charge. We upheld the finding of Wight's constructive possession of the firearm, noting that based on evidence of Wight's leading role in the drug transaction, "[i]t was reasonable for the jury to infer that he, and not [the driver], was in charge of the operation and, as such, exercised control over [the driver], the van, its contents, and the firearm." *Id.* at 1398.

I find more apposite the Seventh Circuit's decision in *United States v. DiNovo,* 523 F.2d 197 (7th Cir.1975). In *DiNovo,* the court reversed a wife's conviction for possession of heroin, notwithstanding her cohabitation with her husband in a trailer where 2 pounds of heroin and other drug paraphernalia were found. *Id.* at 201–02. The court found that even if the wife knew of her husband's drug possession, this did not mean that she possessed the drugs, absent a showing of her right to exercise control over them. *Id.*

To the extent that the court jettisons all idea of legal right or practical claim to the contraband and assesses "power" in terms of physical capacity to seize, it vastly widens the concept of constructive possession. Contraband stored in the locked box of another person could be found within the power of a defendant skilled in the use of lock picking or explosives. Or, in a case like *Wight,* the finding as to constructive possession would turn on whether the driver was bigger and tougher than the passenger.

The same weakness affects the court's reasoning as to the presence of intent to exercise dominion over the drugs. The particular intent is not, as the court would have it, to facilitate transfer of the drugs to their intended recipient, his presumed associate Palestino. The required intent is that defendant intends to exercise his claim of dominion over the drugs, i.e., to take control for himself. So the court, in my view, stretches the contours of both "power" and "intent."

Finally, we should remember why we are of divided views about the propriety of extending the scope of constructive possession beyond that of any apposite authority. It is because . . . Zavala could have been charged with conspiracy to possess drugs with intent to distribute them, or with aiding and abetting Palestino's attempt to possess with intent to distribute. But Zavala was not so charged; and the mere fact that guilt is in the air should not allow us to extend the reach of the criminal possession statute in these circumstances. There needs to be some meaningful distinction between the crime of conspiracy to possess, and possession itself. The rule of the present case, allowing the government to prove constructive possession simply by having a confidential informant deposit contraband in a hotel room shared with a target, and then leave the room with this person, with the arresting officers waiting until the door shuts, would erode any such distinction.

I am uncomfortable in taking this significant step—particularly where the purpose served is to bail out a maladroit prosecution. I therefore respectfully dissent.

DISCUSSION QUESTIONS

1.   Constructive possession requires dominion and control over the item possessed. What is the difference between the nature of the control the majority and the dissent requires in the Maldonado case? Which is the right approach?

2.   Should a court find joint constructive possession for things that are for sale? Should the buyer be found to constructively possess something before he or she pays for it?

3.   Do you agree with both of the two drug possession cases you have read? With neither? If you agree with one but not the other, how do you distinguish them?

J. SPECIAL FOCUS: DIGITAL POSSESSION

The following cases explores the limits of constructive possession in the context of accessing images of child pornography over the internet but the principles articulated might be applied to other types of digital content. Do you possess an image that you access online but do not save? The following two cases reach opposite conclusions and illustrate a split in how courts approach these issues.

STATE OF SOUTH DAKOTA V. TODD DAVID LINSON

Supreme Court of South Dakota
896 N.W.2d 656 (2017)

Opinion

SEVERSON, JUSTICE.

Todd Linson appeals his conviction on five counts of possessing child pornography. We affirm.

Background

On the evening of March 3, 2013, Officers Mertes and Buss were dispatched to Linson's residence to investigate a report of possible child pornography found on a computer. Linson's wife and sister were at the residence when law enforcement arrived. They directed the officers to a computer that required a password to access. When Linson arrived home, he provided the login password so the officers were able to look at web browsing history. After discovering that Linson had searched for pornography using terms associated with child pornography and observing that several websites in the browser's history contained child pornography, the officers decided to seize the computer.

Law enforcement performed a forensic analysis on the computer seized from Linson's home. Two user profiles were found on the computer. Forty-one images of possible child pornography were found in the cache on just one of those profiles—the one belonging to Linson. An additional 360 images of child pornography were found in the unallocated space of the computer. On September 24, 2014, a grand jury indicted Linson on five counts of possessing, distributing, or otherwise disseminating child pornography in violation of SDCL 22–24A–3(3). The five images associated with those five counts were each found in the cache files of the computer. The analysis of the computer also revealed that the person using the computer used the following search terms in internet search engines: "preteen, nude preteen photos, free preteen photos, no tits, [and] Lolita." There were also adult pornography searches that were done around the same time.

A two-day jury trial began on April 13, 2016. Before the case was submitted to the jury, the defense moved for a judgment of acquittal, which the circuit court denied. On April 14, 2016, the jury found Linson guilty on all five counts. . . .

Analysis

1. Whether the evidence was sufficient to prove Linson knowingly possessed the images found in the temporary-internet-file cache of the computer.

"We review the denial of a motion for judgment of acquittal as a question of law under the de novo standard." *State v. Bausch*, 2017 S.D. 1, ¶ 25, 889 N.W.2d 404, 411 (quoting *State v. Overbey*, 2010 S.D. 78, ¶ 12, 790 N.W.2d 35, 40). "We consider the evidence in the light most favorable to the verdict and will not set aside a guilty verdict on appeal 'if the state's evidence and all favorable inferences that can be drawn therefrom support a rational theory of guilt.' " *Id.* (quoting *Overbey*, 2010 S.D. 78, ¶ 12, 790 N.W.2d at 40).

To prove the crime possessing, distributing, or otherwise disseminating child pornography under SDCL 22–24A–3(3), the State needed to establish that Linson "[k]nowingly possesse[d], distribute[d], or otherwise disseminate[d] any visual depiction of a minor engaging in a prohibited sexual act, or in the simulation of such an act." Linson concedes that the images depict child pornography. He only disputes whether he knowingly possessed those images. Although *possession* is not statutorily defined, this Court (in a possession of marijuana case) has stated that it "signifies dominion or right of control over [contraband] with knowledge of its presence and character." *State v. Barry*, 2004 S.D. 67, ¶ 9, 681 N.W.2d 89, 92 (per curiam). "[P]ossession can either be actual or constructive and need not be exclusive." *Id.* It may be proven by circumstantial evidence. *Id.* ¶ 11, 681 N.W.2d at 93.

This Court has not previously considered whether cached images are themselves the contraband that a defendant possesses or whether they are merely evidence of possession of child pornography. Here, where there was no evidence that Linson knew how the cache operated, he cannot be said to have known what images were present in his cache or to have had dominion or control over those cached images. Other courts have held that the presence of cached images or files, standing alone, is not sufficient to establish that a defendant knowingly possessed those cached images or files. *See Marsh v. People*, 389 P.3d 100, 108 (Colo. 2017) ("[T]he presence of photos in the internet cache alone does not automatically establish knowing possession." (citing *United States v. Winkler*, 639 F.3d 692, 698–99 (5th Cir. 2011))). The Colorado Supreme Court explained some of the reasons for such a holding:

> advances in internet technology have made it easier to access child pornography and have also facilitated cyber-attacks like viruses and hacking. Such intrusions could conceivably result in a computer displaying sexually exploitative images without the knowledge of that computer's owner, even where the owner has exclusive physical access to the computer.

Id. The Eighth Circuit has also noted the problematic nature of files such as those that are cached. It explained that "[t]he presence of Trojan viruses and the location of child pornography in inaccessible internet and orphan files can raise serious issues of inadvertent or unknowing possession." *United States v. Kain*, 589 F.3d 945, 949 (8th Cir. 2009) (citing *United States v. Romm*, 455 F.3d 990, 998–1001 (9th Cir. 2006)). The Eighth Circuit concluded that "[t]he presence of child pornography in temporary internet and orphan files on a computer's hard drive is *evidence* of prior possession of that pornography, though of course it is not conclusive evidence of knowing possession and control of the images." *Id.* at 950. And it determined that issues of inadvertent or unknowing possession are "issues of fact, not of law." *Id.* at 949.

We agree with those courts holding that the mere presence of child pornography in a computer's cache is not sufficient to establish that a defendant knowingly possessed it; the cached images are not themselves the contraband. Instead, cached images or files are evidence of possession. The State notes that we have defined constructive possession as the dominion or control over either the contraband or the *premises* in which the contraband was found. *See State v. Riley*, 2013 S.D. 95, ¶ 16, 841 N.W.2d 431, 436. In this case, Linson had dominion or control over the premises where the images were found—the computer and user profile— thus, the State asserts, the element of possession is met. We reject such an approach; it would make a computer owner strictly liable for anything that inadvertently loads on a computer, and it leaves unaddressed the concerns that other courts have highlighted, such as viruses and pop-ups. Those issues are ones reserved for a fact-finder.

Linson contends that using cached images as evidence of possession amounts to the punishment of viewing child pornography, especially here where there was no evidence introduced that Linson exercised his ability to control the images that he retrieved, that he knew about his computer's cache, or that he knew how to access images in the cache. The federal government and other states have prohibited viewing child pornography, but it is not explicitly prohibited by South Dakota's statutes. *See* 18 U.S.C. § 2252A(a)(5)(B) (2012) ("(a) Any person who—(5) either—(B) knowingly possesses, or knowingly accesses with intent to view, any book, magazine, periodical, film, videotape, computer disk, or any other material that contains an image of child pornography . . . shall be punished as provided in subsection (b)."). Linson refers us to various cases in support of his argument that he could not possess images found only in his cache. A couple of the cases he cites determined that their respective legislatures did not intend to criminalize behavior such as Linson's. *See State v. Barger*, 349 Or. 553, 567, 247 P.3d 309, 316 (2011) (concluding "that the acts at issue here—navigating to a website and bringing the images that the site contains to a computer screen—are not acts that the legislature intended to criminalize"); *Worden v. State*, 213 P.3d 144, 147 (Alaska Ct. App. 2009)

("[T]he evidence supported the inference that [defendant] had viewed child pornography on certain websites at some point in the past. . . . But . . . the Alaska Statute prohibiting the knowing possession of child pornography does not criminalize merely viewing images of child pornography on a computer."). The courts in several other cases he has cited considered whether a defendant knew about the computer's cache. Knowledge about the functioning of the cache or how to access the images contained therein is irrelevant when the cached images are evidence of possession and do not themselves conclusively establish possession. *See* Ty E. Howard, *Don't Cache Out Your Case: Prosecuting Child Pornography Possession Laws Based on Images Located in Temporary Internet Files*, 19 Berkeley Tech. L.J. 1227, 1257 (2004) (explaining that under the "evidence of" approach, "criminal liability arises not from the cached images themselves, but rather from the images that the user originally searched for, selected, and placed on his computer screen"). Accordingly, those cases, which do not follow the evidence of possession approach, are largely inapplicable to our analysis.

Drawing a line between the mere viewing of images on a potentially mobile electronic device such as a computer and possessing those images highlights the difficulty of applying older legal concepts rooted in a brick-and-mortar world to today's virtual world. *See generally* Audrey Rogers, *From Peer-to-Peer Networks to Cloud Computing: How Technology is Redefining Child Pornography Laws*, 87 St. John's L. Rev. 1013 (2013). Various courts treating cached images as evidence of possession find relevant whether the defendant navigated to websites containing child pornography (through conduct such as performing searches containing terms associated with child pornography) and the control that technology gives defendant over the images retrieved. The Pennsylvania Supreme Court, using the Black's Law dictionary definition of *control*, explained as follows:

> An individual manifests such knowing control of child pornography when he purposefully searches it out on the internet and intentionally views it on his computer. . . . [T]he viewer may, *inter alia*, manipulate, download, copy, print, save or e-mail the images. It is of no import whether an individual actually partakes in such conduct or lacks the intent to partake in such activity because intentionally seeking out child pornography and purposefully making it appear on the computer screen—for however long the defendant elects to view the image—itself constitutes knowing control.

Commonwealth v. Diodoro, 601 Pa. 6, 970 A.2d 1100, 1107 (2009), *cert. denied*, 558 U.S. 875, 130 S.Ct. 200, 175 L.Ed.2d 127 (2009); *see also New v. State*, 327 Ga.App. 87, 755 S.E.2d 568, 575–76 (2014) ("[A] computer user who intentionally accesses child pornography images on a website 'gains actual control over the images, just as a person who intentionally browses child pornography in a print magazine "knowingly possesses" those images, even if he later puts the magazine down.' " (quoting *Kain*, 589 F.3d at 950)).

Similar to those cases, there was evidence introduced that Linson entered multiple search terms associated with child pornography, repeatedly seeking it out. The officers investigating the computer at his house reported that they had to wait for Linson to arrive before they could access his user profile, which contained the child pornography. Linson's wife testified that those reports were inaccurate and that she and Linson's sister had access to his user profile. But the jury is tasked with making a credibility determination. And based on the evidence introduced, it could infer that Linson had exclusive access to the computer profile on which the images were found. One of the responding officers testified that Linson initially claimed that pop-ups were to blame for the child pornography on his computer's history. He told the officer that he searched for and viewed adult pornography when the child pornography was displayed in a pop-up. The officer further testified that "after some conversation back and forth, I don't recall the exact conversation, but he did admit that he typed some of those terms into there [.]" The detective performing the computer analysis testified that she found an additional 360 images of child pornography in the unallocated space of the computer. Thus, the jury could also infer that Linson consciously sought out and retrieved the images that were introduced. In taking such actions, he gained control over the images that he ultimately accessed and thus knowingly possessed them. *See State v. Mercer*, 324 Wis.2d 506, 782 N.W.2d 125, 139 (Wis. Ct. App. 2010) ("[Defendant's] *repetitive* searches for and navigation within child pornography websites show that this was not a person doing a search for a benign topic who just happened to mistakenly click on a website featuring child pornography."). Some of the various actions that Linson could take in regard to the images include printing, taking a screenshot, emailing, uploading to a cloud-based service, or copying. This is not a case involving mere viewing of child pornography or one in which it was clear that the images found on the computer had been placed there inadvertently. The evidence indicated affirmative actions by Linson to seek out child pornography and place it on his computer at one point in time and for whatever duration he chose, bringing it under his control. *See State v. McKinney*, 2005 S.D. 74, ¶ 13, 699 N.W.2d 460, 465 ("[T]here is no amount of time these images must be in a defendant's possession before a conviction can be upheld."). Such conduct, as found by the jury, amounts to constructive possession of the child pornography.

STATE OF OREGON V. BARRY LOWELL BARGER

Supreme Court of Oregon
349 Or. 553 (2011)

This criminal case involves the following question: Can a person be found guilty of "possess[ing] or control[ling]" digital images of sexually explicit conduct involving a child, as that phrase in used in ORS 163.686(1)(a), based on evidence showing only that the person searched for and found such images through the Internet on his or her computer? Although the trial court in the present case acknowledged that "the world of the Internet presses * * * the boundaries of what we normally understand to be possession and control," it ultimately concluded that a jury *could* find defendant guilty under ORS 163.686(1)(a) based solely on such evidence. As we explain below, we disagree with that conclusion: The statute requires something more than simply accessing and looking at incorporeal material of the kind involved here to "possess" or "control" that material. Accordingly, we reverse both the circuit court judgment and the Court of Appeals decision affirming that judgment.

In the course of investigating a report that defendant had sexually abused a child, a City of Eugene Police Officer, Sullivan, talked to defendant's wife, who told him that there was some "weird" material on the couple's home computer. Defendant's wife showed the computer to Sullivan, who looked at the computer's web-address history and saw three addresses that, based on their titles, seemed suspicious.

A few weeks later, the Eugene police asked defendant's wife if she would allow them to take the computer and examine it. She consented. Thereafter, Eugene police detective Williams, who was certified in computer forensics, took possession of the computer, made a copy of the hard drive, and used certain forensic software to examine that hard drive. Based on Williams's findings, defendant was charged with eight counts of Encouraging Child Sexual Abuse in the Second Degree, ORS 163.686, by possessing or controlling a visual recording of sexually explicit conduct involving a child. Each charge was based on a separate digital image that Williams found in the computer's "temporary internet file cache."

As Williams later explained at defendant's jury trial, temporary Internet files found in a computer are the product of an automatic function of a computer's web browser. Whenever a computer user visits a web page, the browser creates a copy of the web page and stores it in a temporary Internet file "cache," where it remains until the space is used up and written over, or it is erased. If a user calls up the same web page at some later date, the browser simply accesses the copy from the temporary files, rather than going through the slower process of downloading the same information from the web page. Computer users with ordinary skills would not necessarily be aware of that function or know how to go about accessing information stored in the temporary Internet file cache.

Williams testified that, when he received the computer, only one of the three addresses that had triggered Sullivan's suspicions remained in the web-address registry but that, by examining other Internet activity files, he was able to identify two other suspicious web addresses that someone had accessed in the recent past. Williams stated that he checked all three websites and that all appeared to contain pornographic images of prepubescent girls and girls in their early teens.

Williams testified that he then searched for similar images that might be stored on the computer's hard drive, using certain words and phrases commonly used in child pornography. He acknowledged that he did not find any images of that kind that had been purposefully copied and saved in any user's personal files. He did, however, discover sexually explicit images of prepubescent girls in the computer's temporary Internet file cache.

The prosecution then presented the specific evidence that it asserts established defendant's guilt of the eight charges of Encouraging Child Sexual Abuse. The evidence included the eight digital images, all of which Williams had discovered in the temporary Internet file cache of defendant's computer, and which were the bases of the charges. Williams acknowledged that there was nothing about the images that identified what website they had come from and that there was no way to know with absolute certainty whether the images had been accessed intentionally by a user or "were the result of pop-up windows or browser redirects." Williams further explained, however, that pornographic pop-ups and redirects occur almost exclusively when a computer user visits another pornographic website.

After presenting Williams's testimony, the state rested. Defendant then moved for a judgment of acquittal, arguing that there was no evidence that the eight images at issue had made their way onto the hard drive through any intentional or knowing action by him and that, even if it was possible to infer that defendant had *accessed* the images through web browsing, that inference was insufficient to establish defendant's knowing *possession* or *control* of those images. The trial judge denied defendant's motion, and the jury ultimately returned guilty verdicts on all eight charges. On defendant's appeal, the Court of Appeals affirmed without opinion. *State v. Barger,* 233 Or.App. 621, 226 P.3d 718 (2010). We allowed defendant's petition for review.

Before this court, defendant argues that, although the state's evidence might support an inference that he had accessed and viewed the images at issue, the evidence would not support an inference that he ever knowingly "possess[ed] or control[led]" them within the meaning of ORS 163.686(1)(a).

. . . The question for this court thus is a narrow one: Can a computer user be found to have knowingly "possess[ed] or control[led]" digital images of child sexual abuse, within the meaning of ORS 163.686(1)(a)(A)(i), based solely on evidence showing that, at some time in the past, he intentionally accessed those digital images using his computer's Internet browser and—by reasonable inference—looked at them?

The answer to that question depends on what the legislature that enacted ORS 163.686(1)(a) intended by the phrase "possesses or controls" and on whether an activity that is commonplace now but was far less common at the time of the statute's enactment comes within the meaning that the legislature intended for that statute. To determine the legislature's intent, we employ the methodology set out in ORS 174.020 and *State v. Gaines,* 346 Or. 160, 171–73, 206 P.3d 1042 (2009). Specifically, we first consider the text and context of the statute and then, if we so choose, consider any legislative history that the parties might proffer.

We begin with the part of the statutory text that is relevant to the charges against defendant. ORS 163.686 provides, in part:

"(1) A person commits the crime of encouraging child sexual abuse in the second degree if the person:

"(a)(A)(i) Knowingly possesses or controls any photograph, motion picture, videotape or other visual recording of sexually explicit conduct involving a child for the purpose of arousing or satisfying the sexual desires of the person or another person; [and]

"(B) Knows or is aware of and consciously disregards the fact that creation of the visual recording of sexually explicit conduct involved child abuse[.]"

As our synopsis of the arguments suggests, the operative words in the present inquiry are the verbs "possesses" and "controls."

The verb "control" is not statutorily defined, but its common meaning, as set out in *Webster's Third New Int'l Dictionary* 496 (unabridged ed 2002), is "to exercise restraining or directing influence over: REGULATE, CURB." The word "possess," on the other hand, *is* statutorily defined: For purposes of most Oregon criminal statutes, including ORS 163.686, it means "to have physical possession or otherwise to exercise dominion or control over property." ORS 161.015(9). As this court explained in *State v. Fries,* 344 Or. 541, 545–47, 185 P.3d 453 (2008), that definition of the word "possess" encompasses two alternative ways of possessing property that this court traditionally has recognized: (1) *physically* controlling the property ("actual" possession) and (2) exercising some *other* kind of dominion or control over the property ("constructive" possession). Put differently, to "possess" a thing traditionally means to control it, and "actual possession" and "constructive possession" are simply different types of control. *Id.; see also State v. Connally,* 339 Or. 583, 591, 125 P.3d 1254 (2005) (making a similar point about the ordinary dictionary meaning of the term "possession").

Because the idea of control is inherent in the statutory term "possess," it is odd that the legislature chose to define the crime of encouraging child sexual abuse in terms both of "possessing" and of "controlling" certain kinds of images. The state explains that choice as a considered decision to recognize that "control" *itself* may be both actual and constructive, and to define the crime set out in ORS 163.686(1)(a) in terms of (1) actual possession, *i.e.,* physical control of an object; (2) constructive possession, *i.e.,* "dominion or power" over the object that is not necessarily exercised; and (3) actual control, *i.e.,* active restraint or direction of the object.

That explanation is creative, but it is not persuasive. We think it highly unlikely that the legislature engaged in that kind of parsing of terms or that it even recognized that, in light of the statutory definition of the term "possess," the inclusion of the term "control" was duplicative. Instead, we believe it is more logical to conclude that the legislature's choice of words reflects its desire to ensure that the crime not be limited to a narrow, solely physical, concept of possession. In other words, it would appear that the legislature used *two* words to convey the same broad meaning that ORS 161.015(9) actually conveys in the single word "possess" and that, at least in the criminal law context, this court traditionally has ascribed to that word; *viz.,* to *physically or bodily* possess or control something *or* to exercise dominion or control (*i.e.,* a restraining or directing influence) over it *in some other way. See, e.g., State v. Oare,* 249 Or. 597, 599, 439 P.2d 885 (1968) (crime of unlawful possession of marijuana includes actual and constructive possession); *State v. Barnes,* 120 Or. 372, 379–80, 251 P. 305 (1927) (crime of unlawful possession of intoxicating liquor includes actual and constructive possession).

With the foregoing background concerning the meaning of the phrase "possesses or controls" in ORS 163.686(1)(a)(A)(i) in mind, we turn to the specific question that this case presents: Does a computer user's act of accessing an Internet web page and intentionally calling digital images of child sexual abuse onto a computer screen constitute "possess[ion] or control [ ]" of those images within the meaning of that statute? The state asserts that it does, and offers three different explanations for its answer.

First, the state contends that, insofar as a computer user has physical control over a computer screen, he or she has physical control ("actual" possession) of any images that appear on it. The state points to the fact that a computer user can move his or her monitor from one place to another and thereby display the image appearing on the screen wherever he or she chooses. We think, however, that that argument misses the point: The intangible nature of a web image is analogous to seeing something that a visitor has temporarily placed in one's own home. One may be *aware* of it, may even have asked the visitor to bring it for viewing, but one does not thereby *possess* the item.

The state argues, next, that a computer user "controls" a digital image of child pornography by actively navigating to the website where it resides, thereby bringing the image to his computer screen. We think, however, that this argument suffers from some of the same defects as the preceding one: Looking for something on the Internet is like walking into a museum to look at pictures—the pictures are where the person expected them to be, and he can look at them, but that does not in any sense give him possession of them.

Finally, the state argues that, to establish that defendant "controlled" the images at issue at the time that they appeared on his computer screen, the state need only show that, at that time, defendant had the *ability* to direct or influence the images (by, for example, showing that he had the ability to save, copy, print, or e-mail them), and that it need not show that defendant actually *exercised* any such influence or control. . . . Constructive possession in terms of a "right" to control the object in question. *See, e.g., Oare,* 249 Or. at 599, 439 P.2d 885 ("evidence of the control or the right to control is necessary to constructive possession"); *State v. Weller,* 263 Or. 132, 501 P.2d 794 (1972) (quoting *Oare* to same effect); *State v. Barnes,* 120 Or. 372, 380, 251 P. 305 (1926) (jury could conclude that defendant constructively possessed intoxicating liquor to the extent that evidence showed that he "claimed the right and had the power to control, manage and dispose of the same").

A final problem with the state's theory about the meaning of "control" is that it would sweep in more factual scenarios than we believe the legislature could possibly have intended. If the mere *ability* to cause an item to appear on a computer screen is sufficient to constitute "control" or constructive "possession" of the item for purposes of ORS 163.686(1)(a)(A)(i), then *any* person who uses the Internet (and, indeed, any person who is within physical reach of some tangible item of child pornography) can be deemed to be guilty of violating that statute, at least insofar as the element of possession or control is involved. Of course, the state contends that a person who already has accessed an image of child sexual abuse on his computer has a more direct and immediate ability to save, print, or otherwise control that image than does a computer user who has not accessed the image, and that that directness and immediacy makes the difference. But that argument still is nothing more than the assertion, rejected by this court most recently in *Casey,* that the *ability* to possess or control a thing means that one actually *is* possessing or controlling it.

In a final version of that argument, the state insists that a person who uses a computer to look at images of child pornography does more than just *view* the images that he brings to the screen. It contends that, because computers have the *capacity* to save, print, post, and transmit those images "with only a few mouse clicks," web browsing for child pornography is qualitatively different from other methods of "viewing" child pornography, and falls within the intended meaning of the phrase "possesses or controls" in ORS 163.686(1)(a)(A)(i). But we think that our recent holdings in *Casey* and *Daniels* fully answer that argument, particularly where the state fails to explain why existence of those capacities in the viewing device would transform viewing into possession. Neither do we see anything in the statutory wording that would support that idea.

For the foregoing reasons, we are not persuaded by the state's theories as to how and why, in the absence of some additional action by a computer user beyond that proved here, the user could be deemed to "possess" or "control," in any sense that this court heretofore has recognized, a digital image that he or she has called up on a computer screen. Instead, we are satisfied that the statute before us, ORS 163.686(1)(a)(A)(i), when read in the light of its context (particularly ORS 163.686(1)(a)(A)(ii)), embodies a considered legislative choice not to criminalize the mere "obtaining" or "viewing" of child pornography without consideration. Thus, we conclude that the acts at issue here—navigating to a website and bringing the images that the site contains to a computer screen—are not acts that the legislature intended to criminalize.

Applying our conclusions to the record in this case, we hold that defendant's motion for a judgment of acquittal should have been granted. There is no evidence in the record that, at any time, defendant "possess[ed] or control[led]" any of the eight images that are the subject of the charges against him under ORS 163.686(1)(a)(A)(i).

DE MUNIZ, C.J., concurring.

DISCUSSION QUESTIONS

1.   Do you possess an image when you access it on the internet? Do you have sufficient control over the image to satisfy constructive possession? Or should legislatures have to pass separate laws criminalizing such access?

2.   Should legislatures punish accessing an image online if you do not deliberately save it to your computer in some fashion? Should it be punished more or less seriously than actual possession?

3.   Do notions of dominion and control operate differently in the physical and online realms in ways that the law should take into account?

K. MODEL PENAL CODE

Possession, omission liability and the voluntary act doctrine are areas where the Model Penal Code and the common law approach are largely aligned although common law jurisdictions do not always express these doctrines in statutory form. Note that the Model Penal Code offers specific guidance on the amount of time that criminal possession requires.

§ 2.01. Requirement of Voluntary Act; Omission as Basis of Liability; Possession as an Act.

1)   A person is not guilty of an offense unless his liability is based on conduct that includes a voluntary act or the omission to perform an act of which he is physically capable.

2)   The following are not voluntary acts within the meaning of this Section:

a)   a reflex or convulsion;

b) a bodily movement during unconsciousness or sleep;

c) conduct during hypnosis or resulting from hypnotic suggestion;

d) a bodily movement that otherwise is not a product of the effort or determination of the actor, either conscious or habitual.

3) Liability for the commission of an offense may not be based on an omission unaccompanied by action unless:

a) the omission is expressly made sufficient by the law defining the offense; or

b) a duty to perform the omitted act is otherwise imposed by law.

4) Possession is an act, within the meaning of this Section, if the possessor knowingly procured or received the thing possessed or was aware of his control thereof for a sufficient period to have been able to terminate his possession.

Practice Problem 5.2: Left Holding the Bag

Riley is standing next to Jess on a dark street corner when a marked police car drives by. The police recognize Riley as a frequent seller of illegal drugs and shine their floodlight on him. He grabs Jess as if to hug her and in the process she feels him shove something into her pocket. Riley knows that Jess sells drugs and suspects that he has planted drugs in her pocket. Riley then takes off running down the street. By now the two police officers have jumped out of the car with their hands on their guns and yelled "freeze." Riley keeps running and Jess stands still. The officers frisk Jess but do not reach into her pockets. They discover that she is a juvenile and arrest her for being out past curfew. They place her in their police car and drive her to the police station. They tell her they are going to place her in a holding cell by herself in the jail while they summon her parents to the police station. The deputy in charge of the jail searches her jacket and discovers a bag of cocaine.

Jess is charged with possession of cocaine and introduction of a controlled substance into a detention facility. Analyze her liability for these charges.

CHAPTER 6

THE GUILTY MIND

■ ■ ■

Mental states are perhaps the most important part of the criminal law. They are central to our notions of blameworthiness. Oliver Wendel Holmes famously observed once that "even a dog knows the difference between being tripped over and kicked." Deliberately doing a bad thing, for example, is universally seen as worse than accidentally doing a bad thing. Mental states are also central to our notions of dangerousness and deterrence. When people are thinking about doing bad things, we want them to be deterred by the prospect of punishment. Moreover, someone who intentionally hurts people is the sort of dangerous person that we often want to incapacitate through imprisonment. Over time, the criminal law has evolved various definitions of mental states that reflect differing levels of blameworthiness and dangerousness.

Yet, mental states are also deceptively complex. We often talk about intent, but what does it really mean to "intend" to do something? What does it mean to be purposeful, to have knowledge, to be reckless, or to be negligent? The differences between these different mental states are significant when deciding whether and how hard to punish someone. Therefore, the criminal law relies heavily on mental states to determine whether a crime took place and to distinguish more from less serious crimes. To complicate things even further, crimes often involve multiple elements, and judges often must make difficult decisions about which mental states apply to which elements. Various rules have evolved for helping judges make these sorts of decisions, but the rules still leave substantial room for argument.

Finally, two very different approaches to mental states have developed in the United States—the common law approach and the Model Penal Code approach. While some overlap exists, the more modern Model Penal Code diverges sharply from the common law approach on many points and has proven to be very influential—even in some jurisdictions that follow the common law in many other respects.

So, you must learn to do two things to determine what the guilty mind requires for criminal liability. First, you must determine which mental states a crime requires for its various elements. Second, you must analyze whether the defendant had the required mental states. And, you must learn to do this in both a common law and a Model Penal Code jurisdiction. These tasks can be easily mastered if broken down and taken step by step.

A. MODEL PENAL CODE MENTAL STATE DEFINITIONS

The Model Penal Code defines four principal mental states: purpose, knowledge, recklessness, and negligence. The easiest examples involve results, so that is where we will begin.

- Purposely means that it was your conscious effort to bring about the result.

- Knowingly means that you were substantially certain that the result would occur.

- Recklessly means that you consciously disregarded a substantial and unjustifiable risk that the result would occur under circumstances that constituted a gross deviation from the standard of care that a reasonable person would observe in the situation.

- Negligently means that you should have been aware of a substantial and unjustifiable risk that the result would occur under circumstances that constituted a gross deviation from the standard of care that a reasonable person would observe in the situation.

M.P.C. § 2.02. General Requirements of Culpability

2) Kinds of Culpability Defined.

   a) Purposely.

      i) A person acts purposely with respect to a material element of an offense when:

         (1) if the element involves the nature of his conduct or a result thereof, it is his conscious object to engage in conduct of that nature or to cause such a result; and

         (2) if the element involves the attendant circumstances, he is aware of the existence of such circumstances or he believes or hopes that they exist.

   b) Knowingly.

      i) A person acts knowingly with respect to a material element of an offense when:

         (1) if the element involves the nature of his conduct or the attendant circumstances, he is aware that his conduct is of that nature or that such circumstances exist; and

         (2) if the element involves a result of his conduct, he is aware that it is practically certain that his conduct will cause such a result.

c) Recklessly.

i) A person acts recklessly with respect to a material element of an offense when he consciously disregards a substantial and unjustifiable risk that the material element exists or will result from his conduct. The risk must be of such a nature and degree that, considering the nature and purpose of the actor's conduct and the circumstances known to him, its disregard involves a gross deviation from the standard of conduct that a law-abiding person would observe in the actor's situation.

d) Negligently.

i) A person acts negligently with respect to a material element of an offense when he should be aware of a substantial and unjustifiable risk that the material element exists or will result from his conduct. The risk must be of such a nature and degree that the actor's failure to perceive it, considering the nature and purpose of his conduct and the circumstances known to him, involves a gross deviation from the standard of care that a reasonable person would observe in the actor's situation.

Note that the principal difference between recklessness and negligence is whether the defendant foresaw the risk of the prohibited result occurring or ought to have foreseen it. The Model Penal Code (and the common law for that matter) punishes recklessness more severely than negligence because someone who did a risky thing after realizing that it was risky is generally considered more blameworthy and dangerous than someone who didn't realize the risk but should have. Note also that both recklessness and negligence involve gross deviations from the standard care. Simple or ordinary negligence—a mere deviation from a reasonable standard of care—is left to the world of civil liability. The common law also follows this definition of negligence, so whenever you hear criminal negligence, think gross negligence.

We can easily distinguish these four states of mind from one another with a series of hypotheticals about a mad 1L law student. Imagine that a first-year law student has become unhinged and decides to blow up his most hated law professor. He brings a bomb wrapped as a gift to the professor during office hours and sets it down on the professor's desk. He notices, however, that sitting across from his most hated law professor is his most loved law professor. The student leaves and walks down the hall a safe distance before taking the remote detonator switch out of his pocket. He hesitates for a moment, torn between his desire to kill his most hated professor and his deep regret at losing his most loved professor. Then, he pushes the detonator button, sending them both to the law classroom in the sky.

In this first hypothetical, our mad bomber is purposeful as to the death of the hated law professor but only knowing with respect to the death of the loved law professor. It was his conscious objective to kill only the former, although he was substantially certain that the latter would die in the blast.

Now, imagine a variation where after he leaves the office, he sees his first-year study group clustered outside the office waiting for office hours to begin. He loves his study group and pauses to consider whether there is enough explosive in the bomb to harm them, even though the door is closed. He says "Nah" to himself and pushes the button. The blast, contrary to his expectations, blows through the door and kills the study group.

In this second hypothetical, our mad bomber is not knowing but reckless as to the deaths of his study group. Even though, as a matter of physics, it might have been substantially certain that they would be killed in the blast, he was not substantially certain that they would die. Therefore, he was not knowing. He was, however, conscious of the risk—as exemplified by the "nah" moment—which makes him reckless with respect to their deaths.

In our last variation, there is a study group of 2Ls sitting in a courtyard below the window of the law professor's office. (Since they are 2Ls they do their "studying" in the sun.) The blast blows off the external wall of the office, and it falls into the courtyard, killing all of them. Our unhinged bomber is only criminally negligent with respect to their deaths. He was not reckless with respect to their deaths because it never occurred to him that people in the courtyard below could have been harmed. He should have been aware of such a risk, though, and his conduct reflects such unjustifiable and substantially risky behavior that a finder of fact would easily find it to be a gross deviation of the standard of care.[1]

What does the MPC provide if a defendant has a more blameworthy mental state than the law requires? For example, what if a statute defines vandalism as recklessly damaging the property of another? Is it a defense if the person claims that he damaged the property not recklessly, but purposely? Obviously not. The basic rule is that a more culpable mental state satisfies a requirement for a less culpable mental state. So, knowledge is satisfied by purpose, reckless is satisfied by knowledge or purpose, and negligence satisfied by any of the above.

---

[1] These result-oriented examples gets the main idea of the differences between these mental states across. The definition of purpose and knowledge apply differently to conduct elements or to attendant circumstances, however. For conduct elements and attendant circumstances, a person need only be aware of the nature of the conduct or the existence of an attendant circumstance in order to be either knowing or purposeful.

B. COMMON LAW MENTAL STATES

Faulkner once said, "the past is not dead; it is not even the past." In the criminal law, nowhere is this more true than in the area of common law mental states. The moral intuitions that animated the common law's early approach to mental states are powerful and persistent.

Case in Context

The common law term for mental state was mens rea, a Latin phrase that means "guilty mind." The earliest definition of a guilty mind described a general morally blameworthy mental state. Simply put, it meant that the person was "up to no good." The following case illustrates a key point in the evolution of the meaning of mens rea.

REGINA V. FAULKENER
13 Cox. Crim. Cas. 550 (1877)

OPINION

Reserved by Lawson, J. At the Cork Summer Assizes, 1876, the prisoner was indicted for setting fire to the ship Zemindar, on the high seas, on the 26th day of June, 1876. The indictment was as follows: "That Robert Faulkner, on the 26th day of June, 1876, on board a certain ship called the Zemindar, on a certain voyage on the high seas, then being upon the high seas, feloniously, unlawfully, and maliciously, did set fire to the said ship, with intent thereby to prejudice the said Sandback, Parker, and other, the owners of certain goods and chattels then laden, and being on board said ship."

It was proved that the Zemindar was on her voyage home with a cargo of rum, sugar, and cotton, worth 50,0001. That the prisoner was a seaman on board, that he went into the bulk head, and forecastle hold, opened the sliding door in the bulk head, and so got into the hold where the rum was stored; he had no business there, and no authority to go there and went for the purpose of stealing some rum, that he bored hole in the cask with a gimlet, that the rum ran out, that when trying to put a spile in the hole out of which the rum was running, he had a lighted match in his hand; that the rum caught fire; that the prisoner himself was burned on the arms and neck; and that the ship caught fire and was completely destroyed. At the close of the case for the Crown, counsel for the prisoner asked for a direction of an acquittal on the ground that on the facts proved the indictment was not sustained, nor the allegation that the prisoner had unlawfully and maliciously set fire to the ship proved. The Crown contended that inasmuch as the prisoner was at the time engaged in the commission of a felony, the indictment was sustained, and the allegation of the intent was immaterial.

At the second hearing of the case before the Court for Crown Cases Reserved, the learned judge made the addition of the following paragraph to the case stated by him for the court.

"It was conceded that the prisoner had no actual intention of burning the vessel, and I was not asked to leave any question as to the jury as to the prisoner's knowing the probable consequences his act, or as to his reckless conduct."

The learned judge told the jury that although the prisoner had no actual intention of burning the vessel, still if they found he was engaged in stealing the rum, and that the fire took place in the manner above stated, they ought to find him guilty. The jury found the prisoner guilty on both counts, and he was sentenced to seven years penal servitude. The question for the court was whether the direction of the learned judge was right, if not, the conviction should be quashed.

BARRY, J.—A very broad proposition has been contended for by the Crown, namely, that if, while a person is engaged in committing a felony, or, having committed it, is endeavouring to conceal his act, or prevent or spoil waste consequent on that act, he accidently does some collateral act which if done wilfully would be another felony either at common law or by statute, he is guilty of the latter felony. I am by no means anxious to throw any doubt upon, or limit in any way, the legal responsibility of those who engage in the commission of felony, or acts mala in se; but I am not prepared without more consideration to give my assent to so wide a proposition. No express authority either by way of decision or dictum from judge or text writer has been cited in support of it. . . . I shall consider myself bound for the purpose of this case by the authority of Reg. v. Pembliton (12 Cox C. C. 607). That case must be taken as deciding that to constitute an offence under the Malicious Injuries to Property Act, sect. 51, the act done must be in fact intentional and wilful, although the intention and will may (perhaps) be held to exist in, or be proved by, the fact that the accused knew that the injury would be the probable result of his unlawful act, and yet did the act reckless of such consequences. The jury [was] directed to give a verdict of guilty upon the simple ground that the firing of the ship, though accidental, was caused by an act done in the course of, or immediately consequent upon, a felonious operation, and no question of the prisoner's malice, constructive or otherwise, was left to the jury. I am of opinion that, according to Reg. v. Pembliton, that direction was erroneous, and that the conviction should be quashed.

FITZGERALD, J.—I concur in opinion with my brother Barry, and for the reasons he has given, that the direction of the learned judge cannot be sustained in law, and that therefore the conviction should be quashed. I am further of opinion that in order to establish the charge the intention of the accused forms an element in the crime to the extent that it should appear that the defendant intended to do the very act with which he is charged, or that it was the necessary consequence of some other felonious or criminal act in which he was engaged, or that having a probable result which the defendant foresaw, or ought to have foreseen, he, nevertheless, persevered in such other felonious or criminal act. The prisoner did not intend to set fire to the ship; the fire was not the necessary result of the felony he was attempting; and if it was a probable result, which he ought to have foreseen, of the felonious transaction on which he was engaged, and from which a malicious design to commit the injurious act with which he is charged might have been fairly imputed to him, that view of the case was not submitted to the jury. Counsel for the prosecution in effect insisted that the defendant, being engaged in the commission of, or in an attempt to commit a felony, was criminally responsible for every result that was occasioned thereby, even though it was not a probable consequence of his act or such as he could have reasonably foreseen or intended. No authority has been cited for a proposition so extensive, and I am of opinion that it is not warranted by law. . . .

KEOGH, J. I have the misfortune to differ from the other members of the Court. . . . [I am] of [the] opinion that the conviction should stand, as I consider all questions of intentions and malice are closed by the finding of the jury, that the prisoner committed the act whilst engaged in the commission of a substantive felony. . . .

Conviction quashed. (SOURCE: Criminal Law, Cases and Materials, Kaplan)

DISCUSSION QUESTIONS

1.   Using Model Penal Code terminology, what mental state would each judge require for the crime charged?

2.   Should it be enough that the defendant was generally blameworthy in a criminal sense—"up to no good"—to be liable for arson? Why not?

3.   Generally speaking, should criminal liability be limited to behavior that is reckless or worse? Or should it extend to behavior that is grossly negligent?

C. SPECIFIC VS. GENERAL INTENT

The common law has almost always distinguished between a general intent and a specific intent to commit a crime. This distinction has confused generations of judges, lawyers, and law students because it has meant different things at different times in different places. While it is not necessary to discuss all the different meanings of the two terms, a few basic definitions remain important. General intent has been defined in the following three different ways.

1.   A generally blameworthy state of mind.

2.   A general awareness of the nature of what you are doing.

3.   Recklessness or even negligence as to the existence of the element in question.

Specific intent means something more than the above. Specifically, it has been defined as follows.

1.   A further intent beyond what is otherwise required to establish the crime.

2.   An intent to achieve a specific result or condition.

3.   A purposeful or knowing state of mind as to the existence of the element in question.

Assaultive crimes allow us to illustrate both concepts. Battery is an unlawful and offensive touching of another, and it is a general intent crime. Imagine that, in a crowded elevator, a man begins enthusiastically reenacting a mixed martial arts match that he just watched on television. He swings his fists right and left, reenacting a flurry of blows. People next to him edge away, but he accidentally clocks one of them in the face. Is he guilty of criminal battery? Yes, under any of the definitions given above, he has the requisite general intent. He was generally aware of swinging his arms around. Doing so in such a crowded space would be considered by most to be generally blameworthy and reckless or negligent.

But what if he is charged with assault with intent to inflict serious injury? (He hit the guy really hard.) The further intent to inflict serious injury in the crime suggests that there was something "specific" that he had in mind, which means that he was either purposeful or knowing with respect to the result. This would, arguably, not be satisfied on these facts. He was aware of his actions and reckless and negligent with respect to the danger of an injury. But since he did not have the specific intent to injure, he would not be guilty of assault with intent to inflict serious injury.

As you proceed, keep two important considerations in mind. First, specific intent is sometimes interpreted to require not only a knowing but also a purposeful state of mind. Second, whether a specific intent requires purpose or merely knowledge can depend on the element in question. For example, in the Model Penal Code, a specific intent with respect to an attendant circumstance or with respect to conduct—not results—is often interpreted to require only knowledge or awareness.

Cases in Context

The following two cases help illustrate the distinction between general and specific intent.

STATE OF VERMONT V. JAMES RILEY

Supreme Court of Vermont
442 A.2d 1297 (1982)

BARNEY, CHIEF JUSTICE.

The defendant was found guilty after trial by jury on charges of attempting by physical menace to put another in fear of serious bodily injury under Vermont's simple assault statute, 13 V.S.A. s 1023(a)(3). The charge grew out of a confrontation between the defendant and a state trooper on an isolated stretch of I-89 near St. Albans in the early morning hours of October 20, 1979.

The defendant had stopped his car in the breakdown lane of the highway and was seated in the driver's seat with the interior car light on when the officer pulled up behind him and approached his vehicle. When questioned, the defendant stated that he had something like a cramp in his leg, which he was massaging at the time.

During a routine check of the car from the outside, the trooper noticed a handgun on the seat beside the defendant, its barrel pointed toward the passenger door. Opening the door on the defendant's side of the vehicle, the trooper asked the defendant to put both hands on the steering wheel, which the defendant did, and then to get out of the car, which he refused to do.

The trooper then ordered the defendant out of the car, and as he did so the defendant dropped his hand from the steering wheel and reached toward the gun. At this point the trooper drew his own weapon and told the defendant to "hold it right there." The defendant replied "everything is cool, don't shoot," and brushed the gun along the seat until he could place it on the floor in front of the passenger's place. He then got out of the car.

At trial the trooper testified that he had been frightened by the defendant's conduct, and had feared for his life. He said that there was a point at which he could not see the defendant's hand because it was down in front of the seat, and he "knew the gun was with the hand" and "didn't know what the story was."

The defendant claims on appeal that the State failed to prove all the elements of the crime. He maintains that the evidence did not meet our standard for crimes of attempt, as set out in State v. Boutin, 133 Vt. 531 (1975). He claims first, that because the handgun lacked a firing pin it could not put the trooper in actual danger, and second, that because the evidence showed no sudden or threatening moves by the defendant, the requisite criminal intent was never established. The defendant also claims that the court's instruction to the jury on the issue of intent was improper in that it unduly emphasized the weight to be accorded the trooper's perception of what occurred.

With regard to the capacity of the handgun to fire, this Court in State v. Deso, 110 Vt. 1, 6–8 (1938), rejected the notion that present ability to inflict injury upon the person assailed was a prerequisite to a finding of simple assault. In that case we adopted the rule that while there must be some power to do bodily harm, either actual or apparent, apparent power alone would be sufficient. Id. Although the statute has been amended since Deso was decided, the principle has not changed and we find no reason to depart from it in this case.

Vermont's simple assault statute is patterned after the simple assault provision written into the Model Penal Code at s 211.1. (Official Draft and Revised Commentary, 1980). The Comment to that provision explains that the language under which the defendant in this case was charged, 13 V.S.A. s 1023(a)(3), was intended to incorporate into the criminal law the civil notion of assault, that an action may be maintained against a person who places another in fear of bodily injury, even if the alleged assailant acts without purpose to carry out the threat. Id. at 177. The rationale for including this tort aspect within the definition of assault is that a threat of an immediate battery resulting in apprehension, even when intended only as a bluff, is so likely to result in a breach of the peace that it should be a punishable offense.

The question of whether or not the defendant's actions in this instance amounted to a simple assault was properly a question for the jury. Its resolution depended upon all the surrounding circumstances, including the words spoken, the appearance and demeanor of the parties, and their conduct in light of the setting and circumstances. The jury had before it the two participants in the drama, both of whom testified. It was in the best position to determine the issue.

The defendant testified that he slid the gun across the seat of the car and eased it to the floor in an effort to eliminate any possibility that the officer would see it and become so excited that he would shoot the defendant out of fear. The trooper testified that the defendant's actions and his handling of the gun were such that they caused him to feel threatened and to fear for his life. Where contradictory evidence is introduced at trial it is the exclusive province of the jury, as finders of fact, to resolve the contradictions and decide who to believe. State v. Blakeney, 137 Vt. 495, 500–01, 408 A.2d 636, 640 (1979).

The court instructed the jury that in determining whether or not the defendant intended to place the trooper in fear they should consider both the bare actions of the defendant and how those actions were perceived by the officer. This was a correct statement of the law. Criminal intent is not the secret intent of the defendant, but that intent which can be determined from his conduct and all the other circumstances which surround it.

Judgment affirmed.

DISCUSSION QUESTIONS

1.   Why does the court focus on how the defendant's actions were perceived by the officer?

2.   Could you say that the defendant was reckless or negligent with respect to the risk that the officer would feel threatened?

3.   Should simple assault be limited to those whose purpose was to scare or attack?

Case in Context

The court in the following case polices the boundary between specific and general intent.

STATE V. RICHARDSON

Supreme Court of Iowa
162 N.W. 28 (1917)

INDICTMENT charging defendant with the crime of assault with intent to inflict great bodily injury upon one Harry Horn, by operating and running an automobile over said Horn with specific intent to inflict a great bodily injury upon him and otherwise maltreat him, contrary to statute. Defendant appeals from a conviction under this indictment.—Reversed.

II

[Defendant was driving at night in a dust storm without headlights and with faulty brakes at a high rate of speed when he struck Harry Horn, who was at the side of the road repairing a tire on his vehicle. There is no evidence that Defendant saw Horn or had any intention in to injure him or anyone else. The trial judge instructed the jury that if they found the Defendant to be negligent, reckless, or in violation of certain safety laws, they must find specific intent to injure Horn. Defendant was convicted of assault with intent to inflict serious injury and appeals.]

The overshadowing questions, then, are: (a) Whether, as the State claims, if the conduct shown by the evidence "shows a recklessness on the part of defendant that would justify a jury in finding that he was guilty of such carelessness and recklessness as to convict him of the crime with which he was charged;" (b) whether a charge can be sustained which was, in general tenor, that, from finding reckless operation and injury, the jury could find that defendant intended the act charged in the indictment, when in fact he had no such intent in his mind, had no animosity towards the prosecutor, and did not even know he was about to injure or had injured him; and (c)—as a corollary—the still more vital question whether, under all the evidence here, a finding that defendant had such specific intent can be sustained.

Defendant is not being tried under a possible statute which may be conceded to be valid, were it enacted. He is not accused of having feloniously, willfully and unlawfully injured Horn, but of having assaulted Horn with intent to inflict upon him a great bodily injury, and otherwise to maltreat him—an assault which the trial court correctly defined to be one made with the intent to inflict a great bodily injury upon the person assailed, of a more grave and serious nature than an ordinary battery. We have been unable to find a case wherein such an assault is held to have been committed, except where defendant saw the one assaulted, or knew he was present and engaged in the assault with desire to injure seriously. [T]o constitute a criminal assault, there must be some evidence of an attempt or endeavor to do violence to the person. This is on the reasoning that, if the rule were otherwise, mere violent and abusive language or threats, accompanied by violent gestures, would be an assault, whether there was an apparent intention of carrying out the threats or not.

That no cases are found which hold that one who does not know at the time that there is anyone to hurt or who has been hurt, may be guilty of assaulting one in fact injured, with intent to maltreat him and inflict upon him a great bodily injury, is explained by the existence of a very large number of cases which require a specific intent to inflict an aggravated injury upon a specified person, and as many which define what constitutes specific intent. Undoubtedly, there are many cases wherein the sole inquiry is whether an act was willful. State v. Porter, 34 Iowa 131, at 140. There is no doubt that if, in such a case, willfulness is denied by the claim that the act was not intentionally done, the rule applies that sane persons are presumed to intend what will naturally result from what they knowingly do. We may concede, as the State says, that, had Horn been killed under the circumstances here, defendant would have been guilty of manslaughter. All this leaves open whether the rule of natural consequences applies to cases where the State is bound to prove not merely the doing of an unlawful act which inflicted an injury, and that injury to someone might well result from the reckless conduct of defendant, but to prove that he had a specific intent to inflict an aggravated injury upon a named person. Of course, the indictment here is one which requires proof of the specific intent which is essential to the offense charged, and which is specifically charged.

[S]pecific intent may be proven by circumstantial evidence, and by legitimate inference from evidence. The trouble is not with this rule, but with applying it as the State would have us do. Everything may be proven by justified inference. In all cases, the natural and probable consequences of an act tend to show an intent to have these consequences happen. But in every case—and this we think the State overlooks—the finding of intent by inference must rest upon what is relevant to the ultimate question. If that be the existence of a specific intent, the inference must be based upon what is relevant to whether such intent exists. The proof that murder was done is, of itself, nothing upon which to deduce a specific intent to kill. The manner of the murder, the words spoken when it was perpetrated, and conduct immediately preceding, may justify such inference. The fact that defendant has knocked prosecutor down with open hand will justify a finding that he intended to violate the law, but not that he acted with specific intent to inflict a great bodily injury. As said in Commonwealth v. Jeffries, (Mass.) 83 Am. Dec. 712, at 721, 722, the rule permitting the finding of ultimate facts by inference has no limit, except that "it cannot be extended to facts or circumstances which do not naturally or necessarily bear on the issue to be established, precisely as evidence of all collateral facts and circumstances must be confined to the proof of those which have a legitimate and direct connection with the principal transaction;" and the circumstances which can be made a basis must be "significant circumstances bearing on this intent."

If this be not the distinction, then there is no difference between a statute which does and one which does not require a specific intent. And yet a multitude of decisions which affirm that, "when a statute makes an act indictable, irrespective of guilty knowledge, then ignorance of the fact is no defense," and specific intent immaterial, are irresistibly suggestive of the counter-proposition that, when the criminal quality of the act depends upon a specific intent to do what is charged, there must be something which singles out such intent in the proof. On the theory of the State, the defendant stands precisely where he would if he had violated a statute making it a crime to injure another by reckless driving, or to cause injury by disobeying the laws regulating the proper operation of automobiles on the highway. In effect, the position of the court and of the State's counsel is that the statute upon which the indictment rests is not one which punishes for what is in fact an assault with intent to inflict a great bodily injury, but that the law construes it so that it may be read, "whosoever injures another by negligence, or by driving an automobile contrary to the regulations provided by law, is guilty of an assault with intent to inflict a great bodily injury upon that other."

Of course, neither in this nor any other case may the defendant ask that his naked denial of an intent to injure, or injure greatly, be held conclusive against such intent. We are constrained to hold that, if every element upon which the instructions made a finding of specific intent depend, be established, it will not warrant a finding that such intent existed. It follows that it was error to give these instructions.

III

If we assume it to be correct to charge that the jury may find specific intent if they find certain negligences or disregard of the automobile operation laws, it is still error to charge that, upon finding these, they must find a specific intent to injure Horn. Compulsion to find an ultimate fact if certain circumstances are found, differs manifestly from permission to find that ultimate fact upon finding those circumstances. It was for the jury, and not the court, to determine whether, though defendant was reckless and negligent, and whether or not he violated the automobile laws, he was actuated by a specific intent to injure Horn, as the indictment charges. State v. Ledford, 177 Iowa 528, 159 N.W. 187.

The conviction cannot stand. This does not exclude a conviction for assault and battery, or assault.—Reversed

DISCUSSION QUESTIONS

1.   Using the Model Penal Code's terminology, how would you describe the mental state of the defendant?

2.   Why can't a specific intent to injure be inferred from such extreme recklessness as a matter of law?

3.   Why does the common law place such importance on the distinction between general and specific intent?

D. SPECIAL FOCUS: MENTAL STATES AND ONLINE THREATS

The following case required the court to decide the mental state that would apply to a crime committed via Facebook post.

ANTHONY DOUGLAS ELONIS V. UNITED STATES
Supreme Court of the United States
135 S.Ct. 2001 (2015)

CHIEF JUSTICE ROBERTS delivered the opinion of the Court.

Federal law makes it a crime to transmit in interstate commerce "any communication containing any threat . . . to injure the person of another." 18 U.S.C. § 875(c). Petitioner was convicted of violating this provision under instructions that required the jury to find that he communicated what a reasonable person would regard as a threat. The question is whether the statute also requires that the defendant be aware of the threatening nature of the communication, and—if not—whether the First Amendment requires such a showing.

I

A

Anthony Douglas Elonis was an active user of the social networking Web site Facebook. Users of that Web site may post items on their Facebook page that are accessible to other users, including Facebook "friends" who are notified when new content is posted. In May 2010, Elonis's wife of nearly seven years left him, taking with her their two young children. Elonis began "listening to more violent music" and posting self-styled "rap" lyrics inspired by the music. App. 204, 226. Eventually, Elonis changed the user name on his Facebook page from his actual name to a rap-style nom de plume, "Tone Dougie," to distinguish himself from his "on-line persona." *Id.*, at 249, 265. The lyrics Elonis posted as "Tone Dougie" included graphically violent language and imagery. This material was often interspersed with disclaimers that the lyrics were "fictitious," with no intentional "resemblance to real persons." *Id.*, at 331, 329. Elonis posted an explanation to another Facebook user that "I'm doing this for me. My writing is therapeutic." *Id.*, at 329; see also *id.*, at 205 (testifying that it "helps me to deal with the pain").

Elonis's co-workers and friends viewed the posts in a different light. Around Halloween of 2010, Elonis posted a photograph of himself and a co-worker at a "Halloween Haunt" event at the amusement park where they worked. In the photograph, Elonis was holding a toy knife against his co-worker's neck, and in the caption Elonis wrote, "I wish." *Id.*, at 340. Elonis was not Facebook friends with the co-worker and did not "tag" her, a Facebook feature that would have alerted her to the posting. *Id.*, at 175; Brief for Petitioner 6, 9. But the chief of park security was a Facebook "friend" of Elonis, saw the photograph, and fired him. App. 114–116; Brief for Petitioner 9.

In response, Elonis posted a new entry on his Facebook page:

"Moles! Didn't I tell y'all I had several? Y'all sayin' I had access to keys for all the f* * *in' gates. That I have sinister plans for all my friends and must have taken home a couple. Y'all think it's too dark and foggy to secure your facility from a man as mad as me? You see, even without a paycheck, I'm still the main attraction. Whoever thought the Halloween Haunt could be so f* * *in' scary?" App. 332.

This post became the basis for Count One of Elonis's subsequent indictment, threatening park patrons and employees.

Elonis's posts frequently included crude, degrading, and violent material about his soon-to-be ex-wife. Shortly after he was fired, Elonis posted an adaptation of a satirical sketch that he and his wife had watched together. *Id.*, at 164–165, 207. In the actual sketch, called "It's Illegal to Say . . .," a comedian explains that it is illegal for a person to say he wishes to kill the President, but not illegal to explain that it is illegal for him to say that. When Elonis posted the script of the sketch, however, he substituted his wife for the President. The posting was part of the basis for Count Two of the indictment, threatening his wife:

"Hi, I'm Tone Elonis.

Did you know that it's illegal for me to say I want to kill my wife?

. . .

It's one of the only sentences that I'm not allowed to say. . . .

Now it was okay for me to say it right then because I was just telling you that it's illegal for me to say I want to kill my wife. . . .

Um, but what's interesting is that it's very illegal to say I really, really think someone out there should kill my wife. . . .

But not illegal to say with a mortar launcher.

Because that's its own sentence. . . .

I also found out that it's incredibly illegal, extremely illegal to go on Facebook and say something like the best place to fire a mortar launcher at her house would be from the cornfield behind it because of easy access to a getaway road and you'd have a clear line of sight through the sun room. . . .

Yet even more illegal to show an illustrated diagram. [diagram of the house]. . . ." *Id.,* at 333.

The details about the home were accurate. *Id.,* at 154. At the bottom of the post, Elonis included a link to the video of the original skit, and wrote, "Art is about pushing limits. I'm willing to go to jail for my Constitutional rights. Are you?" *Id.,* at 333.

After viewing some of Elonis's posts, his wife felt "extremely afraid for [her] life." *Id.,* at 156. A state court granted her a three-year protection-from-abuse order against Elonis (essentially, a restraining order). *Id.,* at 148–150. Elonis referred to the order in another post on his "Tone Dougie" page, also included in Count Two of the indictment:

"Fold up your [protection-from-abuse order] and put it in your pocket

Is it thick enough to stop a bullet?

Try to enforce an Order

that was improperly granted in the first place

Me thinks the Judge needs an education

on true threat jurisprudence

And prison time'll add zeros to my settlement . . .

And if worse comes to worse

I've got enough explosives

to take care of the State Police and the Sheriff's Department." *Id.,* at 334.

At the bottom of this post was a link to the Wikipedia article on "Freedom of speech." *Ibid.* Elonis's reference to the police was the basis for Count Three of his indictment, threatening law enforcement officers.

That same month, interspersed with posts about a movie Elonis liked and observations on a comedian's social commentary, *id.*, at 356–358, Elonis posted an entry that gave rise to Count Four of his indictment:

"That's it, I've had about enough

I'm checking out and making a name for myself

Enough elementary schools in a ten mile radius to initiate the most heinous school shooting ever imagined

And hell hath no fury like a crazy man in a Kindergarten class

The only question is . . . which one?" *Id.*, at 335.

Meanwhile, park security had informed both local police and the Federal Bureau of Investigation about Elonis's posts, and FBI Agent Denise Stevens had created a Facebook account to monitor his online activity. *Id.*, at 49–51, 125. After the post about a school shooting, Agent Stevens and her partner visited Elonis at his house. *Id.*, at 65–66. Following their visit, during which Elonis was polite but uncooperative, Elonis posted another entry on his Facebook page, called "Little Agent Lady," which led to Count Five:

"You know your s* * *'s ridiculous

when you have the FBI knockin' at yo' door

Little Agent lady stood so close

Took all the strength I had not to turn the b* * * * ghost

Pull my knife, flick my wrist, and slit her throat

Leave her bleedin' from her jugular in the arms of her partner

[laughter]

So the next time you knock, you best be serving a warrant

And bring yo' SWAT and an explosives expert while you're at it

Cause little did y'all know, I was strapped wit' a bomb

Why do you think it took me so long to get dressed with no shoes on?

I was jus' waitin' for y'all to handcuff me and pat me down

Touch the detonator in my pocket and we're all goin'

[BOOM!]

Are all the pieces comin' together?

S* * *, I'm just a crazy sociopath

that gets off playin' you stupid f* * *s like a fiddle

And if y'all didn't hear, I'm gonna be famous

> Cause I'm just an aspiring rapper who likes the attention
>
> who happens to be under investigation for terrorism
>
> cause y'all think I'm ready to turn the Valley into Fallujah
>
> But I ain't gonna tell you which bridge is gonna fall
>
> into which river or road
>
> And if you really believe this s* * *
>
> I'll have some bridge rubble to sell you tomorrow
>
> [BOOM!][BOOM!][BOOM!]" *Id.,* at 336.

B

A grand jury indicted Elonis for making threats to injure patrons and employees of the park, his estranged wife, police officers, a kindergarten class, and an FBI agent, all in violation of 18 U.S.C. § 875(c). App. 14–17. In the District Court, Elonis moved to dismiss the indictment for failing to allege that he had intended to threaten anyone. The District Court denied the motion, holding that Third Circuit precedent required only that Elonis "intentionally made the communication, not that he intended to make a threat." App. to Pet. for Cert. 51a. At trial, Elonis testified that his posts emulated the rap lyrics of the well-known performer Eminem, some of which involve fantasies about killing his ex-wife. App. 225. In Elonis's view, he had posted "nothing . . . that hasn't been said already." *Id.,* at 205. The Government presented as witnesses Elonis's wife and co-workers, all of whom said they felt afraid and viewed Elonis's posts as serious threats. See, *e.g., id.,* at 153, 158.

Elonis requested a jury instruction that "the government must prove that he intended to communicate a true threat." *Id.,* at 21. See also *id.,* at 267–269, 303. The District Court denied that request. The jury instructions instead informed the jury that

> "A statement is a true threat when a defendant intentionally makes a statement in a context or under such circumstances wherein a reasonable person would foresee that the statement would be interpreted by those to whom the maker communicates the statement as a serious expression of an intention to inflict bodily injury or take the life of an individual." *Id.,* at 301.

The Government's closing argument emphasized that it was irrelevant whether Elonis intended the postings to be threats—"it doesn't matter what he thinks." *Id.,* at 286. A jury convicted Elonis on four of the five counts against him, acquitting only on the charge of threatening park patrons and employees. *Id.,* at 309. Elonis was sentenced to three years, eight months' imprisonment and three years' supervised release.

Elonis renewed his challenge to the jury instructions in the Court of Appeals, contending that the jury should have been required to find that he intended his posts to be threats. The Court of Appeals disagreed, holding that the intent required by Section 875(c) is only the intent to communicate words that the defendant understands, and that a reasonable person would view as a threat. 730 F.3d 321, 332 (C.A.3 2013).

We granted certiorari. 573 U.S. ___, 134 S.Ct. 2819, 189 L.Ed.2d 784 (2014).

II

A

An individual who "transmits in interstate or foreign commerce any communication containing any threat to kidnap any person or any threat to injure the person of another" is guilty of a felony and faces up to five years' imprisonment. 18 U.S.C. § 875(c). This statute requires that a communication be transmitted and that the communication contain a threat. It does not specify that the defendant must have any mental state with respect to these elements. In particular, it does not indicate whether the defendant must intend that his communication contain a threat.

. . .

These definitions, however, speak to what the statement conveys—not to the mental state of the author. For example, an anonymous letter that says "I'm going to kill you" is "an expression of an intention to inflict loss or harm" regardless of the author's intent. A victim who receives that letter in the mail has received a threat, even if the author believes (wrongly) that his message will be taken as a joke.

B

The fact that the statute does not specify any required mental state, however, does not mean that none exists. We have repeatedly held that "mere omission from a criminal enactment of any mention of criminal intent" should not be read "as dispensing with it." *Morissette v. United States,* 342 U.S. 246, 250, 72 S.Ct. 240, 96 L.Ed. 288 (1952). This rule of construction reflects the basic principle that "wrongdoing must be conscious to be criminal." *Id.,* at 252, 72 S.Ct. 240. As Justice Jackson explained, this principle is "as universal and persistent in mature systems of law as belief in freedom of the human will and a consequent ability and duty of the normal individual to choose between good and evil." *Id.,* at 250, 72 S.Ct. 240. The "central thought" is that a defendant must be "blameworthy in mind" before he can be found guilty, a concept courts have expressed over time through various terms such as *mens rea,* scienter, malice aforethought, guilty knowledge, and the like. *Id.,* at 252, 72 S.Ct. 240; 1 W. LaFave, Substantive Criminal Law § 5.1, pp. 332–333 (2d ed. 2003). Although there are exceptions, the "general rule" is that a guilty mind is "a necessary element in the indictment and proof of every crime." *United States v. Balint,* 258 U.S. 250, 251, 42 S.Ct. 301, 66 L.Ed. 604 (1922). We therefore generally "interpret [ ] criminal statutes to include broadly applicable scienter requirements, even where the statute by its terms does not contain them." *United States v. X-Citement Video, Inc.,* 513 U.S. 64, 70, 115 S.Ct. 464, 130 L.Ed.2d 372 (1994).

C

Section 875(c), as noted, requires proof that a communication was transmitted and that it contained a threat. The "presumption in favor of a scienter requirement should apply to *each* of the statutory elements that criminalize otherwise innocent conduct." *X-Citement Video,* 513 U.S., at 72, 115 S.Ct. 464 (emphasis added). The parties agree that a defendant under Section 875(c) must know that he is transmitting a communication. But communicating *something* is not what makes the conduct "wrongful." Here "the crucial element separating legal innocence from wrongful conduct" is the threatening nature of the communication. *Id.,* at 73, 115 S.Ct. 464. The mental state requirement must therefore apply to the fact that the communication contains a threat.

Elonis's conviction, however, was premised solely on how his posts would be understood by a reasonable person. Such a "reasonable person" standard is a familiar feature of civil liability in tort law, but is inconsistent with "the conventional requirement for criminal conduct—*awareness* of some wrongdoing." *Staples,* 511 U.S., at 606–607, 114 S.Ct. 1793 (quoting *United States v. Dotterweich,* 320 U.S. 277, 281, 64 S.Ct. 134, 88 L.Ed. 48 (1943); emphasis added). Having liability turn on whether a "reasonable person" regards the communication as a threat—regardless of what the defendant thinks—"reduces culpability on the all-important element of the crime to negligence," *Jeffries,* 692 F.3d, at 484 (Sutton, J., *dubitante*), and we "have long been reluctant to infer that a negligence standard was intended in criminal statutes," *Rogers v. United States,* 422 U.S. 35, 47, 95 S.Ct. 2091, 45 L.Ed.2d 1 (1975) (Marshall, J., concurring).

The Government is at pains to characterize its position as something other than a negligence standard, emphasizing that its approach would require proof that a defendant "comprehended [the] contents and context" of the communication. Brief for United States 29. The Government gives two examples of individuals who, in its view, would lack this necessary mental state—a "foreigner, ignorant of the English language," who would not know the meaning of the words at issue, or an individual mailing a sealed envelope without knowing its contents. *Ibid.* But the fact that the Government would require a defendant to actually know the words of and circumstances surrounding a communication does not amount to a rejection of negligence. Criminal negligence standards often incorporate "the circumstances known" to a defendant. ALI, Model Penal Code § 2.02(2)(d) (1985). See *id.,* Comment 4, at 241; 1 LaFave, Substantive

Criminal Law § 5.4, at 372–373. Courts then ask, however, whether a reasonable person equipped with that knowledge, not the actual defendant, would have recognized the harmfulness of his conduct. That is precisely the Government's position here: Elonis can be convicted, the Government contends, if he himself knew the contents and context of his posts, and a reasonable person would have recognized that the posts would be read as genuine threats. That is a negligence standard.

In light of the foregoing, Elonis's conviction cannot stand. The jury was instructed that the Government need prove only that a reasonable person would regard Elonis's communications as threats, and that was error. Federal criminal liability generally does not turn solely on the results of an act without considering the defendant's mental state. That understanding "took deep and early root in American soil" and Congress left it intact here: Under Section 875(c), "wrongdoing must be conscious to be criminal." *Morissette,* 342 U.S., at 252, 72 S.Ct. 240.

There is no dispute that the mental state requirement in Section 875(c) is satisfied if the defendant transmits a communication for the purpose of issuing a threat, or with knowledge that the communication will be viewed as a threat. See Tr. of Oral Arg. 25, 56. In response to a question at oral argument, Elonis stated that a finding of recklessness would not be sufficient. See *id.,* at 8–9. Neither Elonis nor the Government has briefed or argued that point, and we accordingly decline to address it.

The judgment of the United States Court of Appeals for the Third Circuit is reversed, and the case is remanded for further proceedings consistent with this opinion.

It is so ordered.

JUSTICE ALITO, concurring in part and dissenting in part.

In *Marbury v. Madison,* 1 Cranch 137, 177, 2 L.Ed. 60 (1803), the Court famously proclaimed: "It is emphatically the province and duty of the judicial department to say what the law is." Today, the Court announces: It is emphatically the prerogative of this Court to say only what the law is not.

The Court's disposition of this case is certain to cause confusion and serious problems. Attorneys and judges need to know which mental state is required for conviction under 18 U.S.C. § 875(c), an important criminal statute. This case squarely presents that issue, but the Court provides only a partial answer. The Court holds that the jury instructions in this case were defective because they required only negligence in conveying a threat. But the Court refuses to explain what type of intent was necessary. Did the jury need to find that Elonis had the *purpose* of conveying a true threat? Was it enough if he *knew* that his words conveyed such a threat? Would *recklessness* suffice? The Court declines to say. Attorneys and judges are left to guess.

This will have regrettable consequences. While this Court has the luxury of choosing its docket, lower courts and juries are not so fortunate. They must actually decide cases, and this means applying a standard. If purpose or knowledge is needed and a district court instructs the jury that recklessness suffices, a defendant may be wrongly convicted. On the other hand, if recklessness is enough, and the jury is told that conviction requires proof of more, a guilty defendant may go free. We granted review in this case to resolve a disagreement among the Circuits. But the Court has compounded—not clarified—the confusion.

There is no justification for the Court's refusal to provide an answer. The Court says that "[n]either Elonis nor the Government has briefed or argued" the question whether recklessness is sufficient. *Ante,* at 2012– 2013. But in fact both parties addressed that issue. Elonis argued that recklessness is not enough, and the Government argued that it more than suffices. If the Court thinks that we cannot decide the recklessness question without additional help from the parties, we can order further briefing and argument. In my view, however, we are capable of deciding the recklessness issue, and we should resolve that question now.

I

Section 875(c) provides in relevant part:

"Whoever transmits in interstate or foreign commerce any communication containing . . . any threat to injure the person of another, shall be fined under this title or imprisoned not more than five years, or both."

Thus, conviction under this provision requires proof that: (1) the defendant transmitted something, (2) the thing transmitted was a threat to injure the person of another, and (3) the transmission was in interstate or foreign commerce.

At issue in this case is the *mens rea* required with respect to the second element—that the thing transmitted was a threat to injure the person of another. This Court has not defined the meaning of the term "threat" in § 875(c), but in construing the same term in a related statute, the Court distinguished a "true 'threat' " from facetious or hyperbolic remarks. *Watts v. United States,* 394 U.S. 705, 708, 89 S.Ct. 1399, 22 L.Ed.2d 664 (1969) (*per curiam*). In my view, the term "threat" in § 875(c) can fairly be defined as a statement that is reasonably interpreted as "an expression of an intention to inflict evil, injury, or damage on another." Webster's Third New International Dictionary 2382 (1976). Conviction under § 875(c) demands proof that the defendant's transmission was in fact a threat, *i.e.,* that it is reasonable to interpret the transmission as an expression of an intent to harm another. In addition, it must be shown that the defendant was at least reckless as to whether the transmission met that requirement.

Why is recklessness enough? My analysis of the *mens rea* issue follows the same track as the Court's, as far as it goes. I agree with the Court that we should presume that criminal statutes require some sort of *mens rea* for conviction.

I agree with the Court that we should presume that an offense like that created by § 875(c) requires more than negligence with respect to a critical element like the one at issue here. See *ante,* at 2010–2012. As the Court states, "[w]hen interpreting federal criminal statutes that are silent on the required mental state, we read into the statute 'only that *mens rea* which is necessary to separate wrongful conduct from "otherwise innocent conduct." ' " *Ante,* at 2010 (quoting *Carter v. United States,* 530 U.S. 255, 269, 120 S.Ct. 2159, 147 L.Ed.2d 203 (2000)). Whether negligence is morally culpable is an interesting philosophical question, but the answer is at least sufficiently debatable to justify the presumption that a serious offense against the person that lacks any clear common-law counterpart should be presumed to require more.

Once we have passed negligence, however, no further presumptions are defensible. In the hierarchy of mental states that may be required as a condition for criminal liability, the *mens rea* just above negligence is recklessness. Negligence requires only that the defendant "should [have] be [en] aware of a substantial and unjustifiable risk," ALI, Model Penal Code § 2.02(2)(d), p. 226 (1985), while recklessness exists "when a person disregards a risk of harm of which he is aware," *Farmer v. Brennan,* 511 U.S. 825, 837, 114 S.Ct. 1970, 128 L.Ed.2d 811 (1994); Model Penal Code § 2.02(2)(c). And when Congress does not specify a *mens rea* in a criminal statute, we have no justification for inferring that anything more than recklessness is needed. It is quite unusual for us to interpret a statute to contain a requirement that is nowhere set out in the text. Once we have reached recklessness, we have gone as far as we can without stepping over the line that separates interpretation from amendment.

There can be no real dispute that recklessness regarding a risk of serious harm is wrongful conduct. In a wide variety of contexts, we have described reckless conduct as morally culpable. . . . Someone who acts recklessly with respect to conveying a threat necessarily grasps that he is not engaged in innocent conduct. He is not merely careless. He is aware that others could regard his statements as a threat, but he delivers them anyway.

Accordingly, I would hold that a defendant may be convicted under § 875(c) if he or she consciously disregards the risk that the communication transmitted will be interpreted as a true threat. Nothing in the Court's non-committal opinion prevents lower courts from adopting that standard.

II

There remains the question whether interpreting § 875(c) to require no more than recklessness with respect to the element at issue here would violate the First Amendment. Elonis contends that it would. I would reject that argument.

It is settled that the Constitution does not protect true threats. See *Virginia v. Black,* 538 U.S. 343, 359–360, 123 S.Ct. 1536, 155 L.Ed.2d 535 (2003); *R.A.V. v. St. Paul,* 505 U.S. 377, 388, 112 S.Ct. 2538, 120 L.Ed.2d 305 (1992); *Watts,* 394 U.S., at 707–708, 89 S.Ct. 1399. And there are good reasons for that rule: True threats inflict great harm and have little if any social value. A threat may cause serious emotional stress for the person threatened and those who care about that person, and a threat may lead to a violent confrontation. It is true that a communication containing a threat may include other statements that have value and are entitled to protection. But that does not justify constitutional protection for the threat itself.

Elonis argues that the First Amendment protects a threat if the person making the statement does not actually intend to cause harm. In his view, if a threat is made for a " 'therapeutic' " purpose, "to 'deal with the pain' . . . of a wrenching event," or for "cathartic" reasons, the threat is protected. Brief for Petitioner 52–53. But whether or not the person making a threat intends to cause harm, the damage is the same. And the fact that making a threat may have a therapeutic or cathartic effect for the speaker is not sufficient to justify constitutional protection. Some people may experience a therapeutic or cathartic benefit only if they know that their words will cause harm or only if they actually plan to carry out the threat, but surely the First Amendment does not protect them.

Elonis also claims his threats were constitutionally protected works of art. Words like his, he contends, are shielded by the First Amendment because they are similar to words uttered by rappers and singers in public performances and recordings. To make this point, his brief includes a lengthy excerpt from the lyrics of a rap song in which a very well-compensated rapper imagines killing his ex-wife and dumping her body in a lake. If this celebrity can utter such words, Elonis pleads, amateurs like him should be able to post similar things on social media. But context matters. "Taken in context," lyrics in songs that are performed for an audience or sold in recorded form are unlikely to be interpreted as a real threat to a real person. *Watts, supra,* at 708, 89 S.Ct. 1399. Statements on social media that are pointedly directed at their victims, by contrast, are much more likely to be taken seriously. To hold otherwise would grant a license to anyone who is clever enough to dress up a real threat in the guise of rap lyrics, a parody, or something similar.

The facts of this case illustrate the point. Imagine the effect on Elonis's estranged wife when she read this: " 'If I only knew then what I know now

. . . I would have smothered your ass with a pillow, dumped your body in the back seat, dropped you off in Toad Creek and made it look like a rape and murder.' " 730 F.3d 321, 324 (C.A.3 2013). Or this: "There's one way to love you but a thousand ways to kill you. I'm not going to rest until your body is a mess, soaked in blood and dying from all the little cuts." *Ibid.* Or this: "Fold up your [protection from abuse order] and put it in your pocket[.] Is it thick enough to stop a bullet?" *Id.,* at 325.

JUSTICE THOMAS, dissenting.

We granted certiorari to resolve a conflict in the lower courts over the appropriate mental state for threat prosecutions under 18 U.S.C. § 875(c). Save two, every Circuit to have considered the issue—11 in total—has held that this provision demands proof only of general intent, which here requires no more than that a defendant knew he transmitted a communication, knew the words used in that communication, and understood the ordinary meaning of those words in the relevant context. The outliers are the Ninth and Tenth Circuits, which have concluded that proof of an intent to threaten was necessary for conviction. Adopting the minority position, Elonis urges us to hold that § 875(c) and the First Amendment require proof of an intent to threaten. The Government in turn advocates a general-intent approach.

Rather than resolve the conflict, the Court casts aside the approach used in nine Circuits and leaves nothing in its place. Lower courts are thus left to guess at the appropriate mental state for § 875(c). All they know after today's decision is that a requirement of general intent will not do. But they can safely infer that a majority of this Court would not adopt an intent-to-threaten requirement, as the opinion carefully leaves open the possibility that recklessness may be enough. See *ante,* at 2012–2013.

This failure to decide throws everyone from appellate judges to everyday Facebook users into a state of uncertainty. This uncertainty could have been avoided had we simply adhered to the background rule of the common law favoring general intent. Although I am sympathetic to my colleagues' policy concerns about the risks associated with threat prosecutions, the answer to such fears is not to discard our traditional approach to state-of-mind requirements in criminal law. Because the Court of Appeals properly applied the general-intent standard, and because the communications transmitted by Elonis were "true threats" unprotected by the First Amendment, I would affirm the judgment below.

I

A

Because § 875(c) criminalizes speech, the First Amendment requires that the term "threat" be limited to a narrow class of historically unprotected communications called "true threats." To qualify as a true threat, a communication must be a serious expression of an intention to commit unlawful physical violence, not merely "political hyperbole"; "vehement, caustic, and sometimes unpleasantly sharp attacks"; or "vituperative, abusive, and inexact" statements. *Watts v. United States,* 394 U.S. 705, 708, 89 S.Ct. 1399, 22 L.Ed.2d 664 (1969) (*per curiam*) (internal quotation marks omitted). It also cannot be determined solely by the reaction of the recipient, but must instead be "determined by the interpretation of a *reasonable* recipient familiar with the context of the communication," *United States v. Darby,* 37 F.3d 1059, 1066 (C.A.4 1994) (emphasis added), lest historically protected speech be suppressed at the will of an eggshell observer, cf. *Cox v. Louisiana,* 379 U.S. 536, 551, 85 S.Ct. 453, 13 L.Ed.2d 471 (1965).

Our default rule in favor of general intent applies with full force to criminal statutes addressing speech. Well over 100 years ago, this Court considered a conviction under a federal obscenity statute that punished anyone " 'who shall knowingly deposit, or cause to be deposited, for mailing or delivery,' " any " 'obscene, lewd, or lascivious book, pamphlet, picture, paper, writing, print, or other publication of an indecent character.' " *Rosen v. United States,* 161 U.S. 29, 30, 16 S.Ct. 434, 40 L.Ed. 606 (1896) (quoting Rev. Stat. § 3893). In that case, as here, the defendant argued that, even if "he may have had . . . actual knowledge or notice of [the paper's] contents" when he put it in the mail, he could not "be convicted of the offence . . . unless he knew or believed that such paper could be properly or justly characterized as obscene, lewd, and lascivious." 161 U.S., at 41, 16 S.Ct. 434. The Court rejected that theory, concluding that if the material was actually obscene and "deposited in the mail by one who knew or had notice at the time of its contents, the offence is complete, although the defendant himself did not regard the paper as one that the statute forbade to be carried in the mails." *Ibid.* As the Court explained, "Congress did not intend that the question as to the character of the paper should depend upon the opinion or belief of the person who, with knowledge or notice of [the paper's] contents, assumed the responsibility of putting it in the mails of the United States," because "[e]very one who uses the mails of the United States for carrying papers or publications must take notice of . . . what must be deemed obscene, lewd, and lascivious." *Id.,* at 41–42, 16 S.Ct. 434.

Courts applying this statute shortly after its enactment appeared to require proof of only general intent. In *Ragansky v. United States,* 253 F. 643 (C.A.7 1918), for instance, a Court of Appeals held that "[a] threat is knowingly made, if the maker of it comprehends the meaning of the words uttered by him," and "is willfully made, if in addition to comprehending the meaning of his words, the maker voluntarily and intentionally utters them as the declaration of an apparent determination to carry them into execution," *id.,* at 645. The court consequently rejected the defendant's argument that he could not be convicted when his language "[c]oncededly . . . constituted such a threat" but was meant only "as a joke." *Id.,* at 644. Likewise, in *United States v. Stobo,* 251 F. 689 (Del.1918), a District Court rejected the defendant's objection that there was no allegation "of any facts . . . indicating any intention . . . on the part of the defendant . . . to menace the President of the United States," *id.,* at 693 (internal quotation marks omitted). As it explained, the defendant "is punishable under the act whether he uses the words lightly or with a set purpose to kill," as "[t]he effect upon the minds of the hearers, who cannot read his inward thoughts, is precisely the same." *Ibid.* At a minimum, there is no historical practice requiring more than general intent when a statute regulates speech.

B

Applying ordinary rules of statutory construction, I would read § 875(c) to require proof of general intent. To "know the facts that make his conduct illegal" under § 875(c), see *Staples,* 511 U.S., at 605, 114 S.Ct. 1793, a defendant must know that he transmitted a communication in interstate or foreign commerce that contained a threat. Knowing that the communication contains a "threat"—a serious expression of an intention to engage in unlawful physical violence—does not, however, require knowing that a jury will conclude that the communication contains a threat as a matter of law. Instead, like one who mails an "obscene" publication and is prosecuted under the federal obscenity statute, a defendant prosecuted under § 875(c) must know only the words used in that communication, along with their ordinary meaning in context.

General intent divides those who know the facts constituting the *actus reus* of this crime from those who do not. For example, someone who transmits a threat who does not know English—or who knows English, but perhaps does not know a threatening idiom—lacks the general intent required under § 875(c). . . . Likewise, the hapless mailman who delivers a threatening letter, ignorant of its contents, should not fear prosecution. A defendant like Elonis, however, who admits that he "knew that what [he] was saying was violent" but supposedly "just wanted to express [him]self," App. 205, acted with the general intent required under § 875(c), even if he did not know that a jury would conclude that his communication constituted a "threat" as a matter of law.

C

The majority refuses to apply these ordinary background principles. Instead, it casts my application of general intent as a negligence standard disfavored in the criminal law. *Ante,* at 2010–2013. But that characterization misses the mark. Requiring general intent in this context is not the same as requiring mere negligence. Like the mental-state requirements adopted in many of the cases cited by the Court, general intent under § 875(c) prevents a defendant from being convicted on the basis of any *fact* beyond his awareness. . . . In other words, the defendant must *know*—not merely be reckless or negligent with respect to the fact—that he is committing the acts that constitute the *actus reus* of the offense.

But general intent requires *no* mental state (not even a negligent one) concerning the "fact" that certain words meet the *legal* definition of a threat. That approach is particularly appropriate where, as here, that legal status is determined by a jury's application of the legal standard of a "threat" to the contents of a communication. And convicting a defendant despite his ignorance of the legal—or objective—status of his conduct does not mean that he is being punished for negligent conduct. By way of example, a defendant who is convicted of murder despite claiming that he acted in self-defense has not been penalized under a negligence standard merely because he does not know that the jury will reject his argument that his "belief in the necessity of using force to prevent harm to himself [was] a reasonable one." See 2 W. LaFave, Substantive Criminal Law § 10.4(c), p. 147 (2d ed. 2003).

Elonis nonetheless suggests that an intent-to-threaten element is necessary in order to avoid the risk of punishing innocent conduct. But there is nothing absurd about punishing an individual who, with knowledge of the words he uses and their ordinary meaning in context, makes a threat. For instance, a high-school student who sends a letter to his principal stating that he will massacre his classmates with a machine gun, even if he intended the letter as a joke, cannot fairly be described as engaging in innocent conduct. But see *ante,* at 2006–2007, 2012–2013 (concluding that Elonis' conviction under § 875(c) for discussing a plan to " 'initiate the most heinous school shooting ever imagined' " against " 'a Kindergarten class' " cannot stand without proof of some unspecified heightened mental state).

There is always a risk that a criminal threat statute may be deployed by the Government to suppress legitimate speech. But the proper response to that risk is to adhere to our traditional rule that only a narrow class of true threats, historically unprotected, may be constitutionally proscribed.

The solution is not to abandon a mental-state requirement compelled by text, history, and precedent. Not only does such a decision warp our traditional approach to *mens rea,* it results in an arbitrary distinction between threats and other forms of unprotected speech. Had Elonis mailed obscene materials to his wife and a kindergarten class, he could have been prosecuted irrespective of whether he intended to offend those recipients or recklessly disregarded that possibility. Yet when he threatened to kill his wife and a kindergarten class, his intent to terrify those recipients (or reckless disregard of that risk) suddenly becomes highly relevant. That need not—and should not—be the case.

Nor should it be the case that we cast aside the mental-state requirement compelled by our precedents yet offer nothing in its place. Our job is to decide questions, not create them. Given the majority's ostensible concern for protecting innocent actors, one would have expected it to announce a clear rule—any clear rule. Its failure to do so reveals the fractured foundation upon which today's decision rests.

I respectfully dissent.

DISCUSSION QUESTIONS

1.   What difference does it make in this case and others like it, whether the court reads in a knowing, reckless or general intent standard?

2.   Which mental state do you think is appropriate as a matter of statutory interpretation? As a matter of good policy?

3.   As a general matter, do you think that crimes should require at least a reckless mental state, or is a grossly negligent mental state enough to merit criminal punishment?

E. CONDITIONAL INTENT

Do you intend to do something if you will only do it under certain conditions?

FRANCOIS HOLLOWAY, AKA ABDU ALI V. UNITED STATES

Supreme Court of the United States
526 U.S. 1 (1999)

Opinion

JUSTICE STEVENS delivered the opinion of the Court.

Carjacking "with the intent to cause death or serious bodily harm" is a federal crime. The question presented in this case is whether that phrase requires the Government to prove that the defendant had an unconditional intent to kill or harm in all events, or whether it merely requires proof of an intent to kill or harm if necessary to effect a carjacking. Most of the judges who have considered the question have concluded, as do we, that Congress intended to criminalize the more typical carjacking carried out by means of a deliberate threat of violence, rather than just the rare case in which the defendant has an unconditional intent to use violence regardless of how the driver responds to his threat.

I

A jury found petitioner guilty on three counts of carjacking, as well as several other offenses related to stealing cars. In each of the carjackings, petitioner and an armed accomplice identified a car that they wanted and followed it until it was parked. The accomplice then approached the driver, produced a gun, and threatened to shoot unless the driver handed over the car keys. The accomplice testified that the plan was to steal the cars without harming the victims, but that he would have used his gun if any of the drivers had given him a "hard time." App. 52. When one victim hesitated, petitioner punched him in the face, but there was no other actual violence.

The District Judge instructed the jury that the Government was required to prove beyond a reasonable doubt that the taking of a motor vehicle was committed with the intent "to cause death or serious bodily harm to the person from whom the car was taken." *Id.*, at 29. After explaining that merely using a gun to frighten a victim was not sufficient to prove such intent, he added the following statement over petitioner's objection:

> "In some cases, intent is conditional. That is, a defendant may intend to engage in certain conduct only if a certain event occurs.

> "In this case, the government contends that the defendant intended to cause death or serious bodily harm if the alleged victims had refused to turn over their cars. If you find beyond a reasonable doubt that the defendant had such an intent, the government has satisfied this element of the offense. . . ." *Id.*, at 30.

The specific issue in this case is what sort of evil motive Congress intended to describe when it used the words "with the intent to cause death or serious bodily harm" in the 1994 amendment to the carjacking statute. More precisely, the question is whether a person who points a gun at a driver, having decided to pull the trigger if the driver does not comply with a demand for the car keys, possesses the intent, at that moment, to seriously harm the driver. In our view, the answer to that question does not depend on whether the driver immediately hands over the keys or what the offender decides to do after he gains control over the car. At the relevant moment, the offender plainly does have the forbidden intent.

The opinions that have addressed this issue accurately point out that a carjacker's intent to harm his victim may be either "conditional" or "unconditional." The statutory phrase at issue theoretically might describe (1) the former, (2) the latter, or (3) both species of intent. Petitioner argues that the "plain text" of the statute "unequivocally" describes only the latter: that the defendant must possess a specific and unconditional intent to kill or harm in order to complete the proscribed offense. To that end, he insists that Congress would have had to insert the words "if necessary" into the disputed text in order to include the conditional species of intent within the scope of the statute. See Reply Brief for Petitioner 2. Because Congress did not include those words, petitioner contends that we must assume that Congress meant to provide a federal penalty for only those carjackings in which the offender actually attempted to harm or kill the driver (or at least intended to do so whether or not the driver resisted).

We believe, however, that a commonsense reading of the carjacking statute counsels that Congress intended to criminalize a broader scope of conduct than attempts to assault or kill in the course of automobile robberies. As we have repeatedly stated, " 'the meaning of statutory language, plain or not, depends on context.' When petitioner's argument is considered in the context of the statute, it becomes apparent that his proffered construction of the intent element overlooks the significance of the placement of that element in the statute. The carjacking statute essentially is aimed at providing a federal penalty for a particular type of robbery. The statute's *mens rea* component thus modifies the act of "tak[ing]" the motor vehicle. It directs the factfinder's attention to the defendant's state of mind at the precise moment he demanded or took control over the car "by force and violence or by intimidation." If the defendant has the proscribed state of mind at that moment, the statute's scienter element is satisfied.

Petitioner's reading of the intent element, in contrast, would improperly transform the *mens rea* element from a modifier into an additional *actus reus* component of the carjacking statute; it would alter the statute into one that focuses on attempting to harm or kill a person in the course of the robbery of a motor vehicle. Indeed, if we accepted petitioner's view of the statute's intent element, even Congress' insertion of the qualifying words "if necessary," by themselves, would not have solved the deficiency that he believes exists in the statute. The inclusion of those words after the intent phrase would have excluded the unconditional species of intent—the intent to harm or kill even if not necessary to complete a carjacking. Accordingly, if Congress had used words such as "if necessary" to describe the conditional species of intent, it would also have needed to add something like "or even if not necessary" in order to cover both species of intent to harm. Given the fact that the actual text does not mention either species separately—and thus does not expressly exclude either—that text is most naturally read to encompass the *mens rea* of both conditional and unconditional intent, and *not* to limit the statute's reach to crimes involving the additional *actus reus* of an attempt to kill or harm.

Two considerations strongly support the conclusion that a natural reading of the text is fully consistent with a congressional decision to cover both species of intent. First, the statute as a whole reflects an intent to authorize federal prosecutions as a significant deterrent to a type of criminal activity that was a matter of national concern. Because that purpose is better served by construing the statute to cover both the conditional and the unconditional species of wrongful intent, the entire statute is consistent with a normal interpretation of the specific language that Congress chose. See *John Hancock Mut. Life Ins. Co. v. Harris Trust and Sav. Bank,* 510 U.S. 86, 94–95, 114 S.Ct. 517, 126 L.Ed.2d 524 (1993) (statutory language should be interpreted consonant with "the provisions of the whole law, and . . . its object and policy" (internal quotation marks omitted)). Indeed, petitioner's interpretation would exclude from the coverage of the statute most of the conduct that Congress obviously intended to prohibit.

Second, it is reasonable to presume that Congress was familiar with the cases and the scholarly writing that have recognized that the "specific intent" to commit a wrongful act may be conditional. The facts of the leading case on the point are strikingly similar to the facts of this case. In *People v. Connors,* 253 Ill. 266, 97 N.E. 643 (1912), the Illinois Supreme Court affirmed the conviction of a union organizer who had pointed a gun at a worker and threatened to kill him forthwith if he did not take off his overalls and quit work. The court held that the jury had been properly instructed that the "specific intent to kill" could be found even though that intent was "coupled with a condition" that the defendant would not fire if the victim complied with his demand. That holding has been repeatedly cited with approval by other courts and by scholars. The core principle that emerges from these sources is that a defendant may not negate a proscribed intent by requiring the victim to comply with a condition the defendant has no right to impose; "[a]n intent to kill, in the alternative, is nevertheless an intent to kill."

This interpretation of the statute's specific intent element does not, as petitioner suggests, render superfluous the statute's "by force and violence or by intimidation" element. While an empty threat, or intimidating bluff, would be sufficient to satisfy the latter element, such conduct, standing on its own, is not enough to satisfy § 2119's specific intent element. In a carjacking case in which the driver surrendered or otherwise lost control over his car without the defendant attempting to inflict, or actually inflicting, serious bodily harm, Congress' inclusion of the intent element requires the Government to prove beyond a reasonable doubt that the defendant would have at least attempted to seriously harm or kill the driver if that action had been necessary to complete the taking of the car.

In short, we disagree with petitioner's reading of the text of the Act and think it unreasonable to assume that Congress intended to enact such a truncated version of an important criminal statute. The intent requirement of § 2119 is satisfied when the Government proves that at the moment the defendant demanded or took control over the driver's automobile the defendant possessed the intent to seriously harm or kill the driver if necessary to steal the car (or, alternatively, if unnecessary to steal the car). Accordingly, we affirm the judgment of the Court of Appeals.

It is so ordered.

JUSTICE SCALIA, dissenting.

I dissent from that holding because I disagree with the following, utterly central, passage of the opinion: "[A] carjacker's intent to harm his victim may be either 'conditional' or 'unconditional.'"

I think, to the contrary, that in customary English usage the unqualified word "intent" does not usually connote a purpose that is subject to any conditions precedent except those so remote in the speaker's estimation as to be effectively nonexistent—and it *never* connotes a purpose that is subject to a condition which the speaker hopes will not occur. (It is this last sort of "conditional intent" that is at issue in this case, and that I refer to in my subsequent use of the term.) "Intent" is "[a] state of mind in which a person seeks to accomplish a given result through a course of action." Black's Law Dictionary 810 (6th ed.1990). One can hardly "seek to accomplish" a result he hopes will not ensue.

The Court's division of intent into two categories, conditional and unconditional, makes the unreasonable seem logical. Conditional intent is no more embraced by the unmodified word "intent" than a sea lion is embraced by the unmodified word "lion."

If I have made a categorical determination to go to Louisiana for the Christmas holidays, it is accurate for me to say that I "intend" to go to Louisiana. And that is so even though I realize that there are some remote and unlikely contingencies—"acts of God," for example—that might prevent me. (The fact that these remote contingencies are always implicit in the expression of intent accounts for the humorousness of spelling them out in such expressions as "if I should live so long," or "the Good Lord willing and the creek don't rise.") It is less precise, though tolerable usage, to say that I "intend" to go if my purpose is conditional upon an event which, though not virtually certain to happen (such as my continuing to live), is reasonably likely to happen, and which I hope will happen. I might, for example, say that I "intend" to go even if my plans depend upon receipt of my usual and hoped-for end-of-year bonus.

But it is *not* common usage—indeed, it is an unheard-of usage—to speak of my having an "intent" to do something, when my plans are contingent upon an event that is not virtually certain, and that I hope will not occur. When a friend is seriously ill, for example, I would not say that "I intend to go to his funeral next week." I would have to make it clear that the intent is a conditional one: "I intend to go to his funeral next week if he dies." The carjacker who intends to kill if he is met with resistance is in the same position: He has an "intent to kill if resisted"; he does not have an "intent to kill." No amount of rationalization can change the reality of this normal (and as far as I know exclusive) English usage. The word in the statute simply will not bear the meaning that the Court assigns.

Ultimately, the Court rests its decision upon the fact that the purpose of the statute—which it says is deterring carjacking—"is better served by construing the statute to cover both the conditional and the unconditional species of wrongful intent." *Ante,* at 971. It supports this statement, both premise and conclusion, by two unusually uninformative statements from the legislative history (to stand out in that respect in that realm is quite an accomplishment) that speak generally about strengthening and broadening the carjacking statute and punishing carjackers severely. *Ante,* at 970–971, n. 7. But every statute intends not only to achieve certain policy objectives, but to achieve them by the means specified. Limitations upon the means employed to achieve the policy goal are no less a "purpose" of the statute than the policy goal itself. Under the Court's analysis, any interpretation of the statute that would broaden its reach would further the purpose the Court has found. Such reasoning is limitless and illogical.

The Court confidently asserts that "petitioner's interpretation would exclude from the coverage of the statute most of the conduct that Congress obviously intended to prohibit." It seems to me that one can best judge what Congress "obviously intended" not by intuition, but by the words that Congress enacted, which in this case require intent (not conditional intent) to kill. Is it implausible that Congress intended to define such a narrow federal crime? Not at all. The era when this statute was passed contained well publicized instances of not only carjackings, and not only carjackings involving violence or the threat of violence (as, of course, most of them do); but also of carjackings in which the perpetrators senselessly harmed the car owners when that was entirely unnecessary to the crime. I have a friend whose father was killed, and whose mother was nearly killed, in just such an incident—after the car had already been handed over. It is not at all implausible that Congress should direct its attention to this particularly savage sort of carjacking—where killing the driver is part of the intended crime.

Indeed, it seems to me much more implausible that Congress would have focused upon the ineffable "conditional intent" that the Court reads into the statute, sending courts and juries off to wander through "would-a, could-a, should-a" land. It is difficult enough to determine a defendant's actual intent; it is infinitely more difficult to determine what the defendant planned to do upon the happening of an event that the defendant hoped would not happen, and that he himself may not have come to focus upon. There will not often be the accomplice's convenient confirmation of conditional intent that exists in the present case. Presumably it will be up to each jury whether to take the carjacker ("Your car or your life") at his word. Such a system of justice seems to me so arbitrary that it is difficult to believe Congress intended it. Had Congress meant to cast its carjacking net so broadly, it could have achieved that result—and eliminated the arbitrariness—by defining the crime as "carjacking under threat of death or serious bodily injury." Given the language here, I find it much more plausible that Congress meant to reach—as it said—the carjacker who intended to kill.

DISCUSSION QUESTIONS

1. Which reading of the statute is truer to the plain meaning of the words used in the statute?

2. Which reading of the statute is truer to what Congress probably intended in the statute?

3. Which is more important in interpreting a statute, plain meaning or legislative intent? Why?

F. WILFUL BLINDNESS

Case in Context

What about the criminal who buries her head in the sand—who shields herself from knowledge of a crime?

UNITED STATES V. JEWELL

United States Court of Appeals, Ninth Circuit
532 F.2d 697 (1976)

OPINION

BROWNING, CIRCUIT JUDGE:

Appellant defines "knowingly" in 21 U.S.C. ss 841 and 960 to require that positive knowledge that a controlled substance is involved be established as an element of each offense. On the basis of this interpretation, appellant argues that it was reversible error to instruct the jury that the defendant could be convicted upon proof beyond a reasonable doubt that if he did not have positive knowledge that a controlled substance was concealed in the automobile he drove over the border, it was solely and entirely because of the conscious purpose on his part to avoid learning the truth. The majority concludes that this contention is wrong in principle, and has no support in authority or in the language or legislative history of the statute.

It is undisputed that appellant entered the United States driving an automobile in which 110 pounds of marihuana worth $6,250 had been concealed in a secret compartment between the trunk and rear seat. Appellant testified that he did not know the marijuana was present. There was circumstantial evidence from which the jury could infer that appellant had positive knowledge of the presence of the marijuana, and that his contrary testimony was false. On the other hand there was evidence from which the jury could conclude that appellant spoke the truth that although appellant knew of the presence of the secret compartment and had knowledge of facts indicating that it contained marijuana, he deliberately avoided positive knowledge of the presence of the contraband to avoid responsibility in the event of discovery. If the jury concluded the latter was indeed the situation, and if positive knowledge is required to convict, the jury would have no choice consistent with its oath but to find appellant not guilty even though he deliberately contrived his lack of positive knowledge. Appellant urges this view. The trial court rejected the premise that only positive knowledge would suffice, and properly so.

Appellant tendered an instruction that to return a guilty verdict the jury must find that the defendant knew he was in possession of marihuana. The trial judge rejected the instruction because it suggested that "absolutely, positively, he has to know that it's there. . . ."

The court instructed the jury that the government must prove beyond a reasonable doubt that the defendant "knowingly" brought the marihuana into the United States and that he "knowingly" possessed the marijuana. The court continued:

The Government can complete their burden of proof by proving, beyond a reasonable doubt, that if the defendant was not actually aware that there was marijuana in the vehicle he was driving when he entered the United States his ignorance in that regard was solely and entirely a result of his having made a conscious purpose to disregard the nature of that which was in the vehicle, with a conscious purpose to avoid learning the truth.

The legal premise of these instructions is firmly supported by leading commentators here and in England. Professor Rollin M. Perkins writes, "One with a deliberate antisocial purpose in mind . . . may deliberately 'shut his eyes' to avoid knowing what would otherwise be obvious to view. In such cases, so far as criminal law is concerned, the person acts at his peril in this regard, and is treated as having "knowledge" of the facts as they are ultimately discovered to be." J. Ll. J. Edwards, writing in 1954, introduced a survey of English cases with the statement, "For well-nigh a hundred years, it has been clear from the authorities that a person who deliberately shuts his eyes to an obvious means of knowledge has sufficient mens rea for an offence based on such words as . . . 'knowingly.'" Professor Glanville Williams states, on the basis both English and American authorities, "To the requirement of actual knowledge there is one strictly limited exception. . . . (T)he rule is that if a party has his suspicion aroused but then deliberately omits to make further enquiries, because he wishes to remain in ignorance, he is deemed to have knowledge." Professor Williams concludes, "The rule that willful blindness is equivalent to knowledge is essential, and is found throughout the criminal law."

The substantive justification for the rule is that deliberate ignorance and positive knowledge are equally culpable. The textual justification is that in common understanding one "knows" facts of which he is less than absolutely certain. To act "knowingly," therefore, is not necessarily to act only with positive knowledge, but also to act with an awareness of the high probability of the existence of the fact in question. When such awareness is present, "positive" knowledge is not required.

This is the analysis adopted in the Model Penal Code. Section 2.02(7) states: "When knowledge of the existence of a particular fact is an element of an offense, such knowledge is established if a person is aware of a high probability of its existence, unless he actually believes that it does not exist. . . .

Appellant's narrow interpretation of "knowingly" is inconsistent with the Drug Control Act's general purpose to deal more effectively "with the growing menace of drug abuse in the United States." Holding that this term introduces a requirement of positive knowledge would make deliberate ignorance a defense. It cannot be doubted that those who traffic in drugs would make the most of it. This is evident from the number of appellate decisions reflecting conscious avoidance of positive knowledge of the presence of contraband in the car driven by the defendant or in which he is a passenger, in the suitcase or package he carries, in the parcel concealed in his clothing.

It is no answer to say that in such cases the fact finder may infer positive knowledge. It is probable that many who performed the transportation function, essential to the drug traffic, can truthfully testify that they have no positive knowledge of the load they carry. Under appellant's interpretation of the statute, such persons will be convicted only if the fact finder errs in evaluating the credibility of the witness or deliberately disregards the law.

It begs the question to assert that a "deliberate ignorance" instruction permits the jury to convict without finding that the accused possessed the knowledge required by the statute. Such an assertion assumes that the statute requires positive knowledge. But the question is the meaning of the term "knowingly" in the statute. If it means positive knowledge, then, of course, nothing less will do. But if "knowingly" includes a mental state in which the defendant is aware that the fact in question is highly probable but consciously avoids enlightenment, the statute is satisfied by such proof.

It is worth emphasizing that the required state of mind differs from positive knowledge only so far as necessary to encompass a calculated effort to avoid the sanctions of the statute while violating its substance. "A court can properly find willful blindness only where it can almost be said that the defendant actually knew." In the language of the instruction in this case, the government must prove, "beyond a reasonable doubt, that if the defendant was not actually aware . . . his ignorance in that regard was solely and entirely a result of . . . a conscious purpose to avoid learning the truth."

No legitimate interest of an accused is prejudiced by such a standard, and society's interest in a system of criminal law that is enforceable and that imposes sanctions upon all who are equally culpable requires it.

The conviction is affirmed.

Second, although the majority acknowledges that the statute targets conduct and requires a but-for causal link between the bodily injury and the religion of the victims, it reads into the statute an extra, non-textual element. Specifically, the majority has effectively added to the hate crimes statute proof of faith-based animus, which is nowhere found in the statute. As discussed below, a plain language reading of the "because of" provision in § 249(a) requires only a causal connection between the assailant's conduct and the victim's protected class. Thus, record evidence bearing on the existence (or absence) of this connection is of paramount importance to our harmless error analysis.

I.

A. But-For Causality

As the majority acknowledges, *Burrage,* decided after the trial in this case, provides definitive guidance concerning the appropriate construction of the term "because of" that the trial court simply did not have at the time of trial. At issue in *Burrage* was a statutory enhancement provision that calls for increased penalties "on a defendant who unlawfully distributes a Schedule I or II drug, when 'death or serious bodily injury *results from* the use of such substance.'" 134 S.Ct. at 885 (emphasis added) (quoting 21 U.S.C. § 841(a)(1), (b)(1)(A)–(C) (2012)). The purchaser of the drug died following a binge consisting of five drugs, including heroin, which the defendant had distributed. *Id.* Both of the medical experts testifying at trial opined that the heroin was a contributing factor, but neither could say whether the decedent would have lived had he not taken the heroin. *See id.* at 885–86. The parties disputed the appropriate language for the jury instruction regarding causation. *See id.* at 886.

It is within this context that the *Burrage* Court set about defining the phrase "results from." Within its analysis, the Court reviewed both case law and dictionary definitions of the phrase "because of," noting that the definitions of the phrases "because of" and "results from" "resemble" one another, in that each requires but-for causality. *Id.* at 889. The *Burrage* Court concluded that these phrases "require[ ] proof 'that the harm would not have occurred in the absence of—that is, but for—the defendant's conduct.'" *Id.* at 887–88 (quoting *Univ. of Tex. Sw. Med. Ctr. v. Nassar,* ___ U.S. ___, 133 S.Ct. 2517, 2525, 186 L.Ed.2d 503 (2013) (citation omitted) (internal quotation marks omitted)).

To better explain what but-for causality means, the *Burrage* Court included a number of illustrative examples:

> [W]here A shoots B, who is hit and dies, we can say that A [actually] caused B's death, since but for A's conduct B would not have died. The same conclusion follows if the predicate act combines with other factors to produce the result, so long as the other factors alone would not have done so—if, so to speak, it was

the straw that broke the camel's back. Thus, if poison is administered to a man debilitated by multiple diseases, it is a but-for cause of his death even if those diseases played a part in his demise, so long as, without the incremental effect of the poison, he would have lived.

This but-for requirement is part of the common understanding of cause. Consider a baseball game in which the visiting team's leadoff batter hits a home run in the top of the first inning. If the visiting team goes on to win by a score of 1 to 0, every person competent in the English language and familiar with the American pastime would agree that the victory resulted from the home run. This is so because it is natural to say that one event is the outcome or consequence of another when the former would not have occurred but for the latter. It is beside the point that the victory also resulted from a host of other necessary causes, such as skillful pitching, the coach's decision to put the leadoff batter in the lineup, and the league's decision to schedule the game. By contrast, it makes little sense to say that an event resulted from or was the outcome of some earlier action if the action merely played a nonessential contributing role in producing the event. If the visiting team wound up winning 5 to 2 rather than 1 to 0, one would be surprised to read in the sports page that the victory resulted from the leadoff batter's early, non-dispositive home run.

Id. at 888 (citations omitted) (internal quotation marks omitted); *see id.* at 892 (Ginsburg, J., concurring) ("I do not read 'because of' in the context of antidiscrimination laws to mean 'solely because of.' ").

What these examples demonstrate is that there often exists more than one but-for cause; a number of necessary causes may operate concurrently to produce a given outcome. Such is the case here. The majority submits that the evidence supports an additional but-for cause of the hair sheering, namely, interpersonal and intra-family disagreements. But contrary to the majority's suggestion, neither this Court nor a jury needs to "untangl[e] the role[s]" these various factors played. *Supra* at 595. Nor does it matter whether these other factors were a more significant but for cause or whether one of them played a "starring role" at trial. *Id.* at 594; *see Burrage,* 134 S.Ct. at 888 (the poison was a but-for cause even though it had only an "incremental effect"). Rather, as the *Burrage* Court made clear through its examples, regardless of whether other causes are necessary to the outcome, the pertinent inquiry is always this: in the absence of the cause or factor at issue, would the statutorily prohibited outcome have occurred? As applied in *Burrage,* the Court concluded that the defendant could not be convicted under the enhancement statute because the Government conceded that there was no evidence that the decedent would have lived but for (or in the absence of) his heroin intake. *Id.* at 892.

Under § 249(a), the factor at issue is the victims' protected class—here, the victims' "actual or perceived [Amish] religion." 18 U.S.C. § 249(a)(2). The pertinent but-for causality inquiry, then, is whether, even if all of the other contributing or but-for factors remained, the prohibited conduct (the beard and hair cutting) would have occurred but for or in the absence of the victims' Amish religion. In more concrete terms, would Defendants have cut the victims' hair and beards if the victims were Catholic, atheist, or any other non-Amish faith?

Although the majority recognizes that the phrase "because of" "indicates *a* but-for causal link between the action that comes before it and the circumstance that comes afterwards," *supra* at 591 (emphasis added), the majority endorses a different interpretation of "because of" within its harmless error analysis. In effect, the majority construes the "because of" provision of § 249(a) to require the victim's protected class to be *the* but-for cause rather than *a* but-for cause. This runs afoul of *Burrage. See id.* at 591–92, 594.

The majority identifies no evidence sufficient to support a contrary finding. As discussed above, the interpersonal and intra-family disagreements the majority identifies lend support to the conclusion that there may exist more than one but-for cause in provoking the assaults. But, as the Supreme Court recently held, the existence or demonstration "of *other* necessary causes" "is beside the point." *Burrage,* 134 S.Ct. at 888. Instead, for purposes of our harmless error analysis, what matters is whether Defendants have offered evidence to support the conclusion that they would have cut the victims' hair and beards even if the victims were not Amish. There exists no such evidence, let alone evidence that "could rationally lead to a contrary finding." *Neder,* 527 U.S. at 19, 119 S.Ct. 1827. Accordingly, because the requisite causal link between the beard and hair cuttings and the victims' Amish faith is supported beyond a reasonable doubt, I conclude that the trial court's causation-instruction error was harmless such that all of the convictions must stand.

DISCUSSION QUESTIONS

1.   As to what the words "because of" means, do you agree with the majority or the dissent?

2.   As a matter of public policy, should we distinguish between crimes based on the motive of the person who committed them?

3.   Assume the answer to the last question is yes. As a matter of public policy, how do you think we should define hate crimes?

H. ANALYZING MENTAL STATE REQUIREMENTS

Having determined the definition of various mental states, we turn to the more vexing question of how one figures out which mental states are required for a crime to occur. This question takes different forms. Sometimes a statutory definition of a crime will not contain any mental state language. The question then is whether to read in a mental state requirement and which mental states to read in. More often, the statutory language will contain some mental state terms, but it will be unclear which elements the term modifies.

Imagine, for example, interpreting the following statute.

"A person who purposely transports into the United States animals not indigenous to the United States which he knows to be endangered is guilty of a felony."

Two mental states appear on this statute, purpose and knowledge, but which elements do they modify? Must one simply purposely transport the animals, or must one purposely transport them into the United States? Must one know the animals to be endangered, or must one know them to be not indigenous as well? Is one held strictly liable for any of the elements? In answering such questions, you must first consider whether you are in a Model Penal Code or common law jurisdiction.

1.   MODEL PENAL CODE DEFAULT RULES

M.P.C. § 2.02. General Requirements of Culpability

1)   Minimum Requirements of Culpability. Except as provided in Section 2.05, a person is not guilty of an offense unless he acted purposely, knowingly, recklessly or negligently, as the law may require, with respect to each material element of the offense.

. . . .

3)   Culpability Required Unless Otherwise Provided.

a)   When the culpability sufficient to establish a material element of an offense is not prescribed by law, such element is established if a person acts purposely, knowingly or recklessly with respect thereto.

4)   Prescribed Culpability Requirement Applies to All Material Elements.

a)   When the law, defining an offense, prescribes the kind of culpability that is sufficient for the commission of an offense, without distinguishing among the material elements thereof, such provision shall apply to all the material elements of the offense, unless a contrary purpose plainly appears.

5)   Substitutes for Negligence, Recklessness and Knowledge.

a)   When the law provides that negligence suffices to establish an element of an offense, such element also is established if a person acts purposely, knowingly or recklessly. When recklessness suffices to establish an element, such element also is established if a person acts purposely or knowingly. When acting knowingly suffices to establish an element, such element also is established if a person acts purposely.

6) Requirement of Purpose Satisfied if Purpose Is Conditional.

   a) When a particular purpose is an element of an offense, the element is established although such purpose is conditional, unless the condition negatives the harm or evil sought to be prevented by the law defining the offense.

7) Requirement of Knowledge Satisfied by Knowledge of High Probability.

   a) When knowledge of the existence of a particular fact is an element of an offense, such knowledge is established if a person is aware of a high probability of its existence, unless he actually believes that it does not exist.

8) Requirement of Willfulness Satisfied by Acting Knowingly.

   a) A requirement that an offense be committed willfully is satisfied if a person acts knowingly with respect to the material elements of the offense, unless a purpose to impose further requirements appears.

9) Culpability as to Illegality of Conduct.

   a) Neither knowledge nor recklessness or negligence as to whether conduct constitutes an offense or as to the existence, meaning or application of the law determining the elements of an offense is an element of such offense, unless the definition of the offense or the Code so provides.

10) Culpability as Determinant of Grade of Offense.

   a) When the grade or degree of an offense depends on whether the offense is committed purposely, knowingly, recklessly or negligently, its grade or degree shall be the lowest for which the determinative kind of culpability is established with respect to any material element of the offense.

———————

In this area, the Model Penal Code provides a series of default rules that help judges decide when and where to read various mental states into criminal statutes. First, if no mental state appears on the face of the statute, then the MPC requires at least a reckless mental state as to all material elements. Second, if only one mental state appears in connection with one material element, then the MPC assumes that the legislature intended that term to apply to all material elements absent clear language to the contrary. Third, the MPC precludes strict liability with respect to any material element of a criminal offense and provides that at least negligence will apply to material elements for which no clear legislative intent applies. For example, in the statute described above, if the court did not require the defendant to know that the animals were indigenous, she would at least require the defendant to have been grossly negligent with respect to their native status. These rules do not resolve all interpretive ambiguities, but they cut them down significantly.

What does the MPC provide if a defendant has a more blameworthy mental state than the law requires? For example, what if a statute defines vandalism as recklessly damaging the property of another? Is it a defense if the person claims that he damaged the property not recklessly, but purposely? Obviously not. The basic rule is that a more culpable mental state satisfies a requirement for a less culpable mental state. So, knowledge is satisfied by purpose, reckless is satisfied by knowledge or purpose, and negligence satisfied by any of the above.

Practice Problem 6.1: Home Alone

Kevin has been accidentally left home alone during the holidays by his parents. Harry and Marv break into Kevin's home during the day intending to steal various valuables. Unlike the famous movie, however, Harry and Marv are completely unaware that Kevin is inside the house when they break in. They have every reason to believe that Kevin and his family are away for the holidays. Harry and Marv barely survive a series of deathtraps Kevin created involving electrocution, blowtorches, and potentially paralyzing falls (although both are maimed and traumatized for life). In a Model Penal Code jurisdiction, are they guilty of first degree burglary under the following statute?

A person is guilty of burglary if he purposely enters a dwelling to commit a crime therein and is guilty of a felony in the second degree unless

(a)   the entry is at night in which case the offender is guilty of a felony in the first degree or

(b)   the entry is currently occupied by someone who dwells there, in which case the offender is guilty of a felony in the first degree.

---

2.   COMMON LAW DEFAULT RULES

Mental state ambiguities are much more difficult to resolve in common law jurisdictions, unless those jurisdictions have adopted some default rules.

Absent some clear evidence of legislative intent or purpose, modification questions regarding mental states are resolved primarily based on the text of the statute. A mental state modifies the element that appears immediately after it, but usually does not modify elements that appear before it. Beyond that, however, no clear rules exist to resolve the remaining issues. One must anticipate arguments for and against different interpretations of the statute based on the legislative intent and purpose and the philosophies of punishment.

For example, consider the following statutory language. "A person who purposely transports into the United States items which he knows to be archaeological artifacts which are stolen is guilty of a felony." What mental states would a common law court require, and which elements do they modify? A common law court would require purposeful transport and knowledge that the items were archaeological artifacts. In the absence of the sorts of clear default rules that the Model Penal code provides, a common law jurisdiction court would have to consider legislative intent and policy considerations in deciding whether one had to be purposeful with respect to transport *into the United States* and whether knowledge that the artifacts were stolen is required.

Practice Problem 6.2: Cold-Calling Crime

Imagine that your professor has succeeded in having your legislature make a crime of coming to class unprepared. The statute reads as follows. "It is a misdemeanor to knowingly come to class unprepared when you are on call." What do you have to know in order to be guilty of the crime? Analyze under both common law and Model Penal Code principles.

I. STRICT LIABILITY IN COMMON LAW JURISDICTIONS

To be held strictly liable is to be held liable in the absence of a mental state. As discussed above, the Model Penal Code does not recognize strict liability. The common law was said to generally abhor strict liability. Few strict liability offenses existed at common law. Furthermore, there is no such thing as a "pure" strict liability offenses because some mental state is always required for at least one element of an offense. An offense is considered to be a strict liability offense if no mental state is required for at least one material element.

A relatively familiar strict liability crime is statutory rape. Having sex with a person under the age of consent constitutes statutory rape. Statutory rape is considered a strict liability offense because in most jurisdictions no mental state is required as to the age of the minor. This means that even if a person appeared to be over the age of consent, and even if you examined their passport to verify this, you would still be guilty of statutory rape if they were in, fact, a minor. Wait, you might complain, there was no reasonable way for you to know that they were below the age of consent. And that would be a defense, of course, if negligence were required as to the age of consent. Strict liability, however, means that even a reasonable (and thereby non-negligent) belief is no defense because no state of mind is required for the element to be satisfied. Strict liability means that you act at the peril of being wrong, no matter how reasonable your belief.

Case in Context

The following old English common law case addresses the threshold issue of what mental state, if any, should be read into a statute that contains no mental state terminology. Although the decision deals with an antiquated offense it raises fundamental issues about blameworthiness that continue to be relevant today.

REGINA V. PRINCE
L.R. 2 Cr. Cas. Res. 154 (1875)

Case Reserved for the opinion of the court by DENMAN, J.

At the assizes for Surrey held at Kingston-on-Thames on Mar. 24, 1875, Henry Prince was tried on the charge of having unlawfully taken one Annie Phillips, an unmarried girl being under the age of sixteen years, out of the possession, and against the will of her father, contrary to s. 55 of the Offences against the Person Act, 1861. He was found guilty, but judgment was respited in order that the opinion of the Court for Crown Cases Reserved might be taken. All the facts necessary prima facie to support a conviction existed and were found by the jury to have existed, but the defendant pleaded in defense that the girl Annie Phillips, though proved by her father to be fourteen years old on April 6, 1875, looked very much older than sixteen, and the jury found upon reasonable evidence that before the defendant took her away she had told him that she was eighteen, that the defendant bona fide believed that statement, and that such belief was reasonable.

June 12, 1875.

BRAMWELL, B., read the following judgment, to which KELLY, C.B., CLEASBY, B., GROVE, J., POLLOCK, B., and AMPHLETT, B., assented.—

The question in the case depends on the construction of the statute under which the prisoner is indicted. Section 55 of the Offences against the Person Act, 1861, enacts that:

"Whosoever shall unlawfully take . . . any unmarried girl being under the age of sixteen years, out of the possession and against the will of her father or mother, or any other person having the lawful care or charge of her, shall be guilty of a misdemeanour . . . "

The word "unlawfully" means "not lawfully," "otherwise than lawfully" "without lawful cause"—such as would exist for instance on a taking by a police officer on a charge of felony or a taking by a father of his child from her school. The statute, therefore, may be read thus: "Whosoever shall take etc. without lawful cause." The prisoner had no such cause, and consequently except in so far as it helps the construction of the statute, the word "unlawfully" may, in the present case, be left out, and then the question is: Has the prisoner taken an unmarried girl under the age of sixteen out of the possession of and against the will of her father? In fact he has; but it is said not within the meaning of the statute, and that that must be read as though the word "knowingly" or some equivalent word was in.

The reason given is that as a rule mens rea is necessary to make any act a crime or offence, and that, if the facts necessary to constitute an offence are not known to the alleged offender, there can be no mens rea. I have used the word "knowingly," but it will perhaps be said that here the prisoner not only did not do the act knowingly, but knew, as he would have said, or believed, that the fact was otherwise than such as would have made his act a crime; that here the prisoner did not say to himself: "I do not know how the fact is, whether she is under sixteen or not, and will take the chance," but acted on the reasonable belief that she was over sixteen; and that though, if he had done what he did, knowing or believing neither way, but hazarding it, there would be a mens rea, there is not one when he believes he knows that she is over sixteen. It is impossible to suppose that a person taking a girl out of her father's possession against his will is guilty of no offence within the statute unless he, the taker, knows she is under sixteen—that he would not be guilty if the jury were of opinion he knew neither one way nor the other. Let it be then that the question is whether he is guilty where he knows, as he thinks, that she is over sixteen. This introduces the necessity for reading the statute with some strange words introduced; as thus:

"Whosoever shall take any unmarried girl being under the age of sixteen, and not believing her to be over the age of sixteen, out of the possession," etc. Those words are not there, and the question is whether we are bound to construe the statute as though they were, on account of the rule that mens rea is necessary to make an act a crime.

I am of opinion that we are not, nor as though the word "knowingly" was there, and for the following reasons. The act forbidden is wrong in itself, if without lawful cause. I do not say illegal, but wrong. I have not lost sight of this, that though the statute probably principally aims at seduction for carnal purposes, the taking may be by a female, with a good motive. Nevertheless, though there may be cases which are not immoral in one sense, I say that the act forbidden is wrong.

Let us remember what is the case supposed by the statute. It supposes that there is a girl—it does not say a woman, but a girl something between a child and a woman—it supposes she is in the possession of her father or mother, or other person having lawful care and charge of her, and it supposes there is a taking, and that that taking is against the will of the person in whose possession she is. It is, then, a taking of a girl in the possession of someone, against his will. I say that done without lawful cause is wrong, and that the legislature meant it should be at the risk of the taker, whether or not the girl was under sixteen. I do not say that taking a woman of fifty from her brother's or even father's house is wrong. She is at an age when she has a right to choose for herself; she is not a girl, nor of such tender age that she can be said to be in the possession of or under the care or in the charge of anyone. If I am asked where I draw the line, I answer at when the female is no longer a girl in anyone's possession.

But what the statute contemplates, and what I say is wrong, is the taking of a female of such tender years that she is properly called a girl, and can be said to be in another's possession, and in that other's care or charge. No argument is necessary to prove this; it is enough to state the case. The legislature has enacted that if anyone does this wrong act he does it at the risk of the girl turning out to be under sixteen. This opinion gives full scope to the doctrine of mens rea. If the taker believed he had the father's consent, though wrongly, he would have no mens rea. So if he did not know she was in anyone's possession, nor in the care or charge of anyone. In those cases he would not know he was doing the act forbidden by the statute, an act which, if he knew she was in the possession and care or charge of anyone, he would know was a crime or not according as she was under sixteen or not. He would know he was doing an act wrong itself, whatever was his intention, if done without lawful cause. In addition to these considerations one may add that the statute does use the word "unlawfully," and does not use the words "knowingly or not believing to the contrary." If the question was whether his act was unlawful there would be no difficulty as it clearly was not lawful.

BRETT, J.—It follows from this review that if the facts had been as the prisoner, according to the finding of the jury believed them to be, he would have done no act which has ever been a criminal offence in England; he would have done no act in respect of which an civil action could have ever been maintained against him; he would have done no act for which, if done in the absence of the father, and done with the continuing consent of the girl, the father could have had any legal remedy.

Upon all the cases I think it is proved that there can be no conviction for crime in England in the absence of a criminal mind or mens rea.

Then comes the question: What is the true meaning of the phrase? I do not doubt that it exists where the prisoner knowingly does acts which would constitute a crime if the result were as he anticipated, but in which the result may not improbably end in bringing the offence within a more serious class of crime. As if a man strike with a dangerous weapon with intent to do grievous bodily harm and kills. The result makes the crime murder; the prisoner has run the risk. So, if a prisoner do the prohibited acts without caring to consider what the truth is as to facts, as if a prisoner were to abduct a girl under sixteen without caring to consider whether she was in truth under sixteen, he runs the risk. So, if he without abduction defiles a girl who is in fact under ten years old, with a belief that she is between ten and twelve, if the facts were as he believed he would be committing the lesser crime. Then he runs the risk of his crime resulting in the greater crime. It is clear that ignorance of the law does not excuse. It seems to me to follow that the maxim as to mens rea applies whenever the facts which are present to the prisoner's mind, and which he has reasonable ground to believe, and does believe to be the facts, would, if true, make his acts no criminal offence at all. It may be true to say that the meaning of the word "unlawfully" is without justification or excuse. I, of course, agree that, if there be a legal justification, there can be no crime, but, I come to the conclusion that a mistake of fact on reasonable grounds, to the extent that, if the facts were as believed, the acts of the prisoner would make him guilty of no criminal offence at all, is an excuse, and that such excuse is implied in every criminal charge and every criminal enactment in England. I agree with LORD KENYON that "such is our law," and with COCKBURN, C.J., that "such is the foundation of all criminal justice."

Bearing in mind the previous enactments relating to the abduction of girls under sixteen, the Abduction Act, 1557, s. 2, and the general decisions upon those enactments and upon the present statute, looking at the mischief intended to be guarded against, and for the reasons given in the judgments of BRAMWELL, B., and BLACKBURN, J., it appears to me reasonably clear that the word "unlawfully" in the true sense in which it was used, is fully satisfied by holding that it is equivalent to the words "without lawful excuse," using those words as equivalent to without such an excuse as, being proved, would be a complete legal justification for the act, even where all the facts constituting the offence exist.

Cases may easily be suggested where such a defence might be made out; as, for instance, if it were proved that the prisoner had the authority of a court of competent jurisdiction, or of some legal warrant, or that he acted to prevent some illegal violence, not justified by the relation of parent and child, or schoolmistress or other custodian, and requiring forcible interference by way of protection.

In the present case the jury find that the defendant believed the girl to be eighteen year of age. Even if she had been of that age she would have been in the lawful care and charge of her father as her guardian by nature: see Co. LITT. 88b, n. 12, 19th Edn., recognised in R. v. Howes. Her father had a right to her personal custody up to the age of twenty-one, and to appoint a guardian by deed or will whose right to her personal custody would have extended up to the same age.

The belief that she was eighteen would be no justification to the defendant for taking her out of his possession and against his will. By taking her, even with her own consent, he must at least have been guilty of aiding and abetting her in doing an unlawful act—viz., in escaping against the will of her natural guardian from his lawful care and charge. This, in my opinion, leaves him wholly without lawful excuse or justification for the act he did, even though he believed that the girl was eighteen; and, therefore, unable to allege that what he had done was not unlawfully done within the meaning of the section. In other words, having knowingly done a wrongful act, viz., in taking the girl away from the lawful possession of her father against her will and in violation of his rights as guardian by nature, he cannot be heard to say that he thought the girl was of an age beyond that limited by the statute for the offence charged against him. He had wrongfully done the very thing contemplated by the legislature. He had wrongfully and knowingly violated the father's rights against the father's will, and he cannot set up a legal defense by merely proving that he thought he was committing a different kind of wrong from that which in fact he was committing.

Conviction affirmed.

* * *

DISCUSSION QUESTIONS

1.   Should a court assume that a statutory offense with no mental state terms is a strict liable offense if the conduct described is simply morally wrong, or should a court only so assume if the conduct described is legally wrong? Or should the court not make any assumptions one way or another about missing mental states based on the general blameworthiness of the conduct described?

2.   Should the court simply assume from the fact that the statute states no mental state that the legislature intended the offense to one of strict liability?

3.   Should the court require the legislature to explicitly state that the offense requires no mental state with respect to certain elements?

Case in Context

The following, a much more recent case, also concerns a missing or ambiguous mental state. The analysis is much more elaborate, but arguably the ultimate issue—what role general blameworthiness should play in interpreting mens rea requirements in a criminal statute—is the same the courts confronted in the *Prince* and *Faulkener* cases? Who do you think gets the issue right?

DEAN V. UNITED STATES

Supreme Court of the United States
556 U.S. 568 (2009)

CHIEF JUSTICE ROBERTS delivered the opinion of the Court.

Accidents happen. Sometimes they happen to individuals committing crimes with loaded guns. The question here is whether extra punishment Congress imposed for the discharge of a gun during certain crimes applies when the gun goes off accidentally.

I

Title 18 U.S.C. § 924(c)(1)(A) criminalizes using or carrying a firearm during and in relation to any violent or drug trafficking crime, or possessing a firearm in furtherance of such a crime. An individual convicted of that offense receives a 5-year mandatory minimum sentence, in addition to the punishment for the underlying crime. § 924(c)(1)(A)(i). The mandatory minimum increases to 7 years "if the firearm is brandished" and to 10 years "if the firearm is discharged." §§ 924(c)(1)(A)(ii), (iii).

In this case, a masked man entered a bank, waved a gun, and yelled at everyone to get down. He then walked behind the teller counter and started removing money from the teller stations. He grabbed bills with his left hand, holding the gun in his right. At one point, he reached over a teller to remove money from her drawer. As he was collecting the money, the gun discharged, leaving a bullet hole in the partition between two stations. The robber cursed and dashed out of the bank. Witnesses later testified that he seemed surprised that the gun had gone off. No one was hurt. App. 16–19, 24, 27, 47–48, 79.

Police arrested Christopher Michael Dean and Ricardo Curtis Lopez for the crime. Both defendants were charged with conspiracy to commit a robbery affecting interstate commerce, in violation of 18 U.S.C. § 1951(a), and aiding and abetting each other in using, carrying, possessing, and discharging a firearm during an armed robbery, in violation of § 924(c)(1)(A)(iii) and § 2. App. 11–12. At trial, Dean admitted that he had committed the robbery, id., at 76–81, and a jury found him guilty on both the robbery and firearm counts. The District Court sentenced Dean to a mandatory minimum term of 10 years in prison on the firearm count, because the firearm "discharged" during the robbery. § 924(c)(1)(A)(iii); App. 136.

Dean appealed, contending that the discharge was accidental, and that the sentencing enhancement in § 924(c)(1)(A)(iii) requires proof that the defendant intended to discharge the firearm. The Court of Appeals affirmed, holding that separate proof of intent was not required. 517 F.3d 1224, 1229 (CA11 2008). That decision created a conflict among the Circuits over whether the accidental discharge of a firearm during the specified crimes gives rise to the 10-year mandatory minimum. See United

States v. Brown, 449 F.3d 154 (CADC 2006) (holding that it does not). We granted certiorari to resolve that conflict. 555 U.S. 1028, 129 S. Ct. 593, 172 L. Ed. 2d 452 (2008).

II

Section 924(c)(1)(A) provides:

"[A]ny person who, during and in relation to any crime of violence or drug trafficking crime . . . uses or carries a firearm, or who, in furtherance of any such crime, possesses a firearm, shall, in addition to the punishment provided for such crime of violence or drug trafficking crime—

"(i) be sentenced to a term of imprisonment of not less than 5 years;

"(ii) if the firearm is brandished, be sentenced to a term of imprisonment of not less than 7 years; and

"(iii) if the firearm is discharged, be sentenced to a term of imprisonment of not less than 10 years."

The principal paragraph defines a complete offense and the subsections "explain how defendants are to 'be sentenced.'" Harris v. United States, 536 U.S. 545, 552, 122 S. Ct. 2406, 153 L. Ed. 2d 524 (2002). Subsection (i) "sets a catchall minimum" sentence of not less than five years. Id., at 552–553, 122 S. Ct. 2406, 153 L. Ed. 2d 524. Subsections (ii) and (iii) increase the minimum penalty if the firearm "is brandished" or "is discharged." See id., at 553, 122 S. Ct. 2406, 153 L. Ed. 2d 524. The parties disagree over whether § 924(c)(1)(A)(iii) contains a requirement that the defendant intend to discharge the firearm. We hold that it does not.

A

"We start, as always, with the language of the statute." Williams v. Taylor, 529 U.S. 420, 431, 120 S. Ct. 1479, 146 L. Ed. 2d 435 (2000). The text of subsection (iii) provides that a defendant shall be sentenced to a minimum of 10 years "if the firearm is discharged." It does not require that the discharge be done knowingly or intentionally, or otherwise contain words of limitation. As we explained in Bates v. United States, 522 U.S. 23, 118 S. Ct. 285, 139 L. Ed. 2d 215 (1997), in declining to infer an "'intent to defraud'" requirement into a statute, "we ordinarily resist reading words or elements into a statute that do not appear on its face." Id., at 29, 118 S. Ct. 285, 139 L. Ed. 2d 215.

Congress's use of the passive voice further indicates that subsection (iii) does not require proof of intent. The passive voice focuses on an event that occurs without respect to a specific actor, and therefore without respect to any actor's intent or culpability. Cf. Watson v. United States, 552 U.S. 74, 81, 128 S. Ct. 579, 584, 169 L. Ed. 2d 472, 478 (2007) (use of passive voice in statutory phrase "to be used" in 18 U.S.C. § 924(d)(1) reflects "agnosticism . . . about who does the using"). It is whether something happened—not how or why it happened—that matters.

The structure of the statute also suggests that subsection (iii) is not limited to the intentional discharge of a firearm. Subsection (ii) provides a 7-year mandatory minimum sentence if the firearm "is brandished." Congress expressly included an intent requirement for that provision, by defining "brandish" to mean "to display all or part of the firearm, or otherwise make the presence of the firearm known to another person, in order to intimidate that person." § 924(c)(4). The defendant must have intended to brandish the firearm, because the brandishing must have been done for a specific purpose. Congress did not, however, separately define "discharge" to include an intent requirement. "[W]here Congress includes particular language in one section of a statute but omits it in another section of the same Act, it is generally presumed that Congress acts intentionally and purposely in the disparate inclusion or exclusion." Russello v. United States, 464 U.S. 16, 23, 104 S. Ct. 296, 78 L. Ed. 2d 17 (1983) (internal quotation marks omitted).

Dean argues that the statute is not silent on the question presented. Congress, he contends, included an intent element in the opening paragraph of § 924(c)(1)(A), and that element extends to the sentencing enhancements. Section 924(c)(1)(A)criminalizes using or carrying a firearm "during and in relation to" any violent or drug trafficking crime. In Smith v. United States, 508 U.S. 223, 113 S. Ct. 2050, 124 L. Ed. 2d 138 (1993), we stated that the phrase "in relation to" means "that the firearm must have some purpose or effect with respect to the drug trafficking crime; its presence or involvement cannot be the result of accident or coincidence." Id., at 238, 113 S. Ct. 2050, 124 L. Ed. 2d 138. Dean argues that the adverbial phrase thus necessarily embodies an intent requirement, and that the phrase modifies all the verbs in the statute—not only use, carry, and possess, but also brandish and discharge. Such a reading requires that a perpetrator knowingly discharge the firearm for the enhancement to apply. If the discharge is accidental, Dean argues, it is not "in relation to" the underlying crime.

The most natural reading of the statute, however, is that "in relation to" modifies only the nearby verbs "uses" and "carries." The next verb—"possesses"—is modified by its own adverbial clause, "in furtherance of." The last two verbs—"is brandished" and "is discharged"—appear in separate subsections and are in a different voice than the verbs in the principal paragraph. There is no basis for reading "in relation to" to extend all the way down to modify "is discharged." The better reading of the statute is that the adverbial phrases in the opening paragraph—"in relation to" and "in furtherance of"—modify their respective nearby verbs, and that neither phrase extends to the sentencing factors.

But, Dean argues, such a reading will lead to absurd results. The discharge provision on its face contains no temporal or causal limitations. In the absence of an intent requirement, the enhancement would apply "regardless of when the actions occur, or by whom or for what reason they are taken." Brief for Petitioner 11–12. It would, for example, apply if the gun used during the crime were discharged "weeks (or years) before or after the crime." Reply Brief for Petitioner 11.

We do not agree that implying an intent requirement is necessary to address such concerns. As the Government recognizes, sentencing factors such as the one here "often involve . . . special features of the manner in which a basic crime was carried out." Brief for United States 29 (quoting Harris, 536 U.S., at 553, 122 S. Ct. 2406, 153 L. Ed. 2d 524; internal quotation marks omitted). The basic crime here is using or carrying a firearm during and in relation to a violent or drug trafficking crime, or possessing a firearm in furtherance of any such crime. Fanciful hypotheticals testing whether the discharge was a "special featur[e]" of how the "basic crime was carried out," id., at 553, 122 S. Ct. 2406, 153 L. Ed. 2d 524 (internal quotation marks omitted), are best addressed in those terms, not by contorting and stretching the statutory language to imply an intent requirement.

B

Dean further argues that even if the statute is viewed as silent on the intent question, that silence compels a ruling in his favor. There is, he notes, a presumption that criminal prohibitions include a requirement that the Government prove the defendant intended the conduct made criminal. In light of this presumption, we have "on a number of occasions read a state-of-mind component into an offense even when the statutory definition did not in terms so provide." United States v. United States Gypsum Co., 438 U.S. 422, 437, 98 S. Ct. 2864, 57 L. Ed. 2d 854 (1978). "[S]ome indication of congressional intent, express or implied, is required to dispense with mens rea as an element of a crime." Staples v. United States, 511 U.S. 600, 606, 114 S. Ct. 1793, 128 L. Ed. 2d 608 (1994).

Dean argues that the presumption is especially strong in this case, given the structure and purpose of the statute. In his view, the three subsections are intended to provide harsher penalties for increasingly culpable conduct: a 5-year minimum for using, carrying, or possessing a firearm; a 7-year minimum for brandishing a firearm; and a 10-year minimum for discharging a firearm. Incorporating an intent requirement into the discharge provision is necessary to give effect to that progression, because an accidental discharge is less culpable than intentional brandishment. See Brown, 449 F.3d at 156.

It is unusual to impose criminal punishment for the consequences of purely accidental conduct. But it is not unusual to punish individuals for the unintended consequences of their unlawful acts. See 2 W. LaFave, Substantive Criminal Law § 14.4, pp 436–437 (2d ed. 2003). The felony-murder rule is a familiar example: If a defendant commits an unintended homicide while committing another felony, the defendant can be convicted of murder. See 18 U.S.C. § 1111.

Here the defendant is already guilty of unlawful conduct twice over: a violent or drug trafficking offense and the use, carrying, or possession of a firearm in the course of that offense. That unlawful conduct was not an accident. See Smith, 508 U.S., at 238, 113 S. Ct. 2050, 124 L. Ed. 2d 138.

The fact that the actual discharge of a gun covered under § 924(c)(1)(A)(iii) may be accidental does not mean that the defendant is blameless. The sentencing enhancement in subsection (iii) accounts for the risk of harm resulting from the manner in which the crime is carried out, for which the defendant is responsible. See Harris, supra, at 553, 122 S. Ct. 2406, 153 L. Ed. 2d 524. An individual who brings a loaded weapon to commit a crime runs the risk that the gun will discharge accidentally. A gunshot in such circumstances—whether accidental or intended— increases the risk that others will be injured, that people will panic, or that violence (with its own danger to those nearby) will be used in response. Those criminals wishing to avoid the penalty for an inadvertent discharge can lock or unload the firearm, handle it with care during the underlying violent or drug trafficking crime, leave the gun at home, or—best yet— avoid committing the felony in the first place.

Section 924(c)(1)(A)(iii) requires no separate proof of intent. The 10-year mandatory minimum applies if a gun is discharged in the course of a violent or drug trafficking crime, whether on purpose or by accident. The judgment of the Court of Appeals for the Eleventh Circuit is affirmed.

DISCUSSION QUESTIONS

1.   What mental state language does the statutory provision at issue contain?

2.   Are you persuaded by the court's textual analysis with respect to whether that mental state language modifies the element in question? Did you find the defense's counter hypothetical persuasive?

3.   Is it fair to presume that an accidental discharge of the firearm is enough to trigger the sentencing enhancement? Ultimately the court justifies not reading in a mental state requirement on the grounds that the defendant is already "a criminal twice over." If you were defending Dean, how would you answer that argument? Given that the defendant is already punished for "being a criminal twice over" (i.e. punished for bank robbery and punished for bringing a gun to the bank robbery), should a further mental state be required to impose yet another punishment for the discharge of the gun?

J. PUBLIC WELFARE OFFENSES

Over time a certain class of offenses developed where courts decided not to read in mental state requirements. These offenses came to be known as public welfare offenses. Crimes that are similar to old common law offenses are not public welfare offenses, which means that they are presumed to require at least general criminal intent with respect to all material elements. Even if a statute defines a non-common law criminal offense, a court will only presume strict liability if the court deems the crime a public welfare offense. Public welfare offenses are generally regulatory offenses. While no iron-clad definition exists, courts have over the years identified a number of factors that guide their decisions.

1. The more severe the penalty the less likely the court will find strict liability.

2. The greater the stigma of the offense the less likely the court will find strict liability.

3. The more innocent the nature of the activity the less likely the court will find strict liability.

4. The greater the danger to the public the more likely the court will find strict liability.

5. The more regulated the activity generally the more likely the court will find strict liability.

6. The easier it is for defendants to determine whether the offense element exists through the exercise of ordinary diligence the more likely the court will find strict liability.

7. The harder it will be for the prosecutor to prove a culpable mental state with respect to the element the more likely the court will find strict liability.

With respect to the innocence of the activity in question in this public welfare offense analysis, the basic distinction discussed in the *Prince* decision between moral wrongs and legal wrongs remains important and useful. If the activity in question is either illegal—even if not necessarily criminal—or immoral, courts are more likely to presume that the legislature intended strict liability on the theory that individuals engage in such behavior at their own legal peril.

Case in Context

The following case contains the U.S. Supreme Court's first comprehensive discussion of public welfare offenses—a discussion that has shaped the approach of many state courts to similar issues.

MORISSETTE V. UNITED STATES

Supreme Court of the United States
342 U.S. 246 (1952)

Synopsis

Joseph Edward Morissette was convicted in the United States District Court for the Eastern District of Michigan, Frank A. Picard, J., of knowingly converting to his own use property of the United States, and he appealed. The United States Court of Appeals for the Sixth Circuit, Martin, Circuit Judge, 187 F.2d 427, affirmed the judgment, and Joseph Edward Morissette brought certiorari.

Opinion

MR. JUSTICE JACKSON delivered the opinion of the Court.

This would have remained a profoundly insignificant case to all except its immediate parties had it not been so tried and submitted to the jury as to raise questions both fundamental and far-reaching in federal criminal law, for which reason we granted certiorari.

On a large tract of uninhabited and untilled land in a wooded and sparsely populated area of Michigan, the Government established a practice bombing range over which the Air Force dropped simulated bombs at ground targets. These bombs consisted of a metal cylinder about forty inches long and eight inches across, filled with sand and enough black powder to cause a smoke puff by which the strike could be located. At various places about the range signs read 'Danger—Keep Out—Bombing Range.' Nevertheless, the range was known as good deer country and was extensively hunted.

Spent bomb casings were cleared from the targets and thrown into piles 'so that they will be out of the way.' They were not sacked or piled in any order but were dumped in heaps, some of which had been accumulating for four years or upwards, were exposed to the weather and rusting away.

Morissette, in December of 1948, went hunting in this area but did not get a deer. He thought to meet expenses of the trip by salvaging some of these casings. He loaded three tons of them on his truck and took them to a nearby farm, where they were flattened by driving a tractor over them. After expending this labor and trucking them to market in Flint, he realized $84.

Morissette, by occupation, is a fruit stand operator in summer and a trucker and scrap iron collector in winter. An honorably discharged veteran of World War II, he enjoys a good name among his neighbors and has had no blemish on his record more disreputable than a conviction for reckless driving.

The loading, crushing and transporting of these casings were all in broad daylight, in full view of passers-by, without the slightest effort at concealment. When an investigation was started, Morissette voluntarily, promptly and candidly told the whole story to the authorities, saying that he had no intention of stealing but thought the property was abandoned, unwanted and considered of no value to the Government. He was indicted, however, on the charge that he 'did unlawfully, wilfully and knowingly steal and convert' property of the United States of the value of $84, in violation of 18 U.S.C. s 641, 18 U.S.C.A. s 641, which provides that 'whoever embezzles, steals, purloins, or knowingly converts' government property is punishable by fine and imprisonment. Morissette was convicted and sentenced to imprisonment for two months or to pay a fine of $200. The Court of Appeals affirmed, one judge dissenting.

On his trial, Morissette, as he had at all times told investigating officers, testified that from appearances he believed the casings were cast-off and abandoned, that he did not intend to steal the property, and took it with no wrongful or criminal intent. The trial court, however, was unimpressed, and ruled: '(H)e took it because he thought it was abandoned and he knew he was on government property. * * * That is no defense. * * * I don't think anybody can have the defense they thought the property was abandoned on another man's piece of property.' The court stated: 'I will not permit you to show this man thought it was abandoned. * * * I hold in this case that there is no question of abandoned property.' The court refused to submit or to allow counsel to argue to the jury whether Morissette acted with innocent intention. It charged: 'And I instruct you that if you believe the testimony of the government in this case, he intended to take it. * * * He had no right to take this property. * * * (A)nd it is no defense to claim that it was abandoned, because it was on private property. * * * And I instruct you to this effect: That if this young man took this property (and he says he did), without any permission (he says he did), that was on the property of the United States Government (he says it was), that it was of the value of one cent or more (and evidently it was), that he is guilty of the offense charged here. If you believe the government, he is guilty. * * * The question on intent is whether or not he intended to take the property. He says he did. Therefore, if you believe either side, he is guilty.' Petitioner's counsel contended, 'But the taking must have been with a felonious intent.' The court ruled, however: 'That is presumed by his own act.'

The Court of Appeals suggested that 'greater restraint in expression should have been exercised', but affirmed the conviction because, 'As we have interpreted the statute, appellant was guilty of its violation beyond a shadow of doubt, as evidenced even by his own admissions.' Its construction of the statute is that it creates several separate and distinct offenses, one being knowing conversion of government property. The court ruled that this particular offense requires no element of criminal intent. This conclusion was thought to be required by the failure of Congress to express such a requisite and this Court's decisions in United States v. Behrman,

258 U.S. 280, 42 S.Ct. 303, 66 L.Ed. 619, and United States v. Balint, 258 U.S. 250, 42 S.Ct. 301, 66 L.Ed. 604.

I.

In those cases this Court did construe mere omission from a criminal enactment of any mention of criminal intent as dispensing with it. If they be deemed precedents for principles of construction generally applicable to federal penal statutes, they authorize this conviction. Indeed, such adoption of the literal reasoning announced in those cases would do this and more—it would sweep out of all federal crimes, except when expressly preserved, the ancient requirement of a culpable state of mind. We think a resume of their historical background is convincing that an effect has been ascribed to them more comprehensive than was contemplated and one inconsistent with our philosophy of criminal law.

The contention that an injury can amount to a crime only when inflicted by intention is no provincial or transient notion. It is as universal and persistent in mature systems of law as belief in freedom of the human will and a consequent ability and duty of the normal individual to choose between good and evil. A relation between some mental element and punishment for a harmful act is almost as instinctive as the child's familiar exculpatory 'But I didn't mean to,' and has afforded the rational basis for a tardy and unfinished substitution of deterrence and reformation in place of retaliation and vengeance as the motivation for public prosecution. Unqualified acceptance of this doctrine by English common law in the Eighteenth Century was indicated by Blackstone's sweeping statement that to constitute any crime there must first be a 'vicious will.' Common-law commentators of the Nineteenth Century early pronounced the same principle, although a few exceptions not relevant to our present problem came to be recognized.

Crime, as a compound concept, generally constituted only from concurrence of an evil-meaning mind with an evil-doing hand, was congenial to an intense individualism and took deep and early root in American soil. As the state codified the common law of crimes, even if their enactments were silent on the subject, their courts assumed that the omission did not signify disapproval of the principle but merely recognized that intent was so inherent in the idea of the offense that it required no statutory affirmation. Courts, with little hesitation or division, found an implication of the requirement as to offenses that were taken over from the common law. The unanimity with which they have adhered to the central thought that wrongdoing must be conscious to be criminal is emphasized by the variety, disparity and confusion of their definitions of the requisite but elusive mental element. However, courts of various jurisdictions, and for the purposes of different offenses, have devised working formulae, if not scientific ones, for the instruction of juries around such terms as 'felonious intent,' 'criminal intent,' 'malice aforethought,' 'guilty knowledge,' 'fraudulent intent,' 'wilfulness,' 'scienter,' to denote guilty knowledge, or 'mens rea,' to signify an evil purpose or mental culpability. By use or combination of these various tokens, they have sought to protect those who were not blameworthy in mind from conviction of infamous common-law crimes.

However, the Balint and Behrman offenses belong to a category of another character, with very different antecedents and origins. The crimes there involved depend on no mental element but consist only of forbidden acts or omissions. This, while not expressed by the Court, is made clear from examination of a century-old but accelerating tendency, discernible both here and in England, to call into existence new duties and crimes which disregard any ingredient of intent. The industrial revolution multiplied the number of workmen exposed to injury from increasingly powerful and complex mechanisms, driven by freshly discovered sources of energy, requiring higher precautions by employers. Traffic of velocities, volumes and varieties unheard of came to subject the wayfarer to intolerable casualty risks if owners and drivers were not to observe new cares and uniformities of conduct. Congestion of cities and crowding of quarters called for health and welfare regulations undreamed of in simpler times. Wide distribution of goods became an instrument of wide distribution of harm when those who dispersed food, drink, drugs, and even securities, did not comply with reasonable standards of quality, integrity, disclosure and care. Such dangers have engendered increasingly numerous and detailed regulations which heighten the duties of those in control of particular industries, trades, properties or activities that affect public health, safety or welfare.

While many of these duties are sanctioned by a more strict civil liability, lawmakers, whether wisely or not, have sought to make such regulations more effective by invoking criminal sanctions to be applied by the familiar technique of criminal prosecutions and convictions. This has confronted the courts with a multitude of prosecutions, based on statutes or administrative regulations, for what have been aptly called 'public welfare offenses.' These cases do not fit neatly into any of such accepted classifications of common-law offenses, such as those against the state, the person, property, or public morals. Many of these offenses are not in the nature of positive aggressions or invasions, with which the common law so often dealt, but are in the nature of neglect where the law requires care, or inaction where it imposes a duty. Many violations of such regulations result in no direct or immediate injury to person or property but merely create the danger or probability of it which the law seeks to minimize. While such offenses do not threaten the security of the state in the manner of treason, they may be regarded as offenses against its authority, for their occurrence impairs the efficiency of controls deemed essential to the social order as presently constituted. In this respect, whatever the intent of the violator, the injury is the same, and the consequences are injurious or not according to fortuity. Hence, legislation applicable to such offenses, as a matter of policy, does not specify intent as a necessary element. The accused, if he does not will the violation, usually is in a position to prevent it with no more care than society might reasonably expect and no more exertion than it might reasonably exact from one who assumed his responsibilities. Also, penalties commonly are relatively small, and conviction does not grave damage to an offender's reputation. Under such considerations, courts have turned to construing statutes and regulations which make no mention of intent as dispensing with it and holding that the guilty act alone makes out the crime. This has not, however, been without expressions of misgiving.

The pilot of the movement in this country appears to be a holding that a tavernkeeper could be convicted for selling liquor to an habitual drunkard even if he did not know the buyer to be such. Barnes v. State, 1849, 19 Conn. 398. Later came Massachusetts holdings that convictions for selling adulterated milk in violation of statutes forbidding such sales require no allegation or proof that defendant knew of the adulteration. Commonwealth v. Farren, 1864, 9 Allen 489; Commonwealth v. Nichols, 1865, 10 Allen 199; Commonwealth v. Waite, 1865, 11 Allen 264. Departures from the common-law tradition, mainly of these general classes, were reviewed and their rationale appraised by Chief Justice Cooley, as follows: 'I agree that as a rule there can be no crime without a criminal intent, but this is not by any means a universal rule. * * * Many statutes which are in the nature of police regulations, as this is, impose criminal penalties irrespective of any intent to violate them, the purpose being to require a degree of diligence for the protection of the public which shall render violation impossible.' People v. Roby, 1884, 52 Mich. 577, 579, 18 N.W. 365, 366.

After the turn of the Century, a new use for crimes without intent appeared when New York enacted numerous and novel regulations of tenement houses, sanctioned by money penalties. Landlords contended that a guilty intent was essential to establish a violation. Judge Cardozo wrote the answer: 'The defendant asks us to test the meaning of this statute by standards applicable to statutes that govern infamous crimes. The analogy, however, is deceptive. The element of conscious wrongdoing, the guilty mind accompanying the guilty act, is associated with the concept of crimes that are punished as infamous. * * * Even there it is not an invariable element. * * * But in the prosecution of minor offenses there is a wider range of practice and of power. Prosecutions for petty penalties have always constituted in our law a class by themselves. * * * That is true, though the prosecution is criminal in form.' Tenement House Department of City of New York v. McDevitt, 1915, 215 N.Y. 160, 168, 109 N.E. 88, 90.

Soon, employers advanced the same contention as to violations of regulations prescribed by a new labor law. Judge Cardozo, again for the court, pointed out, as a basis for penalizing violations whether intentional or not, that they were punishable only by fine 'moderate in amount', but cautiously added that in sustaining the power so to fine unintended violations 'we are not to be understood as sustaining to a like length the power to imprison. We leave that question open.' People ex rel. Price v. Sheffield Farms-Slawson-Decker Co., 1918, 225 N.Y. 25, 32–33, 121 N.E. 474, 476, 477.

Thus, for diverse but reconcilable reasons, state courts converged on the same result, discontinuing inquiry into intent in a limited class of offenses against such statutory regulations.

Before long, similar questions growing out of federal legislation reached this Court. Its judgments were in harmony with this consensus of state judicial opinion, the existence of which may have led the Court to overlook the need for full exposition of their rationale in the context of federal law. In overruling a contention that there can be no conviction on an indictment which makes no charge of criminal intent but alleges only making of a sale of a narcotic forbidden by law, Chief Justice Taft, wrote: 'While the general rule at common law was that the scienter was a necessary element in the indictment and proof of every crime, and this was followed in regard to statutory crimes even where the statutory definition did not in terms include it * * *, there has been a modification of this view in respect to prosecutions under statutes the purpose of which would be obstructed by such a requirement. It is a question of legislative intent to be construed by the court. * * *' United States v. Balint, supra, 258 U.S. 251–252, 42 S.Ct. 302.

He referred, however, to 'regulatory measures in the exercise of what is called the police power where the emphasis of the statute is evidently upon achievement of some social betterment rather than the punishment of the crimes as in cases of mala in se,' and drew his citation of supporting authority chiefly from state court cases dealing with regulatory offenses. Id., 258 U.S. at page 252, 42 S.Ct. at page 302.

On the same day, the Court determined that an offense under the Narcotic Drug Act does not require intent, saying, 'If the offense be a statutory one, and intent or knowledge is not made an element of it, the indictment need not charge such knowledge or intent.' United States v. Behrman, supra, 258 U.S. at page 288, 42 S.Ct. at page 304.

It was not until recently that the Court took occasion more explicitly to relate abandonment of the ingredient of intent, not merely with considerations of expediency in obtaining convictions, nor with the malum prohibitum classification of the crime, but with the peculiar nature and quality of the offense. We referred to '* * * a now familiar type of legislation whereby penalties serve as effective means of regulation', and continued, 'such legislation dispenses with the conventional requirement for criminal conduct—awareness of some wrongdoing. In the interest of the larger good it puts the burden of acting at hazard upon a person otherwise innocent but standing in responsible relation to a public danger.' But we warned: 'Hardship there doubtless may be under a statute which thus penalizes the transaction though consciousness of wrongdoing be totally wanting.' United States v. Dotterweich, 320 U.S. 277, 280–281, 284, 64 S.Ct. 134, 136, 88 L.Ed. 48.

Neither this Court nor, so far as we are aware, any other has undertaken to delineate a precise line or set forth comprehensive criteria for distinguishing between crimes that require a mental element and crimes that do not. We attempt no closed definition, for the law on the subject is neither settled nor static. The conclusion reached in the Balint and Behrman cases has our approval and adherence for the circumstances to which it was there applied. A quite different question here is whether we will expand the doctrine of crimes without intent to include those charged here.

Stealing, larceny, and its variants and equivalents, were among the earliest offenses known to the law that existed before legislation; they are invasions of rights of property which stir a sense of insecurity in the whole community and arouse public demand for retribution, the penalty is high and, when a sufficient amount is involved, the infamy is that of a felony, which, says Maitland, is '* * * as bad a word as you can give to man or thing.' State courts of last resort, on whom fall the heaviest burden of interpreting criminal law in this country, have consistently retained the requirement of intent in larceny-type offenses. If any state has deviated, the exception has neither been called to our attention nor disclosed by our research.

Congress, therefore, omitted any express prescription of criminal intent from the enactment before us in the light of an unbroken course of judicial decision in all constituent states of the Union holding intent inherent in this class of offense, even when not expressed in a statute. Congressional silence as to mental elements in an Act merely adopting into federal statutory law a concept of crime already so well defined in common law and statutory interpretation by the states may warrant quite contrary inferences than the same silence in creating an offense new to general law, for whose definition the courts have no guidance except the Act. Because the offenses before this Court in the Balint and Behrman cases were of this latter class, we cannot accept them as authority for eliminating intent from offenses incorporated from the common law. Nor do exhaustive studies of state court cases disclose any well-considered decisions applying the doctrine of crime without intent to such enacted common-law offenses, although a few deviations are notable as illustrative of the danger inherent in the Government's contentions here.

The Government asks us by a feat of construction radically to change the weights and balances in the scales of justice. The purpose and obvious effect of doing away with the requirement of a guilty intent is to ease the prosecution's path to conviction, to strip the defendant of such benefit as he derived at common law from innocence of evil purpose, and to circumscribe the freedom heretofore allowed juries. Such a manifest impairment of the immunities of the individual should not be extended to common-law crimes on judicial initiative.

The spirit of the doctrine which denies to the federal judiciary power to create crimes forthrightly admonishes that we should not enlarge the reach of enacted crimes by constituting them from anything less than the incriminating components contemplated by the words used in the statute. And where Congress borrows terms of art in which are accumulated the legal tradition and meaning of centuries of practice, it presumably knows and adopts the cluster of ideas that were attached to each borrowed word in the body of learning from which it was taken and the meaning its use will convey to the judicial mind unless otherwise instructed. In such case, absence of contrary direction may be taken as satisfaction with widely accepted definitions, not as a departure from them.

We hold that mere omission from s 641 of any mention of intent will not be construed as eliminating that element from the crimes denounced.

Of course, the jury, considering Morissette's awareness that these casings were on government property, his failure to seek any permission for their removal and his self-interest as a witness, might have disbelieved his profession of innocent intent and concluded that his assertion of a belief that the casings were abandoned was an afterthought. Had the jury convicted on proper instructions it would be the end of the matter. But juries are not bound by what seems inescapable logic to judges. They might have concluded that the heaps of spent casings left in the hinterland to rust away presented an appearance of unwanted and abandoned junk, and that lack of any conscious deprivation of property or intentional injury was indicated by Morissette's good character, the openness of the taking, crushing and transporting of the casings, and the candor with which it was all admitted. They might have refused to brand Morissette as a thief. Had they done so, that too would have been the end of the matter.

DISCUSSION QUESTIONS

1. Why does the Court read in mental state requirements for statutory crimes that resemble old common law crimes? Why do people committing traditional crimes receive more mental state protection from the Court than people committing newer crimes?

2. What definition does the Court give public welfare offenses? Don't all crimes affect the public welfare? What should a court do if a crime is neither an old common law crime nor a public welfare offense?

3. Which justification for holding offenders strictly liable for public welfare offenses do you find to be most persuasive?

Practice Problem 6.3: Statutory Smorgasbord

What mental states are required by the following statues in a common law jurisdiction?

- "Whoever destroys the property of another is guilty of a misdemeanor."

- "Except as otherwise provided in this Chapter, it shall be unlawful to operate a vehicle in excess of the following speeds:

  (a) Thirty-five miles per hour inside municipal corporate limits for all vehicles.

  (b) Fifty-five miles per hour outside municipal corporate limits for all vehicles except for school buses and school activity buses."

- "Anyone who unlawfully possesses ricin is guilty of a felony, punishable by up to ten years imprisonment."[2]

K. SPECIAL FOCUS: ENVIRONMENTAL CRIME

Environmental crimes would seem to be the consummate example of a public welfare offense, but application of the public welfare offense factors discussed above raise difficult issues, as the dissent in the following decision describes.

UNITED STATES OF AMERICA V. MICHAEL H. WEITZENHOFF; THOMAS W. MARIANI

United States Court of Appeals, Ninth Circuit
35 F.3d 1275 (1993)

FLETCHER, CIRCUIT JUDGE:

Michael H. Weitzenhoff and Thomas W. Mariani, who managed the East Honolulu Community Services Sewage Treatment Plant, appeal their convictions for violations of the Clean Water Act ("CWA"), 33 U.S.C. §§ 1251 et seq., contending that 1) the district court misconstrued the word "knowingly" under section 1319(c)(2) of the CWA; 2) . . . .

We affirm the convictions and sentence.

---

[2] Ricin is a highly toxic and highly regulated substance made from the concentrated extract of castor beans. The amount of ricin that can be extracted from a single castor bean could potentially kill a thousand people.

FACTS AND PROCEDURAL HISTORY

In 1988 and 1989 Weitzenhoff was the manager and Mariani the assistant manager of the East Honolulu Community Services Sewage Treatment Plant ("the plant"), located not far from Sandy Beach, a popular swimming and surfing beach on Oahu. The plant is designed to treat some 4 million gallons of residential wastewater each day by removing the solids and other harmful pollutants from the sewage so that the resulting effluent can be safely discharged into the ocean. The plant operates under a permit issued pursuant to the National Pollution Discharge Elimination System ("NPDES"), which established the limits on the Total Suspended Solids ("TSS") and Biochemical Oxygen Demand ("BOD")—indicators of the solid and organic matter, respectively, in the effluent discharged at Sandy Beach. During the period in question, the permit limited the discharge of both the TSS and BOD to an average of 976 pounds per day over a 30-day period. It also imposed monitoring and sampling requirements on the plant's management.

The sewage treatment process that was overseen by Weitzenhoff and Mariani began with the removal of large inorganic items such as rags and coffee grounds from the incoming wastewater as it flowed through metal screens and a grit chamber at the head of the plant. The wastewater then entered large tanks known as primary clarifiers, where a portion of the organic solids settled to the bottom of the tanks. The solid material which settled in the primary clarifiers, known as primary sludge, was pumped to separate tanks, known as anaerobic digesters, to be further processed. Those solids that did not settle continued on to aeration basins, which contained microorganisms to feed on and remove the solids and other organic pollutants in the waste stream.

From the aeration basins the mixture flowed into final clarifiers, where the microorganisms settled out, producing a mixture that sank to the bottom of the clarifiers called activated sludge. The clarified stream then passed through a chlorine contact chamber, where the plant's sampling apparatus was, and emptied into the plant's outfall, a long underground pipe which discharged the plant's effluent into the ocean through diffusers 1,100 to 1,400 feet from shore (the "Sandy Beach outfall").

Meanwhile, the activated sludge that had settled in the final clarifiers was pumped from the bottom of the clarifiers. A certain portion was returned to the aeration basins, while the remainder, known as waste activated sludge ("WAS"), was pumped to WAS holding tanks. From the holding tanks, the WAS could either be returned to other phases of the treatment process or hauled away to a different sewage treatment facility.

From March 1987 through March 1988, the excess WAS generated by the plant was hauled away to another treatment plant, the Sand Island Facility. In March 1988, certain improvements were made to the East

Honolulu plant and the hauling was discontinued. Within a few weeks, however, the plant began experiencing a buildup of excess WAS. Rather than have the excess WAS hauled away as before, however, Weitzenhoff and Mariani instructed two employees at the plant to dispose of it on a regular basis by pumping it from the storage tanks directly into the outfall, that is, directly into the ocean. The WAS thereby bypassed the plant's effluent sampler so that the samples taken and reported to Hawaii's Department of Health ("DOH") and the EPA did not reflect its discharge.

The evidence produced by the government at trial showed that WAS was discharged directly into the ocean from the plant on about 40 separate occasions from April 1988 to June 1989, resulting in some 436,000 pounds of pollutant solids being discharged into the ocean, and that the discharges violated the plant's 30-day average effluent limit under the permit for most of the months during which they occurred. Most of the WAS discharges occurred during the night, and none was reported to the DOH or EPA. DOH inspectors contacted the plant on several occasions in 1988 in response to complaints by lifeguards at Sandy Beach that sewage was being emitted from the outfall, but Weitzenhoff and Mariani repeatedly denied that there was any problem at the plant. In one letter responding to a DOH inquiry in October 1988, Mariani stated that "the debris that was reported could not have been from the East Honolulu Wastewater Treatment facility, as our records of effluent quality up to this time will substantiate." (U.S. Excerpts of Record ("U.S.E.R.") at 37.) One of the plant employees who participated in the dumping operation testified that Weitzenhoff instructed him not to say anything about the discharges, because if they all stuck together and did not reveal anything, "they [couldn't] do anything to us." (2 R.T. at 66–67.)

Following an FBI investigation, Weitzenhoff and Mariani were charged in a thirty-one-count indictment with conspiracy and substantive violations of the Clean Water Act ("CWA"), 33 U.S.C. §§ 1251 *et seq.* At trial, Weitzenhoff and Mariani admitted having authorized the discharges, but claimed that their actions were justified under their interpretation of the NPDES permit. The jury found them guilty of six of the thirty-one counts.

Weitzenhoff was sentenced to twenty-one months and Mariani thirty-three months imprisonment. Each filed a timely notice of appeal.

DISCUSSION

A.   Intent Requirement

Section 1311(a) of the CWA prohibits the discharge of pollutants into navigable waters without an NPDES permit. 33 U.S.C. § 1311(a). Section 1319(c)(2) makes it a felony offense to "knowingly violate [ ] section 1311, 1312, 1316, 1317, 1318, 1321(b)(3), 1328, or 1345 . . ., or any permit condition or limitation implementing any of such sections in a permit issued under section 1342."

Prior to trial, the district court construed "knowingly" in section 1319(c)(2) as requiring only that Weitzenhoff and Mariani were aware that they were discharging the pollutants in question, not that they knew they were violating the terms of the statute or permit. According to appellants, the district court erred in its interpretation of the CWA and in instructing the jury that "the government is not required to prove that the defendant knew that his act or omissions were unlawful," (14 R.T. at 117), as well as in rejecting their proposed instruction based on the defense that they mistakenly believed their conduct was authorized by the permit. Apparently, no court of appeals has confronted the issue raised by appellants.

. . .

As with certain other criminal statutes that employ the term "knowingly," it is not apparent from the face of the statute whether "knowingly" means a knowing violation of the law or simply knowing conduct that is violative of the law. We turn, then, to the legislative history of the provision at issue to ascertain what Congress intended.

In 1987, Congress substantially amended the CWA, elevating the penalties for violations of the Act. *See* H.R.Conf.Rep. No. 1004, 99th Cong., 2d Sess. 138 (1986). Increased penalties were considered necessary to deter would-be polluters. S.Rep. No. 50, 99th Cong., 1st Sess. 29 (1985). With the 1987 amendments, Congress substituted "knowingly" for the earlier intent requirement of "willfully" that appeared in the predecessor to section 1319(c)(2). The Senate report accompanying the legislation explains that the changes in the penalty provisions were to ensure that "[c]riminal liability shall . . . attach to any person who is not in compliance with all applicable Federal, State and local requirements and permits *and causes* a POTW [publicly owned treatment works] to violate any effluent limitation or condition in any permit issued to the treatment works." *Id.* (emphasis added). Similarly, the report accompanying the House version of the bill, which contained parallel provisions for enhancement of penalties, states that the proposed amendments were to "provide penalties for dischargers or individuals who knowingly or negligently violate *or cause the violation of* certain of the Act's requirements." H.R.Rep. No. 189, 99th Cong., 1st Sess. 29–30 (1985) (emphasis added). Because they speak in terms of "causing" a violation, the congressional explanations of the new penalty provisions strongly suggest that criminal sanctions are to be imposed on an individual who knowingly engages in conduct that results in a permit violation, regardless of whether the polluter is cognizant of the requirements or even the existence of the permit.

Our conclusion that "knowingly" does not refer to the legal violation is fortified by decisions interpreting analogous public welfare statutes. The leading case in this area is *United States v. International Minerals & Chem. Corp.,* 402 U.S. 558, 91 S.Ct. 1697, 29 L.Ed.2d 178 (1971). In *International Minerals,* the Supreme Court construed a statute which made it a crime to "knowingly violate[ ] any . . . regulation" promulgated by the ICC pursuant to 18 U.S.C. § 834(a), a provision authorizing the agency to formulate regulations for the safe transport of corrosive liquids. *Id.* at 559, 91 S.Ct. at 1699. The Court held that the term "knowingly" referred to the acts made criminal rather than a violation of the regulation, and that "regulation" was a shorthand designation for the specific acts or omissions contemplated by the act. *Id.* at 560–62, 91 S.Ct. at 1699–1700. "[W]here . . . dangerous or deleterious devices or products or obnoxious waste materials are involved, the probability of regulation is so great that anyone who is aware that he is in possession of them or dealing with them must be presumed to be aware of the regulation." *Id.* at 565, 91 S.Ct. at 1701–02.

Appellants seek to rely on the Supreme Court's decision in *Liparota v. United States,* 471 U.S. 419, 105 S.Ct. 2084, 85 L.Ed.2d 434 (1985), to support their alternative reading of the intent requirement. *Liparota* concerned U.S.C. § 2024(b)(1), which provides that anyone who "knowingly uses, transfers, acquires, alters, or possesses [food stamp] coupons or authorization cards in any manner not authorized by [the statute] or regulations" is subject to a fine or imprisonment. *Id.* at 420, 105 S.Ct. at 2085. The Court, noting that the conduct at issue did not constitute a public welfare offense, distinguished the *International Minerals* line of cases and held that the government must prove the defendant knew that his acquisition or possession of food stamps was in a manner unauthorized by statute or regulations. *Id.* at 432–33, 105 S.Ct. at 2092.

Subsequent to the filing of the original opinion in this case, the Supreme Court decided two cases which Weitzenhoff contends call our analysis into question. *See Ratzlaf v. United States,* 510 U.S. 135, 114 S.Ct. 655, 126 L.Ed.2d 615 (1994); *Staples v. United States,* 511 U.S. 600, 114 S.Ct. 1793, 128 L.Ed.2d 608 (1994). We disagree.

The statute in *Ratzlaf* does not deal with a public welfare offense, but rather with violations of the banking statutes. The Court construed the term "willfully" in the anti-structuring provisions of the Bank Secrecy Act to require both that the defendant knew he was structuring transactions to avoid reporting requirements and that he knew his acts were unlawful. The Court recognized that the money structuring provisions are not directed at conduct which a reasonable person necessarily should know is subject to strict public regulation and that the structuring offense applied to all persons with more than $10,000, many of whom could be engaged in structuring for innocent reasons. *Ratzlaf,* 510 U.S. at ___–___, 114 S.Ct. at 660–62. In contrast, parties such as Weitzenhoff are closely regulated and are discharging waste materials that affect public health. The *International Minerals* rationale requires that we impute to these parties knowledge of their operating permit. This was recognized by the Court in *Staples.*

The specific holding in *Staples* was that the government is required to prove that a defendant charged with possession of a machine gun knew that the weapon he possessed had the characteristics that brought it within the statutory definition of a machinegun. But the Court took pains to contrast the gun laws to other regulatory regimes, specifically those regulations that govern the handling of "obnoxious waste materials." *See Staples,* 511 U.S. at ___, 114 S.Ct. at 1798. It noted that the mere innocent ownership of guns is not a public welfare offense. *Id.* at ___, 114 S.Ct. at 1804. The Court focussed on the long tradition of widespread gun ownership in this country and, recognizing that approximately 50% of American homes contain a firearm, *id.* at ___, 114 S.Ct. at 1801, acknowledged that mere ownership of a gun is not sufficient to place people on notice that the act of owning an unregistered firearm is not innocent under the law.

Staples thus explicitly contrasted the mere possession of guns to public welfare offenses, which include statutes that regulate " 'dangerous or deleterious devices or products or obnoxious waste materials,' " *id.* at ___, 114 S.Ct. at 1800, and confirmed the continued vitality of statutes covering public welfare offenses, which "regulate potentially harmful or injurious items" and place a defendant on notice that he is dealing with a device or a substance "that places him in 'responsible relation to a public danger.' " *Id.* "[I]n such cases Congress intended to place the burden on the defendant to ascertain at his peril whether [his conduct] comes within the inhibition of the statute." *Id.* at ___, 114 S.Ct. at 1798 (citations and internal quotations omitted).

Unlike "[g]uns [which] in general are not 'deleterious devices or products or obnoxious waste materials,' *International Minerals, supra* [402 U.S.], at 565 [91 S.Ct. at 1702], that put their owners on notice that they stand 'in responsible relation to a public danger[,]' *Dotterweich,* 320 U.S. at 281 64 S.Ct. at 136]," *Staples,* 511 U.S. at ___, 114 S.Ct. at 1800, the dumping of sewage and other pollutants into our nation's waters is precisely the type of activity that puts the discharger on notice that his acts may pose a public danger. Like other public welfare offenses that regulate the discharge of pollutants into the air, the disposal of hazardous wastes, the undocumented shipping of acids, and the use of pesticides on our food, the improper and excessive discharge of sewage causes cholera, hepatitis, and other serious illnesses, and can have serious repercussions for public health and welfare.

The criminal provisions of the CWA are clearly designed to protect the public at large from the potentially dire consequences of water pollution, *see* S.Rep. No. 99–50, 99th Cong., 1st Sess. 29 (1985), and as such fall within the category of public welfare legislation. *International Minerals* rather than *Liparota* controls the case at hand. The government did not need to prove that Weitzenhoff and Mariani knew that their acts violated the permit or the CWA.

DISSENTING OPINION FROM ORDER REJECTING SUGGESTION FOR REHEARING EN BANC

Aug. 8, 1994

KLEINFELD, CIRCUIT JUDGE, with whom CIRCUIT JUDGES REINHARDT, KOZINSKI, TROTT, and T.G. NELSON join, dissenting from the order rejecting the suggestion for rehearing en banc.

I respectfully dissent from our decision to reject the suggestion for rehearing en banc.

Most of us vote against most such petitions and suggestions even when we think the panel decision is mistaken. We do so because federal courts of appeals decide cases in three judge panels. En banc review is extraordinary, and is generally reserved for conflicting precedent within the circuit which makes application of the law by district courts unduly difficult, and egregious errors in important cases. In my view, this is a case of exceptional importance, for two reasons. First, it impairs a fundamental purpose of criminal justice, sorting out the innocent from the guilty before imposing punishment. Second, it does so in the context of the Clean Water Act. This statute has tremendous sweep. Most statutes permit anything except what is prohibited, but this one prohibits all regulated conduct involving waters and wetlands except what is permitted. 33 U.S.C. § 1311(a); *United States v. Riverside Bayview Homes, Inc.,* 474 U.S. 121, 106 S.Ct. 455, 88 L.Ed.2d 419 (1985). Much more ordinary, innocent, productive activity is regulated by this law than people not versed in environmental law might imagine.

The harm our mistaken decision may do is not necessarily limited to Clean Water Act cases. Dilution of the traditional requirement of a criminal state of mind, and application of the criminal law to innocent conduct, reduces the moral authority of our system of criminal law. If we use prison to achieve social goals regardless of the moral innocence of those we incarcerate, then imprisonment loses its moral opprobrium and our criminal law becomes morally arbitrary.

We have now made felons of a large number of innocent people doing socially valuable work. They are innocent, because the one thing which makes their conduct felonious is something they do not know. It is we, and not Congress, who have made them felons. The statute, read in an ordinary way, does not. If we are fortunate, sewer plant workers around the circuit will continue to perform their vitally important work despite our decision. If they knew they risk three years in prison, some might decide that their pay, though sufficient inducement for processing the public's wastes, is not enough to risk prison for doing their jobs. We have decided that they should go to prison if, unbeknownst to them, their plant discharges exceed permit limits. Likewise for power plant operators who discharge warm water into rivers near their plants, and for all sorts of other dischargers in public and private life. If they know they are discharging into water, have a permit for the discharges, think they are conforming to their permits, but unknowingly violate their permit conditions, into prison they go with the violent criminals.

The statute does not say that. The statute at issue makes it a felony, subject to three years of imprisonment, to "knowingly violate[ ] . . . any permit condition or limitation." 33 U.S.C. § 1319(c)(2)(A). Here is the statutory scheme, with the portion applied in *Weitzenhoff* in boldface:

"Any person who . . .

> "negligently violates [various sections of the Clean Water Act] . . . or any permit condition or limitation . . . [commits a misdemeanor]. 33 U.S.C. § 1319(c)(1)(A);

> "negligently introduces into a sewer system or a publicly owned treatment works any pollutant or hazardous substance which such person knew or reasonably should have known could cause personal injury or property damage or . . . which causes such treatment works to violate any effluent limitation or condition in any permit . . . [commits a misdemeanor]. 33 U.S.C. § 1319(c)(1)(B);

> **"knowingly violates [various sections of the Clean Water Act] . . . or any permit condition or limitation . . . [commits a felony]. 33 U.S.C. § 1319(c)(2)(A);**

> "knowingly introduces into a sewer system or into a publicly owned treatment works any pollutant or hazardous substance which such person knew or reasonably should have known could cause personal injury or property damage or . . . which causes such treatment works to violate any effluent limitation or condition in a permit . . . [commits a felony]. 33 U.S.C. § 1319(c)(2)(B);

> "knowingly violates [various sections of the Clean Water Act] . . . or any permit condition or limitation . . . and who knows at that time that he thereby places another person in imminent danger of death or serious bodily injury . . . [commits a felony punishable by up to 15 years imprisonment]. 33 U.S.C. § 1319(c)(3)(A).

In this case, the defendants, sewage plant operators, had a permit to discharge sewage into the ocean, but exceeded the permit limitations. The legal issue for the panel was what knowledge would turn innocently or negligently violating a permit into "knowingly" violating a permit. Were the plant operators felons if they knew they were discharging sewage, but did not know that they were violating their permit? Or did they also have to know they were violating their permit? Ordinary English grammar, common sense, and precedent, all compel the latter construction.

As the panel opinion states the facts, these two defendants were literally "midnight dumpers." They managed a sewer plant and told their employees to dump 436,000 pounds of sewage into the ocean, mostly at night, fouling a nearby beach. Their conduct, as set out in the panel opinion, suggests that they must have known they were violating their National Pollution Discharge Elimination System (NPDES) permit. *United States v. Weitzenhoff*, 1 F.3d 1523, 1527–28 (9th Cir.1993). But we cannot decide the case on that basis, because the jury did not. The court instructed the jury that the government did not have to prove the defendants knew their conduct was unlawful, and refused to instruct the jury that a mistaken belief that the discharge was authorized by the permit would be a defense. Because of the way the jury was instructed, its verdict is consistent with the proposition that the defendants honestly and reasonably believed that their NPDES permit authorized the discharges.

This proposition could be true. NPDES permits are often difficult to understand and obey. The EPA had licensed the defendants' plant to discharge 976 pounds of waste per day, or about 409,920 pounds over the fourteen months covered by the indictment, into the ocean. The wrongful conduct was not discharging waste into the ocean. That was socially desirable conduct by which the defendants protected the people of their city from sewage-borne disease and earned their pay. The wrongful conduct was violating the NPDES permit by discharging 26,000 more pounds of waste than the permit authorized during the fourteen months. Whether these defendants were innocent or not, in the sense of knowing that they were exceeding their permit limitation, the panel's holding will make innocence irrelevant in other permit violation cases where the defendants had no idea that they were exceeding permit limits. The only thing they have to know to be guilty is that they were dumping sewage into the ocean, yet that was a lawful activity expressly authorized by their federal permit.

The statute says "knowingly violate[s] . . . any permit condition or limitation." "Knowingly" is an adverb. It modifies the verb "violates." The object of the verb is "any permit condition or limitation." The word "knowingly" is placed before "violates" to "explain its meaning in the case at hand more clearly." 1 George O. Curme, A Grammar of the English Language 72 (1935). Congress has distinguished those who knowingly violate permit conditions, and are thereby felons, from those who unknowingly violate permit conditions, so are not. The panel reads the statute as though it says "knowingly discharges pollutants." It does not. If we read the statute on the assumption that Congress used the English language in an ordinary way, the state of mind required is knowledge that one is violating a permit condition.

The panel tries to bolster its construction by categorizing the offense as a "public welfare offense," as though that justified more aggressive criminalization without a plain statutory command. This category is a modernized version of "malum prohibitum." Traditionally the criminal law distinguishes between malum in se, conduct wrong upon principles of natural moral law, and malum prohibitum, conduct not inherently immoral but wrong because prohibited by law. Black's Law Dictionary 1112 (4th ed. 1951). To put this in plain, modern terms, any normal person knows murder, rape and robbery are wrong, and they would be wrong even in a place with no sovereign and no law. Discharging 6% more pollutants than one's permit allows is wrong only because the law says so. Substitution of the modern term "public welfare offense" for the traditional one, malum prohibitum, allows for confusion by rhetorical suggestion. The new term suggests that other offenses might merely be private in their impact, and therefore less serious. The older set of terms made it clear that murder was more vile than violating a federal regulation. The category of malum prohibitum, or public welfare offenses, makes the rule of lenity especially important, most particularly for felonies, because persons of good conscience may not recognize the wrongfulness of the conduct when they engage in it.

Staples v. United States, 511 U.S. 600, 114 S.Ct. 1793, 128 L.Ed.2d 608 (1994), reminds us that "offenses that require no *mens rea* generally are disfavored." *Id.* at ___, 114 S.Ct. at 1797. *Mens rea* may be dispensed with in public welfare offenses, but the penalty is a "significant consideration in determining whether the statute should be construed as dispensing with *mens rea*." *Id.* at ___, 114 S.Ct. at 1802.

> The potentially harsh penalty attached to violation of § 5861(d)— up to 10 years' imprisonment—confirms our reading of the Act. Historically, the penalty imposed under a statute has been a significant consideration in determining whether the statute should be construed as dispensing with *mens rea*. Certainly, the cases that first defined the concept of the public welfare offense almost uniformly involved statutes that provided for only light penalties such as fines or short jail sentences, not imprisonment in the state penitentiary.
>
> As commentators have pointed out, the small penalties attached to such offenses logically complemented the absence of a *mens rea* requirement: in a system that generally requires a "vicious will" to establish a crime, imposing severe punishments for offenses that require no *mens rea* would seem incongruous. Indeed some courts justified the absence of *mens rea* in part on the basis that the offenses did not bear the same punishments as "infamous

crimes," and questioned whether imprisonment was compatible with the reduced culpability required for such regulatory offenses.

Id. at ___–___, 114 S.Ct. at 1802–03 (footnote and citations omitted). If Congress makes a crime a felony, the felony categorization alone is a "factor tending to suggest that Congress did not intend to eliminate a *mens rea* requirement. In such a case, the usual presumption that a defendant must know the facts that make his conduct illegal should apply." *Id.* at ___, 114 S.Ct. at 1804. In the case at bar, "the facts that make his conduct illegal" are the permit violations, not the discharges of pollutants. Discharge of pollutants was licensed by the federal government in the NPDES permit. Under *Staples,* it would be presumed, even if the law did not plainly say so, that the defendant would have to know that he was violating the permit in order to be guilty of the felony.

Precedent cuts strongly against the panel's decision. Two Supreme Court decisions came down this term which should have caused us to rehear the case.

Ratzlaf v. United States, 510 U.S. 135, 114 S.Ct. 655, 126 L.Ed.2d 615 (1994), reversing a decision of ours, holds that to commit the crime of "willfully violating" the law against structuring cash transactions to evade currency transaction reporting requirements, the defendant has to know that his conduct is unlawful. It is not enough that he is engaging in the cash transactions with a purpose of evading currency transaction reporting requirements. *Id.* at ___, 114 S.Ct. at 657. Ignorance of the law generally is no excuse, but "Congress may decree otherwise." *Id.* at ___, 114 S.Ct. at 663. The Court was concerned that a narrower reading of the mental element of the crime would criminalize conduct committed without the criminal motive with which Congress was concerned. *Id.* at ___, 114 S.Ct. at 661.

At issue in *Staples v. United States,* 511 U.S. 600, 114 S.Ct. 1793, 128 L.Ed.2d 608 (1994), was a statute which made it a felony to possess an unregistered "firearm." The statute defined "firearm" to include a fully automatic gun, which would fire more than one bullet on a single pull of the trigger, but not a semiautomatic. The defendant possessed a fully automatic gun, but testified that he did not know it would fire more than one bullet with a single trigger pull. The trial judge had instructed the jury that his ignorance did not matter, so long as the government proved he possessed "a dangerous device of a type as would alert one to the likelihood of regulation." The Supreme Court again rejected dilution of the mental element of the crime. The Court explained that unlike the hand grenades in *United States v. Freed,* 401 U.S. 601, 91 S.Ct. 1112, 28 L.Ed.2d 356 (1971), semiautomatics are innocently possessed by many people. Nor was knowledge that guns are regulated enough to require the owner to ascertain compliance with the regulations at his peril. That might do for a misdemeanor, but the felony status of the offense suggested a more plainly criminal mental state. Nor would the dangerousness of guns suffice to weaken the mens rea requirement:

> If we were to accept as a general rule the Government's suggestion that dangerous and regulated items place their owners under an obligation to inquire at their peril into compliance with regulations, we would undoubtedly reach some untoward results. Automobiles, for example, might also be termed "dangerous" devices and are highly regulated at both the state and federal levels. Congress might see fit to criminalize the violation of certain regulations concerning automobiles, and thus might make it a crime to operate a vehicle without a properly functioning emission control system. But we probably would hesitate to conclude on the basis of silence that Congress intended a prison term to apply to a car owner whose vehicle's emissions levels, wholly unbeknownst to him, began to exceed legal limits between regular inspection dates.

Staples, 511 U.S. at ___–___, 114 S.Ct. at 1801–02.

The panel cites *United States v. International Minerals & Chem. Corp.,* 402 U.S. 558, 91 S.Ct. 1697, 29 L.Ed.2d 178 (1971), . . ., in support of its reading. *International Minerals* was a pre-*Ratzlaf* misdemeanor case. Because of the syntactically similar statute at issue in that case, it is the strongest authority for the panel's decision and raises the most serious question for my own analysis. It held that a shipper of sulfuric acid could be convicted of violating a statute applying to those who "knowingly violate[ ]" regulations governing shipments of corrosive liquids, regardless of whether he had knowledge of the regulations. *International Minerals* expressly limits its holding to "dangerous or deleterious devices or products or obnoxious waste materials." 402 U.S. at 565, 91 S.Ct. at 1702. The Court distinguished materials not obviously subject to regulation:

> Pencils, dental floss, paper clips may also be regulated. But they may be the type of products which might raise substantial due process questions if Congress did not require . . . "*mens rea*" as to each ingredient of the offense. But where, as here . . ., dangerous or deleterious devices or products or obnoxious waste materials are involved, the probability of regulation is so great that anyone who is aware that he is in possession of them or dealing with them must be presumed to be aware of the regulation.

Id. at 564–65, 91 S.Ct. at 1701–02. *International Minerals* would have much persuasive force for *Weitzenhoff,* because of the grammatical similarity of the statute, if (1) the Clean Water Act limited pollutants to "dangerous or deleterious devices or products or obnoxious waste materials;" (2) the crime was only a misdemeanor; and (3) *Staples* had not come down this term. But all three of these conditions are contrary to fact. The pollutants to which the Clean Water Act felony statute applies include many in the "pencils, dental floss, paper clips" category. Hot water, rock, and sand are classified as "pollutants" by the Clean Water Act. *See* 33 U.S.C. § 1362(6). Discharging silt from a stream back into the same stream may amount to discharge of a pollutant. For that matter, so may skipping a stone into a lake. So may a cafeteria worker's pouring hot, stale coffee down the drain. Making these acts a misdemeanor is one thing, but a felony is quite another, as *Staples* teaches.

The panel, finally, asserts that as a matter of policy, the Clean Water Act crimes "are clearly designed to protect the public at large from the dire consequences of water pollution." That is true, but the panel does not explain how the public is to be protected by making felons of sewer workers who unknowingly violate their plants' permits. Provision for sanitary sewage disposal is among the most ancient laws of civilization. Deuteronomy 23:12–13. Sewage workers perform essential work of great social value. Probably nothing has prevented more infant mortality, or freed more people from cholera, hepatitis, typhoid fever, and other disease, than the development in the last two centuries of municipal sewer systems. *See* W.H. Corfield, The Treatment and Utilisation of Sewage 17–27 (1871). Sewage utility workers perform their difficult work in malodorous and dangerous environments. We have now imposed on these vitally important public servants a massive legal risk, unjustified by law or precedent, if they unknowingly violate their permit conditions.

Nor is the risk of prison limited to sewage plant workers. It applies to anyone who discharges pollutants pursuant to a permit, and unknowingly violates the permit. The panel suggests that criminalizing this innocent conduct will protect the public from water pollution. It is at least as likely that the increased criminal risk will raise the cost and reduce the availability of such lawful and essential public services as sewage disposal. We should not deprive individuals of justice, whether the judicial action would serve some desirable policy or not. It is by no means certain that the panel's construction will advance the underlying policy it attributes to Congress. We should apply the words Congress and the President promulgated as law, leaving the difficult policy choices to them.

We undermine the foundation of criminal law when we so vitiate the requirement of a criminal state of knowledge and intention as to make felons of the morally innocent.

> The contention that an injury can amount to a crime only when inflicted by intention is no provincial or transient notion. It is as universal and persistent in mature systems of law as belief in freedom of the human will and a consequent ability and duty of the normal individual to choose between good and evil. A relation between some mental element and punishment for a harmful act is almost as instinctive as the child's familiar exculpatory "But I didn't mean to".... Unqualified acceptance of this doctrine by

English common law in the Eighteenth Century was indicated by Blackstone's sweeping statement that to constitute any crime there must first be a "vicious will."

Morissette v. United States, 342 U.S. 246, 250–51, 72 S.Ct. 240, 243–44, 96 L.Ed. 288 (1952) (footnote omitted). As Justice Jackson explained, "Consequences of a general abolition of intent as an ingredient of serious crimes have aroused the concern of responsible and disinterested students of penology. Of course, they would not justify judicial disregard of a clear command to that effect from Congress, but they do admonish us to caution in assuming that Congress, without clear expression, intends in any instance to do so." *Id.* at 254 n. 14, 72 S.Ct. at 246 n. 14.

Congress made it a serious felony "knowingly" to violate permit limitations on discharge of pollutants. The harsh penalty for this serious crime must be reserved for those who know they are, in fact, violating permit limitations.

DISCUSSION QUESTIONS

1. Based solely on the text of the statute, does the majority or the dissent have the better argument?

2. As a matter of public policy, what mental state should be sufficient for a felony violation of this statute?

3. What could legislatures do to avoid these interpretive battles in the courts? Why don't they?

L. SPECIAL FOCUS: DRUG CRIME AND MENTAL STATES

Are drug crimes public welfare offenses? Should they be? Most jurisdictions require a knowing mental state as an element of the offense which means that it must be proved by the prosecutor. The statute in the following case did not.

STATE OF FLORIDA V. LUKE JARROD ADKINS, ET AL.

Supreme Court of Florida
96 So.3d 412 (2012)

Opinion

CANADY, J.

In this case we consider the constitutionality of the provisions of chapter 893, Florida Statutes (2011), the Florida Comprehensive Drug Abuse Prevention and Control Act, that provide that knowledge of the illicit nature of a controlled substance is not an element of any offenses under the chapter but that the lack of such knowledge is an affirmative defense.

Based on its conclusion that section 893.13, Florida Statutes (2011)—which creates offenses related to the sale, manufacture, delivery, and possession of controlled substances—is facially unconstitutional under the Due Process Clauses of the Florida and the United States Constitutions, the circuit court for the Twelfth Judicial Circuit issued an order granting motions to dismiss charges filed under section 893.13 in forty-six criminal cases. The circuit court reasoned that the requirements of due process precluded the Legislature from eliminating knowledge of the illicit nature of the substance as an element of the offenses under section 893.13. On appeal, the Second District Court of Appeal certified to this Court that the circuit court's judgment presents issues that require immediate resolution by this Court because the issues are of great public importance and will have a great effect on the proper administration of justice throughout the State. We have jurisdiction. *See* art. V, § 3(b)(5), Fla. Const.

For the reasons explained below, we conclude that the circuit court erred in determining the statute to be unconstitutional. Accordingly, we reverse the circuit court's order granting the motions to dismiss.

I.   BACKGROUND

Section 893.13, part of the Florida Comprehensive Drug Abuse Prevention and Control Act, provides in part that except as otherwise authorized "it is unlawful for any person to sell, manufacture, or deliver, or possess with intent to sell, manufacture, or deliver, a controlled substance" or "to be in actual or constructive possession of a controlled substance."

Section 893.13 itself does not specify what mental state a defendant must possess in order to be convicted for selling, manufacturing, delivering, or possessing a controlled substance. In *Chicone v. State,* 684 So.2d 736 (Fla.1996), this Court addressed whether section 893.13 should be interpreted to include a mens rea—that is, a "guilty mind"—element. In reviewing a conviction for possession of cocaine, this Court determined that "guilty knowledge" was one of the elements of the crime of possession of a controlled substance and that the State was required to prove that Chicone knew he possessed the substance and knew of the illicit nature of the substance in his possession. *Id.* at 738–41. This Court reasoned that the common law typically required "scienter or mens rea [as] a necessary element in the indictment and proof of every crime" and that the penalties facing defendants convicted under chapter 893, Florida Statutes, were much harsher than the usual penalties for crimes where a knowledge element is not required. *Chicone,* 684 So.2d at 741. This Court further reasoned that the Legislature "would have spoken more clearly" if it had intended to not require proof of guilty knowledge to convict under section 893.13. *Chicone,* 684 So.2d at 743.

More recently, in *Scott v. State,* 808 So.2d 166 (Fla.2002), this Court clarified that the "guilty knowledge" element of the crime of possession of a controlled substance contains two aspects: knowledge of the presence of the substance and knowledge of the illicit nature of the substance. 808 So.2d at 169. In addition, this Court clarified that the presumption of knowledge set out in *State v. Medlin,* 273 So.2d 394 (Fla.1973), and reiterated in *Chicone*—that a defendant's knowledge of the illicit nature of a controlled substance can be presumed from evidence that the defendant had possession of the controlled substance—can be employed only in cases in which the State proves actual, personal possession of the controlled substance. *Scott,* 808 So.2d at 171–72.

In response to this Court's decisions, the Legislature enacted a statute now codified in section 893.101, Florida Statutes (2011). Section 893.101 provides in full:

> (1) The Legislature finds that the cases of *Scott v. State,* Slip Opinion No. SC94701 [808 So.2d 166] (Fla.2002)[,] and *Chicone v. State,* 684 So.2d 736 (Fla.1996), holding that the state must prove that the defendant knew of the illicit nature of a controlled substance found in his or her actual or constructive possession, were contrary to legislative intent.
>
> (2) The Legislature finds that *knowledge of the illicit nature of a controlled substance is not an element* of any offense under this chapter. *Lack of knowledge of the illicit nature of a controlled substance is an affirmative defense* to the offenses of this chapter.
>
> (3) In those instances in which a defendant asserts the affirmative defense described in this section, the possession of a controlled substance, whether actual or constructive, shall give rise to a permissive presumption that the possessor knew of the illicit nature of the substance. It is the intent of the Legislature that, in those cases where such an affirmative defense is raised, the jury shall be instructed on the permissive presumption provided in this subsection.

(Emphasis added.) The statute thus expressly eliminates knowledge of the illicit nature of the controlled substance as an element of controlled substance offenses and expressly creates an affirmative defense of lack of knowledge of the illicit nature of the substance. The statute does not eliminate the element of knowledge of the presence of the substance, which we acknowledged in *Chicone,* 684 So.2d at 739–40, and *Scott,* 808 So.2d at 169.

Since the enactment of section 893.101, each of the district courts of appeal has ruled that the statute does not violate the requirements of due process.

The United States District Court for the Middle District of Florida recently concluded, however, that section 893.13 is unconstitutional because it does not require sufficient mens rea on the part of the defendant to sustain a conviction. *See Shelton v. Sec'y, Dep't of Corr.*, 802 F.Supp.2d 1289 (M.D.Fla.2011). First, the Middle District reasoned that to withstand constitutional scrutiny, section 893.13 should have provided lighter penalties, "such as fines or short jail sentences, not imprisonment in the state penitentiary." Second, the Middle District reasoned that because of the substantial social stigma associated with a felony conviction, a conviction under section 893.13 should require a guilty mind. And third, assuming that a defendant could be convicted under section 893.13 for delivering or transferring a container without being aware of its contents, the Middle District concluded that section 893.13 violates due process by regulating potentially innocent conduct.

Citing *Shelton* as persuasive—not binding—authority, the circuit court in this case concluded that section 893.13 is facially unconstitutional because it violates the Due Process Clauses of article I, section 9 of the Florida Constitution and the Fourteenth Amendment to the United States Constitution. The circuit court reasoned that the Legislature did not have authority to dispense with a mens rea element for a serious felony crime.

The State now appeals the circuit court's decision in this Court. The State asserts that section 893.13, as modified by section 893.101, is facially constitutional and that the circuit court therefore erred in granting the motions to dismiss.

II. ANALYSIS

"[T]he Legislature generally has broad authority to determine any requirement for intent or knowledge in the definition of a crime." We thus have recognized that generally "[i]t is within the power of the Legislature to declare an act a crime regardless of the intent or knowledge of the violation thereof." "The doing of the act inhibited by the statute makes the crime[,] and moral turpitude or purity of motive and the knowledge or ignorance of its criminal character are immaterial circumstances on the question of guilt."

Given the broad authority of the legislative branch to define the elements of crimes, the requirements of due process ordinarily do not preclude the creation of offenses which lack a guilty knowledge element. This point was recognized long ago in *United States v. Balint*, 258 U.S. 250, 251, 42 S.Ct. 301, 66 L.Ed. 604 (1922), where the Supreme Court considered the imposition of criminal penalties—fines of up to $2000 or imprisonment for up to five years, or both—under section 9 of the Narcotic Act of 1914 where the indictment "failed to charge that [the defendants] had sold the inhibited drugs knowing them to be such." The Narcotic Act required "every person who produces, imports, manufactures, compounds, deals in, dispenses, sells, distributes, or gives away" a substance containing opium or coca leaves to register and pay a tax. Narcotic Act of Dec. 17, 1914, ch. 1, § 1, 38 Stat. 785 (1914). The Narcotic Act prohibited possession of the specified drugs by any unregistered person, subject to certain exceptions—

including an exception for persons to whom the drugs "have been prescribed in good faith" by a registered medical professional. Narcotic Act of Dec. 17, 1914, ch. 1, § 8, 38 Stat. 785 (1914). The Act also provided that "possession or control" of the specified drugs "shall be presumptive evidence of a violation" of the statute. *Id* As recognized by the Supreme Court, the statute did not make "knowledge an element of the offense." *Balint,* 258 U.S. at 251, 42 S.Ct. 301. Despite the substantial penalty for noncompliance with the Narcotic Act, the Supreme Court declined either to read a mens rea element into the Narcotic Act or to conclude that the lack of such an element in the Narcotic Act was unconstitutional.

The *Balint* court specifically rejected the argument that "punishment of a person for an act in violation of law when ignorant of the facts making it so, is an absence of due process of law." *Id.* at 252, 42 S.Ct. 301. The Supreme Court observed that "the state may in the maintenance of a public policy provide 'that he who shall do [proscribed acts] shall do them at his peril and will not be heard to plead in defense good faith or ignorance.'" *Id.* at 252, 42 S.Ct. 301 (quoting *Shevlin-Carpenter Co. v. Minnesota,* 218 U.S. 57, 70, 30 S.Ct. 663, 54 L.Ed. 930 (1910)). The Supreme Court explained that offenses lacking such a knowledge element were commonly "found in regulatory measures in the exercise of what is called the police power where the emphasis of the statute is evidently upon achievement of some social betterment rather than the punishment of crimes as in cases of mala in se." *Id.*

The *Balint* court thus gave effect to the "manifest purpose" of the Narcotic Act—that is, "to require every person dealing in drugs to ascertain at his peril whether that which he sells comes within the inhibition of the statute, and if he sells the inhibited drug in ignorance of its character, to penalize him." 258 U.S. at 254, 42 S.Ct. 301. The Supreme Court recognized that the statutory purpose was properly based at least in part on "considerations as to the opportunity of the seller to find out the fact and the difficulty of proof of knowledge." *Id.*

Since the Supreme Court's decision in *Balint,* both the Supreme Court and this Court have repeatedly recognized that the legislative branch has broad discretion to omit a mens rea element from a criminal offense. For example, in *Staples,* which reviewed a federal law criminalizing the unregistered possession of certain automatic firearms that did not expressly include or exclude a mens rea element, the Supreme Court explained that whether or not a criminal offense requires proof that a defendant knew of the illegal nature of his act "is a question of statutory construction" and that the "definition of the elements of a criminal offense is entrusted to the legislature, particularly in the case of federal crimes, which are solely creatures of statute." Similarly, in *United States v. Freed,* 401 U.S. 601, 91 S.Ct. 1112, 28 L.Ed.2d 356 (1971), and *United States v. International Minerals & Chemical Corp.,* 402 U.S. 558, 91 S.Ct. 1697, 29

L.Ed.2d 178 (1971), the Supreme Court rejected the view that due process required that mens rea elements be read into public safety statutes regulating the possession of unregistered firearms and the shipping of corrosive liquids.

In a limited category of circumstances, the omission of a mens rea element from the definition of a criminal offense has been held to violate due process. A salient example of such circumstance is found in the Supreme Court's decision in *Lambert v. California,* 355 U.S. 225, 78 S.Ct. 240, 2 L.Ed.2d 228 (1957), which addressed a Los Angeles municipal code provision requiring that felons present in the municipality for more than five days register with law enforcement. The code provision applied to "a person who has no actual knowledge of his duty to register." *Id.* at 227, 78 S.Ct. 240. In *Lambert,* the Supreme Court concluded that a legislative body may not criminalize otherwise entirely innocent, passive conduct—such as a convicted felon remaining in Los Angeles for more than five days—without sufficiently informing the population of the legal requirement. As a result, the Supreme Court concluded that the registration requirement then at issue could be enforced only when the defendant was aware of the ordinance. Still, the Supreme Court emphasized that in a situation where the lawmaking body seeks to prohibit affirmative acts, it can do so without requiring proof that the actor knew his or her conduct to be illegal:

> We do not go with Blackstone in saying that "a vicious will" is necessary to constitute a crime, for conduct alone without regard to the intent of the doer is often sufficient. *There is wide latitude in the lawmakers to declare an offense and to exclude elements of knowledge and diligence from its definition.* But we deal here with conduct that is wholly passive—mere failure to register. It is unlike the commission of acts, or the failure to act under circumstances that should alert the doer to the consequences of his deed. The rule that "ignorance of the law will not excuse" is deep in our law, as is the principle that of all the powers of local government, the police power is "one of the least limitable."

Lambert, 355 U.S. at 228, 78 S.Ct. 240 (emphasis added) (citations omitted).

The Supreme Court has also concluded that the omission of a scienter element from the definition of a criminal offense can result in a due process violation where the omission results in criminalizing conduct protected by the First Amendment of the United States Constitution. For example, in *Smith v. California,* 361 U.S. 147, 80 S.Ct. 215, 4 L.Ed.2d 205 (1959), the Supreme Court determined that a scienter element was required in an ordinance making it illegal for any person to have in his possession any obscene or indecent writing in a place of business where books are sold. The Supreme Court reasoned that without such an element, the ordinance would cause a bookseller "to restrict the books he sells to those he has inspected; and thus the State will have imposed a restriction upon the distribution of constitutionally protected as well as obscene literature." *Id.* at 153, 80 S.Ct. 215. Similarly, in *United States v. X-Citement Video, Inc.,* 513 U.S. 64, 115 S.Ct. 464, 130 L.Ed.2d 372 (1994), the Supreme Court construed the modifier "knowing" in the Protection of Children Against Sexual Exploitation Act to apply to the element of the age of the performers. The Supreme Court explained that because nonobscene, sexually explicit materials involving persons over the age of seventeen are protected by the First Amendment, "a statute completely bereft of a scienter requirement as to the age of the performers would raise serious constitutional doubts," and it was "therefore incumbent upon [the court] to read the statute to eliminate those doubts so long as such a reading is not plainly contrary to the intent of Congress." *Id.* at 78, 115 S.Ct. 464.

The provisions of chapter 893 at issue in the present case are readily distinguishable from those cases in which definitions of particular criminal offenses were found to violate the requirements of due process. The rationale for each of those cases is not applicable to the context of controlled substance offenses under Florida law.

Sections 893.13 and 893.101 do not trigger the concern raised in *Lambert* and *Giorgetti.* The statutes do not penalize without notice a "failure to act [that absent the statutes] otherwise amounts to essentially innocent conduct," such as living in a particular municipality without registering. *Giorgetti,* 868 So.2d at 517 (quoting *Oxx,* 417 So.2d at 290). Rather than punishing inaction, to convict under section 893.13 the State must prove that the defendant engaged in the affirmative act of selling, manufacturing, delivering, or possessing a controlled substance. The controlled substance statutes are further distinguishable from the statutes in *Lambert* and *Giorgetti*—which would impose criminal liability for failing to register regardless of the defendant's knowledge of the regulation and his or her status—because in section 893.101 the Legislature has expressly provided that a person charged under chapter 893 who did not have knowledge of the illegality of his or her conduct may raise that fact as an affirmative defense.

Because there is no legally recognized use for controlled substances outside the circumstances identified by the statute, prohibiting the sale, manufacture, delivery, or possession of those substances without requiring proof of knowledge of the illicit nature of the substances does not criminalize innocuous conduct or "impinge[ ] on the exercise of some constitutionally protected freedom." Because the statutory provisions at issue here do not have the potential to curtail constitutionally protected speech, they are materially distinguishable from statutes that implicate the possession of materials protected by the First Amendment, such as those at issue in *Smith* and *X-Citement Video.* There is no constitutional right to possess contraband. "[A]ny interest in possessing contraband cannot be deemed 'legitimate.'"

Nor is there a protected right to be ignorant of the nature of the property in one's possession. *See Turner v. United States,* 396 U.S. 398, 417, 90 S.Ct. 642, 24 L.Ed.2d 610 (1970) (" 'Common' sense tells us that those who traffic in heroin will inevitably become aware that the product they deal in is smuggled, *unless they practice a studied ignorance to which they are not entitled.*") (emphasis added) (citation and footnotes omitted). Just as "common sense and experience" dictate that a person in possession of Treasury checks addressed to another person should be "aware of the high probability that the checks were stolen," a person in possession of a controlled substance should be aware of the nature of the substance as an illegal drug. Because controlled substances are valuable, common sense indicates that they are generally handled with care. As a result, possession without awareness of the illicit nature of the substance is highly unusual.

Any concern that entirely innocent conduct will be punished with a criminal sanction under chapter 893 is obviated by the statutory provision that allows a defendant to raise the affirmative defense of an absence of knowledge of the illicit nature of the controlled substance. In the unusual circumstance where an individual has actual or constructive possession of a controlled substance but has no knowledge that the substance is illicit, the defendant may present such a defense to the jury.

Because we conclude that the Legislature did not exceed its constitutional authority in redefining section 893.13 to not require proof that the defendant knew of the illicit nature of the controlled substance, we likewise conclude that the Legislature did not violate due process by defining lack of such knowledge as an affirmative defense to the offenses set out in chapter 893. The Legislature's decision to treat lack of such knowledge as an affirmative defense does not unconstitutionally shift the burden of proof of a criminal offense to the defendant.

. . .

III. CONCLUSION

In enacting section 893.101, the Legislature eliminated from the definitions of the offenses in chapter 893 the element that the defendant has knowledge of the illicit nature of the controlled substance and created the affirmative defense of lack of such knowledge. The statutory provisions do not violate any requirement of due process articulated by this Court or the Supreme Court. In the unusual circumstance where a person possesses a controlled substance inadvertently, establishing the affirmative defense available under section 893.101 will preclude the conviction of the defendant. Based on the foregoing, we conclude that the circuit court erred in granting the motions to dismiss and we reverse the circuit court's order.

It is so ordered.

PERRY, J., dissenting.

I respectfully dissent. I cannot overstate my opposition to the majority's opinion. In my view, it shatters bedrock constitutional principles and builds on a foundation of flawed "common sense."

Innocent Possession

The majority pronounces that "common sense and experience" dictate that "a person in possession of a controlled substance should be aware of the nature of the substance as an illegal drug" and further that, "[b]ecause controlled substances are valuable, common sense indicates that they are generally handled with care. As a result, possession without awareness of the illicit nature of the substance is highly unusual." Majority op. at 421–22.

But common sense to me dictates that the potential for innocent possession is not so "highly unusual" as the majority makes it out to be.

> [T]he simple acts of possession and delivery are part of daily life. Each of us engages in actual possession of all that we have on our person and in our hands, and in constructive possession of all that we own, wherever it may be located. Each of us engages in delivery when we hand a colleague a pen, a friend a cup of coffee, a stranger the parcel she just dropped.

State v. Washington, 18 Fla. L. Weekly Supp. 1129, 1133 (Fla. 11th Cir.Ct. Aug. 17, 2011) (footnote omitted), *rev'd*, ___ So.3d ___ (Fla. 3d DCA 2012). "[C]arrying luggage on and off of public transportation; carrying bags in and out of stores and buildings; carrying book bags and purses in schools and places of business and work; transporting boxes via commercial transportation—the list extends *ad infinitum*." *Shelton v. Sec'y, Dep't of Corr.*, 802 F.Supp.2d 1289, 1305 (M.D.Fla.2011).

Given this reality, "[i]t requires little imagination to visualize a situation in which a third party hands [a] controlled substance to an unknowing individual who then can be charged with and subsequently convicted . . . without ever being aware of the nature of the substance he was given." *State v. Brown*, 389 So.2d 48, 51 (La.1980) (finding that such a situation offends the conscience and concluding that "the 'unknowing' possession of a dangerous drug cannot be made criminal"). For example,

> [c]onsider the student in whose book bag a classmate hastily stashes his drugs to avoid imminent detection. The bag is then given to another for safekeeping. Caught in the act, the hapless victim is guilty based upon the only two elements of the statute: delivery (actual, constructive, or attempted) and the illicit nature of the substance. *See* FLA. STAT. §§ 893.02(6), 893.13(1)(a). The victim would be faced with the Hobson's choice of pleading guilty or going to trial where he is presumed guilty because he is in fact

guilty of the two elements. He must then prove his innocence for lack of knowledge against the permissive presumption the statute imposes that he does in fact have guilty knowledge. Such an outcome is not countenanced under applicable constitutional proscriptions.

Shelton, 802 F.Supp.2d at 1308. The trial court order presently under review provides even more examples of innocent possession: a letter carrier who delivers a package containing unprescribed Adderall; a roommate who is unaware that the person who shares his apartment has hidden illegal drugs in the common areas of the home; a mother who carries a prescription pill bottle in her purse, unaware that the pills have been substituted for illegally obtained drugs by her teenage daughter, who placed them in the bottle to avoid detection. *State v. Adkins,* Nos. 2011 CF 002001, et al., slip op. at 14 (Fla. 12th Cir.Ct. Sept. 14, 2011).

> As the examples illustrate, even people who are normally diligent in inspecting and organizing their possessions may find themselves unexpectedly in violation of this law, and without the notice necessary to defend their rights. The illegal drugs subject to the statute include tablets which can also be and are commonly and legally prescribed. A medicine which is legally available, can be difficult for innocent parties to recognize as illegal, even if they think they know the contents. For example, the mother of the teenage daughter carries the pill bottle, taking it at face value as a bottle for the pills it ought to contain, even during the traffic stop at which she consents to [a] search of her belongings, confident in her own innocence. These examples represent incidents of innocence which should be protected by the requirement of [a] *mens rea* element, particularly given the serious penalties for the crime of drug possession required under Florida law.

Id. at 14–15. Other examples of innocent possession spring easily and immediately to mind: a driver who rents a car in which a past passenger accidentally dropped a baggie of marijuana under the seat; a traveler who mistakenly retrieves from a luggage carousel a bag identical to her own containing Oxycodone; a helpful college student who drives a carload of a friend's possessions to the friend's new apartment, unaware that a stash of heroin is tucked within those possessions; an ex-wife who is framed by an ex-husband who planted cocaine in her home in an effort to get the upper hand in a bitter custody dispute. The list is endless.

The majority nevertheless states that there is not "a protected right to be ignorant of the nature of the property in one's possession," elaborating that " '[c]ommon' sense tells us that those who traffic in heroin will inevitably become aware that the product they deal in is smuggled, *unless they practice a studied ignorance to which they are not entitled.*" But the above examples, and surely countless others, do not involve such a "studied ignorance." Rather, they involve genuinely innocent citizens who will be snared in the overly broad net of section 893.13. And therein lies the point:

> Section 893.13 does not punish the drug dealer who possesses or delivers controlled substances. It punishes *anyone* who possesses or delivers controlled substances—however inadvertently, however accidentally, however unintentionally.... What distinguishes innocent possession and innocent delivery from guilty possession and guilty delivery is not merely what we possess, not merely what we deliver, *but what we intend.* As to that—as to the state of mind that distinguishes non-culpable from culpable possession or delivery—§ 893.13 refuses to make a distinction. The speckled flock and the clean are, for its purposes, all one.

Washington, 18 Fla. L. Weekly Supp. at 1133.

Presumption of Innocence and Burden of Proof

The majority rather cavalierly offers that, "[i]n the unusual circumstance where a person possesses a controlled substance inadvertently, establishing the affirmative defense available under section 893.101 will preclude the conviction of the defendant." As discussed at length above, I do not agree that innocent possession is such an "unusual circumstance." Moreover, the majority's passing reference to simply "establishing the affirmative defense" implies that it is an inconsequential and easy thing to do. The majority further minimizes the enormity of the task, making it seem even friendly, in stating that "[t]he affirmative defense does not ask the defendant to disprove something that the State must prove in order to convict, but instead provides a defendant with an opportunity to explain why his or her admittedly illegal conduct should not be punished." *Id.* at 423.

But the affirmative defense at issue is hardly a friendly opportunity; rather, it is an onerous burden that strips defendants—including genuinely innocent defendants—of their constitutional presumption of innocence. "The principle that there is a presumption of innocence in favor of the accused is the undoubted law, axiomatic and elementary, and its enforcement lies at the foundation of the administration of our criminal law." *Coffin v. United States,* 156 U.S. 432, 453, 15 S.Ct. 394, 39 L.Ed. 481 (1895). It is as ancient as it is profound:

> Numerius [was on trial and] contented himself with denying his guilt, and there was not sufficient proof against him. His adversary, Delphidius, "a passionate man," seeing that the failure of the accusation was inevitable, could not restrain himself, and exclaimed, "Oh, illustrious Caesar! if it is sufficient to deny, what

hereafter will become of the guilty?" to which Julian replied, "If it suffices to accuse, what will become of the innocent?"

Id. at 455, 15 S.Ct. 394. "What will become of the innocent?" The answer to that question in the present context is as inevitable as it is disturbing. Under the majority's decision and the above examples, the innocent will from the start be presumed guilty. The innocent will be deprived of their right to simply deny the charges and hold the State to its burden of proving them guilty beyond a reasonable doubt. The innocent will instead be forced to assert an affirmative defense, whereupon "the possession of a controlled substance, whether actual or constructive, shall give rise to a permissive presumption that the possessor knew of the illicit nature of the substance."

The innocent will then have no realistic choice but to shoulder the burden of proof and present evidence to overcome that presumption. The innocent will thus have to bear the considerable time and expense involved in conducting discovery, calling witnesses, and otherwise crafting a case for their innocence—all while the State, with its vastly superior resources, should be bearing the burden of proving their guilt.

The innocent will then hear their jury instructed on the permissive presumption that they knew of the illicit nature of the substance in question. § 893.101(3), Fla. Stat. (2011). Finally, the innocent—in I fear far too many cases—may be found guilty, convicted, and sentenced to up to life in prison. *See Shelton,* 802 F.Supp.2d at 1302 ("Sentences of fifteen years, thirty years, and life imprisonment [possible under section 893.13] are not by any measure 'relatively small.' ").

Such convictions and sentences will be a disgrace when, on a profoundly foundational level, "the law holds that it is better that ten guilty persons escape than that one innocent suffer." *Coffin,* 156 U.S. at 456, 15 S.Ct. 394 (quoting 2 William Blackstone, Commentaries *357). The majority opinion breaks that sacred law and, as discussed below, threatens bedrock principles of the presumption of innocence and burden of proof in contexts well beyond the one at hand.

Slippery Slope

As in the present case, the effect of the trial court order in *Washington* would be the dismissal of charges against all the defendants at issue "the overwhelming majority of whom may have known perfectly well that their acts of possession or delivery were contrary to law." 18 Fla. L. Weekly Supp. at 1133.

Viewed in that light, these movants are unworthy, utterly unworthy, of this windfall exoneration. But as no less a constitutional scholar than Justice Felix Frankfurter observed, "It is easy to make light of insistence on scrupulous regard for the safeguards of civil liberties when invoked on behalf of the unworthy. It is too easy. History bears testimony that by such disregard are the rights of liberty extinguished, heedlessly at first, then stealthily, and brazenly in the end."

Id. (quoting *Davis v. United States,* 328 U.S. 582, 597, 66 S.Ct. 1256, 90 L.Ed. 1453 (1946) (Frankfurter, J., dissenting)). In this vein, the court in *Shelton* noted with some consternation that

> if the Florida legislature can by edict and without constitutional restriction eliminate the element of *mens rea* from a drug statute with penalties of this magnitude, it is hard to imagine what other statutes it could not similarly affect. Could the legislature amend its murder statute such that the State could meet its burden of proving murder by proving that a Defendant touched another and the victim died as a result, leaving the Defendant to raise the absence of intent as a defense, overcoming a permissive presumption that murder was the Defendant's intent? Could the state prove felony theft by proving that a Defendant was in possession of an item that belonged to another, leaving the Defendant to prove he did not take it, overcoming a permissive presumption that he did?

Conclusion

"Brave" indeed, in the most foreboding sense of that word. The majority opinion sets alarming precedent, both in the context of section 893.13 and beyond. It makes neither legal nor common sense to me, offends all notions of due process, and threatens core principles of the presumption of innocence and burden of proof. I would find section 893.13 facially unconstitutional and affirm the trial court order under review.

DISCUSSION QUESTIONS

1.   As a matter of public policy, do you think that legislatures should define criminal possession of illegal drugs to include those who do not realize the substance possessed is an illegal drug? How about possession of illegal firearms? Or child pornography?

2.   Should legislatures be constitutionally prohibited from converting knowledge of the illicit nature of a controlled substance from an element of the offense, to be proven by the government, to an affirmative defense to be proved by the defendant? Would the Florida statute still be constitutional if it provided no affirmative defense for lack of such knowledge?

3.   The Florida legislature expressly and directly overruled the Florida courts' prior interpretations of the statute at issue. Does that mean that the courts incorrectly interpreted the statute, or that the legislature failed to express what it intended?

Case in Context

The following drug case raises interesting issues about what "knowingly possess" means in drug cases.

PEOPLE V. RYAN

Court of Appeals of New York
626 N.E.2d 51 (1993)

CHIEF JUDGE KAYE.

Penal Law § 220.18 (5) makes it a felony to "knowingly and unlawfully possess . . . six hundred twenty-five milligrams of a hallucinogen." The question of statutory interpretation before us is whether "knowingly" applies to the weight of the controlled substance. We conclude that it does and that the trial evidence was insufficient to satisfy that mental culpability element.

I.

Viewed in a light most favorable to the People (People v Contes, 60 NY2d 620, 621), the trial evidence revealed that on October 2, 1990 defendant asked his friend David Hopkins to order and receive a shipment of hallucinogenic mushrooms on his behalf. Hopkins agreed, and adhering to defendant's instructions placed a call to their mutual friend Scott in San Francisco and requested the "usual shipment." Tipped off to the transaction, on October 5 State Police Investigator Douglas Vredenburgh located the package at a Federal Express warehouse in Binghamton. The package was opened (pursuant to a search warrant) and resealed after its contents were verified. The investigator then borrowed a Federal Express uniform and van and delivered the package to Hopkins, the addressee, who was arrested upon signing for it.

Hopkins explained that the package was for defendant and agreed to participate in a supervised delivery to him. In a telephone call recorded by the police, Hopkins notified defendant that he got the package, reporting a "shit load of mushrooms in there." Defendant responded, "I know, don't say nothing." At another point Hopkins referred to the shipment containing two pounds. The men agreed to meet later that evening at the firehouse in West Oneonta.

At the meeting, after a brief conversation, Hopkins handed defendant a substitute package stuffed with news-paper. Moments after taking possession, defendant was arrested. He was later indicted for attempted criminal possession of a controlled substance in the second degree.

The case proceeded to trial, where the evidence summarized above was adduced. Additionally, the police chemist testified that the total weight of the mushrooms in Hopkins' package was 932.8 grams (about two pounds), and that a 140-gram sample of the package contents contained 796 milligrams of psilocybin, a hallucinogen (Penal Law § 220.00 [9]; Public Health Law § 3306 [schedule I] [d] [19]). He did not know, however, the process by which psilocybin appears in mushrooms, whether naturally, by injection or some other means. Nor was there any evidence as to how much psilocybin would typically appear in two pounds of mushrooms.

At the close of the People's case, defendant moved to dismiss for insufficient proof that he knew the level of psilocybin in the mushrooms, and also requested a charge-down to seventh degree attempted criminal possession, which has no weight element. Both applications were denied, defendant was convicted as charged, and he was sentenced as a second felony offender to 10 years-to-life.

The Appellate Division affirmed. The court held that a defendant must know the nature of the substance possessed, and acknowledged that the weight of the controlled substance is an element of the crime. The court declined, however, to read the statute as requiring that a defendant have actual knowledge of the weight. Instead, the court held that "the term 'knowingly' should be construed to refer only to the element of possession and not to the weight requirement." (184 AD2d 24, 27.)

We now reverse.

II.

Although the present case involves an attempt, analysis begins with the elements of the completed crime, second degree criminal possession of a controlled substance. Penal Law § 220.18 provides:

"A person is guilty of criminal possession of a controlled substance in the second degree when he knowingly and unlawfully possesses: . . .

"5. six hundred twenty-five milligrams of a hallucinogen."

At issue is whether defendant must similarly know the weight of the material possessed. That is a question of statutory interpretation, as to which the Court's role is clear: our purpose is not to pass on the wisdom of the statute or any of its requirements, but rather to implement the will of the Legislature as expressed in its enactment (People v Smith, 79 NY2d 309, 311).

In effectuating legislative intent, we look first of course to the statutory language. Read in context, it seems evident that "knowingly" does apply to the weight element. Indeed, given that a defendant's awareness must extend not only to the fact of possessing something ("knowingly . . . possesses") but also to the nature of the material possessed ("knowingly . . . possesses . . . a hallucinogen"), any other reading would be strained. Inasmuch as the knowledge requirement carries through to the end of the sentence (see, People v Reisman, 29 NY2d, at 285), eliminating it from the intervening element—weight—would rob the statute of its obvious meaning. We conclude, therefore, that there is a mens rea element associated with the weight of the drug.

That reading is fortified by two rules of construction ordained by the Legislature itself. First, a "statute defining a crime, unless clearly indicating a legislative intent to impose strict liability, should be construed as defining a crime of mental culpability" (Penal Law § 15.15 [2]). If any material element of an offense lacks a mens rea requirement, it is a strict liability crime (Penal Law § 15.10). Conversely, a crime is one of "mental culpability" only when a mental state "is required with respect to every material element of an offense" (id.).

By ruling that a defendant need not have knowledge of the weight, the Appellate Division in effect held, to that extent, that second degree criminal possession is a strict liability crime (see, Penal Law § 15.10). That is an erroneous statutory construction unless a legislative intent to achieve that result is "clearly indicat[ed]" (Penal Law § 15.15 [2]).

In a similar vein, the Legislature has provided in Penal Law § 15.15 (1):

"Construction of statutes with respect to culpability requirements.

"When the commission of an offense defined in this chapter, or some element of an offense, requires a particular culpable mental state, such mental state is ordinarily designated in the statute defining the offense by use of the terms "intentionally," "knowingly," "recklessly" or "criminal negligence," or by use of terms, such as "with intent to defraud" and "knowing it to be false," describing a specific kind of intent or knowledge. When one and only one of such terms appears in a statute defining an offense, it is presumed to apply to every element of the offense unless an intent to limit its application clearly appears."

Accordingly, if a single mens rea is set forth, as here, it presumptively applies to all elements of the offense unless a contrary legislative intent is plain.

We discern no "clear" legislative intent to make the weight of a drug a strict liability element, as is required before we can construe the statute in that manner (Penal Law § 15.15 [1], [2]). Moreover, the overall structure of the drug possession laws supports the view that a defendant must have some knowledge of the weight.

There are six degrees of criminal possession of a controlled substance, graded in severity from a class A misdemeanor (Penal Law § 220.03 [seventh degree]) up to an A-I felony (Penal Law § 220.21 [first degree]). The definition of each begins identically: "A person is guilty of criminal possession of a controlled substance in the degree when he knowingly and unlawfully possesses . . . ." The primary distinctions between one grade or another relate to the type and weight of the controlled substance, and in some instances the existence of an intent to sell (e.g., Penal Law § 220.16 [1]) or intent to sell combined with a prior drug conviction (e.g., Penal Law § 220.09 [13]).

Taking hallucinogens as an example, knowing and unlawful possession of any amount, even a trace (see, People v Mizell, 72 NY2d 651, 655) is seventh degree possession (Penal Law § 220.03); 25 milligrams or more, fourth degree (Penal Law § 220.09 [6]); 125 milligrams or more, third degree (Penal Law § 220.16 [10]; and 625 milligrams, second degree (Penal Law § 220.18 [5]). The maximum penalty for these crimes ranges from one-year incarceration to a life sentence, yet the only statutory difference relates to the weight of the drugs. To ascribe to the Legislature an intent to mete out drastic differences in punishment without a basis in culpability would be inconsistent with notions of individual responsibility and proportionality prevailing in the Penal Law (see, e.g., Penal Law § 1.05 [4]). . .

III.

The People's contrary argument is based in part on a concern that it would be "prohibitively difficult," if not impossible, to secure convictions if they were required to prove that a defendant had knowledge of the weight. We disagree.

Often there will be evidence from which the requisite knowledge may be deduced, such as negotiations concerning weight, potency or price (see, e.g., People v Acosta, 80 NY2d 665, 668, n 1, and 672–673). Similarly, for controlled substances measured on an "aggregate weight" basis (see, e.g., Penal Law § 220.06 [2]), knowledge of the weight may be inferred from defendant's handling of the material, because the weight of the entire mixture, including cutting agents, is counted. . .

By contrast, that same inference may be unavailable for controlled substances measured by "pure" weight, like psilocybin. The effective doses of these drugs may be minuscule, and they are customarily combined with other substances to facilitate handling and use. In these circumstances it may indeed be difficult to show defendant's knowledge of the weight. Although we cannot simply read the knowledge requirement out of the statute, these "compelling practical considerations" may inform our interpretation of that element. . .

. . . A purpose of the knowledge requirement, then, is to avoid overpenalizing someone who unwittingly possesses a larger amount of a controlled substance than anticipated.

That legislative purpose can be satisfied, among other ways, with evidence that the pure weight of the controlled substance possessed by defendant is typical for the particular form in which the drug appears. This correlation between the pure weight typically found, and the pure weight actually possessed, substantially reduces the possibility that a person will unjustly be convicted for a more serious crime. . .

IV.

With the foregoing principles in mind, we consider whether there was sufficient evidence to convict defendant of attempted second degree possession, an A-II felony.

Certainly there was sufficient evidence from which the jury could conclude, beyond a reasonable doubt, that defendant attempted and intended to possess a two-pound box of hallucinogenic mushrooms. It is also undisputed that, upon testing, the mushrooms in the particular box defendant attempted to possess—the one sent to Hopkins by Scott— contained more than 650 milligrams of psilocybin. The issue we must decide, however, is whether sufficient evidence was presented at trial from which it could be inferred that defendant had the requisite knowledge of the weight. . . .We thus conclude on this record that there was insufficient evidence to satisfy the knowledge requirement within the meaning of the statute. . .

DISCUSSION QUESTIONS

1.   Do you think the legislature intended knowledge of the weight of psilocybin to be proved? If so, did they adequately express that intent?

2.   What tools of statutory interpretation did the court employ?

3.   Does the court's decision make it effectively impossible for prosecutors to prove crimes where the weight element of the offense does not refer to the bulk weight of the drugs but to the weight of the psychoactive components? If not, what mistake did the prosecution in this case make?

Practice Problem 6.4: Dubious Downloading

At some point in the not too distant future, a movie studio releases what is widely hoped to be the last movie in the Star Wars franchise ("Star Wars Episode 27: The Search for More Money"). About six months after the movie's release to theatres, just after the movie becomes available for purchase—but not on streaming services, a friend sends you an email. The email contains what she tells you is a link to a website through which you can watch the movie free of charge. You click on the link and watch the movie. The movie is being streamed on the website in violation of copyright, however. Would you be guilty of the crime described in the following statute in a Model Penal Code jurisdiction? In a common law jurisdiction?

"Anyone who accesses a website in order to view a movie displayed in violation of copyright protection is guilty of a misdemeanor punishable by a fine not to exceed $1,000 or imprisonment in a federal correctional facility for up to six months."

CHAPTER 7

MISTAKES AND THE GUILTY MIND

■ ■ ■

What if the defendant was mistaken about one of the elements of the crime? Is that a defense? The concept of mistake seems simple enough, but the legal doctrines dealing with mistake in the criminal law do not always make sense to people. One can iron out these wrinkles if one remembers and understands a few related principles.

1. Mistake of Fact doctrine does not change—but simply reflects—the mental state requirements of a crime.

2. Mistakes of Fact generally do not have to be reasonable.

3. Mistakes of Law usually excuse criminal liability only when the legislature clearly wants them to.

A. MISTAKE OF FACT DOCTRINE REFLECTS BUT DOES NOT CHANGE AN OFFENSE'S MENTAL STATE REQUIREMENTS

This strikes many people as counter-intuitive because people who are mistaken seem less blameworthy, less dangerous, and not as easy to deter as people who know what they are doing. Yet, we decide when we do and don't want mistakes to matter when we decide what mental state is required for the crime., The absence of the required mental state can be described as a "mistake," but whether you call it a mistake or not does not change whether the mental state exists or not.

Theft provides an easy example. At common law and under all modern statutes, theft—or larceny as it is known—requires you to intend to permanently deprive someone of their property. That means that if, as you leave a party, you walk off with someone else's umbrella thinking that it is your own, you are not guilty of theft. This comports with our commonsense understanding of what it means to "steal" something.

Most people would say that you made a mistake. The law would regard this as a mistake of fact because you were mistaken about who owned the umbrella you took. So, at your trial for the theft of the umbrella (it belonged to the chief prosecutor for your county), your lawyer might well ask for a jury instruction that says something like the following. "It is a defense to the crime of larceny if the defendant was mistaken as to whose umbrella he took." Now, imagine that the judge refuses to give this mistake of fact

267

jury instruction. Furthermore, the judge tells your lawyer that she may not use the word "mistake" in her closing argument. Do you still have a defense? Well, the standard jury instruction for theft explains to the jury that they must find beyond a reasonable doubt that you intended to deprive another of their property. Your lawyer argues to the jury that since you thought the umbrella was yours that you did not intend to take the property of another.

The result is the same either way because either you have the mental state required for the crime or you don't—here the belief that the umbrella belonged to someone else. Whether you call the absence of that mental state a mistake or not makes no real difference.

At the end of the day, the question is this: does your mistake mean that you did not have the required mental state? The law's somewhat awkward way of putting this is whether your mistake "negated" the required mental state, but it means the same thing.

What purpose does mistake of fact doctrine serve? In modern courtrooms, a mistake instruction will sometimes help a jury better understand what the mental state required means. Without the mistake instruction, a jury in our umbrella case might scratch their head and wonder about whether it makes a difference that you "made a mistake." Hopefully, though, they would realize that if you thought it belonged to someone else, then you could not intend to take the property of another.

B. MISTAKES OF FACT DO NOT HAVE TO BE REASONABLE

Intuitively, it seems that a mistake should be reasonable for it to matter to criminal liability. In fact, a few jurisdictions tried this approach. When you think it through however, you realize that requiring all mistakes to be reasonable would reduce the mental state for all crimes to simple negligence, something that we obviously don't want to do.

The most dramatic examples involve murder. Imagine that a jurisdiction defines murder as intentionally killing someone and involuntary manslaughter as negligently killing someone. Remember that intentionally generally requires that a person acts purposely or knowingly with respect to results. So, intentionally killing someone requires that you act at least knowing that another human being is substantially certain to die as a result of what you do. Now imagine that a deer hunter accidentally shot and killed another hunter. The defendant shot at what he thought was a deer moving in the underbrush, but it turned out to be another hunter. He intended to kill what he was shooting, but he was mistaken about what it was. He would not seem to have the mental state required for murder because he did not intentionally (knowingly) kill a human being.

Now further assume that it was not reasonable for him to shoot into the underbrush without being sure that it was a deer—not another hunter—that was moving. This means that his mistake was not reasonable. If mistakes of fact must be reasonable to constitute his defense, then his unreasonable mistake about what he was killing cannot be a defense to the charge of murder. Yet, the legislature provided that negligent or reckless killings are not murder but manslaughter. Requiring mistakes to be reasonable would change the mental state required for murder in these sorts of cases from intentional killing to negligent killing. For this reason, most jurisdictions have come around to recognizing that mistakes of fact generally do not have to be reasonable.

Case in Context

Did the defendant's mistake in the next case negate the required mental state?

PEOPLE V. NAVARRO

Appellate Department, Superior Court, Los Angeles County, California
160 Cal.Rptr. 692 (1979)

OPINION

Defendant, charged with a violation of Penal Code section 487, subdivision 1, grand theft, appeals his conviction after a jury trial of petty theft, a lesser but necessarily included offense. His contention on appeal is that the jury was improperly instructed. The only facts set forth in the record on appeal are that defendant was charged with stealing four wooden beams from a construction site and that the state of the evidence was such that the jury could have found that the defendant believed either (1) that the beams had been abandoned as worthless and the owner had no objection to his taking them or (2) that they had substantial value, had not been abandoned and he had no right to take them.

The court refused two jury instructions proposed by defendant reading as follows:

Defendant's A

"If one takes personal property with the good faith belief that the property has been abandoned or discarded by the true owner, he is not guilty of theft. This is the case even if such good faith belief is unreasonable. The prosecutor must prove beyond a reasonable doubt that the defendant did not so believe for you to convict a defendant of theft."

Defendant's B

"If one takes personal property with the good faith belief that he has permission to take the property, he is not guilty of theft. This is the case even if such good faith belief is unreasonable.

The prosecutor must prove beyond a reasonable doubt that the defendant did not so believe for you to convict a defendant of theft."

Instead, the court instructed the jury in the words of the following modified instructions:

Modified-Defendant's A

"If one takes personal property in the reasonable and good faith belief that the property has been abandoned or discarded by the true owner, he is not guilty of theft."

Modified-Defendant's B

"If one takes personal property in the reasonable and good faith belief that he has the consent or permission of the owner to take the property, he is not guilty of theft.

"If you have a reasonable doubt that the defendant had the required criminal intent as specified in these instructions, the defendant is entitled to an acquittal."

Accordingly, the question for determination on appeal is whether the defendant should be acquitted if there is a reasonable doubt that he had a good faith belief that the property had been abandoned or that he had the permission of the owner to take the property or whether that belief must be a reasonable one as well as being held in good faith.

A recent decision by the California Supreme Court throws light on this question. In People v. Wetmore (1978) 22 Cal.3d 318 [149 Cal.Rptr. 265, 583 P.2d 1308], defendant was charged with burglary, like theft a specific intent crime. The Supreme Court held that the trial court had erroneously refused to consider the. . .evidence that, because of mental illness, defendant was incapable of forming the specific intent required for conviction of the crime. . .

The instant case, does not, of course, involve evidence of mental illness. Evidence was presented, however, from which the jury could have concluded that defendant believed that the wooden beams had been abandoned and that the owner had no objection to his taking them, i.e., that he lacked the specific criminal intent required to commit the crime of theft (intent permanently to deprive an owner of his property). . .

In People v. Devine (1892) 95 Cal. 227 [30 P. 378], defendant's conviction of larceny was reversed. He had driven away in a wagon, without any attempt at secrecy, a number of hogs, his own and three bearing another's mark or brand. The Supreme Court pointed out: "There are cases in which all the knowledge which a person might have acquired by due diligence is to be imputed to him. But where a felonious intent must be proven, it can be done only by proving what the accused knew. One cannot intend to steal property which he believes to be his own. He may be careless, and omit to make an effort to ascertain that the property which he thinks his own belongs to another; but so long as he believes it to be his own, he cannot feloniously steal it . . . ."

The proper rule, it seems to us, is set forth in Perkins on Criminal Law (2d ed. 1969) at pages 940–941: "If no specific intent or other special mental element is required for guilt of the offense charged, a mistake of fact will not be recognized as an excuse unless it was based upon reasonable grounds . . . .[On the other hand, because] of the requirement of a specific intent to steal there is no such thing as larceny by negligence. One does not commit this offense by carrying away the chattel of another in the mistaken belief that it is his own, no matter how great may have been the fault leading to this belief, if the belief itself is genuine."

La Fave and Scott, Handbook on Criminal Law (1972) sets forth at page 357 what the authors call the ". . . rather simple rule that an honest mistake of fact or law is a defense when it negates a required mental element of the crime . . . ." As an example they refer to the crime of receiving stolen property, stating ". . . if the defendant by a mistake of either fact or law did not know the goods were stolen, even though the circumstances would have led a prudent man to believe they were stolen, he does not have the required mental state and thus may not be convicted of the crime."

In the instant case the trial court in effect instructed the jury that even though defendant in good faith believed he had the right to take the beams, and thus lacked the specific intent required for the crime of theft, he should be convicted unless such belief was reasonable. In doing so it erred. It is true that if the jury thought the defendant's belief to be unreasonable, it might infer that he did not in good faith hold such belief. If, however, it concluded that defendant in good faith believed that he had the right to take the beams, even though such belief was unreasonable as measured by the objective standard of a hypothetical reasonable man, defendant was entitled to an acquittal since the specific intent required to be proved as an element of the offense had not been established. . .

The judgment is reversed.

DISCUSSION QUESTIONS

1. Why can't you steal something by accident?

2. Does it make sense that an unreasonable mistake can be a defense to a crime of theft?

3. Could a legislature create a crime of taking something by accident? How could it define such a crime?

C. THE COMMON LAW DISTINCTION BETWEEN SPECIFIC AND GENERAL INTENT WITH RESPECT TO MISTAKES

At common law, a mistake of fact did not have to be reasonable to be a defense to a specific intent crime. Since specific intent crimes require that a person act with knowledge or purpose, it makes sense that a genuine but unreasonable mistake would constitute a defense. A mistake of fact does, however, have to be reasonable to be a defense to a general intent crime.

In the hunting example, what effect does the hunter's unreasonable mistake have on the charges of specific intent or general intent crimes? The hunter's unreasonable mistake can constitute a defense to a specific intent crime such as the intentional killing of a person. The hunter's unreasonable mistake, however, is not a defense to a general intent crime. For this reason, our unreasonable deer hunter would be guilty of involuntary manslaughter because that crime requires only negligence.

D. MISTAKES OF LAW GENERALLY ARE NOT A DEFENSE

One must start with a principle that is easy to say but surprisingly hard to accept: ignorance of the law does not excuse. In general, you do not need to prove that a person knew he or she was breaking the law. We are all presumed to know what the law prohibits. We are, in fact, presumed to know not only what is written in criminal statutes, but also every word of every judicial decision interpreting those statutes. It does not matter how complex the law is. It does not even matter that judges themselves might disagree about what the law means. Whatever the highest court determines the law to mean, that is what we are presumed to know. This presumption applies to every single one of us. Whether you be a law professor or a street sweeper, ignorance of even the most arcane, convoluted, and difficult to understand law does not excuse violating it.[1]

There are a couple of related rationales for this rule, but they all basically boil down to choosing utilitarian concerns over blameworthy concerns. The blameworthiness concern is relatively straightforward. Someone who does not realize that what they are doing is illegal is not as blameworthy as someone who knowingly breaks the law. The utilitarian concerns in favor of the rule are numerous. First, if ignorance of the law excused, then there would be an incentive to know as little about the law as possible because only the knowledgeable could be successfully convicted. Second, it would be arguably a lot more difficult to convict people of many types of crime. Presumably, juries would be easily convinced that defendants knew it was against the law to commit murder, theft, and

---

[1]   A law is not unconstitutionally vague if it is complex or difficult to understand. Vagueness and complexity are different things.

common law crimes, but it would be harder to convict people of regulatory crimes that are not obviously criminal. The third argument is a blameworthiness argument. It is blameworthy of you not to know the law, so we will hold you strictly liable for your ignorance of it.

Practice Problem 7.1: A Sharp Distinction

You represent Alan, who has been charged with misdemeanor possession of a switchblade. The statute provides "It shall be a misdemeanor to knowingly possess a switchblade." Case law has interpreted the word switchblade in the statute to mean "a folding knife whose blade may be opened and locked into place by use of a button-activated, spring-loaded mechanism." Alan's knife meets the statutory definition. Alan tells you "I did not know it was a switchblade." Assuming he is telling the truth, can you tell whether he is guilty of the crime from this statement? What further questions might you ask him to determine whether he has a defense or not?

E. MALUM PROHIBITUM CRIMES AND MISTAKES OF LAW

Crimes that are considered to be wrong in and of themselves are often referred to by judges as malum en se, which means bad or evil in itself. Crimes that are considered to be wrong only because the state has decided to prohibit them are often referred to by judges as malum prohibitum, which means prohibited wrong. An easy example of a malum prohibitum crime is the law making it a crime to drive on the left side of the road. There is nothing inherently wrong about driving on the left side of the road (unless you think there is something evil about being left-handed), but we need to pick one side or the other to keep driving safe, so we prohibit driving on the left side.

As the number of malum prohibitum offenses has increased, some argue that judges should reconsider the mistake of law defense since we might not always know that we are breaking the law. Judges, however, have concluded that presuming knowledge of the law in criminal cases is an effective way to ensure that we learn and obey these malum prohibitum offenses.

Case in Context

This case illustrates the harshness of the mistake of law doctrine. What would be the alternative though?

PEOPLE V. MARRERO

Court of Appeals of New York
507 N.E.2d 1068 (1987)

The defense of mistake of law (Penal Law § 15.20 [2] [a], [d]) is not available to a Federal corrections officer arrested in a Manhattan social club for possession of a loaded .38 caliber automatic pistol who claimed he mistakenly believed he was entitled, pursuant to the interplay of CPL 2.10, 1.20 and Penal Law § 265.20, to carry a handgun without a permit as a peace officer.

In a prior phase of this criminal proceeding, defendant's motion to dismiss the indictment upon which he now stands convicted was granted (94 Misc 2d 367); then it was reversed and the indictment reinstated by a divided Appellate Division (71 AD2d 346); next, defendant allowed an appeal from that order, certified to the Court of Appeals, to lapse and be dismissed (Oct. 22, 1980). Thus, review of that aspect of the case is precluded *(People v Corley,* 67 NY2d 105).

On the trial of the case, the court rejected the defendant's argument that his personal misunderstanding of the statutory definition of a peace officer is enough to excuse him from criminal liability under New York's mistake of law statute (Penal Law § 15.20). The court refused to charge the jury on this issue and defendant was convicted of criminal possession of a weapon in the third degree. We affirm the Appellate Division order upholding the conviction. . .

The starting point for our analysis is the New York mistake statute as an outgrowth of the dogmatic common-law maxim that ignorance of the law is no excuse. The central issue is whether defendant's personal misreading or misunderstanding of a statute may excuse criminal conduct in the circumstances of this case.

The common-law rule on mistake of law was clearly articulated in Gardner v People (62 NY 299). In Gardner, the defendants misread a statute and mistakenly believed that their conduct was legal. The court insisted, however, that the "mistake of law" did not relieve the defendants of criminal liability. . .

This is to be contrasted with People v Weiss (276 NY 384) where, in a kidnapping case, the trial court precluded testimony that the defendants acted with the honest belief that seizing and confining the child was done with "authority of law". We held it was error to exclude such testimony since a good-faith belief in the legality of the conduct would negate an express and necessary element of the crime of kidnapping, i.e., intent, without authority of law, to confine or imprison another. Subject to the mistake statute, the instant case, of course, falls within the Gardner rationale because the weapons possession statute violated by this defendant imposes liability irrespective of one's intent.

The desirability of the Gardner-type outcome, which was to encourage the societal benefit of individuals' knowledge of and respect for the law, is underscored by Justice Holmes' statement: "It is no doubt true that there are many cases in which the criminal could not have known that he was breaking the law, but to admit the excuse at all would be to encourage ignorance where the law-maker has determined to make men know and obey, and justice to the individual is rightly outweighed by the larger interests on the other side of the scales" (Holmes, The Common Law, at 48 1881).

The revisors of New York's Penal Law intended no fundamental departure from this common-law rule in Penal Law § 15.20, which provides in pertinent part:

"§ 15.20. Effect of ignorance or mistake upon liability."

2.   A person is not relieved of criminal liability for conduct because he engages in such conduct under a mistaken belief that it does not, as a matter of law, constitute an offense, unless such mistaken belief is founded upon an official statement of the law contained in (a) a statute or other enactment * * * (d) an interpretation of the statute or law relating to the offense, officially made or issued by a public servant, agency, or body legally charged or empowered with the responsibility or privilege of administering, enforcing or interpreting such statute or law."...

The defendant claims as a first prong of his defense that he is entitled to raise the defense of mistake of law under section 15.20 (2) (a) because his mistaken belief that his conduct was legal was founded upon an official statement of the law contained in the statute itself. Defendant argues that his mistaken interpretation of the statute was reasonable in view of the alleged ambiguous wording of the peace officer exemption statute, and that his "reasonable" interpretation of an "official statement" is enough to satisfy the requirements of subdivision (2)(a).

The prosecution. . .counters defendant's argument by asserting that one cannot claim the protection of mistake of law under section 15.20 (2) (a) simply by misconstruing the meaning of a statute but must instead establish that the statute relied on actually permitted the conduct in question and was only later found to be erroneous. To buttress that argument, the People analogize New York's official statement defense to the approach taken by the HN4 Model Penal Code (MPC). Section 2.04 of the MPC provides:

"Section 2.04. Ignorance or Mistake."

"(3) A belief that conduct does not legally constitute an offense is a defense to a prosecution for that offense based upon such conduct when . . . (b) he acts in reasonable reliance upon an official statement of the law, afterward determined to be invalid or erroneous, contained in (i) a statute or other enactment."

Although the drafters of the New York statute did not adopt the precise language of the Model Penal Code provision with the emphasized clause, it is evident and has long been believed that the Legislature intended the New York statute to be similarly construed. In fact, the legislative history of section 15.20 is replete with references to the influence of the Model Penal Code.

It was early recognized that the "official statement" mistake of law defense was a statutory protection against prosecution based on reliance of a statute that did in fact authorize certain conduct. "It seems obvious that society must rely on some statement of the law, and that conduct which is in fact 'authorized' . . . should not be subsequently condemned. The threat of punishment under these circumstances can have no deterrent effect unless the actor doubts the validity of the official pronouncement—a questioning of authority that is itself undesirable" (Note, Proposed Penal Law of New York, 64 Colum L Rev 1469, 1486). While providing a narrow escape hatch, the idea was simultaneously to encourage the public to read and rely on official statements of the law, not to have individuals conveniently and personally question the validity and interpretation of the law and act on that basis. If later the statute was invalidated, one who mistakenly acted in reliance on the authorizing statute would be relieved of criminal liability. That makes sense and is fair. To go further does not make sense and would create a legal chaos based on individual selectivity.

In the case before us, the underlying statute never in fact authorized the defendant's conduct; the defendant only thought that the statutory exemptions permitted his conduct when, in fact, the primary statute clearly forbade his conduct. . .

We recognize that some legal scholars urge that the mistake of law defense should be available more broadly where a defendant misinterprets a potentially ambiguous statute not previously clarified by judicial decision and reasonably believes in good faith that the acts were legal. . .

We conclude that the better and correctly construed view is that the defense should not be recognized, except where specific intent is an element of the offense or where the misrelied-upon law has later been properly adjudicated as wrong. Any broader view fosters lawlessness. . .

If defendant's argument were accepted, the exception would swallow the rule. Mistakes about the law would be encouraged, rather than respect for and adherence to law. There would be an infinite number of mistake of law defenses which could be devised from a good-faith, perhaps reasonable but mistaken, interpretation of criminal statutes, many of which are concededly complex. Even more troublesome are the opportunities for wrongminded individuals to contrive in bad faith solely to get an exculpatory notion before the jury. These are not in terrorem arguments disrespectful of appropriate adjudicative procedures; rather, they are the realistic and practical consequences were the dissenters' views to prevail.

Our holding comports with a statutory scheme which was not designed to allow false and diversionary stratagems to be provided for many more cases than the statutes contemplated. This would not serve the ends of justice but rather would serve game playing and evasion from properly imposed criminal responsibility.

Accordingly, the order of the Appellate Division should be affirmed.

Dissent by: HANCOCK, JR.

DISSENT

HANCOCK, JR., J. (dissenting).

The basic difference which divides the court may be simply put. Suppose the case of a man who has committed an act which is criminal not because it is inherently wrong or immoral but solely because it violates a criminal statute. He has committed the act in complete good faith under the mistaken but entirely reasonable assumption that the act does not constitute an offense because it is permitted by the wording of the statute. Does the law require that this man be punished? The majority says that it does and holds that (1) Penal Law § 15.20 (2) (a) must be construed so that the man is precluded from offering a defense based on his mistake of law and (2) such construction is compelled by prevailing considerations of public policy and criminal jurisprudence. We take issue with the majority on both propositions.

There can be no question that under the view that the purpose of the criminal justice system is to punish blame-worthiness or "choosing freely to do wrong", our supposed man who has acted innocently and without any intent to do wrong should not be punished (see, United States v Barker, 514 F2d 208, 228–229 Bazelon, Ch. J., concurring). Indeed, under some standards of morality he has done no wrong at all (Patterson, Cardozo's Philosophy of Law, Part II, 88 U Pa L Rev 156, 169–171 1939–1940). Since he has not knowingly committed a wrong there can be no reason for society to exact retribution. Because the man is law-abiding and could not have acted but for his mistaken assumption as to the law, there is no need for punishment to deter him from further unlawful conduct. Traditionally, however, under the ancient rule of Anglo-American common law that ignorance or mistake of law is no excuse, our supposed man would be punished.

The maxim "ignorantia legis neminem excusat" finds its roots in Medieval law when the "actor's intent was irrelevant since the law punished the act itself" (United States v Barker, supra, at 228 Bazelon, Ch. J., concurring; see, Keedy, Ignorance and Mistake in the Criminal Law, 22 Harv L Rev 75, 81 1908) and when, for example, the law recognized no difference between an intentional killing and one that was accidental (Ames, Law and Morals, 22 Harv L Rev 97, 98 1908). Although the common law has gradually evolved from its origins in Anglo-Germanic tribal law (adding the element of intent mens rea and recognizing defenses based on the actor's mental state—e.g., justification, insanity and intoxication) the dogmatic rule that ignorance or mistake of law is no excuse has remained unaltered. Various justifications have been offered for the rule, but all are frankly pragmatic and utilitarian—preferring the interests of society (e.g., in deterring criminal conduct, fostering orderly judicial administration, and preserving the primacy of the rule of law) to the interest of the individual in being free from punishment except for intentionally engaging in conduct which he knows is criminal.

Today there is widespread criticism of the common-law rule mandating categorical preclusion of the mistake of law defense (see, e.g., White, op. cit., 77 Colum L Rev 775, 784; Note, Proposed Penal Law of New York, 64 Colum L Rev 1469, 1486; Model Penal Code § 2.04, comment 3, at 274–276 Official Draft and Revised Comments 1985). The utilitarian arguments for retaining the rule have been drawn into serious question (see, LaFave and Scott, Substantive Criminal Law § 5.1; Jeffries, Legality, Vagueness, and the Construction of Penal Statutes, 71 U Va L Rev 189, 208, 209 1985; White, op. cit., at 785–787; Perkins, op. cit., 88 U Pa L Rev 35, 51–53; United States v Barker, 514 F2d 208, 228–231 Bazelon, Ch. J., concurring, supra) but the fundamental objection is that it is simply wrong to punish someone who, in good-faith reliance on the wording of a statute, believed that what he was doing was lawful. It is contrary to "the notion that punishment should be conditioned on a showing of subjective moral blameworthiness" (White, op. cit., at 784). This basic objection to the maxim "ignorantia legis neminem excusat" may have had less force in ancient times when most crimes consisted of acts which by their very nature were recognized as evil (malum in se) (id., at 784). In modern times, however, with the profusion of legislation making otherwise lawful conduct criminal (malum prohibitum), the "common law fiction that every man is presumed to know the law has become indefensible in fact or logic."

With this background we proceed to a discussion of our disagreement with the majority's construction of Penal Law § 15.20 (2) (a) and the policy and jurisprudential arguments made in support of that construction. . .

It is difficult to imagine a case more squarely within the wording of Penal Law § 15.20 (2) (a) or one more fitted to what appears clearly to be the intended purpose of the statute than the one before us. For this reason it is helpful to discuss the statute and its apparent intended effect in the light of what defendant contends was his mistaken belief founded on an official statement of the law contained in a statute.

Defendant's mistaken belief that, as a Federal corrections officer, he could legally carry a loaded weapon without a license was based on the express exemption from criminal liability under Penal Law § 265.02 accorded in Penal Law § 265.20 (a) (1) (a) to "peace officers" as defined in the Criminal Procedure Law and on his reading of the statutory definition for "peace officer" in CPL 2.10 (25) as meaning a correction officer "of *any* penal correctional institution" (emphasis added), including an institution not operated by New York State. Thus, he concluded erroneously that, as a corrections officer in a Federal prison, he was a "peace officer" and, as such, exempt by the express terms of Penal Law § 265.20 (a) (1) (a). This mistaken belief, based in good faith on the statute defining "peace officer" (CPL 2.10 25), is, defendant contends, the precise sort of "mistaken belief * * * founded upon an official statement of the law contained in * * * a statute or other enactment" which gives rise to a mistake of law defense under Penal Law § 15.20 (2) (a). He points out, of course, that when he acted in reliance on his belief he had no way of foreseeing that a court would eventually resolve the question of the statute's meaning against him and rule that his belief had been mistaken, as three of the five-member panel at the Appellate Division ultimately did in the first appeal.

The majority, however, has accepted the People's argument that to have a defense under Penal Law § 15.20 (2) (a) "a defendant must show that the statute permitted his conduct, not merely that he believed it did."

Nothing in the statutory language suggests the interpretation urged by the People and adopted by the majority: that Penal Law § 15.20 (2) (a) is available to a defendant not when he has mistakenly read a statute but only when he has correctly read and relied on a statute which is later invalidated (respondent's brief, at 26). Such a construction contravenes the general rule that penal statutes should be construed against the State and in favor of the accused.

More importantly, the construction leads to an anomaly: only a defendant who is not mistaken about the law when he acts has a mistake of law defense. In other words, a defendant can assert a defense under Penal Law § 15.20 (2) (a) only when his reading of the statute is correct— not mistaken. Such construction is obviously illogical; it strips the statute of the very effect intended by the Legislature in adopting the mistake of law defense. The statute is of no benefit to a defendant who has proceeded in good faith on an erroneous but concededly reasonable interpretation of a statute, as defendant presumably has. . .

It is self-evident that in enacting Penal Law § 15.20 (2) as part of the revision and modernization of the Penal Law (L 1965, ch 1030) the Legislature intended to effect a needed reform by abolishing what had long been considered the unjust archaic common-law rule totally prohibiting mistake of law as a defense.

The majority construes the statute, however, so as to rule out any defense based on mistake of law. In so doing, it defeats the only possible purpose for the statute's enactment and resurrects the very rule which the Legislature rejected in enacting Penal Law § 15.20 (2) (a) as part of its modernization and reform of the Penal Law.

Instead, the majority bases its decision on an analogous provision in the Model Penal Code and concludes that despite its totally different wording and meaning Penal Law § 15.20 (2) (a) should be read as if it were Model Penal Code § 2.04 (3) (b) (i). But New York in revising the Penal Law did not adopt the Model Penal Code. . . New York followed parts of the Model Penal Code provisions and rejected others.

While Penal Law § 15.20 (2) and Model Penal Code § 2.04 are alike in their rejection of the strict common-law rule, they are not alike in wording and differ significantly in substance. . .

Thus, the precise phrase in the Model Penal Code limiting the defense under section 2.04 (3) (b) (i) to reliance on a statute "afterward determined to be invalid or erroneous" which, if present, would support the majority's narrow construction of the New York statute, is omitted from Penal Law § 15.20 (2) (a). How the Legislature can be assumed to have enacted the very language which it has specifically rejected is not explained.

Any fair reading of the majority opinion, we submit, demonstrates that the decision to reject a mistake of law defense is based on considerations of public policy and on the conviction that such a defense would be bad, rather than on an analysis of CPL 15.20 (2) (a) under the usual principles of statutory construction.

A statute which recognizes a defense based on a man's good-faith mistaken belief founded on a well-grounded interpretation of an official statement of the law contained in a statute is a just law. The law embodies the ideal of contemporary criminal jurisprudence "that punishment should be conditioned on a showing of subjective moral blameworthiness".

If defendant's offer of proof is true, his is not the case of a "free agent confronted with a choice between doing right and doing wrong and choosing freely to do wrong" (Pound, Introduction to Sayre, Cases on Criminal Law 1927, quoted in Morissette v United States, 342 U.S. 246, 250, n 4). He carried the gun in the good-faith belief that, as a Federal corrections officer, it was lawful for him to do so under the words of the statute (Penal Law § 265.20 a 1 former a; CPL 2.10, 1.20 see, dissenting opn, at 397, n 7). That his interpretation of the statute as exempting corrections officers (whether or not employed in a State facility) was a reasonable one can hardly be questioned. If the statute does not plainly say that corrections officers are exempt, as defendant contends, the statute at the very least is ambiguous and clearly susceptible to that interpretation. Indeed, Supreme Court in dismissing the indictment (94 Misc 2d 367) and two of the five-member panel in the first appeal to the Appellate Division (71 AD2d 346) read the statute as it was read by defendant and the police officials and others whose opinions he sought. We believe that under our present Penal Law and the policies underlying its revision (L 1965, ch 1030) this defendant should not be found guilty of violating Penal Law § 265.02 if he can establish that his conduct was based on a good-faith mistake of law founded on the wording of the statute.

We do not believe that permitting a defense in this case will produce the grievous consequences the majority predicts. . .Indeed, although the majority foresees "an infinite number of mistake of law defenses" (majority opn, at 392), New Jersey, which adopted a more liberal mistake of law statute in 1978, has apparently experienced no such adversity. Nor is there any reason to believe that courts will have more difficulty separating valid claims from "diversionary stratagems" in making preliminary legal determinations as to the validity of the mistake of law defense than of justification or any other defense.

There should be a reversal and defendant should have a new trial in which he is permitted to assert a defense of mistake of law under Penal Law § 15.20 (2) (a).

DISCUSSION QUESTIONS

1.   Which words in the statute was Marrerro mistaken about?

2.   How many of the judges who adjudicated this case agreed with his interpretation?

3.   Why doesn't the criminal law recognize a "reasonable mistake of law" defense?

F. MISTAKES OF LAW DEFENSES

There are three categories of cases where ignorance of the law can constitute a defense to a criminal charge.

1.   Where knowledge of the law being broken is expressly required by the words of the statute, ignorance of the law is a defense.

Case in Context

Warning: reading this case may make it easier for a prosecutor to convict you of a crime.

UNITED STATES OF AMERICA V. DENNIS MORAN

United States District Court, D. Nebraska
757 F.Supp. 1046 (1991)

MEMORANDUM AND ORDER

RICHARD G. KOPF, UNITED STATES MAGISTRATE JUDGE.

The parties have consented to try this misdemeanor case before me. Trial was held on January 15, 1991, and briefs were received on January 23, 1991. I now find that the defendant is not guilty of the alleged willful infringement of a copyrighted video cassette in violation of 17 U.S.C. § 506(a).

I. FACTS

Dennis Moran (Moran), the defendant, is a full-time Omaha, Nebraska, police officer and the owner of a "mom-and-pop" movie rental business which rents video cassettes of copyrighted motion pictures to the public. On April 14, 1989, agents of the Federal Bureau of Investigation (FBI) executed a court-ordered search warrant on the premises of Moran's business. The FBI seized various video cassettes appearing to be unauthorized copies of copyrighted motion pictures, including "Bat 21," "Big," "Crocodile Dundee II," "The Fourth Protocol," "Hell-Bound: Hellraiser II," and "Mystic Pizza." The parties have stipulated that these six motion pictures are validly copyrighted motion pictures. The parties have further stipulated that each of the six motion pictures was distributed to Moran, with the permission of the copyright holder, between February 1, 1989, and April 14, 1989. The parties have further stipulated that at least one of the movies identified was reproduced by Moran onto a video cassette, without the authorization of the copyright holder, placed into inventory for rental, and subsequently rented.

At the time the FBI executed the search warrant, Moran was fully cooperative. He told the FBI agents he put the "duped" copies out for rental and held the "originals" back because he feared the "original" motion pictures would be stolen or damaged. Moran told the FBI agents at the time they executed the warrant that he believed this practice was legal as long as he had purchased and was in possession of the "original" motion picture. Moran further advised the FBI agents that he would affix to the "duped" copies title labels for the copyrighted motion pictures and a copy of the FBI copyright warning label commonly found on video cassette tapes. Moran advised the FBI agents that he put the title labels and FBI warning on the tapes to stop customers from stealing or duplicating the tapes.

Moran testified at trial. He indicated that he had been employed as an Omaha, Nebraska, police officer for approximately twenty-two-and-a-half years, including service as a narcotics investigator and as a bodyguard to the mayor of the City of Omaha. Moran has a reputation for honesty among his associates.

Moran testified that he began to "insure" copyrighted video cassettes, meaning that he duplicated copyrighted video cassettes which he had validly purchased from distributors, when he realized copyrighted tapes were being vandalized. Moran testified he was under the impression that "insuring" tapes was legal whereas "pirating" tapes was not. For practical purposes, Moran defined "insuring" versus "pirating" as meaning that he could duplicate a copyrighted tape provided he had purchased the copyrighted tape and did not endeavor to rent both the copyrighted tape and the duplicate he had made. Moran testified that he formulated his belief about "insuring" versus "pirating" when talking with various colleagues in the business and from reading trade publications. However, Moran was not able to specifically identify the source of his information.

There was no persuasive evidence that Moran made multiple copies of each authorized version of the copyrighted material. The evidence indicates that Moran purchased more than one copyrighted tape of the same movie, but the persuasive evidence also reveals that Moran made only one copy of each copyrighted tape he purchased. There was no persuasive evidence that Moran endeavored to rent both the copyrighted tape and the duplicate. When Moran made the unauthorized copy, he put the unauthorized copy in a package made to resemble as closely as possible the package containing the original copyrighted motion picture Moran had purchased from an authorized distributor.

II. LAW

Moran makes two arguments. First, Moran argues that the government must prove that he had the specific intent to violate the law, that is, he knew that what he was doing was illegal and he committed the act nevertheless. Secondly, Moran argues that he did not have the specific intent to violate the law and, as a consequence, should be found not guilty.

In pertinent part 17 U.S.C. § 506(a) punishes as a criminal any "person who infringes a copyright willfully and for purposes of commercial advantage or private financial gain." Pursuant to 17 U.S.C. § 106(3), the owner of a copyright has the exclusive right to "distribute copies . . . of the copyrighted work to the public by sale or other transfer of ownership, or by rental, lease, or lending." The "exclusive right" of the owner of a copyright is subject to a variety of exceptions. *See* 17 U.S.C. §§ 107–118.

A.

It must first be determined whether the word "willfully," as used in 17 U.S.C. § 506(a), requires a showing of "bad purpose" or "evil motive" in the sense that there was an "intentional violation of a known legal duty." Adopting the research of the Motion Picture Association of America, the government argues that the term "willful" means only "an intent to copy and not to infringe." (Citations omitted.) On the other hand, Moran argues that the use of the word "willful" implies the kind of specific intent required to be proven in federal tax cases, which is to say, a voluntary, intentional violation of a known legal duty. (Citations omitted.) The general rule is, of course, that ignorance of the law or mistake of the law is no defense to a criminal prosecution. However, when the term "willfully" is used in complex statutory schemes, such as federal criminal tax statutes, the term "willfull" means a "voluntary, intentional violation of a known legal duty." *Cheek v. United States,* 498 U.S. 192, 111 S.Ct. 604, 610, 112 L.Ed.2d 617 (1991) (holding in a criminal tax prosecution that a good faith misunderstanding of the law or a good faith belief that one is not violating the law negates willfulness, whether or not the claimed belief or misunderstanding is objectively reasonable). As the Court recognized in *Cheek, id.* at ___, 111 S.Ct. at 609–611, in *United States v. Murdock,* 290 U.S. 389, 396, 54 S.Ct. 223, 226, 78 L.Ed. 381 (1933), the Supreme Court said that:

> Congress did not intend that a person, by reason of a bona fide misunderstanding as to his liability for the tax, as to his duty to make a return, or as to the adequacy of the records he maintained, should become a criminal by his mere failure to measure up to the prescribed standard of conduct.

> This was evidently so because "[t]he proliferation of statutes and regulations has sometimes made it difficult for the average citizen to know and comprehend the extent of the duties and obligations imposed by the tax law." *Cheek,* 498 U.S. at ___, 111 S.Ct. at 609.

Apparently no case has compared and analyzed the competing arguments, i.e., whether the word "willfully" requires either a showing of specific intent, as suggested by Moran, or the more generalized intent suggested by the government. Indeed, a leading text writer acknowledges that there are two divergent lines of cases, one of which requires specific intent and another which does not. 3 M. Nimmer & D. Nimmer, *Nimmer on Copyright,* § 15.01 at 15–5 n. 13 (1990) (hereinafter *Nimmer*). As pointed out by the government, some courts have suggested that "willful" only means an intent to copy, not to infringe. *Backer,* 134 F.2d at 535; *Taxe,* 380 F.Supp. at 1017. On the other hand, as suggested by Moran, other courts have seemingly required evidence of specific intent. *Heilman,* 614 F.2d at 1137–38; *Wise,* 550 F.2d at 1194. At least two courts have specifically approved jury instructions essentially stating that an act of infringement done "willfully" means an act voluntarily and purposely done with specific intent to do that which the law forbids, that is to say, with bad purpose either to disobey or disregard the law. *Cross,* 816 F.2d at 300–01; *United States v. Rose,* 149 U.S.P.Q. 820 (S.D.N.Y.1966) (quoted in *Nimmer, supra,* § 15.01 at 15–6 n. 13). None of the cases recognize that there are divergent lines of cases on this point, and none of the cases endeavor to explain why one line of cases is more compelling than the other.

I am persuaded that under 17 U.S.C. § 506(a) "willfully" means that in order to be criminal the infringement must have been a "voluntary, intentional violation of a known legal duty." *Cheek,* 498 U.S. at ___, 111 S.Ct. at 610. I am so persuaded because I believe that in using the word "willful" Congress intended to soften the impact of the common-law presumption that ignorance of the law or mistake of the law is no defense to a criminal prosecution by making specific intent to violate the law an element of federal criminal copyright offenses. I came to this conclusion after examining the use of the word "willful" in the civil copyright infringement context and applying that use to the criminal statute. *Wise,*

550 F.2d at 1188 n. 14 (There is a general principle in copyright law of looking to civil authority for guidance in criminal cases).

In the civil context there is "strict liability" for infringement, even where the infringement was "innocent." *United States v. Bily,* 406 F.Supp. 726, 733 (E.D.Pa.1975) (comparing civil and criminal copyright law). In this connection, a plaintiff in a civil case need not prove actual damages, but rather may seek what are called statutory damages. The term "willful" is used in the context of statutory damages, and it is instructive to compare the definition of the term "willful," as used in the civil context regarding statutory damages, with the definition of the term "willful" used in the criminal context.

In the statutory damage context, a civil plaintiff is generally entitled to recover no less than $250.00 nor more than $10,000.00 per act of infringement. 17 U.S.C. § 504(c)(1). But where the infringement is committed "willfully," the court in its discretion may increase the award of statutory damages up to a maximum of $50,000.00 per act of infringement. 17 U.S.C. § 504(c)(2). On the other hand, in the case of "innocent infringement," if the defendant sustains the burden of proving he/she was not aware, and had no reason to believe, that his/her acts constituted an infringement of the copyright, and the court so finds, the court may in its discretion reduce the applicable minimum to $100.00 per act of infringement. 17 U.S.C. § 504(c)(2). *See* H.R.Rep. No. 1476, 94th Cong., 2d Sess. at 162–163, *reprinted in* 1976 U.S.Code Cong. & Admin.News 5659, 5778–79.

As noted text writers have concluded, the meaning of the term "willful," used in 17 U.S.C. § 504, must mean that the infringement was with knowledge that the defendant's conduct constituted copyright infringement. *Nimmer, supra* p. 6, § 14.04[B][3] at 14–40.3–14–40.4 (citations omitted). Otherwise, there would be no point in providing specially for the reduction of awards to the $100.00 level in the case of "innocent" infringement since any infringement which was nonwillful would necessarily be innocent.

The circuit courts of appeal which have considered the issue have all adopted *Nimmer's* formulation with regard to the meaning of the word "willful" for purposes of 17 U.S.C. § 504(c)(2) and statutory civil damages. *Cable/Home Communication v. Network Productions,* 902 F.2d 829, 851 (11th Cir.1990); *Broadcast Music, Inc. v. Xanthas, Inc.,* 855 F.2d 233, 236 (5th Cir.1988); *RCA/Ariola Int'l, Inc. v. Thomas & Grayston Co.,* 845 F.2d 773, 779 (8th Cir.1988); *Fitzgerald Publishing Co., Inc. v. Baylor Publishing Co., Inc.,* 807 F.2d 1110, 1115 (2d Cir.1986). In other words, the term "willful," when used in the civil statutory damage statute, has consistently been interpreted to mean that the infringement must be "with knowledge that the defendant's conduct constitutes copyright infringement." *Nimmer, supra* p. 6, § 14.04[B][3] at 14–40.3–14–40.4.

There is nothing in the text of the criminal copyright statute, the overall scheme of the copyright laws, or the legislative history to suggest that Congress intended the word "willful," when used in the criminal statute, to mean simply, as the government suggests, an intent to copy. Rather, since Congress used "willful" in the civil damage copyright context to mean that the infringement must take place with the defendant being knowledgeable that his/her conduct constituted copyright infringement, there is no compelling reason to adopt a less stringent requirement in the criminal copyright context. Accordingly, I find that "willfully," when used in 17 U.S.C. § 506(a), means a "voluntary, intentional violation of a known legal duty." *Cheek,* 498 U.S. at ___, 111 S.Ct. at 610.

B.

Having determined that the standard enunciated by the Supreme Court in *Cheek,* 498 U.S. 192, 111 S.Ct. 604, applies, it is important to recognize that the rule does not require that a defendant's belief that his conduct is lawful be judged by an objective standard. Rather, the test is whether Moran truly believed that the copyright laws did not prohibit him from making one copy of a video cassette he had purchased in order to "insure" against vandalism. In other words, the test is not whether Moran's view was objectively reasonable, but rather, whether Moran truly believed that the law did not proscribe his conduct. *Cheek,* 498 U.S. 192, 111 S.Ct. at ___. Of course, the more unreasonable the asserted belief or misunderstanding, the more likely it is that the finder of fact will consider the asserted belief or misunderstanding to be nothing more than simple disagreement with known legal duties imposed by the law, and will find that the government has carried its burden of proving knowledge. *Id.* at ___, 111 S.Ct. at ___.

Most of the government's argument that it proved beyond a reasonable doubt that Moran violated the criminal copyright statute, even if the word "willfully" is defined as Moran suggests, is based upon the assumption that Moran's beliefs must be "objectively" reasonable. As indicated above, Moran's beliefs need not have been objectively reasonable; rather, if Moran truly believed that he was not subject to the copyright laws, then his subjective belief would defeat a finding that he "willfully" violated the statute.

First, I note that I had an opportunity to observe Moran when he testified. Moran struck me as an honest, albeit naive, person. I was left with the definite impression that Moran was befuddled and bewildered by the criminal prosecution.

Second, although Moran is a local police officer of long standing, there is nothing in his background to suggest any particular sophistication about business matters, and there is no evidence to suggest that he has any particular knowledge about the intricacies of the copyright laws. When confronted by FBI agents upon the execution of the search warrant, Moran was entirely cooperative. On the day the search warrant was executed, he told his story in the same way he now tells his story.

Third, Moran said he had heard from others and read in various publications that it was legally appropriate to engage in the practice he called "insuring." Moran could not cite the specific source of his information. In this regard, I note that the copyright laws permit libraries and archives to replace a copyrighted article that is damaged, deteriorated, lost, or stolen, if the library or archives have, after reasonable effort, determined that an unused replacement cannot be obtained at a fair price. 17 U.S.C. § 108(c). While Moran obviously did not operate his business as a library or archives, the government's assertion that the practice of "insuring" is patently unreasonable is belied by the recognition that under certain circumstances certain users of copyrighted materials may lawfully engage in copying activity which is similar to Moran's conduct.

Fourth, Moran testified that he made only one copy of the original motion picture purchased from the authorized distributor. The government doubts his testimony, but offers no persuasive evidence to contradict it. Moreover, Moran testified that he never rented both the original copyrighted version of the video cassette purchased from the authorized distributor and the copy he made. Instead, he testified that he always held back the original motion picture. Once again, the government doubts this testimony in its brief, but offers no persuasive evidence to the contrary. Furthermore, the evidence indicates that Moran purchased more than one authorized cassette of a particular motion picture, but made only one duplicate for each authorized cassette purchased.

This evidence suggests that Moran was not acting with a willful intention to violate the copyright laws because if he had such an intention it would make absolutely no sense to purchase multiple authorized video cassettes and then make only one duplicate of each authorized cassette. It would have been far simpler, and certainly more lucrative, for Moran to purchase one authorized cassette of a particular motion picture and make multiple copies from the authorized version. In this way Moran would have had to pay only one fee. The fact that Moran seems to have consistently followed the practice of buying an authorized version, but making only one copy of it, suggests that he was acting in accordance with his belief that to duplicate an authorized version in order to "insure it" was lawful so long as only one copy was made and the authorized version and copy were not both rented.

Fifth, the government argues that Moran must have known that what he was doing constituted a copyright infringement because he had before him the FBI warning label and in fact affixed such labels to the unauthorized copies he made. In pertinent part, the FBI warning states, "Federal law provides severe civil and criminal penalties for the *unauthorized* reproduction, distribution or exhibition of copyrighted motion pictures and video tapes" (emphasis added). Moran explained that he thought these warning labels applied to the renting public, not to him. The use of the word "unauthorized" on the warning label suggested to Moran that vendors who had purchased an authorized version were not subject to the legal restrictions expressed in the warning to the extent that the practice of "insuring" was legal. As Moran suggests, the FBI warning label does not specifically address the claim of legality professed by Moran. Accordingly, Moran's failure to heed the warning label is not determinative.

Sixth, the government further argues that Moran's effort to place the unauthorized copy into a video cassette package displaying a label on its spine and an FBI warning label suggests a sinister motivation. I disagree. Moran's testimony, as I understood it, indicated that when he made a copy he endeavored to make the duplicate look like the original in all respects. After all, the whole purpose of the practice of "insuring" was to use the unauthorized copy in lieu of the original when renting to the public. It was perfectly consistent with Moran's view of the law to make the unauthorized copy look as nearly as possible like the authorized version.

In summary, when Moran's actions were viewed from the totality of the circumstances, the government failed to convince me beyond a reasonable doubt that Moran acted willfully. Moran is a long-time street cop who was fully cooperative with law enforcement authorities. He is obviously not sophisticated and, at least from the record, his business operation of renting movies to the public was not large or sophisticated. Rather, Moran's business appears to have been of the "mom-and-pop" variety. Moran's practice of "insuring," while obviously shifting the risk of loss from Moran to the copyright holder, was conducted in such a way as not to maximize profits, which one assumes would have been his purpose if he had acted willfully. For example, Moran purchased multiple authorized copies of the same movie, but he made only one unauthorized copy for each authorized version purchased. This suggests that Moran truly believed that what he was doing was in fact legal. I therefore find Moran not guilty.

IT IS ORDERED that the Clerk of the United States District Court for the District of Nebraska shall, pursuant to Federal Rule of Criminal Procedure 32(b)(1), enter judgment in favor of the defendant, Dennis Moran, and against the United States of America on the court's finding that the defendant is not guilty.

DISCUSSION QUESTIONS

1.   Does the term "willful" always require proof of knowledge of the law being violated? If not, why does the term require this proof when used in a copyright statute?

2.   As a matter of policy, why should the government have to prove that people know they are breaking the law in order to be guilty of criminal copyright violations? Why should copyright crimes require such a special mental state requirement?

3.   Now that you have read this case, are you easier to prosecute for criminal copyright violations? If so, why should those who are ignorant of the law have an advantage over you in defending themselves?

---

2.   Where the crime contains a mental state element that requires knowledge of some law other than the law defining the offense.

This exception is by far the most perplexing to students. The best example comes from an English case where an evicted tenant was prosecuted for vandalism for removing ceiling tiles from his apartment upon moving out. The vandalism statute required the defendant to knowingly damage the property of another. Since he had purchased and installed the ceiling tiles himself, the tenant had believed that the ceiling tiles belonged to him. Under English real property law, however, a tile attached to a wall or ceiling becomes part of the structure. Since the defendant did not know that the ceiling tiles were the property of the landlord according to the rules of real property law, the court found that he did not have the mental state required for the crime.

Note that the law of which the defendant was ignorant was real property law, not the law defining vandalism. If the defendant had argued that he did not know it was against the law for a tenant to damage the property of the landlord, he would have had no defense. Note, too, that the crime he was charged with required knowledge of the circumstance that was defined by real property law. If the statute had prohibited damaging the property of another regardless of whether you knew it was not your property, then the defendant would also have had no defense.

Case in Context

How do you reconcile this next decision with *Marerro*?

PEOPLE V. BRAY

Court of Appeal, Fourth District, Division 1, California
124 Cal. Rptr. 913 (1975)

James Eugene Bray appeals the judgment following his jury conviction on two counts of being a felon in possession of a concealable firearm.

Bray's meritorious contention is the trial court should have instructed the jury that ignorance or mistake of fact is a defense to the crime.

In 1969 Bray pled guilty in Kansas to being an accessory after the fact (Kansas Statutes Ann. 21–106). At sentencing, the Kansas prosecutor recommended Bray be granted probation because he had no previous criminal record, he had been unwilling to participate in the crime but had gotten involved by driving a friend away from the scene and he had cooperated fully with the district attorney's office. Bray was placed on two years summary probation which he successfully completed before moving to California in 1971. While in California Bray first worked at Convair Aircraft and later was employed by the County of San Diego in the Department of Public Health. Near the end of 1973 he transferred to the district attorney's office.

In January 1972, Bray filled out an application to vote in the State of California. He discussed the problems he had had in Kansas with the deputy of the registrar of voters and asked if he would be allowed to vote. The deputy could not answer the question and suggested he say on the registration form he had been convicted of a felony and fill out a supplementary explanatory form to find out if he, in fact, had committed a felony. This Bray did; he was allowed to vote.

In early July of 1973, Bray applied for a part-time job as a guard with ADT Sterling Security Company. On the application he answered he had been arrested or charged with a crime but had not been convicted of a felony. At the bottom of the page Bray explained the circumstances surrounding his arrest and period of probation. In September he received a notice from the Bureau of Collection and Investigative Services that he had been registered as a guard or patrolman.

Later in July of 1973 Bray bought a .38 caliber revolver from a pawn shop, Western Jewelry and Loan Company, to use in guard assignments requiring an armed patrolman. On one of the required forms he said he had not been convicted of a felony; on another he said he had not been convicted of a crime with a punishment of more than one year. After the statutory five-day waiting period, the gun was delivered to him.

On September 14, 1973, Bray filled out an application for a job as a contract compliance investigator. In response to the question asking whether he had been convicted of a felony or misdemeanor, Bray answered with a "?". He again explained the circumstances surrounding his arrest and the sentence he received.

On November 16, 1973, and April 12, 1974, Bray filled out job applications for positions as an audio-visual technician and as an eligibility worker. . .In each instance he answered he had been convicted of a "felony or misdemeanor;" in each instance he explained his Kansas arrest and sentence.

In July of 1974, two investigators from the district attorney's office conducted a search with a warrant of Bray's house and car. Bray voluntarily led the investigators to a closet where he kept the .38 and a .22 pistol.

In order to gain a conviction under section 12021, the prosecutor must prove: (1) conviction of a felony and (2) ownership, possession, custody or control of a firearm capable of being concealed on the person (People v. Neese, 272 Cal.App.2d 235, 245 77 Cal.Rptr. 314). There was no question here Bray had been in possession of a concealable firearm; there was no question he had been convicted of the crime, "accessory after the fact" in Kansas. Bray says there must be proof he knew he was a felon. Or, in the alternative, he says mistake of fact is a defense and the court erred in denying this requested instruction.

It appears to be a question of first impression whether Penal Code section 12021 requires proof of the defendant's knowledge of his or her felony status, and whether such a prosecution may be defended by showing the defendant lacked knowledge he was a felon. The prevailing trend of decisions is to avoid constructions of penal statutes which would impose strict liability (see People v. Hernandez, 61 Cal.2d 529 39 Cal.Rptr. 361, 393 P.2d 673, 8 A.L.R.3d 1092 statutory rape; People v. Vogel, 46 Cal.2d 798 299 P.2d 850 bigamy; People v. Winston, 46 Cal.2d 151 293 P.2d 40 marijuana possession; People v. Stuart, 47 Cal.2d 167 302 P.2d 5, 55 A.L.R.2d 705 pharmacist misfilling prescriptions). The Attorney General agrees the statute should not be one of strict liability but then says it is not necessary for the People to prove the defendant had knowledge.

In considering the role of knowledge, whether the defendant knew he had committed an offense is irrelevant (People v. Autterson, 261 Cal.App.2d 627, 632 68 Cal.Rptr. 113; People v. Daniels, 118 Cal.App.2d 340, 343 257 P.2d 1038). The question here is whether the defendant must know of the existence of those facts which bring him within the statute's proscription. Even though section 12021 does not explicitly require knowledge, the defendant must know he has possession of a concealable weapon (People v. Burch, 196 Cal.App.2d 754, 771 17 Cal.Rptr. 102). In addition, as to whether a defendant must know he is an alien under section 12021, this court, in dictum, has said:

"Knowledge that one is in the State of California might conceivably be relevant in the case of a person who unwittingly had overstepped the boundary of a neighboring state, who might have been carried into the state against his will, or as the result of mistake in taking some vehicle of public transportation."

"In the present case, defendant knew he was no longer in Mexico." (People v. Mendoza, 251 Cal.App.2d 835, 843 60 Cal.Rptr. 5.)

Likewise, knowledge that one is a felon becomes relevant where there is doubt the defendant knew he had committed a felony. Here, even the prosecution had substantial difficulty in determining whether the offense was considered a felony in Kansas. In arguing to the court the necessity of a Kansas attorney's expert testimony, the district attorney said, ". . . in even our own jurisdiction, let alone a foreign jurisdiction such as the State of Kansas, it's extremely difficult to determine whether a sentence was a felony or a misdemeanor." Although the district attorney had great difficulty in determining whether the Kansas offense was a felony or a misdemeanor, he expects the layman Bray to know its status easily. There was no doubt Bray knew he had committed an offense; there was, however, evidence to the effect he did not know the offense was a felony. Without this knowledge Bray would be ignorant of the facts necessary for him to come within the proscription of section 12021 (People v. Winston, supra, 46 Cal.2d 151, 158). Under these circumstances the requested instructions on mistake or ignorance of fact and knowledge of the facts which make the act unlawful should have been given.

DISCUSSION QUESTIONS

1.   Is this a mistake of fact case or a mistake of law case?

2.   Bray did not think he was a felon, and Marrero thought he was a peace officer within the meaning of the New York statute regulating the carrying of concealed weapons. Why does Bray's mistake afford him a defense but not Marrero's?

3.   Does Bray's mistake about his felon status have to be a reasonable one?

---

3.   Where the legislature creates by statute a limited "reliance" defense on some legal authority other than the statute itself a mistake of law resulting from such reliance is a defense.

Both the Model Penal Code and many common law jurisdictions have created by statute—or sometimes by common law presumption—a limited defense of reasonable reliance on some official interpretation of the criminal statute in question. Such provisions usually recognize three types of legal authority upon which the defendant may reasonably rely.

- A statute later found to be invalid or unconstitutional. Imagine that the legislature exempts certain types of behavior from the reach of a criminal statute, but the legislation is later struck down as unconstitutional. A defendant who relies upon this exemption after the legislature passes the statute and before it is found unconstitutional is legally excused from liability by virtue of his reasonable belief that his conduct was lawful.

- A judicial interpretation of a statute later found to be erroneous. Similarly, in a published opinion, a judge might interpret a statute as allowing a particular type of conduct, but that interpretation might later be overruled by a higher court. If, during the period of time between the publication of the opinion and its overruling, the defendant is prosecuted for that same conduct, he has a defense based on his reasonable reliance.

At first glance, it might strike you as odd that you can only reasonably rely on statutes or judicial decisions that later turn out to be invalid or erroneous. If the statute or judicial decision that you relied on was not erroneous, however, you would not need a mistake of law defense at all. You would simply be not guilty because your understanding of the law was the correct one!

- An official interpretation by an agency or official charged with enforcing the law. Sometimes, law enforcement or regulatory agencies will issue official interpretations of a criminal statute, regulation, or ordinance. If a defendant who relies on such an interpretation is arrested and prosecuted, he too may claim reasonable reliance.

This last exception is an easy one to misinterpret. You cannot rely on an oral or written statement by a police officer on the street, for example, because the interpretation of any one officer is not considered to be an official one. An interpretation by the local district attorney would also not be sufficient. Otherwise, police and prosecutors would essentially be able to usurp the role of the legislature in defining crimes and the role of the courts in interpreting them. Usually, the interpretation must come from the state's Attorney General's office in an official opinion.

It must also be stressed that the official statement must be an interpretation of the law, not a promise not to enforce it. One who relies on the promise of a law enforcement officer or a prosecutor that they will not be prosecuted for violating the criminal law does so at their own peril in all but a very few cases. Moreover, one cannot rely on the opinion of one's own attorney as part of this defense. Otherwise, private attorneys could effectively insulate their clients from criminal prosecution by giving "bad" legal advice.

DISCUSSION QUESTIONS

1.   Why does this reliance defense only apply to official statements of the law later found to be erroneous?

2.   Is it fair that you cannot rely on advice under this defense from police officers or prosecutors about what is legal?

3.   Is it fair that you cannot rely on advice from a lawyer under this defense about what is legal?

G. MODEL PENAL CODE

The Model Penal Code largely tracks the common law's approach to mistake of fact and mistake of law. In addition, the MPC provides that if a mistaken belief would make the defendant guilty of an offense had circumstances been as the defendant believed, then the defendant can be punished for that other offense as long as it is a lesser offense. For example, if a defendant burglarized a store without realizing that it was also a residence, then the defendant would be punished for the lesser crime of commercial burglary. If, on the other hand, he broke into a store believing it to be a home, he would not be prosecuted for the greater crime of residential burglary under the MPC. Some common law jurisdictions, however, apply a "legal-wrong" doctrine that would find the defendant guilty of whatever offense he thought he was committing, whether it is greater or lesser.

§ 2.04. Ignorance or Mistake

1)   Ignorance or mistake as to a matter of fact or law is a defense if:

     a)   the ignorance or mistake negatives the purpose, knowledge, belief, recklessness or negligence required to establish a material element of the offense; or

     b)   the law provides that the state of mind established by such ignorance or mistake constitutes a defense.

2)   Although ignorance or mistake would otherwise afford a defense to the offense charged, the defense is not available if the defendant would be guilty of another offense had the situation been as he supposed. In such case, however, the ignorance or mistake of the defendant shall reduce the grade and degree of the offense of which he may be convicted to those of the offense of which he would be guilty had the situation been as he supposed.

3)   A belief that conduct does not legally constitute an offense is a defense to a prosecution for that offense based upon such conduct when:

     a)   the statute or other enactment defining the offense is not known to the actor and has not been published or otherwise reasonably made available prior to the conduct alleged; or

     b)   he acts in reasonable reliance upon an official statement of the law, afterward determined to be invalid or erroneous, contained in (i) a statute or other enactment; (ii) a judicial decision, opinion or judgment; (iii) an administrative order or grant of permission; or (iv) an official interpretation of the public officer or body charged by law with responsibility for the interpretation, administration or enforcement of the law defining the offense.

4)   The defendant must prove a defense arising under Subsection (3) of this Section by a preponderance of evidence.

Practice Problem 7.2: Monumental Mistakes

Silas and Sam are an elderly couple who have decided to hold a vigil protesting the presence of a statue in the town square of a notorious white supremacist who was one of their town's founding fathers. Because the statue has been defaced during a series of protests the town council passed an ordinance making it a crime to come within twenty-five feet of the statue. Copies of the ordinance are posted all around the square. Silas and Sam arrive at the square with blankets and a protest sign. They tell the officer guarding the statue that they plan to maintain a vigil until the town council orders the statue to be removed. There is a bench fifteen feet in front of the statue, and they ask the officer if they could sit on the bench during their vigil. The officer tells them that that would be fine. She even gives them a copy of her official business card, writes "fine where they are," on the back, and signs her name. A series of different police officers guard the statue over the next twenty-four hours. On day two of Silas and Sam's vigil a different police officer approaches them and tells them to move away from the statue. Silas and Sam refuse to move and are arrested. Discuss their criminal liability for violating the ordinance. (Assume that the ordinance is constitutional.)

CHAPTER 8

INTOXICATION

■ ■ ■

Should intoxication matter to criminal liability? Intoxication has a large role in crime but only a tiny role in the substantive criminal law. It plays a large role in crime because many people commit crimes while intoxicated. Perhaps because intoxicating drugs and alcohol play such a big role in crime, society wants to deter people from becoming intoxicated enough to commit crimes. Society also considers such people blameworthy for getting so intoxicated that they broke the law.

Since the criminal law generally treats intoxicated people as if they were sober, learning the doctrine of intoxication means learning a series of exceptions to this general rule.

A. OVERVIEW

Intoxication can pop up all over the place: voluntary act doctrine, insanity, premeditation, and deliberation for first degree murder, provocation under voluntary manslaughter, and mental states, generally. Among these topics, the most important rule to learn is when and how intoxication is relevant to whether a person had the mental state required for a crime.

The general rule on this point can be stated two different ways, although they essentially mean the same thing.

- *Voluntary intoxication may negate a mental state of purpose or knowledge but not a mental state of criminal recklessness or negligence.*

- *Voluntary intoxication may negate a specific intent but not a general intent to commit a crime.*

There are three important things to note about these two simple rules.

First, they mean essentially the same thing. Generally speaking, specific intent crimes require a purposeful or knowing mental state, whereas general intent crimes usually require a reckless or negligent mental state. So, saying that voluntary intoxication may only negate a specific intent and that it may only negate a purposeful or knowing mental state is basically saying the same thing.

Second, notice that I slipped in the word voluntary before the word intoxication when I stated the rules. We will discuss the difference between voluntary and involuntary intoxication in more detail, but the basic idea is that if you get intoxicated against your will, or through no fault of your own, then you have more possible defenses than these rules describe.

Third, the use of the awkward phrase "negate the capacity" further limits the role that intoxication plays in criminal liability. Alcohol, and many other intoxicating drugs, loosens one's inhibitions in a way that leads to various crimes. This sort of inhibition-loosening effect does not come within the mental state defense these rules describe. Rather, you must be so intoxicated that you are no longer able to form the intent or other mental state required for the crime. Think "really drunk," not just "tipsy." You don't have to be falling down drunk, but you must be way beyond "feeling a buzz."

Apply these rules to a student drinking tequila in the front row of my criminal law classroom. Assume that she was really intoxicated, and that she punched someone in the face, breaking their nose. What is her liability with respect to the general intent offense of simple battery? What is her liability with respect to the charge of assault with intent to inflict serious injury?[1]

B. INTOXICATION AS A GENERAL MENTAL STATE DEFENSE

Let's explore in more depth the majority rule that voluntary intoxication may only negate a purposeful or knowing (specific intent) state of mind. As discussed, this effectively means that, for general intent crimes, the defendant is held to the standard of a sober person when evaluating his mental state. That sounds reasonable from society's point of view because society considers it blameworthy and dangerous to get so intoxicated that you commit crimes. From the defendant's perspective, though, it is completely unreasonable because it often forces the jury to pretend that the defendant was sober.

Let's assume that our tequila-drinking student did not punch her classmate. Rather, imagine that, frustrated by the slowness with which her classmate was moving out of her way (and feeling a rather sudden and uncomfortable need to get to the nearest bathroom), the tequila-drinking student started angrily flailing her arms around and yelling, "Move, move, move." When her puzzled classmate turned around to see what all the fuss was about, she was struck square in the nose by one of the flailing arms.

If this jurisdiction defines battery as including a harmful or offensive touching committed with criminal negligence, then a guilty verdict seems

---

[1] **Answer:** She is out of luck with respect to simple battery because voluntary intoxication may not negate a general intent to commit a crime. Her voluntary intoxication could be a defense, however, to assault with intent to inflict serious injury, which requires specific intent. It is possible that she could have been intoxicated to the point that she was unable to form a specific intent.

fair. Arguably, it was grossly negligent of the tequila-drinker to flail her arms so forcefully and so carelessly in such close proximity to another person. More to the point, it seems intuitively right to most people that being intoxicated should not be a defense to crimes of criminal negligence. Do we want to hold our tequila-drinking student to the standard of care of a reasonable sober person or a reasonable intoxicated person? Putting aside the contradictions implicit in the idea of a "reasonable intoxicated" person, most people accept the idea that part of being reasonable is not getting so intoxicated that you act unreasonably. To put it in more analytical terms, since negligence involves measuring the person's mental state against an objective standard of reasonableness, then it makes sense that we don't allow the jury to take into consideration the defendant's subjective condition of intoxication.

Things change when it comes to recklessness, however. Recklessness is a more culpable mental state usually reserved for more serious crimes. Imagine now that the more serious assault or battery crime with which the tequila-drinking student is charged requires a reckless state of mind. Recklessness requires both a subjective and an objective component. The objective component is that you must disregard a substantial and unjustifiable risk under circumstances that constitute a gross deviation from a reasonable standard of care. The subjective component is that you must consciously disregard this risk. That means that you must have been aware of the risk for at least a moment.

So, to be found guilty of this reckless assault/battery charge, the tequila-drinking law student must have been consciously aware, for at least a moment as she flailed her arms, that she might strike someone inadvertently. This mental state definition requires us to peer inside the brain of the defendant and ask subjectively what she was actually thinking at the moment she committed the prohibited conduct. Once you peer inside the defendant's brain, it is impossible not to notice her intoxication. She might have been too intoxicated to be aware of the risks of her flailing arms. Yet the majority rule does not allow evidence of voluntary intoxication to negate a reckless mental state.

So, the majority rule in effect requires juries to pretend that the defendant is sober when asking whether the defendant was subjectively aware of the risk involved. Most scholars use a fancier word than pretend, of course. They say that the majority rule imputes to the intoxicated defendant a capacity to be conscious of the required risk. It is important to note that on this point the Model Penal Code follows the majority rule.

M.P.C. § 2.08. INTOXICATION

1) Except as provided in Subsection (4) of this Section, intoxication of the actor is not a defense unless it negatives an element of the offense.

2) When recklessness establishes an element of the offense, if the actor, due to self-induced intoxication, is unaware of a risk of which he would have been aware had he been sober, such unawareness is immaterial.

3) Intoxication does not, in itself, constitute mental disease within the meaning of Section 4.01.

4) Intoxication that (a) is not self-induced or (b) is pathological is an affirmative defense if by reason of such intoxication the actor at the time of his conduct lacks substantial capacity either to appreciate its criminality wrongfulness or to conform his conduct to the requirements of law.

5) Definitions. In this Section unless a different meaning plainly is required:

    a) "intoxication" means a disturbance of mental or physical capacities resulting from the introduction of substances into the body;

    b) "self-induced intoxication" means intoxication caused by substances that the actor knowingly introduces into his body, the tendency of which to cause intoxication he knows or ought to know, unless he introduces them pursuant to medical advice or under such circumstances as would afford a defense to a charge of crime;

    c) "pathological intoxication" means intoxication grossly excessive in degree, given the amount of the intoxicant, to which the actor does not know he is susceptible.

Case in Context

How drunk does one have to be to trigger an intoxication defense?

STATE V. CAMERON
Supreme Court of New Jersey
514 A.2d 1302 (1986)

This appeal presents a narrow, but important, issue concerning the role that a defendant's voluntary intoxication plays in a criminal prosecution. The specific question is whether the evidence was sufficient to require the trial court to charge the jury on defendant's intoxication, as defendant requested. The Appellate Division reversed defendant's convictions, holding that it was error not to have given an intoxication charge. We. . .now reverse.

Defendant, Michele Cameron, age 22 at the time of trial, was indicted for second degree aggravated assault, in violation of N.J.S.A. 2C:12–1(b)(1); possession of a weapon, a broken bottle, with a purpose to use it unlawfully, contrary to N.J.S.A. 2C:39–4(d); and fourth degree resisting arrest, a violation of N.J.S.A. 2C:29–2. A jury convicted defendant of all charges. . .The charges arose out of an incident of June 6, 1981, on a vacant lot in Trenton. The unreported opinion of the Appellate Division depicts the following tableau of significant events:

The victim, Joseph McKinney, was playing cards with four other men. Defendant approached and disrupted the game with her conduct. The participants moved their card table to a new location within the lot. Defendant followed them, however, and overturned the table. The table was righted and the game resumed. Shortly thereafter, defendant attacked McKinney with a broken bottle. As a result of that attack he sustained an injury to his hand, which necessitated 36 stitches and caused permanent injury.

Defendant reacted with violence to the arrival of the police. She threw a bottle at their vehicle, shouted obscenities, and tried to fight them off. She had to be restrained and handcuffed in the police wagon.

The heart of the Appellate Division's reversal of defendant's conviction is found in its determination that voluntary intoxication is a defense when it negates an essential element of the offense—here, purposeful conduct. We agree with that proposition. Likewise are we in accord with the determinations of the court below that all three of the charges of which this defendant convicted—aggravated assault, the possession offense, and resisting arrest—have purposeful conduct as an element of the offense; and that a person acts purposely "with respect to the nature of his conduct or a result thereof if it is his conscious object to engage in conduct of that nature or to cause such a result" (quoting N.J.S.A. 2C:2–2(b)(1)). We part company with the Appellate Division, however, in its conclusion that the circumstances disclosed by the evidence in this case required that the issue of defendant's intoxication be submitted to the jury. . .

Under the common law intoxication was not a defense to a criminal charge. . .Notwithstanding the general proposition that voluntary intoxication is no defense, the early cases nevertheless held that in some circumstances intoxication could be resorted to for defensive purposes—specifically, to show the absence of a specific intent.

The principle that developed from the foregoing approach—that intoxication formed the basis for a defense to a "specific intent" crime but not to one involving only "general" intent—persisted for about three-quarters of a century. . .But eventually the problems inherent in the application of the specific-general intent dichotomy surfaced.

Which brings us to the Code. N.J.S.A 2C:2–8 provided:

a.   Except as provided in subsection d. of this section, intoxication of the actor is not a defense unless it negatives an element of the offense.

b. When recklessness establishes an element of the offense, if the actor, due to self-induced intoxication, is unaware of a risk of which he would have been aware had he been sober, such unawareness is immaterial.

c. Intoxication does not, in itself, constitute mental disease within the meaning of chapter 4.

d. Intoxication which (1) is not self-induced or (2) is pathological is an affirmative defense if by reason of such intoxication the actor at the time of his conduct lacks substantial and adequate capacity either to appreciate its wrongfulness or to conform his conduct to the requirement of law.

As is readily apparent, self-induced intoxication is not a defense unless it negatives an element of the offense. Code Commentary at 67–68. Under the common-law intoxication defense, as construed by the Commission, intoxication could either exculpate or mitigate guilt "if the defendant's intoxication, in fact, prevents his having formed a mental state which is an element of the offense and if the law will recognize the proof of the lack of that mental state." Id. at 68. Thus, the Commission recognized that under pre-Code law, intoxication was admissible as a defense to a "specific" intent, but not a "general" intent, crime.

The original proposed Code rejected the specific/general intent distinction, choosing to rely instead on the reference to the four states of culpability for offenses under the Code: negligent, reckless, knowing, and purposeful conduct, N.J.S.A. 2C:2–2(b). Although the Code employs terminology that differs from that used to articulate the common-law principles referable to intoxication, the Commission concluded that the ultimately-enacted statutory intoxication defense would achieve the same result as that reached under the common law. In essence, "that which the cases now describe as a 'specific intent' can be equated, for this purpose, with that which the Code defines as 'purpose' and 'knowledge.' See § 2C:2–2b. A 'general intent' can be equated with that which the Code defines as 'recklessness,' or criminal 'negligence.'" Code Commentary at 68. Therefore, according to the Commissioners, N.J.S.A. 2C:2–8(a) and (b) would serve much the same end as was achieved by the common-law approach. Specifically, HN2 N.J.S.A. 2C:2–8(a) permits evidence of intoxication as a defense to crimes requiring either "purposeful" or "knowing" mental states but it excludes evidence of intoxication as a defense to crimes requiring mental states of only recklessness or negligence. The drafters of the MPC, as did the New Jersey Commission, criticized the specific-general intent distinction.

The policy reasons for requiring purpose or knowledge as a requisite element of some crimes are that in the absence of those states of mind, the criminal conduct would not present a comparable danger, or the actor would not pose as significant a threat. Id. at 357–58. Moreover, the ends of legal policy are better served by subjecting to graver sanctions those who consciously defy legal norms. Ibid. It was those policy reasons that dictated the result that the intoxication defense should be available when it negatives purpose or knowledge. The drafters concluded: "If the mental state which is the basis of the law's concern does not exist, the reason for its non-existence is quite plainly immaterial." Id. at 358.

Thus, when the requisite culpability for a crime is that the person act "purposely" or "knowingly," evidence of voluntary intoxication is admissible to disprove that requisite mental state. . .

The foregoing discussion establishes that proof of voluntary intoxication would negate the culpability elements in the offenses of which this defendant was convicted. The charges—aggravated assault, possession of a weapon with a purpose to use it unlawfully, and resisting arrest—all require purposeful conduct (aggravated assault uses "purposely" or "knowingly" in the alternative). The question is what level of intoxication must be demonstrated before a trial court is required to submit the issue to a jury. What quantum of proof is required?

It is not the case that every defendant who has had a few drinks may successfully urge the defense. The mere intake of even large quantities of alcohol will not suffice. Moreover, the defense cannot be established solely by showing that the defendant might not have committed the offense had he been sober. See Final Report of the New Jersey Criminal Law Revision Commission, Vol. II, Commentary (1971) at 68. What is required is a showing of such a great prostration of the faculties that the requisite mental state was totally lacking. That is, to successfully invoke the defense, an accused must show that he was so intoxicated that he did not have the intent to commit an offense. Such a state of affairs will likely exist in very few cases.

78 N.J. at 495 (PASHMAN, J., concurring and dissenting).

Measured by the foregoing standard and evidence relevant thereto, it is apparent that the record in this case is insufficient to have required the trial court to grant defendant's request to charge intoxication. . .

True, the victim testified that defendant was drunk, and defendant herself said she felt "pretty intoxicated," "pretty bad," and "very intoxicated." But these are no more than conclusory labels, of little assistance in determining whether any drinking produced a prostration of faculties.

More to the point is the fact that defendant carried a quart of wine, that she was drinking (we are not told over what period of time) with other people on the vacant lot, that about a pint of the wine was consumed, and that defendant did not drink this alone but rather "gave most of it out, gave some of it out." Defendant's conduct was violent, abusive, and threatening. But with it all there is not the slightest suggestion that she did not know what she was doing or that her faculties were so beclouded by the wine that she was incapable of engaging in purposeful conduct. That the purpose of the conduct may have been bizarre, even violent, is not the test. The critical question is whether defendant was capable of forming that bizarre or violent purpose, and we do not find sufficient evidence to permit a jury to say she was not.

Defendant's own testimony, if believed, would furnish a basis for her actions. She said she acted in self-defense, to ward off a sexual attack by McKinney and others. She recited the details of that attack and of her reaction to it with full recall and in explicit detail, explaining that her abuse of the police officers was sparked by her being upset by their unfairness in locking her up rather than apprehending McKinney.

Ordinarily, of course, the question of whether a defendant's asserted intoxication satisfies the standards enunciated in this opinion should be resolved by the jury. But here, viewing the evidence and the legitimate inferences to be drawn therefrom in the light most favorable to defendant. . . there is no suggestion. . .that defendant's faculties were so prostrated by her consumption of something less than a pint of wine as to render her incapable of purposeful or knowing conduct. The trial court correctly refused defendant's request. . .

DISCUSSION QUESTIONS

1.   Why did the court refuse to even allow a jury instruction on intoxication for a defendant who was obviously acting under the influence of alcohol?

2.   Why does the law require that one's intoxication negate one's very capacity to form the required mental state? Why isn't it enough that the intoxication affected one's behavior or impaired one's judgment?

3.   Specific intent offense such as the felonious assault in this case are usually more serious crimes than general intent offenses such as her simple assault on the police officers who arrested her. Why do we allow intoxication to serve as a defense to more serious crimes?

C. MINORITY RULES

There are not one but two minority positions that need to be mentioned: one takes a more generous approach to intoxication than the majority approach, and one takes a less generous approach than the majority.

1.   A small number of jurisdictions allow evidence of intoxication to negate recklessness.

2.   A few jurisdictions do not allow evidence of voluntary intoxication to negate any mental state including purpose or knowledge.

Case in Context

The following case from the U.S. Supreme Court discusses the constitutionality of this second minority rule.

MONTANA V. EGELHOFF
Supreme Court of the United States
518 U.S. 37 (1996)

Opinion

JUSTICE SCALIA.

[1A] We consider in this case whether the Due Process Clause is violated by Montana Code Annotated § 45–2–203, which provides, in relevant part, that voluntary intoxication "may not be taken into consideration in determining the existence of a mental state which is an element of a criminal offense."

I

In July 1992, while camping out in the Yaak region of northwestern Montana to pick mushrooms, respondent made friends with Roberta Pavola and John Christenson, who were doing the same. On Sunday, July 12, the three sold the mushrooms they had collected and spent the rest of the day and evening drinking, in bars and at a private party in Troy, Montana. Some time after 9 p.m., they left the party in Christenson's 1974 Ford Galaxy station wagon. The drinking binge apparently continued, as respondent was seen buying beer at 9:20 p.m. and recalled "sitting on a hill or a bank passing a bottle of Black Velvet back and forth" with Christenson. 272 Mont. 114, 118 (1995).

At about midnight that night, officers of the Lincoln County, Montana, sheriff's department, responding to reports of a possible drunk driver, discovered Christenson's station wagon stuck in a ditch along U.S. Highway 2. In the front seat were Pavola and Christenson, each dead from a single gunshot to the head. In the rear of the car lay respondent, alive and yelling obscenities. His blood-alcohol content measured .36 percent over one hour later. On the floor of the car, near the brake pedal, lay respondent's .38 caliber handgun, with four loaded rounds and two empty casings; respondent had gunshot residue on his hands.

Respondent was charged with two counts of deliberate homicide, a crime defined by Montana law as "purposely" or "knowingly" causing the death of another human being. Mont. Code Ann. § 45–5–102 (1995). A portion of the jury charge, uncontested here, instructed that "a person acts purposely when it is his conscious object to engage in conduct of that nature or to cause such a result," and that "a person acts knowingly when he is aware of his conduct or when he is aware under the circumstances his conduct constitutes a crime; or, when he is aware there exists the high probability that his conduct will cause a specific result." Respondent's defense at trial was that an unidentified fourth person must have committed the murders; his own extreme intoxication, he claimed, had rendered him physically incapable of committing the murders, and accounted for his inability to recall the events of the night of July 12. Although respondent was allowed to make this use of the evidence that he was intoxicated, the jury was instructed, pursuant to Mont. Code Ann. § 45–2–203 (1995), that it could not consider respondent's "intoxicated condition . . . in determining the existence of a mental state which is an element of the offense." The jury found respondent guilty on both counts, and the court sentenced him to 84 years' imprisonment.

The Supreme Court of Montana reversed. It reasoned (1) that respondent "had a due process right to present and have considered by the jury all relevant evidence to rebut the State's evidence on all elements of the offense charged," 272 Mont., at 125, and (2) that evidence of respondent's voluntary intoxication was "clearly . . . relevant to the issue of whether respondent acted knowingly and purposely," id., at 122. We granted certiorari.

II

The cornerstone of the Montana Supreme Court's judgment was the proposition that the Due Process Clause guarantees a defendant the right to present and have considered by the jury "all relevant evidence to rebut the State's evidence on all elements of the offense charged." 272 Mont., at 125 (emphasis added). Respondent does not defend this categorical rule; he acknowledges that the right to present relevant evidence "has not been viewed as absolute." As we have said: "The accused does not have an unfettered right to offer evidence that is incompetent, privileged, or otherwise inadmissible under standard rules of evidence." Taylor v. Illinois, 484 U.S. 400, 410 (1988).

Of course, to say that the right to introduce relevant evidence is not absolute is not to say that the Due Process Clause places no limits upon restriction of that right. Respondent's task, then, is to establish that a defendant's right to have a jury consider evidence of his voluntary intoxication in determining whether he possesses the requisite mental state is a "fundamental principle of justice."

Our primary guide in determining whether the principle in question is fundamental is, of course, historical practice. According to Blackstone and Coke, the law's condemnation of those suffering from dementia affectata was harsher still: Blackstone, citing Coke, explained that the law viewed intoxication "as an aggravation of the offence, rather than as an excuse for any criminal behavior." 4 W. Blackstone, Commentaries * 25–26. This stern rejection of inebriation as a defense became a fixture of early American law as well.

Justice Story rejected an objection to the exclusion of evidence of intoxication as follows:

"This is the first time, that I ever remember it to have been contended, that the commission of one crime was an excuse for another. Drunkenness is a gross vice, and in the contemplation of some of our laws is a crime; and I learned in my earlier studies, that so far from its being in law an excuse for murder, it is rather an aggravation of its malignity." United States v. Cornell, 25 F. Cas. 650, 657–658 (No. 14,868) (CC R. I. 1820).

The historical record does not leave room for the view that the common law's rejection of intoxication as an "excuse" or "justification" for crime would nonetheless permit the defendant to show that intoxication prevented the requisite mens rea. Hale's statement that a drunken offender shall have the same judgment "as if he were in his right senses" must be understood as precluding a defendant from arguing that, because of his intoxication, he could not have possessed the mens rea required to commit the crime.

The best argument available to respondent is the one made by his amicus and conceded by the State: Over the course of the 19th century, courts carved out an exception to the common law's traditional across-the-board condemnation of the drunken offender, allowing a jury to consider a defendant's intoxication when assessing whether he possessed the mental state needed to commit the crime charged, where the crime was one requiring a "specific intent." Eventually, however, the new view won out, and by the end of the 19th century, in most American jurisdictions, intoxication could be considered in determining whether a defendant was capable of forming the specific intent necessary to commit the crime charged. See Hall, supra, at 1049; Hopt v. People, 104 U.S. 631, 633–634 (1882) (citing cases).

On the basis of this historical record, respondent's amicus argues that "the old common-law rule . . . was no longer deeply rooted at the time the Fourteenth Amendment was ratified." It is not the State which bears the burden of demonstrating that its rule is "deeply rooted," but rather respondent who must show that the principle of procedure violated by the rule (and allegedly required by due process) is " 'so rooted in the traditions and conscience of our people as to be ranked as fundamental.' " Patterson v. New York, 432 U.S. at 202. Thus, even assuming that when the Fourteenth Amendment was adopted the rule Montana now defends was no longer generally applied. The burden remains upon respondent to show that the "new common-law" rule—that intoxication may be considered on the question of intent—was so deeply rooted at the time of the Fourteenth Amendment (or perhaps has become so deeply rooted since) as to be a fundamental principle which that Amendment enshrined.

That showing has not been made. Instead of the uniform and continuing acceptance we would expect for a rule that enjoys "fundamental principle" status, we find that fully one-fifth of the States either never adopted the "new common-law" rule at issue here or have recently abandoned it. It is not surprising that many States have held fast to or resurrected the common-law rule prohibiting consideration of voluntary intoxication in the determination of mens rea, because that rule has considerable justification—which alone casts doubt upon the proposition that the opposite rule is a "fundamental principle." A large number of crimes, especially violent crimes, are committed by intoxicated offenders; modern studies put the numbers as high as half of all homicides, for example. Disallowing consideration of voluntary intoxication has the effect of increasing the punishment for all unlawful acts committed in that state, and thereby deters drunkenness or irresponsible behavior while drunk. The rule also serves as a specific deterrent, ensuring that those who prove incapable of controlling violent impulses while voluntarily intoxicated go to prison. And finally, the rule comports with and implements society's moral perception that one who has voluntarily impaired his own faculties should be responsible for the consequences.

In sum, not every widespread experiment with a procedural rule favorable to criminal defendants establishes a fundamental principle of justice. Although the rule allowing a jury to consider evidence of a defendant's voluntary intoxication where relevant to mens rea has gained considerable acceptance, it is of too recent vintage, and has not received sufficiently uniform and permanent allegiance, to qualify as fundamental, especially since it displaces a lengthy common law tradition which remains supported by valid justifications today.

III

"The doctrines of actus reus, mens rea, insanity, mistake, justification, and duress have historically provided the tools for a constantly shifting adjustment of the tension between the evolving aims of the criminal law and changing religious, moral, philosophical, and medical views of the nature of man. This process of adjustment has always been thought to be the province of the States." Powell v. Texas, 392 U.S. 514, 535–536 (1968) (plurality opinion). The people of Montana have decided to resurrect the rule of an earlier era, disallowing consideration of voluntary intoxication when a defendant's state of mind is at issue. Nothing in the Due Process Clause prevents them from doing so, and the judgment of the Supreme Court of Montana to the contrary must be reversed.

It is so ordered.

Dissent by: O'CONNOR; SOUTER; BREYER.

Dissent

The Montana Supreme Court unanimously held that Mont. Code Ann. § 45–2–203 (1995) violates due process. I agree. Our cases establish that due process sets an outer limit on the restrictions that may be placed on a defendant's ability to raise an effective defense to the State's accusations. Here, to impede the defendant's ability to throw doubt on the State's case, Montana has removed from the jury's consideration a category of evidence relevant to determination of mental state where that mental state is an essential element of the offense that must be proved beyond a reasonable doubt. Because this disallowance eliminates evidence with which the defense might negate an essential element, the State's burden to prove its case is made correspondingly easier. The justification for this disallowance is the State's desire to increase the likelihood of conviction of a certain class of defendants who might otherwise be able to prove that they did not satisfy a requisite element of the offense. In my view, the statute's effect on the criminal proceeding violates due process.

I

This Court's cases establish that limitations placed on the accused's ability to present a fair and complete defense can, in some circumstances, be severe enough to violate due process. Applying our precedent, the Montana Supreme Court held that keeping intoxication evidence away from the jury, where such evidence was relevant to establishment of the requisite mental state, violated the due process right to present a defense, and that the instruction pursuant to § 45–2–203 was not harmless error. It is true that a defendant does not enjoy an absolute right to present evidence relevant to his defense. But none of the "familiar" evidentiary rules operates as Montana's does. The Montana statute places a blanket exclusion on a category of evidence that would allow the accused to negate the offense's mental-state element. In so doing, it frees the prosecution, in the face of such evidence, from having to prove beyond a reasonable doubt that the defendant nevertheless possessed the required mental state. In my view, this combination of effects violates due process.

Precedent illuminates a simple principle: Due process demands that a criminal defendant be afforded a fair opportunity to defend against the State's accusations. Meaningful adversarial testing of the State's case requires that the defendant not be prevented from raising an effective defense, which must include the right to present relevant, probative evidence. To be sure, the right to present evidence is not limitless. Section 45–2–203 forestalls the defendant's ability to raise an effective defense by placing a blanket exclusion on the presentation of a type of evidence that directly negates an element of the crime, and by doing so, it lightens the prosecution's burden to prove that mental-state element beyond a reasonable doubt.

Because the Montana Legislature has specified that a person commits "deliberate homicide" only if he "purposely or knowingly causes the death of another human being," Mont. Code Ann. § 45–5–102(1)(a) (1995), the prosecution must prove the existence of such mental state in order to convict. That is, unless the defendant is shown to have acted purposely or knowingly, he is not guilty of the offense of deliberate homicide. The Montana Supreme Court found that it was inconsistent with the legislature's requirement of the mental state of "purposely" or "knowingly" to prevent the jury from considering evidence of voluntary intoxication, where that category of evidence was relevant to establishment of that mental-state element.

Where the defendant may introduce evidence to negate a subjective mental-state element, the prosecution must work to overcome whatever doubts the defense has raised about the existence of the required mental state. On the other hand, if the defendant may not introduce evidence that might create doubt in the factfinder's mind as to whether that element was met, the prosecution will find its job so much the easier. A subjective mental state is generally proved only circumstantially. If a jury may not consider the defendant's evidence of his mental state, the jury may impute to the defendant the culpability of a mental state he did not possess.

The State's brief to this Court enunciates a single reason for this bar: Due to the well-known risks related to voluntary intoxication, it seeks to prevent a defendant's use of his own voluntary intoxication as basis for exculpation. That is, its interest is to ensure that even a defendant who lacked the required mental-state element—and is therefore not guilty—is nevertheless convicted of the offense. The final justification proffered by the plurality on Montana's behalf is that Montana's rule perhaps prevents juries, who might otherwise be misled, from being "too quick to accept the claim that the drunk defendant was biologically incapable of forming the requisite mens rea." But this proffered justification is inconsistent with § 45–2–203's exception for persons who are involuntarily intoxicated. That exception makes plain that Montana does not consider intoxication evidence misleading—but rather considers it relevant—for the determination of a person's capacity to form the requisite mental state.

Montana has specified that to prove guilt, the State must establish that the defendant acted purposely or knowingly, but has prohibited a category of defendants from effectively disputing guilt through presentation of evidence relevant to that essential element. And the evidence is indisputably relevant: The Montana Supreme Court held that evidence of intoxication is relevant to proof of mental state, 272 Mont., at 122–123, and furthermore, § 45–2–203's exception for involuntary intoxication shows that the legislature does consider intoxication relevant to mental state. Montana has barred the defendant's use of a category of relevant, exculpatory evidence for the express purpose of improving the State's likelihood of winning a conviction against a certain type of defendant. The purpose of the familiar evidentiary rules is not to alleviate the State's burden, but rather to vindicate some other goal or value—e. g., to ensure the reliability and competency of evidence or to encourage effective communications within certain relationships. Such rules may or may not help the prosecution, and when they do help, do so only incidentally. An evidentiary rule whose sole purpose is to boost the State's likelihood of conviction distorts the adversary process. The sole purpose for this disallowance is to keep from the jury's consideration a category of evidence that helps the defendant's case and weakens the government's case.

It seems to me that a State may not first determine the elements of the crime it wishes to punish, and then thwart the accused's defense by categorically disallowing the very evidence that would prove him innocent.

DISCUSSION QUESTIONS

1.   Given Montana's rule, why was the jury allowed to hear evidence of the defendant's intoxication at all? Do you think that Eglehoff would be more blameworthy if he killed the victims when he was stone cold sober? Or more dangerous?

2.   Arguably Montana's rule requires the jury to pretend that an intoxicated person is sober when deciding whether he knowingly performed an act. Intoxicated people sometimes do not know what they are doing. Why doesn't pretending that Eglehoff is sober violate due process of law according to the majority?

3.   As a matter of public policy, do you think more states should adopt the Montana rule? Or do you think that states should allow intoxication as a defense to crimes requiring a reckless state of mind?

D. INTOXICATION AS A CONDUCT DEFENSE

At this point, it is important to note that intoxication is not always offered as a mental state defense. Sometimes, evidence of intoxication is used to argue that the defendant did not perform the conduct required for the crime. For example, Egelhoff could argue that he was too intoxicated to hold the gun and pull the trigger. Remember to distinguish intoxication as a mental state defense from intoxication as an "it wasn't me" defense.

On a related note, it is possible that an extremely intoxicated person could have performed the prohibited act in a state of "automatism" similar to sleepwalking. A memory "blackout," however, does not necessarily mean that a person was not conscious. In any event, the few cases that discuss this defense seem to reject an automatism defense based on intoxication.

E. INTOXICATION AND MURDER

As will be discussed in the homicide chapter, evidence of intoxication may be used to argue that the defendant did not premeditate and deliberate in killing someone. This would ordinarily have the effect of reducing the murder from first to second degree. Remember though that the defendant must be so intoxicated as to not have the capacity to premeditate and deliberate. Simply realizing after a few drinks that you really do hate this guy and want to kill him does not count.

In contrast, one may not use evidence of intoxication to argue for a voluntary manslaughter verdict on the grounds of provocation. Legally adequate provocation requires, at a minimum, circumstances under which a reasonable person would lose control of his or her emotions. This means a reasonable sober person, not a "reasonable intoxicated" one.

F. INTOXICATION AND TIMING

Not surprisingly, the courts take a rather dim view of people who drink in order to commit crimes. One who knows that he gets violent when drunk and drinks himself drunk for that purpose will not have a defense. A person who decides to kill someone and then intoxicates himself before killing would probably be found to have premeditated and deliberated. You may find your courage to commit a crime in a bottle, but you won't find your defense there.

G. INTOXICATION AND DEFENSIVE FORCE

The legal use of defensive force generally requires a reasonable fear of an imminent harm. This fear must be that of a reasonable sober person. So a person who becomes paranoid on LSD and accidentally shoots a pizza delivery person would not be found to have a reasonable fear.

H. INTOXICATION AND INSANITY

There are three different relationships between intoxication and a mental impairment so profound as to constitute insanity, and each of the three has different legal consequences.

1. TEMPORARY INSANITY

What if you drink so much that you don't know the difference between right and wrong, don't know the nature of what you are doing, or can't control your actions? Temporary insanity resulting from voluntary intoxication is not a defense to a crime. Temporary insanity resulting from *involuntary* intoxication, however, is a different matter, as will be discussed below.

2. SETTLED INSANITY RESULTING FROM INTOXICATING SUBSTANCES

Sometimes people drink or drug themselves into mental illness. Organic brain damage resulting from chronic abuse of alcohol, for example, can produce various mental health impairments that meet the test for insanity. Most—but not all—jurisdictions accept such a "settled" or "fixed" (as opposed to temporary) insanity as a defense, even if it had been created by long-term abuse of alcohol or other drugs. Such settled or non-temporary insanity is treated like any other form of insanity. It provides a complete defense to all crimes but ordinarily results in the involuntary commitment of the defendant to a mental health facility until he is cured.

3.   INTOXICATED WHILE INSANE

Sometimes mentally ill people intoxicate themselves. If someone meets the definition of insanity, independent of their use of an intoxicating substance, the fact that they were intoxicated at the time they committed a crime will not deprive them of their insanity defense.

I.   INVOLUNTARY INTOXICATION

The defense of involuntary intoxication is harder to establish, but it provides a much broader defense than voluntary intoxication. A few cases suggest that involuntary intoxication could negate one's capacity to form a general intent (recklessness or negligence). This would mean that our intoxicated front row student would have a defense to the misdemeanor charge of simple battery if I had slipped tasteless, pure alcohol into her can of coca cola, and she had lost her capacity to be non-negligent or non-reckless.

The law recognizes three types of involuntary intoxication. Courts have generally been very strict about applying these definitions, and examples of successful defenses are rare.

The defendant does not know the intoxicating qualities of the substance consumed. "So that is what Vodka tastes like! I thought it was a strong mouthwash." Someone who unknowingly consumed a tasteless intoxicating substance would have the strongest case for a defense. Think marijuana brownies disguised as regular brownies, LSD laced peanuts, PCP powdered donuts and other similar goodies. This type of involuntary intoxication also includes people taking prescription medication without knowing or having any reason to know about its intoxicating effects. (That is why they put those warning labels on the pill bottles!)

1.   COERCED INTOXICATION

Someone really needs to hold you down and pour the alcohol down your throat or hold a gun to your head. (Not exactly your friendly neighborhood bar.) Simple peer pressure from a fraternity or sorority hazing ritual won't cut it.

2.   PATHOLOGICAL INTOXICATION

Some people have truly excessive reactions to intoxicating substances. One drink and they are off to the races, so to speak. Don't over interpret this defense though. First, the reaction must be truly excessive. Claiming a "bad trip" on a hallucinogen like LSD won't cut it because hallucinations are understood to be one of the risks of taking even one hit of the drug LSD. If our tequila-drinking student became extremely belligerent and uncoordinated after a single shot, that might count as involuntary intoxication. Second, the person must have had no way of knowing that they would have this excessive reaction. Think of this as the "one shot" rule. The first time you learn that tequila turns you into a raving maniac is the last time that you can use this reaction to support a defense of involuntary intoxication.

Case in Context

This case involves the rare scenario of an involuntary intoxication defense to a DWI charge.

COMMONWEALTH OF PENNSYLVANIA V. KAREN SMITH

Superior Court of Pennsylvania
831 A.2d 636 (2003)

Appellant, Karen Smith, appeals from the judgment of sentence of 48 hours to 18 months' incarceration imposed following her conviction of driving under the influence (DUI) and related summary offense. Appellant claims she established the affirmative defense of "involuntary intoxication" thereby negating the state of mind necessary to support a conviction of DUI. After review, we affirm.

The facts and procedural history of this matter may be summarized as follows. On March 29, 2002, Officer James E. Ott, of the Greenfield Township Police Department, observed Appellant driving a Ford truck on State Route 101 in Greenfield Township, Blair County, Pennsylvania. Officer Ott observed Appellant's vehicle drift completely into the oncoming lane and proceed to travel in the lane for oncoming traffic for one tenth of a mile until he activated his emergency lights. Appellant then pulled her vehicle to the side of the road, leaving a large portion of the vehicle protruding into the roadway, even though there was sufficient space to park the vehicle totally off of the roadway. Upon making contact with the Appellant, Officer Ott observed that her eyes were glassy and bloodshot and she emanated a strong odor of alcohol. When asked to exit her vehicle, Appellant stumbled and staggered numerous times. Appellant admitted to consuming beer earlier in the evening.

Officer Ott administered three field sobriety tests, all of which Appellant failed. Appellant was placed under arrest for DUI and transported to the hospital for a blood alcohol test, which she refused. On September 24, 2002, a bench trial was held. On direct examination, Appellant testified that she consumed alcohol while wearing a prescribed "duragesic" patch for pain. She testified that she did not realize that the patch would heighten the effects of alcohol. Appellant admitted that she did not read the directions or warnings for the patch. Moreover, Appellant offered no expert testimony whatsoever to support her allegation that the patch heightened the effects of the alcohol she consumed. The Honorable Thomas J. Peoples, Jr. found Appellant guilty and imposed sentence on October 17, 2002. Appellant filed a post sentence motion that was denied. This timely appeal followed.

Appellant's sole question on appeal reads as follows:

I.   IS THE DEFENSE OF INVOLUNTARY INTOXICATION OR INVOLUNTARY DRUGGED CONDITION A DEFENSE COGNIZABLE IN PENNSYLVANIA?

Initially, we note that Appellant was convicted of driving while under the influence of alcohol to a degree that rendered her incapable of safe driving. 75 Pa.C.S.A. § 3731(a)(1).

> In order to prove a violation of this section, the Commonwealth must show: (1) that the defendant was the operator of a motor vehicle and (2) that while operating the vehicle, the defendant was under the influence of alcohol to such a degree as to render him or her incapable of safe driving. To establish the second element, it must be shown that alcohol has substantially impaired the normal mental and physical faculties required to safely operate the vehicle. Substantial impairment, in this context, means a diminution or enfeeblement in the ability to exercise judgment, to deliberate or to react prudently to changing circumstances and conditions. Evidence that the driver was not in control of himself, such as failing to pass a field sobriety test, may establish that the driver was under the influence of alcohol to a degree which rendered him incapable of safe driving, notwithstanding the absence of evidence of erratic or unsafe driving.

Commonwealth v. Palmer, 751 A.2d 223, 228 (Pa.Super.2000) (citations and footnote omitted).

Appellant asserts that involuntary intoxication is a cognizable affirmative defense in a DUI prosecution. Specifically, she claims that "[i]n the pharmaceutical age, the labeling of drugs places on the physician in Pennsylvania, the duty to warn the patient of the side effects of drugs. When labeling is not on bold print but on minute instructions in tiny print inside of a box, it is not the consumer who is expected to be aware of the consequences, but the physician. Where testimony is offered, unrebutted, nor challenged, that the user was unaware of the polypharmacology of the drug a cognizable defense should be recognized in Pennsylvania." Appellant's brief, at 9. In effect, Appellant urges this Court to find that she was not criminally culpable for her conduct because she was unaware that the newly increased strength of the prescribed duragesic patch she was wearing would heighten the effects of the alcohol she voluntarily ingested. We are not persuaded.

Pennsylvania like many other jurisdictions, either by statute or caselaw, specifically limits the availability of a voluntary intoxication defense but does not specify whether an involuntary intoxication defense is available. *See* 18 Pa.C.S.A. § 308 (stating that evidence of voluntary intoxication is admissible where it is relevant "to reduce murder from a higher to a lower degree of murder."). In *Commonwealth v. Collins*, 810 A.2d 698, 700 (Pa.Super.2002), we recently noted that "the issue of whether involuntary intoxication is a defense to a DUI charge is unclear in Pennsylvania. Moreover, in the context of a DUI prosecution, assuming the defense applies, we have held that the defendant has the burden of proving the affirmative defense of involuntary intoxication by a preponderance of the evidence. *Collins, supra.*

Generally speaking, many of the other jurisdictions that permit an accused to be completely relieved of criminal responsibility based on involuntary intoxication do so premised upon the notion that he or she was temporarily rendered legally insane at the time he or she committed the offense. The defense of involuntary intoxication has been recognized in other jurisdictions in four types of situations: (1) where the intoxication was caused by the fault of another (i.e., through force, duress, fraud, or contrivance); (2) where the intoxication was caused by an innocent mistake on the part of the defendant (i.e., defendant took hallucinogenic pill in reasonable belief it was aspirin or lawful tranquilizer); (3) where a defendant unknowingly suffers from a physiological or psychological condition that renders him abnormally susceptible to a legal intoxicant (sometimes referred to as pathological intoxication); and (4) where unexpected intoxication results from a medically prescribed drug. These widely varying circumstances make it difficult to formulate a comprehensive definition of the defense; nonetheless, it would appear that a key component is lack of culpability on the part of the defendant in causing the intoxication.

Instantly, Appellant's argument is most similar to the situation described above in type number four. This type is premised upon the notion that "because a patient is entitled to assume that an intoxicating dose would not be prescribed or administered by a physician, where intoxication results from medicine which has been prescribed (and taken as prescribed) or administered by a physician, such intoxication is generally considered involuntary." Hassman, *supra*. Significantly, Appellant's argument differs from a pure type four involuntary intoxication defense in that she does not claim that the patch alone caused an unknowing and unexpected intoxicating effect. Rather, she claims that a higher dose of the patch combined with her voluntary ingestion of an allegedly moderate amount of alcohol caused an unexpected intoxication. It would seem, however, that her intoxication was "self-induced" as defined by the Model Penal Code. Clearly, she "knowingly introduce[d]" a substance-alcohol-"the tendency of which to cause intoxication" she "ought to [have known]." Model Penal Code § 2.08(5)(b). In fact, this Court and our Supreme Court have previously rejected similar arguments in *Commonwealth v. Todaro*, 301 Pa.Super. 1, 446 A.2d 1305 (1982) and *Commonwealth v. Hicks*, 483 Pa. 305, 396 A.2d 1183 (1979).

In *Todaro*, the defendant was charged with involuntary manslaughter, recklessly endangering another person, and driving under the influence. This Court held that an instruction on involuntary intoxication was not required where the defendant inadvertently mixed alcoholic beverages with prescribed medication because there was no evidence to support a finding that defendant's intoxication was not voluntary. In *Hicks*, prior to the victim's murder the defendant had consumed a large quantity of alcohol and an amphetamine based diet pill. Defendant asserted that the record did not establish that he was sane so as to be criminally responsible for his conduct. He argued that his mental state was involuntarily induced from a mixture of the prescribed medication and alcohol because he was not warned of the possible effect of such combination. On appeal our Supreme Court held that the trial court properly weighed the evidence and found that defendant's behavior resulted from the voluntary ingestion of alcohol and not mental disease. The Court further noted that "[e]ven accepting the remote possibility of the existence of a pathological disorder, it was at best a passive condition triggered by the ingestion of alcohol. In either event [defendant] was not entitled to escape the responsibility for his conduct under the *M'Naghten* Rule." *Hicks*, at 311–312, 396 A.2d at 1186.

Thus, it would appear that Pennsylvania law is consonant with the Model Penal Code's definition and would not characterize intoxication produced by the voluntary consumption of a prescription drug and alcohol as "involuntary" even if that consumption was without knowledge of a synergistic effect. Here, as in *Todaro* the evidence merely established that Appellant drank alcohol without regard to the effects of its combination with medication she was taking. Thus, even assuming the proffered defense is viable, these facts alone cannot establish involuntary intoxication.

Moreover, upon our careful review of the facts of this case even if we were to assume that such a defense is cognizable under Appellant's theory, she still cannot show that the trial court erred in rejecting this defense because she has failed to establish the necessary factual foundation to support her claimed defense. To absolve Appellant of criminal behavior by the complete defense of involuntary intoxication, she had the burden to show such intoxication by a preponderance of the evidence. *Collins, supra.* If this defense is to be relied upon, Appellant must show that the combination is capable of causing the extreme intoxication which is alleged.

The trial court cannot take judicial notice of this fact. Thus, at a minimum it will be necessary to present expert witnesses to establish this effect. Here, the only evidence of record is Appellant's self-serving statements that she had not read any of the labeling and was not told by her doctor of any possible side effects and thus was unaware of the alleged heightened effect of the patch when combined with alcohol consumption. Appellant did not present her physician or any other medical expert to establish that an increased inebriating effect was even possible. It follows that Appellant has not come close to putting the integrity of the conviction into question. Because Appellant was unable to establish the factual foundation for her proffered defense, it does not bear upon the sufficiency of the evidence in the case, and the trial court properly denied Appellant's motion in arrest of judgment.

Judgment of sentence affirmed.

DISCUSSION QUESTIONS

1. Is it fair to deny defendants an involuntary intoxication defense based on fine print that is not prominently displayed? Or should one be strictly liable for any impairing effects of medication one takes?

2. Does it matter that the medication was combined with alcohol? Would you permit an involuntary intoxication defense in this case if alcohol was not involved?

3. Warning labels tend to be overinclusive in terms of possible side effects. Should the line between voluntary and involuntary intoxication turn upon something other than warning labels?

J. INVOLUNTARY INTOXICATION AND TEMPORARY INSANITY

The case law is very sparse here, so it is not meaningful to identify majority and minority positions. That said, among the few cases and the scholars who write about them, a consensus seems to exist that involuntary intoxication could be a complete defense to any crime if it impaired one's mental state sufficiently to meet the definition of insanity. The advantage of such temporary insanity is that one will not be involuntarily committed to a mental hospital because one is not mentally ill.

Practice Problem 8.0: "Just Take Two Pills and Call Your Lawyer in the Morning"

You work for a legislator who has asked you to draft a model statute defining the defense of involuntary intoxication with respect to prescription medication. She has noticed that most medications advertise extremely long lists of every possible side effect. Your statute should specifically address the role that such lists play in whether or not any resulting intoxication may be considered involuntary as well as any other factors about prescription medication that you deem relevant.

CHAPTER 9

HOMICIDE: AN OVERVIEW

■ ■ ■

Many professors teach the most important parts of the criminal law through the law of homicide. Because the taking of human life has long been considered the gravest crime, homicide law has played a key role in the evolution of criminal law. Judges wrestle with difficult questions in homicide cases, and often write detailed opinions explaining their reasoning, because so much is at stake. These opinions engage student attention because they deal with fundamental issues of criminal law in the context of compelling facts. For these reasons, criminal professors spend far more time in class—and on the exam—on homicide than any other single crime.

Homicide is killing a human being. Note that the word "killing" does a lot of work. To kill someone is to engage in conduct that causes a person's death. So "killing" incorporates three elements: conduct, causation, and a result required by the offense to occur. To put it in quasi-mathematical terms:

Homicide = Conduct Causing Death of a Human Being

Now, not all homicides are crimes. Whether a homicide crime has been committed usually turns on the mental state that accompanied the conduct that caused the death. So, our homicide crime equation looks like this:

Homicide Crime = Conduct Causing Death + Accompanying Mental State

The accompanying mental state, of course, determines not only whether a homicide crime occurred but also which homicide crime occurred. This is a very important distinction because there are almost as many different homicide crimes as there are different mental states.

The first most basic distinction between different types of homicide crimes is the distinction between intentional and unintentional killings. The law in many jurisdictions draws further distinctionsbetween various types of intentional killings and between various types of unintentional killings, as the following overview demonstrates.

A. INTENTIONAL KILLINGS

- Premeditated and Deliberate Killings
- Killing someone intentionally but without premeditation and deliberation

- Killing someone intentionally but in the heat of passion
- Some killings committed during felonies

B. UNINTENTIONAL KILLINGS

- Extremely Reckless/Extremely Indifferent killings
- Reckless killings
- Grossly Negligent killings
- Negligent killings (only in a few jurisdictions)
- Some killings committed during Felonies

Now that we understand the different types of homicide crimes we can discuss how most homicide statutes group them. Homicide statutes by and large group homicide crimes into the two categories of murder and manslaughter. Manslaughter is a less serious category of homicide crime than murder and is punished less severely. As the following overview shows, not all intentional killings are murder, and not all unintentional killings are manslaughter. You can kill someone intentionally in the heat of passion and get convicted of voluntary manslaughter, whereas someone who kills another in an extremely reckless fashion could get murder instead of involuntary manslaughter.

C. MURDER

- Premeditated and Deliberate killings
- Intentional killings
- Extremely reckless, extremely indifferent killings
- Felony Murder

D. MANSLAUGHTER

- Voluntary Manslaughter: intentionally killing someone in the heat of passion
- Involuntary Manslaughter: killing someone recklessly, with gross negligence, or (in a few jurisdictions) with simple negligence.

E. DEGREES OF MURDER

You may wonder at this point about degrees of murder. TV shows love first degree murder, so you have probably heard that term a lot. Most jurisdictions do divide murder up into degrees of murder, but there is a lot of variation in how these divisions are made. The most important thing in practice or on an exam is to read the statute that applies and make sure you understand how that jurisdiction slices up the homicide pie. In the absence of clear statutory definitions, you can rely on the following rough rules of thumb that describe the most common approach.

1. First degree murder is usually reserved for premeditated and deliberate killings and other particularly heinous types of murder.

2. Second degree murder usually includes intentional and extremely reckless killings.

3. Felony murder is a bit of a tossup. Some jurisdictions treat it as first degree, others as second degree, and some split felony murder between both degrees based on the type of felony committed.

F. COMMON LAW MURDER

Understanding the common law definition of murder remains important because a number of common law jurisdictions—though not all—do not define the term "murder" in their statutes. These statutes often define different degrees of murder, but murder itself is never defined. Jurisdictions taking a more modern approach define the different degrees of murder by specifying what mental state must accompany the conduct that caused the death.

You may have heard the colorful phase "killing with malice aforethought." Malice was the common law's definition of murder. If you killed with malice, then it was murder. If you killed with some lesser mental state, then it was manslaughter (assuming it was not completely justified or excused, in which case it was not any crime). Malice, therefore, refers to many different mental states. While modern homicide codes specify which mental states are required, many cases in common law jurisdictions still discuss malice, and a few codes in common law jurisdictions do not specify the mental states required for murder. In these jurisdictions, and on the Multistate Bar Exam (a multiple-choice test that many jurisdictions use as part of their bar exam), you need to know the common law definition of murder.

Malice is divided into two types: express and implied. Express malice refers to an intent to kill. Implied malice refers to everything else.

- Express Malice:
  - Intent to Kill
- Implied Malice:
  - Intent to Commit Grievous Bodily Injury

- Abandoned and Malignant Heart/Depraved heart
- Intent to Commit a Dangerous Felony

The common law implied the malice required for murder in these sorts of cases because it judged the offender to be just as evil or just as dangerous as someone who intended to kill. For example, a bank robber who killed accidentally, an assailant who only wanted to maim his victim, or a person who was so careless that he didn't care whether you lived or died were considered to be murderers if someone died as a result of their conduct. These categories shaped how modern codes draw the line between murder and manslaughter, even though they no longer use the word "malice."

G. MODEL PENAL CODE

The Model Penal Code's approach to homicide will be discussed throughout the chapters that follow, but reviewing the MPC's homicide provision as a whole provides a useful overview of how the code slices up the "homicide pie."

§ 210.2. Murder

1) Except as provided in Section 210.3(1)(b), criminal homicide constitutes murder when:

   a) it is committed purposely or knowingly; or

   b) it is committed recklessly under circumstances manifesting extreme indifference to the value of human life. Such recklessness and indifference are presumed if the actor is engaged or is an accomplice in the commission of, or an attempt to commit, or flight after committing or attempting to commit robbery, rape or deviate sexual intercourse by force or threat of force, arson, burglary, kidnaping or felonious escape.

2) Murder is a felony of the first degree [but a person convicted of murder may be sentenced to death, as provided in Section 210.6].

§ 210.3. Manslaughter

1) Criminal homicide constitutes manslaughter when:

   a) it is committed recklessly; or

   b) a homicide which would otherwise be murder is committed under the influence of extreme mental or emotional disturbance for which there is reasonable explanation or excuse. The reasonableness of such explanation or excuse shall be determined from the viewpoint of a person in the actor's situation under the circumstances as he believes them to be.

2)   Manslaughter is a felony of the second degree.

§ 210.4. Negligent Homicide

1)   Criminal homicide constitutes negligent homicide when it is committed negligently.

2)   Negligent homicide is a felony of the third degree.

Practice Problem 9.0: Interpreting Murder

Here is the homicide statute from North Carolina. How does this jurisdiction handle the different types of homicide crime discussed above?

§ 14–17. Murder in the First and Second Degree defined; punishment

A murder which shall be perpetrated by means of a nuclear, biological, or chemical weapon of mass destruction as defined in G.S. 14–288.21, poison, lying in wait, imprisonment, starving, torture, or by any other kind of willful, deliberate, and premeditated killing, or which shall be committed in the perpetration or attempted perpetration of any arson, rape or a sex offense, robbery, kidnapping, burglary, or other felony committed or attempted with the use of a deadly weapon shall be deemed to be murder in the first degree, a Class A felony, and any person who commits such murder shall be punished with death or imprisonment in the State's prison for life without parole as the court shall determine pursuant to G.S. 15A–2000, except that any such person who was under 17 years of age at the time of the murder shall be punished with imprisonment in the State's prison for life without parole. Provided, however, any person under the age of 17 who commits murder in the first degree while serving a prison sentence imposed for a prior murder or while on escape from a prison sentence imposed for a prior murder shall be punished with death or imprisonment in the State's prison for life without parole as the court shall determine pursuant to G.S. 15A–2000. All other kinds of murder, including that which shall be approximately caused by the unlawful distribution of opium or any synthetic or natural salt, compound, derivative, or preparation of opium, or cocaine or other substance described in G.S. 90–90 (1)d., or methamphetamine when the ingestion of such substance causes the death of the user, shall be deemed murder in the second degree, and any person who commits such murder shall be punished as a Class B2 felon.

§ 14–18. Punishment for Manslaughter

Voluntary manslaughter shall be punishable as a Class D felony, and involuntary manslaughter shall be punishable as a Class F felony.

CHAPTER 10

INTENT TO KILL MURDER

■ ■ ■

A. INTENT TO KILL

Think of intent to kill murder as the baseline of murder. An easy case would be someone who purposely shoots someone else in the head. If you consciously desire that someone die—or are substantially certain that they will die by your conduct—then you intend to kill them. Note that intent to kill includes both purposeful and knowing conduct with respect to death. So, if I blow up a plane to kill you specifically, I will still be found guilty of the murder of all the other passengers since I clearly knew that they would die, as well.

People are generally presumed to intend the natural and probable consequences of what they do. If I push you off the roof of a ten-story building, the natural and probable result would be your death. Additionally, juries are often told that they may infer intent to kill from the use of a deadly weapon directed at a vital part of the human anatomy. So, a baseball bat to the head would do nicely for intent to kill as long as the prosecutor could prove that the defendant intended to hit the victim in the head with the baseball bat.

Obviously, one can intend to kill another in any number of ways. Not only are weapons not required, you don't even have to touch the other person. Telling someone to turn left instead of right with the intent that he walks off a cliff could be murder. Omissions to act in the face of a legal duty can also be murder, although it is often not easy to prove an intent to kill based on something that a person failed to do. Returning to our drowning hypothetical from Chapter 5 if you push me off an ocean pier not knowing that I can't swim, you did not intend to kill me. But failing to throw me a life preserver could be intent to kill murder if you hear me screaming, "I am drowning."

Intentional killings can also be entirely impulsive. Even though the mental state for murder at common law was termed "malice aforethought," intent to kill murder does not require that you have thought about it in advance.

Case in Context

Intent to kill is often straightforward, but not always. Jurors are often instructed that they may (but not must) presume that a defendant intended the natural and probable consequences of his action. Do you think an intent to kill existed in the following case?

ROBERT FRANCIS, WARDEN V. RAYMOND LEE FRANKLIN
Supreme Court of the United States
471 U.S. 307 (1965)

Opinion

JUSTICE BRENNAN delivered the opinion of the Court. . . .

Respondent Raymond Lee Franklin, then 21 years old and imprisoned for offenses unrelated to this case, sought to escape custody on January 17, 1979, while he and three other prisoners were receiving dental care at a local dentist's office. The four prisoners were secured by handcuffs to the same 8-foot length of chain as they sat in the dentist's waiting room. At some point Franklin was released from the chain, taken into the dentist's office and given preliminary treatment, and then escorted back to the waiting room. As another prisoner was being released, Franklin, who had not been reshackled, seized a pistol from one of the two officers and managed to escape. He forced the dentist's assistant to accompany him as a hostage.

In the parking lot Franklin found the dentist's automobile, the keys to which he had taken before escaping, but was unable to unlock the door. He then fled with the dental assistant after refusing her request to be set free. The two set out across an open clearing and came upon a local resident. Franklin demanded this resident's car. When the resident responded that he did not own one, Franklin made no effort to harm him but continued with the dental assistant until they came to the home of the victim, one Collie. Franklin pounded on the heavy wooden front door of the home and Collie, a retired 72-year-old carpenter, answered. Franklin was pointing the stolen pistol at the door when Collie arrived. As Franklin demanded his car keys, Collie slammed the door. At this moment Franklin's gun went off. The bullet traveled through the wooden door and into Collie's chest killing him. Seconds later the gun fired again. The second bullet traveled upward through the door and into the ceiling of the residence.

Hearing the shots, the victim's wife entered the front room. In the confusion accompanying the shooting, the dental assistant fled and Franklin did not attempt to stop her. Franklin entered the house, demanded the car keys from the victim's wife, and added the threat "I might as well kill you." When she did not provide the keys, however, he made no effort to thwart her escape. Franklin then stepped outside and encountered the victim's adult daughter. He repeated his demand for car keys but made no effort to stop the daughter when she refused the demand and fled. Failing to obtain a car, Franklin left and remained at large until nightfall.

Shortly after being captured, Franklin made a formal statement to the authorities in which he admitted that he had shot the victim but emphatically denied that he did so voluntarily or intentionally. He claimed that the shots were fired in accidental response to the slamming of the door. He was tried in the Superior Court of Bibb County, Georgia, on charges of malice murder 1—a capital offense in Georgia—and kidnaping. His sole defense to the malice murder charge was a lack of the requisite intent to kill. To support his version of the events Franklin offered substantial circumstantial evidence tending to show a lack of intent. He claimed that the circumstances surrounding the firing of the gun, particularly the slamming of the door and the trajectory of the second bullet, supported the hypothesis of accident, and that his immediate confession to that effect buttressed the assertion. He also argued that his treatment of every other person encountered during the escape indicated a lack of disposition to use force.

On the dispositive issue of intent, the trial judge instructed the jury as follows:

"A crime is a violation of a statute of this State in which there shall be a union of joint operation of act or omission to act, and intention or criminal negligence. A person shall not be found guilty of any crime committed by misfortune or accident where it satisfactorily appears there was no criminal scheme or undertaking or intention or criminal negligence. The acts of a person of sound mind and discretion are presumed to be the product of the person's will, but the presumption may be rebutted. A person of sound mind and discretion is presumed to intend the natural and probable consequences of his acts but the presumption may be rebutted. A person will not be presumed to act with criminal intention but the trier of facts, that is, the Jury, may find criminal intention upon a consideration of the words, conduct, demeanor, motive and all other circumstances connected with the act for which the accused is prosecuted." App. 8a–9a.

Approximately one hour after the jury had received the charge and retired for deliberation, it returned to the courtroom and requested reinstruction on the element of intent and the definition of accident. Id., at 13a–14a. Upon receiving the requested reinstruction, the jury deliberated 10 more minutes and returned a verdict of guilty. The next day Franklin was sentenced to death for the murder conviction. . . .

A

Franklin levels his constitutional attack at the following two sentences in the jury charge: "The acts of a person of sound mind and discretion are presumed to be the product of the person's will, but the presumption may be rebutted. A person of sound mind and discretion is presumed to intend the natural and probable consequences of his acts but the presumption may be rebutted." App. 8a–9a.4 . . .

The challenged sentences are cast in the language of command. They instruct the jury that "acts of a person of sound mind and discretion are presumed to be the product of the person's will," and that a person "is presumed to intend the natural and probable consequences of his acts," App. 8a–9a These words carry precisely the message of the language condemned in Sandstrom, 442 U.S., at 515, 99 S.Ct., at 2454 (" 'The law presumes that a person intends the ordinary consequences of his voluntary acts"). The jurors "were not told that they had a choice, or that they might infer that conclusion; they were told only that the law presumed it. It is clear that a reasonable juror could easily have viewed such an instruction as mandatory." Ibid. The portion of the jury charge challenged in this case directs the jury to presume an essential element of the offense-intent to kill-upon proof of other elements of the offense-the act of slaying another. In this way the instructions "undermine the factfinder's responsibility at trial, based on evidence adduced by the State, to find the ultimate facts beyond a reasonable doubt." Ulster County Court v. Allen, supra, 442 U.S., at 156, 99 S.Ct., at 2224.

The language challenged here differs from Sandstrom, of course, in that the jury in this case was explicitly informed that the presumptions "may be rebutted." App. 8a–9a. The State makes much of this additional aspect of the instruction in seeking to differentiate the present case from Sandstrom. This distinction does not suffice, however, to cure the infirmity in the charge. Though the Court in Sandstrom acknowledged that the instructions there challenged could have been reasonably understood as creating an irrebuttable presumption, 442 U.S., at 517, 99 S.Ct., at 2455, it was not on this basis alone that the instructions were invalidated. Had the jury reasonably understood the instructions as creating a mandatory rebuttable presumption the instructions would have been no less constitutionally infirm. Id., at 520–524, 99 S.Ct., at 2457–2459.

An irrebuttable or conclusive presumption relieves the State of its burden of persuasion by removing the presumed element from the case entirely if the State proves the predicate facts. A mandatory rebuttable presumption does not remove the presumed element from the case if the State proves the predicate facts, but it nonetheless relieves the State of the affirmative burden of persuasion on the presumed element by instructing the jury that it must find the presumed element unless the defendant persuades the jury not to make such a finding. A mandatory rebuttable presumption is perhaps less onerous from the defendant's perspective, but it is no less unconstitutional. Our cases make clear that "such shifting of the burden of persuasion with respect to a fact which the State deems so important that it must be either proved or presumed is impermissible under the Due Process Clause." Patterson v. New York, 432 U.S., at 215, 97 S.Ct., at 2329. In Mullaney v. Wilbur we explicitly held unconstitutional a mandatory rebuttable presumption that shifted to the defendant a burden of persuasion on the question of intent. 421 U.S., at 698–701, 95

S.Ct., at 1889–1890. And in Sandstrom we similarly held that instructions that might reasonably have been understood by the jury as creating a mandatory rebuttable presumption were unconstitutional. 442 U.S., at 524, 99 S.Ct., at 2459.

When combined with the immediately preceding mandatory language, the instruction that the presumptions "may be rebutted" could reasonably be read as telling the jury that it was required to infer intent to kill as the natural and probable consequence of the act of firing the gun unless the defendant persuaded the jury that such an inference was unwarranted. The very statement that the presumption "may be rebutted" could have indicated to a reasonable juror that the defendant bore an affirmative burden of persuasion once the State proved the underlying act giving rise to the presumption. Standing alone, the challenged language undeniably created an unconstitutional burden-shifting presumption with respect to the element of intent.

B

Sandstrom v. Montana made clear that the Due Process Clause of the Fourteenth Amendment prohibits the State from making use of jury instructions that have the effect of relieving the State of the burden of proof enunciated in Winship on the critical question of intent in a criminal prosecution. 442 U.S., at 521, 99 S.Ct., at 2457. Today we reaffirm the rule of Sandstrom and the wellspring due process principle from which it was drawn. The Court of Appeals faithfully and correctly applied this rule, and the court's judgment is therefore

Affirmed.

DISCUSSION QUESTIONS

1.   What is the difference between the jury instruction that the Court says should have been given from the one that was given? Do you think that most jurors would notice the difference?

2.   Do you believe that Franklin intended to pull the trigger when he fired the fatal shot? If not, should that decision have been left to the jury on these facts?

3.   Can you think of a non-mental state defense for Franklin?

B. INTENT TO GRIEVOUSLY INJURE MURDER

The idea here is that the killer only meant to injure the victim seriously or grievously, not kill them. At common law this was murder, but today only a minority of jurisdictions recognize intent to grievously injure killings as murder.

Imagine that Joey the Loan Shark decides to cut off your pinky finger because you owe him money. You unexpectedly bleed to death. Joey would be guilty of murder at common law. He clearly did not intend for you to die (if you die, he will never get his money). He just wanted to send a message to you and all his other deadbeat customers about the importance of timely payment. He may not even have been reckless with respect to the risk of your death (he handed you a sterile compress bandage as soon as he finished amputating the finger). But the amputation of a pinky finger is a grievous injury, and the common law considered people who would intentionally hurt someone grievously to be just as bad as an intentional killer. If the maimed deadbeat dies unexpectedly, then, it would be murder at common law and under the minority rule.

The more common scenario for this type of murder is a fight or a beating that "gets out of hand." Beating someone to a bloody pulp with your fists or using a deadly weapon against a non-vital part of the human anatomy would suffice. But the mere fact that a grievous injury occurred— which must have happened since the person ended up dying from it—does not necessarily mean that the killer intended the grievous injury. Intent requires at least a knowing state of mind with respect to results, so the assailant must intend that the fight "get out of hand."

How bad must the intended injury be? Definitions vary, but generally something that makes you seriously worry about "life, health or limb." Despite the risk of puncturing a lung, a broken rib might not suffice, even though such an injury would constitute a felonious assault in most jurisdictions. An injury that seriously impairs you in a permanent or semi-permanent way would be enough.

Does this mean that our violent loan shark is safe from a murder charge in the majority of jurisdictions? Not necessarily. Intentionally maiming someone who ends up dying might constitute depraved heart murder.

Practice Problem 10.0: Mezcal Murder?

Addison and Avery have been drinking Mezcal tequila at a bar for the better part of an hour. The more they drink the more they argue. Each remembers various slights and insults suffered at the hands of the other over the long years of their relationship. The argument grows more and more heated until both are yelling red-faced at one another. Finally, Addison tells Avery to hand over the bottle, which contains one last shot in it. Avery says, "sure, I will let you have it." Avery smashes the thick bottle hard enough over Addison's head to break it. The bottle breaks and a shard protruding from the neck of the bottle punctures Addison's carotic artery. (This all happens in one continuous motion.) An ambulance driver who happens to be sitting next to the two immediately jumps up and tries to staunch the bleeding with a bar towel while Avery looks on and the bartender calls 911. Addison loses too much blood before the paramedics arrive and dies. Addison's skull was also fractured by the blow from the bottle, but she probably would have survived that wound had she not bled to death from the wound to her neck. Is Avery guilty of intent to kill murder?

CHAPTER 11

PREMEDITATED AND DELIBERATE MURDER

■ ■ ■

Premeditated and deliberate murder is what you almost always see on TV. Someone has a reason to kill someone, and they think about it before hand. Most jurisdictions today define premeditated and deliberate killings as first degree murder. A killing that one thinks about beforehand is thought to be more blameworthy, and a person who commits such a killing is thought to be more dangerous.

A "hit man" who kills for money is perhaps the clearest example of such a killer. A "mercy killing" where a loving and grief-stricken spouse or other family member who reluctantly takes the life of a loved one to spare them pointless suffering also usually kills after much premeditation and deliberation. This last example makes the point that the people who think before killing are not always more evil than those who do not. The criminal law punishes more harshly killers who reason their way into killing, and it does not distinguish between good and bad reasons unless the killing is justified.

A. PREMEDITATION AND DELIBERATION DEFINED

Premeditation and deliberation require quantity of thought and quality of thought. Quantity of thought refers to the time one spends thinking about killing. Quality of thought refers to how clearly one was able to think about it. Some jurisdictions use premeditation to refer to both requirements, and others use deliberation to refer to the quality of the killer's thinking. Either way, all jurisdictions require you to have both.

There is a broad and a narrow definition of premeditation and deliberation. The broad definition treats premeditation and deliberation as virtually the same thing as intending to kill. Jurisdictions using this broad definition require "no appreciable time" for premeditation, reasoning that "no time is too short for a wicked man" to decide to kill someone. One such court said that one can premeditate and deliberate in the time that it takes to pull a trigger. Most jurisdictions, however, require something more. Their narrower definition requires a period of "brief reflection," although no jurisdiction identifies a minimum period of time. Under the majority approach, you must have enough time to change your mind, to give your decision "a second look."

Time to think about killing is not enough. The jury must conclude that the killer thought about the decision in some meaningful way. For example, imagine a rage filled killer who, after discovering that his best friend had betrayed him, chanted repeatedly, "I am going to kill him, I am going to kill him, I am going to kill him" before killing. Such a killer may have been too caught up in his rage to deliberate his decision, the passage of time notwithstanding.

Deliberation (or the "meditation" part of "premeditation") requires that the killer reflects upon what he is about to do. Some jurisdictions talk about deliberation as a process where one thinks of the reasons for and against. Others emphasize the need for a "cool purpose," free from the influence of passion or excitement. "Cold-blooded killers," such as hit men, are easy examples of such deliberation. Other jurisdictions, however, emphasize that deliberation does not require the absence of "hot blood," only that the killer's capacity to reason remain undisturbed by hot blood.

1. FAILED EXCUSES

Many conditions that do not excuse killing may be enough to prevent a jury from finding that a killer premeditated and deliberated. Voluntary intoxication not sufficient to completely negate an intent to kill, mental defects short of insanity, or provocation that excites hot blood but fails to meet the strict tests for manslaughter might be sufficient to establish that the killer was not capable of the quality of thought required for premeditated and deliberate murder.

2. EARMARKS OF PREMEDITATION AND DELIBERATION

One of the most useful things courts have given us in this area is a list of three "earmarks" of premeditation and deliberation. While not required, the presence of one or more of these earmarks makes the argument for premeditation and deliberation a lot easier.

1. Planning activity

2. Motive

3. Manner of killing suggests passage of time or advance thinking

Planning activity speaks for itself because you can't plan something that you do on the spur of the moment. Motive means that that the killer had a reason that he could have thought about in advance. A husband with a multi-million-dollar insurance policy on his dead wife is easier to convict of premeditated murder because he has millions of reasons that he could have weighed against her life. The manner of killing earmark refers to things such as lying in wait for someone, or acquiring a weapon, which also suggests some advance thinking.

Remember though that premeditation and deliberation does not require good planning or good thinking. Unlike the crafty TV killers that capture everyone's imagination, many of the killers who inhabit the pages of criminal law textbooks are pathetic figures who kill for stupid reasons and in stupid ways. Killing thoughtfully but stupidly can still be first degree murder.

Finally, don't imagine that courts or juries find the line between premeditation and deliberate murder and intentional murder to be clear. Courts have, for example, gone both ways on the issue of whether the manner of killing alone can support a finding of premeditation and deliberation. Do thirty stab wounds reflect a thoughtless frenzy, or a really determined killer who has plenty of time to think between the first and last stab?

B. MODEL PENAL CODE

Some jurisdictions, most notably the Model Penal Code, abandoned or never adopted the distinction between premeditated and deliberate murder and intentional murder. The Model Penal Code, for example, does not divide murder into degrees. A purposeful or knowing killing is murder, whether you thought about it for a second or a year.

ARTICLE 210. CRIMINAL HOMICIDE

§ 210.2. Murder

1) Except as provided in Section 210.3(1)(b), criminal homicide constitutes murder when:

   a) it is committed purposely or knowingly. . .

2) Murder is a felony of the first degree.

C. CASES IN CONTEXT

Is strangulation in and of itself evidence of premeditation and deliberation?

STATE V. BINGHAM
Court of Appeals of Washington
40 Wash. App. 553 (1985)

WORSWICK, C.J.—We are asked to decide whether the time to effect death by manual strangulation is alone sufficient to support a finding of premeditation in the absence of any other evidence supporting such a finding. We hold it is not. Accordingly, we reverse the conviction of Charles Dean Bingham for aggravated first degree murder. . .

Leslie Cook, a retarded adult living at the Laurisden Home in Port Angeles, was raped and strangled on February 15, 1982. Bingham was the last person with whom she was seen. The two of them got off the Port Angeles-Sequim bus together at Sequim about 6 p.m. on February 15. They visited a grocery store and two residences. The last of these was Enid Pratt's where Bingham asked for a ride back to Port Angeles. When he was refused, he said they would hitchhike. They took the infrequently traveled Old Olympic Highway. Three days later, Cook's body was discovered in a field approximately 1/4 mile from the Pratt residence.

At trial, the State's expert testified that, in order to cause death by strangulation, Cook's assailant would have had to maintain substantial and continuous pressure on her windpipe for 3 to 5 minutes. The State contended that this alone was enough to raise an inference that the murder was premeditated. . . Therefore, it allowed the issue of premeditation to go to the jury. The jury convicted Bingham of aggravated first degree murder, rape being the aggravating circumstance. On appeal, counsel for Bingham concedes that a finding of guilty of murder was justified; he challenges only the finding of premeditation, contending that the evidence was insufficient to support it. We agree.

Premeditation is a separate and distinct element of first degree murder. It involves the mental process of thinking over beforehand, deliberation, reflection, weighing or reasoning for a period of time, however short, after which the intent to kill is formed. The time required for manual strangulation is sufficient to permit deliberation. However, time alone is not enough. The evidence must be sufficient to support the inference that the defendant not only had the time to deliberate, but that he actually did so. To require anything less would permit a jury to focus on the method of killing to the exclusion of the mental process involved in the separate element of premeditation.

The concept of premeditation had a slow but sure beginning in Anglo-American legal history. More than 500 years ago, English jurists arrived at the not surprising conclusion that the worst criminals—and those most deserving of the ultimate punishment—were those who planned to kill and then did so. Thus began the movement toward classification of homicides that resulted in restriction of the death penalty to those involving "malice prepensed" or "malice aforethought." When Washington's first criminal code was enacted in 1854, the Territorial Legislature abandoned this archaic language and used the phrase "deliberate and premeditated malice" in defining first degree murder. It thereby made a clear separation between a malicious intent and the process of deliberating before arriving at that intent.

Our Supreme Court recognized the need for evidence of both time for and fact of deliberation in *State v. Arata*, 56 Wash. 185, 189, 105 P. 227 (1909). Although it reversed a first degree murder conviction because a portion of an instruction was erroneous, it approved the remainder of the instruction, saying:

> [I]n the case at bar, the law knows no specific time; if the man reflects upon the act a moment antecedent to the act, it is sufficient; the time of deliberation and premeditation need not be long; if it furnishes room for reflection *and the facts show that such reflection existed*, then it is sufficient deliberation, and closed the instruction upon this point with the statement: "There need be no appreciable space of time between the formation of the intention to kill and the killing." By these few last words the court destroyed at once all that was good in the entire statement, and gave the jury a rule which this court has frequently held was erroneous. This was reversible error.

. . . The subject of premeditation appears frequently in Washington cases. However, it is seldom discussed in a way that affords clear, objective guidance to trial judges in determining the sufficiency of the evidence to support it. Nevertheless, review of these cases reveals that in each one where the evidence has been found sufficient, there has been some evidence beyond time from which a jury could infer the fact of deliberation. This evidence has included, *inter alia*, motive, acquisition of a weapon, and planning directly related to the killing.

Unless evidence of both time for and fact of deliberation is required, premeditation could be inferred in any case where the means of effecting death requires more than a moment in time. For all practical purposes, it would merge with intent; proof of intent would become proof of premeditation. However, the two elements are separate. Premeditation cannot be inferred from intent.

Premeditation can be proved by direct evidence, or it can be proved by circumstantial evidence where the inferences drawn by the jury are reasonable and the evidence supporting the jury's findings is substantial. There was no such evidence here, either direct or circumstantial.

There was no evidence that Bingham had known Cook before February 15 or that he had a motive to kill her. By chance, they took the same bus. When Cook's companion on the bus refused to go to Sequim with her, Bingham offered to see that Cook got back to the Laurisden Home later. That was apparently still his intention when he asked for a ride at the Pratt residence. It could be inferred that between there and the field 1/4 mile away, he decided to rape her. A reasonable jury could not infer from this beyond a reasonable doubt that he also planned to kill her. There is no other evidence to support a finding of premeditation. The fact of strangulation, without more, leads us to conclude that the jury only speculated as to the mental process involved in premeditation. This is not enough. The premeditation finding cannot stand. . . .

Reversed. Remanded for entry of judgment and sentence for second degree murder.

DISCUSSION QUESTIONS

1.   The court frames the issue of whether the time it takes to strangle someone alone is legally sufficient for a finding of premeditation and deliberation. Is that really true? Is there other evidence here from which one could infer premeditation and deliberation? Is there other evidence here that makes premeditation and deliberation less likely?

2.   Do you think that strangling someone to death is a particularly heinous form of killing someone which justifies first degree murder regardless of whether the strangler premeditated and deliberated? How about those who kill as part of a sexual assault? How would you compare Bingham to a contract killer?

3.   In a close case, should judges err on the side of giving jurors the option of finding premeditation and deliberation, or err on the side of not allowing juries to find premeditation and deliberation by not instructing on that crime?

Case in Context

The defendant in the next case killed a police officer. Intentionally killing a police officer who is acting in the line of duty is included within first degree murder in some jurisdictions regardless of whether the killer premeditated and deliberated. But the following jurisdiction required premeditation and deliberation to be proven.

WATSON V. U.S.

District of Columbia Court of Appeals
501 A.2d 791 (1985)

OPINION

Appellant appeals his conviction for first degree murder, D.C. Code § 22–2401 (1981), of Metropolitan Police Officer Donald Lunning on the ground that there was insufficient evidence of premeditation and deliberation. Consistent with our standard of review, we hold that a reasonable jury could reasonably find, from the evidence in the government's case-in-chief, that appellant had formed the decision to kill upon reaching for the loose gun, and that he gave further thought about this decision when the officer pleaded for his life. Accordingly, we affirm.

In reviewing the denial of a motion for a judgment of acquittal notwithstanding the verdict, this court must determine " 'whether there was sufficient evidence from which a reasonable juror could fairly conclude guilt beyond a reasonable doubt.' " Jones v. United States, 477 A.2d 231, 246 (D.C. 1984) (quoting Head v. United States, 451 A.2d 615, 622 (D.C. 1982)). We view the evidence in the "light most favorable to the government, giving full play to the right of the jury to determine credibility, weighing the evidence, and draw justifiable inferences of fact," Hall v. United States, 454 A.2d 314, 317 (D.C. 1982), and do not distinguish between direct and circumstantial evidence. We may reverse only where the government has produced no evidence from which a reasonable mind might infer guilt beyond a reasonable doubt.

First degree murder is a calculated and planned killing while second degree murder is unplanned or impulsive. Hall, supra, 454 A.2d at 317; Harris v. United States, 375 A.2d 505, 507 (D.C. 1977) (quoting Austin v. United States, 127 U.S. App. D.C. 180, 188, 382 F.2d 129, 137 (1967)). The government must therefore prove beyond a reasonable doubt that the accused acted with premeditation and deliberation, the thought processes necessary to distinguish first degree murder from second degree. See Hall, supra, 454 A.2d at 317. As set forth in Frendak, supra, 408 A.2d at 371 (citations omitted):

To prove premeditation, the government must show that a defendant gave "thought before acting to the idea of taking a human life and reached a definite decision to kill." Deliberation is proved by demonstrating that the accused acted with "consideration and reflection upon the preconceived design to kill; turning it over in the mind, giving it second thought." Although no specific amount of time is necessary to demonstrate premeditation and deliberation, the evidence must demonstrate that the accused did not kill impulsively, in the heat of passion, or in an orgy of frenzied activity.

"Some appreciable time must elapse" between the formation of design to kill and actual execution of the design to establish that reflection and consideration amounted to deliberation. Bostic v. United States, 68 App. D.C. 167, 170, 94 F.2d 636, 639 (1937), cert. denied, 303 U.S. 635, 82 L. Ed. 1095, 58 S. Ct. 523 (1938). The time need not be long. Doepel v. United States, 434 A.2d 449, 453 (D.C.), cert. denied, 454 U.S. 1037, 70 L. Ed. 2d 483, 102 S. Ct. 580 (1981). Thus, the government is not required to show that there was a "lapse of days or hours, or even minutes," Bostic, supra, at 170, 94 F.2d at 639, and the time involved may be as brief as a few seconds. Hemphill v. United States, 131 U.S. App. D.C. 46, 48, 402 F.2d 187, 189 (1968). Although reflection and consideration, and not lapse of time, are determinative of deliberation, Bostic, supra, 68 App. D.C. at 169, 94 F.2d at 639, Harris, supra, 375 A.2d at 508, "lapse of time is important because of the opportunity which it affords for deliberation." Bostic, supra, 68 App. D.C. at 169, 94 F.2d at 639 (citation omitted). The evidence of premeditation and deliberation must be sufficient to persuade, not compel, a reasonable juror to a finding of guilty. Crawford v. United States, 126 U.S. App. D.C. 156, 158, 375 F.2d 332, 334 (1967).

Viewing the evidence most favorably to the government, the government's case-in-chief showed that during the investigation of a stolen car, two police officers saw the stolen car pull into the parking lot of 3729 Jay Street, N.E. They ordered the driver to stop by shouting, "Police. Hold it." The driver of the car, appellant, jumped out, looked at the officers, and ran toward an apartment complex; Officer Lunning, with his gun drawn, pursued. Appellant ran through the archway of 3749 Jay Street, N.E. and then through the open door of the Davis' apartment at 3712-A Hayes Street, N.E. Three young girls, ages approximately 14, 13 and 9, were sitting at a table doing their homework. Appellant asked to use the telephone, and after dialing, he asked the responding party "Are they still out there?" He sat down at the table, where the girls were sitting, and held his head in his hands.

Officer Lunning entered the open door of the apartment holding his gun in front of him and told appellant "Police, you are under arrest." Appellant asked, "For what?" When appellant refused to cooperate with being handcuffed, the officer said, "Do you want me to blow your m f head off?" Appellant stood up. As the officer reached for his hand to put on the handcuffs, appellant said, "You are not going to put those things on me." Appellant grabbed the officer in a bear hug around the waist. Eventually the two men fell over a table. The officer's gun, which had been pointed downwards as he had tried to handcuff appellant, dropped onto the floor.

The two men scuffled, rolling over each other, until appellant had the officer in a position where he could not move: appellant had his knee in the officer's chest and, with his hands, held down the officer's hands. At this point, according to two of the girls, the officer told appellant, "It wasn't worth it." Then, with the officer still flat on his back, appellant reached out and grabbed the loose gun. He proceeded to hold the gun to the officer's chest. The officer now repeated, "It wasn't worth it." One of the girls then ran back to the back of the apartment, a distance of approximately twenty feet. She was inside the bathroom when, within seconds, she heard a shot. Another girl ran from the apartment, approximately sixteen feet, and heard a shot while outside. She next saw appellant coming down the steps as he was leaving the apartment complex holding the gun in his hand. The officer followed shortly, holding his chest and eventually fell to the ground.

The gun was fired approximately thirty to thirty-six inches from Officer Lunning's body while he was lying on the floor. The bullet entered at the midline of the top of the officer's abdomen on the right side. Appellant was uninjured when he was arrested at the scene, suffering only scrapes on his kneecap. Appellant was six feet four inches tall and weighed 218 pounds. Officer Lunning was five feet nine inches tall and weighed approximately 220 pounds.

A neighbor testified that when appellant ran into 3694 Hayes Street, N.E. and asked to use her sister's telephone, she heard him say into the telephone, "I just shot the police; could you come and get me." He also said he "had something on him and the police were chasing him so he hit the officer with the gun." The sister who lived in the apartment corroborated this testimony, and also testified that appellant told her he was carrying drugs and offered her money if she would hide him.

"Premeditation and deliberation may be inferred from sufficiently probative facts and circumstances." Hall, supra, 454 A.2d at 317. In the instant case the jury could reasonably find that when appellant sat at the table, after making the telephone call, he was anticipating the officer's arrival and planning how to escape. He knew the officer had drawn his gun, and a juror could infer that appellant realized he would have to disarm the officer in order to escape. Appellant, who was five inches taller, and described by one of the girls as much larger than the officer, initiated the struggle while the officer was pointing his gun at him. He struggled with the officer and caused him to drop his gun. He then continued to struggle with the officer until he gained complete physical control of the officer. One of the girls testified that the officer did not have a chance to get the loose gun. A juror could reasonably find that when the officer said, "It wasn't worth it," and appellant grabbed the gun, the officer was pleading for his life or at least suggesting to appellant that avoiding arrest for stealing a car was not worth assaulting an officer. Since there was nothing blocking appellant's escape from the apartment, a juror could further infer that by grabbing the loose gun and holding it to the officer's chest instead of fleeing, appellant had made the decision to kill the officer.

Before a shot was fired, however, the officer had time to repeat, "It wasn't worth it." Two of the girls also had time to run from the room into another part of the apartment or outside of the apartment building. In addition, appellant rose up and stood over the officer. At no time was anything or anyone impeding appellant's escape from the apartment. Considering the lapse of time before appellant fired the gun, a juror could reasonably infer from all the circumstances that the officer's second plea was asking appellant to reconsider the decision to kill him, and that appellant had sufficient time to, and did reaffirm his decision to kill the officer. Although these events occurred within a short period of time, there was evidence before the jury from which it could find that there were two significant pauses in the action—when appellant had immobilized the officer and when the officer repeated his plea—which afforded appellant time to premeditate and deliberate.

Appellant argues that the absence of eyewitness testimony about the events which occurred from the time appellant had the gun pointed in the officer's chest and the firing of the gun, demonstrates the jury was left to speculate on whether the officer's remarks had any impact on defendant's thought process. He notes that no evidence was presented of his facial gestures or hand movements which would indicate the officer's remarks affected him. Of course, eyewitness testimony is not required for the government to meet its burden of proof; circumstantial evidence will suffice. Jackson v. United States, supra, 395 A.2d at 102. This jurisdiction has long recognized that the jury is entitled to consider all of the circumstances preceding and surrounding the shooting to determine "whether reflection and consideration amounting to deliberation actually occurred." Bostic, supra, 68 App. D.C. at 169–170, 94 F.2d at 638–39 (citations omitted).

Appellant also urges us to hold that like the appellant in Bostic, supra, 68 App. D.C. at 171, 94 F.2d at 640, he acted in fear, panic and self-defense arising from the officer's threat, when he entered the apartment, to shoot appellant's "head off," and the officer's attempt later to grab his gun as appellant pointed it at him. He relies also on the testimony of one of the girls that the officer was acting kind of crazy and appellant looked frightened. Evidence that the officer had tried to grab his gun was not in evidence during the government's case-in-chief. But, in any event, we are satisfied that a juror could reasonably infer from the government's evidence that the totality of the circumstances cast substantial doubt on appellant's claim that he fired out of fear, in a panic, or in self-defense when the officer allegedly reached for the gun.

The government's evidence showed that although he was facing an officer with a drawn gun, appellant, having waited for the officer to arrive, initiated the physical struggle with him. Even after he had immobilized the officer and had grabbed the gun, appellant did not shoot immediately, but held the gun in the officer's chest. When he fired the gun he did not fire a series of shots, as though in a panic, but a single shot, which went directly into the right side of the officer's chest. Combined with the evidence of appellant's motive to escape, these circumstances could cause a reasonable juror to conclude that appellant did not shoot in a panic but acted with deliberation, having decided to kill the officer in order to assure his escape, and that he reflected upon his decision before pulling the trigger, and did not shoot in a frenzy or in the heat-of-passion.

Accordingly, we find no reason to disturb the trial court's implicit finding that the evidence viewed most favorably to the government is not such that a reasonable juror must have a reasonable doubt, and the issue was properly left to the jury.

Affirmed.

DISCUSSION QUESTIONS

1.   Did Watson have time enough to premeditate? Did the circumstances permit deliberation?

2.   Make the best one minute closing argument you can that Watson did premeditate and deliberate when he shot the police officer.

3.   Now make the best one minute closing argument you can that Watson did not premeditate and deliberate when he shot the police officer.

Case in Context

Killings of domestic partners are often emotionally charged. How should this affect how judges and juries think about premeditation and deliberation?

COMMONWEALTH V. CARROLL
Supreme Court of Pennsylvania
412 Pa. 525 (1963)

OPINION

Opinion by MR. CHIEF JUSTICE BELL.

The defendant, Carroll, pleaded guilty generally to an indictment charging him with the murder of his wife, and was tried by a Judge without a jury in the Court of Oyer and Terminer of Allegheny County. That Court found him guilty of first degree murder and sentenced him to life imprisonment. Following argument and denial of motions in arrest of judgment and for a new trial, defendant took this appeal. The only questions involved are thus stated by the appellant:

(1) "Does not the evidence sustain a conviction no higher than murder in the second degree?"

(2) "Does not the evidence of defendant's good character, together with the testimony of medical experts, including the psychiatrist for the Behavior Clinic of Allegheny County, that the homicide was not premeditated or intentional, require the Court below to fix the degree of guilt of defendant no higher than murder in the second degree?"

The defendant married the deceased in 1955, when he was serving in the Army in California. Subsequently he was stationed in Alabama, and later in Greenland. During the latter tour of duty, defendant's wife and two children lived with his parents in New Jersey. Because this arrangement proved incompatible, defendant returned to the United States on emergency leave in order to move his family to their own quarters. On his wife's insistence, defendant was forced first to secure a "compassionate transfer" back to the States, and subsequently to resign from the Army in July of 1960, by which time he had attained the rank of Chief Warrant

Officer. Defendant was a hard worker, earned a substantial salary and bore a very good reputation among his neighbors.

In 1958, decedent-wife suffered a fractured skull while attempting to leave defendant's car in the course of an argument. Allegedly this contributed to her mental disorder which was later diagnosed as a schizoid personality type. In 1959 she underwent psychiatric treatment at the mental hygiene clinic in Aberdeen, Maryland. She complained of nervousness and told the examining doctor "I feel like hurting my children." This sentiment sometimes took the form of sadistic "discipline" toward their very young children. Nevertheless, upon her discharge from the clinic, the doctors considered her much improved. Which this background we come to the immediate events of the crime.

In January, 1962, defendant was selected to attend an electronics school in Winston-Salem, North Carolina, for nine days. His wife greeted this news with violent argument. Immediately prior to his departure for Winston-Salem, at the suggestion and request of his wife, he put a loaded .22 caliber pistol on the window sill at the head of their common bed, so that she would feel safe. On the evening of January 16, 1962, defendant returned home and told his wife that he had been temporarily assigned to teach at a school in Chambersburg, which would necessitate his absence from home four nights out of seven for a ten week period. A violent and protracted argument ensued at the dinner table and continued until four o'clock in the morning.

Defendant's own statement after his arrest details the final moments before the crime: "We went into the bedroom a little before 3 o'clock on Wednesday morning where we continued to argue in short bursts. Generally she laid with her back to me facing the wall in bed and would just talk over her shoulder to me. I became angry and more angry especially what she was saying about my kids and myself, and sometime between 3 and 4 o'clock in the morning I remembered the gun on the window sill over my head. I think she had dozed off. I reached up and grabbed the pistol and brought it down and shot her twice in the back of the head."

When pressed on cross-examination defendant approximated that five minutes elapsed between his wife's last remark and the shooting.

Defendant's testimony at the trial elaborated this theme. He started to think about the children, "seeing my older son's feet what happened to them. I could see the bruises on him and Michael's chin was split open, four stitches. I didn't know what to do. I wanted to help my boys. Sometime in there she said something in there, she called me some kind of name. I kept thinking of this. During this time I either thought or felt—I thought of the gun, just thought of the gun. I am not sure whether I felt my hand move toward the gun—I saw my hand move, the next thing—the only thing I can recollect after that is right after the shots or right during the shots I saw the gun in my hand just pointed at my wife's head. She was still lying on her back—I mean her side. I could smell the gunpowder and I could hear something—it sounded like running water. I didn't know what it was at first, didn't realize what I'd done at first. Then I smelled it. I smelled blood before. . . ." "Q. At the time you shot her, Donald, were you fully aware and intend to do what you did? A. I don't know positively. All I remember hearing was two shots and feeling myself go cold all of a sudden."

Shortly thereafter defendant wrapped his wife's body in a blanket, spread and sheets, tied them on with a piece of plastic clothesline and took her down to the cellar. He tried to clean up as well as he could. That night he took his wife's body, wrapped in a blanket with a rug over it to a desolate place near a trash dump. He then took the children to his parents' home in Magnolia, New Jersey. He was arrested the next Monday in Chambersburg where he had gone to his teaching assignment.

Although defendant's brief is voluminous, the narrow and only questions which he raises on this appeal are as hereinbefore quoted. Both are embodied in his contention that the crime amounted only to second degree murder and that his conviction should therefore be reduced to second degree or that a new trial should be granted. . .

The specific intent to kill which is necessary to constitute in a nonfelony murder, murder in the first degree, may be found from a defendant's words or conduct or from the attendant circumstances together with all reasonable inferences therefrom, and may be inferred from the intentional use of a deadly weapon on a vital part of the body of another human being: Commonwealth v. Tyrrell, 405 Pa., supra; Commonwealth v. Moore, 398 Pa. 198, 157 A.2d 65; Commonwealth v. Nelson, 396 Pa. 359, 152 A.2d 913; Commonwealth v. Ballem, 386 Pa. 20, 123 A.2d 728; Commonwealth v. Heller, 369 Pa. 457, 87 A.2d 287; Commonwealth v. Jones, 355 Pa. 522, 50 A.2d 317.

It is well settled that a jury or a trial Court can believe all or a part of or none of a defendant's statements, confessions or testimony, or the testimony of any witness: Commonwealth v. Melton, 406 Pa. 343, 178 A.2d 728; Commonwealth v. Tyrrell, 405 Pa., supra; Commonwealth v. Ballem, 386 Pa., supra; Commonwealth v. Donough, 377 Pa. 46, 50, 103 A.2d 694; Commonwealth v. Homeyer, 373 Pa. 150, 153, 94 A.2d 743; Commonwealth v. Phillips, 372 Pa. 223, 93 A.2d 455; Commonwealth v. Shults, 221 Pa. 466, 70 Atl. 823.

If we consider only the evidence which is favorable to the Commonwealth, it is without the slightest doubt sufficient in law to prove first degree. However, even if we believe all of defendant's statements and testimony, there is no doubt that this killing constituted murder in the first degree. Defendant first urges that there was insufficient time for premeditation in the light of his good reputation. This is based on an isolated and oft repeated statement in Commonwealth v. Drum, 58 Pa. 9, 16, that " 'no time is too short for a wicked man to frame in his mind his scheme of murder.'" Defendant argues that, conversely, a long time is necessary to find premeditation in a "good man." We find no merit in defendant's analogy or contention. As Chief Justice MAXEY appropriately and correctly said in Commonwealth v. Earnest, 342 Pa. 544, 21 A.2d 38 (pages 549–550): "Whether the intention to kill and the killing, that is, the premeditation and the fatal act, were within a brief space of time or a long space of time is immaterial if the killing was in fact intentional, wilful, deliberate and premeditated. . . . As Justice AGNEW said in Com. v. Drum: 'The law fixes upon no length of time as necessary to form the intention to kill, but leaves the existence of a fully formed intent as a fact to be determined by the jury, from all the facts and circumstances in the evidence.' "

Defendant further contends that the time and place of the crime, the enormous difficulty of removing and concealing the body, and the obvious lack of an escape plan, militate against and make a finding of premeditation legally impossible. This is a "jury argument"; it is clear as crystal that such circumstances do not negate premeditation. This contention of defendant is likewise clearly devoid of merit.

Defendant's most earnestly pressed contention is that the psychiatrist's opinion of what defendant's state of mind must have been and was at the time of the crime, clearly establishes not only the lack but also the legal impossibility of premeditation. Dr. Davis, a psychiatrist of the Allegheny County Behavior Clinic, testified that defendant was "for a number of years . . . passively going along with a situation which he . . . was not controlling and he . . . was not making any decisions, and finally a decision . . . was forced on him . . . . He had left the military to take this assignment, and he was averaging about nine thousand a year; he had a good job. He knew that if he didn't accept this teaching assignment in all probability he would be dismissed from the Government service, and at his age and his special training he didn't know whether he would be able to find employment. More critical to that was the fact that at this point, as we understand it, his wife issued an ultimatum that if he went and gave this training course she would leave him . . . . He was so dependent upon her he didn't want her to leave. He couldn't make up his mind what to do. He was trapped. . . ."

The doctor then gave his opinion that "rage", "desperation", and "panic" produced "an impulsive automatic reflex type of homicide, . . . as opposed to an intentional premeditated type of homicide. . . . Our feeling was that if this gun had fallen to the floor he wouldn't have been able to pick it up and consummate that homicide. And I think if he had to load the gun he wouldn't have done it. This is a matter of opinion, but this is our opinion about it."

There are three answers to this contention. First, as we have hereinbefore stated, neither a Judge nor a jury has to believe all or any part of the testimony of the defendant or of any witness. Secondly, the opinion of the psychiatrists was based to a large extent upon statements made to them by the defendant, which need not be believed and which are in some instances opposed by the facts themselves. Thirdly, a psychiatrist's opinion of a defendant's impulse or lack of intent or state of mind is, in this class of case, entitled to very little weight, and this is especially so when defendant's own actions, or his testimony or confession, or the facts themselves, belie the opinion.

Defendant's own statement after his arrest, upon which his counsel so strongly relies, as well as his testimony at his trail, clearly convict him of first degree murder and justify the finding and sentence of the Court below. Defendant himself described his actions at the time he killed his wife. From his own statements and from his own testimony, it is clear that, terribly provoked by his allegedly nagging, belligerent and sadistic wife, * defendant remembered the gun, deliberately took it down, and deliberately fired two shots into the head of his sleeping wife. There is no doubt that this was a wilful, deliberate and premeditated murder.

DISCUSSION QUESTIONS

1. Make the best one minute closing argument you can that Carroll did premeditate and deliberate.

2. Make the best one minute closing argument you can that Carroll did not premeditate and deliberate.

3. Do you think that the jury in this case based their verdict on an assessment of the timing and quality of Carroll's thinking or on an assessment of his character? Is that inevitable? If so, should we rely on premeditation and deliberation to distinguish degrees of murder?

Exam Tip: Premeditation and Deliberation

Ask three questions of a fact pattern raising this issue. First, when could the killer have begun thinking about killing? Second, what reasons existed to kill? Third, what conditions existed that might have made it hard for the killer to think straight about those reasons?

Practice Problem 11.0: O Pioneers

This assignment is based on the following excerpt from Willa Cather's, *O Pioneer's*. Assume that Frank Shabata has been charged with the murders of Marie Shabata, his wife, and Emil Bergson.[1] Is Frank guilty of premeditated and deliberate murder under the definition given in the

---

[1] You should also assume three additional facts that are not explicitly stated in the excerpt: 1) Marie was Frank's wife; 2) Marie and Emil died as a result of the shots Frank fired; and 3) Frank observed his wife having sexual intercourse with Emil when Frank peered through the mulberry leaves and—literary language to the contrary notwithstanding—he knew that he was shooting at Marie and Emil.

thought he heard a cry simultaneous with the second report, but he was not sure. He peered again through the hedge, at the two dark figures under the tree. They had fallen a little apart from each other, and were perfectly still—No, not quite; in a white patch of light, where the moon shone through the branches, a man's hand was plucking spasmodically at the grass.

Suddenly the woman stirred and uttered a cry, then another, and another. She was living! She was dragging herself toward the hedge! Frank dropped his gun and ran back along the path, shaking, stumbling, gasping. He had never imagined such horror. The cries followed him. They grew fainter and thicker, as if she were choking. He dropped on his knees beside the hedge and crouched like a rabbit, listening; fainter, fainter; a sound like a whine; again—a moan—another—silence. Frank scrambled to his feet and ran on, groaning and praying. From habit he went toward the house, where he was used to being soothed when he had worked himself into a frenzy, but at the sight of the black, open door, he started back. He knew that he had murdered somebody, that a woman was bleeding and moaning in the orchard, but he had not realized before that it was his wife.

The gate stared him in the face. He threw his hands over his head. Which way to turn? He lifted his tormented face and looked at the sky. "Holy Mother of God, not to suffer! She was a good girl—not to suffer!"

Frank had been wont to see himself in dramatic situations; but now, when he stood by the windmill, in the bright space between the barn and the house, facing his own black doorway, he did not see himself at all. He stood like the hare when the dogs are approaching from all sides. And he ran like a hare, back and forth about that moonlit space, before he could make up his mind to go into the dark stable for a horse. The thought of going into a doorway was terrible to him. He caught Emil's horse by the bit and led it out. He could not have buckled a bridle on his own. After two or three attempts, he lifted himself into the saddle and started for Hanover. If he could catch the one o'clock train, he had money enough to get as far as Omaha.

While he was thinking dully of this in some less sensitized part of his brain, his acuter faculties were going over and over the cries he had heard in the orchard. Terror was the only thing that kept him from going back to her, terror that she might still be she, that she might still be suffering. A woman, mutilated and bleeding in his orchard—it was because it was a woman that he was so afraid. It was inconceivable that he should have hurt a woman. He would rather be eaten by wild beasts than see her move on the ground as she had moved in the orchard. Why had she been so careless? She knew he was like a crazy man when he was angry. She had more than once taken that gun away from him and held it, when he was angry with other people. Once it had gone off while they were struggling over it. She was never afraid. But, when she knew him, why hadn't she been more careful? Didn't she have all summer before her to love Emil Bergson in, without taking such chances? Probably she had met the Smirka boy, too, down there in the orchard. He didn't care. She could have met all the men on the Divide there, and welcome, if only she hadn't brought this horror on him.

CHAPTER 12

VOLUNTARY MANSLAUGHTER

■ ■ ■

Manslaughter is the homicide crime below murder. It is punished less harshly than murder in all jurisdictions. The first and simplest thing to get clear is the distinction between voluntary and involuntary manslaughter. Involuntary manslaughter involves an accidental killing, and voluntary manslaughter involves an intentional killing. So group "voluntary" with "intentional" and "involuntary" with "unintentional," and you will be able to keep this distinction straight.

Voluntary manslaughter should be one of the most interesting parts of your criminal law course because it raises fundamental issues that go to the heart of the criminal law. Think of voluntary manslaughter as "discounted murder." You intended to kill someone, which is ordinarily murder, but the crime and your sentence get "discounted" to voluntary manslaughter. Put this way, you can see the grounds for controversy. Why should we give discounts to any murderer? To make things even more interesting, voluntary manslaughter is not some newfangled product of modern sensitivities. It is an old common law doctrine.

The main idea behind voluntary manslaughter is that not all intentional killings are equally blameworthy. Some intentional killers are worse than others, and we should reserve murder for particularly evil intentional killers. The old common law word for this sort of evil was malice. The common law discounts murder down to manslaughter when—in the awkward phrasing of the common law—something "negates the malice" required for murder. What could negate the express malice of an intentional killer? Adequate provocation!

Voluntary manslaughter doctrine is a concession to human frailty, a recognition that we sometimes do things we wish we had not in the heat of the moment. So at common law, an intentional killing committed in a "sudden heat of passion" sometimes constituted voluntary manslaughter instead of murder. Heat of passion would only mitigate murder down to manslaughter if it was a response to "adequate provocation," however, and adequate provocation was very strictly defined.

The main idea behind provocation doctrine is not that a reasonable person would kill under the same circumstances—in which case the defendant should not be guilty of any crime—but rather, whether a reasonable person might lose control of their emotions. Colloquially, we might say that such a person "was not in their right mind," or "not themselves." As a result, their actions don't fully reflect blameworthiness but rather the sort of average human weakness that we want to partially (but not completely) excuse or justify.

A. STATUTORY EXAMPLES

Here are portions of two voluntary manslaughter statutes. How are they similar and how are they different?

Pennsylvania

§ 2503. Voluntary Manslaughter

(a) General rule. A person who kills an individual without lawful justification commits voluntary manslaughter if at the time of the killing he is acting under a sudden and intense passion resulting from serious provocation by:

    (1) the individual killed; or

    (2) another whom the actor endeavors to kill, but he negligently or accidentally causes the death of the individual killed. . .

(c) Grading-Voluntary manslaughter is [punishable by up to 10 years in prison].

Kansas

§ 21–3403. Voluntary Manslaughter

Voluntary manslaughter is the intentional killing of a human being committed:

(a) Upon a sudden quarrel or in the heat of passion; . . .

B. ELEMENTS OF PROVOCATION

Note that the idea has never been to reward the hotheaded. Adequate provocation is limited to those things that would make an ordinary person of average disposition "liable to act rashly" or "incapable of cool reflection." Adequate provocation is for the reasonable person, not for the reasonable drunken, short-tempered, or vengeful person because being drunk, short-tempered, or vengeful is not considered reasonable.

Over time, many common law jurisdictions have loosened and expanded their definitions of provocation, and this is the big story that many criminal law textbooks tell. The Model Penal Code replaces provocation with an even more forgiving doctrine called Extreme Mental or Emotional Disturbance, but that will be discussed a bit later.

Both the strict and looser versions of provocation doctrine follow the same basic structure. Four elements must be satisfied.

    1. The killer must have been actually provoked.

2.   A reasonable person would have been provoked.

3.   The killer must not have cooled off before killing.

4.   A reasonable person would not have cooled off before killing.

Each of these elements deserves further discussion, but let's do a quick overview.

1.   You must, of course, actually be provoked. Someone discovers his spouse engaged in an act of adultery but does not actually care. He kills her anyway to collect on her life insurance policy. This is not voluntary manslaughter because he was not actually provoked. He was not in the heat of passion but coolly killing to collect the insurance money. So this would be murder, not manslaughter.

2.   The grounds for provocation must be reasonable. Our killer becomes enraged and kills after he discovers his wife engaged in a game of "patty cake" with another man. This would also be murder, not manslaughter. Although witnessing your spouse engaged in an act of adultery has always been considered reasonable grounds for provocation, discovering your spouse engaged in an act of patty cake has not.

3.   You can't have cooled off. The spouse is initially enraged by the adultery but then laughs about it before killing the cheating spouse for the insurance money. This would be murder, not manslaughter, because the killer was no longer in the heat of passion when he killed.

4.   The time between the provocation and the killing must also be reasonable. The killer stays enraged about a single act of adultery by his spouse for a year then kills her on the anniversary of the adulterous act. This also would be murder, not manslaughter, because a reasonable person would have cooled off after a year even if he did not.

Note that two of the four elements are what might be described as "objective factors" and two as "subjective factors." The subjective factors are that you must actually have been provoked and that you cannot have actually cooled off. The objective factors—so called because they hold you to an objective standard—are that a reasonable person would have been provoked and that a reasonable person would not have cooled off in time.

Now that we have the basics in mind, let's go through the legal definitions of the two objective factors, noting the differences between the strict and looser approaches in common law jurisdictions. These two approaches go by different names in different textbooks and treatises: traditional v. contemporary and common law v. modern are two of the more common dichotomies. I prefer strict v. loose because it is more descriptively accurate, but make sure that you adopt the terminology of your professor and course.

C. ADEQUACY OF PROVOCATION

Early common law took what many aptly describe as a strict categorical approach. There were five categories of provoking events.

1. Witnessing your spouse in the act of adultery.

2. Witnessing a violent assault on a member of your immediate family.

3. Being violently attacked.

4. Being illegally arrested.

5. Being engaged in mutual combat.

If you were provoked by something not on the list, then you were guilty of murder. Also, these categories were very strictly construed at common law and still are in some common law jurisdictions. For example, with respect to adultery, some courts do not give manslaughter instructions to the jury if the killer didn't actually see the adultery, or if he witnessed oral sex instead of vaginal intercourse, or if it was his girlfriend or boyfriend as opposed to his husband or wife.

Note that the category of illegal arrest has been abandoned in most if not all jurisdictions. If you get illegally arrested, you are supposed to hire a lawyer, not get mad and start fighting with the police. So this no longer seems like a reasonable ground for provocation to most courts.

Over time many common law jurisdictions have moved to a more flexible approach to the evaluating the adequacy of provocation that some scholars refer to as the modern approach. This more flexible approach to provocation expands how these categories are interpreted and sometimes adds new ones. The basic idea is to give the jury the option of returning a manslaughter verdict any time that a reasonable person might lose control. That said, most common law jurisdictions stay close to the two basic types of provoking events that the common law recognized: violent acts and sexual betrayal.

One early common law rule that has survived largely intact in most common law jurisdictions is that "mere words" cannot adequately provoke. Sticks and stones may break your bones, but name-calling won't earn you a manslaughter instruction. Some jurisdictions, however, make an exception for "informational words."

Jurisdictions that have abandoned the strict categorical approach for the looser "reasonableness" standard have had to further define the "reasonable person" for the purposes of the provocation doctrine. What sorts of characteristics do you consider in deciding whether someone was reasonably provoked? Many jurisdictions will instruct juries to take the age and sex of the defendant into account, recognizing that a "reasonable seventeen year old" might be provoked differently than a "reasonable eighty year old woman." Beyond age and gender, however, things get murky. One leading scholar has observed that things that affect the gravity of the provocation are more likely to be considered than things that affect the degree of self-control. So a blind person who was pushed and taunted from different directions would be judged under the standard of a reasonable blind person, rather than a reasonable sighted person. A person with an anger management disorder, though, would be held to the standard of self-control of an average person. In a similar vein, morally idiosyncratic views are completely out of bounds. There is no such thing as a "reasonable racist person" standard, for example.

Case in Context

The following case offers a classic illustration of one common law category of provocation.

ILLINOIS V. WALKER

Appellate Court of Illinois, First District, Fourth Division
204 N.E.2d 594 (1965)

JUDGES: MR. JUSTICE DRUCKER delivered the opinion of the court. McCORMICK, P. J. and ENGLISH, J., concur.

Opinion by: DRUCKER.

OPINION

Defendant appeals from a conviction of murder and the sentence of fourteen years, after a bench trial. He urges that he was not proved guilty beyond a reasonable doubt but that in any event he was guilty of manslaughter and not murder.

The testimony of Albert McClinton, the State's main witness, reveals that on the night of June 2, 1961, he, Claude Jenkins, a Mrs. Brown and the defendant were drinking and talking on a porch at 3310 South Indiana Avenue in Chicago; that a man he did not know, John Stenneth (hereinafter referred to as the deceased), approached and demanded that they gamble; that when he was refused he drew a knife and started toward them; that McClinton grabbed two bottles and told deceased he would hit him if "you comes up on me with that knife"; that defendant and Jenkins told McClinton to come back but that every time he turned deceased ran up and tried to cut him; that defendant and Jenkins came up and backed deceased down the street; that deceased was cutting at both of them but that he did not see either defendant or Jenkins get cut. McClinton further testified that defendant threw a brick which hit deceased and knocked him down; that all three ran up and stood around the deceased; that defendant picked up deceased's hand with the knife in it and said "he would cut his throat with his own knife"; that he cut the deceased and walked away. McClinton then said "You shouldn't have cut the man. I told you not to cut the man, I told you not to cut the man" and defendant answered: "You told me not to cut the man. He cut me."

Defendant's main contention is that, under the law, if a killing occurs during the course of a fight and before the blood of the killer has had time to cool, the offense is not murder but voluntary manslaughter. In support of his view, defendant cites People v. Bissett, 246 Ill 516, 92 NE 949:

... It is indispensable, before one can be convicted of the crime of murder, that the act be done with malice aforethought, either express or implied. Here the element of malice, under the case as made by the People, was wholly wanting. Under our statute the crime committed could not have been more than manslaughter, which to use the language of the statute, "is the unlawful killing of a human being without malice, express or implied, and without any mixture of deliberation whatever. It must be voluntary, upon a sudden heat of passion, caused by a provocation apparently sufficient to make the passion irresistible. ... In cases of voluntary manslaughter, there must be a serious and highly provoking injury inflicted upon the person killing, sufficient to excite an irresistible passion in a reasonable person, or an attempt by the person killed to commit a serious personal injury on the person killing. The killing must be the result of that sudden, violent impulse of passion supposed to be irresistible; for if there should appear to have been an interval between the assault or provocation given, and the killing, sufficient for the voice of reason and humanity to be heard, the killing shall be attributed to deliberate revenge, and punished as murder." That Russell was inflicting upon plaintiff in error a highly provoking injury at the time he voluntarily seized him and demanded he turn over to him the contents of his pocket is clearly shown by the testimony of every witness to the assault. That from the time the affray began until Russell was shot and killed there was not the slightest pause in the activities of the two men engaged, and not the slightest opportunity offered plaintiff in error to deliberate or reason in regard to the matter, is clearly shown. Under this state of facts the plaintiff in error, if guilty at all, is guilty of no graver offense than that of manslaughter, and upon motion for a new trial the verdict of the jury should have been set aside. (246 Ill at 521, 522.)

In the instant case, the deceased was an aggressive, intoxicated belligerent who menaced strangers because they would not gamble with him. According to every witness he kept swinging his knife at one and all. Defendant went to McClinton's aid; defendant had no words with deceased whom he had never seen before; when he was cut by the deceased, he knocked him down by striking him with a brick. It is undisputed that defendant never had a knife. He grabbed deceased's hand with the knife in it and stabbed deceased with the knife in deceased's hand. The affray was a continuous one. It lasted six minutes according to defendant. McClinton testified that:

> I don't know exactly how much time elapsed between the time I first saw this man and when Leroy cut him with his own knife. Everything happened pretty fast. I guess it wasn't as long as 15 minutes. It all happened pretty fast.

In his summation in the trial court, the Assistant State's Attorney said:

> . . . I think the defendant used too much force in attempting to restrain the attack of the deceased. And I think that after he was attacked and was cut by the deceased, that he became impatient and that is when he performed the stabbing on the deceased.

We find that under the evidence defendant was guilty of voluntary manslaughter and remand the cause to the Circuit Court with directions to enter a finding of guilty of voluntary manslaughter and to impose a sentence for that crime appropriate to the facts and circumstances of this cause and to whatever other matters in aggravation or mitigation may be made available to the trial court.

DISCUSSION QUESTIONS

1.   Generally should one who loses his temper and kills immediately after being attacked be eligible for a reduction of murder to manslaughter? If you were on the jury in Walker's case would you have voted for manslaughter or murder?

2.   Do we allow for manslaughter in cases of violent assaults because we understand that being attacked triggers a "fight or "flight" response that leads many people to lose control, or because we believe that an innocent victim of an assault is somewhat justified in retaliating against an aggressor even after the attack has concluded?

3.   What if Walker had not been attacked, but he and his victim had agreed to fight one another after an angry exchange of words? Assume once again that Walker's use of deadly force was not justified by self defense during the fight but that he killed his victim in the same manner while the victim was on the ground. Should provocation include mutual combat? More specifically, should the law permit a manslaughter verdict in such a case?

Case in Context

Many manslaughter cases involve domestic violence, as does the following case. One of the issues discussed was whether words alone can constitute adequate provocation.

GIROUARD V. MARYLAND

Court of Appeals of Maryland
583 A.2d 718 (1991)

Opinion by: COLE.

OPINION

In this case we are asked to reconsider whether the types of provocation sufficient to mitigate the crime of murder to manslaughter should be limited to the categories we have heretofore recognized, or whether the sufficiency of the provocation should be decided by the factfinder on a case-by-case basis. Specifically, we must determine whether words alone are provocation adequate to justify a conviction of manslaughter rather than one of second degree murder.

The Petitioner, Steven S. Girouard, and the deceased, Joyce M. Girouard, had been married for about two months on October 28, 1987, the night of Joyce's death. Both parties, who met while working in the same building, were in the army. They married after having known each other for approximately three months. The evidence at trial indicated that the marriage was often tense and strained, and there was some evidence that after marrying Steven, Joyce had resumed a relationship with her old boyfriend, Wayne.

On the night of Joyce's death, Steven overheard her talking on the telephone to her friend, whereupon she told the friend that she had asked her first sergeant for a hardship discharge because her husband did not love her anymore. Steven went into the living room where Joyce was on the phone and asked her what she meant by her comments; she responded, "nothing." Angered by her lack of response, Steven kicked away the plate of food Joyce had in front of her. He then went to lie down in the bedroom.

Joyce followed him into the bedroom, stepped up onto the bed and onto Steven's back, pulled his hair and said, "What are you going to do, hit me?" She continued to taunt him by saying, "I never did want to marry you and you are a lousy fuck and you remind me of my dad." The barrage of insults continued with her telling Steven that she wanted a divorce, that the marriage had been a mistake and that she had never wanted to marry him. She also told him she had seen his commanding officer and filed charges against him for abuse. She then asked Steven, "What are you going to do?" Receiving no response, she continued her verbal attack. She added that she had filed charges against him in the Judge Advocate General's Office (JAG) and that he would probably be court martialed.

When she was through, Steven asked her if she had really done all those things, and she responded in the affirmative. He left the bedroom with his pillow in his arms and proceeded to the kitchen where he procured a long handled kitchen knife. He returned to Joyce in the bedroom with the knife behind the pillow. He testified that he was enraged and that he kept waiting for Joyce to say she was kidding, but Joyce continued talking. She said she had learned a lot from the marriage and that it had been a mistake. She also told him she would remain in their apartment after he moved out. When he questioned how she would afford it, she told him she would claim her brain-damaged sister as a dependent and have the sister move in. Joyce reiterated that the marriage was a big mistake, that she did not love him and that the divorce would be better for her.

After pausing for a moment, Joyce asked what Steven was going to do. What he did was lunge at her with the kitchen knife he had hidden behind the pillow and stab her 19 times. Realizing what he had done, he dropped the knife and went to the bathroom to shower off Joyce's blood. Feeling like he wanted to die, Steven went back to the kitchen and found two steak knives with which he slit his own wrists. He lay down on the bed waiting to die, but when he realized that he would not die from his self-inflicted wounds, he got up and called the police, telling the dispatcher that he had just murdered his wife.

When the police arrived they found Steven wandering around outside his apartment building. Steven was despondent and tearful and seemed detached, according to police officers who had been at the scene. He was unconcerned about his own wounds, talking only about how much he loved his wife and how he could not believe what he had done. Joyce Girouard was pronounced dead at the scene.

At trial, defense witness, psychologist, Dr. William Stejskal, testified that Steven was out of touch with his own capacity to experience anger or express hostility. He stated that the events of October 28, 1987, were entirely consistent with Steven's personality, that Steven had "basically reach[ed] the limit of his ability to swallow his anger, to rationalize his wife's behavior, to tolerate, or actually to remain in a passive mode with that. He essentially went over the limit of his ability to bottle up those strong emotions. What ensued was a very extreme explosion of rage that was intermingled with a great deal of panic." Another defense witness, psychiatrist, Thomas Goldman, testified that Joyce had a "compulsive need to provoke jealousy so that she's always asking for love and at the same time destroying and undermining any chance that she really might have to establish any kind of mature love with anybody."

Steven Girouard was convicted, at a court trial of second degree murder and was sentenced to 22 years incarceration, 10 of which were suspended.

Petitioner relies primarily on out of state cases to provide support for his argument that the provocation to mitigate murder to manslaughter should not be limited only to the traditional circumstances of: extreme assault or battery upon the defendant; mutual combat; defendant's illegal arrest; injury or serious abuse of a close relative of the defendant's; or the sudden discovery of a spouse's adultery. Petitioner argues that manslaughter is a catchall for homicides which are criminal but that lack the malice essential for a conviction of murder. Steven argues that the trial judge did find provocation (although he held it inadequate to mitigate murder) and that the categories of provocation adequate to mitigate should be broadened to include factual situations such as this one.

The State counters by stating that although there is no finite list of legally adequate provocations, the common law has developed to a point at which it may be said there are some concededly provocative acts that society is not prepared to recognize as reasonable. Words spoken by the victim, no matter how abusive or taunting, fall into a category society should not accept as adequate provocation. According to the State, if abusive words alone could mitigate murder to manslaughter, nearly every domestic argument ending in the death of one party could be mitigated to manslaughter. This, the State avers, is not an acceptable outcome. Thus, the State argues that the courts below were correct in holding that the taunting words by Joyce Girouard were not provocation adequate to reduce Steven's second degree murder charge to voluntary manslaughter.

Initially, we note that the difference between murder and manslaughter is the presence or absence of malice. State v. Faulkner, 301 Md. 482, 485, 483 A.2d 759 (1984); State v. Ward, 284 Md. 189, 195, 396 A.2d 1041 (1978); Davis v. State, 39 Md. 355 (1874). Voluntary manslaughter has been defined as "an intentional homicide, done in a sudden heat of passion, caused by adequate provocation, before there has been a reasonable opportunity for the passion to cool. Cox v. State, 311 Md. 326, 331, 534 A.2d 1333 (1988). See also, State v. Faulkner, supra; State v. Ward, supra; Whitehead v. State, 9 Md.App. 7, 262 A.2d 316 (1970).

There are certain facts that may mitigate what would normally be murder to manslaughter. For example, we have recognized as falling into that group: (1) discovering one's spouse in the act of sexual intercourse with another; (2) mutual combat; (3) assault and battery. See State v. Faulkner, 301 Md. at 486, 483 A.2d 759. There is also authority recognizing injury to one of the defendant's relatives or to a third party, and death resulting from resistance of an illegal arrest as adequate provocation for mitigation to manslaughter. See, e.g., 40 C.J.S. Homicide § 48 at 913 (1944) and 40 C.J.S. Homicide § 50 at 915–16 (1944). Those acts mitigate homicide to manslaughter because they create passion in the defendant and are not considered the product of free will. State v. Faulkner, 301 Md. at 486, 483 A.2d 759.

In order to determine whether murder should be mitigated to manslaughter we look to the circumstances surrounding the homicide and try to discover if it was provoked by the victim. Over the facts of the case we lay the template of the so-called "Rule of Provocation." The courts of this State have repeatedly set forth the requirements of the Rule of Provocation:

1.   There must have been adequate provocation;

2. The killing must have been in the heat of passion;

3. It must have been a sudden heat of passion—that is, the killing must have followed the provocation before there had been a reasonable opportunity for the passion to cool;

4. There must have been a causal connection between the provocation, the passion, and the fatal act.

We shall assume without deciding that the second, third, and fourth of the criteria listed above were met in this case. We focus our attention on an examination of the ultimate issue in this case, that is, whether the provocation of Steven by Joyce was enough in the eyes of the law so that the murder charge against Steven should have been mitigated to voluntary manslaughter. For provocation to be "adequate," it must be " 'calculated to inflame the passion of a reasonable man and tend to cause him to act for the moment from passion rather than reason.' " Carter v. State, 66 Md.App. at 572, 505 A.2d 545 quoting R. Perkins, Perkins on Criminal Law at p. 56 (2d ed. 1969). The issue we must resolve, then, is whether the taunting words uttered by Joyce were enough to inflame the passion of a reasonable man so that that man would be sufficiently infuriated so as to strike out in hot-blooded blind passion to kill her. Although we agree with the trial judge that there was needless provocation by Joyce, we also agree with him that the provocation was not adequate to mitigate second degree murder to voluntary manslaughter.

Although there are few Maryland cases discussing the issue at bar, those that do hold that words alone are not adequate provocation. Words can constitute adequate provocation if they are accompanied by conduct indicating a present intention and ability to cause the defendant bodily harm. Id. Clearly, no such conduct was exhibited by Joyce in this case. While Joyce did step on Steven's back and pull his hair, he could not reasonably have feared bodily harm at her hands. This, to us, is certain based on Steven's testimony at trial that Joyce was about 5'1" tall and weighed 115 pounds, while he was 6'2" tall, weighing over 200 pounds. Joyce simply did not have the size or strength to cause Steven to fear for his bodily safety. Thus, since there was no ability on the part of Joyce to cause Steven harm, the words she hurled at him could not, under the analysis in Lang, constitute legally sufficient provocation.

Other jurisdictions overwhelmingly agree with our cases and hold that words alone are not adequate provocation.

Thus, with no reservation, we hold that the provocation in this case was not enough to cause a reasonable man to stab his provoker 19 times. The standard is one of reasonableness; it does not and should not focus on the peculiar frailties of mind of the Petitioner. That standard of reasonableness has not been met here. We cannot in good conscience countenance holding that a verbal domestic argument ending in the death of one spouse can result in a conviction of manslaughter. We agree with the trial judge that social necessity dictates our holding. Domestic arguments easily escalate into furious fights. We perceive no reason for a holding in favor of those who find the easiest way to end a domestic dispute is by killing the offending spouse.

DISCUSSION QUESTIONS

1.   Do you think that the jury should at least have had the chance to consider whether the words exchanged in this case caused the defendant to lose control? Could you evaluate the reasonableness of losing control without hearing testimony?

2.   What role should expert testimony by psychologists play in finding adequate provocation? Should the jury get to hear it?

3.   The court clearly worries that allowing words alone to conduct adequate provocation would make it too easy to receive a manslaughter verdict in cases of domestic violence. Do you agree?

Case in Context

In the following case—also involving domestic violence—expert psychological evidence was introduced on the issue of the adequacy of the provocation.

BROOKS V. STATE

Court of Criminal Appeals of Alabama
630 So. 2d 160 (1993)

BOWEN, PRESIDING JUDGE.

The appellant, Marguerite Louise Brooks, was convicted of the murder of her husband, Lewis Brooks, and was sentenced to life imprisonment.

I   . . .

The evidence presented at trial tended to show that on September 18, 1992, the appellant was walking down the street with her friend Jeanette McLendon when Lewis Brooks, the appellant's husband, who was accompanied by his friend Yancey Davis, accosted the appellant and told her to "bring [her] ass here." Brooks began "cussing and fussing" at the appellant, grabbed the appellant's blouse, and jerked her toward him. The appellant pulled free. Then she and Ms. McLendon, pursued by Lewis Brooks and Yancey Davis, ran across the street to Ms. McLendon's house. Brooks was drunk and angry and he told Yancey Davis that he was "going to kill that bitch," referring to the appellant.

1.   According to Ms. McLendon, the appellant said "that she needed something . . . she wasn't going to come out that door empty-handed." When McLendon informed the appellant that there was a gun in the dresser drawer, the appellant took

the gun and went outside. Seeing her husband, the appellant told him that "she wasn't going to let him hurt her no more and [to] stay back." Lewis Brooks advanced toward the appellant with his hands raised and she told him again, "Stay back; I will shoot." Brooks said, "You got the gun; go on and do what you got to do." When Brooks continued to move toward the appellant with his hands up, the appellant shot him.[1]

The undisputed evidence at trial established that the appellant was a battered wife who had suffered physical abuse not only at the hands of her current husband, Lewis Brooks, but also at the hands of her former husband and another male companion with whom she had once cohabited. The State's expert witness, Dr. Karl Kirkland, a psychologist and certified forensics examiner, testified that the appellant suffered from "battered woman syndrome," a type of post-traumatic stress disorder characterized by the following symptoms:

> "Depression, a feeling of restricted choice, chronic apprehensiveness, a great deal of anxiety, a tendency to blame oneself, increased dependency. Some people describe a psychological paralysis of the will. That is, it causes a person to stay in a battering relationship. For a long time women who stayed in battering relationships were felt to be either masochistic or to be emotionally disturbed or else why would they stay. And the literature has not supported either of those theories. It basically says they stay because they are afraid."

Dr. Kirkland testified that the appellant's "status as an abused woman or wife played a major role in her behavior at the time of the offense."

II

The appellant . . . contends that the trial court erred by instructing the jury that "battered woman syndrome" did not constitute legal provocation sufficient to reduce murder to manslaughter.

After the jury had been deliberating for some time, it returned to the courtroom to ask the trial judge the following questions: (1) "What is the definition of murder by law?" (2) "What is the definition of manslaughter by law?" (3) "Is 'battered woman syndrome' grounds for manslaughter?" and (4) "Is 'battered woman syndrome' considered provocation?" The court answered the first two questions by reinstructing the jury on murder and heat-of-passion manslaughter. The court answered the third and fourth questions simply by stating, "No."

---

[1] Author's Note: Students sometimes wonder why Brooks was not entitled to shoot her husband in self defense. The jury received a self defense instruction but refused to acquit on those grounds, most likely because they concluded that Brooks left a place of safety and chose to go back outside after arming herself with a gun to confront her husband.

We note that other jurisdictions considering this issue have found provocation and heat-of-passion manslaughter instructions to be appropriate in prosecutions of battered victims who kill their batterers.

In *State v. Vigilante*, 257 N.J.Super. 296, 608 A.2d 425 (1992), the court held that a battered child prosecuted for killing his father was entitled to a heat-of-passion manslaughter instruction. The New Jersey court concluded that the child's past abuse and his contemplation of future abuse, combined with the father's threat to kill the child presented grounds for a provocation and heat-of-passion manslaughter charge.

"It seems to us that a course of ill treatment which can induce a homicidal response in a person of ordinary firmness and which the accused reasonably believes is likely to continue, should permit a finding of provocation. In taking this view, we merely acknowledge the undoubted capacity of events to accumulate a detonating force, no different from that of a single blow or injury. The question is simply one of fact, whether the accused did, because of such prolonged oppression and the prospect of its continuance, experience a sudden episode of emotional distress which overwhelmed her reason, and whether, if she did, she killed because of it and before there had passed time reasonably sufficient for her emotions to yield to reason."

Vigilante, . . . 257 N.J.Super. at 304, 608 A.2d at 429–30 (quoting *State v. Guido*, 40 N.J. 191, 211, 191 A.2d 45, 56 (1963). . . .

In the present case, however, we need not decide this issue because defense counsel made no objection to the court's answers regarding manslaughter and the battered woman syndrome. The appellant has therefore failed to preserve this issue for review. See Rule 21.2, A.R.Crim.P. ("No party may assign as error the court's giving . . . of an erroneous, misleading, incomplete, or otherwise improper oral charge, unless he objects thereto before the jury retires to consider its verdict, stating the matter to which he objects and the grounds of his objection").

The judgment of the circuit court is affirmed.

DISCUSSION QUESTIONS

1.   The court ultimately decides the issues raised in the defendant's favor but does not reverse the conviction and leaves the defendant serving life imprisonment. Why? What lesson do you draw from the answer?

2.   Should battered spouse syndrome evidence be considered in voluntary manslaughter cases?

3.   What constitutes a syndrome? What other syndromes might some defendants wish to raise in voluntary manslaughter cases? Can you come up with a principled basis for deciding which syndromes may be considered and which may not?

D.   REASONABLENESS OF COOLING OFF PERIOD

How long would it take a "reasonable person" to cool off and to regain their ordinary level of self-control after having witnessed an act of sexual betrayal or after having been beaten? Ten minutes, an hour, a day, a week? Courts have been reluctant to put an exact time on such things. Generally speaking, someone might be expected to cool off after an hour and virtually always after a day depending on the gravity of the provocation. Historically, the common law was very strict about this, and judges often refused to give manslaughter instructions to juries if too much time had passed. The modern trend is to leave the issue of how long it should take a reasonable person to cool off to the jury more often.

Case in Context

The following case illustrates how a rigid cooling off requirement can sometimes operate very harshly.

STATE V. GOUNAGIAS

Supreme Court of Washington
153 P. 9 (1915)

The defendant was tried upon an information charging him with murder in the first degree. The jury returned a verdict of guilty as charged. The defendant's motion for a new trial was overruled. Judgment was entered upon the verdict. The defendant appealed.

On May 7, 1914, and for a long time prior thereto, the appellant and one Dionisios Grounas, known also as Dan George, both Greeks, had been employed with a number of their countrymen in a paper mill located at Camas, Clarke county, Wash. The defendant and George had at one time lived in the same house, but prior to the date of the killing the appellant had moved away, and was on the 6th day of May, 1914, living in a house about a quarter of a mile, or, as he testified, six or seven blocks from the house where George lived. At that time the appellant was employed on the evening shift, which began work at 4 o'clock in the afternoon and ceased at midnight. George was employed on a different shift, and on the evening of May 6th went to bed early, apparently remaining there until the time of the shooting. The appellant did not go to work at 4 o'clock as usual on that afternoon, because, as he testified, he was suffering from a severe headache, which lasted all day, the cause of which he was not permitted to relate. He detailed his movements, stating that he visited a pool room, played a little at billiards, made several visits to a coffeehouse in Camas, played a game of cards with the baker, went to the river, intending to commit suicide, but abandoned that idea, visited certain Greeks of his acquaintance and conversed with them for something over an hour, met a man from the old country, took him to his own house, and talked with him for some time, and finally, about 11 o'clock at night, again visited the coffeehouse.

On the 18th day of April, 1914, the day before the Greek Easter, the appellant and two other Greeks, in response to an advertisement in a Greek periodical, each ordered from a mail order house in Chicago a box containing a 32 caliber revolver and certain other articles, which he testified he ordered because he considered the articles cheap. The appellant's box came about the 30th of April, and on that or the following day he procured ammunition for the revolver from a dealer in Camas. He kept the revolver concealed in his house in a slit in the underside of his mattress. He testified that on the evening of May 6th, when he made his last visit to the coffeehouse, there were several of his countrymen there, and something occurred, which he was not permitted to detail, which so excited and enraged him as to cause him to form the design of killing Dan George. He testified that he had never at any time thought of killing George until his last visit to the coffeehouse on the evening of May 6th; that about 10 minutes after 11 o'clock he rushed from the coffeehouse, ran to his own house, made a necessary visit to the toilet, went to his mattress, took out the revolver and loaded it, went rapidly up the hill to the house where George lived, entered the house, and by the light of a match found George asleep in his bed, did not awaken him, but immediately shot him through the head, firing five shots, all that he had in the revolver; that he then returned to his own house, removing the empty shells on the way, put the revolver back in the slit in the mattress, and went to bed, where he was shortly afterwards arrested.

Counsel for the appellant in his opening statement disclaimed any intention of asking an acquittal, but started to detail certain circumstances which he expected to prove in mitigation to reduce the offense from murder to manslaughter. On objection by the state he was not permitted to proceed with this part of the statement. In the progress of the defense counsel offered to prove by the appellant that on the 19th day of April, 1914, the Greek Easter, the appellant, who was then living in the same house with the deceased, had taken several glasses of beer, and either because of the beer, or of some drug therein, had become helpless and almost unconscious, when the deceased, after making many insulting remarks concerning the appellant and his wife, who lived in the old country, finally, while the appellant lay helpless on the floor, committed upon him the unmentionable crime, and went away, leaving the appellant in a state of semiconsciousness; that the appellant thereafter moved to another house, and on the next day, meeting George on the street, upbraided him for his action and asked him why he had done it, to which George in substance laughingly replied, 'You're all right, it did not hurt you;' that the appellant then, in order to avoid the disgrace of the matter, asked George to say nothing about it to their countrymen; that thereafter, wherever the appellant went, he could hear remarks and see signs made by his countrymen indicating that

George had circulated the story, so that the appellant was continuously ridiculed and subjected to insulting remarks and gestures on the part of his fellow countrymen; that these things so preyed upon his mind that he became sick and afflicted with severe headaches, and that the headache on May 6th, which was so severe as to prevent his working, was induced by this cause; that when he entered the coffeehouse at about 11 o'clock on the evening of May 6th there were about 10 men there, who began making laughing remarks and suggestive gestures, which in the appellant's weakened condition so excited and enraged him that he lost all control of his reason and rushed from the house, with the design of avenging himself by killing George. The appellant also offered to prove by other witnesses that Dan George had in fact circulated the report of his treatment of the appellant, and that by reason thereof the insulting remarks, signs, and gestures were often made in the appellant's presence. These offers were made in the absence of the jury, and the evidence was by the court excluded. The appellant was asked in the presence of the jury, 'Why did you kill Dan George?' The court, evidently understanding that in answer to this question he would repeat the story which had been excluded, did not permit him to answer, further than to say that he first thought of killing George 'at the moment when I saw those inhuman things at 11 o'clock.'

After the foregoing offer of evidence had been refused, and after counsel for the appellant had disclaimed any intention of seeking an acquittal on the ground of insanity, or any other ground, he made an offer to show, by the testimony of an alienist, 'what a man would do under these circumstances, or is likely to do.' The court then asked if any question of insanity was raised, and counsel answered, 'No,' further stating, in effect, that the alienist would not say that the man was insane, either at the time of the killing or at the time of the trial, or ever had been, but he would say, from his examination of the appellant, that the appellant acted under an uncontrollable impulse produced by bringing back to his mind the outrage with such vividness and force that it was as real to him on the night of the killing as at the time when the outrage was committed, and even more so, because of his weakened condition. This evidence was also excluded.

The court instructed the jury as to the necessary elements of murder in the first and second degrees, but refused to instruct as to manslaughter. There are many assignments of error, but they are all directed to the exclusion of the offered evidence, which it is claimed should have been admitted in mitigation of the offense from murder to manslaughter, and to the refusal of the court to instruct as to manslaughter upon such evidence.

The offered evidence makes it clear that the appellant knew and appreciated for days before the killing the full meaning of the words, signs, and vulgar gestures of his countrymen, which, as the offer shows, he had encountered from day to day for about three weeks following the original outrage, wherever he went. The final demonstration in the coffeehouse was nothing new. It was exactly what the appellant, from his experience for the prior three weeks, must have anticipated. To say that it alone tended to create the sudden passion and heat of blood essential to mitigation is to ignore the admitted fact that the same thing had created no such condition on its repeated occurrence during the prior three weeks. To say that these repeated demonstrations, coupled with the original outrage, culminated in a sudden passion and heat of blood when he encountered the same character of demonstration in the coffeehouse on the night of the killing, is to say that sudden passion and heat of blood in the mitigative sense may be a cumulative result of repeated reminders of a single act of provocation occurring weeks before, and this, whether that provocation be regarded as the original outrage or the spreading of the story among appellant's associates, both of which he knew and fully realized for three weeks before the fatal night. This theory of the cumulative effect of reminders of former wrongs, not of new acts of provocation by the deceased, is contrary to the idea of sudden anger as understood in the doctrine of mitigation. In the nature of the thing sudden anger cannot be cumulative. A provocation which does not cause instant resentment, but which is only resented after being thought upon and brooded over, is not a provocation sufficient in law to reduce intentional killing from murder to manslaughter, or under our statute to second degree murder, which includes every inexcusable, unjustifiable, unpremeditated, intentional killing.

The evidence offered had no tendency to prove sudden anger and resentment. On the contrary, it did tend to prove brooding thought, resulting in the design to kill. It was therefore properly excluded.

DISCUSSION QUESTIONS

1. Why wouldn't the court admit evidence of Gounigas' rape at the hands of the man he killed?

2. Would Gounigas have received a manslaughter instruction if he killed his rapist immediately after the rape? Are you a more blameworthy person if it takes you a long time to anger and to lose control of your emotions? A more dangerous person?

3. If you were allowed to argue for voluntary manslaughter to the Gounigas' jury, how would you describe the relationship between the ongoing taunts and the rape?

Case in Context

The more flexible standard for evaluating the cooling off element of voluntary manslaughter permitted a manslaughter verdict in the following case.

PEOPLE V. ELLENA STARR NESLER
Supreme Court of California
16 Cal. 4th 561 (1997)

Daniel Driver allegedly raped defendant's son, W., at a Christian camp where Driver worked. Driver told W., who was then seven years of age, that Driver would kill him, his sister, and defendant if W. told anyone what had happened. Several months later, W. disclosed to defendant what Driver had done. In May 1989, a complaint was filed against Driver, alleging seven counts of child molestation involving four boys, including W. Driver, however, had fled and was not apprehended until late 1992 or early 1993.

During this period, W. became hypervigilant and expected Driver to kidnap and kill him. He also began asking defendant questions about suicide, and once defendant found him with a gun. Fearing that W. would kill himself, she obtained counseling for him. Defendant told her sister, Jannette Martinez, that when defendant was a child she had been raped in the same manner as W., and that there was a time when she, too, wanted to die.

Before Driver's preliminary hearing took place in April 1993, defendant protested when she learned that W. would have to face Driver at the hearing. She suggested videotaping W.'s testimony, but that alternative was unavailable; defendant then asked that the hearing at least be closed to the public. On the morning of the hearing, W. began vomiting and continued to do so after he arrived at the courthouse. Defendant appeared nervous, upset, and extremely anxious about W. She told an investigator that W. might not be able to testify, and she attempted to reassure and encourage the boy. When Driver arrived at the courthouse for the hearing, he looked at W. and grinned with a mean, disgusted, and haughty look. Defendant lunged for Driver, but Martinez grabbed her arm. Defendant again asked someone from the district attorney's office whether the courtroom could be closed, but an open hearing was held.

After W. entered the waiting room for witnesses, he continued to vomit. The mother of one of the other boys said that she did not believe her testimony had gone well, and that Driver had smirked at her and her son when they testified. This woman also said that she was convinced Driver was "going to walk," and that she wanted to get a gun and kill him.

She told defendant to try to do better than she and her son had done. After this exchange, defendant became nervous and started pacing.

Defendant and W. were to be the last witnesses to testify at the preliminary hearing. Just before they were called, defendant asked the investigator whether he and other employees in the district attorney's office would get in trouble if "something happened" to Driver. Believing that defendant was referring to a previous assault upon Driver by another inmate in the jail, the investigator gave a negative response. Defendant and Martinez entered the courtroom, and the prosecutor told them to take a seat. The judge was not present, and a shackled Driver was sitting in a chair approximately one foot from defense counsel. Defendant stood behind the defense attorney, drew a gun she had taken from Martinez's purse, and shot Driver five times in the left side of the head and neck; a sixth bullet missed Driver and was found in the wall. The gun's muzzle was within two to three feet of Driver's head, and the shots were fired in rapid succession. Driver was killed almost instantly.

Defendant was taken into custody. She remarked, "You don't understand. He has raped hundreds of boys." The same day, in a tape-recorded statement, defendant said that she had not intended to kill Driver at the hearing and did not know whether she had done the right thing, but was tired of all of the pain Driver had caused, and that he deserved to die. Defendant thought that W.'s pain had destroyed her sense of right and wrong. She said that when Driver smirked at her son outside the courthouse, she would have killed him right there had she already taken possession of the gun.

After completion of the guilt phase of the trial, the jury found defendant not guilty of first or second degree murder, but returned a verdict of guilt on the lesser included offense of voluntary manslaughter.

DISCUSSION QUESTIONS

1. Does this case change your mind one way or the other about how courts should defining the reasonableness of a cooling off period? Do you agree with the common law's original strict approach or the more flexible approach?

2. If you were a juror, would you convict the defendant of murder or voluntary manslaughter?

3. Does it matter to your decision whether Blinder was guilty of raping Nesler's child and the other children or not? Assuming he was guilty, does it matter if he really was smirking at Nesler in the courtroom or not, or whether he often smiled at inappropriate times due to an intellectual disability? Does it matter if Nesler was high on methamphetamine at the time? (Some evidence exists to suggest that both of the latter were true.)

Case in Context

The next case illustrates the more flexible approach both to the cooling off element and to the adequacy of provocation element.

PEOPLE V. ALBERT JOSEPH BERRY

Supreme Court of California
18 Cal. 3d 509 (1976)

OPINION

Defendant Albert Joseph Berry was charged by indictment with one count of murder (Pen. Code, § 187) and one count of assault by means of force likely to produce great bodily injury (Pen. Code, § 245, subd. (a)). The indictment was amended to allege one prior felony conviction which defendant admitted. The assault was allegedly committed on July 23, 1974, and the murder on July 26, 1974. In each count, the alleged victim was defendant's wife, Rachel Pessah Berry. A jury found defendant guilty as charged and determined that the murder was of the first degree. (§ 189.) Defendant was sentenced to state prison for the term prescribed by law. He appeals from the judgment of conviction.

Defendant contends that there is sufficient evidence in the record to show that he committed the homicide while in a state of uncontrollable rage caused by provocation and flowing from a condition of diminished capacity and therefore that it was error for the trial court to fail to instruct the jury on voluntary manslaughter as indeed he had requested. He claims: (1) that he was entitled to an instruction on voluntary manslaughter as defined by statute (§ 192) since the killing was done upon a sudden quarrel or heat of passion; and (2) that he was also entitled to an instruction on voluntary manslaughter in the context of a diminished capacity defense (see People v. Mosher (1969) 1 Cal.3d 379, 385, fn. 1, 389–393 [since malice was negatived by mental defect or disease. (People v. Conley (1966) 64 Cal.2d 310, 316–323.) We agree with defendant as to the first instruction, but not as to the second.

Defendant, a cook, 46 years old, and Rachel Pessah, a 20-year-old girl from Israel, were married on May 27, 1974. Three days later Rachel went to Israel by herself, returning on July 13, 1974. On July 23, 1974, defendant choked Rachel into unconsciousness. She was treated at a hospital where she reported her strangulation by defendant to an officer of the San Francisco Police Department. On July 25, Inspector Sammon, who had been assigned to the case, met with Rachel and as a result of the interview a warrant was issued for defendant's arrest.

While Rachel was at the hospital, defendant removed his clothes from their apartment and stored them in a Greyhound Bus Depot locker. He stayed overnight at the home of a friend, Mrs. Jean Berk, admitting to her that he had choked his wife. On July 26, he telephoned Mrs. Berk and informed her that he had killed Rachel with a telephone cord on that morning at their apartment. The next day Mrs. Berk and two others telephoned the police to report a possible homicide and met Officer Kelleher at defendant's apartment. They gained entry and found Rachel on the bathroom floor. A pathologist from the coroner's office concluded that the cause of Rachel's death was strangulation. Defendant was arrested on August 1, 1974, and confessed to the killing.

At trial defendant did not deny strangling his wife, but claimed through his own testimony and the testimony of a psychiatrist, Dr. Martin Blinder, that he was provoked into killing her because of a sudden and uncontrollable rage so as to reduce the offense to one of voluntary manslaughter. He testified that upon her return from Israel, Rachel announced to him that while there she had fallen in love with another man, one Yako, and had enjoyed his sexual favors, that he was coming to this country to claim her and that she wished a divorce. Thus commenced a tormenting two weeks in which Rachel alternately taunted defendant with her involvement with Yako and at the same time sexually excited defendant, indicating her desire to remain with him. Defendant's detailed testimony, summarized below, chronicles this strange course of events. After their marriage, Rachel lived with defendant for only three days and then left for Israel. Immediately upon her return to San Francisco she told defendant about her relationship with and love for Yako. This brought about further argument and a brawl that evening in which defendant choked Rachel and she responded by scratching him deeply many times. Nonetheless they continued to live together. Rachel kept taunting defendant with Yako and demanding a divorce. She claimed she thought she might be pregnant by Yako. She showed defendant pictures of herself with Yako. Nevertheless, during a return trip from Santa Rosa, Rachel demanded immediate sexual intercourse with defendant in the car, which was achieved; however upon reaching their apartment, she again stated that she loved Yako and that she would not have intercourse with defendant in the future.

On the evening of July 22d defendant and Rachel went to a movie where they engaged in heavy petting. When they returned home and got into bed, Rachel announced that she had intended to make love with defendant, "But I am saving myself for this man Yako, so I don't think I will." Defendant got out of bed and prepared to leave the apartment whereupon Rachel screamed and yelled at him. Defendant choked her into unconsciousness.

Two hours later defendant called a taxi for his wife to take her to the hospital. He put his clothes in the Greyhound bus station and went to the home of his friend Mrs. Berk for the night. The next day he went to Reno and returned the day after. Rachel informed him by telephone that there was a warrant for his arrest as a result of her report to the police about the choking incident. On July 25th defendant returned to the apartment to talk to Rachel, but she was out. He slept there overnight. Rachel returned around 11 a.m. the next day. Upon seeing defendant there, she said, "I suppose you have come here to kill me." Defendant responded, "yes," changed his response to "no," and then again to "yes," and finally stated "I have really come to talk to you." Rachel began screaming. Defendant grabbed her by the shoulder and tried to stop her screaming. She continued. They struggled and finally defendant strangled her with a telephone cord.

Dr. Martin Blinder, a physician and psychiatrist, called by the defense, 3 testified that Rachel was a depressed, suicidally inclined girl and that this suicidal impulse led her to involve herself ever more deeply in a dangerous situation with defendant. She did this by sexually arousing him and taunting him into jealous rages in an unconscious desire to provoke him into killing her and thus consummating her desire for suicide. Throughout the period commencing with her return from Israel until her death, that is from July 13 to July 26, Rachel continually provoked defendant with sexual taunts and incitements, alternating acceptance and rejection of him. This conduct was accompanied by repeated references to her involvement with another man; it led defendant to choke her on two occasions, until finally she achieved her unconscious desire and was strangled. Dr. Blinder testified that as a result of this cumulative series of provocations, defendant at the time he fatally strangled Rachel, was in a state of uncontrollable rage, completely under the sway of passion.

We first take up defendant's claim that on the basis of the foregoing evidence he was entitled to an instruction on voluntary manslaughter as defined by statute which is "the unlawful killing of a human being, without malice . . . upon a sudden quarrel or heat of passion." (§ 192.) In People v. Valentine (1946) 28 Cal.2d 121 this court, in an extensive review of the law of manslaughter, specifically approved the following quotation from People v. Logan (1917) 175 Cal. 45, 48–49 as a correct statement of the law: "In the present condition of our law it is left to the jurors to say whether or not the facts and circumstances in evidence are sufficient to lead them to believe that the defendant did, or to create a reasonable doubt in their minds as to whether or not he did, commit his offense under a heat of passion. The jury is further to be admonished and advised by the court that this heat of passion must be such a passion as would naturally be aroused in the mind of an ordinarily reasonable person under the given facts and circumstances, and that, consequently, no defendant may set up his own standard of conduct and justify or excuse himself because in fact his passions were aroused, unless further the jury believe that the facts and circumstances were sufficient to arouse the passions of the ordinarily reasonable man. . . . For the fundamental of the inquiry is whether or not the defendant's reason was, at the time of his act, so disturbed or obscured by some passion—not necessarily fear and never, of course, the passion for revenge—to such an extent as would render ordinary men of average disposition liable to act rashly or without due deliberation and reflection, and from this passion rather than from judgment." (28 Cal.2d at pp. 138–139.)

We further held in Valentine that there is no specific type of provocation required by section 192 and that verbal provocation may be sufficient. (28 Cal.2d at pp. 141–144.) In People v. Borchers (1958) 50 Cal.2d 321, 329] in the course of explaining the phrase "heat of passion" used in the statute defining manslaughter we pointed out that "passion" need not mean "rage" or "anger" but may be any "[violent], intense, high-wrought or enthusiastic emotion" and concluded there "that defendant was aroused to a heat of 'passion' by a series of events over a considerable period of time. . . ." (50 Cal.2d at p. 328, 329.) Accordingly we there declared that evidence of admissions of infidelity by the defendant's paramour, taunts directed to him and other conduct, "supports a finding that defendant killed in wild desperation induced by [the woman's] long continued provocatory conduct." (50 Cal.2d at p. 329.) We find this reasoning persuasive in the case now before us. Defendant's testimony chronicles a two-week period of provocatory conduct by his wife Rachel that could arouse a passion of jealousy, pain and sexual rage in an ordinary man of average disposition such as to cause him to act rashly from this passion. It is significant that both defendant and Dr. Blinder testified that the former was in the heat of passion under an uncontrollable rage when he killed Rachel.

The Attorney General contends that the killing could not have been done in the heat of passion because there was a cooling period, defendant having waited in the apartment for 20 hours. However, the long course of provocatory conduct, which had resulted in intermittent outbreaks of rage under specific provocation in the past, reached its final culmination in the apartment when Rachel began screaming. Both defendant and Dr. Blinder testified that defendant killed in a state of uncontrollable rage, of passion, and there is ample evidence in the record to support the conclusion that this passion was the result of the long course of provocatory conduct by Rachel, just as the killing emerged from such conduct in Borchers. The Attorney General relies principally on People v. Bufarale (1961) 193 Cal.App.2d 551, 559–563 but the reliance is misplaced. Bufarale merely held that the defendant's killing of a married woman with whom he had been living was not, as a matter of law, upon the heat of passion since the defendant's act was one of vengeance, preceded by neither a quarrel with, nor by adequate provocatory conduct on the part of, the victim, who had decided to return to her husband.

We turn to defendant's second contention that under the evidence in the record he was entitled to an instruction on voluntary manslaughter in the context of a diminished capacity defense. "As we indicated in People v. Conley (1966) 64 Cal.2d 310, 318, the enumeration of nonmalicious homicides contained in section 192 is not complete. Since section 192 was enacted prior to the development of the concept of diminished capacity . . . it did not include those nonmalicious homicides in which there is a lack of malice resulting from a diminished capacity to entertain that mental state . . . . We therefore delineated in Conley a standard to be applied in the determination of whether, in cases involving diminished capacity, the state of mind amounting to malice aforethought is present: 'An intentional act that is highly dangerous to human life, done in disregard of the actor's awareness that society requires him to conform his conduct to the law, is done with malice regardless of the fact that the actor acts without ill will toward his victim or believes that his conduct is justified. . . . If because of mental defect, disease, or intoxication, however, the defendant is unable to comprehend his duty to govern his actions in accord with the duty imposed by law, he does not act with malice aforethought . . . .' (People v. Conley, supra, 64 Cal.2d 310, 322.)" (People v. Morse (1969) 70 Cal.2d 711, 735–736 [76 Cal.Rptr. 391, 452 P.2d 607].) The essence of a showing of diminished capacity is a "showing that the defendant's mental capacity was reduced by mental illness, mental defect or intoxication." (People v. Castillo (1969) 70 Cal.2d 264, 270 [74 Cal.Rptr. 385, 449 P.2d 449].)

Since in the instant case there is no evidence of intoxication, defendant must demonstrate evidence in the record that his mental capacity was reduced by mental disease or mental defect. Of the many cases decided since Conley wherein our courts have reiterated the applicability of diminished capacity evidence to negative malice, the great majority have involved diminished capacity due to voluntary intoxication (e.g., People v. Mosher, supra, 1 Cal.3d 379, 391; People v. Graham (1969) 71 Cal.2d 303, 316 [78 Cal.Rptr. 217, 455 P.2d 153]; People v. Castillo, supra, 70 Cal.2d 264, 270; People v. Small (1970) 7 Cal.App.3d 347, 356 [86 Cal.Rptr. 478]). Conley itself involved voluntary intoxication. Therefore the court in People v. Long (1974) 38 Cal.App.3d 680 [113 Cal.Rptr. 530] felt that it was faced with a question of first impression, namely, whether mental illness or mental defect without intoxication could reduce murder to voluntary or involuntary manslaughter. (But see People v. Gorshen (1959) 51 Cal.2d 716, 726–727 [336 P.2d 492] where diminished capacity based on mental illness was held relevant to negate intent to kill.) Long correctly concluded that mental capacity reduced by mental illness or mental defect without intoxication is sufficient to show diminished capacity.

Nonetheless the sine qua non of such a showing is that there be evidence of either mental illness or mental defect. Defendant fails to point out to us, nor can we find, anywhere in the record, such requisite evidence. Dr. Blinder specifically testified that defendant was sane and that he was neither schizophrenic nor psychotic. He at no time testified that defendant was suffering from a mental illness or mental defect. Rather he stated that at the time of the killing, defendant was in an "altered mental state," which the doctor identified as one of uncontrollable rage and he further explained that this state was "a product of having to contend with what seems to me an incredibly provocative situation, an incredibly provocative young woman, and that this immediate situation was superimposed upon Mr. Berry having encountered the situation time and time again." In sum, Dr. Blinder testified to a heat of passion aroused in defendant by a course of provocatory conduct on the part of Rachel, but never testified to any mental illness or mental defect on the part of defendant. Therefore, defendant was not entitled to an instruction on voluntary manslaughter in the context of diminished capacity and the trial court did not err in refusing such instruction.

However, as we have already explained, the court did commit error in refusing to instruct on voluntary manslaughter based on sudden quarrel or heat of passion. Defendant contends that this constitutes prejudicial error which compels reversal of the judgment as to the murder count. In accordance with the dictates of People v. Sedeno (1974) 10 Cal.3d 703, 720–721 [112 Cal.Rptr. 1, 518 P.2d 913] we have examined the instructions given to determine whether the jury necessarily resolved, although in a different setting, that defendant had not committed the homicide in a heat of passion induced by the provocation of Rachel. While the instructions made passing reference to heat of passion and provocation for the purpose of distinguishing between murder of the first and second degrees, such reference was only casually made. There was no clear direction to the jury to consider the evidence of Rachel's course of provocatory conduct so as to determine whether defendant, as an ordinary man of average disposition (see People v. Logan (1917) 175 Cal. 45, 49 [164 P. 1121]) having been exposed to such conduct, was provoked into committing the homicide under a heat of passion. Therefore we conclude that the jury's determination that defendant was guilty of murder of the first degree under the instructions given did not necessarily indicate that "the factual question posed by the omitted instruction was necessarily resolved adversely to the defendant under other, properly given instructions" (Sedeno at p. 721)—in other words that the jury had found that defendant had not killed Rachel under a heat of passion. Since this theory of provocation constituted defendant's entire defense to the first count, we have no difficulty concluding that the failure to give such instruction was prejudicial error (People v. Watson (1956) 46 Cal.2d 818, 836 [299 P.2d 243]) and requires us to reverse the conviction of murder of the first degree.

DISCUSSION QUESTIONS

1. Do you agree that verbal provocation should be legally sufficient in this case to give the jury the option of returning a verdict of manslaughter and not murder? If not, do you think that verbal provocation (not involving informational words) should ever be sufficient?

2. Do you agree in general with the standard the court articulates for evaluating the reasonableness of a cooling off period? Would Gounigas have received a manslaughter instruction under this standard?

3. The court also considers but rejects an argument for manslaughter based on a finding of diminished capacity, something that California allowed at the time and that a few jurisdictions still do. This is an alternate basis for

reducing murder to manslaughter. Do you agree with it? Why does the court reject Berry's diminished capacity argument?

E. MODEL PENAL CODE AND EMED

The Model Penal Code dispensed with the notion of provocation altogether. Instead, it mitigates murder to voluntary manslaughter when a person kills purposely, knowingly, or extremely recklessly but does so while suffering from an "extreme mental or emotional disturbance," otherwise known by the acronym EMED. A "reasonable explanation or excuse" must exist for this disturbance. The reasonableness of the explanation is to be "determined from the viewpoint of a person in the actor's situation under the circumstances as he believes them to be."

Note first the absence of the word "provocation" in this standard. Instead, the standard asks whether the killer was extremely disturbed for a reason that the jury can understand, in a rational way. Furthermore, by defining reasonable from the perspective of the disturbed person, the MPC creates a hybrid standard that many scholars describe as "objective/subjective." Despite the medical sound of the words "mental or emotional," this condition does not need to rise to the level of a mental disease or defect but requires only an extreme "disturbance." Instead of a cooling off requirement, the MPC requires that he person still be "under the influence" of the disturbance at the time of the killing.

MODEL PENAL CODE SECTION 210.3

MANSLAUGHTER

(1) Criminal homicide constitutes manslaughter when. . . (b) a homicide which would otherwise be murder is committed under the influence of extreme mental or emotional disturbance for which there is reasonable explanation or excuse. The reasonableness of such explanation or excuse shall be determined from the viewpoint of a person in the actor's situation under the circumstances, as he believes them to be.

(2) Manslaughter is a felony of the second degree.

AMERICAN LAW INSTITUTE, MODEL PENAL CODE AND COMMENTARIES
Part II, at 62–63

The critical element in the Model Code formulations is the clause requiring that reasonableness be assessed "from the viewpoint of a person in the actor's situation." The word "situation" is designedly ambiguous. On the one hand, it is clear that personal handicaps and some external circumstances must be taken into account. Thus, blindness, shock from traumatic injury, and extreme grief are all easily read into the term "situation." This result is sound, for it would be morally obtuse to appraise a crime for mitigation of punishment without reference to these factors. On the other hand, it is equally plain that idiosyncratic moral values are not part of the actor's situation. An assassin who kills a political leader because he believes it is right to do so cannot ask that he be judged by the standard of a reasonable extremist. Any other result would undermine the normative message of the criminal law. In between these two extremes, however, there are matters neither as clearly distinct from individual blameworthiness as blindness or handicap nor as integral a part of moral depravity as a belief in the lightness of killing. Perhaps the classic illustration is the unusual sensitivity to the epithet "bastard" of a person born illegitimate. An exceptionally punctilious sense of personal honor or an abnormally fearful temperament may also serve to differentiate an individual actor from the hypothetical reasonable man, yet none of these factors is wholly irrelevant to the ultimate issue of culpability. The proper role of such factors cannot be resolved satisfactorily by abstract definition of what may constitute adequate provocation. The Model Code endorses a formulation that affords sufficient flexibility to differentiate in particular cases between those special aspects of the actor's situation that should be deemed material for purpose of grading and those that should be ignored. There thus will be room for interpretation of the word "situation," and that is precisely the flexibility desired. There will be opportunity for argument about the reasonableness of explanation or excuse, and that too is a ground on which argument is required. In the end, the question is whether the actor's loss of self-control can be understood in terms that arouse sympathy in the ordinary citizen. Section 210.3 faces this issue squarely and leaves the ultimate judgment to the ordinary citizen in the function of a juror assigned to resolve the specific case.

The general effect of the MPC's EMED doctrine is to open voluntary manslaughter to include even more excusing conditions than the looser version of the common law provocation doctrine. Medical conditions that might not satisfy the test for insanity, such as postpartum depression or severe personality disorders that make people react impulsively or aggressively, fit more easily into EMED than into provocation. At the outer boundaries of EMED lie people who get into profound "funks" or "rages" about something that people can understand. Getting unjustly fired from a job, dumped by a longtime boyfriend or girlfriend, or abused or humiliated by someone on an ongoing basis could trigger a jury instruction on this issue.

Dispensing with the provocation element also means that the person killed does not have to have done anything to create the killer's disturbance. EMED makes it easier to find manslaughter when the person killed is blameless because it clearly operates more as an excuse than as a justification.

EMED generally throws more questions to the jury and often with less guidance than provocation instructions provide. Remember, though, that the fact that the jury gets to hear the issue does not mean that they must or will accept the "reasonable explanation or excuse" offered.

Consider a mother who killed her infant while in the throes of postpartum depression. How could the EMED doctrine's rejection of provocation help the jury in this case to find voluntary manslaughter?[2]

Case in Context

The following case illustrates the boundaries of the MPC's EMED approach.

PEOPLE V. CASASSA
Court of Appeals of New York
49 N.Y.2d 668 (1980)

JASEN, JUDGE.

The significant issue on this appeal is whether the defendant, in a murder prosecution, established the affirmative defense of "extreme emotional disturbance" which would have reduced the crime to manslaughter in the first degree.

On February 28, 1977, Victoria Lo Consolo was brutally murdered. Defendant Victor Casassa and Miss Lo Consolo had been acquainted for some time prior to the latter's tragic death. They met in August, 1976 as a result of their residence in the same apartment complex. . . The two apparently dated casually . . . until November, 1976 when Miss Lo Consolo informed defendant that she was not "falling in love" with him. Defendant claims that Miss Lo Consolo's candid statement of her feelings "devastated him."

Miss Lo Consolo's rejection of defendant's advances also precipitated a bizarre series of actions on the part of defendant which, he asserts, demonstrate the existence of extreme emotional disturbance upon which he predicates his affirmative defense. Defendant, aware that Miss Lo Consolo maintained social relationships with others, broke into the apartment below Miss Lo Consolo's on several occasions to eavesdrop. These eavesdropping sessions allegedly caused him to be under great emotional stress. Thereafter, on one occasion, he broke into Miss Lo Consolo's apartment while she was out. Defendant took nothing, but,

---

[2] **Answer:** In a jurisdiction requiring provocation, a jury might never receive a voluntary manslaughter instruction because a crying baby would not satisfy the requirements of provocation. The EMED makes it easier to find voluntary manslaughter when the victim is blameless, however, because the mother's postpartum depression operates as an excuse, rather than a justification.

instead, observed the apartment, disrobed and lay for a time in Miss Lo Consolo's bed. During this break-in, defendant was armed with a knife which, he later told police, he carried "because he knew that he was either going to hurt Victoria or Victoria was going to cause him to commit suicide."

Defendant's final visit to his victim's apartment occurred on February 28, 1977. Defendant brought several bottles of wine and liquor with him to offer as a gift. Upon Miss Lo Consolo's rejection of this offering, defendant produced a steak knife which he had brought with him, stabbed Miss Lo Consolo several times in the throat, dragged her body to the bathroom and submerged it in a bathtub full of water to "make sure she was dead."

Defendant waived a jury and proceeded to trial before the County Court. . . The defendant did not contest the underlying facts of the crime. Instead, the sole issue presented to the trial court was whether the defendant, at the time of the killing, had acted under the influence of "extreme emotional disturbance". (Penal Law, § 125.25, subd 1, par [a].) The defense presented only one witness, a psychiatrist, who testified, in essence, that the defendant had become obsessed with Miss Lo Consolo and that the course which their relationship had taken, combined with several personality attributes peculiar to defendant, caused him to be under the influence of extreme emotional disturbance at the time of the killing.

In rebuttal, the People produced several witnesses. Among these witnesses was a psychiatrist who testified that although the defendant was emotionally disturbed, he was not under the influence of "extreme emotional disturbance" within the meaning of section 125.25 (subd 1, par [a]) of the Penal Law because his disturbed state was not the product of external factors but rather was "a stress he created from within himself, dealing mostly with a fantasy, a refusal to accept the reality of the situation."

The trial court in resolving this issue noted that the affirmative defense of extreme emotional disturbance may be based upon a series of events, rather than a single precipitating cause. In order to be entitled to the defense, the court held, a defendant must show that his reaction to such events was reasonable. In determining whether defendant's emotional reaction was reasonable, the court considered the appropriate test to be whether in the totality of the circumstances the finder of fact could understand how a person might have his reason overcome. Concluding that the test was not to be applied solely from the viewpoint of defendant, the court found that defendant's emotional reaction at the time of the commission of the crime was so peculiar to him that it could not be considered reasonable so as to reduce the conviction to manslaughter in the first degree. Accordingly, the trial court found defendant guilty of the crime of murder in the second degree. . .

On this appeal defendant contends that the trial court erred in failing to afford him the benefit of the affirmative defense of "extreme emotional disturbance". It is argued that the defendant established that he suffered from a mental infirmity not arising to the level of insanity which disoriented his reason to the extent that his emotional reaction, from his own subjective point of view, was supported by a reasonable explanation or excuse. Defendant asserts that by refusing to apply a wholly subjective standard the trial court misconstrued section 125.25 (subd 1, par [a]) of the Penal Law. We cannot agree.

Section 125.25 (subd 1, par [a]) of the Penal Law provides that it is an affirmative defense to the crime of murder in the second degree where "[t]he defendant acted under the influence of extreme emotional disturbance for which there was a reasonable explanation or excuse." This defense allows a defendant charged with the commission of acts which would otherwise constitute murder to demonstrate the existence of mitigating factors which indicate that, although he is not free from responsibility for his crime, he ought to be punished less severely by reducing the crime upon conviction to manslaughter in the first degree.

In enacting section 125.25 (subd 1, par [a]) of the Penal Law, the Legislature adopted the language of the manslaughter provisions of the Model Penal Code. . .

The "extreme emotional disturbance" defense is an outgrowth of the "heat of passion" doctrine which had for some time been recognized by New York as a distinguishing factor between the crimes of manslaughter and murder. However, the new formulation is significantly broader in scope than the "heat of passion" doctrine which it replaced.

For example, the "heat of passion" doctrine required that a defendant's action be undertaken as a response to some provocation which prevented him from reflecting upon his actions. Moreover, such reaction had to be immediate. The existence of a "cooling off" period completely negated any mitigating effect which the provocation might otherwise have had. (See, e.g., *People v Fiorentino*, 197 N.Y. 560, 563.) In *Patterson*, however, this court recognized that "[a]n action influenced by an extreme emotional disturbance is not one that is necessarily so spontaneously undertaken. Rather, it may be that a significant mental trauma has affected a defendant's mind for a substantial period of time, simmering in the unknowing subconscious and then inexplicably coming to the fore."

The thrust of defendant's claim, however, concerns a question arising out of another perceived distinction between "heat of passion" and "extreme emotional disturbance" . . . to wit: whether, assuming that the defense is applicable to a broader range of circumstances, the standard by which the reasonableness of defendant's emotional reaction is to be tested must be an entirely subjective one.

Consideration of the Comments to the Model Penal Code, from which the New York statute was drawn, are instructive. The defense of "extreme emotional disturbance" has two principal components—(1) the particular defendant must have "acted under the influence of extreme emotional disturbance", and (2) there must have been "a reasonable explanation or excuse" for such extreme emotional disturbance, "the reasonableness of which is to be determined from the viewpoint of a person in the defendant's situation under the circumstances as the defendant believed them to be". The first requirement is wholly subjective—i.e., it involves a determination that the particular defendant did in fact act under extreme emotional disturbance, that the claimed explanation as to the cause of his action is not contrived or sham.

The second component is more difficult to describe—i.e., whether there was a reasonable explanation or excuse for the emotional disturbance. It was designed to sweep away "the rigid rules that have developed with respect to the sufficiency of particular types of provocation, such as the rule that words alone can never be enough", and "avoids a merely arbitrary limitation on the nature of the antecedent circumstances that may justify a mitigation." "The ultimate test, however, is objective; there must be 'reasonable' explanation or excuse for the actor's disturbance." In light of these comments and the necessity of articulating the defense in terms comprehensible to jurors, we conclude that the determination whether there was reasonable explanation or excuse for a particular emotional disturbance should be made by viewing the subjective, internal situation in which the defendant found himself and the external circumstances as he perceived them at the time, however inaccurate that perception may have been, and assessing from that standpoint whether the explanation or excuse for his emotional disturbance was reasonable, so as to entitle him to a reduction of the crime charged from murder in the second degree to manslaughter in the first degree. We recognize that even such a description of the defense provides no precise guidelines and necessarily leaves room for the exercise of judgmental evaluation by the jury. This, however, appears to have been the intent of the draftsmen. "The purpose was explicitly to give full scope to what amounts to a plea in mitigation based upon a mental or emotional trauma of significant dimensions, with the jury asked to show whatever empathy it can." (Wechsler, Codification of Criminal Law in the United States: The Model Penal Code, 68 Col L Rev 1425, 1446.).

In the end, we believe that what the Legislature intended in enacting the statute was to allow the finder of fact the discretionary power to mitigate the penalty when presented with a situation which, under the circumstances, appears to them to have caused an understandable weakness in one of their fellows. Perhaps the chief virtue of the statute is that it allows such discretion without engaging in a detailed explanation of individual circumstances in which the statute would apply, thus avoiding the "mystifying cloud of words" which Mr. Justice CARDOZO abhorred.

We conclude that the trial court, in this case, properly applied the statute. The court apparently accepted, as a factual matter, that defendant killed Miss Lo Consolo while under the influence of "extreme emotional disturbance", a threshold question which must be answered in the affirmative before any test of reasonableness is required. The court, however, also recognized that in exercising its function as trier of fact, it must make a further inquiry into the reasonableness of that disturbance. In this regard, the court considered each of the mitigating factors put forward by defendant, including his claimed mental disability, but found that the excuse offered by defendant was so peculiar to him that it was unworthy of mitigation. The court obviously made a sincere effort to understand defendant's "situation" and "the circumstances as defendant believed them to be", but concluded that the murder in this case was the result of defendant's malevolence rather than an understandable human response deserving of mercy. We cannot say, as a matter of law, that the court erred in so concluding. Indeed, to do so would subvert the purpose of the statute.

In our opinion, this statute would not require that the jury or the court as trier of fact find mitigation on any particular set of facts, but, rather, allows the finder of fact the opportunity to do so, such opportunity being conditional only upon a finding of extreme emotional disturbance in the first instance.

DISCUSSION QUESTIONS

1.   The judge in this case was acting as both judge and jury because the defendant waived his right to trial by jury. If it was a jury trial, would the jury have been allowed to consider EMED?

2.   Why did the judge refuse to find EMED?

3.   Which do you prefer? The traditional, strict approach to provocation? The modern, flexible approach to provocation? The Model Penal Code's doctrine of Extreme Mental or Emotional disturbance?

Practice Problem 12.0: A Fatal Reunion

Jay is on trial for the murder of Ted in a Model Penal Code instruction, but the judge has also instructed the jury on EMED, giving them the option to return a manslaughter conviction instead. Prepare a closing argument for the prosecution arguing against EMED and for the defense arguing for EMED.

Bill and Ted, two seniors home from college during spring break, drove into a low-income neighborhood looking to buy some marijuana late on a Friday night. Bill saw Jay, an eighteen-year old youth, whom he had frequently bought marijuana from while in high school, standing on a street corner where Bill had bought drugs from him in the past. Bill drove up to the corner, rolled down the passenger side car window and called out to Jay. When Jay walked over, Bill told Jay that Ted, who was seated in the front passenger seat, wanted to buy a large amount of marijuana to bring back to college with him. Jay told Bill that he didn't sell drugs anymore and was just waiting for a ride. Bill asked Jay where he could go to buy drugs. Jay looked at Ted and asked Bill why he was bringing some guy he had never seen before into his neighborhood to buy drugs. Bill said, "he's cool, he just wants a package, why are you acting so uptight?" Jay started yelling. He said that it looked like Bill was trying to make a deal for the police and told him to "get the fuck out of here." Ted, who was much smaller than Jay but who was slightly intoxicated screamed back "What the fuck you mean are we the police? We came to spend money and you are acting all tough and shit. You ain't that fucking tough. " Jay reached into his pocket for his pistol and began backing away from the car. Ted flung the door open and jumped out. Jay immediately drew the pistol and shot Ted four times in rapid succession, killing him.

Family members and social workers testified to the following events in Jay's earlier life. Jay began selling drugs at age fourteen for what worked out to be minimum wage. With the money he earned he helped pay the rent for the family apartment, and spent the rest of the money on clothes and shoes. He experienced a great deal of violence while selling drugs. During his first month selling drugs, he was badly beaten by the man he sold drugs for when Jay used some of the drugs he was supposed to be selling. He also witnessed frequent beatings of customers who failed to pay their drug debts. During his first two years selling drugs he was robbed twice at gunpoint. The first time he was dragged into an alley with a gun placed at his head while another man went through his pockets and underwear looking for money and drugs. The second time a would-be customer jumped out of his car and pointed a gun at Jay demanding drugs. Jay ran but was shot twice in the leg and once in the foot while escaping. Jay began carrying a gun after the second robbery. Six months later he was arrested for selling drugs to an undercover police officer and placed in juvenile detention. Because he was carrying a gun at the time of the arrest he served two years in juvenile detention.

Employment records confirm that upon being released from detention Jay went to work at Walmart for minimum wage. He had just finished his shift thirty minutes before the shooting. His mother confirmed that she was supposed to pick him up at the corner where the shooting took place on the evening in question but that she was running fifteen minutes late.

A defense psychiatrist who interviewed Jay said that at the time of the shooting Jay was suffering from post-traumatic stress syndrome. Jay reported to the psychiatrist that he had no memory of drawing or firing the pistol but did not dispute that he did so. Jay reported to the psychiatrist that after being shot he constantly feared being shot by customers when he was selling drugs. He took his gun with him everywhere and even slept with it under his pillow. He also had many suicidal thoughts and constantly imagined being shot in the head. His family members found him once late at night holding a loaded shotgun in his mouth. A second time a family member discovered that Jay tried to kill himself by consuming a bottle of what he thought were tranquilizers but which turned out to be only cold medicine.

The defense psychiatrist also testified that Jay reported that he witnessed the rape of several young boys in juvenile detention by older boys. The psychiatrist believed that Jay was also traumatized by this experience. Jay told the psychiatrist that he constantly feared being sexually assaulted, even though he was much larger than most of the other juveniles. Jay reported that after his release, he had nightmares about being sexually assaulted in an adult prison, and this fear lead him to desist from selling drugs upon his release. He also said that the fear of being shot again also never left his mind. His family members confirmed that he continued to sleep with a handgun under his pillow even after his release from juvenile detention. The psychiatrist further testified that research indicated that such a post-traumatic stress syndrome is common among youth who have been shot. Gun crime is widespread in Jay's community. One study showed that over half of those arrested for gun crimes in Jay's community had previously been shot, and youth who had been shot were 132% more likely to carry guns.

A prosecution psychiatrist testified that Jay suffered from anger management problems, not post-traumatic stress syndrome. He further testified that Jay's repeated exposure to violence may have simply desensitized him to violence and made him more willing to engage in violence when angered. He attributed Jay's purported lack of memory of the shooting to an explosive temper that was triggered by Ted challenging him.

Ted and Jay had never met before the shooting. Bill had never been violent in any way towards Jay during their earlier dealings with one another. Jay has no history of violent behavior before this incident apart from the act of carrying a gun.

CHAPTER 13

UNINTENTIONAL KILLINGS

■ ■ ■

A. INVOLUNTARY MANSLAUGHTER

Involuntary manslaughter is the baseline offense for very wrongful but unintentional killings. As discussed above, it is the extraordinary unintentional killing that constitutes extremely reckless murder. Not all unintentional killings constitute manslaughter, however. Virtually all jurisdictions require at least criminal or gross negligence. Some jurisdictions require reckless as opposed to criminal negligence. Recklessness involves a higher level of culpability because it requires that the actor consciously disregard the substantial and unjustifiable risk of death whereas you are criminally negligent if you fail to recognize such a risk.

Modern statutes often specify what state of mind is required for involuntary manslaughter. In the absence of a statutory definition on an exam question, one would ordinarily fall back on majority and minority rules as a default standard. The leading treatises disagree, however, on whether recklessness or criminal negligence is required for involuntary manslaughter in the majority of jurisdictions. (Unless your professor specifies one or the other, you should analyze the fact pattern under both standards in the absence of a statutory definition.) Some jurisdictions, following the Model Penal Code, require recklessness for involuntary manslaughter but create a lesser crime of negligent homicide which only requires criminal negligence. Just a very few jurisdictions allow for some form of reduced homicide liability on the basis of simple or ordinary negligence, but many casebooks include such a case to illustrate the distinction between simple and gross negligence.

What both recklessness and criminal negligence have in common, however, is that the actor was really careless in some aspect. Drunk driving, mishandling firearms, and gross violations of safety regulations are some of the favorite textbook examples. Remember to pay particular attention to crimes of omission in this area. For example, a gross failure to take care of a child or elderly person entrusted to your care is a common manslaughter scenario.

Finally, many jurisdictions recognize a form of involuntary manslaughter called unlawful act manslaughter. Unlawful act manslaughter will be discussed in detail at the end of the chapter on felony murder.

Case in Context

The following case considers whether a skiing accident satisfies Colorado's definition of involuntary manslaughter.

THE PEOPLE OF THE STATE OF COLORADO V. NATHAN HALL

Supreme Court of Colorado, En Banc
999 P.2d 207 (2000)

I.   INTRODUCTION

We hold that Nathan Hall must stand trial for the crime of reckless manslaughter. While skiing on Vail mountain, Hall flew off of a knoll and collided with Allen Cobb, who was traversing the slope below Hall. Cobb sustained traumatic brain injuries and died as a result of the collision. The People charged Hall with felony reckless manslaughter.

At a preliminary hearing to determine whether there was probable cause for the felony count, the county court found that Hall's conduct "did not rise to the level of dangerousness" required under Colorado law to uphold a conviction for manslaughter, and the court dismissed the charges. On appeal, the district court affirmed the county court's decision. The district court determined that in order for Hall's conduct to have been reckless, it must have been "at least more likely than not" that death would result. Because the court found that "skiing too fast for the conditions" is not "likely" to cause another person's death, the court concluded that Hall's conduct did not constitute a "substantial and unjustifiable" risk of death. Thus, the district court affirmed the finding of no probable cause.

The charge of reckless manslaughter requires that a person "recklessly cause the death of another person." For his conduct to be reckless, the actor must have consciously disregarded a substantial and unjustifiable risk that death could result from his actions. We hold that, for the purpose of determining whether a person acted recklessly, a particular result does not have to be more likely than not to occur for the risk to be substantial and unjustifiable. A risk must be assessed by reviewing the particular facts of the individual case and weighing the likelihood of harm and the degree of harm that would result if it occurs. Whether an actor consciously disregarded such a risk may be inferred from circumstances such as the actor's knowledge and experience, or from what a similarly situated reasonable person would have understood about the risk under the particular circumstances.

We hold that under the particular circumstances of this case, whether Hall committed the crime of reckless manslaughter must be determined by the trier of fact. Viewed in the light most favorable to the prosecution,

Hall's conduct—skiing straight down a steep and bumpy slope, back on his skis, arms out to his sides, off-balance, being thrown from mogul to mogul, out of control for a considerable distance and period of time, and at such a high speed that the force of the impact between his ski and the victim's head fractured the thickest part of the victim's skull—created a substantial and unjustifiable risk of death to another person. A reasonable person could infer that the defendant, a former ski racer trained in skier safety, consciously disregarded that risk. For the limited purposes of a preliminary hearing, the prosecution provided sufficient evidence to show probable cause that the defendant recklessly caused the victim's death. Thus, we reverse the district court's finding of no probable cause and we remand the case to that court for trial.

II. FACTS AND PROCEDURAL HISTORY

On April 20, 1997, the last day of the ski season, Hall worked as a ski lift operator on Vail mountain. When he finished his shift and after the lifts closed, Hall skied down toward the base of the mountain. The slopes were not crowded. Hall was skiing very fast, ski tips in the air, his weight back on his skis, with his arms out to his sides to maintain balance. He flew off of a knoll and saw people below him, but he was unable to stop or gain control. [He] then collided with Cobb, who had been traversing the slope below Hall. The collision caused major head and brain injuries to Cobb, killing him. Cobb was taken to Vail Valley Medical Center, where efforts to resuscitate him failed.

The People charged Hall with manslaughter and misdemeanor charges that are not relevant to this appeal.

The county court held a preliminary hearing to determine whether there was probable cause to support the felony charges against Hall. At the preliminary hearing, the People presented testimony from an eyewitness, the coroner who conducted the autopsy on Cobb's body, an investigator from the District Attorney's office, and the detective who investigated the accident for the Eagle County Sheriff's department.

Judge Buck Allen, who serves as a judge for several mountain towns and lives in Vail, testified that he is an expert skier and familiar with Vail's slopes. He was making a final run for the day when he first noticed Hall on the slope. Allen had a direct line of sight to the bottom of the run. Allen said that he could see other skiers traversing the slope below him at least from their waists up and that there were no blind spots on that part of the run.

Hall passed Allen skiing "at a fairly high rate of speed." Allen estimated that Hall was skiing about three times as fast as he was. Allen stated that Hall was "sitting back" on his skis, tips in the air, with his arms out to his sides in an effort to maintain his balance. Hall was skiing straight down the fall line; that is, he was skiing straight down the slope of the mountain without turning from side-to-side or traversing the slope. Hall "bounded off the bumps as he went," and "[t]he terrain was controlling [Hall]" rather than the other way around. In Allen's opinion, Hall was skiing too fast for the skill level he demonstrated, and Hall was out of control "if you define 'out of control' as [not] being able to stop or avoid someone." Although he watched Hall long enough to note Hall's unsafe skiing—approximately two or three seconds—Allen did not see the collision.

Detective McWilliam investigated the collision for the Eagle County Sheriff's office. McWilliam testified that Deputy Mossness said that while Hall could not remember the collision, Hall admitted that as he flew off a knoll and looked down, he saw people below him but could not stop because of the bumps:

> Mr. Hall told [the deputy] that he had been skiing that day, he was an employee of Vail Associates. That he was coming down the mountain and that he—he said he flew off of a knoll, looked down and saw some people below him down the slope, tried to slow down, and that because of the bumps, he wasn't able to stop. And he doesn't remember beyond that point. But he was told that somebody—that he had collided with someone.

McWilliam testified that he interviewed Jonathan Cherin, an eyewitness to the collision between Hall and Cobb. Cherin stated that he saw Hall skiing straight down the slope at a high speed and out of control. He said that Cobb, who appeared to be an inexperienced skier, traversed the slope below Hall when Hall hit some bumps, became airborne, and struck Cobb.

McWilliam said that the trail was 156 feet across at the point of the collision. Cobb's body came to rest slightly to the right of the center of the slope. Hall came to rest in the center of the trail, approximately eighty-three feet below Cobb's body.

Upon cross-examination, McWilliam testified that in eleven years' experience in Eagle County, he was aware of two other collisions between skiers on Vail mountain that resulted in the death of a skier. McWilliam said that deaths on Vail mountain from such collisions are rare.

Sandberg, an investigator for the District Attorney's office, testified that he spoke with Mark Haynes, who had been Hall's high school ski coach. Haynes told Sandberg that in the years he coached Hall, Hall was one of the top two or three skiers on the team and that Hall was "talented and aggressive." Haynes taught his skiers to ski safely and under control.

Dr. Ben Galloway, the coroner who performed the autopsy on Cobb's body, testified that Cobb died from a single and traumatic blow to his head that fractured his skull and caused severe brain injuries. The coroner said that the injury was consistent with the impact from an object, such as a ski, striking Cobb's head on a perpendicular plane. Galloway saw no signs of trauma to any other parts of Cobb's body, indicating that Cobb's head was the sole area of contact.

Galloway testified that Hall struck Cobb just below his right ear, in an area of the skull where the bones are thickest and "it takes more force to fracture those areas" than other areas of the skull. The damage to Cobb's skull resulted in "contusions or bruises" on Cobb's brain, a subdural hemorrhage near the brain stem, and "marked swelling of the brain due to cerebral edema." This trauma to Cobb's brain led to cardiorespiratory failure, the cause of Cobb's death. Galloway found that the severe head injury was the sole cause of Cobb's death.

Galloway testified that "it would take considerable force" to cause such an injury, typically seen in automobile accident victims who sustain basal skull fractures after being thrown from moving vehicles:

> In my experience in my practice spanning some 25 years, you most commonly see this type of fracturing when someone is thrown out of an automobile or a moving vehicle and sustains a basal skull fracture.

Following the presentation of these witnesses, the county court considered whether there was sufficient evidence to find probable cause that Hall recklessly caused Cobb's death. The county court reviewed other Colorado manslaughter cases where courts found substantial and unjustified risks of death resulting from conduct such as firing a gun at a person or kicking an unconscious person in the head. The court found that Hall's conduct—which the court characterized as skiing "too fast for the conditions"—did not involve a substantial and unjustifiable risk of death and "does not rise to the level of dangerousness required under the current case law" to sustain a count of manslaughter. Because Hall's conduct did not, in the court's view, involve a substantial and unjustifiable risk of death, the court found that the prosecution failed to provide sufficient proof that Hall acted recklessly. The county court therefore dismissed the manslaughter count.

The district court agreed with the county court that the prosecution failed to establish probable cause. The court held that Hall's conduct did not involve a substantial risk of death because any risk created by Hall had a less than fifty percent chance of causing another's death. The court ruled that when viewed in the light most favorable to the People, the facts showed that Hall was "skiing too fast for the snow conditions." The district court held that while such conduct may involve a substantial risk of injury, a person of ordinary prudence and caution would not infer that skiing too fast for the conditions creates at least a fifty percent chance of death. Thus, the court held that the prosecution failed to meet its burden and affirmed the county court's finding of no probable cause.

The People petitioned this court pursuant to C.A.R. 49, and we granted certiorari to consider the following:

(1) Whether the district court erred by establishing *"more likely than not"* as the level of substantial risk of death that a defendant must disregard for a finding of probable cause that he caused the death of another recklessly; and

(2) Whether the district court reviewed the wrong criteria and neglected the evidence relating specifically to this case in affirming the county court's dismissal of a manslaughter charge at preliminary hearing.

III. DISCUSSION

[The court held that the defendant's claim that the State violated Colorado Appellate Procedure was incorrect and that the prosecution had a right to appeal.]

B. Manslaughter and Recklessness

To provide background for our explanation of recklessness, we review the history of culpable mental states under our criminal code. We then examine the separate elements of recklessness, which require that an actor consciously disregard a substantial and unjustifiable risk that a result will occur or that a circumstance exists. Based on this review, we hold that to determine whether a risk is substantial and unjustified, a trier of fact must weigh the likelihood and potential magnitude of harm presented by the conduct and consider whether the conduct constitutes a gross deviation from the reasonable standard of care. Whether a person consciously disregards such a risk may be inferred from either the actor's subjective knowledge of the risk or from what a reasonable person with the actor's knowledge and experience would have been aware of in the particular situation.

With the exception of strict liability crimes, a person is not subject to criminal sanctions unless the prosecution establishes that, in addition to committing a proscribed act, the person acted with the culpable mental state required for the particular crime In other words, except for strict liability crimes, our criminal justice system will not punish a defendant for her actions unless she acted with a state of mind that warrants punishment.

In the past, courts and legislatures developed a variety of definitions for different mental states, creating confusion about what the prosecution had to prove in a criminal case. Depending on the specific crime charged and the jurisdiction, juries might be instructed to determine whether the defendant acted with " 'felonious intent,' 'criminal intent,' 'malice aforethought,' 'guilty knowledge,' 'fraudulent intent,' 'wilfulness,' 'scienter,' . . . or 'mens rea,' to signify an evil purpose or mental culpability."

As part of a complete revision of Colorado's criminal code in 1971, the General Assembly followed the Model Penal Code's suggestion and adopted a provision specifically defining four culpable mental states: "intentionally," "knowingly," "recklessly," and "criminal negligence." To be convicted of any crime other than a strict liability crime, a defendant must act with one of these four culpable mental states, depending on the statutory definition of each particular crime. If the elements for the required mental state are not satisfied, the defendant cannot be convicted of the crime charged.

To demonstrate that Hall committed the crime of manslaughter, the prosecution must provide sufficient evidence to show that the defendant's conduct was reckless. Thus, we focus on describing the mental state of recklessness and determining whether Hall's conduct meets that definition.

As Colorado's criminal code defines recklessness, "A person acts recklessly when he consciously disregards a substantial and unjustifiable risk that a result will occur or a that circumstance exists." Thus, in the case of manslaughter, the prosecution must show that the defendant's conduct caused the death of another and that the defendant:

1) *consciously disregarded*

2) *a substantial* and

3) *unjustifiable risk* that he would

4) *cause the death of another*.

We examine these elements in detail.

Substantial and Unjustifiable Risk

To show that a person acted recklessly, the prosecution must establish that the person's conduct created a "substantial and unjustifiable" risk. The district court construed some of our earlier cases as requiring that the risk of death be "at least more likely than not" to constitute a substantial and unjustifiable risk of death. In interpreting our cases, the court relied on an erroneous definition of a "substantial and unjustifiable" risk. Whether a risk is substantial must be determined by assessing both the likelihood that harm will occur and the magnitude of the harm should it occur. We hold that whether a risk is unjustifiable must be determined by assessing the nature and purpose of the actor's conduct relative to how substantial the risk is. Finally, in order for conduct to be reckless, the risk must be of such a nature that its disregard constitutes a gross deviation from the standard of care that a reasonable person would exercise.

A risk does not have to be "more likely than not to occur" or "probable" in order to be substantial. A risk may be substantial even if the chance that the harm will occur is well below fifty percent. Some risks may be substantial even if they carry a low degree of probability because the magnitude of the harm is potentially great. For example, if a person holds a revolver with a single bullet in one of the chambers, points the gun at another's head and pulls the trigger, then the risk of death is substantial even though the odds that death will result are no better than one in six. As one court remarked,

> If the potential of a risk is death, that risk is always serious. Therefore, only some likelihood that death will occur might create for most people a "substantial and unjustifiable" risk. . .

Conversely, a relatively high probability that a very minor harm will occur probably does not involve a "substantial" risk. Thus, in order to determine whether a risk is substantial, the court must consider both the likelihood that harm will occur and the magnitude of potential harm, mindful that a risk may be "substantial" even if the odds of the harm occurring are lower than fifty percent.

Whether a risk is substantial is a matter of fact that will depend on the specific circumstances of each case. Some conduct almost always carries a substantial risk of death, such as engaging another person in a fight with a deadly weapon or firing a gun at another. In such instances, the substantiality of the risk may be evident from the nature of the defendant's conduct and the court will not have to examine the specific facts in detail.

Other conduct requires a greater inquiry into the facts of the case to determine whether it creates a substantial risk of death. In *Moore v. People*, we affirmed a manslaughter conviction where the defendant kicked the victim to death. While "kicking another" may not necessarily involve a substantial risk of death, a trier of fact can find that repeatedly kicking the head and torso of someone already beaten unconscious can create a substantial risk of death. A court cannot generically characterize the actor's conduct (e.g., "driving a truck") in a manner that ignores the specific elements of the conduct that create a risk (e.g., driving a truck with failing brakes on a highway). Thus, to determine whether the conduct created a substantial risk of death, a court must inquire beyond the general nature of the defendant's conduct and consider the specific conduct in which the defendant engaged.

As well as being substantial, a risk must be unjustifiable in order for a person's conduct to be reckless. Whether a risk is justifiable is determined by weighing the nature and purpose of the actor's conduct against the risk created by that conduct. If a person consciously disregards a substantial risk of death but does so in order to advance an interest that justifies such a risk, the conduct is not reckless. For example, if a surgeon performs an operation on a patient that has a seventy-five percent chance of killing the patient, but the patient will certainly die without the operation, then the conduct is justified and thus not reckless even though the risk is substantial.

In addition to the separate analyses that are applied to determine whether a risk is both "substantial" and "unjustified," the concept of a "substantial and unjustifiable risk" implies a risk that constitutes a gross deviation from the standard of care that a reasonable law-abiding person would exercise under the circumstances. Both the Model Penal Code and the New York Code, which the General Assembly followed in drafting the Colorado criminal code, expressly define a "substantial and unjustifiable risk" as one that is a gross deviation from the reasonable standard of care. A substantial and unjustifiable risk must constitute a "gross deviation" from the reasonable standard of care in order to justify the criminal sanctions imposed for criminal negligence or reckless conduct.

Whether a risk is substantial and unjustified is a question of fact. In the limited context of a preliminary hearing, the court must determine whether a risk was substantial and unjustified by considering the evidence presented in the light most favorable to the prosecution, and the court must ask whether a reasonable person could "entertain" the belief—though not necessarily conclude beyond a reasonable doubt—that the defendant's conduct was reckless based on that evidence.

Conscious Disregard

In addition to showing that a person created a substantial and unjustifiable risk, the prosecution must demonstrate that the actor "consciously disregarded" the risk in order to prove that she acted recklessly. A person acts with a conscious disregard of the risk created by her conduct when she is aware of the risk and chooses to act despite that risk. In contrast to acting "intentionally" or "knowingly," the actor does not have to intend the result or be "practically certain" that the result will occur, he only needs to be "aware" that the risk exists. The statutory definitions of culpable mental states make these distinctions clear.

Although recklessness is a less culpable mental state than intentionally or knowingly, it involves a higher level of culpability than criminal negligence. Criminal negligence requires that, "through a gross deviation from the standard of care that a reasonable person would exercise," the actor fails to perceive a substantial and unjustifiable risk that a result will occur or a circumstance exists. An actor is criminally negligent when he should have been aware of the risk but was not, while recklessness requires that the defendant actually be aware of the risk but disregard it. Thus, even if she should be, a person who is not actually aware that her conduct creates a substantial and unjustifiable risk is not acting recklessly.

A court or trier of fact may infer a person's subjective awareness of a risk from the particular facts of a case, including the person's particular knowledge or expertise. For example, a court may infer a person's subjective awareness of the risks created by firing a gun from the facts that the person served an extended tour of duty in the military as a rifleman and machine gunner and was instructed by both the army and his father not to point a gun at another person.

In addition to the actor's knowledge and experience, a court may infer the actor's subjective awareness of a risk from what a reasonable person would have understood under the circumstances. When a court infers the defendant's subjective awareness of a risk from what a reasonable person in the circumstances would have known, the court may consider the perspective of a reasonable person in the situation and with the knowledge and training of the actor. Although a court can infer what the defendant actually knew based on what a reasonable person would have known in the circumstances, a court must not confuse what a reasonable person would have known in the circumstances with what the defendant actually knew. Thus, if a defendant engaged in conduct that a reasonable person would have understood as creating a substantial and unjustifiable risk of death, the court may infer that the defendant was subjectively aware of that risk, but the court cannot hold the defendant responsible if she were actually unaware of a risk that a reasonable person would have perceived.

Hence, in a reckless manslaughter case, the prosecution must prove that the defendant acted despite his subjective awareness of a substantial and unjustifiable risk of death from his conduct. Because absent an admission by the defendant such awareness cannot be proven directly, the court or trier of fact may infer the defendant's awareness of the risk from circumstances such as the defendant's training, knowledge, and prior experiences, or from what a reasonable person would have understood under the circumstances.

Risk of Death

The final element of recklessness requires that the actor consciously disregard a substantial and unjustifiable risk of a particular result, and in the case of manslaughter the actor must risk causing death to another person. The risk can be a risk of death to another generally; the actor does not have to risk death to a specific individual. Because the element of a "substantial and unjustifiable risk" measures the likelihood and magnitude of the risk disregarded by the actor, any risk of death will meet the requirement that the actor, by his conduct, risks death to another. That is, only a slight risk of death to another person is necessary to meet this element.

IV. APPLICATION OF LEGAL PRINCIPLES
TO HALL'S CONDUCT

B.   Review of Hall's Conduct

The district court's conclusion that Hall's conduct did not represent a substantial and unjustifiable risk of death rested on an erroneous construction of recklessness. Relying on two of our earlier cases, the court found that for a risk to be "substantial" it must "be *at least more likely than not* that death would result." As discussed, a risk of death that has less than a fifty percent chance of occurring may nonetheless be a substantial risk depending on the circumstances of the particular case. Because the district court applied a flawed interpretation of the law, we hold that the district court's assessment of probable cause was in error.

Because the district court relied on an erroneous legal standard, we consider this case in light of the standard we explain above. Because this case was dismissed at the preliminary hearing, we must consider the facts in the light most favorable to the prosecution and we must draw all inferences against the defendant. Furthermore, the prosecution does not have to satisfy the much higher burden of proof necessary to convict Hall of reckless manslaughter. Rather, it need only establish sufficient evidence so that a reasonably prudent and cautious person could entertain the belief that Hall committed the crime.

We first ask whether the prosecution presented sufficient evidence to show that Hall's conduct created a substantial and unjustifiable risk of death. "[S]kiing too fast for the conditions" is not widely considered behavior that constitutes a high degree of risk. However, we hold that the specific facts in this case support a reasonable inference that Hall created a substantial and unjustifiable risk that he would cause another's death.

Several witnesses stated that Hall was skiing very fast. Allen and the other eyewitnesses all said that Hall was travelling too fast for the conditions, at an excessive rate of speed, and that he was out of control. Sandberg presented testimony that Hall was a ski racer, indicating that Hall was trained to attain and ski at much faster speeds than even skilled and experienced recreational skiers. The witnesses said that Hall was travelling straight down the slope at such high speeds that, because of his lack of control, he would not have been able to stop or avoid another person.

In addition to statements of witnesses, the nature of Cobb's injuries and other facts of the collision support the inference that Hall was skiing at an inordinately high speed when he struck Cobb. As Dr. Galloway testified, the severe injuries Cobb sustained were consistent with a person being thrown from a moving automobile during a crash. Hall came to rest over eighty feet past Cobb's body, further suggesting that Hall was skiing at exceptionally high speeds. Thus, based on the testimony of the witnesses and the coroner's examination of Cobb's body, a reasonable person could conclude that Hall was skiing at very high speeds, thereby creating a risk of serious injury or death in the event of a skier-to-skier collision.

In addition to Hall's excessive speed, Hall was out of control and unable to avoid a collision with another person. All the witnesses said Hall was not traversing the slope and that he was skiing straight down the fall line. Hall admitted to Deputy Mossness that he first saw Cobb when he was airborne and that he was unable to stop when he saw people below him just before the collision. Hence, in addition to finding that Hall was skiing at a very high rate of speed, a reasonably prudent person could have concluded that Hall was unable to anticipate or avoid a potential collision with a skier on the trail below him.

While skiing ordinarily carries a very low risk of death to other skiers, a reasonable person could have concluded that Hall's excessive speed, lack of control, and improper technique significantly increased both the likelihood that a collision would occur and the extent of the injuries that might result from such a collision, including the possibility of death, in the event that a person like Cobb unwittingly crossed Hall's downhill path.

We next ask whether a reasonable person could have concluded that Hall's creation of a substantial risk of death was unjustified. To the extent that Hall's extremely fast and unsafe skiing created a risk of death, Hall was serving no direct interest other than his own enjoyment. [A] reasonable person could determine that the enjoyment of skiing does not justify skiing at the speeds and with the lack of control Hall exhibited. Thus, a reasonable person could have found that Hall's creation of a substantial risk was unjustifiable.

In addition to our conclusion that a reasonable person could have entertained the belief that Hall's conduct created a substantial and unjustifiable risk, we must ask whether Hall's conduct constituted a "gross deviation" from the standard of care that a reasonable law-abiding person (in this case, a reasonable, law-abiding, trained ski racer and resort employee) would have observed in the circumstances.

As we noted, the nature of the sport involves moments of high speeds and temporary losses of control. However, the General Assembly imposed upon a skier the duty to avoid collisions with any person or object below him. Although this statute may not form the basis of criminal liability, it establishes the minimum standard of care for uphill skiers and, for the purposes of civil negligence suits, creates a rebuttable presumption that the skier is at fault whenever he collides with skiers on the slope below him. A violation of a skier's duty in an extreme fashion, such as here, may be evidence of conduct that constitutes a "gross deviation" from the standard of care imposed by statute for civil negligence. Hall admitted to Deputy Mossness that as he flew off a knoll, he saw people below him but was unable to stop; Hall was travelling so fast and with so little control that he could not possibly have respected his obligation to avoid skiers below him on the slope. Additionally, Hall skied in this manner for some time over a considerable distance, demonstrating that his high speeds and lack of control were not the type of momentary lapse of control or inherent danger associated with skiing, a reasonable person could conclude that Hall's conduct was a gross deviation from the standard of care that a reasonable, experienced ski racer would have exercised.

Having determined that Hall's conduct created a substantial and unjustified risk of death that is a gross deviation from the reasonable standard of care under the circumstances, we next ask whether a reasonably prudent person could have entertained the belief that Hall consciously disregarded that risk. Hall is a trained ski racer who had been coached about skiing in control and skiing safely. Hall's knowledge and training could give rise to the reasonable inference that he was aware of the possibility that by skiing so fast and out of control he might collide with and kill another skier unless he regained control and slowed down.

In addition to inferring Hall's awareness of the risk from Hall's training and experience, a reasonable person with expert training and knowledge of skiing may have realized that skiing at very high speeds without enough control to stop or avoid a collision could seriously injure or kill another skier. Both Hall's subjective knowledge and the awareness that a reasonable person with Hall's background would have had support the inference that Hall consciously disregarded the risk he created by acting despite his awareness of the risk.

Although the risk that he would cause the death of another was probably slight, Hall's conduct created a risk of death. Hall's collision with Cobb involved enough force to kill Cobb and to simulate the type of head injury associated with victims in car accidents. Based on the evidence presented at the preliminary hearing, a reasonable person could conclude that Hall's conduct involved a risk of death.

Thus, interpreting the facts presented in the light most favorable to the prosecution, we hold that a reasonably prudent and cautious person could have entertained the belief that Hall consciously disregarded a substantial and unjustifiable risk that by skiing exceptionally fast and out of control he might collide with and kill another person on the slope.

Obviously, this opinion does not address whether Hall is ultimately guilty of any crime. Rather, we hold only that the People presented sufficient evidence to establish probable cause that Hall committed reckless manslaughter, and the court should have bound Hall's case over for trial.

V. CONCLUSION

The prosecution provided sufficient evidence at the preliminary hearing to induce a person of reasonable prudence and caution to entertain the belief that Hall consciously disregarded a substantial and unjustifiable risk that he might collide with and kill another skier. A court must inquire into the specific facts of each case to determine whether a risk was substantial and unjustified based on the likelihood of the risk, the potential magnitude of the harm, and the nature and purpose of the actor's conduct. In most instances, "skiing too fast for the conditions" does not create a substantial and unjustifiable risk of death, but the facts in this case are sufficient to lead a reasonable person to determine that Hall consciously disregarded such a risk. Although a reasonable person would not necessarily conclude that the evidence proves beyond a reasonable doubt that Hall committed reckless manslaughter, the evidence is sufficient to meet the limited purpose and low threshold at a preliminary hearing to establish probable cause. Thus, we remand this case to the district court for trial.

DISCUSSION QUESTIONS

1.   Do you think it occurred to Hall that he might kill someone when he started down the slope?

2.   How does the court use Hall's training and experience against him in finding that he did possess the required mental state?

3.   Does recklessness require too much for involuntary manslaughter? Should gross negligence be sufficient?

Practice Problem 13.1: Texting and Dying

You work for a legislator who is considering legislation addressing the use of handheld electronic communications devices while driving. Recently, a middle-aged driver crossed the center line while checking a news alert and crashed into a car full of high school graduates on senior night, killing all of them. Your boss wants your recommendations on two related questions. First, what sort of uses of handheld electronic communications devices during driving should be prohibited as criminal? Second, under what circumstances, if any, should deaths resulting from the use of such devices while driving be prosecuted as manslaughter or as murder, and what factors should distinguish manslaughter from murder cases? Your legislator is interested in both specific recommendations about statutory language as well as a discussion of the general policy considerations behind your recommendations.

Case in Context

The following case involves a tragic death of a child at the hands of loving but disadvantaged parents.

THE STATE OF WASHINGTON V. WILLIAMS
Court of Appeals of Washington
484 P.2d 1167 (1971)

Defendants, husband and wife, were charged by information filed October 3, 1968, with the crime of manslaughter for negligently failing to supply their 17-month child with necessary medical attention, as a result of which he died on September 12, 1968. Upon entry of findings, conclusions and judgment of guilty, sentences were imposed on April 22, 1969. Defendants appeal.

The defendant husband, Walter Williams, is a 24-year-old full-blooded Sheshont Indian with a sixth-grade education. His sole occupation is that of laborer. The defendant wife, Bernice Williams, is a 20-year-old part Indian with an 11th grade education. At the time of the marriage, the wife had two children, the younger of whom was a 14-month son. Both parents worked and the children were cared for by the 85-year-old mother of the defendant husband. The defendant husband assumed parental responsibility with the defendant wife to provide clothing, care and medical attention for the child. Both defendants possessed a great deal of love and affection for the defendant wife's young son.

The court expressly found [t]hat both defendants were aware that William Joseph Tabafunda was ill during the period September 1, 1968 to September 12, 1968. They did not realize how sick the baby was. They thought that the baby had a toothache and no layman regards a toothache as dangerous to life. They loved the baby and gave it aspirin in hopes of improving its condition. They did not take the baby to a doctor because of fear that the Welfare Department would take the baby away from them. They knew that medical help was available because of previous experience. They had no excuse that the law will recognize for not taking the baby to a doctor.

The defendants Walter L. Williams and Bernice J. Williams were negligent in not seeking medical attention for William Joseph Tabafunda [and] as a proximate result of this negligence, William Joseph Tabafunda died.

From these and other findings, the court concluded that the defendants were each guilty of the crime of manslaughter as charged.

Defendants take no exception to findings but contend that the findings do not support the conclusions that the defendants are guilty of manslaughter as charged. The contentions raise two basic issues, (1) the existence of the duty to furnish medical aid charged by the information to be violated and the seriousness of the breach required; and (2) the issue of proximate cause, i.e., whether defendants were put on notice, in time to save the child's life, that medical care was required. Because the nature of the duty and the quality or seriousness of the breach are closely interrelated, our discussion of the first issue involved will embrace both matters.

Parental duty to provide medical care for a dependent minor child was recognized at common law and characterized as a natural duty. In Washington, the existence of the duty is commonly assumed and is stated at times without reference to any particular statute. The existence of the duty also is assumed, but not always defined, in statutes that provide special criminal and civil sanctions for the performance of that duty. RCW 26.16.205 imposes civil liability on parental property for the 'expenses of the family and education of the children.' The quoted language is broad enough to include 'necessaries,' and necessaries include necessary medical expense of dependent minor children which it is the duty of a parent to provide. On the question of the quality or seriousness of breach of the duty, at common law, in the case of involuntary manslaughter, the breach had to amount to more than mere ordinary or simple negligence—gross negligence was essential. In Washington, however, RCW 9.48.060 (since amended by Laws of 1970, ch. 49, § 2) and RCW 9.48.150 supersede both voluntary and involuntary manslaughter as those crimes were defined at common law. Under these statutes the crime is deemed committed even though the death of the victim is the proximate result of only simple or ordinary negligence.

The concept of simple or ordinary negligence describes a failure to exercise the 'ordinary caution' necessary to make out the defense of excusable homicide. RCW 9.48.150. Ordinary caution is the kind of caution that a man of reasonable prudence would exercise under the same or similar conditions. If, therefore, the conduct of a defendant, regardless of his ignorance, good intentions and good faith, fails to measure up to the conduct required of a man of reasonable prudence, he is guilty of ordinary negligence because of his failure to use 'ordinary caution. If such negligence proximately causes the death of the victim, the defendant, as pointed out above, is guilty of statutory manslaughter.

In the instant case, defendants contend that the only duty to provide medical care for the infant child is the statutory duty set forth in RCW 26.20.030; that the court having concluded that the defendants were not guilty of 'willful . . . misconduct,' that no duty to furnish medical care was violated and that, accordingly, defendants are not guilty of the crime of statutory manslaughter charged in the information.

RCW 26.20.030(1) (b) makes it a felony for a person who 'willfully omits, without lawful excuse, to furnish necessary . . . medical attendance for his or her child . . .' The words 'willfully omits' are, used in two senses, namely, (1) 'an act or omission done intentionally . . .' or (2) when used in statutes making nonsupport a crime, 'an absence of lawful excuse or justification on the part of the accused parent.' It was further pointed out that, by reason of RCW 26.20.080, the state meets its burden of proving willfulness and absence of lawful excuse on a prima facie basis when the evidence, directly or circumstantially, reveals a failure on the part of a physically or vocationally able parent to furnish the required medical attendance. Hence, RCW 26.20.030 is presumptively violated either because a defendant intentionally omits to furnish necessary medical care, or omits so to do without lawful excuse.

Defendants' contention misconceives the significance of the words 'willful . . . misconduct' contained in the conclusions because of defendants' failure to recognize that 'willful' is a phrase of double meaning. Since the trial court expressly found that the defendants 'had no excuse that the law will recognize for not taking the baby to a doctor,' it is reasonable to conclude that the phrase 'willful . . . misconduct,' contained in the conclusion, merely means intentional misconduct. The conclusion, in light of the findings, means merely that the conduct, although not intentional, was without lawful excuse and therefore willful in the second sense. Even if it is assumed that the information charging the crime of manslaughter relied upon a violation of RCW 26.20.030(1) (b), the conviction must stand since the findings and supporting evidence are sufficient to support the conclusion that, in the second sense of the term, the defendants willfully violated the duty owing their deceased child.

Furthermore, the significance of the words 'willful . . . misconduct' contained in the conclusion is overstated. If it be assumed that RCW 26.20.030(1) (b) can be said to create a duty to furnish medical care otherwise not existing, as distinguished from a mere statement of a condition precedent to the imposition of a criminal sanction, then a duty may be said to exist even if the conditions permitting imposition of the criminal sanction do not. Hence, a conclusion that defendants' conduct was not willful does not mean that the duty has not been violated.

We need not, however, rest our decision solely on the above-mentioned grounds. The information charging statutory manslaughter made no mention of and did not purport to restrict itself to the violation of the duty set forth in RCW 26.20.030 (1) (b). The information charged the violation of 'the legal duty of providing necessary . . . medical attention to said . . . minor child . . .' This general language permits reliance upon the existence of the legal duty no matter from what source derived. We have already pointed out that such a parental duty is recognized in the decisions of this state and has been characterized as a natural duty existing independently of statutes. [S]hould RCW 26.20.030(1) (b) be repealed, it could not reasonably be claimed that parents were thereby absolved from their natural duty to provide necessary medical care for their minor dependent children. We therefore hold that the violation of the parental duty to furnish medical care to a minor dependent child, the other elements of manslaughter being present, is a sufficient basis on which to rest a conviction of the crime of manslaughter.

In the instant case, however, the defendant husband is not the father of the minor child, nor has he adopted that child. Nevertheless, the evidence shows that he had assumed responsibility with his wife for the care and maintenance of the child, whom he greatly loved. Such assumption of responsibility, characterized in the information as that required of a 'guardian and custodian,' is sufficient to impose upon him the duty to furnish necessary medical care.

The remaining issue of proximate cause requires consideration of the question of when the duty to furnish medical care became activated. If the duty to furnish such care was not activated until after it was too late to save the life of the child, failure to furnish medical care could not be said to have proximately caused the child's death. Timeliness in the furnishing of medical care also must be considered in terms of 'ordinary caution.' The law does not mandatorily require that a doctor be called for a child at the first sign of any indisposition or illness. The indisposition or illness may appear to be of a minor or very temporary kind, such as a toothache or cold. If one in the exercise of ordinary caution fails to recognize that his child's symptoms require medical attention, it cannot be said that the failure to obtain such medical attention is a breach of the duty owed.

We quite agree that the Code does not contemplate the necessity of calling a physician for every trifling complaint with which the child may be afflicted which in most instances may be overcome by the ordinary household nursing by members of the family; that a reasonable amount of discretion is vested in parents, charged with the duty of maintaining and bringing up infant children; and that the standard is at what time would an ordinarily prudent person, solicitous for the welfare of his child and anxious to promote its recovery, deem it necessary to call in the services of a physician.

It remains to apply the law discussed to the facts of the instant case.

Defendants have not assigned error to the findings either on the ground that the evidence is insufficient to prove negligence or proximate cause, or that the state has failed to prove the facts found by failing to apply the required standard of proof beyond a reasonable doubt. They contended below and on appeal that they are not guilty of the crime charged. Because of the serious nature of the charge against the parent and stepparent of a well-loved child, and out of our concern for the protection of the constitutional rights of the defendants, we have made an independent examination of the evidence to determine whether it substantially supports the court's express finding on proximate cause and its implied finding that the duty to furnish medical care became activated in time to prevent death of the child.

Dr. Gale Wilson, the autopsy surgeon and chief pathologist for the King County Coroner, testified that the child died because an abscessed tooth had been allowed to develop into an infection of the mouth and cheeks, eventually becoming gangrenous. This condition, accompanied by the child's inability to eat, brought about malnutrition, lowering the child's resistance and eventually producing pneumonia, causing the death. Dr. Wilson testified that in his opinion the infection had lasted for approximately 2 weeks, and that the odor generally associated with gangrene would have been present for approximately 10 days before death. He also expressed the opinion that had medical care been first obtained in the last week before the baby's death, such care would have been obtained too late to have saved the baby's life. Accordingly, the baby's apparent condition between September 1 and September 5, 1968 became the critical period for the purpose of determining whether in the exercise of ordinary caution defendants should have provided medical care for the minor child.

The defendant husband testified that he noticed the baby was sick about 2 weeks before the baby died. The defendant wife testified that she noticed the baby was ill about a week and a half or 2 weeks before the baby died. The evidence showed that in the critical period the baby was fussy; that he could not keep his food down; and that a cheek started swelling up. The swelling went up and down, but did not disappear. In that same period, the cheek turned 'a bluish color like.' The defendants, not realizing that the baby was as ill as it was or that the baby was in danger of dying, attempted to provide some relief to the baby by giving the baby aspirin during the critical period and continued to do so until the night before the baby died. The defendants thought the swelling would go down and were waiting for it to do so; and defendant husband testified, that from what he had heard, neither doctors nor dentists pull out a tooth 'when it's all swollen up like that.' There was an additional explanation for not calling a doctor given by each defendant. Defendant husband testified that 'the way the cheek looked, . . . and that stuff on his hair, they would think we were neglecting him and take him away from us and not give him back.' Defendant wife testified that the defendants were 'waiting for the swelling to go down,' and also that they were afraid to take the child to a doctor for fear that the doctor would report them to the welfare department, who, in turn, would take the child away. 'It's just that I was so scared of losing him.' They testified that they had heard that the defendant husband's cousin lost a child that way. The evidence showed that the defendants did not understand the significance or seriousness of the baby's symptoms. However, there is no evidence that the defendants were physically or financially unable to obtain a doctor, or that they did not know an available doctor, or that the symptoms did not continue to be a matter of concern during the critical period. Indeed, the evidence shows that in April 1968 defendant husband had taken the child to a doctor for medical attention.

In our opinion, there is sufficient evidence from which the court could find, as it necessarily did, that applying the standard of ordinary caution, i.e., the caution exercisable by a man of reasonable prudence under the same or similar conditions, defendants were sufficiently put on notice concerning the symptoms of the baby's illness and lack of improvement in the baby's apparent condition in the period from September 1 to September 5, 1968 to have required them to have obtained medical care for the child. The failure so to do in this case is ordinary or simple negligence, and such negligence is sufficient to support a conviction of statutory manslaughter.

The judgment is affirmed.

DISCUSSION QUESTIONS

1.   Why does it matter when the point of no return was reached in terms of the treatment of the child's infection?

2.   Negligence turns on what a reasonable person would do. But who is the reasonable person? What age, gender, sexual orientation, race, ethnicity, level of education, economic class? What standard of reasonableness should these parents be held to?

3.   Is simple negligence too low a standard for manslaughter liability? Or is gross negligence too high?

Practice Problem 13.2: Ember Alert

Casey is a thirty-year-old man whose wife and three small children were killed in a fire in their home. Casey testified to the following facts. That night Casey and some friends had been having a party in the basement of Casey's home. They drank alcohol and snorted cocaine. At 2:00 a.m. the party ended when they ran out of beer. His friends left. Casey was intoxicated but also wide-awake from the cocaine he had snorted. Because the furnace in their home was broken, his wife had left a fire burning in the fireplace in the living room to keep the bedrooms upstairs warm during the cold winter night. Casey noticed that the night was particularly cold and that the fire was almost out. He removed the screen from the fireplace and added a big pile of logs to the fire. He then remembered that he had promised to make his children pancakes in the morning but that they were out of syrup. He was afraid that he was too intoxicated to drive, so he decided to walk to a mini-mart that was open all night and only twenty minutes away by foot, in order to get some syrup for the pancakes and some beer to help him sleep.

Halfway to the mini-mart Casey realized that he could not remember whether he had replaced the fire screen after adding the logs. Casey decided not to worry about it. He said that he and his wife often left the screen off because the kids loved stirring up sparks with the fire poker. Casey had never once seen an ember or spark of any size escape the fire place. Casey continued walking to the mini-mart, bought the beer and the syrup, and headed back home. As soon as he saw the fire on his street he began running toward his house. By the time he reached the house the fire department was on the scene but the house was completely engulfed in flames.

> The fire chief testified to the following: From the remaining ashes around the fireplace it appeared that a log had rolled out across the stone floor and onto a rug that caught fire. The fire spread, and Casey's wife and children were overcome with smoke before they could flee the burning home. The chief admitted that he had never heard of a log rolling that far out of a fireplace before, but he also said that the screen would have easily stopped the log from rolling out of the fireplace. The chief also testified that a fire could easily start from embers escaping an unscreened fireplace that did not have adequate ventilation to create a strong updraft. A burning ember can be easily stomped out if someone is present, but embers from unattended fires can start a house fire. For this reason it is dangerous to leave a fire burning unattended without a screen in place. Finally, the chief testified that it took three firefighters to stop Casey from running into his burning home and that he was screaming the names of his wife and children as they dragged him away. The police found the mini-mart bag with a bottle of pancake syrup and a six pack of beer where Casey said he had dropped it.
>
> Casey is on trial in a Model Penal Code jurisdiction for manslaughter and negligent homicide. Make closing arguments for the defense and for the prosecution. The prosecution must make arguments for both crimes in the alternative. The defense must make arguments against both crimes in the alternative.

B. DEPRAVED HEART MURDER

Imagine someone so utterly careless that they seem just as evil and just as dangerous as someone who actually intended to kill. You need to imagine the sort of carelessness that makes you yell, "Oh my God," or "Damn," or worse. A bank robber who uses a child as a human shield during a gunfight. A dentist who killed not one, not two, but three patients in a row by being mind-bogglingly careless about infection procedures. A driver who drove ninety miles an hour down the sidewalk of a busy street. Someone who adopted a pit bull that had been trained to fight and who left the gate on his pen open, despite the fact that preschool children lived next door. An airline captain and copilot who show up drunk to fly a 747. You now have the main idea behind depraved heart murder.

Depraved heart murder has its roots in the common law. This next case is an old example of this doctrine in action. At the end of the day, why did the court find this man guilty? What philosophy of punishment did it serve?

Common law had all sorts of colorful labels for this sort of extreme carelessness.

- Depraved Heart
- Abandoned and Malignant Heart
- Wicked Disposition

- Wanton, Cruel, Callous

- Hard Hearted

These phrases tried to get at the same thing: this was as bad a person as someone who actually intended to kill and thereby deserved the label and penalty of a murderer. Notice how many of the phrases use the word "heart," and how much they allude to not only mental state but also character.

Beyond the extreme cases that are easy to identify, there is not a clear line between the sort of carelessness that constitutes murder as opposed to involuntary manslaughter. How reckless or indifferent do you have to be? What about your garden-variety drunk driver who has too much to drink and misses a stop sign? Or your garden-variety idiot who plays Russian Roulette with his friends? Should murder or manslaughter be the crime if death results? Cases go both ways, although the recent trend has been decidedly in favor of prosecuting aggravated drunk driving cases as murder.

Case in Context

This nineteenth century case illustrates the original idea behind depraved heart murder.

MAYES V. ILLINOIS

Supreme Court of Illinois
46 Am. Rep. 698 (1883)

MR. JUSTICE SCHOLFIELD delivered the opinion of the Court: Plaintiff in error, by the judgment of the court below, was convicted of the crime of murder, and sentenced to the penitentiary for the term of his natural life. . .

It is contended the facts proved do not constitute murder. They are, briefly, these: The deceased was the wife of plaintiff in error, and came to her death by burning, resulting from plaintiff in error throwing a beer glass against a lighted oil lamp which she was carrying, and thereby breaking the lamp and scattering the burning oil over her person. Plaintiff in error came into the room where his wife, his mother-in-law and his young daughter were seated around a table engaged in domestic labors, about nine o'clock at night. He had been at a saloon near by, and was, to some extent, intoxicated,—not, however, to the degree of unconsciousness, for he testifies to a consciousness and recollection of all that occurred. When he sat down, the deceased, noticing that one side of his face was dirty, asked him if he had fallen down. He replied that it was none of her business. She then directed the daughter to procure water for him with which to wash his face, which being done, he washed his face, and he then directed the daughter to procure him a clean beer glass, which she did. He had brought some beer with him from the saloon, and he then proceeded to fill the glass with the beer and handed it to the deceased. She took a sup of it, and then offered it to her mother, who declined tasting it. The deceased then brought plaintiff in error his supper, but he declined eating it, and was about to throw a loaf of bread at the deceased when she took it from his hands and returned it to the cupboard. After this, having sat quietly for a few minutes, he asked for arsenic. No reply was made to this request, and thereupon he commenced cursing, and concluded by saying that he would either kill deceased or she should kill him. He wanted a fire made, but deceased told him it was bed time and they did not need any fire. He then picked up a tin quart measure and threw it at the daughter. Thereupon deceased started, with an oil lamp in her hand, toward a bed-room door, directing the daughter to go to bed, and as the deceased and daughter were advancing toward the bed-room door, he picked up the beer glass, which is described as being a large beer glass, with a handle on one side, and threw it with violence at the deceased. It struck the lamp in her hand and broke it, scattering the burning oil over her person and igniting her clothes. Plaintiff in error made no effort to extinguish the flames, but seems to have caught hold of the deceased, temporarily, by her arms. This occurred on Monday night, and on Saturday of that week she died of the wounds caused by this burning.

The plaintiff in error claims that he was only intending to pitch the beer glass out of doors—that he did not design hitting the deceased, and that the striking of the lamp was therefore purely an accident. In this he is positively contradicted by his daughter and mother-in-law, the only witnesses of the tragedy besides himself. He says, to give plausibility to his story, that the door leading into the yard was open, and that deceased and daughter had to pass between him and that door in going to the bed-room, and that deceased was near the edge of the door and moving across the door when he pitched the glass. They both say this door was closed, and that he threw the glass. The language of his mother-in-law, in regard to the throwing, is: "He threw at her with vengeance a heavy tumbler;" and his daughter's language is: "He picked up a tumbler and threw it with such force that it struck the lamp." We can not say the jury erred in believing the mother-in-law and daughter, and disbelieving plaintiff in error.

. . .The plaintiff in error asked the court to instruct the jury, "that to constitute a murder there is required an union of act and intent, and the jury must believe, beyond a reasonable doubt, both that the weapon used was thrown with the intent to inflict bodily injury upon the person of Kate Mayes, and if they have a reasonable doubt as to whether his intent was to strike his wife or not, the jury should give the prisoner the benefit of such doubt, and acquit him." The court refused to give this as asked, but modified it by adding: "Unless the jury further believe, from the evidence, beyond a reasonable doubt, that all the circumstances of the killing of Kate Mayes, (if the evidence shows that she was killed by defendant,) shows an abandoned and malignant heart on the part of the defendant," and then gave it. Plaintiff in error then also asked the court to instruct the jury as follows:

> "The court instructs the jury, for the defendant, that intention to commit a crime is one of the especial ingredients of an offence, and the People are bound to show, beyond a reasonable doubt, that the defendant threw the glass in question at the deceased with the intention to do her bodily injury, and if you believe, from the evidence, that there is a reasonable doubt as to the defendant having thrown said glass with intent to do her bodily injury, the jury will give the defendant the benefit of said doubt, and acquit the defendant."

This, also, the court refused to give as asked, but modified it by adding: "Unless all the circumstances of the killing of Mrs. Mayes (if she is shown, beyond a reasonable doubt, to have been killed by defendant,) show an abandoned and malignant heart on the part of the defendant," and then gave it. Exceptions were taken to the rulings in these modifications, so the question whether they were erroneous is properly before us.

We perceive no objection to these rulings. Malice is an indispensable element to the crime of murder. But our statute, repeating the common law rule, says: "Malice shall be implied when no considerable provocation appears, or when all the circumstances of the killing show an abandoned and malignant heart." (Rev. Stat. 1874, p. 374, sec. 140.) And hence it is said: "When an action, unlawful in itself, is done with deliberation, and with intention of mischief or great bodily harm to particulars, or of mischief indiscriminately, fall where it may, and death ensue, against or beside the original intention of the party, it will be murder." (Wharton on Homicide, 45.) And as illustrative of the principle, the author says: "Thus, if a person, breaking in an unruly horse, willfully ride him among a crowd of persons, the probable danger being great and apparent, and death ensue from the viciousness of the animal, it is murder. * * * So, if a man mischievously throw from a roof into a crowded street, where passengers are constantly passing and repassing, a heavy piece of timber, calculated to produce death on such as it might fall, and death ensue, the offence is murder at common law. And upon the same principle, if a man, knowing that people are passing along the street, throw a stone likely to do injury, or shoot over a house or wall with intent to do hurt to people, and one is thereby slain, it is murder on account of previous malice, though not directed against any particular individual. It is no excuse that the party was bent upon mischief generally." To like effect is, also, 1 Russell on Crimes, (7th Am. ed.) 540, 541; 1 Wharton on Crim. Law, (7th ed.) sec. 712 b. So, here, it was utterly immaterial whether plaintiff in error intended the glass should strike his wife, his mother-in-law, or his child, or whether he had any specific intent, but acted solely from general malicious recklessness, disregarding any and all consequences. It is sufficient that he manifested a reckless, murderous disposition,—in the language of the old books, "A heart void of social duty, and fatally bent on mischief." A strong man who will violently throw a tin quart measure at his daughter—a tender child—or a heavy beer glass in a direction that he must know will probably cause it to hit his wife, sufficiently manifests malice in general to render his act murderous when death is the consequence of it. He may have intended some other result, but he is responsible for the actual result. Where the act is, in itself, lawful, or, even if unlawful, not dangerous in its character, the rule is different. In cases like the present, the presumption is the mind assented to what the hand did, with all the consequences resulting therefrom, because it is apparent he was willing that any result might be produced, at whatever of harm to others. In the other case, the result is accidental, and, therefore, not presumed to have been within the contemplation of the party, and so not to have received the assent of his mind.

Judgment affirmed.

DISCUSSION QUESTIONS

1.   Do you believe beyond a reasonable doubt that Mayes intended to kill his wife when he threw the beer glass at her? Do you think that it occurred to him as he threw the glass that he might kill her?

2.   How does this court define depraved heart murder?

3.   Was Mayes found guilty of murder because he was a very bad man who caused a freak accident? Is that a good or bad result?

Case in Context

In the following case, depraved heart murder is defined in less colorful, more analytical language.

PEOPLE V. MARJORIE KNOLLER

Supreme Court of California
158 P. 3d 731 (2007)

KENNARD, J.

I.   FACTS AND PROCEEDINGS

In 1998, Pelican Bay State Prison inmates Paul Schneider and Dale Bretches, both members of the Aryan Brotherhood prison gang, sought to engage in a business of buying, raising, and breeding Presa Canario dogs. This breed of dog tends to be very large, weighing over 100 pounds, and reaching over five feet tall when standing on its hind legs. A document found in defendants' apartment describes the Presa Canario as "a gripping dog . . . always used and bred for combat and guard . . . and used extensively for fighting . . . ."

Prisoners Schneider and Bretches relied on outside contacts, including Brenda Storey and Janet Coumbs, to carry out their Presa Canario business. Schneider told Coumbs that she should raise the dogs.

As of May 1998, Coumbs possessed four such dogs, named Bane, Isis, Hera, and Fury. Hera and Fury broke out of their fenced yard and attacked Coumbs's sheep. Hera killed at least one of the sheep and also a cat belonging to Coumbs's daughter. Coumbs acknowledged that Bane ate his doghouse and may have joined Fury in killing a sheep.

Defendants Knoller and Noel, who were attorneys representing a prison guard at Pelican Bay State Prison, met inmate Schneider at the prison sometime in 1999. In October 1999, defendants filed a lawsuit on behalf of Brenda Storey against Coumbs over the ownership and custody of the four dogs. Coumbs decided not to contest the lawsuit and to turn the dogs over to defendants. Coumbs warned Knoller that the dogs had killed Coumbs's sheep, but Knoller did not seem to care.

Defendant Knoller thereafter contacted Dr. Donald Martin, a veterinarian for 49 years, and on March 26, 2000, he examined and vaccinated the dogs. With his bill to Knoller, Dr. Martin included a letter, which said in part: "I would be professionally amiss sic if I did not mention the following, so that you can be prepared. These dogs are huge, approximately weighing in the neighborhood of 100 pounds each. They have had no training or discipline of any sort. They were a problem to even get to, let alone to vaccinate. You mentioned having a professional hauler gather them up and taking them. . . . Usually this would be done in crates, but I doubt one could get them into anything short of a livestock trailer, and if let loose they would have a battle. To add to this, these animals would be a liability in any household, reminding me of the recent attack in Tehama County to a boy by large dogs. He lost his arm and disfigured his face. The historic romance of the warrior dog, the personal guard dog, the gaming dog, etc. may sound good but hardly fits into life today." Knoller thanked Dr. Martin for the information and said she would pass it on to her client.

On April 1, 2000, both defendants and a professional dog handler took custody of the dogs from Coumbs. Bane then weighed 150 pounds and Hera 130 pounds. Coumbs told both defendants that she was worried about the dogs, that Hera and Fury should be shot, and that she was also concerned about Bane and Isis.

Hera remained for a short time at a kennel in San Mateo County while Bane was sent to a facility in Los Angeles County. Both defendants soon became concerned for the health of the two dogs. On April 30, 2000, defendants brought Hera to their sixth-floor apartment at 2398 Pacific Avenue in San Francisco. Bane arrived in September 2000. Codefendant Noel purchased dog licenses, registering himself and Knoller as the dogs' owners.

A later search of defendants' apartment showed that they frequently exchanged letters with Pelican Bay inmates Schneider and Bretches. Over 100 letters were sent and received between March and December 2000, apparently under the guise of attorney-client correspondence. In the letters, defendants discussed a commercial breeding operation, considering various names such as GuerraHund Kennels, Wardog, and finally settling on Dog-O-War. Prisoners Schneider and Bretches's notes on a Web site for the business described Bane as "Wardog," and "Bringer of Death: Ruin: Destruction."

Between the time defendants Noel and Knoller brought the dogs to their sixth-floor apartment in San Francisco and the date of the fatal mauling of Diane Whipple on January 26, 2001, there were about 30 incidents of the two dogs being out of control or threatening humans and other dogs. Neighbors mentioned seeing the two dogs unattended on the sixth floor and running down the hall. Codefendant Noel's letters to prisoner Schneider confirmed this, mentioning one incident when defendant Knoller had to let go of the two dogs as they broke from her grasp and ran to the end of the hall. Noel described how the dogs even pushed past him and "took off side by side down the hall toward the elevator in a celebratory stampede!! 240 lbs. of Presa wall to wall moving at top speed!!!" In a letter to inmate Schneider, defendant Knoller admitted not having the upper body strength to handle Bane and having trouble controlling Hera.

When neighbors complained to defendants Noel and Knoller about the two dogs, defendants responded callously, if at all. In one incident, neighbors Stephen and Aimee West were walking their dog in a nearby park when Hera attacked their dog and "latched on" to the dog's snout. Noel was unable to separate the dogs, but Aimee threw her keys at Hera, startling Hera and causing Hera to release her grip on the Wests' dog. On another day, Stephen West was walking his dog when he encountered Noel with Bane. Bane lunged toward West's dog, but Noel managed to pull Bane back. When Stephen West next saw Noel, West suggested that Noel muzzle the dogs and talk to dog trainer Mario Montepeque about training them; Noel replied there was no need to do so. Defendants Knoller and Noel later encountered Montepeque, who advised defendants to have their dogs trained and to use a choke collar. Defendants disregarded this advice. On still another occasion, when dog walker Lynn Gaines was walking a dog, Gaines told Noel that he should put a muzzle on Bane; Noel called her a "bitch" and said the dog Gaines was walking was the problem.

There were also instances when defendants' two dogs attacked or threatened people. David Moser, a fellow resident in the apartment building, slipped by defendants Knoller and Noel in the hallway only to have their dog Hera bite him on the "rear end." When he exclaimed, "Your dog just bit me," Noel replied, "Um, interesting." Neither defendant apologized to Moser or reprimanded the dog. Another resident, Jill Cowen

Davis, was eight months pregnant when one of the dogs, in the presence of both Knoller and Noel, suddenly growled and lunged toward her stomach with its mouth open and teeth bared. Noel jerked the dog by the leash, but he did not apologize to Davis. Postal carrier John Watanabe testified that both dogs, unleashed, had charged him. He said the dogs were in a "snarling frenzy" and he was "terrified for his life." When he stepped behind his mail cart, the dogs went back to Knoller and Noel. On still another occasion, the two dogs lunged at a six-year-old boy walking to school; they were stopped less than a foot from him.

One time, codefendant Noel himself suffered a severe injury to his finger when Bane bit him during a fight with another dog. The wound required surgery, and Noel had to wear a splint on his arm and have two steel pins placed in his hand for eight to 10 weeks.

Mauling victim Diane Whipple and her partner Sharon Smith lived in a sixth-floor apartment across a lobby from defendants. Smith encountered defendants' two dogs as often as once a week. In early December 2000, Whipple called Smith at work to say, with some panic in her voice, that one of the dogs had bitten her. Whipple had come upon codefendant Noel in the lobby with one of the dogs, which lunged at her and bit her in the hand. Whipple did not seek medical treatment for three deep, red indentations on one hand. Whipple made every effort to avoid defendants' dogs, checking the hallway before she went out and becoming anxious while waiting for the elevator for fear the dogs would be inside. She and Smith did not complain to apartment management because they wanted nothing to do with defendants Knoller and Noel.

On January 26, 2001, Whipple telephoned Smith to say she was going home early. At 4:00 p.m., Esther Birkmaier, a neighbor who lived across the hall from Whipple, heard dogs barking and a woman's "panic-stricken" voice calling, "Help me, help me." Looking through the peephole in her front door, Birkmaier saw Whipple lying face down on the floor just over the threshold of her apartment with what appeared to be a dog on top of her. Birkmaier saw no one else in the hallway. Afraid to open the door, Birkmaier called 911, the emergency telephone number, and at the same time heard a voice yelling, "No, no, no" and "Get off." When Birkmaier again approached her door, she could hear barking and growling directly outside and a banging against a door. She heard a voice yell, "Get off, get off, no, no, stop, stop." She chained her door and again looked through the peephole. Whipple's body was gone and groceries were strewn about the hallway. Birkmaier called 911 a second time.

At 4:12 p.m., San Francisco Police Officers Sidney Laws and Leslie Forrestal arrived in response to Birkmaier's telephone calls. They saw Whipple's body in the hallway; her clothing had been completely ripped off, her entire body was covered with wounds, and she was bleeding profusely. Defendant Knoller and the two dogs were not in sight.

The officers called for an ambulance. Shortly thereafter, defendant Knoller emerged from her apartment. She did not ask about Whipple's condition but merely told the officers she was looking for her keys, which she found just inside the door to Whipple's apartment.

An emergency medical technician administered first aid to Whipple, who had a large, profusely bleeding wound to her neck. The wound was too large to halt the bleeding, and Whipple's pulse and breathing stopped as paramedics arrived. She was revived but died shortly after reaching the hospital.

An autopsy revealed over 77 discrete injuries covering Whipple's body "from head to toe." The most significant were lacerations damaging her jugular vein and her carotid artery and crushing her larynx, injuries typically inflicted by predatory animals to kill their prey. The medical examiner stated that although earlier medical attention would have increased Whipple's chances of survival, she might ultimately have died anyway because she had lost one-third or more of her blood at the scene. Plaster molds of the two dogs' teeth showed that the bite injuries to Whipple's neck were consistent with Bane's teeth.

Animal control officer Andrea Runge asked defendant Knoller to sign over custody of the dogs for euthanasia. Knoller, whom Runge described as "oddly calm," agreed to sign over Bane, but she refused to sign over Hera for euthanasia and she refused to help the animal control officers with the animals, saying she was "unable to handle the dogs."

At trial, Noel did not testify, but he presented evidence of positive encounters between the two dogs and veterinarians, friends, and neighbors. Defendant Knoller did testify in her own defense. She referred to herself, her husband, and Pelican Bay prisoner Schneider as the "triad," and she spoke of Schneider as her "son." The two dogs had become a focal point in the relationship. She denied reading literature in the apartment referring to the vicious nature of the dogs. She thought the dogs had no personality problems requiring a professional trainer. She denied receiving or otherwise discounted any warnings about the two dogs' behavior and she maintained that virtually all the witnesses testifying to incidents with the dogs were lying. She said she never walked both dogs together. Ordinarily, she would walk Hera and codefendant Noel would walk Bane, because she had insufficient body strength to control Bane. But after Noel was injured while breaking up a fight between Bane and another dog, Knoller would sometimes walk Bane, always on a leash. She said she had just returned from walking Bane on the roof of the apartment building, and had opened the door to her apartment while holding Bane's leash, when Bane dragged her back across the lobby toward Whipple, who had just opened the door to her own apartment. The other dog, Hera, left defendants' apartment and joined Bane, who attacked Whipple. Knoller said she threw herself on

Whipple to save her. She denied that Hera participated in the attack. She acknowledged not calling 911 to get help for Whipple.

Asked whether she denied responsibility for the attack on Whipple, Knoller gave this reply: "I said in an interview that I wasn't responsible but it wasn't for the—it wasn't in regard to what Bane had done, it was in regard to knowing whether he would do that or not. And I had no idea that he would ever do anything like that to anybody. How can you anticipate something like that? It's a totally bizarre event. I mean how could you anticipate that a dog that you know that is gentle and loving and affectionate would do something so horrible and brutal and disgusting and gruesome to anybody? How could you imagine that happening?"

In rebuttal, the prosecution presented evidence that the minor character of defendant Knoller's injuries—principally bruising to the hands—indicated that she had not been as involved in trying to protect mauling victim Whipple as she had claimed. Dr. Randall Lockwood, the prosecution's expert on dog behavior, testified that good behavior by a dog on some occasions does not preclude aggressive and violent behavior on other occasions, and he mentioned the importance of training dogs such as Bane and Hera not to fight.

The jury found Knoller guilty of second degree murder; it also found Noel guilty of involuntary manslaughter and owning a mischievous animal that caused the death of a human being. Both defendants moved for a new trial. The trial court denied Noel's motion. We quote below the pertinent statements by the trial court in granting Knoller's motion for a new trial on the second degree murder count.

The trial court observed: "The law requires that there be a subjective understanding on the part of the person that on the day in question—and I do not read that as being January 26th, 2001 because by this time, with all of the information that had come out dealing with the dogs, the defendants were fully on notice that they had a couple of wild, uncontrollable and dangerous dogs that were likely going to do something bad. Is the 'something bad' death? That is the ultimate question in the case. There is no question but that the something bad was going to be that somebody was going to be badly hurt. I defy either defendant to stand up and tell me they had no idea that those dogs were going to hurt somebody one day. But can they stand up and say that they knew subjectively—not objectively and that's an important distinction—that these dogs were going to stand up and kill somebody?"

The trial court continued: "I am guided by a variety of principles. One of them is that public emotion, public outcry, feeling, passion, sympathy do not play a role in the application of the law. The other is that I am required to review all of the evidence and determine independently rather than as a jury what the evidence showed. I have laid out most of the evidence as it harms the defendants in this case. Their conduct from the time that they got the dogs to the time—to the weeks after Diane Whipple's death was despicable.

"There was one time on the stand, Ms. Knoller, when I truly believed what you said. You broke down in the middle of a totally scripted answer and you actually, instead of crying, you actually got mad and you said you had no idea that this dog could do what he did and pounded the table. I believed you. That was the only time, but I did believe you." The court then described the definition of second degree murder as requiring that one "subjectively knows, based on everything, that the conduct that he or she is about to engage in has a high probability of death to another human being."

The trial court went on: "What we have in this case as it relates to Ms. Knoller is the decision to take the dog outside, into the hallway, up to the roof, go to the bathroom, bring it back down and put it in the apartment. There was no question but that taking the dog out into the hallway by that very act exposed other people in the apartment, whether they are residents there or guests, invitees to what might happen with the dog. When you take everything as a totality, the question is whether or not as a subjective matter and as a matter of law Ms. Knoller knew that there was a high probability that day, or on the day before on the day after,—I reject totally the argument of the defendants that she had to know when she walked out the door—she was going to kill somebody that morning. The Court finds that the evidence does not support it."

The trial court concluded it had "no choice, . . . taking the Legislature's scheme, the evidence that was received, as despicable as it is, but to determine not that defendant Knoller is acquitted of second degree murder but to find that on the state of the evidence, I cannot say as a matter of law that she subjectively knew on January 26th that her conduct was such that a human being was likely to die."

The trial court mentioned another consideration: "The Court also notes a great troubling feature of this case that Mr. Noel was never charged with murder as Ms. Knoller was. In the Court's view, given the evidence, Mr. Noel is more culpable than she. Equality of sentencing and the equal administration of justice is an important feature in any criminal court. That played a role as well." The trial court then granted defendant Knoller's motion for a new trial on the second degree murder count.

II.   THE ELEMENTS OF IMPLIED MALICE

Murder is the unlawful killing of a human being, or a fetus, with malice aforethought. Malice may be express or implied. At issue here is the definition of "implied malice."

Defendant Knoller was convicted of second degree murder as a result of the killing of Diane Whipple by defendant's dog, Bane. Second degree murder is the unlawful killing of a human being with malice aforethought but without the additional elements, such as willfulness, premeditation, and deliberation, that would support a conviction of first degree murder. Section 188 provides: "Malice may be either express or implied. It is express when there is manifested a deliberate intention to take away the life of a fellow creature. It is implied, when no considerable provocation appears, or when the circumstances attending the killing show an abandoned and malignant heart."

The statutory definition of implied malice, a killing by one with an "abandoned and malignant heart", is far from clear in its meaning. Indeed, an instruction in the statutory language could be misleading, for it "could lead the jury to equate the malignant heart with an evil disposition or a despicable character" instead of focusing on a defendant's awareness of the risk created by his or her behavior. "Two lines of decisions developed, reflecting judicial attempts 'to translate this amorphous anatomical characterization of implied malice into a tangible standard a jury can apply.'" Under both lines of decisions, implied malice requires a defendant's awareness of the risk of death to another.

IV. THE TRIAL COURT'S GRANT OF A NEW TRIAL ON THE SECOND DEGREE MURDER CHARGE

We now turn to ...whether the trial court abused its discretion in granting defendant Knoller a new trial on the second degree murder charge. Such an abuse of discretion arises if the trial court based its decision on impermissible factors or on an incorrect legal standard.

In granting Knoller a new trial, the trial court properly viewed implied malice as requiring a defendant's awareness of the danger that his or her conduct will result in another's death and not merely in serious bodily injury. (See, ante, at pp. 149–151.) But the court's ruling was legally flawed in other respects. As we explain below, the trial court based its ruling on an inaccurate definition of implied malice, and it inappropriately relied on the prosecutor's failure to charge codefendant Noel with murder.

As discussed earlier this court had defined implied malice in two similar but somewhat different ways. Under the Thomas test, malice is implied when "the defendant for a base, antisocial motive and with wanton disregard for human life, does an act that involves a high degree of probability that it will result in death." Under the Phillips test, malice is implied when the killing is proximately caused by " 'an act, the natural consequences of which are dangerous to life, which act was deliberately performed by a person who knows that his conduct endangers the life of another and who acts with conscious disregard for life.' " In People v. Dellinger, we observed that although these two tests "articulated one and the same standard" the Thomas test contained "obscure phraseology" and had "become a superfluous charge," so that the "better practice in the future" would be for trial courts to instruct juries in the "straightforward language" of the Phillips test.

Here, the trial court properly instructed the jury in accordance with the Phillips test. But when the court evaluated defendant Knoller's new trial motion, it relied on language from the Thomas test, and as explained below, its description of that test was inaccurate. The court stated that a killer acts with implied malice when the killer "subjectively knows, based on everything, that the conduct that he or she is about to engage in has a high probability of death to another human being" and thus the issue in this case was "whether or not as a subjective matter and as a matter of law Ms. Knoller knew that there was a high probability" that her conduct would result in someone's death. (Italics added.) But the * * * Phillips test does not require a defendant's awareness that his or her conduct has a high probability of causing death. Rather, it requires only that a defendant acted with a " 'conscious disregard for human life.' "

In ruling on Knoller's motion for a new trial, the trial court also commented that, in its view, codefendant Noel was more culpable than defendant Knoller, and that the district attorney's failure to charge Noel with murder was a "troubling feature of this case" that "played a role as well" in the court's decision to grant Knoller a new trial on the second degree murder charge. Dissimilar charging of codefendants, however, is not among the grounds for a new trial in section 1181.

Even assuming a new trial could be granted on such a ground, it is not justified here. Defendant Knoller and codefendant Noel were not similarly situated with regard to their dog Bane's fatal mauling of Whipple in the hallway of the apartment building where they all lived. The immediate cause of Whipple's death was Knoller's own conscious decision to take the dog Bane unmuzzled through the apartment building, where they were likely to encounter other people, knowing that Bane was aggressive and highly dangerous and that she could not control him. Bringing a more serious charge against the person immediately responsible for the victim's death was a permissible exercise of prosecutorial discretion, not grounds for a new trial.

DISCUSSION QUESTIONS

1. Why do you think jurisdictions like California stopped using phrases such as "abandoned and malignant heart" and "base and anti-social purpose" to define depraved heart murder? What difference does it make? Should they have stopped using them?

2. The trial judge believed the defendant to be somewhat oblivious to the danger involved. Does this mean that she is not guilty of murder, or is such obliviousness itself murderous?

3. The defendant who testified got convicted of murder, and the defendant who did not testify got convicted of manslaughter by the jury. The trial judge found the defendant not guilty in part based on her affect while testifying. How much importance do you think a factfinder would place on a

defendant's affect in choosing between manslaughter and murder in a case like this? Is affect a reliable way to judge a defendant's regard for human life? What is the alternative?

1. MODEL PENAL CODE AND RECKLESS MURDER

Today many jurisdictions, especially those that follow the Model Penal Code, use more analytical and less emotional language to define depraved heart murder. These jurisdictions often speak in terms of "extreme recklessness." The MPC uses the following definition of "reckless" murder.

Section 210.2. Murder

1) Except as provided in Section 210.3(1)(b), criminal homicide constitutes murder when:

     b) it is committed recklessly under circumstances manifesting extreme indifference to the value of human life.

Case in Context

The jurisdiction in this next case applied the Model Penal Code definition of reckless murder, to a driving under the influence killing.

KANSAS V. JOHN P. DOUB, III

Court of Appeals of Kansas
95 P.3d 116 (2004)

GREENE, J.

Following a party for his softball team at a club where he admitted drinking six beers, Doub admitted that his pickup struck two parked vehicles and that he left the scene because he was concerned that he had been drinking. Doub ultimately admitted that, approximately 2 hours after striking the parked cars, he drove his pickup into the rear of a Cadillac in which 9-year-old Jamika Smith was a passenger. According to the State's accident investigator, the collision occurred as Doub's pickup, "going tremendously faster," drove "up on top of the Cadillac," initially driving it down into the pavement, and ultimately propelling it off the street and into a tree. Doub offered no aid to the victims, left the scene of the accident, and initially denied any involvement in the collision, suggesting that his pickup had been stolen. Some 15 hours after the collision, Smith died as a result of blunt traumatic injuries caused by the collision.

Approximately 6 months after these events, Doub admitted to a former girlfriend that he had a confrontation with his second ex-wife the evening of the collision, had been drinking alcohol and smoking crack, and had subsequently caused the collision. The girlfriend approached the authorities with Doub's statements, which suggested that Doub left the softball party, caused the collisions with the parked vehicles, left that scene, subsequently consumed the additional alcohol and crack cocaine, and then caused the collision resulting in Smith's death, all within a 2- to 3-hour period.

Doub was charged with: (1) second-degree depraved heart murder. Doub appeals. When the sufficiency of the evidence is challenged in a criminal case, the standard of review is whether, after review of all the evidence, viewed in the light most favorable to the prosecution, the appellate court is convinced that a rational factfinder could have found the defendant guilty beyond a reasonable doubt.

Elements of Second-degree "Depraved Heart" Murder

K.S.A. 2003 Supp. 21–3402 defines second-degree murder as follows:

"Murder in the second-degree is the killing of a human being committed:

(a) Intentionally; or

(b) unintentionally but recklessly under circumstances manifesting extreme indifference to the value of human life."

When the offense is committed pursuant to subsection (b), our courts have employed the common-law nomenclature of "depraved heart" second-degree murder. * * *

In State v. Robinson, 261 Kan. 865, 876–78, 934 P.2d 38 (1997), our Supreme Court discussed the requirements for depraved heart murder:

"Both depraved heart murder and reckless involuntary manslaughter require recklessness—that the killing be done under circumstances showing a realization of the imminence of danger and a conscious disregard of that danger. Depraved heart murder requires the additional element that the reckless killing occur under circumstances manifesting extreme indifference to the value of human life.

"We hold that depraved heart second-degree murder requires a conscious disregard of the risk, sufficient under the circumstances, to manifest extreme indifference to the value of human life. Recklessness that can be assimilated to purpose or knowledge is treated as depraved heart second-degree murder, and less extreme recklessness is punished as manslaughter. Conviction of depraved heart second-degree murder requires proof that the defendant acted recklessly under circumstances manifesting extreme in-difference to the value of human life. This language describes a kind of culpability that differs in degree but not in kind from the ordinary recklessness required for manslaughter." 261 Kan. at 876–78.

Overview of Depraved Heart Murder by Vehicle in Other Jurisdictions

The state of mind or mens rea required for second-degree murder has been somewhat problematic throughout the history of Anglo-American jurisprudence. As early as 1762, Sir Michael Foster termed the requisite mental state for the common-law offense as a "heart regardless of social duty and fatally bent upon mischief." Foster, Crown Law 257 (1762). Since the advent of the automobile in the nineteenth century, many jurisdictions have struggled with the application of second-degree murder statutes in this context, and the debate seems to have been focused largely on whether malice, whether express or implied, should be required. See, e.g., State v. Chalmers, 100 Ariz. 70, 411 P.2d 448 (1966). We need not enter this debate, however, since our Supreme Court has determined that the 1993 amendment to the second-degree murder statute eliminated malice as an element of second-degree murder in Kansas.

Instead, our focus is the statutory language adopted in Kansas that apparently had its genesis in the Model Penal Code first proposed in 1962, which required killing "recklessly under circumstances manifesting extreme indifference to the value of human life." A.L.I., Model Penal Code § 210.2 (Proposed Official Draft 1962).

Since 1975 the appellate courts of many states have acknowledged that the required state of mind for depraved heart murder can be attributed to the driver of an automobile.

Our review of such cases reveals that most jurisdictions with statutory provisions patterned after the Model Penal Code have acknowledged that the offense may be committed by automobile. Cases to the contrary generally construe and apply statutes that retain some requirement of malice.

One commentator surveyed 20 cases between 1975 and 1986 and found the following factors as persuasive of the requisite state of mind:

1.   Intoxication. The driver was using alcohol, illegal drugs, or both.

2.   Speeding. Usually excessive rates are recorded.

3.   Near or nonfatal collisions shortly before the fatal accident. Courts believe that collisions should serve as a warning to defendants that their conduct is highly likely to cause an accident. Failure to modify their driving is viewed as a conscious indifference to human life.

4.   Driving on the wrong side of the road. Many cases involve head-on collisions. Included here is illegally passing or veering into oncoming traffic.

5.   Failure to aid the victim. The driver left the scene of the accident and/or never attempted to seek aid for the victim.

6.   Failure to heed traffic signs. Usually more than once prior to the fatal accident, the driver ran a red light and/or stop sign.

7.   Failure to heed warnings about reckless driving. In Pears v. State, for example, the court cited as proof of Pears' extreme indifference to life the fact that he continued driving after he had been warned by police

officers not to drive because he was intoxicated. In other cases a police pursuit of the driver for earlier traffic violations was an implicit warning that the defendant's driving was dangerous.

8.   Prior record of driving offenses (drunk or reckless driving or both). The relevance of a defendant's prior record for reckless or intoxicated driving is, as United States v. Fleming pointed out, not to show a propensity to drive while drunk but 'to establish that defendant had grounds to be aware of the risk his drinking and driving while intoxicated presented to others.' "

Application of these factors seems appropriate to determine whether evidence in a particular case meets the requisite state of mind, but we are mindful that no precise universal definition or exclusive criteria is appropriate. The comments to the Model Penal Code declare that "recklessness" must be of such an extreme nature that it demonstrates an indifference to human life similar to that held by one who commits murder purposely or knowingly, but precise definition is impossible.

"The significance of purpose of knowledge as a standard of culpability is that, cases of provocation or other mitigation apart, purposeful or knowing homicide demonstrates precisely such indifference to the value of human life. Whether recklessness is so extreme that it demonstrates similar indifference is not a question, it is submitted, that can be further clarified. It must be left directly to the trier of fact under instructions which make it clear that recklessness that can fairly be assimilated to purpose or knowledge should be treated as murder and that less extreme recklessness should be punished as manslaughter." A.L.I., Model Penal Code & Commentaries Part II § 210.2, Comment. 4, pp. 21–22 (1980).

The evidence against Doub is particularly damning considering that (a) he admits that his driving was preceded by drinking; (b) he admits that he struck two parked cars and ignored commands to stop because he was concerned that he had been drinking; (c) he then consumed additional alcohol and used crack cocaine; (d) he then resumed driving and caused a fatal collision, due in part to excessive speed; (e) he failed to render aid to the victims; and (f) he fled the scene in order to avoid criminal liability. We conclude that these facts clearly demonstrate an extreme indifference to human life.

Affirmed.

DISCUSSION QUESTIONS

1.   How do you compare "extreme indifference to human life" to the other definitions of reckless or depraved heart murder discussed so far? What is captured and what is lost by this phrase?

2.   Deaths caused by those driving while impaired had historically been prosecuted as manslaughter rather than murder. Of the factors that the court

discusses in distinguishing the two in DWI cases which do you think are the most important? Would you rule out murder for a driver who had no prior history of driving while intoxicated, for example, or would it depend on the other circumstances?

3.   What other types of driving-related deaths do you think should be prosecuted as murder, if any? Driving while texting? Driving while sleepy? What principle can you articulate for distinguishing driving while impaired from these other categories of conduct for the purposes of assigning murder liability?

Exam Tip: Reckless Murder

Reckless murder issues are common exam issues because they test the student's ability to argue both sides of an issue, since no clear line exists between murder and manslaughter. The best way to sort your way through this confusion on an exam is by working your way through the elements of recklessness.

- Conscious Disregard of a

- Substantial (magnitude of the harm times probability of harm) and

- Unjustifiable Risk that constitutes a

- Gross Deviation from the standard of care of a reasonable person

What almost always distinguishes murder from manslaughter is that the evidence supporting one or more of the elements will be overwhelming to the point that it is disturbing. Risks about food poisoning in a restaurant or fire exits in a crowded building are very substantial because many people will die even if they might not be very probable. Driving a car down a busy sidewalk is murderous because of the high probability that someone will die, even if you are racing to take a sick child to the hospital. Playing Russian roulette is arguably murderous because even though the possibility of the gun going off is only one in six, the risk is completely unjustifiable since the participants do it "just for kicks."

The easiest cases for extreme recklessness murder are often ones that involve risks that are not only unjustifiable but also involve "base or anti-social purposes." Think of someone training a dangerous animal for fighting competitions or a drug dealer cutting his illegal drugs with toxic substances. What is considered base or anti-social (fancy words for evil or super dangerous) changes over time. Drunk driving, for example, has gone from being considered mischievous, to criminal, to potentially murderous in many jurisdictions over the last thirty or forty years.

Practice Problem 13.3: A Murderous Beef?

Bovine spongiform encephalopathy—better known as mad cow disease—has come to the U.S.A. Mad cow disease is a fatal and incurable neurological disease that occurs in cattle. You should assume for the purposes of this question that people can and in this case did die from eating meat from a cow infected with mad cow disease. An outbreak occurred in a small Midwestern town where 200 people came down with the disease and died. The outbreak was traced back to a single cow from a nearby cattle ranch that provided organic beef for local restaurants and a farmer's market.

Agricultural regulators have long been concerned about mad cow disease. An outbreak of mad cow disease in Europe devastated the cattle industry there, and people died from eating infected beef. For this reason, agricultural regulations require that any cow that cannot walk unassisted may not be slaughtered for food and specifically prohibits the use of cattle prods to force cows to walk into a slaughter pen. Mad cow disease was first discovered in 1986. Since then only six cows have been diagnosed with the disease in the United States.

Investigation of the outbreak has revealed the following. The infected cow first showed symptoms of the disease when it had difficulty walking out of a pen to the slaughterhouse. The owner of the ranch then told one of his employees to use electric cattle prods to force the cow in question into the slaughterhouse, a direct violation of the applicable regulations. When his employee initially refused to comply with the instruction, the owner said "Look, that cow is just tired. It spent all last night standing up in the cattle truck. If we waste every cow that is a little sleepy, I will go broke and we will all be out of business." His employee then prodded the infected cow into the slaughter pen. That cow was the source of the outbreak.

The owner of the infected cattle has been charged with murder under the Model Penal Code. Discuss his liability for this crime.

CHAPTER 14

FELONY MURDER

∎ ∎ ∎

Felony murder is a very important doctrine because it is widely used by prosecutors. The doctrine can be a challenging one to learn because it requires students to work through a complex set of interlocking rules and definitions.

Under the basic felony murder rule one is guilty of murder if a death results from a felony one commits or attempts to commit. That basic rule is subject to a number of important exceptions and limitations, however.

Felony murder is a sweeping homicide crime because it covers so much ground. For starters, it involves both intentional and unintentional killings. Think of the butterfingered bank robber who drops his gun during the robbery, and the gun goes off and kills a bank teller. What is the bank robber guilty of? Negligent handling of a firearm during a bank robbery? Involuntary manslaughter because he was careless with the gun and someone died? No, the butterfingered bank robber is guilty of murder under the felony murder doctrine, and in many jurisdictions, he is guilty of first degree murder.

Let's take it a step further. Assume that the butterfingered bank robber was not careless with the gun. He wore special sticky gloves and practiced drawing the gun to avoid mishaps. He still is guilty of felony murder in most jurisdictions. (And as we will learn when we deal with complicity, so is his hapless driver who is waiting outside the bank in the getaway car when the gun goes off.)

What sets felony murder apart from all other homicide crimes is that, strictly speaking, the law does not care what your mental state was with respect to the conduct causing the death. Whether the bank robber was careful or careless with the gun does not matter under a classic felony murder rule. What matters is whether the killer had the mental state required for the felony. If he committed (or was attempting to commit) a felony covered by the rule and death resulted, then he is guilty of felony murder. For this reason, many describe felony murder as a form of strict liability because felons are held strictly liable for resulting deaths regardless of their culpability with respect to the specific acts causing death.

A. POLICIES BEHIND THE FELONY MURDER DOCTRINE

Why do we allow such strict liability for murder when the common law is generally so hostile to strict liability? The short answer is because we really don't like felons. The longer answer consists of the following three policy arguments in favor of felony murder liability.

1.   To deter felonies.

2.   To deter accidental deaths during felonies.

3.   To ease proof of homicide during felonies.

Obviously, the fact that you will be executed or go to prison for life if someone dies during your felony might discourage you from committing the felony in the first place. Less obvious, but equally important, is the idea that the felony murder rule creates an additional incentive to avoid accidental deaths during your felony. Felony murder applies to both intentional killings as well as accidental ones, but an intentional killing will already be prosecuted as murder. Accidental killings might otherwise be prosecuted as involuntary manslaughter if they involved only grossly negligent conduct. They might not be prosecuted as homicide crimes at all if they involved only simple negligence. Imagine that your kidnapping victim suffocates in the trunk of your car while you are driving to your hideout. Was that negligent? Grossly negligent? Reckless? Extremely reckless? Who cares! Under most versions of the felony murder rule, you will be guilty of first degree murder, not "negligent transport of a kidnapping victim."

Finally, the felony murder rule often eliminates proof problems when dealing with multiple felons. Imagine that a hostage gets executed during a botched bank robbery. There are three bank robbers. Which one killed the hostage? What if the bank robber who killed the hostage did so without consulting with his colleagues? Who cares! Under felony murder, the prosecutor need only prove that each defendant participated in the bank robbery, and the death resulted from that felony. All three robbers are guilty of felony murder.

B. STATUTORY VARIATIONS

There are a number of variations in how different jurisdictions define felony murder. Here are some sample felony murder statutes. How are they different, and how are they similar?

Kansas

§ 21–3401. Murder in the First Degree

Murder in the first degree is the killing of a human being committed:

(b) in the commission of, attempt to commit, or flight from an inherently dangerous felony including kidnapping, robbery, rape, burglary, or arson. Murder in the first degree is a class A felony punishable by death or by life imprisonment.

North Carolina

§ 14–17. Murder in the First and Second Degree defined; punishment

A murder which shall be ... committed in the perpetration or attempted perpetration of any arson, rape or a sex offense, robbery, kidnapping, burglary, or other felony committed or attempted with the use of a deadly weapon shall be deemed to be murder in the first degree.

C. THE BASIC RULE

Case in Context

Note the strict nature of the liability that results from the felony murder rule in the following case.

WEST VIRGINIA V. PAUL EMERSON SIMS

Supreme Court of Appeals of West Virginia
162 W. Va. 212 (1978)

OPINION

Paul Sims, after pleading guilty to first degree murder, contends that he was coerced into the plea as a result of the trial court's ruling in connection with the felony-murder rule.

The claimed coercion occurred when the trial court ruled preliminarily to the trial that as a matter of law Sims' defense of an accidental discharge of his shotgun during the commission of a burglary would not permit the jury to reduce the crime below first degree murder. We refuse to overturn the guilty plea.

The operative facts are these: Around 2:00 a.m. on January 16, 1976, the defendant Paul Sims, Clay Grimmer and Arthur Burns went to the home of Mr. and Mrs. Oscar Schmidt located in Brooke County, West Virginia. After cutting the telephone wires on the outside of the house, Sims and Burns proceeded onto the front porch of the home. Both men were armed. Sims carried a 20-gauge sawed-off shotgun and Burns had a pistol.

The Schmidts' bedroom adjoined the porch. While Sims remained on the porch adjacent to the windows, his companion Burns broke the windows and stepped through them into the bedroom. Sims pointed his shotgun and a flashlight into the bedroom. Shortly after Burns had entered the bedroom, Walter Schmidt, the son of Oscar Schmidt, entered the bedroom from another portion of the house.

Apparently as a result of this distraction, Oscar Schmidt was able to seize his pistol and fire it at Sims. The bullet struck Sims' right arm, and he claimed this caused an involuntary muscle spasm in his trigger finger which resulted in the discharge of the shotgun, killing Walter Schmidt.

In support of the defendant's theory that the bullet wound caused an involuntary muscle reaction, his attorneys took a deposition from the neurologist who treated him for the injury. Since the doctor was not available for testimony at the trial, the prosecuting and defense attorneys stipulated that his deposition would be read at trial.

Based upon his examination and treatment of the defendant's wound, together with his expert knowledge of the involved nerves and muscles, the doctor concluded it was possible that the bullet wound caused an involuntary muscle reflex resulting in the discharge of the shotgun.

It is to be noted that the State did not agree with the involuntary reflex theory and vigorously cross-examined the doctor, who conceded that the same type of wound might instead have caused the defendant to drop the gun.

The trial court proceeded to rule in limine that even assuming the defendant's theory to be true, it would not present a factual defense to mitigate the first degree murder verdict required under this State's felony-murder rule.

I

The issue before us on this direct appeal relates to the voluntariness of the guilty plea based on the theory that the plea was coerced as a result of the court's preliminary ruling that deprived the defendant of a key factual defense. However, the focus is not upon the court's ruling, but the competency of defendant's counsel in advising the guilty plea in light of the court's ruling.

II

The guilty plea in this case can only be invalidated if it can be found that Sims' counsel was not acting with reasonable competency when he advised that an involuntary homicide would not mitigate the crime of felony-murder. There is no dispute that the killing occurred during the course of an attempted burglary. There is also no dispute that the guilty plea was prompted by defendant's belief that he had no defense to the felony-murder crime.

Our inquiry is narrowed to a consideration of whether our felony-murder rule, which by statute makes the crime first degree murder, admits any amelioration from first degree by virtue of the fact that the homicide was accidental.

Our felony-murder statute alters the scope of the common law rule by confining its application to the crimes of arson, rape, robbery and burglary or the attempt to commit such crimes. W.Va. Code, 61–2–1. Traditionally at common law, the commission of, or the attempt to commit, any felony which resulted in a homicide was deemed murder.

Our statute enumerates three broad categories of homicide constituting first degree murder: (1) murder by poison, lying in wait, imprisonment, starving; (2) by any wilful, deliberate and premeditated killing; (3) in the commission of, or attempt to commit, arson, rape, robbery or burglary.

It is defendant's contention that this State's felony-murder statute warrants the conclusion that malice is an element of the crime and that an accidental homicide committed during one of the designated felonies will not invoke the felony-murder rule. The third syllabus of State ex rel. Peacher v. Sencindiver, W.Va., 233 S.E.2d 425 (1977), is cited as supporting this point.

But in each of the cases cited by Peacher the courts found that the felony-murder crime historically did not require malice, premeditation or deliberate intent to kill as an element of proof.

From a review of the law of other jurisdictions two salient facts emerge: First, in those jurisdictions having felony-murder statutes similar to ours, the courts recognize that their statutes embody the common law concept of the crime of felony-murder. Second, the common law created this substantive crime so as not to include the element that the homicide has to be committed with malice or an intent to kill.

The defendant argues, however, that a literal reading of our statute would suggest that by the use of the term "murder" as the initial subject of the sentence setting out the categories of first degree murder, it was intended that the State must initially prove what amounts to a common law murder before it can invoke the felony-murder rule. Stripping the statute of its other categories of first degree murder, the defendant presents the statute as follows:

He submits that this is a fair reading of the third syllabus of Peacher. From a purely grammatical standpoint, it would have been better usage to begin the independent clause defining the crime of felony-murder with the term "homicide." However this may be, we do not approach the question of what the statute means as if we were on a maiden voyage and were forced upon uncharted seas without compass or sextant.

The felony-murder rule was a part of our substantive criminal law long before this State was formed. No case, either from this Court or from the

Virginia court, has ever broken from the historical common law precedent to suggest that proof of an intentional killing is an element of the felony-murder crime. This principle is not only settled in the Virginias, but exists uniformly in all other states which have similar statutes.

In the few cases where such argument, as here advanced, has been considered, it has been flatly rejected as violating the historical common law concepts of the crime of felony-murder.

The use of the term "murder" in the statute, W.Va. Code, 61–2–1, and in the third syllabus of Peacher as it relates to the crime of felony-murder, means nothing more than it did at common law—a homicide.

The defendant's trial counsel competently advised him as to the guilty plea, as there could be no reasonable expectation under the settled principles of our law that an unintended homicide committed in the course of an attempted burglary would constitute a defense to first degree murder arising out of the felony-murder rule.

For these reasons, we affirm the judgment of the Circuit Court of Brooke County.

DISCUSSION QUESTIONS

1.   Whose interpretation of West Virginia's felony murder provision makes more sense in terms of the plain meaning of the statutory text? The defendant's or the court's? Whose interpretation makes more sense in terms of what the legislature probably intended? Which approach to statutory interpretation is more appropriate in the context of felony murder provisions?

2.   Why isn't the absence of a voluntary act a defense to felony murder?

3.   If felony murder were not available in this case, and the jury believed that Sims pulled the trigger involuntarily, what theory of murder could the prosecution still pursue?

Case in Context

The judge in the following case expresses serious reservations about the wide application of the felony murder rule.

PEOPLE V. ARCHIE FULLER

Court of Appeal, Fifth District, California
86 Cal. App. 3d 618 (1978)

JUDGES: Opinion by FRANSON, ACTING P. J.

This appeal challenges the California felony-murder rule as it applies to an unintentionally caused death during a high speed automobile chase following the commission of a nonviolent, daylight burglary of an unattended motor vehicle. Solely by force of precedent we hold that the felony-murder rule applies and respondents can be prosecuted for first degree murder.

The pertinent facts are as follows: On Sunday, February 20, 1977, at about 8:30 a.m., uniformed Cadet Police Officer Guy Ballesteroz was on routine patrol in his vehicle. As the officer approached the Fresno Dodge car lot, he saw an older model Plymouth parked in front of the lot. He also saw respondents rolling two tires apiece toward the Plymouth. His suspicions aroused, the officer radioed the dispatcher and requested that a police unit be sent.

Ballesteroz kept the respondents under observation as he proceeded past the car lot and stopped at the next intersection. As he reached that point he saw the respondents stop rolling the tires and walk to the Plymouth on the street. Ballesteroz made a U-turn and headed northbound on Blackstone. The respondents got into the Plymouth and drove away "really fast." Thereafter, a high speed chase ensued which eventually resulted in respondents' car running a red light and striking another automobile which had entered the intersection. The driver of the other automobile was killed. Respondents were arrested at the scene. The chase from the car lot covered some 7 miles and lasted approximately 10 to 12 minutes.

Later investigation revealed that four locked Dodge vans at the car lot had been forcibly entered and the spare tires removed. Fingerprints from both of the respondents were found on the jack stands in some of the vans.

Penal Code section 189 provides, in pertinent part: "All murder . . . which is committed in the perpetration of, or attempt to perpetrate, arson, rape, robbery, burglary, mayhem, or lewd acts with a minor, is murder of the first degree; . . ." This statute imposes strict liability for deaths committed in the course of one of the enumerated felonies whether the killing was caused intentionally, negligently, or merely accidentally.

Burglary falls expressly within the purview of California's first degree felony-murder rule. Any burglary within Penal Code section 459 is sufficient to invoke the rule.

Thus, the trial court erred in striking the murder count premised upon the felony-murder rule.

We deem it appropriate, however, to make a few observations concerning the irrationality of applying the felony-murder rule in the present case.

If we were writing on a clean slate, we would hold that respondents should not be prosecuted for felony murder since viewed in the abstract, an automobile burglary is not dangerous to human life. The present case demonstrates why this is so. Respondents committed the burglary on vans parked in a dealer's lot on a Sunday morning. There were no people inside the vans or on the lot at the time. The respondents were not armed and presumably had no expectation of using violence during the burglary.

Under the felony-murder statute if a merchant in pursuit of a fleeing shoplifter is killed accidentally (by falling and striking his head on the curb or being hit by a passing automobile), the thief would be guilty of first degree felony murder assuming the requisite intent to steal at the time of the entry into the store. (Cf. People v. Earl, supra, 29 Cal.App.3d 894.) Such a harsh result destroys the symmetry of the law by equating an accidental killing resulting from a petty theft with a premeditated murder. In no sense can it be said that such a result furthers the ostensible purpose of the felony-murder rule which is to deter those engaged in felonies from killing negligently or accidentally.

DISCUSSION QUESTIONS

1.   What mental state is required for felony murder in this case?

2.   What difference would it have made if they stole a spare tire that was lying next to a car instead of inside a trunk?

3.   The court points out that one can be liable for felony murder if a pursuer is hit by a passing automobile. Should first degree murder turn upon such accidental circumstances?

D. OVERVIEW OF FELONY MURDER LIMITS

Now that you see how sweeping felony murder can potentially be in its scope, you are in a better position to understand the need for ways to limit the resulting murder liability. There are lots of limits on felony murder liability (although none would spare the butterfingered bank robber or his hapless driver from first degree murder liability in most jurisdictions). What makes this area particularly tricky for first year law students is that some of these limitations will be written in the statute, and other limitations will be read into a statute by a judge who interprets the law against the background of the common law. Here is a quick preview of these limitations and exceptions.

1.   Limits on the types of felonies that trigger the felony murder rule.

2.   Exceptions for felonies that are not independent from the homicide itself.

3.   Limits on the causal relationship between the felony and the resulting death.

4.   Limits on the duration of the felony.

One important point needs to be made about these limitations: they are creatures of the common law that have been incorporated into modern homicide schemes by judges or legislatures. These limitations often operate as presumptions by judges who assume that the legislature intended to incorporate the common law's limits on felony murder into the jurisdiction's statutory scheme. They are not constitutional principles, though. This means that where the legislature clearly intends to ignore one of these limits, a judge will abandon a contrary common law presumption and apply the statue as the legislature wrote it. This idea will become clearer after we discuss the first two limitations on felony murder liability.

E. LIMITS ON TYPES OF FELONIES

In the song "Alice's Restaurant," the narrator commits "felony littering" by dumping a truckload of garbage where he shouldn't. Imagine that a homeless person was sleeping where the trash was dumped and suffocated as a result. (You might want to further imagine that the dumper reasonably had no way of anticipating that a person would have been sleeping in that spot to rule out murder or manslaughter on the grounds of recklessness or negligence.) Could the dumper be convicted of felony murder for his felony littering? The answer is almost always no because very few jurisdictions would allow this type of felony to support felony murder.

1. ENUMERATION

There are two ways that jurisdictions limit the type of felonies that create felony murder liability. The first way is "enumeration." Enumeration means that the statute lists the felonies that suffice for felony murder and limits felony murder liability to that list. The following felonies all created felony murder liability at common law and are also the most commonly enumerated felonies in those jurisdictions that list them in their statute.

- Rape
- Robbery
- Burglary
- Arson
- Kidnapping

Note that enumeration can work in a couple of different ways. Some statutes enumerate felonies but do not limit felony murder liability to that list. Others create first degree felony murder liability for enumerated felonies and second degree murder liability for non-enumerated felonies. Read your statute with care on this point!

2. THE INHERENTLY DANGEROUS FELONY RULE

The second type of limitation is the inherently dangerous felony rule. At common law, only felonies that were inherently dangerous to human life supported felony murder. Importantly, the inherently dangerous rule is not applied to felonies that are enumerated in the statute. The fact that the legislature listed the felony precludes the need for further analysis on this point.

Many jurisdictions interpret inherently dangerous in an abstract or per se way. This means that a felony is inherently dangerous only if there is no way the felony can be committed without creating a substantial risk that someone will die. This means that you disregard the facts of the case before you (in which someone obviously did die) and ask whether there exists some possible way for the felony to be committed safely. Even felonies that are often considered dangerous fail to satisfy this test because there is a safe way to commit the offense.

Many other jurisdictions (treatise writers don't say which is the majority and which is the minority camp) interpret inherently dangerous by manner of commission. This means that a felony is inherently dangerous if it was committed in a dangerous manner in the case before the court. In the felony littering example, a judge would ask whether the dumping of the litter created a substantial risk of death. Now, a death does not necessarily constitute a substantial risk. But although the defense would argue that the death was a freak accident, that argument can be a hard one to make. A judge might see even a slight risk of death as a substantial one, especially in light of the fact that someone was sleeping there and did die as a result of the felony littering.

Case in Context

The next case is not what most people imagine when they think about felony murder.

HINES V. THE STATE OF GEORGIA
Supreme Court of Georgia
578 S.E.2d 868 (2003)

While hunting, Robert Lee Hines mistook his friend Steven Wood for a turkey and shot him dead. A jury convicted Hines of felony murder based on the underlying crime of possession of a firearm by a convicted felon, but acquitted him of felony murder based on the underlying felony of misuse of a firearm while hunting.

Hines contends that a convicted felon's possession of a firearm while turkey hunting cannot be one of the inherently dangerous felonies required to support a conviction for felony murder. "The only limitation on the type of felony that may serve as an underlying felony for a felony murder conviction is that the felony must be inherently dangerous to human life." A felony is "inherently dangerous" when it is " 'dangerous per se' " or "by its circumstances creates a foreseeable risk of death." Depending on the facts, possession of a firearm by a convicted felon can be an inherently dangerous felony.

In Ford v. State, the defendant was a convicted felon who was unloading a handgun when it accidentally discharged, went through the floor, and killed an occupant of the apartment below. A jury convicted Ford for felony murder based on his felonious possession of a firearm. This Court reversed, finding that, because no evidence showed the defendant knew there was an apartment below him or that the victim was present, his possession of a firearm could not support a conviction for felony murder.

In contrast to Ford, Hines intentionally fired his shotgun intending to hit his target. He had been drinking before he went hunting, and there was evidence that he had been drinking while hunting. He knew that other hunters were in the area and was unaware of their exact location. He also knew that other people visited the area in which he was hunting. He took an unsafe shot at dusk, through heavy foliage, at a target eighty feet away that he had not positively identified as a turkey. Under these circumstances, we conclude that Hines's illegal possession of a firearm created a foreseeable risk of death. Accordingly, Hines's violation of the prohibition against convicted felons possessing firearms was an inherently dangerous felony that could support a felony murder conviction. Judgment affirmed.

SEARS, PRESIDING JUSTICE, dissenting.

Because I conclude that circumstances surrounding Hines's commission of the status felony of possessing a firearm were not inherently dangerous within the meaning of our decision in Ford v. State, I dissent to the majority's affirmance of Hines's conviction of felony murder.

In Ford, this Court held that for a felony to serve as the basis for a felony murder conviction, it had to be inherently dangerous by its very nature or had to be committed under circumstances creating a foreseeable risk of death. We also held that the imputation of malice that justifies the felony murder rule is dependent on the "perpetrator's life-threatening state of mind accompanying the commission of the underlying felony." In Ford, however, we did not specify how to determine whether a particular felony, either by its nature or as it was committed, was inherently dangerous to human life. Because of the severe punishments that accompany a conviction of murder and because it is illogical to impute malice for purposes of felony murder "from the intent to commit a felony not foreseeably dangerous to human life," I conclude that for purposes of our felony-murder doctrine, a felony is inherently dangerous per se or as committed if it carries 'a high probability' that a human death will result." This standard will ensure that our felony murder rule is not inappropriately expanded by "reducing the seriousness of the act which a defendant must commit in order to be charged with murder."

In the present case, I conclude that the possession of a firearm by Hines was not committed in a fashion that was inherently dangerous and that carried a high probability that death would result. The fact that Hines was hunting, a dangerous sport; the fact that he had been drinking before he went hunting; the fact that he was hunting at dusk; and the fact that he fired a shot when he knew other hunters were in the general area in which he was hunting may establish that Hines was negligent, but do not establish that his acts created a high probability that death to a human being would result, or that he had a "life-threatening state of mind." Moreover, as for the fatal shot, Hines testified that he heard a turkey gobble, that he "saw it fan out," and that he then fired at the object. Even though Hines may not, as stated by the majority, have positively identified his target as a turkey, he had to make a split-second decision regarding his target and concluded, based on hearing a gobble and seeing something "fan out," that the object was a turkey. I cannot conclude that, under these circumstances, the failure of the hunter to identify his target beyond doubt carried a high probability that a human being would be killed or that he acted with a "life-threatening state of mind." The death in this case is clearly a tragic incident, and Hines's conduct before and after the shooting was reprehensible. But the sanction of life in prison for murder should be reserved for cases in which the defendant's moral failings warrant such punishment. Here, the application of the felony murder statute to Hines's actions punishes him more severely than his culpability merits. In this regard, Hines will be serving the same punishment—life in prison—as an arsonist convicted of felony murder who firebombed an apartment that he knew was occupied, causing the death of two young children, and the same punishment as an armed robber convicted of felony murder who entered a store with a firearm and shot and killed a store employee. This result is unwarranted and unnecessary, as Hines could be prosecuted and convicted of an appropriate lesser crime, such as involuntary manslaughter or the misuse of a firearm while hunting.

One final note. Hunting is a time-honored recreational activity encouraged by the State of Georgia and enjoyed by many of our State's citizens. No doubt a number of hunters have probably engaged in negligent hunting practices similar to those in this case. Although I do not condone such careless practices, neither can I agree with subjecting so many hunters to the possibility of spending life in prison when they do not fastidiously follow proper hunting procedures and accidentally shoot a fellow hunter.

For the foregoing reasons, I dissent to the majority opinion.

DISCUSSION QUESTIONS

1. Ordinarily, do you believe that someone should receive life in prison for a hunting accident? If not, should the fact that the defendant is a felon who is not allowed to possess a gun make a difference?

2. What is the difference between how the majority and the dissent define inherently dangerous by manner of commission?

3. Does the fact that Hines intended to hit what he shot at mean that death to a human being was a foreseeable result?

Case in Context

The following case nicely illustrates the strictness of the "per se" approach to defining inherently dangerous.

THE PEOPLE V. EVERT KEITH HOWARD
Supreme Court of California
34 Cal. 4th 1129 (2005)

KENNARD, J.—Murder is the unlawful killing of a human being, with malice aforethought. (Pen. Code, § 18d7, subd. (a).) But under the second degree felony-murder rule, the prosecution can obtain a conviction without showing malice if the killing occurred during the commission of an inherently dangerous felony. Is the crime of driving with a willful or wanton disregard for the safety of persons or property while fleeing from a pursuing police officer (Veh. Code, § 2800.2) an inherently dangerous felony for purposes of the second degree felony-murder rule? We conclude it is not.

At 12:40 a.m. on May 23, 2002, California Highway Patrol Officer Gary Stephany saw defendant driving a Chevrolet Tahoe (a sport utility vehicle) without a rear license plate, and signaled him to pull over. Defendant stopped on the side of the road. But when Officer Stephany and his partner got out of their patrol car, defendant restarted the engine and sped to a nearby freeway. The officers gave chase at speeds of up to 90 miles per hour and radioed for assistance. Defendant left the freeway and drove onto a surface street, turning off his car's headlights. He ran two stop signs and a red light, and he drove on the wrong side of the road. His speed was 15 to 20 miles over the posted speed limit of 50 miles per hour. At some point, he made a sharp turn onto a small dirt road and escaped.

Minutes later, Officer Anthony Arcelus and his partner saw the Tahoe with its headlights on again and took up the chase. Officer Arcelus estimated the Tahoe's speed at more than 80 miles per hour, and he saw it run a stop sign and a traffic light. By then, the car's headlights were again turned off. Up to that point, the chase had taken place in rural parts of Fresno County. When the Tahoe started heading toward downtown Fresno,

Officer Arcelus gave up the pursuit, fearing that the high-speed chase might cause an accident.

About a minute after Officer Arcelus stopped chasing the Tahoe, he saw it run a red light half a mile ahead of him and collide with a car driven by Jeanette Rodriguez. Rodriguez was killed. It turned out that the Tahoe that defendant was driving had been stolen earlier that day. Defendant was arrested and charged with murder and with evading a police officer in willful or wanton disregard for the safety of persons or property (§ 2800.2).

The jury convicted defendant of both counts.

The Court of Appeal affirmed. As pertinent here, it rejected defendant's contention that he could not be convicted under the second degree felony-murder rule because section 2800.2 is not an inherently dangerous felony.

II

Because the second degree felony-murder rule is a court-made rule, it has no statutory definition. This court has described it thusly: "A homicide that is a direct causal result of the commission of a felony inherently dangerous to human life (other than the . . . felonies enumerated in Pen. Code, § 189) constitutes at least second degree murder." The rule "eliminates the need for proof of malice in connection with a charge of murder." It is a substantive rule based on the theory that "when society has declared certain inherently dangerous conduct to be felonious, a defendant should not be allowed to excuse himself by saying he was unaware of the danger to life because, by declaring the conduct to be felonious, society has warned him of the risk involved."

Because the second degree felony-murder rule is "a judge-made doctrine without any express basis in the Penal Code", its constitutionality has been questioned. And, as we have noted in the past, legal scholars have criticized the rule for incorporating "an artificial concept of strict criminal liability that 'erodes the relationship between criminal liability and moral culpability.' " Therefore, we have repeatedly stressed that the rule " 'deserves no extension beyond its required application.' "

"In determining whether a felony is inherently dangerous under the second degree felony-murder rule, the court looks to the elements of the felony in the abstract, 'not the "particular" facts of the case,' i.e., not to the defendant's specific conduct." That is, we determine whether the felony "by its very nature . . . cannot be committed without creating a substantial risk that someone will be killed. . ."

Felonies that have been held inherently dangerous to life include shooting at an inhabited dwelling, poisoning with intent to injure, arson of a motor vehicle, grossly negligent discharge of a firearm, manufacturing methamphetamine, kidnapping, and reckless or malicious possession of a destructive device.

Felonies that have been held not inherently dangerous to life include practicing medicine without a license under conditions creating a risk of great bodily harm, serious physical or mental illness, or death; false imprisonment by violence, menace, fraud, or deceit; possession of a concealable firearm by a convicted felon; possession of a sawed-off shotgun; escape; grand theft; conspiracy to possess methedrine; extortion and child endangerment or abuse.

III

In determining whether section 2800.2 is an offense inherently dangerous to life, we begin by reviewing the statutory scheme.

Section 2800.1 states that any motorist who "with the intent to evade, willfully flees or otherwise attempts to elude" a peace officer pursuing on a motor vehicle or bicycle is, under specified circumstances, guilty of a misdemeanor.

Section 2800.2, which was the basis for defendant's conviction under the second degree felony-murder rule, provides:

> "(a) If a person flees or attempts to elude a pursuing peace officer in violation of Section 2800.1 and the pursued vehicle is driven in a willful or wanton disregard for the safety of persons or property, the person driving the vehicle, upon conviction, shall be punished by imprisonment in the state prison, or by confinement in the county jail .... The court may also impose a fine ... or may impose both that imprisonment or confinement and fine.

> "(b) For purposes of this section, a willful or wanton disregard for the safety of persons or property includes, but is not limited to, driving while fleeing or attempting to elude a pursuing peace officer during which time either three or more violations that are assigned a traffic violation point count under Section 12810 occur, or damage to property occurs."

In concluding that section 2800.2 is an inherently dangerous felony, the Court of Appeal relied heavily on People v. Johnson (1993) 15 Cal.App.4th 169 18 Cal. Rptr. 2d 650. There the Court of Appeal, construing an earlier version of section 2800.2 that was essentially the same as what is now subdivision (a) of that section, held that driving with "willful or wanton disregard for the safety of persons or property" was inherently dangerous to life. We need not decide, however, whether Johnson was correct, because in 1996, three years after Johnson was decided, the Legislature amended section 2800.2 to add subdivision (b). (Stats. 1996, ch. 420, § 1.) Subdivision (b) very broadly defines the term "willful or wanton disregard for the safety of persons or property," as used in subdivision (a), to include any flight from an officer during which the motorist commits three traffic violations that are assigned a "point count" under section 12810, or which results in "damage to property."

Violations that are assigned points under section 12810 and can be committed without endangering human life include driving an unregistered vehicle owned by the driver (§§ 40001, 12810, subds. I, (g)(1)), driving with a suspended license (§§ 14601, 12810, subd. (i)), driving on a highway at slightly more than 55 miles per hour when a higher speed limit has not been posted (§§ 22349, subd. (a), 12810, subd. I), failing to come to a complete stop at a stop sign (§§ 22450, 12810, subd. I), and making a right turn without signaling for 100 feet before turning.

The Court of Appeal concluded that subdivision (b) "did not change the elements of the section 2800.2 offense, in the abstract, or its inherently dangerous nature." (Sewell, at p. 694.) But, as we pointed out in the preceding paragraph, subdivision (b) greatly expanded the meaning of the quoted statutory phrase to include conduct that ordinarily would not be considered particularly dangerous.

In the absence of any evidence of legislative intent, we assume that the Legislature contemplated that we would determine the application of the second degree felony-murder rule to violations of section 2800.2 based on our long-established decisions holding that the rule applies only to felonies that are inherently dangerous in the abstract. (People v. Robertson, supra, 34 Cal.4th at p. 166; People v. Hansen, supra, 9 Cal.4th at p. 309; People v. Phillips, supra, 64 Cal.2d at p. 582; People v. Williams, supra, 63 Cal.2d at p. 458, fn. 5.) As we have explained, a violation of section 2800.2 is not, in the abstract, inherently dangerous to human life. Therefore, the second degree felony-murder rule does not apply when a killing occurs during a violation of section 2800.2.

Thus, the trial court here erred when it instructed the jury that it should find defendant guilty of second degree murder if it found that, while violating section 2800.2,

Conclusion

Nothing here should be read as saying that a motorist who kills an innocent person in a hazardous, high-speed flight from a police officer should not be convicted of murder. A jury may well find that the motorist has acted with malice by driving with conscious disregard for the lives of others, and thus is guilty of murder. (See generally People v. Watson (1981) 30 Cal.3d 290 179 Cal. Rptr. 43, 637 P.2d 279.) But, as we have explained, not all violations of section 2800.2 pose a danger to human life. Therefore, the prosecution may not (as it did here) resort to the second degree felony murder rule to remove from the jury's consideration the question whether a killing that occurred during a violation of section 2800.2 was done with malice.

DISCUSSION QUESTIONS

1. The felony charged in this case requires wanton disregard for the safety of others. Why doesn't the court consider it to be inherently dangerous?

2. There are many dangerous ways to commit the felony charged in this case. Why isn't that enough to support a charge of felony murder?

3. The court expresses open hostility to the felony murder rule. Should the court simply abolish the doctrine? How might the legislature respond?

F. LIMITING FELONY MURDER TO INDEPENDENT FELONIES

While death must result from a felony in order to support felony murder, the felony must be independent from the resulting homicide. This confuses many students initially, but the rule makes sense once the alternative is considered.

Imagine that one person has badly beaten another, and the victim dies. Ordinarily, the prosecutor must prove an intent to kill to obtain a murder conviction. If the evidence suggested that he intended to hurt, not kill, the victim, then the jury would return a not guilty verdict on the murder charge if they harbored a reasonable doubt as to whether he intended to kill. Now imagine what would happen if a clever prosecutor could charge felony murder based on the felonious assault. (An assault committed with the intent to seriously injure another is usually a felony assault.) Even if the prosecutor could not prove intent to kill, he could use the felony murder rule to "bootstrap" a felonious assault into a murder conviction. For that matter, why would a prosecutor ever try to prove intent to kill if he could rely instead on an intent to seriously injure under the felony murder rule? Murder liability would quickly expand to cover many unintended deaths. The same paradox results if the law allows criminally negligent or reckless conduct to satisfy felony murder requirements on the grounds that such conduct constitutes the felony of involuntary manslaughter.

To avoid this result, judges limited felony murder to felonies that were independent of the resulting homicide. Assaultive crimes, were said to "merge" into the resulting homicide and did not constitute felony murder.

At this point many students scratch their heads and wonder how can a felony that is independent of the homicide result in the homicide? A felony is considered independent if it has an independent felonious purpose. The easiest examples of felonies that can easily result in death but that have such an independent purpose are the felonies most commonly enumerated: rape, robbery, burglary, arson, and kidnapping. Ordinarily, you don't rape, or rob, or kidnap someone in order to kill them. These crimes are committed for their own reasons. So, they do not merge into any homicides that result from their commission, and they create felony murder liability. An intent to seriously injure someone, on the other hand, is not considered to have a purpose independent of any resulting homicide.

Case in Context

The felony in the following case is horrific, but the court rules out felony murder liability.

THE PEOPLE V. LINDA LEE SMITH

Supreme Court of California
35 Cal. 3d 798 (1984)

Defendant appeals from a judgment convicting her of second degree murder (Pen. Code, § 187), felony child abuse (§ 273a, subd. (1)), and child beating (§ 273d).

Defendant and her two daughters, three-and-a-half-year-old Bethany (Beth) and two-year-old Amy, lived with David Foster. On the day Amy died, she refused to sit on the couch instead of the floor to eat a snack. Defendant became angry, took Amy into the children's bedroom, spanked her and slapped her in the face. Amy then went towards the corner of the bedroom which was often used for discipline; defendant hit her repeatedly, knocking her to the floor. Foster then apparently joined defendant to "assist" in Amy's discipline. Eventually, defendant knocked the child backwards and she fell, hitting her head on the closet door.

Amy stiffened and went into respiratory arrest. Defendant and Foster took her to the hospital. . . Amy died that evening.

Our opinions have repeatedly emphasized that felony murder, although the law of this state, is a disfavored doctrine: Accordingly, we have reiterated that this "highly artificial concept" (Phillips, supra, at p. 582) "should not be extended beyond any rational function that it is designed to serve." (Washington, supra, at p. 783.) "Applying this principle to various concrete factual circumstances, we have sought to insure that the doctrine . . . be given the narrowest possible application consistent with its ostensible purpose—which is to deter those engaged in felonies from killing negligently or accidentally" (People v. Satchell (1971) 6 Cal.3d 28, 34 98 Cal.Rptr. 33, 489 P.2d 1361, 50 A.L.R.3d 383).

In accord with this policy, we restricted the scope of the felony-murder rule in Ireland by holding it inapplicable to felonies that are an integral part of and included in fact within the homicide. In that case the defendant and his wife were experiencing serious marital difficulties which eventually culminated in defendant's drawing a gun and killing his wife. The jury was instructed that it could find the defendant guilty of second degree felony murder if it determined that the homicide occurred during the commission of the underlying felony of assault with a deadly weapon. We reasoned that "the utilization of the felony-murder rule in circumstances such as those before us extends the operation of that rule 'beyond any rational function that it is designed to serve.' (Citation omitted.) To allow such use of the felony-murder rule would effectively preclude the jury from considering the issue of malice aforethought in all cases wherein homicide has been committed as a result of a felonious assault—a category which includes the great majority of all homicides. This kind of bootstrapping finds support neither in logic nor in law. We therefore hold that a second degree felony-murder instruction may not properly be given when it is based upon a felony which is an integral part of the homicide and which the evidence produced by the prosecution shows to be an offense included in fact within the offense charged."

Very soon after Ireland we again had occasion to consider the question of merger in People v. Wilson (1969) 1 Cal.3d 431 82 Cal.Rptr. 494, 462 P.2d 22. There the defendant forcibly entered his estranged wife's apartment carrying a shotgun. Once inside the apartment, he proceeded to break into the bathroom where he killed his wife.

The jury was instructed on first degree felony murder on the theory that the homicide was committed in the course of a burglary because the defendant had entered the premises with intent to commit a felony, i.e., assault with a deadly weapon. We held that the felony-murder rule cannot apply to burglary-murder cases in which "the entry would be non-felonious but for the intent to commit the assault, and the assault is an integral part of the homicide and is included in fact in the offense charged . . . ." Because under Ireland the "elements of the assault were necessary elements of the homicide" (Id., at p. 441), the felony of burglary based on an intent to commit assault was included in fact in the homicide. We reasoned that "Where a person enters a building with an intent to assault his victim with a deadly weapon, he is not deterred by the felony-murder rule. That doctrine can serve its purpose only when applied to a felony independent of the homicide."

In People v. Sears (1970) 2 Cal.3d 180 84 Cal.Rptr. 711, 465 P.2d 847, we followed Wilson in a slightly different factual situation. There the defendant entered a cottage with the intent to assault his estranged wife. In the course of the assault, her daughter intervened and was killed by the defendant. The People argued that this situation was distinguishable on the ground that the felony of burglary with intent to assault the wife was "independent of the homicide" of the daughter and therefore the felony-murder rule could apply. We rejected the theory, holding that "It would be anomalous to place the person who intends to attack one person and in the course of the assault kills another inadvertently or in the heat of battle in a worse position than the person who from the outset intended to attack both persons and killed one or both."

In addition to the offenses of assault with a deadly weapon and burglary with intent to assault, the felony of discharging a firearm at an inhabited dwelling (§ 246) has also been held to merge into a resulting homicide; thus, application of the felony-murder rule in this situation is similarly prohibited.

Cases in which the second degree felony-murder doctrine has withstood an Ireland attack include those in which the underlying felony was furnishing narcotics (Health & Saf. Code, § 11501; People v. Taylor (1970) 11 Cal.App.3d 57 89 Cal.Rptr. 697); driving under the influence of narcotics (Veh. Code, § 23105; People v. Calzada (1970) 13 Cal.App.3d 603, 606 91 Cal.Rptr. 912); poisoning food, drink or medicine (§ 347; People v. Mattison (1971) 4 Cal.3d 177, 185–186 93 Cal.Rptr. 185, 481 P.2d 193); armed robbery (§ 211; People v. Burton (1971) 6 Cal.3d 375, 387 99 Cal.Rptr. 1, 491 P.2d 793); kidnaping (§ 207; People v. Kelso (1976) 64 Cal.App.3d 538, 542 134 Cal.Rptr. 364); and finally, felony child abuse by malnutrition and dehydration (§ 273a, subd. (1); People v. Shockley (1978) 79 Cal.App.3d 669 145 Cal.Rptr. 200) and felony child endangering by beating (§ 273a, subd. (1); People v. Northrop (1982) 132 Cal.App.3d 1027 182 Cal.Rptr. 197). With the exception of Northrop, however, none of these decisions involved an underlying felony that has as its principal purpose an assault on the person of the victim.

In People v. Burton, supra, we refined the Ireland rule by adding the caveat that the felony-murder doctrine may nevertheless apply if the underlying offense was committed with an "independent felonious purpose." (6 Cal.3d at p. 387.) Even if the felony was included within the facts of the homicide and was integral thereto, a further inquiry is required to determine if the homicide resulted "from conduct for an independent felonious purpose" as opposed to a "single course of conduct with a single purpose" (ibid.). In cases like Ireland, the "purpose of the conduct was the very assault which resulted in death"; on the other hand, "in the case of armed robbery* * * there is an independent felonious purpose, namely to acquire money or property belonging to another." (Ibid.; italics deleted.)

(1b) Our task is to apply the foregoing rules to the offense at issue here—felony child abuse defined by section 273a, subdivision (1).

The language of Ireland, Wilson and Burton bars the application of the felony-murder rule "where the purpose of the conduct was the very assault which resulted in death." (People v. Burton, supra, 6 Cal.3d at p. 387.) In cases in which the violation of section 273a, subdivision (1), is a direct assault on a child that results in death (i.e., causing or permitting a child to suffer or inflicting thereon unjustifiable physical pain), it is plain that the purpose of the child abuse was the "very assault which resulted in death." It would be wholly illogical to allow this kind of assaultive child abuse to be bootstrapped into felony murder merely because the victim was a child rather than an adult, as in Ireland.

In the present case the homicide was the result of child abuse of the assaultive variety. Thus, the underlying felony was unquestionably an "integral part of" and "included in fact" in the homicide within the meaning of Ireland. Furthermore, we can conceive of no independent purpose for the conduct, and the People suggest none; just as in Ireland, the purpose here was the very assault that resulted in death. To apply the felony-murder rule in this situation would extend it "beyond any rational function that it is designed to serve." (People v. Washington, supra, 62 Cal.2d 777, 783.) We reiterate that the ostensible purpose of the felony-murder rule is not to deter the underlying felony, but instead to deter negligent or accidental killings that may occur in the course of committing that felony. (Id., at p. 781.) When a person willfully inflicts unjustifiable physical pain on a child under these circumstances, it is difficult to see how the assailant would be further deterred from killing negligently or accidentally in the course of that felony by application of the felony-murder rule.

DISCUSSION QUESTIONS

1.   Why is felony murder allowed for a death resulting from an auto burglary (see *Fuller* above) but not for beating a child to death?

2.   What role does an "independent felonious purpose" play in the merger analysis?

3.   What options does the legislature have in light of this doctrine if it wishes first degree murder liability to result from the death of any child from child abuse?

G. LIMITS ON THE CAUSAL RELATIONSHIP BETWEEN THE FELONY AND THE RESULTING DEATH

There are several different types of rules that define the relationship that must exist between the death and the underlying felony for felony murder. Don't feel confused if they seem to overlap in a couple of places because they do overlap, and even judges and scholars don't always keep them straight.

The simplest way to organize your thinking in this area is to divide these rules into the following three groups.

1.   Time and Place Rules

2.   Logical Relationship Rules

3.   Causal Rules

All three types of rules have been referred to by the Latin phrase res gestae, which is Latin for the words "thing done." (Not exactly a phrase that one uses all the time in casual conversation.) The idea was that felony murder required that the killing be within the "thing done" by the felony.

1. TIME AND PLACE RULES

Central to res gestae was the idea that the death must be related in time and place to the underlying felony. Time is the more important of these two factors. Many courts describe the common law felony murder rule as applying to deaths occurring during the commission or attempted commission of the felony, and this language has been incorporated into many modern statutes.

Courts have generally held that the felony begins with conduct sufficient to constitute an attempt and ends when a defendant reaches a place of temporary safety. Beginning felony murder liability with the attempt is logical given the deterrent purposes of the rule. Deciding when to end felony murder liability is more difficult. Many felons flee the scene of the crime, and some remain "in flight" for days, months, or even years. Extending felony murder liability to any death they cause during their flight seemed to be too open-ended to many courts, and the temporary safety rule seemed a reasonable place to end liability.

Imagine that a bank robber runs over and kills a pedestrian as he pulls his car into the bank parking lot and then runs over and kills a second pedestrian several miles away as he is fleeing the robbery. Having safely eluded the police, he stops at a motel to check into a room and take a nap. (All that stress has him worn out.) When he wakes up, he turns on the TV and learns that there is a manhunt underway, using a perfect description of him and his car. As he is hurriedly pulling his car out of the parking lot, he hits and kills a third pedestrian. Under conventional res gestae rules he would be guilty of felony murder of the first pedestrian (his attempt began when he became dangerously proximate to committing the offense) and the second pedestrian (distance from the scene notwithstanding, he was still fleeing the crime) but not the third pedestrian (he may not have been completely safe in the motel room, but he was temporarily and relatively safe). So, two counts of felony murder and one count of involuntary manslaughter for our bad-driving bank robber.

Case in Context

The next case fashions a new approach to deciding when a felony ends for the purposes of the felony murder rule.

THE PEOPLE OF THE STATE OF NEW YORK V. GLADMAN

Court of Appeals of New York
359 N.E.2d 420 (1976)

Opinion by: JASEN.

At trial, the People submitted overwhelming evidence. . . that on the night of December 29, 1971, the defendant shot and killed Nassau County Police Officer Richard Rose in a bowling alley parking lot. The events of that evening can be briefly recited. At approximately 8:00 p.m., defendant obtained a ride to the County Line Shopping Center in Amityville, New York. Ten minutes later, he entered a delicatessen, produce a gun, and demanded money from the clerk. The clerk turned over about $ 145 in cash and checks. After the robbery, Gladman left the shopping center and walked through the surrounding neighborhood, eventually arriving at the County Line Bowling Alley. In the meantime, the robbery had been reported to the Nassau County Police Department and an alert was transmitted over the police radio. Two officers arrived at the delicatessen at 8:16 p.m., just minutes after the defendant had left. A description of the robber was obtained and broadcast over the police radio. Normal police procedure required that unassigned patrol cars proceed to the vicinity of the crime area and any nearby major intersections in an effort to seal off potential avenues of escape. As Gladman walked onto the parking lot of the bowling alley, he saw a police car turn and enter the lot. He hid under a parked car. Patrolman Rose, the lone officer in the car, emerged from his vehicle and walked over to defendant's hiding place. The defendant got up from underneath the car with his gun concealed between his legs. The officer ordered the defendant to put his weapon on the car hood; instead, the defendant turned and fired. Patrolman Rose, mortally wounded, struggled to his police car and attempted to use the radio to summon the assistance of brother officers. He collapsed on the seat. The defendant commandeered the automobile of a bowling alley patron and made good his escape. An off-duty New York City police officer used Rose's radio to broadcast a signal for help. The report of the shooting went over the police radio at 8:24 p.m. Eyewitnesses fixed the time of the altercation at approximately 8:25 p.m. The bowling alley was located less than one-half mile from the robbed delicatessen.

Defendant was subsequently captured, identified by eyewitnesses . . . indicted and convicted.

The principal issue on this appeal is whether the jury was properly permitted to conclude that the shooting of Officer Rose occurred in the immediate flight from the delicatessen robbery. . .

Under older statutes which did not specifically address the issue, it was early held that a killing committed during an escape could. . .constitute a felony murder. . .where the defendants got away with some loot. A different result was reached in People v Huter (184 NY 237), where . . . hot pursuit . . . "did not operate to continue the burglary after the defendant had abandoned the property that he undertook to carry away and had escaped from the premises burglarized." These kinds of analyses soon led to the development of some rather arbitrary rules.

The later New York cases indicate some dissatisfaction with the strict legal rules that had developed and tended to leave the question of escape killings to the jury as a question of fact, under appropriate instructions.

The change was to point out "generally that the killing to be felony murder must occur while the actor or one or more of his confederates is engaged in securing the plunder or in doing something immediately connected with the underlying crime (Dolan v. People, 64 N. Y. 485); that escape may, under certain unities of time, manner and place, be a matter so immediately connected with the crime as to be part of its commission (People v. Giro, 197 N. Y. 152); but that where there is no reasonable doubt of a complete intervening desistance from the crime, as by the abandonment of the loot and running away, the subsequent homicide is not murder in the first degree without proof of deliberation and intent. (People v. Marwig, 227 N. Y. 382)." (People v Walsh, 262 NY 140, 148, supra; People v Jackson, 20 NY2d 440, 454, cert den 391 U.S. 928.) The question of termination of the underlying felony was then left to the jury as a fact question. (People v Jackson, supra.)

The New York approach was more rigid than that developed in other jurisdictions. The majority of the States tended to follow the "res gestae" theory—i.e., whether the killing was committed in, about and as a part of the underlying transaction. (See Ann., 58 ALR3d 851.) California had adopted the res gestae theory, at least insofar as robbery is concerned, holding that a robbery is not complete if the "conspirators have not won their way even momentarily to a place of temporary safety and the possession of the plunder is nothing more than a scrambling possession.

The 1967 Penal Law limited the application of the felony murder concept to nine serious and violent predicate felonies. At the same time, it was provided that the doctrine would apply to a killing committed in "immediate flight". This change was intended to do away with many of the old technical distinctions relating to "abandonment" or "completion". (See Hechtman, Practice Commentaries, McKinney's Cons Laws of NY, Book 39, Penal Law, § 125.25, p 400; Gegan, Criminal Homicide in the Revised New York Penal Law, HN5 12 NYLF 565, 589.)

Under the new formulation, the issue of whether the homicide occurred in "immediate flight" from a felony is only rarely to be considered as a question of law for resolution by the court. (People v Carter, 50 AD2d 174, 176.) Only where the record compels the inference that the actor was not in "immediate flight" may a felony murder conviction be set aside on the law. Rather, the question is to be submitted to the jury, under an appropriate charge. The jury should be instructed to give consideration to whether the homicide and the felony occurred at the same location or, if not, to the distance separating the two locations. Weight may also be placed on whether there is an interval of time between the commission of the felony and the commission of the homicide. The jury may properly consider such additional factors as whether the culprits had possession of the fruits of criminal activity, whether the police, watchmen or concerned citizens were in close pursuit, and whether the criminals had reached a place of temporary safety. These factors are not exclusive; others may be appropriate in differing factual settings. If anything, past history demonstrates the fruitlessness of attempting to apply rigid rules to virtually limitless factual variations. No single factor is necessarily controlling; it is the combination of several factors that leads to a justifiable inference.

In this case, the jury could properly find, as a question of fact, that the killing of Officer Rose occurred in immediate flight from the delicatessen robbery. The shooting occurred less than 15 minutes after the robbery and less than a half mile away. The defendant had made off with cash proceeds and was attempting to secure his possession of the loot. The police had reason to believe that the robber was still in the immediate vicinity and had taken steps to seal off avenues of escape. In this regard, the absence of proof as to why Officer Rose turned into the bowling alley parking lot is no deficiency. The standard is not whether the police officer subjectively believed that the defendant was the robber. Indeed, the defendant's own apprehension may be more valuable. The defendant's response to the observation of the police car was to seek an immediate hiding place. This indicates that the defendant perceived that the police were on his trail. The record does not indicate that the officer knew or supposed, that defendant committed a crime; it does indicate that the defendant feared that the officer possessed such knowledge.

Additionally, the defendant had not reached any place of temporary safety. In short, there is evidence from which the jury could conclude, as it did, that the defendant was in immediate flight from the robbery and that he shot the officer in order to make good his escape with the loot. The jury was properly charged as to the relevant considerations and we see no basis for disturbing its findings.

Order affirmed.

DISCUSSION QUESTIONS

1. What new rule does the court announce?

2. Do you think juries or judges should make this decision?

3. Should the court favor clear, bright line rules in this area or more flexible, contextual standards? Why?

––––––––––

One unusual twist that courts sometimes see in this area is the homicide that precedes a felony. Imagine that you see your hated college roommate from freshman year, and you immediately shoot him dead over some trivial past slight that bubbles up into your consciousness (you are a bit of a grudge-holder). After you shoot him, you decide to go through his pockets for spare change. You find a wallet stuffed full of hundred dollar bills (he may have been a jerk, but he did pretty well for himself), and you take the money. On these facts, you are guilty of second degree murder for an unpremeditated intentional killing, but not first degree felony murder because the killing preceded and was not "within the thing done." If you shot him hoping to get the money back that you lent him freshman year that, of course, would be an easy case of felony murder because the killing was simply the first step in the felony robbery.

2. LOGICAL RELATIONSHIP RULES

Duration rules only take us so far. What if you see your hated freshman roommate while you are robbing a bank and shoot him? One might argue that you killed him out of fear that he recognized you and could identify you to the police. Let's put a ski mask on you, though, to rule out that possibility and assume that you killed him out of spite. That would not be felony murder because the killing was not logically related in any way to the felony. (Something that means a lot to your accomplices who would otherwise be on the hook for a murder that truly had nothing to do with the felony they committed.)

At common law, it was sometimes said that felony murder liability applied to acts committed in furtherance of the felony, language that many jurisdictions have adopted by statute or by court decision. The mere fact that a killing coincided in time and place with a felony does not mean that the act causing the death was necessarily committed in furtherance of the felony. Similarly, many courts have found that the language in the commission or attempted commission of a felony also implies a logical or causal relationship to the felony. Note that the death itself need not further the felony, just the act that caused the death. In the case of the butter-fingered bank robber, the accidental death of the teller does not necessarily further the felony of robbery in any way but the carrying of the gun did.

Some courts have gone beyond requiring a logical relationship between the death and the felony and have replaced the time and place rules discussed above with a "logical nexus" test. Such courts say that time and place are only factors to be considered when assessing whether a killing was logically related to the felony.

In the next case, try to identify the procedural posture of the appeal. How was the jury instructed and how did the defense want it to be? Why did the court find the way it did? How does the role of the factfinder play in deciding appeals like this?

Case in Context

Keep your eye on the differences between the defendants' and the prosecutor's version of how the victim died in the following case.

PEOPLE V. CAVITT

Supreme Court of California
91 P.3d 222 (2004)

Opinion by: BAXTER.

BAXTER, J.—Defendants James Freddie Cavitt and Robert Nathaniel Williams were convicted in separate trials of the felony murder of 58-year-old Betty McKnight, the stepmother of Cavitt's girlfriend, Mianta McKnight. Defendants admitted plotting with Mianta to enter the McKnight home, to catch Betty unawares and tie her up, and to steal Betty's jewelry and other property. On the evening of December 1, 1995, with Mianta's assistance, the plan went forward. Defendants entered the house, threw a sheet over Betty's head, bound this hooded sheet to her wrists and ankles with rope and duct tape, and escaped with guns, jewelry, and other valuables from the bedroom. Betty was beaten and left hog-tied, facedown on the bed. Her breathing was labored. Before leaving, defendants made it appear that Mianta was a victim by pretending to tie her up as well. By the time Mianta untied herself and called her father to report the burglary-robbery, Betty had died from asphyxiation.

The evidence at trial amply supported a finding that defendants were the direct perpetrators of the murder. However, there was also evidence that tended to support the defense theory—namely, that Mianta deliberately suffocated Betty, for reasons independent of the burglary-robbery, after defendants had escaped and reached a place of temporary safety. Defendants assert that the felony-murder rule would not apply to this scenario and that the trial court's instructions erroneously denied the jury the opportunity to consider their theory.

Because the jury could have convicted defendants without finding they were the direct perpetrators of the murder, we granted review to clarify a nonkiller's liability for a killing "committed in the perpetration" of an inherently dangerous felony under Penal Code section 189's felony-murder rule. (See People v. Pulido (1997) 15 Cal.4th 713, 720–723 63 Cal. Rptr. 2d 625, 936 P.2d 1235 (Pulido).) We hold that, in such circumstances, the felony-murder rule requires both a causal relationship and a temporal relationship between the underlying felony and the act resulting in death. The causal relationship is established by proof of a logical nexus, beyond mere coincidence of time and place, between the homicidal act and the underlying felony the nonkiller committed or attempted to commit. The temporal relationship is established by proof the felony and the homicidal act were part of one continuous transaction. Applying these rules to the facts here, we affirm the judgment of the Court of Appeal.

This case involves the "complicity aspect" of the felony-murder rule. Defendants contend that a nonkiller can be liable for the felony murder committed by another only if the act resulting in death facilitated the commission of the underlying felony. . .The Attorney General, on the other hand, asserts that no causal relationship need exist between the underlying felony and the killing. In his view, it is enough that the act resulting in death occurred at the same time as the burglary and robbery.

After reviewing our case law, we find that neither formulation satisfactorily describes the complicity aspect of California's felony-murder rule. We hold instead that the felony-murder rule does not apply to nonkillers where the act resulting in death is completely unrelated to the underlying felony other than occurring at the same time and place. Under California law, there must be a logical nexus—i.e., more than mere coincidence of time and place—between the felony and the act resulting in death before the felony-murder rule may be applied to a nonkiller. Evidence that the killing facilitated or aided the underlying felony is relevant but is not essential. . .

Defendants contend that a nonkiller's liability for the felony murder committed by a co-felon depends on proof of a very specific causal relationship between the homicidal act and the underlying felony—namely, that the killer intended thereby to advance or facilitate the felony. Yet, defendants cite no case in which we have relieved a nonkiller of felony-murder liability because of insufficient proof that the killer actually intended to advance or facilitate the underlying felony. Indeed, the felony-murder rule is intended to eliminate the need to plumb the parties' peculiar intent with respect to a killing committed during the perpetration of the felony. (Burton, supra, 6 Cal.3d at p. 388.) Defendants' formulation, which finds no support in the statutory text, would thwart that goal.

Moreover, defendants' formulation is at odds with a fundamental purpose of the felony-murder rule, which is "to deter felons from killing negligently or accidentally by holding them strictly responsible for killings they commit." (People v. Billa (2003) 31 Cal.4th 1064, 1069 6 Cal. Rptr. 3d 425, 79 P.3d 542.) It is difficult to imagine how homicidal acts that are unintentional, negligent, or accidental could be said to have advanced or facilitated the underlying felony when those acts are, by their nature, unintended.

Defendants make little effort to grapple with the policies underlying the felony-murder rule and rely instead almost entirely on our oft-repeated observation in People v. Vasquez (1875) 49 Cal. 560 (Vasquez) that "if the homicide in question was committed by one of the nonkiller's associates engaged in the robbery, in furtherance of their common purpose to rob, he is as accountable as though his own hand had intentionally given the fatal blow, and is guilty of murder in the first degree." (Id. at p. 563.) However, in the century and a quarter since Vasquez was decided, we have never construed it to require a killing to advance or facilitate the felony, so long as some logical nexus existed between the two.

Indeed, even jurisdictions whose felony-murder statutes require the homicidal act to be "in furtherance" of an enumerated felony do not require proof that the act furthered or aided the felony. People v. Lewis (1981) 111 Misc.2d 682, 686 444 N.Y.S.2d 1003, 1006, which construed a New York felony-murder statute that included this language, is instructive: "This equation of 'in furtherance' with 'in aid of' or 'in advancement of' has the virtue of linguistic accuracy, but is at odds with both the history and purpose of the 'in furtherance' requirement. The phrase can best be understood as the third logical link in the triad which must be present to connect a felony with a consequent homicide. Just as 'in the course of' imposes a duration requirement, and 'causes the death' a causation requirement, 'in furtherance' places a relation requirement between the felony and the homicide. More than the mere coincidence to time and place, the nexus must be one of logic or plan. Excluded are those deaths which are so far outside the ambit of the plan of the felony and its execution as to be unrelated to them." In sum, it is "a misinterpretation of the phrase to require that the murder bring success to the felonious purpose." (Id. at p. 687; see also State v. Young (1983) 191 Conn. 636 469 A.2d 1189, 1193 "New York courts have construed the phrase to impose the requirement of a logical nexus between the felony and the homicide"; see also State v. Montgomery (2000) 254 Conn. 694 759 A.2d 995, 1020 ("The phrase 'in furtherance of' was intended to impose the requirement of a relationship between the underlying felony and the homicide beyond that of mere causation in fact".) We likewise construe Penal Code section 189 to require only a logical nexus between the felony and the homicide.

Substantial evidence of a logical nexus between the burglary-robbery and the murder exists in this case . . .The record supports a finding that defendants and/or Mianta killed Betty to eliminate the sole witness to the burglary-robbery or that Betty died accidentally as a result of being bound and gagged during the burglary-robbery. Either theory is sufficient to support the judgment. (E.g., People v. Kimble (1988) 44 Cal.3d 480, 502 244 Cal. Rptr. 148, 749 P.2d 803 (Kimble).) Even if the jury believed that defendants did not want to kill Betty or that they conditioned their participation in the burglary-robbery on the understanding that Betty not get hurt, it would not be a defense to felony murder. (People v. Boss, supra, 210 Cal. at p. 249; Vasquez, supra, 49 Cal. at pp. 562–563.)

As defendants point out, however, the record might also have supported a finding that Mianta killed Betty out of a private animus and not to aid or promote the burglary-robbery. Defendants contend that the jury instructions, by omitting any requirement that the homicidal act be "in furtherance of" the burglary-robbery, failed to apprise the jury of this latter possibility and therefore mandate reversal of their convictions.

We disagree. The instructions adequately apprised the jury of the need for a logical nexus between the felonies and the homicide in this case. To convict, the jury necessarily found that "the killing occurred during the commission or attempted commission of robbery or burglary" by "one of several persons engaged in the commission" of those crimes. The first of these described a temporal connection between the crimes; the second described the logical nexus. A burglar who happens to spy a lifelong enemy through the window of the house and fires a fatal shot. . . may have committed a killing while the robbery and burglary were taking place but cannot be said to have been "engaged in the commission" of those crimes at the time the shot was fired. . .

Defendants apparently assume that Mianta's personal animus towards the victim of the felony, if credited, should somehow absolve the other participants of their responsibility for the victim's death. They are mistaken. . . One would hardly be surprised to discover that targets of inherently dangerous felonies are selected precisely because one or more of the participants in the felony harbors a personal animus towards the victim. But it would be novel indeed if that commonplace fact could be used to exculpate the parties to a felonious enterprise of a murder committed in the perpetration of that felony, where a logical nexus between the felony and the murder exists.

The judgment of the Court of Appeal is affirmed.

DISCUSSION QUESTIONS

1.   What relationship does the prosecutor say should be required between the death and the felony? How broadly would that sweep? What relationship would the defense have the court require? How would that help them?

2.   How does logical nexus differ from cause, and how does it apply in this case?

3.   Do you think courts should require a causal relationship or only a logical nexus?

———————

In the freshman roommate scenario, imagine that you did not wear the ski mask. Your former roommate recognized you, but you did not shoot him in the bank. A year later, while you are still on the run, your former roommate recognizes you in the parking lot of a local supermarket (maybe you should have moved somewhere else), and you shoot him. Would you have felony murder liability in a jurisdiction using the logical nexus test? Would you have felony murder liability under traditional res gestae rules?

Using a logical nexus test, a court would infer that you killed him to stop him from reporting you to the police, which is logically related to the bank robbery. Therefore, using a logical nexust test, you would have felony murder liability. Under traditional res gestae rules, however, your felony murder liability would have ended long ago when you reached a place of temporary safety.

Don't be confused if res gestae and logical relation seem to be closely related to ideas of causation. They are! The cases, however, often speak of them separately, so it is important to be able to do the same in arguing to a judge or writing for an exam. Remember that your job as a student—and as a lawyer—is often not to make the law simpler or more logical than it is, but to learn to make arguments using the concepts and rules as they have been developed.

3. CAUSATION RULES

As has been discussed, requiring a logical relationship between the death and the felony implies causation. Two types of causal rules come into play with felony murder: general causal requirements applicable to all deaths and special rules dealing with killings committed by non-felons.

The general causal rules are critically important to the scope of felony murder liability. Two approaches exist. One requires only actual causation, also known as factual or but for causation. But for causation means that but for the felony the death would not have occurred. The second requires not just actual causation but proximate causation. Proximate causation for felony murder essentially means that the death was a foreseeable or natural result of the felonious act. (These types of causation will be discussed in much greater detail in the chapter on causation that follows, but these rough definitions will do for now.)

Requiring only actual causation greatly expands the scope of felony murder liability. In one widely noted case, an armed robber was found guilty of felony murder when one of the people in the store he robbed had a heart attack and died after the robber left. Instead of straining to call the death foreseeable, the court said that the deaths need only be actually caused to come within felony murder. Had proximate cause been required, most courts would not have found felony murder on these facts because, while it is conceivable that someone might have a heart attack as a result of an armed robbery, it is sufficiently improbable.

While some jurisdictions require only actual causation, most also require proximate causation. That said, those jurisdictions typically define proximate cause broadly. Our butter-fingered bank robber would probably be found guilty of felony murder under both actual and proximate causation. But for the felony the death would not have occurred. Moreover, the death would be considered a natural and foreseeable result of waiving a gun during an armed robbery.

Don't be too troubled if you find both examples to be equally foreseeable or unforeseeable. First, these rules of causation don't always produce predictable results. Courts from different jurisdictions and even within a jurisdiction often differ in how they apply them. Second, further nuances about the rules of causation will be discussed in the chapter on causation. (I put the causation chapter after the homicide chapters because that is where it appears in many textbooks and because homicide crimes provide the best illustrations of causation principles.)

For example, one important difference between the two examples given is that death by gunshot is the same general type of harm contemplated by one who engages in an armed robbery, whereas death by heart attack is not. Some courts might also see the heart attack as the sort of intervening cause that "breaks the chain of causation" between the defendant's acts and the resulting death where the butter-fingered bank robber's dropping of his gun more directly caused the death of the teller. Each of these principles will be discussed in more detail later. Consider the causation analysis in the following felony murder case.

Case in Context

How does foreseeability play into felony murder liability? Where should the cutoff be?

STATE V. MARTIN

Supreme Court of New Jersey
573 A.2d 1359 (1990)

POLLOCK, J. On June 29, 1983, defendant and four others from Keyport attended a party in the apartment of Lois Baker on the third floor of a three-story wood-framed building in Keansburg. Defendant, who claimed he was intoxicated, stated that he had smoked marijuana and consumed four beers before the party, and four more beers and four shots of Southern Comfort at the party. Paul Wade, one member of the Keyport group, became involved in two altercations with other guests, including Mike Kilpatrick. After the second altercation, Baker told everyone from Keyport to leave. On leaving, defendant and Wade vandalized a motorcycle that they thought belonged to Kilpatrick. . .

Within fifteen minutes after defendant left Baker's apartment, another guest noticed that the building was on fire. Everyone escaped, except Barbara Quartz, who had fallen asleep after drinking alcoholic beverages at the party. She died of asphyxiation due to smoke inhalation and carbon monoxide intoxication.

According to defendant, he set the fire by lighting a paper bag containing trash that he found in the hallway by Lois Baker's door. Defendant testified:

> I picked up the bag and walked down the steps with it. I was just, you know, throwing it around making a mess, you know, and I set it down and I lit up a cigarette. And the match—I lit the paper bag on fire, you know, 'cause I thought maybe it would burn up the garbage, you know, not to spread or anything, just make, like make a mess of the bottom of the landing. And then, then I left. . .I put the match on the bag and lit the bag, the top of the bag on fire.

I thought it would make a mess of things. I didn't understand. I mean I didn't figure that it would, you know, cause a fire and spread or catch on anything. I thought it would just, you know, burn the garbage and go right out. I didn't mean to hurt nobody.

The State's version of the setting of the fire differed materially from that of defendant. According to the State's experts, Frederick Dispensiere of the Monmouth County Prosecutor's Office, and Daniel Slowick, a fire insurance investigator, the fire was set by spreading kerosene between the ground floor and the second floor. . .

Defendant, Daniel Martin, was found guilty of . . . felony murder, arson, and aggravated arson arising out of the death of a woman in a building that he set on fire . . . The Appellate Division affirmed . . . Because the charge incorrectly instructed the jury on the standard for finding that defendant's act caused the death of the victim, we reverse the defendant's murder conviction.

Under the New Jersey Penal Code, causation . . . is a term of art, the meaning of which varies with the mental state of the actor. It means one thing when an offense is committed knowingly or purposely, and something else for a crime of strict or absolute liability, such as felony murder . . . The New Jersey Code is based substantially on the Model Penal Code. The underlying premise of both codes is that problems regarding variations between the actual and designed or contemplated results are problems of culpability rather than metaphysical problems of causation. Consequently, in assessing whether a defendant's conduct is the cause of a remote result, both codes focus on whether the actual result justly bears on the defendant's culpability for the offense. . .

The felony-murder verdict arose under N.J.S.A. 2C:11–3a(3), which imposes liability when

the actor, acting either alone or with one or more other persons, is engaged in the commission of arson or robbery, sexual assault, burglary, kidnapping, carjacking or criminal escape and in the course of such crime . . . any person causes the death of a person other than one of the participants; except that in any prosecution under this subsection, in which the defendant was not the only participant in the underlying crime, it is an affirmative defense that the defendant:

(a) Did not commit the homicidal act or in any way solicit, request, command, importune, cause or aid the commission thereof; and

(b) Was not armed with a deadly weapon, or any instrument, article or substance readily capable of causing death or serious physical injury and of a sort not ordinarily carried in public places by law-abiding persons; and

(c) Had no reasonable ground to believe that any other participant was armed with such a weapon, instrument, article or substance; and

(d) Had no reasonable ground to believe that any other participant intended to engage in conduct likely to result in death or serious physical injury.

At common law, if the victim died during the course of the commission of the felony, the perpetrator was guilty of murder. Theoretically, the intent to commit the felony, even in the absence of an intent to kill, was transferred to the death of the victim. . .More recently, felony murder has been viewed not as a crime of transferred intent, but as one of absolute or strict liability. . .The historical justification for the rule is that it serves as a general deterrent against the commission of violent crimes. The rationale is that if potential felons realize that they will be culpable as murderers for a death that occurs during the commission of a felony, they will be less likely to commit the felony. . .

To the extent that the felony-murder rule holds an actor liable for a death irrespective of the actor's mental state, the rule cuts across the grain of criminal law. Generally, people are not criminally culpable for the consequences of their acts unless those consequences were intended, contemplated, or foreseeable. Because the felony-murder rule runs counter to normal rules of criminal culpability, it received careful consideration from the drafters of the Model Penal Code and from the New Jersey Commission. The drafters of the Model Penal Code objected to the rule as "a form of strict liability to which we are opposed." Model Penal Code § 2.01.1 (Tent. Draft No. 9 (1959)). Although it ultimately recommended retention of the rule, the New Jersey Commission stated that "principled justification in its defense is hard to find." II N.J.Code § 2C:11–3 commentary at 157. Ultimately, the Commission incorporated the advice of Oliver Wendell Holmes, Jr., who wrote:

If experience shows, or is deemed by the lawmaker to show, that somehow or other deaths which the evidence makes accidental happen disproportionately often in connection with other felonies, or with resistance to officers, or if on any other ground of policy it is deemed desirable to make special efforts for the prevention of such deaths, the law-maker may consistently treat acts which, under the known circumstances, are felonious, or constitute resistance to officers, as having a sufficiently dangerous tendency to put under a special ban. The law may, therefore, throw on the actor the peril, not only of the consequences foreseen by him, but also of consequences which, although not predicted by common experience, the legislator apprehends. The Common Law 49 (1963).

To comprehend the New Jersey Code's approach to felony murder, one must consider the pre-existing law, the Model Penal Code, and the New Jersey Commission's modifications of that Code. Before the enactment of the New Jersey Code, this State recognized a broad felony-murder rule. The predecessor statute provided:

> any person, who in committing or attempting to commit arson, burglary, kidnapping, rape, robbery, sodomy or any unlawful act of which the probable consequences may be bloodshed, kills another, or if the death of anyone ensues from the committing or attempting to commit any such crime or act was guilty of murder.

Even under that statute, the State was required to prove not only that the felony was the cause-in-fact or "but-for" cause, but also that it was the proximate cause of the victim's death. Thus, the proximate-cause test limited the harsh effect of the common-law felony-murder rule. Because of its vagueness, however, the test created problems of its own.

The Model Penal Code took a different approach. Under the Model Penal Code, felony murder was treated as a form of negligent or reckless homicide. Instead of treating felony murder as an absolute-liability offense, the Model Penal Code created a presumption of recklessness when a homicide occurred in the course of the commission of certain felonies, including arson...If not rebutted, that presumption would support a conviction for murder.

Initially, the New Jersey Commission agreed with that approach. In a tentative draft of the New Jersey Code, the Commission recommended adoption of the Model Penal Code's treatment of felony murder, concluding that "beyond this, we submit that the felony-murder doctrine, as a basis for establishing the criminality of homicide, should be abandoned." New Jersey Law Commission (Tentative Draft at 310 (Jan. 1971)). As an alternative, the Commission mentioned the New York Code, id. at 313–14, which "allows a limited affirmative defense as to the non-perpetrator participant in the felony where that person is able to demonstrate that he did not assume a homicidal risk." II N.J.Code § 2C:11–3 commentary at 157.

In its final report, the New Jersey Commission rejected the Model Penal Code's approach...but provided an affirmative defense, similar to that provided in New York, for perpetrators who did not assume a homicidal risk...Consequently, an accomplice, as distinguished from the primary actor, may establish the defense by proving that he or she did not commit the homicidal act, was not armed with a deadly weapon, and had no reason to believe that any other participant was so armed or "intended to engage in conduct likely to result in death or serious physical injury."

N.J.S.A. 2C:11–3a(3)(a) to –3a(3)(d). Those four factors focus on whether the accomplice undertook a homicidal risk or could have foreseen that the commission of the felony might result in death. . .

Amendments, enacted in 1979 and 1981 in response to this Court's decision in State v. Canola, 73 N.J. 206, 374 A.2d 20 (1977), extend the reach of the statute. In Canola, four perpetrators attempted to rob a jewelry store. During the course of the robbery, the owner killed one of the perpetrators and then was himself killed. The defendant was convicted of felony murder of both the owner and the other perpetrator. This court reversed the conviction for the death of the other perpetrator. . .According to the Court, a felon could not be liable for any death, even of a non-felon, when the death was caused by someone other than a participant in the commission of the felony because the statute punished only deaths caused by a "participant" and "in the course of and in furtherance of" the felony. . .The Legislature responded by eliminating the requirement that the death be caused by one of the participants. . .and that the death occur "in furtherance of" the commission of the felony. . . .

Concerning absolute-liability offenses, the New Jersey Code states:

> When causing a particular result is a material element of an offense for which absolute liability is imposed by law, the element is not established unless the actual result is a probable consequence of the actor's conduct. N.J.S.A. 2C:2–3e.

In effect, subsection e provides that the actual result—death, in the case of felony murder—"is not established unless" it is the "probable consequence of the commission of the felony." However, a question remains about the meaning of "probable consequences."

The term "probable consequence" is undefined in the Model Penal Code or Commentary, the New Jersey Com-mission Report, the New Jersey Code, or anywhere else in the legislative history. Our review of that history leads us to conclude that the Legislature. . . did not intend a drastic change in the law of felony murder. . .

Pre-Code cases originally employed the term "probable consequence" or the equivalent when referring to the risk of death created by the felon's acts. In State v. Cooper, the former Supreme Court stated that an unintentional killing occurring during the commission or attempt to commit a felony constitutes a felony murder, "especially if death were a probable consequence of the act." 13 N.J.L. 360, 370 (1833). . .

In an attempt to focus more closely on the meaning of "probable consequence," we listed this case for re-argument. . .At oral argument, defendant urged that probable consequence in the felony-murder context means variously that the victim's death must not be too remote or depend on the act of another, and that the death cannot be accidental, unanticipated, or remote. By comparison, the State contended that "probable consequence" means that the victim's death need be only foreseeable, and not the result of an independent or intervening cause. Significantly, both counsel urge that probable consequences means something more than "but for" causation. The point to be derived from prior law, the language and history of the Code, and the argument of counsel is that some deaths are too remotely related to the commission of the felony to justify holding the actor responsible not only for the commission of the felony, but for murder. . .

. . .The Model Penal Code Commentary supports the proposition that the meaning of "probable consequence" is closely related to the concept of foreseeability. In the commentary to the accomplice-liability section of the Model Penal Code, 2.06, the commentators recognize that the "probable consequence" test is substantially similar to a test of foreseeability. As they observe: "To say that the accomplice is liable if the offense committed is 'reasonably foreseeable' or the 'probable consequence' of another crime is to make him liable for negligence." Model Penal Code and Commentaries § 2.06 at 312 n. 42 (1985). Although not directly related to felony-murder analysis, the commentary lends support to the interchangeability of the terms "probable consequence" and "reasonable foreseeability."

Keeping in mind that the New Jersey Commission predicated its version of the felony-murder rule on New York law, the causation test developed by the New York courts is illuminating. Those courts have rejected the notion that "but-for" causation is sufficient to sustain a felony-murder conviction. To find a defendant guilty of felony murder, New York courts require that the "death be a reasonably foreseeable and non-accidental consequence" of the felony. Flores, supra, 124 Misc.2d at 481, 476 N.Y.S.2d at 480. . .

In sum, pre-Code case law and the Model Penal Code draw on notions of foreseeability. To the extent that the Legislature looked to those sources, "probable consequence" may be interpreted in their light. . .We can define . . . "probable consequence" by recourse to the terms used to define causation in 2C:2–3 for crimes committed knowingly, purposely, or recklessly, or with criminal negligence. For those offenses, in addition to other prescribed requirements, the result must "not be too remote, accidental in its occurrence, or dependent on another's volitional act to have a just bearing on the actor's liability or the gravity of his offense." N.J.S.A. 2C:2–3b and –3c. As previously noted, however, the Legislature amended N.J.S.A. 2C:11–3 to provide that culpability for felony murder may attach when the killing is committed by one other than the felon, such as the victim or a police officer. As that amendment intimates, such killings are not "too dependent on another's volition to have a just bearing on the actor's liability." In brief, deaths occurring as a result of self-defense or retaliation are not "too dependent on another's volition," but are the foreseeable result of the risk created by the felon. Although the legislative intent is not entirely clear, we conclude that the Legislature recognized that some deaths will occur in the course of a felony that are too remotely related or accidental to warrant holding the actor liable.

The court should instruct the jury that the defendant, whether a sole perpetrator or an accomplice, is liable for felony murder only if the death is not too remote, accidental in its occurrence, or too dependent on another's volitional act to have a just bearing on the defendant's culpability.

Two examples define the outer limits of the problem. On the one hand, a bank robber would not be liable for felony murder if at "the moment a bank robber stepped into the bank, an employee pushing the button for a burglar alarm was electrocuted." Model Penal Code and Commentaries § 2.03(4) comment at 264 (1985). On the other hand, in a robbery of a store in which "the shopkeeper fires at the robber but instead kills an innocent bystander," the death would not be too remote for the defendant to be guilty of felony murder. Senate Judiciary Committee, Statement to Senate Committee Substitute, No. 1537, § 14 (1981). . .

As the foregoing examples illustrate, in a multiple-perpetrator felony, the focus should be on the relationship between the victim's death and the felony, not the individual roles of the various perpetrators. Hence, in such a felony, an otherwise culpable accomplice may be liable for the death of the victim even if he or she was not the gunman who killed the victim, but was merely a lookout for the driver of a getaway car. The point is that a defendant should be exculpated only when a death occurs in a manner that is so unexpected or unusual that he or she could not justly be found culpable for the result. . .

In the instant case, the trial court failed to instruct the jury that defendant would not be liable for the felony murder of the victim if her death was "too remote, accidental in its occurrence, or too dependent on another's volitional act to have a just bearing on the defendant's culpability." Supra at 32, 573 A.2d at 1375. Instead, the trial court instructed the jury:

> Now, under this law felony murder it does not matter whether the act which caused death is committed recklessly or unintentionally or accidentally. The perpetrator is as guilty of murder as he would be if he had purposely or knowingly committed the act which caused the death. . .

Because the trial court did not adequately charge the jury on causation under N.J.S.A. 2C:2–3, we reverse the judgment of conviction for murder, and remand the cause to the Law Division.

DISCUSSION QUESTIONS

1.   What type of causation does the court require for felony murder? What type of causation do you think felony murder should require?

2.   If a bank teller committed suicide upon being handed a "this is a robbery" note by a bank robber, would that death be included under the felony murder rule under the traditional approach? Under the approach of this court? What if the teller has a heart attack and dies when the robber presses a gun against his head and demands money?

3.   What do you think of the justification for felony murder offered in the passage from the writings of Oliver Wendell Holmes'? (p. 464)

H. KILLINGS COMMITTED BY NON-FELONS

Does felony murder liability include killings by people reacting to the felony? The classic examples involve a police officer, crime victim, or bystander who kills someone in the process of trying to foil an armed robbery.

The majority of jurisdictions, however, refuse to extend felony murder liability to killings by non-felons. They employ what is sometimes called an agency theory of felony murder reasoning that the act causing death must be performed by an "agent" of the felony, not someone resisting it.

A minority of jurisdictions, however, hold the felons liable for felony murder for such deaths under a proximate causation theory. So, if the store owner shoots at one of the robbers and accidentally kills an innocent customer, the robber gets convicted of felony murder for the death of the customer on the theory that it is foreseeable that people might resist an armed robbery with deadly force and that a bystander might get killed.

Within the minority of jurisdictions that extend felony murder liability to killings by non-felons, most of those states do not include within felony murder killings of a co-felon by a non-felon. So if the store owner kills your accomplice to the robbery, you will not be found guilty of felony murder for his death, even though you would be found guilty if the bullet had hit and killed a customer. (So as an armed robber, you actually want straight-shooting store owners as long as you are not the felon being shot!)

Within the minority of jurisdictions that extend felony murder liability to killings by non-felons, a few jurisdictions include killings of co-felons by non-felons within felony murder. So not only do you lose your accomplice to the straight-shooting storeowner, but you get convicted of murder for his death. Talk about adding insult to injury!

Case in Context

Note where the defendant was and in what condition when the killing occurred in the following case.

KANSAS V. SANEXAY SOPHOPHONE
Supreme Court of Kanas
270 Kan. 703 (2001)

Opinion by: LARSON.

LARSON, J.: This is Sanexay Sophophone's direct appeal of his felony-murder conviction for the death of his co-felon during flight from an aggravated burglary in which both men participated.

The facts are not in dispute. Sophophone and three other individuals conspired to and broke into a house in Emporia. The resident reported the break-in to the police.

Police officers responded to the call, saw four individuals leaving the back of the house, shined a light on the suspects, identified themselves as police officers, and ordered them to stop. The individuals, one being Sophophone, started to run away. One officer ran down Sophophone, hand-cuffed him, and placed him in a police car.

Other officers arrived to assist in apprehending the other individuals as they were running from the house. An officer chased one of the suspects later identified as Somphone Sysoumphone. Sysoumphone crossed railroad tracks, jumped a fence, and then stopped. The officer approached with his weapon drawn and ordered Sysoumphone to the ground and not to move. Sysoumphone was lying face down but raised up and fired at the officer, who returned fire and killed him. It is not disputed that Sysoumphone was one of the individuals observed by the officers leaving the house that had been burglarized.

Sophophone was charged with conspiracy to commit aggravated burglary, K.S.A. 21–3302; aggravated burglary...and felony murder, K.S.A. 21–3401(b).

Sophophone moved to dismiss the felony-murder charges, contending the complaint was defective because the police officer and not he or his co-felons had killed Sysoumphone and further because he was in custody and sitting in the police car when the deceased was killed and therefore not attempting to commit or even fleeing from an inherently dangerous felony. His motion to dismiss was denied by the trial court.

Sophophone was convicted by a jury of all counts. His motion for judgment of acquittal was denied. He was sentenced on all counts.

The applicable provisions of K.S.A. 21–3401 read as follows:

"Murder in the first degree is the killing of a human being committed:

"(b) in the commission of, attempt to commit, or flight from an inherently dangerous felony as defined in K.S.A. 21–3436 and amendments thereto."

Aggravated burglary is one of the inherently dangerous felonies as enumerated by K.S.A. 21–3436(10).

Sophophone does not dispute that aggravated burglary is an inherently dangerous felony which given the right circumstances would support a felony-murder charge. His principal argument centers on his being in custody at the time his co-felon was killed by the lawful act of the officer which he contends was a "break in circumstances" sufficient to insulate him from further criminal responsibility.

This "intervening cause" or "break in circumstances" argument has no merit under the facts of this case. We have held in numerous cases that "time, distance, and the causal relationship between the underlying felony and a killing are factors to be considered in determining whether the killing occurs in the commission of the underlying felony and the defendant is therefore subject to the felony-murder rule."

We look to the prevailing views concerning the applicability of the felony-murder doctrine where the killing has been caused by the acts of a third party.

In Dressler, Understanding Criminal Law the question is posed of whether the felony-murder rule should apply when the fatal act is performed by a non-felon. Dressler states:

"This issue has perplexed courts. Two approaches to the question have been considered and applied by the courts.

"b   The 'Agency' Approach

"The majority rule is that the felony-murder doctrine does not apply if the person who directly causes the death is a non-felon. . . .

"The reasoning of this approach stems from accomplice liability theory. Generally speaking, the acts of the primary party (the person who directly commits the offense) are imputed to an accomplice on the basis of the agency doctrine. It is as if the accomplice says to the primary party: 'Your acts are my acts.' It follows that a co-felon cannot be convicted of the homicides because the primary party was not the person with whom she was an accomplice. It is not possible to impute the acts of the antagonistic party—the non-felon or the police officer—to a co-felon on the basis of agency.

"c   The 'Proximate Causation' Approach

"An alternative theory, followed by a few courts for a while, holds that a felon may be held responsible under the felony-murder rule for a killing committed by a non-felon if the felon set in motion the acts which resulted in the victim's death.

"Pursuant to this rule, the issue becomes one of proximate causation: if an act by one felon is the proximate cause of the homicidal conduct by the non-felon or the police officer, murder liability is permitted."

The leading case adopting the agency approach is Commonwealth v. Redline, 391 Pa. 486, 495, 137 A.2d 472 (1958), where the underlying principle of the agency theory is described as follows:

"In adjudging a felony-murder, it is to be remembered at all times that the thing which is imputed to a felon for a killing incidental to his felony is malice and not the act of killing. The mere coincidence of homicide and felony is not enough to satisfy the felony-murder doctrine."

The following statement from Redline is more persuasive for Sophophone:

"In the present instance, the victim of the homicide was one of the robbers who, while resisting apprehension in his effort to escape, was shot and killed by a policeman in the performance of his duty. Thus, the homicide was justifiable and, obviously, could not be availed of, on any rational legal theory, to support a charge of murder. How can anyone, no matter how much of an outlaw he may be, have a criminal charge lodged against him for the consequences of the lawful conduct of another person? The mere question carries with it its own answer." 391 Pa. at 509.

The minority of the states whose courts have adopted the proximate cause theory believe their legislatures intended that any person, co-felon, or accomplice who commits an inherently dangerous felony should be held responsible for any death which is a direct and foreseeable consequence of the actions of those committing the felony. These courts apply the civil law concept of proximate cause to felony-murder situations.

It appears to the majority that to impute the act of killing to Sophophone when the act was the lawful and courageous one of a law enforcement officer acting in the line of his duties is contrary to the strict construction we are required to give criminal statutes. There is considerable doubt about the meaning of K.S.A. 21–3401(b) as applied to the facts of this case, and we believe that making one criminally responsible for the lawful acts of a law enforcement officer is not the intent of the felony-murder statute as it is currently written.

We hold that under the facts of this case where the killing resulted from the lawful acts of a law enforcement officer in attempting to apprehend a co-felon, Sophophone is not criminally responsible for the resulting death of Somphone Sysoumphone, and his felony-murder conviction must be reversed.

Reversed.

DISSENT

ABBOTT, J., dissenting:

When an issue requires statutory analysis and the statute is unambiguous, we are limited by the wording chosen by the legislature. We are not free to alter the statutory language, regardless of the result. In the present case, the felony-murder statute does not require us to adopt the "agency" theory favored by the majority. Indeed, there is nothing in the statute which establishes an agency approach. The statute does not address the issue at all. The requirements, according to the statute, are: (1) there must be a killing, and (2) the killing must be committed in the commission, attempt to commit, or flight from an inherently dangerous felony. The statute simply does not contain the limitations discussed by the majority. The facts in this case, in my opinion, satisfy all of the requirements set forth in K.S.A. 21–3401(b).

Here, Sophophone set in motion acts which would have resulted in the death or serious injury of a law enforcement officer had it not been for the highly alert law enforcement officer. This set of events could have very easily resulted in the death of a law enforcement officer, and in my opinion this is exactly the type of case the legislature had in mind when it adopted the felony-murder rule.

DISCUSSION QUESTIONS

1.   Do you think that felony murder should include killings by non-felons?

2.   What about killings of co-felons by non-felons?

3.   What other type of murder liability might exist for killings by non-felons that were committed in response to a defendant's felony?

I.   OTHER TYPES OF FELONY MURDER LIABILITY

Up to this point, we have discussed the felony murder rule in its "classic form," which is largely based on common law. Many jurisdictions, however, have modified the rule to make it less harsh. Generally, they include a requirement that the defendant have a culpable mental state with respect to the conduct that caused the death. You might think of this as "felony-murder-lite." Some jurisdictions require that the felon perform an act "inherently dangerous" or "clearly dangerous" to human life. Other jurisdictions use felony murder only as a "grading provision. These statues require proof of some form of express or implied malice but then provide that such murders shall be first degree murders if committed in the course of certain types of felonies.

The Model Penal Code, for example, contains a felony murder provision that "felony murder purists" would not even consider to be felony

J. MISDEMEANOR OR UNLAWFUL ACT MANSLAUGHTER

Many jurisdictions provide for involuntary manslaughter liability when death results from an unlawful act that does not satisfy the jurisdiction's felony murder rule. These provisions often include unenumerated felonies, felonies that are not inherently dangerous, and misdemeanors. Our felony litterer, for example, could be found guilty of misdemeanor manslaughter along with a driver who kills not recklessly or even negligently but through some minor traffic infraction.

Case in Context

Note the accidental nature of the death in the following case but the strictness of the liability that results.

U.S. v. Earl E. Walker
District of Columbia Court of Appeals
380 A.2d 1388 (1977)

Opinion by: KERN.

Appellee was charged with two counts of involuntary manslaughter and one count of carrying a pistol without a license (D.C. Code 1973, § 22–3204). The government appeals from the trial court's dismissal of the count in the indictment which charged that appellee feloniously, in perpetrating and attempting to perpetrate the crime of carrying a pistol without a license, involving danger of injury, did shoot Ernestine Curry with a pistol, thereby causing injuries from which the said Ernestine Curry died . . .

At the hearing on appellee's motion to dismiss this count of the indictment, the government's proffer of evidence was that appellee, while carrying a pistol without a license, dropped it in the stairwell of an apartment building, and that the gun went off, fatally wounding a bystander. Appellee's proffer was that a firearms expert had determined that when the hammer of the pistol was not cocked, it would fire on impact only if dropped at a particular angle. These proffers constitute the only explanation in the record of the incident underlying the indictment.

There is no statutory definition of manslaughter in this jurisdiction; In an earlier opinion on involuntary manslaughter, we said:

Involuntary manslaughter is an unlawful killing which is unintentionally committed. By unintentionally it is meant that there is no intent to kill or to do bodily injury. The crime may occur as the result of an unlawful act which is a misdemeanor involving danger of injury. . . The requisite intent in involuntary manslaughter is supplied by the intent to commit the misdemeanor, or by gross or criminal negligence . . .

The state of mind in involuntary manslaughter is characterized, on the one hand, by a lack of intent to cause death or injury and, on the other, by a lack of awareness of the consequences of the act amounting to an unreasonable failure of perception criminal negligence . . . or the intention to do an act which is a misdemeanor and is in some way dangerous. . .

We defined the elements of involuntary manslaughter as: "(1) an unlawful killing of a human being (2) with either (a) the intent to commit a misdemeanor dangerous in itself or (b) an unreasonable failure to perceive the risk of harm to others." Id. at 216; emphasis added.

This appeal therefore presents for our determination the question whether the unlawful act of carrying a pistol without a license is also a dangerous act. Id. at 216 n.24. The pertinent statute provides:

No person shall within the District of Columbia carry either openly or concealed on or about his person, except in his dwelling house or place of business or on other land possessed by him, a pistol without a license therefor issued as hereinafter provided . . . D.C. Code 1973, § 22–3204.

Appellee, citing Mitchell v. United States, D.C.App., 302 A.2d 216, 217 (1973), argues that the plain intent of Section 3204 is to stop the prohibited conduct before danger of injury arises, and that such danger is not a necessary concomitant of the offense. Appellee proceeds to illustrate what he deems to be the "essence" of the offense of carrying a pistol without a license by the following hypothetical (Brief at 6–7):

Two persons are walking peaceably on a public street carrying holstered pistols. One . . . has a license to carry a pistol, but the other has no license. The second person is violating section 3204, and the first is not. Yet there is no difference between them in terms of the danger presented to others.

Appellee's hypothetical and argument notwithstanding, we conclude that carrying a pistol without a license exposes the community to such inherent risk of harm that when death results, even though an unintended consequence, the defendant may be nonetheless charged with involuntary manslaughter. Appellee in the instant case was carrying a loaded handgun, which, so far as the record shows, had no purpose other than its use as a weapon. See Scott v. United States, D.C.App., 243 A.2d 54, 56 (1968). Implicit in the statutory proscription of carrying a pistol without a license outside the possessor's "dwelling house or place of business" is a congressional recognition of the inherent risk of harm to the public of such dangerous instrumentality being carried about the community and away from the residence or business of the possessor. Indeed, the history of the statute evinces congressional concern with the need to control the introduction of pistols into the community by licensing all those who do so.

Additionally, we think it significant in assessing the dangerousness vel non of the unlawful act of carrying a pistol without a license that

Congress has expressly required one who seeks the license to be "a suitable person to be so licensed." D.C. Code 1973, § 22–3206. Issuance of these licenses is the responsibility of the Chief of the Metropolitan Police Department, id., and is subject to restrictive regulations which, among other things, require the applicant to be of sound mind, to be without a prior criminal record, not to be an alcoholic or user of narcotics, to "be trained and experienced in the use, functioning and safe operation of the pistol," and finally, "to be free from physical defects which would impair his safe use of the weapon." 21 D.C.Reg. 413–21 (1974).

Thus, taking up appellee's hypothetical of the two persons carrying pistols on a public street, one of whom is licensed and the other of whom is not, we conclude that Congress intended to preclude the non-licensee from being on the street with his weapon because of the danger he posed to the community as a result (1) of the inherent dangerousness of the weapon he carried, and (2) of the absence of any evidence of his capability to carry safely such a dangerous instrumentality.

To summarize, this court in Bradford defined involuntary manslaughter as the killing of another "as the result of an unlawful act which is a misdemeanor involving danger of injury." Bradford, supra at 215. In Mitchell, we declared the object of Section 3204, which proscribes carrying a pistol outside the residence or place of business without a license, to be "to forestall the temptation to use it the pistol as such," thereby recognizing the danger of injury arising from the unlicensed carrying of the pistol. Mitchell, supra at 217. We now hold that a charge of violation of Section 3204 resulting in the shooting and death of another validly charges involuntary manslaughter because the misdemeanor of carrying a pistol without a license is dangerous in and of itself. Accordingly, the trial court's order must be reversed and the count at issue restored to the indictment.

So ordered.

DISCUSSION QUESTIONS

1.　Should involuntary manslaughter always require at least criminal negligence? Is it just or efficient to impose manslaughter liability if the defendant committed the misdemeanor without being criminally negligent as to the risk of death?

2.　Conversely, should misdemeanor manslaughter liability be limited to misdemeanors dangerous to human life, or does the commission of any misdemeanor justify imposing manslaughter liability if death results?

3.　Do you agree with the court's response to the defendant's hypothetical about two people walking down the street?

Practice Problem 14.2: Deadly Dealings

You work for the governor of a state in a common law jurisdiction that has seen deaths from drug overdoses skyrocket. The increase in overdoses is evenly divided between prescription painkillers and heroin although about half the time the prescription overdoses involve one person illegally using drugs that were prescribed for another or drugs that were illegally supplied in excess of the doctor's prescription. Some of the overdose deaths are clear acts of suicide (where notes or messages were left to that effect), but most of the overdose deaths appear to be accidental. Currently defendants in such cases are charged with either depraved heart murder or involuntary manslaughter as defined by common law.

The governor is greatly concerned about the overdose problem. She wants to take some action that will reduce the number of people dying from drug overdoses, but she also wants the criminal punishment given to be fair.

Recently one legislator has proposed the following piece of legislation.

Any person who manufactures, distributes or dispenses an illegal drug or who unlawfully distributes or dispenses a legal drug is strictly liable for a death which results from the injection, inhalation or ingestion of that substance, and is guilty of involuntary manslaughter. It shall not be a defense to a prosecution under this section that the decedent contributed to his own death by his purposeful, knowing, reckless or negligent injection, inhalation or ingestion of the substance, or by his consenting to the administration of the substance by another.

The Governor has asked you for your advice. She wants to know how the proposed legislation would change the law and whether it is a good idea or not. She wants you to explain the pro's and con's of this proposal as well as the current approach. She would also welcome your thoughts on any proposed amendments to the legislation as well as any entirely new proposal that you think would better serve the needs of the state.

Exam Tips: Felony Murder

Felony murder fact patterns are favorite exam topics for many criminal law professors because they test a student's ability to apply a complex set of interlocking rules and doctrines. Even the most complex fact pattern can be broken into the following steps.

- Determine who is guilty of the felony
- Determine whether the felony resulted in a death
- Determine whether the felony satisfies that jurisdiction's felony murder.

Depending on the call of the question, you might want to switch around the order of these questions. Are you asked to analyze liability for all crimes? Then start with the analysis of whether the person is guilty of the felony, and then work your way up to felony murder. Are you asked to analyze liability for only homicide crimes? Then determine whether that felony would satisfy the felony murder rule before spending time analyzing whether the felony was committed or not.

If you are asked to analyze liability for all crimes in a fact pattern that raises felony murder issues, don't forget to include reckless murder and involuntary manslaughter in your analysis. Many a "failed felony murder" fact pattern will support a reckless murder theory. For example, imagine that you conclude that an "evading the police" felony does not satisfy felony murder in a jurisdiction because the felony is not inherently dangerous in the abstract. The actual driving involved in the case at hand might be so reckless and indifferent to human life that it might constitute reckless murder. You would get points on the exam for discussing both theories for murder liability, so make sure you discuss both.

Practice Problem 14.3: 911 Murder

Wayne and Garth were archrivals in a multi-player, online video game. Wayne began taunting Garth online that he was going to have Garth "swatted," a term that refers to calling in a false report of a violent shooter to the police that results in a SWAT team being dispatched to someone's home to deal with what they believe to be an ongoing violent incident. Garth taunted Wayne back saying that Wayne did not have the guts to do it and that in any event Garth was not afraid of a SWAT team. Wayne responded by daring Garth to provide his address. Garth responded by giving an old address. (All of these communications took place online.) Wayne called 911 pretending to be Garth. He claimed that he had just killed his wife and wanted the police to come and stop him before he killed their three children. He gave the address that Garth had provided.

Ben, the resident at the address that Wayne had given 911 was just getting ready to go paintballing when the SWAT team arrived. As a serious paintballer, Ben was wearing protective vests and leg plates that at a distance roughly resemble the body armor that soldiers, law enforcement, and some highly prepared active shooters wear. He was also carrying his paintball rifle, which roughly appears to be an assault rifle at a distance. As he was locking his front door, the startled SWAT team appeared at the end of his very long driveway and ordered him to freeze. Ben had his back to the officers when they called out to him. As Ben turned around in surprise his paint ball rife pointed at the officers, and they shot him dead.

Discuss the criminal liability of Wayne for homicide crimes. The state is a common law jurisdiction and its homicide statute and one other relevant statute follows.

Murder in the first degree is the killing of a human being committed:

(a) intentionally and with premeditation and deliberation or

(b) in the commission of, attempt to commit, or flight from kidnapping, robbery, rape, burglary, arson or any inherently dangerous felony.

Murder in the second degree is the killing of a human being intentionally or recklessly under circumstances evincing a depraved indifference to human life.

Voluntary Manslaughter is the intentional killing of a human being in the heat of passion.

Involuntary Manslaughter is the reckless killing of a human being.

Negligent Homicide is the killing of a human being through gross negligence or through the commission of an unlawful act.

False Reporting of an Emergency: It is a misdemeanor for an individual to report to any government agency that an emergency exists involving an act of violence, knowing that the report is false. It is a felony do so if death or serious bodily injury results.

Practice Problem 14.4: Murderous Beef Redux

Assume that the owner of the infected cattle in the Murderous Beef problem described in the last chapter has been charged with felony murder in a common law jurisdiction under the Kansas felony murder statute reproduced at the beginning of this chapter (p. 433). Discuss his liability.

CHAPTER 15

CAUSATION

■ ■ ■

While most crimes only require a guilty hand moved by a guilty mind, some crimes require results. These crimes require a result *caused* by the conduct defined by the crime, and, therefore, result crimes are governed by principles of causation.

A. OVERVIEW OF THE ELEMENTS

Two types of causation are required: actual causation, also known as cause-in-fact, and proximate causation, sometimes referred to as legal causation. Never forget that you need both for criminal liability.

Most people think of cause-in-fact as "but for" causation: "but for" the act the result would not have occurred. If you shoot at my head with the intent to kill and the bullet misses, yet at that moment I die from an unrelated brain aneurysm, you cannot be guilty of murder. You did not "actually" cause my death. I would have been dead anyway, even if you hadn't fired your shot. If your bullet strikes me and kills me, however, then we have an easy case of actual causation because but for your shot I would not have died.

The central principle of proximate cause is foreseeability, and we limit criminal liability to foreseeable harms. For example, if a hunter shot me after I parachuted on top of him as he was firing at a flock of ducks, then he would most likely not be found to have proximately caused my death because we don't foresee people falling out of the sky on top of us. Moreover, the distinction between mental states and causation deserves mention here. While you might say that the duck hunter was not reckless or grossly negligent, his mental state is irrelevant. If the result was not proximately caused, then it does not matter what mental state the defendant had with respect to his conduct.

What complicates both types of causation is the reality that all results have multiple causes. How do we select the causes that count for the purposes of criminal liability? Actual causation *rules out* possible causes. If you were not a but for cause, then you can't be a cause. The problem is trickier for proximate causation because proximate causation "does more work," as the philosophers like to say. Proximate causation rules out causes whose results were not foreseeable.

B. ACTUAL CAUSATION

Actual causation seems simpler than it is. Any result has many causes. Let's go back to the shooting example. What if you only found me in my office to shoot me because one of my colleagues had delayed my departure from work that day by chatting with me about a particularly exciting college basketball game that had been played the night before. If I had not been chatting with him then I would not have been in my office when you came looking for me. But for my colleague's actions I would still be alive. So, you could say that my colleague is a but for cause of my death. For that matter though, so are the people who made your gun and bullets. You could even say that the basketball players who played the exciting game the night before actually caused my death. For that matter, if my mother had never given birth to me, then I could not have ever been killed!

Ultimately, actual causation relies on our sense of the ordinary. No person would say that my mother caused my death by giving birth to me because that is what mothers do. Likewise, there is nothing out of the ordinary about chatting with a colleague or playing in an exciting basketball game. People who see guns and bullets as inherently evil might be tempted to look there for the cause of my death, but unless there was something unusual about the gun, the bullets, or the way in which they were distributed or sold, it would be hard to argue that the manufacture caused my death. Scholars refer to these ordinary events that form part of the background of daily life as "conditions," not causes. Walking up to someone and shooting them, however, is anything but ordinary, so your doing so will be an actual cause of my death.

1. MULTIPLE ACTUAL CAUSES AND SUBSTANTIAL FACTORS

Often, criminal results have multiple concurrent causes. For example, a group of people might attack someone, resulting in the victim's death. The people are almost always working together. As you will see when you learn the doctrine of complicity, any one accomplice can be held liable for the acts of another. If two of you, working together, attack me with baseball bats and cause my death, the criminal law does not have to worry whether either or both of you actually caused my death. Under complicity, each of you is responsible for the acts of the other, and together you killed me. So complicity liability fills in any gaps in causation that occur when more than one person causes the bad result.

The tricky questions arise (usually in treatises and law review articles, not in actual cases) when you have multiple, independent causes of the result. Sometimes these are successive acts where one accelerates the required results, and other times they are concurrent acts where each contributes to it. Actual court decisions confronting such issues are so rare that the law is a little sketch here. The important general principal to keep firmly in mind, however, is that **an actual cause does not have to be an exclusive cause but can be a substantial factor**.

1. *Accelerating Causes.* An accelerating cause is an actual cause. Imagine someone stabs me and leaves me along the road dying. Before I actually die a "Bad Samaritan" finds me in the road and shoots me. The Bad Samaritan actually caused my death by accelerating it. (Courts have gone both ways on whether the stabber can be found to have caused my death under these circumstances, with some courts finding that the shooting was an "obstructing cause" that stopped the initial cause from being realized.)

2. *Concurrent Sufficient Causes.* What if two people acting independently stab and shoot me at the same time, with either wound being enough to kill me. One could say that neither was a but for cause of my death since the other concurrent cause would have killed me anyway. In such cases, courts often fudge by simply saying that each act was a "substantial factor" in bringing about my death. (I say "fudge" because these courts usually don't define substantial factor or explain the principle behind the test clearly.)

3. *Concurrent Insufficient Causes.* What if neither wound would have been fatal in and of itself, but both wounds cumulatively resulted in my death? Paradoxically, this is an easier case for the law because now each act clearly satisfies the but for test. But for the stabbing, I would not have died. But for the shooting I would not have die. Everyone is happy! (Except for me.)

2. THE YEAR AND A DAY RULE

At common law, one could not be guilty of a homicide crime unless the victim died within a year and a day of the homicidal act. The period of time has been increased or the rule has been abolished altogether in a majority of jurisdictions.

Case in Context

In the following case the court took a very strict approach to the question of actual causation.

REGINA V. MARTIN DYOS

Central Criminal Court
Crim. L. Rev. 660–62 (1979)

CANTLEY, J. A Friday night dance at a Community Center was attended by a group of seven youths. The deceased, RM, was one of these as was also SK who at one stage danced near two girls—"he was cocky and showing off."

The boyfriend, BT, of one of the girls was incensed by this; when the seven left shortly before the end of the dance he encouraged the four friends with him to follow to "give a hand."

At the exit to the dance hall there was some general abuse and threats directed at SK.

The seven went towards the railway station to find a taxi; the five followed at a distance continuing their abuse and threats. When the seven crossed the road the five followed, and were by now closing up.

One of the five, MD, and possibly others, were seen to pick up stones/bricks and throw them. One stone thrown by MD hit PS, one of the seven, on the back of the head. Momentarily stunned, he turned, took off his jacket, challenged the five, advanced, and hit BT.

This immediately turned into a scuffle or fight involving for certain PS, SK, MB, and RM from the seven and BT, IS, and KW of the five. The fight lasted no more than a minute or so as RM was spotted lying in the road by his twin brother GM, bleeding from severe head injuries— whereupon the five fled and emergency services was called.

One of RM's Injuries, that to his right forehead, was caused by a brick held by MD. What had happened, in MD's own words to the police was this:

Matey threw a punch at me and I ran away. . . . I was hit in back by brick as I was going to jump on wall. . . . I picked up a brick and started towards one I thought had chucked brick at me. . . . [H]e started to run and I went to throw it but I was running and I hit him before I could let it go. I misjudged the distance.

RM survived nine days before succumbing to his injuries; in the meantime all involved were questioned. No evidence was offered against any of the seven; all of the five were indicted with unlawful assembly to which they pleaded guilty, affray which they all denied, MD alone being charged with murder and grievous bodily harm . . . to RM.

At the post mortem it was found that apart from a very few slight marks on the right hand side of the body, legs, and arms, all the injuries were confined to the head, of which the two principal were the one caused by MD to the right forehead and one behind the right ear for which there was no evidence as to the cause.

As to the cause of death the following is a summary of the pathologist's conclusions:

1. The cause of death was cerebnral contusion due to a fractured skull.

2. RM received two more separate blows. There was no evidence as to whether they were caused by the same or different objects, be it metal, wood, masonry, and/or a shod foot.

3. Both wounds were potentially fatal

4. No distinction was made as to the seriousness of either wound.

5. Either wound would "very probably" cause death.

6. There was no certain way of telling which injury came first.

7. There was a "reasonable and sensible" possibility that the deceased might have recovered from the first injury, whichever that was.

In addition to the medical evidence, there was no evidence as to how the second injury was caused, apart from speculation at the time of RM hitting one of the many passing vehicles or of his being swung around and thrown into traffic. Likewise apart from traces of blood on at least one of the five's shoes (which probably came from kicking SK in the mouth) there was no evidence of blood being found on any blunt object, shoe, brick or kerb. Nor were there any traces of material such as the brick dust in the wounds.

The only evidence against MD was that he struck the one blow to the right forehead; and there was no evidence of joint enterprise as to either wound.

On the count of murder the trial judge upheld the defence submission at the close of the prosecution that it would be unsafe to leave the count to the jury.

These submissions were as follows:

The Crown had failed to prove that MD was responsible for the cause of death because,

(a) the pathologist's evidence was that it was a reasonable and sensible possibility that the injury behind the ear caused the death, and . . . there was no evidence that MD was responsible for it,

(b) and conversely there was no evidence that the injury which MD (admitted) having caused, was in fact beyond a reasonable doubt the cause of death. MD could only be guilty if death was a natural and probable consequence of his act.

Even if the forehead injury caused by MD was the first injury there was a reasonable and sensible possibility of recovery.

MD's act cannot be held to be the cause of death if that event would or could have occurred without it.

Before the count of murder could go to the jury the Crown had to exclude the possibility . . . that death was . . . caused by another injury.

It was conceded by the defence that if as a result of what MD did the Crown could show, e.g., that RM was struck by a passing car, then MD's act would have been a substantial cause of death. There was no evidence of this (and in fact the Crown sought to exclude this possibility).

If the ear injury was caused by a brick and that was the cause of death (and the pathologist said both were reasonable possibilities) there was no evidence that MD (or anyone else) did it.

Therefore, in sum:

1. there was another injury

2. that injury may reasonably have been the cause of death

3. that injury cannot be shewn not to have been the cause of death. . . .

After the judge's ruling MD changed his plea to guilty on Count 1 (affray) and Count 4 (grievous bodily harm). . . .

DISCUSSION QUESTIONS

1. Why can't the court find cause in fact if either injury would "very probably cause death?"

2. Would it have made a difference if the coroner had said that the cumulative effect of both blow's caused death?

3. Is it just that potentially no one might be held responsible for the victim's death?

C. PROXIMATE CAUSE

They say that variety is the spice of life. Well, variety is the source of the more difficult issues of proximate cause in the criminal law. Specifically, variety in how a result occurs creates the need for principles that deal with 1) results that involve unintended or unexpected victims; and 2) results that occur in unintended or unexpected ways.

Harms often result in unintended or unexpected ways due to causes that "intervene" between the defendant's actions and the required result. Whether such intervening causes "break the chain" of causation between the defendant's act and the required result generally depends on the foreseeability of the intervening cause. The causal chain between the defendant and the criminal result is less likely to be broken if the intervening cause was a response to—and not independent of—something the defendant did.

1. UNEXPECTED VICTIMS AND TRANSFERRED INTENT

Harming the wrong person does not ordinarily break the chain of causation between the defendant and the result. When the result requires intent, this principle is called transferred intent. Imagine I try to shoot a student in my class who is never prepared, but the unprepared student ducks, and the bullet kills the unfortunate student sitting behind him. The law transfers my intent to kill from the intended to the actual victim for the purposes of causation and intent.

2. INTERVENING CAUSES

Sometimes, the intended or expected victim of a person's criminal conduct suffers harm in an unexpected way. Figuring out whether to hold the actor causally responsible in such cases gets a little complicated. Let's introduce the legal terms used, and then we will illustrate how the rules work.

1. Intervening Cause. The force or event that causes the harm to occur in the unexpected way.

2. Chain of Causation. A metaphorical term that refers to a sequence of causally related actions or events. When we say that the chain of causation is broken, we mean that we no longer consider the defendant's earlier acts to be responsible for the results after the break.

3. Dependent Intervening Cause. An intervening cause that was a response to something that the defendant did. (Usually does not break the chain of causation.)

4. Independent Intervening Cause. An intervening cause that operated completely independently of the defendant's actions. (Often breaks the chain of causation.)

5. Superseding Cause. An intervening cause that is not only unexpected but also sufficiently unforeseeable that the law finds the chain of causation between the defendant's act and the criminal result to be broken.

Consider the following example. While you are robbing a bank, you fire a warning shot in the air (just to show everyone that you mean business), but the bullet ricochets off the ceiling and kills a bank teller. Were your actions the proximate cause of the bank teller's death? Yes, this would be a straightforward case of proximate causation, which requires foreseeability. It was reasonably foreseeable that shooting into an enclosed room could cause the death of someone in that room.

3. DEPENDENT INTERVENING CAUSES

What if the bullet instead hit the bank teller's arm, and he died in surgery when his doctor nicked an artery trying to remove it? Although you still have actual/but for causation, do you also have proximate causation? Or, has the intervening cause of the surgical error broken the chain of causation between the shot you fired and the resulting death?

Probably not. The surgical error is a dependent intervening cause because the surgery itself was a reaction or response to your wrongful act of firing the shot. **Generally, a responsive/dependent intervening cause will only break the chain of causation if it is not just unforeseeable but highly unusual.** Surgical errors are neither unforeseeable nor highly unusual. Even medical negligence is considered foreseeable. For the surgical error to become a superseding intervening cause that would break the chain of causation, it would need to be gross negligence. If the bullet only nicked the teller's arm, and then a drunk surgeon picked up the wrong instrument, sliced through the arm's major artery, and failed to stop the bleeding in time to prevent death, that would be not only unforeseeable but also highly unusual. The surgeon's superseding actions would relieve you of liability for the teller's death by breaking the chain of causation.

Responsive/dependent intervening causes also include actions by the victim. Now imagine that the bank teller runs screaming out of the bank after getting nicked in the arm and gets run over by a car when he dashes across the street. Once again, the negligence of the teller in not looking both ways would not break the chain of causation because it is foreseeable that victims might panic and act unreasonably under such circumstances. **Negligent acts by the victim that respond to the defendant's acts do not break the chain of causation.** To relieve the defendant of causal responsibility the victim's actions must be bizarre. (e.g. The teller decides to kill himself when he sees you pull out the gun.)

4. PRE-EXISTING WEAKNESS OF THE VICTIM

What if the bullet kills the bank teller because he has a rare clotting disorder that makes it unusually easy for him to bleed to death? A victim's pre-existing weakness or particular vulnerability does not break the chain of causation between the defendant's act and the resulting harm. In criminal law, a wrongful actor "takes the victim as he finds him." Torts has a catchy but gruesome metaphor that makes this idea easy to remember. The "eggshell plaintiff" is someone whose skull is as thin as an eggshell, and knocking down such a person might kill him. So, remember this as the "eggshell victim" rule in criminal law.

Before you protest against murder liability for knocking someone down, remember that the eggshell victim rule only establishes causation, not mental state. Even if you deliberately knocked the person down, it would impossible to prove an intent to kill or a reckless or criminally negligent state of mind with respect to the risk of death. You might be guilty of misdemeanor manslaughter, however, since all that is required is guilt of a misdemeanor (or unlawful act) that causes death. Just your bad luck to have shoved someone with an eggshell skull!

5. INDEPENDENT (OR COINCIDENTAL) INTERVENING CAUSES

Let's go back to the bank. Now imagine that the bullet only nicked the arm of the teller, but that while he was in the waiting area of the emergency room, an enraged patient goes on a shooting rampage, killing everyone. (That is one way to get to the front of the line.) **Forces that do not respond to or depend on the defendant's acts usually break the chain of causation unless they are foreseeable**. The enraged patient is not responding to what you did in the bank. His actions do not depend on what you did in the bank. While it is true that the bank teller would not be in the emergency room but for being shot by you, this establishes only cause-in-fact. So, you would not be criminally liable for the death of the teller because the enraged patient is a superseding intervening cause.

Foreseeable independent intervening causes, on the other hand, are rare but not unheard of. Imagine now that you take the teller hostage, and leave him wandering the road on the outskirts of town near a dangerous neighborhood in the middle of the night. He is then robbed and killed by someone who sees him wandering down the street. On these facts, the force that killed him was truly independent but not unforeseeable, and you could be found to have caused his death for the purposes of homicidal liability.

6. PULLING THE PLUG ON LIFE SUPPORT

Not infrequently, victims of homicidal acts who have lapsed into coma's or other vegetative states are taken off life support by doctors acting in accordance with established principles and procedures. In such cases, defendants often argue that the doctor caused the death, not the defendant. Usually, such arguments fail because courts find that the termination of life support in such a state is a foreseeable consequence of the injuries inflicted.

Case in Context

In the following case the court wrestles with the difference between causation in criminal and tort law.

COMMONWEALTH V. ROOT
Supreme Court of Pennsylvania
170 A.2d 310 (1961)

JONES, C.T. The appellant was found guilty of involuntary manslaughter for the death of his competitor in the course of an automobile race between them on a highway. The trial court overruled the defendant's demurrer to the Commonwealth's evidence and, after verdict, denied his motion in arrest of judgment. On appeal from the judgment of sentence entered on the jury's verdict, the Superior Court affirmed. We granted allocatur because of the important question present as to whether the defendant's unlawful and reckless conduct was a sufficiently direct cause of the death to warrant his being charged with criminal homicide.

The testimony, which is uncontradicted in material part, discloses that, on the night of the fatal accident, the defendant accepted the deceased's challenge to engage in an automobile race; that the racing took place on a rural 3-lane highway; that the night was clear and dry, and traffic light; that the speed limit on the highway was 50 miles per hour; that, immediately prior to the accident, the two automobiles were being operated at varying speeds of from 70 to 90 miles per hour; that the accident occurred in a no-passing zone on the approach to a bridge where the highway narrowed to two directionally-opposite lanes; that, at the time of the accident, the defendant was in the lead and was proceeding in his right-hand lane of travel; that the deceased, in an attempt to pass the defendant's automobile, when a truck was closely approaching from the opposite direction, swerved his car to the left, crossed the highway's white dividing line and drove his automobile on the wrong side of the highway head-on into the oncoming truck with resultant fatal effect to himself.

This evidence would of course amply support a conviction of the defendant for speeding, reckless driving and, perhaps, other violations of The Vehicle Code. . . . In any event, unlawful or reckless conduct is only one ingredient of the crime of involuntary manslaughter. Another essential and distinctly separate element of the crime is that the unlawful or reckless conduct charged to the defendant was the *direct* cause of the death in issue. The first ingredient is obviously present in this case but, just as plainly, the second is not.

While precedent is to be found for application of the tort law concept of "proximate cause" in fixing responsibility for criminal homicide, the want of any rational basis for its use in determining criminal liability can no longer be properly disregarded. When proximate cause was first borrowed from the field of tort law and applied to homicide prosecutions in Pennsylvania, the concept connoted a much more direct causal relation in producing the alleged culpable result than it does today. Proximate cause, as an essential element of a tort founded in negligence, has undergone in recent times, and is still undergoing, a marked extension. More specifically, this area of civil law has been progressively liberalized in favor of claims for damages for personal injuries to which careless conduct of others can in some way be associated. To persist in applying the tort liability concept of proximate cause to prosecutions for criminal homicide after the marked expansion of *civil* liability of defendants in tort actions for negligence would be to extend possible *criminal* liability to persons chargeable with unlawful or reckless conduct in circumstances not generally considered to present the likelihood of a resultant death.

In this very case the Superior Court mistakenly opined that "The concept of proximate cause as applied in tort cases is applicable to similar problems of causation in criminal cases. Commonwealth v. Almeida." It is indeed strange that the *Almeida* case should have been cited as authority for the above quoted statement; the rationale of the *Almeida* case was flatly rejected by this Court in *Commonwealth v. Redline*, where we held that the tort liability concept of proximate cause is not a proper criterion of causation in a criminal homicide case. True enough, *Commonwealth v. Redline* was a murder case, but the distinction between murder and involuntary manslaughter does not rest upon a differentiation in causation; it lies in the state of mind of the offender. If one kills with malice aforethought, he is chargeable with murder; and if death, though unintentional, results directly from his unlawful or reckless conduct, he is chargeable with involuntary manslaughter. In either event, the accused is not guilty unless his conduct was a cause of death sufficiently direct as to meet the requirements of the *criminal*, and not the *tort*, law.

The instant case is one of first impression in this State; and our research has not disclosed a single instance where a district attorney has ever before attempted to prosecute for involuntary manslaughter on facts similar to those established by the record now before us. The closest case, factually, would seem to be *Commonwealth v. Levin*, which affirmed the defendant's conviction of involuntary manslaughter. In the *Levin* case two cars were racing on the streets of Philadelphia at speeds estimated at from 85 to 95 miles per hour. The defendant's car, in the left-hand lane, was racing alongside of the car in which the deceased was a passenger when the defendant turned his automobile sharply to the right in front of the other car, thereby causing the driver of the latter car to lose control and smash into a tree, the passenger being thrown to the road and killed as a result of the impact. It is readily apparent that the elements of causation in the *Levin* case were fundamentally different from those in the present case. Levin's act of cutting his automobile sharply in front of the car in which the deceased was riding directly forced that car off of the road and into the tree. The defendant's reckless and unlawful maneuver was the direct cause of the crucial fatality. In the instant case, the defendant's conduct was not even remotely comparable. Here, the action of the deceased driver in recklessly and suicidally swerving his car to the left lane of a 2-lane highway into the path of an oncoming truck was not forced upon him by any act of the defendant; it was done by the deceased and by him alone, who thus directly brought about his own demise. The *Levin* case was properly decided but it cannot, by any ratiocination, be utilized to justify a conviction in the present case.

Legal theory which makes guilt or innocence of criminal homicide depend upon such accidental and fortuitous circumstances as are now embraced by modern tort law's encompassing concept of proximate cause is too harsh to be just. . .

Even if the tort liability concept of proximate cause were to be deemed applicable, the defendant's conviction of involuntary manslaughter in the instant case could not be sustained under the evidence. The operative effect of a supervening cause would have to be taken into consideration: *Commonwealth v. Redline*, supra, at p. 505. But, the trial judge refused the defendant's point for charge to such effect and erroneously instructed the jury that "negligence or want of care on the part of [the deceased] is no defense to the criminal responsibility of the defendant . . . ."

The Superior Court, in affirming the defendant's conviction in this case, approved the charge above mentioned, despite a number of decisions in involuntary manslaughter cases holding that the conduct of the deceased victim must be considered in order to determine whether the defendant's reckless acts were the proximate (i.e., sufficiently direct) cause of his death. The Superior Court dispensed with this decisional authority by expressly overruling [past decisions] . . . on the ground that there can be more than one proximate cause of death. The point is wholly irrelevant. Of course there can be more than one proximate cause of death just as there can also be more than one *direct* cause of death. For example, in the so-called "shield" cases where a felon interposes the person of an innocent victim between himself and a pursuing officer, if the officer should fire his gun at the felon to prevent his escape and fatally wound the person used as a shield, the different acts of the policeman and the felon would each be a direct cause of the victim's death.

If the tort liability concept of proximate cause were to be applied in a criminal homicide prosecution, then the conduct of the person whose death is the basis of the indictment would have to be considered, not to prove that it was merely an *additional* proximate cause of the death, but to determine, under fundamental and long recognized law applicable to proximate cause, whether the subsequent wrongful act *superseded* the original conduct chargeable to the defendant. If it did in fact supervene, then the original act is so insulated from the ensuing death as not to be its proximate cause.

Under the uncontradicted evidence in this case, the conduct of the defendant was not the proximate cause of the decedent's death as a matter of law. In *Kline v. Moyer and Albert*, the rule is stated as follows: "Where a second actor has become aware of the existence of a potential danger created by the negligence of an original tort-feasor, and thereafter, by an independent act of negligence, brings about an accident, the first tort-feasor is relieved of liability, because the condition created by him was merely a circumstance of the accident and not its proximate cause."

In the case last above cited, while Angretti was driving his truck eastward along a highway, a bus, traveling in the same direction in front of him, stopped to take on a passenger. Angretti swerved his truck to the left into the lane of oncoming traffic in an attempt to pass the bus but collided with a tractor-trailer driven by the plaintiff's decedent, who was killed as a result of the collision. In affirming the entry of judgment n.o.v. in favor of the defendant bus company, we held that any negligence on the part of the bus driver, in suddenly bringing his bus to a halt in order to pick up a passenger, was not a proximate cause of the death of the plaintiff's decedent since the accident "was due entirely to the intervening and superseding negligence of Angretti in allowing his truck to pass over into the pathway of the westbound tractor-trailer . . . ."

In the case now before us, the deceased was aware of the dangerous condition created by the defendant's reckless conduct in driving his automobile at an excessive rate of speed along the highway but, despite such knowledge, he recklessly chose to swerve his car to the left and into the path of an oncoming truck, thereby bringing about the head-on collision which caused his own death.

To summarize, the tort liability concept of proximate cause has no proper place in prosecutions for criminal homicide and more direct causal connection is required for conviction: *Commonwealth v. Redline*, supra, at pp. 504–505. In the instant case, the defendant's reckless conduct was not a sufficiently direct cause of the competing driver's death to make him criminally liable therefor.

The judgment of sentence is reversed and the defendant's motion in arrest of judgment granted.

EAGEN, J., dissenting.

The opinion of the learned Chief Justice admits, under the uncontradicted facts, that the defendant, at the time of the fatal accident involved, was engaged in an unlawful and reckless course of conduct. Racing an automobile at 90 miles per hour, trying to prevent another automobile going in the same direction from passing him, in a no-passing zone on a two-lane public highway, is certainly all of that. Admittedly also, there can be more than one direct cause of an unlawful death. To me, this is self-evident. But, says the majority opinion, the defendant's recklessness was not a direct cause of the death. With this, I cannot agree.

If the defendant did not engage in the unlawful race and so operate his automobile in such a reckless manner, this accident would never have occurred. He helped create the dangerous event. He was a vital part of it. The victim's acts were a natural reaction to the stimulus of the situation.

The race, the attempt to pass the other car and forge ahead, the reckless speed, all of these factors the defendant himself helped create. He was part and parcel of them. That the victim's response was normal under the circumstances, that his reaction should have been expected and was clearly foreseeable, is to me beyond argument. That the defendant's recklessness was a substantial factor is obvious. All of this, in my opinion, makes his unlawful conduct a direct cause of the resulting collision.

The cases cited in support of the majority opinion are not in point. For instance, in *Johnson v. Angretti*, this Court, in affirming the trial court, found that the bus driver *was not guilty of any negligence or violation of The Vehicle Code* in bringing the bus to a stop. The Court, as dicta, then went on to say, "Moreover it is clear that such alleged violation bore no causal relation whatever to the happening of the accident which was due entirely to the intervening and superseding negligence of Angretti in allowing his truck to pass over into the pathway of the westbound tractor-trailer instead of bringing his vehicle to a stop as Osterling [the driver of the truck directly behind the bus and in front of Angretti] had done and *as he admitted he could readily have done without colliding with the truck ahead of him.* The situation created by the stopping of the bus was merely a circumstance of the accident and not its proximate cause: (citing cases)." It is readily apparent that the instant case and the *Angretti* case are distinguishable in all the important factors. In the present case there was, (1) recklessness and a violation of The Vehicle Code; (2) a joint venture or common enterprise of racing; (3) no proof that Hall could have guided his car back into the right-hand lane behind Root after he became aware of the danger of the oncoming truck. . .

In the present case, there wasn't any evidence that Hall saw the oncoming truck when he pulled out to pass Root. This would have been suicide, against which there is a presumption. The act of passing was not an "extraordinary negligent" act, but rather a "normal response" to the act of "racing." Furthermore, as Hall pulled out to pass, Root "dropped off" his speed to 90 miles an hour. Such a move probably prevented Hall from getting back into the right-hand lane since he was alongside of Root at the time and to brake the car at that speed would have been fatal to both himself and Root. Moreover, the dangerous condition of which the deceased had to become aware of before the defendant was relieved of his direct causal connection with the ensuing accident, was not the fact that the defendant was driving at an excessive rate of speed along the highway. He knew that when the race began many miles and minutes earlier. *The dangerous condition necessary was an awareness of the oncoming truck and the fact that at the rate of speed Root was traveling he couldn't safely pass him.* This important fact was not shown and, therefore, was a question for the fact-finders and not a question that could be decided as a matter of law.

The majority opinion states, "Legal theory which makes guilt or innocence of criminal homicide depend upon such *accidental and fortuitous circumstances* as are now embraced by modern tort law's encompassing concept is . . . too harsh to be just." If the resulting death had been dependent upon "accidental and fortuitous circumstances" or, as the majority also say, "in circumstances not generally considered to present the likelihood of a resultant death," we would agree that the defendant is not criminally responsible. However, acts should be judged by their tendency under the known circumstances, not by the actual intent, which accompanies their performance. Every day of the year, we read that some teen-agers, or young adults, somewhere in this country, have been killed or have killed others, while racing their automobiles. Hair-raising, death-defying, lawbreaking rides, which encompass "racing" are the rule rather than the exception, and endanger not only the participants, but also every motorist and passenger on the road. To call such resulting accidents "accidental and fortuitous," or unlikely to result in death, is to ignore the cold and harsh reality of everyday occurrences. Root's actions were as direct a cause of Hall's death as those in the "shield" cases. Root's shield was his high speed and any approaching traffic in his quest to prevent Hall from passing, which he knew Hall would undertake to do, the first time he thought he had the least opportunity. . . .

But, says the majority opinion, these are principles of tort law and should not in these days be applied to the criminal law. But such has been the case since the time of Blackstone. These same principles have always been germane to both crimes and tort. They have been repeatedly so applied throughout the years and were employed in a criminal case in Pennsylvania as long as one hundred and seventeen years ago. . .

While the victim's foolhardiness in this case contributed to his own death, he was not the only one responsible and it is not he alone with whom we are concerned. It is the people of the Commonwealth who are harmed by the kind of conduct the defendant pursued. Their interests must be kept in mind.

DISCUSSION QUESTIONS

1. Do you think the death was foreseeable in this case?

2. Does it matter how you "frame" the risk? Can you come up with a broad framing and a narrow framing of the risk in this case? Does a narrow framing of the risk in a case where death has resulted usually benefit the prosecution or the defense?

3. Should causation requirements in criminal cases be stricter than those in tort cases?

Case in Context

The following case involves an unintended result from an intended crime.

STATE V. ECHOLS

Court of Criminal Appeals of Tennessee
919 S. W.2d 634 (1995)

SUMMERS, JUDGE.

The defendant Robert L. Echols was convicted by a jury of aggravated robbery, and the trial court entered judgment. On appeal, he claims that the evidence is insufficient to support his conviction because his conduct was not the cause of the victim's injury.

We affirm the judgment of the trial court.

Shortly after 6:00 a.m. on June 17, 1993, the victim unlocked her door and an outer wrought iron security door to take out the garbage. Meanwhile, the defendant who had "been up all night smoking drugs" was walking home. As he walked past the victim's house he saw her purse. While the victim was gathering the garbage, the defendant opened the door and grabbed the victim's purse. When the victim went outside to scream for help and look for the defendant, she fell. She was later admitted to the hospital where she was diagnosed with a fractured bone in her hip. The victim remained in the hospital for four days and later underwent three weeks of rehabilitation. She testified that she was in a "lot of pain."

One element of aggravated robbery is that the alleged victim suffer serious bodily injury. This offense requires a defendant to cause a certain result—serious bodily injury. The necessary causal relationship between the conduct and the result is that the defendant's conduct be both 1) the "but for" cause or "cause in fact" and 2) the "proximate" or "legal cause" of the result.

The defendant essentially contends that the evidence fails to establish that his conduct was the proximate cause of the victim's serious bodily injury. Rather, he appears to assert that the victim's own conduct was the cause of her injury. A defendant's conduct is the proximate cause of the natural and probable consequences of his conduct.

Where sufficiency of the evidence is challenged, the relevant question for an appellate court is whether, after viewing the evidence in the light most favorable to the prosecution, any rational trier of fact could have found the essential elements of the crime or crimes beyond a reasonable doubt. This standard applies to evidence of causation. The evidence amply supports a finding that the defendant's conduct was the proximate cause of the victim's injury. The victim's act of quickly exiting the house to scream for help and look for the defendant is a natural and probable response to the defendant's conduct. Her actions were normal and instinctive under the circumstances. That the victim's own conduct may also be a proximate cause of her injury is of no consequence to the defendant's situation. "[O]ne whose wrongdoing is a concurrent proximate cause of an injury may be criminally liable the same as if his wrongdoing were the sole proximate cause of the injury."

AFFIRMED.

DISCUSSION QUESTIONS

1.   How probable was it that stealing the purse would result in the broken hip?

2.   Do you agree with finding proximate cause in this case?

3.   What role does the fact that defendant was intentionally committing a crime play in your assessment of foreseeability?

D. MODEL PENAL CODE

Not surprisingly, the Model Penal Code simplifies causation by relying on its defined mental states. Only actual causation is required, and actual causation is defined as but for causation. The MPC also substitutes a simpler standard for the common law's rules of proximate causation. Section 2.03 provides that no culpable mental state exists if the injury or harm was "too remote or accidental in its occurrence to have a [just] bearing on the actor's liability or on the gravity of his offense," For good and for bad, this language frees up the finder of fact to do what they think is fair when more complicated issues of causation arise.

§ 2.03. Causal Relationship Between Conduct and Result; Divergence Between Result Designed of Contemplated and Actual Result or Between Probable and Actual Result.

1)   Conduct is the cause of a result when:

   a.   it is an antecedent but for which the result in question would not have occurred; and

   b.   the relationship between the conduct and result satisfies any additional causal requirements imposed by the Code or by the law defining the offense.

2)   When purposely or knowingly causing a particular result is an element of an offense, the element is not established if the actual result is not within the purpose or the contemplation of the actor unless:

   a.   the actual result differs from that designed or contemplated, as the case may be, only in the respect that a different property is injured or affected or that the injury or harm designed or contemplated would have been more serious or more extensive than that caused; or

    b.   the actual result involves the same kind of injury or harm as that designed or contemplated and is not too remote or accidental in its occurrence to have a [just] bearing on the actor's liability or on the gravity of his offense.

3)   When recklessly or negligently causing a particular result is an element of an offense, the element is not established if the actual result is not within the risk of which the actor is aware or, in the case of negligence, of which he should be aware unless:

    a.   the actual result differs from the probable result only in the respect that a different property is injured or affected or that the probable injury or harm would have been more serious or more extensive than that caused; or

    b.   the actual result involves the same kind of injury or harm as the probable result and is not too remote or accidental in its occurrence to have a [just] bearing on the actor's liability or on the gravity of his offense.

4)   When causing a particular result is a material element of an offense for which absolute liability is imposed by law, the element is not established unless the actual result is a probable consequence of the actor's conduct.

Exam Tip: Look for the Strange

The good news is that difficult causation issues are hard to miss in an exam fact pattern. Causal chains usually jump out because they are so unusual. Instead of simply dying from the gunshot wound, the victim staggers to a window and jumps out of it, is run over by a speeding motorist, or is hit by a meteorite . . . you get the idea. When you see a result crime such as homicide and a crazy story about one thing leading to another, remember to apply the rules of proximate causation. Alternately, when you see multiple actors and multiple causes hammering the same poor victim ("the really bad day scenario" where you are being shot, stabbed, and bit by a rabid dog all at once), analyze cause-in-fact issues. Finally, always remember to keep your eye out for complicity theories that simplify many potentially difficult causation issues. If the actors are working together as accomplices, then each can be held criminally responsible for harms caused by the group.

E. SPECIAL FOCUS: ASSISTED SUICIDE

Assisted suicide raises important and vexing issues of causation.

PEOPLE V. KEVORKIAN
Supreme Court of Michigan
527 N.W. 2d 714 (1994)

Before ... [Michigan's Assisted Suicide] statute was enacted, defendant [Dr. Jack] Kevorkian allegedly assisted in the deaths of Sherry Miller and Marjorie Wantz on October 23, 1991 .... Each woman was said to be suffering from a condition that caused her great pain or was severely disabling. Each separately had sought defendant Kevorkian's assistance in ending her life. The women and several friends and relatives met the defendant at a cabin in Oakland County on October 23, 1991.

According to the testimony presented at the defendant's preliminary examination, the plan was to use his "suicide machine." The device consisted of a board to which one's arm is strapped to prevent movement, a needle to be inserted into a blood vessel and attached to IV tubing, and containers of various chemicals that are to be released through the needle into the bloodstream. Strings are tied to two of the fingers of the person who intends to die. The strings are attached to clips on the IV tubing that control the flow of the chemicals. As explained by one witness, the person raises that hand, releasing a ... fast-acting barbiturate.... "When the person falls asleep, the hand drops, pulling the other string, which releases another clip and allows potassium chloride to flow into the body in concentrations sufficient to cause death."

The defendant tried several times, without success, to insert the suicide-machine needle into Ms. Miller's arm and hand. He then left the cabin, returning several hours later with a cylinder of carbon monoxide gas and a mask apparatus. He attached a screw driver to the cylinder, and showed Ms. Miller how to use the tool as a lever to open the gas valve.

The defendant then turned his attention to Ms. Wantz. He was successful in inserting the suicide-machine needle into her arm. The defendant explained to Ms. Wantz how to activate the device so as to allow the drugs to enter her bloodstream. The device was activated, and Ms. Wantz died.

The defendant then placed the mask apparatus on Ms. Miller. The only witness at the preliminary examination who was present at the time said that Ms. Miller opened the gas valve by pulling on the screwdriver. The cause of her death was determined to be carbon-monoxide poisoning.

The defendant was indicted on two counts of open murder. He was bound over for trial following a preliminary examination. However, in circuit court, the defendant moved to quash the information and dismiss the charges, and the court granted the motion.

A divided Court of Appeals reversed. . . . The Court of Appeals majority relied principally on *People v. Roberts*, 178 N.W. 690 (1920).

In *Roberts*, the defendant's wife was suffering from advanced multiple sclerosis and in great pain. She previously had attempted suicide and, according to the defendant's statements at the plea proceeding, requested that he provide her with poison. He agreed, and placed a glass of poison within her reach. She drank the mixture and died. The defendant was charged with murder. He pleaded guilty, and the trial court determined the crime to be murder in the first degree.

The defendant appealed [unsuccessfully] . . . [T]he *Roberts* Court concluded: We are of the opinion that when defendant mixed the paris green with water and placed it within reach of his wife to enable her to put an end to her suffering by putting an end to her life, he was guilty of murder by means of poison within the meaning of the statute, even though she requested him to do so. By this act, he deliberately placed within her reach the means of taking her own life, which she could have obtained in no other way by reason of her helpless condition. [178 N.W. 690.] . . .

We must determine . . . whether *Roberts* remains viable. . . Under the common-law definition, "[m]urder is where a person of sound memory and discretion unlawfully kills any reasonable creature in being, in peace of the state, with malice prepense or aforethought, either express or implied." Implicit in this definition is a finding that the defendant performed an act that caused the death of another. To convict a defendant of criminal homicide, it must be proven that death occurred as a direct and natural result of the defendant's act. . .

Early decisions indicate that a murder conviction may be based on merely providing the means by which another commits suicide. However, few jurisdictions, if any, have retained the early common-law view that assisting in a suicide is murder. The modern statutory scheme in the majority of states treats assisted suicide as a separate crime, with penalties less onerous than those for murder.

Recent decisions draw a distinction between active participation in a suicide and involvement in the events leading up to the suicide, such as providing the means. Frequently, these cases arise in the context of a claim by the defendant that the prosecution should have been brought under an assisted suicide statute. The courts generally have held that a person may be prosecuted for murder if the person's acts went beyond the conduct that the assisted suicide statute was intended to cover.

For example, in *People v. Cleaves,* 229 Cal. App. 3d 367, 280 Cal. Rptr. 146 (1991), the defendant was charged with first-degree murder in the strangulation death of another man. [The decedent in *Cleaves* was suffering from AIDS and wanted the defendant's assistance in strangling himself.] The trial court had refused a defense request to instruct the jury on the statutory offense of aiding and abetting a suicide, and the jury convicted him of second-degree murder.

. . . In holding that the trial judge properly refused to instruct the jury under the assisted suicide stature, the appeals court said:

[The stature] provides: "Every person who deliberately aids, or advises, or encourages another to commit suicide, is guilty of a felony." As explained by our Supreme Court, the "key to distinguishing between the crimes of murder and of assisting suicide is the active or passive role of the defendant in the suicide. If the defendant merely furnishes the means, he is guilty of aiding a suicide; if he actively participates in the death of the suicide victim, he is guilty of murder." [*In re* Joseph G, 34 Cal. 3d 429, 236 (1983).] The statue providing for a crime less than murder " 'Does not contemplate active participation by one in the overt act directly causing death. It contemplates some participation in the events leading up to the commission of the final overt act, such as furnishing the means for bringing about death, the gun the knife, the poison, or providing the water, for the use of the person who himself commits the act of self-murder. But where a person actually performs, or actively assists in performing, the overt act resulting in death, such as shooting or stabbing the victim, administering the poison, or holding one underwater until death takes place by drowning, his act constitutes murder, and it is wholly immaterial whether this act is committed pursuant to an agreement with the victim . . .' " [quoting *People v. Matlock*, 51 Cal. 2d 682, 694 (1959).]

In the years since 1920, when *Roberts* was decided, interpretation of causation in criminal cases has evolved in Michigan to require closer nexus between an act and a death than was required in *Roberts*. . .

In the context of participation in a suicide, the distinction recognized in In re Joseph G constitute the view most consistent with the overwhelming trend of modern authority. There, the California Supreme Court explained that the conviction of a murder is proper if a defendant participates in the final overt act that causes death, such as firing a gun or pushing the plunger on a hypodermic needle. However, where a defendant is involved merely "in the events leading up to the commission of the final overt act, such as furnishing the means . . .," a conviction of assisted suicide is proper. *Id.*

. . . [T]his Court has modified the common law when it perceives a need to tailor culpability to fit the crime more precisely than is achieved through application of existing interpretations of the common law. . . For the reasons given, we perceive such a need here. Accordingly, we would overrule *Roberts* to the extent that it can be read to support the view that the common-law definition of murder encompasses the act of intentionally providing the means by which a person commits suicide. Only where there is probable cause to believe death was the direct and natural result of a defendant's act can the defendant be properly bound over on a charge of murder. Where a defendant merely is involved in the events leading up to the death, such as providing the means, the proper charge is assisting in a suicide.

. . . [W]e remand this matter to the circuit court for reconsideration of the defendant's motion to quash in light of the principles discussed in this opinion.

BOYLE, JUSTICE, dissenting in part.

I do not agree with the lead opinion's redefinition of the statutory offense of murder to exclude participation in the events leading up to death, including, without limitation, providing the means and all other acts save that of the final act precipitating death. A person who participates in the death of another may be charged with murder, irrespective of the consent of the deceased. . . The acts shown in the Oakland County case establish causation as a matter of law for purposes of bindover. Thus, the trial court erred in quashing the information, and the decision of the Court of Appeals should be affirmed.

Criminal homicide has been a statutory offense in Michigan since 1846. The crime is not defined by reference to its elements but by reference to the common law. . . There is no dispute that at the time these offenses were committed, the Legislature had shown no disposition to depart from the common-law definition of murder as including assisted suicide. The lead opinion today would alter the definition of murder by changing the causation requirement in the context of suicide to exclude from liability for criminal homicide those who intentionally participate in the events that directly cause death with the intention that death occur.

However, the intended results of the plaintiff's acts were the results actually obtained, and the acts were both the cause in fact and the proximate or foreseeable cause of the decedents' deaths. The lead opinion would thus redefine murder as it is defined in our statutes and has created a special causation standard, unknown in any other jurisdiction. . .

The fact that an active participant in the death of another risks jury determination that the circumstances are not so compelling as to benefit from their mercy-dispensing power tests the situation and the actions by the only repository of authority within the judicial reach. Whether death has been caused for good, bad, or mixed reasons, or whether the person is in fact presently incurable or suffering intolerable and unmanageable pain, and has a fixed and rational desire to die, are issues that should be addressed by a jury or the Legislature, not by this Court as a matter of law. . .

In a society that draws a line that dictates that it is better that many go free than that one innocent person should be convicted, something approaching the principles protecting against error that are extended to the criminally accused should be extended to the victims of those who are willing to participate in suicide and to cause death, as long as they do not pull the final trigger. . . To the extent that this Court reduces culpability for those who actively participate in acts that produce death, we do so at the risk of the most vulnerable members of our society—the elderly, the ill, the chronically depressed, those suffering from a panoply of stressful situations: adolescence, loss of employment, the death of a child or spouse, divorce, alcoholism, the abuse of other mind-altering substances, and the burden of social stigmatization.

DISCUSSION QUESTIONS

1.   How does the court define "active participation" in a suicide?

2.   Do you think assisting suicide should be treated as murder? If so, how broadly would you define it? If not, should assisted suicide be a crime at all?

3.   If a person makes a fully informed and voluntary decision to end their life does it make sense to say that someone else caused their death?

Practice Problem 15.0: Death by Text Message

A recent teen suicide has resulted in a manslaughter prosecution against the dead teen's girlfriend. Charlotte and Werner were both eighteen years old when they began dating in the fall of their senior year of high school. Both suffered from clinical depression. Charlotte had been briefly hospitalized over the summer for depression and persistent suicidal thoughts and was under the care of a clinical psychologist. Under the psychologist's care Charlotte had been doing very well when she began dating Werner. Despite the fact that they were romantically involved, however, they spent relatively little time together and in fact often only spoke to each other in person or by phone once a week. Instead, they conducted their relationship largely though text messages that were numerous, frequent and often very long.

Initially their relationship seemed to play a positive role in both of their lives. Charlotte encouraged Werner to talk to his parents about seeing a psychologist and getting treatment. Werner refused, and his depression persisted. When he began expressing suicidal thoughts to Charlotte she encouraged him to seek hospitalization. A representative text message from this phase follows. ("W" stands for Werner, "C" stands for Charlotte, and all of the text appearing in italics are text messages sent and received.)

W: No one is going to give me confidence, no one will give me strength, no one will give me perseverance, no one can make me feel smart, funny or cool. No one can help me but me but I don't believe in myself so I'm stuck.

C: You only believe no one will give you all that because you don't let yourself open up to the help people are trying to give you. You never really give yourself a chance to heal and get better. But the mental hospital would help you. I know you don't think it would but I'm telling you, if you give them a chance, they can save your life.

Charlotte and Werner texted back and forth along these lines for weeks. Charlotte's attitude toward Werner's depression eventually became somewhat ambivalent.

C: Part of me wants you to try something and fail just so you can get help.

W: It doesn't help. Trust me.

C: So what are you gonna do then? Keep being all talk and no action and everyday go thru saying how badly you wanna kill yourself? Or are you gonna try to get better?

W: I can't get better I already made my decision. If you were in my position honestly what would you do?

C: I would get help. That's just me though. When I have a serious problem like that, my first instinct is to get help because I know I can't do it on my own

W: Well it's too late I already gave up.

After another month of similar text exchanges Charlotte began to agree that Werner should commit suicide.

C: I think your parents know you're in a really bad place. I'm not saying they want you to do it but I honestly feel like they can accept it. They know there is nothing they can do. They've tried helping. Everyone's tried but there is a point that comes where there isn't anything anyone can do to save you, not even yourself. And you've hit that point and I think your parents know you've hit that point.

For two weeks Werner kept telling Charlotte that he was going to kill himself and then postponing his suicide. Charlotte then began pressing him to "get it over with."

C: You already made this decision and if you don't do it tonight you're gonna be thinking about it all the time and stuff all the rest of your life and be miserable. You're finally going to be happy in heaven. You can' think about it. You just have to do it. You said you were gonna do it. Like I don't get why you aren't.

W: I don't get it either. I don't know.

C: So I guess you aren't gonna do it then. All that for nothing. Im just confused. Like you were so ready and determined.

W: I am gonna eventually. I really don't know what I'm waiting for but I have everything lined up.

C: You kept pushing it off and you say you'll do it, but you never do. It's always gonna be that way if you don't take action. You're just making it harder on yourself by pushing it off. You just have to do it.

When Werner suggested killing himself by pumping carbon monoxide into his car Charlotte responded with the following advice.

C: Yeah, it will work. If you emit 3200 ppm of it for five or ten minutes you will die within a half hour. You lose consciousness with no pain. You just fall asleep and die. You can just take a hose and run that from the exhaust pipe to the rear window and seal it with duct tape.

Werner took Charlotte's advice and rigged the hose in the manner Charlotte suggested. When the time came to start the engine, however, Werner hesitated. He and Charlotte had the following exchange.

W: I don't know. I am sitting in the car, and everything is all set, but I'm freaking out again. I'm over thinking.

C: I thought you wanted to do this. This time is right and you're ready. You just need to do it, or I'm gonna get you help. You can't keep doing this everyday.

W: Okay. I'm gonna do it.

C: You promise?

W: I promise, babe. I have to now.

C: Like right now?

G: Yeah, I got this.

C: Yes, you do. I believe in you. Did you delete my messages?

G: Yes. But you're going to keep messaging me?

C: I will until you turn on the engine.

G: Ok, here I go.

C: Ok, you can do this.

G: I'm almost there.

Werner's dead body was subsequently found in his car with the engine running. An autopsy indicated that he died from carbon monoxide poisoning from the exhaust in the car. Charlotte was charged with involuntary manslaughter for her role in Werner's suicide in a common law jurisdiction that does not recognize a separate crime of assisted suicide. Analyze her liability for Werner's death.[1]

---

[1]   The texts in this case are taken from the court records of an actual case, but some of the surrounding facts have been changed.

CHAPTER 16

INCHOATE CRIMES OVERVIEW
AND SOLICITATION

■ ■ ■

A. OVERVIEW

Criminal law has always recognized liability for inchoate—incomplete—crimes as well. Something inchoate is something not fully completed or realized. The three inchoate crimes that first-year criminal law courses typically touch upon are solicitation, conspiracy, and attempt.

- Solicitation is the crime of seriously asking someone to commit a crime.

- Conspiracy is the crime of agreeing to commit a crime or to do something illegal.

- Attempt is beginning to commit a crime.

While each of these crimes deserve their own special consideration, it is helpful to understand a few points before we delve into the details. First of all, we don't want to prosecute people for "thinking bad thoughts." If I admit to you that I am seriously thinking of stealing a candy bar, I am not admitting to any inchoate crime. We don't prosecute thought crimes for a number of reasons. For instance, people who think bad thoughts often don't act on them, and so they are neither dangerous nor blameworthy enough to punish. Second, it would be particularly disturbing to allow the government to punish people based on their thoughts alone. Finally, we believe that we are entitled to our "mental freedom" to think in whichever ways we prefer.

Therefore, defining inchoate offenses requires a balancing act. On the one hand, if we require too much conduct to establish guilt, then we lose an opportunity to prevent crime by prosecuting potentially dangerous conduct and punishing people who are sufficiently blameworthy. On the other hand, if we require too little to establish guilt, then we risk punishing people who would have never done anything further and who are not sufficiently blameworthy. In the end, the law makes a tradeoff. To be guilty of an inchoate offense, you must have a very guilty mind since you have a less guilty hand. For this reason, all inchoate offenses are specific intent offenses.

B. SOLICITATION

Solicitation means asking, inviting, requesting, commanding, or even encouraging another to commit a crime with the intent that they do so. At common law, the solicited crime had to be a felony or a misdemeanor that constituted obstruction of justice or a "breach of the peace" (which generally meant a crime of violence or public disorder). The guilty hand is the solicitation, and the guilty mind is the purpose that the crime be committed.

1. AN HISTORICAL EXAMPLE

Solicitation is a very compact crime. It is complete once the words leave the solicitor's mouth. Let's take an example from history. In 1170, England's King Henry II got into a serious quarrel with Thomas Becket, the Archbishop of Canterbury for excommunicating another Archbishop who was loyal to Henry. This was very serious stuff, and everyone knew it. One day at court, Henry yelled out "Will someone not rid me of this troublesome priest?" Four knights who heard this concluded that Henry wanted Becket dead, so they went and killed Becket.

Let's play around with this story to illustrate the ins and outs of solicitation as a crime. Assume Henry is on trial for solicitation.

- What if Henry was joking? He is not guilty of solicitation because he lacks intent. It does not matter that the knights thought Henry was serious and that someone died as a result.

- What if Henry was serious, but the knights did not respond to Henry's request? Henry is guilty of solicitation. No agreement or response is required.

- What about the fact that Henry did not direct the request to any particular person? Henry is guilty as long as he solicited someone and was not talking to himself in an empty room.

- What if Henry was serious, but everyone thought he was joking? Still guilty. As long as Henry intended the crime to be committed, it does not matter what those solicited thought.

- What if no one killed Becket, even though they thought Henry was serious? Still guilty because the crime is complete once the solicitation is made with the required intent.

- What if Henry was serious, but no one heard him? Henry would not be guilty of solicitation under the common law because he would not actually have solicited anyone. You might argue that he was guilty of attempted solicitation, but few if any common law jurisdictions recognize "attempted solicitation."

In these hypotheticals, everything depends on Henry's state of mind. He must intend that Thomas be killed. It would not be enough if he were joking but had been reckless or negligent with respect to the risk that someone might think he was serious. As long as Henry intends for Thomas to be killed, the law does not care whether anyone believed or acted on his request. Solicitation doctrine punishes people who seriously ask others to commit a crime without respect to what does or does not happen next.

2. FIRST AMENDMENT LIMITS

Solicitation statutes must be carefully crafted to avoid constitutional scrutiny—prohibit too much speech, and you run afoul of the First Amendment. An unclear statute may be open to a challenge on vagueness or overbreadth grounds (remember *Chicago v. Morales*?)

Case in Context

Before there was an internet, people used more primitive means to encourage lots of people to commit crimes, as the next case illustrates.

NEW YORK V. ROBERT QUENTIN & JOHN GARCIA

District Court of Nassau County, First District
58 Misc. 2d 601 (1968)

OPINION

The defendants, Robert Quentin and John Garcia, have been charged [with] criminal solicitation in the third degree in violation of section 100.00 of the Penal Law. The defendants move for leave to withdraw their not guilty pleas and interpose a demurrer to the information on the ground that it does not state facts sufficient to constitute a crime.

The brochure in question is worthy of note. The inside front cover concisely describes the philosophy of the defendants. In part it reads: "America is carnivorous. She eats the world for dessert. Behind slick pictures of pretty-suburban-middle-church-going-family lie hamburgers seasoned with napalm, race crimes too brutal to recall, cultures plundered, and triviality elevated into a way of life. The rich are rich because they are thieves and the poor because they are victims, and the future will condemn those who accept the present as reality. Break down the family, church, nation, city, economy. Subversiveness saves us our professors are spies; let us close the schools and flow into the streets. Grow hair long and become too freaky to fit into the machine culture. What's needed is a generation of people who are freaky, crazy, irrational, sexy, angry, irreligious, childish and mad: people who burn draft cards, burn high school and college degrees: people who say: 'To hell with your goals'; people who lure the youth with music, pot and acid: people who re-define reality, who re-define the normal; The white youth of America have more in common with Indians plundered, than they do with their own parents. Burn their house down, and you will be free."

This is followed by a paragraph entitled "How to make a fire bomb", and a recipe for Tryptamine, a psychedelic agent. The recipe ends with the statements: "This last (Tetrahydrofurane) is a very powerful reducing agent; wear safety glasses, add very cautiously, and perform this step with ventilation, away from flames (H2 is evolved). The yield is about 40 grams of DMT, in tetrahydrofurane solution. This cannot be drunk or injected, but may be smoked by sprinkling on mint or cannabis leaves and letting the solution evaporate. It's evaporated when it starts smelling like DMT instead of tetrahydrofurane."

Count three alleges a violation of section 100.00 of the Penal Law which is criminal solicitation in the third degree. It charges that the defendants violated the section in that they attempted to cause persons to whom a brochure was distributed to possess a chemical compound known as DET and DMT which violates section 229 (429) of the Mental Hygiene Law. The brochure on one of its pages gives a formula for making a fire bomb. Below that is also a formula for making both DET and DMT. On the page with the formula is no other solicitation, request or advocacy concerning the drugs. The formula taken alone appears to be such as would be found in a chemistry book or encyclopedia. It is clear that section 100.00 was intended to cover a situation where a particular person importunes another specified individual to do a specific act which constitutes a crime. The purpose was to hold the solicitor criminally responsible even if the one solicited fails to commit the act. It does not appear that section 100.00 was designed to cover a situation where the defendant makes a general solicitation (however reprehensible) to a large indefinable group to commit a crime.

The defendants' motion is granted and all counts of the information are dismissed with leave to the District Attorney to file for new information.

DISCUSSION QUESTIONS

1. What crimes were solicited? What were the words of solicitation?

2. Do you agree that general solicitations of criminal activity should not be a crime? Does it depend on the crime solicited?

3. What constitutes a "definable group?" What types of online solicitations would fit within your definition?

Case in Context

The following case analyzes solicitation in the context of "doxing," the vindictive disclosure of personal information online

UNITED STATES OF AMERICA V. WILLIAM WHITE

United States District Court, N.D. Illinois
779 F.Supp.2d 775 (2011)

In 2003, a jury in the Northern District of Illinois convicted white supremacist leader Matthew Hale of soliciting the murder of District Judge Joan Lefkow, who had presided over a civil case involving Hale's organization, the World Church of the Creator. The district court sentenced Hale to 480 months in prison, and the Seventh Circuit affirmed Hale's conviction and sentence on direct appeal.

In 2008, Hale filed a motion challenging his conviction and sentence on various grounds, including the alleged ineffectiveness of his trial counsel. Among other errors, Hale alleged that his lawyer botched jury selection, failing to challenge or strike a juror named Mark Hoffman, a gay man with an African-American partner who ended up serving as the jury foreperson. On September 11, 2008, after an article about Hale's motion appeared in the *Chicago Sun-Times,* defendant William White (hereafter "defendant"), also a white supremacist and the leader of an organization called the American National Socialist Workers Party ("ANSWP"), posted an article about Hale's motion on his website, Overthrow.com. The article was entitled "Hale Seeks To Have Sentence Overturned," with the sub-headline "Gay Jewish Anti-Racist Led Jury." (Govt. Ex. 2 at 1.) Below the headline, defendant posted Hoffman's picture with the caption:

> Gay Jewish anti-racist Mark P Hoffmann was a juror who played a key role in convicting Hale. Born August 24, 1964, he lives at 6915 HAMILTON # A CHICAGO, IL 60645 with his gay black lover and his cat "homeboy". His phone number is (773)274-1215, cell phone is (773)426-5676 and his office is (847) 491-3783.

(Govt. Ex. 2 at 1.) Defendant also displayed Hoffman's picture and the above caption on the blog section of the website. (Govt. Ex. 1.) The following day, after Hoffman's employer removed the picture to which defendant had linked, defendant posted a "Mark P Hoffman Update," with the sub-heading, "Since They Blocked the First Photo." (Govt. Ex. 4 at 1.) The post contained the same photo and caption, with the additional text: "Note that Northwestern University blocked much of Mr. Hoffman's information after we linked to his photograph." (Govt. Ex. 4 at 1.)

Based on these posts, the government charged defendant with soliciting or otherwise endeavoring to persuade another person to injure Hoffman based on his jury service in the Hale case, in violation of 18 U.S.C. § 373. Section 373(a) provides:

> Whoever, with intent that another person engage in conduct constituting a felony that has as an element the use, attempted use, or threatened use of physical force against property or against the person of another in violation of the laws of the United States,

and under circumstances strongly corroborative of that intent, solicits, commands, induces, or otherwise endeavors to persuade such other person to engage in such conduct, shall be imprisoned not more than . . .

18 U.S.C. § 373.

III. DISCUSSION

In order to obtain a conviction in this case, the government had to prove two things. First, the government had to show that defendant solicited, commanded, induced or otherwise endeavored to persuade another person to commit a violent federal crime against Mark Hoffman. As I instructed the jury and as the parties agreed, whether a particular statement is a solicitation is determined by an objective standard. That is, a statement is a solicitation if a reasonable person hearing or reading it and familiar with its context would understand it as a serious expression that another person commit a violent felony. Second, the government had to prove, with strongly corroborative evidence, that defendant intended that another person commit a violent federal crime against Hoffman. (Tr. at 551–54.)

C.   The First Amendment

[T]he First Amendment protects vehement, scathing, and offensive criticism of others, including individuals involved in the criminal justice system, such as Juror Hoffman. *See id.* at 945 (collecting cases). Speech is "protected unless both the intent of the speaker and the tendency of his words was to produce or incite an imminent lawless act, one likely to occur." *Freeman,* 761 F.2d at 552 (citing *Brandenburg v. Ohio,* 395 U.S. 444, 447–48, 89 S.Ct. 1827, 23 L.Ed.2d 430 (1969)). Knowledge or belief that one's speech, even speech advocating law breaking, might cause others to act does not remove the speech from the protection of the First Amendment, unless the speech is directed to inciting imminent lawless action and is likely to produce such action. *See Brandenburg,* 395 U.S. at 447, 89 S.Ct. 1827; *see also Ashcroft v. Free Speech Coalition,* 535 U.S. 234, 245, 122 S.Ct. 1389, 152 L.Ed.2d 403 (2002) ("The prospect of crime . . . by itself does not justify laws suppressing protected speech."). Nor may the government, consistent with the First Amendment, penalize speech approving of past violence by others. *Planned Parenthood of Columbia/Willamette, Inc. v. American Coalition of Life Activists* (hereafter *PPCW*), 290 F.3d 1058, 1091 n. 3 (9th Cir.2002) (Kozinski, J., dissenting) And this highly protective standard applies to the type of speech at issue here—internet communications disclosing personal information about others—even when that speech may tend to alarm or intimidate the persons so identified or expose them to unwanted attention from others.).

Applying these standards, it is clear that defendant's posts about Hoffman are protected by the First Amendment. Even reading them within the overall context of Overthrow.com, the Hoffman posts are not directed to inciting or producing imminent lawless action. Neither these posts—nor any of the other content on Overthrow.com—solicit, command, request, or even suggest that anyone do anything to Hoffman, presently or in the future. The fact that the posts may have singled Hoffman out for the attention of unrelated, potentially violent third parties does not remove them from the protection of the First Amendment. *Sheehan,* 272 F.Supp.2d at 1150 (citing *Planned Parenthood of Columbia/Willamette, Inc.,* 290 F.3d at 1063). Like the *Sheehan* court, I do not "intend to minimize the real fear of harm and intimidation" that those involved in the court system may experience based on disclosure of personal information about them.

However, we live in a democratic society founded on fundamental constitutional principles. In this society, we do not quash fear by increasing government power, proscribing those constitutional principles, and silencing those speakers of whom the majority disapproves. Rather, as Justice Harlan eloquently explained, the First Amendment demands that we confront those speakers with superior ideas:

> The constitutional right of free expression is powerful medicine in a society as diverse and populous as ours. It is designed and intended to remove governmental restraints from the arena of public discussion, putting the decision as to what views shall be voiced largely into the hands of each of us, in the hope that use of such freedom will ultimately produce a more capable citizenry and more perfect polity and in the belief that no other approach would comport with the premise of individual dignity and choice upon which our political system rests. To many, the immediate consequence of this freedom may often appear to be only verbal tumult, discord, and even offensive utterance. These are, however, within established limits, in truth necessary side effects of the broader enduring values which the process of open debate permits us to achieve. That the air may at times seem filled with verbal cacophony is, in this sense not a sign of weakness but of strength. We cannot lose sight of the fact that, in what otherwise might seem a trifling and annoying instance of individual distasteful abuse of a privilege, these fundamental societal values are truly implicated.

Id. at 1150 (quoting *Cohen v. California,* 403 U.S. 15, 24–25, 91 S.Ct. 1780, 29 L.Ed.2d 284 (1971)).

For the reasons stated, no reasonable jury could have found defendant's posts about Hoffman unprotected, and I conclude based on the entire trial record that as a matter of law they were covered by the First Amendment. Therefore, defendant's Rule 29 motion must be granted.

A final note: In remanding the case, the court of appeals stated that if defendant's intent was to make a political point about sexual orientation or to facilitate opportunities for other people to make such views known to the Juror, or to permit electronic or verbal harassment, he would not be guilty of solicitation because he did not have the requisite intent required for the crime. *White,* 610 F.3d at 961–62. While it is true that the crime of solicitation is complete at the time the words are spoken with the requisite intent, and no further action need follow, it is worth noting that "electronic and verbal harassment" is exactly what happened here. Hoffman received crude text massages and one harassing phone call. But no one threatened him, and no attempts were made to harm him.

DISCUSSION QUESTIONS

1.   Why do you think the defendant disclosed his victim's personal information?

2.   Should solicitations of crime have to be express, or should the law permit "implied" solicitations?

3.   Do you agree that the First Amendment should protect speech such as this?

C. SOLICITATION AS AN ATTEMPT?

We will return to this point when we discuss attempt liability, but the majority of jurisdictions do not consider a solicitation by itself to be an attempt of the crime solicited. A minority of jurisdictions will treat solicitations as attempts in and of themselves.

MODEL PENAL CODE

§ 5.02. Criminal Solicitation

1)   Definition of Solicitation. A person is guilty of solicitation to commit a crime if with the purpose of promoting or facilitating its commission he commands, encourages or requests another person to engage in specific conduct which would constitute such crime or an attempt to commit such crime or which would establish his complicity in its commission or attempted commission.

2)   Uncommunicated Solicitation. It is immaterial under Subsection (1) of this Section that the actor fails to communicate with the person he solicits to commit a crime if his conduct was designed to effect such communication.

3)   Renunciation of Criminal Purpose. It is an affirmative defense that the actor, after soliciting another person to commit a crime, persuaded him not to do so or otherwise prevented the commission of the crime, under circumstances manifesting a complete and voluntary renunciation of his criminal purpose.

The MPC creates wider criminal liability for solicitation. First, it applies to any crime, not just felonies or certain misdemeanors. Second, it extends not only to solicitations to commit a crime but also to any conduct that would constitute an attempt or make the other person an accomplice. So, if I ask you to hand me a gun so that I can shoot someone, I am not soliciting a crime under the common law because handing me a gun is not a crime. Under the MPC, however, I would be guilty of solicitation because handing me a gun knowing that I intend to shoot someone makes you an accomplice to the shooting (as we will discuss later).

The Model Penal Code offers would-be solicitors one consolation prize. It allows them to "undo" their solicitation by renouncing it. Under the common law, the crime is complete once the words leave your mouth. Yet, under the MPC, a person who completely and voluntarily renounces his criminal intent, and either persuades the solicited person to abandon the crime or prevents them from committing it, will not be guilty of solicitation.

The Model Penal Code is not currently adopted in any jurisdiction in its entirety—instead, many jurisdictions pick and choose the parts they like.

D. MERGER

Merger doctrine for inchoate offenses aims to avoid punishing someone twice for what is essentially the same conduct. Whenever we want to stop the state from "double dipping in the punishment bowl" we say that the lesser offense merges into the greater offense. Assume you solicit someone to commit a crime, they agree, and they commit the crime. Can you be found guilty of solicitation, conspiracy, and the completed crime? No, the crime of solicitation merges into the conspiracy and merges into the completed crime. Moreover, if you solicited someone to commit a crime, and were found guilty of attempting that crime, your solicitation would also merge into your attempt if both were based on the same conduct.

Practice Problem 16.0: "Do You Want to Go?"

Watch the Key and Peele skit "Text Message Confusion" online. Do either of them commit a crime?

CHAPTER 17

CONSPIRACY

∎ ∎ ∎

A. THE CRIME IS THE AGREEMENT

The first thing to understand about conspiracy is that the crime is the agreement. Fans of the TV show "The Office" might appreciate the following example. In one episode Dwight, a dweebishly evil character, is confronted by another employee who tells him "I know about your diabolical plan!" Dwight feigns ignorance and says, "I don't know what you are talking about." His co-worker says, "You left it in the printer," and hands Dwight the paper titled "Dwight's Diabolical Plan." "What do you want?" Dwight asks. "I want in," his co-worker replies, and they both shake hands. At common law, the crime of conspiracy was complete once they shook hands (assuming that the diabolical plan was to do something unlawful). They do not need to do anything more because *the crime is the agreement.*

The idea of a criminal agreement makes conspiracy doctrine tricky. The guilty mind required is the intent to agree and the intent to achieve the object of the agreement. The guilty hand required at common law is the agreement itself. Most people think of an agreement as something that exists in people's minds, though. This makes conspiracy's conduct requirement what I would call a "mentalish" one.

Conspiracy is a crime unto itself. You might *also* be guilty of the crime you conspired to commit, but this liability exists separate and apart from your liability for the crime of conspiracy. Always analyze conspiracy separately from liability for other crimes and attempted crimes.

B. POLICIES BEHIND CONSPIRACY DOCTRINE

Why do we punish people for agreeing to do bad things before any of them have attempted to do a bad thing? We might punish people who might never do anything because they either had a change of heart or were too lazy, fearful, or incompetent to get things going.

One reason we punish conspiracies is crime prevention. Making it a crime to agree to commit a crime allows the police to arrest people before they can get close to doing something bad. Police surveillance and investigation is an imperfect enterprise conducted with limited resources. Following conspirators until they begin their attempt consumes police time that is better spent doing other things. Also, continued surveillance might be detected or circumvented, running the risk that the crime will be successfully completed at some point. If a group of people agree to blow up a building, do we really want to try following them around until they buy their explosives?

The second reason we punish conspiracies is the "special danger of group activity." The criminal law considers people who agree to commit crimes in groups to be more likely to see things through to the end and more likely to be successful. Teamwork makes things easy, including crime. A group of people can encourage one another, pool their resources, and efficiently divide up tasks. Moreover, groups can commit more elaborate crimes. They can also continue their criminal activities longer as new members add to or replace the old ones. Historically, the criminal law has had good reason to fear crime committed by groups: think of organized crime syndicates, terrorist organizations, and insurrectionary movements. The government relied heavily on conspiracy law in prosecuting the Ku Klux Klan, the Mafia, and Al Qaeda.

But conspiracy law also involves special dangers to civil liberties. Criminal conspiracy law is defined so broadly that one noted judge aptly called it the "darling of the modern prosecutor's nursery." The same features that make conspiracy a great weapon against the evil and the dangerous also make it a handy club against the unpopular. Critics of conspiracy law fear that it promotes guilt by association and chills our First Amendment Right of Free Assembly by making it possible to be convicted for meeting with people the government deems suspicious. Because conspiracy requires little or no action, it also confers great power onto informants who can make up a conversation about an agreement that never existed. Finally, broad conspiracy liability may waste government resources in the war against terrorism or organized crime by unleashing prosecutions against hapless groups of incompetent individuals who talk big but who could never bring themselves to organize a luncheon, much less an elaborate crime.

The law strikes the balance between these competing concerns in how it defines the elements and scope of conspiracy law.

C. THE ELEMENTS OF CONSPIRACY: AN OVERVIEW

A criminal conspiracy may be defined in the following way.

- An Agreement, express or implied
  - Agreement may be inferred from circumstances
- Where the fact finder must find a "communion of understanding"

- To commit a crime or—at common law and in a few jurisdictions—an unlawful act

- To which the defendant intended to agree

- With the further intent that the object of the agreement be achieved

- Many jurisdictions, including the MPC (but unlike the common law), also require an overt act in furtherance of the conspiracy.

Ordinarily the distinction between conduct elements and mental state elements is pretty clear cut. The agreement element of conspiracy blurs that distinction. An agreement is the conduct required for a conspiracy to occur, but the act of agreeing to something is inextricably bound up with the mental state that accompanies an agreement. In this sense, conspiracy requires conduct that one might call "mentalish." That said, one should be sure to consider and discuss each of the elements described above separately.

D. THE GUILTY HAND: THE AGREEMENT

Almost all jurisdictions today (including the Model Penal Code) limit conspiracy to agreements to commit a crime. At common law and in a few remaining jurisdictions, one could be convicted of the crime of conspiracy if one agreed to commit an unlawful act. This older, broader understanding of conspiracy meant that an agreement to violate some aspect of civil law could be prosecuted criminally. For most jurisdictions today, however, this broader version of conspiracy is far too sweeping. An aggressive prosecutor could use it to obliterate the distinction between civil and criminal wrongs. Garden variety breaches of contract or tort violations could be prosecuted as crimes if two or more people agreed on the conduct constituting the civil wrong.

The most important thing to learn about the agreement element of conspiracy is that it may be implied from the circumstances. No signed contract, handshake, or express words of agreement are required. Even more perplexing, no direct communication between conspirators is required. A mere coincidence of purpose is not enough for an agreement, though. There must be a communion of purpose by which the courts mean that the actors are mutually aware of their shared purpose.

Imagine that a mob descends on an unlucky few. People in the crowd never speak to one another, but they can clearly see one another as they surround the victims. Acting in concert permits the inference that they share an understanding that each wishes the crime to be committed, and that could be enough to find an agreement for the purposes of criminal conspiracy. Note, though, that simple awareness of one another's purpose should not even be enough for an agreement (although this distinction is razor thin). The understanding must be mutual in the sense that each takes the other person's purpose into account and intends the other person to take his shared purpose into account. This idea of a mutual understanding brings us into the realm of a tacit agreement. "Yeah," people in the crowd think, "we are all agreed on doing this thing." Now you have communion of purpose, not just a coincidence of purpose.

Contrast that scenario with an unlucky law professor who faces assassination by not one but two of his disgruntled first-year law students. One student walks up behind him with a knife while the other (more forthright) student walks up to his face with a gun. Each share a purpose, but because they are not mutually aware they cannot enjoy the communion of purpose necessary for conspiracy.

Remember that while an agreement may be implied from very little, it still must be proved. Just because a judge allows a conspiracy charge to go to the jury does not mean that the jury will find the agreement to have been proved beyond a reasonable doubt. If a jury returns a verdict of guilty, however, it may be hard for a judge to set aside the verdict as a matter of law because it is often very easy to imply an agreement from actions that work together towards a criminal objective.

1. THE GUILTY HAND: OVERT ACT

While the crime of conspiracy is the agreement, a majority of common law jurisdictions, as well as the Model Penal Code, require an overt act in furtherance of the conspiracy in addition to the acts that constituted the agreement. (Although the Model Penal Code dispenses with this requirement for conspiracies to commit the most serious felonies.) In such a jurisdiction Dwight and his co-worker in the scenario described at the beginning of this chapter would not become guilty of conspiracy as soon as they shook hands. The shaking of hands would be an express act of agreement, not an overt act in furtherance of the agreement.

The purpose of the overt act requirement is to make sure that the conspiracy is not something that will exist only in the minds of the conspirators. The fact that someone has taken some action after the agreement is formed provides a modest guarantee that the agreement to commit a crime is a serious one.

This overt act does not have to be the beginning of an attempt to commit the crime. It need only be performed by one member of the group and need not be a criminal act in and of itself. Imagine that, after Dwight and his co-worker shake hands on Dwight's diabolical plan, his co-worker says, "I am going to make a copy of your diabolical plan." That would satisfy the overt act requirement in these jurisdictions even though copying the plan is neither a crime nor enough to constitute an attempt to commit the crime in many jurisdictions.

Case in Context

In the following case the court infers an agreement from circumstances.

COMMONWEALTH OF PENNSYLVANIA V. CHARLES AZIM

Superior Court of Pennsylvania
313 Pa.Super. 310 (1983)

PER CURIAM:

Appellant Charles Azim seeks dismissal of all the charges brought against him. Appellant was arrested, along with Mylice James and Thomas Robinson, on September 18, 1977 for simple assault, robbery, and conspiracy. The victim of the robbery was Jerry Tennenbaum, a Temple University student. Appellant drove a car in which the other two men were passengers. Appellant stopped the car, Robinson called Tennenbaum over to the curb, the two passengers got out of the car, inflicted bodily injury on Tennenbaum, took his wallet which had fallen to the ground, and immediately left the scene in the same car driven by appellant. Robinson and appellant were tried to a jury and convicted as co-defendants in April 1978.

In this appeal, appellant. . . argues that because his conspiracy conviction was not supported by sufficient evidence against him, the charges of assault and robbery must also fail.

In Commonwealth v. Volk, 298 Pa.Super. 294, 444 A.2d 1182 (1982). . . our Court maintained that:

> "The essence of criminal conspiracy is a common understanding, no matter how it came into being, that a particular criminal objective be accomplished." By its very nature, the crime of conspiracy is frequently not susceptible of proof except by circumstantial evidence. And although a conspiracy cannot be based upon mere suspicion or conjecture, a conspiracy "may be inferentially established by showing the relationship, conduct or circumstances of the parties, and the overt acts on the part of the co-conspirators have uniformly been held competent to prove that a corrupt confederation has in fact been formed.

At trial, the prosecution presented evidence that established that appellant was the driver of the car in which James and Robinson (the men who demanded money from Tennenbaum and beat and choked him) rode. Robinson was seated on the front seat, next to appellant. Robinson rolled down the car window, twice beckoned to the victim to come close to the car, and when Tennenbaum refused, the two passengers got out, assaulted Tennenbaum, and took his wallet. Appellant sat at the wheel, with the engine running and lights on, and the car doors open, while the acts were committed in the vicinity of the car. He then drove James and Robinson from the scene.

Among those circumstances relevant to proving conspiracy are association with alleged conspirators, knowledge of the commission of the crime, presence at the scene of the crime, and, at times, participation in the object of the conspiracy. . . Conspiracy to commit burglary has been found where the defendant drove codefendants to the scene of a crime and then later picked them up. . . We find no merit in appellant's claim that he was merely a hired driver, with no knowledge of his passengers' criminal activity.

We hold that a rational factfinder could find, beyond a reasonable doubt, that appellant conspired with James and Robinson to commit assault and robbery.

Once conspiracy is established and upheld, a member of the conspiracy is also guilty of the criminal acts of his co-conspirators, even if he is not present at the time the acts are committed.

DISCUSSION QUESTIONS

1. Is Azim being prosecuted simply for being with the wrong people at the wrong time? For failing to stop the robbery or at least to drive away when he saw it beginning?

2. Assume that Azim had no idea his companions were about to commit a robbery. Does driving them away afterwards necessarily mean that he is a conspirator?

3. How much latitude should jurors be given to find an implied agreement?

Case in Context

In contrast, the court finds insufficient evidence from which to infer an agreement in the following drug case.

UNITED STATES V. FITZ
United States Court of Appeals, Eighth Circuit
317 F.3d 878 (2003)

Opinion

HEANEY, CIRCUIT JUDGE.

After a trial by jury, Edwardo Flores Fitz, also known as Victor Manuel Crespo-Garcia, was found guilty of conspiracy to distribute and possess with intent to distribute methamphetamine and possession with intent to distribute and distribution of the same, and was sentenced to two concurrent terms of 188 months imprisonment.

Fitz [argues] that there was insufficient evidence to support the verdicts... After careful review of the record, we hold there was insufficient evidence to support Fitz's convictions.

" 'In reviewing the sufficiency of the evidence to support a guilty verdict, we look at the evidence in the light most favorable to the verdict and accept as established all reasonable inferences supporting the verdict.' In a conspiracy case, the government must prove there was a conspiracy with an illegal purpose, that the defendant was aware of the conspiracy, and that he knowingly became a part of it. Moreover, there must be evidence that the defendant entered into an agreement with at least one other person and that the agreement had as its objective a violation of law. It is not necessary to prove an overt act in furtherance of a conspiracy. The conspiracy may be proved through circumstantial evidence and may be implied by the surrounding circumstances or by inference from the actions of the parties. 'Once the government establishes the existence of a drug conspiracy, only slight evidence linking the defendant to the conspiracy is required to prove the defendant's involvement and support the conviction.' "

With this background, we turn to a detailed discussion of the evidence and the reasons why we conclude there was insufficient evidence to establish Fitz's guilt on either count. Applying the principles outlined above and reviewing the evidence in the light most favorable to the verdict, the only evidence in the record that could be said to support the view that Fitz knowingly participated in the conspiracy was the following: Fitz, Vega, and Preciado traveled from Minneapolis to Grand Forks in a Honda Civic and a Nissan Pathfinder, in which the drugs were hidden; Fitz was observed in the presence of Preciado and Vega in Grand Forks at various locations between 6:00 p.m. and 9:30 p.m.; Fitz gave a false name when he was arrested; and Fitz was present during a recorded conversation between the confidential informant and Preciado in the Burger King parking lot in Grand Forks, in which Preciado said he wanted everything and wanted to return to the motel to discuss the matter. Thereafter, Preciado and Fitz left the parking lot in a Honda Civic when they were stopped by the Grand Forks Narcotics Task Force officers and arrested.

On the other hand, there is considerable evidence that casts into serious doubt whether Fitz knowingly participated in the conspiracy. The confidential informant never talked to Fitz. Moreover, the conversation that occurred in Fitz's presence between the confidential informant and Preciado was conducted in English, and there is no evidence in the record that shows that Fitz spoke or understands English. He was provided with an interpreter during the entire trial and the sentencing hearing. Further, there is no evidence in the record to indicate that Fitz knew there were drugs in a secret compartment in the Pathfinder's gas tank. Also, when Preciado, Vega, and Fitz first arrived in Grand Forks, a hotel room was rented in the name of Antonio Mendoza. This name was used in the past by Preciado at the same motel.

Nothing in the record indicates that Fitz had been in Grand Forks at an earlier date, and Fitz had no prior criminal record or any record of dealing in drugs. The confidential informant had Preciado's pager number and could reach Preciado at any time. Between June 26 and June 28, seven calls were made between the confidential informant and Preciado. There is no evidence, however, that the informant knew how to contact Fitz or ever sought to do so. There is no evidence Fitz ever rode in or drove the Pathfinder. Even if Fitz had been in the Pathfinder, the methamphetamine was well hidden in the Pathfinder, and there was no evidence in the record that Fitz was aware of the existence of the drugs.

Perhaps most importantly, the government failed to call the confidential informant as a witness even though the confidential informant was available and known only to the government. In short, while the government can prove that a conspiracy existed between Preciado and Vega, the government failed to prove that Fitz was aware of the conspiracy, or that Fitz knowingly agreed to join the conspiracy. As the government cannot prove two of the three necessary elements of Fitz's alleged crimes, we cannot affirm his convictions.

There is no evidence in the record that would tend to show by inference or otherwise that Fitz was a knowing participant in the drug conspiracy or that he constructively possessed the methamphetamine because he was a passenger in a car that accompanied the Pathfinder from Minneapolis to Grand Forks. A verdict based on unsupported speculation cannot stand. Under these circumstances, we have no alternative but to reverse Fitz's convictions.

DISCUSSION QUESTIONS

1.   What special rule about drug conspiracies does the court note in its discussion? In light of that rule, why doesn't the court find sufficient evidence of a conspiracy here?

2.   Can you reconcile this case with the *Azim* case?

3.   Was the court too strict in the inferences it allowed to be drawn in this case?

E. THE GUILTY MIND: INTENT TO AGREE AND INTENT TO ACHIEVE

The two intents required for conspiracy should be kept separate although the distinction seems a bit fuzzy to many. One must both intend to agree with one another as well as intend to achieve the object of the agreement.

Intent to agree is difficult to separate from intent to achieve the criminal objective. An undercover police officer posing as a hit man may intend to agree with the person asking him to kill someone for money but not intend to carry out the crime. For this reason, undercover policeman officers ordinarily can't be found guilty for conspiracy for their actions in sting operations. Conversely, a "lone wolf" mob member in the crowd scenario might intend to attack the victims but not intend to enter into any agreement with anyone else in the mob.

If the intent to agree issue seems to blend into the conduct issue of whether an agreement exists, don't worry. It does! This is what I meant earlier by saying that the "act" of agreeing is a "mentalish" act. The intent to agree is the mental state side of the "mentalish" act of agreement.

The intent to achieve the object of the conspiracy has its own wrinkles. At a minimum, it means that you must have the mental state required for the crime. Imagine that you, my roommate, and I agree to borrow your roommate's Ferrari without his permission. You plan to return it in mint condition after speeding around for a while, whereas my roommate and I plan to sell the car to cover our gambling debts. You are not guilty of conspiracy to steal the car because you lack the mental state required by theft—the intent to permanently deprive the owner of the property. My roommate and I are guilty of conspiracy because we both have that intent.

This mental state requirement also effectively rules out conspiracy for crimes that create liability for reckless or negligent results. What if you and I agree to use the Ferrari in a game of chicken with another car, where we speed toward a cliff with another car in order to see who "chickens out" first? The drivers in the other car cut things too close and drive off the cliff to their deaths. Have you and I conspired to commit reckless murder or involuntary manslaughter? We intended to do something at least criminally negligent and possibly extremely reckless depending on the circumstances. But we did not intend for anyone to die. Death is a required result for any homicide crime. Conspiracy requires you to intend that the objective of the conspiracy occur, and, in this case, that crime requires death. For this reason, many commentators observe that the only sorts of homicide one can conspire to commit are intentional killings, and probably only ones that are premeditated and deliberate.

Case in Context

This case considers the special mental state requirements that conspiracy entails.

PEOPLE V. SWAIN

Supreme Court of California
12 Cal.4th 593 (1996)

BAXTER, ASSOCIATE JUSTICE.

Defendants Jamal K. Swain and David Chatman were each convicted of conspiracy to commit murder and other crimes, stemming from the drive-by shooting death of a 15-year-old boy. As we shall explain, we hold that HN1 intent to kill is a required element of the crime of conspiracy to commit murder. In light of the jury instructions given, and general verdicts returned, we cannot determine beyond a reasonable doubt whether the jury found that the defendants conspired with an intent to kill. That conclusion requires us to reverse defendants' conspiracy convictions.

FACTS AND PROCEDURAL BACKGROUND

The question before us is one of law; the facts found by the Court of Appeal, summarized below, are not disputed.

Prosecution evidence established that a brown van passed through the Hunter's Point neighborhood of San Francisco about 2 a.m. on January 13, 1991. It slowed down near the spot where the young victim, who was of Samoan descent, and his friends were listening to music on the street.

A young Black male who appeared to have no hair was driving the van. Suddenly several shots were fired from the front of the van. Defendant Chatman and another young man also fired guns from the rear of the van. One of the intended victims had yelled out "drive-by" as a warning of the impending shooting, so most of the people on the street ducked down. The 15-year-old victim, Hagbom Saileele, who was holding the radio from which music was playing, was shot twice from behind. He later died in surgery.

Afterward, defendant Swain was in jail and boasted to jailmates about what good aim he had with a gun: "He was talking about what a good shot he was. He was saying he had shot that Samoan kid when they were in the van going about 30 miles an hour up a hill." The area where the shooting occurred is hilly; the van would have had to have been traveling uphill as it passed by the scene of the shooting. . .

The abandoned brown van was recovered by police; in the van and nearby were found surgical gloves, expended cartridges, a hooded ski mask, and two handguns—a .380-caliber semiautomatic and a. 25-caliber automatic. Defendant Swain's fingerprint was on the inside of the driver's side window. The forensic evidence established that whoever had used the .380-caliber semiautomatic handgun, from which the fatal shots were fired, had been sitting in the driver's side front seat of the van.

The .380-caliber gun was traced, through a series of owners and transactions involving narcotics, to defendant Chatman. Chatman was interrogated by police; he denied any knowledge of the van and claimed he had not purchased the gun. When this story proved false, Chatman admitted he had bought the gun, but claimed it had been stolen from him. Still later, he claimed he had sold it to someone else.

A warrant was obtained for Chatman's arrest. After waiving his rights, Chatman told police he and two other people, not including Swain, had driven the van to the crime scene in order to get revenge for a car theft by a rival gang. Chatman insisted, to the police and at trial, that Swain had not been in the van. He could not, however, explain Swain's fingerprint inside the van.

The owner of the van testified Swain had never been inside his van prior to the incident, but that Swain had intimidated him into telling police he (Swain) had previously been inside the vehicle, since otherwise "he was going to have something done to him."

At trial, Chatman admitted he had been in the van, which was driven to Hunter's Point to retaliate for a car theft attributed to a neighborhood youth who was not the victim of the shooting. The original plan was allegedly to steal the car of the thief. Chatman admitted he had fired shots, but claimed he fired wildly and only in self-defense. In support of this self-defense theory, he testified he heard an initial shot and thought it was fired by someone outside the van shooting at him, so he returned the fire. As noted, Chatman claimed Swain was not in the van.

Swain testified he was not in the van during the shooting and did not do any shooting. He claimed he had entered the van earlier in the evening, but had left because "the smell of marijuana bothered him." He claimed he took BART (Bay Area Rapid Transit) to Berkeley, where he spent the evening at a relative's home. He denied boasting about shooting the victim and denied having threatened any witnesses.

The jury first returned a verdict finding defendant Chatman guilty of second degree murder and conspiracy. As instructed, the jury also made a finding that the target offense of the conspiracy was murder in the second degree. Several days later, the jury returned verdicts against defendant Swain, finding him not guilty of murder or its lesser included offenses, but guilty of conspiracy and of attempting to dissuade a witness from testifying by threats. Once again, the jury made a finding under the conspiracy count that the target offense of the conspiracy was murder in the second degree. . .

Both defendants appealed on several grounds, including the question of whether intent to kill is a required element of the crime of conspiracy to commit murder. More particularly, where, as here, the target offense is determined to be murder in the second degree, does conviction of conspiracy to commit murder necessarily require proof of express malice—the functional equivalent of intent to kill—or can one conspire to commit implied malice murder?. . .

DISCUSSION

Defendants contend the jury should have been instructed that proof of intent to kill is required to support a conviction of conspiracy to commit murder, whether the target offense of the conspiracy—murder—is determined to be in the first or second degree. More particularly, defendants assert it was error to instruct the jury on the principles of implied malice second degree murder in connection with the determination of whether they could be found guilty of conspiracy to commit murder, since implied malice does not require a finding of intent to kill. As we shall explain, we agree.

We commence our analysis with a brief review of the elements of the crime of conspiracy, and of murder, the target offense of the conspiracy here in issue.

Conspiracy is an inchoate crime. It does not require the commission of the substantive offense that is the object of the conspiracy. "As an inchoate crime, conspiracy fixes the point of legal intervention at [the time of] agreement to commit a crime," and "thus reaches further back into preparatory conduct than attempt. . ." (Model Pen. Code & Commentaries (1985) com. 1 to § 5.03, pp. 387–388.)

The crime of conspiracy is defined in the Penal Code as "two or more persons conspir[ing]" "[t]o commit any crime," together with proof of the commission of an overt act "by one or more of the parties to such agreement" in furtherance thereof. "Conspiracy is a 'specific intent' crime. . .

The specific intent required divides logically into two elements: (a) the intent to agree, or conspire, and (b) the intent to commit the offense which is the object of the conspiracy. . . To sustain a conviction for conspiracy to commit a particular offense, the prosecution must show not only that the conspirators intended to agree but also that they intended to commit the elements of that offense." In some instances, the object of the conspiracy "is defined in terms of proscribed conduct." In other instances, it "is defined in terms of. . . a proscribed result under specified attendant circumstances."

Turning next to the elements of the target offense of the conspiracy here in issue, Penal Code section 187 defines the crime of murder as the "unlawful killing of a human being. . . with malice aforethought." Malice aforethought "may be express or implied." "It is express when there is manifested a deliberate intention unlawfully to take away the life of a fellow creature. It is implied, when no considerable provocation appears, or when the circumstances attending the killing show an abandoned and malignant heart."

This court has observed that proof of unlawful "intent to kill" is the functional equivalent of express malice. . .

As noted, the jury in this case was instructed on the elements of murder, including principles of implied malice second degree murder. Under the instructions given, the jury could have based its verdicts finding defendants guilty of conspiracy to commit murder in the second degree on a theory of implied malice murder. . .

We have noted that conspiracy is a specific intent crime requiring an intent to agree or conspire, and a further intent to commit the target crime, here murder, the object of the conspiracy. Since murder committed with intent to kill is the functional equivalent of express malice murder, conceptually speaking, no conflict arises between the specific intent element of conspiracy and the specific intent requirement for such category of murders. Simply put, where the conspirators agree or conspire with specific intent to kill and commit an overt act in furtherance of such agreement, they are guilty of conspiracy to commit express malice murder. The conceptual difficulty arises when the target offense of murder is founded on a theory of implied malice, which requires no intent to kill.

Implied malice murder, in contrast to express malice, requires instead an intent to do some act, the natural consequences of which are dangerous to human life. "When the killing is the direct result of such an act," the requisite mental state for murder—malice aforethought—is implied. . . In such circumstances, ". . . it is not necessary to establish that the defendant intended that his act would result in the death of a human being." Hence, under an implied malice theory of second degree murder, the requisite mental state for murder—malice aforethought—is by definition "implied," as a matter of law, from the specific intent to do some act dangerous to human life together with the circumstance that a killing has resulted from the doing of such act. . .

The element of malice aforethought in implied malice murder cases is therefore derived or "implied," in part through hindsight so to speak, from (i) proof of the specific intent to do some act dangerous to human life and (ii) the circumstance that a killing has resulted therefrom. It is precisely due to this nature of implied malice murder that it would be illogical to conclude one can be found guilty of conspiring to commit murder where the requisite element of malice is implied. Such a construction would be at odds with the very nature of the crime of conspiracy—an "inchoate" crime that "fixes the point of legal intervention at [the time of] agreement to commit a crime," and indeed "reaches further back into preparatory conduct than [the crime of] attempt" (Model Pen. Code & Commentaries, supra, com. 1 to § 5.03, pp. 387–388)—precisely because commission of the crime could never be established, or be deemed complete, unless and until a killing actually occurred.

By analogy, we have reached similar conclusions respecting the nature of proof of the element of malice required to establish the inchoate crimes of assault with intent to commit murder and attempted murder. . .

We conclude that a conviction of conspiracy to commit murder requires a finding of intent to kill, and cannot be based on a theory of implied malice. . .

That portion of the Court of Appeal's judgment affirming defendants' convictions of conspiracy to commit murder must therefore be reversed.

DISCUSSION QUESTIONS

1.   What can we infer from the fact that the jury did not find Swain guilty of murder?

2.   What mental state did the jury instructions for conspiracy to commit murder require with respect to the death of the victim? What is wrong with this instruction?

3.   Do you agree that one conspiracy cannot encompass unintended results?

1. PURPOSEFUL VS. KNOWING ASSISTANCE

Intent can mean either purposeful or knowing behavior. Since agreeing is a purposeful act, one cannot intend to agree without it being one's purpose to agree. Whether intent to achieve the object of the agreement requires purpose or knowledge, however, is a more difficult question.

Consider a supplier of goods and services. If he knows that one of his customers uses his supplies to commit a crime, and he agrees to supply his customer, has he conspired to commit that crime? He could claim "I don't care how my customers use my stuff as long as I get paid." A prosecutor, however, might argue that people who knowingly profit from criminal activity should be found to intend that activity. Whether the supplier "intends" the crime to be committed depends on whether his knowledge alone constitutes intent or whether it must be his purpose that his supplies be used to commit the crime.

There is a split among jurisdictions as to whether knowledge alone in such cases suffices for criminal conspiracy. The split is less consequential than one might think, however, because the jurisdictions that require purpose often define it in a way that comes very close to knowledge plus some sort of special stake in the outcome. If a supplier provides something that can only be used illegally, provides it at greatly inflated prices, or if his criminal buyers constitute a disproportionate share of his business, then courts seem likely to find that to be legally sufficient evidence of purpose.

One leading Supreme Court case suggests that providing assistance in closely regulated areas also supports a finding of purposeful assistance of illegal activities when the assistance circumvents those regulations. Assume that you have a hand-held scanner that can rapidly scan the pictures of a textbook, and that you rent the scanner out to other students in the library whom you know use it to make bootleg copies of the very expensive textbooks that law school courses often require. Whether you might be found to have conspired to violate the copyright laws (which do contain limited criminal provisions) would probably depend on whether the success of your rental business seemed to depend on—or do particularly well as a result of—the illegal nature of what was being scanned. While scanners are not per se illegal, the copying of material published under copyright is sufficiently regulated, and a court might find your agreements with your customers to be purposeful with respect to the violation those copyright laws. (So, don't agree to let anyone use your scanner to scan this book!)

Case in Context

The following case proved to be very influential. Many courts have followed its approach.

PEOPLE V. LAURIA

Court of Appeal, Second District, Division 2, California
251 Cal. App. 2d 471 (1967)

FLEMING, J.

In an investigation of call-girl activity the police focused their attention on three prostitutes actively plying their trade on call, each of whom was using Lauria's telephone answering service, presumably for business purposes.

On January 8, 1965, Stella Weeks, a policewoman, signed up for telephone service with Lauria's answering service. Mrs. Weeks, in the course of her conversation with Lauria's office manager, hinted broadly that she was a prostitute concerned with the secrecy of her activities and their concealment from the police. She was assured that the operation of the service was discreet and "about as safe as you can get." It was arranged that Mrs. Weeks need not leave her address with the answering service, but could pick up her calls and pay her bills in person.

On February 11, Mrs. Weeks talked to Lauria on the telephone and told him her business was modelling and she had been referred to the answering service by Terry, one of the three prostitutes under investigation. She complained that because of the operation of the service she had lost two valuable customers, referred to as tricks. Lauria defended his service and said that her friends had probably lied to her about having left calls for her. But he did not respond to Mrs. Weeks' hints that she needed customers in order to make money, other than to invite her to his house for a personal visit in order to get better acquainted. In the course of his talk he said "his business was taking messages."

On February 15, Mrs. Weeks talked on the telephone to Lauria's office manager and again complained of two lost calls, which she described as a $ 50 and a $ 100 trick. On investigation the office manager could find nothing wrong, but she said she would alert the switchboard operators about slip-ups on calls.

On April 1 Lauria and the three prostitutes were arrested. Lauria complained to the police that this attention was undeserved, stating that Hollywood Call Board had 60 to 70 prostitutes on its board while his own service had only 9 or 10, that he kept separate records for known or suspected prostitutes for the convenience of himself and the police. When asked if his records were available to police who might come to the office to investigate call girls, Lauria replied that they were whenever the police had a specific name. However, his service didn't "arbitrarily tell the police about prostitutes on our board. As long as they pay their bills we tolerate them." In a subsequent voluntary appearance before the grand jury Lauria testified he had always cooperated with the police. But he admitted he knew some of his customers were prostitutes, and he knew Terry was a prostitute because he had personally used her services, and he knew she was paying for 500 calls a month.

Lauria and the three prostitutes were indicted for conspiracy to commit prostitution, and nine overt acts were specified. Subsequently the trial court set aside the indictment as having been brought without reasonable or probable cause. (Pen Code, § 995.) The People have appealed, claiming that a sufficient showing of an unlawful agreement to further prostitution was made.

To establish agreement, the People need show no more than a tacit, mutual understanding between coconspirators to accomplish an unlawful act. Here the People attempted to establish a conspiracy by showing that Lauria, well aware that his codefendants were prostitutes who received business calls from customers through his telephone answering service, continued to furnish them with such service. This approach attempts to equate knowledge of another's criminal activity with conspiracy to further such criminal activity, and poses the question of the criminal responsibility of a furnisher of goods or services who knows his product is being used to assist the operation of an illegal business. Under what circumstances does a supplier become a part of a conspiracy to further an illegal enterprise by furnishing goods or services which he knows are to be used by the buyer for criminal purposes?

The two leading cases on this point face in opposite directions. In United States v. Falcone, the sellers of large quantities of sugar, yeast, and cans were absolved from participation in a moonshining conspiracy among distillers who bought from them, while in Direct Sales Co. v. United States, a wholesaler of drugs was convicted of conspiracy to violate the federal narcotic laws by selling drugs in quantity to a codefendant physician who was supplying them to addicts. The distinction between these two cases appears primarily based on the proposition that distributors of such dangerous products as drugs are required to exercise greater discrimination in the conduct of their business than are distributors of innocuous substances like sugar and yeast.

In the earlier case, Falcone, the sellers' knowledge of the illegal use of the goods was insufficient by itself to make the sellers participants in a conspiracy with the distillers who bought from them. Such knowledge fell short of proof of a conspiracy, and evidence on the volume of sales was too vague to support a jury finding that respondents knew of the conspiracy from the size of the sales alone.

In the later case of Direct Sales, the conviction of a drug wholesaler for conspiracy to violate federal narcotic laws was affirmed on a showing that it had actively promoted the sale of morphine sulphate in quantity and had sold codefendant physician, who practiced in a small town in South Carolina, more than 300 times his normal requirements of the drug, even though it had been repeatedly warned of the dangers of unrestricted sales of the drug. The court contrasted the restricted goods involved in Direct Sales with the articles of free commerce involved in Falcone: "All articles of commerce may be put to illegal ends," said the court. "But all do not have inherently the same susceptibility to harmful and illegal use. . . This difference is important for two purposes. One is for making certain that the seller knows the buyer's intended illegal use. The other is to show that by the sale he intends to further, promote, and cooperate in it. This intent, when given effect by overt act, is the gist of conspiracy. While it is not identical with mere knowledge that another purposes unlawful action it is not unrelated to such knowledge. . . The step from knowledge to intent and agreement may be taken. There is more than suspicion, more than knowledge, acquiescence, carelessness, indifference, lack of concern. There is informed and interested cooperation, stimulation, instigation. And there is also a 'stake in the venture' which, even if it may not be essential, is not irrelevant to the question of conspiracy."

While Falcone and Direct Sales may not be entirely consistent with each other in their full implications, they do provide us with a framework for the criminal liability of a supplier of lawful goods or services put to unlawful use. Both the element of knowledge of the illegal use of the goods or services and the element of intent to further that use must be present in order to make the supplier a participant in a criminal conspiracy.

Proof of knowledge is ordinarily a question of fact and requires no extended discussion in the present case. The knowledge of the supplier was sufficiently established when Lauria admitted he knew some of his customers were prostitutes and admitted he knew that Terry, an active subscriber to his service, was a prostitute. In the face of these admissions he could scarcely claim to have relied on the normal assumption an operator of a business or service is entitled to make, that his customers are behaving themselves in the eyes of the law. Because Lauria knew in fact that some of his customers were prostitutes, it is a legitimate inference he knew they were subscribing to his answering service for illegal business purposes and were using his service to make assignations for prostitution. On this record we think the prosecution is entitled to claim positive knowledge by Lauria of the use of his service to facilitate the business of prostitution.

The more perplexing issue in the case is the sufficiency of proof of intent to further the criminal enterprise. The element of intent may be proved either by direct evidence, or by evidence of circumstances from which an intent to further a criminal enterprise by supplying lawful goods or services may be inferred. Direct evidence of participation, such as advice from the supplier of legal goods or services to the user of those goods or services on their use for illegal purposes, such evidence as appeared in a companion case we decide today, People v. Roy, ante, provides the simplest case. When the intent to further and promote the criminal enterprise comes from the lips of the supplier himself, ambiguities of inference from circumstance need not trouble us. But in cases where direct proof of complicity is lacking, intent to further the conspiracy must be derived from the sale itself and its surrounding circumstances in order to establish the supplier's express or tacit agreement to join the conspiracy.

In the case at bench the prosecution argues that since Lauria knew his customers were using his service for illegal purposes but nevertheless continued to furnish it to them, he must have intended to assist them in carrying out their illegal activities. Thus through a union of knowledge and intent he became a participant in a criminal conspiracy. Essentially, the People argue that knowledge alone of the continuing use of his telephone facilities for criminal purposes provided a sufficient basis from which his intent to participate in those criminal activities could be inferred.

In examining precedents in this field we find that sometimes, but not always, the criminal intent of the supplier may be inferred from his knowledge of the unlawful use made of the product he supplies. Some consideration of characteristic patterns may be helpful.

1.   Intent may be inferred from knowledge, when the purveyor of legal goods for illegal use has acquired a stake in the venture. For example, in Regina v. Thomas, a prosecution for living off the earnings of prostitution, the evidence showed that the accused, knowing the woman to be a convicted prostitute, agreed to let her have the use of his room between the hours of 9 p.m. and 2 a.m. for a charge of # 3 a night. The Court of Criminal Appeal refused an appeal from the conviction, holding that when the accused rented a room at a grossly inflated rent to a prostitute for the purpose of carrying on her

trade, a jury could find he was living on the earnings of prostitution.

In the present case, no proof was offered of inflated charges for the telephone answering services furnished the codefendants.

2. Intent may be inferred from knowledge, when no legitimate use for the goods or services exists. The leading California case is *People v. McLaughlin*, in which the court upheld a conviction of the suppliers of horse-racing information by wire for conspiracy to promote bookmaking, when it had been established that wire-service information had no other use than to supply information needed by bookmakers to conduct illegal gambling operations.

In *Rex v. Delaval*, the charge was unlawful conspiracy to remove a girl from the control of Bates, a musician to whom she was bound as an apprentice, and place her in the hands of Sir Francis Delaval for the purpose of prostitution. Lord Mansfield not only upheld the charges against Bates and Sir Francis, but also against Fraine, the attorney who drew up the indentures of apprenticeship transferring custody of the girl from Bates to Sir Francis. Fraine, said Lord Mansfield, must have known that Sir Francis had no facilities for teaching music to apprentices so that it was impossible for him to have been ignorant of the real intent of the transaction.

In Shaw v. Director of Public Prosecutions, the defendant was convicted of conspiracy to corrupt public morals and of living on the earnings of prostitution, when he published a directory consisting almost entirely of advertisements of the names, addresses, and specialized talents of prostitutes. Publication of such a directory, said the court, could have no legitimate use and serve no other purpose than to advertise the professional services of the prostitutes whose advertisements appeared in the directory. The publisher could be deemed a participant in the profits from the business activities of his principal advertisers.

Other services of a comparable nature come to mind: the manufacturer of crooked dice and marked cards who sells his product to gambling casinos; the tipster who furnishes information on the movement of law enforcement officers to known lawbreakers, where the furnisher of signaling equipment used to warn gamblers of the police was convicted of aiding the equipping of a gambling place. In such cases the supplier must necessarily have an intent to further the illegal enterprise since there is no known honest use for his goods.

However, there is nothing in the furnishing of telephone answering service which would necessarily imply assistance in the performance of illegal activities. Nor is any inference to be derived from the use of an answering service by women, either in any particular volume of calls, or outside normal working hours. Night-club entertainers, registered nurses, faith healers, public stenographers, photographic models, and free lance substitute employees, provide examples of women in legitimate occupations whose employment might cause them to receive a volume of telephone calls at irregular hours.

3. Intent may be inferred from knowledge, when the volume of business with the buyer is grossly disproportionate to any legitimate demand, or when sales for illegal use amount to a high proportion of the seller's total business. In such cases an intent to participate in the illegal enterprise may be inferred from the quantity of the business done. For example, in Direct Sales, supra, the sale of narcotics to a rural physician in quantities 300 times greater than he would have normal use for provided potent evidence of an intent to further the illegal activity. In the same case the court also found significant the fact that the wholesaler had attracted as customers a disproportionately large group of physicians who had been convicted of violating the Harrison Act. In *Shaw v. Director of Public Prosecutions*, almost the entire business of the directory came from prostitutes.

No evidence of any unusual volume of business with prostitutes was presented by the prosecution against Lauria.

Inflated charges, the sale of goods with no legitimate use, sales in inflated amounts, each may provide a fact of sufficient moment from which the intent of the seller to participate in the criminal enterprise may be inferred. In such instances participation by the supplier of legal goods to the illegal enterprise may be inferred because in one way or another the supplier has acquired a special interest in the operation of the illegal enterprise. His intent to participate in the crime of which he has knowledge may be inferred from the existence of his special interest.

Yet there are cases in which it cannot reasonably be said that the supplier has a stake in the venture or has acquired a special interest in the enterprise, but in which he has been held liable as a participant on the basis of knowledge alone. Some suggestion of this appears in Direct Sales, supra, where both the knowledge of the illegal use of the drugs and the intent of the supplier to aid that use were inferred. In Regina v. Bainbridge, a supplier of oxygen-cutting equipment to one known to intend to use it to break into a bank was convicted as an accessory to the crime. In Sykes v. Director of Public Prosecutions, one having knowledge of the theft of 100 pistols, 4 submachine guns, and 1,960 rounds of ammunition was convicted of misprision of felony for failure to disclose the theft to the public authorities. It seems apparent from these cases that a supplier who furnishes equipment which he knows will be used to commit a serious crime may be deemed from that knowledge alone to have intended to produce the result. Such proof may justify an inference that the furnisher intended to aid the execution of the crime and that he thereby became a participant. For instance, we think the operator of a telephone answering service with positive knowledge that his service was being used to facilitate the extortion of ransom, the distribution of heroin, or the passing of counterfeit money who continued to furnish the service with knowledge of its use, might be chargeable on knowledge alone with participation in a scheme to extort money, to distribute narcotics, or to pass counterfeit money. The same result would follow the seller of gasoline who knew the buyer was using his product to make Molotov cocktails for terroristic use.

Logically, the same reasoning could be extended to crimes of every description. Yet we do not believe an inference of intent drawn from knowledge of criminal use properly applies to the less serious crimes classified as misdemeanors. The duty to take positive action to dissociate oneself from activities helpful to violations of the criminal law is far stronger and more compelling for felonies than it is for misdemeanors or petty offenses. In this respect, as in others, the distinction between felonies and misdemeanors, between more serious and less serious crime, retains continuing vitality. In historically the most serious felony, treason, an individual with knowledge of the treason can be prosecuted for concealing and failing to disclose it. In other felonies, both at common law and under the criminal laws of the United States, an individual knowing of the commission of a felony is criminally liable for concealing it and failing to make it known to proper authority. Sykes v. Director of Public Prosecutions. But this crime, known as misprision of felony, has always been limited to knowledge and concealment of felony and has never extended to misdemeanor. A similar limitation is found in the criminal liability of an accessory, which is restricted to aid in the escape of a principal who has committed or been charged with a felony. We believe the distinction between the obligations arising from knowledge of a felony and those arising from knowledge of a misdemeanor continues to reflect basic human feelings about the duties owed by individuals to society. Heinous crime must be stamped out, and its suppression is the responsibility of all. Venial crime and crime not evil in itself present less of a danger to society, and perhaps the benefits of their suppression through the modern equivalent of the posse, the hue and cry, the informant, and the citizen's arrest, are outweighed by the disruption to everyday life brought about by amateur law enforcement and private officiousness in relatively inconsequential delicts which do not threaten our basic security. . .

With respect to misdemeanors, we conclude that positive knowledge of the supplier that his products or services are being used for criminal purposes does not, without more, establish an intent of the supplier to participate in the misdemeanors. With respect to felonies, we do not decide the converse, viz., that in all cases of felony knowledge of criminal use alone may justify an inference of the supplier's intent to participate in the crime.

The implications of Falcone make the matter uncertain with respect to those felonies, which are merely prohibited wrongs. See also Holman v. Johnson (1775) 98 Eng.Rep. 1120 (sale and delivery of tea at Dunkirk known to be destined for smuggling into England not an illegal contract). But decision on this point is not compelled, and we leave the matter open.

From this analysis of precedent we deduce the following rule: the intent of a supplier who knows of the criminal use to which his supplies are put to participate in the criminal activity connected with the use of his supplies may be established by (1) direct evidence that he intends to participate, or (2) through an inference that he intends to participate based on, (a) his special interest in the activity, or (b) the aggravated nature of the crime itself.

When we review Lauria's activities in the light of this analysis, we find no proof that Lauria took any direct action to further, encourage, or direct the call-girl activities of his codefendants and we find an absence of circumstance from which his special interest in their activities could be inferred. Neither excessive charges for standardized services, nor the furnishing of services without a legitimate use, nor an unusual quantity of business with call girls, are present. The offense which he is charged with furthering is a misdemeanor, a category of crime which has never been made a required subject of positive disclosure to public authority. Under these circumstances, although proof of Lauria's knowledge of the criminal activities of his patrons was sufficient to charge him with that fact, there was insufficient evidence that he intended to further their criminal activities, and hence insufficient proof of his participation in a criminal conspiracy with his codefendants to further prostitution. Since the conspiracy centered around the activities of Lauria's telephone answering service, the charges against his codefendants likewise fail for want of proof.

In absolving Lauria of complicity in a criminal conspiracy we do not wish to imply that the public authorities are without remedies to combat modern manifestations of the world's oldest profession. Licensing of telephone answering services under the police power, together with the revocation of licenses for the toleration of prostitution, is a possible civil remedy. The furnishing of telephone answering service in aid of prostitution could be made a crime. (Cf. Pen. Code, § 316, which makes it a misdemeanor to let an apartment with knowledge of its use for prostitution.) Other solutions will doubtless occur to vigilant public authorities if the problem of call-girl activity needs further suppression.

The order is affirmed.

DISCUSSION QUESTIONS

1.   Do you think knowing assistance should be enough to make one a conspirator?

2.   What factors does the court announce for determining whether purpose can be inferred from knowledge? Do you think a provider of legal services should ever be found guilty of conspiracy without explicit evidence of purpose?

3.   Play with these factors by creating your own hypotheticals. Imagine that a friend has asked you to drive him to a party at which you know he will be selling drugs. What facts would you have to add to make you liable for conspiracy under the *Lauria factors*?

2.   ATTENDANT CIRCUMSTANCES

What does it mean to intend a crime be committed if the crime does not require knowledge of all the circumstances that attend its commission? The answer varies from state to state and even from offense to offense within states. The following case illustrates one approach.

Case in Context

Concerns about general blameworthiness play an important part in the court's decision in the following case.

UNITED STATES V. FEOLA
Supreme Court of the United States
420 U.S. 671 (1975)

Opinion

MR. JUSTICE BLACKMUN delivered the opinion of the Court.

This case presents the issue whether knowledge that the intended victim is a federal officer is a requisite for the crime of conspiracy, under 18 U.S.C. s 371, to commit an offense violative of 18 U.S.C. s 111, that is, an assault upon a federal officer while engaged in the performance of his official duties.

Respondent Feola and three others (Alsondo, Rosa, and Farr) were indicted for violations of ss 371 and 111. A jury found all four defendants guilty of both charges. [T]he United States Court of Appeals for the Second affirmed the judgment of conviction on the substantive charges, but reversed the conspiracy convictions. Because of a conflict among the federal Circuits on the scienter issue with respect to a conspiracy charge, we granted the Government's petition for a writ of certiorari in Feola's case.

I

The facts reveal a classic narcotics 'rip-off.' [T]he evidence shows that Feola and his confederates arranged for a sale of heroin to buyers who turned out to be undercover agents for the Bureau of Narcotics and Dangerous Drugs. The group planned to palm off on the purchasers, for a substantial sum, a form of sugar in place of heroin and, should that ruse fail, simply to surprise their unwitting buyers and relieve them of the cash they had brought along for payment. The plan failed when one agent, his suspicions being aroused, drew his revolver in time to counter an assault upon another agent from the rear. Instead of enjoying the rich benefits of a successful swindle, Feola and his associates found themselves charged, to their undoubted surprise, with conspiring to assault, and with assaulting, federal officers.

At the trial, the District Court, without objection from the defense, charged the jurors that, in order to find any of the defendants guilty on either the conspiracy count or the substantive one, they were not required to conclude that the defendants were aware that their quarry were federal officers.

The Court of Appeals reversed the conspiracy convictions on a ground not advanced by any of the defendants. Although it approved the trial court's instructions to the jury on the substantive charge of assaulting a federal officer, it nonetheless concluded that the failure to charge that knowledge of the victim's official identity must be proved in order to convict on the conspiracy charge amounted to plain error. 486 F.2d, at 1344. The court perceived itself bound by a line of cases, commencing with Judge Learned Hand's opinion in United States v. Crimmins, 123 F.2d 271 (CA2 1941), all holding that scienter of a factual element that confers federal jurisdiction, while unnecessary for conviction of the substantive offense, is required in order to sustain a conviction for conspiracy to commit the substantive offense.

II

The Government's plea is for symmetry. It urges that since criminal liability for the offense described in 18 U.S.C. s 111 does not depend on whether the assailant harbored the specific intent to assault a federal officer, no greater scienter requirement can be engrafted upon the conspiracy offense, which is merely an agreement to commit the act proscribed by s 111.

This interpretation poses no risk of unfairness to defendants. It is no snare for the unsuspecting. Although the perpetrator of a narcotics 'rip-off,' such as the one involved here, may be surprised to find that his intended victim is a federal officer in civilian apparel, he nonetheless knows from the very outset that his planned course of conduct is wrongful. The situation is not one where legitimate conduct becomes unlawful solely because of the identity of the individual or agency affected. In a case of this kind the offender takes his victim as he finds him. The concept of criminal intent does not extend so far as to require that the actor understand not only the nature of his act but also its consequence for the choice of a judicial forum.

We hold, therefore, that in order to incur criminal liability under s 111 an actor must entertain merely the criminal intent to do the acts therein specified. We now consider whether the rule should be different where persons conspire to commit those acts.

III

Our decisions establish that in order to sustain a judgment of conviction on a charge of conspiracy to violate a federal statute, the Government must prove at least the degree of criminal intent necessary for the substantive offense itself. . . Respondent Feola urges upon us the proposition that the Government must show a degree of criminal intent in the conspiracy count greater than is necessary to convict for the substantive offense; he urges that even though it is not necessary to show that he was aware of the official identity of his assaulted victims in order to find him guilty of assaulting federal officers, in violation of 18 U.S.C. s 111, the Government nonetheless must show that he was aware that his intended victims were undercover agents, if it is successfully to prosecute him for conspiring to assault federal agents. And the Court of Appeals held that the trial court's failure to charge the jury to this effect constituted plain error.

The general conspiracy statute, 18 U.S.C. s 371,20 offers no textual support for the proposition that to be guilty of conspiracy a defendant in effect must have known that his conduct violated federal law. The statute makes it unlawful simply to 'conspire. . . to commit any offense against the United States.' A natural reading of these words would be that since one can violate a criminal statute simply by engaging in the forbidden conduct, a conspiracy to commit that offense is nothing more than an agreement to engage in the prohibited conduct. Then where, as here, the substantive statute does not require that an assailant know the official status of his victim, there is nothing on the face of the conspiracy statute that would seem to require that those agreeing to the assault have a greater degree of knowledge.

With no support on the face of the general conspiracy statute or in this Court's decisions, respondent relies solely on the line of cases commencing with United States v. Crimmins, 123 F.2d 271 (CA2 1941), for the principle that the Government must prove 'antifederal' intent in order to establish liability under s 371. In Crimmins, the defendant had been found guilty of conspiring to receive stolen bonds that had been transported in interstate commerce. Upon review, the Court of Appeals pointed out that the evidence failed to establish that Crimmins actually knew the stolen bonds had moved into the State. Accepting for the sake of argument the assumption that such knowledge was not necessary to sustain a conviction on the substantive offense, Judge Learned Hand nevertheless concluded that to permit conspiratorial liability where the conspirators were ignorant of the federal implications of their acts would be to enlarge their agreement beyond its terms as they understood them. He capsulized the distinction in what has become well known as his 'traffic light' analogy:

> 'While one may, for instance, be guilty of running past a traffic light of whose existence one is ignorant, one cannot be guilty of conspiring to run past such a light, for one cannot agree to run past a light unless one supposes that there is a light to run past.' Id., at 273.

Judge Hand's attractive, but perhaps seductive, analogy has received a mixed reception in the Courts of Appeals. The Second Circuit, of course, has followed it; others have rejected it. It appears that most have avoided it by the simple expedient of inferring the requisite knowledge from the scope of the conspiratorial venture. We conclude that the analogy, though effective prose, is, as applied to the facts before us, bad law.

One may run a traffic light 'of whose existence one is ignorant,' but assaulting another 'of whose existence one is ignorant,' probably would require unearthly intervention. Thus, the traffic light analogy, even if it were a correct statement of the law, is inapt, for the conduct proscribed by the substantive offense, here assault, is not of the type outlawed without regard to the intent of the actor to accomplish the result that is made criminal. If the analogy has any vitality at all, it is to conduct of the latter variety; that, however, is a question we save for another day. We hold here only that where a substantive offense embodies only a requirement of mens rea as to each of its elements, the general federal conspiracy statute requires no more.

Our decisions have identified two independent values served by the law of conspiracy. The first is protection of society from the dangers of concerted criminal activity. . . .That individuals know that their planned joint venture violates federal as well as state law seems totally irrelevant to that purpose of conspiracy law which seeks to protect society from the dangers of concerted criminal activity. Given the level of criminal intent necessary to sustain conviction for the substantive offense, the act of agreement to commit the crime is no less opprobrious and no less dangerous because of the absence of knowledge of a fact unnecessary to the formation of criminal intent.

The second aspect is that conspiracy is an inchoate crime. This is to say, that, although the law generally makes criminal only antisocial conduct, at some point in the continuum between preparation and consummation, the likelihood of a commission of an act is sufficiently great and the criminal intent sufficiently well formed to justify the intervention of the criminal law. . . The law of conspiracy identifies the agreement to engage in a criminal venture as an event of sufficient threat to social order to permit the imposition of criminal sanctions for the agreement alone, plus an overt act in pursuit of it, regardless of whether the crime agreed upon actually is committed... Criminal intent has crystallized, and the likelihood of actual, fulfilled commission warrants preventive action.

We hold, then, that assault of a federal officer pursuant to an agreement to assault is not, even in the words of Judge Hand, 'beyond the reasonable intendment of the common understanding,' United States v. Crimmins, 123 F.2d, at 273. The agreement is not thereby enlarged, for knowledge of the official identity of the victim is irrelevant to the essential nature of the agreement, entrance into which is made criminal by the law of conspiracy.

DISCUSSION QUESTIONS

1.   What are the mental state requirements for assaulting a federal officer? Should they be higher?

2.   Why doesn't the court agree with Judge Learned Hand's approach?

3.   Do you think that conspiracy should require knowledge of attendant circumstances of the target offense even if simply committing that target offense requires no such knowledge? If not, why should the rule be different for results than for attendant circumstances?

3. THE CORRUPT MOTIVE DOCTRINE

Can you conspire to violate a law that you don't know about? Ignorance of the law is ordinarily no excuse, but some courts require what is called a "corrupt motive" for conspiracy liability. These courts reason that the very idea of a conspiracy implies that you are agreeing to something with an evil purpose. The cases distinguish between regulatory offenses, which are wrong because society has legally prohibited them (malum prohibitum), and other offenses which are clearly understood to be wrong in and of themselves (malum en se). One can always be guilty of conspiring to commit a malum en se offense such as theft. To be guilty of conspiring to commit a malum prohibitum offense, such as certain regulatory reporting or disclosure requirements, jurisdictions recognizing this doctrine will require either proof of knowledge of the law to be broken or proof of a corrupt or evil motive.

F. LIABILITY FOR OTHER CRIMES

Conspiracy is its own crime, but the federal courts and many jurisdictions also hold a conspirator liable for certain crimes committed as a result of the conspiracy. This additional liability is known as Pinkerton liability, taking its name from the Supreme Court case that announced the rule for the federal courts. Under this rule, a conspirator is responsible for crimes committed by other conspirators if

1. The crime was committed in furtherance of the conspiracy and

2. The crime was a foreseeable consequence of the unlawful agreement.

Pinkerton liability often overlaps with ordinary complicity liability, which will be discussed in a subsequent chapter. The Pinkerton doctrine, however, can create liability for a crime that the conspirator did not aid or assist (the basis for complicity liability). For example, in the original case, Pinkerton was held liable for crimes committed by his co-conspirators while he was in jail.

Most crimes that are committed in furtherance of a conspiracy will be considered foreseeable. A bank robber, for example, who kills a resisting teller satisfies both elements. The killing was committed in furtherance of the conspiracy and the crime was a foreseeable consequence of the agreement to rob the bank.

What if, during the robbery, the bank robber sees someone who bullied him in high school and executes the former bully without warning? Would liability for the killing be imputed to the other conspirators? This killing would likely not be a foreseeable consequence of the agreement to rob the bank. On the one hand, one could argue that killing the bully eliminates a witness, furthering the conspiracy by reducing the chances of apprehension. On the other hand, the risk that one of the robbers would be recognized and then take it upon himself to kill the witness would not be foreseeable. In that case, liability for the killing would not be imputed to the other conspirators.

Case in Context

This case shows the Pinkerton doctrine in action.

UNITED STATES OF AMERICA V. DIAZ

United States Court of Appeals, Seventh Circuit
864 F.2d 544 (1988)

Opinion

RIPPLE, CIRCUIT JUDGE.

This is a direct appeal from a federal criminal conviction. After a jury trial, the appellant, Reynaldo Diaz, was convicted of conspiracy to distribute cocaine, possession and distribution of cocaine, and use of a firearm in relation to the commission of a drug trafficking crime. Mr. Diaz alleges that his conviction for use of a firearm was based improperly on his conviction on the conspiracy charge. For the following reasons, we affirm the judgment of the district court.

The testimony at trial revealed the following. A DEA agent purchased cocaine from Carmen Diaz (no relation to the appellant) and Perez on July 23, 1987. There was no testimony that Reynaldo Diaz was involved in this sale. Perez was just beginning to deal in drugs and contacted Rodriguez in an effort to find a supplier of cocaine. Rodriguez testified that he knew somebody who could "help [Perez] out" and arranged a meeting between himself, Perez, and Mr. Diaz. R.166 at 160. Rodriguez had known Mr. Diaz since 1977. After the meeting, Mr. Diaz agreed to supply drugs to Perez.

On August 21, 1987, and again on September 3, 1987, Perez sold two ounces of cocaine to DEA Agent Patricia Collins. Perez testified that he obtained these drugs from Mr. Diaz. Although Mr. Diaz was not present for either sale, Perez testified that the second sale occurred a half-block from Mr. Diaz's house so that Mr. Diaz could see the buyer. Rodriguez and Perez also testified that they dropped the money off at Mr. Diaz's house after the second sale. This assertion could not be verified by agents circulating in the neighborhood at the time.

On September 9, 1987, Perez and Rodriguez went to a designated location; they were to meet with Mr. Diaz to sell one kilogram of cocaine to Agent Collins. Upon their arrival, Mr. Diaz was not present. Telephone records introduced at trial corroborated that Perez and Rodriguez telephoned Mr. Diaz. Testimony of Perez and Rodriguez at trial revealed that Mr. Diaz thought the deal was going to take place closer to his home but agreed to join the men in ten to fifteen minutes. Approximately five minutes after Mr. Diaz arrived, Peirallo arrived. Peirallo had brought the kilogram of cocaine from Miami, Florida to Chicago, Illinois earlier that same day.

The parties waited an hour for Agent Collins. Peirallo became impatient and decided to leave the scene. He asked to be paged telephonically when Agent Collins arrived. Almost as soon as Peirallo left, Agent Collins arrived. Telephone records and testimony confirmed that Mr. Diaz telephoned Peirallo's pager. Perez joined Agent Collins in her car, counted the money, and then met with Mr. Diaz to confirm that Peirallo was on his way. Perez returned to Agent Collins' car to await Peirallo's arrival. Almost immediately, Mr. Diaz sent Rodriguez to Agent Collins' car to announce that Peirallo was arriving. After Peirallo had arrived and parked, the cars were lined up so that Peirallo's was first in line, Mr. Diaz's was the middle car and Agent Collins' car was the last car parked in line.

The officers engaged in surveillance testified that there was a great deal of movement and conversation among Mr. Diaz, Peirallo, and Rodriguez. When Peirallo arrived, Mr. Diaz and Rodriguez moved to Mr. Diaz's car; Mr. Diaz opened the hood of his car. The government and the appellant have conflicting theories about why the hood of the car was opened. Mr. Diaz claims the hood was opened because he was having car trouble. The government, in contrast, asserts that opening a car hood is a standard method by which drug dealers prevent their buyers from seeing the supplier of the drugs. Around the time the hood was raised, Perez left Agent Collins' car and went to Peirallo's car. Peirallo told Perez that he had a gun which he intended to use if anyone tried to steal the drugs. While Perez was with Peirallo, Mr. Diaz and Rodriguez continued to stand by Mr. Diaz's car watching Agent Collins. Perez took the drugs to Agent Collins. Agent Collins then gave the arrest signal.

Mr. Diaz was convicted of using and carrying a firearm during and in relation to the commission of drug trafficking crimes. As a result of this conviction, Mr. Diaz was sentenced to an additional five years in prison. The government did not submit evidence at trial that Mr. Diaz was armed. Rather, it contended that Peirallo's carrying of a firearm could be imputed to Mr. Diaz because of their joint membership in the conspiracy.

Our law has long acknowledged the "special and continuing dangers incident to group activity." W. Lafave & A. Scott, Jr., Substantive Criminal Law § 6.4 (1986). As the Supreme Court noted in Callanan v. United States, 364 U.S. 587, 81 S.Ct. 321, 5 L.Ed.2d 312 (1961):

> Concerted action both increases the likelihood that the criminal object will be successfully attained and decreases the probability that the individuals involved will depart from their path of criminality. Group association for criminal purposes often, if not normally, makes possible the attainment of ends more complex than those which one criminal could accomplish. Nor is the danger of a conspiratorial group limited to the particular end toward which it has embarked. Combination in crime makes more likely the commission of crimes unrelated to the original purpose for which the group was formed. In sum, the danger which a conspiracy generates is not confined to the substantive offense which is the immediate aim of the enterprise.

The firearm violation under section 924(c)(1) may be imputed to other members of the conspiracy, including Mr. Diaz, under Pinkerton v. United States, 328 U.S. 640, 66 S.Ct. 1180, 90 L.Ed. 1489 (1946). In Pinkerton, the Supreme Court held that a party to a continuing conspiracy may be responsible "when the substantive offense is committed by one of the conspirators in furtherance of the [conspiracy]," even though he does not participate in the substantive offense or have any knowledge of it. The jury was instructed that:

> To sustain the charge in Count Six as to defendant Reynaldo Diaz, of using and carrying a firearm during and in relation to a drug trafficking crime, the government must prove the following propositions:

> First, the defendant David Peirallo is guilty of the offense charged in Count Six of the indictment;

Second, the defendant David Peirallo committed the offense charged in Count Six in furtherance of or as a natural and foreseeable consequence of the conspiracy charged in Count one [sic] of the indictment; and

Third, defendant Reynaldo Diaz was a member of the conspiracy at the time defendant David Peirallo committed the offense charged in Count Six.

If you find from your consideration of all the evidence that each of these propositions has been proved beyond a reasonable doubt, then you should find the defendant Reynaldo Diaz guilty of Count Six of the indictment.

If, on the other hand, you find from your consideration of all the evidence that any of these propositions has not been proved beyond a reasonable doubt, then you should find defendant Reynaldo Diaz not guilty of Count Six.

R. 145. This circuit has interpreted "Pinkerton to mean that each conspirator may be liable for 'acts of every other conspirator done in furtherance of the conspiracy.'" . . . Therefore, Peirallo's possession of a gun during the cocaine sale may be imputed to Mr. Diaz.

There is, of course, one established exception to the Pinkerton doctrine. A conspirator may be found guilty of a substantive crime unless that crime "could not be reasonably foreseen as a necessary or natural consequence of the unlawful agreement." Pinkerton, 328 U.S. at 648, 66 S.Ct. at 1184. However, the illegal drug industry is, to put it mildly, a dangerous, violent business. When an individual conspires to take part in a street transaction involving a kilogram of cocaine worth $39,000, it certainly is quite reasonable to assume that a weapon of some kind would be carried.

DISCUSSION QUESTIONS

1.   What mental state did the court require for Diaz with respect to the firearm offense? Is every member of the conspiracy liable for this offense?

2.   Should the prosecution have to prove that Diaz at least knew about the firearm in order to be guilty of the firearm offense?

3.   Under the Pinkerton doctrine could you be guilty of crimes committed by someone whom you did not even know belonged to the conspiracy? Is that just?

G. ABANDONING OR WITHDRAWING FROM A CONSPIRACY

Until someone invents a time machine, you cannot "undo" your criminal liability for conspiracy by withdrawing from the agreement or abandoning the effort once the crime of conspiracy has been committed in the majority of jurisdictions or at common law. If your jurisdiction requires an overt act, however, you can avoid conspiracy liability if you withdraw before the overt act is committed. Even if an overt act is not required—or has already been performed if the jurisdiction does require one—withdrawal is still worth doing. While it may not eliminate your *past* liability for conspiracy, it will cut off your *future* liability for crimes committed in furtherance of the conspiracy under the Pinkerton doctrine. Withdrawal requires you to effectively communicate to all conspirators that you are withdrawing. In most jurisdictions, you do not have to report the conspiracy to the police.

The Model Penal Code and a small minority of jurisdictions will allow you to withdraw in a way that not only cuts off future liability but also constitutes a defense to your past crime of conspiracy. Not surprisingly, you must do more than just break the bad news to all your co-conspirators. The Model Penal Code requires that you "thwart the success of the conspiracy." (Some of these minority jurisdictions require only that you make timely warning to the authorities.)

So, if you change your mind after agreeing with your roommates to rob a bank to pay your law school bills, make sure you call each and every one of them before they get to the bank lest they do something really bad while they are inside. If you are in an MPC/Minority jurisdiction, you might want to also call the police before they get there to avoid being held liable for the conspiracy itself.

Case in Context

The defendant in the following case abandons a conspiracy he set in motion.

THE PEOPLE V. DAVID WAYNE SCONCE
Court of Appeal, Second District, Division 3, California
279 Cal.Rptr. 59 (1991)

KLEIN, P. J.

The People filed an information charging defendant and respondent David Wayne Sconce (Sconce) with conspiracy to commit murder. (Pen. Code, §§ 182, 187, subd. (a).)1 The trial court set the information aside because it found Sconce effectively had withdrawn from the conspiracy. (§ 995.) The People appeal.

Because withdrawal cannot insulate Sconce from criminal liability for conspiracy after an overt act in furtherance of the conspiracy has been committed, the order must be reversed.

Factual Background

1.   Preliminary hearing testimony.

This case involves Sconce's alleged formation of a conspiracy to kill Elie Estephan (Estephan).

In 1985 Estephan and Cindy Strunk (Cindy) were separated. Cindy testified she worked for her father, Frank Strunk, at his business, the Cremation Society of California (CSC). In the course of her duties at CSC, she met Sconce whose family owned the Lamb Funeral Home (LFH) and the Pasadena Crematorium. In 1985, Cindy met Sconce's brother-in-law, Brad Sallard (Sallard). She and Sallard dated and began to live together in May 1985.

When Estephan served divorce papers on Cindy in June, 1985, Sconce offered her the services of LFH's attorney. Sconce and Sallard accompanied Cindy to the first meeting with the lawyer. One of the assets she mentioned during the meeting was a $250,000 insurance policy on Estephan's life which named her as beneficiary.

At some point thereafter, Cindy argued with Estephan at CSC in front of Frank Strunk and others including an LFH employee, John Pollerana (Pollerana). Estephan chased Cindy and pushed her down a number of stairs. She was upset but not hurt.

Pollerana testified that in late summer of 1985, the day after the argument between Estephan and Cindy, Sconce asked Pollerana "if he gave me $10,000, would I get rid of Elie [Estephan], but, you know, I just shook my head, and we just walked by. That was the end of the conversation."

Pollerana further testified Sconce did not like Estephan because he had slapped Cindy. Pollerana did not take Sconce's offer seriously. However, two weeks later Pollerana had a conversation with Bob Garcia (Garcia) in which Garcia said Sconce had offered him $10,000 to kill Estephan. Pollerana told Garcia, " 'I wouldn't do it.' " A few days later, Garcia showed Pollerana the address to Estephan's house and Pollerana drove Garcia there.

Garcia testified he also worked for Sconce. One day at the crematorium Sconce asked Garcia "about someone being murdered, and if I knew anyone who would do it." Sconce told him "a friend wanted someone killed." Sconce offered Garcia $10,000 or $15,000 to commit the murder. Garcia told Sconce he would either find someone to do it or that he would do it himself.

In a telephone conversation a few days later, Sconce told Garcia that Estephan "had a large insurance policy and he just wanted him murdered to collect the insurance money." Sconce gave Garcia the impression that Sconce, Sallard and Cindy were plotting Estephan's murder.

Approximately one week later Sconce and Garcia went to a Jack-In-The-Box across the street from Estephan's gas station. CSC is on another corner of the same intersection. They sat next to the window and, as they ate lunch, Sconce used binoculars to point Estephan out to Garcia. Sconce later gave Estephan's address to Garcia. One night shortly thereafter, Garcia and Pollerana drove to Estephan's house.

Garcia then contacted Herbert Dutton (Dutton), an ex-convict who lived next door to him, about committing the offense. Dutton agreed to do the job for $5,000. That same night Garcia and Dutton drove to Estephan's house. On the way there they discussed whether to blow up Estephan's car or shoot him on the freeway. They settled on the former because Dutton had explosives and no one would have to pull the trigger. They intended to plant the bomb, run a wire to it from three houses away, and wait for Estephan.

Conversations between Sconce and Garcia about the matter were brief but continued over a three-week period. Sconce would ask Garcia, "Is he still walking today[?]" Garcia would respond that "we" would take care of it. Approximately three weeks after Sconce's initial conversation with Garcia, Sconce "just called it off. He said just forget about it, disregard doing it." Garcia did not see Dutton after the night they drove to Estephan's house. Although Garcia did not know it at the time Sconce told him not to kill Estephan, Dutton had been arrested on a parole violation.

Dutton testified that in mid-September, 1985, Garcia asked him if he knew anyone who would kill someone his boss wanted killed. Dutton said he would do it for "about $2,500." Dutton suggested explosives or a 12-gauge shotgun. That same evening they drove to the home of the victim "to see if it would be suitable to wire the car out there." Dutton told Garcia to give him half the money up front and to let him know. However, Dutton, who was on federal parole for bank robbery, was arrested for parole violation stemming from heroin abuse shortly after discussing the matter with Garcia. Dutton did not see Garcia again after that night and had never met Sconce.

Frank Strunk testified that sometime after the argument between Cindy and Estephan at CSC, he saw Sconce and another person at the Jack-In-The-Box across the street from CSC making gestures and looking at Estephan through binoculars. Frank Strunk went to the restaurant and asked Sconce why he was watching Estephan. Sconce said he was just pointing out the gas station. Frank Strunk told Cindy about this incident.

Cindy testified that after speaking with her father, she confronted Sallard and asked him why Sconce had been looking at Estephan with binoculars. Sallard made statements to her which the trial court excluded as hearsay. However, after this conversation, Cindy feared for her life and left Sallard immediately. Sallard told her not to repeat their conversation, that no one would believe her, and that if she did repeat it she would have to "watch. . . [her] back."

Contentions

The People contend the trial court erroneously set aside the information because Sconce's withdrawal from the conspiracy, although it might insulate him from liability for future conspiratorial acts, does not constitute a defense to liability for the conspiracy itself. Further, the People assert Sconce failed to demonstrate effective withdrawal from the conspiracy.

Discussion

" 'Once the defendant's participation in the conspiracy is shown, it will be presumed to continue unless he is able to prove, as a matter of defense, that he effectively withdrew from the conspiracy. Although a defendant's arrest and incarceration may terminate his participation in an alleged conspiracy, his arrest does not terminate, or constitute a withdrawal from, the conspiracy as a matter of law. Withdrawal from, or termination of, a conspiracy is a question of fact.

Withdrawal from a conspiracy requires "an affirmative and bona fide rejection or repudiation of the conspiracy, communicated to the coconspirators.

Under California law withdrawal is a complete defense to conspiracy only if accomplished before the commission of an overt act, or, where it is asserted in conjunction with the running of the statute of limitations.

"The requirement of an overt act before conspirators can be prosecuted and punished exists. . . to provide a locus p[o]enitentiae-an opportunity for the conspirators to reconsider, terminate the agreement, and thereby avoid punishment for the conspiracy.

Obviously, the inverse of this rule is that once an overt act has been committed in furtherance of the conspiracy the crime of conspiracy has been completed and no subsequent action by the conspirator can change that.

Thus, even if it be assumed Sconce effectively withdrew from the conspiracy or, as Sconce argues, that the People conceded withdrawal before the trial court, withdrawal merely precludes liability for subsequent acts committed by the members of the conspiracy. The withdrawal does not relate back to the criminal formation of the unlawful combination. In sum, conspiracy is complete upon the commission of an overt act.

This rule is consistent with the traditional view that the crime of conspiracy is complete with the agreement and an overt act, and no subsequent action can exonerate the conspirator of that crime.

The rationale in favor of terminating liability is the one relied upon by the trial court, i.e., the reasons for allowing withdrawal as a defense to conspiracy-encouraging abandonment and thereby weakening the group-continue to apply after the commission of an overt act.

However, the rule remains that withdrawal avoids liability only for the target offense, or for any subsequent act committed by a coconspirator in pursuance of the common plan. "[I]n respect of the conspiracy itself, the individual's change of mind is ineffective; he cannot undo that which he has already done.

Even if this court were inclined to agree with the trial court, we are bound to follow the foregoing settled rule. Any change in the law is a matter for the Legislature.

Because we conclude Sconce's withdrawal from the conspiracy is not a valid defense to the completed crime of conspiracy, we need not determine whether the evidence showed that Sconce, in fact, withdrew from the conspiracy and communicated that withdrawal to each coconspirator.

DISCUSSION QUESTIONS

1. Under this court's approach, when, if ever, could a conspirator withdraw in a way that would "undo" his liability for the crime of conspiracy itself?

2. Did Sconce do enough to cut off his liability for future crimes committed in furtherance of the conspiracy?

3. Should the law make it easier to withdraw from a conspiracy? Should it provide greater incentives for those who do?

H. DURATION OF THE CONSPIRACY

Determining when a conspiracy ends can be important for terminating Pinkerton liability for other crimes and also for running of the statute of limitations (the time period within which the state must prosecute you for the crime). Conspiracies end when the goal of the conspiracy is successfully achieved (although that achievement sometimes includes activities after the fact to avoid detection). Withdrawal from a conspiracy also ends the duration of the conspiracy for the person withdrawing.

Case in Context

The next case considers whether a conspiracy exists if it cannot possibly succeed.

UNITED STATES V. RECIO

Supreme Court of the United States
537 U.S. 270 (2003)

JUSTICE BREYER delivered the opinion of the Court.

We here consider the validity of a Ninth Circuit rule that a conspiracy ends automatically when the object of the conspiracy becomes impossible to achieve—when, for example, the Government frustrates a drug conspiracy's objective by seizing the drugs that its members have agreed to distribute. In our view, conspiracy law does not contain any such "automatic termination" rule.

I

In United States v. Cruz, 127 F.3d 791, 795 (CA9 1997), the Ninth Circuit, following the language of an earlier case, United States v. Castro, 972 F.2d 1107, 1112 (CA9 1992), wrote that a conspiracy terminates when " 'there is affirmative evidence of abandonment, withdrawal, disavowal or defeat of the object of the conspiracy' " (emphasis added). It considered the conviction of an individual who, the Government had charged, joined a conspiracy (to distribute drugs) after the Government had seized the drugs in question. The Circuit found that the Government's seizure of the drugs guaranteed the "defeat" of the conspiracy's objective, namely, drug distribution. The Circuit held that the conspiracy had terminated with that "defeat," i.e., when the Government seized the drugs. Hence the individual, who had joined the conspiracy after that point, could not be convicted as a conspiracy member.

In this case the lower courts applied the Cruz rule to similar facts: On November 18, 1997, police stopped a truck in Nevada. They found, and seized, a large stash of illegal drugs. With the help of the truck's two drivers, they set up a sting. The Government took the truck to the drivers' destination, a mall in Idaho. The drivers paged a contact and described the truck's location. The contact said that he would call someone to get the truck. And three hours later, the two defendants, Francisco Jimenez Recio and Adrian Lopez-Meza, appeared in a car. Jimenez Recio drove away in the truck; Lopez-Meza drove the car away in a similar direction. Police stopped both vehicles and arrested both men.

A federal grand jury indicted Jimenez Recio, Lopez-Meza, and the two original truck drivers, charging them with having conspired, together and with others, to possess and to distribute unlawful drugs. A jury convicted all four. But the trial judge then decided that the jury instructions had been erroneous in respect to Jimenez Recio and Lopez-Meza. The judge noted that the Ninth Circuit, in Cruz, had held that the Government could not prosecute drug conspiracy defendants unless they had joined the conspiracy before the Government seized the drugs. See Cruz, supra, at 795–796. That holding, as applied here, meant that the jury could not convict Jimenez Recio and Lopez-Meza unless the jury believed they had joined the conspiracy before the Nevada police stopped the truck and seized the drugs. The judge ordered a new trial where the jury would be instructed to that effect. The new jury convicted the two men once again.

Jimenez Recio and Lopez-Meza appealed. They pointed out that, given Cruz, the jury had to find that they had joined the conspiracy before the Nevada stop, and they claimed that the evidence was insufficient at both trials to warrant any such jury finding. The Ninth Circuit panel, by a vote of 2 to 1, agreed. All three panel members accepted Cruz as binding law. Two members concluded that the evidence presented at the second trial was not sufficient to show that the defendants had joined the conspiracy before the Nevada drug seizure. One of the two wrote that the evidence at the first trial was not sufficient either, a circumstance she believed independently warranted reversal. The third member, dissenting, believed that the evidence at both trials adequately demonstrated preseizure membership. He added that he, like the other panel members, was bound by Cruz, but he wrote that in his view Cruz was "totally inconsistent with long established and appropriate principles of the law of conspiracy," and he urged the Circuit to overrule it en banc "at the earliest opportunity."

The Government sought certiorari. It noted that the Ninth Circuit's holding in this case was premised upon the legal rule enunciated in Cruz. And it asked us to decide the rule's validity, i.e., to decide whether "a conspiracy ends as a matter of law when the government frustrates its objective." Pet. for Cert. I. We agreed to consider that question.

II

In Cruz, the Ninth Circuit held that a conspiracy continues " 'until there is affirmative evidence of abandonment, withdrawal, disavowal or defeat of the object of the conspiracy.' " The critical portion of this statement is the last segment, that a conspiracy ends once there has been "defeat of [its] object." The Circuit's holdings make clear that the phrase means that the conspiracy ends through "defeat" when the Government intervenes, making the conspiracy's goals impossible to achieve, even if the conspirators do not know that the Government has intervened and are totally unaware that the conspiracy is bound to fail. In our view, this statement of the law is incorrect. A conspiracy does not automatically terminate simply because the Government, unbeknownst to some of the conspirators, has "defeated" the conspiracy's "object."

Two basic considerations convince us that this is the proper view of the law. First, the Ninth Circuit's rule is inconsistent with our own understanding of basic conspiracy law. The Court has repeatedly said that the essence of a conspiracy is "an agreement to commit an unlawful act." That agreement is "a distinct evil," which "may exist and be punished whether or not the substantive crime ensues." The conspiracy poses a "threat to the public" over and above the threat of the commission of the relevant substantive crime—both because the "combination in crime makes more likely the commission of [other] crimes" and because it "decreases the probability that the individuals involved will depart from their path of criminality." Where police have frustrated a conspiracy's specific objective but conspirators (unaware of that fact) have neither abandoned the conspiracy nor withdrawn, these special conspiracy-related dangers remain. Cf. 2 W. LaFave & A. Scott, Substantive Criminal Law § 6.5, p. 85 (1986) ("impossibility" does not terminate conspiracy because "criminal combinations are dangerous apart from the danger of attaining the particular objective"). So too remains the essence of the conspiracy—the agreement to commit the crime. That being so, the Government's defeat of the conspiracy's objective will not necessarily and automatically terminate the conspiracy.

Second, the view we endorse today is the view of almost all courts and commentators but for the Ninth Circuit. No other Federal Court of Appeals has adopted the Ninth Circuit's rule. Three have explicitly rejected it. . . One treatise, after surveying lower court conspiracy decisions, has concluded that "impossibility of success is not a defense." 2LaFave & Scott, Substantive Criminal Law § 6.5, at 85; see also id., § 6.5(b), at 90–93. And the American Law Institute's Model Penal Code § 5.03, p. 384 (1985), would find that a conspiracy "terminates when the crime or crimes that are its object are committed" or when the relevant "agreement. . . is abandoned." It would not find "impossibility" a basis for termination.

The Cruz majority argued that the more traditional termination rule threatened "endless" potential liability. To illustrate the point, the majority posited a sting in which police instructed an arrested conspirator to go through the "telephone directory. . . [and] call all of his acquaintances" to come and help him, with the Government obtaining convictions of those who did so. The problem with this example, however, is that, even though it is not necessarily an example of entrapment itself, it draws its persuasive force from the fact that it bears certain resemblances to entrapment. The law independently forbids convictions that rest upon entrapment. And the example fails to explain why a different branch of the law, conspiracy law, should be modified to forbid entrapment-like behavior that falls outside the bounds of current entrapment law. At the same time, the Cruz rule would reach well beyond arguable police misbehavior, potentially threatening the use of properly run law enforcement sting operations. See Lewis v. United States, 385 U.S. 206, 208–209, 17 L. Ed. 2d 312, 87 S. Ct. 424 (1966) (Government may "use decoys" and conceal agents' identity); see also M. Lyman, Criminal Investigation 484–485 (2d ed. 1999) (explaining the importance of undercover operations in enforcing drug laws). . .

III

We conclude that the Ninth Circuit's conspiracy-termination law holding set forth in Cruz is erroneous in the manner discussed. We reverse the present judgment insofar as it relies upon that holding. Because Jimenez Recio and Lopez-Meza have raised other arguments not here considered, we remand the case, specifying that the Court of Appeals may consider those arguments, if they were properly raised.

The judgment of the Ninth Circuit is reversed, and the case is remanded for further proceedings consistent with this opinion.

DISCUSSION QUESTIONS

1.   Are the defendants equally blameworthy or dangerous whether they joined the drug conspiracy before or after law enforcement seized the drugs?

2.   Should the law punish those who conspire to do something that is impossible?

3.   The entrapment defense requires a defendant to show that he was not at all predisposed to commit the crime that law enforcement agents encouraged or enabled him to commit. There may be people who were somewhat predisposed but who may not have committed a crime unless the law enforcement agent approached him. Is this good police work that prevents future crime, or bad police work that "creates" crime and criminals?

I. MERGER

More bad news for would-be conspirators. Conspiracy (unlike solicitation and attempt) does not merge into either an attempt to commit the crime or the completed crime. Why the difference? The conspiracy itself is considered a "distinct evil" separate and apart from any crimes that are committed as a result, so you can get punished twice—once for the crime and once for the conspiracy. So, if you are still thinking about robbing that bank, you might want to consider doing it solo.

J. WHARTON'S RULE

What if the offense you agree to commit requires at least two people to commit it by its very nature? Can you be convicted of both the conspiracy and the intended offense? Many offenses cannot be committed alone: bigamy, dueling, selling illegal drugs, bribery. The traditional version of Wharton's rule was that you could not prosecute people for conspiracy to commit such offenses. The modern rule is that the government has "fielder's choice." They can prosecute you for conspiracy or for the target offense, but not for both. Wharton's rule is a presumption of legislative intent, not a constitutional principle, so the legislature can provide for liability for both conspiracy and the target offense if it expresses its intent clearly. The Model Penal Code does not recognize Wharton's rule at all.

K. UNILATERAL VS. BILATERAL CONSPIRACIES

What if your roommate with whom you agree to rob the bank is working for the police or (worse yet) is an undercover police officer herself? Since a police agent does not intend to rob the bank (or let you do the same), they are not really agreeing with you. You may think that they are, but no actual agreement exists since one of you is faking it. Justice Cardozo expressed the common law's view when he said that "it was impossible for a man to conspire with himself." The law describes such a one-sided-pretend agreement as a "unilateral" conspiracy. The common law recognized only bilateral conspiracies. Think if this as the "it takes at least two to tango" approach. The Model Penal Code recognizes unilateral conspiracies, and the modern trend has been to do the same. So, check out your roommate carefully before you bring up the whole bank robbing idea.

L. SCOPE OF THE CONSPIRACY

Professors who really love conspiracy will take the time to dip into a complex set of rules that determine the scope and nature of very elaborate conspiracies. Even touching on these intricate rules is beyond the scope of a short and happy guide. The fundamental issue is "who is conspiring with whom and about what?" The way most books and cases explore these issues is by three visual references: chain, spoke and wheel conspiracies.

A chain conspiracy is one where people work together in one connected process. A typical example of a chain conspiracy can be the manufacture and sale of an illegal drug that might involve a producer, a smuggler, and then a distributor. A wheel or spoke conspiracy, on the other hand, involves a hub that sits at the center of all activity. For example, a hub may be the distributor of illegal drugs who sells drugs to a number of people who then sell it on the streets. In a wheel conspiracy, each street seller works as part of a single organization and, therefore, as members of a single conspiracy. In a spoke conspiracy, each street seller is akin to an independent contractor who enters into his own separate conspiracy with the distributor and is not connected to the other sellers.

Correctly determining the scope and shape of the conspiracy affects numerous issues, most importantly Pinkerton liability for crimes committed in furtherance of the conspiracy. In wheel and chain conspiracies, you are on the hook for all crimes committed by anyone in the chain or anyone on the wheel. A spoke conspiracy means that you will be responsible only for the acts of those in your own separate conspiracy.

No simple rule of thumb distinguishes one conspiratorial structure from another, but a few general observations can be usefully made. Not every member of a single conspiracy needs to communicate with every other member. More importantly, not every member of a single conspiracy needs to either know the identity of or even be aware of the existence of every other member. Each conspirator must be generally aware of the scope and nature of the conspiracy, however. So, don't expect every conspirator to be able to fill out an organizational chart, but do expect each one to have the sense that "we are all in this together," the sense that the fortunes of each rise and fall with the success or failure of the larger enterprise. It is this "community of interest" that the courts seem to be guided by in deciding who belongs to which conspiracy.

M. MODEL PENAL CODE

Distinctions between the Model Penal Code approach to conspiracy and common law approaches have been noted above. Note in particular that the MPC does require an overt act, requires purpose with respect to the commission of the target offense, allows for withdrawal under certain conditions, recognizes unilateral conspiracies, and does not recognize Pinkerton liability.

SECTION 5.03. CRIMINAL CONSPIRACY

(1) Definition of Conspiracy. A person is guilty of conspiracy with another person or persons to commit a crime if with the purpose of promoting or facilitating its commission he:

(a) agrees with such other person or persons that they or one or more of them will engage in conduct which constitutes such crime or an attempt or solicitation to commit such crime; or

(b) agrees to aid such other person or persons in the planning or commission of such crime or of an attempt or solicitation to commit such crime.

(2) Scope of Conspiratorial Relationship. If a person guilty of conspiracy, as defined by Subsection (1) of this Section, knows that a person with whom he conspires to commit a crime has conspired with another person or persons to commit the same crime, he is guilty of conspiring with such other person or persons, whether or not he knows their identity, to commit such crime.

(3) Conspiracy With Multiple Criminal Objectives. If a person conspires to commit a number of crimes, he is guilty of only one conspiracy so long as such multiple crimes are the object of the same agreement or continuous conspiratorial relationship.

(5) Overt Act. No person may be convicted of conspiracy to commit a crime, other than a felony of the first or second degree, unless an overt act in pursuance of such conspiracy is alleged and proved to have been done by him or by a person with whom he conspired.

(6) Renunciation of Criminal Purpose. It is an affirmative defense that the actor, after conspiring to commit a crime, thwarted the success of the conspiracy, under circumstances manifesting a complete and voluntary renunciation of his criminal purpose.

(7) Duration of Conspiracy. For purposes of Section 1.06(4):

(a) conspiracy is a continuing course of conduct which terminates when the crime or crimes which are its object are committed or the agreement that they be committed is abandoned by the defendant and by those with whom he conspired; and

(b) such abandonment is presumed if neither the defendant nor anyone with whom he conspired does any overt act in pursuance of the conspiracy during the applicable period of limitation; and

(c) if an individual abandons the agreement, the conspiracy is terminated as to him only if and when he advises those with whom he conspired of his abandonment or he informs the law enforcement authorities of the existence of the conspiracy and of his participation therein.

Practice Problem 17.0: The Long Game

Huey Long is running for Governor of her state as an independent. Waging a highly emotional, populist campaign centered on the economic grievances of the middle class she attracts thousands of people to her rallies. She tells her crowds that the middle class has been pushed around and taken advantage of by both major parties. "Hit back twice as hard!" is the theme of her campaign, and she says that the middle class needs to stop playing by the unfair rules of the party system. She has developed a routine way of beginning and ending her rallies to reinforce this theme. At the beginning of her rallies she asks the crowd "what are you going to do the next time you get pushed around?," to which the crowd answers on cue "hit back twice as hard." In a similar vein she asks them at the end of the rally, "what do we bring to a fist fight?," to which they answer "a knife." She then asks "what do we bring to a knife fight," to which they answer, "lots of guns."

As Long's poll numbers have risen protesters from both major parties have begun heckling Long at the rallies. Fights have often broken out before security personnel could intervene and remove the protesters. It is often not clear who had thrown the first punch. Since the protesters are always outnumbered they have been badly beaten more than once. These fights have brought Long's candidacy even greater publicity, which seems to have driven her poll numbers even higher. The police have warned Long that her fiery rhetoric and violent chants may be encouraging the violence. Long disputes this, saying that her supporters show up angry for good reason and that giving them a voice makes violence less likely.

At Long's last rally, she stopped speaking as one fight broke out between protesters and supporters in the seats right in front of her. As the police arrested individuals on both sides of the fight, Long publically announced that she had seen the protesters start the fight. She said she would happily pay the legal fees of any of her supporters who were charged with a crime for fighting during a rally as long as they "hit back twice as hard." The crowd roared its approval. In reply Long said that if she had her way, people who tried to stop other people from speaking would be "taken out and shot." Long then asked the crowd what would they do if they saw that one of the protesters had a weapon, to which they roared in reply "shoot them." (Guns are actually banned from Long's rallies though.) Just then a second group of protesters jumped to their feet in a different part of the stadium and started yelling insults at Long. Long turned towards the group and yelled to the crowd "remember what I said—twice as hard!" The next moment one of her supporters rushed one of the protesters who had a megaphone and knocked him over a railing. The protester fell 30 feet to the seats below and died.

Long has been charged with conspiracy, murder, and manslaughter in a common law jurisdiction that consistently follows the majority approach. Analyze her liability for these crimes.

CHAPTER 18

ATTEMPT

■ ■ ■

In the science fiction movie *Minority Report*, the government develops a "pre-crime program" that uses psychics to stop murders before they are committed. Once the psychics give the word, a SWAT team swoops in and arrests the would-be killers for the crimes they were about to commit. While no such psychics exist in real life (if there were, they'd probably be in Vegas) the doctrine of attempt is our pre-crime program. Through attempt law we try to identify those who are going to commit a crime and subject them to arrest and prosecution for criminal liability before the crime is completed.

Attempt doctrine raises a number of interesting issues, including some of the metaphysical ones raised in science fiction tales such as *Minority Report*. Is it prudent to punish people for something they have not yet done? How do we know they were going to go through with it? Are they blameworthy for beginning to commit the crime? Should we allow them to back out and "undo" their attempt liability if they change their mind? Alternately, why don't we just punish someone who attempts a crime the same as someone who completes it?

More concretely:

1. Where and when should attempt liability begin?

2. Should we require a more culpable state of mind for an attempt than a completed crime?

3. Are there some crimes for which attempt liability should not exist at all?

4. What do we do about attempts that were "impossible" to begin with for one reason or another?

Attempt doctrine is important as well as interesting. As the poet said, "the best laid plans of mice and men often go awry." So too with crime. Many attempt crimes fail or do not finish, so drawing these lines around attempt liability is not just an interesting academic enterprise.

A. AN OVERVIEW OF THE ELEMENTS

As is the case with the other inchoate offenses, attempt law requires a highly culpable mental state to compensate for the fact that less conduct is required of the offender. The common law generally defined a criminal attempt as an intentional act that crossed the line from preparation to perpetration of a crime with the intent that the crime be committed. The Model Penal Code modified this definition by including the purposeful commission of a "substantial step" towards commission of a crime taken with the mental state required for the offense attempted. The Model Penal Code approach generally expands attempt liability by allowing a conviction on the basis of less and earlier conduct than is possible under the common law approach. While many jurisdictions still follow the common law approach, the Model Penal Code's approach has become very influential. Many states—even ones that generally follow the common law—have adopted the MPC's definition of attempt.

B. SENTENCING

By statute, an attempt of a crime is almost always punished less than the completion of the crime. The only exceptions are crimes where the legislature writes into the definition of the crime "commits or attempts to commit" and, even then, the sentencing judge may use whatever discretion she has to sentence towards the lower end of the permissible range.

C. COMPLETE ATTEMPTS AND "MORAL LUCK"

One distinction has fallen largely by the way side but is still worth noting because it reveals something important about our moral intuitions about attempts. At common law, one had to complete "the last act necessary" for the crime to occur in order to be guilty of attempt. For example, to be guilty of an attempted murder involving a firearm you actually had to pull the trigger. If someone grabbed the gun away from you before you pulled the trigger, then no attempt would have been committed. Only such "complete attempts" triggered criminal liability under the original common law rule.

No common law jurisdiction follows the "last act necessary" approach anymore. Here is a question worth a moment's reflection though. Why don't we punish such complete attempts just as harshly as the completed crime? If you only miss killing me because you sneezed as you pulled the trigger, why should your hay fever result in a less severe punishment? You are just as blameworthy and just as dangerous (setting your hay fever aside) as if you had not missed.

The answer is that our intuitions about punishment are heavily influenced notions of harm. The actual social harm of your missed shot is much less than the actual social harm of a successful shot. Sure, I might have a few sleepless nights thinking about what a close call I had (and worrying about how many other students might be stalking me), but I am a lot better off than if I was dead. It does not seem fair to punish you the same, even though the harm is a lot less. "No harm, no foul," is not something that we just say in sports.

Philosophers describe this sort of paradox as "moral luck," a situation where consequences turn upon factors beyond your control. Defendants who commit complete attempts enjoy moral luck because they have done everything within their control to be guilty of the complete crime but end up only being guilty of an attempt. So, they should really feel lucky as they serve their lesser prison sentences.

D. CONDUCT REQUIRED FOR ATTEMPT

So, you now know that jurisdictions permit attempt liability for incomplete attempts. But how incomplete can it be? How close does one have to come to actually committing the intended crime to be guilty of an attempt? Or to look at things from the other end, what is the earliest point in time at which the police can swoop in and arrest someone with confidence that the person will be convicted?

Remember that bad thoughts alone cannot constitute a crime, not even a crime of attempt. So conclusive proof that someone had decided to commit a crime would not alone constitute an attempt. The defendant must do something. But what?

Let me repeat that the line we are talking about is between preparation to commit an offense (which is not attempting it) and beginning to perpetrate an offense. Unfortunately, that rule does not really tell us anything although it is worth repeating at the beginning of your exam answer. "An act of perpetration" is a really a label for a conclusion about where attempt liability begins.

This is a messy area. There are a lot of different tests for drawing the line between preparation and perpetration. Sometimes different tests will even be used within the same jurisdiction. It sometimes seems like judges are "mixing and matching" between different types of cases and the different tests. As a law student, this just creates more different ways for you to earn points on an attempt question because there are a number of different rules that you can apply to the fact pattern. As a practitioner, you just need to spend a little time in the library figuring out which tests are most often used in your jurisdiction.

Remember also that the earlier we draw the line the easier it is to keep society safe but the greater the risk that we are punishing someone for attempting something that she might never have gone through with. With that in mind, let's now learn the different conduct tests for attempt.

1. *Physical Proximity*. Considers the closeness to the commission of the offense in terms of time, place, and ability to carry out the crime. This test focuses not on what has been done but on what remains to be done. In its strictest form, this test requires the actor to have it within his or her power to complete the crime almost immediately.

2. *Dangerous Proximity*. A variation on the physical proximity test that takes a "sliding scale approach." The more the conduct involves a danger to human life the less the proximity required. So, attempting to pick a man's pocket might require me to get close enough to put my hand into his pocket, but attempting to kill the same man might easily be satisfied if I sat in the last row of a large auditorium in which he was speaking with a knife in my pocket. Focus on the nearness of the danger, the magnitude of the harm, and the degree of apprehension felt.

3. *Indispensable Element*. Has the actor obtained control over everything that he needs to commit the offense? A sniper needs his rifle, a con artist his "mark," and a bootlegger his raw materials to be guilty of an attempt under this rule.

4. *Probable Desistance*. Has the actor reached the point where an ordinary person would probably have already desisted if he were not going to complete the crime? This is not the point of no return necessarily. It might still be possible for someone to pull out without incident, but it is not probable that the average person would do so. It is the point beyond which the actor is not likely to quit, absent some sort of outside intervention. Bringing a prostitute to one's room, for example, would be enough conduct for an attempt to commit prostitution under this test. Like the swimmer who swam half way across the English Channel before pondering whether to turn back, the actor is considered likely to keep going.

5. *Unequivocality*. (Sometimes called the res ipsa loquitor test, which is Latin for the thing speaks for itself.) This test requires conduct to reach a point where it becomes clear from the person's actions alone that they intend to commit the crime. In requiring that the conduct "unambiguously manifest" criminal intent, this test essentially asks whether you can imagine some innocent explanation for what has been done. A person going through the pockets of an unconscious homeless person lying in the street, for example, might be looking for some information about who might be called to aid the person, not attempting to rob him.

Some jurisdictions strictly ignore any separate evidence of the person's actual intent (such as a confession) in applying this test. That would mean that our would-be pickpocket in the above example would not be held guilty of attempted larceny even if they admit that they were bent on stealing what was found in the pockets because their conduct was not unequivocal. Other jurisdictions will consider independent evidence of mental state such as confessions in deciding whether the person's conduct unequivocally manifested a criminal intent and was thereby sufficient for an attempt. So, keep your mouth shut about your attempts to commit crimes!

6. *Substantial Step*. This is the Model Penal Code test that applies to incomplete attempts. Under MPC section 5.01, a "substantial step in a course of conduct planned to culminate in commission of the crime" is sufficient conduct for an attempt if it is "strongly corroborative of the actor's criminal purpose." The MPC further provides a list of examples of conduct which would constitute a substantial step if strongly corroborative of the actor's purpose:

   a. Lying in wait for or searching for the victim or trying to lure them somewhere.

   b. Scouting out the place where the crime is to be committed.

   c. Unlawful entry of a place where the crime will be committed.

   d. Possession of materials to be used in the crime which have no lawful purpose or are specially designed for the crime, especially if possessed at what is to be the scene of the crime.

   e. Soliciting an innocent agent to engage in conduct constituting an element of the crime.

   The substantial step test has been widely adopted, including in many common law jurisdictions. As will be illustrated in the following example, it also greatly expands attempt liability by allowing attempt convictions on lesser and earlier conduct than any of the common law tests.

Case in Context

The following case illustrates an earlier approach to conduct requirements for attempt.

PEOPLE V. MURRAY
Supreme Court of California
14 Cal. 159 (1859)

JUDGES: FIELD, C. J. delivered the opinion of the Court. COPE, J. and BALDWIN, J. concurring.

Opinion by: FIELD.

OPINION

The evidence in this case entirely fails to sustain the charge against the defendant of an attempt to contract an incestuous marriage with his niece. It only discloses declarations of his determination to contract the marriage, his elopement with the niece for that avowed purpose, and his request to one of the witnesses to go for a magistrate to perform the ceremony. It shows very clearly the intention of the defendant, but something more than mere intention is necessary to constitute the offense charged. Between preparation for the attempt and the attempt itself, there is a wide difference. The preparation consists in devising or arranging the means or measures necessary for the commission of the offense; the attempt is the direct movement toward the commission after the preparations are made. To illustrate: a party may purchase and load a gun, with the declared intention to shoot his neighbor; but until some movement is made to use the weapon upon the person of his intended victim, there is only preparation, and not an attempt. For the preparation, he may be held to keep the peace; but he is not chargeable with any attempt to kill. So in the present case, the declarations, and elopement, and request for a magistrate, were preparatory to the marriage; but until the officer was engaged, and the parties stood before him, ready to take the vows appropriate to the contract of marriage, it cannot be said, in strictness, that the attempt was made. The attempt contemplated by the statute must be manifest by acts which would end in the consummation of the particular offense, but for the intervention of circumstances independent of the will of the party.

Judgment reversed and cause remanded.

DISCUSSION QUESTIONS

1.   The court says that the defendant's conduct very clearly showed his intent to engage in the incestuous marriage. Why shouldn't that be enough for attempt liability?

2.   What standard for attempt conduct does the court articulate? Under this standard just how close to having the person officiating pronounce them man and wife would the court let the defendant get before finding attempt liability?

3.   Do you agree that a person who buys a gun to shoot his neighbor cannot be found guilty until he "used the weapon upon the person of his

intended victim." Under this standard he could wait for the victim with the gun on his person without incurring attempt liability. Do you think conduct requirements for attempt should depend to some extent upon the nature of the crime being committed?

Case in Context

The following decision applies the Model Penal Code standard to an attempt where the defendants came very close to actually committing the offense.

U.S. v. JACKSON, SCOTT, & ALLEN

United States Court of Appeals, Second Circuit
560 F.2d 112 (1977)

Opinion by: BRYAN.

OPINION

BRYAN, SENIOR DISTRICT JUDGE:

Robert Jackson, William Scott, and Martin Allen appeal from judgments of conviction entered on November 23, 1976 in the United States District Court for the Eastern District of New York after a trial before Chief Judge Jacob Mishler without a jury.

Count one of the indictment alleged that between June 11 and June 21, 1976 the appellants conspired to commit an armed robbery of the Manufacturers Hanover Trust branch located at 210 Flushing Avenue, Brooklyn, New York, in violation of 18 U.S.C. § 371. Counts two and three each charged appellants with an attempted robbery of the branch on June 14 and on June 21, 1976, respectively, in violation of 18 U.S.C. §§ 2113(a) and 2. Count four charged them with possession of two unregistered sawed-off shotguns on June 21, 1976, in violation of 26 U.S.C. § 5861(d) and 18 U.S.C. § 2.

After a suppression hearing on July 23, 1976 and a one-day trial on August 30, 1976,

CHIEF JUDGE MISHLER filed a memorandum of decision finding each defendant guilty on all four counts.

Appellants' principal contention is that the court below erred in finding them guilty on counts two and three. While they concede that the evidence supported the conspiracy convictions on count one, they assert that, as a matter of law, their conduct never crossed the elusive line which separates "mere preparation" from "attempt.

I.

The Government's evidence at trial consisted largely of the testimony of Vanessa Hodges, an unindicted co-conspirator, and of various FBI agents who surveilled the Manufacturers Hanover branch on June 21, 1976. Since the facts are of critical importance in any attempt case, United States v. Stallworth, supra, at 1039, we shall review the Government's proof in considerable detail.

On June 11, 1976, Vanessa Hodges was introduced to appellant Martin Allen by Pia Longhorne, another unindicted co-conspirator. Hodges wanted to meet someone who would help her carry out a plan to rob the Manufacturers Hanover branch located at 210 Flushing Avenue in Brooklyn, and she invited Allen to join her. Hodges proposed that the bank be robbed the next Monday, June 14th, at about 7:30 A.M. She hoped that they could enter with the bank manager at that time, grab the weekend deposits, and leave. Allen agreed to rob the bank with Hodges, and told her he had access to a car, two sawed-off shotguns, and a .38 caliber revolver.

The following Monday, June 14, Allen arrived at Longhorne's house about 7:30 A.M. in a car driven by appellant Robert Jackson. A suitcase in the back seat of the car contained a sawed-off shotgun, shells, materials intended as masks, and handcuffs to bind the bank manager. While Allen picked up Hodges at Longhorne's, Jackson filled the car with gas. The trio then left for the bank.

When they arrived, it was almost 8:00 A. M. It was thus too late to effect the first step of the plan, viz., entering the bank as the manager opened the door. They rode around for a while longer, and then went to a restaurant to get something to eat and discuss their next move. After eating, the trio drove back to the bank. Allen and Hodges left the car and walked over to the bank. They peered in and saw the bulky weekend deposits, but decided it was too risky to rob the bank without an extra man.

Consequently, Jackson, Hodges, and Allen drove to Coney Island in search of another accomplice. In front of a housing project on 33rd Street they found appellant William Scott, who promptly joined the team. Allen added to the arsenal another sawed-off shotgun obtained from one of the buildings in the project, and the group drove back to the bank.

When they arrived again, Allen entered the bank to check the location of any surveillance cameras, while Jackson placed a piece of cardboard with a false license number over the authentic license plate of the car. Allen reported back that a single surveillance camera was over the entrance door. After further discussion, Scott left the car and entered the bank. He came back and informed the group that the tellers were separating the weekend deposits and that a number of patrons were now in the bank. Hodges then suggested that they drop the plans for the robbery that day, and reschedule it for the following Monday, June 21. Accordingly, they left the vicinity of the bank and returned to Coney Island where, before splitting up, they purchased a pair of stockings for Hodges to wear over her head as a disguise and pairs of gloves for Hodges, Scott, and Allen to don before entering the bank.

Hodges was arrested on Friday, June 18, 1976 on an unrelated bank robbery charge, and immediately began cooperating with the Government. After relating the events of June 14, she told FBI agents that a robbery of the Manufacturers branch at 210 Flushing Avenue was now scheduled for the following Monday, June 21. The three black male robbers, according to Hodges, would be heavily armed with hand and shoulder weapons and expected to use a brown four-door sedan equipped with a cardboard license plate as the getaway car. She told the agents that Jackson, who would drive the car, was light-skinned with a moustache and a cut on his lip, and she described Allen as short, dark-skinned with facial hair, and Scott as 5 feet 9 inches, slim build, with an afro hair style and some sort of defect in his right eye.

At the request of the agents, Hodges called Allen on Saturday, June 19, and asked if he were still planning to do the job. He said that he was ready. On Sunday she called him again. This time Allen said that he was not going to rob the bank that Monday because he had learned that Hodges had been arrested and he feared that federal agents might be watching. Hodges nevertheless advised the agents that she thought the robbery might still take place as planned with the three men proceeding without her.

At about 7:00 A. M. on Monday, June 21, 1976, some ten FBI agents took various surveilling positions in the area of the bank. At about 7:39 A. M. the agents observed a brown four-door Lincoln, with a New York license plate on the front and a cardboard facsimile of a license plate on the rear, moving in an easterly direction on Flushing Avenue past the bank, which was located on the southeast corner of Flushing and Washington Avenues. The front seat of the Lincoln was occupied by a black male driver and a black male passenger with mutton-chop sideburns. The Lincoln circled the block and came to a stop at a fire hydrant situated at the side of the bank facing Washington Avenue, a short distance south of the corner of Flushing and Washington.

A third black male, who appeared to have an eye deformity, got out of the passenger side rear door of the Lincoln, walked to the corner of Flushing and Washington, and stood on the sidewalk in the vicinity of the bank's entrance. He then walked south on Washington Avenue, only to return a short time later with a container of coffee in his hand. He stood again on the corner of Washington and Flushing in front of the bank, drinking the coffee and looking around, before returning to the parked Lincoln.

The Lincoln pulled out, made a left turn onto Flushing, and proceeded in a westerly direction for one block to Waverly Avenue. It stopped, made a U-turn, and parked on the south side of Flushing between Waverly and Washington—a spot on the same side of the street as the bank entrance but separated from it by Washington Avenue. After remaining parked in this position for approximately five minutes, it pulled out and cruised east on Flushing past the bank again. The Lincoln then made a right onto Grand Avenue, the third street east of the bank, and headed south. It stopped halfway down the block, midway between Flushing and Park Avenues, and remained there for several minutes. During this time Jackson was seen working in the front of the car, which had its hood up.

The Lincoln was next sighted several minutes later in the same position it had previously occupied on the south side of Flushing Avenue between Waverly and Washington. The front license plate was now missing. The vehicle remained parked there for close to thirty minutes. Finally, it began moving east on Flushing Avenue once more, in the direction of the bank.

At some point near the bank as they passed down Flushing Avenue, the appellants detected the presence of the surveillance agents. The Lincoln accelerated down Flushing Avenue and turned south on Grand Avenue again. It was overtaken by FBI agents who ordered the appellants out of the car and arrested them. The agents then observed a black and red plaid suitcase in the rear of the car. The zipper of the suitcase was partially open and exposed two loaded sawed-off shotguns, a toy nickelplated revolver, a pair of handcuffs, and masks. A New York license plate was seen lying on the front floor of the car. All of these items were seized.

In his memorandum of decision, Chief Judge Mishler concluded that the evidence against Jackson, Scott, and Allen was "overwhelming" on counts one and four. In contrast, he characterized the question of whether the defendants had attempted a bank robbery as charged in counts two and three or were merely engaged in preparations as "a close one." After canvassing the authorities on what this court one month later called a "perplexing problem," United States v. Stallworth, supra, at 1039, Chief Judge Mishler applied the following two-tiered inquiry formulated

First, the defendant must have been acting with the kind of culpability otherwise required for the commission of the crime which he is charged with attempting. . .

Second, the defendant must have engaged in conduct which constitutes a substantial step toward commission of the crime. A substantial step must be conduct strongly corroborative of the firmness of the defendant's criminal intent.

He concluded that on June 14 and again on June 21, the defendants took substantial steps, strongly corroborative of the firmness of their criminal intent, toward commission of the crime of bank robbery and found the defendants guilty on each of the two attempt counts. These appeals followed.

II.

"There is no comprehensive statutory definition of attempt in federal law." United States v. Heng Awkak Roman, 356 F. Supp. 434, 437 (S.D.N.Y.), aff'd, 484 F.2d 1271 (2d Cir. 1973), cert. denied, 415 U.S. 978, 39 L. Ed. 2d 874, 94 S. Ct. 1565 (1974). Fed. R. Crim. P. 31(c), however, provides in pertinent part that a defendant may be found guilty of "an attempt to commit either the offense charged or an offense necessarily included therein if the attempt is an offense." 18 U.S.C. § 2113(a) specifically makes attempted bank robbery an offense.

Appellant Scott argues that the very wording of 18 U.S.C. § 2113(a) precludes a finding that the actions charged in counts two and three reached the level of attempts. Relying on United States v. Baker, 129 F. Supp. 684 (S.D. Cal. 1955), he contends that since the statute only mentions attempted taking and not attempted force, violence, or intimidation, it clearly contemplates that actual use of force, violence, or intimidation must precede an attempted taking in order to make out the offense of attempted bank robbery.

The Stallworth court faced a similar statutory construction argument which also relied heavily on United States v. Baker, supra. In response to the assertion that the defendants in that case could not be convicted of attempted bank robbery because they neither entered the bank nor brandished weapons, Chief Judge Kaufman stated:

We reject this wooden logic. Attempt is a subtle concept that requires a rational and logically sound definition, one that enables society to punish malefactors who have unequivocally set out upon a criminal course without requiring law enforcement officers to delay until innocent bystanders are imperiled.

CHIEF JUDGE KAUFMAN, writing for the court, selected the two-tiered inquiry of United States v. Mandujano, supra, "properly derived from the writings of many distinguished jurists," 543 F.2d at 1040, as stating the proper test for determining whether the foregoing conduct constituted an attempt. He observed that this analysis "conforms closely to the sensible definition of an attempt proffered by the American Law Institute's Model Penal Code."

The draftsmen of the Model Penal Code recognized the difficulty of arriving at a general standard for distinguishing acts of preparation from acts constituting an attempt. They found general agreement that when an actor committed the "last proximate act," i.e., when he had done all that he believed necessary to effect a particular result which is an element of the offense, he committed an attempt. They also concluded, however, that while the last proximate act is sufficient to constitute an attempt, it is not necessary to such a finding. The problem then was to devise a standard more inclusive than one requiring the last proximate act before attempt liability would attach, but less inclusive than one which would make every act done with the intent to commit a crime criminal. . .

The formulation upon which the draftsmen ultimately agreed required, in addition to criminal purpose, that an act be a substantial step in a course of conduct designed to accomplish a criminal result, and that it be strongly corroborative of criminal purpose in order for it to constitute such a substantial step. The following differences between this test and previous approaches to the preparation-attempt problem were noted:

First, this formulation shifts the emphasis from what remains to be done—the chief concern of the proximity tests—to what the actor has already done. The fact that further major steps must be taken before the crime can be completed does not preclude a finding that the steps already undertaken are substantial. It is expected, in the normal case, that this approach will broaden the scope of attempt liability.

Second, although it is intended that the requirement of a substantial step will result in the imposition of attempt liability only in those instances in which some firmness of criminal purpose is shown, no finding is required as to whether the actor would probably have desisted prior to completing the crime. Potentially the probable desistance test could reach very early steps toward crime—depending upon how one assesses the probabilities of desistance—but since in practice this test follows closely the proximity approaches, rejection of probable desistance will not narrow the scope of attempt liability.

Finally, the requirement of proving a substantial step generally will prove less of a hurdle for the prosecution than the res ipsa loquitur approach, which requires that the actor's conduct must itself manifest the criminal purpose. The difference will be illustrated in connection with the present section's requirement of corroboration. Here it should be noted that, in the present formulation, the two purposes to be served by the res ipsa loquitur test are, to a large extent, treated separately. Firmness of criminal purpose is intended to be shown by requiring a substantial step, while problems of proof are dealt with by the requirement of corroboration (although, under the reasoning previously expressed, the latter will also tend to establish firmness of purpose).

Model Penal Code § 5.01, Comment at 47 (Tent. Draft No. 10, 1960).

The draftsmen concluded that, in addition to assuring firmness of criminal design, the requirement of a substantial step would preclude attempt liability, with its accompanying harsh penalties, for relatively remote preparatory acts. At the same time, however, by not requiring a "last proximate act" or one of its various analogues it would permit the apprehension of dangerous persons at an earlier stage than the other approaches without immunizing them from attempt liability.

. . .

On two separate occasions, appellants reconnoitered the place contemplated for the commission of the crime and possessed the paraphernalia to be employed in the commission of the crime—loaded sawed-off shotguns, extra shells, a toy revolver, handcuffs, and masks—which was specially designed for such unlawful use and which could serve no lawful purpose under the circumstances. Under the Model Penal Code formulation, supra at 4816–18, approved by the Stallworth court, either type of conduct, standing alone, was sufficient as a matter of law to constitute a "substantial step" if it strongly corroborated their criminal purpose. Here both types of conduct coincided on both June 14 and June 21, along with numerous other elements strongly corroborative of the firmness of appellants' criminal intent. The steps taken toward a successful bank robbery thus were not "insubstantial" as a matter of law, and Chief Judge Mishler found them "substantial" as a matter of fact. We are unwilling to substitute our assessment of the evidence for his, and thus affirm the convictions for attempted bank robbery on counts two and three.

The judgments of conviction are affirmed.

DISCUSSION QUESTIONS

1.   What is the earliest point in time when attempt liability could be found under the Model Penal Code test in this case?

2.   Is it possible that these procrastinating robbers might never have actually committed this robbery? Should that matter as to their criminal liability?

3.   Which conduct test for attempt liability do you think society should use?

Practice Problem 18.1: Fatal Feedback

Assume that one of my students decides to kill me after a particularly terrible class. Between the boredom and the bad jokes, she decides that she would rather kill me than sit through another class session. At what point in the following chronology does she have enough conduct for attempt liability under the various tests?

1.   She thinks about different ways of killing me and decides to shoot me as I get out of my car the next morning in the faculty parking lot.

2.   She makes a to-do list in her computer of things she will need to do to prepare for the crime.

3.   She scouts out the faculty parking lot immediately after class and finds a nice big rock concealed in a wooded area adjacent to the lot from which she could shoot anyone in the parking lot.

4. She buys a hunting rifle and ammunition.

5. That night she parks her car in a parking lot on the opposite side of the woods adjacent to the faculty parking lot. She takes the rifle and hides behind the rock she picked out.

6. The next morning she loads the rifle.

7. When she sees me drive up she picks up the rifle.

8. When I get out of my car she aims the rifle at me, and switches off the safety.

9. She pulls the trigger but misses her shot.

E. MENTAL STATE REQUIRED FOR ATTEMPT

Intent lies at the conceptual heart of attempt. When you say that you "tried to do something" you almost always mean that you acted with purpose. "Accidentally attempting" something is a contradiction in terms.

As with conspiracy, there are two distinct intents required at common law. One must intend the actions that constitute the conduct for the attempt and intend that the crime committed be carried out. With respect to intending one's actions, you obviously can't attempt to kill someone by accidentally bumping into them by the edge of a steep cliff. What if you intentionally bumped into them, however, but did so only to give them a good scare? That also would not be attempted murder because you did not intend to kill them by bumping into them.

1. ATTEMPTED RESULT CRIMES

The requirement that you intend the crime to be committed requires more than might be apparent. One must intend "the whole crime," even the parts which the crime itself do not require to be intentional. Homicide crimes provide the easiest example, although the same principle comes into play in all result crimes. Depraved heart murder, for example, does not require that you intend anyone's death, only that you are recklessly indifferent to it. Depraved heart murder does require the result of someone's death, of course. Since attempt requires that you intend the "whole crime" you must also intend someone's death. For this reason, most jurisdictions conclude that one cannot really attempt a reckless or negligent killing. Since you must intend death—not be reckless or negligent with respect to it—the only type of attempted murder possible is an intentional killing under this view.

This requirement sometimes creates a paradox. Imagine that two disgruntled students independently decide to attack me after they get their exam grades back. One student decides to shoot me dead. The other student decides to maim me with a knife. If the shooter kills me, he would obviously be guilty of intentional murder. If I end up dying from the knife wounds then the student with the knife would probably be found guilty of intent to grievously injure murder in a common law jurisdiction that recognized that offense. But what if I live? Only the shooter gets convicted of attempted murder, because only the shooter intended my death. The student with the knife cannot be convicted of any attempted homicide crime because he did not intend my death. (Although he will do a nice long prison sentence for aggravated assault.)

Case in Context

The opinions in the next case present both sides of the debate about "attempted recklessness."

SOUTH DAKOTA V. LYERLA

Supreme Court of South Dakota
424 N.W.2d 908 (1988)

Opinion by: KONENKAMP.

OPINION

A jury convicted Gerald K. Lyerla (Lyerla) of second degree murder and two counts of attempted second degree murder. We affirm the second degree murder conviction, but reverse the convictions for attempted second degree murder.

On the night of January 18, 1986, while driving east on Interstate 90 in Haakon County, Lyerla fired three shots with his .357 magnum pistol at a pickup truck carrying three teenage girls. One was killed, the other two were injured. Only one bullet entered the pickup cab, the one that killed seventeen-year-old Tammy Jensen. Another bullet was recovered from the engine block; the third was never found. Lyerla fled the scene, but was later apprehended. He was charged in the alternative with first degree murder or second degree murder for the death of Tammy Jensen and two counts each of attempted first degree murder and alternatively two counts of attempted second degree murder of the two surviving girls.

Before the shooting, the teenagers and Lyerla were traveling in the same direction. The vehicles passed each other a few times. At one point when Lyerla tried to pass the girls, their truck accelerated so that he could not overtake them. Lyerla decided to leave the interstate. When he exited, the Jensen pickup pulled to the side of the road near the entry ramp. Lyerla loaded his pistol, reentered the interstate and passed the Jensen pickup. When the girls attempted to pass him, he fired at the passenger side of their truck.

At his trial, Lyerla told the jury that the teenagers were harassing him to such an extent that he feared for his life and fired the shots to disable their pickup. The two girls gave a different rendition of the events leading up to the shooting, but the prosecutor conceded in closing argument that

Tammy Jensen was "trying to play games" with Lyerla by not letting him pass. . .

Lyerla argues that it is a legal impossibility to attempt to commit murder in the second degree and his two convictions for this offense should be reversed.

In order to attempt to commit a crime, there must exist in the mind of the perpetrator the specific intent to commit the acts constituting the offense. State v. Primeaux, 328 N.W.2d 256 (S.D. 1982); State v. Poss, 298 N.W.2d 80 (S.D. 1980); State v. Rash, 294 N.W.2d 416 (S.D. 1980); State v. Martinez, 88 S.D. 369, 220 N.W.2d 530 (1974); State v. Judge, 81 S.D. 128, 131 N.W.2d 573 (1964). To attempt second degree murder one must intend to have a criminally reckless state of mind, i.e. perpetrating an imminently dangerous act while evincing a depraved mind, regardless of human life, but without a design to kill any particular person.

A death occurred here, but the jury obviously decided that Lyerla did not intend the death of the deceased since he was found guilty of the lesser count of second degree murder. Nor did he intend to kill the other two girls as the verdicts for attempted second degree murder confirm.

Other courts have likewise found attempted reckless homicide a logical impossibility. In *People v. Perez*, 108 Misc. 2d 65, 437 N.Y.S.2d 46, 48 (1981) it was stated:

> However, murder in the second degree under PL 125.25 subdivision 2, involves no intent but instead requires a culpable mental state of recklessness. One may not intentionally attempt to cause the death of another by a reckless act. (Citations omitted.)

The Colorado Supreme Court held:

> An attempt to commit criminal negligent homicide thus requires proof that the defendant intended to perpetrate an unintended killing—a logical impossibility. The words "attempt" and "negligence" are at war with one another; they are internally inconsistent and cannot sensibly co-exist.

Defendant's convictions for attempted second degree murder are reversed.

SABERS, JUSTICE (dissenting).

I agree with the majority that the jury obviously decided that Lyerla did not intend the death of the deceased since he was found guilty of the lesser count of second-degree murder. Nor did he intend to kill the other two girls as the verdicts for attempted second-degree murder confirm. However, had his acts resulted in their deaths, either directly as in the case of Tammy Jensen, or indirectly, through a resulting car accident, he would have been guilty of second-degree murder. Since deaths did not result he was guilty of attempted second-degree murder under South Dakota law.

SDCL 22–4–1 provides:

"Any person who attempts to commit a crime and in the attempt does any act toward the commission of the crime, but fails or is prevented or intercepted in the perpetration thereof, is punishable where no provision is made by law for the punishment of such attempt[.]"

SDCL 22–16–7 provides:

"Homicide is murder in the second degree when perpetrated by any act imminently dangerous to others and evincing a depraved mind, regardless of human life, although without any premeditated design to effect the death of any particular individual."

This statute deals with "homicide" which is named "murder in the second degree." Neither statute contains an element of specific intent. SDCL 22–16–7 simply requires an act. The act required must be dangerous to others (or stupid) under South Dakota law. If one attempts a "dangerous" or "stupid" act it is sufficient. The only "intent" or "attempt" necessary is a voluntary as opposed to a non-volitional or forced act. In this case, Lyerla clearly attempted the dangerous and stupid act of pulling the trigger and shooting the gun at or near the people or the car in which they were riding. This is sufficient for attempted second-degree murder under South Dakota law.

The majority opinion cites People v. Perez, 108 Misc.2d 65, 437 N.Y.S.2d 46, 48 (1981) and People v. Hernandez, 44 Colo. App. 161, 614 P.2d 900, 901 (1980), for the proposition that one cannot intentionally attempt to cause the death of another by a reckless act and for the proposition that the perpetration of an unintended killing is a logical impossibility. Further, these cases are cited to support the proposition that the words "attempt" and "negligence" are at war with one another; that they are internally inconsistent and cannot sensibly co-exist. These cases place emphasis on the word "intentional" contrary to the South Dakota statute on attempt. As previously indicated, the "intent" or "attempt" required under the South Dakota statute is simply to voluntarily act as opposed to an involuntary or forced action. In other words, an attempt to pull the trigger and shoot the gun is enough. This type of "attempt" and the "dangerous" or "stupid" act are not at war with one another; they are internally consistent and can sensibly co-exist.

Much of the confusion in this matter results from the use of the word murder, which implies an intent to take life. What we are really dealing with under South Dakota law is homicide, named second-degree murder. To intentionally pull the trigger and shoot a gun in this dangerous manner was not homicide because neither Gropper girl died, but it was attempted homicide, also known as attempted second-degree murder. Accordingly, attempted second-degree murder is a crime in South Dakota, and Lyerla's convictions for attempted second-degree murder should be affirmed.

DISCUSSION QUESTIONS

1. Why didn't the jury find Lyerla guilty of first degree murder?

2. As a matter of statutory interpretation, do you agree with the majority or the dissent?

3. As a matter of policy, do you agree with the majority or the dissent?

Practice Problem 18.2: Hunter's Squabble

Bill and Ted are avid deer hunters who do all their hunting with crossbows. While hunting together Bill kills a large trophy buck. Ted is enraged because under the rules that they have agreed upon he was supposed to have first shot at the buck because he spotted him first. Bill laughs, turns his back on Ted as he walks towards the fallen buck. He shouts over his shoulder that Ted was waiting too long to take the shot and needs to be quicker on the trigger. Bill decides to teach Ted a lesson by giving him a good scare. He aims his cross bow at the center of Ted's back and shouts "how is this for being quick on the trigger?" Bill turns around, sees Ted pointing the crossbow and shouts "you haven't got the guts to do it!" Further enraged, Ted takes the safety off the crossbow and carefully aims it right at Bill's heart to further scare him. In the process of aiming it, however, Ted's finger slips onto the trigger and the crossbow fires. Even though Ted is standing only ten feet away from Bill, the arrow hits Bill but miraculously misses his heart and all other vital organs and blood vessels. Bill survives. Can Ted be convicted of attempted reckless murder or attempted involuntary manslaughter?

---

2. ATTEMPTED FELONY MURDER

All but a very few states have concluded that there is no such thing as attempted felony murder. (Imagine that the butter-fingered bank robber drops his gun and it seriously wounds a bank employee.) Felony murder includes unintentional killings, but to prove an attempted felony murder you would have to prove an intent to kill. If you have proved an intent to kill, then you have already proved attempted intent to kill murder. Since the butter fingered bank robber did not intend to kill, he cannot be guilty of attempted felony murder.

3. ATTEMPTED MANSLAUGHTER

There is more of a split in jurisdictions as to whether one can attempt voluntary manslaughter. Imagine that you are adequately provoked, fly into a rage, and take a shot at someone with a gun. You are so angry, though, that you miss the person. Are you guilty of attempted murder or a lesser crime of attempted voluntary manslaughter? A great majority of states have concluded that attempted voluntary manslaughter does not exist because you cannot "intend to lose control in the heat of passion," which is essentially what voluntary manslaughter requires. A minority of states reason, however, that the only intent you must have is the intent to kill. They reason that it makes no sense to convict someone who intentionally attempts to kill after having been adequately provoked of the same crime as one who intentionally attempts to kill for no good reason at all.

Attempted involuntary manslaughter is generally not recognized as possible for the same reasons described earlier. Since manslaughter requires the result of death, one must intend—not be grossly negligent with respect to—death in order to be guilty of attempting that crime. Attempting to intentionally kill someone is murder, not involuntary manslaughter.

4. ATTEMPTED RECKLESS OR NEGLIGENT CONDUCT CRIMES

Things get more complicated with respect to whether one can attempt a crime that requires reckless or negligent conduct but not any sort of result. If the police arrest someone who was about to engage in a dangerous drag race on city streets should the driver be convicted of attempted reckless driving? Here, there are just not enough eggs to make an omelet, by which I mean that there are too few cases to describe either position as majority or minority. The few reported cases go both ways. Some cases allow attempted reckless or negligent conduct offenses on the grounds that one need only intend the conduct that constitutes the reckless or negligent conduct. In the drag racing example, that would be intending to drive a car really fast through city streets just for thrills. Other cases reason that you can't intend to be unaware of a risk or intend to consciously disregard it.

5. PURPOSE VS. KNOWLEDGE

Does intent to commit a crime mean that you do so knowing or purposefully? What if you tried to detonate a bomb to blow up your worst enemy knowing that the blast will kill innocent bystanders. Are you guilty of just one count of attempted murder or many? The answer is unclear in common law jurisdictions.

6. ATTENDANT CIRCUMSTANCES

Do you have to be intentional with respect to all the circumstances that must attend the offense that you are charged with attempting? Returning to the hypo concerning assaulting a federal law enforcement officer, do you have to intend to assault a federal officer or just intend to assault someone who turns out to be a federal officer unbeknownst to you? There are precious few cases on this point, but the scholarly consensus seems to be that the mental state requirements for attempt do not require anything more with respect to attendant circumstances than is required for complete commission of the offense. So, if assaulting a federal officer does not require proof that you knew the person you were assaulting was a federal officer (as in the *Feola* case discussed earlier), then neither does attempting to assault a federal officer.

7. MODEL PENAL CODE MENTAL STATE REQUIREMENTS FOR ATTEMPT

The Model Penal Code diverges from the common law approach to mental state requirements for attempt in a few ways. First, belief that a result will occur is sufficient for an attempt of an offense that requires a result. So, in the bomber hypothetical, a defendant who knew that bystanders would be killed would be liable under the MPC for attempted murder of all such bystanders. Second, the MPC makes clear that attempt imposes no additional mental states for attendant circumstances than exist for the complete commission of the offense.

F. RENUNCIATION OR WITHDRAWAL

Thomas Wolfe said that you can't go back home. Can you go effectively go back in time and "undo" your criminal liability for an attempt you have already committed? What if you have already crossed the line separating perpetration from preparation but have a change of heart? Imagine that the law school assassin described above gets as far as pointing her rifle at me before deciding not to go through with it. If she goes home and confesses all to her roommate, can she still be convicted of attempted murder?

The common law did not recognize a defense of renunciation or withdrawal to attempt liability, and most common law jurisdictions that have ruled on the matter do the same. So, our soft-hearted or indecisive would-be sniper described above probably needs to pack her toothbrush for prison. Those few jurisdictions that recognize the defense (which includes the Model Penal Code) require the withdrawal to be complete and voluntary. Complete means that you have decided to never commit the offense, not to postpone or reschedule it. Voluntary means essentially that you had a true change of heart, not that you were discouraged or frustrated by some setback or difficulty. So, in the example above, if my disgruntled law student decided not to shoot me because she saw me pet a kitten, then she would have a defense if she were in a jurisdiction that permitted withdrawal. If she changed her mind because she noticed a surveillance camera over the parking lot, then that would not count as a truly voluntary withdrawal. In no event, however, can one withdraw once one has completed an attempt. So, if she takes one shot and misses, and then changes her mind when she sees me shield the kitten with my body from the next shot, she is still stuck with the attempt liability for the first shot. (Although it is lucky for me that she is a cat person.)

Even in a jurisdiction that does not recognize withdrawal you should remember that a decision not to complete an attempt can be used to argue that the person never really intended to commit the crime in the first place and therefore had never really attempted the crime. If I were defending my would-be-parking-lot assassin I would argue that even though she pointed the rifle at me she never really did so with the intent to kill me. She was still wrestling with her conscience and thinking about it all along. The farther along one gets with the attempt conduct the harder it becomes to make this argument, but it is "worth a shot."

Case in Context

The defendant in the next case had second thoughts about his crime.

PEOPLE V. STAPLES

Court of Appeal, Second District, Division 5, California
6 Cal. App. 3d 61 (1970)

REPPY, J.

Defendant was charged in an information with attempted burglary. Trial by jury was waived, and the matter submitted on the testimony contained in the transcript of the preliminary hearing together with exhibits. Defendant was found guilty. . .

I.   The Facts

In October 1967, while his wife was away on a trip, defendant, a mathematician, under an assumed name, rented an office on the second floor of a building in Hollywood which was over the mezzanine of a bank. Directly below the mezzanine was the vault of the bank. Defendant was aware of the layout of the building, specifically of the relation of the office he rented to the bank vault. Defendant paid rent for the period from October 23 to November 23. The landlord had 10 days before commencement of the rental period within which to finish some interior repairs and painting. During this prerental period defendant brought into the office certain equipment. This included drilling tools, two acetylene gas tanks, a blow torch, a blanket, and a linoleum rug. The landlord observed these items when he came in from time to time to see how the repair work was progressing. Defendant learned from a custodian that no one was in the building on Saturdays. On Saturday, October 14, defendant drilled two groups of holes into the floor of the office above the mezzanine room. He stopped drilling before the holes went through the floor. He came back to the office several times thinking he might slowly drill down, covering the holes with the linoleum rug. At some point in time he installed a hasp lock on a closet, and planned to, or did, place his tools in it. However, he left the closet keys on the premises. Around the end of November, apparently after

November 23, the landlord notified the police and turned the tools and equipment over to them. Defendant did not pay any more rent. It is not clear when he last entered the office, but it could have been after November 23, and even after the landlord had removed the equipment. On February 22, 1968, the police arrested defendant. After receiving advice as to his constitutional rights, defendant voluntarily made an oral statement which he reduced to writing.

Among other things which defendant wrote down were these:

"Saturday, the 14th. . . I drilled some small holes in the floor of the room. Because of tiredness, fear, and the implications of what I was doing, I stopped and went to sleep.

"At this point I think my motives began to change. The actual [sic] commencement of my plan made me begin to realize that even if I were to succeed a fugitive life of living off of stolen money would not give the enjoyment of the life of a mathematician however humble a job I might have.

"I still had not given up my plan however. I felt I had made a certain investment of time, money, effort and a certain pschological [sic] commitment to the concept.

"I came back several times thinking I might store the tools in the closet and slowly drill down (covering the hole with a rug of linoleum square. As time went on (after two weeks or so). My wife came back and my life as bank robber seemed more and more absurd."

II. Discussion of Defendant's Contentions

Defendant's position in this appeal is that, as a matter of law, there was insufficient evidence upon which to convict him of a criminal attempt under Penal Code section 664. Defendant claims that his actions were all preparatory in nature and never reached a stage of advancement in relation to the substantive crime which he concededly intended to commit (burglary of the bank vault) so that criminal responsibility might attach.

In order for the prosecution to prove that defendant committed an attempt to burglarize as proscribed by Penal Code section 664, it was required to establish that he had the specific intent to commit a burglary of the bank and that his acts toward that goal went beyond mere preparation.

The required specific intent was clearly established in the instant case. Defendant admitted in his written confession that he rented the office fully intending to burglarize the bank, that he brought in tools and equipment to accomplish this purpose, and that he began drilling into the floor with the intent of making an entry into the bank.

The question of whether defendant's conduct went beyond "mere preparation" raises some provocative problems. The briefs and the oral argument of counsel in this case point up a degree of ambiguity and uncertainty that permeates the law of attempts in this state. Each side has cited us to a different so-called "test" to determine whether this defendant's conduct went beyond the preparatory stage. Predictably each respective test in the eyes of its proponents yielded an opposite result. . .

We suggest that the confusion in this area is a result of the broad statutory language of section 664, which reads in part: "Any person who attempts to commit any crime, but fails, or is prevented or intercepted in the perpetration thereof, is punishable. . ." This is a very general proscription against all attempts not specifically made a crime. The statute does not differentiate between the various types of attempts which may be considered culpable. Reference must be made to case law in order to determine precisely what conduct constitutes an attempt. However, the statute does point out by the words "fails," "prevented," and "intercepted," those conditions which separate an attempt from the substantive crime. . .

Our courts have come up with a variety of "tests" which try to distinguish acts of preparation from completed attempts. "The preparation consists in devising or arranging the means or measures necessary for the commission of the offense; the attempt is the direct movement toward the commission after the preparations are made." " '[The] act must reach far enough towards the accomplishment of the desired result to amount to the commencement of the consummation.' " "[Where] the intent to commit the substantive offense is. . . clearly established. . . [,] acts done toward the commission of the crime may constitute an attempt, where the same acts would be held insufficient to constitute an attempt if the intent with which they were done is equivocal and not clearly proved."

None of the above statements of the law applicable to this category of attempts provide a litmus-like test, and perhaps no such test is achievable. Such precision is not required in this case, however. There was definitely substantial evidence entitling the trial judge to find that defendant's acts had gone beyond the preparation stage. Without specifically deciding where defendant's preparations left off and where his activities became a completed criminal attempt, we can say that his "drilling" activity clearly was an unequivocal and direct step toward the completion of the burglary. It was a fragment of the substantive crime contemplated, i.e., the beginning of the "breaking" element. Further, defendant himself characterized his activity as the actual commencement of his plan. The drilling by defendant was obviously one of a series of acts which logic and ordinary experience indicate would result in the proscribed act of burglary. . .

The order is affirmed.

DISCUSSION QUESTIONS

1. Why didn't the court even consider abandonment or withdrawal as a defense?

2. Do you think Staples ever would have gone through with his plan? Should that matter as to his criminal liability?

3. Do you think the law should allow defendants to "undo" their liability for attempts by withdrawing? What should be required for such a withdrawal?

G. IMPOSSIBILITY

This doctrine really is a bit of a mind bender. The issue is whether someone should be guilty of attempt if success was impossible. The short version of the story is that judges originally thought factual impossibility was not a defense and legal impossibility was a defense. Over time, however, it eventually became clear that the distinction between factual and impossibility was not workable. Now most jurisdictions have come to recognize that impossibility is not a defense, and whether you think of it as factual or legal does not matter. But, I am getting ahead of myself. To really understand how this doctrine works, we must retrace the steps of common law judges as they wrestled with this issue.

1. FACTUAL VS. LEGAL IMPOSSIBILITY

Assume that my homicidal law student decides to sneak into my house and shoot me to death while I sleep. She bursts into my bedroom in the dead of night, and shoots into my bed at the form beneath the blankets. Unbeknownst to her I have become quite paranoid after years of thinking up homicidal hypotheticals for my criminal law class, and I have taken to sleeping in my bedroom closet while leaving a manikin under my blankets to fool would be assassins.

Has my homicidal student committed attempted murder? Early common law judges said yes. They would concede that it is impossible to kill me (or anyone) by shooting a manikin but would point out that the law student was as morally blameworthy as a murderer. The only thing that made the crime impossible was the fact that I was not in the bed as she pulled the trigger, and this fact makes no difference to her blameworthiness or dangerousness. These common law judges called this sort of situation factual impossibility, and they ruled that factual impossibility was not a defense to an attempt charge.

Now consider a second type of case. A man buys a horse at a really cheap price and believes that the price is so low because the horse is stolen. If the horse was in fact stolen he would be guilty of the property crime of knowingly receiving stolen property. He is wrong though. The horse is not stolen; the seller is just desperate. Is the buyer of the horse guilty of attempted receipt of stolen property? Common law judges used to say no.

This was a case of legal impossibility because whether the property was stolen or not is a matter of law. These judges reasoned that you can't be guilty of attempting something that is not a crime, and it was not a crime to buy this horse. So, legal impossibility, they reasoned, was a defense to an attempt charge.

Case in Context

Lest you think that all of these questions are hypothetical ones, the next case involves shooting a corpse.

PEOPLE V. DLUGASH
Court of Appeals of New York
41 N.Y.2d 725 (1977)

JASEN, JUDGE.

The 1967 revision of the Penal Law approached the impossibility defense to the inchoate crime of attempt in a novel fashion. The statute provides that, if a person engages in conduct which would otherwise constitute an attempt to commit a crime, "it is no defense to a prosecution for such attempt that the crime charged to have been attempted was, under the attendant circumstances, factually or legally impossible of commission, if such crime could have been committed had the attendant circumstances been as such person believed them to be." (Penal Law, § 110.10.) This appeal presents to us, for the first time, a case involving the application of the modern statute. We hold that, under the proof presented by the People at trial, defendant Melvin Dlugash may be held for attempted murder, though the target of the attempt may have already been slain, by the hand of another, when Dlugash made his felonious attempt.

On December 22, 1973, Michael Geller, 25 years old, was found shot to death in the bedroom of his Brooklyn apartment. The body, which had literally been riddled by bullets, was found lying faceup on the floor. An autopsy revealed that the victim had been shot in the face and head no less than seven times. Powder burns on the face indicated that the shots had been fired from within one foot of the victim. Four small caliber bullets were recovered from the victim's skull. The victim had also been critically wounded in the chest. One heavy caliber bullet passed through the left lung, penetrated the heart chamber, pierced the left ventricle of the heart upon entrance and again upon exit, and lodged in the victim's torso. A second bullet entered the left lung and passed through to the chest, but without reaching the heart area. Although the second bullet was damaged beyond identification, the bullet tracks indicated that these wounds were also inflicted by a bullet of heavy caliber. A tenth bullet, of unknown caliber, passed through the thumb of the victim's left hand. The autopsy report listed the cause of death as "[multiple] bullet wounds of head and chest with brain injury and massive bilateral hemothorax with penetration of [the] heart." Subsequent ballistics examination established that the four bullets recovered from the victim's head were .25 caliber bullets and that the heart-piercing bullet was of .38 caliber.

. . .[During police questioning,] Defendant stated that, on the night of December 21, 1973, he, [Joe] Bush and Geller had been out drinking. Bush had been staying at Geller's apartment and, during the course of the evening, Geller several times demanded that Bush pay $100 towards the rent on the apartment. According to defendant, Bush rejected these demands, telling Geller that "you better shut up or you're going to get a bullet". All three returned to Geller's apartment at approximately midnight, took seats in the bedroom, and continued to drink until sometime between 3:00 and 3:30 in the morning. When Geller again pressed his demand for rent money, Bush drew his .38 caliber pistol, aimed it at Geller and fired three times. Geller fell to the floor. After the passage of a few minutes, perhaps two, perhaps as much as five, defendant walked over to the fallen Geller, drew his .25 caliber pistol, and fired approximately five shots in the victim's head and face. Defendant contended that, by the time he fired the shots, "it looked like Mike Geller was already dead". After the shots were fired, defendant and Bush walked to the apartment of a female acquaintance. Bush removed his shirt, wrapped the two guns and a knife in it, and left the apartment, telling Dlugash that he intended to dispose of the weapons. Bush returned 10 or 15 minutes later and stated that he had thrown the weapons down a sewer two or three blocks away.

After [police detective] Carrasquillo had taken the bulk of the statement, he asked the defendant why he would do such a thing. According to Carrasquillo, the defendant said, "gee, I really don't know." Carrasquillo repeated the question 10 minutes later, but received the same response. After a while, Carrasquillo asked the question for a third time and defendant replied, "well, gee, I guess it must have been because I was afraid of Joe Bush."

At approximately 9:00 p.m., the defendant repeated the substance of his statement to an Assistant District Attorney. Defendant added that the time he shot at Geller, Geller was not moving and his eyes were closed. While he did not check for a pulse, defendant stated that Geller had not been doing anything to him at the time he shot because "Mike was dead."

Defendant was indicted by the Grand Jury of Kings County on a single count of murder in that, acting in concert with another person actually present, he intentionally caused the death of Michael Geller. At the trial, there were four principal prosecution witnesses: Detective Carrasquillo, the Assistant District Attorney who took the second admission, and two physicians from the office of the New York City Chief Medical Examiner. For proof of defendant's culpability, the prosecution relied upon defendant's own admissions as related by the detective and the prosecutor. From the physicians, the prosecution sought to establish that Geller was still alive at the time defendant shot at him. Both physicians testified that each of the two chest wounds, for which defendant alleged Bush to be responsible, would have caused death without prompt medical attention. However, the victim would have remained alive until such time as his chest cavity became fully filled with blood. Depending on the circumstances, it might take 5 to 10 minutes for the chest cavity to fill. Neither prosecution witness could state, with medical certainty, that the victim was still alive when, perhaps five minutes after the initial chest wounds were inflicted, the defendant fired at the victim's head.

The defense produced but a single witness, the former Chief Medical Examiner of New York City. This expert stated that, in his view, Geller might have died of the chest wounds "very rapidly" since, in addition to the bleeding, a large bullet going through a lung and the heart would have other adverse medical effects. "Those wounds can be almost immediately or rapidly fatal or they may be delayed in there, in the time it would take for death to occur. But I would say that wounds like that which are described here as having gone through the lungs and the heart would be fatal wounds and in most cases they're rapidly fatal."

The trial court declined to charge the jury, as requested by the prosecution, that defendant could be guilty of murder on the theory that he had aided and abetted the killing of Geller by Bush. Instead, the court submitted only two theories to the jury: that defendant had either intentionally murdered Geller or had attempted to murder Geller.

The jury found the defendant guilty of murder. The defendant then moved to set the verdict aside. He submitted an affidavit in which he contended that he "was absolutely, unequivocally and positively certain that Michael Geller was dead before [he] shot him." Further, the defendant averred that he was in fear for his life when he shot Geller. "This fear stemmed from the fact that Joseph Bush, the admitted killer of Geller, was holding a gun on me and telling me, in no uncertain terms, that if I didn't shoot the dead body I, too, would be killed." This motion was denied.

On appeal, the Appellate Division reversed the judgment of conviction on the law and dismissed the indictment. The court ruled that "the People failed to prove beyond a reasonable doubt that Geller had been alive at the time he was shot by defendant; defendant's conviction of murder thus cannot stand." Further, the court held that the judgment could not be modified to reflect a conviction for attempted murder because "the uncontradicted evidence is that the defendant, at the time he fired the five shots into the body of the decedent, believed him to be dead, and there is not a scintilla of evidence to contradict his assertion in this regard."

Preliminarily, we state our agreement with the Appellate Division that the evidence did not establish, beyond a reasonable doubt, that Geller was alive at the time defendant fired into his body. To sustain a homicide conviction, it must be established, beyond a reasonable doubt, that the defendant caused the death of another person. . . Whatever else it may be, it is not murder to shoot a dead body. . .

Turning to the facts of the case before us, we believe that there is sufficient evidence in the record from which the jury could conclude that the defendant believed Geller to be alive at the time defendant fired shots into Geller's head. Defendant admitted firing five shots at a most vital part of the victim's anatomy from virtually point blank range. Although defendant contended that the victim had already been grievously wounded by another, from the defendant's admitted actions, the jury could conclude that the defendant's purpose and intention was to administer the coup de grace. . .

Defendant argues that the jury was bound to accept, at face value, the indications in his admissions that he believed Geller dead. Certainly, it is true that the defendant was entitled to have the entirety of the admissions, both the inculpatory and the exculpatory portions, placed in evidence before the trier of facts. . .

However, the jury was not required to automatically credit the exculpatory portions of the admissions. The general rule is, of course, that the credibility of witnesses is a question of fact and the jury may choose to believe some, but not all, of a witness' testimony. . .

The jury convicted the defendant of murder. Necessarily, they found that defendant intended to kill a live human being. Subsumed within this finding is the conclusion that defendant acted in the belief that Geller was alive. Thus, there is no need for additional fact findings by a jury. Although it was not established beyond a reasonable doubt that Geller was, in fact, alive, such is no defense to attempted murder since a murder would have been committed "had the attendant circumstances been as [defendant] believed them to be." (Penal Law, § 110.10.) The jury necessarily found that defendant believed Geller to be alive when defendant shot at him.

The Appellate Division erred in not modifying the judgment to reflect a conviction for the lesser included offense of attempted murder. An attempt to commit a murder is a lesser included offense of murder and the Appellate Division has the authority, where the trial evidence is not legally sufficient to establish the offense of which the defendant was convicted, to modify the judgment to one of conviction for a lesser included offense which is legally established by the evidence. (CPL 470.15, subd 2, par [a]; 470.20, subd 4.) Thus, the Appellate Division, by dismissing the indictment, failed to take the appropriate corrective action. . .

DISCUSSION QUESTIONS

1. If Dlugash thought Gellar to be alive as he fired his shots, why not punish him the same as you would punish someone for murder?

2.   If Gellar was dead, there was no chance of Dlugash hurting him. Why punish Dlugash at all for such an attempt?

3.   Is there such a crime as "murder of a corpse" or "attempted murder of a corpse?"

2.   THE BREAKDOWN OF THE DISTINCTION BETWEEN FACTUAL AND LEGAL IMPOSSIBILITY

Well, a middle category of cases soon developed. And common law judges applying this rule came to different conclusions as to whether the impossibility was legal or factual. One man tried to pick another man's pocket, but the pocket was empty. Was the first man guilty of attempted pickpocketing? (Technically this would have been called attempted grand larceny because it involved trying to steal something from another's person, but we will just call it pickpocketing for present purposes.) Think about this for a minute before you read on. Whatever you decide, can you see why some people might decide it differently?

Some judges decided this was a clear case of factual impossibility and would find the person guilty of attempted pickpocketing. Like the student shooting the manikin, this crime was not possible because the pocket was empty. Not so fast, said a number of other judges. They said this was a case of legal impossibility because there is no such crime as picking an empty pocket. (Putting your hand into someone else's pocket is a minor physical trespass but pickpocketing/grand larceny requires that you take something.) Since you can't be guilty of attempting something that is not a crime, it is not a crime to try to pick an empty pocket under this view.

More examples of this middle categories of cases came along over the years, and judges realized that you could characterize just about any type of impossibility as legal or factual. Was my homicidal student's attempt factually impossible because the bed was empty or legally impossible because there is no such crime as murdering a manikin? Was the circumstance that the horse was not stolen factual or legal circumstance?

3.   THE MODEL PENAL CODE AND PURE LEGAL IMPOSSIBILITY

The drafters of the Model Penal Code eventually cut through this confusion with a simple principle. We should take the circumstances of the act as the attempter believes them to be in deciding whether they have committed an attempt. If I was in the bed instead of the manikin—as the homicidal student believed—then she would have been guilty of murder, so she becomes guilty of attempted murder. If the horse was in fact stolen— as the horse buyer believed—then he would have been guilty of receiving stolen property, so he becomes guilty of attempted receipt of stolen property.

There is one limit to the Model Penal Code's principle of taking the world as the actor imagined it to be, however. We will take the world as the actor imagines it to be, but we won't take the law itself as the actor imagines it to be. Let's assume, for example, that, after taking some sort of professionalism pledge on the first day of law school, you believe that it is a crime to come to class unprepared. Are you guilty of the crime of attempting to come to class unprepared if you do so? No, because there is no such crime. Well, are you guilty of the crime of attempted coming to class unprepared because you thought you were committing a crime? No, that would be crazy. There is no such crime, and we are not going to invent one just to indulge your paranoid conscience. Wait, you might ask, aren't you blameworthy and perhaps dangerous because you committed what you thought to be a crime? No, society answers, you are only blameworthy or dangerous if you think you are doing something that actually is a crime. What if you thought that singing out of tune was a crime? Are we going to prosecute you for that, too? (I would be in a lot of trouble because I can't carry a tune to save my life.)

The coming-to-class-unprepared/singing-out-of-tune category is what the Model Penal Code commentary calls instances of pure legal impossibility. This is the only type of impossibility that the Model Penal Code recognizes. The crime contemplated is impossible because it is imaginary in all respects.

Case in Context

The investigative techniques used in the next case may be familiar, having been featured on countless procedural cop shows and primetime investigative shows.

PEOPLE V. THOUSAND
Supreme Court of Michigan
465 Mich. 149 (2001)

YOUNG, J.

We granted leave in this case to consider whether the doctrine of "impossibility" provides a defense to a charge of attempt to commit an offense prohibited by law under MCL 750.92. . . The circuit court granted defendant's motion to quash and dismissed [the charge]. . . against him on the basis that it was legally impossible for him to have committed. . .the charged crime. . .

I.   FACTUAL AND PROCEDURAL BACKGROUND

Deputy William Liczbinski was assigned by the Wayne County Sheriff's Department to conduct an undercover investigation for the department's Internet Crimes Bureau. Liczbinski was instructed to pose as a minor and log onto "chat rooms" on the Internet for the purpose of identifying persons using the Internet as a means for engaging in criminal activity.

On December 8, 1998, while using the screen name "Bekka," Liczbinski was approached by defendant, who was using the screen name "Mr. Auto-Mag," in an Internet chat room. Defendant described himself as a twenty-three-year-old male from Warren, and Bekka described herself as a fourteen-year-old female from Detroit. Bekka indicated that her name was Becky Fellins, and defendant revealed that his name was Chris Thousand. During this initial conversation, defendant sent Bekka, via the Internet, a photograph of his face.

From December 9 through 16, 1998, Liczbinski, still using the screen name "Bekka," engaged in chat room conversation with defendant. During these exchanges, the conversation became sexually explicit. Defendant made repeated lewd invitations to Bekka to engage in various sexual acts, despite various indications of her young age.

During one of his online conversations with Bekka, after asking her whether anyone was "around there," watching her, defendant indicated that he was sending her a picture of himself. Within seconds, Liczbinski received over the Internet a photograph of male genitalia. Defendant asked Bekka whether she liked and wanted it and whether she was getting "hot" yet, and described in a graphic manner the type of sexual acts he wished to perform with her. Defendant invited Bekka to come see him at his house for the purpose of engaging in sexual activity. Bekka replied that she wanted to do so, and defendant cautioned her that they had to be careful, because he could "go to jail." Defendant asked whether Bekka looked "over sixteen," so that if his roommates were home he could lie.

The two then planned to meet at an area McDonald's restaurant at 5:00 p.m. on the following Thursday. Defendant indicated that they could go to his house, and that he would tell his brother that Bekka was seventeen. Defendant instructed Bekka to wear a "nice sexy skirt," something that he could "get [his] head into." Defendant indicated that he would be dressed in black pants and shirt and a brown suede coat, and that he would be driving a green Duster. Bekka asked defendant to bring her a present, and indicated that she liked white teddy bears.

On Thursday, December 17, 1998, Liczbinski and other deputy sheriffs were present at the specified McDonald's restaurant when they saw defendant inside a vehicle matching the description given to Bekka by defendant. Defendant, who was wearing a brown suede jacket and black pants, got out of the vehicle and entered the restaurant. Liczbinski recognized defendant's face from the photograph that had been sent to Bekka. Defendant looked around for approximately thirty seconds before leaving the restaurant. Defendant was then taken into custody. . .

Following a preliminary examination, defendant was bound over for trial on charges of. . . attempted distribution of obscene material to a minor.

Defendant brought a motion to quash the information, arguing that, because the existence of a child victim was an element of each of the charged offenses, the evidence was legally insufficient to support the charges. The circuit court agreed and dismissed the case, holding that it was legally impossible for defendant to have committed the charged offenses. The Court of Appeals affirmed the dismissal of the charges. . .

III. ANALYSIS

A. THE "IMPOSSIBILITY" DOCTRINE

The doctrine of "impossibility" as it has been discussed in the context of inchoate crimes represents the conceptual dilemma that arises when, because of the defendant's mistake of fact or law, his actions could not possibly have resulted in the commission of the substantive crime underlying an attempt charge. Classic illustrations of the concept of impossibility include: (1) the defendant is prosecuted for attempted larceny after he tries to "pick" the victim's empty pocket; (2) the defendant is prosecuted for attempted rape after he tries to have nonconsensual intercourse, but is unsuccessful because he is impotent; (3) the defendant is prosecuted for attempting to receive stolen property where the property he received was not, in fact, stolen; and (4) the defendant is prosecuted for attempting to hunt deer out of season after he shoots at a stuffed decoy deer. In each of these examples, despite evidence of the defendant's criminal intent, he cannot be prosecuted for the completed offense of larceny, rape, receiving stolen property, or hunting deer out of season, because proof of at least one element of each offense cannot be derived from his objective actions. The question, then, becomes whether the defendant can be prosecuted for the attempted offense, and the answer is dependent upon whether he may raise the defense of "impossibility."

Courts and legal scholars have drawn a distinction between two categories of impossibility: "factual impossibility" and "legal impossibility." It has been said that, at common law, legal impossibility is a defense to a charge of attempt, but factual impossibility is not. See American Law Institute, Model Penal Code and Commentaries (1985), comment to § 5.01, pp 307–317; Perkins & Boyce, Criminal Law (3d ed), [158] p 632; Dressler, Understanding Criminal Law (1st ed), § 27.07[B], p 349. However, courts and scholars alike have struggled unsuccessfully over the years to articulate an accurate rule for distinguishing between the categories of "impossibility."

"Factual impossibility," which has apparently never been recognized in any American jurisdiction as a defense to a charge of attempt, "exists when [the defendant's] intended end constitutes a crime but she fails to consummate it because of a factual circumstance unknown to her or beyond her control." Dressler, supra, § 27.07[C][1], p 350. An example of a "factual impossibility" scenario is where the defendant is prosecuted for attempted murder after pointing an unloaded gun at someone and pulling the trigger, where the defendant believed the gun was loaded.

The category of "legal impossibility" is further divided into two subcategories: "pure" legal impossibility and "hybrid" legal impossibility. Although it is generally undisputed that "pure" legal impossibility will bar an attempt conviction, the concept of "hybrid legal impossibility" has proven problematic. As Professor Dressler points out, the failure of courts to distinguish between "pure" and "hybrid" legal impossibility has created confusion in this area of the law.

"Pure legal impossibility exists if the criminal law does not prohibit D's conduct or the result that she has sought to achieve." Id., § 27.07[D][2], p 352 [159] (emphasis in original). In other words, the concept of pure legal impossibility applies when an actor engages in conduct that he believes is criminal, but is not actually prohibited by law: "There can be no conviction of criminal attempt based upon D's erroneous notion that he was committing a crime." Perkins & Boyce, supra, p 634. As an example, consider the case of a man who believes that the legal age of consent is sixteen years old, and who believes that a girl with whom he had consensual sexual intercourse is fifteen years old. If the law actually fixed the age of consent at fifteen, this man would not be guilty of attempted statutory rape, despite his mistaken belief that the law prohibited his conduct.

When courts speak of "legal impossibility," they are generally referring to what is more accurately described as "hybrid" legal impossibility.

Most claims of legal impossibility are of the hybrid variety. Hybrid legal impossibility exists if D's goal was illegal, but commission of the offense was impossible due to a factual mistake by her regarding the legal status of some factor relevant to her conduct. This version of impossibility is a "hybrid" because, as the definition implies and as is clarified immediately below, D's impossibility claim includes both a legal and a factual aspect to it.

Courts have recognized a defense of legal impossibility or have stated that it would exist if D receives unstolen property believing it was stolen; tries to pick the pocket of a stone image of a human; offers a bribe to a "juror" who is not a juror; tries to hunt deer out of season by shooting a stuffed animal; shoots a corpse believing that it is alive; or shoots at a tree stump believing that it is a human.

That each of the mistakes in these cases affected the legal status of some aspect of the defendant's conduct. The status of property as "stolen" is necessary to commit the crime of "receiving stolen property with knowledge it is stolen"-i.e., a person legally is incapable of committing this offense if the property is not stolen. The status of a person as a "juror" is legally necessary to commit the offense of bribing a juror. The status of a victim as a "human being" (rather than as a corpse, tree stump, or statue) legally is necessary to commit the crime of murder or to "take and carry away the personal property of another." Finally, putting a bullet into a stuffed deer can never constitute the crime of hunting out of season.

On the other hand, in each example of hybrid legal impossibility D was mistaken about a fact: whether property was stolen, whether a person was a juror, whether the victims were human or whether the victim was an animal subject to being hunted out of season. [Dressler, supra].

As the Court of Appeals panel in this case accurately noted, it is possible to view virtually any example of "hybrid legal impossibility" as an example of "factual impossibility":

> "Ultimately any case of hybrid legal impossibility may reasonably be characterized as factual impossibility... By skillful characterization, one can describe virtually any case of hybrid legal impossibility, which is a common law defense, as an example of factual impossibility, which is not a defense."

See also. . .United States v Thomas, 13 U.S.C.M.A. 278, 283; 32 C.M.R. 278, 283 (1962) ("what is abundantly clear. . . is that it is most difficult to classify any particular state of facts as positively coming within one of these categories to the exclusion of the other"); State v. Moretti, 52 N.J. 182, 189; 244 A.2d 499 (1968) ("our examination of [authorities discussing the doctrine of impossibility] convinces us that the application of the defense of impossibility is so fraught with intricacies and artificial distinctions that the defense has little value as an analytical method for reaching substantial justice").

It is notable that "the great majority of jurisdictions have now recognized that legal and factual impossibility are 'logically indistinguishable'. . . and have abolished impossibility as a defense." United States v Hsu, 155 F.3d 189, 199 (CA 3, 1998). For example, several states have adopted statutory provisions similar to Model Penal Code, § 5.01(1) [abolishing defense of legal impossibility.]

In other jurisdictions, courts have considered the "impossibility" defense under attempt statutes that did not include language explicitly abolishing the defense. Several of these courts have simply declined to participate in the sterile academic exercise of categorizing a particular set of facts as representing "factual" or "legal" impossibility, and have instead examined solely the words of the applicable attempt statute.

B. ATTEMPTED DISTRIBUTION OF OBSCENE MATERIAL TO A MINOR

The Court of Appeals panel in this case, after examining Professor Dressler's exposition of the doctrine of impossibility, concluded that it was legally impossible for defendant to have committed the charged offense of attempted distribution of obscene material to a minor. The panel held that, because "Bekka" was, in fact, an adult, an essential requirement of the underlying substantive offense was not met (dissemination to a minor), and therefore it was legally impossible for defendant to have committed the crime.

We begin by noting that the concept of "impossibility," in either its "factual" or "legal" variant, has never been recognized by this Court as a valid defense to a charge of attempt.

Finding no recognition of impossibility in our common law, we turn now to the terms of the statute. MCL 750.92 provides, in relevant part:

Any person who shall attempt to commit an offense prohibited by law, and in such attempt shall do any act towards the commission of such offense, but shall fail in the perpetration, or shall be intercepted or prevented in the execution of the same, when no express provision is made by law for the punishment of such attempt, shall be punished as follows:

If the offense so attempted to be committed is punishable by imprisonment in the state prison for a term less than 5 years, or imprisonment in the county jail or by fine, the offender convicted of such attempt shall be guilty of a misdemeanor. . .

Under our statute, then, an "attempt" consists of (1) an attempt to commit an offense prohibited by law, and (2) any act towards the commission of the intended offense. We have further explained the elements of attempt under our statute as including "an intent to do an act or to bring about certain consequences which would in law amount to a crime; and. . . an act in furtherance of that intent which, as it is most commonly put, goes beyond mere preparation."

In determining whether "impossibility," were we to recognize the doctrine, is a viable defense to a charge of attempt under MCL 750.92, our obligation is to examine the statute in an effort to discern and give effect to the legislative intent that may reasonably be inferred from the text of the statute itself. . .

We are unable to discern from the words of the attempt statute any legislative intent that the concept of "impossibility" provide any impediment to charging a defendant with, or convicting him of, an attempted crime, notwithstanding any factual mistake-regarding either the attendant circumstances or the legal status of some factor relevant thereto-that he may harbor. The attempt statute carves out no exception for those who, possessing the requisite criminal intent to commit an offense prohibited by law and taking action toward the commission of that offense, have acted under an extrinsic misconception.

Defendant in this case is not charged with the substantive crime of distributing obscene material to a minor in violation of MCL 722.675. It is unquestioned that defendant could not be convicted of that crime, because defendant allegedly distributed obscene material not to "a minor," but to an adult man. Instead, defendant is charged with the distinct offense of attempt, which requires only that the prosecution prove intention to commit an offense prohibited by law, coupled with conduct toward the commission of that offense. The notion that it would be "impossible" for the defendant to have committed the completed offense is simply irrelevant to the analysis. Rather, in deciding guilt on a charge of attempt, the trier of fact must examine the unique circumstances of the particular case and determine whether the prosecution has proven that the defendant possessed the requisite specific intent and that he engaged in some act "towards the commission" of the intended offense.

Because the nonexistence of a minor victim does not give rise to a viable defense to the attempt charge in this case, the circuit court erred in dismissing this charge on the basis of "legal impossibility.". . .

KELLY, J. (. . .dissenting. . .)

I respectfully disagree with the majority's conclusion that the doctrine of "legal impossibility" has never been adopted in Michigan. There is ample evidence to the contrary in the case law of the state. Because "legal impossibility" is a viable defense, I would affirm the Court of Appeals decision affirming the circuit court's dismissal of attempted distribution of obscene material to a minor. . .

Even if "legal impossibility" were not part of Michigan's common law, I would disagree with the majority's interpretation of the attempt statute. It does not follow from the fact that the statute does not expressly incorporate the concept of impossibility that the defense is inapplicable.

Examination of the language of the attempt statute leads to a reasonable inference that the Legislature did not intend to punish conduct that a mistake of legal fact renders unprohibited. The attempt statute makes illegal an ". . . attempt to commit an offense prohibited by law. . .". It does not make illegal an action not prohibited by law. Hence, one may conclude, the impossibility of completing the underlying crime can provide a defense to attempt.

This reasoning is supported by the fact that the attempt statute codified the common-law rule regarding the elements of attempt. At common law, "legal impossibility" is a defense to attempt. Absent a statute expressly abrogating "legal impossibility," this common-law rule continues to provide a viable defense.

This state's attempt statute, unlike the Model Penal Code and various state statutes that follow it, does not contain language allowing for consideration of a defendant's beliefs regarding "attendant circumstances." Rather, it takes an "objective" view of criminality, focusing on whether the defendant actually came close to completing the prohibited act. The impossibility of completing the offense is relevant to this objective approach because impossibility obviates the state's "concern that the actor may cause or come close to causing the harm or evil that the offense seeks to prevent."

The majority's conclusion, that it is irrelevant whether it would be impossible to have committed the completed offense, contradicts the language used in the attempt statute. If an element of the offense cannot be established, an accused cannot be found guilty of the prohibited act. The underlying offense in this case, disseminating or exhibiting sexual material to a minor, requires a minor recipient. Because the dissemination was not to a minor, it is legally impossible for defendant to have committed the prohibited act.

This Court should affirm the Court of Appeals decision, determining that it was legally impossible for defendant to have committed the charged offense of attempted distribution of obscene material to a minor. . .

As judges, we often decide cases involving disturbing facts. However repugnant we personally find the criminal conduct charged, we must decide the issues on the basis of the law. I certainly do not wish to have child predators loose in society. However, I believe that neither the law nor society is served by allowing the end of removing them from society to excuse unjust means to accomplish it. In this case, defendant raised a legal impossibility argument that is supported by Michigan case law. The majority, in determining that legal impossibility is not a viable defense in this state, ignores that law. . .

DISCUSSION QUESTIONS

1.   Should it matter that the intended victim of child abuse is in fact a fully grown sheriff's deputy? Why isn't this a case of legal impossibility?

2.   Should law enforcement engage in these types of sting operations? Are the police preventing crime or creating crime?

3.   Do you agree with the Model Penal Code's approach to impossibility?

4. THE MODERN APPROACH

The end of this long and complicated story is that judges in most common law jurisdictions have come to realize that the MPC got it right. Impossibility (legal or factual) is not a defense to an attempt charge. In figuring out whether they are guilty of an attempt we take everything as they imagine it to be except the law itself. This means, by the way, that the guy who thought he was buying the stolen horse that was actually not stolen is now considered guilty of attempting to receive stolen property.

Imagine that you believe it to be a crime to sell alcohol to someone who is under the age of 30. (You have seen those signs in the supermarket saying that they card people who are under the age of 30, so you assume that 30, not 21, is the drinking age.) Consider the following hypotheticals.

You sell someone alcohol whom you believe to be 29 and who is 29. Are you guilty of attempting to sell alcohol to someone who is under the age of 21? No, because you did not believe them to be under the age of 21 and selling someone alcohol who is 29 is not a crime.

Now imagine that they are 29 but that you believed them to be 20. (Lucky them, they must really have stayed out of the sun.) Now you would be guilty of attempting to sell someone who is under the age of 21 alcohol because while we won't take the law as you imagine it to be (i.e. the drinking age) we will take the world as you imagine it to be (i.e. the age of the person you sold to), and that makes what you did an attempted crime.

5. INHERENT IMPOSSIBILITY

There is one final rule worth mentioning, not because it is ever likely to come up in your practice, but because you may wake up in the middle of the night wondering about it the night before your final. What about someone who just got into the Harry Potter stories a little too much and who came to believe that he, like Harry, has magical powers? Unlike Harry, however, he is not blessed with a saintly disposition. He uses a killing curse against someone fully believing that the curse will kill. Is Evil Wannabe-Harry guilty of attempted murder? The answer would seem to be yes because 1) killing someone is a crime so he is not committing an imaginary crime; and 2) if his curse had the power to kill then the person would be dead. This situation is referred to as a case of "inherent impossibility" because it is inherently impossible to commit murder in this way. The MPC provides that while such an actor is guilty of attempted murder the sentencing judge should take the inherent impossibility of success of such a scheme into consideration during sentencing. So, Evil Wannabe-Harry gets a reduced sentence but not an acquittal. Maybe he can earn money making wands in prison.

H. MODEL PENAL CODE

The Model Penal Code's attempt provisions have been discussed throughout this chapter. As you review them in their entirety below note the consistent emphasis on the culpability of the actor in defining when attempt liablity begins and ends.

§ 5.01. Criminal Attempt

1) Definition of Attempt. A person is guilty of an attempt to commit a crime if, acting with the kind of culpability otherwise required for commission of the crime, he:

   a) purposely engages in conduct that would constitute the crime if the attendant circumstances were as he believes them to be; or

   b) when causing a particular result is an element of the crime, does or omits to do anything with the purpose of causing or with the belief that it will cause such result without further conduct on his part; or

   c) purposely does or omits to do anything that, under the circumstances as he believes them to be, is an act or omission constituting a substantial step in a course of conduct planned to culminate in his commission of the crime.

2) Conduct That May Be Held Substantial Step Under Subsection (1)(c). Conduct shall not be held to constitute a substantial step under Subsection (1)(c) of this Section unless it is strongly corroborative of the actor's criminal purpose. Without negativing the sufficiency of other conduct, the following, if strongly corroborative of the actor's criminal purpose, shall not be held insufficient as a matter of law:

   a) lying in wait, searching for or following the contemplated victim of the crime;

   b) enticing or seeking to entice the contemplated victim of the crime to go to the place contemplated for its commission;

   c) reconnoitering the place contemplated for the commission of the crime;

   d) unlawful entry of a structure, vehicle or enclosure in which it is contemplated that the crime will be committed;

   e) possession of materials to be employed in the commission of the crime, that are specially designed for such unlawful use or that can serve no lawful purpose of the actor under the circumstances;

   f) possession, collection or fabrication of materials to be employed in the commission of the crime, at or near the place contemplated for its commission, if such possession, collection or fabrication serves no lawful purpose of the actor under the circumstances;

   g) soliciting an innocent agent to engage in conduct constituting an element of the crime.

3)   Conduct Designed to Aid Another in Commission of a Crime. A person who engages in conduct designed to aid another to commit a crime that would establish his complicity under Section 2.06 if the crime were committed by such other person, is guilty of an attempt to commit the crime, although the crime is not committed or attempted by such other person.

4)   Renunciation of Criminal Purpose. When the actor's conduct would otherwise constitute an attempt under Subsection (1)(b) or (1)(c) of this Section, it is an affirmative defense that he abandoned his effort to commit the crime or otherwise prevented its commission, under circumstances manifesting a complete and voluntary renunciation of his criminal purpose. The establishment of such defense does not, however, affect the liability of an accomplice who did not join in such abandonment or prevention. Within the meaning of this Article, renunciation of criminal purpose is not voluntary if it is motivated, in whole or in part, by circumstances, not present or apparent at the inception of the actor's course of conduct, that increase the probability of detection or apprehension or that make more difficult the accomplishment of the criminal purpose. Renunciation is not complete if it is motivated by a decision to postpone the criminal conduct until a more advantageous time or to transfer the criminal effort to another but similar objective or victim.

Practice Problem 18.3: Criminal Collaboration

In the state of Joeland violating the Honor Code at any institution of higher learning that receives federal funds (which is virtually all institutions of higher learning) is a misdemeanor. The Honor Code at Joeland University states that a student may not consult an outline that the student has not contributed to herself in any way during an exam. Pat is a second-year student who emails four first-year students Pat's criminal law outline very late the night before the criminal law exam. Lee reads over the outline but does not print it out. Riley prints out the exam but does not bring it to the exam the next day. Casey brings the outline into the exam room but does not take it out. Kerry places the outline on the desk but then reports the entire group to the exam proctor fifteen minutes later without having consulted the outline at all. Joeland is a Model Penal Code jurisdiction. Which students, if any, are guilty of attempting this crime if Joeland is a Model Penal Code jurisdiction? A common law jurisdiction?

CHAPTER 19

COMPLICITY AND LIABILITY FOR CRIMES OF OTHERS

■ ■ ■

Complicity is not a crime in and of itself like conspiracy: it is a way of being guilty of a crime. This simple point is worth belaboring at the outset. If you are an accomplice to a bank robbery, then you are guilty of the crime of. . . wait for it. . . bank robbery! And you receive the same prison sentence as a. . . wait for it again. . . bank robber! This might strike you as uncontroversial because you probably imagine a team of armed robbers running around in the bank waiving guns around. What you will soon learn, however, is that you don't need to do much to become an accomplice to a bank robbery or any other crime as long as you do it with the right frame of mind. Even bit players in the cast of characters get the same full liability for the crime being committed as those enjoying the starring roles (although a judge might sentence them differently within the range permitted for the offense). Your chicken-hearted getaway driver parked at the curb outside will also be guilty of armed robbery. So will your sainted mother who made you a bag lunch before you set out to rob the bank that day. At least you will have a lot of company in prison.

A. OVERVIEW OF THE ELEMENTS

Complicity has both guilty hand and guilty mind requirements. In the simplest terms, an accomplice is one who:

- Even slightly Assists or Encourages

- Another in the commission of a crime

- With the Intent to Assist or Encourage and

- With the Intent that the Crime assisted or encouraged be Committed.

Timing is of the essence for a would-be accomplice. You cannot be an accomplice if you come into the picture after the crime has already been committed. On the other hand, if you have intentionally assisted in or encouraged the commission of a crime and change your mind, you are generally out of luck because your complicity was complete at the moment of assistance or encouragement.

B. PHILOSOPHICAL AND POLICY CONSIDERATIONS

Why do we expand criminal liability so greatly through complicity? Why would even a slight act of assistance or encouragement subject one to the full weight of punishment for a crime that someone else committed? The utilitarian answer is that we fear the effectiveness and dangerousness of group criminality, and defining complicity broadly allows us to deter group crime by making sure that all members of the group can be fully punished. In terms of blameworthiness, broad complicity prevents highly culpable individuals from hiding their guilt behind the work of others.

Yet broad complicity liability raises many troubling issues. So little conduct is required that complicity depends very heavily on getting the mental state of the offender right. Since mental states are often inferred from circumstances, a danger exists that some hapless individual who was helping the wrong people at the wrong time will suffer criminal liability that he does not deserve. Moreover, by failing to distinguish between great and small acts of assistance and between mere encouragement and real action, complicity arguably fails to distinguish the half-hearted offender from the committed criminal, the merely bad from the truly evil. The man who points the gun is arguably a worse and more dangerous person than the person who writes the bank robbery note, but each share equally in liability for bank robbery under the complicity doctrine.

C. COMMON LAW TERMINOLOGY

The modern approach is to treat anyone who intentionally assists or encourages the crime equally and to not make distinctions between types of accomplices. The common law took a different approach. Learning the different types of accomplices at common law is useful both because the old terminology still crops up in cases from time to time and because these terms describe the full range of accomplice liability.

- *Principal in the First Degree.* This is the main actor, the one who often "does the crime," although he may be assisted by others. Ordinarily, he will be present at the scene of the crime during its commission. There also may be more than one principal in the first degree. If three men run into a bank waiving guns and demanding money, all three would be considered principals in the first degree at common law.

- *Principal in the Second Degree.* These are the "helpers" or encouragers of the principals in the first degree. They also generally must be present at the scene when the crime is committed. The getaway driver who sits behind the wheel of the car outside of the bank would be a principal in the second degree. So would a lookout who stood outside looking for police cars and listening for sirens. Neither threatens anyone with a gun nor takes anything from anyone—necessary elements for armed robbery—but they help people who do and are guilty of armed robbery as a result.

- *Accessory Before the Fact.* These are the "helpers" or encouragers who are not present at the scene of the crime and who ordinarily did their part before the crime began. So, your loud mouth roommate who got you all fired up on the idea of robbing the bank would fit the bill. So might your otherwise saintly mother who worried that you might not take the time to eat a nutritious lunch the day of the robbery unless she packed one for you. Neither could be bothered going with you to the bank, so neither would be considered principals in the second degree. Think of them as the "stay-at-home" types.

It bears repeating that all would be considered accomplices both at common law and in all modern jurisdictions. They are all bank robbers.

There is one final category of "helper" at common law that needs to be discussed so that you will understand one of the important limits of complicity liability.

- *Accessory After the Fact.* This is the "Johnny-Come-Lately" crime. An accessory after the fact is someone who knowingly and intentionally helps another to avoid arrest, trial, or conviction of a crime after it has been convicted. Imagine your old college roommate drops by your apartment after the bank robbery. You mention that you just robbed a bank and that the police are looking all over for you. Your former roommate says that he does not think you would do very well in prison and offers to let you spend the night at his place. He is an accessory after the fact because he knows you committed the bank robbery, and he intends by letting you spend the night to help you avoid arrest.

You must remember that an accessory after the fact is not an accomplice. As willing and helpful (and blameworthy and dangerous) as they are, they came into the picture too late to be an accomplice. (At common law they were accomplices, but this is not the rule anywhere anymore.) Since accessories after the fact are not accomplices, they cannot be liable for the crime that has already been committed, so your good old college roommate is not guilty of bank robbery. What do we have as a consolation prize for our Johnny-Come-Lately helper? An accessory after the fact is guilty of the separate crime of being an accessory after the fact, a crime that has been created in many jurisdictions just for this purpose.

Once you have learned the common law terminology, remember to burn the main point into your brain. Principals in the first degree, principals in the second degree, and accessories before the fact are all considered accomplices today and are therefore all equally guilty of whatever crime has been committed.

1. ACQUITTAL OF THE PRINCIPAL

These old common law distinctions made a difference when some but not all the accomplices were acquitted. Specifically, acquittal of the principal in the first degree—the primary "doer" of the crime—barred conviction of the principal in the second degree and the accessories. Virtually all jurisdictions have abandoned this rule, although a few may still bar conviction of a second degree principal or an accessory before the fact if the principal in the first degree was acquitted in the same trial in order to avoid an inconsistent verdict. So today any sort of accomplice can be tried and convicted regardless of whether other accomplices have been convicted or acquitted just as long as the prosecution proves that the crime assisted or encouraged did take place.

So, your mother can be put on trial for making your lunch before the bank robbery even though you are safely—and selfishly—counting your ill-gotten gains in some country from which you cannot be extradited. The prosecution must prove, of course, that the bank was robbed to convict your mother of bank robbery, so your name will definitely come up. But you don't have to be convicted for your mother to go to prison for bank robbery. Just imagine though all the nasty things the jury will say about you before they send your Mom packing off to prison.

D. THE GUILTY HAND: ASSISTANCE

The basic rule is that even a slight act of assistance will make one an accomplice, but you must actually assist. Your assistance, though, does not need to be essential to the crime. So the prosecutor does not have to prove that but for your assistance the crime would not have been committed.

Let's imagine that I am present during your robbery of the bank, and that I recognize you as a former student who has obviously fallen on hard times (and who probably is going to end up doing hard time). You have your hands full with your shotgun as you are walking into the bank, and I realize that you are going to have to put the shotgun down in order to open the door. I helpfully open the door for you. That slight act of assistance, if done with the requisite mental state, would be sufficient to make me an accomplice to your bank robbery. Now, would you have gone ahead and robbed the bank anyway even if I had not opened the door for you? Of course! It is very unlikely that, having walked up to a bank carrying a shotgun, you would have let an unlocked door stand in your way. But my act of assistance need not be a but for cause of your crime (i.e. but for my assistance the crime would not have been committed). My act need only slightly assist you, which it did since you did not have to put down and pick up your shotgun.

Note that while it might be of slight assistance, the act must actually assist. Imagine now that I ran and opened one door while you went through the other door oblivious to my efforts to assist. This attempt to assist would not make me an accomplice in the vast majority of jurisdictions (MPC jurisdictions being the exception, which we will discuss later). Even though I have an equally blameworthy mental state in both cases, and even though even slight assistance is enough to make one an accomplice, I would not be guilty of anything since I did not actually assist.

Case in Context

The following case discusses complicity in the context of crowd violence.

STATE V. OCHOA

Supreme Court of New Mexico
41 N.M. 589 (1937)

Opinion by: SADLER.

The defendants were convicted of murder in the second degree in a trial before the district court of San Juan county on change of venue from McKinley county. They prosecute this appeal from the judgment of conviction pronounced upon them at such trial. The victim of the homicide was M. R. Carmichael, sheriff of McKinley county. He was slain while accompanying a prisoner from the office of the local justice of the peace to the county jail.

The homicide occurred about 9:30 o'clock in the forenoon of April 4, 1935. A few days previously one Esiquel Navarro, one Victor Campos, and a Mrs. Lovato had been arrested on warrants charging the unlawful breaking and entering of a certain house. Theretofore the house had been occupied by said Campos who was evicted in forcible entry and detainer proceedings. Following eviction, so the charge ran, the three persons just mentioned forcibly re-entered the house and replaced Campos' furniture therein. The preliminary hearing for Navarro, who was confined in jail, was set for 9 a.m., April 4th.

The house in question was located in a section of Gallup known locally as Chihuahuita, largely occupied by former employees of a coal mining company. Considerable excitement had been engendered among them by the eviction proceedings and the approaching trial of Navarro. . . .

. . .

The sheriff, accompanied by several deputies, left the jail with the prisoner, Navarro, shortly before 9 o'clock the morning of April 4th and proceeded to the office of Justice of the Peace William H. Bickel on Coal avenue, a distance of one and one-half blocks. Arriving there, they found the justice engaged in the hearing of another matter and were compelled to await the conclusion of that hearing. Soon after they arrived a crowd of approximately 125 people, included in which were many women and children, gathered on the sidewalk and in the street in front of the office of the justice of the peace. The crowd was made up largely of friends of the prisoner, Navarro. The officers, even before leaving the jail with the prisoner, had become apprehensive that an effort might be made to rescue him. So that, when the crowd sought admittance to the justice's chambers which had seating capacity for not more than 25 spectators, none except witnesses were permitted to enter.

The crowd in front grew threatening. They pressed against the plate glass windows to the extent that one of them was cracked; pounded on the windows with their fists; shouted, cursed; and some threatened to kick the door down if they were not admitted. After some delay incident to completion of the other hearing, and upon Navarro's objection that he had no attorney, the hearing of his case was postponed for the purpose of enabling him to secure an attorney to represent him.

Apprehensive of trouble in attempting to make their exit from the office of the justice through the crowd at the front entrance en route back to the jail, the sheriff directed that Navarro should be removed through the rear door [into an alley thus avoiding the crowd].

About the time it was appreciated by the crowd in front that the prisoner was to be removed through the rear door into the alley, the defendant Leandro Velarde was seen going through the crowd motioning toward the west, the direction to be taken to reach the alley, and he went into the alley practically at the head of the crowd.

The three defendants, Leandro Velarde, Manuel Avitia, and Juan Ochoa, along with certain other defendants acquitted at the trial, were identified as being in the crowd in front of the justice's office and also in the crowd at the rear of the office in the alley after it had hastened there upon discovering that the prisoner, Navarro, was to be removed through the rear door and thence via the alley to the jail. The present defendants, along with Ignacio Velarde and Solomon Esquibel, slain during the affray, were in the forefront of the crowd formed in a semicircle around the rear entrance as the officers prepared to emerge with their prisoner.

Just before they took the prisoner through the rear entrance, former Deputy Fred Montoya, who formed one of the sheriff's party at the justice's office, at the sheriff's request, opened the rear door. He took one step outside. There confronting him among those recognized were Ignacio Velarde, Leandro Velarde, and Solomon Esquibel. Leandro Velarde, clenching his fist and raising it in a threatening manner, said to Montoya: "Now you shall see what happens disgraced (one)." Solomon Esquibel, reaching his right hand into a partially open blue jacket worn at the time as if to draw a weapon, said: "You move back, leave them to us alone." Montoya being unarmed immediately moved back inside the office of the justice of the peace.

Contemporaneously with Montoya's return to the inside of the office, Sheriff Carmichael and Undersheriff Dee Roberts emerged therefrom with the prisoner. As they did so and started pushing their way out into the alley, the defendant Juan Ochoa, from a distance of about three feet, struck at Undersheriff Dee Roberts with a claw hammer. The officers, nevertheless, succeeded in getting their prisoner into the alley, pushing their way through the crowd, and proceeded eastwardly toward the jail with the prisoner. Sheriff Carmichael was on the prisoner's right, holding him by the right arm, and Undersheriff Dee Roberts was on the prisoner's left, holding him by the left arm, walking eastwardly toward the jail. As they proceeded up the alley toward the jail they were surrounded by the crowd, some of whom were ahead of them, some on either side and some to their rear. The officers with the prisoner were followed by Deputies E. L. "Bobcat" Wilson and Hoy Boggess in the order named. An unidentified person in the crowd had been heard to shout: "We want Navarro."

When the officers had advanced a short distance up the alley with their prisoner, the defendant Manuel Avitia drew a pistol from his pocket and rushed from the rear through the crowd toward the officers.

When they were about forty feet from the rear exit of the justice's office, Deputy Hoy Boggess observed someone, unknown to him, grab at the prisoner as if to take him from the custody of the officers. Thereupon, he raised his arm and hurled a tear gas bomb to the rear and westwardly into the crowd in the alley.

After hurling the tear gas bomb, and just before being struck and rendered unconscious, Deputy Boggess observed the defendant Leandro Velarde only a few feet from him on the right; Solomon Esquibel, later slain, not far away; and the defendant Manuel Avitia running toward him (Boggess). When Boggess fell unconscious from a blow on the head delivered by some unidentified person in the crowd, his pistol fell from his belt to the pavement. Two members of the crowd were seen to spring toward same and to be bent over as if to recover it. . .

While Deputy Boggess was down on the paving and after the firing had begun, the defendants Avitia and Ochoa, with two or three other persons, were seen beating and kicking him.

Almost simultaneously with the detonation from explosion of the bomb, a shot was fired somewhat to the rear of the officers accompanying the prisoner. Then a second shot followed the first, apparently fired by Ignacio Velarde, a brother of the defendant Leandro Velarde, from a point at the northeast corner of the Independent Building, some fifteen feet from Sheriff Carmichael. This shot struck the sheriff in the left side of the face and passed out of his body on the right side of his neck. The first shot fired had struck the sheriff in the left side, just under the left arm, passed through his chest and out into his right shoulder. He died instantly, his undersheriff, Dee Roberts, catching hold of his right arm and lowering his body to the pavement. The latter then looking to the west observed two men firing toward him. One was on his left at the corner of the Independent Building, perhaps fifteen feet distant. This proved to be Ignacio Velarde. The other was farther down the alley about twenty feet and to his right. This was Solomon Esquibel. Their fire was returned by Undersheriff Roberts, and both Ignacio Velarde and Solomon Esquibel were killed.

In the meantime the firing had become more general, the total number of shots fired during the affray being twelve to fifteen. When the shooting had ceased Avitia ran west out of the alley with a pistol in his hand. When the firing ceased, besides Sheriff Carmichael and the two others named being killed, Deputy Wilson had been seriously wounded by a bullet which entered his body about an inch below the armpit and was later extracted. Two other members of the crowd had received wounds, a woman by a shot through the leg. Both of these wounded, as well as Deputy Wilson, subsequently recovered.

The pistols with which Ignacio Velarde and Solomon Esquibel were seen firing were never located after the affray. The pistol which dropped from Deputy Boggess' belt when he was knocked unconscious was never recovered. Sheriff Carmichael's pistol was removed from its scabbard on his body after his death. It had never been fired. The bullet which had entered the body of Sheriff Carmichael under the left armpit was later extracted from his right shoulder. The bullet which had wounded Deputy Wilson likewise was later extracted. The pistol which Deputy Boggess lost during the affray and which had not been fired by him when lost was a forty-five Smith and Wesson double action. The bullet removed from the body of Sheriff Carmichael and that extracted from Deputy Wilson were both fired from the same pistol and it was of the same make and caliber as that lost by Deputy Boggess, using the same type of ammunition as that then employed in the Boggess gun.

The defendants were proceeded against by information, the State electing to employ the short form authorized by Trial Court Rule 35–4407. Ten were thus accused of the murder of Sheriff Carmichael, of whom seven were acquitted by the jury. The three defendants above named having been convicted of second degree murder, they alone prosecute this appeal. The most serious claim of error is directed at the action of the trial court in submitting to the jury the issue of second degree murder. It is claimed the evidence does not warrant submission of second degree. If this claim be good as to all of the defendants it is decisive. Hence, we give it first consideration. The facts as we have recited them are within the verdicts of guilty returned against defendants. Do they support second degree? That is the issue.

The Attorney General in the State's brief says: we still have two theories presented by the evidence shown (under) which the jury might find the appellants guilty of second degree murder. First, that one of the appellants actually shot and killed Sheriff Carmichael. Second, that the appellants or any of them aided and abetted the person or persons who actually shot and killed Sheriff Carmichael.

The distinction between an accessory before the fact and a principal and between principals in the first and second degree, in cases of felony, has been abolished in New Mexico and every person concerned in the commission thereof, whether he directly commits the offense or procures, counsels, aids, or abets in its commission, must be prosecuted, tried, and punished as a principal. Laws 1933, c. 105; Trial Court Rule 35–4439. The evidence of aiding and abetting may be as broad and varied as are the means of communicating thought from one individual to another; by acts, conduct, words, signs, or by any means sufficient to incite, encourage or instigate commission of the offense or calculated to make known that commission of an offense already undertaken has the aider's support or approval. State v. Wilson, supra. Mere presence, of course, and even mental approbation, if unaccompanied by outward manifestation or expression of such approval, is insufficient.

Before an accused may become liable as an aider and abettor, he must share the criminal intent of the principal. There must be community of purpose, partnership in the unlawful undertaking.

"To aid and abet another in a crime one must share the intent or purpose of the principal. If two or more acting independently assault another, and one of them inflicts a mortal wound, the other is not guilty as an aider and abettor. An aider and abettor is a partner in the crime, the chief ingredient of which is always intent. There can be no partnership in the act where there is no community of purpose or intent."

"To render one an aider or abettor and, as a consequence, guilty in like degree with the principal in the commission of a crime, there should be evidence of his knowledge of the intention or purpose of the principal to commit the assault. In other words, there must have been a 'common purpose' by which is meant a like criminal intent in the minds of Mills and the appellant, to render the latter guilty as charged, and hence authorize the giving of the instruction." State v. Porter, 276 Mo. 387, 207 S.W. 774, 776.

With these preliminary observations, we shall proceed to apply them to the facts of the instant case. As to the defendant Leandro Velarde there is no evidence which sufficiently connects him with the unlawful design of the slayer of Sheriff Carmichael. The last time seen prior to the hurling of the tear gas bomb and the firing of the first shot, he was in the crowd a few feet removed from Deputy Boggess. There apparently was nothing about his actions when then seen to excite suspicion. If so, it was not testified to by any witness.

He is not shown to have taken part in the assault on Deputy Boggess, as were Avitia and Ochoa.

The defendants Avitia and Ochoa are differently situated. After Deputy Boggess hurled the tear gas bomb, he was knocked down and rendered unconscious for a time. Firing from the party of which they formed a part started almost instantly and continued until a total of as many as 12 or 15 shots had been exchanged between members of the two parties. Even if it be assumed that these two defendants were without previous knowledge of the purpose of the slayer or slayers of deceased to make an attempt on his life, the evidence abundantly supports an inference that with the firing of the first shot they became apprised of that purpose. The intent to kill, or to aid and abet in the commission thereof, may be formed at the scene of the crime, even though the accused may have gone there without such intention. People v. Will, 79 Cal. App. 101, 248 P. 1078. If, with knowledge that one of their party was using or was about to use a deadly weapon, they or either of them rendered aid or assistance to him or them engaged in the deadly assault, they are equally guilty as aiders and abettors. The aider under such circumstances adopts the criminal intent of the principal. State v. Powell, 168 N.C. 134, 83 S.E. 310. Both Avitia and Ochoa are identified in the testimony as being still engaged in an assault upon the fallen Boggess after two bullets had entered the body of the deceased. Boggess was a deputy of the slain sheriff and, of course, would be expected to come to the aid of his chief in peril. The fact that they were thus engaged in a vicious assault upon him (Boggess), after firing upon the sheriff's party commenced, left it within the jury's province to infer, if it saw fit, not alone that these defendants shared the intent of the slayer, but also that they aided and abetted him in his unlawful undertaking.

Nor would it seem an unwarranted inference, if the jury should elect so to find, that these defendants saw the sheriff's assailant in the act of drawing or aiming his gun and commenced the assault on Deputy Boggess momentarily before or simultaneously with the first outburst of gunfire. Particularly is this true in view of the fact that the assault on Boggess did not cease when it must have become known to the defendants that a member of their party was firing on the sheriff's party. Such an inference, however, is not essential to sustain the verdicts.

However free from felonious intent a participant in the combat of opposing parties may have been in the beginning, once it becomes known to him that another member of his party is employing a deadly weapon, he exposes himself to an inference of sharing the latter's intent if, except in necessary defense of his own person, he continues his participation. The question of whether the alleged aider and abettor did share the principal's criminal intent, and whether he knew the latter acted with criminal intent, is one of fact for the jury and may be inferred from circumstances.

It was unnecessary for the State to show who actually fired the fatal shot if the proof was sufficient to warrant the inference as to a given defendant that, if he did not fire it, he aided and abetted him who did.

Morally, there never has been a distinction in the degree of culpability. The law long since has ceased to recognize any. All are subject to prosecution, trial, and punishment as principals. Laws 1933, c. 105; Trial Court Rule 35–4439. The aider and abettor may be tried and convicted even though the actual slayer is never apprehended or has been tried and acquitted.

It follows from what has been said that the judgment of the district court must stand affirmed as to the defendants Avitia and Ochoa. As to the defendant Velarde, it is reversed, with a direction to the trial court to set aside the judgment of conviction pronounced upon him and to discharge the prisoner.

DISCUSSION QUESTIONS

1. Could the defendants have been accomplices to the shooting if the shooter did not know that they were helping him?

2. Could the defendants have been accomplices to the shooting if they did not know about the shooting before they attacked the deputy? What if they learned about the shooting while they were beating the deputy?

3. Could everyone in the crowd be charged with complicity in the shooting? What about all the people who were standing between the deputy and the sheriff?

Case in Context

Under what circumstances can one be a "secret accomplice"?

STATE V. TALLY

Supreme Court of Alabama
102 Ala. 25 (1894)

Opinion by: MCCLELLAN.

Briefly stated, the information in this case contains two charges against John B. Tally as Judge of the Ninth Judicial Circuit. The second count charges complicity on the part of Tally in the murder of Ross, by the hands of said Skeltons. Tally was a brother-in-law to all of the Skeltons named the grievance they had against Ross lay in the fact that the latter had seduced or been criminally intimate with a sister of three of them and of Mrs. Tally.

[Ross, after a period of hiding from the Skeltons out of town, returned to Scottsboro for a few days. On January 30, 1894, Ross traveled from Scottsboro to Stevenson by carriage. That morning, James Skelton, who lived with the defendant, armed himself and followed by horse, along with Robert and John Skelton. Walter Skelton had already preceded them].

The flight of Ross and the pursuit of the Skeltons at once became generally known in the town of Scottsboro, and was well-nigh the sole topic of conversation that Sunday morning. Everybody knew it. Everybody talked only about it. Everybody was impressed with the probability of a terrible tragedy to be enacted on the road to Stevenson, or at the latter point. The respondent was soon abroad. He went to the depot where the telegraph office was. He remained about there most of that morning. About nine o'clock that morning Dr. Rorex saw him there, and this, in the language of the witness, passed between them: "I said to Judge Tally that I thought we had better send a hack and a physician to their assistance up the road [referring to the Ross and Skelton parties then on the road to Stevenson]; that these parties might get hurt and they might need assistance. Judge Tally replied that his folks or friends could take care of themselves. I also said to him that I reckoned we ought to send a telegram to Stevenson and have all of them arrested, to which he made no reply. He said that he was waiting to see if anybody sent a telegram—or words to that effect—waiting or watching to see if anybody sent a telegram." And he did wait and watch. He was seen there by Judge Bridges just before the passenger train going west at 10:17 passed. He was there after it passed. E. H. Ross, a kinsman of the Ross who had fled and was being pursued, meeting the telegraph operator, Whitner, at the passenger station walked with him down to the freight depot where the telegraph office was. Judge Tally followed them. They went into the telegraph office and so did he. Ross was sitting at a table writing a message. It was addressed to R. C. Ross, Stevenson, Alabama. Its contents were: "Four men on horseback with guns following. Look out." Ross handed it to the operator to be sent. Tally either saw this message or in some way very accurately divined its contents. He called for paper and immediately wrote a message himself. Judge Bridges was still in the office. At this juncture Tally spoke to him, took him into a corner of the room and, calling him by his given name, said: "What do you reckon that fellow [the operator] would think if I told him I should put him out of that office before he should send that message?" referring to the message quoted above which E. H. Ross had just given the operator. Judge Bridges replied: "Judge, I wouldn't do that. That might cause you very serious trouble, and besides that might cause the young man to lose his position with the company he is working for." Judge Tally then remarked: "I don't want him to send the message he has, and I am going to send this one." He then showed Judge Bridges a message addressed to William Huddleston at Stevenson, containing these words: "Do not let the party warned get away." This message was signed by Tally. Huddleston was the operator at Stevenson and a friend of Tally. The respondent then handed this telegram to the operator, remarked to him "this message has something to do with that one you just received," said he wanted it sent, and paid for it. He then started toward the door, but turned to the operator and said: "Just add to that message, 'say nothing.'" Tally then left the office. This message was sent just after that of E. H. Ross to R. C. Ross. The original of it was placed on a file in the office at Scottsboro. These telegrams of Ed. Ross and Tally were sent about 10:25 A. M. Tally then, his watch to prevent the sending or delivery of a telegram to R. C. Ross being over, went home.

[When Ross alighted in Stevenson he was shot at by Robert, James, and Walter Skelton. Wounded, Ross ran for cover behind a building, where he was ambushed and shot in the head from behind by John Skelton. Robert Skelton then telegraphed Tally that Ross was dead and the Skeltons unhurt]

The second specification charges that the Skeltons "unlawfully and with malice aforethought killed Robert C. Ross by shooting him with a gun," and "that the said John B. Tally, did aid or abet the said" Skeltons, naming them, "in the commission of the said felony and murder." These charges of aiding or abetting murder and of murder direct, which amount to the same thing under our statute (Code, § 3704), are, upon considerations, to which we have already adverted, to be sustained, if at all, by evidence of the respondent's connection with the homicide after the Skeltons had left Scottsboro in pursuit of Ross, since we do not find any incriminating connection up to that point of time. Being without conviction that Tally knew of the Skeltons' intention to take Ross's life until after they had departed on their errand of death, and there being no evidence or pretense that between this time and the homicide any communication passed between them and Tally, we reach and declare the conclusion that the respondent did not command, direct, counsel, instigate or encourage the Skeltons to take the life of Ross, and that in whatever and all that was done by them and him, respectively, there was no understanding, preconcert or conspiracy between them and him.

This narrows the issues to three inquiries—two of fact, and one of law: First—a question of fact—Did Judge Tally on Sunday, February 4, 1894, knowing the intention of the Skeltons to take the life of Ross, and after they had gone in pursuit of him, do any act intended to further their design and aid them in the taking of his life? If he did, then, second—a question of law—Is it essential to his guilt that his act should have contributed to the effectuation of their design—to the death of Ross? And if so, third—another inquiry of fact—Did his act contribute to the death of Ross?

There can be no reasonable doubt that Judge Tally knew soon after the Skeltons had departed that they had gone in pursuit of Ross, and that they intended to take his life. Within a few minutes he was informed by his wife that Ross had fled and that the four Skeltons were pursuing him. He had seen three of them mounted and heavily armed. He knew the fourth, even keener on the trail than these, had gone on before. He knew their grievance. The fact that they intended to wreak vengeance in the way they did upon overtaking Ross, was known to all men in Scottsboro, as soon as the flight and pursuit became known. It was in the minds and on the tongues of everybody there. Nothing else was thought or talked of. When Dr. Rorex, voicing the universal apprehension, suggested to him that aid be sent up the road to the dead and wounded, Judge Tally, taking in the full force of the implication that there would be a fight to the death with the Skeltons as assailants, and not dissenting therefrom at all, said with the ken of prophesy, as a reason why he would not be a party to the execution of this humane suggestion, that his folks—the Skeltons—would take care of themselves. . . . This was the situation: Ross was in what he supposed to be secret flight from the Skeltons. He was unaware that his early departure had been seen by one of them. He did not know they were all in full pursuit to take his life. Under these circumstances, the pursuers had every advantage of the pursued. They could come upon him unawares. Being on horse back while he was in a vehicle, coming up to him they could well get beyond and waylay him. This they actually did. Tally's telegram to Huddleston was: "Do not let party warned get away. Say nothing." "Get away" from what or from whom? From whom indeed and in all common sense but from the four men on horseback following with guns to take his life. . . . "Say nothing." Say nothing about what? Clearly about the subject matter of the two dispatches, nothing about the pursuit of the four men on horseback with guns, nothing about the warning to Ross. . . . In other words and in short, the substance and effect of what Tally said to Huddleston, taking the two dispatches and all the circumstances into the account, was simply this, no more or less: "Ross has fled in the direction of Stevenson. The four Skeltons are following him on horseback with guns to take his life. Ross does not know of the pursuit. An effort is being made to get the word to Ross through you that he is thus pursued in order that he may get away from them. If you do not deliver this word to him he cannot escape them. Do not deliver that message, say nothing about it, and thereby prevent his getting away from them." A most careful analysis of the voluminous testimony in this case convinces us beyond a reasonable doubt that this was what Tally intended to convey to Huddleston, and that his message means this and only this to all reasonable comprehension.

And we are next to consider and determine the second inquiry stated above, namely: Whether it is essential to the guilt of Judge Tally as charged in the second count of the information that the said acts, thus adapted, intended and committed by him, should in fact have aided the said Skeltons to take the life of the said Ross, should have in fact contributed to his death at their hands.

We have already stated our conclusion—and the considerations which led us to it—that Judge Tally did not command, direct, incite, counsel, or encourage the Skeltons to the murder of Ross. . . .To be guilty of murder, therefore, not being a common law principal and not being an accessory before the fact—to be concerned in the commission of the offense within the meaning of our statute—he must be found to have aided or abetted the Skeltons in the commission of the offense in such sort as to constitute him at common law a principal in the second degree. A principal in this degree is one who is present at the commission of a felony by the hand of the principal in the first degree, and who being thus present aids or abets, or aids and abets the latter therein. The presence which this definition requires need not be actual, physical juxtaposition in respect of the personal perpetrator of the crime. It is enough, so far as presence is concerned, for the principal in the second degree to be in a position to aid the commission of the crime by others. It is enough if he stands guard while the act is being perpetrated by others, to prevent interference with them or to warn them of the approach of danger; and it is immaterial how distant from the scene of the crime his vigil is maintained provided it gives some promise of protection to those engaged in its active commission. At whatever distance he may be, he is present in legal contemplation if he is at the time performing any act in furtherance of the crime, or is in a position to give information to the principal which would be helpful to the end in view, or to prevent others from doing any act, by way of warning the intended victim or otherwise, which would be but an obstacle in the way of the consummation of the crime, or render its accomplishment more difficult.

We are therefore clear to the conclusion that before Judge Tally can be found guilty of aiding and abetting the Skeltons to kill Ross, it must appear that his vigil at Scottsboro to prevent Ross from being warned of his danger . . . aided them to kill Ross, contributed to Ross's death in point of physical fact by means of the telegram he sent to Huddleston.

The assistance given, however, need not contribute to the criminal result in the sense that but for it the result would not have ensued. It is quite sufficient if it facilitated a result that would have transpired without it. It is quite enough if the aid merely renders it easier for the principal actor to accomplish the end intended by him and the aider and abettor, though in all human probability the end would have been attained without it. If the aid in homicide can be shown to have put the deceased at a disadvantage, to have deprived him of a single chance of life, which but for it he would have had, he who furnishes such aid is guilty though it cannot be known or shown that the dead man, in the absence thereof, would have availed himself of that chance. . . . [S]o where he who facilitates murder, even by so much as destroying a single chance of life the assailed might otherwise have had, he thereby supplements the efforts of the perpetrator, and he is guilty as principal in the second degree at common law, and is principal in the first degree under our statute, notwithstanding it may be found that in all human probability the chance would not have been availed of, and death would have resulted anyway.

And so we are come to a consideration of the effect, if any, produced upon the situation at Stevenson by the message of Judge Tally to Huddleston. Its effect upon the situation could only have been through Huddleston, and upon his action in respect of the delivery to Ross of the message of warning sent by Ed. Ross. This latter message reached Huddleston for Ross, we suppose, about five minutes—certainly not more than ten minutes—before Ross arrived at Stevenson. Immediately upon the heels of it, substantially at the same time, Tally's message to Huddleston was received by the latter. Ross's message imported extreme urgency in its delivery, and Tally's to Huddleston, though by no means so intended, emphasized the necessity and importance, from the standpoint of duty, for the earliest possible delivery of Ed. Ross's message to Robert C. Ross; and it was the manifest duty of Huddleston to deliver it at the earliest practicable moment of time.—Law of Telegraphy, Scott & Jernigan, § 188. Huddleston appears to have appreciated the urgency of the case, and at first to have intended doing his duty. Upon receiving the two messages, he went at once without waiting to copy them to the Stevenson Hotel, which is located very near the telegraph office, in quest of Ross, upon the idea that he might have already arrived. We are to presume a purpose to do what duty enjoins until the contrary appears; and we, therefore, shall assume that Huddleston intended to deliver the message to Ross, or to inform him of its contents had he been in the hotel. Not finding him there, for he had not yet reached Stevenson, Huddleston returned to the door of the depot up stairs in which was the telegraph office. By this time the command which Judge Tally had laid upon him had overmastered his sense of duty and diverted him from his purpose to deliver Ed. Ross's message to Robert. Standing there at the door he saw a hack approaching from the direction of Scottsboro. He said then that he supposed Ross was in that hack. We do not think it was incumbent upon him, inasmuch as the hack was being driven directly to the depot, to go down the road to meet it, though the situation was then more urgent than was indicated by the telegrams in that the Skeltons were at that time skulking on the flanks of and immediately behind the hack; but there is no evidence that Huddleston knew this. But we do not doubt that it was Huddleston's duty to go out to the road along which the hack was being driven, at a point opposite his own position at the depot, and near to it, and there and then have delivered the message or made known its contents to Ross. The only explanation he offers for not then delivering the message or making known its contents to Ross was—not that he could not have done it, that was entirely practicable—but that he had not taken a copy of it; a consideration which did not prevent his going to the hotel for the purpose of delivery before he saw Ross approaching, and which, had his original purpose continued, we cannot believe would have swerved him from his plain duty at this juncture. Presuming that he would have done this because it was his duty to do it— a duty which he at first appreciated—and finding as a fact that he did not do it, the reason for his default is found in the injunction laid upon him by Judge Tally. He did not warn Ross because he did not want Ross to get away, and this because Judge Tally had asked him not to let Ross get away. . . .

It remains to be determined whether the unwarranted delay in the delivery of the message to Ross, or in advising him of its contents, thus caused by Judge Tally with intent thereby to aid the Skeltons to kill Ross, did in fact aid them or contribute to the death of Ross by making it easier than it would otherwise have been for the Skeltons to kill him, by depriving him of some advantage he would have had had he been advised of its contents when his carriage stopped or immediately upon his alighting from it, or by leaving him without some chance of life which would have been his had Huddleston done his duty.

The telegram, we have said, should have been delivered, or its contents made known, to Ross at the time the hack came opposite where Huddleston was and stopped. Huddleston and William Tally were equidistant from this point when the former called to the latter, at which time also Huddleston had seen the hack approaching this point. Tally, going to Huddleston, reached this middle point between them, unhastened as Huddleston should have been by the urgency of the message, just as the carriage got there and stopped. It is, therefore, clear that had Huddleston, instead of calling Tally and going into the depot, himself gave gone out to the road along which the carriage was approaching, and which was not more than one hundred feet from him, he would have gotten there certainly by the time it stopped, and have acquainted Ross with the contents of the message, with the fact that four men were pursuing him with guns to take his life, before Ross alighted from the hack.

Being thus advised, and not knowing of the immediate proximity of the Sheltons, it may be that Ross would have alighted as he did, exposed himself to the Skeltons' fire as he did and been killed as he was. But on the other hand, the Skeltons were at that time dismounted, and two of them at least, a long way from their horses, and none of them were in his front up the road, and he had a chance of escape by continued flight in the vehicle. Again, he might then and there have put himself under the protection of Huddleston as an officer of the law and had the bystanders, those in the immediate neighborhood, of whom there were several, summoned to help protect him. This might have saved his life; it was a chance that he had. But, if it be conceded that, as he would not have known of the proximity of the Skeltons from mere knowledge that they were in pursuit, he would have alighted precisely as and when he did, yet when the first shot was fired Ross would have known that the man who fired it was one of the

Skeltons, and that three others of them were present in ambush armed with guns to take his life. Knowing this, the hopelessness of standing his ground and attempting to defend himself from his enemies, overpowering in number and secure in their hiding places, while he stood in the open street, would have been at once manifest to him; and instead of standing there as he did, knowing only as he did that some one man, whom he did not know, had fired a gun, and peering and craning his neck to see whence the shot came and who fired it, he could and doubtless would have sought safety by flight in the opposite direction, in which was the Union Hotel scarce an hundred feet away. And in view of the fact that he was hit only once by the numerous shots that were fired at him while he stood there in the open, and that not in a vital or disabling part, it is very probable that had he attempted that mode of escape, as soon as the first shot was fired, he would have reached the hotel in perfect safety. Certain it is that in making that effort he would have gone away from the lurking places of his enemies, and he would not, as he did in his ignorance of the true situation, have placed himself where John Skelton at close quarters could and did shoot him to death from behind his back. But whether he would or would not have reached a place of refuge, we need not inquire or find. The knowledge that he would have had, if the telegram of Ed. Ross had been delivered to him when it could and should have been delivered, of the pursuit of the Skeltons, together with the knowledge which would have been imparted to him by the report of the first gun in connection with the contents of the message, would instantly have advised him of the extent of his danger—a danger which he could not combat, which was deadly in character and from which, as he would naturally have been at once impressed, the only hope of escape lay in immediate flight. That was a chance for his life that this knowledge would have given him. That was a chance of which the withholding of this knowledge deprived him. Tally's telegram to Huddleston deprived him of that knowledge. Tally through Huddleston deprived him of that chance. . . . Can it be doubted in any case that murder by lying in wait is facilitated by the unconsciousness of the victim? . . . It is inconceivable to us, after the maturest consideration, reflection and discussion, but that Ross's predicament was rendered infinitely more desperate, his escape more difficult and his death of much more easy and certain accomplishment by the withholding from him of the message of Ed. Ross. . . . And we are impelled to find that John B. Tally aided and abetted the murder of Robert C. Ross, as alleged in the second specification of the second count of the information; and to adjudge that he is guilty as charged in that specification, and guilty of murder as charged in said second count. And judgment deposing him from office will be entered on the records of this court.

Dissent by: HEAD.

HEAD, J., dissenting.—I am of opinion the respondent should be acquitted of both charges. I do not believe, beyond a reasonable doubt, that respondent intended, in sending the telegram to Huddleston, to aid or abet in the murder of Ross. I do not believe, beyond a reasonable doubt, that the telegram of warning would have been delivered to Ross by Huddleston, before the shooting began, if the telegram of the respondent had not been sent.

DISCUSSION QUESTIONS

1.   How can you be an accomplice to a crime when none of the other perpetrators know you are involved?

2.   Ross probably would have been killed even if Tally hadn't sent his telegram. Why find Tally guilty of a murder that probably would have happened anyway?

3.   Alternately, why require Tally's telegram to have had some effect on Ross' chance of survival?

Case in Context

The following case explores the complexities of complicity as a "lookout."

STATE OF WEST VIRGINIA V. KEVIN DWAYNE HOSELTON

Supreme Court of Appeals of West Virginia
179 W. Va. 645 (1988)

Opinion by: PER CURIAM.

This case is before the Court upon the appeal of Kevin Wayne Hoselton from his conviction of entering without breaking a vessel, with intent to commit larceny, pursuant to W. Va. Code, 61–3–12 [1923].

The accused was charged as a principal in the first degree for either breaking and entering or entering without breaking a storage unit on a docked barge with intent to commit larceny. He was eighteen years old at the time, and was with several friends, each of whom was separately indicted as a principal in the first degree. The accused was convicted of entering without breaking, as charged in the indictment.

The indictment reads:

That on or about the day of April, 1985, in Wood County, West Virginia, KEVIN DWAYNE HOSELTON, committed the offense of 'entering without breaking' by unlawfully and feloniously entering without breaking a vessel owned by Dravo Corporation, more particularly described as a crane barge located in Wood County on the Little Kanawha River at a place commonly known as Merrill Landing, with intent to commit larceny therein, against the peace and dignity of the State.

The only evidence used to link the accused to the crime was his voluntary statement. The pertinent answers given by the accused in his voluntary statement were, as follows:

Q.   Were you with some individuals that broke into the barge?

A.   Yes, sir.

Q.   Once you got to the barges, what happened?

A.   We all walked up on that, and I was standing outside there. Mike, he tried to get the big door open, and he couldn't do it.

Q.   M[. . .] A[. . .]? [Sic]

A.   Yes, sir. And I heard a couple of other people back there—I don't know who it was—trying to get in.

Q.   Why couldn't you see them?

A.   Because I was standing at the end of the barge there.

Q.   Were you keeping a look-out?

A.   You could say that. I just didn't want to go down in there.

Q.   Do you know who actually gained entry to the barge.

A.   No, sir, I'm not sure.

Q.   Kevin, did you know at the time that you were down there that you all were committing a crime?

A.   Yes, I did know that, but—

The items stolen from the storage unit were tools, grease guns, grease and a battery charger. None of these items, or profits on their resale, were given to the accused. In both his statement and his trial testimony, the accused stated that he, standing at one end of the barge, with an obstructed view of the storage unit, was unaware of his friends' intent to steal the items until he heard the opening of the storage unit door. He then walked to the unit and saw his friends handling the goods. He then returned to the other end of the barge and went to an automobile, owned and operated by one of his friends, who remained in the storage facility. His friends returned to the automobile with the goods. The accused did not assist the others in placing the goods in the automobile. He was then immediately driven home.

The accused testified that he and his friends frequently trespassed upon the barge for fishing.

On appeal, the accused contends that the evidence is insufficient to support a conviction for entering with intent to commit larceny. Therefore, the trial judge erred when he denied the accused's motions for acquittal and new trial.

The State contends there was sufficient evidence to establish that the accused was a lookout, therefore, the conviction for breaking and entering as a principal in the first degree should stand.

A lookout is one who is "by prearrangement, keeping watch to avoid interception or detection or to provide warning during the perpetration of the crimes and thereby participating in the offenses charged. . ." People v. Small, 55 A.D.2d 994, 391 N.Y.S.2d 192, 194 (1977).

This Court has consistently held that lookouts are aiders and abettors, principals in the second degree.

Principals in the second degree are punishable as principals in the first degree. W. Va. Code, 61–11–6 [1923].

An aider and abettor, or principal in the second degree must "in some sort associate himself with the venture, that he participate in it as something that he wishes to bring about, that he seek[s] by his action to make it succeed." State v. Harper, W. Va., 365 S.E.2d 69, 73 (1987), quoting Learned Hand in U.S. v. Peoni, 100 F.2d 401, 402 (2nd Cir. 1938).

It is well established that in order for a defendant to be convicted as an aider and abettor, and thus a principal in the second degree, the prosecution must demonstrate that he or she shared the criminal intent of the principal in the first degree. [citations omitted] Of course we also recognize that the defendant is not required to possess the identical intent as the principal in the first degree. State v. Harper, W. Va., 365 S.E.2d 69, 74 (1987).

See also LaFave & Scott, Substantive Criminal Law, § 6 (1986), using the Model Penal Code definition of accomplices (principals in the second degree and accessories before the fact), Professor Scott writes:

[I]t is useful to give separate consideration to whether a person has engaged in the requisite acts (or omissions) and to whether he had the requisite mental state. . . It may generally be said that one is liable as an accomplice to the crime of another if he (a) gave assistance or encouragement or failed to perform a legal duty to prevent it (b) with the intent thereby to promote or facilitate commission of the crime. There is a split of authority as to whether some lesser mental state will suffice for accomplice liability, such as mere knowledge that one is aiding a crime or knowledge that one is aiding reckless or negligent conduct which may produce a criminal result.

. . . [Acts or omissions which establish accomplice liability must exhibit] sufficient encouragement that the accomplice is standing by at the scene of the crime ready to give some aid if needed, although in such a case it is necessary that the principal actually be aware of the accomplice's intentions. An undisclosed intention to render aid if needed will not suffice, for it cannot encourage the principal in his commission of the crime. Quite clearly, mere presence at the scene of the crime is not enough, nor is mental approval of the actor's conduct. Also, in the absence of unique circumstances giving rise to a duty to do so, one does not become an accomplice by refusing to intervene in the commission of a crime. [§ 6.7(a)]

. . . [A mental state must be evinced which establishes that] the accomplice intentionally encourages or assists, in the sense that his purpose is to encourage or assist another in the commission of a crime as to which the accomplice has the requisite mental state. . . liability without fault does not obtain in this area. [§ 6.7(b)]

Therefore, if the State establishes evidence that an accused acted as a lookout, it has necessarily established the requisite act and mental state to support a conviction of aiding and abetting.

In this case, the only evidence that suggested the accused was a lookout was his response to the investigating officer's questioning: "Q. Were you a lookout? A. You could say that. I just didn't want to go down there."

In both his voluntary statement and during his testimony at trial, the accused stated that he had no prior knowledge of his friends' intentions to steal anything from the barge. When he heard the door open to the storage unit and saw his friends removing the goods, the accused left the barge and returned to the car. The accused never received any of the stolen property, which was later retrieved by the police from the other defendants.

[T]he accused's response that "you could say" he was a lookout, standing completely alone, does not establish that the accused was an aider and abettor by participating in, and wishing to bring about the entering with intent to commit larceny.

Viewed in the light most favorable to the prosecution, the State did not prove that the accused was a lookout.

We therefore reverse and set aside the accused's conviction for entering without breaking. Because of our ruling that the evidence was insufficient to support a conviction, we need not discuss the appellant's contention that local police officers were required to read the accused his Miranda rights for the third time prior to signing his voluntary statement which was taken in a non-custodial atmosphere, or his assignment of instructional error. Furthermore, as to the principles relating to a second trial, see State v. Frazier, 162 W. Va. 602, 252 S.E.2d 39 (1979).

DISCUSSION QUESTIONS

1.   Can a lookout be an accomplice if the principals do not know he is looking out?

2.   Can a lookout be an accomplice if no one ever comes and he never has to alert the principals?

3.   Should it matter if the lookout never sees anyone coming? Or if the principals do not know he is looking out?

E. THE GUILTY HAND: ACTS OF ENCOURAGEMENT

This one throws a lot of people for a loop. You can be guilty of a crime just for applauding. Now imagine that instead of opening the door I loudly applauded your efforts once you announced, "this is a robbery." (How melodramatic of you.) I do nothing to help, but I clap wildly as I deliver a rambling speech about the vices of capitalism, high finance, and banks that are "too big to jail." Assuming the requisite mental state, I have just committed bank robbery along with you.

The rule is simple. Inciting, soliciting, inducing, or encouraging is sufficient conduct for complicity. Once again, the encouragement need not be a but-for cause of the crime. "Thank you very much for the applause," you say, "but I am not your student anymore and don't need your approval to rob this bank." An attempted act of encouragement is not enough, however. If I am standing outside the bank, waiving at you through the window and cheering wildly, but if you neither hear nor see me I am, once again, not an accomplice.

One less obvious issue arises when an actor is encouraged by an attempt to assist. As discussed earlier, attempting to assist someone does not alone make one an accomplice. If you know of my attempted assistance, however, you may be encouraged by my failed attempt. So, if you see me open the other door to the bank, that could be enough to make me an accomplice even if you go through a different door. The resulting encouragement of a failed effort to assist can be enough to make one an accomplice.

1.   SOLICITATION AND CONSPIRACY

At this point, you may be asking yourself about the relationship between the crime of solicitation and complicity. Asking or inducing someone to commit a crime is enough conduct to make you an accomplice to the crime. As you may remember from an earlier chapter, the crime of solicitation merges into any crime in which you are complicit. So, Henry's guilt of solicitation when he implicitly asked someone to kill Thomas

Becket merged into his guilt of murder once the knights acted on his request.

2. MERE PRESENCE NOT ENOUGH

Some of the most difficult cases in this area deal with people whose presence is alleged to assist or encourage the crime. The basic rule is simple enough. Mere presence is insufficient conduct for complicity. Indeed, one might quibble about whether being somewhere is actually conduct or a state of being. But deciding when presence is mere is not always so easy.

Imagine now that I am standing in the bank when you come in to rob it. Seeing me there you immediately feel encouraged. You remember my anti-bank diatribes in class and feel encouraged knowing that at least some people might approve of what you are doing. Perhaps you also think that if things go badly that I might pitch in and help out in some way. Do your thoughts about my presence make me an accomplice? No, that would not be very fair to me. Do my prior anti-bank diatribes combined with my presence make me an accomplice? No, unless I specifically encouraged you to rob a bank, in which case my presence might actually be superfluous to my complicity (see above).

Even if I were secretly glad that you were robbing the bank or were secretly planning to help you if things went badly I would still not be an accomplice. Secret wishes or plans do not change the fact that I am merely present and doing nothing as you rob the bank.

Presence can be enough for complicity when coupled with some prior statement or understanding that encourages the principal actor. If I told you previously that I would help out if needed my presence would make me an accomplice even if I never ended up doing anything. Similarly, telling someone during a crime that you won't interfere could be seen as an act of encouragement that could also be sufficient for complicity (if the statement was made with the required mental state).

Imagine now that I am standing in the bank when you come into rob it. Seeing me there you immediately feel encouraged. You remember my anti-bank diatribes in class and feel encouraged knowing that at least some people might approve of what you are doing. Perhaps you also think that if things go badly that I might pitch in and help out in some way. Do your thoughts about my presence make me an accomplice? No, that would not be very fair to me. Do my prior anti-bank diatribes combined with my presence make me an accomplice? No, unless I specifically encouraged you to rob a bank, in which case my presence might actually be superfluous to my complicity (see above).

Even if I were secretly glad that you were robbing the bank or were secretly planning to help you if things went badly I would still not be an accomplice. Secret wishes or plans do not change the fact that I am merely present and doing nothing as you rob the bank.

Presence can be enough for complicity when coupled with some prior statement or understanding that encourages the principal actor. If I told you previously that I would help out if needed my presence would make me an accomplice even if I never ended up doing anything. Similarly, telling someone during a crime that you won't interfere could be seen as an act of encouragement that could also be sufficient for complicity (if the statement was made with the required mental state).

3.   ASSISTANCE BY OMISSION

As discussed previously, no general duty exists to prevent a crime or to interfere with one in progress. Absent one of the legal duties described in the earlier chapter on the voluntary act requirement, you can just sit and watch a crime take place without fear of becoming an accomplice. Just as failure to act in the face of a legal duty can sometimes constitute a crime, so too can failure to act in the face of a legal duty make someone an accomplice. A police officer who watches a shoplifting unfold, a mother who watches her child being beaten, and even a property owner who watches criminal activity take place on his premises may become an accomplice to the crimes committed if they have the requisite mental states.

Case in Context

If the following case does not make you at least smile—if not laugh out loud—you did not read it carefully enough. The defendant and his friends were not exactly criminal masterminds.

STATE EX REL. V.T.
Court of Appeals of Utah
5 P.3d 1234 (2000)

BACKGROUND

On June 12, 1998, V.T. and two friends, "Moose" and Joey, went to a relative's apartment to avoid being picked up by police for curfew violations. The boys ended up spending the entire night at the apartment.

The next morning, the relative briefly left to run an errand, while the boys remained in her apartment. She returned about fifteen minutes later to find the boys gone, the door to her apartment wide open, and two of her guns missing. She immediately went in search of the group and found them hanging out together near her apartment complex. She confronted the boys about the theft of her guns and demanded that they return them to her. When they failed to do so, she reported the theft to the police.

Two days after the theft of her guns, she discovered that her camcorder, which had been in the apartment when the boys visited, was also missing, and she immediately reported its theft to the police. The police found the camcorder at a local pawn shop, where it had been pawned on the same day the guns were stolen.

Still inside the camcorder was a videotape featuring footage of V.T., Moose, and Joey. The tape included a segment where Moose telephoned a friend, in V.T.'s presence, and discussed pawning the stolen camcorder. V.T. never spoke or gestured during any of this footage.

V.T. was charged with two counts of theft of a firearm; one count of theft, relating to the camcorder;

V.T. was tried [in juvenile court] under an accomplice theory on the three theft charges. The court found that V.T. had committed class A misdemeanor theft of the camcorder.

The sole issue presented by V.T. is whether there was sufficient evidence to support the adjudication that he was an accomplice in the theft of the camcorder.

Utah's accomplice liability statute, Utah Code Ann. § 76–2–202 (1999), provides:

> Every person, acting with the mental state required for the commission of an offense who directly commits the offense, who solicits, requests, commands, encourages, or intentionally aids another person to engage in conduct which constitutes an offense shall be criminally liable as a party for such conduct.

As with any other crime, the State must prove the elements of accomplice liability beyond a reasonable doubt. See State v. Lopes, 1999 UT 24, P11, 980 P.2d 191; State v. Labrum, 959 P.2d 120, 123 (Utah Ct. App. 1998).

The State argues that V.T.'s continued presence during the theft and subsequent phone conversation about selling the camcorder, coupled with his friendship with the other two boys, is enough evidence to support the inference that he had "encouraged" the other two in committing the theft and that he is therefore an accomplice to the crime. Black's Law Dictionary defines encourage as: "to instigate; to incite to action; to embolden; to help." Black's Law Dictionary 547 (7th ed. 1999). The plain meaning of the word confirms that to encourage others to take criminal action requires some form of active behavior, or at least verbalization, by a defendant. Passive behavior, such as mere presence—even continuous presence—absent evidence that the defendant affirmatively did something to instigate, incite, embolden, or help others in committing a crime is not enough to qualify as "encouragement" as that term is commonly used.

The case law in Utah is consistent "Mere presence, or even prior knowledge, does not make one an accomplice" to a crime absent evidence showing that defendant "advised, instigated, encouraged, or assisted in perpetuation of the crime."

The juvenile court's conclusion that V.T. was an accomplice to the camcorder theft was not supported by the evidence in this case. No evidence whatsoever was produced indicating V.T. had encouraged—much less that he solicited, requested, commanded or intentionally aided—the other two boys in the theft of the camcorder.

We would, of course, conclude otherwise had the evidence shown, for example, that V.T. had suggested to his two friends that they go rob the apartment, that he had pointed out where the camcorder was kept, that he had helped carry the stolen goods out, or that he helped select the pawn shop at which to sell the camcorder.

DISCUSSION QUESTIONS

1.   Do you think that his friends felt emboldened to steal from VT's relative by VT's failure to object? Why shouldn't this be enough for complicity?

2.   Why not require people at the scene of a crime to dissociate themselves from the crime if they can safely do so?

3.   Under what circumstances, if any, do you think that a person should be found complicit for a failure to act?

4. AIDING AND ABETTING

Why use simple, easy to understand words when fancy legal ones are at hand? Doubtless you have heard the terms "aid and abet" to describe conspiracy. Originally the two words each meant something different. Aid meant to assist, and abet meant to encourage or incite. (The root of abet literally comes from the word "bait" and referred to the practice of "baiting" animals to get them to do something.) Alas, the two terms have come to be used largely synonymously, so things are not quite that simple anymore.

Case in Context

Note the nature of the acts of encouragement in the following case.

WILCOX V. JEFFERY

King's Bench Division
1 All ER 464 (1951)

LORD GODDARD, C.J. HERBERT WILLIAM WILCOX, the proprietor of a periodical called "Jazz Illustrated" was charged on information that "on Dec. 11, 1949, he did unlawfully aid and abet one Coleman Hawkins in contravening art. 1(4) of the Aliens Order, 1920, by failing to comply with a condition attached to a grant of leave to land, to wit, that the said Coleman Hawkins should take no employment paid or unpaid while in the United Kingdom, contrary to art. 18(2) of the Aliens Order, 1920".

Under the Aliens Order, art. 1 (1), it is provided that

". . . an alien coming. . . by sea to a place in the United Kingdom—a) shall not land in the United Kingdom without the leave of an Immigration officer. . ."

It is provided by art 1 (4) that:

"An immigration officer, in accordance with general or special directions of the Secretary of State, may, by general order or notice or otherwise, attach such conditions as he may think fit to the grant of leave to land, and the Secretary of State may at any time vary such conditions in such manner as he thinks fit, and the alien shall comply with the conditions so attached or varied. . ."

If the alien fails to comply, he is to be in the same position as if he has landed without permission, i.e., he commits an offence.

The case is concerned with the visit of a celebrated professor of the saxophone, a gentleman by the name of Hawkins who was a citizen of the United States. He came here at the invitation of two gentlemen of the name of Curtis and Hughes, connected with a jazz club which enlivens the neighbourhood of Willesden. They, apparently, had applied for permission for Mr. Hawkins and and it was refused, but, nevertheless, this professor of the saxophone arrived with four French musicians. When they came to the airport, among the people who were there to greet them was the appellant. He had not arranged their visit, but he knew they were coming and he was there to report the arrival of these important musicians for his magazine. So, evidently, he was regarding the visit of Mr. Hawkins as a matter which would be of interest to himself and the magazine which he was editing and selling for profit. Messrs. Curtis and Hughes arranged a concert at the Princes Theatre, London. The appellant attended that concert as a spectator. He paid for his ticket. Mr. Hawkins went on the stage and delighted the audience by playing the saxophone. The appellant did not get up and protest in the name of the musicians of England that Mr. Hawkins ought not to be here competing with them and taking the bread out of their mouths or the wind out of their instruments. It is not found that he actually applauded, but he was there having paid to go in, and, no doubt, enjoying the performance, and then, lo and behold, out comes his magazine with a most, laudatory description, fully illustrated, of this concert. On those facts the magistrate has found that he aided and abetted.

There was not accidental presence in this case. The appellant paid to go to the concert and he went there because he wanted to report it. He must, therefore, be held to have been present, taking part, concurring, or encouraging, whichever word you like to use for expressing this conception. The appellant clearly knew that it was an unlawful act for him to play. He had gone there to hear him, and his presence and his payment to go there was an encouragement. He went there to make use of the performance, because he went there, as the magistrate finds and was justified in finding, to get "copy" for his newspaper. It might have been entirely different, as I say, if he had gone there and protested, saying: "The musicians' union do not like you foreigners coming here and playing and you ought to get off the stage." [F]or these reasons I am of opinion that the appeal fails.

DISCUSSION QUESTIONS

1. Did the performer know that the reporter was present or that he was going to write up the performance? If not, how can the court find the reporter to be an accomplice?

2. Was everyone in the crowd at the concert an accomplice? All those who applauded?

3. How would you apply the complicity principle illustrated in this case to the online activity?

Practice Problem 19.1: Facebook Dead

Recently a man caught an armed intruder in his home. He gagged the intruder and tied him up in a chair. He then broadcast a live video of himself and the intruder using Facebook Live (a social media platform that allows a person to broadcast video live on the internet). On the broadcast he said that there had been a number of home invasion robberies in his neighborhood (which was true) and that he was sick and tired of living in fear of violent criminals. Visibly distraught and enraged, he asked people watching the video to tell him whether he should kill the intruder or not. Because he was using the Facebook page of a neighborhood watch group the video reached many people and quickly went viral. Within fifteen minutes the video received over a hundred likes, and he received a dozen comments urging him to kill the intruder. He killed the intruder before the police could arrive, and he then took his own life. Who has sufficient conduct to be an accomplice to the killing?

F. THE GUILTY MIND

There is a bit of confusion here among the courts. To be specific, there are two different ways of stating complicity's mental state requirement in common use, a traditional rule and an alternate one that takes into account special issues arising from crimes requiring only a reckless or negligent state of mind. Most professors spare you as much of that confusion as they can. Following that approach, we will learn the traditional rule and then learn the alternate rule. To paraphrase Einstein, we make things as simple as possible but no simpler.

The traditional rule is that an accomplice must intend to assist or encourage the person in the conduct that constitutes the crime and further intend that the crime encouraged or assisted be committed. So, when I open the door for you as you go into the bank, I can't be doing it absent-mindedly; I must be opening the door for you. I must further intend by so doing that you are going to rob the bank. So, when your Mom makes your lunch the morning of the bank robbery she does not become a bank robber unless she intends that you rob the bank. (That should make you feel a little better.) Note that it is practically impossible to have the second mental state if you don't have the first. It is hard even for law professors to come up with realistic examples where someone did not intend their act of assistance or encouragement but intends a crime to be committed.

1. PURPOSE VS. KNOWLEDGE

Once again, we confront the issue of what intent means. Is it enough if you know that you are assisting a crime or must it be your purpose to assist a crime? If your Mom knows that you are robbing a bank the day that she makes your lunch, should that be enough? Let's assume she does not want you to rob the bank—what mother would?—but she does want you to eat lunch—what mother wouldn't?—yet she knows that having your lunch made in advance will make it easier for you to rob the bank (hard to do drive through at a fast food restaurant when the police are chasing you). Should this knowledge be enough to make her an accomplice to bank robbery?

While early cases held that knowledge that you were helping someone commit a crime was sufficient, the majority of courts now hold that purpose is required. The line between purpose and knowledge becomes blurry in many cases, though (as it does with respect to the meaning of intent in conspiracy).

The cases that typically raise this issue concern providers of legal services to people who use them for illegal purposes with the full knowledge of the provider. A hotel owner rents rooms to prostitutes, or a merchant sells sugar to a moonshiner, each knowing full well that they are assisting illegal activity. The position of the provider is that they are indifferent to what paying customers use their goods or services for and therefore cannot be purposeful with respect to the crimes committed as a result.

While the case law is a bit of a muddle, two trends are evident. First, courts tend to find providers of legal goods and services to be purposeful with respect to resulting crimes—and thereby to be complicit—when the provider can be said to have some sort of stake in the venture. Perhaps criminals constitute a disproportionate share of his business, or he charges inflated prices, or he literally gets paid out of the proceeds from the crime. Second, some courts require only knowledge with respect to serious crimes that involve danger to life.

Even where a jurisdiction does not specifically lower the requirement for complicity from purpose to knowledge for more serious crimes, juries are much more likely to find purpose when danger to human life is involved. Imagine that I ask you to give me directions to someone's house after telling you that I plan to kill the person who lives there. If you give me the directions, a jury would doubt whether you were purely indifferent to whether I killed the person and would more likely conclude that you also wanted the person dead. So, the purpose required for complicity is more likely to be found from knowing assistance for serious crimes than for minor ones.

Some jurisdictions deal with the knowledge issue by creating a standalone offense of "knowingly facilitating a criminal offense." Such crimes are offenses onto themselves, however, and do not make the facilitator guilty of the crime assisted.

Case in Context

The next question might be called the case of the indifferent accomplice.

THE PEOPLE V. TIMOTHY MARK BEEMAN
Supreme Court of California
35 Cal. 3d 547 (1984)

Opinion by: REYNOSO.

Timothy Mark Beeman appeals from a judgment of conviction of robbery, burglary, false imprisonment, destruction of telephone equipment and assault with intent to commit a felony. Appellant was not present during commission of the offenses. His conviction rested on the theory that he aided and abetted his acquaintances James Gray and Michael Burk.

The primary issue before us is whether the standard California Jury Instructions (CALJIC Nos. 3.00 and 3.01) adequately inform the jury of the criminal intent required to convict a defendant as an aider and abettor of the crime.

We hold that instruction No. 3.01 is erroneous. Sound law, embodied in a long line of California decisions, requires proof that an aider and abettor rendered aid with an intent or purpose of either committing, or of encouraging or facilitating commission of, the target offense.

James Gray and Michael Burk drove from Oakland to Redding for the purpose of robbing appellant's sister-in-law, Mrs. Marjorie Beeman, of valuable jewelry, including a 3.5 carat diamond ring. They telephoned the residence to determine that she was home. Soon thereafter Burk knocked at the door of the victim's house, presented himself as a poll taker, and asked to be let in. When Mrs. Beeman asked for identification, he forced her into the hallway and entered. Gray, disguised in a ski mask, followed.

The two subdued the victim, placed tape over her mouth and eyes and tied her to a bathroom fixture. Then they ransacked the house, taking numerous pieces of jewelry and a set of silverware. The jewelry included a 3.5 carat, heart-shaped diamond ring and a blue sapphire ring. The total value of these two rings was over $ 100,000. In the course of the robbery, telephone wires inside the house were cut.

Appellant was arrested six days later in Emeryville. He had in his possession several of the less valuable of the stolen rings. He supplied the police with information that led to the arrests of Burk and Gray. With Gray's cooperation appellant assisted police in recovering most of the stolen property.

Burk, Gray and appellant were jointly charged. After the trial court severed the trials, Burk and Gray pled guilty to robbery. At appellant's trial they testified that he had been extensively involved in planning the crime.

[They testified that Beeman had supplied them with information about the contents and layout of the house, discussed the method used, made suggestions about how Burk and Gray should dress, and agreed to sell the loot for 20 percent of the proceeds. Gray's testimony did indicate that shortly before the robbery Beeman said he wanted no part of it, and afterward expressed anger that the robbery had been committed and Burk had not disguised himself].

Appellant Beeman's testimony contradicted that of Burk and Gray as to nearly every material element of his own involvement.

Appellant requested that the jury be instructed that aiding and abetting liability requires proof of intent to aid. The request was denied.

After three hours of deliberation, the jury submitted two written questions to the court: "We would like to hear again how one is determined to be an accessory and by what actions can he absolve himself"; and "Does inaction mean the party is guilty?" The jury was reinstructed in accord with the standard instructions, CALJIC Nos. 3.00 and 3.01. The court denied appellant's renewed request that the instructions be modified as suggested in Yarber, explaining that giving another, slightly different instruction at this point would further complicate matters. The jury returned its verdicts of guilty on all counts two hours later.

Penal Code section 31 provides in pertinent part: "All persons concerned in the commission of a crime. . . whether they directly commit the act constituting the offense, or aid and abet in its commission, or, not being present, have advised and encouraged its commission. . . are principals in any crime so committed." Thus, those persons who at common law would have been termed accessories before the fact and principals in the second degree as well as those who actually perpetrate the offense, are to be prosecuted, tried and punished as principals in California. (See Pen.

Code, § 971.) The term "aider and abettor" is now often used to refer to principals other than the perpetrator, whether or not they are present at the commission of the offense.

CALJIC No. 3.00 defines principals to a crime to include "Those who, with knowledge of the unlawful purpose of the one who does directly and actively commit or attempt to commit the crime, aid and abet in its commission. . .or. . . Those who, whether present or not at the commission or attempted commission of the crime, advise and encourage its commission. . ." CALJIC No. 3.01 defines aiding and abetting as follows: "A person aids and abets the commission of a crime if, with knowledge of the unlawful purpose of the perpetrator of the crime, he aids, promotes, encourages or instigates by act or advice the commission of such crime."

Prior to 1974 CALJIC No. 3.01 read: "A person aids and abets the commission of a crime if he knowingly and with criminal intent aids, promotes, encourages or instigates by act or advice, or by act and advice, the commission of such crime." (See, People v. Cabral (1975) 51 Cal.App.3d 707, 714, fn. 5 [124 Cal.Rptr. 418].)

Appellant asserts that the current instructions, in particular CALJIC No. 3.01, substitute an element of knowledge of the perpetrator's intent for the element of criminal intent of the accomplice, in contravention of common law principles and California case law. He argues that the instruction given permitted the jury to convict him of the same offenses as the perpetrators without finding that he harbored either the same criminal intent as they, or the specific intent to assist them, thus depriving him of his constitutional rights to due process and equal protection of the law. Appellant further urges that the error requires reversal because it removed a material issue from the jury and on this record it is impossible to conclude that the jury necessarily resolved the same factual question that would have been presented by the missing instruction.

The People argue that the standard instruction properly reflects California law, which requires no more than that the aider and abettor have knowledge of the perpetrator's criminal purpose and do a voluntary act which in fact aids the perpetrator. The People further contend that defendants are adequately protected from conviction for acts committed under duress or which inadvertently aid a perpetrator by the limitation of the liability of an aider and abettor to those acts knowingly aided and their natural and reasonable consequences. (People v. Beltran (1949) 94 Cal.App.2d 197, 205 [210 P.2d 238]; People v. King (1938) 30 Cal.App.2d 185, 203 [85 P.2d 928].) Finally, the People argue that the modification proposed by Yarber, supra, is unnecessary because proof of intentional aiding in most cases can be inferred from aid with knowledge of the perpetrator's purpose. Thus, respondent argues, it is doubtful that the requested modification would bring about different results in the vast majority of cases.

There is no question that an aider and abettor must have criminal intent in order to be convicted of a criminal offense. The act of encouraging or counseling itself implies a purpose or goal of furthering the encouraged result. "An aider and abettor's fundamental purpose, motive and intent is to aid and assist the perpetrator in the latter's commission of the crime." (People v. Vasquez (1972) 29 Cal.App.3d 81, 87 [105 Cal.Rptr. 181].)

The essential conflict in current appellate opinions is between those cases which state that an aider and abettor must have an intent or purpose to commit or assist in the commission of the criminal offenses and those finding it sufficient that the aider and abettor engage in the required acts with knowledge of the perpetrator's criminal purpose.

The facts from which a mental state may be inferred must not be confused with the mental state that the prosecution is required to prove. Direct evidence of the mental state of the accused is rarely available except through his or her testimony. The trier of fact is and must be free to disbelieve the testimony and to infer that the truth is otherwise when such an inference is supported by circumstantial evidence regarding the actions of the accused. Thus, an act which has the effect of giving aid and encouragement, and which is done with knowledge of the criminal purpose of the person aided, may indicate that the actor intended to assist in fulfillment of the known criminal purpose. However, as illustrated by Hicks v. U.S. (1893) 150 U.S. 442 [37 L.Ed. 1137, 14 S.Ct. 144] (conviction reversed because jury not instructed that words of encouragement must have been used with the intention of encouraging and abetting crime in a case where ambiguous gesture and remark may have been acts of desperation) and People v. Bolanger (1886) 71 Cal. 17 [11 P. 799] (feigned accomplice not guilty because lacks common intent with the perpetrator to unite in the commission of the crime), the act may be done with some other purpose which precludes criminal liability.

If the jury were instructed that the law conclusively presumes the intention of the accused solely from his or her voluntary acts, it would " 'effectively eliminate intent as an ingredient of the offense' " and would " 'conflict with the overriding presumption of innocence with which the law endows the accused and which extends to every element of the crime.' " (Sandstrom v. Montana (1979) 442 U.S. 510, 522 [61 L.Ed.2d 39, 49–50, 99 S.Ct. 2450], quoting from Morissette v. United States (1952) 342 U.S. 246, 274–275 [96 L.Ed. 288, 306–307, 72 S.Ct. 240]; original italics omitted.)

Thus, we conclude that the weight of authority and sound law require proof that an aider and abettor act with knowledge of the criminal purpose of the perpetrator and with an intent or purpose either of committing, or of encouraging or facilitating commission of, the offense.

When the definition of the offense includes the intent to do some act or achieve some consequence beyond the actus reus of the crime (see People v. Hood (1969) 1 Cal.3d 444, 456–457 [82 Cal.Rptr. 618, 462 P.2d 370]), the aider and abettor must share the specific intent of the perpetrator. By "share" we mean neither that the aider and abettor must be prepared to commit the offense by his or her own act should the perpetrator fail to do so, nor that the aider and abettor must seek to share the fruits of the crime. (See People v. Terry, supra, at p. 401.) Rather, an aider and abettor will "share" the perpetrator's specific intent when he or she knows the full extent of the perpetrator's criminal purpose and gives aid or encouragement with the intent or purpose of facilitating the perpetrator's commission of the crime. (See People v. Terry, supra; Model Pen. Code, § 2.06; generally, Perkins, Criminal Law, supra, at pp. 662–663.) The liability of an aider and abettor extends also to the natural and reasonable consequences of the acts he knowingly and intentionally aids and encourages.

CALJIC No. 3.01 inadequately defines aiding and abetting because it fails to insure that an aider and abettor will be found to have the required mental state with regard to his or her own act. While the instruction does include the word "abet," which encompasses the intent required by law, the word is arcane and its full import unlikely to be recognized by modern jurors. Moreover, even if jurors were made aware that "abet" means to encourage or facilitate, and implicitly to harbor an intent to further the crime encouraged, the instruction does not require them to find that intent because it defines an aider and abettor as one who "aids, promotes, encourages or instigates." Thus, as one appellate court recently recognized, the instruction would "technically allow a conviction if the defendant knowing of the perpetrator's unlawful purpose, negligently or accidentally aided the commission of the crime." (People v. Patrick (1981) 126 Cal.App.3d 952, 967, fn. 10 [179 Cal.Rptr. 276].)

Both the instruction suggested by Yarber, supra, 90 Cal.App.3d 895, 912 ("A person aids and abets the commission of a crime if, with knowledge of the unlawful purpose of the perpetrator of the crime, he intentionally aids, promotes, encourages or instigates by act or advice the commission of such crime") and the version of CALJIC used prior to 1974 ("A person aids and abets the commission of a crime if he knowingly and with criminal intent aids, promotes, encourages or instigates by act or advice, or by act and advice, the commission of such crime") seek to include the required intent element. However, both are sufficiently ambiguous to conceivably permit conviction upon a finding of an intentional act which aids, without necessarily requiring a finding of an intent to encourage or facilitate the criminal offense. We suggest that an appropriate instruction should inform the jury that a person aids and abets the commission of a crime when he or she, acting with (1) knowledge of the unlawful purpose of the perpetrator; and (2) the intent or purpose of committing, encouraging, or facilitating the commission of the offense, (3) by act or advice aids, promotes, encourages or instigates, the commission of the crime.

Respondent urges that any instructional error was harmless

Appellant did not deny that he had given information to Burk and Gray which aided their criminal enterprise, but he claimed his purposes in doing so were innocent. Appellant admitted that he was at some time made aware of his friends' intent to rob Mrs. Beeman, but insisted that he had repeatedly stated that he wanted nothing to do with a robbery of his relatives. He testified that he didn't think Burk would really go through with the robbery or that Gray would help. Two days before the incident, he again told Gray that he didn't want to be involved. Gray's testimony confirmed that appellant had twice said he did not want to be involved. Finally, appellant claimed to have taken possession of the jewelry and feigned attempts to sell it in order to recover the property and return it to the victims. Thus, the essential point of his defense was that although he acted in ways which in fact aided the criminal enterprise, he did not act with the intent of encouraging or facilitating the planning or commission of the offenses.

Under these circumstances, where the defense centered on the very element as to which the jury was inadequately instructed and the jurors' communication to the court indicated confusion on the same point, we cannot find the error harmless. Even applying the most lenient Watson standard, we find that in this case it is reasonably probable that the jury would have reached a result more favorable to appellant had it been correctly instructed upon the mental element of aiding and abetting. (People v. Watson, supra, 46 Cal.2d 818.) Because we reverse under Watson we do not in this case decide whether failure to correctly instruct on the element of criminal intent should as a general rule be reviewed under a stricter rule of harmless error.

The convictions are reversed.

DISCUSSION QUESTIONS

1.   What was the flaw with the jury instruction used? Why might that flaw have made a difference in this case?

2.   How likely is it that one would knowingly assist a crime without being purposeful?

3.   Should knowing assistance be enough for complicity in this case? Generally?

Practice Problem 19.2: A Felonious Ride?

You are on your way out the door to drive to a party when your roommate asks you for a ride. You agree. On the way there he asks you to make a detour so that he can pick up some ecstasy (an illegal drug) to bring to the party. This is the first time you have been invited to a party with this particular group of people, and you complain that the detour will make you later than you want to be to the party. He tells you that your drugs will be free this night. You tell him that you are not going to use the drugs. He then tells you that these drugs will make the party one that everyone will remember and will make the two of you the hit of the party. You make the detour, he picks up the drugs and distributes them at the party. Are you an accomplice to the distribution of an illegal drug? Would it make a difference if the drug were an opiod such as fentanyl?

2. COMPLICITY FOR RECKLESSNESS OR NEGLIGENCE

Can you be an accomplice to a crime that requires only recklessness? If you give your car keys to someone you know to be drunk, are you an accomplice to involuntary manslaughter if they kill someone while driving your car? Involuntary manslaughter requires recklessness or criminal negligence depending on the jurisdiction. It was reckless or at least negligent of your friend to drive drunk. Can you be said to have intended him to be reckless or negligent when you gave him your keys? If you intended him to kill someone when you gave him your keys that would be murder, not manslaughter. Many have argued that you cannot be an accomplice to his negligence because it is conceptually not possible for you to intend recklessness or negligence. A number of courts have found complicity in such cases, however. One leading treatise even states that the overwhelming majority rule is to recognize complicity for reckless or negligence crimes. Another treatise, however, describes the cases as more mixed. So, pay attention to how your professor characterizes this split and adopt whatever terminology she uses to characterize it.

Case in Context

One might flippantly title the following case "friends don't let friends commit manslaughter."

THE STATE OF WASHINGTON V. CHRISTINE HOPKINS
Supreme Court of Washington
147 Wash. 198 (1928)

Opinion by: PARKER.

The defendant, Mrs. Hopkins, was by information filed in the superior court for King county jointly, with one John Doe, charged with the crime of manslaughter. The information charges, in substance, that John Doe, his true name being unknown, by his wilful, reckless and unlawful driving of an automobile on a public highway in King county, caused the death of Lois Ames. Mrs. Hopkins was, by the concluding language of the information, charged with aiding and abetting John Doe in the death of Lois Ames, as follows:

"And she, said Christine Hopkins, being then and there present, and being then and there the owner of said Studebaker automobile and a passenger therein and knowing said John Doe to be intoxicated, wilfully and unlawfully entrusted the operation of said automobile to said John Doe and permitted him to drive the same upon said highway and did then and there wilfully, unlawfully and feloniously aid, encourage, assist, advise, counsel and abet him, the said John Doe, in said unlawful acts as hereinbefore set forth and in the said unlawful operation of said Studebaker automobile aforesaid."

Trial in the superior court sitting with a jury resulted in a verdict of guilty and a judgment thereon being rendered against Mrs. Hopkins, from which she has appealed to this court.

The principal question here presented is as to the sufficiency of the evidence to sustain the verdict and judgment. That question was presented to the trial court by appropriate timely motions which were overruled, and is here presented by appropriate assignments of error. At the time in question, Mrs. Hopkins was proprietor of, and lived at, a small hotel situated in the southerly portion of the main business district of Seattle. She was then, and had been for about three years, the owner of an enclosed Studebaker automobile which she was accustomed and well qualified to drive. Shortly before ten o'clock of the night in question, her friend "Jimmie Burns," as she called him, came to the hotel to see her. They then agreed to take an automobile ride northerly to a so-called "chicken dinner" resort beyond the city limits on the Bothell Highway. It was agreed that they would go in her automobile and that he would drive. Accordingly they proceeded northerly through the city some six or seven miles to a point very near and just inside the northerly city limits.

There is no direct evidence as to what occurred during this portion of their journey, nor is there any direct evidence as to the condition of either of them as to being intoxicated up to that time, other than she admitted to the police officers that she had taken two or three drinks of whiskey earlier in the evening. According to the evidence of a witness, who was driving north on the highway, just before reaching the city limits, the Hopkins' car passed close to the left of the car the witness was driving, going in the same direction. The witness noticed this particularly, because the car passed dangerously close and turned quickly to the right in front of the car of the witness, requiring some care on the part of the witness to avoid a collision at that time. The witness' car was going about twenty miles per hour; the Hopkins' car probably about twenty-five miles per hour. According to this witness and some other witnesses, the Hopkins' car was, upon and after passing that car, driven in a very erratic and apparently reckless manner. It proceeded in this manner so that, in going approximately a distance of two or three blocks farther, it, for the most part, proceeded on its left, the west, side of the somewhat wide pavement, its speed continuing at from twenty-five to thirty miles per hour.

While so proceeding for a distance of about two blocks to a short distance north of the city limits, it came in collision with the Ames car which was then being driven south on its right, the west, side of the pavement. When the driver of the Ames' car saw the approach of the Hopkins' car on its wrong side of the pavement, he checked his speed, which had previously been about twenty-five miles per hour, and finally seeing that he would have a head-on collision with the Hopkins' car, as it was proceeding on his side of the pavement, and there being a bank on that side preventing his turning off the pavement, to avoid the impending collision, if possible, he turned his car east to his left. The driver of the Hopkins' car, an instant later, turned his car east to its right, and struck the right side of the Ames' car back of the front wheel, forcing the Ames' car to the east side of the pavement and in some manner causing Mrs. Ames and her daughter Lois Ames to fall from their car to the pavement and come to rest partly under the Hopkins' car which was a much heavier car than the Ames' car. From the injuries so received Lois Ames died a few hours later.

There is practically no room for controversy over the facts we have thus far summarized. We think they leave no room for seriously arguing that they are not sufficient to warrant the jury in believing beyond a reasonable doubt that John Doe (Jimmie Burns), the driver of the Hopkins' car, was guilty of such reckless and unlawful acts on his part causing the death of Lois Ames as to make him guilty of manslaughter. This, of course, is but a part of our problem here.

We now notice facts, as the jury were warranted in believing them to exist, touching more particularly Mrs. Hopkins' relation to the reckless and unlawful acts of Jimmie Burns resulting in the death of Lois Ames. Jimmie Burns, as Mrs. Hopkins called the driver of her car, disappeared from the scene of the collision very soon after its occurrence, while others present were intent on and busily engaged in extricating Mrs. Ames and Lois Ames from the wreck. He has not been seen since then, hence the trial of Mrs. Hopkins alone. Mrs. Hopkins had been acquainted with Jimmie Burns some two or three months only. She did not know what his business or vocation was, or where he lived, only that he had come to her hotel occasionally.

Mrs. Hopkins sat in her car for some time immediately following the collision. One witness testified to talking to her there as follows:

"I informed her that she had been in a very bad wreck and had probably killed my little girl.

Q. What did she say then?

A. Well, she said—for a minute she didn't say anything, and then she said, 'I told him that he could not drive.' "

The jury could well believe from the evidence that Mrs. Hopkins was considerably under the influence of intoxicating liquor, though she apparently knew what she was doing and was conscious of her surroundings. That was apparently about an hour after she had the drinks of whiskey, as admitted by her.

We think, under all the circumstances shown, that the jury might well conclude that the intoxicated man leaning against Mrs. Hopkins' car, while she was sitting therein, very soon after the collision, was the driver of that car; that his intoxicated condition was such that he was unfit to drive a car; that it was not of sudden acquiring; that in time it extended back at least over the period of the approximately one half hour elapsing from the time that Mrs. Hopkins placed her car in his charge upon leaving her hotel; and that his intoxication was, or should have been, known to Mrs. Hopkins had she used due care in deciding whether or not she would entrust the driving of her car to him. Our opinion is that the evidence is sufficient to sustain the verdict and judgment.

It is contended in behalf of Mrs. Hopkins that the information does not state facts constituting the crime of manslaughter as against her. This, as we understand her counsel, is rested upon the theory that manslaughter is a crime of such nature as to preclude the possibility of there being an accessory before the fact to such crime. There does seem to be language of that purport in the decisions of this court in State v. Robinson, 12 Wash. 349, 41 P. 51, and State v. McFadden, 48 Wash. 259, 93 P. 414, 14 L.R.A. (N.S.) 1140. However, Judge Hadley, speaking for the court in the latter case, said:

> "It is argued that such facts can in no event amount to other than a charge that appellant was an accessory before the fact, whereas the authorities hold that there cannot be such an accessory to the crime of manslaughter. This court so held in State v. Robinson, 12 Wash. 349, 41 P. 51. Our statute, Bal. Code, § 6782, however, abolishes all distinctions between an accessory before the fact and a principal, and provides that 'all persons concerned in the commission of an offense, whether they directly counsel the act constituting the offense, or counsel, aid and abet in its commission, though not present, shall hereafter be indicted, tried, and punished as principals.' Under the said statute appellant may be, and is, charged here as a principal and not as an accessory."

> "Every person concerned in the commission of a felony, gross misdemeanor or misdemeanor, whether he directly commits the act constituting the offense, or aids or abets in its commission, and whether present or absent; and every person who directly or indirectly counsels, encourages, hires, commands, induces or otherwise procures another to commit a felony, gross misdemeanor or misdemeanor, is a principal, and shall be

proceeded against and punished as such. The fact that the person aided, abetted, counseled, encouraged, hired, commanded, induced or procured, could not or did not entertain a criminal intent, shall not be a defense to any person aiding, abetting, counseling, encouraging, hiring, commanding, inducing or procuring him."

It is now the settled law in this state that intent to cause the death of another is not an element in the crime of manslaughter. [Citations omitted.] This plainly does not mean that intent to do an unlawful or grossly negligent act resulting in the unintentional death of another, is not an element of the crime of manslaughter. We think these are elements in the crime of manslaughter. So it seems to us that Mrs. Hopkins was by this information charged with negligence, in a criminal sense, in the placing of her car in the charge of John Doe, as driver, while he was intoxicated, she then knowing him to be intoxicated, and in then permitting him to drive it in the reckless, unlawful manner that resulted in the death of Lois Ames. So we conclude that the information sufficiently charged her, in contemplation of our law, as principal, though somewhat in form charging her as an accessory before the fact.

The judgment is affirmed.

Dissent by: FRENCH.

FRENCH, J.

In the case of State v. Robinson, 12 Wash. 349, 41 P. 51, a prosecution under the aiding and abetting statute, this court laid down the rule:

"We think that § 1319 [Code Proc.], supra, contains but the usual provisions in force in all, or nearly all, of the states, and we have been cited to no case, nor have we found one in which a conviction for manslaughter has been sustained under circumstances similar to those disclosed by the record here. The offense of manslaughter from its legal character excludes the possibility of an accessory before the fact as an element in its composition." (Citing cases).

The doctrine announced in the above cases is that the killing of a human being in order to constitute manslaughter must be involuntary and unintentional. I am unable to understand how a person can be aided and abetted in the doing of an unintentional and involuntary act by another person who has no intent.

In many cases of recklessness or negligence involving multiple actors, however, complicity is not the only or even the best way of finding criminal liability. For example, arguably you were negligent or reckless to give your car keys to an obviously intoxicated driver and could be found directly liable for involuntary manslaughter without resort to a theory of complicity.

DISCUSSION QUESTIONS

1.   Why can't you be an accessory before the fact to manslaughter in the view of the court?

2.   Why does the court nonetheless find the defendant guilty of involuntary manslaughter? What does court mean that she was essentially charged as a principal?

3.   Would it confuse or clarify things for the jury to argue that the defendant was an accomplice?

3.   THE ALTERNATE RULE FOR COMPLICITY MENTAL STATES

Some courts, professors, and textbook authors favor a different way of expressing the mental state requirements of complicity because of the issues raised by complicity for reckless/negligent crimes.

- Intentionally assist or encourage with

- The mental state required for the crime assisted or encouraged

By changing the second requirement from "intending that the crime assisted or encouraged by committed" to "with the mental state required for the crime assisted or encouraged," these sources eliminate the apparent paradox involved in "intending" recklessness/negligence. Such a statement allows for complicity in recklessness/negligence by importing the mental state requirement from the underlying crime into the mental state required for the accomplice. So, you could be an accomplice to involuntary manslaughter in the drunk driving case if you were grossly negligent in giving the driver your keys.

It is important to recognize that the traditional rule already required that an accomplice have the mental state required for the crime assisted or encouraged. You can't intend for someone to engage in larceny, for example, without knowing that the property taken is the property of another. By not requiring that the underlying crime be intended, however, this alternate rule reduces the mental state required for complicity to the mental state required for the offense itself, something that does not matter when the underlying crime requires intentional conduct, but does matter when it only requires reckless or negligent conduct.

G. NATURAL AND PROBABLE CONSEQUENCES

At common law, an accomplice was said to be liable not only for the crime assisted or encouraged but also for any other crimes that were the "natural and probable consequence" of the crime assisted or encouraged. Under this rule, an accomplice to an armed bank robbery would be liable for murder if one of the robbers shot a bank teller. An accomplice to shoplifting, however, would not be liable for murder if his accomplice killed a security guard who tried to apprehend him, as one would not think of lethal violence as a natural and probable consequence of what is usually a stealthy crime of theft typically punishable as a misdemeanor.

The leading treatises seem to agree that this remains the established rule today in the majority of jurisdictions but one treatise questions how widely it really applies. The easiest examples are ones that are already covered by the felony murder rule like the bank robbery example described above. One author notes that application of the natural and probable consequences rule, outside the context of felony murder or misdemeanor manslaughter, tends to involve very special cases involving unusual circumstances. Some courts have clearly rejected the rule in cases that don't involve dangerous felonies. For example, a defendant who helped falsify a company's books was not found liable for the subsequent filing of a false tax return using the falsified records, an offense that most would agree is a natural and probable consequence of accounting fraud. (Once you have cooked your books you might run a greater risk of being caught if you did not incorporate them into your tax return.) Look to see how widely your professor or textbook applies this rule.

Also, don't forget about possible Pinkerton liability under conspiracy law if crimes are committed in furtherance of a conspiratorial agreement (see the chapter on conspiracy). A conspirator will often, but not always, also be an accomplice. Someone who agreed to a crime, but did not assist in anyway and did not offer any direct encouragement to any of those who committed it, might nonetheless be liable for the crime in a jurisdiction that recognized Pinkerton liability. The harsh nature of expanding criminal liability so widely is, of course, one of the reasons why so many jurisdictions reject this sort of conspiracy-based complicity.

Case in Context

The following case illustrates the natural and probable consequences rule in the context of a violent felony.

STATE OF MAINE V. WILLIAM LINSCOTT

Supreme Judicial Court of Maine
520 A.2d 1067 (1987)

Opinion by: SCOLNIK.

William Linscott appeals from a judgment following a jury-waived trial convicting him of one count of murder, 17–A M.R.S.A. § 201(1)(A) (1983), and one count of robbery, 17–A M.R.S.A. § 651(1)(D) (1983). He contends that his conviction of intentional or knowing murder as an accomplice under the accomplice liability statute, 17–A M.R.S.A. § 57(3)(A) (1983), violated his constitutional right to due process of law in that he lacked the requisite intent to commit murder.

The facts are not in dispute. On December 12, 1984, the defendant, then unemployed, and two other men—the defendant's step-brother, Phillip Willey, and Jeffrey Colby—drove to the house of a friend, Joel Fuller. Fuller, with a sawed-off shotgun in his possession, joined the others. The defendant drove to the residence of Larry Ackley, where Fuller obtained 12-gauge shotgun shells.

Later that evening, Fuller suggested that the four men drive to the house of a reputed cocaine dealer, Norman Grenier of Swanville, take Grenier by surprise, and rob him. The defendant agreed to the plan, reasoning that Grenier, being a reputed drug dealer, would be extremely reluctant to call the police and request they conduct a robbery investigation that might result in the discovery of narcotics in his possession. Fuller stated that Grenier had purchased two kilograms of cocaine that day, and that Grenier had been seen with $50,000 in cash. Fuller guaranteed the defendant $10,000 as his share of the proceeds of the robbery.

The four drove up to Grenier's house, which was situated in a heavily wooded rural area on a dead-end road in Swanville. The defendant and Fuller left the car and approached the house. The defendant carried a hunting knife and switchblade, and Fuller was armed with the shotgun. The defendant and Fuller walked around to the back of Grenier's house. At that time, Grenier and his girlfriend were watching television in their living room. The defendant and Fuller intended to break in the back door in order to place themselves between Grenier and the bedroom, where they believed Grenier kept a loaded shotgun. Because the back door was blocked by snow, the two men walked around to the front of the house. Under their revised plan the defendant was to break the living room picture window whereupon Fuller would show his shotgun to Grenier, who presumably would be dissuaded from offering any resistance.

The defendant subsequently broke the living room window with his body without otherwise physically entering the house. Fuller immediately fired a shot through the broken window, hitting Grenier in the chest. Fuller left through the broken window after having removed about $1,300 from Grenier's pants pocket, later returning to the house to retrieve an empty shotgun casing.

At a jury-waived trial, the defendant testified that he knew Fuller to be a hunter and that it was not unusual for Fuller to carry a firearm with him, even at night. He nevertheless stated that he had no knowledge of any reputation for violence that Fuller may have had. The defendant further testified that he had no intention of causing anyone's death in the course of the robbery.

At the completion of the trial the trial justice found the defendant guilty of robbery and, on a theory of accomplice liability, found him guilty of murder. The court specifically found that the defendant possessed the intent to commit the crime of robbery, that Fuller intentionally or at least knowingly caused the death of Grenier, and that this murder was a reasonably foreseeable consequence of the defendant's participation in the robbery. However, the court also found that the defendant did not intend to kill Grenier, and that the defendant probably would not have participated in the robbery had he believed that Grenier would be killed in the course of the enterprise.

The sole issue raised on appeal is whether the defendant's conviction pursuant to the second sentence of subsection 3–A of the accomplice liability statute, 17–A M.R.S.A. § 57 (1983), unconstitutionally violates his right to due process under Article I, section 6–A of the Maine Constitution and the Fourteenth Amendment of the United States Constitution. "The Due Process Clause protects the accused against conviction except upon proof beyond a reasonable doubt of every fact necessary to constitute the crime with which he is charged." In re Winship, 397 U.S. 358, 364, 25 L. Ed. 2d 368, 90 S. Ct. 1068 (1970). The defendant contends that the accomplice liability statute impermissibly allows the State to find him guilty of murder, which requires proof beyond a reasonable doubt that the murder was committed either intentionally or knowingly, without having to prove either of these two culpable mental states. Instead, the defendant argues, the accomplice liability statute permits the State to employ only a mere negligence standard in convicting him of murder in violation of his right to due process. We find the defendant's argument to be without merit.

17–A M.R.S.A. § 57(3)(A) (1983) provides: A person is an accomplice of another person in the commission of a crime if:

> A.   With the intent of promoting or facilitating the commission of the crime, he solicits such other person to commit the crime, or aids or agrees to aid or attempts to aid such other person in planning or committing the crime. A person is an accomplice under this subsection to any crime the commission of which was a reasonably foreseeable consequence of his conduct. . .

The second sentence of section 57(3)(A) endorses the "foreseeable consequence" rule of accomplice liability. See State v. Goodall, 407 A.2d 268, 278 (Me. 1979). In that case we stated that the history of the statute demonstrates that the legislature indeed intended to impose liability upon accomplices for those crimes that were the reasonably foreseeable consequence of their criminal enterprise, notwithstanding an absence on their part of the same culpability required for conviction as a principal to the crime.

Id. Accordingly, we have stated that section 57(3)(A) is to be interpreted as follows: Under the first sentence of that section, which is to be read independently of the second sentence, liability for a "primary crime". . . [here, robbery] is established by proof that the actor intended to promote or facilitate that crime. Under the second sentence, liability for any "secondary crime". . . [here, murder] that may have been committed by the principal is established upon a two-fold showing: (a) that the actor intended to promote the primary crime, and (b) that the commission of the secondary crime was a "foreseeable consequence" of the actor's participation in the primary crime.

Id. at 277–278 (footnote omitted; emphasis in original). We have consistently upheld this interpretation of section 57(3)(A). See State v. Armstrong, 503 A.2d 701, 703 (Me. 1986); State v. Johnson, 434 A.2d 532, 538 (Me. 1981); State v. Kimball, 424 A.2d 684, 693 (Me. 1981); State v. Anderson, 409 A.2d 1290, 1303 (Me. 1979). We discern no compelling reason to depart from this construction of the statute.

The "foreseeable consequence" or "natural and probable consequence" rule in complicity law has been stated as follows: "an accessory is liable for any criminal act which in the ordinary course of things was the natural or probable consequence of the crime that he advised or commanded, although such consequence may not have been intended by him." 22 C.J.S. Criminal Law § 92 (1961) (footnote omitted). The rule has also been adopted in several other jurisdictions. . . .

Furthermore, the foreseeable consequence rule as stated in Section 57(3)(A) merely carries over the objective standards of accomplice liability as used in the common law. (Citation omitted.) Thus, a rule allowing for a murder conviction under a theory of accomplice liability based upon an objective standard, despite the absence of evidence that the defendant possessed the culpable subjective mental state that constitutes an element of the crime of murder, does not represent a departure from prior Maine law.

We also do not find fundamentally unfair or disproportionate the grading scheme for sentencing purposes [of] murder premised on a theory of accomplice liability.

The potential penalty of life imprisonment for murder under a theory of accomplice liability based on an objective standard "does not denote such punitive severity as to shock the conscience of the public, nor our own respective or collective sense of fairness."

For the foregoing reasons, we find no constitutional defect in this statutory provision, nor any fundamental unfairness in its operation.

DISCUSSION QUESTIONS

1.   Felony murder would ordinarily account for murder liability in this case. What if the victim did not die, however? Would the defendant have been found guilty of anything but burglary?

2.   Is the defendant correct in arguing that the natural and probable consequences doctrine essentially imposes murder liability in this case for simple negligence?

3. What purpose of punishment does the natural and probable consequence doctrine best serve? Retribution? Deterrence?

Exam Tip: Felony Murder and Complicity

One of the reasons law professors love felony murder exam questions is because they require knowledge of many different doctrines. Felony murder fact patterns involving multiple defendants require you to apply both felony murder and complicity doctrines. Could your Mom be guilty of felony murder for making your lunch the day of the robbery if one of your fellow robbers kills someone during the robbery? If she intended to assist in the robbing of the bank when she packed the lunch, the answer is yes in most jurisdictions that have a classic felony murder rule. You only come up with this answer if you see how these various doctrines connect with one another, and that is one of the principle challenges of a criminal law exam.

H. ABANDONMENT/WITHDRAWAL

Unlike conspiracy, some jurisdictions will allow an accomplice to "undo" their crime by withdrawing from or abandoning the crime assisted or encouraged. Such withdrawal requires you to do everything you can to "undo" your acts of assistance or encouragement. If you have supplied materials, you must get them back. If you have offered shelter, you must revoke the invitation. If you only encouraged the commission of the crime, then you need only communicate your change of heart to those involved. So, yes, this means that your poor mother is going to have to chase you through the street to get the bag lunch back to escape liability for bank robbery. If you can't take back the assistance or encouragement given, you may have to try to thwart the crime by informing the police or taking equivalent preventative measures on your own. So, if Mom can't catch up to you before you rob the bank, she will have to "drop a dime" on you and call the police. If the crime is already complete or reached a point where it simply can't be stopped, then withdrawal has come too late to constitute a defense.

Some jurisdictions impose additional requirements upon such a withdrawal. In such jurisdictions, withdrawal must be truly voluntary in the sense that it is not motivated by new developments that make the crime more difficult or dangerous. It also must be complete in the sense that one is not postponing or rescheduling the crime.

Even if a jurisdiction does not accept withdrawal as a defense to complicity, it may allow it to cut off liability for further criminal acts by one's accomplices. This means that the withdrawing accomplice would not be held liable for crimes that are the natural and probable consequence of the crimes committed. Many courts take this approach.

Case in Context

The following case illustrates the difficulties of successfully withdrawing once complicity has been achieved.

THE STATE OF NEW HAMPSHIRE V. PAUL FORMELLA

Supreme Court of New Hampshire
960 A.2d 722 (2008)

Opinion by: GALWAY.

GALWAY, J. The defendant, Paul Formella, appeals his conviction following a bench trial in the Lebanon District Court (Cirone, J.) for criminal liability for the conduct of another. See RSA 626:8 (2007). We affirm.

On the afternoon of Wednesday, June 13, 2007, the defendant, then a junior at Hanover High School, and two friends, were studying at the Howe Library near the school. After studying for approximately two hours, the defendant and his friends returned to the school to retrieve some books from their second-floor lockers. Upon entering the school, they encountered another group of students who said they intended to steal mathematics exams from the third floor. The defendant and his companions were asked to serve as lookouts during the theft, which they agreed to do. They were instructed to yell something like "did you get your math book?" up to the third floor as a code to alert the thieves if someone was coming.

The defendant and his friends then proceeded to their second-floor lockers. The defendant testified that on their way to their lockers they looked around to "confirm or dispel" whether anyone was there. Once the defendant and his friends had retrieved their books, they "were all feeling like this was the wrong thing to do," and decided to head back down to the first floor to wait for the other group. On their way down the stairs, they encountered some janitors who told them that they ought to leave the school. The defendant and his friends left the school building, but waited in the parking lot for approximately five to ten minutes for the other group. Eventually, the other students exited the school with the stolen examinations and all of the students shared the exam questions.

The next week, someone informed the dean of students that some students had stolen the exams. The police were called, and in connection with their investigation they interviewed the defendant, who admitted his involvement in the theft. He was later charged with criminal liability for conduct of another. See RSA 626:8. Following his conviction, the defendant appealed to this court.

On appeal, the defendant contends that the trial court erred in failing to make findings of fact relative to the timing of his withdrawal from the theft and the completion of the theft because, he argues, without such findings the trial court could not properly apply RSA 626:8.

RSA 626:8 provides, in relevant part, that an individual is criminally liable for the conduct of another when he acts as an accomplice in the commission of an offense. RSA 626:8, II(c). A person is an accomplice when with the purpose of promoting or facilitating the commission of an offense, he aids or agrees or attempts to aid another person in planning or committing the offense. RSA 626:8, III(a). RSA 626:8 further provides, however, that a person is not an accomplice if he "terminates his complicity prior to the commission of the offense and wholly deprives it of effectiveness in the commission of the offense or gives timely warning to the law enforcement authorities or otherwise makes proper effort to prevent the commission of the offense." RSA 626:8, VI(c).

The defendant does not dispute that he became an accomplice in the first instance when he agreed to act as a lookout. Accordingly, we are concerned only with whether the defendant's later acts terminated his liability as an accomplice. We note that the defendant does not contend that he gave timely warning to law enforcement or otherwise made "proper effort" to prevent the offense. See RSA 626:8, VI(c). Thus, under RSA 626:8, VI(c) the defendant was not an accomplice if: (1) he terminated his complicity in the crime; (2) his termination occurred prior to the commission of the offense; and (3) he wholly deprived his complicity of effectiveness in the commission of the offense.

As regards the third factor, the statute does not define what is required for a person to "wholly deprive" his complicity of effectiveness in the commission of an offense. According to the State, an overt act aimed at undermining the prior complicity is required, while the defendant argues that, at least in this case, no such act is necessary. As the statute does not clarify whether such an act is necessary, we conclude that it is ambiguous, and we look to other sources to determine legislative intent.

RSA 626:8 tracks the provisions of section 2.06 of the Model Penal Code. Comment 9(c) to section 2.06 addresses situations where liability may be averted if the accomplice's complicity is terminated prior to the commission of the crime. MODEL PENAL CODE § 2.06 cmt. 9(c) at 326 (1985). The comment notes that the actions sufficient to deprive the prior complicity of effectiveness vary with the type of accessorial behavior. Id. Relevant to the analysis here, the comment states that if "complicity inhered in request or encouragement, countermanding disapproval may suffice to nullify its influence, providing it is heard in time to allow reconsideration by those planning to commit the crime." Id. The comments thus indicate that in order to deprive the prior complicity of effectiveness, one who has encouraged the commission of an offense may avoid liability by terminating his or her role in the commission of the crime and by making his or her disapproval known to the principals sufficiently in advance of the commission of the crime to allow them time to reconsider as well.

The view that an accomplice must make some affirmative act, such as an overt expression of disapproval to the principals, accords with that of other jurisdictions with statutes mirroring the provisions of the Model Penal Code. See People v. Lacey, 49 Ill. App. 2d 301, 200 N.E.2d 11, 14 (Ill. App. Ct. 1964) ("A person who encourages the commission of an unlawful act cannot escape responsibility by quietly withdrawing from the scene."); People v. Brown, 26 Ill. 2d 308, 186 N.E.2d 321, 324 (Ill. 1962); Commonwealth v. Spriggs, 463 Pa. 375, 344 A.2d 880, 883 (Pa. 1975). Additionally, the relevant authorities weigh in favor of requiring any withdrawal to be communicated far enough in advance to allow the others involved in the crime to follow suit. See Lacey, 200 N.E.2d at 14 ("[I]t must be possible for the trier of fact to say that the accused had wholly and effectively detached himself from the criminal enterprise before the act with which he is charged is in the process of consummation or has become so inevitable that it cannot reasonably be stayed."); see also LAFAVE, supra at 366 ("A mere change of heart, flight from the crime scene, apprehension by the police, or an uncommunicated decision not to carry out his part of the scheme will not suffice."). This is not to say that the terminating accomplice must actually prevent the crime from occurring. Instead, he need only make some act demonstrating to the principals of the crime that he has withdrawn, and he must do so in a manner, and at such a time, that the principals could do likewise.

To extricate himself from accomplice liability, the defendant needed to make an affirmative act, such as communicating his withdrawal to the principals. Here, the defendant made no such act. The defendant testified that he and his companions simply left the scene. He did not communicate his withdrawal, discourage the principals from acting, inform the custodians, or do any other thing which would deprive his complicity of effectiveness. In fact, the principals remained unaware of his exit. Thus, the defendant did not do that which was necessary to undo his complicity.

The defendant contends that because he had been acting as a lookout, leaving the scene so as to no longer be "looking out" deprived his complicity of its effectiveness, and, therefore, findings regarding the timing of the offense were required. We disagree. While at the point he left the scene he was no longer an effective lookout, the defendant did nothing to counter his prior complicity. According to the defendant, the principals had requested aid in committing the offense, he agreed to provide it, and he agreed to warn the principals if anyone approached, thus encouraging the act. Further, upon reaching the second floor the defendant looked around to "confirm or dispel" whether anyone was around who might have apprehended the thieves or otherwise spoiled the crime. Thus, it was the complicity of agreeing to aid the primary actors and then actually aiding them that needed to be undone; silently withdrawing from the scene did not, in any way, undermine the encouragement the defendant had provided. As there was no evidence that the defendant had wholly deprived his complicity of its effectiveness, it was not error for the trial court to refuse to make findings on the timing of the offense because such findings would not have altered the result.

DISCUSSION QUESTIONS

1.	Why did the court find that the defendant failed to withdraw? What more would the defendant have had to do?

2.	What if the defendant had not withdrawn before the other students emerged from the teacher's office with the stolen exams? What would the defendant have to do at that point to successfully withdraw?

3.	Should withdrawal be permitted as a defense to complicity?

I.   MODEL PENAL CODE

MPC § 2.06. Liability for Conduct of Another; Complicity

1.	A person is guilty of an offense if it is committed by his own conduct or by the conduct of another person for which he is legally accountable, or both.

2.	A person is legally accountable for the conduct of another person when:

	a.	acting with the kind of culpability that is sufficient for the commission of the offense, he causes an innocent or irresponsible person to engage in such conduct; or

	b.	he is made accountable for the conduct of such other person by the Code or by the law defining the offense; or

	c.	he is an accomplice of such other person in the commission of the offense.

3.	A person is an accomplice of another person in the commission of an offense if:

	a.	with the purpose of promoting or facilitating the commission of the offense, he

		i.	solicits such other person to commit it, or

		ii.	aids or agrees or attempts to aid such other person in planning or committing it, or

		iii.	having a legal duty to prevent the commission of the offense, fails to make proper effort so to do; or

	b.	his conduct is expressly declared by law to establish his complicity.

4.	When causing a particular result is an element of an offense, an accomplice in the conduct causing such result is an accomplice in the commission of that offense if he acts with the kind of culpability, if any, with respect to that result that is sufficient for the commission of the offense.

The Model Penal Code departs from the common law approach in a number of important ways. The common theme among these differences is the greater importance that the MPC places on the mental state of the offender. In places, the MPC requires more in the way of mental state and less in the way of conduct than the common law.

As noted earlier, the MPC rejects Pinkerton liability for foreseeable crimes committed in furtherance of a conspiracy of which the defendant was a member. The MPC also rejects liability for crimes that are the natural and probable consequences of the crime assisted or encouraged. The MPC specifically provides for complicity liability, however, for one who agrees to aid, but the resulting liability is for the crime one agreed to aid, not all crimes in furtherance of that crime as would be the case under Pinkerton liability.

Unlike the common law, the MPC creates complicity liability for one who merely attempts to aid. So, if you don't even see the lunch your mother packed for you on the kitchen counter, she can still go down the river for bank robbery because she was trying to aid you in your bank robbery.

On the bright side (for defendants, that is), complicity under the MPC requires purpose. It is not enough to knowingly assist or encourage; one must do so with "the purpose of promoting or facilitating the commission of the crime." (MPC 2.06(3)(a).) This means that the prosecutor must prove that your mother did not just know that you were going to rob the bank the day she made your lunch. It must be proved that she provided you with lunch for the purpose of helping you rob the bank. Maybe there is a Thanksgiving dinner in your (post-prison) future after all!

The MPC came down on the side of the prosecutor, however, with respect to the issue of reckless and negligent crimes. The MPC specifically provides that, with respect to results, an accomplice need only have the mental state required for the offense assisted or encouraged. So, you could easily be an accomplice to involuntary manslaughter if you handed your car keys to an intoxicated driver and he killed someone as a result.

Finally, the MPC clearly provides for a defense of abandonment. To qualify one must:

1. neutralize their assistance or encouragement or

2. warn the police in a timely manner or

3. try some other way to prevent the crime assisted or encouraged.

J. VICARIOUS AND ENTERPRISE LIABILITY DISTINGUISHED

Two different types of criminal liability need to be distinguished from complicity liability. (Neither gets much attention in first year courses.)

Vicarious liability refers to the situation where one person is held criminally responsible for the acts of another. Such vicarious liability is today created by statute. The most common scenario is an employer being liable for the criminal acts of his employees. One such statute holds one who runs a liquor store criminally responsible for any sales by his employees of alcohol to those under the legal drinking age. Such statutes often create only misdemeanor liability. Other statutes create liability for certain employee actions only when the employer knows or should know of those actions.

Enterprise liability, on the other hand, refers to the criminal liability of corporations and other such legal entities. The corporation itself is found guilty despite there being "no body to kick and no soul to damn." Ordinarily, such liability exists only when the board of directors or high—ranking officers engage in criminal conduct.

Vicarious and enterprise liability may exist alongside of complicity liability in a fact pattern, but remember to analyze each separately.

Practice Problem 19.3: The Spice Boys

Chip is the President of Omega Alpha, an on-campus fraternity at Faber College. He asks Skip, the fraternity officer in charge of the entering pledge class to devise a hazing ritual to initiate the incoming pledge class. (Pledges are the probationary members of a fraternity who seek full admission.) In past years these initiation rituals required the incoming pledges to drink enough alcohol to make everyone physically sick. The previous year, however, a pledge in another fraternity died from alcohol poisoning during an initiation ritual. Subsequently the state legislature passed the anti-hazing statute excerpted below, and the university instituted a strict prohibition on the drinking of alcohol by students on campus. Chip tells Skip that it is important that the hazing ritual be just as challenging and memorable as the previous year to build the solidarity of the incoming pledge class, but orders him not to use alcohol or drugs in any way.

Skip hears from friends about "The Cinnamon Challenge." The cinnamon challenge simply involves swallowing one teaspoon of cinnamon within sixty seconds without drinking any water. Skip googles "cinnamon challenge." The search results include a series of links to articles discussing health risks associated with the cinnamon challenge. Skip passes over these links and goes straight to a series of You Tube clips showing young people completing or attempting to complete the challenge. In one or two clips, the person completes the challenge without incident but in all of the rest the person ends up sputtering, coughing spasmodically or partially choking—although everyone seems fine in the end. Skip starts to tell Chip about the cinnamon challenge but Chip holds up his hands and says, "just as long as it does not involve drugs or alcohol I don't care and I don't want to know."

Although no one had up to this point ever died from the cinnamon challenge, the game has well known health risks that were described in the articles that Skip did not read. People who cough initially and try to breath in through their mouths sometimes inhale a fine dust of cinnamon that can burn the lungs and that in some cases could cause a lung to collapse. Doctors have speculated that a person with asthma doing the challenge might choke to death before medical help arrived.

During initiation, Skip orders the pledges to complete the cinnamon challenge. One of the pledges, Todd, has asthma, and he chokes after swallowing the cinnamon and dies.

Discuss Skip and Chip's criminal liability for Todd's death under the following statutory scheme. Assume that you are in a common law jurisdiction.

First Degree Hazing: A person is guilty of hazing in the first degree when, in the course of another person's initiation into any organization, he intentionally or recklessly engages in conduct which creates a substantial risk of physical injury to such other person through the use of alcohol, illegal drugs or dangerous substances. Hazing in the first degree is a felony.

Second Degree Hazing: A person is guilty of hazing in the second degree when, in the course of another person's initiation into any organization, he intentionally or recklessly engages in conduct which creates a substantial risk of physical injury to such other person. Hazing in the second degree is a misdemeanor.

Definition of Hazing: Hazing is an activity that a high-status member orders other members to engage that produces mental or physical discomfort, embarrassment, harassment, or ridicule.

First Degree Murder: A person who intentionally kills with premeditation and deliberation is guilty of murder in the first degree.

Second Degree Murder: A person who kills intentionally or who causes the death of another in the commission of an inherently dangerous felony is guilty of murder in the second degree.

Third Degree Murder: A person who causes the death of another during the commission of a non-inherently dangerous felony or under circumstances manifesting an extreme indifference to human life.

Voluntary Manslaughter: A person who intentionally kills in the heat of passion is guilty of voluntary manslaughter.

Involuntary Manslaughter: A person who kills recklessly or who causes the death of another in the commission of a misdemeanor is guilty of involuntary manslaughter.

Practice Problem 19.4: 911 Murder Redux

Evaluate Garth's liability for homicide crimes in Practice Problem 14.3 (p. 480).

CHAPTER 20

DEFENSIVE FORCE

■ ■ ■

Self-defense is the classic justification defense. People intuitively believe that the innocent have a right to protect themselves from violence. People also intuitively understand that there is an important difference between self-defense and retaliation, between attacking someone out of fear and attacking someone out of anger. One of the main purposes of the criminal law is to reduce violence by stopping people from taking the law into their own hands, but the law cannot be everywhere. A person should not have to choose between allowing himself to be hurt and breaking the law. So, the criminal law justifies what it usually forbids—private violence—when a person is rightfully protecting him or herself or another innocent party.

Distinguishing self-defense from ordinary violence is all very fine in theory. In practice, however, drawing the line between justified and unjustified force is often far from easy. First of all, fear and anger go hand in hand. When we are afraid of people we often also hate them. Also, deciding how early people can use force to protect themselves is a very tricky business. If we make it too easy to lawfully use force, people will become more afraid of one another, and more likely to use force in anticipation of the other person using force. We could easily spiral into the sort of chaos that the criminal law is supposed to prevent.

These issues, among others, make the doctrines justifying defensive force interesting and important. Lawyers who practice criminal law deal with self-defense issues all the time. Don't be lulled by the intuitive nature of these doctrines, though. You must think systematically through a range of issues—not just latch onto the first one that jumps out at you.

A. JUSTIFICATION VS. EXCUSE

Before we work through the elements, let's review the distinction between justifications and excuses. We refer to a defense as a justification when society approves or tolerates your conduct. We say that you were justified in your actions because you did not do anything wrong. An excuse, in contrast, involves a wrongful act committed under circumstances that relieve you of criminal (but usually not civil) liability for what you did.

Self-defense is generally thought of as the paradigm example of a justification. Society approves of defensive force. We want you to defend yourself against wrongful force. We will eventually see, however, that the

659

distinction is not always clear depending on how we define some of the elements of self-defense.

B. OVERVIEW OF THE ELEMENTS

Defensive force doctrines cover both the justified use of force to defend others as well as oneself. The rules for each are largely the same, with a few important differences. To avoid the cumbersome repetition of the phrase "defense of self or of others," we will refer to both as "self-defense" until later in the chapter when we learn the special rules that apply to using force to protect others.

Generally speaking, you can only use force when you reasonably fear an imminent harm. The amount of force you use must be reasonably proportionate and necessary under the circumstances. You also must not be in the wrong to begin with, which means that you did not start a fight with someone else and were not a crime. So, violent bullies and criminals can't claim self-defense when they are attacking or stealing from someone.

With that very general understanding, let's use the following checklist to systematically analyze the issues raised.

Justifiable Defensive Force Must. . .

- *Be used against an unlawful force*
- *Be used as the result of a reasonable fear*
- *Be used as the result of an actual fear*
- *Be used in the face of an imminent harm*
- *Be necessary*
- *Be reasonable in the amount of force used*
- *Not be used by an initial aggressor*
- *Not be used when you should retreat*

Once you learn to use this checklist, you will be able to defend yourself against any self-defense fact pattern on an exam!

1. USED AGAINST AN UNLAWFUL FORCE

If you go shoplifting and get caught, you don't get to punch the security guard in order to get away. When the security guard tells you to stop and you run, he can lawfully grab you by the arm. You can't lawfully use any force in response because his force is lawful. What if the security guard throws you to the ground and starts kicking you? Now you can defend yourself because his excessive force has ceased to be lawful.

The basic idea here is that only one person can be lawfully using force at a time. If the security guard could lawfully grab you, and you could lawfully punch him, then society would end up with a lawful fist fight. This is not desirable since a goal of the criminal law is to reduce violence.

The security guard example is intended to be obvious, but the principle can apply to any conflict between two private citizens. If someone puts some hard but legal blocks on you during an intramural football game, you cannot lawfully punch them in self-defense. Their blocks are lawful because the law implies your consent when you agree to play football.

2. ACTUAL FEAR

Fear must not only be reasonable but actual. Usually, the two go hand in hand, but occasionally one comes across a fact pattern where a person has a reason other than fear to use force against another.

3. REASONABLE FEAR

The reasonableness of one's fear is the moral foundation of self-defense. There are all sorts of reasons one might be afraid, but we don't want to license force based on unreasonable fear. Imagine that someone goes to the door on Halloween night after hearing his doorbell ring and opens fire on a group of teenagers wearing masks. Perhaps this is an exceptionally timorous person who forgot that it was Halloween. He may have been in fear for his life, but his use of force would not be justified because we would not consider his fear to be reasonable. Without the reasonableness requirement, we would legally be at the mercy of the most fearful people in our society.

a. A Reasonable Fear Does Not Have to Be Correct

On the other hand, your fear need only be reasonable, not right. Now imagine that, as you walk across campus one night, you are confronted by someone in a ski mask who points a gun at you and tells you to get down on your knees to pray for your life. You happen to be carrying your field hockey stick, so you smash him over the head with it. It turns out that he is a participant in a role-playing game called "Assassin," and he mistook you for the game player he was supposed to attack. The "gun" was a completely realistic looking toy. You are not guilty of felonious assault (or even murder if he dies) because you reasonably feared that he was going to kill you.

We justify force used reasonably but mistakenly because we don't want you to take the chance of facing a real gun in the hope that it is a toy. If everyone must wait until the first shot is fired, then innocent people may die out of fear of criminal liability. So, while no one is happy about "reasonable mistakes" where people are hurt or killed, society has decided to tolerate—if not approve—such reasonably mistaken uses of defensive force.

b. A Fear Cannot Be Unreasonable Even if Correct

To be reasonable, the grounds for fear need to be apparent to the defendant. Sometimes a fear can be reasonable in retrospect, yet it does not support the use of force at the time. This occurs when the defendant does not know what makes his fear reasonable. The criminal law takes this position to stop people from "gambling" unreasonably when they use force.

c. Who Is the Reasonable Person, and What Is Reasonable Fear?

Any time you see a reasonableness standard you should ask the question, "reasonable to who?" Whose fear must be reasonable to enjoy a right of self-defense? A person of what age, gender, physical size, and strength? Is the reasonable person a frail 98 pound weakling, a heavyweight Mixed Martial Arts fighting champion, or some mythical "average" person in between? And under what circumstances is your fear to be judged? What time and place? Asking someone for money on the first tee of a golf course at an elite country club is one thing; asking someone for change in a dark alley of a high crime neighborhood is another. Do we imagine some fear-neutral time and place? Most of these questions find no clear answer in the law. Instead, we look to jurors or prosecutors to exercise reasonable discretion.

The reasonableness of one's fear becomes an issue when force is used pre-emptively. Once an attack is ongoing, the reasonableness of one's fear is beyond question. One need not wait until an attack begins, however, to have a fear that the criminal law recognizes as reasonable. In movies set in the wild west, the "good guy" would wait until the "bad guy" reached for his gun before shooting. The criminal law does not always require you to wait that long because it does not assume that the good guys will always be faster than the bad. Deciding how long you must wait before your fear becomes reasonable, however, is difficult.

Much ink has been spilt by judges and legislators trying to define reasonable fear in a way that is both sensitive enough to context to be fair and yet clear enough to be predictable. The consensus view allows the following factors to be taken into consideration in determining whether a fear is reasonable.

- Physical attributes of the defendant using the defensive force
- Physical attributes of the person against whom defensive force was used
- Knowledge the defendant has about the person against whom defensive force was used
- Any relevant past experiences of the defendant

For example, a woman who has been raped before in a dark alley sees a man walking behind her in a dark alley approach her. She recognizes him as a heavy drinker in a bar she just visited. He is much bigger than she is and made sexually threatening remarks to her that night in the bar. She quickens her pace, and he breaks into a run, catching up to her. She turns and shoots him in the face with pepper spray. Was her fear of being sexually assaulted reasonable? Juries in most jurisdictions would be invited to take all of the above facts into account in deciding whether she was reasonable in fearing that he would sexually assault her. It is widely accepted that differing sizes can be taken into account when evaluating reasonableness of fear—a 250 pound man threatened by an unarmed 120 pound man may find it difficult to get a jury to find his fear reasonable. But should gender be considered in this equation? What issues are inherent in allowing juries to consider the genders of actors in determining reasonableness?

Case in Context

Does the following case involve a subway robbery successfully thwarted or a murderous overreaction?

PEOPLE V. GOETZ

Court of Appeals of New York
68 N.Y.2d 96 (1986)

WACHTLER, C.J.

A Grand Jury has indicted defendant on attempted murder, assault, and other charges for having shot and wounded four youths on a New York City subway train after one or two of the youths approached him and asked for $ 5. The lower courts, concluding that the prosecutor's charge to the Grand Jury on the defense of justification was erroneous, have dismissed the attempted murder, assault and weapons possession charges. We now reverse and reinstate all counts of the indictment.

I.

The precise circumstances of the incident giving rise to the charges against defendant are disputed, and ultimately it will be for a trial jury to determine what occurred. We feel it necessary, however, to provide some factual background to properly frame the legal issues before us. Accordingly, we have summarized the facts as they appear from the evidence before the Grand Jury. We stress, however, that we do not purport to reach any conclusions or holding as to exactly what transpired or whether defendant is blameworthy. The credibility of witnesses and the reasonableness of defendant's conduct are to be resolved by the trial jury.

On Saturday afternoon, December 22, 1984, Troy Canty, Darryl Cabey, James Ramseur, and Barry Allen boarded an IRT express subway train in The Bronx and headed south toward lower Manhattan. The four youths rode together in the rear portion of the seventh car of the train. Two of the four, Ramseur and Cabey, had screwdrivers inside their coats, which they said were to be used to break into the coin boxes of video machines.

Defendant Bernhard Goetz boarded this subway train at 14th Street in Manhattan and sat down on a bench towards the rear section of the same car occupied by the four youths. Goetz was carrying an unlicensed .38 caliber pistol loaded with five rounds of ammunition in a waistband holster. The train left the 14th Street station and headed towards Chambers Street.

It appears from the evidence before the Grand Jury that Canty approached Goetz, possibly with Allen beside him, and stated "give me five dollars." Neither Canty nor any of the other youths displayed a weapon. Goetz responded by standing up, pulling out his handgun and firing four shots in rapid succession. The first shot hit Canty in the chest; the second struck Allen in the back; the third went through Ramseur's arm and into his left side; the fourth was fired at Cabey, who apparently was then standing in the corner of the car, but missed, deflecting instead off of a wall of the conductor's cab. After Goetz briefly surveyed the scene around him, he fired another shot at Cabey, who then was sitting on the end bench of the car. The bullet entered the rear of Cabey's side and severed his spinal cord.

All but two of the other passengers fled the car when, or immediately after, the shots were fired. The conductor, who had been in the next car, heard the shots and instructed the motorman to radio for emergency assistance. The conductor then went into the car where the shooting occurred and saw Goetz sitting on a bench, the injured youths lying on the floor or slumped against a seat, and two women who had apparently taken cover, also lying on the floor. Goetz told the conductor that the four youths had tried to rob him.

While the conductor was aiding the youths, Goetz headed towards the front of the car. The train had stopped just before the Chambers Street station and Goetz went between two of the cars, jumped onto the tracks and fled. Police and ambulance crews arrived at the scene shortly thereafter. Ramseur and Canty, initially listed in critical condition, have fully recovered. Cabey remains paralyzed, and has suffered some degree of brain damage.

On December 31, 1984, Goetz surrendered to police in Concord, New Hampshire, identifying himself as the gunman being sought for the subway shootings in New York nine days earlier. Later that day, after receiving Miranda warnings, he made two lengthy statements, both of which were tape recorded with his permission. In the statements, which are substantially similar, Goetz admitted that he had been illegally carrying a handgun in New York City for three years. He stated that he had first purchased a gun in 1981 after he had been injured in a mugging. Goetz also revealed that twice between 1981 and 1984 he had successfully warded off assailants simply by displaying the pistol.

According to Goetz's statement, the first contact he had with the four youths came when Canty, sitting or lying on the bench across from him, asked "how are you," to which he replied "fine". Shortly thereafter, Canty, followed by one of the other youths, walked over to the defendant and stood to his left, while the other two youths remained to his right, in the corner of the subway car. Canty then said "give me five dollars". Goetz stated that he knew from the smile on Canty's face that they wanted to "play with me." Although he was certain that none of the youths had a gun, he had a fear, based on prior experiences, of being "maimed".

Goetz then established "a pattern of fire," deciding specifically to fire from left to right. His stated intention at that point was to "murder [the four youths], to hurt them, to make them suffer as much as possible". When Canty again requested money, Goetz stood up, drew his weapon, and began firing, aiming for the center of the body of each of the four. Goetz recalled that the first two he shot "tried to run through the crowd [but] they had nowhere to run". Goetz then turned to his right to "go after the other two". One of these two "tried to run through the wall of the train, but he had nowhere to go". The other youth (Cabey) "tried pretending that he wasn't with [the others]" by standing still, holding on to one of the subway hand straps, and not looking at Goetz. Goetz nonetheless fired his fourth shot at him. He then ran back to the first two youths to make sure they had been "taken care of". Seeing that they had both been shot, he spun back to check on the latter two. Goetz noticed that the youth who had been standing still was now sitting on a bench and seemed unhurt. As Goetz told the police, "I said '[you] seem to be all right, here's another' ", and he then fired the shot which severed Cabey's spinal cord. Goetz added that "if I was a little more under self-control I would have put the barrel against his forehead and fired." He also admitted that "if I had had more [bullets], I would have shot them again, and again, and again.". . .

III.

Penal Law article 35 recognizes the defense of justification, which "permits the use of force under certain circumstances". One such set of circumstances pertains to the use of force in defense of a person, encompassing both self-defense and defense of a third person. Penal Law § 35.15 (1) sets forth the general principles governing all such uses of force: "[a] person may use physical force upon another person when and to the extent he reasonably believes such to be necessary to defend himself or a third person from what he reasonably believes to be the use or imminent use of unlawful physical force by such other person".

Section 35.15 (2) sets forth further limitations on these general principles with respect to the use of "deadly physical force": "A person may not use deadly physical force upon another person under circumstances specified in subdivision one unless (a) He reasonably believes that such other person is using or about to use deadly physical force or (b) He reasonably believes that such other person is committing or attempting to commit a kidnapping, forcible rape, forcible sodomy or robbery."

Thus, consistent with most justification provisions, Penal Law § 35.15 permits the use of deadly physical force only where requirements as to triggering conditions and the necessity of a particular response are met. As to the triggering conditions, the statute requires that the actor "reasonably believes" that another person either is using or about to use deadly physical force or is committing or attempting to commit one of certain enumerated felonies, including robbery. As to the need for the use of deadly physical force as a response, the statute requires that the actor "reasonably believes" that such force is necessary to avert the perceived threat.

Because the evidence before the second Grand Jury included statements by Goetz that he acted to protect himself from being maimed or to avert a robbery, the prosecutor correctly chose to charge the justification defense in section 35.15 to the Grand Jury (see, CPL 190.25 [6]; People v Valles, 62 NY2d 36, 38). The prosecutor properly instructed the grand jurors to consider whether the use of deadly physical force was justified to prevent either serious physical injury or a robbery, and, in doing so, to separately analyze the defense with respect to each of the charges. He elaborated upon the prerequisites for the use of deadly physical force essentially by reading or paraphrasing the language in Penal Law § 35.15. The defense does not contend that he committed any error in this portion of the charge.

When the prosecutor had completed his charge, one of the grand jurors asked for clarification of the term "reasonably believes". The prosecutor responded by instructing the grand jurors that they were to consider the circumstances of the incident and determine "whether the defendant's conduct was that of a reasonable man in the defendant's situation". It is this response by the prosecutor—and specifically his use of "a reasonable man"—which is the basis for the dismissal of the charges by the lower courts. As expressed repeatedly in the Appellate Division's plurality opinion, because section 35.15 uses the term "he reasonably believes", the appropriate test, according to that court, is whether a defendant's beliefs and reactions were "reasonable to him". Under that reading of the statute, a jury which believed a defendant's testimony that he felt that his own actions were warranted and were reasonable would have to acquit him, regardless of what anyone else in defendant's situation might have concluded. Such an interpretation defies the ordinary meaning and significance of the term "reasonably" in a statute, and misconstrues the clear intent of the Legislature, in enacting section 35.15, to retain an objective element as part of any provision authorizing the use of deadly physical force.

Penal statutes in New York have long codified the right recognized at common law to use deadly physical force, under appropriate circumstances, in self-defense. These provisions have never required that an actor's belief as to the intention of another person to inflict serious injury be correct in order for the use of deadly force to be justified, but they have uniformly required that the belief comport with an objective notion of reasonableness. . .

Had the drafters of section 35.15 wanted to adopt a subjective standard, they could have simply used the language of section 3.04. "Believes" by itself requires an honest or genuine belief by a defendant as to the need to use deadly force. Interpreting the statute to require only that the defendant's belief was "reasonable to him," as done by the plurality below, would hardly be different from requiring only a genuine belief; in either case, the defendant's own perceptions could completely exonerate him from any criminal liability.

We cannot lightly impute to the Legislature an intent to fundamentally alter the principles of justification to allow the perpetrator of a serious crime to go free simply because that person believed his actions were reasonable and necessary to prevent some perceived harm. To completely exonerate such an individual, no matter how aberrational or bizarre his thought patterns, would allow citizens to set their own standards for the permissible use of force. It would also allow a legally competent defendant suffering from delusions to kill or perform acts of violence with impunity, contrary to fundamental principles of justice and criminal law.

We can only conclude that the Legislature retained a reasonableness requirement to avoid giving a license for such actions. . . Statutes or rules of law requiring a person to act "reasonably" or to have a "reasonable belief" uniformly prescribe conduct meeting an objective standard measured with reference to how "a reasonable person" could have acted. . .

Goetz also argues that the introduction of an objective element will preclude a jury from considering factors such as the prior experiences of a given actor and thus, require it to make a determination of "reasonableness" without regard to the actual circumstances of a particular incident. This argument, however, falsely presupposes that an objective standard means that the background and other relevant characteristics of a particular actor must be ignored. To the contrary, we have frequently noted that a determination of reasonableness must be based on the "circumstances" facing a defendant or his "situation." Such terms encompass more than the physical movements of the potential assailant. As just discussed, these terms include any relevant knowledge the defendant had about that person. They also necessarily bring in the physical attributes of all persons involved, including the defendant. Furthermore, the defendant's circumstances encompass any prior experiences he had which could provide a reasonable basis for a belief that another person's intentions were to injure or rob him or that the use of deadly force was necessary under the circumstances.

Accordingly, a jury should be instructed to consider this type of evidence in weighing the defendant's actions. The jury must first determine whether the defendant had the requisite beliefs under section 35.15, that is, whether he believed deadly force was necessary to avert the imminent use of deadly force or the commission of one of the felonies enumerated therein. If the People do not prove beyond a reasonable doubt that he did not have such beliefs, then the jury must also consider whether these beliefs were reasonable. The jury would have to determine, in light of all the "circumstances," as explicated above, if a reasonable person could have had these beliefs.

The prosecutor's instruction to the second Grand Jury that it had to determine whether, under the circumstances, Goetz's conduct was that of a reasonable man in his situation was thus essentially an accurate charge. . .

Accordingly, the order of the Appellate Division should be reversed, and the dismissed counts of the indictment reinstated.

DISCUSSION QUESTIONS

1. Did Goetz have a reasonable fear of being robbed at the moment he fired the first shot? Assume that the youths were actually going to rob Goetz. At what point in time could he have reasonably used deadly force? Must he wait until he threaten them or begin using force against him? Should he have to warn them first?

2. Does it matter that Goetz has been mugged on the subway before? Should it? Should the race of the muggers matter?

3. The opinion does not mention race. Goetz was white, and the youths were all people of color. Do you think racial fear played a role in his conduct? How should the law of self defense deal with racial fear?

Practice Problem 20.1: Hating History

James is a slightly built African American man whose African American teenage son Bernard calls him in terror late one Friday night, telling him that some white youths are after him and threatening to kill him over a misunderstanding about his relationship with a white teenage girl. James tells Bernard to come straight home. James then arms himself with a pistol and stands on the front porch of his house. Bernard pulls his car into the driveway, and James tells Bernard to go inside. Within seconds another car pulls up to the bottom of James's driveway with its headlights illuminating James as he stands on the porch. Three obviously intoxicated white teenagers jump out of the car and start screaming for Bernard to come out. James advances to the end of his driveway with the gun in his hand—but pointed at the ground—telling the youths to leave him and his family alone. The youths scream profanities and racial epithets at James who returns them in kind. A standoff ensues with James standing at the bottom of his driveway and the youths standing on the sidewalk. The youths taunt James about the gun telling him that it won't do him any good. James tells them that they better leave if they know what is good for them. Steven, the oldest and largest of the four teens, steps up right in front of James and tells him "we are going to f---k up that son of yours." James points the gun at Steven's head, and Steven slaps or grabs at the gun with his long arms. The gun fires, killing Steven.

James is on trial for murder and manslaughter. He claims that he did not intentionally pull the trigger but that the gun went off because of the contact with Steven's hand. James also wishes to introduce the following evidence in support of a claim of self defense and defense of others. James was very close to his grandfather, who was forced to leave the deep south with his family as a child after a murderous attack by members of the Ku Klux Klan. James grew up hearing his grandfather tell stories of that attack. He specifically remembers his grandfather telling him how the klansmen had pulled their cars up to the front of his grandfather's house blinding everyone inside with their headlights before the attack. James has always lived with a fear of racial violence by whites against his family even though he lives in a racially integrated neighborhood. He also maintains that when he was illuminated with the headlights of the youths' car he became convinced that his life and the lives of his family were in imminent danger. You are the trial judge. The prosecution has moved to exclude James's grandfather's story on grounds of relevance. What is your ruling on the prosecution's motion to exclude?

4. SUBJECTIVE REASONABLENESS AS A STANDARD FOR AN EXCUSE

"I'm pretty much not afraid of anything. Except clowns. . . I'm
not really sure where the fear comes from. My mother
says it's because when I was a kid I found a dead
clown in the woods. But who knows."

—Phil Dunphy, *Modern Family*

A few courts go even farther and incorporate even more subjective factors. Such courts tell juries to see things from the defendant's perspective, and that perspective includes more of the defendant's individual characteristics. Under such a standard, a person who was the victim of and witness to extensive abuse as a child would be held to a different (and probably lower) standard than one who had never suffered violence. In the hands of these courts, the "reasonable person" standard would become the "reasonable person who had been violently abuse as a child" standard.

Granted, the line between of these two approaches may seem thin. Under the first approach, the alley rape of the woman leaving the bar would be taken into account but the prior child abuse of the second defendant would not be. The difference is that the woman in the first hypo finds herself once again vulnerable to attack in a dark alley, which makes her past experience relevant to our assessment to the reasonableness of her fear in the current case. The child abuse of the second defendant would not ordinarily be considered relevant to the reasonableness of his fears as an adult, even though the fearfulness of his early childhood might have stayed within throughout his adult life.

Many have noted that as a jurisdiction allows the reasonable person standard to become more individualized, self-defense becomes more of an excuse rather than a justification. For instance, imagine that Phil Dunphy punches a circus clown who gets too close to him during a birthday party. Since society does not consider clowns to be dangerous or "clown fear" to be reasonable, such an act is not something that society can approve of or tolerate. The rationale for incorporating Phil Dunphy's fear of clowns into the reasonable person standard is to excuse him for his unjustified use of force out of sympathy and understanding for the childhood trauma that created his irrational fear.

One difficulty with excusing people for using force on such a basis, however, is finding a principle upon which one can distinguish good unreasonable fears from bad ones. What if the fearful defendant had been traumatized as a child not by a clown but by someone of a different race? Transforming self-defense from a justification into an excuse also removes an important incentive for people to master the fears that society does not find to be reasonable. It also subjects the sources of those fears to force that is considered unreasonable by society in general. Clowns are people, too!

All courts, however, draw a line against what the MPC might call "morally idiosyncratic" beliefs or traits. Someone excessively fearful of people of other races, for instance, would not be entitled to a "reasonable racist person" standard because "reasonable racism" would be considered a contradiction in terms.

Most courts draw the line against incorporating the personal characteristics of the defendant into the reasonable person standard because doing so makes the reasonable person standard too subjective. We all have our fears, but the criminal law requires us to master our irrational ones. The Model Penal Code goes as far as to instruct jurors to assess reasonableness from the point of view of a person "in the actor's situation," but leaves it up to the jury to decide exactly what that should include.

Case in Context

The next case introduces gender into the mix of factors to be assessed in determining the reasonableness of one's fear.

STATE V. WANROW

Supreme Court of Washington, En Banc
88 Wash.2d 221 (1977)

UTTER, ASSOCIATE JUDGE.

Yvonne Wanrow was convicted by a jury of second-degree murder and first-degree assault. She appealed her conviction to the Court of Appeals. The Court of Appeals reversed and remanded the case. . . We granted review and affirm the Court of Appeals.

We order a reversal of the conviction on two grounds. The first is the ground stated by the Court of Appeals regarding the erroneous admission of the tape recording. The second ground is error committed by the trial court in improperly instructing the jury on the law of self-defense as it related to the defendant.

On the afternoon of August 11, 1972, defendant's (respondent's) two children were staying at the home of Ms. Hooper, a friend of defendant. Defendant's son was playing in the neighborhood and came back to Ms. Hooper's house and told her that a man tried to pull him off his bicycle and drag him into a house. Some months earlier, Ms. Hooper's 7-year-old daughter had developed a rash on her body which was diagnosed as venereal disease. Ms. Hooper had been unable to persuade her daughter to tell her who had molested her. It was not until the night of the shooting that Ms. Hooper discovered it was William Wesler (decedent) who allegedly had violated her daughter. A few minutes after the defendant's son related his story to Ms. Hooper about the man who tried to detain him, Mr. Wesler appeared on the porch of the Hooper house and stated through the door, "I didn't touch the kid, I didn't touch the kid." At that moment, the Hooper girl, seeing Wesler at the door, indicated to her mother that Wesler was the man who had molested her. Joseph Fah, Ms. Hooper's landlord, saw Wesler as he was leaving and informed Shirley Hooper that Wesler had tried to molest a young boy who had earlier lived in the same house, and that Wesler had previously been committed to the Eastern State Hospital for the mentally ill. Immediately after this revelation from Mr. Fah, Ms. Hooper called the police who, upon their arrival at the Hooper residence, were informed of all the events which had transpired that day. Ms. Hooper requested that Wesler be arrested then and there, but the police stated, "We can't, until Monday morning." Ms. Hooper was urged by the police officer to go to the police station Monday morning and "swear out a warrant." Ms. Hooper's landlord, who was present during the conversation, suggested that Ms. Hooper get a baseball bat located at the corner of the house and "conk him over the head" should Wesler try to enter the house uninvited during the weekend. To this suggestion, the policeman replied, "Yes, but wait until he gets in the house." (A week before this incident Shirley Hooper had noticed someone prowling around her house at night. Two days before the shooting someone had attempted to get into Ms.

Hooper's bedroom and had slashed the window screen. She suspected that such person was Wesler.)

That evening, Ms. Hooper called the defendant and asked her to spend the night with her in the Hooper house. At that time she related to Ms. Wanrow the facts we have previously set forth. The defendant arrived sometime after 6 p.m. with a pistol in her handbag. The two women ultimately determined that they were too afraid to stay alone and decided to ask some friends to come over for added protection. The two women then called the defendant's sister and brother-in-law, Angie and Chuck Michel. The four adults did not go to bed that evening, but remained awake talking and watching for any possible prowlers. There were eight young children in the house with them. At around 5 a.m., Chuck Michel, without the knowledge of the women in the house, went to Wesler's house, carrying a baseball bat. Upon arriving at the Wesler residence, Mr. Michel accused Wesler of molesting little children. Mr. Wesler then suggested that they go over to the Hooper residence and get the whole thing straightened out. Another man, one David Kelly, was also present, and together the three men went over to the Hooper house. Mr. Michel and Mr. Kelly remained outside while Wesler entered the residence.

The testimony as to what next took place is considerably less precise. It appears that Wesler, a large man who was visibly intoxicated, entered the home and when told to leave declined to do so. A good deal of shouting and confusion then arose, and a young child, asleep on the couch, awoke crying. The testimony indicates that Wesler then approached this child, stating, "My what a cute little boy," or words to that effect, and that the child's mother, Ms. Michel, stepped between Wesler and the child. By this time Hooper was screaming for Wesler to get out. Ms. Wanrow, a 5-foot 4-inch woman who at the time had a broken leg and was using a crutch, testified that she then went to the front door to enlist the aid of Chuck Michel. She stated that she shouted for him and, upon turning around to reenter the living room, found Wesler standing directly behind her. She testified to being gravely startled by this situation and to having then shot Wesler in what amounted to a reflex action.

After Wesler was shot, Ms. Hooper called the police via a Spokane crime check emergency phone number, stating, "There's a guy broke in, and my girlfriend shot him." The defendant later took the phone and engaged in a conversation with the police operator. The entire conversation was tape recorded.

At trial, over defense counsel's objection, the tape was admitted into evidence. After presentation of the evidence, the jury was instructed on the law and commenced deliberations. Deliberations progressed for a time, and the jurors requested to hear the tape again. The request was granted. Not long after reviewing the tape, the jury reached its verdict of guilty as to both counts. . .

[The court concludes that the tape recording should not have been admitted into evidence.]

Reversal of respondent's conviction is also required by a second serious error committed by the trial court. Instruction No. 10, setting forth the law of self-defense, incorrectly limited the jury's consideration of acts and circumstances pertinent to respondent's perception of the alleged threat to her person. . .

In the opening paragraph of instruction No. 10, the jury, in evaluating the gravity of the danger to the respondent, was directed to consider only those acts and circumstances occurring "at or immediately before the killing. . ." This is not now, and never has been, the law of self-defense in Washington. On the contrary, the justification of self-defense is to be evaluated in light of all the facts and circumstances known to the defendant, including those known substantially before the killing. . .

The second paragraph of instruction No. 10 contains an equally erroneous and prejudicial statement of the law. That portion of the instruction reads:

> However, when there is no reasonable ground for the person attacked to believe that his person is in imminent danger of death or great bodily harm, and it appears to him that only an ordinary battery is all that is intended, and all that he has reasonable grounds to fear from his assailant, he has a right to stand his ground and repel such threatened assault, yet he has no right to repel a threatened assault with naked hands, by the use of a deadly weapon in a deadly manner, unless he believes, and has reasonable grounds to believe, that he is in imminent danger of death or great bodily harm.

In our society, women suffer from a conspicuous lack of access to training in and the means of developing those skills necessary to effectively repel a male assailant without resorting to the use of deadly weapons. Instruction No. 12 does indicate that the "relative size and strength of the persons involved" may be considered; however, it does not make clear that the defendant's actions are to be judged against her own subjective impressions and not those which a detached jury might determine to be objectively reasonable. . .

The second paragraph of instruction No. 10 not only establishes an objective standard, but through the persistent use of the masculine gender leaves the jury with the impression the objective standard to be applied is that applicable to an altercation between two men. The impression created—that a 5-foot 4-inch woman with a cast on her leg and using a crutch must, under the law, somehow repel an assault by a 6-foot 2-inch intoxicated man without employing weapons in her defense, unless the jury finds her determination of the degree of danger to be objectively reasonable—constitutes a separate and distinct misstatement of the law and, in the context of this case, violates the respondent's right to equal protection of the law. The respondent was entitled to have the jury consider her actions in the light of her own perceptions of the situation, including those perceptions which were the product of our nation's "long and unfortunate history of sex discrimination." Frontiero v. Richardson, 411 U.S. 677, 684, 36 L. Ed. 2d 583, 93 S. Ct. 1764 (1973). Until such time as the effects of that history are eradicated, care must be taken to assure that our self-defense instructions afford women the right to have their conduct judged in light of the individual physical handicaps which are the product of sex discrimination. To fail to do so is to deny the right of the individual woman involved to trial by the same rules which are applicable to male defendants. The portion of the instruction above quoted misstates our law in creating an objective standard of "reasonableness." It then compounds that error by utilizing language suggesting that the respondent's conduct must be measured against that of a reasonable male individual finding himself in the same circumstances.

We conclude that the instruction here in question contains an improper statement of the law on a vital issue in the case, is inconsistent, misleading, and prejudicial when read in conjunction with other instructions pertaining to the same issue, and therefore is a proper basis for a finding of reversible error. . .

In light of the errors in admission of evidence and instruction of the jury, the decision of the Court of Appeals is affirmed, the conviction reversed, and the case remanded for a new trial.

DISCUSSION QUESTIONS

1.   Putting gender completely aside for a moment but taking size and physical power into account, how reasonable was Wanroe's shooting of Wesler? What alternatives did she have?

2.   Does Wanroe's gender make her shooting of Wesler more reasonable?

3.   Should juries be given guidance about how to factor gender into the reasonableness of one's fear and actions? What should they be told?

C. MODEL PENAL CODE

The Model Penal Code follows the common law approach to self-defense in many respects. The MPC also takes the following positions on the variations among common law jurisdictions discussed earlier.

- A person must retreat if he can safely do so before he uses deadly force.

- An initial aggressor who initially uses non-deadly force regains his right of self-defense if the victim of his initial aggression escalates the conflict from non-deadly to deadly force.

- A person may use force when it is immediately necessary, even if the actual harm feared is not yet imminent.

- The reasonableness of a person's fear is to be judged on the basis of a person in the actor's situation.

These differences have been explained in the sections dealing with reasonableness, imminence, retreat, and initial aggressors. The most important difference between the Model Penal Code and common law jurisdictions deals with actual but unreasonable fears.

1. ACTUAL BUT UNREASONABLE FEARS

An actual but unreasonable fear is a partial defense to criminal liability under the MPC. As discussed earlier, some common law jurisdictions recognize an imperfect form of self-defense in homicide cases that results in not murder but manslaughter liability. The Model Penal Code goes several steps further, applying the concept of imperfect self-defense to all crimes and making distinctions between different degrees of unreasonableness.

Under the MPC, an actor cannot be guilty of a crime requiring purpose or knowledge if he used force out of an actual fear of unlawful harm. If that fear was recklessly formed, however, the actor can be guilty of a crime requiring a reckless state of mind. If the fear was formed with gross negligence, then the actor can be found guilty of a crime requiring gross negligence. The result is a rejection of the all or nothing approach of many common law jurisdictions in favor of an approach that calibrates one's liability to the culpability of one's mental state.

Return to the scenario of the fearful resident who kills the trick-or-treating teenager at his doorstep on Halloween night. Assume the jury accepts that the resident was actually afraid that the masked teenager was a deranged killer. If the jury concludes that the resident was criminally (grossly) negligent in not realizing that the teenager was a harmless trick-or-treater, then the jury can find the resident guilty of negligent homicide. If the jury concludes that the resident consciously disregarded a substantial and unjustifiable risk that the teenager was harmless, then the jury could find the resident guilty of reckless homicide (manslaughter under the MPC). If the jury concludes that the resident was so reckless as to be extremely indifferent to human life, then they could find him guilty of extremely reckless murder under the MPC.

Therefore, instead of facing the all or nothing choice between a conviction for murder and a not guilty verdict, the MPC permits the jury to convict the defendant of a crime that matches how unreasonable his fear was.

D. IMMINENCE OF HARM

Timing is everything in self-defense. You cannot use force against harms that took place in the past or that will not occur in the immediate future.

In the movie "Pulp Fiction," John Travolta's and Samuel Jackson's characters survive a fusillade of bullets from an attacker. Their attacker empties his gun, and they can clearly hear it clicking as he pulls the trigger again and again after he is out of bullets. All his bullets missed. After Travolta and Jackson's characters exchange a momentary look of surprise they shoot their attacker dead. Their use of force is clearly not self-defense but simple retaliation because the harm is past, not imminent.

The more difficult issue is how close a future harm must be to justify defensive force. Generally, we don't want people to act rashly and engage in unnecessary violence, yet we also don't want them to have to wait until it is too late to avoid injury. Forcing lawful defenders to absorb the first blow in a fight might put them at a disadvantage from which they might never recover.

While imminence does not require you to wait until an attack begins, it does preclude responding with force to an attack that is not going to happen right now. The farther in the future the threatened harm the greater the possibility that it will never happen or that you have some reasonable recourse other than violence. Having someone tell you that they are going to kill you the next time they see you clearly does not justify using defensive force that very moment. It might justify using it the very next time you see them, although, if you have not sought the police in the interim, the finder of fact may wonder whether you believed the initial threat was real. Even having an irate fan tell you during the seventh inning stretch of a baseball game that they are going to beat you up after the game does not justify hitting them preemptively. Especially given how slow baseball games can be! Somewhere between the next inning and the next pitch, however, things get murky and imminence becomes a jury question.

1. IMMEDIACY VS. NECESSITY

What if someone threatens you in the future, but your only chance to respond to the threat comes long before that? Fans of the book and movie *The Princess Bride* may think of this as the "Dread Pirate Roberts" problem. Every night for a number of years, the Dread Pirate Roberts told Wesley, his cabin boy, "Good night, Wesley, nice work today, I'll most likely kill you in the morning." Now imagine that Wesley could have easily killed Roberts in his sleep, but that he was no match for Roberts once he was awake. Does Wesley have to wait until the harm is imminent, or does the necessity of imminent action satisfy the requirement? It seems unfair and unwise to force Wesley to let sleeping pirates lie, although Roberts never followed through on his threat and eventually groomed Wesley to be his replacement.

This fanciful example illustrates a real issue that arises in a number of contexts. A hostage whose life is being held for ransom would be justified in killing his captor long before the ransom was due if it seemed to be the only way to avoid being killed. The necessity of taking immediate action would justify not waiting until the actual harm was more imminent. This only works because the ransom makes the prospect of death sufficiently likely and the captivity of the hostage rules out obtaining help from the police. A far more controversial application of this same principle involves a battered spouse who effectively believes herself to be hostage to her batterer. This specific issue will be discussed along with other domestic violence issues below.

Some jurisdictions (including those that follow the Model Penal Code) deal with this issue by requiring that the use of force be only immediately necessary instead of requiring that the harm be imminent. Such a standard allows the hostage, and in some cases the battered spouse, to use force more pre-emptively than they might be able to under a strict interpretation of imminence.

E. DOMESTIC VIOLENCE AND SYNDROME EVIDENCE

Domestic violence has raised difficult issues for self-defense doctrine. The most common scenario involves women who kill the husbands and boyfriends who batter and abuse them. Such killings can be divided up into two categories: confrontational and non-confrontational homicides.

Confrontational homicides occur when the woman kills while she is being assaulted or just before she believes she is going to be assaulted. These killings can usually be analyzed under ordinary self-defense principles. Evidence of the man's prior violence against the woman is ordinarily admitted to establish that the woman's fear on this occasion was a reasonable one.

The more difficult self-defense issues arise in the relatively rare non-confrontational homicide cases. In these cases, women kill their batterers during a lull in the violence or sometimes even while their batterers are asleep. Ordinarily, nothing could seem less imminent than an attack from someone who is asleep and nothing less necessary than killing him instead of calling the police.

Self-defense cases involving actors who suffer from a syndrome are great subjects for policy-oriented exam questions. Post-traumatic stress syndrome based on military service, early child abuse, or sexual assault are three subjects that raise interesting and difficult questions.

Case in Context

The non-confrontational homicide in the following case involved battered spouse syndrome evidence.

STATE OF NORTH CAROLINA V. JUDY ANN LAWS NORMAN

Supreme Court of North Carolina
324 N.C. 253 (1989)

Opinion by: MITCHELL.

The Court of Appeals granted a new trial, citing as error the trial court's refusal to submit a possible verdict of acquittal by reason of self-defense. Notwithstanding the uncontroverted evidence that the defendant shot her husband three times in the back of the head as he lay sleeping in his bed, the Court of Appeals held that the defendant's evidence that she exhibited what has come to be called "the battered wife syndrome" entitled her to have the jury consider whether the homicide was an act of self-defense and, thus, not a legal wrong.

We conclude that the evidence introduced in this case would not support a finding that the defendant killed her husband due to a reasonable fear of imminent death or great bodily harm, as is required before a defendant is entitled to jury instructions concerning self-defense. Therefore, the trial court properly declined to instruct the jury on the law relating to self-defense. Accordingly, we reverse the Court of Appeals.

The right to kill in self-defense is based on the necessity, real or reasonably apparent, of killing an unlawful aggressor to save oneself from imminent death or great bodily harm at his hands. State v. Gappins, 320 N.C. 64, 357 S.E. 2d 654 (1987). Our law has recognized that self-preservation under such circumstances springs from a primal impulse and is an inherent right of natural law.

The killing of another human being is the most extreme recourse to our inherent right of self-preservation and can be justified in law only by the utmost real or apparent necessity brought about by the decedent. For that reason, our law of self-defense has required that a defendant claiming that a homicide was justified and, as a result, inherently lawful by reason of perfect self-defense must establish that she reasonably believed at the time of the killing she otherwise would have immediately suffered death or great bodily harm. Only if defendants are required to show that they killed due to a reasonable belief that death or great bodily harm was imminent can the justification for homicide remain clearly and firmly rooted in necessity. The imminence requirement ensures that deadly force will be used only where it is necessary as a last resort in the exercise of the inherent right of self-preservation.

The term "imminent," as used to describe such perceived threats of death or great bodily harm as will justify a homicide by reason of perfect self-defense, has been defined as "immediate danger, such as must be instantly met, such as cannot be guarded against by calling for the assistance of others or the protection of the law." Black's Law Dictionary 676 (5th ed. 1979).

The evidence in this case did not tend to show that the defendant reasonably believed that she was confronted by a threat of imminent death or great bodily harm. The evidence tended to show that no harm was "imminent" or about to happen to the defendant when she shot her husband. The uncontroverted evidence was that her husband had been asleep for some time when she walked to her mother's house, returned with the pistol, fixed the pistol after it jammed and then shot her husband three times in the back of the head. The defendant was not faced with an instantaneous choice between killing her husband or being killed or seriously injured. Instead, all of the evidence tended to show that the defendant had ample time and opportunity to resort to other means of preventing further abuse by her husband.

Additionally, the lack of any belief by the defendant—reasonable or otherwise—that she faced a threat of imminent death or great bodily harm from the drunk and sleeping victim in the present case was illustrated by her own expert witnesses when testifying about her subjective assessment of her situation at the time of the killing.

Dr. Tyson testified that the defendant "believed herself to be doomed. . . to a life of the worst kind of torture and abuse, degradation that she had experienced over the years in a progressive way; that it would only get worse, and that death was inevitable." Such evidence of the defendant's speculative beliefs concerning her remote and indefinite future, while indicating she had felt generally threatened, did not tend to show that she killed in the belief—reasonable or otherwise—that her husband presented a threat of imminent death or great bodily harm.

We are not persuaded by the reasoning of our Court of Appeals in this case that when there is evidence of battered wife syndrome, neither an actual attack nor threat of attack by the husband at the moment the wife uses deadly force is required to justify the wife's killing of him in perfect self-defense. The Court of Appeals concluded that to impose such requirements would ignore the "learned helplessness," meekness and other realities of battered wife syndrome and would effectively preclude such women from exercising their right of self-defense. 89 N.C. App. 384, 392–393, 366 S.E. 2d 586, 591–592 (1988). See Mather, The Skeleton in the Closet: The Battered Woman Syndrome, Self-Defense, and Expert Testimony, 39 Mercer L. Rev. 545 (1988); Eber, The Battered Wife's Dilemma: To Kill Or To Be Killed, 32 Hastings L.J. 895 (1981). Other jurisdictions which have addressed this question under similar facts are divided in their views, and we can discern no clear majority position on facts closely similar to those of this case.

[S]tretching the law of self-defense to fit the facts of this case would require changing the "imminent death or great bodily harm" requirement to something substantially more indefinite than previously required and would weaken our assurances that justification for the taking of human life remains firmly rooted in real or apparent necessity. That result in principle could not be limited to a few cases decided on evidence as poignant as this. The relaxed requirements proposed by our Court of Appeals would tend to categorically legalize the opportune killing of abusive husbands by their wives solely on the basis of the wives' testimony concerning their subjective speculation as to the probability of future felonious assaults by their husbands. Homicidal self-help would then become a lawful solution, and perhaps the easiest and most effective solution, to this problem.

Reversed.

Dissent by: MARTIN.

JUSTICE MARTIN dissenting.

At the outset it is to be noted that the peril of fabricated evidence is not unique to the trials of battered wives who kill. The possibility of invented evidence arises in all cases in which a party is seeking the benefit of self-defense. Moreover, in this case there were a number of witnesses other than defendant who testified as to the actual presence of circumstances supporting a claim of self-defense. This record contains no reasonable basis to attack the credibility of evidence for the defendant.

Defendant does not seek to expand or relax the requirements of self-defense and thereby "legalize the opportune killing of allegedly abusive husbands by their wives," as the majority overstates. Rather, defendant contends that the evidence as gauged by the existing laws of self-defense is sufficient to require the submission of a self-defense instruction to the jury. The proper issue for this Court is to determine whether the evidence, viewed in the light most favorable to the defendant, was sufficient to require the trial court to instruct on the law of self-defense. I conclude that it was.

Evidence presented by defendant described a twenty-year history of beatings and other dehumanizing and degrading treatment by her husband. In his expert testimony a clinical psychologist concluded that defendant fit "and exceed[ed]" the profile of an abused or battered spouse, analogizing this treatment to the dehumanization process suffered by prisoners of war under the Nazis during the Second World War and the brainwashing techniques of the Korean War. The psychologist described the defendant as a woman incarcerated by abuse, by fear, and by her conviction that her husband was invincible and inescapable:

This, in fact, is a state of mind common to the battered spouse, and one that dramatically distinguishes Judy Norman's belief in the imminence of serious harm from that asserted by [defendants in other cases] For the battered wife, if there is no escape, if there is no window of relief or momentary sense of safety, then the next attack, which could be the fatal one, is imminent. In the context of the doctrine of self-defense, "imminent" is a term the meaning of which must be grasped from the defendant's point of view. Properly stated, the question is not whether the threat was in fact imminent, but whether defendant's belief in the impending nature of the threat, given the circumstances as she saw them, was reasonable in the mind of a person of ordinary firmness.

Defendant's intense fear evident in the testimony of witnesses who recounted events of the last three days of the decedent's life could have led a juror to conclude that defendant reasonably perceived a threat to her life as "imminent," even while her husband slept.

In State v. Wingler, 184 N.C. 747, 115 S.E. 59 (1922), in which the defendant was found guilty for the murder of his wife, Justice Stacy recognized the pain and oppression under which a woman suffers at the hands of an abusive husband: "The supreme tragedy of life is the immolation of woman. With a heavy hand, nature exacts from her a high tax of blood and tears." Id. at 751, 115 S.E. at 61. By his barbaric conduct over the course of twenty years, J. T. Norman reduced the quality of the defendant's life to such an abysmal state that, given the opportunity to do so, the jury might well have found that she was justified in acting in self-defense for the preservation of her tragic life.

In both of these types of cases, battered spouse syndrome evidence has been accepted by some courts to provide the jury with a better understanding of how the principles of reasonable fear, imminence, and necessity should be applied to such violence. Battered spouse syndrome is a complex phenomenon, but generally describes a state of learned helplessness in which the battered woman feels that her abuser is all powerful. Expert evidence in this area also usually describes a cycle of violence with distinct phases that involves a buildup of tension followed by battering. Cycle of violence testimony can help woman establish that they reasonably believed violence was imminent because of the telltale signs of building tension. The learned helplessness testimony explains to the juror why a battered woman reasonably might believe that no one can help her and that her only chance of defending herself against her spouse is through a pre-emptive attack before he assaults her or in extreme cases when he is asleep. Such evidence is used in different ways in different jurisdictions and remains controversial when used in non-confrontational homicides.

DISCUSSION QUESTIONS

1.   Should a self defense instruction be given in a case of non-confrontational homicide? When the victim is asleep?

2.   Should battered spouse syndrome evidence be admitted in self defense cases?

3.   Battered spouse syndrome evidence aside, can you come up with a principle for determining which syndromes should and shouldn't be considered in self defense cases?

Case in Context

The jurisdiction in the next case follows the Model Penal Code's approach to self defense and takes a different position on battered spouse syndrome evidence.

STATE OF NORTH DAKOTA V. JANICE LEIDHOLM

Supreme Court of North Dakota
334 N.W.2d 811 (1983)

Opinion by: VANDEWALLE.

Janice Leidholm was charged with murder for the stabbing death of her husband, Chester Leidholm, in the early morning hours of August 7, 1981, at their farm home near Washburn. She was found guilty by a McLean County jury of manslaughter and was sentenced to five years' imprisonment in the State Penitentiary with three years of the sentence suspended. Leidholm appealed from the judgment of conviction. We reverse and remand the case for a new trial.

I

According to the testimony, the Leidholm marriage relationship in the end was an unhappy one, filled with a mixture of alcohol abuse, moments of kindness toward one another, and moments of violence. The alcohol abuse and violence was exhibited by both parties on the night of Chester's death.

Early in the evening of August 6, 1981, Chester and Janice attended a gun club party in the city of Washburn where they both consumed a large amount of alcohol. On the return trip to the farm, an argument developed between Janice and Chester which continued after their arrival home just after midnight. Once inside the home, the arguing did not stop; Chester was shouting, and Janice was crying.

A Breathalyzer test administered to Janice shortly after the stabbing, at approximately 3:30 a.m., showed her blood-alcohol content was .17 of 1 percent. The analysis of a blood sample from Chester showed his blood-alcohol content was .23 of 1 percent.

At one point in the fighting, Janice tried to telephone Dave Vollan, a deputy sheriff of McLean County, but Chester prevented her from using the phone by shoving her away and pushing her down. At another point, the argument moved outside the house, and Chester once again was pushing Janice to the ground. Each time Janice attempted to get up, Chester would push her back again.

A short time later, Janice and Chester re-entered their home and went to bed. When Chester fell asleep, Janice got out of bed, went to the kitchen, and got a butcher knife. She then went back into the bedroom and stabbed Chester. In a matter of minutes Chester died from shock and loss of blood.

II

The first, and controlling, issue we consider is whether or not the trial court correctly instructed the jury on self-defense. Our resolution of the issue must of necessity begin with an explanation of the basic operation of the law of self-defense as set forth in Chapter 12.1–05 of the North Dakota Century Code.

[12.1–05.03. Self Defense. A Person is justified in using force upon another person to defend himself against danger of imminent unlawful bodily injury. . .

12.1–05.07. Limits on the use of force—excessive force—Deadly force

1.   A person is not justified in using more force than is necessary and appropriate under the circumstances.

2.   Deadly force is justified. . . .

b.   When it is used in lawful self-defense, or in lawful defense of others, if such force is necessary to protect the actor or anyone else against death, serious bodily injury, of the commission of a felony involving violence. The use of deadly force is not justified if it can be avoided, with safety to the actors and others, by retreat or other conduct involving minimal interference with the freedom of the person menaced. . .but. . . (2) no person is required to retreat from his dwelling or place of work unless he was the original aggressor or is assailed by a person who he knows also dwells or works there.]

Conduct which constitutes self-defense may be either justified [Section 12.1–05–03, N.D.C.C.] or excused [Section 12.1–05–08, N.D.C.C.]. Although the distinction between justification and excuse may appear to be theoretical and without significant practical consequence, because the distinction has been made in our criminal statutes we believe a general explanation of the difference between the two concepts—even though it requires us to venture briefly into the pathway of academicism—is warranted.

A defense of justification is the product of society's determination that the actual existence of certain circumstances will operate to make proper and legal what otherwise would be criminal conduct. A defense of excuse, contrarily, does not make legal and proper conduct which ordinarily would result in criminal liability; instead, it openly recognizes the criminality of the conduct but excuses it because the actor believed that circumstances actually existed which would justify his conduct when in fact they did not.

In short, had the facts been as he supposed them to be, the actor's conduct would have been justified rather than excused.

In the context of self-defense, this means that a person who believes that the force he uses is necessary to prevent imminent unlawful harm is justified in using such force if his belief is a correct belief; that is to say, if his belief corresponds with what actually is the case. If, on the other hand, a person reasonably but incorrectly believes that the force he uses is necessary to protect himself against imminent harm, his use of force is excused.

The distinction is arguably superfluous because whether a person's belief is correct and his conduct justified, or whether it is merely reasonable and his conduct excused, the end result is the same, namely, the person avoids punishment for his conduct. Furthermore, because a correct belief corresponds with an actual state of affairs, it will always be a reasonable belief; but a reasonable belief will not always be a correct belief, viz., a person may reasonably believe what is not actually the case. Therefore, the decisive issue under our law of self-defense is not whether a person's beliefs are correct, but rather whether they are reasonable and thereby excused or justified.

For example, a person may reasonably, but mistakenly, believe that a gun held by an assailant is loaded.

Section 12.1–05–08, N.D.C.C., which sets forth the general conditions that excuse a person's conduct, states:

> "A person's conduct is excused if he believes that the facts are such that his conduct is necessary and appropriate for any of the purposes which would establish a justification or excuse under this chapter, even though his belief is mistaken. However, if his belief is negligently or recklessly held [i.e., unreasonably], it is not an excuse in a prosecution for an offense for which negligence or recklessness, as the case may be, suffices to establish culpability. Excuse under this section is a defense or affirmative defense according to which type of defense would be established had the facts been as the person believed them to be."

The first sentence of Section 12.1–05–08, N.D.C.C., in combination with Section 12.1–05–03, N.D.C.C., which contains the kernel statement of self-defense, yields the following expanded proposition: A person's conduct is excused if he believes that the use of force upon another person is necessary and appropriate to defend himself against danger of imminent unlawful harm, even though his belief is mistaken. Thus we have a statement of the first element of self-defense, i.e., a person must actually and sincerely believe that the conditions exist which give rise to a claim of self-defense.

If the danger against which a person uses force to defend himself is "death, serious bodily injury, or the commission of a felony involving violence," the person may use deadly force [Section 12.1–05–07, N.D.C.C.], which is defined as that force "which a person uses with the intent of causing, or which he knows creates a substantial risk of causing, death or serious bodily injury." Sec. 12.1–05–12(2), N.D.C.C.

From the next sentence of Section 12.1–05–08 we may infer that, besides being actual and sincere, a person's belief that the use of force is necessary to protect himself against imminent unlawful harm must be reasonable. Here, we have the second element of self-defense, namely, a person must reasonably believe that circumstances exist which permit him to use defensive force.

If, therefore, a person has an actual and reasonable belief that force is necessary to protect himself against danger of imminent unlawful harm, his conduct is justified or excused. . . . If, on the other hand, a person's actual belief in the necessity of using force to prevent imminent unlawful harm is unreasonable, his conduct will not be justified or excused. . . . Instead, he will be guilty of an offense for which negligence or recklessness suffices to establish culpability. See Sec. 12.1–05–08, N.D.C.C. For example, if a person recklessly believes that the use of force upon another person is necessary to protect himself against unlawful imminent serious bodily injury and the force he uses causes the death of the other person, he is guilty of manslaughter. . . . And if a person's belief is negligent in the same regard, he is guilty of negligent homicide.

Under both approaches, if a person reasonably believes self-defense is necessary, his conduct is excused or justified. And even though under our view an unreasonable belief may result in a conviction for either manslaughter or negligent homicide, and under theirs an unreasonable belief may result only in a conviction for manslaughter, they are the same to the extent that an honest but unreasonable belief will never result in a conviction for murder.

It must remain clear that once the factfinder determines under a claim of self-defense that the actor honestly and sincerely held the belief that the use of defensive force was required to protect himself against imminent unlawful injury, the actor may not be convicted of more than a crime of recklessness or negligence; but, if the factfinder determines, to the contrary, that the actor did not honestly and sincerely hold the requisite belief under a claim of self-defense, the actor may not appeal to the doctrine of self-defense to avoid punishment, but will be subject to conviction for the commission of an intentional and knowing crime.

As stated earlier, critical issue which a jury must decide in a case involving a claim of self-defense is whether or not the accused's belief that force is necessary to protect himself against imminent un-lawful harm was reasonable. However, before the jury can make this determination, it must have a standard of reasonableness against which it can measure the accused's belief.

Courts have traditionally distinguished between standards of reasonableness by characterizing them as either "objective" or "subjective." E.g., State v. Simon, 231 Kan. 572, 646 P.2d 1119 (1982). An objective standard of reasonableness requires the factfinder to view the circumstances surrounding the accused at the time he used force from the standpoint of a hypothetical reasonable and prudent person. E.g., Mendoza, supra, 258 N.W.2d at 272. Ordinarily, under such a view, the unique physical and psychological characteristics of the accused are not taken into consideration in judging the reasonableness of the accused's belief.

This is not the case, however, where a subjective standard of reasonableness is employed. See State v. Wanrow, 88 Wash.2d 221, 559 P.2d 548 (1977). Under the subjective standard the issue is not whether the circumstances attending the accused's use of force would be sufficient to create in the mind of a reasonable and prudent person the belief that the use of force is necessary to protect himself against immediate unlawful harm, but rather whether the circumstances are sufficient to induce in the accused an honest and reasonable belief that he must use force to defend himself against imminent harm.

Neither Section 12.1–05–03, N.D.C.C., nor Section 12.1–05–08, N.D.C.C., explicitly states the viewpoint which the factfinder should assume in assessing the reasonableness of an accused's belief. Moreover, this court has not yet decided the issue of whether Sections 12.1–05–03 and 12.1–05–08 should be construed as requiring an objective or subjective standard to measure the reasonableness of an accused's belief under a claim of self-defense. Finally, the legislative history of our self-defense statutes, as well as the commentaries to the codified criminal statutes which form the basis of the North Dakota Criminal Code, give no indication of a preference for an objective standard of reasonableness over a subjective standard, or vice versa.

Because (1) the law of self-defense as developed in past decisions of this court has been interpreted to require the use of a subjective standard of reasonableness, and (2) we agree with the court in Hazlett that a subjective standard is the more just, and (3) our current law of self-defense as codified in Sections 12.1–05–03, 12.1–05–07, and 12.1–05–08 does not require a contrary conclusion, that is to say, our current law of self-defense is consistent with either a subjective or objective standard, we now decide that the finder of fact must view the circumstances attending an accused's use of force from the standpoint of the accused to determine if they are sufficient to create in the accused's mind an honest and reasonable belief that the use of force is necessary to protect himself from imminent harm.

The practical and logical consequence of this interpretation is that an accused's actions are to be viewed from the standpoint of a person whose mental and physical characteristics are like the accused's and who sees what the accused sees and knows what the accused knows. ... For example, if the accused is a timid, diminutive male, the factfinder must consider these characteristics in assessing the reasonableness of his belief. If, on the other hand, the accused is a strong, courageous, and capable female, the factfinder must consider these characteristics in judging the reasonableness of her belief.

In its statement of the law of self-defense, the trial court instructed the jury:

> "The circumstances under which she acted must have been such as to produce in the mind of reasonably prudent persons, regardless of their sex, similarly situated, the reasonable belief that the other person was then about to kill her or do serious bodily harm to her."

In view of our decision today, the court's instruction was a misstatement of the law of self-defense. A correct statement of the law to be applied in a case of self-defense is: "[A] defendant's conduct is not to be judged by what a reasonably cautious person might or might not do or consider necessary to do under the like circumstances, but what he himself in good faith honestly believed and had reasonable ground to believe was necessary for him to do to protect himself from apprehended death or great bodily injury." Hazlett, supra, 113 N.W. at 380.

The significance of the difference in viewing circumstances from the standpoint of the "defendant alone" rather than from the standpoint of a "reasonably cautious person" is that the jury's consideration of the unique physical and psychological characteristics of an accused allows the jury to judge the reasonableness of the accused's actions against the accused's subjective impressions of the need to use force rather than against those impressions which a jury determines that a hypothetical reasonably cautious person would have under similar circumstances.

Hence, a correct statement of the law of self-defense is one in which the court directs the jury to assume the physical and psychological properties peculiar to the accused, viz., to place itself as best it can in the shoes of the accused, and then decide whether or not the particular circumstances surrounding the accused at the time he used force were sufficient to create in his mind a sincere and reasonable belief that the use of force was necessary to protect himself from imminent and unlawful harm.

Leidholm argued strongly at trial that her stabbing of Chester was done in self-defense and in reaction to the severe mistreatment she received from him over the years. Because the court's instruction in question is an improper statement of the law concerning a vital issue in Leidholm's defense, we conclude it amounts to reversible error requiring a new trial.

DISCUSSION QUESTIONS

1.   Do you think this court's approach to self defense in cases of domestic violence will increase or decrease violence in the home? Will it make life better or worse for battered spouses?

2.   Do you prefer the Model Penal Code's approach to defining the reasonable fear element or the common law's?

3.   In what ways does the Model Penal Code give a prosecutor and a jury more options in self defense homicide cases than under the common law's approach? Which is better?

F. NECESSITY OF FORCE

One may not use force in the face of an imminent harm if one does not have to. Returning to the seventh inning stretch scenario described above, imagine that the enraged fan who threatens to beat you up after the game is an intoxicated, elderly, and somewhat infirm person. After the game, while you are standing next to each other and hemmed in on all sides by the fans standing around you, he throws a punch at you. He is so slow, though, that you easily duck the punch. Now visibly out of breath, he takes a second, slower swing, but you easily duck that punch, too. He is now even more out of breath, and you see the police approaching him from behind. As he begins a third, even slower swing, you punch him right in the face, knocking him down. Now you shouldn't feel very good about yourself (even if he is a Yankees fan), but you will feel even worse when the police officer (who has been going to law school at night and read this book) arrests you for misdemeanor battery. You don't have a valid claim of self-defense, even though you reasonably feared an imminent harm, because your use of force was not necessary. You could have easily ducked the third punch, and the police were about to grab him, so your punch was not necessary.

This necessity requirement makes sense if you remember that self-defense legalizes violence, something that the criminal law generally forbids and tries to reduce. So, self-defense limits a person to using only what force is necessary, even though that person faces a wrongful, unlawful attack. You don't "get to hit the old man" just because he swung at you. We don't want you hitting people just because they made you mad, even if the other person "has it coming to them," in society's view. Instead, we want you to report that person to the police and have them prosecuted. That way, private violence goes down, not up. Self-defense is not a license for righteous retaliation. It is an exception to the criminal law's general prohibition on violence, narrowly drawn to keep violence to a minimum while allowing the righteous to do what is necessary to protect themselves.

Exam Tip: Reading Fact Patterns Carefully

I imagined the above scenario in the crowded stands of a major league baseball game because I wanted to avoid dealing with the issue of retreat. If you imagine yourself hemmed in by people in the seats around you, then running away is not an option (although ducking clearly was). The reason I wrote a possible retreat out of the problem was to isolate the general requirement of necessity from the particular sub-issue of retreat, or "stand your ground." I draw attention to this not to show you how clever I am (although it was a little clever, wasn't it?) but to demonstrate a big part of how law school professors write their questions.

Law professors create fact patterns specifically to raise some issues and to exclude others. This is important because it makes a difference as to how we grade your answers. If you write on and on about whether a duty of retreat exists and what the scope of that duty would be, you probably would not be earning any points because this fact pattern was written to exclude that issue. Instead, you should briefly describe why retreat was not an option to show me that you did consider the issue before writing about necessity—the issue that I wrote into the problem.

G. STAND YOUR GROUND AND THE DUTY TO RETREAT

So what if you weren't hemmed in by people all around you in the baseball problem described above? Do you have to run away from the old man rather than hit him? Or let's make things a little more dramatic. Imagine that you see your former college roommate at your 60 year college reunion. He hated you then, and he hates you still. After you have been arguing for a while about old slights, he grabs a sharp carving knife from the meat tray at the buffet and screams that he is going to kill you. Time has not been kind to him, however, because he is now wheelchair bound. He begins to wheel quickly toward you, waiving the carving knife. As luck would have it, you have kept in pretty good shape and just won the 100, 400, and 800 meter races in your state's "Senior Olympics." As luck would also have it, you are lawfully carrying a concealed handgun. Can you shoot him dead, or do you have to run away?

Applying the principle of necessity, it would seem that self-defense law should require you to "retreat" in both instances even though you did nothing wrong and face a wrongful aggressor. This in fact was the position that the early common law took. One had to "retreat to the wall" before using deadly force.

American jurisdictions have always taken a different view. Retreat was considered ignominious and dishonorable. No jurisdiction requires one to retreat in the face of an imminent, wrongful harm before using non-deadly force. So, even if you could run away from the elderly intoxicated baseball fan, you don't have to in any jurisdiction because the punch you threw is not ordinarily considered deadly force. A majority of jurisdictions do not even require you to retreat before using deadly force. You could shoot your knife-wielding former roommate as he wheels towards you in his wheel chair. In these jurisdictions, requiring retreat is considered to be inflicting a second wrong on the wronged party. Why should you have to run away from your hateful former roommate when you did nothing wrong?

A minority of jurisdiction (including the Model Penal Code) require you to retreat before using deadly force only if you can safely do so. You could be prosecuted for murder if you shot your former roommate instead of running away from him. These jurisdictions reason that even the life of a wrongful aggressor is worth sparing, and a safe retreat by an innocent victim of aggression is not too big a price to pay for avoiding an unnecessary loss of life.

It bears emphasis that only a minority of American jurisdictions ever required retreat under any circumstances, and that no jurisdictions have ever required someone to endanger themselves by retreating. (This is why I made you a track star in the hypo above so that there would be no doubt that you could safely get away if you wanted to.) Furthermore, you must be aware of your safe avenue of retreat for the obligation to exist. Retreat, then, is usually not an issue if you are facing a gun because no one can safely outrun a bullet.

A number of states have recently passed "Stand Your Ground" laws eliminating any obligation to retreat and sometimes expanding one's right to stand one's ground, so one might be forgiven for assuming that most jurisdictions previously required retreat. In some cases, these new laws expanded the right to stand your ground and not retreat by creating pretrial hearings at which one's immunity from civil and criminal prosecution on self-defense grounds could be established.

1. THE CASTLE EXCEPTION

Your home is your castle, and no one has to run out of their castle. Even the minority of jurisdictions that require you retreat before using deadly force do not require you to retreat if you are in your own home. Some jurisdictions have broadened this exception to include one's car and one's place of work. What if the person attacking you lives or works with you? While some jurisdictions require retreat before using deadly force against a co-occupant, the recent trend is decidedly in favor of not requiring retreat from the home in cases of domestic violence. (Some of these same jurisdictions require a workplace retreat from a co-worker, though.)

H. PROTECTION OF PROPERTY AND HOME

You can use reasonable force to protect property. This means that you can't use deadly force to protect your property, since human life is considered more valuable than property (even the life of a would-be thief or vandal). So, you can run out and grab someone you see breaking into your car, but you can't shoot them on sight.

What if you grab someone who is breaking into your car, and they start punching you. Can you punch them back? Of course! You are not an initial aggressor because your initial use of force (grabbing them) was legally justified by your right to use reasonable force to protect property. Your auto burglar does not legally get to punch you for grabbing him because he has no right to defend himself against your lawful use of force.

The line between protection of property and protection of self becomes blurry when the property at issue is one's home, however. Depending on the circumstances, a person breaking into one's home may or may not also create a reasonable fear of imminent harm to your safety. Details matter here. If you wake up in the middle of the night to find an intruder looming over your bed holding a knife, all juries would find use of deadly force justified on the grounds that you reasonably feared for your life. If, on the other hand, you discover your no-good-crack-addicted neighbor stealing a bicycle out of your garage one morning, you can't shoot him because these circumstances don't present the same fear of imminent death or serious bodily injury. Many jurisdictions, however, have created a rebuttable presumption of a reasonable fear of serious bodily injury if you confront someone who has broken into your home. If the burglar raised his hands and said "don't shoot," or if he was a clearly unarmed child, the jury might find this presumption to be rebutted, and your use of deadly force would not be lawful self-defense.

Along similar lines, "spring guns" or other lethal traps that expose intruders to death or serious bodily injury are not lawful means of protecting your property. Since they ordinarily operate automatically in your absence, it is not possible for you to claim that you were in reasonable fear at the time, and the death or serious injury involved is not justified by the protection of mere property.

Case in Context

The following case wrestles with the boundaries of the *castle doctrine*.

STATE OF NEW MEXICO V. CECIL BOYETT

Supreme Court of New Mexico
144 N.M. 184 (2008)

Opinion by: PATRICIO M. SERNA.

Defendant Cecil Boyett appeals from his conviction for the first degree murder of Deborah Rhodes (Victim) He alleges that the trial court erred in refusing to instruct the jury on his theory of the case.

I. BACKGROUND

Defendant and Victim had a rancorous history. The enmity that each harbored for the other apparently had its roots in a romantic interest that both had in Renate Wilder (Wilder).

Wilder and Victim were childhood friends who eventually moved in together and started an intimate relationship. Although their romance ended, the two remained close friends, living and working together. Wilder later met Defendant, and the two became romantically involved. Wilder eventually supplanted Victim's presence in her life with that of Defendant. She fired Victim from her bar and gave Victim's former job to Defendant. She ousted Victim from her home with the help of a restraining order and invited Defendant to move in. At one point, Victim discovered the entwined couple near the hot tub behind Wilder's house. Enraged, Victim retrieved a gun from the house and used it to threaten the couple. Disdain developed between Defendant and Victim, and Victim only occasionally returned to Wilder's home after she was forced out.

Following a protracted courtship, Wilder and Defendant planned to marry on February 6, 2004. A few days prior to her wedding, Wilder absconded from the home that she shared with Defendant. She spent that time with Victim and did not tell Defendant where she was or what she was doing. Wondering as to her whereabouts, Defendant engaged in a variety of activities aimed at locating her but was unsuccessful in his attempts; he rightfully suspected that she was with Victim although he was unable, at that time, to confirm his suspicions.

On the afternoon of February 5, 2004, Wilder departed Victim's company to return to her own home but had a car accident along the way. The accident occurred near Victim's residence and, for a variety of reasons, Victim offered to claim responsibility for it. Wilder accepted and departed the scene on foot, walking back to the house that she shared with Defendant. Shortly after Wilder returned to the house, Victim arrived. Victim's visit concluded when Defendant shot her in the head with a .357 revolver from approximately four feet away, but the events leading to that end were disputed at trial.

[The prosecutor argued that Victim arrived at the house to return Wilder's car keys, that Defendant opened the front door, shouted at her to leave, and then immediately shot her.]

Defendant's version of events was quite different. He claimed that Victim came to the house that day intent on killing him to prevent his impending marriage to Wilder. Defendant testified that he heard a loud banging at the front door, grabbed the gun that he kept nearby, and opened the door only to find a furious Victim on the doorstep. Defendant said that he shouted at Victim, telling her to get off his property, but in the process of trying to run her off, he observed her draw the gun that he knew she routinely carried. In fear for his life, Defendant raised his revolver and shot Victim. Defendant asserted that if he had not shot her, she would have fired her gun and fatally wounded him.

Defendant argued that he was not guilty because he acted lawfully in shooting Victim, either in self-defense, defense of another, or defense of habitation.

The trial court concluded that the jury instruction related to defense of habituation did not apply in this case because Defendant did not shoot Victim inside his home.

II. DEFENDANT WAS NOT ENTITLED TO THE REQUESTED JURY INSTRUCTIONS

The trial court denied the defense of habitation instruction based on its conclusion that the defense applies to only those situations in which an intruder is killed within the home. Picking up the torch lit by the trial court, the State now argues that the defense should be limited to situations in which a person forcibly enters a home and is killed while intruding therein. By that argument, the State seeks our endorsement of a bright line rule that would require an intruder to cross the threshold before an occupant's use of force to repel that entry could be justified by defense of habitation. Despite the State's contention, we are unwilling to draw such a bright line.

Defense of habitation has long been recognized in New Mexico. See, e.g., State v. Bailey, 27 N.M. 145, 162–63, 198 P. 529, 534 (1921). It gives a person the right to use lethal force against an intruder when such force is necessary to prevent the commission of a felony in his or her home. Id. at 162, 198 P. at 534; see also UJI 14–5170. The defense is grounded in the theory that "[t]he home is one of the most important institutions of the state, and has ever been regarded as a place where a person has a right to stand his [or her] ground and repel, force by force, to the extent necessary for its protection." State v. Couch, 52 N.M. 127, 134, 193 P.2d 405, 409 (1946) (quoted authority omitted). Ultimately, in every purported defense of habitation, the use of deadly force is justified only if the defendant reasonably believed that the commission of a felony in his or her home was immediately at hand and that it was necessary to kill the intruder to prevent that occurrence.

This Court has refused to extend the defense to situations in which the victim was fleeing from the defendant, Gonzales, 2007 NMSC 59, P 22, 143 N.M. 25, 172 P.3d 162, as well as situations in which the victim had lawfully entered the defendant's home, see State v. Abeyta, 1995 NMSC 52, 120 N.M. 233, 244, 901 P.2d 164, 175 (1995) (abrogated on other grounds by State v. Campos, 1996 NMSC 43, 122 N.M. 148, 921 P.2d 1266). But our courts have never held that entry into the defendant's home is a prerequisite for the defense. On the contrary, the seminal New Mexico case on defense of habitation was clear that, in certain circumstances, it may justify an occupant's use of lethal force against an intruder who is outside the home. Bailey, 27 N.M. at 162, 198 P. at 534.

In addition to providing a defense for the killing of an intruder already inside the defendant's home, Bailey explained that defense of habitation justifies killing an intruder who is assaulting the defendant's home with the intent of reaching its occupants and committing a felony against them. Id. Protecting a defendant's right to prevent forced entry necessitates that the defense apply when an intruder is outside the home but endeavoring to enter it. See id. This interpretation of defense of habitation is supported by Couch, where the defendant fired a shotgun from within his home at an intruder who was outside, pelting the home with rocks. 52 N.M. at 130, 193 P.2d at 406. Prior to the night of the shooting, the defendant's home had repeatedly been broken into, which caused he and his wife to "suffer intensely from apprehension of violence at the hands of the unknown intruder." Id. at 130, 139, 193 P.2d at 406, 412. When the later assault on their home occurred, both the defendant and his wife believed that the attackers were the same people who had previously broken in. Id. at 139, 193 P.2d at 412. This Court concluded that, even though the victim was killed outside the home, the defendant was entitled to an instruction on defense of habitation because he could reasonably have believed that the person attacking it intended to enter and commit violence against the occupants.

The proposition that defense of habitation allows one to kill to prevent an intruder's forced entry is well supported by the law in other jurisdictions and treatises on the subject. See, e.g., People v. Curtis, 30 Cal. App. 4th 1337, 37 Cal.Rptr.2d 304, 318 (Ct. App. 1994) ("Defense of habitation applies where the defendant uses reasonable force to exclude someone he or she reasonably believes is trespassing in, or about to trespass in, his or her home." State v. Avery, 120 S.W.3d 196, 204 (Mo. 2003) (en banc) ("[D]efense of premises. . . authorizes protective acts to be taken. . . at the time when and place where the intruder is seeking to cross the protective barrier of the house." (quoted authority omitted)); State v. Blue, 356 N.C. 79, 565 S.E.2d 133, 139 (N.C. 2002) ("[U]nder the defense of habitation, the defendant's use of force. . . would be justified to prevent the victim's entry. . ." State v. Rye, 375 S.C. 119, 651 S.E.2d 321, 323 (S.C. 2007) ("[T]he defense of habitation provides that where one attempts to force himself into another's dwelling, the law permits an owner to use reasonable force to expel the trespasser."); see also 40 C.J.S. Homicide § 164 (2006) ("People may defend their dwellings against those who endeavor by violence to enter them and who appear to intend violence to persons inside. . ."); 2 Wharton's Criminal Law § 131 (15th ed. 1994) ("When a dwelling house is entered or attempted to be entered by force. . . the occupant may use deadly force, if reasonably necessary, to prevent or terminate such entry."

Based on our precedent and the authorities cited above, we cannot accept the position that defense of habitation requires an intruder to cross the threshold of the defendant's home. Instead, we emphasize that a person has a right to defend his or her residence not only when an intruder is already inside the home, but also when an intruder is outside the home and attempting to enter to commit a violent felony.

We recognize that "[t]he term felony in former times carried a connotation of greater threat than" it does today. State v. Pellegrino, 1998 SD 39, 577 N.W.2d 590, 596 (S.D. 1998). "In the common law, the rule developed that use of lethal force to prevent a felony was only justified if the felony was a forcible and atrocious crime." Id. (quoted authority omitted). Felonies are no longer constrained to forcible and atrocious crimes, and were we not to update Bailey's "felony" language, defense of habitation may apply to situations in which an intruder attempts to force entry into a home with the purpose of committing a non-violent felony, such as bribing a public official therein. See NMSA 1978, § 30–24–1 (1963) (bribing a public official is a third degree felony). Seeking to avoid such absurdity, we turn to our prior decisions to determine the meaning of "felony" as it is used in the defense of habitation context.

As noted above, the defendant in Couch was entitled to an instruction on defense of habitation because he could have reasonably believed that the people who were attacking his home intended violence against its occupants. See 52 N.M. at 140, 193 P.2d at 412–13. Later this Court held that the defendant did not qualify for a defense of habitation instruction because, among other things, no evidence had been presented that the victim "enter[ed] the house in order to commit a felony involving violence." 120 N.M. at 244, 901 P.2d at 175. Those authorities show that the term "felony" in the defense of habitation context is properly limited to those felonies involving violence. In other words, the felony that the defendant acted to prevent must have been one that would have resulted in violence against the occupants were it not prevented; in the event of any other felony, a defense of habitation instruction would be unwarranted.

Because defense of habitation is not restricted to instances in which the victim is killed inside the defendant's home, the trial court in this case erred when it excluded the instruction on that ground. Defendant would have been entitled to an instruction on the defense if some evidence reasonably tended to show that he killed Victim to prevent her from forcing entry into his home and committing a violent felony once inside. Thus, the question we must now answer is whether, when viewed in the light most favorable to giving the instruction, the evidence supports that theory. We decide that it does not.

Defendant asserts that the following evidence is enough to support his theory that he had a reasonable belief that killing Victim was necessary to prevent a felony from occurring within his home: (1) Victim hated Defendant; (2) she knocked on the door to Defendant's home; (3) she had threatened him with a gun in the past; (4) she was furious that the couple was to be married the next day; and (5) she always carried a loaded gun. Absent from that evidence is any demonstration that Victim was "endeavor[ing] by violence to enter" his home or that she "intend[ed] violence to persons inside." 40 C.J.S. Homicide § 164. Assuming that Defendant reasonably believed that Victim intended to commit a felony in his home, defense of habitation would have justified his actions only if he could show that Victim was attempting to force entry to his home. For example, if the evidence showed that Victim was trying to break through Defendant's front door at the time he killed her, defense of habitation would apply. However, under the facts of this case, there is no evidence reasonably tending to support the theory that Victim was attempting to force entry at the time Defendant killed her. After knocking on the door, Victim had retreated some four feet from it and was waiting for it to open. No evidence shows that, at the time she was killed, Victim was attempting to gain entry to Defendant's home with the intent to commit a violent felony therein.

Defendant's argument justifies the instructions that Defendant received on self-defense, see UJI 14–5171 NMRA, and defense of another, see UJI 14–5172 NMRA, it does not give rise to an instruction on defense of habitation because it does not allege any attempted forced entry on Victim's part.

Because there is no evidence to support the theory that Defendant killed Victim in defense of his habitation, refusing the instruction was not in error.

DISCUSSION QUESTIONS

1. What instructions on self defense were given and not given by the trial court, and what difference does it make?

2. Do you have to wait until an intruder is inside in order to receive a habitation instruction? Why isn't the defendant entitled to one?

3. Are habitation instructions just? A good idea?

I. PROPORTIONATE FORCE

A corollary to the necessity requirement is that force used in lawful self-defense must be necessary and proportionate to the harm that is imminent. Even if you could not safely duck the old man's punches in the baseball hypothetical, punching him might have been unnecessary if you could have safely restrained him until the police got hold of him. You cannot use deadly force against non-deadly force, and fact-finders will sometimes draw further distinctions between levels of non-deadly force. So, you may not be able to punch someone who is pushing you, and you ordinarily can't stab someone who is punching you. Any force that threatens death or serious bodily injury may be lawfully met with deadly force. You can shoot your college roommate who is going to stab you, though, because force does not have to be exactly equal to be proportionate. (It is his problem that he brought a knife to a gunfight.)

Whether force is deadly will sometimes depend on the circumstances. Deadly weapons aren't always required. Age, size, strength, and training all matter, as does the specific nature of the attack. Details matter. An unarmed attack by Chuck Norris, the former martial arts star who is the subject of numerous jokes about his power ("when the bogey man goes to sleep he checks under his bed for Chuck Norris"), could constitute deadly force even though Norris is now in his seventies.

J. INITIAL AGGRESSOR RULES

If you start it, you don't get to end it, or—to be a little more precise—you ordinarily don't get to claim self-defense against someone you have attacked. The person who "starts it" is called the "initial aggressor" in the law of self-defense. Aggressors ordinarily don't enjoy a right of self-defense. So, if it was necessary to punch the old man at the baseball game who attacked you (maybe the old man was Chuck Norris!) then he can't claim self-defense with respect to any subsequent punches he throws since he was the initial aggressor.

Note that being an initial aggressor does not mean that you are just being a jerk. If you insult a Yankee's fan, and he throws a punch at you, he is the initial aggressor, not you. Being an initial aggressor does not always require actual violence, though. One can become an initial aggressor by threatening imminent harm. If, midway through your heated argument with the hated Yankees fan, he raises a clenched fist and says he is going to "knock your block off," then he is the initial aggressor. If his punch reasonably seemed imminent, then you can punch him in self-defense, and he won't be able to legally punch you back.

Can an initial aggressor ever regain his right of self-defense? This is where things get a bit more complicated. It is a lot easier for the enraged old man than it is for your knife-wielding college roommate because there is only one way for a "deadly initial aggressor" (one who uses deadly force) to regain his right of self-defense. A deadly initial aggressor must completely withdraw from the conflict and communicate that withdrawal to the victim of his initial aggression.

So, assume that your college roommate has been slashing away at you with his knife. You pick up another carving knife from one of the other trays. Your college roommate wheels back away from you and tells you that he quits. You have been cut, however, and are very mad. You chase after him with your knife. Your college roommate can now legally stab you with his knife because he has regained his right of self-defense through his complete and clearly communicated withdrawal. To allow you to kill him with impunity would be to legalize a retaliatory killing because you no longer face an imminent harm.

Note, however, that most jurisdictions require you to both withdraw and clearly communicate that withdrawal. This reduces the chance of a misunderstanding. You might otherwise think that your opponent is just resting up for another attack. Note that you don't necessarily have to put down your weapon and accept the initial aggressor's withdrawal at face value. (He might be a liar as well as an initial aggressor.) But you do need to cease your attack unless and until you have a reasonable fear that he is going to continue the attack.

A non-deadly initial aggressor has a second way of regaining his right of self-defense (in addition to the sort of withdrawal just described). A non-deadly initial aggressor may regain his right of self-defense if the victim of his initial aggression responds with deadly force. Some jurisdictions (including the Model Penal Code) immediately restore the initial aggressor's right of self-defense at this point. So, if you shove someone for no reason, and they pull out a knife and try to stab you, you can pull out a gun and shoot him, even though they were the initial victim. You, of course, can still be prosecuted for the misdemeanor battery you initially committed, but at least you don't have to choose between letting him stab you and going to prison for murder.

Other jurisdictions, however, require a non-deadly initial aggressor to retreat if possible when faced with deadly force from his victim. In these jurisdictions you would need to run away from your knife-wielding, shove-victim. You could only use deadly force if he chases you down, and you have no other choice. Some jurisdictions will find a non-deadly initial aggressor who faces a deadly force response guilty not of murder but of manslaughter if he kills his victim without first retreating. Such "split-the-baby" manslaughter is one form of what is called "imperfect self-defense."

Things get more serious when deadly force is involved and when one of the two parties involved makes a mistake. Imagine that your bone-headed friend decides to break into your house late at night and stand over your bed with an axe as a Halloween prank. If you start shooting at him out of reasonable fear, he cannot defend himself with the axe because your use of force is lawful, even though mistaken.

Case in Context

Regaining your right of self defense is easier said than done, as the next case illustrates.

THE PEOPLE V. KELSEY DRU GLEGHORN

Court of Appeal, Second District, California
193 Cal. App. 3d 196 (1987)

Opinion by: STONE.

May a person who enters the habitat of another at 3 o'clock in the morning for the announced purpose of killing him, and who commences to beat the startled sleeper's bed with a stick and set fires under him, be entitled to use deadly force in self defense after the intended victim shoots him in the back with an arrow? Upon the basis of these bizarre facts, we hold that he may not, and instead, must suffer the slings and arrows of outrageous fortune (with apologies to William Shakespeare and Hamlet, Act III, sc. 1).

Kelsey Dru Gleghorn appeals his conviction by jury of one count of simple assault (Pen. Code, § 240) and one count of battery with the infliction of serious bodily injury (Pen. Code, § 243, subd. (d)). He contends the trial court erred in denying his motion for mistrial based on his allegation of inconsistent verdicts and insufficient evidence to support the conviction on count II and erred in instructing the jury pursuant to CALJIC No. 5.42. We find no error and affirm the judgment.

Facts

This case is a parable of the dangers of weaponry in the hands of unreasonable powers who become unduly provoked over minor irritations. Melody Downes shared her house with several persons, including appellant. She rented her garage to Michael Fairall for $ 150 per month. She believed he was to give her a stereo as part of the rent. He believed her intent was only to borrow it. He asked for the return of the stereo; she said she sold it.

Fairall, a man of obvious sensitivity, smashed all the windows of her automobile, slashed the tires, and dented the body. Not quite mollified, he kicked in her locked door, scattered her belongings in the bedroom, and broke an aquarium, freeing her snake. (It was scotched, not killed. See Macbeth, W. Shakespeare.) Ms. Downes advised appellant of Fairall's behavior; he apparently took umbrage. On the fateful night in question, Fairall, having quaffed a few, went to the garage he called home and then to bed, a mattress laid upon a lofty perch in the rafters. He was rudely awakened by a pounding on the garage door accompanied by appellant's request that he come out so that appellant might kill him. Fairall wisely advised him that they could exchange pleasantries in the morning.

Undeterred, appellant opened the garage door, entered with stick in hand and began beating on the rafters, yelling for Fairall to come down. In the darkness, Fairall claimed he could see sparks where the board hit the rafters. Appellant said that if Fairall did not come down, he would burn him out. No sooner said than done, appellant set a small fire to some of Fairall's clothes.

Fairall, who happened to have secreted a bow and quiver of arrows in the rafters to prevent its theft, loosed one but did not see where it landed. Fairall, abandoning his weapons, swung down from the rafters and was immediately hit from behind. He yelled for someone to bring a hose and attempted to extinguish the fire with his hands. Meanwhile, appellant, in an ill humor from the gash in his back caused by the arrow, continued to beat him, causing a two-inch-wide vertical break in Fairall's lower jaw, tearing his lips, knocking out six to ten teeth, mangling two fingers, and lacerating his arm, stomach and back. Fairall also suffered burns on the palms of his hands.

Fairall testified under a grant of immunity given concerning the vandalism of the car.

The jury returned verdicts of guilty of simple assault as a lesser included offense of assault by means of force likely to incur great bodily injury (Pen. Code. § 245, subd. (a)(1)) on count I and of battery with the infliction of serious bodily injury on count II. Appellant moved for a new trial (Pen. Code, § 1181) on grounds that the verdicts were contrary to the law or evidence. He contends that since the jury found his acts prior to being shot constituted only simple assault, Fairall was not justified in replying with deadly force. Since the victim responded with deadly force, he continues, he was entitled to defend himself with deadly force. Ergo, he could not be convicted of battery with the infliction of serious bodily injury.

Not every assault gives rise to the right to kill in self-defense. Penal Code section 197 explains when homicide is justifiable, i.e., "When committed in defense of habitation, property, or person, against one who manifestly intends or endeavors, by violence or surprise, to commit a felony, or against one who manifestly intends and endeavors, in a violent, riotous or tumultuous manner, to enter the habitation of another for the purpose of offering violence to any person therein; or, [para.] . . . when there is reasonable ground to apprehend a design to commit a felony or to do some great bodily injury, and imminent danger of such design being accomplished. . ." However, to repel a slight assault, the person assaulted is not authorized to resort to unduly violent measures. (People v. Mesa (1932) 121 Cal.App. 345, 349 [8 P.2d 920].)

Generally, if one makes a felonious assault upon another, or has created appearances justifying the other to launch a deadly counterattack in self-defense, the original assailant cannot slay his adversary in self-defense unless he has first, in good faith, declined further combat, and has fairly notified him that he has abandoned the affray. (People v. Hecker (1895) 109 Cal. 451, 463 [42 P. 307].) However, when the victim of simple assault responds in a sudden and deadly counterassault, the original aggressor need not attempt to withdraw and may use reasonably necessary force in self-defense.

Appellant contends that, since he initially committed only a simple assault, he was legally justified as a matter of law in standing his ground, even though he was the initial attacker, and in utilizing lethal force against Fairall. He asserts that the jury did not follow special instruction number 5, which stated: "Where the original aggressor is not guilty of a deadly attack, but of a simple assault or trespass, the person assaulted has no right to use deadly or other excessive force. [para.] And, where the counter assault is so sudden and perilous that no opportunity be given to decline further to fight and he cannot retreat with safety he is justified in slaying in self-defense."

The right of self-defense is based upon the appearance of imminent peril to the person attacked. (People v. Smith (1981) 122 Cal.App.3d 581, 590 [176 Cal.Rptr. 73].) The right to defend one's person or home with deadly force depends upon the circumstances as they reasonably appeared to that person. (People v. Loustaunau (1986) 181 Cal.App.3d 163, 171 [226 Cal.Rptr. 216].) That right cannot depend upon the appellant's supposedly nonfelonious secret intent. (Ibid.; People v. Walker (1973) 32 Cal.App.3d 897, 902–903 [108 Cal.Rptr. 548].) Similarly, justification does not depend upon the existence of actual danger but rather upon appearances, i.e., if a reasonable person would be placed in fear for his or her safety, and defendant acted out of that fear. (People v. Clark (1982) 130 Cal.App.3d 371, 377 [181 Cal.Rptr. 682].)

Moreover, even though a person is mistaken in judgment as to the actual necessity for the use of extreme measures, if he was misled through no fault or carelessness on his part and defends himself correctly according to what he supposed the facts to be, his act is justifiable. (Id., at p. 377.) These are usually questions of fact for the jury to resolve. (Id., at p. 378.) It is beyond the province of this court to reweigh the evidence.

Here, the jury could reasonably infer from the evidence that: (1) Fairall acted reasonably upon the appearances that his life was in danger or (2) even if Fairall acted unreasonably in shooting appellant with the arrow and appellant was justified in responding with deadly force, appellant continued to beat his attacker long after the attacker was disabled. If a person attacked defends himself so successfully that his attacker is rendered incapable of inflicting injury, or for any other reason the danger no longer exists, there is no justification for further retaliation. (1 Witkin, Cal. Crimes, § 163, p. 156 (1963); see People v. Perez (1970) 12 Cal.App.3d 232, 236 [90 Cal.Rptr. 521]; People v. Smith, supra, 122 Cal.App.3d 581, 588.) This principle is embodied in CALJIC Nos. 5.52 and 5.53 (1983 rev.), both of which were given to the jury.

The evidence supports a finding that Fairall did not threaten or take any action against appellant after Fairall descended from the loft. On the other hand, if the jury found, as it could have, that Fairall was justified in reasonably fearing for his life on the appearances of appellant's actions, appellant never obtained the right of self-defense in the first place. We find no error.

DISCUSSION QUESTIONS

1.   Why couldn't the defendant regain his right of self defense?

2.   Why did the defendant argue that the jury's verdicts were inconsistent?

3.   Even if the defendant had won his initial aggressor argument, he would have still lost this appeal. Why?

Case in Context

The next case illustrates two different elements of self-defense doctrine.

UNITED STATES OF AMERICA V. BENNIE L. PETERSON

United States Court of Appeals, District of Columbia Circuit
483 F.2d 1222 (1973)

Opinion by: ROBINSON.

Indicted for second-degree murder, and convicted by a jury of manslaughter as a lesser included offense, Bennie L. Peterson [appeals]. He complains that the judge twice erred in the instructions given the jury in relation to his claim that the homicide was committed in self-defense. One error alleged was an instruction that the jury might consider whether Peterson was the aggressor in the altercation that immediately foreran the homicide. The other was an instruction that a failure by Peterson to retreat, if he could have done so without jeopardizing his safety, might be considered as a circumstance bearing on the question whether he was justified in using the amount of force which he did. We affirm Peterson's conviction.

I

The events immediately preceding the homicide are not seriously in dispute. Charles Keitt, the deceased, and two friends drove in Keitt's car to the alley in the rear of Peterson's house to remove the windshield wipers from the latter's wrecked car. While Keitt was doing so, Peterson came out of the house into the back yard to protest. After a verbal exchange, Peterson went back into the house, obtained a pistol, and returned to the yard. In the meantime, Keitt had reseated himself in his car, and he and his companions were about to leave.

Upon his reappearance in the yard, Peterson paused briefly to load the pistol. "If you move," he shouted to Keitt, "I will shoot." He walked to a point in the yard slightly inside a gate in the rear fence and, pistol in hand, said, "If you come in here I will kill you." Keitt alighted from his car, took a few steps toward Peterson and exclaimed, "What the hell do you think you are going to do with that?" Keitt then made an about-face, walked back to his car and got a lug wrench. With the wrench in a raised position, Keitt advanced toward Peterson, who stood with the pistol pointed toward him. Peterson warned Keitt not to "take another step" and, when Keitt continued onward, shot him in the face from a distance of about ten feet. Death was apparently instantaneous.

III

More than two centuries ago, Blackstone, best known of the expositors of the English common law, taught that "all homicide is malicious, and of course, amounts to murder, unless. . . justified by the command or permission of the law; excused on the account of accident or self-preservation; or alleviated into manslaughter, by being either the involuntary consequence of some act not strictly lawful, or (if voluntary) occasioned by some sudden and sufficiently violent provocation."

Tucked within this greatly capsulized schema of the common law of homicide is the branch of law we are called upon to administer today. No issue of justifiable homicide, within Blackstone's definition is involved. But Peterson's consistent position is that as a matter of law his conviction of manslaughter—alleviated homicide—was wrong, and that his act was one of self-preservation—excused homicide.

By the early common law, justification for homicide extended only to acts done in execution of the law, such as homicides in effecting arrests and preventing forcible felonies, and homicides committed in self-defense were only excusable. See, generally, authorities cited supra note 34. The distinction between justifiable and excusable homicide was important because in the latter case the slayer, considered to be not wholly free from blame, suffered a forfeiture of his goods. F. Wharton, Homicide § 3 at 211 (1855). However, with the passage of 24 Henry VIII, ch. 5 (1532), the basis of justification was enlarged, and the distinction has largely disappeared. More usually the terms are used interchangeably, each denoting a legally non-punishable act, entitling the accused to an acquittal.

Self-defense, as a doctrine legally exonerating the taking of human life, is as viable now as it was in Blackstone's time, and in the case before us the doctrine is invoked in its purest form. But "the law of self-defense is a law of necessity"; the right of self-defense arises only when the necessity begins, and equally ends with the necessity; and never must the necessity be greater than when the force employed defensively is deadly. The "necessity must bear all semblance of reality, and appear to admit of no other alternative, before taking life will be justifiable as excusable." Hinged on the exigencies of self-preservation, the doctrine of homicidal self-defense emerges from the body of the criminal law as a limited though important exception to legal outlawry of the arena of self-help in the settlement of potentially fatal personal conflicts.

When we speak of deadly force, we refer to force capable of inflicting death or serious bodily harm.

So it is that necessity is the pervasive theme of the well-defined conditions which the law imposes on the right to kill or maim in self-defense. There must have been a threat, actual or apparent, of the use of deadly force against the defender. The threat must have been unlawful and immediate. The defender must have believed that he was in imminent peril of death or serious bodily harm, and that his response was necessary to save himself therefrom. These beliefs must not only have been honestly entertained, but also objectively reasonable in light of the surrounding circumstances. It is clear that no less than a concurrence of these elements will suffice.

IV

The first of Peterson's complaints centers upon an instruction that the right to use deadly force in self-defense is not ordinarily available to one who provokes a conflict or is the aggressor in it. Mere words, the judge explained, do not constitute provocation or aggression; and if Peterson precipitated the altercation but thereafter withdrew from it in good faith and so informed Keitt by words or acts, he was justified in using deadly force to save himself from imminent danger or death or grave bodily harm. Peterson contends that there was no evidence that he either caused or contributed to the conflict, and that the instructions on that topic could only mislead the jury.

It has long been accepted that one cannot support a claim of self-defense by a self-generated necessity to kill. The right of homicidal self-defense is granted only to those free from fault in the difficulty; it is denied to slayers who incite the fatal attack, encourage the fatal quarrel or otherwise promote the necessitous occasion for taking life. The fact that the deceased struck the first blow, fired the first shot or made the first menacing gesture does not legalize the self-defense claim if in fact the claimant was the actual provoker. In sum, one who is the aggressor in a conflict culminating in death cannot invoke the necessities of self-preservation. Only in the event that he communicates to his adversary his intent to withdraw and in good faith attempts to do so is he restored to his right of self-defense.

This body of doctrine traces its origin to the fundamental principle that a killing in self-defense is excusable only as a matter of genuine necessity. Quite obviously, a defensive killing is unnecessary if the occasion for it could have been averted, and the roots of that consideration run deep with us.

In the case at bar, the trial judge's charge fully comported with these governing principles. The remaining question, then, is whether there was evidence to make them applicable to the case. A recapitulation of the proofs shows beyond peradventure that there was.

It was not until Peterson fetched his pistol and returned to his back yard that his confrontation with Keitt took on a deadly cast. Prior to his trip into the house for the gun, there was, by the Government's evidence, no threat, no display of weapons, no combat. There was an exchange of verbal aspersions and a misdemeanor against Peterson's property was in progress but, at this juncture, nothing more.

It is well settled that deadly force cannot be employed to arrest or prevent the escape of a misdemeanant.

The law never tolerates the use of deadly force in the protection of one's property.

The evidence is uncontradicted that when Peterson reappeared in the yard with his pistol, Keitt was about to depart the scene. Richard Hilliard testified that after the first argument, Keitt reentered his car and said "Let's go." This statement was verified by Ricky Gray, who testified that Keitt "got in the car and. . . they were getting ready to go;" he, too, heard Keitt give the direction to start the car. The uncontroverted fact that Keitt was leaving shows plainly that so far as he was concerned the confrontation was ended. It demonstrates just as plainly that even if he had previously been the aggressor, he no longer was.

Not so with Peterson, however, as the undisputed evidence made clear. Emerging from the house with the pistol, he paused in the yard to load it, and to command Keitt not to move. He then walked through the yard to the rear gate and, displaying his pistol, dared Keitt to come in, and threatened to kill him if he did. While there appears to be no fixed rule on the subject, the cases hold, and we agree, that an affirmative unlawful act reasonably calculated to produce an affray foreboding injurious or fatal consequences is an aggression which, unless renounced, nullifies the right of homicidal self-defense. We cannot escape the abiding conviction that the jury could readily find Peterson's challenge to be a transgression of that character.

The situation at bar is not unlike that presented in Laney. There the accused, chased along the street by a mob threatening his life, managed to escape through an areaway between two houses. In the back yard of one of the houses, he checked a gun he was carrying and then returned to the areaway. The mob beset him again, and during an exchange of shots one of its members was killed by a bullet from the accused's gun. In affirming a conviction of manslaughter, the court reasoned:

It is clearly apparent. . . that, when defendant escaped from the mob into the back yard. . . he was in a place of comparative safety, from which, if he desired to go home, he could have gone by the back way, as he subsequently did. The mob had turned its attention to a house on the opposite side of the street. According to Laney's testimony, there was shooting going on in the street. His appearance on the street at that juncture could mean nothing but trouble for him. Hence, when he adjusted his gun and stepped out into the areaway, he had every reason to believe that his presence there would provoke trouble. We think his conduct in adjusting his revolver and going into the areaway was such as to deprive him of any right to invoke the plea of self-defense.

Similarly, in Rowe v. United States, the accused was in the home of friends when an argument, to which the friends became participants, developed in the street in front. He left, went to his nearby apartment for a loaded pistol and returned. There was testimony that he then made an insulting comment, drew the pistol and fired a shot into the ground. In any event, when a group of five men began to move toward him, he began to shoot at them, killing two, and wounding a third. We observed that the accused "left an apparently safe haven to arm himself and return to the scene," and that "he inflamed the situation with his words to the men gathered there, even though he could have returned silently to the safety of the [friends'] porch." We held that these facts could have led the jury to conclude that [the accused] returned to the scene to stir up further trouble, if not actually to kill anyone, and that his actions instigated the men into rushing him. Self-defense may not be claimed by one who deliberately places himself in a position where he has reason to believe "his presence. . . would provoke trouble."

We noted the argument "that a defendant may claim self-defense if he arms himself in order to proceed upon his normal activities, even if he realizes that danger may await him"; we responded by pointing out "that the jury could have found that the course of action defendant here followed was for an unlawful purpose." We accordingly affirmed his conviction of manslaughter over his objection that an acquittal should have been directed.

We are brought much the readier to the same conclusion here. We think the evidence plainly presented an issue of fact as to whether Peterson's conduct was an invitation to and provocation of the encounter which ended in the fatal shot. We sustain the trial judge's action in remitting that issue for the jury's determination.

V

The second aspect of the trial judge's charge as to which Peterson asserts error concerned the un-disputed fact that at no time did Peterson endeavor to retreat from Keitt's approach with the lug wrench. The judge instructed the jury that if Peterson could have safely retreated but did not do so, that failure was a circumstance which the jury might consider, together with all others, in determining whether he went further in repelling the danger, real or apparent, than he was justified in going.

Peterson contends that this imputation of an obligation to retreat was error, even if he could safely have done so. He points out that at the time of the shooting he was standing in his own yard, and argues he was under no duty to move. We are persuaded to the conclusion that in the circumstances presented here, the trial judge did not err in giving the instruction challenged.

Within the common law of self-defense there developed the rule of "retreat to the wall," which ordinarily forbade the use of deadly force by one to whom an avenue for safe retreat was open. This doctrine was but an application of the requirement of strict necessity to excuse the taking of human life, and was designed to insure the existence of that necessity. Even the innocent victim of a vicious assault had to elect a safe retreat, if available, rather than resort to defensive force which might kill or seriously injure.

In a majority of American jurisdictions, contrarily to the common law rule, one may stand his ground and use deadly force whenever it seems reasonably necessary to save himself. While the law of the District of Columbia on this point is not entirely clear, it seems allied with the strong minority adhering to the common law.

That is not to say that the retreat rule is without exceptions. Even at common law it was recognized that it was not completely suited to all situations. Today it is the more so that its precept must be adjusted to modern conditions nonexistent during the early development of the common law of self-defense. One restriction on its operation comes to the fore when the circumstances apparently foreclose a withdrawal with safety. The doctrine of retreat was never intended to enhance the risk to the innocent; its proper application has never required a faultless victim to increase his assailant's safety at the expense of his own. On the contrary, he could stand his ground and use deadly force otherwise appropriate if the alternative were perilous, or if to him it reasonably appeared to be.

Time, place, and conditions may create a situation which would clearly justify a modification of the rule. For example, the common-law rule, which required the assailed to retreat to the wall, had its origin before the general introduction of firearms. If a person is threatened with death or great bodily harm by an assailant, armed with a modern rifle, in open space, away from safety, it would be ridiculous to require him to retreat. Indeed, to retreat would be to invite almost certain death." Laney v. United States, supra note 53, 54 App.D.C. at 58–59, 294 F. at 414–15.

The trial judge's charge to the jury incorporated each of these limitations on the retreat rule. Peterson, however, invokes another—the so-called "castle" doctrine. It is well settled that one who through no fault of his own is attacked in his home is under no duty to retreat therefrom. The oft-repeated expression that "a man's home is his castle" reflected the belief in olden days that there were few if any safer sanctuaries than the home. The "castle" exception, moreover, has been ex-tended by some courts to encompass the occupant's presence within the curtilage outside his dwelling. Peterson reminds us that when he shot to halt Keitt's advance, he was standing in his yard and so, he argues, he had no duty to endeavor to retreat.

Despite the practically universal acceptance of the "castle" doctrine in American jurisdictions wherein the point has been raised, its status in the District of Columbia has never been squarely decided. But whatever the fate of the doctrine in the District law of the future, it is clear that in absolute form it was inapplicable here. The right of self-defense, we have said, cannot be claimed by the aggressor in an affray so long as he retains that unmitigated role. It logically follows that any rule of no-retreat which may protect an innocent victim of the affray would, like other incidents of a forfeited right of self-defense, be unavailable to the party who provokes or stimulates the conflict. Accordingly, the law is well settled that the "castle" doctrine can be invoked only by one who is without fault in bringing the conflict on. That, we think, is the critical consideration here.

We need not repeat our previous discussion of Peterson's contribution to the altercation which culminated in Keitt's death. It suffices to point out that by no interpretation of the evidence could it be said that Peterson was blameless in the affair.

DISCUSSION QUESTIONS

1.   Why doesn't the *castle doctrine* apply to Peterson's use of force?

2.   Why isn't the windshield wiper thief the initial aggressor?

3.   Why didn't Peterson regain his right to self defense once his victim angrily advanced upon Peterson with a wrench?

Practice Problem 20.2: Concealed Culpability

You work for a member of the state legislature in the state of Kennedicut. Kennedicut is a common law jurisdiction that follows the majority approach consistently. Recently Kennedicut greatly expanded the availability of permits to carry concealed handguns (concealed carry permits). Kennedicut is now a "shall issue" state which means that local sheriff's department are legally obliged to issue concealed permits to anyone who does not have a criminal record or a history of being involuntarily committed for mental illness, and who passes a written exam and pays a modest fee. Your boss is an ardent supporter of gun rights and does not want to restrict the availability of concealed carry permits in any way. She believes, however, that self-defense and homicide law in Kennedicut needs to change in response to the fact that many more people are now carrying concealed handguns.

By way of example, your boss described the following case. Two men got into an argument after a minor traffic accident. The older man challenged the younger man to a fight. The younger man pulled back his jacket to display his holstered gun. The older man lifted up his sweatshirt and put his hand on his holstered gun. The younger man then drew his gun but kept it pointed at the ground. The older man drew and pointed his gun at the younger man. When the younger man raised his gun and pointed it at the older man, both men fired, killing each other. Both guns were being legally carried. Your boss believes that these killings were tragic and unnecessary. She wants to know who was at fault under current law and how the laws of self-defense and the law of homicide should be reformed to reduce the likelihood of people being unnecessarily shot or killed. She would like you to propose specific changes to the law and to explain the pros and cons of making such changes.

K. PROTECTION OF OTHERS

The principles discussed with respect to self-defense apply to the defense of others. The most important distinction between self-defense and the defense of others concerns the mistaken use of force. A typical fact pattern involves a Good Samaritan who uses force to help someone he mistakenly believes to be the victim of a wrongful aggression. You punch a scruffy-looking man whom you saw tackle someone else to the ground but soon discover that the man you punched was an undercover police officer chasing a purse snatcher.

A minority of jurisdictions apply what is called the alter ego rule, which means that the Good Samaritan steps into the shoes of the person she was defending. Since the undercover officer was using lawful and non-excessive force against the fleeing purse snatcher, the purse snatcher had no right of self-defense against the officer. Since the purse snatcher had no right of self-defense, neither doe his alter ego, the Good Samaritan who steps into his shoes. Without a lawful basis for self-defense, the Good Samaritan is guilty of the crime of hitting the police officer.

The majority of jurisdictions now find the alter ego rule to be too harsh. They base the Good Samaritan's liability on the reasonableness of his belief in the need for defensive force, so one using defensive force on behalf of another needs to just be reasonable, not correct, in their fear of imminent harm to the party protected. Under that standard, the scruffiness of the undercover officer would work in favor of the Good Samaritan by suggesting that it was reasonable that he thought the officer was a mugger or wrongful assailant. This is also the Model Penal Code's rule.

L. IMPERFECT SELF DEFENSE

Usually, self-defense operates as an all-or-nothing defense. If one acts in lawful self-defense, one is guilty of no crime; if not, then one suffers the full weight of criminal liability for the force used. This principal can operate harshly in homicide cases. One who shoots another out of a genuine but unreasonable fear becomes guilty of murder for an intentional killing. Some jurisdictions have created a middle category of liability between guilty and not guilty in homicide cases that is called imperfect self-defense and which results in a conviction for manslaughter, not murder.

Different types of imperfect self-defense exist in different jurisdictions, although all create manslaughter liability. These are the three most common versions.

1. One who kills out of an actual but unreasonable fear. You shoot the mask wearing treat-or-treating teenager at your doorstep on Halloween night out of a sincere but unreasonable fear.

2. One who unreasonably but actually believes that deadly force is necessary. A police officer shoots a charging unarmed assailant because the officer forgot that he had his Taser on his gun belt.

3. A non-deadly-force initial aggressor who fails to retreat in the face of deadly force from his victim. You shove someone, they pull a knife, and you fail to run before shooting them in a jurisdiction that requires retreat under these circumstances.

Jurisdictions that follow the Model Penal Code create more than one type of imperfect self-defense liability by distinguishing reckless fears from unreasonable ones.

Exam Tip: Look for Breadth and Depth

As will be discussed in the final chapter, some exam questions contain many issues and other contain fewer issues that require more in-depth discussions. (Impossible questions require both, but remember that they are equally impossible for the person writing next to you.) Self-defense fact patterns lend themselves easily to both types of question. A fight sequence can contain multiple moments at which the reasonableness of fears can change over time, the role of initial aggressor can change, obligations to retreat can come and go, and questions about the necessity and proportionality of the amount of force used can arise. Self-defense fact patterns can also raise interesting questions about how individualized our standard of reasonable fear should be, how imminent the harm must be, and what role psychological syndromes should play in reasonable fear. Don't be afraid of these issues! See them as opportunities for you to show what you know.

M. MODEL PENAL CODE SECTIONS

§ 3.04. Use of Force in Self-Protection

1. Use of Force Justifiable for Protection of the Person. Subject to the provisions of this Section and of Section 3.09, the use of force upon or toward another person is justifiable when the actor believes that such force is immediately necessary for the purpose of protecting himself against the use of unlawful force by such other person on the present occasion.

2. Limitations on Justifying Necessity for Use of Force.

    a. The use of force is not justifiable under this Section:

        i. to resist an arrest that the actor knows is being made by a peace officer, although the arrest iss unlawful; or

        ii. to resist force used by the occupier or possessor of property or by another person on his behalf, where the actor knows that the person using the force is doing so under a claim of right to protect the property, except that this limitation shall not apply if:

            A. the actor is a public officer acting in the performance of his duties or a person lawfully assisting him therein or a person making or assisting in a lawful arrest; or

            B. the actor has been unlawfully dispossessed of the property and is making a re-entry or recaption justified by Section 3.06; or

            C. the actor believes that such force is necessary to protect himself against death or serious bodily injury.

b. The use of deadly force is not justifiable under this Section unless the actor believes that such force is necessary to protect himself against death, serious bodily injury, kidnaping or sexual intercourse compelled by force or threat; nor is it justifiable if:

    i. the actor, with the purpose of causing death or serious bodily injury, provoked the use of force against himself in the same encounter; or

    ii. the actor knows that he can avoid the necessity of using such force with complete safety by retreating or by surrendering possession of a thing to a person asserting a claim of right thereto or by complying with a demand that he abstain from any action that he has no duty to take, except that:

        A. the actor is not obliged to retreat from his dwelling or place of work, unless he was the initial aggressor or is assailed in his place of work by another person whose place of work the actor knows it to be; and

        B. a public officer justified in using force in the performance of his duties or a person justified in using force in his assistance or a person justified in using force in making an arrest or preventing an escape is not obliged to desist from efforts to perform such duty, effect such arrest or prevent such escape because of resistance or threatened resistance by or on behalf of the person against whom such action is directed.

c. Except as required by paragraphs (a) and (b) of this Subsection, a person employing protective force may estimate the necessity thereof under the circumstances as he believes them to be when the force is used, without retreating, surrendering possession, doing any other act that he has no legal duty to do or abstaining from any lawful action.

* * *

§ 3.05. Use of Force for the Protection of Other Persons

1. Subject to the provisions of this Section and of Section 3.09, the use of force upon or toward the person of another is justifiable to protect a third person when:

a. the actor would be justified under Section 3.04 in using such force to protect himself against the injury he believes to be threatened to the person whom he seeks to protect; and

b. under the circumstances as the actor believes them to be, the person whom he seeks to protect would be justified in using such protective force; and

c. the actor believes that his intervention is necessary for the protection of such other person.

Practice Problem 20.3: Fatal Flashback

Marcel recently left the army. During her last posting she was the victim of prolonged sexual harassment by one of her superior officers. This officer threatened her with unfavorable fitness reports and undesirable assignments unless she engaged in a sexual relationship with him. After several months of enduring this pressure she complained to other officers but was told that her superior officer was merely joking around with her and that she should just ignore him. Late one night her superior officer confronted her in a deserted corner of the warehouse where she worked and demanded that she have sex with him. When she refused and turned her back on him, he grabbed her from behind around the waist. She broke free and slapped him hard across the face with an open hand. Enraged, the officer, who was much larger, began choking her. Luckily two other soldiers entered the warehouse just in time to witness Marcel's slap and her superior officer's response. They pulled the officer off of Marcel but not before he was able to choke her into unconsciousness. On the strength of their testimony the officer was convicted of felonious assault and imprisoned.

After recovering from her physical injuries Marcel had trouble performing her duties as before. She was constantly irritable, continually questioned orders and argued with her superiors. She was diagnosed by Army psychiatrists with post-traumatic stress disorder as the result of the sexual harassment and assault that she suffered. She disputed the diagnosis, saying "I am not crazy; I was just stupid to let myself become a victim." She further claimed that the officers were conspiring against her because she had stood up to one of their fellow officers. She accepted a medical discharge from the Army but refused the counseling for post-traumatic stress disorder that was offered through the veteran's administration.

After leaving the army, Marcel got a job in a warehouse driving a forklift. Bill, her direct supervisor immediately began asking her to go out with him. When she complained about this to her coworkers, she was told that Bill was a big practical joker and teased all the female employees. Marcel said that she knew all about men like Bill and that everyone always covered up for people like him. She grew increasingly irritable at work and got into frequent arguments with her coworkers. Bill warned her several times that she needed to loosen up a bit or that she would be out of a job. Bill asked her to undergo workplace counseling with someone from the human resources department. She refused, saying that "counseling is for nutjobs, not for me." He said that if she refused counseling that he had no choice but to assign her to the night shift so that she could do most of her work alone.

Late one night when Marcel was working Bill entered the warehouse as he sometimes did as part of his job duties. Warehouse security cameras recorded what happened next. Bill tiptoed up behind Marcel where she was standing alone in narrow aisle in a deserted part of the warehouse and grabbed her around the waist yelling "now I have got you," mugging for the security camera as he did so. Marcel broke free and punched Bill hard in the face, breaking his nose. Bill, who was much larger, shoved Marcel back hard. He then wiped the blood that was beginning to run out of his nose with his hand and yelled "you psycho bitch, now you have had it." Marcel immediately looked to her left and right, picked up a crow bar that was on a shelf next to her and hit Bill hard across the head with the claw end of the crow bar. Bill collapsed and Marcel continued hitting him on the head with the crowbar until a security guard who had witnessed the entire incident on his security monitor ran up to Marcel a minute later and told her to put the crow bar down.

With respect to Bill's death, Marcel has been charged in the alternative with Murder, Manslaughter, and Negligent Homicide in a Model Penal Code jurisdiction. At trial Marcel testified that she did not remember anything from the moment when Bill grabbed her from behind until the moment when security guard told her to put the crowbar down. Psychiatrists for the defense and prosecution agreed that Marcel suffered from post-traumatic stress disorder but offered conflicting testimony as to whether and how it affected her behavior at the time of the killing. The defense psychiatrist testified that she probably had a flashback in which she re-experienced the attack by her superior officer when she was in the army. He attributed her failure to remember her response to being grabbed as evidence of a dissociative disorder. A dissociative disorder impairs the normal state of awareness and limits or alters one's sense of identity, memory, or consciousness. The prosecution psychiatrist testified that Marcel simply had anger management issues as the result of her refusal to undergo counseling. He said that a dissociative episode involving memory loss could simply be the result of an explosive temper, something that he described as a character trait, not a mental disease or defect.

Analyze Marcel's liability for homicide crimes under the Model Penal Code.

CHAPTER 21

DURESS AND NECESSITY

■ ■ ■

Duress and necessity are two different doctrines that law students and judges sometimes confuse.

Duress is generally thought of as an excuse. Here is a classic example of duress. Your first-year criminal law professor becomes progressively more annoyed at the person sitting next to you in class, who smirks whenever the professor gets particularly serious about something and— even worse—never laughs at any of the professor's jokes. One day when this student is being particularly dismissive, the professor pulls out a gun, points it at you and orders you to slap the student across the face. To make things perfectly clear, the professor says that he is going to shoot you if you don't slap the student. You slap the student. After the cheering from your classmates dies down (the student really did get on everyone's nerves), someone calls the police. The professor and you are both arrested. You have a perfect defense, though. Your criminal responsibility for the misdemeanor battery is excused because you committed the crime under duress. The professor, on the other hand, is guilty not only of felonious assault for pointing a gun at you but also of the misdemeanor battery he forced you to commit.

Necessity is generally thought of as a justification. Here is a classic example of necessity. Imagine that, to recover from the stress of having your life threatened by one of your first-year professors, you go cross-country skiing. A freak storm suddenly develops, and you get caught in a terrible blizzard. Unable to see your hand in front of your face, you become hopelessly lost. Night begins to fall. Just when you think all is lost, you see a cabin in the woods. (Not the one from all the horror movies; that would be for a homicide fact pattern.) You stagger up to it and bang on all the doors and windows, but no one answers. Once night falls, it gets unbelievably cold. Realizing that you could freeze to death if you sleep outside, you break into the cabin and survive the night watching Netflix and drinking some beer you find in the refrigerator. Under the doctrine of necessity, you would be found not guilty of criminal trespass because breaking into the cabin is considered to be a lesser evil than dying in the snow. (You are guilty of stealing the beer, however, because no one ever died of lack of beer.)

At the outset, one must distinguish duress and necessity from other defenses that arise from a failure of proof with respect to one of the required elements. The law student committed a voluntary act when she slapped her fellow student and when she broke into the cabin. She also had the mental state required for assault/battery and for trespass. Duress and necessity come into play after the prosecutor proves the guilty hand, the guilty mind, and any required result.

A. ELEMENTS OF DURESS

The defense of duress is sometimes referred to as the defense of coercion. The defense existed at common law. A number of jurisdictions have reduced it to statutory form, but there is a great deal of variation from one state to another. States that are common law jurisdictions generally apply it even in the absence of a statute. For these reasons, it is harder than usual to generalize about the elements of duress. That said, the following description tracks how common law jurisdictions define the elements of duress.

1. A threat to kill or seriously injure the defendant or a third party unless the defendant commits the crime. At common law, the threat had to be to the defendant or to a member of his family, but many modern statues include any innocent third party.

2. The defendant reasonably believed that the threat would be carried out if he did not commit the crime.

3. The threat coerced the defendant to commit the crime. Not all jurisdictions require this element. Some require only that the defendant reasonably believed the threat as mentioned above.

4. The threat was of an imminent/immediate/instant/impending harm. Lots of variation in the words used here, but you get the idea. A threat of harm in the non-immediate future is insufficient because then you could presumably get help. (See below.)

5. No reasonable alternative existed. No time to call the police, and no other way to nullify the threatened harm or warn the intended victim.

6. The defendant has "clean hands." This means that the defendant did not do something wrong in the first place that exposed him to the threat, such as participating with others in committing a crime or joining a criminal organization. The idea here is that you should have known when you signed up to commit a crime with others that they might threaten you at some point if you did not do your part.

The common law was quite clear that duress could not be a defense to murder. So, if your crazy law professor puts the gun to your head and puts a knife on the desk in front of you and tells you to kill not slap the smirking student, then you have to take the bullet! If this last limitation on the defense seems a bit harsh to you, you have plenty of company. A number of jurisdictions have abandoned this limitation and allow duress to be a defense to a homicide crime.

Most jurisdictions also limit duress to harms emanating from human forces. In these jurisdictions, one cannot be "under duress" from natural forces or from a situation. Someone must threaten you, not something. Note also that orders from a boss or a commanding officer do not constitute duress (unless he points a gun at your head as he gives them).

1. DURESS UNDER THE MODEL PENAL CODE

§ 2.09. Duress

1. It is an affirmative defense that the actor engaged in the conduct charged to constitute an offense because he was coerced to do so by the use of, or a threat to use, unlawful force against his person or the person of another, that a person of reasonable firmness in his situation would have been unable to resist.

2. The defense provided by this Section is unavailable if the actor recklessly placed himself in a situation in which it was probable that he would be subjected to duress. The defense is also unavailable if he was negligent in placing himself in such a situation, whenever negligence suffices to establish culpability for the offense charged.

A number of jurisdictions have followed the MPC's lead.

- Duress is not limited to imminent threats of death or serious bodily injury but includes any coercion that a "person of ordinary firmness" would be unable to resist. This also opens duress to include threats of future harms although the harm must be of bodily injury or death.

- The person endangered does not have to be the defendant or a member of his family.

- Duress can be a defense to murder or a defense to a crime other than the one required by the person making the threat. (See below under prison escapes.)

The MPC also deals with the common law's clean hands/no fault requirement in a more nuanced way. If one recklessly or negligently exposed one's self to the threat, then one can be found guilty of a crime requiring a reckless or negligent mental state. As with self-defense, the MPC's aim here is to calibrate one's criminal liability to match the culpability of one's mental state. So check the membership rules next time you join a criminal street gang!

2. PRISON ESCAPES

Duress defenses are not infrequently raised in certain types of prison escapes. An inmate will claim that he had to escape custody (often a minimum-security facility where he can just walk away) in order to avoid being killed, badly beaten, or sexually assaulted. Jurisdictions are split on whether the defense raised is one of duress or necessity. The fact that human forces are at work suggests duress, but the threatened inmate is also committing the lesser evil of escaping to avoid the greater evil of death or felonious assault, which suggests necessity. In either event, most courts require the inmate to promptly turn themselves in once they have escaped the facility and also require some showing that the inmate could not have eliminated the threat by reporting it earlier.

The Model Penal Code also facilitates the use of duress in prison escapes by applying it to any crime that the threatened harm causes someone to commit. So, if your prison gang orders you to kill someone, you can escape instead and raise duress as a defense to the escape. You don't have to kill the person in order to raise the defense.

B. ELEMENTS OF THE NECESSITY DEFENSE

Necessity is messier and vaguer than duress. It did not seem to exist at English common law but has always been a part of American criminal law. In the absence of a statutory definition, courts apply a general definition from American common law. Some states have defined it by statute, although many of those definitions are vague. A once clear line between duress and necessity has blurred as the MPC and a number of jurisdictions have expanded the defense.

Necessity can generally be broken down into three interconnected elements.

1. The defendant faces an immediate danger that presents a "greater evil" than the "lesser evil" of the crime he is committing. Note that the evil avoided must be greater in the eyes of society, not just in the eyes of the actor. So, our blizzard-stranded law student is ok since society considers her life more important than the integrity of the cabin.

2. The crime committed must be the most reasonable way of averting the greater evil. If our law student could have safely called for help on her cell phone (what a cell phone

commercial that would make!) then she would not have a defense to breaking into the cabin.

3.   The defendant must have "clean hands." This means that the defendant neither created the emergency herself nor was otherwise at fault. I made the blizzard a freak storm to write this issue out of the hypo. If the storm had been predicted in a weather report that the law student failed to check, she would not have a defense to the trespass charge.

Note that a necessity defense can be ruled out by statute. The legislature can balance the evils on behalf of society. For example, a legislature's explicit decision to prohibit the use of marijuana even for medical purposes rules out an argument by users that their medical use of marijuana is the lesser evil than the greater evil of suffering without it.

Necessity defenses have been raised in a variety of different situations with varying degrees of success. Some of the more notable examples include the following:

- Needle exchange programs to control the spread of AIDS that violate restrictions on the distribution of hypodermic needles.

- Homeless people violating city ordinances against sleeping outside.

- Inmates escaping prisons to avoid dangerous or intolerable conditions.

- Parents kidnapping adult children from brainwashing cults.

- Some acts of civil disobedience.

Relatively few necessity defenses are successful, although the outcomes can be difficult to predict given the vagueness of the standards and the fact-specific nature of the inquiry. A city without homeless shelters might be hard-pressed to overcome the defense brought by the homeless because of the lack of reasonable alternatives to sleeping on the streets. Needle exchange activists, on the other hand, might have a difficult time establishing the imminence of the harm when infection by a shared needle is a matter of probability, not certainty.

Sometimes the line between necessity and duress becomes hard to draw. As discussed above, courts have split on whether the prison escape cases come within necessity, the key point being whether necessity is restricted to responses to human forces or only natural ones.

Practice Problem 21.1: A Turn for the Worse?

Your driving alone on a mountain road at a legal rate of speed. As you come around a sharp bend you see a crowd of small children standing in the road directly in front of you and a lone cyclist to your left in the opposite lane riding towards you. To the right of the children is the side of a mountain and there is no room for your vehicle to avoid the children. To the left of the cyclist is a cliff without a guardrail. There is no room for you to avoid the cyclist without either hitting some of the childen or driving off the steep cliff to your certain death. There is no time to brake. You turn away from the children killing the cyclist. Do you have a defense? Otherwise, what crime are you guilty of?

C. CASES IN CONTEXT

The following case explores the boundaries between duress and necessity.

UNITED STATES OF AMERICA V. JUAN MANUEL CONTENTO-PACHON
United States Court of Appeals, Ninth Circuit
723 F.2d 691 (1984)

Opinion by: BOOCHEVER.

This case presents an appeal from a conviction for unlawful possession with intent to distribute a narcotic controlled substance in violation of 21 U.S.C. § 841(a)(1) (1976). At trial, the defendant attempted to offer evidence of duress and necessity defenses. The district court excluded this evidence on the ground that it was insufficient to support the defenses. We reverse because there was sufficient evidence of duress to present a triable issue of fact.

I.   FACTS

The defendant-appellant, Juan Manuel Contento-Pachon, is a native of Bogota, Colombia and was employed there as a taxicab driver. He asserts that one of his passengers, Jorge, offered him a job as the driver of a privately-owned car. Contento-Pachon expressed an interest in the job and agreed to meet Jorge and the owner of the car the next day.

Instead of a driving job, Jorge proposed that Contento-Pachon swallow cocaine-filled balloons and transport them to the United States. Contento-Pachon agreed to consider the proposition. He was told not to mention the proposition to anyone, otherwise he would "get into serious trouble." Contento-Pachon testified that he did not contact the police because he believes that the Bogota police are corrupt and that they are paid off by drug traffickers.

Approximately one week later, Contento-Pachon told Jorge that he would not carry the cocaine. In response, Jorge mentioned facts about Contento-Pachon's personal life, including private details which Contento-Pachon had never mentioned to Jorge. Jorge told Contento-Pachon that his failure to cooperate would result in the death of his wife and three year-old child.

The following day the pair met again. Contento-Pachon's life and the lives of his family were again threatened. At this point, Contento-Pachon agreed to take the cocaine into the United States.

The pair met two more times. At the last meeting, Contento-Pachon swallowed 129 balloons of cocaine. He was informed that he would be watched at all times during the trip, and that if he failed to follow Jorge's instruction he and his family would be killed.

After leaving Bogota, Contento-Pachon's plane landed in Panama. Contento-Pachon asserts that he did not notify the authorities there because he felt that the Panamanian police were as corrupt as those in Bogota. Also, he felt that any such action on his part would place his family in jeopardy.

When he arrived at the customs inspection point in Los Angeles, Contento-Pachon consented to have his stomach x-rayed. The x-rays revealed a foreign substance which was later determined to be cocaine.

At Contento-Pachon's trial, the government moved to exclude the defenses of duress and necessity. The motion was granted. We reverse.

A. DURESS

There are three elements of the duress defense: (1) an immediate threat of death or serious bodily injury, (2) a well-grounded fear that the threat will be carried out, and (3) no reasonable opportunity to escape the threatened harm.

We examine the elements of duress.

Immediacy: The element of immediacy requires that there be some evidence that the threat of injury was present, immediate, or impending. "[A] veiled threat of future unspecified harm" will not satisfy this requirement. Rhode Island Recreation Center v. Aetna Casualty and Surety Co., 177 F.2d 603, 605 (1st Cir. 1949). See also United States v. Atencio, 586 F.2d 744, 746 (9th Cir. 1978) (per curiam) (citing United States v. Patrick, 542 F.2d 381 (7th Cir. 1976)). The district court found that the initial threats were not immediate because "they were conditioned on defendant's failure to cooperate in the future and did not place defendant and his family in immediate danger."

Evidence presented on this issue indicated that the defendant was dealing with a man who was deeply involved in the exportation of illegal substances. Large sums of money were at stake and, consequently,

Contento-Pachon had reason to believe that Jorge would carry out his threats. Jorge had gone to the trouble to discover that Contento-Pachon was married, that he had a child, the names of his wife and child, and the location of his residence. These were not vague threats of possible future harm. According to the defendant, if he had refused to cooperate, the consequences would have been immediate and harsh.

Contento-Pachon contends that he was being watched by one of Jorge's accomplices at all times during the airplane trip. As a consequence, the force of the threats continued to restrain him. Contento-Pachon's contention that he was operating under the threat of immediate harm was supported by sufficient evidence to present a triable issue of fact.

Escapability: The defendant must show that he had no reasonable opportunity to escape. See United States v. Gordon, 526 F.2d 406, 407 (9th Cir. 1975). The district court found that because Contento-Pachon was not physically restrained prior to the time he swallowed the balloons, he could have sought help from the police or fled. Contento-Pachon explained that he did not report the threats because he feared that the police were corrupt. The trier of fact should decide whether one in Contento-Pachon's position might believe that some of the Bogota police were paid informants for drug traffickers and that reporting the matter to the police did not represent a reasonable opportunity of escape.

If he chose not to go to the police, Contento-Pachon's alternative was to flee. We reiterate that the opportunity to escape must be reasonable. To flee, Contento-Pachon, along with his wife and three year-old child, would have been forced to pack his possessions, leave his job, and travel to a place beyond the reaches of the drug traffickers. A juror might find that this was not a reasonable avenue of escape. Thus, Contento-Pachon presented a triable issue on the element of escapability.

B. NECESSITY

The defense of necessity is available when a person is faced with a choice of two evils and must then decide whether to commit a crime or an alternative act that constitutes a greater evil. United States v. Richardson, 588 F.2d 1235, 1239 (9th Cir. 1978), cert. denied, 441 U.S. 931, 99 S. Ct. 2049, 60 L. Ed. 2d 658, cert. denied, 440 U.S. 947, 59 L. Ed. 2d 636, 99 S. Ct. 1426 (1979). Contento-Pachon has attempted to justify his violation of 21 U.S.C. § 841(a)(1) by showing that the alternative, the death of his family, was a greater evil.

Traditionally, in order for the necessity defense to apply, the coercion must have had its source in the physical forces of nature. The duress defense was applicable when the defendant's acts were coerced by a human force. W. LaFave & A. Scott, Handbook on Criminal Law § 50 at 383 (1972). This distinction served to separate the two similar defenses. But modern courts have tended to blur the distinction between duress and necessity.

It has been suggested that, "the major difference between duress and necessity is that the former negates the existence of the requisite mens rea for the crime in question, whereas under the latter theory there is no actus reus." United States v. Micklus, 581 F.2d 612, 615 (7th Cir. 1978). The theory of necessity is that the defendant's free will was properly exercised to achieve the greater good and not that his free will was overcome by an outside force as with duress.

The defense of necessity is usually invoked when the defendant acted in the interest of the general welfare.

Contento-Pachon's acts were allegedly coerced by human, not physical forces. In addition, he did not act to promote the general welfare. Therefore, the necessity defense was not available to him. Contento-Pachon mischaracterized evidence of duress as evidence of necessity. The district court correctly disallowed his use of the necessity defense.

II. CONCLUSION

Contento-Pachon presented credible evidence that he acted under an immediate and well-grounded threat of serious bodily injury, with no opportunity to escape. Because the trier of fact should have been allowed to consider the credibility of the proffered evidence, we reverse.

Concur by: COYLE (In Part).

Dissent by: COYLE (In Part).

DISSENT

COYLE, DISTRICT JUDGE (dissenting in part and concurring in part):

In excluding the defense of duress, the trial court specifically found Contento-Pachon had failed to present sufficient evidence to establish the necessary elements of immediacy and inescapability. In its Order the district court stated:

The first threat made to defendant and his family about three weeks before the flight was not immediate; the threat was conditioned upon defendant's failure to cooperate in the future and did not place the defendant and his family in immediate danger or harm. Moreover, after the initial threat and until he went to the house where he ingested the balloons containing cocaine, defendant and his family were not physically restrained and could have sought help from the police or fled. See United States v. Gordon, 526 F.2d 406 (9th Cir. 1975). No such efforts were attempted by defendant. Thus, defendant's own offer of proof negates two necessary elements of the defense of duress.

This finding is adequately supported by the record.

I agree with the majority, however, that the district court properly excluded Contento-Pachon's necessity defense.

DISCUSSION QUESTIONS

1. Do you agree with the court's interpretation of the necessity defense?

2. Do you agree with the court's interpretation of the duress defense?

3. How do you strike the balance between utilitarian and blameworthiness concerns in a case like this?

Practice Problem 21.2: Desert in the Desert

A group of humanitarian aid workers have been leaving water bottles in remote areas of desert that span the border between the United States and Mexico. They leave the bottles so that people crossing the border illegally into the United States will not die of thirst. A number of migrants have died in the desert from thirst during these illegal crossings. The workers have been charged with the crime of assisting people to enter the United States illegally. Do the aid workers have a necessity defense? What further facts would you need to know?

Case in Context

The next case explores similar issues in the context of a prison escape.

ILLINOIS V. UNGER

Supreme Court of Illinois
66 Ill. 2d 333 (1977)

Opinion by: RYAN.

Defendant, Francis Unger, was charged with the crime of escape (Ill. Rev. Stat. 1971, ch. 108, par. 121), and was convicted following a jury trial. The conviction was reversed upon appeal. We affirm the judgment of the appellate court.

At the time of the present offense, the defendant was confined at the Illinois State Penitentiary in Joliet, Illinois. Defendant was serving a one- to three-year term as a consequence of a conviction for auto theft in Ogle County. Defendant began serving this sentence in December of 1971. On February 23, 1972, the defendant was transferred to the prison's minimum security, honor farm. It is undisputed that on March 7, 1972, the defendant walked off the honor farm. Defendant was apprehended two days later in a motel room in St. Charles, Illinois.

At trial, defendant testified that prior to his transfer to the honor farm he had been threatened by a fellow inmate. This inmate allegedly brandished a six-inch knife in an attempt to force defendant to engage in homosexual activities. Defendant was 22 years old and weighed approximately 155 pounds. He testified that he did not report the incident to the proper authorities due to fear of retaliation. Defendant also testified that he is not a particularly good fighter.

Defendant stated that after his transfer to the honor farm he was assaulted and sexually molested by three inmates, and he named the assailants at trial. The attack allegedly occurred on March 2, 1972, and from that date until his escape defendant received additional threats from inmates he did not know. On March 7, 1972, the date of the escape, defendant testified that he received a call on an institution telephone. Defendant testified that the caller, whose voice he did not recognize, threatened him with death because the caller had heard that defendant had reported the assault to prison authorities. Defendant said that he left the honor farm to save his life and that he planned to return once he found someone who could help him. None of these incidents were reported to the prison officials.

Defendant's first trial for escape resulted in a hung jury. The jury in the second trial returned its verdict after a five-hour deliberation. The following instruction (People's Instruction No. 9) was given by the trial court over defendant's objection.

"The reasons, if any, given for the alleged escape are immaterial and not to be considered by you as in any way justifying or excusing, if there were in fact such reasons."

The appellate court majority found that the giving of People's Instruction No. 9 was reversible error. (33 Ill. App. 3d 770, 777.) Two instructions which were tendered by defendant but refused by the trial court are also germane to this appeal. Defendant's instructions Nos. 1 and 3 were predicated upon the affirmative defenses of compulsion and necessity. (Ill. Rev. Stat. 1971, ch. 38, pars. 7–11 (compulsion), 7–13 (necessity).) Defendant's instructions Nos. 1 and 3 read as follows:

"It is a defense to the charge made against the Defendant that he left the Honor Farm of the Illinois State Penitentiary by reason of necessity if the accused was without blame in occasioning or developing the situation and reasonably believed such conduct was necessary to avoid a public or private injury greater than the injury which might reasonably result from his own conduct."

"It is a defense to the charge made against the Defendant that he acted under the compulsion of threat or menace of the imminent infliction of death or great bodily harm, if he reasonably believed death or great bodily harm would be inflicted upon him if he did not perform the conduct with which he is charged."

The principal issue in the present appeal is whether it was error for the court to instruct the jury that it must disregard the reasons given for defendant's escape and to conversely refuse to instruct the jury on the statutory defenses of compulsion and necessity. The State contends that, under the facts and circumstances of this case, the defenses of compulsion and necessity are, as a matter of law, unavailable to defendant.

Proper resolution of this appeal requires some preliminary remarks concerning the law of compulsion and necessity as applied to prison escape situations. Traditionally, the courts have been reluctant to permit the defenses of compulsion and necessity to be relied upon by escapees. (See 1975 U. Ill. L.F. 271, 274–75 & n.23, and the cases cited therein.) This reluctance appears to have been primarily grounded upon considerations of public policy. Several recent decisions, however, have recognized the applicability of the compulsion and necessity defenses to prison escapes. In People v. Harmon (1974), 53 Mich. App. 482, 220 N.W.2d 212, the defense of duress was held to apply in a case where the defendant alleged that he escaped in order to avoid repeated homosexual attacks from fellow inmates. In People v. Lovercamp (1974), 43 Cal. App. 3d 823, 118 Cal. Rptr. 110, a limited defense of necessity was held to be available to two defendants whose escapes were allegedly motivated by fear of homosexual attacks.

As illustrated by Harmon and Lovercamp, different courts have reached similar results in escape cases involving sexual abuse, though the question was analyzed under different defense theories. A certain degree of confusion has resulted from the recurring practice on the part of the courts to use the terms "compulsion" (duress) and "necessity" interchangeably, though the defenses are theoretically distinct. (Gardner, The Defense of Necessity and the Right to Escape from Prison—A Step Towards Incarceration Free From Sexual Assault, 49 S. Cal. L. Rev. 110, 115 (1975); Note, Duress—Defense to Escape, 3 Am. J. Crim. L. 331, 332 (1975).) It has been suggested that the major distinction between the two defenses is that the source of the coercive power in cases of compulsion is from human beings, whereas in situations of necessity the pressure on the defendant arises from the forces of nature. (LaFave and Scott, Handbook on Criminal Law 381 (1972).) Also, as noted in the dissenting opinion in the appellate court, the defense of compulsion generally requires an impending, imminent threat of great bodily harm together with a demand that the person perform the specific criminal act for which he is eventually charged. (33 Ill. App. 3d 770, 777 (Stengel, J., dissenting); People v. Terry (1975), 30 Ill. App. 3d 713; People v. Davis (1974), 16 Ill. App. 3d 846.) Additionally, where the defense of compulsion is successfully asserted the coercing party is guilty of the crime.

It is readily discernible that prison escapes induced by fear of homosexual assaults and accompanying physical reprisals do not conveniently fit within the traditional ambits of either the compulsion or the necessity defense. However, it has been suggested that such cases could best be analyzed in terms of necessity. (LaFave and Scott, Handbook on Criminal Law 381–82 n.2 (1972).) One commentator has stated that the relevant consideration should be whether the defendant chose the lesser of two evils, in which case the defense of necessity would apply, or whether he was unable to exercise a free choice at all, in which event compulsion would be the appropriate defense.

In our view, the defense of necessity, as defined by our statute (Ill. Rev. Stat. 1971, ch. 38, par. 7–13), is the appropriate defense in the present case. In a very real sense, the defendant here was not deprived of his free will by the threat of imminent physical harm which appears to be the intended interpretation of the defense of compulsion as set out in the Criminal Code. Rather, if defendant's testimony is believed, he was forced to choose between two admitted evils by the situation which arose from actual and threatened homosexual assaults and fears of reprisal. Though the defense of compulsion would be applicable in the unlikely event that a prisoner was coerced by the threat of imminent physical harm to perform the specific act of escape, no such situation is involved in the present appeal. We, therefore, turn to a consideration of whether the evidence presented by the defendant justified the giving of an instruction on the defense of necessity.

The defendant's testimony was clearly sufficient to raise the affirmative defense of necessity. Defendant testified that he was subjected to threats of forced homosexual activity and that, on one occasion, the threatened abuse was carried out. He also testified that he was physically incapable of defending himself and that he feared greater harm would result from a report to the authorities. Defendant further testified that just prior to his escape he was told that he was going to be killed, and that he therefore fled the honor farm in order to save his life. It is clear that defendant introduced some evidence to support the defense of necessity. [T]hat is sufficient to justify the giving of an appropriate instruction.

The State, however, would have us apply a more stringent test to prison escape situations. The State refers to the Lovercamp decision, where only a limited necessity defense was recognized. In Lovercamp, it was held that the defense of necessity need be submitted to the jury only where five conditions had been met. (43 Cal. App. 3d 823, 831, 118 Cal. Rptr. 110, 115.) Those conditions are:

"(1) The prisoner is faced with a specific threat of death, forcible sexual attack or substantial bodily injury in the immediate future;

(2) There is no time for a complaint to the authorities or there exists a history of futile complaints which make any result from such complaints illusory;

(3) There is no time or opportunity to resort to the courts;

(4) There is no evidence of force or violence used towards prison personnel or other 'innocent' persons in the escape; and

(5) The prisoner immediately reports to the proper authorities when he has attained a position of safety from the immediate threat."

The State correctly points out that the defendant never informed the authorities of his situation and failed to report immediately after securing a position of safety. Therefore, it is contended that, under the authority of Lovercamp, defendant is not entitled to a necessity instruction. We agree with the State and with the court in Lovercamp that the above conditions are relevant factors to be used in assessing claims of necessity. We cannot say, however, that the existence of each condition is, as a matter of law, necessary to establish a meritorious necessity defense.

The preconditions set forth in Lovercamp are, in our view, matters which go to the weight and credibility of the defendant's testimony. The absence of one or more of the elements listed in Lovercamp would not necessarily mandate a finding that the defendant could not assert the defense of necessity.

By way of example, in the present case defendant did not report to the authorities immediately after securing his safety. However, defendant testified that he intended to return to the prison upon obtaining legal advice from an attorney and claimed that he was attempting to get money from friends to pay for such counsel. Regardless of our opinion as to the believability of defendant's tale, this testimony, if accepted by the jury, would have negated any negative inference which would arise from defendant's failure to report to proper authorities after the escape. The absence of one of the Lovercamp preconditions does not alone disprove the claim of necessity and should not, therefore, automatically preclude an instruction on the defense.

DISCUSSION QUESTIONS

1. Do you agree with the court's interpretation of the necessity defense?

2. Do you agree with the court's interpretation of the duress defense?

3. Should the criminal law assume that prison conditions may sometimes justify or excuse escapes? If so, what should happen to an inmate who successfully prevails on such a defense?

1. NECESSITY UNDER THE MODEL PENAL CODE

The MPC roughly follows the common law approach but expands the defense in a number of ways. First, the defense is not limited to natural forces but also includes human ones, so prison escape cases may qualify. Second, the need not be imminent, although it still must not be reasonably avoidable. Finally, whether fault on the part of the defendant in creating the impending harm bars raising the defense depends on the degree of fault involved and the mental state required for the crime. One who recklessly creates a hazard remains criminally liable for any crime requiring a reckless state of mind, and one who is grossly negligent remains liable for crimes requiring gross negligence. Finally, commentary to the Code suggests that necessity might justify taking one life to save more lives, although no case so holding yet exists.

§ 3.02. Justification Generally: Choice of Evils

1. Conduct that the actor believes to be necessary to avoid a harm or evil to himself or to another is justifiable, provided that:

    a. the harm or evil sought to be avoided by such conduct is greater than that sought to be prevented by the law defining the offense charged; and

    b. neither the Code nor other law defining the offense provides exceptions or defenses dealing with the specific situation involved; and

    c. a legislative purpose to exclude the justification claimed does not otherwise plainly appear.

When the actor was reckless or negligent in bringing about the situation requiring a choice of harms or evils or in appraising the necessity for his conduct, the justification afforded by this Section is unavailable in a prosecution for any offense for which recklessness or negligence, as the case may be, suffices to establish culpability.

Return to the case of *Regina v. Dudley and Stephens*. One of the principle issues raised was whether the killing of one was a "lesser evil" than the "greater evil" of the death of the remaining sailors and thereby justified under the doctrine of necessity. The court denied the defense. Although acknowledging that the temptation of the starving, dying men was overwhelming and conceding that the man killed would have died anyway, the court refused to either justify or excuse the killing. The court's opinion can be read many ways, but one of the simpler points was that necessity stops short of justifying the killing of an innocent person. The idea that necessity is not a defense to an intentional killing seems to be generally accepted. Although troubling counterexamples have been raised from time to time (including the unexecuted decision on 9/11 to shoot down a hijacked plane filled with innocent passengers before it could be crashed into a government building in the nation's capital), no judicial case has yet ruled to the contrary.

Practice Problem 21.3: Going Viral

Doctor Poe is charged in a Model Penal Code jurisdiction with Murder, Manslaughter, and Negligent Homicide. Poe was the ship doctor on a South Pacific cruise ship that suffered an outbreak of the Dbola virus.

The Dbola virus is highly dangerous. It is 100% lethal if untreated. Early detection and treatment only reduces the average mortality rate to 60%. People who are younger or in good health are somewhat more likely to survive the virus. The first symptom is a high fever. The first stage of treatment requires that patients immediately and continuously receive a hydrating fluid containing blood plasma through an intravenous ("IV") drip to keep them stable. Without the plasma IV patients often die in a few hours. Dbola is also agonizingly painful although the pain can be managed by the pain killing drug morphine. Dbola can easily spread through contact with an infected person's bodily fluids once the patient has become feverish. For this reason, patients are immediately quarantined. Health care providers are at high risk for infection unless they carefully follow stringent infection control procedures.

All agree that Poe acted diligently and effectively in diagnosing and containing the outbreak. Three passengers were afflicted. Making the most of the limited facilities on board, Poe created a quarantine zone in the ship's sick bay, immediately began administering the plasma IV to keep the patients stable, and had the captain radio for a helicopter to evacuate the patients to the nearest hospital. She was assisted by a single male nurse who possessed the specialized training required for dealing with Dbola. Both observed the infection control procedures as well as they could, given the limited protective equipment available.

The three patients ranged in age and health. Michael, a teenage boy, was in excellent physical condition. May, an elderly woman in her seventies who was an avid swimmer was in excellent physical condition for her age. Don, a middle-aged lawyer, was an obese ex-smoker in generally poor health.

Unfortunately, the outbreak struck when the ship was far out to sea and just as a sudden storm made helicopter flight impossible. These weather conditions were predicted to last for 72 hours. After 24 hours Poe's nurse informed her that there would not be enough plasma to keep all three patients stable until the storm passed and that they were also running out of morphine. While speaking with the nurse about the lack of plasma and morphine Poe noticed that she, herself, was feeling feverish. Poe immediately took her own temperature and realized that she was running a temperature of 105 degrees, the first symptom of the Dbola virus. Poe immediately dismissed the nurse from sick bay with orders that he remain under quarantine in his quarters and that he have no direct contact with anyone else until he could be evacuated along with the patients. Poe told the nurse that she would tend to the patients alone and would summon the nurse only if she could function no longer. When the nurse protested, Poe insisted, arguing that obviously the virus was spreading and that she did not want to risk the nurse becoming infected as well. Reluctantly the nurse agreed but first asked what Poe would do about the diminishing supplies of plasma and morphine. Poe said that she would save as many people as possible.

Up to this point in time the morphine and plasma had been equally allocated between all three patients. After the nurse left, Poe removed Don's plasma IV. She allocated 80% of Don's plasma equally between Michael and May and placed the remaining 20% in a small intravenous drip bag that she administered to herself. After an hour, Don became delirious with pain and began screaming incoherently, yelling that Poe was going to kill them all. Poe combined the remaining portions of Michael and May's pain medication and administered all of it to Don. Michael and May immediately began to experience agonizing pain, which continued until they were evacuated by helicopter. Don's pain immediately abated, but he died within two hours.

The storm blew over 24 hours earlier than expected and Michael, May, Poe, and the nurse were all evacuated to a hospital in American Samoa where their treatment continued. Michael died, and May survived. Neither Poe nor the male nurse turned out to be infected with Dbola. Poe's fever was the result of a common flu virus.

Expert medical testimony at the trial established the following: It was extremely unlikely that either Don or May would have survived if the storm had lasted 48 more hours as expected because all three would have run out of plasma and Don's obesity and May's age would have made their survival extremely unlikely. Reallocating 80% of Don's fluids to Michael and May would have been sufficient to keep them stable for the remaining 48 hours that the storm was expected to last. If the plasma had continued to be equally allocated among all three patients for the remaining 24 hours that the storm lasted, all three patients would probably have remained stable. If all three patients were stable at the time of evacuation, May would have had a 45% chance of surviving, Don a 50% chance and Michael a 75% chance. Without the plasma drip Don had virtually no chance of surviving for more than twelve hours. The extra dose of pain medication administered by Poe to Don after his plasma was cut off was necessary to manage his pain but was highly likely to stop his breathing within a few hours given his poor health and the absence of the plasma. Without the pain medication, however, he would have been in unspeakable agony for the remaining hours of his life. Testimony also established that, if Poe had been infected with Dbola, the modest plasma drip she self-administered would have made it more likely that she would remain functional until the storm passed, and would have increased the chance of her eventual survival from five percent to fifty per cent. Any competent doctor under the circumstances would be expected to know all of the above, and Poe admitted to knowing all of the above in a statement to the police investigators.

Doctor Poe has been charged in the alternative with Murder, Manslaughter, and Negligent Homicide with respect to Don's death under the Model Penal Code. Analyze her criminal liability for these charges.

CHAPTER 22

INSANITY AND RELATED DEFENSES

■ ■ ■

Should someone be criminally punished if as the result of mental illness he believes that God has ordered him to kill someone, or if he kills a person he believes has been beaming radio waves into his head, or if he feels an overwhelming compulsion to attack the next person who speaks to him? Insanity is the classic excuse. Retribution and deterrence both presume a person's ability to make rational choices. How can a person be morally responsible for his behavior when his mind tricks him into seeing, hearing, and thinking things that are not real or rational? And how can such a person be deterred?

Insanity seems like the perfect excuse because it destroys the ability to make meaningful choices. Yet, America's individualistic culture has always been very skeptical of excuses. "It is not my fault that I never learned to accept responsibility," the joke goes. We have also been particularly hard on those claiming excuses based on mental illness. Opinion surveys consistently show that most people see insanity as a "fake excuse" built on fabricated evidence of mental illness. Yet mental illness is all too real, and the idea that it makes a difference to criminal responsibility is not a modern notion but a very old one.

The insanity defense is hard to establish, rarely asserted, and even more rarely successful. Still, it remains an important doctrine to study because it describes an outer boundary to our notions of personal responsibility and raises fundamental issues about the purposes of punishment.

Related to insanity but different in its standards and consequences are the doctrines of diminished capacity and partial responsibility. They operate in a small minority of jurisdictions but are worthy of brief discussion.

A. DIMINISHED CAPACITY AND PARTIAL RESPONSIBILITY

Diminished capacity and partial responsibility are two terms that have sometimes been used interchangeably to refer to doctrines that mitigate or rule out guilt on the basis of mental health conditions that fall short of insanity. The broad version of this doctrine allows for a defense to any crime. The narrow form allows for arguments that may reduce premeditated and deliberate murder down to intentional murder or intentional murder down to voluntary manslaughter. Following one leading treatise and a trend among some courts we will refer to the broad form of this defense that potentially applies to all crimes as diminished capacity and the narrow form that potentially applies only to homicide crimes as partial responsibility since the very term "partial responsibility" admits of some remaining criminal liability.

1. DIMINISHED CAPACITY

A small number of jurisdictions follow the Model Penal Code in allowing evidence of some mental condition, short of insanity, to establish that the defendant did not have the capacity to form the mental state required for the offense. It is difficult to find examples in the cases, however, of conditions which, if proved, would not support a finding of lack of cognition or lack of volition sufficient to establish insanity. The significance of this doctrine may lie in the different allocations of the burden of proof involved. Imagine that a defendant wishes to put on evidence of a mental condition that leads him to lash out violently at people when he is in a crowd. Since many jurisdictions put the burden of proof of an insanity defense on the defendant, he might have to prove his lack of volition if pleading insanity. In a diminished capacity jurisdiction, however, the prosecution would have to prove his general or specific intent (depending on the charge) beyond a reasonable doubt and would have to in the process disprove the defense's evidence that he possessed no such intent.

Some jurisdictions will admit evidence of diminished mental capacity to disprove specific intent (usually requiring purpose or knowledge) but not general intent crimes (usually requiring recklessness or negligence).

While one may think of diminished capacity as disproving mental states, the actual standard is a bit different. Diminished capacity means that the mental condition prevented the defendant from forming the required mental state or "negated his capacity" to form it.

MODEL PENAL CODE

§ 4.02. Evidence of Mental Disease or Defect Admissible When Relevant to Element of the Offense

1. Evidence that the defendant suffered from a mental disease or defect is admissible whenever it is relevant to prove that the defendant did or did not have a state of mind that is an element of the offense.

2. PARTIAL RESPONSIBILITY

In practice, use of mental diseases or defects short of insanity to disprove one's capacity to form a required mental state is most common in the context of homicide, and a few jurisdictions have limited such evidence to the homicide context. Evidence of a brain disorder that impaired a person's ability to plan or deliberate might be admitted to disprove (or negate) premeditation and deliberation in a first degree murder case. Similarly, a mental condition that resulted in explosive anger might be used to negate the malice of intentional murder and permit a verdict of only voluntary manslaughter in these jurisdictions.

B. OVERVIEW OF THE ELEMENTS OF INSANITY

Insanity is a legal concept, not a medical one. Doctors diagnose patients with various mental illnesses and disorders, but medical science does not define sanity or insanity because it has no need for such a definition.

Society needs a definition of insanity for two different purposes. First, society needs a civil definition of insanity to determine when a person may be committed involuntarily to a mental institution (although people who are subject to involuntary commitment are not generally referred to as insane anymore). This definition is a somewhat empty one: it generally provides that a person may be involuntarily committed when they are a danger to themselves or others. Second, society needs a criminal definition of insanity to decide when a person should be excused from criminal responsibility for their actions. Law, not medicine, supplies both definitions because the question is ultimately a philosophical and policy question. For your criminal law class, you need only learn the second definition, which continues to be referred to as insanity.

Although variations of each test exist, most jurisdictions have settled on one of two definitions of insanity: the M'Naghten test and the Model Penal Code test (also referred to as the "ALI" or American Law Institute test).

The M'Naghten test dates from the common law and defines as insane one who as a result of mental disease or defect fails to

1.   Know the Nature and Quality of his Act or who fails to

2.   Know the Difference between Right and Wrong.

The M'Naghten test is generally described as a cognitive test because it defines insanity solely in terms of a defendant's ability to know things.

In contrast, the MPC test adds a volitional test which concerns a defendant's ability to control his actions. The MPC test defines as insane one who as the result of mental disease or defect lacks the

1. Substantial Capacity to Appreciate the Criminality or Wrongfulness of his act or who lacks the

2. Substantial Capacity to Conform his Conduct to the requirements of the law.

In addition to adding a volitional component, the MPC also requires less of an impairment than the M'Naghten test. Under M'Naghten, one must not know, which implies a complete lack of capacity to know. In contrast, the MPC test is satisfied if one lacks the substantial capacity to satisfy either the cognitive or volitional prong. Note that both tests require an element in addition to a mental disease or defect. Although you can't be insane without a mental illness, the existence of a mental illness alone does not necessarily make you insane.

C. PROCEDURAL BACKGROUND

A variety of procedural issues surround the insanity defense. While outside the scope of what is taught in most first-year criminal law courses, these issues provide useful background. Substantial variation exists between jurisdictions, but a few general observations can be made.

First, those found to be insane during criminal proceedings are usually involuntarily committed to a mental institution. This essentially means that a person is confined to a mental hospital. You might wonder how society can confine a person if they have been found not guilty on grounds of insanity. The answer is that this confinement is civil in nature and not considered criminal punishment. We confine a defendant, not to punish him, but to treat the mental disease or defect that produced his insanity. Additionally, mental illness is not the only ground for such civil commitments. A person with a dangerous contagious disease can also be civilly confined for treatment under certain circumstances. Like a patient with a contagious disease, the criminally insane will also be released from civil confinement when he is no longer a danger to himself or others. Thus, the nature of involuntary commitment is one reason why so few defendants present insanity defenses. For a variety of reasons, many would rather face imprisonment for a definite term than an open-ended commitment to a hospital that only ends once they have been "cured."

The other important procedural consideration is burden of proof. Insanity is an affirmative defense. In all states, a defendant must present some initial mental health evidence in order to raise the defense. The burden would then switch to the prosecution to prove the defendant's sanity at the time of the crime beyond a reasonable doubt. This is still the case in a minority of jurisdictions. A majority of jurisdictions, however, now require the defendant to prove insanity by a preponderance of the evidence (which means roughly a 51% probability), and the federal courts and some others require proof by clear and convincing evidence.

Whatever the burden of proof, most jurisdictions allow for three different verdicts in an insanity case: guilty, not guilty, and not guilty by reason of insanity. The not guilty verdict is necessary because the state might not be able to prove the defendant guilty beyond a reasonable doubt, regardless of the defendant's sanity. (The defendant might not be the person who committed the crime, for example.) Not guilty by reason of insanity means that the prosecution proved beyond a reasonable doubt that the defendant committed the crime except for the defendant's insanity. A guilty verdict means that the defendant committed the crime and was sane.

A substantial minority of jurisdictions have created a different, fourth option: guilty but mentally ill. This verdict subjects the defendant to a prison sentence but allows the defendant to be treated while in prison. Even if cured, however, the defendant must finish his sentence. Proponents of this fourth option argue that it reduces improper insanity verdicts by giving the jury a way to recognize the mental illness of the offender while still finding him to be sane and criminally responsible. Critics point out that it is at best unnecessary—since all inmates found guilty may receive psychiatric care—and at worst a cruel trick since the jury may believe that the verdict not just allows but entitles the inmate to psychiatric care (which it does not). Critics also argue that the temptation to use this verdict to "split the baby" between guilty and insane will encourage juries to find insane defendants to be sane.

1. COMPETENCY DISTINGUISHED

Insanity should be distinguished from mental incompetence. Insanity deals with one's mental condition at the time the crime was committed. In contrast, incompetency concerns one's mental condition at the time of trial. It is a violation of constitutional due process to put a mentally incompetent person on trial. The standards for incompetency and insanity are also different. A defendant is incompetent if he 1) is unable to assist his attorney prepare or present his defense or if he 2) does not understand the nature of the proceedings against him. To use some extreme examples, a mentally ill defendant who was incapable of coherent speech would fail the first prong, and a defendant who believed that he was a king and the trial was an effort to depose him from the throne would fail the second prong.

Being found incompetent to stand trial does not result in one's release. One is confined and treated until one is competent and then put on trial. A person who never regains competency might never be tried or released.

D. MENTAL DISEASE OR DEFECT

Under any of the tests, the foundation for an insanity defense requires the defendant to fail the cognitive or volitional test as the result of a mental disease or defect. Generally, a person might be unable to distinguish right from wrong or control his impulses due to reasons other than a mental disease or defect. For example, he may have been raised by evil parents to become an evil person. Such a condition, however, would not make a person insane because it is not a mental disease or defect.

While no clear legal definition of mental disease or defect exists, disease is generally considered to be something that can be cured or managed by treatment (such as schizophrenia) and a defect is a permanent condition (such as a condition caused by a traumatic brain injury). In this area, the law defers largely to medical science, and some widely recognized diagnosis is generally required. Any mental disorder would suffice, including organic brain damage, a brain tumor that impairs thinking, and basic intellectual deficiencies (e.g. extremely low IQ).

Although in theory, syndromes such as postpartum depression or post-traumatic stress disorder could suffice, in practice, only extreme forms of psychosis tend to satisfy the M'Naghten or the MPC test. One may be grossly impaired by any number of conditions, but to not know one's actions or to not know right from wrong requires a gross distortion of reality. Similarly, to be unable to control one's self requires a gross impairment of control.

One group of disorders has been expressly excluded from the definition of mental disease or defect in all jurisdictions: psychopathy, sociopathy, and any condition whose only symptom is the tendency to commit criminal or anti-social acts. Criminality itself does not constitute insanity. Also, some jurisdictions require a "severe" mental disease or defect in order to rule out mere neuroses, personality disorders, or low-level impairments resulting from the habitual use of alcohol or illegal drugs.

E. M'NAGHTEN TEST

The M'Naghten test is the majority rule and a version of it is used in the federal system. The test has two cognitive prongs. A person is insane if he satisfies either prong. Once again, the predicate for either prong is that your lack of knowledge is the result of a mental disease or defect.

- Not know the Nature and Quality of the act or

- Not know the Wrongfulness of the Act

These prongs are distinct, but the first can affect the second. If you don't know what you are doing, you clearly cannot know that it is wrong, but it is possible to know what you are doing but not know that it is wrong. Imagine that you shoot a police officer who approaches your car because you believe she is an alien invader. If you don't know that you are shooting a human being, the question of whether you know that it is wrongful to kill a human being under these circumstances becomes moot. Now, imagine that you believe that the police officer is a human being who is working with the alien forces to kill or enslave human beings. You know that you are killing a human being, but arguably you can't know the wrongfulness of that act if you believe that you are protecting yourself and other human beings from death or enslavement at the hands of an alien race.

Narrow and broad definitions of knowledge exist among the states applying this test. The narrow definition interprets knowledge as an intellectual awareness. A person is considered to "know" the nature and quality of the act if he can describe in mechanical terms what he did, and he is considered to "know" its wrongfulness if he can acknowledge the act is considered to be wrong. Additionally, the broader interpretation of "know" requires that a person is able to appreciate the significance more fully, to grasp its consequences and meaning in the grand scale of things. Some refer to this broader meaning of "know" as affective or emotional knowledge. Although most M'Naghten jurisdictions have not defined "know" with any specificity, some research suggests that the broader understanding of "know" is usually applied.

For example, in the early eighties John Hinckley tried to assassinate President Ronald Reagan in order to attract the attention and affection of the actress Jodie Foster, with whom Hinckley had become deeply obsessed as the result of a mental illness. Hinckley clearly satisfied the narrow definition of knowledge. He knew that he was trying to kill the President of the United States. He also knew that he would be imprisoned for it. That may, in fact, have been part of his plan to win the affections (or at least the attention) of Ms. Foster. But one could argue that Hinckley failed the broader definition of knowledge under M'Naghten. Did he really think that killing the President was going to get him a date with Jodie Foster? That a famous actress, or anyone for that matter, would be romantically intrigued with someone just because they assassinated the head of our government? Hinckley's failure to "see the big picture" through his psychosis arguably makes him insane under the broader—but not the narrower—definition of knowledge under M'Naghten.

Different interpretations also exist as to whether "wrongful" in M'Naghten's second prong refers to legal or moral wrongfulness. Imagine a defendant kills his nextdoor neighbor because of a paranoid delusion that his neighbor has been poisoning his food. The defendant might recognize that the killing would be considered legally wrong but not consider it morally wrongful because of the danger and pain he suffered at the hands of his neighbor. Jurisdictions are split on whether legal or moral wrongfulness is required for insanity under M'Naghten. In any event, the difference may be minimal because courts that use moral wrongfulness define wrongful in terms of societal standards, not the defendant's personal sense of right or wrong. So, if our delusional defendant understands that society would consider the killing of his neighbor to be wrongful, then he would not be insane even though he personally believes the killing to be righteous.

Case in Context

The next case involves both insanity and diminished capacity.

ERIC MICHAEL CLARK V. ARIZONA

Supreme Court of the United States
548 U.S. 735 (2006)

JUSTICE SOUTER delivered the opinion of the Court.

The case presents two questions: whether due process prohibits Arizona's use of an insanity test stated solely in terms of the capacity to tell whether an act charged as a crime was right or wrong; and whether Arizona violates due process in restricting consideration of defense evidence of mental illness and incapacity to its bearing on a claim of insanity, thus eliminating its significance directly on the issue of the mental element of the crime charged (known in legal shorthand as the *mens rea,* or guilty mind). We hold that there is no violation of due process in either instance.

I

In the early hours of June 21, 2000, Officer Jeffrey Moritz of the Flagstaff Police responded in uniform to complaints that a pickup truck with loud music blaring was circling a residential block. When he located the truck, the officer turned on the emergency lights and siren of his marked patrol car, which prompted petitioner Eric Clark, the truck's driver (then 17), to pull over. Officer Moritz got out of the patrol car and told Clark to stay where he was. Less than a minute later, Clark shot the officer, who died soon after but not before calling the police dispatcher for help. Clark ran away on foot but was arrested later that day with gunpowder residue on his hands; the gun that killed the officer was found nearby, stuffed into a knit cap.

Clark was charged with first-degree murder for intentionally or knowingly killing a law enforcement officer in the line of duty. In March 2001, Clark was found incompetent to stand trial and was committed to a state hospital for treatment, but two years later the same trial court found his competence restored and ordered him to be tried. Clark waived his right to a jury, and the case was heard by the court.

At trial, Clark did not contest the shooting and death, but relied on his undisputed paranoid schizophrenia at the time of the incident in denying that he had the specific intent to shoot a law enforcement officer or knowledge that he was doing so, as required by the statute. Accordingly, the prosecutor offered circumstantial evidence that Clark knew Officer Moritz was a law enforcement officer. The evidence showed that the officer was in uniform at the time, that he caught up with Clark in a marked police car with emergency lights and siren going, and that Clark acknowledged the symbols of police authority and stopped. The testimony for the prosecution indicated that Clark had intentionally lured an officer to the scene to kill him, having told some people a few weeks before the incident that he wanted to shoot police officers. At the close of the State's evidence, the trial court denied Clark's motion for judgment of acquittal for failure to prove intent to kill a law enforcement officer or knowledge that Officer Moritz was a law enforcement officer.

In presenting the defense case, Clark claimed mental illness, which he sought to introduce for two purposes. First, he raised the affirmative defense of insanity, putting the burden on himself to prove by clear and convincing evidence, § 13–502(C) (West 2001), that "at the time of the commission of the criminal act [he] was afflicted with a mental disease or defect of such severity that [he] did not know the criminal act was wrong," § 13–502(A). Second, he aimed to rebut the prosecution's evidence of the requisite *mens rea,* that he had acted intentionally or knowingly to kill a law enforcement officer.

The trial court ruled that Clark could not rely on evidence bearing on insanity to dispute the *mens rea.* The court cited *State v. Mott,* 187 Ariz. 536, 931 P.2d 1046, cert. denied, 520 U.S. 1234, 117 S.Ct. 1832, 137 L.Ed.2d 1038 (1997), which "refused to allow psychiatric testimony to negate specific intent," 187 Ariz., at 541, 931 P.2d, at 1051, and held that "Arizona does not allow evidence of a defendant's mental disorder short of insanity . . . to negate the *mens rea* element of a crime," *ibid.*

As to his insanity, then, Clark presented testimony from classmates, school officials, and his family describing his increasingly bizarre behavior over the year before the shooting. Witnesses testified, for example, that paranoid delusions led Clark to rig a fishing line with beads and wind chimes at home to alert him to intrusion by invaders, and to keep a bird in his automobile to warn of airborne poison. There was lay and expert testimony that Clark thought Flagstaff was populated with "aliens" (some impersonating government agents), the "aliens" were trying to kill him, and bullets were the only way to stop them. A psychiatrist testified that Clark was suffering from paranoid schizophrenia with delusions about "aliens" when he killed Officer Moritz, and he concluded that Clark was incapable of luring the officer or understanding right from wrong and that he was thus insane at the time of the killing. In rebuttal, a psychiatrist for the State gave his opinion that Clark's paranoid schizophrenia did not keep him from appreciating the wrongfulness of his conduct, as shown by his actions before and after the shooting (such as circling the residential block with music blaring as if to lure the police to intervene, evading the police after the shooting, and hiding the gun).

At the close of the defense case consisting of this evidence bearing on mental illness, the trial court denied Clark's renewed motion for a directed verdict grounded on failure of the prosecution to show that Clark knew the victim was a police officer. The judge then issued a special verdict of first-degree murder, expressly finding that Clark shot and caused the death of Officer Moritz beyond a reasonable doubt and that Clark had not shown that he was insane at the time. The judge noted that though Clark was indisputably afflicted with paranoid schizophrenia at the time of the shooting, the mental illness "did not . . . distort his perception of reality so severely that he did not know his actions were wrong." App. 334. For this conclusion, the judge expressly relied on "the facts of the crime, the evaluations of the experts, [Clark's] actions and behavior both before and after the shooting, and the observations of those that knew [Clark]." *Id.,* at 333. The sentence was life imprisonment without the possibility of release for 25 years.

When the Arizona Legislature first codified an insanity rule, it adopted the full *M'Naghten* statement (subject to modifications in details that do not matter here):

> "A person is not responsible for criminal conduct if at the time of such conduct the person was suffering from such a mental disease or defect as not to know the nature and quality of the act or, if such person did know, that such person did not know that what he was doing was wrong." Ariz.Rev.Stat. Ann. § 13–502 (West 1978).

In 1993, the legislature dropped the cognitive incapacity part, leaving only moral incapacity as the nub of the stated definition. See 1993 Ariz. Sess. Laws ch. 256, §§ 2–3. Under current Arizona law, a defendant will not be adjudged insane unless he demonstrates that "at the time of the commission of the criminal act [he] was afflicted with a mental disease or defect of such severity that [he] did not know the criminal act was wrong," Ariz.Rev.Stat. Ann. § 13–502(A) (West 2001).

A

Clark challenges the 1993 amendment excising the express reference to the cognitive incapacity element. He insists that the side-by-side *M'Naghten* test represents the minimum that a government must provide in recognizing an alternative to criminal responsibility on grounds of mental illness or defect, and he argues that elimination of the *M'Naghten* reference to nature and quality " 'offends [a] principle of justice so rooted in the traditions and conscience of our people as to be ranked as fundamental,' " *Patterson v. New York,* 432 U.S. 197, 202 (1977).

The claim entails no light burden, see *Montana v. Egelhoff,* 518 U.S. 37, 43, 116 S.Ct. 2013, 135 L.Ed.2d 361 (1996) (plurality opinion), and Clark does not carry it. History shows no deference to *M'Naghten* that could elevate its formula to the level of fundamental principle, so as to limit the traditional recognition of a State's capacity to define crimes and defenses.

Even a cursory examination of the traditional Anglo-American approaches to insanity reveals significant differences among them, with four traditional strains variously combined to yield a diversity of American standards. The main variants are the cognitive incapacity, the moral incapacity, the volitional incapacity, and the product-of-mental-illness tests.

With this varied background, it is clear that no particular formulation has evolved into a baseline for due process, and that the insanity rule, like the conceptualization of criminal offenses, is substantially open to state choice. Indeed, the legitimacy of such choice is the more obvious when one considers the interplay of legal concepts of mental illness or deficiency required for an insanity defense, with the medical concepts of mental abnormality that influence the expert opinion testimony by psychologists and psychiatrists commonly introduced to support or contest insanity claims. For medical definitions devised to justify treatment, like legal ones devised to excuse from conventional criminal responsibility, are subject to flux and disagreement. There being such fodder for reasonable debate about what the cognate legal and medical tests should be, due process imposes no single canonical formulation of legal insanity.

B

Nor does Arizona's abbreviation of the *M'Naghten* statement raise a proper claim that some constitutional minimum has been shortchanged.

Though Clark is correct that the application of the moral incapacity test (telling right from wrong) does not necessarily require evaluation of a defendant's cognitive capacity to appreciate the nature and quality of the acts charged against him, his argument fails to recognize that cognitive incapacity is itself enough to demonstrate moral incapacity. Cognitive incapacity, in other words, is a sufficient condition for establishing a defense of insanity, albeit not a necessary one. As a defendant can therefore make out moral incapacity by demonstrating cognitive incapacity, evidence bearing on whether the defendant knew the nature and quality of his actions is both relevant and admissible. In practical terms, if a defendant did not know what he was doing when he acted, he could not have known that he was performing the wrongful act charged as a crime. Indeed, when the two-part rule was still in effect, the Supreme Court of Arizona held that a jury instruction on insanity containing the moral incapacity part but not a full recitation of the cognitive incapacity part was fine, as the cognitive incapacity part might be " 'treated as adding nothing to the requirement that the accused know his act was wrong.' " *State v. Chavez,* 143 Ariz. 238, 239 (1984).

Clark, indeed, adopted this very analysis himself in the trial court: "[I]f [Clark] did not know he was shooting at a police officer, or believed he had to shoot or be shot, even though his belief was not based in reality, this would establish that he did not know what he was doing was wrong." Record, Doc. 374, at 1. The trial court apparently agreed, for the judge admitted Clark's evidence of cognitive incapacity for consideration under the State's moral incapacity formulation. And Clark can point to no evidence bearing on insanity that was excluded. His psychiatric expert and a number of lay witnesses testified to his delusions, and this evidence tended to support a description of Clark as lacking the capacity to understand that the police officer was a human being. There is no doubt that the trial judge considered the evidence as going to an issue of cognitive capacity, for in finding insanity not proven he said that Clark's mental illness "did not . . . distort his perception of reality so severely that he did not know his actions were wrong," App. 334.

We are satisfied that neither in theory nor in practice did Arizona's 1993 abridgment of the insanity formulation deprive Clark of due process.

III

Clark's second claim of a due process violation challenges the rule adopted by the Supreme Court of Arizona in *State v. Mott,* 187 Ariz. 536 (1997). This case ruled on the admissibility of testimony from a psychologist offered to show that the defendant suffered from battered women's syndrome and therefore lacked the capacity to form the *mens rea* of the crime charged against her. The state court held that testimony of a professional psychologist or psychiatrist about a defendant's mental incapacity owing to mental disease or defect was admissible, and could be considered, only for its bearing on an insanity defense; such evidence could not be considered on the element of *mens rea,* that is, what the State must show about a defendant's mental state (such as intent or understanding) when he performed the act charged against him. See *id.,* at 541, 544, 931 P.2d, at 1051, 1054.

A

Understanding Clark's claim requires attention to the categories of evidence with a potential bearing on *mens rea.* First, there is "observation evidence" in the everyday sense, testimony from those who observed what Clark did and heard what he said; this category would also include testimony that an expert witness might give about Clark's tendency to think in a certain way and his behavioral characteristics. This evidence may support a professional diagnosis of mental disease and in any event is the kind of evidence that can be relevant to show what in fact was on Clark's mind when he fired the gun. Observation evidence in the record covers Clark's behavior at home and with friends, his expressions of belief around the time of the killing that "aliens" were inhabiting the bodies of local people (including government agents), his driving around the neighborhood before the police arrived, and so on.

Second, there is "mental-disease evidence" in the form of opinion testimony that Clark suffered from a mental disease with features described by the witness. As was true here, this evidence characteristically but not always comes from professional psychologists or psychiatrists who testify as expert witnesses and base their opinions in part on examination of a defendant, usually conducted after the events in question. The thrust of this evidence was that, based on factual reports, professional observations, and tests, Clark was psychotic at the time in question, with a condition that fell within the category of schizophrenia.

Third, there is evidence we will refer to as "capacity evidence" about a defendant's capacity for cognition and moral judgment (and ultimately also his capacity to form *mens rea*). This, too, is opinion evidence. Here, as it usually does, this testimony came from the same experts and concentrated on those specific details of the mental condition that make the difference between sanity and insanity under the Arizona definition. In their respective testimony on these details the experts disagreed: the defense expert gave his opinion that the symptoms or effects of the disease in Clark's case included inability to appreciate the nature of his action and to tell that it was wrong, whereas the State's psychiatrist was of the view that Clark was a schizophrenic who was still sufficiently able to appreciate the reality of shooting the officer and to know that it was wrong to do that.

B

It is clear that *Mott* itself imposed no restriction on considering evidence of the first sort, the observation evidence. We read the *Mott* restriction to apply, rather, to evidence addressing the two issues in testimony that characteristically comes only from psychologists or psychiatrists qualified to give opinions as expert witnesses: mental-disease evidence (whether at the time of the crime a defendant suffered from a mental disease or defect, such as schizophrenia) and capacity evidence (whether the disease or defect left him incapable of performing or experiencing a mental process defined as necessary for sanity such as appreciating the nature and quality of his act and knowing that it was wrong).

Mott was careful to distinguish this kind of opinion evidence from observation evidence generally and even from observation evidence that an expert witness might offer, such as descriptions of a defendant's tendency to think in a certain way or his behavioral characteristics; the Arizona court made it clear that this sort of testimony was perfectly admissible to rebut the prosecution's evidence of *mens rea,* 187 Ariz., at 544, 931 P.2d, at 1054. Thus, only opinion testimony going to mental defect or disease, and its effect on the cognitive or moral capacities on which sanity depends under the Arizona rule, is restricted.

In this case, the trial court seems to have applied the *Mott* restriction to all evidence offered by Clark for the purpose of showing what he called his inability to form the required *mens rea,* see, *e.g.,* Record, Doc. 406, at 7–10 (that is, an intent to kill a police officer on duty, or an understanding that he was engaging in the act of killing such an officer, see Ariz.Rev.Stat. Ann. § 13–1105(A)(3) (West Supp.2005)). Thus, the trial court's restriction may have covered not only mental-disease and capacity evidence as just defined, but also observation evidence offered by lay (and expert) witnesses who described Clark's unusual behavior. Clark's objection to the application of the *Mott* rule does not, however, turn on the distinction between lay and expert witnesses or the kinds of testimony they were competent to present.

The . . . principle implicated by Clark's argument is a defendant's right as a matter of simple due process to present evidence favorable to himself on an element that must be proven to convict him. As already noted, evidence tending to show that a defendant suffers from mental disease and lacks capacity to form *mens rea* is relevant to rebut evidence that he did in fact form the required *mens rea* at the time in question; this is the reason that Clark claims a right to require the factfinder in this case to consider testimony about his mental illness and his incapacity directly, when weighing the persuasiveness of other evidence tending to show *mens rea,* which the prosecution has the burden to prove.

As Clark recognizes, however, the right to introduce relevant evidence can be curtailed if there is a good reason for doing that. "While the Constitution . . . prohibits the exclusion of defense evidence under rules that serve no legitimate purpose or that are disproportionate to the ends that they are asserted to promote, well-established rules of evidence permit trial judges to exclude evidence if its probative value is outweighed by certain other factors such as unfair prejudice, confusion of the issues, or potential to mislead the jury." And if evidence may be kept out entirely, its consideration may be subject to limitation, which Arizona claims the power to impose here. State law says that evidence of mental disease and incapacity may be introduced and considered, and if sufficiently forceful to satisfy the defendant's burden of proof under the insanity rule it will displace the presumption of sanity and excuse from criminal responsibility. But mental-disease and capacity evidence may be considered only for its bearing on the insanity defense, and it will avail a defendant only if it is persuasive enough to satisfy the defendant's burden as defined by the terms of that defense. The mental-disease and capacity evidence is thus being channeled or restricted to one issue and given effect only if the defendant carries the burden to convince the factfinder of insanity; the evidence is not being excluded entirely, and the question is whether reasons for requiring it to be channeled and restricted are good enough to satisfy the standard of fundamental fairness that due process requires. We think they are.

A State's insistence on preserving its chosen standard of legal insanity cannot be the sole reason for a rule like *Mott,* however, for it fails to answer an objection the dissent makes in this case. An insanity rule gives a defendant already found guilty the opportunity to excuse his conduct by showing he was insane when he acted, that is, that he did not have the mental capacity for conventional guilt and criminal responsibility. But, as the dissent argues, if the same evidence that affirmatively shows he was not guilty by reason of insanity also shows it was at least doubtful that he could form *mens rea,* then he should not be found guilty in the first place; it thus violates due process when the State impedes him from using mental-disease and capacity evidence directly to rebut the prosecution's evidence that he did form *mens rea.*

Are there, then, characteristics of mental-disease and capacity evidence giving rise to risks that may reasonably be hedged by channeling the consideration of such evidence to the insanity issue on which, in States like Arizona, a defendant has the burden of persuasion? We think there are: in the controversial character of some categories of mental disease, in the potential of mental-disease evidence to mislead, and in the danger of according greater certainty to capacity evidence than experts claim for it.

To begin with, the diagnosis may mask vigorous debate within the profession about the very contours of the mental disease itself. See, *e.g.,* American Psychiatric Association, Diagnostic and Statistical Manual of Mental Disorders xxxiii (4th ed. text rev.2000) (hereinafter DSM-IV-TR) ("DSM-IV reflects a consensus about the classification and diagnosis of mental disorders derived at the time of its initial publication. New knowledge generated by research or clinical experience will undoubtedly lead to an increased understanding of the disorders included in DSM-IV, to the identification of new disorders, and to the removal of some disorders in future classifications. . . . Though we certainly do not "condem[n mental-disease evidence] wholesale," the consequence of this professional ferment is a general caution in treating psychological classifications as predicates for excusing otherwise criminal conduct.

Next, there is the potential of mental-disease evidence to mislead jurors (when they are the factfinders) through the power of this kind of evidence to suggest that a defendant suffering from a recognized mental disease lacks cognitive, moral, volitional, or other capacity, when that may not be a sound conclusion at all. Even when a category of mental disease is broadly accepted and the assignment of a defendant's behavior to that category is uncontroversial, the classification may suggest something very significant about a defendant's capacity, when in fact the classification tells us little or nothing about the ability of the defendant to form *mens rea* or to exercise the cognitive, moral, or volitional capacities that define legal sanity. . . . The limits of the utility of a professional disease diagnosis are evident in the dispute between the two testifying experts in this case; they agree that Clark was schizophrenic, but they come to opposite conclusions on whether the mental disease in his particular case left him bereft of cognitive or moral capacity. Evidence of mental disease, then, can easily mislead; it is very easy to slide from evidence that an individual with a professionally recognized mental disease is very different, into doubting that he has the capacity to form *mens rea,* whereas that doubt may not be justified. And of course, in the cases mentioned before, in which the categorization is doubtful or the category of mental disease is itself subject to controversy, the risks are even greater that opinions about mental disease may confuse a jury into thinking the opinions show more than they do. Because allowing mental-disease evidence on *mens rea* can thus easily mislead, it is not unreasonable to address that tendency by confining consideration of this kind of evidence to insanity, on which a defendant may be assigned the burden of persuasion.

There are, finally, particular risks inherent in the opinions of the experts who supplement the mental-disease classifications with opinions on incapacity: on whether the mental disease rendered a particular defendant incapable of the cognition necessary for moral judgment or *mens rea* or otherwise incapable of understanding the wrongfulness of the conduct charged. Unlike observational evidence bearing on *mens rea,* capacity evidence consists of judgment, and judgment fraught with multiple perils: a defendant's state of mind at the crucial moment can be elusive no matter how conscientious the enquiry, and the law's categories that set the terms of the capacity judgment are not the categories of psychology that govern the expert's professional thinking. Although such capacity judgments may be given in the utmost good faith, their potentially tenuous character is indicated by the candor of the defense expert in this very case. Contrary to the State's expert, he testified that Clark lacked the capacity to appreciate the circumstances realistically and to understand the wrongfulness of what he was doing, App. 48–49, but he said that "no one knows exactly what was on [his] mind" at the time of the shooting, *id.,* at 48.

JUSTICE KENNEDY, with whom JUSTICE STEVENS and JUSTICE GINSBURG join, dissenting.

In my submission the Court is incorrect in holding that Arizona may convict petitioner Eric Clark of first-degree murder for the intentional or knowing killing of a police officer when Clark was not permitted to introduce critical and reliable evidence showing he did not have that intent or knowledge.

I

The Court's error, of course, has significance beyond this case. It adopts an evidentiary framework that, in my view, will be unworkable in many cases. The Court classifies Clark's behavior and expressed beliefs as observation evidence but insists that its description by experts must be mental-disease evidence or capacity evidence. These categories break down quickly when it is understood how the testimony would apply to the question of intent and knowledge at issue here. The most common type of schizophrenia, and the one Clark suffered from, is paranoid schizophrenia. The existence of this functional psychosis is beyond dispute, but that does not mean the lay witness understands it or that a disputed issue of fact concerning its effect in a particular instance is not something for the expert to address. Common symptoms of the condition are delusions accompanied by hallucinations, often of the auditory type, which can cause disturbances of perception. *Ibid.* Clark's expert testified that people with schizophrenia often play radios loudly to drown out the voices in their heads. See App. 32. Clark's attorney argued to the trial court that this, rather than a desire to lure a policeman to the scene, explained Clark's behavior just before the killing. *Id.,* at 294–295. The observation that schizophrenics play radios loudly is a fact regarding behavior, but it is only a relevant fact if Clark has schizophrenia.

Even if this evidence were, to use the Court's term, mental-disease evidence, because it relies on an expert opinion, what would happen if the expert simply were to testify, without mentioning schizophrenia, that people with Clark's symptoms often play the radio loudly? This seems to be factual evidence, as the term is defined by the Court, yet it differs from mental-disease evidence only in forcing the witness to pretend that no one has yet come up with a way to classify the set of symptoms being described. More generally, the opinion that Clark had paranoid schizophrenia—an opinion shared by experts for both the prosecution and defense—bears on efforts to determine, as a factual matter, whether he knew he was killing a police officer. The psychiatrist's explanation of Clark's condition was essential to understanding how he processes sensory data and therefore to deciding what information was in his mind at the time of the shooting. Simply put, knowledge relies on cognition, and cognition can be affected by schizophrenia. See American Psychiatric Association, Diagnostic and Statistical Manual of Mental Disorders 299 (4th ed. text rev. 2000) ("The characteristic symptoms of Schizophrenia involve a range of cognitive and emotional dysfunctions that include perception"); *ibid.* (Symptoms include delusions, which are "erroneous beliefs that usually involve a misinterpretation of perceptions or experiences"). The mental-disease evidence at trial was also intertwined with the observation evidence because it lent needed credibility. Clark's parents and friends testified Clark thought the people in his town were aliens trying to kill him. These claims might not be believable without a psychiatrist confirming the story based on his experience with people who have exhibited similar behaviors. It makes little sense to divorce the observation evidence from the explanation that makes it comprehensible.

States have substantial latitude under the Constitution to define rules for the exclusion of evidence and to apply those rules to criminal defendants. This authority, however, has constitutional limits.

The central theory of Clark's defense was that his schizophrenia made him delusional. He lived in a universe where the delusions were so dominant, the theory was, that he had no intent to shoot a police officer or knowledge he was doing so. It is one thing to say he acted with intent or knowledge to pull the trigger. It is quite another to say he pulled the trigger to kill someone he knew to be a human being and a police officer. If the trier of fact were to find Clark's evidence sufficient to discount the case made by the State, which has the burden to prove knowledge or intent as an element of the offense, Clark would not be guilty of first-degree murder under Arizona law.

The *mens rea* element of intent or knowledge may, at some level, comprise certain moral choices, but it rests in the first instance on a factual determination. That is the fact Clark sought to put in issue. Either Clark knew he was killing a police officer or he did not.

The issue is not, as the Court insists, whether Clark's mental illness acts as an "excuse from customary criminal responsibility," but whether his mental illness, as a factual matter, made him unaware that he was shooting a police officer. If it did, Clark needs no excuse, as then he did not commit the crime as Arizona defines it. For the elements of first-degree murder, where the question is knowledge of particular facts—that one is killing a police officer—the determination depends not on moral responsibility but on empirical fact. Clark's evidence of mental illness had a direct and substantial bearing upon what he knew, or thought he knew, to be the facts when he pulled the trigger; this lay at the heart of the matter.

The trial court's exclusion was all the more severe because it barred from consideration on the issue of *mens rea* all this evidence, from any source, thus preventing Clark from showing he did not commit the crime as defined by Arizona law.

This is not to suggest all general rules on the exclusion of certain types of evidence are invalid. If the rule does not substantially burden the defense, then it is likely permissible.

In the instant case Arizona's proposed reasons are insufficient to support its categorical exclusion. While the State contends that testimony regarding mental illness may be too incredible or speculative for the jury to consider, this does not explain why the exclusion applies in all cases to all evidence of mental illness. "A State's legitimate interest in barring unreliable evidence does not extend to *per se* exclusions that may be reliable in an individual case." States have certain discretion to bar unreliable or speculative testimony and to adopt rules to ensure the reliability of expert testimony. Arizona has done so, and there is no reason to believe its rules are insufficient to avoid speculative evidence of mental illness. This is particularly true because Arizona applies its usual case-by-case approach to permit admission of evidence of mental illness for a variety of other purposes.

The risk of jury confusion also fails to justify the rule. The State defends its rule as a means to avoid the complexities of determining how and to what degree a mental illness affects a person's mental state. The difficulty of resolving a factual issue, though, does not present a sufficient reason to take evidence away from the jury even when it is crucial for the defense. "We have always trusted juries to sort through complex facts in various areas of law." *United States v. Booker,* 543 U.S. 220, 289, 125 S.Ct. 738, 160 L.Ed.2d 621 (2005) (STEVENS, J., dissenting in part). Even were the risk of jury confusion real enough to justify excluding evidence in most cases, this would provide little basis for prohibiting all evidence of mental illness without any inquiry into its likely effect on the jury or its role in deciding the linchpin issue of knowledge and intent. Indeed, Arizona has a rule in place to serve this very purpose.

The Court undertakes little analysis of the interests particular to this case. By proceeding in this way it devalues Clark's constitutional rights. The reliability rationale has minimal applicability here. The Court is correct that many mental diseases are difficult to define and the subject of great debate. Schizophrenia, however, is a well-documented mental illness, and no one seriously disputes either its definition or its most prominent clinical manifestations. The State's own expert conceded that Clark had paranoid schizophrenia and was actively psychotic at the time of the killing. The jury-confusion rationale, if it is at all applicable here, is the result of the Court's own insistence on conflating the insanity defense and the question of intent. Considered on its own terms, the issue of intent and knowledge is a straightforward factual question. A trier of fact is quite capable of weighing defense testimony and then determining whether the accused did or did not intend to kill or knowingly kill a human being who was a police officer. True, the issue can be difficult to decide in particular instances, but no more so than many matters juries must confront.

The Court says mental-illness evidence "can easily mislead," *ante,* at 2735, and may "tel[l] us little or nothing about the ability of the defendant to form *mens rea*." These generalities do not, however, show how relevant or misleading the evidence in this case would be. As explained above, the evidence of Clark's mental illness bears directly on *mens rea,* for it suggests Clark may not have known he was killing a human being. It is striking that while the Court discusses at length the likelihood of misjudgment from placing too much emphasis on evidence of mental illness, it ignores the risk of misjudging an innocent man guilty from refusing to consider this highly relevant evidence at all. Clark's expert, it is true, said no one could know exactly what was on Clark's mind at the time of the shooting. The expert testified extensively, however, about the effect of Clark's delusions on his perceptions of the world around him, and about whether Clark's behavior around the time of the shooting was consistent with delusional thinking. This testimony was relevant to determining whether Clark knew he was killing a human being. It also bolstered the testimony of lay witnesses, none of which was deemed unreliable or misleading by the state courts.

Contrary to the Court's suggestion, see *ante,* at 2735, the fact that the state and defense experts drew different conclusions about the effect of Clark's mental illness on his mental state only made Clark's evidence contested; it did not make the evidence irrelevant or misleading. The trial court was capable of evaluating the competing conclusions, as factfinders do in countless cases where there is a dispute among witnesses. In fact, the potential to mislead will be far greater under the Court's new evidentiary system, where jurors will receive observation evidence without the necessary explanation from experts.

The fact that mental-illness evidence may be considered in deciding criminal responsibility does not compensate for its exclusion from consideration on the *mens rea* elements of the crime. Cf. *ante,* at 2733–2734. The evidence addresses different issues in the two instances. Criminal responsibility involves an inquiry into whether the defendant knew right from wrong, not whether he had the *mens rea* elements of the offense. While there may be overlap between the two issues, "the existence or nonexistence of legal insanity bears no necessary relationship to the existence or nonexistence of the required mental elements of the crime."

Future dangerousness is not, as the Court appears to conclude, see *ante,* at 2737, n. 45, a rational basis for convicting mentally ill individuals of crimes they did not commit. Civil commitment proceedings can ensure that individuals who present a danger to themselves or others receive proper treatment without unfairly treating them as criminals. The State presents no evidence to the contrary, and the Court ought not to imply otherwise.

While defining mental illness is a difficult matter, the State seems to exclude the evidence one would think most reliable by allowing unexplained and uncategorized tendencies to be introduced while excluding relatively well-understood psychiatric testimony regarding well-documented mental illnesses. It is unclear, moreover, what would have happened in this case had the defendant wanted to testify that he thought Officer Moritz was an alien. If disallowed, it would be tantamount to barring Clark from testifying on his behalf to explain his own actions. If allowed, then Arizona's rule would simply prohibit the corroboration necessary to make sense of Clark's explanation. In sum, the rule forces the jury to decide guilt in a fictional world with undefined and unexplained behaviors but without mental illness. This rule has no rational justification and imposes a significant burden upon a straightforward defense: He did not commit the crime with which he was charged.

These are the reasons for my respectful dissent.

DISCUSSION QUESTIONS

1.   Do you agree with the majority's argument that Arizona's changes to its definition of insanity doesn't make much of a difference? Do you agree that they don't implicate due process? Are they a good idea as a matter of policy?

2.   Is denying admission of diminished capacity evidence fundamentally unfair to mentally ill defendants? Would you be better off claiming voluntary intoxication in the majority of jurisdictions?

3.   How many people in prison do you think suffer from mental health problems? How should this affect whether we consider diminished capacity evidence?

F. ARGUING ABOUT DELUSIONAL BELIEFS

Often, lawyers and students find themselves making arguments from within the delusional belief system of the mentally ill defendant. Riffing off the TV show "Heroes," a person who believes that he must "kill the cheerleader to save the world" would be acting morally by subjecting himself to life imprisonment or execution to save the rest of humanity. Here, the delusional beliefs make the defendant incapable of knowing that killing the cheerleader is wrongful because it can't be wrongful to save the world!

Prosecutors sometimes also argue from within a defendant's delusional complex. Arguably, Hinckley was not insane but sociopathic in being willing to kill Ronald Reagan just to get Jodie Foster to answer his love letters. Hinckley had something he wanted, and he attempted to kill to get it. Such behavior does not mean that he was incapable of distinguishing right from wrong; it means that he disregarded right from wrong to pursue his own selfish ends. Under this view, the fact that his means and ends were delusional does not change the fact that he knew he was doing wrong.

Arguing within a delusional complex can be dangerous for a prosecutor, however, because it draws even more attention to the utter irrationality of the defendant's thinking. Actresses don't date assassins. People who think otherwise seem "crazy." Often, a stronger argument for the prosecution is to point out non-delusional although not entirely rational reasons for the defendant's behavior. For example, mentally ill people sometimes kill those who annoy or offend them. If a defendant claims a delusional complex of persecution by a neighbor he kills, a prosecutor could argue that the defendant killed the neighbor because the defendant was short-tempered and overly sensitive, not delusional. Remember that a criminal act need not be entirely rational to be sane (If mere irrationality was a defense, we would have to let a whole lot of people out of prison).

1. DEIFIC COMMANDS

Courts have often wrestled with the psychotic delusion that God has commanded someone to perform a criminal act, and they have applied M'Naghten to "deific commands" in different ways. First, some jurisdictions treat deific commands as an exception to the requirements of M'Naghten. For example, this interpretation would find Abraham to be insane if he labors under a psychotic delusion that God wants him to sacrifice his son Isaac, even though Abraham understands that society will consider the killing to be morally and legally wrong. This reading interprets the deific command as an exception to the knowledge of the wrongful act.

The alternate interpretation treats deific commands as falling squarely within M'Naghten's definition of insanity. On this reading, one who believes he is carrying out a command of God will believe that his act will be seen as morally right by society, and the actor is therefore incapable of understanding its wrongfulness. This reading treats God as the ultimate source of moral standards.

Deific commands also raise interesting philosophical questions about the relationship between religious thought and conventional notions of rationality. One person's devoutly held religious belief might be another person's psychotic delusion. Many people talk to God, but claiming that he or she talks back can either be an authentic religious experience or an auditory hallucination, depending on one's point of view. Ultimately, such claims are evaluated not philosophically but sociologically. A deific command that you kill or commit a criminal act is more likely to be considered evidence of mental disease than divine inspiration.

This next case showcases a M'Naghten jurisdiction's treatment of an insanity defense built around a deific command. How does the court treat Serravo's defense? What is their attitude towards his "communications" with God? Should the case have turned out the way it did or is there another way you would have approached this question?

Case in Context

The next case involves a delusional complex that is religious in nature.

COLORADO V. ROBERT PASQUAL SERRAVO

Supreme Court of Colorado, En Banc
823 P.2d 128 (1992)

Opinion by: QUINN.

JUSTICE QUINN delivered the Opinion of the Court.

We granted certiorari to review the decision of the court of appeals in People v. Serravo, 797 P.2d 782 (Colo. App. 1990), in order to determine the meaning of the phrase "incapable of distinguishing right from wrong" in Colorado's statutory definition of insanity codified at section 16–8–101(1), 8A C.R.S. (1986). The trial court, in the insanity phase of a criminal prosecution, instructed the jury that the phrase "incapable of distinguishing right from wrong" refers to a person who appreciates that his conduct is criminal but, due to a mental disease or defect, believes that the conduct is morally right. The prosecution, pursuant to section 16–12–102(1), 8A C.R.S. (1986), appealed the trial court's ruling on the question of law.

I.

Serravo was charged in a multi-count information with crimes of attempt to commit first degree murder after deliberation, assault in the first degree, and the commission of crimes of violence. The charges arose out of the stabbing his wife, Joyce Serravo, on May 10, 1987. After the charges were filed, Serravo entered a plea of not guilty by reason of insanity and was thereafter examined by several psychiatrists. The issue of legal insanity was tried to a jury, which returned a verdict of not guilty by reason of insanity.

The evidence at the insanity trial established that the stabbing occurred under the following circumstances. On the evening of May 9, 1987, Serravo, who was a King Soopers union employee, visited striking employees at the King Soopers store near his home. Serravo returned home at approximately 12:30 a.m. on May 10. After sitting in the kitchen and reading the Bible, he went upstairs to the bedroom where his wife was sleeping, stood over her for a few minutes, and then stabbed her in the back just below the shoulder blade. When his wife awoke, Serravo told her that she had been stabbed by an intruder and that she should stay in bed while he went downstairs to call for medical help.

Police officers were later dispatched to the home. Serravo told the officers that he had gone to the King Soopers store and had left the garage door open, that the door leading to the house from the garage was unlocked, that when he returned from King Soopers and was reading the Bible he heard his front door slam, and that he went upstairs to check on his wife and children and saw that his wife was bleeding from a wound in her back. Serravo signed a consent to search his home and gave the police clothes that he was wearing at the time of his discovery of his wife's injury.

Several weeks after the stabbing Serravo's wife found letters written by Serravo. In these letters Serravo admitted the stabbing, stating that "our marriage was severed on Mother's Day when I put the knife in your back," that "I have gone to be with Jehovah in heaven for three and one-half days," and that "I must return for there is still a great deal of work to be done." After reading the letters, Serravo's wife telephoned him in order to confront him about the letters. Serravo told his wife that God had told him to stab her in order to sever the marriage bond. Mrs. Serravo informed the police of these facts and Serravo was thereafter arrested and charged.

The prosecution presented expert psychiatric testimony on Serravo's sanity at the time of the stabbing. Doctor Ann Seig, a resident psychiatrist in training at the University of Colorado Health Sciences Center, examined Serravo pursuant to a court ordered evaluation of his mental state. Serravo gave the doctor a history of having worked on a plan, inspired by his relationship to God, to establish a multi-million dollar sports complex called Purely Professionals. This facility, according to Serravo, would enable him to achieve his goal of teaching people the path to perfection. On the night of the stabbing, Serravo, according to the history given to Doctor Seig, was excited because he finally believed that he had received some positive encouragement in his endeavor from some King Soopers union members, but he was discouraged by some inner "evil spirits" who kept raising troublesome questions about how he would deal with his wife's lack of encouragement and support. Doctor Seig diagnosed Serravo as suffering either from an organic delusional disorder related to left temporal lobe damage as a result of an automobile accident some years ago or paranoid schizophrenia. Either diagnosis, in Doctor Seig's opinion, would adequately account for Serravo's delusional belief that he had a privileged relationship with God as the result of which he was in direct communication with God. Doctor Seig testified that Serravo was operating under this delusional system when he stabbed his wife and these delusions caused him to believe that his act was morally justified. Doctor Seig, however, was of the view that Serravo, because he was aware that the act of stabbing was contrary to law, was sane at the time of the stabbing.

A standard mental health diagnostic manual published by the American Psychiatric Association, Diagnostic and Statistical Manual of Mental Disorders, Third Edition Revised (1987) (DSM IIIR), defines paranoid schizophrenia as a "major disturbance in the content of thought involving delusions that are often multiple, fragmented or bizarre. . ." Id. at 188. A preoccupation with grandiose or religious delusions is a symptom of paranoid schizophrenia. Id. The DSM IIIR defines a delusional disorder as the presence of a persistent thematic delusion. A person laboring under a grandiose delusion is convinced that he or she has a great talent or insight, or has a special relationship with a prominent person or deity. Id. at 199–200.

Serravo presented four psychiatrists and a clinical psychologist on the issue of his legal insanity. The first psychiatrist, Doctor Frederick Miller, was of the opinion that on the night of the stabbing Serravo was under the psychotic delusion that it was his divine mission to kill his wife and that he was morally justified in stabbing her because God had told him to do so. Doctor Miller was not quite certain whether Serravo's psychotic disorder was paranoid schizophrenia, a paranoid delusional disorder, or an organic delusional disorder. Although uncertain of the exact diagnostic label applicable to Serravo, Doctor Miller was of the opinion that Serravo's mental illness made it impossible for him to distinguish right from wrong even though Serravo was probably aware that such conduct was legally wrong.

Another psychiatrist, Doctor Eric Kaplan, was the attending psychiatrist at the University of Colorado Health Services and a member of the faculty of the medical school. Doctor Kaplan supervised Doctor Ann Seig during her examination of Serravo and also made an independent evaluation of Serravo's mental condition. It was Doctor Kaplan's opinion that Serravo was suffering from paranoid schizophrenia at the time of the stabbing and was laboring under the paranoid delusion that his wife stood in the way of his divine mission of completing the large sports complex, that Serravo believed that the stabbing was the right thing to do, and that Serravo, as a result of his mental illness, was unable to distinguish right from wrong with respect to the stabbing. Two other psychiatrists, Doctor Geoffrey Heron and Doctor Seymour Sundell, offered the opinion that Serravo, at the time of the stabbing, was suffering from paranoid schizophrenia and a paranoid delusion about God which so affected his cognitive ability as to render him incapable of distinguishing right from wrong as normal people would be able to do in accordance with societal standards of morality.

Doctor Leslie Cohen, a clinical psychologist, also testified about Serravo's mental condition at the time of the stabbing. Having conducted extensive psychological testing of Serravo, Doctor Cohen was able to offer an opinion on Serravo's reality testing, his emotional reactivity, and his volition, all of which were relevant to the functioning of his conscience. The doctor was of the opinion that Serravo's conscience was based on a false belief or delusion about his magical powers as a result of his direct communication with God. Serravo, in the doctor's view, was suffering from a psychotic disorder that rendered him incapable of distinguishing right from wrong at the time of the stabbing. Although Doctor Cohen acknowledged that Serravo appeared to cover up his conduct when the police arrived at his home, the doctor explained that conduct as the product of a small part of his still intact reality testing. According to Doctor Cohen, Serravo is "not an incoherent man who can't figure out what's going on," but rather "senses that people don't understand his reasoning very well" and thus apparently believed that the police "wouldn't understand the complex reasoning that went behind the stabbing and that it would be better if he kept it to himself."

At the conclusion of the evidence, the trial court instructed the jury, in accordance with the statutory definition of insanity, that a person "is not accountable who is so diseased or defective in mind at the time of the commission of the act as to be incapable of distinguishing right from wrong, with respect to the act." The court also gave the following jury instruction, to which the prosecution objected, on the meaning of the phrase "incapable of distinguishing right from wrong":

Instruction No. 5

As used in the context of the statutory definition of insanity as a criminal defense, the phrase "incapable of distinguishing right from wrong" includes within its meaning the case where a person appreciates that his conduct is criminal, but, because of a mental disease or defect, believes it to be morally right.

In objecting to the jury instruction, the prosecution stated that it would permit the jury to return an insanity verdict based solely on a purely subjective moral standard rather than a legal standard of right and wrong. The trial court, however, was of the view that, because the statutory definition of insanity was not cast in terms of either legal or moral wrong, it was appropriate to instruct the jury that legal insanity included an incapacity, due to a mental disease or defect, to distinguish right from wrong in a moral sense.

The jury returned a verdict of not guilty by reason of insanity at the time of the commission of the alleged crimes, and the court committed Serravo to the custody of the Department of Institutions until such time as he is found to be eligible for release.

II.

We initially consider whether the phrase "incapable of distinguishing right from wrong" should be measured by legal right and wrong, as argued by the People, or instead, should be measured by a societal standard of morality. The phrase in question appears in section 16–8–101, 8A C.R.S. (1986), which defines legal insanity as follows:

> The applicable test of insanity shall be, and the jury shall be so instructed: "A person who is so diseased or defective in mind at the time of the commission of the act as to be incapable of distinguishing right from wrong with respect to that act is not accountable. But care should be taken not to confuse such mental disease or defect with moral obliquity, mental depravity, or passion growing out of anger, revenge, hatred, or other motives, and kindred evil conditions, for when the act is induced by any of these causes the person is accountable to the law."

A person may be considered legally sane as long as the person commits an act contrary to law and knows that the act is morally wrong without regard to the person's actual knowledge of its legality under positive law.

We acknowledge that some cases subsequent to M'Naghten have interpreted the right-wrong test as limiting the insanity defense to a cognitive inability to distinguish legal right from legal wrong, with the result that a person's simple awareness that an act is illegal is a sufficient basis for finding criminal responsibility. We believe, however, that such an analysis injects a formalistic legalism into the insanity equation to the disregard of the psychological underpinnings of legal insanity. A person in an extremely psychotic state, for example, might be aware that an act is prohibited by law, but due to the overbearing effect of the psychosis may be utterly without the capacity to comprehend that the act is inherently immoral. . . . A standard of legal wrong would render such person legally responsible and subject to imprisonment for the conduct in question notwithstanding the patent injustice of such a disposition. Conversely, a person who, although mentally ill, has the cognitive capacity to distinguish right from wrong and is aware that an act is morally wrong, but does not realize that it is illegal, should nonetheless be held responsible for the act, as ignorance of the law is no excuse. Id.

Construing the term "wrong" as moral wrong finds support in several cases which have basically followed the well-reasoned opinion of the New York Court of Appeals in People v. Schmidt, 216 N.Y. 324, 110 N.E. 945 (N.Y. 1915). . . . The Schmidt opinion, written by then Judge Benjamin Cardozo, rejected the view that the term "wrong" means "contrary to the law of the state." 110 N.E. at 946. After a careful analysis of M'Naghten and the history of the insanity defense, Judge Cardozo remarked:

> The [M'Naghten] judges expressly held that a defendant who knew nothing of the law would none the less be responsible if he knew that the act was wrong, by which, therefore, they must have meant, if he knew that it was morally wrong. Whether he would also be responsible if he knew that it was against the law, but did not know it to be morally wrong, is a question that was not considered. In most cases, of course, knowledge that an act is illegal will justify the inference of knowledge that it is wrong. But none the less it is the knowledge of wrong, conceived of as moral wrong, that seems to have been established by that decision as the controlling test. That must certainly have been the test under the older law when the capacity to distinguish between right and wrong imported a capacity to distinguish between good and evil as abstract qualities. There is nothing to justify the belief that the words right and wrong, when they became limited by M'Naghten's Case to the right and wrong of the particular act, cast off their meaning as terms of morals, and became terms of pure legality.

In resolving the ostensible tension between the legal standard of wrong . . . (i.e., a person is legally responsible if the person acted with knowledge that an act is contrary to the "law of the land") and the moral . . . (i.e., actual knowledge of codified law is not required for a conviction, but rather a person may be punished for conduct if the person knows that the act is one that "he ought not do"), the Schmidt opinion stated that the first answer "presupposes the offender's capacity to understand that violation of the law is wrong" and that the offender is sane except for a delusion that his act will redress a supposed grievance or attain some public benefit. 110 N.E.2d at 948. . . . The delusion that an act will redress a supposed grievance or result in a public benefit, in Cardozo's words, "has no such effect in obscuring moral distinctions as a delusion that God himself has issued a command," inasmuch as "the one delusion is consistent with knowledge that the act is a moral wrong, [but] the other is not." Id.

Because the delusion emanating from an imagined grievance or public benefit does not obscure moral distinctions—as would an insane belief that God has issued a command—there is really no conflict between "the commands of law and morals" in a case where a defendant knows that the act is morally wrong but commits the act because he believes that either personal or public good will result. Id. There is an obvious difference in kind, however, between that case and the person who suffers from an insane delusion that virtually destroys the cognitive ability to distinguish the morality or immorality of an act, even though the person may be aware the act is contrary to law. Although in most instances the very same forms of criminal conduct classified as felonies would also be considered violative of basic ethical norms, we are of the view that limiting the definition of "wrong" to "legal wrong" results in stripping legal insanity of a significant part of its psychological components. Various forms of mental diseases or defects can impair a person's cognitive ability to distinguish moral right from moral wrong and yet have no effect whatever on the person's rather sterile awareness that a certain act is contrary to law. To be sure, a person should not be judged legally insane merely because that person has personal views of right or wrong at variance with those which find expression in the law. It is quite another matter, however, to say that a mentally ill person suffering from an insane delusion that overbears the mental capacity to distinguish right from wrong should nonetheless be held criminally responsible for conduct solely because the person was aware that the act charged in the criminal prosecution was contrary to law. Such a result, in our view, proceeds from a narrowly legalistic interpretation that accords little weight to the baneful effects of various forms of mental illness on the cognitive capacity of the human mind.

We thus conclude that the term "wrong" in the statutory definition of insanity refers to moral wrong.

C.

Moral wrong can be measured either by a purely personal and subjective standard of morality or by a societal and presumably more objective standard. We believe that the better reasoned interpretation of "wrong" in the term "incapable of distinguishing right from wrong" refers to a wrongful act measured by societal standards of morality.

The concepts of "right" and "wrong" are essentially ethical in character and have their primary source in the existing societal standards of morality, as distinguished from the written law. A person's awareness and appreciation of right and wrong derive primarily from a variety of experiences and relationships including, but not necessarily limited to, behavioral rules endorsed by the social culture as well as ethical principles transmitted through the family, the community, the formal educational process, and religious associations. Simply put, legal insanity combines concepts of law, morality and medicine with the moral concepts derived primarily from the total underlying conceptions of ethics shared by the community at large. See United States v. Brawner, 153 App. D.C. 1, 471 F.2d 969, 976 982 (D.C. Cir. 1972). Defining "wrong" in terms of a purely personal and subjective standard of morality ignores a substantial part of the moral culture on which our societal norms of behavior are based.

The traditional reluctance to hold children under a certain age responsible for criminal acts is a good illustration of the fact that moral standards are learned through a dynamic societal process. Society has determined that both insane persons and children under a certain age are not responsible moral agents, in the former case because a mental disease or defect has prevented an adequate assimilation of societal moral standards, and in the latter case because immaturity has prevented an adequate opportunity for acquiring a moral sense of right and wrong. Like the M'Naghten test, the test for measuring infant incapacity has generally involved the inquiry of whether the child could distinguish between right and wrong.

Construing the term "wrong" in accordance with societal standards of morality results in a substantially more objective standard of moral wrong than the purely personal and subjective moral standard, under which an accused could be adjudicated insane even if he knew that the act in question was both forbidden by law and condemned by society, but nonetheless harbored a personal belief that the act was right. A personal and subjective standard of morality should not be permitted to exonerate a defendant any more than an ignorance of the law, engendered by a mental illness, should be equated with legal insanity. In sum, the appropriate construction of the term "incapable of distinguishing right from wrong with respect to [the] act" in section 16–8–101 should be measured by existing societal standards of morality rather than by a defendant's personal and subjective understanding of the legality or illegality of the act in question.

D.

We turn then to Jury Instruction No. 5, which stated that the phrase "incapable of distinguishing right from wrong" includes the case of a person who "appreciates that his conduct is criminal but, because of a mental disease or defect, believes it to be morally right." Although the court of appeals concluded that this instruction did not incorporate a "subjective moral standard to the determination of whether defendant understood right from wrong," Serravo, 797 P.2d at 782–83, we are of a contrary view. Jury Instruction No. 5 was cast in terms so general that it well could have been interpreted by the jury to incorporate a personal and subjective standard of moral wrong rather than a societal standard of right and wrong.

We emphasize here that in most cases involving the defense of legal insanity there will be no practical difference between a definition of "wrong" in terms of legal wrong and a definition of "wrong" in terms of societal standards of morality. This is so because, for the most part, the proscriptions of the criminal law generally reflect the moral prohibitions of the social order. As previously discussed, however, the concept of legal insanity, while part of our positive law, incorporates psychological and moral components that are not necessarily limited by the confines of positive law. A clarifying instruction on the definition of legal insanity, therefore, should clearly state that, as related to the conduct charged as a crime, the phrase "incapable of distinguishing right from wrong" refers to a person's cognitive inability, due to a mental disease or defect, to distinguish right from wrong as measured by a societal standard of morality, even though the person may be aware that the conduct in question is criminal. Any such instruction should also expressly inform the jury that the phrase "incapable of distinguishing right from wrong" does not refer to a purely personal and subjective standard of morality.

III.

We next consider the relationship between the so-called "deific-decree" delusion and Colorado's test of legal insanity. The court of appeals, after holding that the term "wrong" in the statutory definition of insanity refers not to legal wrong but moral wrong under societal standards of morality, held that the "deific-decree" delusion was an exception to the societal standards of moral wrong. Drawing on the opinion of the Washington Supreme Court in State v. Crenshaw, 98 Wash. 2d 789, 659 P.2d 488 (Wash. 1983), the court of appeals limited the so-called deific-decree exception to those situations "in which a person commits a criminal act, knowing it is illegal and morally wrong according to society's standards but, because of a mental defect, believes that God has decreed the act." Serravo, 797 P.2d at 783. This exception, the court of appeals went on to conclude, must be distinguished from the case "in which a person acts in accordance with a duty imposed by a particular faith." Id. In our view, the "deific-decree" delusion is not so much an exception to the right-wrong test measured by the existing societal standards of morality as it is an integral factor in assessing a person's cognitive ability to distinguish right from wrong with respect to the act charged as a crime.

In Crenshaw, the Supreme Court of Washington carved out the deific exception from Justice Cardozo's reference in Schmidt, 110 N.E. at 949, to a mother insanely obeying God's command to kill her child. The Crenshaw court, citing Schmidt, stated that although the woman who kills her infant child under an insane delusion that God has ordered the act might know "that the law and society condemn the act, it would be unrealistic to hold her responsible for the crime, since her free will has been subsumed by her belief in the deific decree." 659 P.2d at 494. Crenshaw appears to have judicially embrodered the Schmidt opinion, since Schmidt contains no reference to the volitional or free will aspect of the insanity defense. On the contrary, Judge Cardozo in Schmidt specifically states that New York's test of insanity does not contain an irresistible impulse component. It thus appears that the Crenshaw court added a volitional component to the "deific-decree" exception which is not supported by Schmidt.

In discussing the deific-decree delusion in Schmidt, the court stated:

> We must not. . . exaggerate the rigor of the rule by giving the word "wrong" a strained interpretation, at war with its broad and primary meaning, and least of all, if in so doing, we rob the rule of all relation to the mental health and true capacity of the criminal. The interpretation placed upon the statute by the trial judge may be tested by its consequences. A mother kills her infant child to whom she has been devotedly attached. She knows the nature and quality of the act; she knows that the law condemns it; but she is inspired by an insane delusion that God has appeared to her and ordained the sacrifice. It seems a mockery to say that, within the meaning of the statute, she knows that the act is wrong. If the definition propounded by the trial judge is right, it would be the duty of a Jury to hold her responsible for the crime. We find nothing either in the history of the rule, or in its reason and purpose, or in judicial exposition of its meaning, to justify a conclusion so abhorrent. . .

> . . . Knowledge that an act is forbidden by law will in most cases permit the inference of knowledge that, according to the accepted standards of mankind, it is also condemned as an offense against good morals. Obedience to the law is itself a moral duty. If, however, there is an insane delusion that God has appeared to the defendant and ordained the commission of a crime, we think it cannot be said of the offender that he knows the act to be wrong.

If a person insanely believes that "he has a command from the Almighty to kill, it is difficult to understand how such a man can know that it is wrong for him to do it." Schmidt, 110 N.E. at 948 (quoting Guiteau's Case, 10 Fed. 161, 182 (1882)). A person acting under such a delusion is no less insane even though the person might know that murder is prohibited by positive law. Schmidt, 110 N.E.2d at 948. It thus seems clear to us that a person is legally insane if that person's cognitive ability to distinguish right from wrong with respect to the act has been destroyed as a result of a psychotic delusion that God has commanded the act.

We thus conclude that, although the court of appeals mischaracterized the deific-decree delusion as an exception to the right-wrong test for legal insanity, a defendant nonetheless may be judged legally insane where, as here, the defendant's cognitive ability to distinguish right from wrong with respect to the act has been destroyed as a result of a psychotic delusion that God has decreed the act.

We recognize, as did the court in People v. Schmidt, 216 N.Y. 324, 110 N.E. 945, 950 (N.Y. 1915), that some defendants may attempt to hide behind "a professed belief that their crime was ordained by God." The Schmidt court, however, went on to observe that "we can safely leave such fabrications to the common sense of juries." Id.; see also State v. Crenshaw, 98 Wash. 2d 789, 659 P.2d 488, 494 (Wash. 1983) (jury properly found that defendant's adherence to the Muscovite faith which requires husbands to kill unfaithful wives was a personal subjective belief rather than a "deific decree"). We agree with the Schmidt court's observation. The jury, functioning as the conscience of the community, is well-suited to the task of determining whether a defendant in a given case had the mental capacity to distinguish right from wrong in accordance with societal standards of morality with respect to an act charged as a crime.

IV.

[W]e disapprove the trial court's jury instruction which defined the phrase "incapable of distinguishing right from wrong" in such a general manner as likely to be interpreted by a jury as including a purely subjective and personal standard of morality; we approve of the court of appeals' construction of the phrase "incapable of distinguishing right from wrong" as referring to an incapacity, due to a mental disease or defect, to know that an act is wrong under existing societal standards of morality; and we disapprove of the court of appeals' characterization of the deific-decree delusion as an exception to the right-wrong test for legal insanity rather than as an integral factor in assessing a person's cognitive ability to distinguish right from wrong with respect to the act charged as a crime. The judgment of the court of appeals is accordingly approved in part and disapproved in part.

DISCUSSION QUESTIONS

1. Do you believe that Serravo should be excused from criminal responsibility for stabbing his wife?

2. Do you believe that insanity should require only an incapacity to understand moral wrongfulness or should an incapacity to understand legal wrongfulness also be required?

3. Should a belief in deific commands provide a legal basis for insanity?

G. M'NAGHTEN CRITICISMS AND RESPONSES

It is easier to understand the MPC test if one understands the two tests that developed in response to criticisms of M'Naghten. The MPC test can be understood as an attempt to find a middle ground between these two approaches.

1. THE IRRESISTIBLE IMPULSE TEST AND THE ROLE OF VOLITION

One of the principal criticisms of M'Naghten is that it ignored the way in which mental illness often impairs volition as opposed to cognition. Regardless of what you know to be true or right, your ability to control your behavior might be impaired by your disease or defect. A person tortured by continual auditory and visual hallucinations, for example, may lose the necessary willpower to resist impulses they know to be irrational. Organic brain damage may also directly impair impulse control. Even milder neurological conditions may create a fractured, disordered interior world that weakens a person's ability to govern their emotions.

Since your ability to control your behavior is an essential foundation for moral blameworthiness and deterrability, an insanity test that ignores control is, arguably, deeply flawed. In response to these criticisms, some jurisdictions added a volitional test. Some courts described this as the irresistible impulse test, which means that the defendant suffered a disease or defect that disabled him from controlling his conduct. Other courts phrased this volitional test in terms of the loss of one's power to choose between right and wrong or the destruction of one's will.

These volitional tests were criticized from two directions. Some argued that they demanded too much by seeming to require a complete loss of self-control. Others argued that any impulse or urge is capable of being resisted and that the degree of one's self control is too difficult to medically assess. Advocates of deterrence argued that the harder an impulse is to control the greater the need to reinforce control with the threat of criminal punishment. In turn, critics of deterrence argued that people who lack the ability to control their behavior can not be deterred by any amount of punishment.

2. THE DURHAM "PRODUCT" TEST AND THE SCOPE OF PSYCHIATRIC EXPERTISE

A second and distinct criticism of M'Naghten is that it restricted psychiatric testimony. Rather than confining psychiatric testimony to narrow, semi-philosophical questions about one's ability to know right from wrong or the nature and quality of acts, an insanity test should invite medical experts to share the full range of their understanding of how a mental disease or defect affected the defendant. In response to these criticisms, some jurisdictions experimented with a cause and effect test. A person was insane if their unlawful act was the product of mental disease or defect. The product test greatly widened the scope of psychiatric testimony in insanity cases because any symptom or condition that might have caused the behavior was now relevant. Since many mental health conditions involve a range of symptoms, this test allowed expert witnesses to give a jury the fullest possible picture of the defendant's mental condition.

The principal problem with the product test, however, was its "emptiness." It asked the jury to decide whether an act was or was not a product of mental illness. This seemed too open-ended. Some described it as a "non-rule." For one thing, the test failed to define whether the mental illness could be one cause among many, a primary cause, or an exclusive cause of the defendant's behavior. John Hinckley would never have shot Reagan but for his obsessions and delusions about Jodie Foster. Does this mean that his act was "a product" of his mental illness? Should that alone make him insane? The rule provides no guidance to the jury on these key questions. Ultimately calling an act a "product" of mental illness operates more as a label for a conclusion than as a standard for evaluating behavior.

Many feared that expert psychiatric testimony would now play too great a role in the juror's deliberations because they might focus solely on whether the defendant had a mental disease of defect. Others feared that the absence of more definite criteria to guide the deliberations of the jury would result in arbitrary and inconsistent verdicts. Before abandoning it altogether, some jurisdictions narrowed this test by defining mental disease or defect in a way that foreshadowed what would become the MPC test.

H. THE MODEL PENAL CODE

§ 4.01. Mental Disease or Defect Excluding Responsibility

1. A person is not responsible for criminal conduct if at the time of such conduct as a result of mental disease or defect he lacks substantial capacity either to appreciate the criminality [wrongfulness] of his conduct or to conform his conduct to the requirements of law.

2. As used in this Article, the terms "mental disease or defect" do not include an abnormality manifested only by repeated criminal or otherwise antisocial conduct.

The MPC's substantial capacity test, which emerged from the debate regarding the limitations of M'Naghten, defines insanity in a minority of jurisdictions. In addition to adding a volitional component, it also made a series of other, more nuanced changes. Section 4.01 of the Model Penal Code defines insanity in the following terms.

1. A person is not responsible for criminal conduct if at the time of such conduct as a result of mental disease or defect he lacks substantial capacity either to appreciate the criminality [wrongfulness] of his conduct or to conform his conduct to the requirements of law.

2. As used in this Article, the terms "mental disease or defect" do not include an abnormality manifested only by repeated criminal or otherwise anti-social conduct.

Unlike M'Naghten, the MPC test only requires a lack of a substantial capacity, not a complete lack of capacity, with respect to the defendant's ability to appreciate the wrongfulness of his conduct. Similarly, the use of the word "appreciate" invites a full consideration of the emotional and affective nature of a defendant's mental condition. Since the mentally ill are often plagued by conflicting and sometimes incoherent thoughts and emotions, these changes invite a more nuanced assessment of criminal responsibility. Note that the MPC put "wrongfulness" in brackets to avoid taking a stand on the controversy over whether legal or moral wrongfulness was at issue, leaving it up to each jurisdiction to decide which was appropriate.

Likewise, the volitional prong of the MPC test requires a lack of a substantial capacity to conform one's conduct to the requirements of the law. First, this test only requires a lack of substantial capacity, rather than a complete inability, as was the case with some of the other volitional tests. In addition, this volitional prong speaks to an actor's ability to *conform* rather than to control his conduct. Practically speaking, these changes mean that a mentally ill person need not "snap" or "explode" to be found insane under this prong. A brooding, confused defendant who wrestled with himself before acting could be found insane more easily under this test. The lengthier, conflicted nature of his thought-process arguably reveals *some* capacity to conform his behavior, but not a substantial capacity. Moreover, some ability to control his behavior (by lying in wait for a victim, for example) would not be inconsistent with his ultimate inability to conform his behavior to the law.

Furthermore, the second paragraph of the MPC test rules out sociopathy or psychopathy as a basis for insanity. Arguably, a classic sociopath or psychopath—one unable to experience empathy towards another—lacks substantial capacity to appreciate the wrongfulness of his actions (although he may still be intellectually aware that they are illegal and criminal). The best way of understanding the exemption of sociopathy and psychopathy is that such a complete lack of empathy is itself the core of both dangerousness and blameworthiness. It is what most people think of as the essence of evil, something that we choose not to excuse even if it is the result of a mental disease or defect.

1. THE HINCKLEY VERDICT AND THE RETURN OF M'NAGHTEN

Rarely does one criminal case have as big an effect on criminal law doctrine as the Hinckley case did. Hinckley was tried for the attempted murder of Ronald Reagan in federal court, which used the MPC's substantial capacity test. After Hinckley was found not guilty by reason of insanity, an enormous backlash against the MPC test ensued. Congress changed the federal standard and a number of states switched back to the M'Naghten test.

The Hinckley case provides a nice illustration of the difference between the two tests. As discussed earlier, one could argue under M'Naghten that Hinckley did not "know" what he was doing or understand its wrongfulness in the sense that he did not appreciate its significance. Such an argument is much easier under the MPC's substantial capacity test, however.

The prosecution argued that Hinckley wanted to kill Reagan to become famous. Using the MPC test, however, the defense argued that Hinckley could not fully appreciate just how wrongful his act was because of his delusional obsession with Jodie Foster. On the one hand, Hinckley believed that killing the president would make him infamous, revealing that he had some capacity to understand the wrongfulness of the act. Hinckley, however, was unable to appreciate that killing Reagan would not make him attractive or interesting to Jodie Foster. Therefore, although he did not completely lack the capacity, Hinckley lacked a substantial capacity to appreciate the wrongfulness of his conduct.

Case in Context

This case discussed the volitional component of an insanity standard.

UNITED STATES OF AMERICA V. ROBERT LYONS

United States Court of Appeals, Fifth Circuit
731 F.2d 243 (1984)

Defendant Robert Lyons was indicted on twelve counts of knowingly and intentionally securing controlled narcotics by misrepresentation, fraud, deception and subterfuge in violation of 21 U.S.C. § 843(a)(3) (1976) and 18 U.S.C. § 2 (1976). Before trial Lyons informed the Assistant United States Attorney that he intended to rely on a defense of insanity: that he had lacked substantial capacity to conform his conduct to the requirements of the law because of drug addiction. Lyons proffered evidence that in 1978 he began to suffer from several painful ailments, that various narcotics were prescribed to be taken as needed for his pain, and that he became addicted to these drugs. He also offered to present expert witnesses who would testify that his drug addiction affected his brain both physiologically and psychologically and that as a result he lacked substantial capacity to conform his conduct to the requirements of the law.

In response to the government's motion *in limine,* the district court excluded any evidence of Lyon's drug addiction, apparently on the ground that such an addiction could not constitute a mental disease or defect sufficient to support an insanity defense. A panel of this Court reversed, holding that it was the jury's responsibility to decide whether involuntary drug addiction could constitute a mental disease or defect depriving Lyons of substantial capacity to conform his conduct to the requirements of the law. *United States v. Lyons,* 704 F.2d 743 (5th Cir.1983). We agreed to rehear the case en banc. *Id.* at 748.

I.

For the greater part of two decades our Circuit has followed the rule that a defendant is not to be held criminally responsible for conduct if, at the time of that conduct and as a result of mental disease or defect, he lacked substantial capacity either to appreciate the wrongfulness of his conduct *or to conform his conduct to the requirements of the law. Blake v. United States,* 407 F.2d 908, 916 (5th Cir.1969) (en banc).

Today the great weight of legal authority clearly supports the view that evidence of mere narcotics addiction, standing alone and without other physiological or psychological involvement, raises no issue of such a mental defect or disease as can serve as a basis for the insanity defense. [Case citations omitted.) *See also* Fingarette, *Addiction and Criminal Responsibility,* 84 Yale L.J. 413, 424–25 (1975) ("there is no consensus in the medical profession that addiction is a mental disease").

There are a number of reasons why. In the first place, there is an element of reasoned choice when an addict knowingly acquires and uses drugs; he could instead have participated in an addiction treatment program. *Moore,* 486 F.2d at 1183 (opinion of Leventhal, J.). A person is not to be excused for offending "simply because he wanted to very, very badly." *Bailey,* 386 F.2d at 4. Second, since the defense of insanity is "essentially an acknowledgement on the part of society that because of mental disease or defect certain classes of wrongdoers are not properly the subjects of criminal punishment," *Freeman,* 357 F.2d at 625, it seems anomalous to immunize narcotics addicts from other criminal sanctions when Congress has decreed severe penalties for mere possession and sale of narcotics. *Id.* In addition, Congress has dealt with the problem of responsibility of narcotics addicts for their crimes by providing for civil commitment and treatment of addicts in lieu of prosecution or sentencing.

Finally, what definition of "mental disease or defect" is to be employed by courts enforcing the criminal law is, in the final analysis, a question of legal, moral and policy—not of medical—judgment. Among the most basic purposes of the criminal law is that of preventing a person from injuring others or, perhaps to a lesser degree, himself. This purpose and others appropriate to law enforcement are not necessarily served by an uncritical application of definitions developed with medical considerations of diagnosis and treatment foremost in mind. Indeed, it would be coincidental indeed should concepts deriving from such disparate sources correspond closely, one to the other. Thus it is, for example, that the law has not greatly concerned itself with medical opinion about such mental states as accompany the commission of crimes of passion or of those done while voluntarily intoxicated; whatever that opinion may be, policy considerations have been thought to forbid its cutting much of a figure in court.

Although mere narcotics addiction is not itself to be acknowledged as a mental disease or defect, evidence of narcotics addiction has been received by some courts as evidence of such an underlying condition. *Green v. United States,* 383 F.2d 199, 201 (D.C.Cir.1967), *cert. denied,* 390 U.S. 961, 88 S.Ct. 1061, 19 L.Ed.2d 1158 (1968). In addition, if addiction has caused actual physical damage to the structures of a defendant's body, evidence of that addiction has been admitted to show any mental defect resulting from that damage. *Cf. Brinkley v. United States,* 498 F.2d 505, 511–12 (8th Cir.1974) (remanding to explore possible physiological and psychological effects of long term LSD use on appellant and whether these effects might amount to insanity).

We view the reasoning of such rulings as *Green* with profound misgivings. To us it seems to rest on the proposition that, assuming drug addiction itself is neither a mental disease nor a defect, yet the two are often to be found in association, so that an addicted person is more likely to suffer from some mental disorder than is one who is not addicted. By a parity of reasoning, since combat veterans as a group are self-evidently more likely to have suffered the loss of a physical member than is the populace at large, evidence of whether a party is a combat veteran should be received on the issue whether he has lost a leg. Or, to take a less extreme example, since because of light skin pigmentation persons of Scandinavian ancestry are more subject to skin cancer than are others, the family tree of a suitor should be received in evidence when his skin cancer is at legal issue. The flaw in both illustrations seems evident: where evidence bearing directly on a legal question is available, that involving tangential matters, even though perhaps logically relevant in theory, is of small practical value.

Our review of numerous records over the course of years has revealed no dearth of experts ready and willing to testify squarely on the issue of insanity in criminal trials: direct evidence on the issue seems all but too readily available. Since this is so, receiving evidence of drug addiction in addition seems to us an exercise seldom likely to prove more probative than prejudicial in practice.

Nor do we see how matters are clarified by reference to the condition of addiction as one involving "psychological damage" to the addict, *e.g., Brinkley v. United States, supra.* As nearly as we can determine, the psychological condition so described is simply one of drug addiction to one degree or another, a condition that we have already declined to view as a mental disease or defect for legal purposes. An actual drug-induced or drug-aggravated psychosis, or physical damage to the brain or nervous system would, however, be another matter.

We do not doubt that actual physical damage to the brain itself falls within the ambit of "mental disease or defect." To refuse to recognize that a congenital microcephalic, or one who has suffered, say, extensive brain damage from a gunshot wound or other physical trauma, may be thereby rendered unable to appreciate the character of his conduct as wrongful would be presumptuous. Here, within the limits of appropriate legal and policy considerations, the medical model must have its day. The same is true of the question whether such organic brain pathology or psychosis can be caused by drugs.

Lyons asserted by his proffer of evidence that his drug addiction caused physiological damage to his brain and that this damage caused him to lack substantial capacity to conform his conduct to the requirements of the law. 704 F.2d at 746. Since he did so, he should—under our subsisting *Blake* test—have been allowed to introduce evidence of any physical brain damage and consequent mental disease or defect. Because the proffer offers evidence tending to suggest such damage, that evidence should have been submitted to the jury. *Blake,* 407 F.2d at 911. And although we today withdraw our recognition of the volitional prong of *Blake*—that as to which such evidence has usually been advanced—we also conclude that should Lyons wish to offer such evidence in an attempt to satisfy the remaining cognitive prong, fairness demands that we afford him an opportunity to do so.

II.

Because the concept of criminal responsibility in the federal courts is a congeries of judicially-made rules of decision based on common law concepts, it is usually appropriate for us to reexamine and reappraise these rules in the light of new policy considerations. *Wion v. United States,* 325 F.2d 420, 425 (10th Cir.1963). We last examined the insanity defense in *Blake v. United States,* 407 F.2d 908 (5th Cir.1969) (en banc), where we adopted the ALI Model Penal Code definition of insanity: that a person is not responsible for criminal conduct if, at the time of such conduct and as a result of mental disease or defect, he lacks substantial capacity either to appreciate the wrongfulness of his conduct or to conform his conduct to the requirements of the law. *Id.* at 916. Following the example of sister circuits, we embraced this standard in lieu of our former one, defined in *Howard v. United States,* 232 F.2d 274, 275 (5th Cir.1956) (en banc), because we concluded that then current knowledge in the field of behavioral science supported such a result. 407 F.2d at 909, 914–15. Unfortunately, it now appears our conclusion was premature-that the brave new world that we foresaw has not arrived.

Reexamining the *Blake* standard today, we conclude that the volitional prong of the insanity defense—a lack of capacity to conform one's conduct to the requirements of the law—does not comport with current medical and scientific knowledge, which has retreated from its earlier, sanguine expectations. Consequently, we now hold that a person is not responsible for criminal conduct on the grounds of insanity only if at the time of that conduct, as a result of a mental disease or defect, he is unable to appreciate the wrongfulness of that conduct.

We do so for several reasons. First, as we have mentioned, a majority of psychiatrists now believe that they do not possess sufficient accurate scientific bases for measuring a person's capacity for self-control or for calibrating the impairment of that capacity. Bonnie, *The Moral Basis of the Insanity Defense*, 69 ABA J. 194, 196 (1983). "The line between an irresistible impulse and an impulse not resisted is probably no sharper than between twilight and dusk." *American Psychiatric Association Statement on the Insanity Defense*, 11 (1982) [APA Statement]. Indeed, Professor Bonnie states:

> There is, in short, no objective basis for distinguishing between offenders who were undeterrable and those who were merely undeterred, between the impulse that was irresistible and the impulse not resisted, or between substantial impairment of capacity and some lesser impairment.

Bonnie, *supra*, at 196.

In addition, the risks of fabrication and "moral mistakes" in administering the insanity defense are greatest "when the experts and the jury are asked to speculate whether the defendant had the capacity to 'control' himself or whether he could have 'resisted' the criminal impulse." Bonnie, *supra*, at 196. Moreover, psychiatric testimony about volition is more likely to produce confusion for jurors than is psychiatric testimony concerning a defendant's appreciation of the wrongfulness of his act. APA Statement at 12. It appears, moreover, that there is considerable overlap between a psychotic person's inability to understand and his ability to control his behavior. Most psychotic persons who fail a volitional test would also fail a cognitive test, thus rendering the volitional test superfluous for them. *Id.* Finally, Supreme Court authority requires that such proof be made by the federal prosecutor beyond a reasonable doubt, an all but impossible task in view of the present murky state of medical knowledge. *Davis v. United States,* 160 U.S. 469, 16 S.Ct. 353, 40 L.Ed. 499 (1895).

One need not disbelieve in the existence of Angels in order to conclude that the present state of our knowledge regarding them is not such as to support confident conclusions about how many can dance on the head of a pin. In like vein, it may be that some day tools will be discovered with which reliable conclusions about human volition can be fashioned. It appears to be all but a certainty, however, that despite earlier hopes they do not lie in our hands today. When and if they do, it will be time to consider again to what degree the law should adopt the sort of conclusions that they produce. But until then, we see no prudent course for the law to follow but to treat all criminal impulses—including those not resisted—as resistible. To do otherwise in the present state of medical knowledge would be to cast the insanity defense adrift upon a sea of unfounded scientific speculation, with the palm awarded case by case to the most convincing advocate of that which is presently unknown—and may remain so, because unknowable.

III.

Thus, Lyons' claim that he lacked substantial capacity to conform his conduct to the requirements of the law will not raise the insanity defense. It would be unfair, however, to remit him retroactively to our newly restricted insanity defense without allowing him the opportunity to plan a defense bearing its contours in mind. Consequently, we vacate his conviction and remand for a new trial in accordance with our new insanity standard. As for other cases, today's holding shall have prospective application only, commencing thirty days from the date of its publication.

VACATED and REMANDED.

JOHNSON, CIRCUIT JUDGE, dissenting.

This dissent is necessitated by the mischaracterization of the panel opinion by both the majority and the dissenting opinion of Judges Rubin and Williams; by the mischaracterization of Lyons' contentions on appeal by both opinions; and because of the sincere belief that the Court is here choosing a particularly inopportune time to delve into the quagmire of the insanity defense.

The issue on appeal in the Lyons case was quite clear; it was not whether Lyons was indeed insane. The issue was simply whether Lyons should have been permitted to submit his insanity argument and defense to the jury. The jury, of course, was fully entitled to reject or accept his contentions. The panel concluded that Lyons should have been permitted to submit his argument and defense to the jury under existing precedent and I continue to believe that the existing precedent of this circuit requires such a result.

It is noted at the outset that Lyons' proffer goes far beyond a mere allegation of iatrogenic drug addiction. The majority's and Judge Rubin's and Judge Williams' characterization of Lyons' contentions as alleging *mere* drug addiction is, in my judgment, inaccurate. An examination of

Lyons' proffer demonstrates that Lyons' addiction became so extreme that he lost over forty pounds and suffered from drastic malnutrition. The proffer notes that "[h]is decalcified bones had become so brittle that during the course of [a] convulsion, he broke three [3] ribs, three [3] vertebrae, and his left hip was completely torn from the socket." Moreover, Lyons offered to present two expert witnesses, indeed medical witnesses, that would testify that Lyons' addiction had damaged his brain, both physiologically and psychologically.

When Lyons' proffer is viewed in its true form, it becomes clear that he was entitled to submit his insanity defense to the jury under existing precedent. The reasons for this conclusion were set forth in the panel opinion:

> [T]his Court has held that involuntary drug addiction may constitute a "mental disease or defect" bearing on the defendant's criminal responsibility. *United States v. Bass,* 490 F.2d 846 (5th Cir.1974). In *Bass,* a case strikingly similar to the case at bar, this Court concluded that evidence of involuntary drug addiction could, and did in the particular circumstances of that case, constitute relevant evidence on the issue of the defendant's sanity. In *Bass,* as in the instant case, the defendant was charged, *inter alia,* with obtaining narcotics by misrepresentation, deception, fraud, and subterfuge. More importantly, *Bass* and the case *sub judice* both dealt with defendants *involuntarily* addicted to the narcotics they illegally obtained. In *Bass,* the defendant had become involuntarily addicted to Demerol as a result of medical treatment aimed at alleviating the defendant's regional enteritis, an acutely painful disease of the lower gastro-intestinal tract. *Bass,* 490 F.2d at 849.

> > In the instant case, the defendant's proffer indicates that Lyons became involuntarily addicted to pain medication, including Demerol, as a result of medical treatment designed to alleviate the barrage of illnesses suffered by Lyons during the three-year period prior to the commission of the charged offenses. No meaningful distinction between *Bass* and the case *sub judice* can be discerned. In both cases, the defendant embarked upon a course of narcotics use not by choice, but pursuant to doctor's orders—orders presumably aimed at treating an admittedly painful physical disorder. Additionally, in both cases, the defendant offered expert testimony, which, if believed by the jury, would establish that the defendant lacked substantial capacity to conform his conduct to the requirements of applicable law due to his involuntary drug addiction.

United States v. Lyons, 704 F.2d 743, 747 (5th Cir.1983). For these reasons, the reasons which are more fully explained in the panel opinion, it is my belief that Lyons should be permitted to present his insanity defense to the jury under the law of this Circuit.

DISCUSSION QUESTIONS

1.   Should insanity include a volitional prong?

2.   Should addiction be considered a basis for insanity? If so, should it matter how the addiction developed?

3.   Should incapacity or a lack of substantial capacity be the requirement for insanity under either a cognitive or a volitional test?

Practice Problem 22.0: Friends, Lovers, and Zombies

Rick and Laurie had just become engaged when Rick developed schizophrenia. He started to believe that he could detect a disease of the human spirit that signaled the coming of a zombie plague. As a result, he became obsessed with depictions of a zombie apocalypse in movies, TV shows, and books. Rick believed that a person infected with the virus would die, turn into a zombie, and then spread the virus by biting other people. Only by completely destroying the brains of the zombies could they be killed. Sometimes, however, Rick had moments of doubts about the reality of his beliefs. Because of these doubts, and when Laurie threatened to leave Rick, Laurie was able to convince him to see a therapist. Rick began taking medication for his condition, and the intensity of his delusions diminished. With the help of his therapist, he began to see his beliefs about zombies as obsessions to be resisted.

Around this time, Rick's coworker Shane began to torment him. At first, Shane would shuffle around with his mouth open, staring vacantly. Rick would yell at him to stop joking. One day, Shane asked Rick if he was feeling lethargic and emotionally flat. Rick admitted that he was feeling that way but said that his doctor had told him that this was an effect of his medication. Shane instead suggested that Rick was succumbing to the zombie virus. Shane said that the medication was possibly weakening his mind, and that he was feeling "deader" because the virus was starting to grow in his brain. Shane further suggested that he go without medication for seventy-two hours to determine what was real and what was not.

Rick took Shane's suggestion. After seventy-two hours, he feared his beliefs of a coming zombie plague were real, and he simultaneously feared that he had made a terrible mistake by stopping his medication. In addition, when Laurie realized that Rick had stopped taking his medication, she broke off their engagement and told him that she never wanted to see him again. Having no one to turn to for advice, Rick drove to Shane's apartment. When Laurie emerged from Shane's bedroom, Rick discovered that they had become romantically involved. Shane laughed at Rick and told him that Laurie had no use for a lunatic boyfriend.

Rick punched Shane hard, knocking him momentarily unconscious. When Shane regained consciousness, he jumped up and pretended to be a zombie, grabbing Rick, and opening his mouth as if to bite him. While holding Shane with one hand, Rick grabbed a heavy paper weight that was within reach and began smashing Shane over the head until Shane fell to the ground.

By this time, Laurie had called the police. When they arrived, they found Rick sitting dazed on the floor. He stared at Shane who had died from the blows to his head. While he was being handcuffed, Rick noticed for the first time that Shane had bit him during the fight. As Rick was lead out of the apartment by the police, Laurie jumped on him. She screamed that she loved Shane, and slapped him across the face. Rick then bit her hard on her hand, and only released his bite when one of the officers sprayed him with mace.

Assume that these events happened in a jurisdiction that has adopted all of the Model Penal Code. Discuss Rick's liability for all homicide crimes.

CHAPTER 23

RAPE

∎ ∎ ∎

Rape law is a fascinating, important, and difficult subject, both to teach and to learn. The special challenges of rape law shape how most professors approach it, so this chapter begins with a discussion of those challenges before proceeding with an overview of the elements of rape.

A. THE CHALLENGES AND REWARDS OF RAPE LAW

Rape is not an easy topic to talk about. Statistically, it is very likely that someone in your class has been raped. It is much less likely but not inconceivable that someone in your class may have been falsely accused of rape. That obviously makes the topic a sensitive one to discuss. These same facts, however, make rape law an important and potentially rewarding topic to explore.

Rape law also raises profoundly difficult issues of gender, autonomy, and the role of the criminal law in the most intimate areas of our lives. The law of rape was formed during an openly patriarchal time when woman were subjugated by law in numerous ways. At common law men were legally incapable of being guilty of the rape of their wives because the consent of the wife to intercourse with her husband was conclusively presumed as a matter of law. Since adultery and sex outside of marriage were each crimes in their own right, common law judges worried that a woman would "cry rape" to avoid criminal liability herself. This skepticism towards rape complainants continued into modern times, often in the form of procedural requirements such as corroboration of the woman's claims, a prompt complaint, and admission of evidence of the rape complainant's past sexual history to rebut the claim of non-consent. In sum, rape law often protected men too much and women too little, and it still does in some jurisdictions.

Race also complicates discussion of rape in a different way. Historically rape allegations played a large role in the oppression of racial and ethnic minorities. Rape allegations against men of color often were the pretext for lynchings and other racial violence. Rape carried the death penalty in some southern states, and rape charges were often brought against African American men for raping white women. Rape and sexual violence against African American women by white men in contrast often went unreported and unprosecuted. Rape prosecutions also played a role in enforcing prohibitions against sexual relations between races. A white woman discovered to have had sexual intercourse with a man of color faced ostracism and possible criminal prosecution if the intercourse was consensual. If she alleged rape, however, all-white juries often returned convictions on the basis of an assumption that a white woman would not willingly engage in sex with a man of color.

Recent reform efforts have made some headway, but ongoing attempts to redefine rape remain deeply controversial. Even putting issues of patriarchy and gender discrimination aside, the definition of rape requires the law to essentially take a stand on how people should and should not speak to and touch one another when engaged in intimate sexual activity. Deciding how much or how little the criminal law should regulate sexual activity would not be easy for any society, much less one with the gendered baggage that our own and most other societies carry. Figuring out where and how to draw this line is both interesting and important though.

Finally, rape is very complex legally. Most serious crimes place great importance on mental state requirements. Rape law, historically, does not, despite the fact that the one thing that separates rape from perfectly lawful sexual activity is the presence or absence of freely formed consent, a circumstance that obviously is mental in nature. To make matters even worse, rape law is incredibly varied. The rape law reform movement did not generate a consensus approach. While all jurisdictions have reformed their rape laws, they have done so in many different ways.

So professors teaching rape law face multiple challenges. They must untangle a complicated legal doctrine and lead discussions that are both respectful of the various sensitivities involved as well as robust in engaging the deeper, truly difficult issues that demand resolution. These challenges shape how many professors a teach rape law in a couple of different ways.

First, the sensitive nature of the topic leads many professors to abandon or limit use of hypotheticals because such hypotheticals often require a student to put themselves in the position of someone who is being raped (a particularly disturbing experience for someone who has actually been raped). Instead, professors will often substitute policy questions that ask students to approach the legal issues as legislators with an eye to deciding what the law of rape should be.

Second, most professors find themselves giving students more latitude during classroom discussion. Discussing rape law is difficult enough for many students without having the professor question them closely about what they have just said. Students can also learn much from hearing what their classmates say in these more free flowing discussions, although the conversation is not always a comfortable one.

Third, the incredible variety of rape law statutes means that any selection of cases or statutes will provide at best a partial and selective view of how rape law operates. Professors who emphasize black letter rules will usually settle on a few examples of different approaches. Professors who emphasize statutory interpretation might expose students to a wider variety of rape definitions to develop their ability to read statutes carefully. With this in mind, this chapter tries to give you a feel for the major issues of rape law without any pretense of describing a consensus approach that simply does not exist.

B. OVERVIEW OF ELEMENTS

The traditional elements of rape are easy to list but hard to define.

- Sexual intercourse
- Committed by
  - Force or
  - Threat of Force or
  - When the victim is unconscious or lacks capacity
- Without the Victim's Consent

Rape then can be usefully divided into three different conduct elements: a sexual act, force, and non-consent. The definition of the sexual act that lies at the heart of rape has been expanded to include more than just sexual intercourse, as will be discussed below. The greatest difficulty in rape law comes from defining force and non-consent.

Rape is a general intent crime, which means that the defendant must be generally aware of his or her conduct. More specifically, many jurisdictions hold that the only mental state required is that one be generally aware that one is having intercourse. This means that technically *even a reasonable mistake as to whether the victim consents to the intercourse would not create a mental state defense to rape under the traditional view.*

The absence of an explicit requirement of a more blameworthy mental state for such a serious felony is both very confusing to most students and the key to understanding the elements of rape. *Rape did not traditionally require a more blameworthy mental state because the conduct elements were defined in such a way that only a wrongful actor could satisfy them.*

Consent in rape law is defined objectively, not subjectively. Whether consent exists or not does not depends not on what the victim thinks or what the defendant thinks, but on what the victim and defendant say and do (or fail to say or do). Since consent is determined from the observable circumstances, a victim's purely private or "secret" lack of consent will not satisfy the lack of consent element. A defendant who had intercourse under circumstances where consent reasonably seemed to exist would not be found guilty of rape because consent would be found to have existed *regardless of the subjective beliefs or thoughts of the victim.*

Similarly, force has often been defined in such a way that it would be impossible for a person to reasonably believe that the victim consented to the intercourse. Often it meant the use of violent force or the threat of violent force. It would not have been possible for a defendant to use such force and reasonably believe that the victim consented to the intercourse.

So despite the absence of a culpable mental state requirement, the traditional definition of rape did not involve a risk that men who reasonably believed that the woman consented to the intercourse would be wrongfully convicted. In fact, the elements of force and non-consent were defined in a way that made it far too easy for a man who forced intercourse upon a woman against her will to escape conviction. When jurisdictions reformed their rape definitions to make it less difficult to prosecute blameworthy men for rape, most did not add mental state requirements. Instead, they strove to redefine the force and non-consent elements in ways that made it easier to prosecute the blameworthy while still protecting the blameless. Drawing that line in a clear way has been difficult, however, and remains controversial.

One further point needs to be made before each element is discussed in turn. Force and non-consent operate in what might be described as a symbiotic relationship: each must be defined in light of the other. The more you require of one, the less you need of the other.

For example, assume for the sake of argument that you defined consent in purely subjective terms. This would mean that even a victim's private or "secret" lack of consent would satisfy the element. Such a definition would not endanger blameless defendants if force were defined to require actual violence or the threat of violence because blameless defendants do not ordinarily threaten or commit violence against their sexual partners. Alternately, imagine that force is defined in such a way that simply the physical force required to achieve sexual intercourse were sufficient for that element. Again, the risk of convicting blameless defendants would not exist if non-consent were defined to require observable acts of resistance, even if only verbal.

This symbiotic relationship between force and consent obviously affects the victim's interest just as directly. For example, a definition of force that required not threatened but actual violence would leave unprotected many victims who do not wish to engage in intercourse but who feared physical injury too much to resist, regardless of how consent were defined. Similarly, a definition of non-consent that required victims to physically resist the defendant would force victims to choose between the physical and mental violation that rape entails and the physical injury that resisting rape might precipitate, regardless of how force was defined.

So the division of labor between the elements of force and non-consent in ensuring that the blameworthy, but only the blameworthy, are convicted is key to the definition of rape. Unfortunately for the student of criminal law, jurisdictions varied widely in how they reformed rape law. Some leaned on the force requirement to do the hard work; others use the non-consent element to do the heavy lifting.

A few observations can be made on a very general level about current state of rape law. Traditionally force was required for rape, and the victim had to resist to establish non-consent. Today force is not always required, and verbal resistance (or in some jurisdictions the absence of affirmative consent) is sufficient to establish non-consent.

C. THE PREDICATE SEXUAL ACT

All definitions of rape or serious sexual offense have as their predicate some form of sexual act. At common law the only sexual act that could constitute rape was sexual intercourse defined as the penetration of a female's vagina by a male's penis. Many modern statutes have broadened this definition in a number of different ways. The predicate sexual act for rape has been variously defined as including the penetration of the anus with a penis, the penetration of any bodily orifice with the penis or any body part or even mechanical objects, and various forms of oral sex. In some jurisdictions these acts are considered rape when performed forcibly or without the victim's consent; in other jurisdictions the term rape is reserved for some subset of these acts with the other acts called a felonious sex offense of a degree that is often equivalent to rape for sentencing purposes.

The early definition of the required sexual act as the penetration of a vagina by a penis essentially limited rape to a crime committed by a man against a woman. Many modern statutes with broader definitions of the required sex act are written in gender neutral language and allow any gender to be capable of raping any other gender or even the same gender.

D. FORCE

At common law rape often required the use or threatened use of force that was likely to cause great bodily harm. In the presence of such extreme force or an explicit threat of the same, no resistance was required. Lesser force—which could easily include punching, hitting and holding a woman down—required some resistance which the man's force overcame. Such "resistance to the utmost," required a woman to fight until she was too exhausted, injured or frightened to continue.

No jurisdiction require such "resistance to the utmost" anymore. Some have abolished the resistance requirement altogether. "Earnest resistance" or resistance that is "reasonable under the circumstances" is required by others. Verbal resistance is often sufficient. Some critics argue that the force and resistance requirements should be abolished altogether.

Even in the absence of an explicit resistance requirement, difficult questions remain as to how much force should be required for a rape to occur. One line of cases requires no more force than is necessary to accomplish the act of penetration. Other cases require some greater degree of force, although usually not force likely to cause great bodily harm. So choking someone while one penetrates them (or threatening to do so) is no longer required. Holding someone down while one penetrates them would likely be sufficient, but simply holding onto someone while one penetrates them would not be. A factfinder might find the difference between holding someone down and holding onto someone to lie in whether the person being held physically resists.

Finally, jurisdictions that eliminate or reduce the force requirement often shift the hard questions over to the non-consent requirement. Alternately, jurisdictions that retain the force requirement tend to require more force than is necessary to accomplish penetration when a genuine issue exists as to whether the intercourse was without consent.

E. LACK OF CAPACITY

Even at common law certain individuals were presumed to lack the capacity to consent to sexual intercourse, and this category of individuals has been expanded over time. Intercourse with individuals under the age of 18 is defined as statutory rape in many jurisdictions. As previously discussed, statutory rape is a strict liability offense with respect to the age of the victim, although a minority of jurisdictions recognize a defense of reasonable mistake as to this element. Intercourse with people who are unconscious is also presumed to be nonconsensual. Likewise, intercourse or equivalent sexual acts with individuals who otherwise lack mental capacity to consent as a result of mental disabilities is also defined as rape or an equivalent sex offense in some jurisdictions. Intercourse with a person too intoxicated to consent is considered rape in a minority of jurisdictions. If the defendant administered the intoxicants without the victim's knowledge and consent, however, all jurisdictions find rape to have occurred.

F. NON-CONSENT

At common law, intercourse had to be without the victim's consent in order to be rape. At common law and in a majority of jurisdictions until relatively recently, non-consent had to be demonstrated by the victim's active physical resistance. While resistance to the utmost is not required anymore, defining non-consent remains a difficult issue. Doing away with resistance requirements does not resolve the issue of what conduct and circumstances are necessary to establish a lack of consent.

Rape is unique among crimes against the person in being founded on a physical act that is ordinarily consensual. People don't ordinarily consent to being punched in the face. If someone punches you in the face, people generally don't presume you consented to the punch, unless you are participating in a boxing match. Sexual activity between people is ordinarily consensual though. If you have sexual intercourse with someone, the presence or absence of consent is a much more open question. So the definition of the non-consent element in rape is uniquely important and uniquely difficult among violent crimes.

The fact that intercourse is ordinarily consensual, however, does not necessarily mean that consent should be considered the default position. Some rape reform advocates argue for a "yes means yes" standard that requires the giving of explicit affirmative permission for the sexually regulated act, although some take the position that explicit affirmative permission could be physical, not verbal. Others argue that a "no means no" rule would be sufficient to guarantee the autonomy of would be victims of rape. Still others argue for the elimination of the non-consent element altogether. They would define rape solely in terms of the amount and nature of the force used to accomplish the sexual act in order to keep the jury's focus on what the defendant did, not what the victim failed to do.

The policy questions that lie at the heart of defining non-consent in rape are not easy to resolve. Feminist scholars disagree about whether consent must be affirmative and verbal, with some arguing that such a requirement is the only way to effectively protect rape victims, while others argue that such a requirement is paternalistic and treats woman as incapable of expressing their unwillingness to engage in sexual intercourse.

Gender concerns aside, the definition of non-consent in rape also raises questions of privacy and autonomy and the government's role in regulating sexual relations.

Some strongly believe that requiring such explicit communication during sexual activity robs sexual intimacy of a natural and spontaneous quality that is important. These critics believe that an affirmative consent requirement imposes by fiat one particular way of relating to one another sexually. Some argue further that the criminal law is too blunt and powerful an instrument with which to regulate our most private moments with such particularity.

Others argue equally strongly that requiring a verbal or physical indication of affirmative consent is a small price to pay to both reduce the possibility of misunderstandings and to make easier the prosecution of individuals who would violate the sexual autonomy of their partners. They argue that nothing would be lost by requiring affirmative consent because sexual intimacy is at its best when grounded in mutual sexual autonomy realized through clear communication.

No easy answers are to be found here.

G. ACQUAINTANCE RAPE AND MARITAL RAPE

In an earlier era, consent would often be presumed in cases where the defendant and the victim were acquainted with one another. With the growing recognition that "acquaintance rape" was both prevalent and a serious problem this presumption no longer seemed reasonable. While few rape statutes make explicit distinctions between acquaintance and stranger rape, the existence of a prior relationship of some sort between the defendant and the victim continues to play an important role in the thinking of prosecutors, judges, and juries in deciding whether non-consent existed in any particular case. While it no longer seems reasonable to presume that you consented to sexual intercourse with someone just because you were dating him or her, it continues to seem reasonable to presume that you did not consent to sex with a complete stranger in a deserted parking lot in the middle of the night. So while prior acquaintance does not rule out rape as it once often did, it is usually not irrelevant to determining non-consent either.

That said, all jurisdictions have abolished the common law's marital exemption for rape liability. Consent to acts of intercourse between people who are married is no longer conclusively presumed. To be sure, marital status, like prior acquaintance, is not irrelevant to a fact-finder's deliberations about whether consent existed as to any particular sexual act, but it is no longer the basis for a conclusive presumption.

H. MENTAL STATE AS TO CONSENT

Contrary to the strong trend described earlier, a few states recognize a reasonable mistake of fact as to whether the victim consented as a defense to rape, although some states will only give such an instruction in the face of substantial evidence of equivocal conduct on the victim's part.

I. DEGREES OF RAPE

Many jurisdictions recognized degrees of rape to distinguish more serious from less serious violations. First degree rape in many jurisdictions is reserved for defendants who commit rape with weapons, or with accomplices, or who inflict serious bodily injury on their victims.

J. THE MPC

Discussion of the Model Penal Code has been noticeably absent up to this point because the Model Penal Code has had a negligible influence on how jurisdictions define rape and related sexual offenses. Even huge fans of the MPC usually acknowledge that the MPC got rape wrong. Most notably the MPC failed to abolish the marital exemption for rape and retained the early common law's requirement that claims of rape be corroborated.

K. CASES IN CONTEXT

The following case shows the law of rape in transition in the jurisdiction in which it occurred. Decisions by both the initial and final appellate courts are included.

RUSK V. STATE
Court of Special Appeals of Maryland
406 A.2d 624 (1979)

THOMPSON, JUDGE.

We are called upon to review the sufficiency of the evidence to convict for rape. Whatever the law may have been before, it is now clear that our standard must be: Is the evidence sufficient for a finder of fact to conclude that the accused was guilty beyond a reasonable doubt? We hold that the evidence was not sufficient. In making this review we must look at the evidence in the light most favorable to the prosecution.

Edward Salvatore Rusk, the appellant, was convicted . . . of rape in the second degree and of assault. . . . The appellant does not challenge the conviction for assault.

The prosecutrix was a twenty-one year old mother of a two-year old son. She was separated from her husband but not yet divorced. Leaving her son with her mother, she attended a high school reunion after which she and a female friend, Terry, went bar hopping in the Fells Point area of Baltimore. They drove in separate cars. At the third bar the prosecutrix met appellant. They had a five or ten minute conversation in the bar; at the end of which the prosecutrix said she was ready to leave. Appellant requested a ride home and she agreed. When they arrived at appellant's home, the prosecutrix parked at the curb on the side of the street opposite his rooming house but did not turn off the ignition. She put the car in park and appellant asked her to come up to his apartment. She refused. He continued to ask her to come up, and she testified she then became afraid. While trying to convince him that she didn't want to go to his apartment she mentioned that she was separated and if she did, it might cause her marital problems particularly if she were being followed by a detective. The appellant then took the keys out of the car and walked over to her side of the car, opened the door and said, "Now will you come up?" The prosecutrix then told him she would. She stated:

> "At that point, because I was scared, because he had my car keys. I didn't know what to do. I was someplace I didn't even know where I was. It was in the city. I didn't know whether to run. I really didn't think, at that point, what to do. Now, I know that I

should have blown the horn. I should have run. There were a million things I could have done. I was scared, at that point, and I didn't do any of them."

The prosecutrix followed appellant into the rowhouse, up the stairs, and into the apartment. When they got into appellant's room, he said that he had to go to the bathroom and left the room for a few minutes. The prosecutrix made no attempt to leave. When appellant came back, he sat on the bed while she sat on the chair next to the bed. He turned the light off and asked her to get on the bed with him. He started to pull her onto the bed and also began to remove her blouse. She stated she took off her slacks and removed his clothing because "he asked [her] to do it." After they both undressed, prosecutrix stated:

> "I was still begging him to please let, you know, let me leave. I said, 'you can get a lot of other girls down there, for what you want,' and he just kept saying, 'no,' and then I was really scared, because I can't describe, you know, what was said. It was more the look in his eyes; and I said, at that point I didn't know what to say; and I said, 'If I do what you want, will you let me go without killing me?' Because I didn't know, at that point, what he was going to do; and I started to cry; and when I did, he put his hands on my throat, and started lightly to choke me; and I said, 'If I do what you want, will you let me go?' And he said, yes, and at that time, I proceeded to do what he wanted me to."

She stated that she performed oral sex and they then had sexual intercourse.[1]

---

[1]   If we could say at this point that there is enough evidence for a reasonable fact finder to say such threat of force is solely that which overcame her will to resist, the conduct of both following intercourse would belie that conclusion:

> "Q. All right. Now, after the sexual intercourse came to conclusion, what is the very next thing that took place?
>
> A. I asked him if I could leave now, and he said, 'Yes;' and I got up and got dressed; and he got up and got dressed; and he walked me to my car, and asked if he could see me again; and I said, 'Yes;' and he asked me for my telephone number; and I said, 'No, I'll see you down Fell's Point sometime,' just so I could leave.
>
> Q. What was the reason that you said that you would meet him the next day?
>
> A. I didn't say the next day, and I just said I would see him down there only so I could leave. I didn't know what else to say. I had no intention of meeting him again."

After arriving home she said:

> > "I sat in the car, thinking about it a while, and I thought I wondered what would happen if I hadn't of done what he wanted me to do. So I thought the right thing to do was to go report it, and I went from there to Hillendale to find a police car."

If, in quiet contemplation after the act, she had to wonder what would have happened, her submission on the side of prudence seems hardly justified. Indeed, if *she* had to wonder afterward, how can a fact finder reasonably conclude that she was justifiably in fear sufficient to overcome her will to resist, at the time.

The Court of Appeals of Maryland last spoke on the amount of force required to support a rape conviction in *Hazel v. State*, 221 Md. 464, 469, 157 A.2d 922, 925 (1960), when the Court said:

"Force is an essential element of the crime and to justify a conviction, the evidence must warrant a conclusion either that the victim resisted and her resistance was overcome by force or that she was prevented from resisting by threats to her safety."[2]

In all of the victim's testimony we have been unable to see any resistance on her part to the sex acts and certainly can we see no fear as would overcome her attempt to resist or escape as required by *Hazel*. Possession of the keys by the accused may have deterred her vehicular escape but hardly a departure seeking help in the rooming house or in the street. We must say that "the way he looked" fails utterly to support the fear required by *Hazel*. . . .

Appellee argues . . . that the issue as to whether or not intercourse was accompanied by force or threats of force is one of credibility to be resolved by the triers of the fact. We cannot follow the argument. As we understand the law, the trial judge in ruling on a motion to acquit must first determine that there is legally sufficient evidence for the jury to find the victim was reasonably in fear. That is the rule set forth in *Hazel*. . . .

Cases from other jurisdictions have followed the rule that the victim's fear which overcomes her will to resist must be a reasonable fear. . . .

. . . [W]e find the evidence legally insufficient to warrant a conclusion that appellant's words or actions created in the mind of the victim a reasonable fear that if she resisted, he would have harmed her, or that faced with such resistance, he would have used force to overcome it. The prosecutrix stated that she was afraid, and submitted because of "the look in his eyes." After both were undressed and in the bed, and she pleaded to him that she wanted to leave, he started to lightly choke her. At oral argument it was brought out that the "lightly choking" could have been a heavy caress. We do not believe that "lightly choking" along with all the facts and circumstances in the case, were sufficient to cause a reasonable fear which overcame her ability to resist. In the absence of any other evidence showing force used by appellant, we find that the evidence was insufficient to convict appellant of rape.

---

[2] *Since Hazel*, the Maryland Legislature has codified extensively the law pertaining to sexual offenses providing in Md. Code, Art. 27, § 463 as follows:

"(a) What constitutes.—A person is guilty of rape in the second degree if the person engages in vaginal intercourse with another person:

(1) By force or threat of force against the will and without the consent of the other person. . . ."

The statute has made no change in the force as required by *Hazel*.

WILNER, JUDGE, dissenting:

The majority's error, in my judgment, is not in their exposition of the underlying principles of law that must govern this case, but rather in the manner that they have applied those principles. . . .

Under the guise of judging the sufficiency of the evidence presented against appellant, they have tacitly—perhaps unwittingly, but nonetheless effectively—substituted their own view of the evidence (and the inferences that may fairly be drawn from it) for that of the judge and jury. In so doing, they have not only improperly invaded the province allotted to those tribunals, but, at the same time, have perpetuated and given new life to myths about the crime of rape that have no place in our law today. . . .

Md. Annot. Code art. 27, § 463 (a) considers three types of conduct as constituting second degree rape. We are concerned only with the first: a person is guilty of rape in the second degree if he (1) engages in vaginal intercourse with another person, (2) by force or threat of force, (3) against the will, and (4) without the consent of the other person. There is no real question here as to the first, third, or fourth elements of the crime. The evidence was certainly sufficient to show that appellant had vaginal intercourse with the victim, and that such act was against her will and without her consent. The point at issue is whether it was accomplished by force or threat of force; and I think that in viewing the evidence, that point should remain ever clear. *Consent is not the issue here, only whether there was sufficient evidence of force or the threat of force.*

Unfortunately, courts, including in the present case a majority of this one, often tend to confuse these two elements—force and lack of consent—and to think of them as one. They are not. They mean, and require, different things. What seems to cause the confusion—what, indeed, has become a common denominator of both elements—is the notion that the victim must actively resist the attack upon her. If she fails to offer sufficient resistance (sufficient to the satisfaction of the judge), a court is entitled, or at least presumes the entitlement, to find that there was no force or threat of force, or that the act was not against her will, or that she actually consented to it, or some unarticulated combination or synthesis of these elements that leads to the ultimate conclusion that the victim was not raped. Thus it is that the focus is almost entirely on the extent of resistance—*the victim's acts, rather than those of her assailant.* Attention is directed not to the wrongful stimulus, but to the victim's reactions to it. Right or wrong, that seems to be the current state of the Maryland law; and, notwithstanding its uniqueness in the criminal law, and its illogic, until changed by statute or the Court of Appeals, I accept it as binding.

But what is required of a woman being attacked or in danger of attack? How much resistance must she offer? Where is that line to be drawn between requiring that she either risk serious physical harm, perhaps death, on the one hand, or be termed a willing partner on the other? Some answers were given in Hazel v. State, 221 Md. 464 (1960), although, as in so many cases, they

From . . . pronouncements in *Hazel*, this Court has articulated what the majority refers to as a "rule of reason"—i.e., that "where the victim's story could not be corroborated by wounds, bruises or disordered clothing, the lack of consent could be shown by fear based upon reasonable apprehension." *Winegan v. State*, 10 Md. App. 196, 200 (1970); Goldberg v. State, 41 Md. App. 58 (1979). As so phrased, I do not consider this to be a rule of reason at all; it is highly unreasonable, and again mixes the element of consent with that of force. But what I do accept is what the Court of Appeals said in *Hazel*: (1) if the acts and threats of the defendant were reasonably calculated to create in the mind of the victim having regard to the circumstances in which she was placed a real apprehension, due to fear, of imminent bodily harm, serious enough to impair or overcome her will to resist, then such acts and threats are the equivalent of force; (2) submission is not the equivalent of consent; and (3) the real test is whether the assault was committed without the consent and against the will of the prosecuting witness.

Upon this basis, the evidence against appellant must be considered. . . . The victim—I'll call her Pat—attended a high school reunion. . . . We know nothing about Pat and appellant. We don't know how big they are, what they look like, what their life experiences have been. We don't know if appellant is larger or smaller than she, stronger or weaker. We don't know what the inflection was in his voice as he dangled her car keys in front of her. We can't tell whether this was in a jocular vein or a truly threatening one. We have no idea what his mannerisms were. The trial judge and the jury could discern some of these things, of course, because they could observe the two people in court and could listen to what they said and how they said it. But all we know is that, between midnight and 1:00 a.m., in a neighborhood that was strange to Pat, appellant took her car keys, demanded that she accompany him, and most assuredly implied that unless she did so, at the very least, she might be stranded. . . .

How does the majority Opinion view these events? It starts by noting that Pat was a 21-year old mother who was separated from her husband but not yet divorced, as though that had some significance. To me, it has none, except perhaps (when coupled with the further characterization that Pat and Terry had gone "bar hopping") to indicate an underlying suspicion, for which there is absolutely no support in the record, that Pat was somehow "on the make". Even more alarming, and unwarranted, however, is the majority's analysis [in footnote 1] of Pat's initial reflections on whether to report what had happened.

It is this type of reasoning—if indeed "reasoning" is the right word for it—that is particularly distressing. The concern expressed by Pat, made even more real by the majority Opinion of this Court, is one that is common among rape victims, and largely accounts for the fact that most incidents of forcible rape go unreported by the victim. If appellant had desired, and Pat had given, her wallet instead of her body, there would be no question about appellant's guilt of robbery. Taking the car keys under those circumstances would certainly have supplied the requisite threat of force or violence and negated the element of consent. No one would seriously contend that because she failed to raise a hue and cry she had consented to the theft of her money. Why then is such life-threatening action necessary when it is her personal dignity that is being stolen?

Rape has always been considered a most serious crime, one that traditionally carried the heaviest penalty. But until recently, it remained shrouded in the taboos and myths of a Victorian age, and little real attention was given to how rapes occur, how they may be prevented, and how a victim can best protect herself from injury when an attack appears inevitable. . . .

As the result of the Battelle Study[8] we now know some things about this crime that we could only guess at before. . .

Of particular significance is what was learned about resistance. The most common type of resistance offered by victims is verbal. Note: verbal resistance is resistance! In cases arising in the large cities, only 12.7% of the victims attempted flight, and only 12% offered physical resistance. The reason for this is apparent from the next thing learned: that *"[r]ape victims who resisted were more likely to be injured than ones who did not."* . . .

Where does this leave us but where we started? A judge and a jury, observing the witnesses and hearing their testimony, concluded without dissent that there was sufficient evidence to find beyond a reasonable doubt that appellant had sexual intercourse with Pat by force or threat of force against her will and without her consent; in other words, that the extent of her resistance and the reasons for her failure to resist further were reasonable. No claim is made here that the jury was misinstructed on the law of rape. Yet a majority of this Court, without the ability to see and hear the witnesses, has simply concluded that, in their judgment, Pat's fear was not a reasonable one, or that there was no fear at all. . . .

. . . Brushing all of this aside, they have countermanded the judgment of the trial court and jury and declared Pat to have been, in effect, an adulteress.[17] . . .

---

[8] This was a study conducted by the Battelle Memorial Institute Law and Justice Study Center under grant from LEAA (National Institute of Law Enforcement and Criminal Justice). The Report of the study was published during 1977 and 1978. . . .

[17] Interestingly, appellant was convicted of assault arising out of the same incident, but did not contest the sufficiency of the evidence supporting that conviction. It would seem that if there was not enough evidence of force, or lack of consent, to permit the rape conviction, there was an equal insufficiency to support the assault conviction. The majority is spared, in this case, the need to deal with that thorny dilemma.

STATE V. RUSK

Court of Appeals of Maryland
424 A.2d 720 (1981)

MURPHY, CHIEF JUDGE.

We think the reversal of Rusk's conviction by the Court of Special Appeals was in error for the fundamental reason so well expressed in the dissenting opinion by Judge Wilner that the reasonableness of Pat's apprehension of fear was plainly a question of fact for the jury to determine.

Judgement of the Court of Special Appeals reversed case remanded to that court with directions that it affirm the judgment of the Criminal Court of Baltimore.

COLE, JUDGE, dissenting:

I agree with the Court of Special Appeals that the evidence adduced at the trial of Edward Salvatore Rusk was insufficient to convict him of rape.

While courts no longer require a female to resist to the utmost or to resist where resistance would be foolhardy, they do require her acquiescence in the act of intercourse to stem from fear generated by something of substance. She many not simply say, "I was really scared," and thereby transform consent or mere unwillingness into submission by force. These words do not transform a seducer into a rapist. She must follow the natural instinct of every proud female to resist, by more than mere words, the violation of her person by a stranger or an unwelcomed friend. She must make it plain that she regards such sexual acts as abhorrent and repugnant to her natural sense of pride. She must resist unless the defendant has objectively manifested his intent to use physical force to accomplish his purpose. The law regards rape as a crime of violence. The majority today attenuates this proposition. It declares the innocence of an at best distraught young woman. It does not demonstrate the defendant's guilt of the crime of rape.

My examination of the evidence in a light most favorable to the State reveals no conduct by the defendant reasonably calculated to cause the prosecutrix to be so fearful that she should fail to resist and thus, the element of force is lacking in the State's proof.

I find it incredible for the majority to conclude that on these facts, without more, a woman was forced to commit oral sex upon the defendant and then to engage in vaginal intercourse. In the absence of any verbal threat to do her grievous bodily harm or the display of any weapon and threat to use it, I find it difficult to understand how a victim could participate in these sexual activities and not be willing.

DISCUSSION QUESTIONS

1.　What definition of force should be applied to a case such as this? What definition of consent should be applied to a case such as this?

2.　At the heart of the clash between the majority and dissenting opinions in both decisions lie differing visions about how people usually engage in consensual intercourse. Is it possible to define rape without relying on some default conception of consensual intercourse?

3.　To what degree should issues of consent be left to the jury and to what degree should the judge play a gatekeeper role?

Case in Context

The defendant in the following case was a complete stranger to the victim, but issues of force and consent were still raised and litigated.

THE PEOPLE OF THE STATE OF NEW YORK V. ERIC DORSEY

Supreme Court, Bronx County, New York, Criminal Term, Part 16
429 N.Y.S.2d 828 (1980)

WALTER M. SCHACKMAN, JUSTICE.

The sole issue to be decided in this motion to dismiss at the end of the People's case is whether or not forcible rape and sodomy have been committed when a woman submits to these acts, without physical resistance on her part, and without an explicit threat by a man with whom she is trapped in an elevator that is stalled between floors.

The defendant in the instant case was indicted on charges of Rape in the First Degree and Sodomy in the First Degree. Upon the completion of the People's case, and again upon completion of the entire case, the defense moved for a trial order of dismissal as to both counts of the indictment, pursuant to Criminal Procedure Law s 290.10. The defense claimed that the People had failed to present sufficient evidence upon which the jury could find beyond a reasonable doubt that the defendant exercise forcible compulsion in the commission of the crimes charged, this being an essential element of each of them.

This Court reserved decision on this motion and the jury ultimately returned a verdict of guilty as to both counts. The motion to dismiss must now be decided.

THE INCIDENT

On August 27, 1979, the complainant, a forty-nine year old woman, who was five feet tall and who weighed 130 pounds, entered the lobby of her apartment building at about 6:00 P.M., returning home from work. When an elevator arrived, the complainant entered and pressed the button for the tenth floor, on which her apartment was located. A young male entered the elevator with her and pressed the button for another floor.

The next thing the complainant noticed was the elevator stopping. Upon looking up to see if it was her floor, she saw the defendant standing by the elevator buttons, manipulating them. She also saw that the elevator was stopped between floors, with the door to the elevator shaft being open. However, the alarm bell of the elevator did not go off.

The complainant testified that the defendant, a fifteen year old male approximately five feet seven inches tall and weighing in excess of two hundred pounds, turned around and told her to take her clothes off, and undress. When the complainant did not respond the defendant repeated this demand. The complainant then complied and was subjected to acts of sexual intercourse and sodomy during the next ten to fifteen minutes.

Following this, the defendant told the complainant to get dressed, and he started the elevator back up, eventually getting out at the twenty-second floor. The complainant testified that she was then able to get the elevator back down to her floor, where she got out, went into her apartment, and called the development's security police force. They then contacted the New York City Police Department. The defendant was identified by the complainant later that evening at the security police offices, and he was then arrested.

The complainant testified that she had not attempted to scream at any time before or during the incident because she felt that no one outside the elevator could have heard her, or helped her. She also testified that the defendant did not use any overt physical force against her, either before or during the incident, other than what was necessary for completion of the sexual acts. She further testified that the only express threat made by the defendant came after completion of the incident, as he was leaving the elevator, in which he stated that if anything "happened" to him in the next couple of days, his friends would "get her".

THE LAW

Since 1965, New York's statutes dealing with non-consensual sex offenses that were committed by forcible compulsion, have spoken in terms of the use by the perpetrator of either a sufficient amount of physical force, or of threats. In addition, the courts were also required to judge the sufficiency of the resultant behavior and emotions of the victim. Therefore, where physical force was used by the defendant, the question was whether the resistance of the victim was sufficient to indicate lack of consent, and when the defendant resorted to the use of threats, either express or implied, the question was whether the victim sustained a sufficient degree of fear, either of death, serious physical injury or of being kidnapped.

Many jurisdictions have similar forcible rape and sodomy statutes, and many of them have had as much difficulty applying them to the changing societal standards and viewpoints as New York has had.

"As might be expected, the use of the outward manifestation of the subjective state of mind of the victim has proved an unsure index to the conduct of rapists. How much resistance indicates nonconsent? Some states require resistance to the utmost, an unenlightened attitude that has been repudiated elsewhere. Where utmost resistance is not required, great confusion exists. Some cases seem to impose a reasonableness standard, while others emphasize decision by the woman without requiring that her fears be reasonable * * * Still other cases require sufficient resistance to make nonconsent reasonably manifest. The amount of resistance required depends on all of the circumstances of the case." (The Resistance Standard in Rape Legislation, 18 Stan.L.Rev. 680, 682–683 (1966).)

The cases in New York seemed to fluctuate on a case-by-case basis, each judge and jury having to decide for themselves whether or not the resistance offered by the victim was sufficient. Many cases used the "reasonable resistance" standard, in which the judge and jury decided whether or not the resistance of the woman in each case was of a type which reasonably indicated, in light of all the circumstances of the incident, that she did not consent to the sexual advances of the man. This standard was based on the rationale that "obviously the degree of force required to place somebody in fear will vary with the person involved. It may take a great deal of force * * * or a great deal of threat to overcome resistance in some people. It may require far lesser degree to overcome the resistance of others." (People v. Yanik (Sup.Ct., N.Y.Co., 1975).)

The use in New York of the "reasonable resistance" standard seemed to come to a definitive end, however, when the Appellate Division, First Department, issued a pronouncement that "(R)ape is not committed unless the woman opposed the man to the utmost limit of her power. A feigned or passive or perfunctory resistance is not enough. It must be genuine and active and proportioned to the outrage." (People v. Yanik, 55 A.D.2d 164, 167, 390 N.Y.S.2d 98, 101.)

Many civil rights and women's rights groups were outraged at this seeming retrenchment by the courts to the old "utmost resistance" standard. They put forth two major arguments in their fight to change this law in New York.

First, they pointed out that "reports concerning violent crimes support the concept that resistance offered by the victim often causes the attacker to escalate the level of violence he is using to effectuate the crime." (Snyder, Reform of New York's Rape Law Proposed, N.Y.L.J., December 13, 1978, at p. 6, col. 1.) To illustrate this point, the public was referred to the notorious New York case, People v. Allweiss, 401 N.Y.S.2d 501 (1st Dept., 1978), which dealt with a defendant who had earlier pleaded guilty to a series of six rapes, four of the victims of which he had threatened with a knife, and all of whom he had grabbed by the throat during the assault. This case dealt with a homicide, however, since the seventh rape victim was the first to struggle and to cry out, as a result of which she was manually strangled to death, and also stabbed viciously and repeatedly, by the defendant.

The argument that resistance by a rape victim greatly increased the likelihood of increased violence by the perpetrator, was borne out by a study authorized by the Department of Justice. This comprehensive analysis of rape incidents declared that "victims who resisted were more likely to be injured than victims who did not. This result was observed across counties of all sizes. The likelihood of receiving injuries which required hospitalization was almost doubled in those cases in which the victims resisted their attackers. These results indicated an important danger in the popular notion (and some statutory requirements) that a victim of an attack should resist to her utmost." (Forcible Rape: A National Survey of the Response by Prosecutors, National Institute of Law Enforcement and Criminal Justice, Law Enforcement Assistance Administration, March 1977 at p. 14).

This fact has also been recognized by the New York City Police Department, and other law enforcement agencies, who "advise women who are threatened with rape to use their judgment as to how much physical resistance it is safe to offer. They recognize that submission might be the only alternative open to the victim as a means of saving her life, and that in some instances futile attempts at physical resistance may very well place the victim's life in further jeopardy." Accordingly, this information has been incorporated in "Rape Alert: Safety Measures," a joint publication of the New York City Police Department and the organization "New York Women Against Rape," in which women are advised, once an attacker makes known his demands, to follow their instincts. They must check out how they match up physically and psychologically with their assailant and decide if they can safely run, scream or fight. They are advised to do what they are told, since that is the safest course to follow, and that they should do what it takes to stay alive.

The second major argument put forth in favor of the proposed changes in the penal law of New York, was the fact that awareness of women's rights was rapidly changing in today's society, and it was time to discard the anachronistic concept that women who are raped had probably "asked for it," a concept which held them to be equally guilty in the eyes of many. Many women's groups sought changes in the law in order "to focus attention exclusively on the actor's conduct. In every other crime, except a sex crime, the only factor that is considered important is the behavior of the defendant. It is only in sex crimes that the victim has had to 'prove' himself or herself, and in many cases, the victim has been, effectively, put on trial along with the defendant, to have his or her conduct judged."

The New York State Legislature did not delay long in taking action to remedy this situation. The legislators realized that "the existing law places women in a cruel dilemma, forcing them to choose to follow either the advice of law enforcement experts not to resist where personal safety would be jeopardized, on the one hand, or (to follow) the legal resistance mandate on the other." (An Act to amend the penal law, in relation to the definition of "forcible compulsion" in sex offenses: Memorandum in Support, New York State Senate, June, 1977). They realized that women in New York were faced with a decision, not to resist in order to save their lives, but destroying any possibility of obtaining a rape conviction against their assailants. This was not demanded of the victim of any other crime.

Therefore, barely six months after the decision by the Appellate Division, First Department in Yanik, the New York State Legislature passed a law amending New York Penal Law s 130.00(8), the definition of forcible compulsion, by explicitly stating that a woman has to exert only "earnest resistance," and that earnest resistance does not mean utmost resistance. Rather, earnest resistance means "resistance of a type 'reasonably' to be expected from a person who genuinely refuses to participate in sexual intercourse, deviate sexual intercourse, or sexual contact, under all the attendant circumstances." (L.1977, c. 692, s 2).

The intent behind this legislation was set forth in the preamble of the new law, in which it was decreed that;

> "It is the legislature's intention to modify the resistance requirement in the definition of forcible compulsion so that the victim needed only offer so much resistance as is reasonable under the circumstances." (id., s 1).

The legislature had clearly decided to modify "the requirement in forcible rape cases so that the amount of resistance must be proportional to the circumstances of the attack, (taking into account factors) such as the relative strength of the parties, and the futility of resistance. Under * * * (this) standard, the perpetrator of a sex crime would no longer be excused from culpability because his victim, in fear of death or serious physical injury, had ceased to resist, and had therefore survived." (Senate memo, supra).

Some states, such as Michigan (Mich.Comp.Laws Ann. s 750.520(i)) and Ohio (Ohio Rev.Code Ann. s 2907.02) have gone further and have recently passed statutes relieving the prosecution of the need to show any resistance as proof of non-consent, an enlightened viewpoint which would eliminate this problem altogether. However, New York was brought in line with the majority of other states, such as California, of whose law it was written:

> "The resistance must be such as might be expected from a woman in the victim's circumstances. This, plus the reasonableness

required removes the victim's opinion from the case. The concern is not with what she thought was necessary, but what would reasonably appear necessary to a woman in her position. The reasonableness-under-the-circumstances approach with language to make clear that the woman need not incur serious risk of death or serious bodily injury, is as low as the standard can be set and remain consistent with fair treatment of defendants." (Stan.Law R., supra at p. 685.)

Therefore, in the instant case, this court must decide whether the People presented sufficient evidence from which a jury could conclude, beyond a reasonable doubt, that the defendant's sexual acts with the complainant had been committed by the use of forcible compulsion, that is, "physical force which is capable of overcoming earnest resistance; or a threat, express or implied, that places a person in fear of immediate death or serious physical injury to himself or another person, or in fear that he or another person will immediately be kidnapped." (New York Penal Law s 130.00(8)). Included in this is the definition of earnest resistance as mentioned previously.

That the complainant's freedom was violated there is no doubt. The United States Supreme Court long ago said that "the inviolability of a person is as much invaded by a compulsory stripping and exposure as by a blow. To compel anyone, and especially a woman, to lay bare the body, or to submit to the touch of a stranger, without lawful authority, is an indignity, an assault, and a trespass. The issue before this court is more complex, however, since it must determine from the facts of this case whether the defendant either exerted physical force capable of overcoming this complainant's reasonable, earnest resistance, or whether the complainant was overcome by fear of immediate death or serious physical injury due to threat from the defendant. Both of these questions must be measured by all of the attendant circumstances of this case.

Taking the latter question first, it is clear that there was no express threat issued by the defendant. It is just as clear to this court, however, that there was a definite implied threat from the defendant to the complainant, from which she could reasonably have concluded that she was faced with immediate death or serious physical injury. The defense argued that the defendant never once threatened her expressly, and that there was also no implied threat, because the defendant did not mention or display any gun, knife or other weapon. How then could the complainant have been put in fear of immediate death or serious physical injury?

The answer, in part, is that it is a well-settled point of law that a threat can be implied, as well as being express. A California court stated over thirty-five years ago that:

"We are unable to agree with the view that there can be no threat
* * * unless it is expressed in words or through the exhibition of a

gun, knife or other deadly weapon. A threat may be expressed by acts and conduct as well as by words. If one were met in a lonely place by four big men and told to hold up his hands or to do anything else, he would be doing the reasonable thing if he obeyed, even if they did not say what they would do to him if he refused. Their actions and manner might well indicate their purpose and intention and it would be a mere play on words to say that these actions and circumstances did not constitute, and were not the expression of, a threat. In fact, it would be a very compelling one." (People v. Flores, 62 Cal.App.2d 700, 145 P.2d 318 (1944).)

Here, instead of being faced with four big men in a lonely place, the complainant was faced with a husky teenager, who was seven inches taller and who outweighed her by over seventy pounds. She was trapped in a stalled elevator, between floors, with no place to retreat to, or from which help could arrive. The law, and common sense, did not require that she ascertain what the defendant would do to her if she refused to take off her clothes. Nor does it take but a brief recognition of the everyday events in this City to reasonably conclude that a gun, knife or other deadly weapon might quickly and savagely be used if she did not yield to the defendant.

Therefore, this Court finds, as a matter of law, that the People presented sufficient trial evidence from which the jury could conclude, beyond a reasonable doubt, that the defendant engaged in sexual acts with the complainant by means of forcible compulsion, in that there was an implied threat which placed the complainant in fear of immediate death or serious physical injury.

Although this alone would be enough to deny the defendant's motion, the "physical force" aspect of this case would lead this Court to the same conclusion. While the defendant did not actually grab or hit the complainant, his act of manipulating the elevator to stop it between floors was certainly a physical act directed against the complainant. That act, plus the physical advantages that the defendant enjoyed, constituted the use of physical force which is capable of overcoming earnest resistance.

There are many instances where no resistance could reasonably be expected from a person who genuinely refuses to participate in sexual activities, and it is difficult for this Court to imagine one clearer than the case at hand. The fact that the defendant would have inevitably succeeded in forcing himself on the complainant, able to overcome any possible resistance she could have offered, plus the fact that she was totally at his mercy in the stalled elevator, clearly indicates to this Court, under all the attendant circumstances, that total compliance by the complainant was all that earnest resistance could reasonably require. In a similar situation, the New York Court of Appeals declared that "at the time she capitulated she was virtually imprisoned and isolated in the elevator * * *." (People v. Coleman, 42 N.Y.2d 500, 505–506, 399 N.Y.S.2d 185, 187, 369 N.E.2d 742,

744.) In that case, the complainant was sexually attacked in an elevator by two men, who had jammed open the elevator doors (on a regular floor stop) with a shopping cart. As a matter of fact, toward the end of the incident the complainant was able to push away the cart and run out of the elevator and down the corridor. The fact that this could not have happened in the instant case illustrates the true level of hopelessness this victim faced.

Therefore, this Court finds, as a matter of law, that the People presented sufficient trial evidence from which the jury could conclude, beyond a reasonable doubt, that the defendant engaged in sexual acts with the complainant by means of forcible compulsion, in that he used physical force capable of overcoming the earnest resistance of the complainant.

Having decided that the trial evidence presented by the People in the instant case was legally sufficient to establish the offenses charged in the indictment, it was for the jury to decide the question of the guilt or innocence of the defendant. "Unlike most other human activities, rape is an encounter the nature and dynamics of which can be perceived by the average person, including a juror." (People v. Yanik, 43 N.Y.2d 97, 100, 400 N.Y.S.2d 778, 780, 371 N.E.2d 497, 499.) As mentioned previously, the jury returned a guilty verdict on both counts of the indictment, and this Court finds no grounds to set aside that verdict.

WHEREFORE the defendant's motion to dismiss the indictment, on the ground that the trial evidence was not legally sufficient to establish the offenses charged therein, is denied.

DISCUSSION QUESTIONS

1.   What do you think of the earnest resistance standard? Is it sufficiently protective of rape victims? Is it sufficiently protective of rape defendants?

2.   Do you agree that this standard was met in this case?

3.   Is it a mistake to rely on the force requirement to define rape? Should rape be defined solely in terms of consent?

Case in Context

Even jurisdictions that have reformed their rape law continue to struggle with defining rape when dealing with rape cases involving acquaintances.

COMMONWEALTH OF PENNSYLVANIA
V. ROBERT A. BERKOWITZ

Superior Court of Pennsylvania
415 Pa.Super. 505 (1992)

PER CURIAM:

Appellant appeals from judgment of sentence imposed following convictions of rape and indecent assault. We are called upon to determine the degree of physical force necessary to complete the act of rape in Pennsylvania. We find that under the totality of the circumstances, evidence of sufficient force was not adduced herein. . . . Accordingly, we discharge appellant on the rape conviction and reverse and remand for a new trial on the indecent assault conviction.

I. FACTS AND PROCEDURAL HISTORY

In the spring of 1988, appellant and the victim were both college sophomores at East Stroudsburg State University, ages twenty and nineteen years old, respectively. They had mutual friends and acquaintances. On April nineteenth of that year, the victim went to appellant's dormitory room. What transpired in that dorm room between appellant and the victim thereafter is the subject of the instant appeal.

During a one day jury trial held on September 14, 1988, the victim gave the following account during direct examination by the Commonwealth. At roughly 2:00 on the afternoon of April 19, 1988, after attending two morning classes, the victim returned to her dormitory room. There, she drank a martini to "loosen up a little bit" before going to meet her boyfriend, with whom she had argued the night before. N.T. 9/14/88 at 24. Roughly ten minutes later she walked to her boyfriend's dormitory lounge to meet him. He had not yet arrived.

Having nothing else to do while she waited for her boyfriend, the victim walked up to appellant's room to look for Earl Hassel, appellant's roommate. She knocked on the door several times but received no answer. She therefore wrote a note to Mr. Hassel, which read, "Hi Earl, I'm drunk. That's not why I came to see you. I haven't seen you in a while. I'll talk to you later, [victim's name]." *Id.* at 27. She did so, although she had not felt any intoxicating effects from the martini, "for a laugh." *Id.*

After the victim had knocked again, she tried the knob on the appellant's door. Finding it open, she walked in. She saw someone lying on the bed with a pillow over his head, whom she thought to be Earl Hassel. After lifting the pillow from his head, she realized it was appellant. She asked appellant which dresser was his roommate's. He told her, and the victim left the note.

Before the victim could leave appellant's room, however, appellant asked her to stay and "hang out for a while." *Id.* at 31. She complied because she "had time to kill" and because she didn't really know appellant and wanted to give him "a fair chance." *Id.* Appellant asked her to give him a back rub but she declined, explaining that she did not "trust" him. *Id.* Appellant then asked her to have a seat on his bed. Instead, she found a seat on the floor, and conversed for a while about a mutual friend.[1] No physical contact between the two had, to this point, taken place.

Thereafter, however, appellant moved off the bed and down on the floor, and "kind of pushed [the victim] back with his body. It wasn't a shove, it was just kind of a leaning-type of thing." *Id.* at 32. Next appellant "straddled" and started kissing the victim. The victim responded by saying, "Look, I gotta go. I'm going to meet [my boyfriend]." *Id.* Then appellant lifted up her shirt and bra and began fondling her. The victim then said "no." *Id.*

After roughly thirty seconds of kissing and fondling, appellant "undid his pants and he kind of moved his body up a little bit." *Id.* at 34. The victim was still saying "no" but "really couldn't move because [appellant] was shifting at [her] body so he was over [her]." *Id.* Appellant then tried to put his penis in her mouth. The victim did not physically resist, but rather continued to verbally protest, saying "No, I gotta go, let me go," in a "scolding" manner. *Id.* at 36.

Ten or fifteen more seconds passed before the two rose to their feet. Appellant disregarded the victim's continual complaints that she "had to go," and instead walked two feet away to the door and locked it so that no one from the outside could enter.[2]

Then, in the victim's words, "[appellant] put me down on the bed. It was kind of like—he didn't throw me on the bed. It's hard to explain. It was kind of like a push but no. . . ." *Id.* at 38. She did not bounce off the bed. "It wasn't slow like a romantic kind of thing, but it wasn't a fast shove either. It was kind of in the middle." *Id.* at 39.

Once the victim was on the bed, appellant began "straddling" her again while he undid the knot in her sweatpants. *Id.* He then removed her sweatpants and underwear from one of her legs. The victim did not physically resist in any way while on the bed because appellant was on top of her, and she "couldn't like go anywhere." *Id.* She did not scream out at anytime because, "[i]t was like a dream was happening or something." *Id.*

Appellant then used one of his hands to "guide" his penis into her vagina. *Id.* at 41. At that point, after appellant was inside her, the victim began saying "no, no to him softly in a moaning kind of way . . . because it

---

[1]   On cross-examination, the victim testified that during this conversation she had explained she was having problems with her boyfriend. N.T. 9/14/88 at 54.

[2]   The victim testified that she realized at the time that the lock was not of a type that could lock people inside the room. N.T. 9/14/88 at 61.

was just so scary." *Id.* at 40. After about thirty seconds, appellant pulled out his penis and ejaculated onto the victim's stomach. *Id.* at 42.

Immediately thereafter, appellant got off the victim and said, "Wow, I guess we just got carried away." *Id.* at 43. To this the victim retorted, "No, we didn't get carried away, you got carried away." *Id.* The victim then quickly dressed, grabbed her school books and raced downstairs to her boyfriend who was by then waiting for her in the lounge.

Once there, the victim began crying. Her boyfriend and she went up to his dorm room where, after watching the victim clean off appellant's semen from her stomach, he called the police.

Defense counsel's cross-examination elicited more details regarding the contact between appellant and the victim before the incident in question. The victim testified that roughly two weeks prior to the incident, she had attended a school seminar entitled, "Does 'no' sometimes means 'yes'?" *Id.* at 50, 74. Among other things, the lecturer at this seminar had discussed the average length and circumference of human penises. *Id.* at 50, 75. After the seminar, the victim and several of her friends had discussed the subject matter of the seminar over a speaker-telephone with appellant and his roommate Earl Hassel. *Id.* at 76. The victim testified that during that telephone conversation, she had asked appellant the size of his penis. *Id.* at 50, 76. According to the victim, appellant responded by suggesting that the victim "come over and find out." *Id.* at 76. She declined. *Id.*

When questioned further regarding her communications with appellant prior to the April 19, 1988 incident, the victim testified that on two other occasions, she had stopped by appellant's room while intoxicated. *Id.* at 51–52. During one of those times, she had laid down on his bed. *Id.* at 51. When asked whether she had asked appellant again at that time what his penis size was, the victim testified that she did not remember.[3]

Appellant took the stand in his own defense and offered an account of the incident and the events leading up to it which differed only as to the consent involved. According to appellant, the victim had begun communication with him after the school seminar by asking him of the size of his penis and of whether he would show it to her. *Id.* at 124. Appellant had suspected that the victim wanted to pursue a sexual relationship with him because she had stopped by his room twice after the phone call while intoxicated, laying down on his bed with her legs spread and again asking to see his penis. *Id.* at 125, 127. He believed that his suspicions were confirmed when she initiated the April 19, 1988 encounter by stopping by his room (again after drinking), and waking him up. *Id.* at 128–129.

---

[3] The victim was unsure of exactly what date these events took place. *See* N.T. 9/14/88 at 51.

Appellant testified that, on the day in question, he did initiate the first physical contact, but added that the victim warmly responded to his advances by passionately returning his kisses. *Id.* at 130. He conceded that she was continually "whispering . . . no's," *id.* at 134, but claimed that she did so while "amorously . . . passionately" moaning. *Id.* at 132–133. In effect, he took such protests to be thinly veiled acts of encouragement. When asked why he locked the door, he explained that "that's not something you want somebody to just walk in on you [doing.]" *Id.* at 139.

According to appellant, the two then laid down on the bed, the victim helped him take her clothing off, and he entered her. He agreed that the victim continued to say "no" while on the bed, but carefully qualified his agreement, explaining that the statements were "moaned passionately." *Id.* at 140–142. According to appellant, when he saw a "blank look on her face," he immediately withdrew and asked "is anything wrong, is something the matter, is anything wrong." *Id.* at 143–44. He ejaculated on her stomach thereafter because he could no longer "control" himself. *Id.* at 144. Appellant testified that after this, the victim "saw that it was over and then she made her move. She gets right off the bed . . . she just swings her legs over and then she puts her clothes back on." *Id.* Then, in wholly corroborating an aspect of the victim's account, he testified that he remarked, "Well, I guess we got carried away," to which she rebuked, "No, we didn't get carried, you got carried away' " *Id.* at 145.

After hearing both accounts, the jury convicted appellant of rape and indecent assault Appellant was then sentenced to serve a term of imprisonment of one to four years for rape and a concurrent term of six to twelve months for indecent assault. Post-trial bail was granted pending this timely appeal.

II.   SUFFICIENCY OF THE EVIDENCE

Appellant's argument in this regard was well summarized by appellant's counsel in his brief. * * *

> Mr. Berkowitz prays that this Court overturns his rape conviction. He asks that this Court define the parameters between what may have been unacceptable social conduct and the criminal conduct necessary to support the charge for forcible rape.
>
> We contend that upon review, the facts show no more than what legal scholars refer to as "reluctant submission". The complainant herself admits that she was neither hurt nor threatened at any time during the encounter. She admits she never screamed or attempted to summon help. The incident occurred in a college dormitory in the middle of the afternoon.
>
> There has never been an affirmed conviction for forcible rape under similar circumstances. Not one factor which this Court has

considered significant in prior cases, exists here. The uncontroverted evidence fails to establish forcible compulsion.

Appellant's Brief at 10.

The Commonwealth counters:

Viewing the evidence and its inferences in the light most favorable to the Commonwealth, the jury's conclusion that the Defendant's forcible conduct overcame [the victim's] will is reasonable. The assault was rapid and the victim was physically overcome. Because she was acquainted with the Defendant, [the victim] had no reason to be fearful or suspicious of him and her resorting to verbal resistance only is understandable. More importantly, perhaps, it is only her lack of consent that is truly relevant. It is entirely reasonable to believe that the Defendant sat on her, pushed her on the bed and penetrated her before she had time to fully realize her plight and raise a hue and cry. If the law required active resistance, rather the simple absence of consent, speedy penetration would immunize the most violent attacks and the goal-oriented rapist would reap an absurd reward. Certainly a victim must communicate her objections. But, contrary to the Defendant's arguments, Pennsylvania law says she can "just say no." [The victim] said "no." She said it repeatedly, clearly and sternly. She was rapidly, forcibly raped and deserves the protection of the law.

Commonwealth's Brief at 6. With the Commonwealth's position, the trial court agreed. We cannot.

In viewing the evidence, we remain mindful that credibility determinations were a matter solely for the fact finder below. On appeal, we must examine the evidence in the light most favorable to the Commonwealth drawing all reasonable inferences therefrom. If a jury could have reasonably determined from the evidence adduced that all of the necessary elements of the crime were established, then the evidence will be deemed sufficient to support the verdict.

In Pennsylvania, the crime of rape is defined by statute as follows:

A person commits a felony of the first degree when he engages in sexual intercourse with another person not his spouse:

(1) by forcible compulsion;

(2) by threat of forcible compulsion that would prevent resistance by a person of reasonable resolution;

(3) who is unconscious; or

(4) who is so mentally deranged or deficient that such person is incapable of consent.

18 Pa.C.S.A. § 3121. A statutory caveat to this rule may be found in section 3107 of title 18.

Resistance Not Required

The alleged victim need not resist the actor in prosecution under this chapter: Provided, however, that nothing in this section shall be construed to prohibit a defendant from introducing evidence that the alleged victim consented to the conduct in question.

The contours of Pennsylvania's rape statute, however, are not immediately apparent. As our Supreme Court explained in the landmark case, *Commonwealth v. Rhodes,* 510 Pa. 537, 510 A.2d 1217 (1986):

"[F]orcible compulsion" as used in section 3121(1) includes not only physical force or violence but also moral, psychological or intellectual force used to compel a person to engage in sexual intercourse against that person's will.

Closely related to section 3121(1) is section 3121(2) which applies to the situation where "forcible compulsion" is not actually used but is threatened. That section uses the phrase "by threat of forcible compulsion that would prevent resistance by a person of reasonable resolution." The Model Penal Code used the terminology "compels her to submit by any threat that would prevent resistance by a woman of ordinary resolution" and graded that offense as gross sexual imposition, a felony of the third degree. The Pennsylvania legislature rejected the concept that sexual intercourse compelled by "gross imposition" should be graded as a less serious offense and, therefore, enacted section 3121(2). By use of the phrase "person of reasonable resolution," the legislature introduced an objective standard regarding the use of *threats* of forcible compulsion to prevent resistance (as opposed to actual application of "forcible compulsion.")

The determination of whether there is sufficient evidence to demonstrate beyond a reasonable doubt that an accused engaged in sexual intercourse by forcible compulsion (which we have defined to include "not only physical force or violence, but also moral, psychological or intellectual force used to compel a person to engage in sexual intercourse against that person's will," *supra,* at 1226), or by the threat of such forcible compulsion that would prevent resistance by a person of reasonable resolution *is, of course, a determination that will be made in each case based upon the totality of the circumstances that have been presented to the fact finder.* Significant factors to be weighed in that determination would include the respective ages of the victim and the accused, the respective mental and physical conditions of the victim and the accused, the atmosphere and physical setting in which the incident was alleged to have taken place, the extent to which the accused may have been in a position of authority, domination or custodial control over the victim, and whether the victim was under duress. This list of possible factors is by no means exclusive.

Id., 510 Pa. at 557, 510 A.2d at 1226–27 n. 15 (footnote 14 omitted) (emphasis added).

Before us is not a case of mental coercion. There existed no significant disparity between the ages of appellant and the victim. They were both college sophomores at the time of the incident. Appellant was age twenty; the victim was nineteen. The record is devoid of any evidence suggesting that the physical or mental condition of one party differed from the other in any material way. Moreover, the atmosphere and physical setting in which the incident took place was in no way coercive. The victim walked freely into appellant's dorm room in the middle of the afternoon on a school day and stayed to talk of her own volition. There was no evidence to suggest that appellant was in any position of authority, domination or custodial control over the victim. Finally, no record evidence indicates that the victim was under duress. Indeed, nothing in the record manifests any intent of appellant to impose "moral, psychological or intellectual" coercion upon the victim. *See and compare Commonwealth v. Rhodes, supra* (position of authority, isolated area of the incident and explicit commands sufficient to prove mental coercion); *Commonwealth v. Ables, supra,* 404 Pa.Superior Ct. at 177–179, 590 A.2d at 338 (position of trust and confidence coupled with emotional exploitation sufficient to establish moral coercion); *Commonwealth v. Ruppert,* 397 Pa.Super. 132, 579 A.2d 966 (1990) (father-daughter relationship coupled with showing of sexually explicit pictures sufficient to establish psychological coercion); *Commonwealth v. Frank,* 395 Pa.Super. 412, 577 A.2d 609 (1990) (therapist-patient relationship coupled with threat sufficient for psychological coercion); *Commonwealth v. Dorman, supra* (appellant's position of authority and trust and remote location of the incident sufficient to establish psychological coercion).

Nor is this a case of a threat of forcible compulsion. When asked by defense counsel at trial whether appellant had at any point threatened her in any manner, the victim responded, "No, he didn't." N.T. 9/14/88 at 67, 71. Moreover, careful review of the record fails to reveal any express or even implied threat that could be viewed as one which, by the objective standard applicable herein, "would prevent resistance by a person of reasonable resolution." 18 Pa.C.S.A. § 3121(2). *Compare Commonwealth v. Poindexter,* 372 Pa.Super. 566, 539 A.2d 1341 (1989) (father's reproaches and threats sufficient to establish coercion toward daughters); *Commonwealth v. Williams,* 294 Pa.Super. 93, 439 A.2d 765 (1982) (threat that victim would be killed if she resisted sufficient to establish forcible compulsion).

Rather, the Commonwealth contends that the instant rape conviction is supported by the evidence of actual physical force used to complete the act of intercourse. Essentially, the Commonwealth maintains that, viewed in the light most favorable to it, the record establishes that the victim did not consent to engage in the intercourse, and thus, any force used to complete the act of intercourse thereafter constituted "forcible compulsion."

In response, appellant urges that the victim's testimony itself precludes a finding of "forcible compulsion." Appellant essentially argues that the indisputable lack of physical injuries and physical resistance proves that the evidence was insufficient to establish rape.

In beginning our review of these arguments, it is clear that any reliance on the victim's absence of physical injuries or physical resistance is misplaced. Although it is true that the instant victim testified that she was not "physically hurt in any fashion," N.T. 9/14/88 at 68, and that it was "possible that [she] took no physical action to discourage [appellant]," *id.* at 59, such facts are insignificant in a sufficiency determination. As our Supreme Court has made clear, " 'rape . . . is defined, not in terms of the physical injury to the victim, but in terms of the effect it has on the victim's volition.' " Similarly, our legislature has expressly commanded that the "victim *need not resist* the actor in prosecutions under" As the *Rhodes* Court observed, this legislative mandate was intended to make it clear that "lack of consent is not synonymous with lack of resistance." *Commonwealth v. Rhodes, supra,* 510 Pa. at 557, 510 A.2d at 1227 n. 14. Thus, while the *presence* of actual injury or physical resistance might well indicate "forcible compulsion," we are compelled to conclude that the absence of either or both is not fatal to the Commonwealth's case.[5]

---

[5] That the victim need not resist "forcible compulsion" to later prove rape may be seen through an examination of the history of the resistance requirement in Pennsylvania. Traditionally, Pennsylvania law looked with peculiar suspicion upon the rape complaint. Due in part perhaps to Lord Chief Justice Matthew Hale's now infamous seventeenth century remonstration: "Rape is an accusation easily to be made and hard to be proved, and harder still to be defended by the party accused, tho never so innocent," Hale, *History of the Pleas of the Crown,* vol. 1, 634 (R.H. Small 1847), accusations of rape were reviewed with a scrutiny unparalleled by the review given to any other criminal complaint. For example, in 1875, our Supreme Court upheld an instruction that, "in order to guard against false charges in cases of this kind—it has been deemed an important test of the sincerity of the woman, that while the commission of the offense was in progress, she cried aloud, struggled and complained on the first opportunity, and prosecuted the offender without delay." *Stevick v. Commonwealth,* 78 Pa. 460, 460 (1875) (referring vaguely to Lord Chief Justice Hale's remonstration). Thereafter, countless reporters contained admonitions to the trial courts to bring to the attention of jurors the significance of actual "bona fide" resistance, outcry and prompt complaint. *See e.g. Commonwealth v. Berklowitz,* 133 Pa.Super. 190, 193–94, 2 A.2d 516 (1938) (conviction, based on evidence that the defendants, who were strangers to the victim, kidnapped the victim, drove her to a club seven miles away where she sipped drinks with the defendants and roughly 150 others, drove her thereafter to a vacant lot and had intercourse with her forcibly and against her will, reversed for failure to charge on significance of the absence of a prompt complaint and resistance); *Commonwealth v. Moran,* 97 Pa.Super. 120 (1929) (conviction, based on evidence that the defendants, with whom the victim had been acquainted, forced the victim into the grandstand of a baseball park, held down her shoulders and had intercourse with her, reversed for failure to charge on meaning of "bona fide" resistance).

In 1973 and 1976, however, our Legislature enacted several amendments to the Crimes Code which removed many of the obstacles in the path of rape prosecutions. The effect of

What is comparatively uncertain, however, in the absence of either an injury or resistance requirement, is the precise degree of actual physical force necessary to prove "forcible compulsion." As the *Rhodes* Court has made clear, no precise definition of the term "forcible compulsion" may be found.

> The "force necessary to support convictions for rape and involuntary deviate sexual intercourse *need only be such as to establish lack of consent and to induce the woman to submit without additional resistance* . . . The degree of force required to constitute rape [or involuntary deviate sexual intercourse] is *relative* and *depends upon the facts and particular circumstances of the case.*"

The *Rhodes* Court specifically refused to "delineate all of the possible circumstances that might tend to demonstrate that sexual intercourse was engaged in by forcible compulsion or by threat of forcible compulsion within the meaning of [title 18] section 3121(1) and (2)." *Commonwealth v. Rhodes, supra,* 510 Pa. at 556,510 A.2d at 1226. Rather, the Court left that delineation to evolve "in the best tradition of the common law—by development of a body of case law. . . . [W]hether there is sufficient evidence to demonstrate . . . that an accused engaged in sexual intercourse by forcible compulsion . . . is, of course, a determination that will be made in each case based on the *totality of the circumstances.* . . ." Thus, the ultimate task for the fact finder remains the question of whether, under the totality of circumstances, "the victim . . . was forced to . . . engage in sexual intercourse . . . *against his or her will.*"

Here, the victim testified that the physical aspects of the encounter began when appellant "kind of pushed me back with his body. It wasn't a shove, it was just kind of a leaning-type thing." N.T. 9/14/88 at 32. *Compare Commonwealth v. Rough, supra* (victim forced to floor and struck). She did not testify that appellant "pinned" her to the floor with his hands thereafter; she testified that he "started kissing me . . . [and] lift [ing] my shirt [and] bra . . . straddling me kind of . . . shifting at my body so that he was over me." N.T. 9/14/88 at 32–34. *Compare Commonwealth v. Meadows,* 381 Pa.Super. 354, 356–60, 553 A.2d 1006, 1008–09 (1989) (victim "pinned" to the ground despite physical resistance). When he attempted to have oral sex with her, appellant "knelt up straight . . . [and] tried to put his penis in

---

the reforms was dramatic. The "pernicious 'special rules' " governing rape prosecutions which had become a tradition in Pennsylvania were effectively abrogated by these amendments. *Commonwealth v. Rhodes, supra,* 510 A.2d at 1223 n. 11. As our Supreme Court made clear, "[m]odern social, legal and psychological thinking has thoroughly discredited these 'special rules,' and our Crimes Code, with amendments in 1973 and 1976, has finally discarded the last vestiges of these ill-conceived rules." *Id.*

Among the changes in rape law brought about by the amendments is that which annulled the resistance requirement. *See* 18 Pa.C.S.A. § 3107. Thus, for us to hold that a victim must resist "forcible compulsion" would be to ignore the history and defy the intent of the present no resistance requirement. This we cannot do.

my mouth . . . and after he obviously couldn't . . . he, we got up." N.T. 9/14/88 at 34–36. Although appellant then locked the door, his act cannot be seen as an attempt to imprison the victim since she knew and testified that the type of lock on the door of appellant's dorm room simply prevented those on the outside from entering but could be opened from the inside without hindrance. *Id.* at 61. *Compare Commonwealth v. Rhodes, supra* (victim imprisoned in car brought to isolated area). Appellant did not push, shove or throw the victim to his bed; he "put" her on the bed, not in a "romantic" way, but not with a "fast shove either." N.T. 9/14/88 at 39. Once on the bed, appellant did not try to restrain the victim with his hands in any fashion. *Id.* at 64. *Compare Commonwealth v. Irvin* (victim choked and her screams muffled by defendant's hands). Rather, while she was "just kind of laying there," he "straddled" her, "quick[ly] undid" the knot in her sweatpants, "took off" her sweatpants and underwear, placed the "weight of his body" on top of her and "guided" his penis inside her vagina. N.T. 9/14/88 at 39–41.

Even in the light most favorable to the Commonwealth, the victim's testimony as to the physical aspects of the encounter cannot serve as a basis to prove "forcible compulsion." The cold record is utterly devoid of any evidence regarding the respective sizes of either appellant or the victim. As such, we are left only to speculate as to the coercive effect of such acts as "leaning" against the victim or placing the "weight of his body" on top of her. This we may not do. Moreover, even if the record indicated some disparity in the respective weights or strength of the parties, such acts are not themselves inconsistent with consensual relations. Except for the fact that appellant was on top of the victim before and during intercourse, there is no evidence that the victim, if she had wanted to do so, could not have removed herself from appellant's bed and walked out of the room without any risk of harm or danger to herself whatsoever. These circumstances simply cannot be bootstrapped into sexual intercourse by forcible compulsion.

Similarly inconclusive is the fact that the victim testified that the act occurred in a relatively brief period of time. The short time frame might, without more, indicate that the victim desired the sexual encounter as easily as it might that she didn't, given the fact that no threats or mental coercion were alleged. At most, therefore, the physical aspects of the encounter establishes that appellant's sexual advances may have been unusually rapid, persistent and virtually uninterrupted. However inappropriate, undesirable or unacceptable such conduct may be seen to be, it does not, standing alone, prove that the victim was "forced to engage in sexual intercourse against her will."

The only evidence which remains to be considered is the fact that both the victim and appellant testified that throughout the encounter, the victim repeatedly and continually said "no."[6] Unfortunately for the Commonwealth, under the existing statutes, this evidence alone cannot suffice to support a finding of "forcible compulsion."

Evidence of verbal resistance is unquestionably relevant in a determination of "forcible compulsion." At least twice previously this Court has given weight to the failure to heed the victim's oral admonitions. *See Commonwealth v. Meadows, supra,* 381 Pa.Superior Ct. at 358553 A.2d at 1009 (evidence sufficient to convict for rape where "appellant pinned [the victim] to the ground and *knowingly disregarded her efforts to communicate the idea that she did not want to have intercourse.*") (emphasis added); *see also Commonwealth v. Dorman, supra,* 547 A.2d at 761 (finding evidence of rape sufficient where "[d]espite the victim's protests, appellant ... disrobed her, pushed her down on the seat of the car and had intercourse with her.") (emphasis added). In each such case, however, evidence of verbal resistance was only found sufficient where coupled with a sufficient threat of forcible compulsion, mental coercion, or actual physical force of a type inherently inconsistent with consensual sexual intercourse. Thus, although evidence of verbal protestations may be relevant to prove that the intercourse was against the victim's will, it is not dispositive or sufficient evidence of "forcible compulsion."

If the legislature had intended to define rape, a felony of the first degree, as non-consensual intercourse, it could have done so. It did not do this. It defined rape as sexual intercourse by "forcible compulsion." If the legislature means what it said, then where as here no evidence was adduced by the Commonwealth which established either that mental coercion, or a threat, or force inherently inconsistent with consensual intercourse was used to complete the act of intercourse, the evidence is insufficient to support a rape conviction.[7] Accordingly, we hold that the

---

[6]   The accounts differed in this respect only as to the tone in which the word was spoken. Appellant claimed it was whispered "passionately." N.T. 9/14/88 at 134. The victim testified that she voiced her objections *before* the intercourse in a "scolding" manner. *Id.* at 36. At trial, it was peculiarly for the jury to determine the credibility of the parties. *Commonwealth v. Murray, supra.* On appeal, we must view the record in the light most favorable to the Commonwealth. *Commonwealth v. Bryant, supra.* Viewed in this way, we must consider the victim's admonitions *before* the intercourse to be sincere protests. Although the victim testified that *during* the intercourse she "moaned" the word "no," N.T. 9/14/88 at 40, the degree of the ambiguity of her protests at that point is inconsequential for a *sufficiency* determination. By that time, penetration had occurred and the crime, if any, was complete. *See* Pa.C.S.A. § 3121. Such evidence merely went to the *weight* to attach to the victim's credibility. *See Commonwealth v. Pearsall,* 368 Pa.Super. 327, 329–30, 534 A.2d 106, 108 (1987). Moreover, the victim carefully explained that her "moaning" during intercourse was in no way "passionate." N.T. 9/14/88 at 65.

[7]   It may be argued that our conclusion requires the victim, whose *verbal* resistance did not deter the sexual advances, to *physically* resist, in violation of the "no resistance requirement," 18 Pa.C.S.A. § 3107. *See* note 5, *supra.* In this regard, we note the following. Although the "no resistance requirement" does not, on its face, in any way restrict the situations to which it may apply, it appears that the statute must have limits. Section 3121(2) of title 18, which describes the threat element of rape, states that rape occurs when a person "engages in sexual intercourse with another ... by threat of forcible compulsion *that would prevent resistance* by a person of reasonable resolution" (emphasis added). If the "no resistance requirement" were applied in that setting, the description of the type of threat which is sufficient would be rendered wholly meaningless. To be

trial court erred in determining that the evidence adduced by the Commonwealth was sufficient to convict appellant of rape. * * *

IV. CONCLUSION

For the foregoing reasons, we conclude that the evidence adduced by the Commonwealth was insufficient to convict appellant of rape, and that a new trial is warranted on the indecent assault charge. . . .

DISCUSSION QUESTIONS

1. Do you agree with the legal definitions of the elements of rape that the court used?

2. Do you agree with how the court applied those elements to the facts of this case?

3. Should the law of rape make any explicit distinctions between defendants who are acquainted with the victim and defendants who are strangers to the victim?

Case in Context

The jurisdiction in the following case redefined rape in a way that many places of higher education have adopted in defining sexual misconduct.

IN THE INTEREST OF M.T.S.

New Jersey Supreme Court
609 A.2d 1266 (1992)

HANDLER, J. Under New Jersey law a person who commits an act of sexual penetration using physical force or coercion is guilty of second-degree sexual assault. The sexual assault statute does not define the words "physical force." The question posed by this appeal is whether the element of "physical force" is met simply by an act of non-consensual penetration involving no more force than necessary to accomplish that result.

The issue is presented in the context of what is often referred to as "acquaintance rape." The record in the case discloses that the juvenile, a seventeen-year-old boy, engaged in consensual kissing and heavy petting with a fifteen-year-old girl and thereafter engaged in actual sexual penetration of the girl to which she had not consented. There was no evidence or suggestion that the juvenile used any unusual or extra force or threats to accomplish the act of penetration. The trial court determined that the juvenile was delinquent for committing a sexual assault. The

---

consistent, therefore, the "no resistance requirement" must be applied only to prevent any *adverse inference* to be drawn against the person who, *while* being "forcibly compelled" to engage in intercourse, chooses not to physically resist. *See* note 5, *supra.* Since there is no evidence that the instant victim was at any time "forcibly compelled" to engage in sexual intercourse, our conclusion is not at odds with the "no resistance requirement."

Appellate Division reversed the disposition of delinquency, concluding that non-consensual penetration does not constitute sexual assault unless it is accompanied by some level of force more than that necessary to accomplish the penetration.

I

On Monday, May 21, 1990, fifteen-year-old C.G. was living with her mother, her three siblings, and several other people, including M.T.S. and his girlfriend. A total of ten people resided in the three-bedroom town home at the time of the incident. M.T.S., then age seventeen, was temporarily residing at the home with the permission of the C.G.'s mother; he slept downstairs on a couch. C.G. had her own room on the second floor. At approximately 11:30 P.M. on May 21, C.G. went to bed, she was wearing underpants, a bra, shorts, and a shirt.

At trial, C.G. and M.T.S. offered very different accounts concerning the nature of their relationship and the events that occurred after C.G. had gone upstairs. The trial court did not credit fully either teenager's testimony.

C.G. stated that earlier in the day, M.T.S. had told her three or four times that he "was going to make a surprise visit up in [her] bedroom." She said that she had not taken M.T.S. seriously and considered his comments a joke because he frequently teased her. She testified that M.T.S. had attempted to kiss her on numerous other occasions and at least once had attempted to put his hands inside of her pants, but that she had rejected all of his previous advances. C.G. testified that on May 22, at approximately 1:30 A.M., she awoke to use the bathroom. As she was getting out of bed, she said, she saw M.T.S., fully clothed, standing in her doorway. According to C.G, M.T.S. then said that "he was going to tease [her] a little bit." C.G. testified that she "didn't think anything of it"; she walked past hum, used the bathroom, and then returned to bed, falling into a "heavy" sleep within fifteen minutes.

The next event C.G. claimed to recall of that morning was waking up with M.T.S. on top of her, her underpants and shorts removed. She said "his penis was into [her] vagina." As soon as C.G. realized what had happened, she said, she immediately slapped M.T.S. once in the face, then "told him to get off [her], and get out." She did not scream or cry out. She testified that M.T.S. complied in less than one minute after being struck; according to C.G., "he jumped right off of [her]." She said she did not know how long M.T.S. had been inside of her before she awoke. C.G. said that after M.T.S. left the room, she "fell asleep crying" because "[she] couldn't believe that he did what he did to [her]." she Explained that she did not immediately tell her mother or anyone else in the house of the events of that morning because she was "scared and in shock." According to C.G., M.T.S. engaged in intercourse with her "without [her] wanting it or telling him to come up [to her bedroom]." By her own account, C.G. was not otherwise harmed by M.T.S. At about 7:00 A.M., C.G. went downstairs and told her mother about her encounter with M.T.S. earlier in the morning and said that they would have to "get [him] out of the house." While M.T.S. was out on an errand, C.G.'s mother gathered his clothes and put them outside in his car; when he returned, he was told that "[he] better not even get near the house." C.G. and her mother then filed a complaint with the police.

According to M.T.S., he and C.G. had been good friends for a long time, and their relationship "kept leading on to more and more." He had been living at C.G.'s home for about five days before the incident occurred; he testified that during the three days preceding the incident they had been "kissing and necking" and had discussed having sexual intercourse. The first time M.T.S. kissed C.G., he said, she "didn't want him to, but she did after that." He said C.G. repeatedly had encouraged him to "make a surprise visit up in her room." M.T.S. testified that at exactly 1:15 A.M. on May 22, he entered C.G.'s bedroom as she was walking to the bathroom. He said C.G. soon returned from the bathroom and the two began "kissing and all," eventually moving to the bed. Once they were in bed, he said, they undressed each other and continued to kiss and touch for about five minutes. M.T.S., who was on top of C.G., he "stuck it in" and "did it [thrust] three times, and then the fourth time [he] stuck it in, that's when [she] pulled [him] off of her." M.T.S. said that as C.G. pushed him off, she said "stop, get off," and he "hopped off right away."

According to M.T.S., after about one minute, he asked C.G. what was wrong; she replied with a back-hand to his face. He recalled asking C.G. what was wrong a second time, and her replying "how can you take advantage of me or something like that." M.T.S. said that he proceeded to get dressed and told C.G. to calm down, but that she then told him to get away from her and began to cry. Before leaving the room, he told C.G., "I'm leaving. . . . I'm going with my real girlfriend, don't talk to me. . . . I don't want nothing to do with you or anything, stay out of my life . . . don't tell anybody about this . . . it would just screw everything up." He then walked downstairs and went to sleep.

On May 23, 1990, M.T.S. was charged with conduct that if engaged in by an adult would constitute second-degree sexual assault of the victim, contrary to N.J.S.A 2C:14–2c(1). . . . After reviewing the testimony, the court concluded that the victim had consented to a session of kissing and heavy petting with M.T.S. The Trial court did not find that C.G. had been sleeping at the time of penetration, but nevertheless found that she had not consented to the actual sexual act. Accordingly, the court concluded that the State had proven second-degree sexual assault beyond a reasonable doubt. On appeal, following the imposition of suspended sentences on the sexual assault and the other remaining charges, the Appellate Division determined that the absence of force beyond that involved in the act of sexual penetration precluded a finding of second-degree sexual assault. It therefore reversed the juvenile's adjudication of delinquency for that offense.

II

The New Jersey Code of Criminal Justice, N.J.S.A 2C:14–2c(1), defines "sexual assault" as the commission of "sexual penetration" "with another person" with the use of "physical force or coercion."[1] An unconstrained reading of the statutory language indicates that both the act of "sexual penetration" and the use of "physical force" are separate and distinct elements of the offense. . . . The trial court held that "physical force" had been established by the sexual penetration of the victim without her consent. The Appellate Division believed that the statute requires some amount of force more than that necessary to accomplish penetration.

The parties offer two alternative understandings of the concept of "physical force" as it is used in the statute. The State would read "physical force" to mean force "used to overcome lack of consent." That definition equates force with violence and leads to the conclusion that sexual assault requires the application of some amount of force in addition to the act of penetration. Current judicial practice suggests an understanding of "physical force" to mean "any degree of physical power or strength used against the victim, even though it entails no injury and leaves no mark." Model Jury Charges, Criminal 3 (revised Mar. 29, 1989). Resort to common experience or understanding does not yield a conclusive meaning. The dictionary provides several definitions of "force," among which are the following: (1) "power, violence, compulsion, or constraint exerted upon or against a person or thing," (2) "a general term for exercise of strength or power, esp. physical, to overcome resistance," or (3) "strength or power of any degree that is exercised without justification or contrary to law upon a person or thing." Webster's Third New International Dictionary 887 (1961). Thus, as evidenced by the disagreements among the lower courts and the parties, and the variety of possible usages, the statutory words "physical force" do not evoke a single meaning that is obvious and plain. . . . Under traditional rape law, in order to prove that a rape had occurred, the state had to show both that force had been used and that penetration had been against the woman's will. Force was identified and determined not as an independent factor but in relation to the response of the victim, which in turn implicated the victim's own state of mind. "Thus, the perpetrator's use of force became criminal only if the victim's state of mind met the statutory requirement. The perpetrator could use all the force imaginable and no

---

[1] The sexual assault statue, N.J.S.A 2C:14–2c(1) reads as follows:

   c. An actor is guilty of sexual assault if he commits an act of sexual penetration with another person under any one of the following circumstances:

     1. The actor uses physical force or coercion, but the victim does not sustain severe personal injury; . . .

Sexual Assault is a crime of the second degree.

crime would be committed if the state could not prove additionally that the victim did not consent." National Institute of Law Enforcement and Criminal Justice, Forcible Rape—An Analysis of Legal Issues 5 (March 1978) (Forcible Rape). Although the terms "non-consent" and "against her will" were often treated as equivalent, under the traditional definition of rape, both formulations squarely placed on the victim the burden of proof and of action. Effectively, a woman who was above the age of consent had actively and affirmatively to withdraw that consent for the intercourse to be against her will. . . . The presence or absence of consent often turned on credibility. To demonstrate that the victim had not consented to the intercourse, and also that sufficient force had been used to accomplish the rape, the state had to prove that the victim had resisted. According to the oft-quoted Lord Hale, to be deemed a credible witness, a woman had to be of good fame, disclose the injury immediately, suffer signs of injury, and cry out for help. 1 Matthew Hale, History of the Pleas of the Crown 633 (1st ed. 1847). . . . Evidence of resistance was viewed as a solution to the credibility problem; it was the "outward manifestation of nonconsent, [a] device for determining whether a woman actually gave consent." Note, The Resistance Standard in Rape Legislation, 18 Stan. L. Rev. 680, 689 (1966). . . .

At lease by 1960s courts in New Jersey followed a standard for establishing resistance that was somewhat less drastic than the traditional rule. Thus, in 1965 the Appellate Division stated: "[W]e have rejected the former test that a woman must resist 'to the uttermost.' We only require that she resist as much as she possibly can under the circumstances." State v. Terry, 215 A.2d 374 (N.J. Super.). . . .

Resistance was necessary not only to prove non-consent but also to demonstrate that the force used by the defendant had been sufficient to overcome the victim's will. The amount of force used by the defendant was assessed in relation to the resistance of the victim. In New Jersey the amount of force necessary to establish rape was characterized as "the degree of force sufficient to overcome any resistance that had been put up by the female.' State v. Terry, supra, 215 A.2d 374 (N.J. Super.) (quoting jury charge by trial court). Resistance, often demonstrated by torn clothing and blood, was a sign that the defendant had used significant force to accomplish the sexual intercourse. Thus, if the defendant forced himself on a woman, it was her responsibility to fight back, because force was measured in relation to the resistance she put forward. Only if she resisted, causing him to use more force than was necessary to achieve penetration, would his conduct be criminalized. . . .

Critics of rape law agreed that the focus of the crime should be shifted from the victim's behavior to the defendant's conduct, and particularly to its forceful and assaultive, rather than sexual, character. Reformers also shared the goals of facilitating rape prosecutions and of sparing victims much of the degradation involved in bringing and trying a charge of rape. There were, however, differences over the best way to redefine the crime. Some reformers advocated a standard that defined rape as unconsented-to sexual intercourse; others urged the elimination of any reference to consent from the definition of rape. Nonetheless, all proponents of reform shared a central premise: that the burden of showing non-consent should not fall on the victim of the crim. In dealing with the problem of consent, the reform goal was not so much to purge the entire concept of consent from the law as to eliminate the burden that had been placed on victims to prove they had not consented.

Similarly, with regard to force, rape law reform sough to give independent significance to the forceful or assaultive conduct of the defendant and to avoid a definition of force that depended on the reaction of the victim. Traditional interpretations of force were strongly criticized for failing to acknowledge that force may be understood simply as the invasion of "bodily integrity." Susan Estrich, Rape, 95 Yale L.J. 1087, 1105 (1986). In urging that the "resistance" requirement be abandoned, reformers sought to break the connection between force and resistance.

III

[T]he New Jersey Code of Criminal Justice does not refer to force in relation to "overcoming the will" of the victim, or to the "physical overpowering" of the victim. It does not require the demonstrated non-consent of the victim. As we have noted, in reforming the rape laws, the Legislature placed primary emphasis on the assaultive nature of the crime, altering its constituent elements so that they focus exclusively on the forceful or assaultive conduct of the defendant. The Legislature's concept of sexual assault and the role of force was significantly colored by its understanding of the law of assault and battery. As a general matter, criminal battery is defined as "the unlawful application of force to the person of another." 2 Wayne LaFave & Austin Scott, Criminal Law, § 7.15 at 301 (1986). The application of force is criminal when it results in either (a) a physical injury or (b) an offensive touching. Id. at 301–02. Any "unauthorized touching of another [is] a battery." Perna v. Pirozzi, 457 A.2d 431 (N.J. 1983).

Thus, by eliminating all references to the victim's state of mind and conduct, and by broadening the definition of penetration to cover not only sexual intercourse between a man and a woman but a range of acts that invade another's body or compel intimate contact, the Legislature emphasized the affinity between sexual assault and other forms of assault and battery. . . .

The understanding of sexual assault as a criminal battery, albeit one with especially serious consequences, follows necessarily from the Legislature's decision to eliminate nonconsent and resistance from the substantive definition of the offense. Under the new law, the victim no longer is required to resist and therefore need not have said or done anything in order for the sexual penetration to be unlawful. The alleged victim is not put on trial, and his or her responsive or defensive behavior is rendered immaterial. We are thus satisfied that an interpretation of the statutory crime of sexual assault to require physical force in addition to that entailed in an act of involuntary or unwanted sexual penetration would be fundamentally inconsistent with the legislative purpose to eliminate any consideration of whether the victim resisted or expressed non-consent. . . .

Because the statute eschews any reference to the victim's will or resistance, the standard defining the role of force in sexual penetration must prevent the possibility that the establishment of the crime will turn on the alleged victim's state of mind or responsive behavior. We conclude, therefore, that any act of sexual penetration engaged in by the defendant without the affirmative and freely-given permission of the victim to the specific act of penetration constitutes the offense of sexual assault. Therefore, physical force in excess of that inherent in the act of sexual penetration is not required for such penetration to be unlawful. The definition of "physical force" is satisfied under N.J.S.A 2C:14–2c(1) if the defendant applies any amount of force against another person in the absence of what a reasonable person would believe to be affirmative and freely given permission to the act of sexual penetration. Under the reformed statute, permission to engage in sexual penetration must be affirmative and it must be given freely, but that permission may be inferred either from acts or statements reasonably viewed in the light of the surrounding circumstances. Persons need not, of course, expressly announce their consent to engage in intercourse for there to be affirmative permission. Permission to engage in an act of sexual penetration can be and indeed often is indicated through physical actions rather than words. Permission is demonstrated when the evidence, in whatever form, is sufficient to demonstrate that a reasonable person would have believed that the alleged victim had affirmatively and freely given authorization to the act.

. . . Although it is possible to imagine a set of rules in which persons must demonstrate affirmatively that sexual contact is unwanted or not permitted, such a regime would be inconsistent with modern principled of personal autonomy. . . .

IV

In a Case such as this one, in which the State does not allege violence or force extrinsic to the act of penetration, the factfinder must decide whether the defendant's act of penetration was undertaken in circumstances that led the defendant reasonably to believe that the alleged victim had freely given affirmative permission to the specific act of sexual penetration. Such permission can be indicated either through words or through her words or actions. We conclude that the record provides reasonable support for the trail court's disposition.

Accordingly, we reverse the judgement of the Appellate Division and reinstate the disposition of juvenile delinquency for the commission of second-degree assault.

DISCUSSION QUESTIONS

1.   How does the definition of force used by the court differ from the definitions used in the other cases we have studied? Is it a better or worse definition?

2.   How does the definition of consent used differ from the definitions used in the other cases we have studied. Is it a better or worse definition?

3.   If you had to rely on only force or consent to define rape, which would you choose?

Exam Tip: Think Through Both Sides of a Policy Question

As mentioned earlier, exam questions dealing with rape are often framed as policy questions. As is always the case, the most important thing to demonstrate on a policy question is your ability to think deeply through both sides of a question. This does not mean that you cannot ultimately reach a strong conclusion one way or the other. It does mean that you should only arrive there after dealing with the opposite's side's very best arguments. Because rape law involves so many difficult and deeply controversial questions it is a great vehicle for assessing your ability to do so.

Practice Problem 23.0: Defining Rape

Draft a model statute defining the crime of rape. You may create degrees as well as lesser or alternate crimes of sexual assault. Be sure you specify as clearly as possible the predicate sexual act required as well as what role force and/or consent play as well as how these elements are to be defined.

CHAPTER 24

MISCELLANEOUS CRIMES
AGAINST THE PERSON

■ ■ ■

A. ASSAULT AND BATTERY DISTINGUISHED

Strictly speaking a battery is very distinct from an assault. As originally understood a battery required a touching whereas an assault did not. This distinction has broken down in some jurisdictions that include battery within assault. Generally assault statutes are more numerous and include more serious crimes than battery statutes. This puzzles some because assaults by definition typically don't require even a touching or contact much less an injury. What you will soon realize, however, is that assaultive crimes focus more on the culpable intent of the assailant and make important distinctions about the level of harm intended. The absence of an injury or contact requirement also makes them easier to prove.

B. BATTERY

- A Harmful or Offensive
- Application of Force against the Person of another
- Committed either Intentionally or with at least Criminal Negligence
- That is Unlawful

When I was a child, commercials for toys often carried the warning, "Batteries not included." If you see a fact pattern that contains some violence but not actual *contact* against the victim, then you should think "battery not included" among the possible crimes.

The application of force required for battery requires contact with the victim. A simple shove is enough because even though the person might not be harmed most would be offended by being shoved. The defendant need not actually touch the victim, however. You could batter someone by throwing a rock or a paper clip at them. For that matter you can batter someone by spitting at them (definitely offensive), but the spit must actually hit them. I can also commit a battery by setting a force in motion, like releasing an angry dog to attack someone or even taking the parking brake off a car that will roll downhill towards a crowd of people.

Note that battery is a general intent crime, which means that criminal/gross negligence is all that is required. So if I am swinging my fists around in a crowded space while watching a prize fight on TV and end up hitting you, then I could be guilty of battery, although gross negligence would require me to be taking really big swings in a really crowded space.

The application of force must, of course, be unlawful. People consent to be tackled when they play football; security guards are legally authorized to grab running shoplifters; everyone is legally justified in using force in self defense. All of these applications of force would be lawful, and none of them would constitute battery.

Aggravated batteries are usually defined by statute, often classified as felonies, and typically involve one of three aggravating factors.

1. An especially vulnerable type of victim such as a child, or elderly person, or police officer.

2. Use of a deadly weapon.

3. The actual infliction of serious bodily harm or worse.

Note that the third aggravating creates a result crime. The prosecution must prove the occurrence of the harm as well as causation.

C. ASSAULT

Assault is a bit trickier because there are generally two types of assaults: an attempted battery and an intentional attempt to frighten.

1. ATTEMPTED BATTERY ASSAULT

Assault as an attempted battery is more straightforward. Think if it as "a swing and a miss." Imagine that I see former NBA basketball star Shaquille O'Neal walking down the street and decide that I am going to punch him in the face. Shaq is, of course, over 7 feet tall, whereas I am just under six feet and have a two inch vertical leap. I miss Shaq completely. I am guilty of assault, not battery.

Like all crimes of attempt, an attempted battery requires intent to commit the crime. So even though a battery is a general intent crime requiring only criminal negligence, the attempted battery type of assault requires me to intend to apply force against his person, which is, of course, a specific intent. If I was not trying to hit O'Neal but was jumping up to waive my autograph book in his face and came inches from hitting him, I would not be guilty of an assault. (If I hit him with the book, though, I would be guilty of an actual battery because it was arguably grossly negligent of me to do so.)

A minority of jurisdictions require for this type of assault that the defendant have the present ability to commit the attempted act. Assume instead that I was trying to hit former NBA star Yao Ming in the nose. Ming is 7′6″ tall. If I can't reach his nose with my fist, then I would not be guilty of assault for taking a swing at him on a theory of attempted battery in such a jurisdiction (although they will get me under the next type of assault). Most jurisdictions don't care whether the defendant has the present ability to succeed in the attempted battery.

Finally, assault as an attempted battery does not require any sort of mental state on the part of the victim. The victim does not need to be afraid and does not even need to be aware of the attempted battery. So assume again that I was trying to hit O'Neal, but he did not even see or otherwise notice the swing. I am nonetheless still guilty of the attempted battery version of assault.

2.   INTENT TO FRIGHTEN ASSAULT

The more sweeping and more common type assault could be thought of as a "scare crime," although actual fear as we will see is not required.

- Intentionally
- Causing the Victim to Reasonably Expect
- An Imminent Battery
- By More than Mere Words

This type of assault covers much more ground. Pointing a gun or a knife at someone would obviously do. Angrily shaking my (comparatively small) fist in O'Neal's face would also be enough. Simply yelling angrily at O'Neal that I am going to punch him in the nose would not be enough. If my "mere words" were accompanied by the clenching of one of my fists, however, that would be enough to satisfy the elements of an attempt to frighten assault.

One important point of difference between intent to frighten assault and an attempted battery assault is the subjective awareness of the victim. For the attempted battery the victim need not be aware of "the swing and the miss." The "scare crime" assault requires the defendant to cause the victim to expect an imminent battery. So if I jump up and shake my fist at Neal yelling that I am going to punch him, but he neither sees nor hears me, then I would not be guilty of an assault under the intent to frighten theory. (I would also not be guilty of assault under the attempted battery theory since I arguably had not begun the attempt.)

Note that fear is not actually required for this type of assault, merely the reasonable expectation of an imminent battery. Can you imagine Shaquille O'Neal being actually afraid of me? (Did I mention that he weighs over 300 lbs. and that his arms are probably thicker than my legs?) The only way that he could get hurt by me would be if he fell down laughing. Actual fear of bodily harm is not required, however. He need merely reasonably expect an imminent battery, which includes of course not just a harmful touching but an offensive one.

Finally, the fear must be of an imminent battery. Telling him that I going to punch him in the nose tomorrow as I shake my fist will not cut it.

Case in Context

The defendant in the next case gives meaning to the phrase "felony stupid," but should he have been found guilty of the crime he was charged with?

COMMONWEALTH V. ALBERT J. HENSON
Supreme Judicial Court of Massachusetts, Suffolk
357 Mass. 686 (1970)

QUIRICO, JUSTICE.

These are appeals from convictions on two complaints charging the defendant, respectively, with the crimes of assault on Theodore Finochio by means of a dangerous weapon, to wit: a revolver, and carrying a loaded revolver without a valid license so to do. In argument before this court and in his brief the defendant waived his appeal on the charge of carrying the revolver. The only issue before us is whether there was error in denying a motion by the defendant for a directed verdict on the complaint charging the crime of assault by means of a dangerous weapon.

The evidence would permit the jury to find the following facts. On December 24, 1968, Theodore Finochio, an off-duty police officer was at a gasoline station in Boston. He was not in uniform, but he had his service revolver in a holster under his coat. Another man and woman also were in the station at that time. The defendant and a female companion entered the station and the female used profane language. Finochio asked the defendant to keep the woman quiet. The defendant reached in his pocket, pulled out a revolver, aimed it at Finochio's stomach and said 'Why should I?' Finochio put up his hands and said 'No reason at all.' He described his state of mind at that time by saying 'I thought I was done for.' The defendant then turned to go out of the station, holding the revolver at his side. Finochio took out his revolver, pointed it at the defendant and said, 'Hold it there, buddy. I am a police officer.' The defendant, who was then partially out of the door, turned and fired two shots at Finochio from a distance of about five feet. Finochio fired back and chased the defendant out to the street. They exchanged further shots in that chase which lasted about twenty to thirty seconds until the defendant was captured, subdued and handcuffed, and his revolver taken from his hand. The defendant fired a total of five or more shots, and Finochio fired six, one of which struck the defendant. Finochio was not struck by any projectile, and he received no injuries or powder burns in the incident. No projectiles were recovered at the scene. The defendant had taken the revolver from his female companion before going to the gasoline station. Before the shooting he noticed that it was loaded. He removed one shell from the cylinder and recognized it as a blank. He described the revolver as a 'phony' gun or 'play' gun.

On the evidence the jury could find that the defendant, without any legal justification, suddenly drew his revolver from his pocket, pointed it at Finochio's stomach in a threatening manner and thereafter fired it at Finochio five or more times. They could also find that the defendant intended to create, and did create, the impression on the persons present that he had a loaded revolver which was capable of shooting Finochio, and that until the defendant's running gun battle with Finochio was over and he was subdued, no one present except the defendant knew that the defendant's revolver was loaded with blanks. Finally, they could find that all persons present, except the defendant, reasonably believed that the defendant's revolver was loaded with live bullets which he was firing at Finochio.

It is at least relevant, even if not an essential element of the crime charged, that 'the objectively menacing conduct of the defendant, despite an actual inability to do harm, produced the fear of harm which it was intended to produce, with the same consequential tendency to provoke a breach of the peace as if he had the actual ability to do harm.' Commonwealth v. Slaney, 345 Mass. 135, 140, 185 N.E.2d 919, 923.

Despite this factual situation, the defendant contends that although he carried the revolver in violation of G.L. c. 269, s 10, as found by the jury, and used it against Finochio thereby committing an assault upon him, his conduct could not, and did not, constitute the aggravated offence of assault by means of a dangerous weapon since the shells in the revolver at the time were blanks. He equates his position to that of a person using a revolver which is capable of firing a bullet, but which is in fact not loaded, or to that of a person using a toy or imitation revolver which in fact cannot fire a bullet. Basically, he argues that because the revolver was not loaded with live ammunition, he did not have the ability to accomplish a battery by means of the revolver, and thus cannot be convicted of assault by means of the revolver.

It had previously been held in Commonwealth v. White, 110 Mass. 407, decided in 1872, that the inability to commit a battery with an unloaded gun was no defence to a charge of simple assault. There, although the defendant was charged with a simple assault, the complaint included reference to a threat 'to shoot with a gun * * * pointed and aimed at (the victim).' The court said, at 409: 'It is not the secret intent of the assaulting party, nor the undisclosed fact of his ability or inability to commit a battery, that is material; but what his conduct and the attending circumstances denote at the time to the party assaulted. If to him they indicate an attack, he is justified in resorting to defensive action. The same rule applies to the proof necessary to sustain a criminal complaint for an assault. It is the outward demonstration that constitutes the mischief which is punished as a breach of the peace.'

If this test were applied to the present case, the jury could find that the defendant's conduct and the attending circumstances indicated that the defendant was attacking Finochio by means of a loaded revolver. Thus the defendant's secret intent not to shoot Finochio based on his undisclosed inability to do so with the blank shells is not material. The defendant's acts, judged without the benefit of his secret knowledge that he was firing blanks, constituted a reasonably obvious case of an assault by means of a loaded revolver, involving a violent breach of the public order and setting in motion the normal reaction thereto by Finochio. The issue before us is whether this test should be applied to a case of assault by means of a dangerous weapon. Put another way, should the defendant now be allowed to avoid criminal responsibility for his conduct on the ground that he had only blank shells in his revolver, or that the revolver was only a 'phony' gun or 'play' gun?

Our answer to the question before us would seem to depend on whether, under the law of this Commonwealth, proof of a charge of the crime of simple assault or of aggravated assault requires proof of the present ability to accomplish the battery which is threatened or attempted in the assault. As we have indicated above, it was held as to simple assault that '(i)t is not the secret intent of the assaulting party, nor the undisclosed fact of his ability or inability to commit a battery, that is material; but what his conduct and the attending circumstances denote at the time to the party assaulted. * * * It is the outward demonstration that constitutes the mischief which is punished as a breach of the peace.' Commonwealth v. White, 110 Mass. 407, 409. That language has been quoted and the decision cited on many occasions in the discussion of 'apparent' ability to commit the battery threatened or attempted. In Perkins on Criminal Law (1957) 91, the author poses the questions: 'If one has tried to apply force to the person of another unlawfully, or has made a menacing gesture causing apprehension thereof, what will be the effect of proof that at the moment he did not have the actual ability to do what he tried or offered to do? * * * Suppose there is apparent ability but not actual ability; suppose it is apparent to one but not to the other; will it make any difference?' He then answers the questions by writing further, at 91–93: 'Where an assault may be committed either by an attempt to commit a battery or by an unlawful act placing the other in reasonable apprehension of receiving an immediate battery, it is clear that apparent ability will suffice. * * * There must be some power, actual or apparent, or doing bodily harm but apparent power is sufficient. * * * Hence in jurisdictions giving full scope to the modern rule of criminal assault, this offense may be committed where the battery itself is actually impossible, if it reasonably seems possible either to the assailant or to his victim; * * * and the assailant could place the other in apprehension of an immediate battery by means that appeared to be effective although the assailant himself knew otherwise. * * * In jurisdictions giving full scope to the modern rule of criminal assault it is possible to commit this offense by pointing an unloaded weapon at another within normal range.' The author cites Commonwealth v. White, supra, as well as many other decisions as the basis for his statements on the doctrine of 'apparent ability.'

The fundamental reason for permitting a conviction for simple assault on proof of apparent ability of the assailant to accomplish the attempted or threatened battery is that the public peace and order is affected by and dependent upon what is reasonably apparent, and not upon secret fact or reason rendering the assailant incapable of accomplishing the battery. The reason applies with even greater force to a case of apparent ability to accomplish a battery attempted or threatened by means of a firearm. The threat to the public peace and order is greater, and natural reactions thereto by the intended victim and others may be more sudden and violent than in cases where no weapon is involved. There is no reason why the rule of apparent ability should not apply to charges of aggravated assaults by means of weapons. It is sufficient to prove such a charge if the evidence shows an apparent ability to accomplish the battery by means of the particular weapon used. Thus, the mere fact that a firearm brandished by an assailant is known by him to be unloaded, or to be loaded with blank cartridges, does not entitle him to an acquittal on a charge of the aggravated offence of assault by means of a dangerous weapon.

Judgments affirmed.

DISCUSSION QUESTIONS

1. Why should courts define assault to include those with an apparent but not actual ability to accomplish the threatened battery?

2. Was Henson as blameworthy or as dangerous as someone pointing and firing a loaded gun? Should a separate and lesser offense be created for such crimes?

3. Was the court right to apply the rule for simple assaults to aggravated assaults in this case?

3. AGGRAVATED ASSAULTS

Once again, these are often defined by statute and usually classified as felonies. The list of aggravating factors is slightly longer than for aggravated batteries.

1. An especially vulnerable type of victim such as a child, or elderly person, or police officer.

2. Use of a deadly weapon.

3. The actual infliction of serious bodily harm or worse.

4. The intent to inflict serious injury.

Note in particular the fourth type of aggravated assault. Any assault committed with the intent to seriously injure someone suffices. Definitions of serious injury vary, but broken bones, injuries requiring stitches and even knocked out teeth easily count.

Case in Context

The following aggravated assault case required the court to make decisions about both the mental state and result element of the offense.

THE PEOPLE OF THE STATE OF ILLINOIS
V. WILLIAM J. CONLEY

Appellate Court of Illinois, First District, Third Division
187 Ill.App.3d 234 (1989)

JUSTICE CERDA delivered the opinion of the court:

The defendant, William J. Conley, was charged with two counts of aggravated battery based on permanent disability and great bodily harm. (Ill.Rev.Stat.1983, ch. 38, par. 12–4(a).) He was found guilty after a jury trial of aggravated battery based solely on permanent disability on July 17, 1986. The defendant's motions for judgment notwithstanding the verdict or a new trial were denied, and the defendant was sentenced to thirty months probation including forty days of periodic imprisonment. On appeal, it is contended that: The State failed to prove beyond a reasonable doubt that the victim incurred a permanent disability and that the defendant intended to inflict a permanent disability.

The defendant was charged with aggravated battery in connection with a fight which occurred at a party on September 28, 1985, in unincorporated Orland Township. Approximately two hundred high school students attended the party and paid admission to drink unlimited beer. One of those students, Sean O'Connell, attended the party with several friends. At some point during the party, Sean's group was approached by a group of twenty boys who apparently thought that someone in Sean's group had said something derogatory. Sean's group denied making a statement and said they did not want any trouble. Shortly thereafter, Sean and his friends decided to leave and began walking toward their car which was parked a half block south of the party.

A group of people were walking toward the party from across the street when someone from that group shouted "There's those guys from the party." Someone emerged from that group and approached Sean who had been walking with his friend Marty Carroll ten to fifteen steps behind two other friends, Glen Mazurowski and Dan Scurio. That individual demanded that Marty give him a can of beer from his six-pack. Marty refused, and the individual struck Sean in the face with a wine bottle causing Sean to fall to the ground. The offender attempted to hit Marty, but missed as Marty was able to duck. Sean had sustained broken upper and lower jaws and four broken bones in the area between the bridge of his nose and the lower left cheek. Sean lost one tooth and had root canal surgery to reposition ten teeth that had been damaged. Expert testimony revealed that Sean has a permanent condition called mucosal mouth and permanent partial numbness in one lip. The expert also testified that the life expectancy of the damaged teeth might be diminished by a third or a half.

The defendant initially contends on appeal that the State failed to prove beyond a reasonable doubt that Sean O'Connell incurred a permanent disability. Section 12–4(a) of the Criminal Code of 1961 provides that: "[a] person who, in committing a battery, intentionally or knowingly causes great bodily harm, or permanent disability or disfigurement commits aggravated battery." (Ill.Rev.Stat. (1983) ch. 38, par. 12–4(a).) The defendant contends there must be some disabling effect for an aggravated battery conviction based on permanent disability. The defendant does not dispute that Sean lost a tooth or that surgery was required to repair damaged teeth. The defendant also does not dispute that Sean will have permanent partial numbness in one lip or suffer from a condition called mucosal mouth. The defendant maintains, however, that there is no evidence as to how these injuries are disabling because there was no testimony of any tasks that can no longer be performed as a result of these injuries.

The function of the courts in construing statutes is to ascertain and give effect to the intent of the legislature. The starting point for this task is the language itself and the language should be given its plain and ordinary meaning. The defendant urges the court to adopt the definition found in Webster's Third New International Dictionary which defines disability as an "inability to do something." The State refers to additional language from the same source that a disability is a "physical or mental illness, injury or condition that incapacitates in any way." There is some support for defendant's proposed definition in an old Illinois decision. In *Dahlberg v. People* (1907), 225 Ill. 485, a woman was convicted of assault with intent to commit mayhem (aggravated battery incorporates the earlier offense of mayhem) after she threw red pepper at someone's eyes and missed, hitting an innocent bystander in the eyes instead. Her conviction was reversed because the crime of attempt requires that the offender employ adequate means to accomplish the attempted result, and the evidence revealed that blindness could not have resulted had she succeeded. Thus, by necessary implication, anything short of blindness would not have supported a conviction for mayhem.

In arriving at a definition, however, it is also proper to consider the statute's purpose and the evils sought to be remedied. The Committee Comment explains that section 12–4(a) incorporates the old offense of mayhem. (Ill.Ann.Stat., ch. 38, par. 12–4(a), Committee Comment at 465 (Smith-Hurd 1979).) At common law the offense of mayhem required the dismemberment or disablement of some bodily part. Initially, the law sought to protect the King's right to the military services of his subjects. However, modern criminal codes have expanded their protection against a wider range of injuries.

Under this view, it seems apparent that for an injury to be deemed disabling, all that must be shown is that the victim is no longer whole such that the injured bodily portion or part no longer serves the body in the same manner as it did before the injury. Applying this standard to the case at hand, the injuries Sean O'Connell suffered are sufficient to constitute a permanent disability. Sean will endure permanent partial numbness in one lip and mucosal mouth. He lost one tooth and there is also a chance he may loose some teeth before attaining the age of seventy.

The defendant further argues that the State failed to prove beyond a reasonable doubt that he intended to inflict any permanent disability. The thrust of defendant's argument is that under section 12–4(a), a person must intend to bring about the particular harm defined in the statute. The defendant asserts that while it may be inferred from his conduct that he intended to cause harm, it does not follow that he intended to cause permanent disability. The State contends it is not necessary that the defendant intended to bring about the particular injuries that resulted. The State maintains it met its burden by showing that the defendant intentionally struck Sean.

For proper resolution of this issue, it is best to return to the statutory language. Section 12–4(a) employs the terms "intentionally or knowingly" to describe the required mental state. The relevant statutes state:

> "4–4. Intent. A person intends, or acts intentionally or with intent, to accomplish a result or engage in conduct described by the statute defining the offense, when his conscious objective or purpose is to accomplish that result or engage in that conduct." (Ill.Rev.Stat.1987, ch. 38, par. 4–4.)

> "4–5. Knowledge. A person knows or acts knowingly or with knowledge of: (b) The result of his conduct, described by the statute defining the offense, when he is consciously aware that such result is practically certain to be caused by his conduct." (Ill.Rev.Stat.1987, ch. 38, par. 4–5.)

Section 12–4(a) defines aggravated battery as the commission of a battery where the offender intentionally or knowingly causes great bodily harm, or permanent disability or disfigurement. Because the offense is defined in terms of result, the State has the burden of proving beyond a reasonable doubt that the defendant either had a "conscious objective" to achieve the harm defined, or that the defendant was "consciously aware" that the harm defined was "practically certain to be caused by his conduct." This is the identical construction which we conclude is the correct statement of the law.

Although the State must establish the specific intent to bring about great bodily harm, or permanent disability or disfigurement under section 12–4(a), problems of proof are alleviated to the extent that the ordinary presumption that one intends the natural and probable consequences of his actions shifts the burden of production, though not persuasion, to the defendant. If the defendant presents evidence contrary to the presumption, then the presumption ceases to have effect, and the trier of fact considers all the evidence and the natural inferences drawn therefrom. Intent can be inferred from the surrounding circumstances, the offender's words, the weapon used, and the force of the blow. If Conley had denied any intention to inflict permanent disability, the surrounding circumstances, the use of a bottle, the absence of warning and the force of the blow are facts from which the jury could reasonably infer the intent to cause permanent disability. Therefore, we find the evidence sufficient to support a finding of intent to cause permanent disability beyond a reasonable doubt.

DISCUSSION QUESTIONS

1. As a matter of statutory interpretation, do you think that the injuries in this case were sufficiently serious to constitute a disability? As a matter of policy?

2. Do you believe that the prosecution met its burden on intent in this case? Does "natural and probable consequences" refer to what is probable as a matter of physics and science or what seems natural to most people?

3. Why should we treat an assault that inflicts a serious injury more seriously than an assault that intends to inflict such an injury? Conversely, why not treat an assault that inflicts a serious injury more seriously regardless of whether a serious injury was intended?

D. STALKING

Case in Context

As the next case demonstrates, stalking is an offense that is easy to recognize but hard to define.

THE STATE OF NEW HAMPSHIRE v. FRANK SIMONE

Supreme Court of New Hampshire
152 N.H. 755 (2005)

DALIANIS, J.

Following a trial in the Superior Court (*Hicks*, J.), a jury convicted the defendant, Frank Simone, of stalking in violation of RSA 633:3–a, I(a). We affirm.

The jury could have found the following facts. In 2001, Coral Olson was employed by the U.S. Census Bureau as a field service representative. Olson traveled door-to-door to conduct census surveys. She would then re-contact the same respondents by telephone and by personal visit until she had obtained sufficient survey information. In January 2001, Olson went to the defendant's home to conduct a census survey. Olson gave the defendant her business card with her home phone number, and conducted several follow-up telephone calls and one follow-up personal visit to complete the census survey. After the defendant completed his census survey, however, he continued to call Olson. The defendant told Olson that he was interested in her; Olson responded that she was married and not interested in him. Nevertheless, the defendant persisted in calling her. He told Olson that he had "serious personal problems" and felt suicidal and out of control. Olson did not initiate any of these personal telephone calls. She felt extremely uncomfortable and did not want to talk to the defendant. She told him not to contact her. If she did not answer the telephone, the defendant would call repeatedly and leave messages each time until she finally answered. The defendant threatened to ruin Olson's marriage and sabotage her employment.

In August 2001, Olson contacted the Temple Police Department. She met with Officer Steven Duval and expressed her desire that the defendant cease contact. On August 18, 2001, Officer Duval spoke with the defendant about the situation. Nonetheless, the defendant continued to pursue contact with Olson.

In October 2001, Olson obtained a protective order prohibiting the defendant from contacting her. Notwithstanding the protective order, the defendant continued to call her. Olson testified that between the fall of 2001 and June 2003, the defendant placed more unwanted calls to her than she could estimate. The defendant also sent Olson packages, which she did not open. As a result, Olson frequently contacted the Temple police.

On June 11, 2003, the defendant called Olson. She again told the defendant not to contact her. Nevertheless, he called back and left several lengthy messages on Olson's answering machine. In a 7:15 p.m. message on June 11, the defendant said, among other things, that the anger he had shown in court was not towards Olson, but that he "had a lot of anger towards [her]." He also acknowledged that he said and wrote "a lot of things."

In a 7:18 p.m. message on June 11, the defendant admitted that he had previously misrepresented himself to Olson's husband in order to obtain personal information about her and about her marriage. The defendant then said:

> I don't care if the police come and arrest me. I don't care if I go to court. And I don't care if I get seven years or 70 years. This means so much to me to tell, tell you that I'm terribly sorry and remorseful and I don't care if I rot in hell. And I know I will die in, in jail. I do not have to worry about spending seven years of my life in jail because I know unequivocally that I will die within a few months. I will die in prison because my health is very poor, and I'm not saying that for sympathy. I've lost a lot of weight. I haven't been eating a thing since Tuesday after I got out of court with you. I have not—

At 7:21 p.m. on June 11, the defendant called again and continued:

> You know, as I was saying before, I don't, I honestly don't care and I've made the decision now, I know this is very severe and even stupid of me to call you, but I basically don't care because I, I consider on August the 13th of 2001, when you broke up with me, that my life had changed drastically. It's not gotten any better and I realize that was like, you know, that was like the nail in the coffin for me. I, I'm already dead and jail is just a place to finalize that act.

The defendant then said he "was terribly, terribly sorry over the bad things that he did, then [*sic*] it was worth rotting in jail for, and [he] would do it again in a heartbeat." The defendant said that "he had a lot of demons inside" but that he was not a violent person and "never entertained the thoughts of hurting [Olson]." He also admitted that he was stopped while traveling to her home late at night.

After listening to these messages, Olson called the police department and Officer Duval came to her home. Olson received another telephone call from the defendant just as Officer Duval arrived. Officer Duval took the telephone and spoke with the defendant for about twenty minutes. Even after speaking with Officer Duval, the defendant called again and left a fourth message at 7:55 p.m. on June 11. In that message, the defendant said, "I just had a lengthy conversation with that moron, Duval. They're coming to arrest me." The defendant also said that he would be "prosecuted and face a felony charge" and stated that he would pray for Olson every night. Officer Duval left the residence at approximately 8:11 p.m. However, Officer Duval returned at 8:49 p.m. to respond to a 911 call made by Olson.

While the record is silent as to what Olson reported to Officer Duval, he observed that Olson appeared upset.

Olson arrived home on June 17, 2003, to find twenty new messages from the defendant on her answering machine. At 12:15 p.m., the defendant left a message that he "was not going to jail for seven years." At 12:23 p.m., the defendant said he was "sorry it had to come to this." At 12:28 p.m., he implored Olson "not to return the things that are coming in the mail." At 12:32 p.m., 12:36 p.m., 12:39 p.m., 12:45 p.m. and 12:47 p.m., the defendant asked whether Olson was home and begged her to answer the telephone. At 12:53 p.m., the defendant said that he was sorry that he did not have her anymore, that he lost everything that he loved and that he caused her "so much pain and anguish." At 12:56 p.m., 12:58 p.m., 1:02 p.m., 1:05 p.m., 1:19 p.m., 1:25 p.m., 1:32 p.m., 1:39 p.m., 1:51 p.m., 1:59 p.m. and 2:15 p.m., the defendant again asked whether Olson was home and begged her to answer his calls. She immediately called the police department and Officer Duval came to her home. The next day, Olson called Officer Duval to report that she had received two packages from the defendant. On June 24, Olson reported to Officer Duval that she had received yet another package and a letter from the defendant. The defendant continued to call Olson and, on one occasion, the defendant said "I love you" to her.

In October 2003, a Hillsborough County Grand Jury indicted the defendant on one count of stalking under RSA 633:3–a, I(a), which criminalizes "knowingly . . . engag[ing] in a course of conduct targeted at a specific person which would cause a reasonable person to fear for his or her personal safety . . . and the person is actually placed in such fear." RSA 633:3–a, I(a) (Supp.2005). The State had to prove at trial that: (1) the defendant knowingly engaged in a course of conduct; (2) targeted at Olson; (3) which would cause a reasonable person to fear for his or her personal safety; and (4) which actually placed Olson in fear for her personal safety. *See id.*

After the State rested, the defendant moved to dismiss the charge, contending that the State failed to prove the elements of the crime. The trial court denied the motion. The court denied the defendant's renewed motion on the same grounds at the conclusion of the evidence. After the jury found the defendant guilty, the defendant moved to set aside the verdict, asserting essentially the same grounds. The trial court denied the motion.

On appeal, the defendant argues: (1) the State failed to present sufficient evidence to support the jury's verdict; and (2) the trial court erred in denying his motions to dismiss and/or to set aside the verdict.

We first examine the defendant's argument that there was insufficient evidence to support a finding that his conduct: (1) would cause a reasonable person to fear for his or her personal safety; and (2) actually placed Olson in fear for her personal safety. The defendant carries the burden of proving that no rational trier of fact, viewing the evidence in the light most favorable to the State, could have found guilt beyond a reasonable doubt. *State v. Littlefield,* 152 N.H. 331, 350, 876 A.2d 712 (2005) (reviewing sufficiency of evidence underlying the trial court's denial of defendant's motion to dismiss); *State v. Small,* 150 N.H. 457, 464, 843 A.2d 932 (2004) (reviewing sufficiency of evidence underlying the jury verdict).

The defendant argues that we must interpret the phrase, "fear for his or her personal safety," as used in the stalking statute, to require a fear of physical violence. *See* RSA 633:3–a, I(a). We need not reach the defendant's argument, however, because even if the term "fear for his or her personal safety" means a fear of physical violence, the evidence was sufficient to prove that the defendant's conduct would cause a reasonable person, and actually caused Olson, to fear physical violence by the defendant.

The defendant contends that his conduct would not cause a reasonable person to fear physical violence because he never assaulted Olson or explicitly threatened her with violence, and he "mostly apologized and expressed his continuing love" in his repeated telephone calls to her. We disagree.

Even in the absence of an explicit verbal threat of physical violence, a reasonable person could view the defendant's unrelenting telephone calls and gifts to Olson, especially in light of the defendant's articulated history of emotional instability, as evidence that the defendant was obsessed with Olson and posed a threat of physical violence to her. The defendant and Olson never had a personal relationship. In the fall of 2001, the defendant started repeatedly calling her. If she did not answer the telephone, he left message after message until she answered. Olson told the defendant to stop, and finally resorted to calling the police. In August 2001, Officer Duval spoke to the defendant but he continued to call Olson anyway. Olson obtained a restraining order in October 2001, but the defendant continued to call her. In fact, Olson testified that she could not estimate the number of unwanted telephone calls that the defendant initiated between the fall of 2001 and June 2003. He told Olson that he felt suicidal and out of control. During this time, the defendant obtained highly personal information about Olson by misrepresenting himself to her husband. He was also stopped while traveling to her home late at night.

On June 11, 2003, the defendant left several lengthy telephone messages on her answering machine, prompting Olson again to call the police department. Even after Officer Duval arrived at Olson's home and spoke with the defendant on the telephone, the defendant continued to call Olson. No more than thirty minutes after Officer Duval left Olson's home, the defendant again upset Olson, prompting her to call 911.

The defendant's conduct continued to escalate. On June 17, 2003, the defendant left twenty messages for Olson on her answering machine between 12:15 p.m. and 2:15 p.m. In sixteen of those calls, the defendant repeatedly asked Olson if she was present in her home and begged her to answer the telephone. Olson immediately called the police. In the ensuing days, the defendant also sent Olson multiple packages and at least one letter, and continued to call her.

The evidence demonstrates that the defendant obsessively called and sent packages to Olson for several years even though Olson, the police, and the courts repeatedly and explicitly told him not to do so. He also communicated that he was emotionally unstable and suicidal. Viewing all of the evidence and reasonable inferences therefrom in the light most favorable to the State, we conclude that there was sufficient evidence to prove beyond a reasonable doubt that the defendant's conduct would cause a reasonable person to fear for his or her personal safety.

Next, the defendant argues the State failed to prove that his conduct caused Olson actually to fear for her personal safety. At trial, the State asked Olson about the impact of the defendant's conduct upon her. Olson answered, "I live in fear every day. I don't know—I don't know what's going to happen next, or what [the defendant is] going to do." Both Olson and Officer Duval testified that Olson frequently contacted the police between August 2001 and June 2003 as a result of the defendant's conduct. In denying the defense motion to dismiss, the trial court twice noted that Olson's testimony and demeanor on the witness stand, particularly when testifying as to the effect of the defendant's conduct, gave rise to a reasonable inference that Olson actually feared the defendant.

Viewing all of the evidence and reasonable inferences drawn therefrom in the light most favorable to the State, we conclude that there was sufficient evidence to prove beyond a reasonable doubt that the defendant's conduct actually caused Olson to fear for her personal safety. See Small, 150 N.H. at 465, 843 A.2d 932. Accordingly, the jury properly convicted the defendant of stalking in violation of RSA 633:3–a, I(a) and the trial court properly denied the defendant's motions to dismiss and to set aside the verdict.

Affirmed.

DISCUSSION QUESTIONS

1.   What is the mental state required for this offense?

2.   How broadly does this offense apply? What if a stalker never made any sort of threat? Should some sort of threatening behavior be required?

3.   What role, if any, should understandings about mental illness play in the definition of this offense? In charging decisions by the prosecutor?

E. FALSE IMPRISONMENT

- Unlawful

- Intentional

- Confinement of Another Person

- Without his or her Consent

Assume you decide to lock your roommate in her room until she finally catches up to you in binge-watching your favorite Netflix show. (You really hate to watch those episodes alone.) Unless she agrees to be locked in, you have committed the crime of false imprisonment, even though she is being locked in her own room.

F. KIDNAPPING

All the elements of false imprisonment are contained within the crime of kidnapping (making it a lesser included offense), but an additional element is required.

- False Imprisonment AND

- Movement of Victim OR

- Concealment of the Victim

If you drag your roommate out of her bedroom and lock her in your room you have graduated from false imprisonment (often just a misdemeanor) up to kidnapping (usually a felony). That is it! No ransom notes or guns or secret hideouts required. Also, note that you only have to forcibly move the victim a short distance for false imprisonment to morph into kidnapping. Shame that they won't let you watch Netflix in prison.

Remember that kidnapping is one of the felonies that support felony murder liability. It is considered inherently dangerous, does not merge, and is often enumerated in any event. So if your roommate bumps her (eggshell) head and dies as you drag her to her Netflix session you may just have committed felony murder.

Remember though that felonious assaults or batteries generally do not support felony murder because they "merge" into the homicide and involve no independent felonious purpose.

Practice Problem 24.0: Just for Kicks

Billy is a sixteen-year-old public high school student. He has been placed in a "Special Needs" class for students with cognitive or emotional disorders. Billy's special needs involve difficulties in concentration and poor impulse control. He has a particular problem controlling his anger. He has been in therapy and on medication for these conditions since he was ten.

As part of his therapy, Billy has been intensively studying Karate for the last four years. Karate has improved Billy's concentration, self-confidence, and sense of security. He has developed a high level of proficiency in Karate for a sixteen-year-old, and he has recently taken to staging impromptu demonstrations for his classmates. They are particularly impressed by his ability to make high acrobatic kicks. Billy is quite small for his age and otherwise very poor at sports, so he very much enjoys being able to show his fellow students what he is capable of. At no point during any of these demonstrations has he ever struck or even aimed a kick at another person. He simply delivers a series of high-flying kicks into the air.

Billy's Special Needs Teacher, Ms. Daisy, has seen Billy give these demonstrations during lunchtime on several occasions. After the first demonstration she counseled and warned him that martial arts displays violated the school's written antiviolence policy. She expressly forbade him from performing any more demonstrations in the lunchroom. Billy persisted in giving these lunchroom demonstrations, however, and she disciplined him several times for this behavior. After the last demonstration, she had him arrested by the school deputy sheriff. He was charged and convicted with Misdemeanor Disorderly Conduct in a school. Since that arrest he has stopped doing the lunchroom demonstrations, but he has become sullen and somewhat surly around Ms. Daisy.

One day during class time, Ms. Daisy has to leave the classroom suddenly because she begins to feel faint. With no adult in the room, Billy walks to the front of the class and challenges any student in the class to try and punch him without getting kicked. Nick, a tall seventeen-year-old who is a good friend of Billy's, accepts the challenge but says that he wants to make sure that this is just a game and not a fight. Billy and Nick agree that they will pull their punches and kicks and that no one will get hurt.

Nick repeatedly tries to dart in and tap Billy with his fists. Billy drives him back with high swinging kicks. The kicks are at head level but fall several inches short and have the effect of keeping Nick back. Everyone is having a good time although things seem to be happening faster and faster, and the on looking students have now crowded around occasionally bumping into the two boys.

Suddenly, one of Billy's kicks connects squarely with Nick's jaw breaking it and knocking him down. It is unclear whether Billy miscalculated, or whether Nick miscalculated, or whether Nick was jostled forward into the path of the kick. At the moment Billy's kick connects, Ms. Daisy walks back into the room. While Billy is walking with a stunned look on his face towards the fallen Nick, Ms. Daisy grabs Billy from behind as she starts to speak. (Billy had his back towards her and did not see her walk into the room; Ms. Daisy could not see Billy's face as he approached Nick.) Without turning around, Billy instantly strikes her hard with his elbow in the rib cage.

Nick suffered a broken jaw but only a very mild concussion. His jaw is expected to mend completely although there is a possibility that he may experience a little "clicking sound" when he opens his mouth widely. He has also lost three teeth that will have to be replaced by either a bridge or implants.

Ms. Daisy has a broken rib. While her broken rib will heal, the great force of this blow to her torso aggravated her Muscular Sclerosis. Before the attack she experienced pain as the result of her MS only on an intermittent basis. During the weeks since the attack she has experienced MS related pain on a daily basis, and her doctor cannot say whether or when the pain will subside.

Billy has been charged with each of the following crimes against Ms. Daisy and Nick: 1) Assault; 2) Assault with Intent to Inflict Serious Injury; 3) Assault Inflicting Grave Bodily Harm. The relevant statutory provisions follow.

Assault: A person is guilty of this offense if they unlawfully strike another.

Assault with Intent to Inflict Serious Injury: A person is guilty of this offense if they commit an assault with the intent to inflict serious injury. Serious injury is defined as any injury that causes great pain or suffering, even if temporary.

Assault Inflicting Grave Bodily Harm: A person is guilty of this offense if they intentionally commit an assault that inflicts grave bodily harm. Grave bodily harm is defined as bodily injury that creates a substantial risk of death, or that causes serious permanent disfigurement, coma, a permanent or protracted condition that causes extreme pain, or permanent or protracted loss or impairment of the function of any bodily member or organ, or that results in prolonged hospitalization.

Case law has in the past defined "serious injury" to include a broken bone, a cut that required several or more stitches, and a lost tooth. "Grave bodily harm" is a new term and has not yet been interpreted in the case law. Discuss Billy's liability for these charges in a common law jurisdiction.

CHAPTER 25

PROPERTY CRIMES

■ ■ ■

Property crimes are a staple of criminal law practice (and most bar exams). People like to mess with other people's stuff, but there are more ways of messing with other people's stuff than you might think. The result is a series of different types of crime against property, and the trick is to distinguish one from the other.

Most property crimes orbit around behavior that the common person would simply consider to be different forms of "stealing." These are the different crimes that constitute "stealing."

- Larceny

- Embezzlement

- Obtaining Property by False Pretenses

- Forgery

- Robbery

Sometimes the difference lies in the nature of the thing taken, sometimes in the nature of the taking. In the case of robbery, the difference is the combination of assault and larceny. We all know stealing when we see it; we just need to learn the different labels for it that the law uses.

In an attempt to simplify things, a number of jurisdictions (including the Model Penal Code) have passed into law a consolidated theft statute which covers all of this ground. Such statutes can be somewhat unwieldy, however, and this is one reform that has not really caught on.

The two other important crimes in this area are crimes *against* property as opposed to crimes *of* property.

- Burglary

- Arson

Burglary, as we have discussed earlier is basically the combination of trespassing with a felonious or larcenous intent. Arson is a particularly serious and dangerous form of destruction of property.

As is always the case, each of these crimes can be understood in terms of the elements of a guilty hand moved by a guilty mind. Keeping an eye on the finer points of the definitions of conduct and mental state is particularly important.

A. LARCENY

- Wrongful Taking and

- Carrying Away of

- Personal Property of

- Another with the

- Intent to Permanently Deprive the Owner of It.

Larceny is simply the heart of what most people think of as stealing or theft. Shoplifters commit larceny. So did that kid in the fifth grade who used to steal the cookies out of your lunch when you were not looking.

That said, each of the elements listed above does important work, so you don't want to take larceny for granted.

1. TAKING

Larceny first requires that you take something. Picking it up could be taking it, but destroying something would not be taking it. Taking also means that you take it from someone else's possession. The person possessing the thing need not be the owner, but it can't of course be you. If you already have possession of something you may end up being guilty of a property crime, but it won't be larceny. (See embezzlement below.) Property that is abandoned is in no one's possession and cannot be "taken," but property that is merely lost can be taken because the law considers it to be in the "constructive possession" of the owner.

The taking must be wrongful or "trespassory." If your roommate told you that you could borrow her dress anytime you wanted to, then you can't be guilty of larceny when you remove it from her closet.

2. LARCENY BY TRICK

You can't "trick" your way out of larceny by deceit. Say you deceive someone at a party that the last umbrella left in the umbrella stand is yours, not theirs. They hand you the umbrella, and you run outside laughing about how gullible they are. Don't laugh too hard because in addition to being quite a jerk you have just committed the crime of "larceny by trick," a crime created by law to deal with people who do not "take" things but lie their way into being given them.

3. ASPORTATION

Let's go back to you and your roommate's dress. If she did not give you permission to take the dress but happened upon you just as you picked it up you are not yet guilty of larceny. While you have taken it you have not yet carried it away. The fancy legal term for the carrying away requirement is "asportation." (Try throwing that one around at the next party you go to.) "Where did you "asport" my coat when I came in.) Asportation requires some slight movement, but it does require movement from one place to another. If she caught you walking out of the door to her room with it you would now have taken *and* "asported" it.

4. PERSONAL PROPERTY

One cannot commit larceny against land or its fixtures. One also cannot commit larceny of intangible things. If you sneak into the next big (fill in your favorite band's name here) concert without paying you are not guilty of larceny because the experience of the performance is not tangible property. You better take off running if you see security coming after you though because you are guilty of other crimes (just not ones you are likely to study or be tested on in law school).

5. ANOTHER'S PROPERTY

This trips people up because you actually can be guilty under some circumstances of stealing stuff you own. Imagine that your property is in the lawful *possession* of another. Let's say that you left your suit at the dry cleaner's to get a stain removed before a big interview. After you inspect the suit you decide to run out the door without paying. Well, I am sure you looked great at your interview, but if hired you may have to explain a larceny conviction to your new employer because you just committed larceny. Even though the dry cleaner does not own your suit state law in many jurisdictions gives him the right to retain *custody* and *possession*. That confers upon you the dubious distinction of having stolen your own stuff!

6. INTENT TO PERMANENTLY DEPRIVE

There are a number of ways this intent might be satisfied and a few ways that it can't. Remember that each of the following assumes that the thing was wrongfully taken to begin with.

Equals Intent to Permanently Deprive

- Keeping something.
- Giving or selling it to someone else.
- Destroying it.
- Exposing it to Substantial Risk.

Does Not Equal an Intent to Permanently Deprive

- Borrowing it.
- Slightly using it.

Let's play around with these distinctions a bit. A teenager borrows his Mom's car against his Mom's wishes. That would not be larceny since the teenager is only borrowing it. (Many states have a separate offense for "joyriding" when someone uses another's automobile without permission.) The teenager would be guilty of larceny, however, if at the time of the taking she plans to drag race the car because this would be a substantial risk. Now assume that the teenager borrows her Mom's dress without permission and plans to dance the night away in it. That also would not be larceny since such slight and non-risky use is not the equivalent of permanent deprivation.

7. GOOD FAITH MISTAKES

You cannot intend to permanently deprive another of their property if you believe that what you take is rightfully yours. Assume that as I leave a party I grab the wrong umbrella from the umbrella stand. If I honestly believe that the umbrella is mine then I am not guilty of larceny. What if my umbrella is black and the umbrellas I grab is pink? That would be an unreasonable mistake, but I am still not guilty as long as I *believed in good faith* that the umbrella was mine. In common law terminology, larceny is a *specific intent* crime that requires you to specifically intend to take something that does not belong to you. That means that people who are unreasonably stupid have a complete defense. There is no such thing as recklessly or negligently stealing something. We all understand intuitively that one who steals *knows* that they are taking something that does not belong to them.

Remember though that the more unreasonable your belief the less likely that a jury would believe that you did really believe that you were entitled to possession of the thing. A pink umbrella is pretty far from a black one. Hopefully the jury will believe that I am the stereotypical absent-minded professor.

8. DOCTRINE OF CONTINUING TRESPASS

The requirement that a crime's mental state exist concurrently with a crime's conduct would seem to create a loophole for a certain type of thief. Imagine that you borrow your roommate's dress without her permission fully intending to return it after you wear it once or twice. It looks so darn good on you though that you decide to keep it after receiving just one compliment too many on how it matches your eyes. You would seem to be guilty only of a trespass, not larceny, since you did not intend to permanently deprive your roommate of the dress at the time you took it. Only later did you form the intent required for larceny. Well, the law contains what is really a legal fiction to close that loophole. The law bridges the gap in time between your initial wrongful taking and your subsequent larcenous mental state by finding that the trespass continued until you decided to steal the dress at which point your crime changed from trespass to larceny. Under the doctrine of continuing trespass you would be guilty of larceny.

B. EMBEZZLEMENT

Embezzlement is a trust offense. Basically, it means that you are messing with stuff that other people have entrusted to you. The law calls "messing with stuff" *conversion*. There is no taking involved because the owner entrusted the thing to you.

- Conversion of the
- Personal Property of Another
- By One in lawful Possession
- With the Intent to Defraud

Conversion means any significant interference with the owner's rights in the property and includes selling, consuming, discarding, or badly damaging it. Slight use is not enough. One need not personally gain by the conversion. Donating someone else's property to charity could constitute conversion. Once again property means something tangible, so letting your friends in free into the movie theatre where you work would be some crime other than embezzlement.

Finally, the reason why embezzlement is truly a trust offense is that the element of lawful possession means more than just lawful custody. The owner must have given you some sort of authority over the property. The fraudulent intent requirement is satisfied when you intentionally violate the terms under which the property was entrusted to you.

Say that I park my Ferrari (yeah right!) on a public street and leave the keys in it. If someone jumps in and drives off then that would be larceny. If I park it in a paid parking lot and the valet parking attendant takes it for a hundred mile spin around the outskirts of Chicago (shades of "Ferris Bueller's Day Off") then that would be embezzlement. When I handed the parking attendant the keys I invested him with the authority to drive the car to a parking space. When he abused that trust by heavily using and thereby converting the car to his own use he committed the crime of embezzlement.

C. OBTAINING PROPERTY BY FALSE PRETENSES

The difference here is what you get and how you get it. First, this crime requires that you obtain *ownership*, not just custody or possession, of something. Second, you don't take it but trick someone into giving it to you.

- Knowingly False Representation of
- Present or Past (but *Not* Future) Fact

- Causing Victim to Pass Title to Defendant

Essentially the defendant gets the victim to give the defendant ownership of something by lying about something important. The lie cannot be a false promise, however. The fact falsely represented must be a present or past one. So if I drop by the car dealership and convince a gullible salesperson to give me the pink slip to a new Ferrari (the parking attendant really banged up mine) by telling the salesperson that I paid his colleague in cash the previous week then the crime would be complete. If I tell him instead that I will pay him next week (knowing full well that I can't on a professor's salary) then we have a breach of contract or possibly a fraud case but not this crime.

Note that this crime does important work that larceny ordinarily does not. When the police pull me over in *my* new Ferrari after my lie has been discovered it will not do me any good to waive the pink slip at them and tell them that the car is not stolen. I am not going to jail for larceny but for obtaining property by false pretenses. Oh, what tangled webs we weave when we deceive in order to get those shiny, flashy things we covet!

1. LARCENY BY TRICK DISTINGUISHED

Earlier I mentioned that stealing something by tricking them into giving it to you is considered larceny by trick in many jurisdictions. The difference between larceny by trick and obtaining property by false pretenses is that you only obtain possession in larceny by trick—not title and ownership.

What crime occurs when you obtain ownership by knowingly writing a bad check? Most jurisdictions treat that as larceny by trick on the grounds that title does not pass until the check is successfully cashed. So the bad-check writer walks out of the store with possession but not ownership.

On a related note, obtaining property by use of an unauthorized or stolen credit card is deal with in most jurisdictions by a specific statute.

D. FORGERY AND WRITING BAD CHECKS

Speaking of bad checks, two different crimes ordinarily come into play here. First, many jurisdictions have specific statutory crimes for writing a check against insufficient funds in one's bank account. These statutes require that you *know* that the check will "bounce" and that you *intend to defraud* the recipient of the check thereby. So bad arithmetic in balancing your checkbook is a defense!

Writing a bad check also is included within forgery ordinarily although forgery encompasses lots of other types of behavior as well, obviously.

- Making or Altering
- A Legally Significant Writing

- With the Intent to Defraud

Note that forgery includes altering as well as making a document. So you don't need to steal someone's checkbook and write out a check from scratch in order to be guilty. Just wait for them to write you a check and add a couple of zeroes to the amount! Both count equally as forgeries under the criminal law.

E. CONSOLIDATED THEFT STATUTES

Not surprisingly some jurisdictions have grown weary of keeping all of these common law crimes straight for judges, prosecutors, juries and the public. These jurisdictions have consolidated the theft crimes discussed into a single "theft" statute. Sometimes these consolidations change the requirements of the particular crimes in order to iron out inconsistencies or gaps. Other times the statutes simply create different sections for each type of theft crime under one omnibus statute in order to simplify charging and proof at trial.

Case in Context

The following case illustrates how a consolidated theft statute operates in practice.

COMMONWEALTH V. JAMES O. MILLS

Supreme Judicial Court of Massachusetts, Suffolk
436 Mass. 387 (2002)

Following a jury trial, the defendant was found guilty of three counts of larceny from the city of Boston, in violation of G.L. c. 266, § 30; two counts of larceny by false pretenses from the Committee for Public Counsel Services (CPCS), in violation of G.L. c. 266, § 30; three counts of perjury, in violation of G.L. c. 268, § 1A; three counts of pension fraud, in violation of G.L. c. 32, § 18; two counts of procurement fraud, in violation of G.L. c. 266, § 67A; two counts of making false claims, in violation of G.L. c. 266, § 67B; and four counts of failure to make tax returns, in violation of G.L. c. 62C, § 73(c). Based on the five larceny convictions, the judge adjudicated the defendant a "common and notorious thief" pursuant to G.L. c. 266, § 40, and sentenced him to serve not less than eighteen and not more than twenty years in prison with various lesser concurrent sentences on the remaining charges. The defendant filed a timely notice of appeal. The Appeals Court (1) reversed the judgment as to the indictment alleging three counts of larceny from the retirement board of the city of Boston (board), set aside those verdicts, and entered judgment for the defendant on those counts; (2) reversed the adjudication of the defendant as a common and notorious thief and vacated the sentence under G.L. c. 266, § 40; and (3) remanded the case to the Superior Court for resentencing by a different judge on the remaining indictments. *Commonwealth v. Mills,* 51

Mass.App.Ct. 366, 745 N.E.2d 981 (2001). We granted the Commonwealth's application for further appellate review. The issues now before us are whether the judge (1) erred in denying the defendant's motion for a required finding of not guilty with respect to the three counts of larceny from the board; (2) erred by adjudicating the defendant a common and notorious thief; and (3) considered improper factors, including the defendant's exercise of his right to remain silent, when sentencing the defendant. We reverse the judgments as to the three counts of larceny from the board (no. 96-11037-002), and remand those matters for a new trial; we vacate the adjudication of the defendant as a common and notorious thief, which was dependent on the three counts of larceny from the board; and we remand the remaining convictions to the Superior Court for resentencing by a different judge.

1. *Background.* The defendant retired in 1978 from the Boston police department after he was diagnosed with hypertensive heart disease. He applied for and received from the board a nontaxable accidental disability pension of approximately $15,500 per year. The defendant then began to run a private investigation business, Mills Investigations, Inc. (Mills Investigations), out of his home in New Hampshire.

During 1993, 1994, and 1995, the defendant spent every business day at the Middlesex Superior Court, either in the court room assigned to clerk-magistrate Joseph Marshall or in Marshall's office. Beginning in April, 1994, Marshall handled most of the appointments of counsel for indigent defendants and motions for investigation funds. When the designated bar advocate was not in the courtroom, Marshall would deviate from the master list and appoint one attorney from among a group of four who were typically in the courtroom. Those four attorneys moved for investigation funds in every one of their cases and always retained the services of Mills Investigations. Marshall "rubber-stamped" his allowance of these motions off the record and in his back office where the defendant usually spent three hours a day socializing with Marshall.

For fiscal year 1993, the defendant billed CPCS for approximately $107,000 for investigative services. For fiscal year 1994, the defendant billed CPCS for approximately $197,000, representing 5,483 hours of investigative services. On forty-four occasions, the defendant submitted bills with more than twenty-four hours of work attributed to a single day. For fiscal year 1995, the defendant billed CPCS for approximately $359,000, representing 10,057 hours of investigative services. The defendant submitted 211 bills in which he claimed to have worked well over twenty-four hours in a single day (with some days as long as seventy-two hours).

Between 1992 and 1994, the defendant received approximately $45,000 in nontaxable accidental disability benefits from the board. Once approved for a disability pension, the only limitation to keeping the full amount received each year is the amount of income the recipient earns, if any, during that same time period. Following receipt of pension benefits, every disability pensioner is required by statute to file with the board a yearly earnings report, signed under the pains and penalties of perjury. See G.L. c. 32, § 91A. The board calculates an earned income limitation for each disability pensioner, and the pensioner must refund a dollar's worth of pension for each dollar of income over the established limit. To collect money owed as a refund, the board sends bills to pensioners requesting remittance of a check in the appropriate amount. If the pensioner does not respond, the board withholds the amount due from the current pension distribution as security until payment is properly received.

The board estimated that the defendant could earn up to $30,228 in 1992, $30,820 in 1993, and $32,484 in 1994 before being liable for any refunds. For 1992, the defendant withdrew $89,637 from the corporate account of Mills Investigations for his own personal use; he reported to the board that he had earned a total of $25,000. For 1993, the defendant withdrew $65,640 from the corporate account of Mills Investigations for his own personal use; he reported to the board that he had earned a total of $17,500. For 1994, the defendant withdrew $104,494 from the corporate account of Mills Investigations for his own personal use; he reported to the board that he had earned a total of $30,000. As a result of the defendant under-reporting his earnings, the board never sought a refund of any pension money.

2. *Motion for required finding of not guilty.* At the close of the Commonwealth's case, the defendant presented a general motion for required findings of not guilty. The motion was denied. The defense rested without presenting any evidence, the defendant renewed his motion, and it was again denied.

The defendant now asserts that the Superior Court judge erred in denying his motion for a required finding of not guilty with respect to the larceny indictment charging him with three counts of stealing the property of the city of Boston when he submitted false earnings reports to the board. He contends that while making such fraudulent statements would violate criminal statutes for perjury, see G.L. c. 268, § 1A, and pension fraud, see G.L. c. 32, § 18, such conduct did not constitute larceny. The defendant argues that he obtained his accidental disability pension payments lawfully. What he did was make it unlikely that the board would demand a refund and hold his future pension payments as security therefor. See G.L. c. 32, § 91A. The defendant also asserts that because the judge erred in denying his motion for required findings of not guilty, his adjudication as a common and notorious thief should be vacated because only two larceny convictions (from CPCS) would remain. See note 2, *supra.*

In his general motion for a required finding of not guilty, the defendant stated that the evidence produced by the Commonwealth was insufficient to prove beyond a reasonable doubt that he had committed the offenses as charged in the indictments. Pursuant to Mass. R.Crim. P. 25, as amended, 420 Mass. 1502 (1995), "[t]he judge on motion of a defendant . . . shall enter a finding of not guilty of the offense charged in an indictment . . . after the evidence on either side is closed if the evidence is insufficient as a matter of law to sustain a conviction on the charge." See *Commonwealth v. Andrews,* 427 Mass. 434, 440, 694 N.E.2d 329 (1998). The pertinent indictment herein, for three counts of larceny under G.L. c. 266, § 30, charged the defendant with *stealing* the property of the city of Boston, namely "money or a release of a claim to money, the value of which exceeded $250." "[T]he word 'steal' has become 'a term of art and includes the criminal taking or conversion' by way either of larceny, embezzlement or obtaining by false pretenses." *Commonwealth v. King,* 202 Mass. 379, 385, 88 N.E. 454 (1909), quoting *Commonwealth v. Kelley,* 184 Mass. 320, 324, 68 N.E. 346 (1903). These three formerly separate crimes have been merged into the one crime of larceny as defined in G.L. c. 266, § 30. See *Commonwealth v. King, supra* at 388, 88 N.E. 454. Larceny can be established by evidence that would have warranted a conviction upon any one of the three formerly separate charges. *Id.* See *Commonwealth v. Nadal-Ginard,* 42 Mass.App.Ct. 1, 5 n. 6, 674 N.E.2d 645 (1997) ("Despite the merger of all types of larcenies in a single statute, G.L. c. 266, § 30, the distinctions among the former separate crimes of larceny, obtaining property by false pretenses and embezzlement may not have been wholly obliterated, but at the very least the evidence adduced must be sufficient to prove the elements of one or the other of the former separate crimes"); *Commonwealth v. Kelly,* 24 Mass.App.Ct. 181, 183, 507 N.E.2d 777 (1987) (one who commits any of three offenses of stealing, embezzlement, or obtaining property by false pretenses shall be guilty of "larceny"). The purpose of the merger of these three common-law crimes of "stealing" into one statutory crime was to eliminate the possibility that a defendant indicted for one of the crimes would escape punishment if the proof at trial established another of the crimes. See *Commonwealth v. King, supra* at 388, 88 N.E. 454; *Commonwealth v. Kelly, supra* at 184, 507 N.E.2d 777.

General Laws c. 277, § 41, provides: "In an indictment for criminal dealing with personal property with intent to steal, an allegation that the defendant stole said property shall be sufficient; and such indictment may be supported by proof that the defendant committed larceny of the property, or embezzled it, or obtained it by false pretenses." Thus, "[t]he statute explicitly permits convictions to be supported by evidence that the defendant's theft was committed in any manner condemned by the law." *Commonwealth v. Nadal-Ginard, supra* at 6, 674 N.E.2d 645. See *Commonwealth v. Corcoran,* 348 Mass. 437, 440–441, 204 N.E.2d 289 (1965); *Commonwealth v. Kenneally,* 10 Mass.App.Ct. 162, 172, 176, 406 N.E.2d 714 (1980), *S.C.,* 383 Mass. 269, 418 N.E.2d 1224, cert. denied, 454 U.S. 849, 102 S.Ct. 170, 70 L.Ed.2d 138 (1981).

The Commonwealth was not ordered to elect its theory of the manner in which the alleged larcenies were committed. See *Commonwealth v. Monahan,* 349 Mass. 139, 171, 207 N.E.2d 29 (1965). Cf. *Commonwealth v. Liberty,* 27 Mass.App.Ct. 1, 9, 533 N.E.2d 1383 (1989) "Where a crime can be committed in any one of several ways, an indictment properly charges its commission in all those ways. . . . Then the defendant should be convicted if it is proved that he committed the crime in any of those ways"). To require the Commonwealth to elect a particular theory of larceny would be to continue to afford an opportunity to frustrate the ends of justice in derogation of the specific legislative intent to eliminate the merely technical differences between three cognate and similar offenses. See *Commonwealth v. King, supra* at 388–389, 88 N.E. 454. Here, there was no restriction in the indictment as to what legal theory of the statutory crime of larceny would be established by the evidence. As such, the proof offered by the Commonwealth with respect to the three counts of "stealing" from the board could be used to support any of the theories of larceny. See *Commonwealth v. Corcoran, supra* at 442, 204 N.E.2d 289 (while evidence offered was relevant to proof of embezzlement, it was also adequate to support charge of obtaining title by false pretenses); *Commonwealth v. Kenneally, supra* at 176, 406 N.E.2d 714 (even where Commonwealth proceeded on theory that defendant committed larceny by false pretenses, Commonwealth could prove its case by showing embezzlement or false pretenses).

Our well-established standard of review of the denial of a motion for a required finding of not guilty is "whether, after viewing the evidence in the light most favorable to the prosecution, *any* rational trier of fact could have found the essential elements of the crime beyond a reasonable doubt" (emphasis in original). *Commonwealth v. Latimore,* 378 Mass. 671, 677, 393 N.E.2d 370 (1979), quoting *Jackson v. Virginia,* 443 U.S. 307, 318–319, 99 S.Ct. 2781, 61 L.Ed.2d 560 (1979). Where, as here, a defendant submits a generally expressed motion for a required finding of not guilty, the motion applies to any offense properly charged in the indictment and is correctly denied when the evidence supports any such properly charged offense. See *Commonwealth v. Kalinowski,* 360 Mass. 682, 686, 277 N.E.2d 298 (1971); *Commonwealth v. Domanski,* 332 Mass. 66, 76, 123 N.E.2d 368 (1954). Therefore, we examine whether the Commonwealth presented sufficient evidence to establish the essential elements of at least one form of "stealing," namely larceny, embezzlement, or larceny by false pretenses, beyond a reasonable doubt. If so, then the Superior Court judge did not err in denying the defendant's motion for a required finding of not guilty.

"To support a conviction of larceny under G.L. c. 266, § 30, the Commonwealth is required to prove the 'unlawful taking and carrying away of the personal property of another with the specific intent to deprive the person of the property permanently'" (footnote omitted). *Commonwealth v. Donovan,* 395 Mass. 20, 25–26, 478 N.E.2d 727 (1985), quoting *Commonwealth v. Johnson,* 379 Mass. 177, 181, 396 N.E.2d 974 (1979). See G.L. c. 277, § 39. We agree with the well-reasoned analysis of the Appeals Court that filing false earnings reports with the board does not constitute a trespassory taking of money, and the "release of a claim to money" is not property within the meaning of G.L. c. 266, § 30(2), or the common law. See *Commonwealth v. Mills, supra* at 371–372, 745 N.E.2d 981.

With respect to embezzlement, the evidence should establish that the defendant "fraudulently converted" to his personal use property that was under his control by virtue of a position of "trust or confidence" and did so with the intent to deprive the owner of the property permanently. See *Commonwealth v. Nadal-Ginard, supra* at 7–8, 674 N.E.2d 645. See also *Commonwealth v. Hays,* 80 Mass. 62, 14 Gray 62, 64 (1859) ("The statutes relating to embezzlement . . . do not apply to cases where the element of a breach of trust or confidence in the fraudulent conversion of money or chattels is not shown to exist"). Contrary to the Commonwealth's argument that the Appeals Court added a new element to the crime of embezzlement, the existence of a confidential or fiduciary relationship between the embezzler and the victim has always been at the heart of this crime. See *Mickelson v. Barnet,* 390 Mass. 786, 790, 460 N.E.2d 566 (1984) (conversion was embezzlement where nature of relationship was that of agent and principal); *Commonwealth v. King, supra* at 391–392, 88 N.E. 454 relationship necessary to crime of embezzlement one of trust and confidence); *Commonwealth v. Ryan,* 155 Mass. 523, 526–527, 530, 30 N.E. 364 (1892) (fraudulent conversion of property by one entrusted with its possession constitutes embezzlement). Compare *Commonwealth v. Barry,* 124 Mass. 325, 327 (1878) ("If a person honestly receives the possession of the goods, chattels or money of another upon any trust, express or implied, and, after receiving them, fraudulently converts them to his own use, he may be guilty of the crime of embezzlement"); *Commonwealth v. Kenneally, supra* at 177, 406 N.E.2d 714 (defendant who legally obtains money from client and later forms intent to keep it may be guilty of embezzlement). The fraudulent conversion of property by parties who merely have a debtor-creditor relationship does not constitute embezzlement. See *Mickelson v. Barnet, supra* at 790, 460 N.E.2d 566; *Commonwealth v. King, supra* at 391–392, 88 N.E. 454; *Commonwealth v. Snow,* 284 Mass. 426, 430–432, 187 N.E. 852 (1933).

The defendant's filing of false earnings reports with the board, conduct intended to eliminate the possibility that the board would demand a refund of a portion of his annual accidental disability pension because of his earned income, does not establish the essential elements of embezzlement. Pursuant to G.L. c. 32, § 13(1)(*b*), "[p]ayments under any annuity, pension or retirement allowance . . . shall be due and payable for the month on the last day of each month during the continuance of such annuity, pension or retirement allowance, as the case may be." General Laws c. 32, § 91A, provides that "[e]very person pensioned or retired under any general or special law for disability, including accidental disability, shall in each year on or before April fifteenth subscribe, under the penalties of perjury, and file with the [public employee retirement administration] commission a statement . . . certifying the full amount of his earnings from earned income during the preceding year." If such earnings exceed a predetermined amount, said person "shall refund the portion of his retirement allowance for such preceding year equal to such excess and until such refund is made, his pension or retirement allowance shall be held as security therefor." *Id.* This procedure establishes a debtor-creditor relationship between the recipient of a disability retirement allowance and the board. The recipient is lawfully entitled to a specified amount on a monthly basis. If, after submitting an earned income statement, it is determined that the recipient should have received a smaller disability retirement allowance because of other earned income, the recipient then must refund a portion of it to the board and future distributions will be withheld until that debt has been satisfied.

At the time the defendant filed his annual earnings reports with the board on or about April 15, 1993, April 4, 1994, and April 28, 1995, he was not "fraudulently converting" money that was under his control by virtue of a position of "trust or confidence." The money he received was merely the distribution of a government benefit to which he was lawfully entitled each month for his own personal use and to which, at the time of receipt, he obtained complete title and possession. By filing false earnings reports, the defendant was ensuring that he would not have to pay a reimbursement to the board and would not be subjected to any subsequent withholdings. While such conduct certainly constitutes perjury, see G.L. c. 268, § 1A, and pension fraud, see G.L. c. 32, § 18, it is not embezzlement.

The Commonwealth contends that the nature of the relationship between an alleged embezzler and a victim is one of fact that falls within the province of the jury to decide. See *Commonwealth v. Snow, supra* at 430–432, 187 N.E. 852 (duty of fact finder to determine whether trust relationship or debtor-creditor relationship existed between mortgage trust company officer and depositors). This would ordinarily be true where, to establish the essential elements of embezzlement, the Commonwealth must show that the defendant acquired control of property through a position of "trust or confidence." See *Commonwealth v. King, supra* at 391–392, 88 N.E. 454 (question of fact for jury was whether dealings between investment broker and customers made him their debtor for money or property, or made him their agent under a trust and confidence to use their money only as specifically directed). In this case, the relationship between the defendant and the board is established, as a matter of law, pursuant to G.L. c. 32, § 91A, to be that of debtor and creditor.

The final "stealing" offense that falls under the larceny statute, G.L. c. 266, § 30, is larceny by false pretenses. A prosecution for larceny by false pretenses requires proof that (1) a false statement of fact was made; (2) the defendant knew or believed that the statement was false when he made it; (3) the defendant intended that the person to whom he made the false statement would rely on it; and (4) the person to whom the false statement was made did rely on it and, consequently, parted with property. See *Commonwealth v. Leonard,* 352 Mass. 636, 644–645, 227 N.E.2d 721 (1967); *Commonwealth v. Monahan,* 349 Mass. 139, 150–151, 207 N.E.2d 29 (1965). See also G.L. c. 277, § 39.

Following his diagnosis of hypertensive heart disease, the defendant applied for, and the board made a determination that he was entitled to, an accidental disability retirement allowance. The Commonwealth has not contested the defendant's lawful entitlement to this benefit. However, when the defendant filed annual earnings reports with the board in 1993, 1994, and 1995, he stated that he had earned far less income than he had actually withdrawn from the corporate account of Mills Investigations for his own personal use. The evidence warrants a finding that the defendant knowingly made such false statements with the intent that the board would rely on them, would determine that he had not exceeded his annual earned income limitations, and, consequently, would continue to pay him the full amount of his accidental disability retirement allowance every year. This is exactly what happened; the defendant's expectations were fulfilled. The defendant's actions resulted in his receiving a greater allowance from the board than that to which he was lawfully entitled and constituted larceny by false pretenses.

We conclude that the judge did not err in denying the defendant's motion for required findings of not guilty with respect to the three counts of larceny from the board. After viewing the evidence in the light most favorable to the Commonwealth, a rational trier of fact could have found the essential elements of larceny by false pretenses beyond a reasonable doubt.

3. *Jury instructions.* The defendant's convictions of "stealing" from the board were based on a theory of traditional larceny because that was the only instruction given to the jury. The jury were not instructed on larceny by false pretenses with respect to this indictment. The Commonwealth did not request further instructions on any other theory of larceny, and the defendant, understandably, did not object to the instructions as given.

"The primary purpose of instructions to a jury is to assist them in the discharge of their responsibility for finding the facts in issue and then in applying to the facts found the applicable rules of law to enable them to render a proper verdict. The instructions should be full, fair and clear as to the issues to be decided by the jury, the rules to be followed by the jury in deciding the facts, and the law they are to apply to the facts found." *Pfeiffer v. Salas,* 360 Mass. 93, 100, 271 N.E.2d 750 (1971). See *Commonwealth v. Key,* 381 Mass. 19, 27, 407 N.E.2d 327 (1980) (jury should be clearly presented with issues of fact raised by evidence and with careful explanation of applicable law). A criminal conviction cannot be affirmed on appeal where the jury were not instructed on the elements of the theory of the crime. See *Commonwealth v. Claudio,* 418 Mass. 103, 117–119, 634 N.E.2d 902 (1994) (omission of essential element from instruction on underlying felony to felony-murder charge, not raised as error below, was of sufficient magnitude, together with omission in joint venture instruction, to warrant relief to avoid miscarriage of justice); *Commonwealth v. Watson,* 388 Mass. 536, 546, 447 N.E.2d 1182 (1983), *S.C.,* 393 Mass. 297, 471 N.E.2d 88 (1984) (judge's failure to instruct jury, in absence of objection, that defendant could be found guilty of felony-murder based on armed robbery only if he knew that accomplice had gun resulted in substantial risk of miscarriage of justice within meaning of G.L. c. 278, § 33E, and necessitated new trial); *Commonwealth v. Colon,* 52 Mass.App.Ct. 725, 730–731, 756 N.E.2d 615 (2001) (judge's failure to instruct jury on essential element of crime of armed robbery based on joint venture theory, in absence of objection, resulted in substantial risk of miscarriage of justice).

Precise instructions to the jury on the Commonwealth's *theory* of how the defendant "stole" from the board were critical because traditional larceny, embezzlement, and larceny by false pretenses have different required elements. The jury herein did not have the benefit of the applicable law, namely the elements of larceny by false pretenses, so as to be able to render a proper verdict. Because the jury were only given instructions as to traditional larceny, pursuant to which they found the defendant guilty, and because we have already concluded that the filing of false earnings reports with the board does not constitute traditional larceny (only larceny by false pretenses), the defendant's larceny convictions cannot stand. A new trial is required with respect to the indictment charging the defendant with three counts of larceny from the board. In light of this conclusion, the defendant may not be adjudicated a common and notorious thief pursuant to G.L. c. 266, § 40.

. . .

5.   *Conclusion.* The judgments are reversed as to the indictment alleging three counts of larceny from the board (no. 96-11037-002), the verdicts set aside, and the cases remanded for a new trial. The adjudication of the defendant as a common and notorious thief is vacated. The remaining convictions are remanded to the Superior Court for resentencing.

DISCUSSION QUESTIONS

1.   Why did the court reverse one of the larceny convictions?

2.   Do consolidated theft statutes make it easier or harder for juries to make the right decisions?

3.   Should the law treat larceny the same as embezzlement and obtaining property by false pretenses?

Practice Problem 25.1: Drunken Dealings at Downton Abbey

Downton Abbey, a fine English estate, has fallen on hard times. The staff has been greatly reduced, and morale among the servants is very low. Mr. Carson, the head butler is particularly despondent. As head butler his duties include acting as the wine steward for the abbey. The wine steward is responsible for ensuring the quality of wine served, so he is expected to take a small taste of wine before it is served. One night Mr. Carson drowns his sorrows with half of the wine bottle. He gives the rest to Mr. Barrow, a head footman who is responsible for serving the wine at dinner. Seeing that Mr. Carson has partaken so freely, Barrow drinks a glass of the fine wine as soon as he is out of Mr. Carson's sight. What crimes have Carson and Barrow committed?

F. ROBBERY

Think of robbery as a particular type of larceny with a particular type of assault added on. Robbery includes someone walking into a store or bank and demanding money at gunpoint and a mugger who hits you over the head in an alley and takes your money. For reasons that will become apparent, it does not include a pickpocket or someone who grabs money off a store counter and runs out the door.

- Taking the Personal Property of Another
- From their Person or Presence
- Through Force OR
- Through Intimidation
- With the Intent to Permanently Deprive the Victim of the Property

Note first that taking another's property with the intent to permanently deprive is ordinarily larceny. So robbery is simply a more serious form of larceny. It is typically classified as a felony although unarmed robberies are sometimes classified as high level misdemeanors in some jurisdictions.

1. FROM PERSON OR PRESENCE

Robberies can only occur from someone's person or presence. Something in your hand or in a pocket or in contact in some other way with your body or clothing that you are wearing is considered to be on your body. Presence is a bit more complex. The key factors are proximity and control. The basic idea is that had the victim not been threatened or harmed he could have stopped the taking. Pulling a handbag from a little old lady's arm is taking it from her person. Grabbing if off the park bench that she is sitting on is taking it from her presence. Note that a number of modern statutes (including the Model Penal Code) do not require that the taking be from the person or presence.

2. THROUGH FORCE OR INTIMIDATION

Simply snatching the little old lady's handbag from the park bench where she is feeding the pigeons is not enough by itself to make my larceny a robbery at common law. I must either use force intimidation. Note the "or." You need one or the other, not both.

Force is more than simply the physical effort necessary to take and move the object. This is why a pickpocket is not ordinarily a robber. I don't need a gun or a knife or any sort of weapon though. Punching the little old lady in the nose would be enough although I also do not need to inflict any sort of harm upon her. The tougher case is if I just snatch the bag off of her arm. Most cases hold that simply snatching something from another's grasp is not enough. If, however, the victim resists or struggles during the taking, then any amount of force sufficient to overcome that resistance will be enough for a robbery. Even a momentary tug of war would be enough. Again, no injury or harm to the victim is required—simply momentary resistance that is successfully overcome. So make sure that you make a clean grab the next time you decide to go purse snatching.

Intimidation is something entirely different. Here you do not need to even touch the victim. One must simply create a fear of harm. So if I shake my fist in the little old lady's face as I snatch her purse from the park bench she is sitting on then I have probably committed a robbery. I say probably because the law requires for a robbery to occur that the victim *actually be in fear*. Fear here means the apprehension of bodily harm though, not necessarily a state of fright. Imagine that instead of robbing a little old lady I grab the "man purse" of Shaquille O'Neal (a former NBA player who is 7'1" tall and over 300 pounds) from the bench he is sitting on. When I shake my fist at Shaquille he will probably start to laugh, but as long as he expects me to punch him in the face if he tries to rescue his "moorse" a robbery has still occurred. (I better get clean away though or there will be nothing left of me to try.)

3. MENTAL STATE

Mental state is typically not an issue in robbery cases because the conduct essentially speaks for itself. It is hard to imagine someone accidentally threatening someone else and taking their money. Not surprisingly robbery is a general intent offense in common law terms. One need only be aware that one is threatening or hurting another and taking their property. One need not have any particular purpose to be a robber. Sorry Robin Hood, the law does not care why you rob or what you do with the money.

4. ATTEMPTED ROBBERY

Many jurisdictions have defined robbery to include an attempted robbery on the grounds that robbers should not be rewarded with a lesser conviction if their victims successfully resist or otherwise thwart the taking. So if the little old lady wins the tug of war over her purse you still get convicted of a robbery in these jurisdictions.

5. AGGRAVATED ROBBERY

Not surprisingly, many jurisdictions have defined by statute more aggravated forms of robbery by that entail harsher punishments. Typically the aggravating factors include use of a deadly weapon, infliction of bodily harm or the presence of at least one accomplice.

Case in Context

The following case explores the boundaries between robbery and mere larcency.

LEAR V. STATE
Supreme Court of Arizona.
39 Ariz. 313 (1931)

ROSS, J.

The appellant was convicted of robbery. He appeals and assigns as error the insufficiency of the evidence to sustain the conviction and the giving of erroneous instructions.

The prosecuting witness, George Gross, testified that around 7 o'clock on the morning of August 12, 1931, he opened the Campbell Quality Shop, located in Buckeye, Maricopa county; that just about that time appellant entered the store and inquired about purchasing some shirts and shoes; that in the meantime he had taken a box of currency and a bag of silver out of the store safe; had placed the currency in the cash register and the bag of silver on the counter; that, while he was in the act of untying or unrolling the bag of silver, and while it was on the counter, appellant grabbed it from his hands and ran out of the back door; that appellant said no word at the time, exhibited no arms, and used no force other than to grab the bag as stated above. Appellant admitted taking the bag of silver and that it contained $33.

It was the contention of appellant at the trial, and is his contention here, that the facts do not show that he committed the crime of robbery. This crime is defined by our statute, section 4602, Revised Code of 1928, as follows: 'Robbery is the felonious taking of personal property in the possession of another, from his person or immediate presence and against his will, accomplished by means of force or fear. The fear may be either of an unlawful injury to the person or property of the person robbed, or of a relative or member of his family; or of an immediate and unlawful injury to the person or property of any one in the company of the person robbed at the time of the robbery.'

The crimes of robbery and larceny are not the same. The former is classified as a crime against the person and the latter as a crime against property. In robbery there is, in addition to a felonious taking, a violent invasion of the person. If the person is not made to surrender the possession of the personal property by means of force of fear, the dominant element of robbery is not present. The mere taking of property in possession of another, from his person or immediate presence and against his will, is not robbery. Such taking must be accomplished by force or fear to constitute robbery.

The element of fear is not in the case. Appellant made no threat or demonstration. He simply grabbed the bag of silver from the hands of the prosecuting witness and ran away with it. There was no pulling or scrambling for possession of the bag. Was the force employed by appellant the kind of force necessary to constitute robbery? We think not. As we read the cases and text-writers, 'the force used must be either before, or at the time of the taking, and must be of such a nature as to shew that it was intended to overpower the party robbed, and prevent his resisting, and not merely to get possession of the property stolen.' Rex v. Gnosil (1824) 1 Car. & P. 304, 171 Eng. Reprint, 1206.

It is said in State v. Parsons, 44 Wash. 299, 87 P. 349, 350, 7 L. R. A. (N. S.) 566, 120 Am. St. Rep. 1003, 12 Ann. Cas. 61: 'The courts generally hold that it is not robbery to merely snatch from the hand or person of another, or to surreptitiously take from another's pocket, money or some other thing of value, as such taking lacks the element of force, or putting in fear, one or the other of which being essential to constitute the crime of burglary.'

Wharton in his work on Criminal Law (11th Ed.) vol. 2, p. 1297, says: 'The snatching a thing is not considered a taking by force, but if there be a struggle to keep it, or any violence, or disruption, the taking is robbery, the reason of the distinction being that, in the former case, we can infer neither fear nor the intention violently to take in face of resisting force.'

Grigsby's Criminal Law, p. 644, § 694a, says: 'The force must be of such a nature as to overcome the person robbed regardless of his resistance-that is, the robber's intention must be to overcome resistance at all events. The violence must be used before and at the time of the robbery. The degree or extent of force is so closely allied to that of 'apprehended force producing fear,' that it is rather a metaphysical deduction to draw the distinction. 'No sudden taking unawares from the person, even done with force, as by snatching a thing from one's hand, or out of his pocket, is sufficient to constitute robbery."

Bishop on Criminal Law (9th Ed.) vol. 2, p. 864, § 1167, states the force necessary for robbery as follows: 'Snatching-which is a sufficient asportation in simple larceny, may or may not carry with it the added violence of robbery, according as it is met or not by resistance. * * * The true distinction is that in the absence of active opposition, it will be robbery if the article is so attached to the person or clothes as to create resistance however slight.'

In Ramirez v. Territory, 9 Ariz. 177, 80 P. 391, the prosecuting witness testified that he felt somebody come up behind him and run his hands in his pockets and then run off. The conviction of the defendant was set aside; the court holding that the mere taking of money by stealth from the person of another did not constitute robbery. Of similar tenor is Reynolds v. State, 14 Ariz, 537, 132 P. 434.

The Attorney General, while expressing doubt as to whether the facts shown constitute robbery, calls our attention to the case of Brown v. State, 34 Ariz. 150, 268 P. 618, as authority that possibly robbery was committed. In that case the defendant and one Jefferson had gone to the home of the prosecuting witness, and, after she had sold them some beer, represented to her that they were prohibition officers, and that they were going to 'throw her in' for violation of the prohibition law. Jefferson seized her and started towards the door. Brown intervened and suggested that, if she paid him $150, the matter could be 'fixed up.' The prosecuting witness went to her bedroom, obtained her purse, and dumped its contents in her lap, and while she was counting the momey Brown snatched the roll of bills from her and left the premises. We held this constituted robbery. We think the Brown Case falls within the rule announced by many courts to the effect that threats to accuse, arrest, or prosecute, when supplemented by force, actual or constructive, will support a charge of robbery. Montsdoca v. State, 84 Fla. 82, 93 So. 157, 27 A. L. R. 1291, and note II at page 1301. In the Brown Case the defendants actually took hold of the prosecuting witness and started with her towards the door as though they would place her in jail. This demonstration of force no doubt put her in fear.

The judgment of the lower court is reversed, and the cause remanded for such further action as may seem advisable in the premises.

DISCUSSION QUESTIONS

1.   Where would you draw the line between larceny and robbery in this sort of case? Should it be enough that you take something from the victim's person? Conversely, should robbery require some sort of actual or threatened violence against the victim apart from the force necessary to accomplish the taking?

2.   What would the victim have had to do differently for the defendant's taking to constitute a robbery? What would the defendant have had to do differently?

3.   Should the line between larceny and robbery depend upon how the victim reacts to the taking? Upon how the defendant reasonably expects the victim to react?

G. BURGLARY

Burglary was a narrowly defined offense at common law that has since been expanded by statute in a number of different ways. We will begin with the narrow common law definition.

- Breaking and
- Entering
- A Dwelling
- At Night
- With the Intent to Commit a Felony or Larceny Therein.

The elements that have been dropped or modified over time are the dwelling and nighttime requirements. Many jurisdictions define burglary as the breaking and entering of any structure with the requisite intent; others created different degrees of burglary depending on whether the structure was dwelling or not. Similarly, many jurisdictions have abolished the night time requirement, and others treat night time burglaries as a more serious offense. Finally, some jurisdictions have largely eliminated the breaking requirement.

1. BREAKING

Breaking requires a trespass. One who enters with either express or implied consent is not breaking although the law will find a "constructive breaking" if the consent was obtained by fraud or coercion. So you can't escape a burglary charge by tricking or threatening your way inside. Breaking otherwise requires some use of force against the structure itself. One does not have to actually "break" down the door or break through a window. Simply opening a door or window is enough. Even the slight enlargement of an existing opening is enough: pushing a door that is already ajar just a little bit more or lifting up an already open window would suffice. That said, many jurisdictions have simply done away with the breaking requirement although they still require the entry to be without consent.

2. ENTERING

One need not step completely inside the structure to accomplish the burglary in order to enter. Inserting any part of the human anatomy would be enough. Imagine that you smell your favorite pie through the open window of someone's kitchen. You lift up the already open window (breaking!) in order to fit your hand in and then reach through the window to grab the pie. As soon as your hand passes through the open window you have committed the burglary. You don't even need to touch the pie! You can also accomplish the required entry with a tool or instrument, but the insertion of the tool must be to accomplish the felony or larceny intended. Using a crowbar to open the window would not count, but using a "grabber" to grab the pie (messy!) would.

3. FELONIOUS OR LARCENOUS INTENT

This intent must exist concurrently with the breaking and entering. Breaking into a house just to get out of the cold is a criminal trespass, not a burglary, even if you subsequently decide while inside to steal something. On the other hand, you become guilty of burglary at the moment you and break and enter with the requisite intent. Changing your mind later does not undo your liability. So if you so much as set foot inside a structure that you "broke" into with the requisite intent, the crime is complete.

This element is satisfied if the defendant intended to commit any felony inside the structure, or if they intended to commit larceny. Don't be confused if you see this element stated as simply with the intent to commit a felony inside. At common law all larceny was a felony. Larceny aside, other misdemeanors won't suffice. If you break and enter to commit a misdemeanor act of vandalism, you are not guilty of burglary but of trespass (and of vandalism if you follow through).

4. BURGLARY AS AN ANTICIPATORY OFFENSE

Burglary is a great example of what scholars and judges refer to as an anticipatory offense. Like the crime of attempt, burglary is punished seriously because it anticipates a greater social harm that might happen. We all feel violated if someone intrudes into our home, but we feel a greater sense of violation if the intruder has come to do us harm or take things from us. So the law allows persons who break and enter under circumstances suggesting that they meant to do either of these things to be punished far more severely than an ordinary trespasser.

Case in Context

The following case reviews the approaches of various jurisdictions to defining the crime of burglary.

STATE OF MAINE V. DALE THIBEAULT

Supreme Judicial Court of Maine
402 A.2d 445 (1979)

Opinion

DELAHANTY, JUSTICE.

A Superior Court jury, Penobscot County, found Dale Thibeault guilty of Class B burglary. 17–A M.R.S.A. s 401(B). On April 24, 1978, Thibeault was sentenced to a term of six years at the Maine State Prison. On appeal, the defendant attacks the legality of his conviction on numerous grounds. * * *

The prosecution introduced ample evidence tending to show that on the evening of December 9, 1977, the defendant entered an apartment leased by David and Debbie Gardner with the intent, later consummated, to abscond with certain valuables. On his case-in-chief, the defendant called one of the cotenants, David Gardner, to the stand. Gardner testified that he had been friendly with the defendant for several years and that prior to the December 9 incident he had given the defendant blanket permission to enter his apartment at any time. On cross-examination, Gardner allowed that he had not given the defendant permission to remove any property from the apartment.

On appeal, as at his trial, the defendant directs his attack at that segment of the jury instructions in which the presiding Justice discussed the evidence pertinent to the "license or privilege" language found in Section 401.[1] The challenged passage reads as follows:

Now as to the license and privilege. There's not much of a dispute that Mr. Gardner, one of the co-tenants, gave permission but it becomes your duty under the law and considering all the facts whether or not the State has sustained its burden which I have given you beyond a reasonable doubt that the Defendant, Mr. Thibeault, knew that he was not licensed and privileged or privileged to do so with the intent to commit this crime of theft which I have defined to you. Was that a license? Was it a privilege? Was it a qualified license or privilege? It's for you to say what was in the mutual contemplation of the parties when permission to enter was given by Mr. Gardner. There is no dispute that Mr. Gardner, himself, says, I never gave him consent to steal or to rip off the apartment, so the facts are not much

---

[1]   The pertinent portion of Section 401 provides:

A person is guilty of burglary if he enters or surreptitiously remains in a structure, knowing that he is not licensed or privileged to do so, with the intent to commit a crime therein.

in dispute. Therefore, you must decide whether or not from all the testimony, from all the facts, and under the law which I have given to you, whether or not the Defendant, in whatever condition he was, knew that he was not licensed or privileged when he went in those premises to commit the crime of theft.

　　　* * *

The defendant argues that under Section 401 a person cannot validly be convicted of burglary if the individual rightfully in possession has given that person permission to enter the structure. He contends that the jury instruction was erroneous to the extent that it gave the jury the impression that if it found that the defendant had intended to commit a crime within the apartment that intention would negative, for the purposes of the burglary statute, Gardner's permission to enter.

At common law, consent to enter was a complete defense to a burglary prosecution. Burglary, like arson, was conceived of as an invasion of the "right of habitation." Thus, mere entry upon the dwelling of another in the nighttime with intent to commit a felony therein was insufficient to constitute the common-law crime of burglary. The prosecution additionally had to prove a "breaking": "the actual or constructive use of some force against a part of a building in effectuating an Unconsented entry." State v. High, 281 So.2d 356, 357 (Fla.1973). (emphasis in original.) That the initial entry must be trespassory[2] was established in Maine in State v. Newbegin, 25 Me. 500 (1846), where the defendant was convicted of burglarizing a dry goods store which, at the time in question, was open for trade. The defendant lifted an unlocked latch, opened a door, stole some cloth, and escaped all without attracting the attention of the store attendants. The Court reversed the burglary conviction finding that the State had failed to establish a breaking.

The offence of breaking is a violation of the security designed to exclude. And coupled with an entrance into a shop with a felonious intent, it constitutes (burglary). The opening of a shop door . . . which had been closed only to exclude the dust or cold air, with a design that it should be opened by all, who should be inclined to enter, could not be a violation of any security designed to exclude, and therefore not a breaking. Id. at 504.

Since the common law required a "violation of the security designed to exclude," it was axiomatic that a person entering with the permission of the lawful possessor could not be guilty of burglary. As one authority explains,

> (t)he law was not ready to punish one who had been "invited" in
> any way to enter the dwelling. The law sought only to keep out

---

[2]   Indeed, the English common law considered burglary to be essentially a heinous form of trespassing. 5 Eng. Comm'rs Reports on the Criminal Law 4 (1840).

intruders, and thus anyone given authority to come into the house could not be committing a breaking when he so entered.

Although we have not had occasion to deal with a consent defense to a burglary prosecution since Newbegin was decided in 1846, it is nevertheless clear that consent remained a valid defense at least until such time as Maine's Criminal Code became effective in 1976. The former burglary statutes, all included or incorporated by reference the familiar breaking element. Furthermore, our interpretations of that element were entirely consistent with the "security-designed-to-exclude" rationale put forth in Newbegin.[3]

Although few quarreled with the logic of including the requirement of a trespassory entry for a law designed to protect the security of the habitation, judicial interpretations of the "force" aspect of the breaking element rightly attracted the criticism of reformers. In interpreting the "force" aspect, the judges of the common law perhaps wishing to constrict the application of what was then a capital crime created a host of fine distinctions and bewildering qualifications.[4]

With burglary no longer a capital offense, the irrationality of these interpretations became manifest. Many state legislatures have reacted by excising the breaking element from their statutes entirely. In these jurisdictions, burglary has been reduced to a three-element crime: (1) entry (2) of a structure (3) with the intent to commit a crime. Under such a statute, it is clear that consent to enter is not a defense since, no vestige of the breaking element remaining, the entry need not be trespassory to be burglarious.

In other jurisdictions, Maine among them, the word "breaking" has been eliminated and a word or phrase such as "unlawful," "unauthorized," or "without license or privilege" has been inserted in the statute to qualify "entry." Where such language has been employed in a burglary statute, the result has generally been to retain so much of the breaking element as required a trespassory entry while at the same time eliminating the illogical rules stemming from the "force" aspect of breaking. Of course,

---

[3]   In State v. Cookson, Me., 293 A.2d 780, 784–85 (1972), for example, Justice Weatherbee declared:

It appears clear that the offense of burglary is one primarily against the security of the habitation. It marks the state's determination to safeguard in his dwelling the homeowner, his family and guests from the dangers that accompany felonious invasions of their sanctuaries during the particularly vulnerable periods of darkness. (footnote omitted.)

[4]   For example, if the defendant entered through an open door or window, no breaking occurred since no force was used: the occupant, it was said, had not sufficiently secured his dwelling and was therefore not entitled to the protection of the law. 2 E. East, Pleas of the Crown 485 (1803); W. LaFave & A. Scott, Supra at s 96. Worse still, courts were divided over the question of whether pushing open a partly open door or window was a sufficient use of force to satisfy the breaking element.

where the statute requires a trespassory entry, the lawful possessor's consent is a complete defense.

New York's burglary statute and the judicial interpretations thereof are particularly instructive since that statute makes use of the same "license or privilege" language found in our Section 401.[5] N.Y. Penal Law ss 140.00(5), 140.20 (McKinney 1975). . . . The New York courts have held that the "license or privilege" language included in Section 140.00(5) requires a trespassory entry.

We hold that the "license or privilege" language in Maine's Section 401 requires a like construction. The portion of the statute relevant to this appeal provides that "(a) person is guilty of burglary if he enters . . . a structure, knowing that he is not licensed . . . to do so, with the intent to commit a crime therein." Breaking the statute down to its constituent parts, we discern four elements: (1) entry (2) of a structure (3) with the knowledge that the entry is not licensed and (4) with the intent to commit a crime within the structure. Obviously, the "license" referred to in the statute means the license to enter a particular structure. The "do so" clearly refers back to "enters." Accordingly, the prosecution must, as an independent proposition, prove beyond reasonable doubt that the accused knew that he was not "licensed" to enter the structure.

The State argues that since the defendant entered the Gardners' apartment for the unlawful purpose of stealing certain valuables, any permission he may have secured from Gardner would be negated. We find no room in Section 401 for this argument. Whether or not the defendant had permission to enter is a question that must be resolved without reference to his alleged intent, another separate and distinct element of the crime. The Louisiana Supreme Court, construing that state's "unauthorized entry" statute, responded to the same argument as follows:

> As we construe the burglary statute, the entry must be unauthorized and this must be determined as a distinct element of the offense separate and apart from the intent to steal. If the legislature desired that burglary consist only of an entry with intent to steal, they would have omitted the word Unauthorized.

Much the same can be said of Maine's Section 401. If we construed the statute to allow the existence of a criminal intent upon entry to negate the permission of the lawful possessor, the result would be, for all practical purposes, the expungement of the "license" language from the statute. If the State's argument is accepted, a burglary defendant would have to prevail on the question of his intent to commit a crime in order to prevail on the "license or privilege" issue. The State's interpretation would thus render the "license or privilege" language mere surplusage, and Section 401

---

[5] Both New York and Maine appear to have adopted modified versions of the Model Penal Code's definition of burglary. Model Penal Code s 221.1 (1974).

would be little more than a variation on the typical three-element statute discussed earlier. We have no reason to believe that the Legislature would inject unnecessary language into any of the Code's provisions. Indeed, our familiar rule has been to construe statutes, particularly criminal ones, as being free of superfluous language.

It is true that the Comment appended to Section 401 declares that the statute eliminates "the common law requirement . . . that there be a 'breaking.'" However, the next sentence, "(t)he crime loses nothing in seriousness if the burglar enters a door inadvertently left open, rather than through a door he breaks open," indicates that the revisers intended to draft the statute in such a way as to eliminate only the "force" aspect of breaking together with the irrational judicial interpretations that accompanied it. The "license or privilege" language inserted in the statute itself indicates that the trespassory aspect of the breaking element was retained.

Turning to the instruction given by the presiding Justice, we conclude that the jury was given the mistaken impression that it could find the defendant guilty of burglary whether or not David Gardner gave him permission to enter the apartment. "There's not much of a dispute," stated the court, "that Mr. Gardner, one of the co-tenants, gave permission . . . ." That being the case, the jury's function, according to the court, was to determine whether or not the defendant "knew that he was not licensed (to enter) with the intent to commit this crime of theft . . . ." The instruction invited the jury to consider whether, in the words of the presiding Justice, a "qualified license" existed. As our analysis here indicates, Section 401 does not contemplate the kind of qualification outlined by the presiding Justice. A remand will therefore be necessary.

Case remanded for a new trial.

DISCUSSION QUESTIONS

1.   How do you think burglary should be defined? Must the entry itself be wrongful? Should there also be a "breaking?"

2.   Should a separate offense be created for what the defendant in this case did? How would you define it? Would you punish it more or less than a burglary?

3.   What is your conception of a "burglar?" What do you think the public imagines when they hear the word "burglary?" What role, if any, should such public conceptions play in how burglary is defined?

Case in Context

Restraining orders raise interesting issues in burglary cases, as the following case demonstrates.

STATE OF MINNESOTA V. PETER ALLEN COLVIN
Supreme Court of Minnesota
645 N.W.2d 449 (2002)

LANCASTER, JUSTICE.

This appeal presents the question of whether a criminal defendant's violation of an order for protection (OFP) is sufficient to establish first-degree burglary, absent the commission of or intent to commit a crime other than a violation of the order for protection.

Michelle Colvin applied for and obtained an emergency (ex parte) OFP pursuant to Minn.Stat. § 518B.01 (2000), against her ex-husband, Peter Colvin, on October 14, 1998. The order, which was valid for one year and was served on Colvin on the date obtained, provided that "Respondent [Colvin] must not enter Petitioner's [Michelle Colvin's] residence located at [address] or any future residence. Respondent must not enter or stay at Petitioner's residence for any reason, even if invited to do so." The order also provided that Colvin could not commit acts of domestic abuse against Michelle Colvin, have any contact with her, or enter or call her workplace.

On February 25, 1999, Michelle Colvin telephoned the Rochester Police Department to report a violation of the OFP. According to the police report, a fifteen-year-old girl, A.M.E., who was staying with Michelle Colvin, returned to their home in Rochester that evening at 6:10 p.m. A.M.E. found Colvin inside the residence, watching television and drinking a beer. A.M.E. asked Colvin to leave, and he complied. She then telephoned Michelle Colvin at work and left a message about Colvin's presence in the home. The police officer responding to Michelle Colvin's call later that evening found no sign of forced entry. Michelle Colvin reported to the officer that she believed Colvin entered the residence through a window in the dining area because the blinds were disturbed and because that window would not lock.

As a result of the events of February 25, 1999, Colvin was charged with first-degree burglary in violation of Minn.Stat. § 609.582, subd. 1(a) (2000), and violation of an OFP in violation of Minn.Stat. § 518B.01, subd. 14(d)(1). Because Colvin had been convicted of two prior order for protection violations in the past five years, this OFP violation was charged at the felony level. Colvin brought a motion to dismiss the burglary charge, arguing that violation of an OFP could not form the basis of a burglary charge because burglary required commission of or intent to commit a crime other than illegal entry. At the July 29, 1999, pretrial hearing on Colvin's motion, the parties stipulated to the facts as represented in the police report and complaint and further agreed that there was no allegation that Colvin committed or attempted to commit any crime independent of the OFP violation.

After the district court denied Colvin's motion on September 29, 1999, the parties reached a plea agreement that included dismissal of the OFP violation and resolution of other unrelated charges. Under that agreement, the burglary charge was submitted to the court on the same stipulated facts as agreed to in the pretrial hearing. On April 10, 2000, the district court found Colvin guilty of first-degree burglary. The court made written findings of guilt, specifically finding: That Colvin entered a building; that he did so without consent; that the building was a residence; that another person, not an accomplice, was present in the building during some of the time Colvin was present; and that in entering the building Colvin intended to commit and did commit the crime of violating the valid October 14, 1998, OFP.

Colvin appealed, arguing that intent to violate an OFP cannot satisfy the element of intent to commit a crime while in the building. The court of appeals affirmed the district court, holding that violation of an OFP, unlike trespass, satisfies the independent crime element of first-degree burglary. Colvin additionally argued that the evidence in the stipulated facts was insufficient to prove intent to violate the OFP. The court of appeals rejected this argument as well.

On appeal to this court, Colvin raises only the question of whether intent to violate an OFP is sufficient to establish burglary, absent the commission of or intent to commit a crime other than the OFP violation.

Colvin was charged with first-degree burglary in violation of Minn.Stat. § 609.582, subd. 1(a). Subdivision 1 provides:

Whoever enters a building without consent and with intent to commit a crime, or enters a building without consent and commits a crime while in the building, either directly or as an accomplice, commits burglary in the first degree and may be sentenced to imprisonment for not more than 20 years or to payment of a fine of not more than $35,000, or both, if:

(a) the building is a dwelling and another person, not an accomplice, is present in it when the burglar is in the building.

Violation of an OFP, however, can be accomplished in many ways. It is the nature of the OFP violation that will determine whether the OFP violation constitutes an independent crime under the burglary statute. For example, the OFP in this case prohibited Colvin from: (1) committing acts of domestic abuse against his ex-wife; (2) having any contact with his ex-wife; (3) entering her residence; and (4) entering or calling her workplace. If Colvin had acted in contravention of either the first, second, or fourth provision, his conduct would not resemble trespass, while violation of the no-entry provision clearly does bear such a resemblance.

The state argues that Colvin committed two violations of the OFP—by entering his ex-wife's residence, he violated the no-entry prohibition in the order, and evidence of this conduct satisfied the illegal entry element of burglary. Second, by intending to contact his ex-wife in violation of the order's prohibition against "any contact" with his ex-wife, Colvin violated the order a second time. Evidence of this second method of violating the OFP, the state contends, satisfies the intent to commit an independent crime element of burglary.

We disagree, because the district court's findings and the stipulated facts fail to support the state's allegation that Colvin intended to contact his ex-wife in violation of the OFP. The district court in its written findings of guilt specifically found that the independent crime committed by Colvin was violation of the no-entry part of the OFP. The district court stated: "In entering the building, [Colvin] intended to and did commit a crime— specifically violation of the October 14, 1998 Order for Protection which excluded [Colvin] from that building * * *." The district court made no other finding related to the no-contact provision of the order. Further, nothing in the stipulated facts—comprised of the police report, the complaint, and the parties' agreement at the pretrial hearing that there was no allegation that Colvin committed or attempted to commit any crime independent of the OFP violation—establishes that Colvin intended to contact Michelle. In fact, because the parties agreed that "there is no allegation that *any* crime independent of the OFP violation was committed or attempted to be committed" by Colvin, and because this statement refers to a single method of violating the OFP, this suggests that only one OFP violation method was contemplated during the district court proceedings. (Emphasis added.)

Because the district court found that Colvin violated the no-entry provision of the OFP, but made no other finding of additional OFP violations, we conclude that Colvin was not charged with violation of the no-contact provision of the OFP. Thus, the state's argument that Colvin's intention to violate the no-contact provision of the order was the basis for satisfying the independent crime element of burglary is unsupported by the record.

Likewise, the dissent's venture into factfinding based on a default OFP order and petition in this case is improper. This case is before us on stipulated facts and admittedly cryptic district court findings. However, as an appellate court those findings are our only foundation. Appellate courts have no more business finding facts after a court trial than after a jury trial. Just as we must defer to a jury's findings, we are bound by the district court determination that Colvin's intent, "[i]n entering the building," was to violate the OFP, "which excluded Defendant from that building." The dissent erroneously states that we conclude that Colvin's sole intent was to enter the home. We made no such independent factual conclusion. Accordingly, the narrow issue presented is whether Colvin's violation of the no-entry provision of the OFP is sufficient to establish the independent crime element of burglary.

In *Larson,* this court held that trespass cannot serve as the crime committed or intended to be committed to establish burglary. 358 N.W.2d at 670. We explained: "To allow an intent to commit a trespass to satisfy the requirement of intent to commit a crime would mean that a mere trespasser who had no intent other than to enter or remain in a building without the consent of the owner could be convicted of burglary." *Id.* The court concluded that the state is required to "do more than establish an intent to commit the crime of trespass" to fall within the parameters of the burglary statute. *Id.*

Colvin argues that the OFP violation he committed was so similar to trespass that the same result is required here as in *Larson.* The only identifiable criminal act in both cases was the illegal entry, and in neither case is there evidence of intent to commit a crime other than illegal entry. Colvin acknowledges that the cases differ in that Colvin's entry was made illegal not simply because of the prohibition against trespass, but by operation of the valid October 14, 1998, order for protection. But Colvin contends that the OFP simply establishes the illegal entry element of burglary, not the element of intent to commit a crime independent of the illegal entry.

We conclude that violation of a no-entry provision of an OFP, like trespass, is excluded from the crimes that can be the bases for the independent crime element of burglary. Both offenses are designed to protect the interests that are invaded by the unauthorized entry that the burglar makes. Thus both trespass and violation of the no-entry provision of an OFP satisfy the illegal entry element of burglary. Further, both offenses are complete upon entry. But we conclude that the same entry is insufficient to satisfy both the illegal entry element of the burglary statute and the independent-crime requirement.

Freed from the district court findings, the dissent paints a picture of an intruder who is more than a mere trespasser to support the conclusion that a burglary charge is appropriate. In addition to failing to give proper deference to the district court's findings, the dissent misses the point. To hold that a burglary charge here was not supported by the district court's findings is not to say that Colvin is a mere trespasser. Colvin may well have violated the OFP in ways other than mere entry; we simply have no district court findings to support that conclusion. More importantly, given our holding in *Larson,* a court adjudicating a burglary charge based on a violation of an OFP must determine that the OFP violation constituted something more than mere entry into the home in order to support the burglary charge.

Finally, we note that the legislature has created a statutory scheme to address the serious problem of domestic abuse. Minn.Stat. ch. 518B (2000). Among other remedies, the statutes address the significant danger inherent in domestic abuse by ratcheting up the penalties for repeat violations. *See* Minn.Stat. § 518B.01, subd. 14(c), (d). Unlike the crime of trespass, repeat violations of orders for protection are designated as felonies. *Id.,* subd. 14(d). A defendant convicted of violating three orders for protection in five years—such as the defendant here—is guilty of a felony level offense carrying a presumptive prison sentence. *Id.* Had the defendant been convicted of simple trespass for a third time, the crime would be a misdemeanor. Minn.Stat. § 609.605 (2000). Such disparate treatment of domestic abuse based on unauthorized entry as compared to trespass underscores the legislature's intent to treat domestic abuse seriously and severely. If the legislature chooses to sanction violation of an OFP based solely on entering a home similarly to first-degree burglary—with a presumptive sentence of 48 months for a first-time offender—it can do so by amending the appropriate statutes.

In summary, we hold that because the stipulated facts establish that there is no allegation that Colvin committed or intended to commit a crime other than the OFP violation, and because the district court specifically found that Colvin's OFP violation was a violation of the prohibition against entry onto his ex-wife's residence, Colvin's unconsented entry in violation of the OFP cannot be the basis for a burglary charge.

Reversed.

RUSSELL A. ANDERSON, JUSTICE (dissenting).

I respectfully dissent. I disagree with the majority's conclusion that entry into a home with intent to violate an order for protection (OFP) is the equivalent of entry into a home with intent to trespass. I also disagree with the majority's characterization of the district court's written findings of fact. By improperly focusing on two short phrases in the district court's findings, the court not only ignores the fundamental finding of the court that the felony underlying the burglary was violation of the OFP and not a mere trespass, but fails to appreciate the significant difference between entry into a home and entry into a home where a person protected by an OFP resides.

The entirety of the district court's findings in this case is as follows:

1. On February 25, 1999, Defendant entered the building located at [address];

2. He did so without consent;

3. In entering the building, he intended to and did commit a crime—*specifically violation of the October 14, 1998 Order for Protection* which excluded Defendant from that building;

4. The building was a dwelling, and;

5. Another person, not an accomplice, was present in the building during some of the time that Defendant was in the building.

(Emphasis added.) The majority focuses exclusively on the phrases, "In entering the building," and "which excluded Defendant from that building" to conclude that the district court found that the independent crime committed was a violation of the "no-entry part of the order for protection." However, the district court stated that the *specific violation* was simply violation of the OFP, not the "no-entry part" of the order.

The majority strains to construe the district court order as finding a violation of only the "no-entry" aspect of the OFP so that it can characterize Colvin as a mere trespasser. In *Larson,* we stated: "[t]o allow an intent to commit a trespass to satisfy the requirement of intent to commit a crime would mean that a mere trespasser who had no intent other than to enter or remain in a building without the consent of the owner could be convicted of burglary." *State v. Larson,* 358 N.W.2d 668, 670 (Minn.1984). The majority's characterization of Colvin as a mere trespasser is not supported by the record nor is it supported by our previous case law, which permits circumstantial evidence to determine an intruder's intent.

The record in this case belies the majority's characterization of Colvin as a mere trespasser. This mere trespasser had twice previously broken into Michelle Colvin's home, stealing money and personal belongings. This mere trespasser had threatened violence against Michelle and their children. This mere trespasser appeared at Michelle's home every day for a 30-day period, intoxicated. This mere trespasser brought drugs and alcohol to Michelle's home. This mere trespasser brought his friends to the home, which resulted in an allegation of inappropriate contact with the children. About this mere trespasser, Michelle stated, "I am afraid."

In addition, the majority ignores the case law, acknowledged in *Larson,* that permits the consideration of circumstantial evidence to determine the intent of an unlawful intruder; that is the consideration of circumstantial evidence to determine if one is a "mere trespasser." When consideration is given to the circumstantial evidence in this case—that is Colvin's history of domestic violence towards Michelle—a perfectly reasonable inference from Colvin's occupation of Michelle's home was that Colvin intended contact with Michelle and their children, and that Colvin intended to cause Michelle and the children fear of harm. The court is unwilling to consider the circumstantial evidence, provided by the very order that Colvin violated, that Colvin intended to do more than merely enter into the home without consent. The court's analysis that Colvin is a mere trespasser is contrary to both the law and the facts.

The majority finds support for its conclusion in the stipulation that there was no allegation that Colvin committed or attempted to commit any crime independent of the OFP violation. However, while actual conduct can be indicative of intent, what is relevant to a burglary charge is the intruder's intent *at the time of entry,* not whether Colvin committed or attempted to commit a crime independent of the OFP violation once inside the home. Minn.Stat. § 609.582, subd. 1 (2000). The intent that the district court found was the simple intent to violate the OFP, not the intent that the majority surmises, the intent to enter into the home. While the record is sparse, one can easily surmise that Colvin's intent was to have contact with Michelle and the children and to cause fear of harm. In *State v. Crosby,* we affirmed a burglary conviction that relied upon circumstantial evidence of intent, stating:

> [W]hether they found what they expected to find in the building does not detract from the fact that they had an intent to commit a felony or gross misdemeanor; and if that intent existed it is sufficient, even though they did not actually find in the building what they expected to take.

277 Minn. at 26, 151 N.W.2d at 300. Our holding in *Crosby* applies with equal force here. It is irrelevant that Colvin did not find Michelle when he unlawfully entered her home, staying for two hours while drinking a beer and watching TV. His intent, as found by the district court, was to violate the OFP, which, in addition to prohibiting entry into the home, prohibited Colvin from causing fear of harm to Michelle and prohibited contact with her "in any other way."

The effect of the majority's ruling is to erase any distinction between a court-prohibited entry into a home by a person with a court-identified propensity to harm or cause fear of harm to the home-owner and a mere trespass into a building by a stranger. The two, one an offense against a person and the other an offense against property, certainly are not the same and should not be merged indiscriminately, as the majority does today.

In addition, the effect of the majority's analysis—parsing out what aspect of an OFP has been violated—requires the state to allege and the factfinder to find in burglary cases exactly what aspect of the OFP the intruder intended to violate upon entry. In other contexts, we do not require a jury to agree unanimously on exactly how a law was violated, but only to agree on the "bottom line"—that the particular violation alleged was proved beyond a reasonable doubt. The majority analysis subverts this principle by requiring a jury to agree on which aspect of an OFP an intruder intended to violate where burglary is charged. This result appears to inject unnecessary complexity into a relatively simple charge.

I suspect the majority's true concern, a valid one, is whether a burglary charge, a severity level 6 offense, should be charged when the perhaps more accurate characterization of the offense is felony violation of the order for protection, a severity level 4 offense. However, if the state has misused its charging authority given the facts in this case, that action should be addressed directly rather than through a strained interpretation of the district court's straightforward ruling. The effect of the court's ruling will be to discourage the state from charging similar offenses as burglaries, perhaps contrary to legislative intent.

In sum, the majority analysis, which parses out and requires proof of the particular aspect of the OFP an intruder intended to violate upon entry in order to determine whether a burglary charge will stand, is simply unworkable. Moreover, it is unnecessary in this case, given that the district court found that the felony underlying the burglary charge was violation of the order for protection and not the *"no-entry part"* of the OFP, and given that Colvin was much more than a mere trespasser.

I would affirm.

DISCUSSION QUESTIONS

1.   Why do you think the prosecutor charged this case as a burglary as opposed to a felony violation of a restraining order? Was this a "misuse" of charging authority as the dissent suggests?

2.   Do you agree with the court's interpretation of the district court's findings?

3.   How should a court interpret a crime that overlaps with other crimes? Should the existence of one affect the interpretation of the other?

Practice Problem 25.2: Murderous Munchies?

Amber has convinced herself (against the advice of all of her professors) that the best way to outline is to pull a series of all-nighters. She is on night two of this marathon study session when she realizes that she is running out of caffeinated energy drinks and sugary snacks and that her law school's snack shop may be closing. She runs to the shop only to see the iron grill at the entrance to the shop pulled half way down, a clear indication that the store has closed but that Ben, the shop clerk, is still inside. She ducks under the grill and sees Ben sitting on the floor stocking energy drinks into the refrigerated display. Amber grabs a handful of energy drinks from the floor next to Ben. Ben yells at her telling her that he has already closed out the cash register and that she needs to put those back. Desperate to complete her criminal law outline that night Amber turns and runs out of the shop dropping a few cans along the way as she ducks under the gate. Ben springs to his feet and runs after her but he trips on one of the energy drink cans and smacks his head hard on the gate. His brain hemmorrahges as he lies unconscious on the floor, and he dies. Discuss Amber's liability for felony murder in a jurisdiction in which burglary and robbery are enumerated felonies.

APPENDIX

THE ULTIMATE PRACTICE PROBLEM

■ ■ ■

If you treat this as a practice exam question you may lose your mind because there is no way anyone could address all of the issues raised fully in three or even four hours. Instead, use it as the mother-of-all-review problems. If you work through it step by step you will have covered a great deal of the first year course in criminal law.

Psycho-Survivor

The deaths of four participants have given new meaning to the phrase "Reality Television." Last week four participants in a reality show died on live, prime time national television when they fell off the tower they were climbing during the final competition of the show "Psycho Survivor."

Team Sesame Street was locked in a three-way tie with Team Barney and Team Teletubby going into the final event of the show's competition. At stake was a cash prize of an undisclosed amount (but which was rumored to exceed $1 million). The final event was a climbing race to see which team would be the first to reach the top of a three-sided, hundred-foot-tall climbing tower. At the start of the competition all team members were tied together with a fifty-foot rope. Fastened to each of the three sides of the climbing tower were the sorts of artificial hand and footholds used on climbing walls. Each team was pre-assigned a side of the climbing tower the day before the competition so that they could map out a climbing strategy.

The night before the climbing competition each team retreated to their "privacy cabin" where they were allowed to converse with one another without being recorded by the show's video cameras. Team Sesame Street consisted of four members, Bert, Ernie, Ms. Piggy, and Kermit. That night in the privacy cabin Bert, who had been drinking heavily all night and was intoxicated, suggested that they sabotage the climbing walls of the other two teams in order to gain an advantage during the competition.

Ernie immediately proclaimed that he wanted nothing to do with such a scheme. He put on the earphones from his ipod and turned up the music so loud that he could not hear anything said by anyone else for the rest of the conversation. Secretly, he hoped that Bert succeeded in his sabotage because Ernie desperately wanted to win the competition's prize money at all costs. He feared that the privacy tent was secretly bugged with microphones and surveillance cameras, however, and did not want to be observed participating in the plot lest he be disqualified.

Bert, used to being ignored by Ernie, proceeded to explain his plan. He said that the bolts securing some of the handholds on the other teams' climbing wall could be loosened using the screw driver on the Swiss Army knife issued to the team at the beginning of the competition. Bert suggested that he sneak out in the middle of the night and loosen just enough handholds on each of the other two walls to slow down the other teams. He had picked out key handholds on the other walls that were ten feet off the ground. Bert was willing to do the loosening but wanted someone to serve as lookout for him.

Kermit spoke next and expressed horror that Bert would cheat in order to win the competition. He said that he was morally opposed to any cheating.

Ms. Piggy spoke next and reprimanded Kermit for being such a wimp. Ms. Piggy pointed out that acts of sabotage had been committed by the other two teams during earlier rounds of the competition and that it was about time that Team Sesame Street got in the game. Ms. Piggy also observed that no one was likely to be hurt by a ten-foot fall. She explained that she was night blind, however. She would not go with Bert to loosen the bolts because she was afraid that she would stumble in the dark and draw attention to what they were doing.

Ms. Piggy, however, had a secret reason for wanting to win the competition. She had long suffered from schizophrenia complicated by a narcissistic personality disorder. She had stopped taking her medication during the competition because she did not want to disclose her condition to anyone else. Her beliefs about the results of winning the competition had become progressively more grandiose and delusional as a result of her not taking her medication, however. She now believed that if she was seen on television standing at the top of the tower as part of the winning team that she would be worshipped as a God by her fans who would realize that she had become a divine being.

Kermit spoke again. He repeated that he was morally opposed to cheating. He also said that he would not serve as Bert's lookout. Bert said that he would loosen the bolts without a lookout in that case. At that point, Kermit threatened to report Bert to the show's producer unless Bert promised not to loosen any handholds that were higher than five feet off the ground. Kermit said that he was worried that someone might get seriously injured by a ten-foot fall.

Bert said that he would not loosen handholds higher than five feet off the ground. He said this just to keep Kermit quiet, however. Bert secretly decided that he would still loosen handholds ten feet off the ground. Bert feared that loosened handholds that were only five feet off the ground might be discovered before the competition began. He realized that someone might get seriously hurt if they fell from ten feet off the ground and had in fact once seen someone get paralyzed from a ten foot fall off of a climbing wall. He did not care about people getting injured, however. His only concern was avoiding getting caught. He assumed that unless someone died there would not be a criminal investigation. Bert believed that it was simply impossible for anyone to die from a ten-foot fall.

After Bert left the privacy cabin, Ernie took off his MP3 player and loudly proclaimed that he was going to go for a walk. Once outside, however, he stealthily approached the climbing tower to see what Bert was up to. In the darkness, he could only see that Bert seemed to be doing something to the other team's climbing walls. He realized that the entire team would be disqualified if Bert was caught, so he stood look out while Bert worked. His plan was to alert Bert if anyone else approached so that they could avoid discovery. If no one approached, he would not alert Bert to his presence, however, because he still wanted to be able to deny involvement in whatever Bert was doing if at all possible. He was careful not to let Bert see him. Since no one else approached he never had to reveal himself to Bert. Ernie slipped back to the cabin once Bert had finished working on the tower and never revealed his activities to anyone on the Team.

Bert had partially changed his mind during his sabotage. He loosened the handholds on Team Teletubby's wall as he had planned. Almost immediately after he began loosening the first screw on a handhold on Team Barney's wall, however, he decided that malfunctions on two different climbing walls would look too suspicious. Bert also believed that Team Barney were wimps and had no chance of beating Team Sesame Street in the competition. He returned to the Privacy Cabin and said nothing further about the sabotage.

The next day all four members of Team Sesame Street roped themselves together and participated in the competition. All did not go according to plan, however. The loosened handhold on the wall of Team Teletubby did not come loose until, Tinky Winky, the last of the four climbers pulled on it. The team's lead climber, Dipsy, was fifty-five feet off the ground at this point, with the next climber ten feet below him and the remaining third climber ten feet further below. Unfortunately, Tinky Winky's fall created a chain reaction pulling each of the three climbers above him off the wall. The three climbers above Tinky Winky were all killed by the fall. Tinky Winky survived his ten-foot fall only to be crushed to death by his falling Teletubby teammates.

Despite the fact that the one handhold on the climbing wall of Team Barney had been barely loosened at all, Baby Bop, the lead climber for Team Barney, felt it wiggle slightly when she grasped it. She climbed on but noted it as something suspicious. Baby Bop and her Team climbed fast. In fact, she and Bert, the lead climber for Team Sesame Street, were both just about to gain the top of the tower when Team Teletubby began to fall. Hearing the screams of the falling Teletubbies, Baby Bop immediately concluded that Team Sesame Street had sabotaged both of the other climbing walls. On gaining the top, Baby Bop threw herself in a furious rage at Bert who had just gained the top himself She tried to push Bert off the top. Just as Baby Bop appeared to be gaining the advantage in the struggle Kermit and Ernie reached the top. Fearing that Bert would pull him off the tower if Bert fell off (remember all team members were roped together) Kermit grabbed at one of Baby Bop's legs to try to stop her from pushing Bert off the edge. This grab in combination with Bert's continued struggling was enough to cause Baby Bop to lose her balance. Enraged at having come so close to being pushed off the top, Bert took this opportunity to give Baby Bop one last shove to push her off the top. Ms. Piggy had a chance to grab Baby Bop and stop her from falling but decided to let her and the rest of her team die in the hope that this would guarantee Team Sesame Street the prize money. (She was heard to exclaim "C'est la vie"[1] as Baby Bop disappeared from view.)

Fortunately, however, Baby Bop's rope had become hooked on a handhold near the top of the tower. This arrested her fall and saved both her and the rest of Team Barney from what would have been certain death.

All of the preceding took place in the state of Kennedicut. Kennedicut is a jurisdiction that generally takes the common law approach to questions of criminal law. Some relevant Kennedicut penal code provisions are provided on the following page for your use in answering questions the following questions. Discuss the criminal liability of Bert, Ernie, Kermit and Ms. Piggie for the following crimes.

Kennedicut Penal Code Provisions

<u>Game Show Fraud</u>: It shall be a felony for any person to knowingly obtain an unfair advantage in a competition televised for the public where the monetary reward exceeds one thousand dollars in value.

<u>Recreational Climbing Endangerment</u>: It shall be a felony for any person to interfere with the proper operation of a structure designed for recreational climbing in a way that may cause serious injury or death.

<u>Criminal Conspiracy:</u> A person is guilty of conspiracy with another person or persons to commit a crime if with the purpose of promoting or facilitating its commission he:

---

[1]   French for "that's life."

(a) agrees with such other person or persons that they or one or more of them will engage in conduct that constitutes such crime or an attempt to commit such crime; or

(b) agrees to aid such other person or persons in the planning or commission of such crime or of an attempt to commit such crime.

Criminal Homicide

Offense Defined: A person is guilty of criminal homicide if he intentionally, knowingly, recklessly, or negligently causes the death of another human being.

Classification: Criminal homicide shall be classified as murder, voluntary manslaughter, or involuntary manslaughter.

Murder

Murder of the first degree: A criminal homicide constitutes murder of the first degree when it is committed with premeditation and deliberation.

Murder of the second degree: A criminal homicide constitutes murder of the second degree when it is committed while the defendant was engaged as a principal or an accomplice in the perpetration of a felony or when it was committed by an intentional killing.

Murder of the third degree: A criminal homicide constitutes murder of the third degree when a defendant does an act with a high probability that it will result in death and does it with a base antisocial motive and with a wanton disregard for human life.

Voluntary Manslaughter

A person who kills an individual without lawful justification commits voluntary manslaughter if at the time of the killing he is acting under a sudden and intense passion resulting from serious provocation by the person killed.

Involuntary Manslaughter

A person is guilty of involuntary manslaughter when as a direct result of doing an unlawful act in a reckless or grossly negligent manner, or the doing of a lawful act in a reckless or grossly negligent manner, he causes the death of another person.

INDEX

References are to Pages

A

Actual Causation, 484
Addiction, 43
Aggravated Assaults, 825
Appeals by the Prosecution, 10
Appellate, 8, 9
Asportation, 840
Assault, 819, 820, 821, 825
Assault and Battery Distinguished, 819
Assisted Suicide, 501
Attempt, 563, 565, 576, 601
Attendant Circumstances, 541, 581

B

Battery, 819, 820
Burglary, 859, 860

C

Causation, 483
Common Law Mental States, 171
Common Law Murder, 323
Complicity, 603, 653
Conditional Intent, 195
Consent, 784
Consolidated Theft Statutes, 845
Conspiracy, 519, 520, 549
Constitutional Constraints, 95
Constitutional Law and Federal Criminal
    Law, 57
Corrupt Motive Doctrine, The, 545
Criminal Process, The, 7

D

Defensive Force, 659
Depraved Heart Murder, 411
Digital Possession, 154
Diminished Capacity, 734
Domestic Violence and Syndrome Evidence,
    677
Drug Crime and Mental States, 249
Drug Possession, 145
Duress, 715

E

Embezzlement, 843
EMED, 381
Environmental Crime, 236
Evidentiary Rulings, 10

F

False Imprisonment, 835
False Pretenses, Obtaining Property, 843
Felonious or Larcenous Intent, 860
Felony Murder, 431
First Amendment Limits, 511
Forgery, 844

H

Hate Crimes, 204
How the Voluntary Act Doctrine Often
    Operates in Practice, 128

I

Imperfect Self Defense, 710
Independent Felonies, 447
Initial Aggressor Rules, 697
Intent to Frighten, 821
Intent to Grievously Injure, 331
Intent to Kill Murder, 327
Intentional Killings, 321
Intervening Causes, 489
Intoxication, 297
Involuntary Manslaughter, 391

J

Jury Nullification, 11

K

Kidnapping, 835

L

Larceny, 840
Legality, 95

M

M'Naghten Criticisms and Responses, 764
M'Naghten Test, 738
Malum Prohibitum Crimes, 273
Manslaughter, 322, 324, 355, 391
Mental Disease, 734
Mental Disease or Defect, 737, 766
Mental State Definitions, 168
Mental State Requirements, 267, 576, 582
Merger, 517
Miscellaneous Crimes Against the Person, 819
Mistake of Fact Doctrine, 267
Mistakes of Fact, 268
Mistakes of Law, 272, 281
Model Penal Code Mental State
    Definitions, 168
Motions to Dismiss, 9
Murder, 322

N

Natural and Probable Consequences, 644
Necessity, 715, 718
Necessity of Force, 688
Non-Consent, 782

O

Obtaining Property by False Pretenses, 843
Omission Liability, 139
Online Threats, 180
Overbreadth, 95

P

Partial Responsibility, 733, 735
Philosophies of Punishment, 29
Plea Bargaining, 12
Possessory Offenses, 145
Premeditation and Deliberation Defined, 335
Prison Escapes, 718
Professional Ethics, 13
Property Crimes, 839
Prosecutorial Discretion, 12
Prostitution and Sex Trafficking, 17
Protection of Others, 709
Protection of Property and Home, 691
Proximate Cause, 488
Public Welfare Offenses, 226

R

Rape, 777
Rape, Acquaintence, 784
Rape, Marital, 784
Reasonable Fear, 661
Retribution, 30
Robbery, 854, 856

S

Sentencing, 12, 36
Sexual Autonomy, 118
Solicitation, 510, 516
Stalking, 829
Stand Your Ground, 689
Status Offenses, 127
Statutory Examples, 356
Statutory Interpretation, 58
Strict Liability, 216
Syndrome Evidence, 677

T

Taking, 840

U

Unexpected Victims and Transferred
    Intent, 489
Unilateral vs. Bilateral Conspiracies, 558
Unintentional Killings, 322, 391
Unlawful Act Manslaughter, 476
Use of Force for the Protection of Other
    Persons, 25, 712
Use of Force in Self-Protection, 25, 711
Utilitarian Theories of Punishment, 32, 34

V

Vagueness, 95
Vicarious and Enterprise Liability
    Distinguished, 655
Voluntary Act, 125
Voluntary Act Doctrine, 128
Voluntary Manslaughter, 355

W

Wharton's Rule, 558
White Collar Crime, 75
Wilful Blindness, 201
Writing Bad Checks, 844